# Managerial Accounting

# Managerial Accounting

**8th** edition

**John J. Wild**

University of Wisconsin—Madison

**Ken W. Shaw**

University of Missouri—Columbia

McGraw Hill

**To my students and family, especially Kimberly, Jonathan, Stephanie, and Trevor.
To my wife Linda and children Erin, Emily, and Jacob.**

MANAGERIAL ACCOUNTING, EIGHTH EDITION

Published by McGraw Hill LLC, 1325 Avenue of the Americas, New York, NY 10121. Copyright ©2022 by McGraw Hill LLC. All rights reserved. Printed in the United States of America. Previous editions ©2019, 2017, and 2015. No part of this publication may be reproduced or distributed in any form or by any means, or stored in a database or retrieval system, without the prior written consent of McGraw Hill LLC, including, but not limited to, in any network or other electronic storage or transmission, or broadcast for distance learning.

Some ancillaries, including electronic and print components, may not be available to customers outside the United States.

This book is printed on acid-free paper.

3 4 5 6 7 8 9 LWI 24 23 22

ISBN 978-1-260-72784-5 (bound edition)
MHID 1-260-72784-X (bound edition)
ISBN 978-1-264-11192-3 (loose-leaf edition)
MHID 1-264-11192-4 (loose-leaf edition)

Portfolio Manager: *Steven Schuetz*
Product Developers: *Michael McCormick, Christina Sanders*
Marketing Manager: *Claire McLemore*
Content Project Managers: *Fran Simon, Brian Nacik*
Buyer: *Sandy Ludovissy*
Designer: *Matt Diamond*
Content Licensing Specialist: *Melissa Homer*
Cover Image: *Michael DeYoung/Blend Images LLC*
Compositor: *Aptara®, Inc.*

All credits appearing on page or at the end of the book are considered to be an extension of the copyright page.

Library of Congress Control Number: 2020949687

The Internet addresses listed in the text were accurate at the time of publication. The inclusion of a website does not indicate an endorsement by the authors or McGraw Hill LLC, and McGraw Hill LLC does not guarantee the accuracy of the information presented at these sites.

mheducation.com/highered

# About the Authors

Courtesy of John J. Wild

**JOHN J. WILD** is a distinguished professor of accounting at the University of Wisconsin at Madison. He previously held appointments at Michigan State University and the University of Manchester in England. He received his BBA, MS, and PhD from the University of Wisconsin.

John teaches accounting courses at both the undergraduate and graduate levels. He has received numerous teaching honors, including the Mabel W. Chipman Excellence-in-Teaching Award and the departmental Excellence-in-Teaching Award, and he is a two-time recipient of the Teaching Excellence Award from business graduates at the University of Wisconsin. He also received the Beta Alpha Psi and Roland F. Salmonson Excellence-in-Teaching Award from Michigan State University. John has received several research honors, is a past KPMG Peat Marwick National Fellow, and is a recipient of fellowships from the American Accounting Association and the Ernst and Young Foundation.

John is an active member of the American Accounting Association and its sections. He has served on several committees of these organizations, including the Outstanding Accounting Educator Award, Wildman Award, National Program Advisory, Publications, and Research Committees. John is author of *Financial Accounting Fundamentals, Managerial Accounting, Fundamental Accounting Principles,* and *Financial and Managerial Accounting,* all published by McGraw Hill.

John's research articles on accounting and analysis appear in *The Accounting Review; Journal of Accounting Research; Journal of Accounting and Economics; Contemporary Accounting Research; Journal of Accounting, Auditing and Finance; Journal of Accounting and Public Policy; Accounting Horizons;* and other journals. He is past associate editor of *Contemporary Accounting Research* and has served on several editorial boards including *The Accounting Review* and the *Journal of Accounting and Public Policy.*

In his leisure time, John enjoys hiking, sports, boating, travel, and spending time with family and friends.

Courtesy of Ken W. Shaw

**KEN W. SHAW** is the KPMG/Joseph A. Silvoso Distinguished Professor of Accounting at the University of Missouri at Columbia. He previously was on the faculty at the University of Maryland at College Park. He has also taught in international programs at the University of Bergamo (Italy) and the University of Alicante (Spain). He received a B.S. in accounting from Bradley University and an MBA and PhD from the University of Wisconsin. He is a Certified Public Accountant with audit experience at KPMG.

Ken teaches managerial and financial accounting. He teaches in online, flipped classroom, and face-to-face modes. He has received numerous School of Accountancy, College of Business, and university-level awards for teaching excellence and for teaching with technology. He is the past advisor to his school's Beta Alpha Psi and Association of Certified Fraud Examiners chapters.

Ken is an active member of the American Accounting Association and its sections. He has served on many committees of these organizations. Ken has presented his research papers at international and national conferences and workshops. Ken's research appears in the *Journal of Accounting Research; The Accounting Review; Contemporary Accounting Research; Journal of Financial and Quantitative Analysis; Journal of the American Taxation Association; Strategic Management Journal; Journal of Accounting, Auditing, & Finance;* and other journals. He has served on the editorial boards of *Issues in Accounting Education; Journal of Business Research;* and *Research in Accounting Regulation.* Ken is co-author of *Fundamental Accounting Principles, and Managerial Accounting,* all published by McGraw Hill.

In his leisure time, Ken enjoys tennis, cycling, music, and travel.

# Author note

## Applying Learning Science and Data Analytics

**Learning science** reveals that students better learn and retain information when text is presented in a direct, concise, and systematic manner within a blocked format. Our new edition delivers the content in that format and in fewer pages. Visual aids and numerous demonstrations and videos offer additional learning support. Summary *Cheat Sheets* conclude each chapter to visually reinforce key concepts and procedures, and provide a mapping for students as they search and learn.

Our new edition has over 650 videos aimed to captivate students and improve outcomes.

- **Concept Overview Videos**—cover each chapter's learning objectives with multimedia presentations that include interactive Knowledge Checks to engage students and assess comprehension.
- **Need-to-Know Demos**—walk-through demonstrations of key procedures and analysis for each text block to ensure success with assignments and tests.
- **Hint (Guided Example) Videos**—step-by-step walk-through of assignments that mimic Quick Studies, Exercises, and General Ledger assignments. Instructors can turn the Hint on or off for each assignment.

**Data analytics and visualizations** skills are increasingly in demand. Our new edition has 3 Tableau Dashboard Activities per chapter to develop those skills. They are in Connect and are auto-graded. No knowledge of Tableau or analytics is required. Introductory students can begin immediately.

# Developing Career Readiness . . .

## Tableau Dashboard Activities

Tableau Dashboard Activities expose students to accounting analytics using visual displays. These assignments (1) do not require instructors to know Tableau, (2) are accessible to introductory students, (3) do not require Tableau software, and (4) run in **Connect**. All analytics and visualization activities are familiar to instructors as they consist of introductory concepts and procedures applied in our current assignments.

A quick study, exercise, and mini-case are available for each chapter. All are auto-gradable. Tableau is a great tool to excite students and show the relevance of accounting.

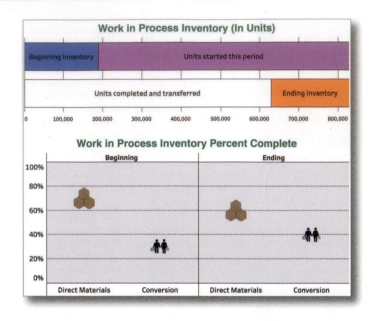

## Analytics Insight

**Analytics Insight**

**For Our Eyes Only** Retail businesses use big data to understand shopping behavior and attract new customers. **Amazon**'s "recommendation engine" tailors recommendations based on customers' browsing and buying habits. A consulting firm estimates that 35% of Amazon's revenue is generated from its recommendations. ∎

**Analytics Insight**

**Sam-apple?** **Apple** buys its component parts from over 200 different suppliers, including competitors. For example, **Samsung** supplies screens for iPhones and iPads. Apple relies on data analytics to manage its vast supply chain and to analyze its incremental costs and revenues for production decisions. ∎

## NEW! Analytics Insight

In an NVP survey of executives, 97% report they are investing in data analytics, big data, and AI. In a Robert Half survey of CFOs, 61% felt that knowledge of data analytics and visualization is mandatory for some or all of their accounting employees. Accounting students with analytics skills are highly sought after and are commanding higher salaries.

Analytics Insight boxes show students the importance of accounting analytics and visualization in business. These boxes educate students on how businesses are utilizing these competencies to improve business decisions.

## Accounting Analysis

**Accounting Analysis** assignments have students evaluate managerial accounting data from Apple, Google, and Samsung. Students compute key metrics and compare performance across companies and the industry.

These three types of assignments—Company Analysis, Comparative Analysis, Extended Analysis—are auto-gradable in **Connect** and are included after Problem Set B in each chapter.

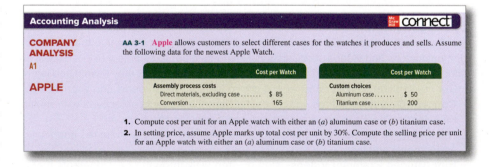

## General Ledger Problems

**General Ledger Problems** expose students to general ledger software similar to that in practice, without the expense and hassle of downloading additional software. They offer students the ability to work with transactions and see how these transactions flow into managerial reports and financial statements. Easy minimal-scroll navigation, instant "Check My Work" feedback, and fully integrated hyperlinking across tabs show how inputted data affect each stage of the accounting process. Algorithmic versions are available. **All are auto-gradable.**

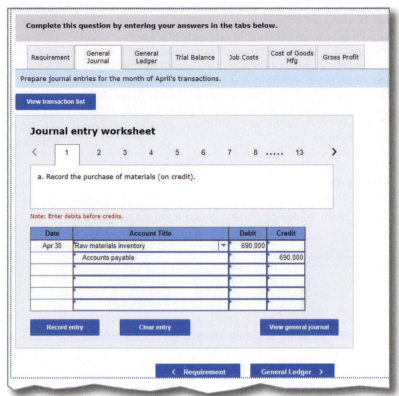

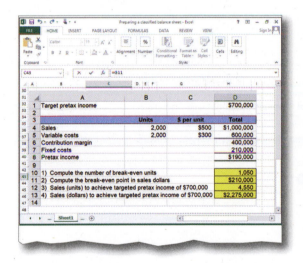

## Applying Excel

**Applying Excel** enables students to work select chapter problems or examples in Excel. These problems are assignable in **Connect** and give students instant feedback as they work through assignments in Excel.

Accompanying Excel videos teach students how to use Excel and the primary functions needed to complete each assignment. Short assessments can be assigned to test student comprehension of key Excel skills.

## Excel Simulations

**Excel Simulations,** assignable in **Connect,** allow students to practice their Excel skills—such as basic formulas and formatting—within the context of accounting. These questions feature animated, narrated Help and Show Me tutorials (when enabled), as well as automatic feedback and grading for both students and professors. These questions differ from **Applying Excel** in that students work in a simulated version of Excel. *Downloading the Excel application is not required to complete Excel Simulations.*

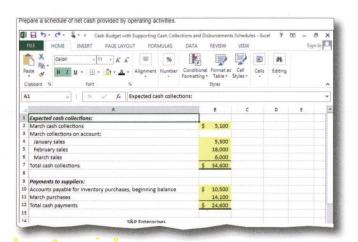

# Enhancing Learning . . .

## Learning Science

Learning science shows that students learn better when material is broken into "blocks" of content. Each chapter opens with a visual preview of the content blocks. Learning objectives highlight the location of content. Each "block" of content concludes with a Need-to-Know (NTK) demo to aid and reinforce student learning. Visual aids along with concise, bullet-point discussions further help students learn.

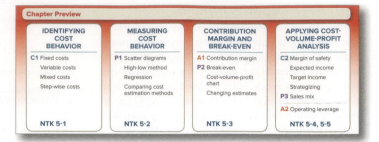

## Up-to-Date

This text reflects trending topics in managerial accounting, including lean production, supply chain, triple bottom line, and digitial manufacturing.

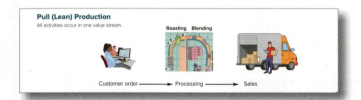

**Supply Chain Management**

**Supply chain management** or *logistics* is the control of materials, information, and finances as they move between suppliers, manufacturers, and customers. Lean businesses use supply chain management to ensure raw materials arrive just-in-time for production and customers receive their orders on schedule.

**Digital Manufacturing**   **Digital manufacturing** combines machines, computers, and human control to manufacture products. On the factory floor, machines replace much of direct labor. Computers collect information on these automated processes, including product quality,

## Assignments in Connect with Algos

**Connect** helps students learn more efficiently by providing feedback and practice material when they need it, where they need it. **Connect** grades homework automatically and gives immediate feedback.

- Wild has auto-gradable and algorithmic assignments; most focus on one learning objective and are targeted at introductory students.
- 99% of Wild's Quick Study, Exercise, and Problem Set A assignments are available with algorithmic options.
- 100% of Wild's Accounting Analysis assignments are in **Connect**.
- Over 95 assignments are new to this edition—all available in **Connect** with algorithmic options. Most are Quick Studies and Exercises.

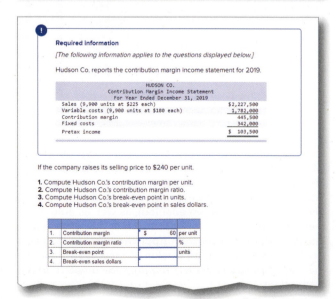

## Updated Learning Videos

- **Wild offers over 650** videos that increase student engagement and improve outcomes.
- Hundreds of **Hint** videos or **Guided Examples** provide a narrated, animated, step-by-step walk-through of most Quick Studies and Exercises similar to those assigned. These short presentations, which can be turned on or off by instructors, provide reinforcement when students need it most. (Exercise PowerPoints are available for instructors.)
- **Concept Overview Videos** cover each chapter's learning objectives with narrated, animated presentations that frequently assess comprehension using interactive Knowledge Checks. Grading of Knowledge Checks can be turned on or off by instructors.

## Need-to-Know Demos

Need-to-Know demonstrations are located at the end of each learning block. There are multiple learning blocks within each chapter. These demonstrations pose questions about the material just presented—content that students "need to know" to learn accounting. Accompanying solutions walk students through key procedures and analyses necessary to be successful with homework and test materials.

Need-to-Know demonstrations are supplemented with narrated, animated, step-by-step walk-through videos led by an instructor, which are available via **Connect**.

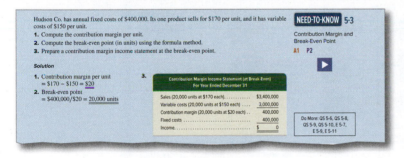

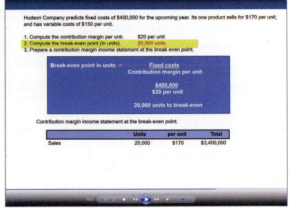

## Remote Proctoring & Browser-Locking

New remote proctoring and browser-locking capabilities, hosted by Proctorio within Connect, provide control of the assessment environment by enabling security options and verifying the identity of the student.

Seamlessly integrated within Connect, these services allow instructors to control students' assessment experience by restricting browser activity, recording activity during assessment, and verifying students are doing their own work.

Instant and detailed reporting gives instructors an at-a-glance view of potential academic integrity concerns, thereby avoiding personal bias and supporting evidence-based claims.

# Engaging Content...

## Business Decisions

Whether we prepare, analyze, or apply accounting information, one skill remains essential: decision making. To help develop good decision-making habits and to show the relevance of accounting, we use a decision-learning framework.

- **Decision Insight** offers context for business decisions.
- **Decision Ethics** and **Decision Maker** are role-playing scenarios that show the relevance of accounting.
- **Decision Analysis** provides key tools and ratios to assess company performance.

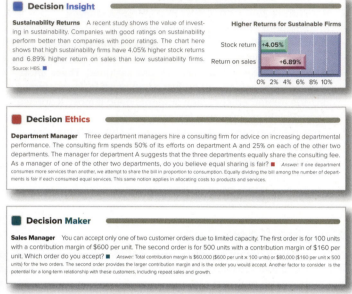

**Decision Insight**

**Sustainability Returns** A recent study shows the value of investing in sustainability. Companies with good ratings on sustainability perform better than companies with poor ratings. The chart here shows that high sustainability firms have 4.05% higher stock returns and 6.89% higher return on sales than low sustainability firms. Source: HBS. ■

*Higher Returns for Sustainable Firms*

Stock return +4.05%

Return on sales +6.89%

0% 2% 4% 6% 8% 10%

**Decision Ethics**

**Department Manager** Three department managers hire a consulting firm for advice on increasing departmental performance. The consulting firm spends 50% of its efforts on department A and 25% on each of the other two departments. The manager for department A suggests that the three departments equally share the consulting fee. As a manager of one of the other two departments, do you believe equal sharing is fair? ■ *Answer: If one department consumes more services than another, we attempt to share the bill in proportion to consumption. Equally dividing the bill among the number of departments is fair if each consumed equal services. This same notion applies to allocating costs to products and services.*

**Decision Maker**

**Sales Manager** You can accept only one of two customer orders due to limited capacity. The first order is for 100 units with a contribution margin of $600 per unit. The second order is for 500 units with a contribution margin of $160 per unit. Which order do you accept? ■ *Answer: Total contribution margin is $60,000 ($600 per unit × 100 units) or $80,000 ($160 per unit × 500 units) for the two orders. The second order provides the larger contribution margin and is the order you would accept. Another factor to consider is the potential for a long-term relationship with these customers, including repeat sales and growth.*

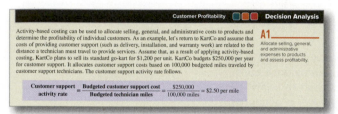

Customer Profitability | Decision Analysis

Activity-based costing can be used to allocate selling, general, and administrative costs to products and determine the profitability of individual customers. As an example, let's return to KartCo and assume that costs of providing customer support (such as delivery, installation, and warranty work) are related to the distance a technician must travel to provide services. Assume that, as a result of applying activity-based costing, KartCo plans to sell its standard go-kart for $1,200 per unit. KartCo budgets $250,000 per year for customer support. It allocates customer support costs based on 100,000 budgeted miles traveled by customer support technicians. The customer support activity rate follows.

**A1** Allocate selling, general, and administrative expenses to products and assess profitability.

$$\frac{\text{Customer support}}{\text{activity rate}} = \frac{\text{Budgeted customer support cost}}{\text{Budgeted technician miles}} = \frac{\$250,000}{100,000 \text{ miles}} = \$2.50 \text{ per mile}$$

## Visual Learning

Learning science tells us today's students learn better with visual aids supporting blocks of text. Wild has adapted to student needs by having informative visual aids throughout. Many visuals and exhibits are new to this edition.

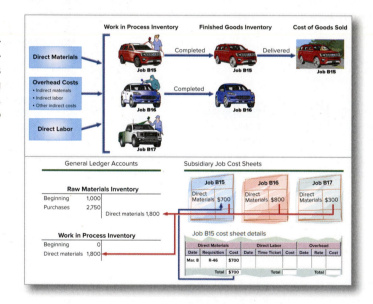

## Exercise Presentations

Animated PowerPoints, created from text assignments, enable instructors to be fully prepared for in-class demonstrations. Instructors can use these animated PowerPoints along with their own audio to record personalized online lectures.

## Less Is More

Wild is more direct, concise, and systematic than competing books covering the same content.

- The text is to the point and uses visuals to aid student learning.
- Bullet-point discussions and active writing aid learning.

## Cheat Sheets

Cheat Sheets are provided at the end of each chapter to reinforce student learning. Cheat Sheets are roughly one page in length and include key procedures, concepts, entries, and formulas.

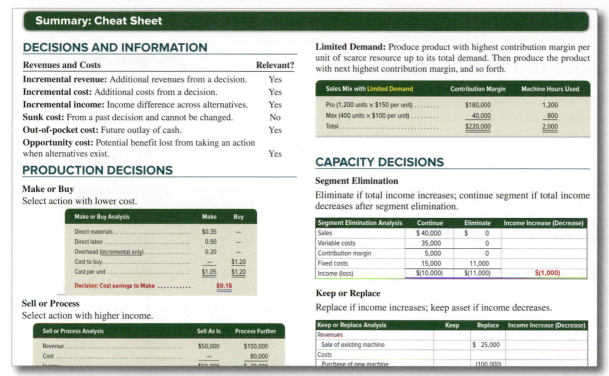

**Summary: Cheat Sheet**

### DECISIONS AND INFORMATION

| Revenues and Costs | Relevant? |
|---|---|
| **Incremental revenue:** Additional revenues from a decision. | Yes |
| **Incremental cost:** Additional costs from a decision. | Yes |
| **Incremental income:** Income difference across alternatives. | Yes |
| **Sunk cost:** From a past decision and cannot be changed. | No |
| **Out-of-pocket cost:** Future outlay of cash. | Yes |
| **Opportunity cost:** Potential benefit lost from taking an action when alternatives exist. | Yes |

### PRODUCTION DECISIONS

**Make or Buy**
Select action with lower cost.

| Make or Buy Analysis | Make | Buy |
|---|---|---|
| Direct materials | $0.35 | — |
| Direct labor | 0.50 | — |
| Overhead (incremental only) | 0.20 | — |
| Cost to buy | — | $1.20 |
| Cost per unit | $1.05 | $1.20 |
| **Decision: Cost savings to Make** | | $0.15 |

**Sell or Process**
Select action with higher income.

| Sell or Process Analysis | Sell As Is | Process Further |
|---|---|---|
| Revenue | $50,000 | $150,000 |
| Cost | — | 80,000 |

**Limited Demand:** Produce product with highest contribution margin per unit of scarce resource up to its total demand. Then produce the product with next highest contribution margin, and so forth.

| Sales Mix with Limited Demand | Contribution Margin | Machine Hours Used |
|---|---|---|
| Pro (1,200 units × $150 per unit) | $180,000 | 1,200 |
| Max (400 units × $100 per unit) | 40,000 | 800 |
| Total | $220,000 | 2,000 |

### CAPACITY DECISIONS

**Segment Elimination**

Eliminate if total income increases; continue segment if total income decreases after segment elimination.

| Segment Elimination Analysis | Continue | Eliminate | Income Increase (Decrease) |
|---|---|---|---|
| Sales | $ 40,000 | $ 0 | |
| Variable costs | 35,000 | 0 | |
| Contribution margin | 5,000 | 0 | |
| Fixed costs | 15,000 | 11,000 | |
| Income (loss) | $(10,000) | $(11,000) | $(1,000) |

**Keep or Replace**

Replace if income increases; keep asset if income decreases.

| Keep or Replace Analysis | Keep | Replace | Income Increase (Decrease) |
|---|---|---|---|
| Revenues | | | |
| Sale of existing machine | | $ 25,000 | |
| Costs | | | |
| Purchase of new machine | | (100,000) | |

## Keep It Real

Research shows that students learn best when using current data from real companies. Wild uses the most current data from real companies for assignments, examples, and analysis in the text. See Chapter 13 for samples on the use of real data.

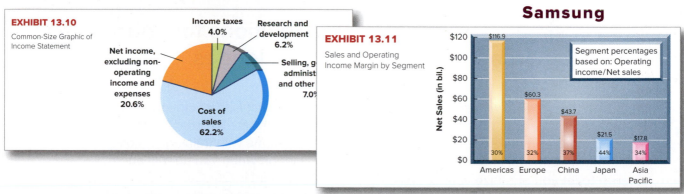

**EXHIBIT 13.10**

Common-Size Graphic of Income Statement

Income taxes 4.0%
Research and development 6.2%
Net income, excluding non-operating income and expenses 20.6%
Selling, g administ and other 7.0%
Cost of sales 62.2%

**EXHIBIT 13.11**

Sales and Operating Income Margin by Segment

Segment percentages based on: Operating income/Net sales

Net Sales (in bil.)

| | Americas | Europe | China | Japan | Asia Pacific |
|---|---|---|---|---|---|
| Net Sales | $116.9 | $60.3 | $43.7 | $21.5 | $17.8 |
| | 30% | 32% | 37% | 44% | 34% |

---

**CORPORATE SOCIAL RESPONSIBILITY**

Food processor **General Mills** needs a steady supply of high-quality corn, oats, and sugarcane. These agricultural inputs face risks due to water scarcity and climate change that could disrupt General Mills's process operations and hurt profits.

Buying from suppliers that follow sustainable principles reduces risk of reputational damage. The Sustainability Accounting Standards Board (SASB) recommends that food processors disclose information on *priority food ingredients* (those that are essential to the company's products), including details on the company's strategies to address strategic risks.

Consistent with SASB guidelines, General Mills disclosed the following in its recent *Global Responsibility Report.*

## Doing What's Right

Companies increasingly issue corporate social responsibility reports, and accountants are being asked to prepare, analyze, and audit them. Wild includes brief Corporate Social Responsibility sections in the managerial chapters that show the importance of corporate social responsibility.

## You're in the driver's seat.

Want to build your own course? No problem. Prefer to use our turnkey, prebuilt course? Easy. Want to make changes throughout the semester? Sure. And you'll save time with Connect's auto-grading too.

## 65%
**Less Time Grading**

Laptop: McGraw-Hill; Woman/dog: George Doyle/Getty Images

## They'll thank you for it.

Adaptive study resources like SmartBook® 2.0 help your students be better prepared in less time. You can transform your class time from dull definitions to dynamic debates. Find out more about the powerful **personalized learning** experience available in SmartBook 2.0 at **www.mheducation.com/highered/ connect/smartbook**

## Make it simple, make it affordable.

Connect makes it easy with seamless integration using any of the major Learning Management Systems— Blackboard®, Canvas, and D2L, among others—to let you organize your course in one convenient location. Give your students access to digital materials at a discount with our inclusive access program. Ask your McGraw-Hill representative for more information.

Padlock: Jobalou/Getty Images

## Solutions for your challenges.

A product isn't a solution. Real solutions are affordable, reliable, and come with training and ongoing support when you need it and how you want it. Our Customer Experience Group can also help you troubleshoot tech problems— although Connect's 99% uptime means you might not need to call them. See for yourself at **status. mheducation.com**

Checkmark: Jobalou/Getty Images

## Effective, efficient studying.

Connect helps you be more productive with your study time and get better grades using tools like SmartBook 2.0, which highlights key concepts and creates a personalized study plan. Connect sets you up for success, so you walk into class with confidence and walk out with better grades.

## Study anytime, anywhere.

Download the free ReadAnywhere app and access your online eBook or SmartBook 2.0 assignments when it's convenient, even if you're offline. And since the app automatically syncs with your eBook and SmartBook 2.0 assignments in Connect, all of your work is available every time you open it. Find out more at **www.mheducation.com/readanywhere**

> *"I really liked this app—it made it easy to study when you don't have your textbook in front of you."*
>
> - Jordan Cunningham, Eastern Washington University

## No surprises.

The Connect Calendar and Reports tools keep you on track with the work you need to get done and your assignment scores. Life gets busy; Connect tools help you keep learning through it all.

Calendar: owattaphotos/Getty Images

## Learning for everyone.

McGraw-Hill works directly with Accessibility Services Departments and faculty to meet the learning needs of all students. Please contact your Accessibility Services office and ask them to email accessibility@mheducation.com, or visit **www.mheducation.com/about/accessibility** for more information.

Top: Jenner Images/Getty Images, Left: Hero Images/Getty Images, Right: Hero Images/Getty Images

# Leading Edge Content...

Instructors and students guided this edition's revisions. Those revisions include the following.

- New **Tableau Dashboard Activities** expose students to accounting analytics and visualizations with 3 assignments per chapter.
- New **Analytics Insight** boxes highlight accounting analytics in business.
- New coverage of artificial intelligence, lean accounting, digital manufacturing, data analytics, and other emerging topics.
- New **Applying Excel** and **Excel Simulations** enhance skills for career readiness.
- Expanded **General Ledger** assignments let students engage with general ledger software tools similar to those in practice.

- Content is concise and succinct; new edition has fewer pages with no loss of content and text organized into learning blocks.
- More than 95 new assignments—all in Connect with static and algorithmic options.
- **Cheat Sheets** at each chapter-end visually reinforce key chapter content and provide a search map for students.
- Updated Accounting Analysis assignments—all in Connect and auto-gradable—use data from **Apple**, **Google**, and **Samsung**.
- Auto-gradable Concept Overview Videos for each learning objective.

## Chapter 1

NEW Opener—**Sweet Tea Cosmetics** and entrepreneurial assignment.
Streamlined learning objectives.
NEW Analytics Insight on **Kickstarter** crowdfunding.
Postponed fixed vs variable cost classifications to later chapters.
NEW Exhibit 1.6 on prime and conversion costs.
Improved Exhibits 1.7 and 1.8 on product versus period costs.
NEW Exhibit 1.9 on cost classifications for service company.
Simplified Exhibit 1.12 on reporting Cost of Goods Sold.
NEW NTK 1-3 on reporting for manufacturers.
Simplified Exhibits 1.13 and 1.15 on cost flows.
Simplified Schedule of Cost of Goods Manufactured in Exhibit 1.14 and 1.15.
New Part B to NTK 1-4 on preparing schedule of cost of goods manufactured.
NEW coverage of digital manufacturing, data analytics, and data visualization.
Revised NTK 1-5.
Added four new Quick Studies, one new Exercise, and one new Problem.
Revised analysis assignments: Company Analysis, Comparative Analysis, and Extended Analysis.

## Chapter 2

NEW Opener—**Wallace Detroit Guitars** and entrepreneurial assignment.
Combined C1 and C2 LOs.
Simplified job order costing example from five jobs to three jobs.
Revised Exhibits 2.2, 2.3, 2.5, 2.6, 2.7, 2.9, 2.10, 2.13, 2.14, 2.16, and 2.17.
Revised NTK 2-1, 2-2 and 2-3.
NEW systematic way to apply estimated overhead costs.
Enhanced Exhibit 2.15 on cost flows.
NEW coverage of financial statements.
Revised Adjusting Overhead section for consistency with Road Warriors example.

NEW Analytics Insight on risk scores for health-care providers.
Revised Decision Analysis section and added *gross profit ratio*.
Enhanced and clarified NTK 2-7.
Added five new Quick Studies, seven new Exercises, one new Problem.
Revised analysis assignments: Company Analysis, Comparative Analysis, and Extended Analysis.

## Chapter 3

UPDATED Opener—**Azucar Ice Cream Company**.
Streamlined learning objectives.
Modernized Exhibit 3.1.
NEW Exhibit 3.2 is simple overview of GenX operations.
Moved coverage of EUP to step 2 of process costing demo.
Simplified process costing demo into 4-steps.
Revised Exhibits 3.7, 3.10 and 3.11 to match Connect assignments.
Simplified Exhibit 16.8 on cost data.
Improved NTKs 3-2, 3-3, 3-5, 3-6 to match Connect assignments.
Renamed Process Cost Summary to Production Cost Report for consistency with practice.
Simplified Production Cost Report in Exhibit 3.11.
NEW coverage of reporting on financial statements.
NEW discussion of computing cost per completed unit.
NEW Analytics Insight on machine learning at **Hershey**.
Revised hybrid costing systems and added manufacturing *yield* to Decision Analysis.
Simplified FIFO process costing demo into 4-steps in Appendix 3A.
NEW section on determining units started and completed for FIFO.
Revised Exhibits 3A.3, 3A.6, and 3A.9 to match Connect assignments.
Simplified Exhibit 3A.7 on cost data.
Improved NTKs 3-8 and 3-9 to match Connect assignments.

Renamed (FIFO) Process Cost Summary to Production Cost Report.
Simplified Production Cost Report in Exhibit 3A.10.
Added three new Quick Studies and five new Exercises.
Revised analysis assignments: Company Analysis, Comparative Analysis, and Extended Analysis.

## Chapter 4

NEW Opener—**Grimm Artisanal Ales** and entrepreneurial assignment.
Streamlined learning objectives.
Revised Exhibit 4.4 (previously 4.5).
Enhanced NTK 4-1 for consistency with assignment materials.
Simplified and improved ABC section.
NEW Exhibit 4.10 gives a step-by-step allocation table for ABC.
Revised NTK 4-2 using new step-by-step allocation approach for ABC.
Postponed Cost of Quality and Lean Manufacturing coverage to later chapters.
Supported ABC for Service Providers with step-by-step allocation example.
NEW NTK 4-3 on ABC for Service Providers.
NEW Analytics Insight on cost allocation at **DHL Express.**
Improved NTK 4-4 using step-by-step ABC allocation approach.
Enhanced and revised multiple choice quiz.
Three new Quick Studies and eight new Exercises.
Revised analysis assignments: Company Analysis, Comparative Analysis, and Extended Analysis.

## Chapter 5

NEW opener—**SmartSweets** and entrepreneurial assignment.
Streamlined procedural learning objectives.
Removed income taxes and pretax income for clarity.
Postponed coverage of curvilinear costs to advanced courses.
Simplified Exhibit 5.2 on step-wise costs.

Added examples of step-wise costs to Exhibit 5.3.
Revised formula for variable cost per unit using high-low method.
Enhanced NTK 5-2 to show solution in steps.
Added NEW alternative to compute contribution margin ratio.
Simplified Exhibit 5.13 on contribution margin in reporting.
Streamlined CVP changes in estimates for Exhibits 5.15, 5.16 and 5.17.
NEW coverage of sales mix and break-even using *Weighted-Average Contribution Margin per Unit*.
Revised Exhibits 5.27, 5.28, 5.29 for weighted-average contribution margin per unit and contribution margin in dollars.
Revised NTK 5-5 for weighted-average contribution margin per unit.
NEW Analytics Insight on big data at **Amazon**.
Simplified degree of operating leverage formulas in Exhibits 5.31 and 5.32.
Simplified NTK 5-6.
Added six new Quick Studies and four new Exercises.
Revised analysis assignments: Company Analysis, Comparative Analysis, and Extended Analysis.

## Chapter 6

NEW Opener—**Da Bomb** and Entrepreneurial assignment.
Streamlined learning objectives.
Revised account titles in Exhibit 6.4, 6.5, and 6.6 for consistency and simplicity.
Removed *previous edition* Exhibits 6.5, 6.7, and 6.9 based on student and instructor feedback.
Improved NTK 6-2 with more consistent terminology.
Moved 'Converting Income from Variable Costing to Absorption Costing' to Appendix 6A.
Simplified Exhibit 6.9 by shortening the selling and administrative expenses section.
Moved Analyzing Special Orders into text following Setting Target Price section.

Postponed CVP analysis coverage to later chapters.
NEW Decision Analysis section on using Contribution Margin Ratio to make decisions.
Simplified computations in NTK 6-4 to focus on the accounting.
Six new Quick Studies and six new Exercises.
Revised analysis assignments: Company Analysis, Comparative Analysis, and Extended Analysis.

### Chapter 7

NEW opener—**Ellis Island Tropical Tea** and entrepreneurial assignment.
NEW LO on direct labor budget for a service firm and revenue per employee.
Simplified Production Budget in Exhibit 7.6.
Slightly revised direct materials budget in Exhibit 7.7.
Slightly revised direct labor budget in Exhibit 7.8.
Revised NTK 7-3 solution formatting.
Simplified factory overhead budget in Exhibit 7.9.
NEW cost of goods sold budget.
Revised NTK 7-4 solution for consistency with Connect assignments.
Improved schedule of cash receipts from sales in Exhibit 7.14.
NEW table for capital expenditures budget.
NEW tables to budget cash receipts of credit sales and with uncollectibles.
Enhanced schedule of cash payments for direct materials in Exhibit 7.15.
Revised NTK 7-5 solution for consistency with Connect assignments.
NEW Decision Analysis on direct labor budget for service firms and revenue per employee.
Revised NTK 7-6 and 7-7.
Improved merchandise purchases budget in Exhibit 7A.3.
NEW schedule of cash payments for merchandise purchases in Exhibit 7A.4.
Added one new Exercise.
Revised analysis assignments: Company Analysis, Comparative Analysis, and Extended Analysis.

### Chapter 8

NEW opener—**True Fit** and entrepreneurial assignment.
Revised Exhibit 8.1 to better show fixed vs flexible budgets.
Simplified Exhibit 8.2 for a fixed budget performance report.
Simplified Exhibits 8.3 and 8.4.
Added Part B to Need-to-Know 8-1.
Modernized Exhibit 8.5.
Revised cost variance example and tables.
Revised NTK 8-2.
Modified direct labor variances example from 1 direct labor hour per unit to ½ direct labor hour per unit to clarify steps.
NEW Analytics Insight on predictive analysis.

Enhanced and revised NTK 8-4.
Revised Exhibit 8.12 on Flexible Overhead Budget, so that variable overhead rate per unit differs from $1.
NEW section on overhead controllable and volume variances.
NEW formulas for Variable overhead rate and Fixed overhead rate.
Revised Exhibit 8.15 to show volume and controllable variances for overhead.
Revised Exhibit 8.16 to better explain the overhead variance report.
Simplified NTK 8-6.
NEW numbers and exhibits in Appendix 8A.
Expanded and improved NTK 8-7.
Added five new Exercises.
Revised analysis assignments: Company Analysis, Comparative Analysis, and Extended Analysis.

### Chapter 9

NEW opener—**Teysha** and entrepreneurial assignment.
Streamlined conceptual learning objectives.
Removed Appendix A; cost allocations simplified and moved into chapter.
Removed Appendix B; transfer pricing streamlined and moved into chapter.
NEW demo company, Outdoor Gal, with new department examples beginning with Exhibit 9.8.
Reduced five departments to three departments in Departmental Income Statement to simplify demonstration.
Revised Exhibits 9.9, 9.10, 9.11 and 9.12.
Simplified return on investment example and formula in Exhibit 9.13.
Simplified residual income example and formula in Exhibit 9.14.
Combined and updated NTKs 9-3 and 9-4.
Postponed Measurement Issues to advanced courses.
Simplified profit margin and investment turnover examples and formulas in Exhibits 9.15 and 9.16.
Refined balance scorecard in Exhibit 9.18.
Changed joint cost demonstration in Appendix 9A to milk types.
Postponed physical basis allocation to advanced courses.
Added three new Quick Studies and one new Exercise.
Revised analysis assignments: Company Analysis, Comparative Analysis, and Extended Analysis.

### Chapter 10

NEW opener—**Eye Symmetry** and entrepreneurial assignment.
Added *avoidable cost* in distinguishing between relevant and irrelevant costs.
Improved NTK 10-1.
Enhanced Make or Buy analysis with a decision row in Exhibit 10.2.
Revised NTK 10-2.

Enhanced Sell or Process Further demo to focus on one product and to include a decision row in Exhibit 10.3.
Improved Scrap or Rework analysis with a decision row in Exhibit 10.4.
Revised NTK 10-3.
Revised Sales Mix section with electric scooters example.
Updated Exhibit 10.5 to apply new scooters example.
NEW Exhibits 10.6 and 10.7 for sales mix decisions with unlimited and limited demand.
Revised NTK 10-4.
NEW and improved Segment Elimination with Exhibits 10.8, 10.9 and 10.10.
NEW and improved Keep or Replace with Exhibit 10.11.
Revised NTK 10-5.
New visual aid for price takers versus price setters.
New formula for selling price per unit.
New illustration of three-step total cost method to determine price.
Simplified Special Offer analysis and Exhibits 10.12 and 10.13.
Revised NTK 10-6.
Revised and improved Decision Analysis section on Time and Materials Pricing.
Improved NTK 10-7 to include all decision scenarios.
Added two new Quick Studies and three new Problems.
Revised analysis assignments: Company Analysis, Comparative Analysis, and Extended Analysis.

### Chapter 11

NEW opener—**Gecko Robotics** and entrepreneurial assignment.
Removed income taxes and pretax income for clarity.
Simplified Payback Period with numbers not requiring rounding.
Simplified Payback Period with unequal cash flows from 8 to 5 years.
Revised accounting rate of return formula in Exhibit 11.6.
Simplified calculations for accounting rate of return in Exhibit 11.7.
Revised NTK 11-2 to not require rounding.
Simplified NPV demo from 8 to 3 years in Exhibit 11.8.
Simplified numbers in NPV of annuity in Exhibit 11.9.
Streamlined NPV with unequal cash flows in Exhibit 11.10 by removing Project C.
NEW table on NPV for investments with salvage value.
Postponed accelerated depreciation, inflation, and capital rationing in NPV to advanced courses.
Revised IRR to simplify calculations, limit rounding, and work with App B present value tables.

Postponed Postaudit coverage to advanced courses.
Simplified Break-even time demo from 8 to 5 years in Exhibit 11.14.
Added one new Quick Study, one new Exercise, two new Problems.
Revised analysis assignments: Company Analysis, Comparative Analysis, and Extended Analysis.

### Chapter 12

Slightly revised infographics on cash flows from operating, investing, and financing.
Updated cash flow on total assets analysis using **Nike** and **Under Armour**.
Added one new Quick Study.
Added two new Exercises.
Updated analysis assignments: Company Analysis, Comparative Analysis, and Extended Analysis.

### Chapter 13

Streamlined conceptual learning objectives.
Updated data for all analyses of **Apple** using horizontal, vertical, and ratio analysis.
Updated comparative analysis using **Google** and **Samsung**.
Updated data visualizations with current data.
Added gross margin ratio to profitability analysis.
Revised and simplified return on equity calculation.
Added seven new Quick Studies.
Added one new Exercise.
Updated analysis assignments: Company Analysis, Comparative Analysis, and Extended Analysis.

### Appendix A

New financial statements for **Apple**, **Google**, and **Samsung**.

### Appendix C

Revised Exhibit C.1 on lean business model.
Updated coverage of lean principles.
Added P2 learning objective on costs of quality and cost of quality report.
Revised Exhibit C.3 on push versus pull production.
NEW section on Lean Overhead Costs and the 80-20 rule.
NEW exhibit with real-world example of using lean techniques to reduce overhead costs.
Revised exhibit on components of cycle efficiency.
NEW example of computing revised days' sales in WIP from lean techniques.
NEW section on costs of quality and cost of quality report.
New Exhibit C.8 on quality costs.
New Exhibit C.9 on a Cost of Quality Report.
Added two new Quick Studies and two new Exercises.

# Acknowledging Our Friends...

John J. Wild, Ken W. Shaw, and McGraw Hill Education recognize the following instructors for their valuable feedback and involvement in the development of *Managerial Accounting*. We are thankful for their suggestions, counsel, and encouragement.

**Darlene Adkins,** University of Tennessee–Martin

**Peter Aghimien,** Indiana University South Bend

**Janice Akao,** Butler Community College

**Nathan Akins,** Chattahoochee Technical College

**John Alpers,** Tennessee Wesleyan University

**Sekhar Anantharaman,** Indiana University of Pennsylvania

**Karen Andrews,** Lewis-Clark State College

**Ruqayyah T. Archie,** Community College of Philadelphia

**Chandra D. Arthur,** Cuyahoga Community College

**Steven Ault,** Montana State University

**Victoria Badura,** Metropolitan Community College

**Felicia Baldwin,** City College of Chicago

**Richard Barnhart,** Grand Rapids Community College

**Ellie Baumgartner,** University of Missouri

**Reb Beatty,** Anne Arundel Community College

**Robert Beebe,** Morrisville State College

**Mark Bell,** Bluegrass Community and Technical College

**George Henry Bernard,** Seminole State College of Florida

**Cynthia Bird,** Tidewater Community College, Virginia Beach

**Pascal Bizarro,** Bowling Green State University

**Martin Blaine,** Columbus State Community College

**Amy Bohrer,** Tidewater Community College, Virginia Beach

**William Bond,** Des Moines Area Community College

**John Bosco,** North Shore Community College

**Nicholas Bosco,** Suffolk County Community College

**Anna Boulware,** St. Charles Community College

**Jerold K. Braun,** Daytona State College

**Doug Brown,** Forsyth Technical Community College

**Tracy L. Bundy,** University of Louisiana at Lafayette

**Marci Butterfield,** University of Utah

**Mark Camma,** Atlantic Cape Community College

**Ann Capion,** Scott Community College

**Amy Cardillo,** Metropolitan State University of Denver

**Anne Cardozo,** Broward College

**Crystal Carlson-Myer,** Indian River State College

**Julie Chasse,** Des Moines Area Community College

**Patricia Chow,** Grossmont College

**Maria Coclin,** Community College of Rhode Island

**Michael Cohen,** Lewis-Clark State College

**Jerilyn Collins,** Herzing University

**Scott Collins,** Penn State University, University Park

**William Conner,** Tidewater Community College

**Shawna Coram,** Florida State College at Jacksonville

**Erin Cornelsen,** University of South Dakota

**Karen Crisonino,** County College of Morris

**Mariah Dar,** John Tyler Community College

**Nichole Dauenhauer,** Lakeland Community College

**Janet Dausey,** Northeast Wisconsin Technical College

**Laurence Degaetano,** Montclair State University

**Donna DeMilia,** Grand Canyon University

**Tiffany DeRoy,** University of South Alabama

**Susan Dickey,** Motlow State Community College

**Erin Dischler,** Milwaukee Area Technical College–West Allis

**Holly Dixon,** State College of Florida

**Vicky Dominguez,** College of Southern Nevada

**David Doyon,** Southern New Hampshire University

**Chester Drake**, Central Texas College

**Jerrilyn Eisenhauer,** Tulsa Community College

**Christopher Eller,** Appalachian State University

**Cynthia Elliott,** Southwest Tennessee Community College–Macon

**Kim Everett,** East Carolina University

**Corinne Frad,** Eastern Iowa Community College

**Krystal Gabel,** Southeast Community College

**Harry Gallatin,** Indiana State University

**Rena Galloway,** State Fair Community College

Rick Gaumer, University of Wisconsin–Green Bay

Tammy Gerszewski, University of North Dakota

Pradeep Ghimire, Rappahannock Community College

Kari Gingrich, University of Missouri

Marc Giullian, Montana State University, Bozeman

Nelson Gomez, Miami Dade College–Kendall

Robert Goodwin, University of Tampa

Marina Grau, Houston Community College

Donald Green, Farmington State College

Steve G. Green, U.S. Air Force Academy

Darryl Greene, Muskegon Community College

Lisa Hadley, Southwest Tennessee Community College–Macon

Penny Hahn, KCTCS Henderson Community College

Yoon Han, Bemidji State University

Becky Hancock, El Paso Community College

Paul Haugen, Wisconsin Indianhead Technical College

Amie Haun, University of Tennessee–Chattanooga

Michelle Hays, Kalamazoo Valley Community College

Brian Hefty, University of Wisconsin

Sueann Hely, West Kentucky Community and Technical College

Rhonda Henderson, Olive Harvey College

Youngwon Her, California State University, Northridge

Lora Hines, John A. Logan College

Rob Hochschild, Ivy Tech Community College of Indiana–South Bend

Yongtao Hong, North Dakota State University

John Hoover, Volunteer State Community College

Zach Houck, Des Moines Area Community College

Roberta Humphrey, Southeast Missouri State University

Carley Hunzeker, Metro Community College, Elkhorn

Kay Jackson, Tarrant County College South

Elizabeth Jennison, Saddleback College

Todd Jensen, Sierra College

Mary Jepperson, Saint John's University

Vicki Jobst, Benedictine University

Kevin Jones, University of California Santa Cruz

Odessa Jordan, Calhoun Community College

Susan Juckett, Victoria College

Amanda Kaari, Central Georgia Technical College

Dmitriy Kalyagin, Chabot College

Ramadevi Kannan, Owens Community College

Anne Kenner, Eastern Florida State College

Angela King, Johnson County Community College

Jan Klaus, University of North Texas

Phillip Klaus, University of North Texas

Aaron P. Knape, The University of New Orleans

Jennifer Knauf, Grand Rapids Community College

Eric Knight, Southeastern Louisiana University

Cedric Knott, Henry Ford Community College

Robin Knowles, Texas A&M International University

Kimberly Kochanny, Central Piedmont Community College

Sergey Komissarov, University of Wisconsin–La Crosse

Stephanie Lareau Kroeger, Ocean County College

Joseph Krupka, Lander University

Tara Laken, Joliet Junior College

Suzanne Lay, Colorado Mesa University

Brian Lazarus, Baltimore City Community College

Christy Lefevers, Catawba Valley Community College

Kevin Leifer, Long Island University, CW Post Campus

Harold Levine, Los Angeles Valley College

Philip Lee Little, Coastal Carolina University

Yuebing Liu, University of Tampa

Delores Loedel, Miracosta College

Rebecca Lohmann, Southeast Missouri State University

Ming Lu, Santa Monica College

Annette C. Maddox, Georgia Highlands College

Natasha Maddox, KCTCS Maysville Community and Technical College

Rich Mandau, Piedmont Technical College

Diane Marker, University of Toledo

Robert Maxwell, College of the Canyons

Karen McCarron, Georgia Gwinnett College

Michael McDonald, College of Southern Neveda

Gwendolyn McFadden-Wade, North Carolina A&T University

Allison McLeod, University of North Texas

Kate McNeil, Johnson County Community College

Jane Medling, Saddleback College

Heidi H. Meier, Cleveland State University

Tammy Metzke, Milwaukee Area Technical College

Jeanine Metzler, Northampton Community College

Michelle Meyer, Joliet Junior College

Pam Meyer, University of Louisiana at Lafayette

Deanne Michaelson, Pellissippi State Community College

Susan Miller, County College of Morris

Carmen Morgan, Oregon Tech

Karen Satterfield Mozingo, Pitt Community College

Haris Mujahid, South Seattle College

Andrea Murowski, Brookdale Community College

Jaclynn Myers, Sinclair Community College

Lisa Nash, University of North Georgia

Joseph Nicassio, Westmoreland County Community College

Micki Nickla, Ivy Tech Community College of Indiana–Gary

Lisa Novak, Mott Community College

Dan O'Brien, Madison College

Jamie O'Brien, South Dakota State University

Grace Odediran, Union County College

Danica Olson, Milwaukee Area Technical College

Ashley Parker, Grand Canyon University

Pamela Parker, NOVA Community College Alexandria

Margaret Parrish, John Tyler Community College

Lori Parry, Eastern Gateway Community College

Reed Peoples, Austin Community College

Rachel Pernia, Essex County College

Dawn Peters, Southwestern Illinois College

Brandis Phillips, North Carolina A&T University

Debbie Porter, Tidewater Community College–Virginia Beach

Jeff M. Quinlan, Madison College

James E. Racic, Lakeland Community College

Ronald de Ramon, Rockland Community College

Robert J. Rankin, Texas A&M University–Commerce

Robert Rebman, Benedictine University

Susan Reeves, University of South Carolina

Jenny Resnick, Santa Monica Community College

DeAnn Ricketts, York Technical College

Renee Rigoni, Monroe Community College

Cecile M. Roberti, Community College of Rhode Island

Jan Rose, Cleveland State University

Kevin Rosenberg, Southeastern Community College

David Rosser, University of Texas at Arlington

Michael J. Rusek, Eastern Gateway Community College

Alfredo Salas, El Paso Community College

Carolyn Satz, Tidewater Community College–Chesapeake

Kathy Saxton, Bryant & Stratton College

Brian Schmoldt, Madison College

Wilson Seda, Lehman College–CUNY

Perry Sellers, Lonestar College–North Harris

James Shimko, Ferris State University

Philip Slater, Forsyth Technical Community College

Clayton Smith, Columbia College Chicago

Patricia Smith, DePaul University

Jane Stam, Onondaga Community College

Tracy Stant, Indian River State College

Natalie Strouse, Notre Dame College

Erica Teague-Friend, Gwinnett Technical College

Louis Terrero, Lehman College

Geoff Tickell, Indiana University of Pennsylvania

Judith A. Toland, Bucks County Community College

Debra Touhey, Ocean County College

Jim Ulmer, Angelina College

Bob Urell, Irvine Valley College

Kevin Veneskey, Ivy Tech Community College

Teresa Walker, North Carolina A&T University

Terri Walsh, Seminole State College of Florida

Eric Weinstein, Suffolk County Community College, Brentwood

Andy Welchel, Greenville Technical College

Joe Welker, College of Western Idaho

Jean Wells, Howard University

Denise White, Austin Community College

**Jonathan M. Wild,** Oklahoma State University

**Lynne Wisdom,** Mineral Area College

**Kenneth Wise,** Wilkes Community College

**Shondra Woessner,** Holyoke Community College

**Mindy Wolfe,** Arizona State University

**Wanda Wong,** Chabot College

**Jan Workman,** East Carolina University

**Ray Wurtzburger,** New River Community College

**Lori Zaher,** Bucks County Community College

**Judith Zander,** Grossmont College

**Jessie Zetnick,** Texas Woman's University

**Laurence Zuckerman,** Fulton-Montgomery Community College

Many talented educators and professionals have worked hard to create the materials for this text, and for their efforts, we're grateful. **We extend a special thank you to our contributing and technology supplement authors, who have worked so diligently to support this text.**

**Contributing Author, Connect Content, Applying Excel, General Ledger Problems,** and **Exercise PowerPoints:**
Kathleen O'Donnell, *Onondaga Community College*

**Smartbook Author, Concept Overview Videos, PowerPoint Presentations,** and **Instructor Resource Manual:**
April Mohr, *Jefferson Community and Technical College, SW*

**Text and Supplements Accuracy Checkers:** Dave Krug, *Johnson County Community College;* Mark McCarthy, *East Carolina University;* Helen Roybark, *Radford University;* and Brian Schmoldt, *Madison College*

Special recognition extends to the entire team at McGraw Hill Education: Tim Vertovec, Steve Schuetz, Natalie King, Claire McLemore, Julie Wolfe, Michele Janicek, Christina Sanders, Michael McCormick, Fran Simon, Xin Lin, Kevin Moran, Brian Nacik, Missy Homer, Sandy Ludovissy, and Matt Diamond. We could not have published this new edition without your efforts.

*John J. Wild     Ken W. Shaw*

# Brief Contents

# Contents

# Managerial Accounting

# 1 Managerial Accounting Concepts and Principles

## Chapter Preview

### MANAGERIAL ACCOUNTING BASICS

**C1** Introducing managerial accounting

Fraud and ethics

Career paths

**NTK 1-1**

### COST CONCEPTS

**C2** Direct vs. indirect

Manufacturing costs

Prime vs. conversion

Product vs. period

**NTK 1-2**

### REPORTING

**P1** Manufacturer vs. merchandiser vs. service company

Balance sheet

Income statement

**NTK 1-3**

### COST FLOWS

**C3** Flow of activities

**P2** Schedule of cost of goods manufactured

**C4** Trends

**A1** Inventory analysis

**NTK 1-4**

## Learning Objectives

### CONCEPTUAL

**C1** Explain the roles and ethics of managerial accounting.

**C2** Describe accounting concepts useful in classifying costs.

**C3** Explain manufacturing activities and the flow of manufacturing costs.

**C4** Describe trends in managerial accounting.

### ANALYTICAL

**A1** Assess raw materials inventory management using raw materials inventory turnover and days' sales in raw materials inventory.

### PROCEDURAL

**P1** Prepare an income statement and balance sheet for a manufacturer.

**P2** Prepare a schedule of cost of goods manufactured and explain its purpose and links to financial statements.

# Best Face Forward

*"Use digital media to drive business"*—**TEANNA BASS**

ST. LOUIS—Teanna Bass dreamed of her own cosmetics business. After some research, and a company name from her twin sister, Teanna launched **Sweet Tea Cosmetics** in her college's student union. Teanna's goal: "Give the customer the best experience."

Getting the right materials was Teanna's first step. She chose to buy her cosmetics rather than make them herself. "Sourcing is very important," explains Teanna. She chose her supplier in part for its sustainable business practices such as using glass containers instead of plastic.

Teanna next set up her accounting system, which required basic managerial principles and cost classifications. Though not an accounting major, Teanna drew on her introductory accounting courses, and guidance from her aunt (an accountant), to keep her records. "I do it all," admits Teanna.

Analytics and visualization through social media are key to Teanna's strategy. She uses analytics—likes per post, comments per post, profile visits, website clicks—to measure follower engagement. This helped Teanna double her Instagram followers and increase revenues. "The right picture at the right time" is crucial, says Teanna.

Teanna continues to study business-to-business development and is considering a subscription model. She uses a *four-H model*—"be humble, have a heart, ask for help, and be hungry." Adds Teanna, "Be passionate about what you do."

Courtesy of Teanna Bass/photographer Chelsea Priebe

Sources: Sweet Tea Cosmetics *Facebook*, January 2021; *Columbia Missourian*, November 2018; *Vox magazine*, December 2018; Author interview, July 2019

## MANAGERIAL ACCOUNTING BASICS

**Managerial accounting** provides financial and nonfinancial information to an organization's managers. Managers control or direct a company or one of its many parts. Examples are an employee in charge of a company division, the head of marketing, the information technology officer, the human resources head, and top-level managers such as the chief executive officer (CEO) and chief financial officer (CFO). This section explains the purpose of managerial accounting (also called *management accounting*) and compares it with financial accounting.

**C1**
Explain the roles and ethics of managerial accounting.

### Purpose of Managerial Accounting

Managerial accounting provides useful information to aid in

- Determining the costs of an organization's products and services.
- Planning future activities.
- Comparing actual results to planned results.

For example, managerial accounting helps marketing managers decide whether to advertise on social media such as **Twitter**. Managerial accounting also helps **Google**'s information technology manager decide whether to buy new computers.

The managerial accounting system collects cost information and assigns it to an organization's products and services. Costs are important to managers because they impact the financial position and profitability of a business. Costs are also important for decisions such as product pricing, profitability analysis, and whether to make or buy a product.

Much of managerial accounting involves gathering information for planning and control. **Planning** is the process of setting goals and making plans to achieve them. Companies make long-term strategic plans that usually span 5 to 10 years. Strategic plans are then turned into short-term *action plans,* which are more concrete with better-defined goals. A short-term action plan that includes dollar amounts is known as a *budget.*

**Control** is the process of monitoring and evaluating an organization's activities and employees. Feedback from the control function helps managers compare actual results with planned results and take corrective actions. Exhibit 1.1 shows the relation between planning and control and the types of questions managerial accounting helps answer.

**EXHIBIT 1.1**

Planning and Control

**Planning**
- Build a new factory?
- Develop new products?
- Expand into new markets?

Strategy

Evaluation

**Control**
- Are costs too high?
- Are services profitable?
- Are customers satisfied?

# Nature of Managerial Accounting

Exhibit 1.2 highlights key differences between managerial accounting and financial accounting.

**EXHIBIT 1.2**

Managerial Accounting vs.
Financial Accounting

| Attribute | Financial Accounting | Managerial Accounting |
|---|---|---|
| | "This company's outlook is good. I'll buy its stock." | "This product is selling well. We'll make more." |
| Users | External users: Investors, creditors, and others outside of the company's managers | Internal users: Managerial and executive employees inside the company |
| Purpose | Help external users make investment, credit, and other decisions | Help managers make planning and control decisions |
| Flexibility of reporting | Structured and controlled by GAAP | Relatively flexible (no GAAP rules) |
| Timeliness | Often available only after an audit | Available quickly without an audit |
| Time dimension | Past performance using historical information. | Current performance and future projections using mostly real-time information |
| Focus | The whole company | A company's projects, processes, and divisions |
| Nature | Monetary information | Mostly monetary; some nonmonetary |

**Users of Accounting Information**   Companies report to different groups of decision makers. Financial accounting information is provided primarily to external users including investors, creditors, and regulators. Managerial accounting information is provided primarily to internal managerial and executive employees who are in charge of a company's business activities.

**Purpose of Information**   External users of financial accounting information often decide whether to invest in or lend to a company. Internal decision makers use managerial accounting information to understand, analyze, plan, and control company activities.

**Flexibility of Reporting**   Financial accounting follows concepts and rules known as generally accepted accounting principles (GAAP) to provide consistency and comparability of financial statements across companies. Managerial accounting provides internal information and is more flexible (not rules-based), reflecting the needs of managers to analyze, plan, and control products and processes.

**Timeliness of Information**   Financial accounting provides information to external users following required time periods (such as annual and quarterly). Many financial statements are delayed until an audit is done. Managerial accounting provides information to internal users as they request it. This can be as immediate and frequent as demanded.

**Time Dimension**   External users of financial accounting information get historical reports using information that is often months old. Internal users of managerial accounting information often get real-time reports that are used to evaluate current performance, plan future activities, and make projections.

**Focus of Information**   External users of financial accounting information often focus on the performance of a company as a whole for investing and lending decisions. Internal users of managerial accounting information often focus on a specific activity, product, department, or division for which they are responsible. For example, an investor of **Apple** might focus on income growth. An Apple production manager might focus on cost control at its Mac production facility.

**Nature of Information**   Both financial and managerial accounting reports have monetary information. Managerial accounting reports also have *nonmonetary* information, which includes customer and employee satisfaction data, percentage of on-time deliveries, product defect rates, energy from renewable sources, and employee diversity.

## Fraud and Ethics in Managerial Accounting

Fraud affects all business and it is costly: The Association of Certified Fraud Examiners (ACFE) estimates the average U.S. business loses 5% of its revenues to fraud.

The fraud triangle in Exhibit 1.3 shows *three* factors that push a person to commit fraud.

- **Opportunity**. A person must be able to commit fraud with a low risk of getting caught.
- **Pressure**, or incentive. A person must feel pressure or have incentive to commit fraud.
- **Rationalization**, or attitude. A person justifies fraud or does not see its criminal nature.

### Implications of Fraud for Managerial Accounting   The key to stopping fraud is prevention. It is less expensive and more effective to prevent fraud than to detect it. To help prevent fraud, managers set up internal controls. An **internal control system** is procedures managers use to

- Ensure reliable accounting.
- Protect assets.
- Uphold company policies.
- Promote efficiency.

Combating fraud requires ethics in accounting. **Ethics** are beliefs that distinguish right from wrong. They are accepted standards of good and bad behavior. The **Institute of Management Accountants (IMA)** requires that management accountants be competent, maintain confidentiality, act with integrity, and communicate information in a fair and credible manner.

## Career Paths

Managerial accountants are highly regarded, and their professional standing is sometimes denoted by a certificate. Certified management accountants (CMAs) must meet education and experience requirements, pass an exam, and be ethical. Many accounting specialists hold certificates in addition to or instead of the CMA. One of the most common is certified public accountant (CPA). Employers also want specialists with designations such as certified financial manager (CFM), certified internal auditor (CIA), certified bookkeeper (CB), certified payroll professional (CPP), certified fraud examiner (CFE), and certified forensic accountant (CrFA).

Managerial accountants are in demand. Exhibit 1.4 reports average annual salaries for several accounting positions. Salaries vary based on location, company size, and other factors.

**EXHIBIT 1.3**

Fraud Triangle

Joe Prachatree/Shutterstock

**EXHIBIT 1.4**

Accounting Salaries

| Top-Level Managers | Annual Salary |
|---|---|
| Chief financial officer (CFO) | $290,000 |
| Controller/Treasurer | 180,000 |

| Senior-Level Managers | Annual Salary |
|---|---|
| Division controller | $130,000 |
| General manager | 105,000 |

| Mid- and Entry-Level Jobs | Annual Salary |
|---|---|
| Financial analyst | $85,000 |
| Senior accountant | 85,000 |
| Junior accountant | 60,000 |

Managerial accounting skills are highly valued and are useful in many careers.

- **Marketing** uses sales and cost data to decide which products to promote.
- **Management** uses sales staff performance data for bonuses.
- **Entrepreneurs** use costs, budgets, and financial reports for financing.
- **Decision makers** in both for-profit and non profit organizations use accounting data to make informed decisions and secure financing from donors.

Caia Image/Image Source

### Analytics Insight

**Jump Start** Kickstarter's crowdfunding site allows budding entrepreneurs to seek financing. Analytics can be used to tailor one's pitch—most successfully funded projects seek less than $10,000. About 37% of all projects are fully funded, with over 60% of theater and dance projects funded, but less than 30% of fashion and food projects funded. ■

---

**NEED-TO-KNOW 1-1**

Managerial Accounting Basics

**C1**

Do More: QS 1-1, E 1-1

Following are aspects of accounting information. Classify each as relating more to financial accounting or to managerial accounting.

1. Primary users are external
2. Includes more nonmonetary information
3. Focuses more on the future
4. Uses many estimates and projections
5. Controlled by GAAP
6. Used in managers' planning decisions
7. Focuses on the whole organization
8. Not constrained by GAAP

***Solution***

| | Financial | Managerial |
|---|---|---|
| 1. Primary users are external . . . . . . . . . . . . . . | X | |
| 2. Includes more nonmonetary information. . . | | X |
| 3. Focuses more on the future . . . . . . . . . . . . | | X |
| 4. Uses many estimates and projections . . . . . | | X |

| | Financial | Managerial |
|---|---|---|
| 5. Controlled by GAAP. . . . . . . . . . . . . . . . . . | X | |
| 6. Used in managers' planning decisions . . . | | X |
| 7. Focuses on the whole organization . . . . . . | X | |
| 8. Not constrained by GAAP . . . . . . . . . . . . . | | X |

---

# COST CONCEPTS

**C2**

Describe accounting concepts useful in classifying costs.

This section explains how to classify costs. We demonstrate these cost classifications with Rocky Mountain Bikes, a manufacturer of bicycles.

## Direct versus Indirect

Costs can be classified as direct or indirect, depending on their link to a cost object. A **cost object** is a product, process, department, or customer to which costs are assigned. Rocky Mountain Bikes' cost object is a bicycle.

- **Direct costs** are costs that *can* be cost-effectively traced to a cost object and consist of direct materials and direct labor. *Direct materials* for a bicycle include tires, frame, seat, chain, and so on. *Direct labor* for a bicycle includes wages and benefits of the workers making the bikes. See Exhibit 1.5.
- **Indirect costs** are costs that *cannot* be cost-effectively traced to a cost object. Indirect costs include the salary of a manufacturing supervisor, who monitors production but does not actually make bikes. That supervisor's salary cannot be directly traced to bikes. Another example of indirect costs is the wages of maintenance department employees who clean the factory. These wages cannot be directly traced to bikes.

Exhibit 1.5 lists examples of direct and indirect costs for a bicycle manufacturer.

**EXHIBIT 1.5**

Direct and Indirect Costs

| Direct Costs (for bicycle) | | Indirect Costs (for bicycle) |
|---|---|---|
| • Tires | • Frames | • Factory accounting |
| • Seats | • Chains | • Factory administration |
| • Handlebars | • Brakes | • Factory rent |
| • Cables | • Pedals | • Factory manager's salary |
| • Bike maker | • Bike maker | • Factory light and heat |
|   wages |   benefits | • Factory insurance |
| | | • Factory equipment depreciation* |
| | | *Except units-of-production. |

## Manufacturing Costs

### Direct Materials
**Direct materials** are materials that are crucial parts of a finished product. **Direct materials costs** are costs for direct materials that *can* be cost-effectively traced through the manufacturing process to finished goods. Examples of direct materials in manufacturing a bike include its tires, seat, frame, pedals, brakes, cables, gears, and handlebars.

### Direct Labor
**Direct labor** refers to employees who directly convert materials to finished goods. **Direct labor costs** are the wages and benefits for direct labor that *can* be cost-effectively traced through the manufacturing process to finished goods. Examples of direct labor in manufacturing a bike include operators directly converting raw materials into finished goods (welding, painting, forming) and assembly workers who attach materials such as tires, seats, pedals, and brakes.

### Factory Overhead
**Factory overhead,** also called *manufacturing overhead* or *overhead,* includes all manufacturing costs that are not direct materials or direct labor. **Factory overhead costs** are manufacturing costs that *cannot* be cost-effectively traced to finished goods. Factory overhead costs include indirect materials, indirect labor, and other indirect costs.

- **Indirect materials** are materials used in manufacturing that *cannot* be cost-effectively traced to finished goods. Materials are often classified as indirect materials when their costs are low. Examples include screws and nuts used in assembling bikes, and staples and glue used in manufacturing shoes.
- **Indirect labor** is labor needed in manufacturing that *cannot* be cost-effectively traced to finished goods. Indirect labor costs are the costs of workers who assist in or supervise manufacturing. Examples include costs for employees who maintain and repair manufacturing equipment and salaries of production supervisors. Those workers do not assemble products but are indirectly involved in production.
- *Other indirect costs* include factory utilities (water, gas, electricity), factory rent, depreciation on factory buildings and equipment, factory insurance, and property taxes on factory buildings.

**Typical Manufacturing Costs**

Direct materials
+ Direct labor
+ Factory overhead
= Total manufacturing costs

## Prime and Conversion Costs

We can classify product costs into prime costs or conversion costs as in Exhibit 1.6.

- **Prime costs** consist of direct materials costs and direct labor costs.
- **Conversion costs** are costs incurred in converting raw materials to finished goods. Conversion costs consist of direct labor and factory overhead.

Conversion Costs

Direct Materials    Direct Labor    Overhead

Prime Costs

**EXHIBIT 1.6**

Prime Costs and Conversion Costs

Conversion costs =
Direct labor + Factory overhead

Prime costs =
Direct materials + Direct labor

# Product versus Period Costs

Costs can be classified as product costs or period costs. Exhibit 1.7 lists product and period costs for a bicycle manufacturer.

- **Product costs** are production costs necessary to create a product and consist of direct materials, direct labor, and factory overhead. Product costs are added to inventory, or *capitalized*, during manufacturing of products. When products are sold, these costs are expensed as cost of goods sold.

- **Period costs** are nonproduction costs linked to a time period (not to specific products). Period costs are expensed in the period when incurred and reported on the income statement as either selling expenses or general and administrative expenses. Common examples of selling expenses are advertising, delivery, and salesperson salaries, commissions, and travel expenses. Common examples of general and administrative expenses are office accounting expenses, office employee wages, office rent, depreciation on office equipment, and office manager salaries. For a manufacturer, period costs are also called *nonmanufacturing costs*.

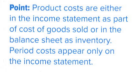

**EXHIBIT 1.7**

Product and Period Costs

| Product Costs (for bicycle) | | | Period Costs (for bicycle) | |
|---|---|---|---|---|
| **Direct Costs** | | **Indirect Costs** | **Selling Expenses** | **General & Administrative Expenses** |
| • Tires<br>• Seats<br>• Handlebars<br>• Cables<br>• Bike maker wages | • Frames<br>• Chains<br>• Brakes<br>• Pedals<br>• Bike maker benefits | • Factory accounting<br>• Factory rent<br>• Factory manager's salary<br>• Factory light and heat<br>• Factory Insurance<br>• Factory equipment depreciation*<br>*Except units-of-production. | • Advertising<br>• Promotional materials<br>• Salesperson salaries<br>• Salesperson commissions<br>• Salesperson travel<br>• Salesperson smartphone | • Office accounting<br>• Office employee wages<br>• Office rent<br>• Office equipment depreciation<br>• Office insurance<br>• Office manager's salary |

**Reporting Product and Period Costs**   Exhibit 1.8 shows the financial statement effects of product and period costs.

- Period costs go directly to the current income statement as expenses.
- Product costs are first assigned to inventory. They move to cost of goods sold when inventory is sold.

**Point:** Product costs are either in the income statement as part of cost of goods sold or in the balance sheet as inventory. Period costs appear only on the income statement.

Product costs assigned to inventory that is sold in 2021 are reported on the 2021 income statement as cost of goods sold. Product costs assigned to inventory not sold in 2021 are reported on the 2021 balance sheet. If this inventory is sold in 2022, product costs assigned to it are reported as cost of goods sold in the 2022 income statement.

**EXHIBIT 1.8**

Product and Period Costs in Financial Statements

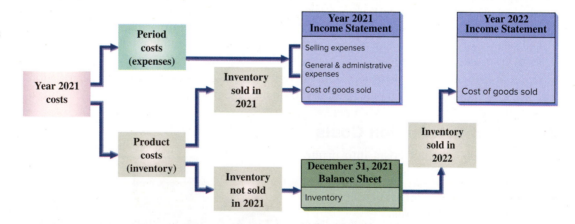

# Cost Concepts for Service Companies

Managers in service companies apply cost concepts. A **Southwest Airlines** manager traces flight crew salaries, food, fuel, and oil costs to specific flights. These are *direct costs* of a flight. Southwest does not trace *indirect costs* such as ground crew wages to specific flights. (Classification as product versus period costs is not relevant to service companies as costs of services are not reported in inventory.) Travel agent fees and office manager salaries are neither directly nor indirectly related to flights.

Service companies can also classify costs into direct materials, direct labor, overhead, selling, or general and administrative costs. Selling expenses and General and administrative expenses for a service company are period costs unrelated to performing its services.

Exhibit 1.9 lists cost classifications for an airline when the cost object is a flight. No matter how each cost is classified, all service company costs are expensed when incurred.

Digital Vision/PunchStock

**EXHIBIT 1.9**

Service Company Cost Classification

| Costs for Airline Company | Direct or Indirect | Cost Classification |
|---|---|---|
| Beverages and snacks . . . . . . . . . | Direct | Direct materials |
| Pilot salaries . . . . . . . . . . . . . . . . | Direct | Direct labor |
| Flight attendant salaries. . . . . . . . | Direct | Direct labor |
| Fuel and oil costs . . . . . . . . . . . . . | Direct | Direct materials |
| Travel agent fees . . . . . . . . . . . . . | Neither | Selling |
| Ground crew wages . . . . . . . . . . . | Indirect | Overhead |
| Maintenance crew wages . . . . . . | Indirect | Overhead |
| Office manager salary . . . . . . . . . | Neither | General and administrative |

### Decision Maker

**Entrepreneur**   You wish to trace as many of your assembly department's direct costs as possible. You can trace 90% of them in a cost-effective manner. To trace the other 10%, you need sophisticated and costly accounting software. Do you buy this software? ■   *Answer:* Tracing costs directly to cost objects is desirable if it is cost-effective. If the cost of purchasing and maintaining the software is greater than the benefit of tracing the other 10%, do not buy the software.

Following are selected costs of a computer chip manufacturer. Classify each as either a product cost or a period cost. Then classify each of the product costs as direct material, direct labor, or overhead.

1. Plastic boards used to mount chips
2. Advertising
3. Factory maintenance salaries
4. Sales office rent
5. Factory rent
6. Factory supervisor salary
7. Depreciation on factory equipment
8. Assembly worker hourly pay to make chips

**NEED-TO-KNOW 1-2**

Cost Classification

C2

***Solution***

| | Product Cost | | | Period Cost |
|---|---|---|---|---|
| | Direct Material | Direct Labor | Overhead | |
| 1. Plastic boards used to mount chips . . . . . . . . | X | | | |
| 2. Advertising . . . . . . . . . . . . . . . . . . . . . . . . . | | | | X |
| 3. Factory maintenance salaries. . . . . . . . . . . . . | | | X | |
| 4. Sales office rent . . . . . . . . . . . . . . . . . . . . . . | | | | X |
| 5. Factory rent. . . . . . . . . . . . . . . . . . . . . . . . . . | | | X | |
| 6. Factory supervisor salary . . . . . . . . . . . . . . . . | | | X | |
| 7. Depreciation on factory equipment . . . . . . . . . | | | X | |
| 8. Assembly worker hourly pay to make chips . . . | | X | | |

Do More: QS 1-2, QS 1-3, QS 1-4, E 1-5, E 1-6

## REPORTING

Companies with manufacturing activities differ from both merchandising and service companies.

- **Target** is a merchandiser. It buys and sells goods without physically changing them.
- **Adidas** is a manufacturer of shoes and apparel. It purchases materials such as cloth, dye, plastic, glue, and laces and converts them to products.

**P1**

Prepare an income statement and balance sheet for a manufacturer.

- **Southwest Airlines** is a service company that transports people.
- **Best Buy** is a merchandiser that also provides services via Geek Squad, showing that some companies pursue multiple activities.

Because manufacturing activities are different than those for merchandising and service companies, their reporting is different.

## Reporting Inventory on the Balance Sheet

**Point:** Materials that *cannot* be cost-effectively traced to a product (such as staples or glue) are called indirect materials and included in overhead.

Manufacturers report three types of inventories: raw materials, work in process, and finished goods.

### Raw Materials Inventory
**Raw materials inventory** is the cost of materials a company acquires to use in making products. Raw materials that *can* be cost-effectively traced to a product are called *direct materials* and are included in raw materials inventory.

### Work in Process Inventory
**Work in process inventory,** also called *goods in process inventory,* consists of the costs of direct materials, direct labor, and overhead for partially completed products.

### Finished Goods Inventory
**Finished goods inventory** consists of the costs of direct materials, direct labor, and overhead of completed products ready for sale.

### Manufacturer Balance Sheet
The current assets section of the balance sheet for a manufacturer is different than that for merchandising and service companies. A manufacturer reports three types of inventory, a merchandiser reports only merchandise inventory, and a service company usually reports no inventory. Exhibit 1.10 shows the current assets section of the balance sheet for a service company, a merchandiser, and a manufacturer.

**EXHIBIT 1.10**

Balance Sheets

| Service Company | | Merchandising Company | | Manufacturing Company | |
|---|---|---|---|---|---|
| **NORTHEAST AIR** Current assets section of Balance Sheet December 31 | | **TELE-MART** Current assets section of Balance Sheet December 31 | | **ROCKY MOUNTAIN BIKES** Current assets section of Balance Sheet December 31 | |
| **Assets** | | **Assets** | | **Assets** | |
| Current assets | | Current assets | | Current assets | |
| Cash | $11,000 | Cash | $11,000 | Cash | $11,000 |
| Accounts receivable, net | 30,150 | Accounts receivable, net | 30,150 | Accounts receivable, net | 30,150 |
| | | Merchandise inventory | 21,000 | Raw materials inventory | 9,000 |
| | | | | Work in process inventory | 7,500 |
| | | | | Finished goods inventory | 10,300 |
| Supplies | 350 | Supplies | 350 | Supplies | 350 |
| Prepaid insurance | 300 | Prepaid insurance | 300 | Prepaid insurance | 300 |
| Total current assets | $41,800 | Total current assets | $62,800 | Total current assets | $68,600 |

## Reporting Cost of Goods Sold on the Income Statement

The main difference between the income statement of a manufacturer and that of a merchandiser is the content of cost of goods sold.

### Computing Cost of Goods Sold
Exhibit 1.11 compares the calculation of cost of goods sold for a merchandiser with that for a manufacturer.

- *Merchandisers* add cost of merchandise purchased to beginning merchandise inventory and then subtract ending merchandise inventory to compute cost of goods sold.
- *Manufacturers* add cost of goods manufactured to beginning finished goods inventory and then subtract ending finished goods inventory to compute cost of goods sold.

| Merchandiser | Beginning merchandise inventory | + | Cost of merchandise purchased | − | Ending merchandise inventory | = | Cost of goods sold |
| Manufacturer | Beginning finished goods inventory | + | Cost of goods manufactured | − | Ending finished goods inventory | = | Cost of goods sold |

**EXHIBIT 1.11**

Cost of Goods Sold Computation

Key differences in computing cost of goods sold between merchandisers and manufacturers follow.

- Merchandisers have *merchandise inventory*. Manufacturers have *finished goods inventory*.
- Merchandisers have cost of merchandise *purchased*. This is the cost of buying products to sell.
- Manufacturers have cost of goods *manufactured*. This is the cost of direct materials, direct labor, and factory overhead in making finished goods.

### Reporting Cost of Goods Sold

Exhibit 1.12 highlights differences in the reporting of cost of goods sold on the income statement for a service, a merchandising, and a manufacturing company. Because a service company does not make or buy inventory to sell, it does not report cost of goods sold.

**EXHIBIT 1.12**

Income Statements

| Service Company | Merchandising Company | Manufacturing Company |

**NORTHEAST AIR**
Income Statement
For Year Ended December 31

| | |
|---|---|
| Revenues | $310,000 |
| | |
| | |
| | |
| | |
| | |
| | |
| | |
| Selling expenses | 209,600 |
| Gen. & admin. exp. | 54,400 |
| Net income | $ 46,000 |

**TELE-MART**
Income Statement
For Year Ended December 31

| | |
|---|---|
| Sales | $310,000 |
| Cost of goods sold | |
| Merchandise inventory, beginning | 14,200 |
| Cost of merchandise purchased | 169,300 |
| Goods available for sale | 183,500 |
| Less merchandise inventory, ending | 12,100 |
| Cost of goods sold | 171,400 |
| Gross profit | 138,600 |
| Selling expenses | 38,200 |
| General and admin. expenses | 54,400 |
| Net income | $ 46,000 |

**ROCKY MOUNTAIN BIKES**
Income Statement
For Year Ended December 31

| | |
|---|---|
| Sales | $310,000 |
| Cost of goods sold | |
| Finished goods inventory, beginning | 11,200 |
| Cost of goods manufactured | 170,500 |
| Goods available for sale | 181,700 |
| Less finished goods inventory, ending | 10,300 |
| Cost of goods sold | 171,400 |
| Gross profit | 138,600 |
| Selling expenses | 38,200 |
| General and admin. expenses | 54,400 |
| Net income | $ 46,000 |

Use the following information for the month ended April 30 from a manufacturing company and from a merchandising company to prepare an income statement for each company.

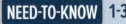 **NEED-TO-KNOW 1-3**

Preparing an Income Statement

**P1**

**Built-Rite Manufacturer**

| | |
|---|---|
| Sales | $360 |
| Cash | 750 |
| Selling expenses | 65 |
| General and admin. expenses | 55 |
| Finished goods inventory, ending | 20 |
| Cost of goods manufactured | 120 |
| Finished goods inventory, beginning | 105 |

**SaveMart Merchandiser**

| | |
|---|---|
| Merchandise inventory, ending | $100 |
| Selling expenses | 50 |
| Sales | 325 |
| General and admin. expenses | 28 |
| Cost of merchandise purchased | 180 |
| Accounts receivable | 125 |
| Merchandise inventory, beginning | 110 |

**Solution**

| Built-Rite Manufacturer Income Statement For Month Ended April 30 | | |
|---|---:|---:|
| Sales......................... | | $360 |
| Cost of goods sold | | |
| Finished goods inventory, beginning..... | $105 | |
| Cost of goods manufactured ........... | 120 | |
| Goods available for sale.............. | 225 | |
| Less finished goods inventory, ending.... | 20 | |
| Cost of goods sold ................... | | 205 |
| Gross profit........................... | | 155 |
| Selling expenses ..................... | | 65 |
| General and admin. expenses ......... | | 55 |
| Net income........................... | | $ 35 |

| SaveMart Merchandiser Income Statement For Month Ended April 30 | | |
|---|---:|---:|
| Sales......................... | | $325 |
| Cost of goods sold | | |
| Merchandise inventory, beginning..... | $110 | |
| Cost of merchandise purchased....... | 180 | |
| Goods available for sale............. | 290 | |
| Less merchandise inventory, ending ... | 100 | |
| Cost of goods sold ................. | | 190 |
| Gross profit.......................... | | 135 |
| Selling expenses ..................... | | 50 |
| General and admin. expenses .......... | | 28 |
| Net income........................... | | $ 57 |

Do More: QS 1-7 through QS 1-11, E 1-10, E 1-11

# COST FLOWS AND COST OF GOODS MANUFACTURED

**C3**

Explain manufacturing activities and the flow of manufacturing costs.

## Flow of Manufacturing Activities

Exhibit 1.13 shows the flow of manufacturing activities and their cost flows. Looking across the top row, the activities flow consists of *materials activity* followed by *production activity* followed by *sales activity*.

**EXHIBIT 1.13**

Activities and Cost Flows in Manufacturing

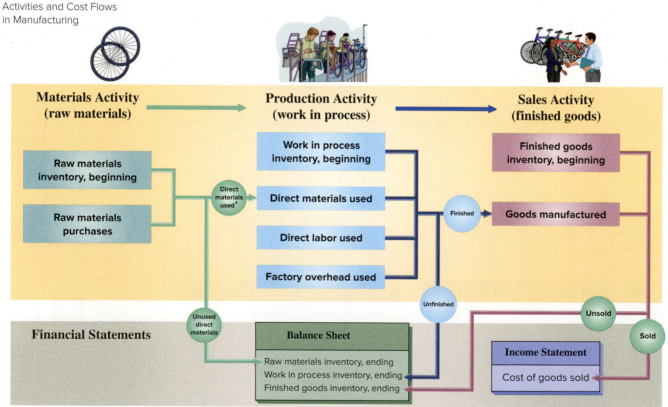

†Indirect materials are $0 in this example. If there were indirect materials used, another line would extend from Raw materials to Factory overhead.

**Materials Activity**    The left side of Exhibit 1.13 shows the flow of raw materials. Manufacturers usually start a period with beginning raw materials inventory left over from the prior period. The company then buys more raw materials in the current period. Adding these purchases to beginning inventory gives *total raw materials available for use* in production. These raw materials are then either used in production in the current period or remain in raw materials inventory at the end of the period for use in future periods.

RM Inventory, beginning
+ RM Purchases
= Total RM available for use

**Production Activity**    The middle section of Exhibit 1.13 describes production activity. Manufacturers usually start a period with beginning work in process inventory, which equals the costs of partially complete products from prior periods. Production then adds the costs of direct materials, direct labor, and factory overhead for the current period. Production activity results in products that are either finished or unfinished at the end of the period.

- Total cost of direct materials, direct labor, and factory overhead for *finished* products makes up the **cost of goods manufactured.** That amount is carried over to the current period income statement in the computation of cost of goods sold.
- Total cost of direct materials, direct labor, and factory overhead for *unfinished* products makes up ending work in process inventory. That amount is carried over to the current period balance sheet.

**Sales Activity**    The right side of Exhibit 1.13 shows the flow of finished goods. Manufacturers usually start a period with beginning finished goods inventory, which is the cost of unsold finished goods from prior periods. Adding this to the cost of newly completed units (goods manufactured) equals *total finished goods available for sale* in the current period. The cost of finished goods sold is reported on the income statement. The cost of any finished goods not sold is reported as a current asset, *finished goods inventory,* on the balance sheet.

FG Inventory, beginning
+ Cost of goods manufactured
= Total FG available for sale

## Schedule of Cost of Goods Manufactured

Manufacturing activities are described in a report called a **schedule of cost of goods manufactured** (also called a *manufacturing statement* or a *statement of cost of goods manufactured*). This schedule lists the types and amounts of costs incurred in manufacturing. Exhibit 1.14 shows the schedule of cost of goods manufactured for Rocky Mountain Bikes.

**P2**

Prepare a schedule of cost of goods manufactured and explain its purpose and links to financial statements.

**EXHIBIT 1.14**

Schedule of Cost of Goods Manufactured

**Point:** Indirect materials are $0 in this example. If there were indirect materials, we would subtract that from materials used to get direct materials used *and* indirect materials would be listed under factory overhead.

| ROCKY MOUNTAIN BIKES Schedule of Cost of Goods Manufactured For Year Ended December 31 | | |
|---|---:|---:|
| **Direct materials** | | |
| Raw materials inventory, beginning ...... | $ 8,000 | |
| Raw materials purchases............... | 86,500 | |
| Raw materials available for use ......... | 94,500 | |
| Less raw materials inventory, ending ..... | 9,000 | |
| Direct materials used................. | | $ 85,500 |
| **Direct labor** ......................... | | 60,000 |
| **Factory overhead** | | |
| Indirect labor ....................... | 15,000 | |
| Factory utilities...................... | 2,600 | |
| Repairs—Factory equipment .......... | 2,500 | |
| Property taxes—Factory .............. | 4,400 | |
| Depreciation expense—Factory ......... | 5,500 | |
| Total factory overhead ............... | | 30,000 |
| Total manufacturing costs ............... | | 175,500 |
| Add work in process inventory, beginning ... | | 2,500 |
| Total cost of work in process ............. | | 178,000 |
| Less work in process inventory, ending ..... | | 7,500 |
| **Cost of goods manufactured**............ | | $170,500 |

The schedule has four parts: *direct materials, direct labor, overhead,* and *cost of goods manufactured.*

**Raw Materials Inventory**

| Beginning | 8,000 | | |
|---|---|---|---|
| Purchases | 86,500 | | |
| | | Direct Mtls. | 85,500 |
| Ending | 9,000 | | |

**Point:** This chapter's raw materials inventory excludes indirect materials. This aids students by simplifying the flow of costs in the first managerial chapter. The next chapter includes indirect materials.

**Work in Process Inventory**

| Beginning | 2,500 | | |
|---|---|---|---|
| Mfg. costs | 175,500 | | |
| | | COGM | 170,500 |
| Ending | 7,500 | | |

① **Compute direct materials used.** Add beginning raw materials inventory of $8,000 to the purchases of $86,500 to get $94,500 of raw materials available for use. A year-end count of inventory shows $9,000 of ending raw materials inventory. If $94,500 of materials were available for use and $9,000 of materials remain in inventory, then $85,500 of direct materials were used in the period.

② **Compute direct labor used.** Total direct labor costs are $60,000 for the period. This includes wages, payroll taxes, and benefits for workers who make bikes.

③ **Compute factory overhead used.** The schedule lists each factory overhead cost. All of these costs are *indirectly* related to manufacturing activities. (Period expenses, such as selling expenses and general and administrative expenses, are *not* reported on this schedule.) Total factory overhead is $30,000.

④ **Compute cost of goods manufactured.** Total manufacturing costs are $175,500 ($85,500 + $60,000 + $30,000), the sum of direct materials, direct labor, and overhead. We take the $175,500 total manufacturing costs and add the $2,500 beginning work in process inventory to get total work in process of $178,000. We then subtract the $7,500 ending work in process inventory to get cost of goods manufactured of $170,500. Cost of goods manufactured (COGM) is also called *net cost of goods manufactured* or *cost of goods completed.*

Key calculations in the schedule of costs of goods manufactured follow.

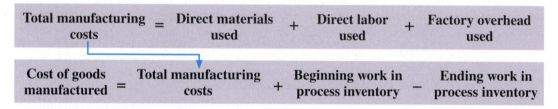

$$\text{Total manufacturing costs} = \text{Direct materials used} + \text{Direct labor used} + \text{Factory overhead used}$$

$$\text{Cost of goods manufactured} = \text{Total manufacturing costs} + \text{Beginning work in process inventory} - \text{Ending work in process inventory}$$

Management uses the schedule of cost of goods manufactured to plan and control manufacturing activities. To provide timely information for business decisions, the schedule is often prepared monthly, weekly, or even daily.

**Estimating Cost per Unit**   Managers can use the schedule of cost of goods manufactured to estimate per unit costs. For example, if Rocky Mountain Bikes makes 1,000 bikes during the year, the average manufacturing cost per unit is $170.50 (computed as $170,500/1,000).

## Manufacturing Cost Flows across Accounting Reports

Cost information is used in financial statements. Exhibit 1.15 shows how product costs affect financial statements. Direct materials, direct labor, and overhead costs are in the schedule of cost of goods manufactured. The cost of goods manufactured from that schedule is used to compute cost of goods sold

**EXHIBIT 1.15**

Manufacturing Cost Flows across Reports

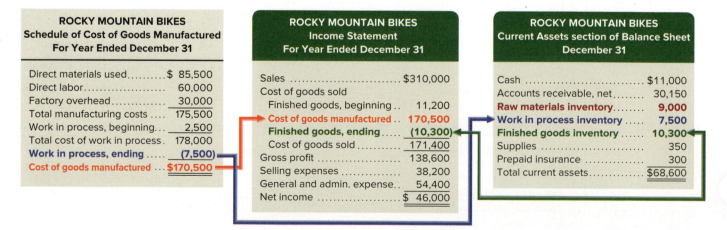

| ROCKY MOUNTAIN BIKES Schedule of Cost of Goods Manufactured For Year Ended December 31 | |
|---|---|
| Direct materials used......... | $ 85,500 |
| Direct labor.................... | 60,000 |
| Factory overhead............. | 30,000 |
| Total manufacturing costs .... | 175,500 |
| Work in process, beginning... | 2,500 |
| Total cost of work in process. | 178,000 |
| Work in process, ending ..... | (7,500) |
| Cost of goods manufactured ... | $170,500 |

| ROCKY MOUNTAIN BIKES Income Statement For Year Ended December 31 | |
|---|---|
| Sales ........................... | $310,000 |
| Cost of goods sold | |
| Finished goods, beginning .. | 11,200 |
| Cost of goods manufactured .. | 170,500 |
| Finished goods, ending ..... | (10,300) |
| Cost of goods sold .......... | 171,400 |
| Gross profit................. | 138,600 |
| Selling expenses ............. | 38,200 |
| General and admin. expense.. | 54,400 |
| Net income ................... | $ 46,000 |

| ROCKY MOUNTAIN BIKES Current Assets section of Balance Sheet December 31 | |
|---|---|
| Cash ............................ | $11,000 |
| Accounts receivable, net........ | 30,150 |
| Raw materials inventory........ | 9,000 |
| Work in process inventory ..... | 7,500 |
| Finished goods inventory ...... | 10,300 |
| Supplies ........................ | 350 |
| Prepaid insurance .............. | 300 |
| Total current assets............. | $68,600 |

on the income statement. The ending work in process inventory is carried from that schedule to the balance sheet, and the ending finished goods inventory is used in computing cost of goods sold on the income statement and is also part of current assets on the balance sheet.

**NEED-TO-KNOW 1-4**

Cost of Goods Manufactured

**P2  C3**

**Part A:** Compute the following three cost amounts using the information below.

    **1.** Direct materials used   **2.** Cost of goods manufactured   **3.** Cost of goods sold

| | | | | |
|---|---|---|---|---|
| Raw materials inventory, beginning . . . . . | $15,500 | Raw materials inventory, ending . . . . . . . . | $10,600 |
| Work in process inventory, beginning . . . . | 29,000 | Work in process inventory, ending . . . . . . | 44,000 |
| Finished goods inventory, beginning . . . . . | 24,000 | Finished goods inventory, ending . . . . . . . | 37,400 |
| Raw materials purchased . . . . . . . . . . . . . . | 66,000 | Direct labor used . . . . . . . . . . . . . . . . . . . . | 38,000 |
| Total factory overhead used . . . . . . . . . . . | 60,000 | | |

**Solution**

**1.** $70,900    **2.** $153,900    **3.** $140,500

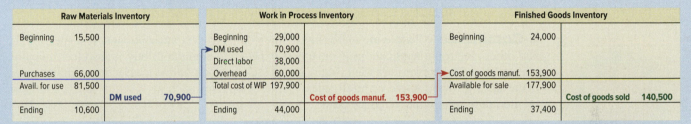

**Part B:** Prepare a schedule of cost of goods manufactured using information in Part A. Total factory overhead used of $60,000 consists of Indirect labor of $25,000, Depreciation expense—Factory of $32,000, and Factory utilities of $3,000.

**Solution**

| Schedule of Cost of Goods Manufactured | | |
|---|---:|---:|
| **Direct materials** | | |
|   Raw materials inventory, beginning . . . . . . | $15,500 | |
|   Raw materials purchases . . . . . . . . . . . . . . | 66,000 | |
|   Raw materials available for use . . . . . . . . . | 81,500 | |
|   Less raw materials inventory, ending . . . . . | 10,600 | |
|   Direct materials used . . . . . . . . . . . . . . . . . | | $ 70,900 |
| **Direct labor** . . . . . . . . . . . . . . . . . . . . . . . . | | 38,000 |
| **Factory overhead** | | |
|   Indirect labor . . . . . . . . . . . . . . . . . . . . . . . | 25,000 | |
|   Depreciation expense—Factory . . . . . . . . . | 32,000 | |
|   Factory utilities . . . . . . . . . . . . . . . . . . . . . | 3,000 | |
|   Total factory overhead . . . . . . . . . . . . . . . . | | 60,000 |
| Total manufacturing costs . . . . . . . . . . . . . . | | 168,900 |
| Add work in process inventory, beginning . . . | | 29,000 |
| Total cost of work in process . . . . . . . . . . . . | | 197,900 |
| Less work in process inventory, ending . . . . . | | 44,000 |
| **Cost of goods manufactured** . . . . . . . . . . . | | $153,900 |

Do More: QS 1-15, QS 1-16, E 1-7, E 1-13, E 1-15

# Trends in Managerial Accounting

Tools and techniques of managerial accounting evolve due to changes in business. This section describes some of these changes.

**C4**

Describe trends in managerial accounting.

## Digital Manufacturing

**Digital manufacturing** combines machines, computers, and human control to manufacture products. On the factory floor, machines replace much of direct labor. Computers collect information on these automated processes, including product quality, equipment performance, and maintenance demands. Humans then use data analytics and data visualization to plan and control operations. Growth of digital manufacturing means employers seek employees with data analytics and visualization skills.

- *Data analytics* is a process of analyzing data to identify meaningful relations and trends.
- *Data visualization* is a graphical depiction of data to help people interpret their meaning.

### Customer Orientation

There is increased emphasis on *customers*. Customers expect value for the money spent to buy products and services. They want the right service (or product) at the right time and the right price. This **customer orientation** means that managers and employees understand the changing needs of customers and align operations accordingly.

### Global Economy

Our *global economy* expands competitive boundaries and provides customers more choices. One notable case that reflects changes in customer demand and global competition is auto manufacturing. The top three Japanese auto manufacturers (**Honda**, **Nissan**, and **Toyota**) once controlled more than 40% of the U.S. auto market. Customers perceived that Japanese manufacturers provided value not available from others. Many European and North American manufacturers responded and regained much of the lost market share.

### E-Commerce

People are increasingly interconnected via smartphones, text messaging, and other electronic applications. Consumers expect and demand to buy items electronically, whenever and wherever they want. Many businesses focus on online transactions. Online sales make up a growing share of retail sales. Some companies such as **BucketFeet**, a footwear retailer, only sell online to reduce costs.

### Service Economy

Businesses that provide services, such as telecommunications and health care, constitute an ever-growing part of our economy. Service businesses typically account for over 60% of total economic activity. Many service companies, such as **Uber**, employ part-time workers. The "gig economy" changes cost structures.

### Lean Principles

Many companies have adopted a **lean business model,** whose goal is to *eliminate waste* while "satisfying the customer" and "providing a positive return" to the company. This is often paired with continuous improvement. **Continuous improvement** rejects the notion of "good enough" and challenges employees and managers to continuously improve operations. This has led companies to adopt practices such as total quality management (TQM) and just-in-time (JIT) manufacturing.

**Point:** Goals of a TQM process include reduced waste, better inventory control, fewer defects, and continuous improvement. JIT concepts have similar aims.

**Point:** Quality control standards include the International Organization for Standardization (ISO). To be certified under **ISO 9000 standards,** a company must use a quality control system and provide documentation.

**Point:** The time between buying raw materials and selling finished goods is called *throughput time*.

- **Total quality management** focuses on quality improvement to business activities. Managers and employees seek to uncover waste in business activities, including accounting activities such as payroll and disbursements. **Ritz Carlton Hotel** applies a set of values, called *The Gold Standards,* to improve customer service.
- **Just-in-time manufacturing** is a system that acquires inventory and produces products only after it receives an order (a *demand-pull* system) and then delivers orders on time. Processes are aligned to eliminate delays and inefficiencies. Companies must establish good communications with suppliers. On the downside, JIT is more susceptible to disruption. Several **General Motors** plants were temporarily shut down due to a strike at a supplier that provided components *just in time* to the assembly division.

### Value Chain

The **value chain** is the series of activities that add value to a company's products or services. Exhibit 1.16 illustrates a possible value chain for a retail cookie company.

**EXHIBIT 1.16**

Value Chain
(cookie retailer)

Acquire raw materials          Baking          Sales          Service

**How Lean Principles Impact the Value Chain**   Companies can use lean practices across the value chain to increase efficiency and profits. Managerial accounting is important in providing accurate cost and performance information to measure the "value" to customers. The price that customers pay for goods and services reflects on that value.

## Corporate Social Responsibility

**Corporate social responsibility (CSR)** is a concept that goes beyond shareholder value and the law. Corporations must consider the demands of other stakeholders, including employees, suppliers, and society. To reduce its impact on the environment, **Three Twins Ice Cream** uses only cups and spoons made from organic ingredients. **United By Blue**, an apparel and jewelry company, removes one pound of trash from waterways for every product sold. Many companies extend CSR to include sustainability, which considers future generations when making business decisions.

**Point:** Companies like **Microsoft**, **Google**, and **Walt Disney** disclose CSR results on their websites.

## Triple Bottom Line

**Triple bottom line** focuses on three measures: financial ("profits"), social ("people"), and environmental ("planet"). Adopting a triple bottom line impacts how businesses report. The **Sustainability Accounting Standards Board (SASB)** sets reporting standards for businesses' sustainability activities. The SASB has developed reporting standards for several sectors including health care, nonrenewable resources, and renewable resources and alternative energy.

■ **Decision Insight** ▬▬▬▬▬▬▬▬▬▬▬▬▬▬▬▬▬▬▬▬▬▬

**Balanced Scorecard**   The *balanced scorecard* aids continuous improvement by augmenting financial measures with information on the "drivers" (indicators) of future financial performance along four dimensions: **(1)** *financial*—profitability and risk, **(2)** *customer*—value creation and product and service differentiation, **(3)** *internal processes*—business activities that create customer and owner satisfaction, and **(4)** *innovation and learning*—organizational change, innovation, and growth. ■

 ## CORPORATE SOCIAL RESPONSIBILITY

The Sustainability Accounting Standards Board (SASB) considers sustainability information as *material* if its disclosure would affect the views of equity investors on a company's financial condition or operating performance. Material information can vary across industries. While environmental "planet" issues such as air quality, wastewater management, and biodiversity impacts are important for investments in the nonrenewable resources sectors, such issues are likely not as important for investments in banks. "People" issues such as diversity and inclusion, fair labor practices, and employee health are considered material for most sectors, and especially for sectors having high direct labor use.

**Sweet Tea Cosmetics**, this chapter's feature company, focuses on inclusivity and sustainability. "My makeup is for everybody," explains Teanna. Her makeup supplier uses safe, nontoxic ingredients; does not do animal testing; and aims to reduce its carbon footprint. Although this increases costs, Teanna believes her company's focus on "consciously sustaining the earth" appeals to her target market and helps drive sales.

Courtesy of Teanna Bass/ photographer Chelsea Priebe

■ **Decision Insight** ▬▬▬▬▬▬▬▬▬▬▬▬▬▬▬▬▬▬▬▬▬▬

**Sustainability Returns**   A recent study shows the value of investing in sustainability. Companies with good ratings on sustainability perform better than companies with poor ratings. The chart here shows that high sustainability firms have 4.05% higher stock returns and 6.89% higher return on sales than low sustainability firms. Source: HBS. ■

**Higher Returns for Sustainable Firms**

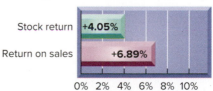

**Decision Analysis**     Raw Materials Inventory Turnover and Days' Sales in Raw Materials Inventory

## A1

Assess raw materials inventory management using raw materials inventory turnover and days' sales in raw materials inventory.

Managerial accounting information helps managers perform analyses to improve operations and profitability. Inventory management is one example.

### Raw Materials Inventory Turnover

A manager can assess how effectively a company manages its *raw materials* inventory by computing the **raw materials inventory turnover** ratio as defined in Exhibit 1.17. Average raw materials inventory is (Beginning raw materials inventory + Ending raw materials inventory) ÷ 2.

**EXHIBIT 1.17**

Raw Materials Inventory Turnover

$$\text{Raw materials inventory turnover} = \frac{\text{Raw materials used}}{\text{Average raw materials inventory}}$$

This ratio reveals how many times a company turns over (uses in production) its raw materials inventory during a period. A high ratio of raw materials inventory turnover is preferred, as long as raw materials inventory levels are adequate to meet demand. To demonstrate, Rocky Mountain Bikes reports direct (raw) materials used of $85,500 for the year, with a beginning raw materials inventory of $8,000 and an ending raw materials inventory of $9,000 (from Exhibit 1.14). Raw materials inventory turnover for Rocky Mountain Bikes is computed below.

$$\text{Raw materials inventory turnover} = \frac{\$85,500}{(\$8,000 + \$9,000)/2} = 10.1 \text{ (rounded)}$$

### Days' Sales in Raw Materials Inventory

A manager can measure the adequacy of raw materials inventory to meet production demand. **Days' sales in raw materials inventory** reveals how much raw materials inventory is available in terms of the number of days' sales. It is a measure of how long it takes raw materials to be used in production. It is defined and computed for Rocky Mountain Bikes in Exhibit 1.18.

**EXHIBIT 1.18**

Days' Sales in Raw Materials Inventory Turnover

$$\text{Days' sales in raw materials inventory} = \frac{\text{Ending raw materials inventory}}{\text{Raw materials used}} \times 365$$

$$= \frac{\$9,000}{\$85,500} \times 365 = 38.4 \text{ days (rounded)}$$

This shows that it will take about 38 days for raw materials inventory to be used in production. Assuming production needs can be met, companies prefer a *low* number of days' sales in raw materials inventory. Just-in-time manufacturing can help lower days' sales in raw materials inventory. For example, **Dell** keeps less than seven days of production needs in raw materials inventory for most of its computer components.

### ■ Decision Maker

**Chief Financial Officer**   Your company regularly reports days' sales in raw materials of 20 days, which is similar to that of competitors. A manager argues that profit can be increased if the company applies just-in-time principles and cuts it down to 2 days. Do you drop it to 2 days? ■ *Answer:* Cutting days' sales in raw materials to 2 days *might* increase profits. Having less money tied up in inventory is a positive. However, if the company loses customers over out-of-stock inventory or if production is delayed (with costs), then the increase in profit might be outweighed by the increase in costs.

The following information is from SUNN Company's records for the current year-end December 31. Prepare (1) a schedule of cost of goods manufactured and (2) an income statement.

NEED-TO-KNOW 1-5

**COMPREHENSIVE**

Schedule of Cost of Goods Manufactured, and Income Statement

| | | | |
|---|---|---|---|
| Depreciation expense—Factory | $211,000 | Indirect labor | $ 100,000 |
| Direct labor | 250,000 | Property taxes on factory | 51,000 |
| Factory insurance expired | 62,000 | Raw materials inventory, beginning | 60,000 |
| Factory utilities | 115,000 | Raw materials inventory, ending | 78,000 |
| Finished goods inventory, beginning | 15,000 | Raw materials purchases | 313,000 |
| Finished goods inventory, ending | 12,000 | Repairs expense—Factory | 31,000 |
| General and administrative expenses | 200,000 | Sales | 1,630,000 |
| Work in process inventory, beginning | 8,000 | Selling expenses | 230,000 |
| Work in process inventory, ending | 9,000 | | |

## SOLUTION

**SUNN COMPANY**
**Schedule of Cost of Goods Manufactured**
**For Year Ended December 31**

| | | |
|---|---|---|
| Direct materials | | |
| Raw materials inventory, beginning | $ 60,000 | |
| Raw materials purchases | 313,000 | |
| Raw materials available for use | 373,000 | |
| Less raw materials inventory, ending | 78,000 | |
| Direct materials used | | $ 295,000 |
| Direct labor | | 250,000 |
| Factory overhead | | |
| Depreciation expense—Factory | 211,000 | |
| Factory insurance expired | 62,000 | |
| Factory utilities | 115,000 | |
| Indirect labor | 100,000 | |
| Property taxes on factory | 51,000 | |
| Repairs expense—Factory | 31,000 | |
| Total factory overhead | | 570,000 |
| Total manufacturing costs | | 1,115,000 |
| Add work in process inventory, beginning | | 8,000 |
| Total cost of work in process | | 1,123,000 |
| Less work in process inventory, ending | | 9,000 |
| Cost of goods manufactured | | **$1,114,000** |

**SUNN COMPANY**
**Income Statement**
**For Year Ended December 31**

| | | |
|---|---|---|
| Sales | | $1,630,000 |
| Cost of goods sold | | |
| Finished goods inventory, beginning | $ 15,000 | |
| Cost of goods manufactured | **1,114,000** | |
| Goods available for sale | 1,129,000 | |
| Less finished goods inventory, ending | 12,000 | |
| Cost of goods sold | | 1,117,000 |
| Gross profit | | 513,000 |
| Selling expenses | | 230,000 |
| General and administrative expenses | | 200,000 |
| Net income | | $ 83,000 |

**Raw Materials Inventory**

| | | | |
|---|---|---|---|
| Beginning | 60,000 | | |
| Purchases | 313,000 | | |
| Available | 373,000 | | |
| | | Direct Mtls. | 295,000 |
| Ending | 78,000 | | |

**Finished Goods Inventory**

| | | | |
|---|---|---|---|
| Beginning | 15,000 | | |
| COGM | 1,114,000 | | |
| Available | 1,129,000 | | |
| | | COGS | 1,117,000 |
| Ending | 12,000 | | |

**Work in Process Inventory**

| | | | |
|---|---|---|---|
| Beginning | 8,000 | | |
| Direct Materials | 295,000 | | |
| Direct Labor | 250,000 | | |
| Overhead | 570,000 | | |
| | 1,123,000 | | |
| | | COGM | 1,114,000 |
| Ending | 9,000 | | |

## Summary: Cheat Sheet

### MANAGERIAL ACCOUNTING BASICS

**Planning:** Process of setting goals and making plans to achieve them.
**Control:** Process of monitoring and evaluating an organization's activities and employees.
**Managerial Accounting:** Focused on the needs of internal managerial and executive employees.
**Financial Accounting:** Focused on the needs of external users including investors and creditors.

### COST CONCEPTS

**Direct costs:** Costs that *can* be cost-effectively traced to a cost object. Examples for a bicycle include wages of bike maker, tires, seats, handlebars, cables, frames, pedals, and brakes.
**Indirect costs:** Costs that *cannot* be cost-effectively traced to a cost object. Examples for a bicycle include factory accounting, factory rent, factory supervisor salary, and factory insurance.

**Direct materials:** Materials that are crucial parts of a finished product and that *can* be cost-effectively traced to finished goods. Examples for a bicycle include tires, seats, handlebars, cables, frames, pedals, and brakes.

**Direct labor:** Employees who directly convert materials to finished product and whose costs *can* be cost-effectively traced to finished goods. Examples for a bicycle include workers who convert raw materials into finished products (welding, painting, forming) and assembly workers who attach materials such as tires, seats, pedals, and brakes.

**Factory overhead:** All manufacturing costs that are not direct materials or direct labor. Costs include manufacturing costs that *cannot* be cost-effectively traced to finished goods. Factory overhead includes indirect materials, indirect labor, and other indirect costs such as staples, glue, supervisor salaries, and factory insurance.

- **Indirect materials:** Materials used in manufacturing that *cannot* be cost-effectively traced to finished goods. Their costs are often low. Examples include staples, glue, nuts, and screws.
- **Indirect labor:** Labor needed in manufacturing that *cannot* be cost-effectively traced to finished goods. Examples include costs for employees who maintain and repair manufacturing equipment and salaries of production supervisors.
- *Other indirect costs* include factory utilities (water, gas, electricity), factory rent, depreciation on factory buildings and equipment, and factory insurance.

**Prime costs:** Direct materials costs + Direct labor costs.
**Conversion costs:** Overhead costs + Direct labor costs.

**Product costs:** Consist of direct materials, direct labor, and factory overhead. Product costs are added to inventory during production. After products are sold, these costs become cost of goods sold.

**Period costs:** *Nonproduction* costs linked to a time period rather than to completed products. Examples include sales staff salaries, office worker wages, advertising expenses, and depreciation on office furniture. Period costs are expensed in the period when incurred and reported on the income statement as either selling expenses or general and administrative expenses.

## REPORTING

**Raw materials inventory:** Materials a company acquires to use in making products.
**Work in process inventory:** Products in the process of being manufactured but not yet complete.
**Finished goods inventory:** Completed products ready for sale.

**Manufacturer Balance Sheet (current assets section):**

| ROCKY MOUNTAIN BIKES<br>Current Assets section of Balance Sheet<br>December 31 | |
| --- | ---: |
| **Assets** | |
| Current assets | |
| Cash | $11,000 |
| Accounts receivable, net | 30,150 |
| **Raw materials inventory** | **9,000** |
| **Work in process inventory** | **7,500** |
| **Finished goods inventory** | **10,300** |
| Supplies | 350 |
| Prepaid insurance | 300 |
| Total current assets | $68,600 |

**Cost of Goods Sold:**

Merchandiser

Beginning merchandise inventory **+** Cost of merchandise purchased **−** Ending merchandise inventory **=** Cost of goods sold

Manufacturer

Beginning finished goods inventory **+** Cost of goods manufactured **−** Ending finished goods inventory **=** Cost of goods sold

**Manufacturer Income Statement:**

| ROCKY MOUNTAIN BIKES<br>Income Statement<br>For Year Ended December 31 | | |
| --- | ---: | ---: |
| Sales | | $310,000 |
| **Cost of goods sold** | | |
| Finished goods inventory, beginning | $ 11,200 | |
| Cost of goods manufactured | 170,500 | |
| Goods available for sale | 181,700 | |
| Less finished goods inventory, ending | 10,300 | |
| Cost of goods sold | | 171,400 |
| **Gross profit** | | 138,600 |
| Selling expenses | | 38,200 |
| General and administrative expenses | | 54,400 |
| Net income | | $ 46,000 |

## COST FLOWS

**Cost of goods manufactured:** Total of direct materials used, direct labor, and factory overhead costs for finished goods manufactured.

**Cost of Goods Manufactured Computation:**

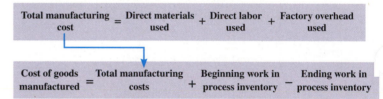

**Schedule of Cost of Goods Manufactured:**

| ROCKY MOUNTAIN BIKES<br>Schedule of Cost of Goods Manufactured<br>For Year Ended December 31 | | |
| --- | ---: | ---: |
| **Direct materials** | | |
| Raw materials inventory, beginning | $ 8,000 | |
| Raw materials purchases | 86,500 | |
| Raw materials available for use | 94,500 | |
| Less raw materials inventory, ending | 9,000 | |
| Direct materials used | | $ 85,500 |
| **Direct labor** | | 60,000 |
| **Factory overhead** | | |
| Indirect labor | 15,000 | |
| Factory utilities | 2,600 | |
| Repairs—Factory equipment | 2,500 | |
| Property taxes—Factory | 4,400 | |
| Depreciation expense—Factory | 5,500 | |
| Total factory overhead | | 30,000 |
| Total manufacturing costs | | $175,500 |
| Add work in process inventory, beginning | | 2,500 |
| Total cost of work in process | | 178,000 |
| Less work in process inventory, ending | | 7,500 |
| **Cost of goods manufactured** | | $170,500 |

## Key Terms

Continuous improvement (16)
Control (4)
Conversion costs (7)
Corporate social responsibility (CSR) (17)
Cost object (6)
Cost of goods manufactured (13)
Customer orientation (16)
Days' sales in raw materials inventory (18)
Digital manufacturing (15)
Direct costs (6)
Direct labor (7)
Direct labor costs (7)
Direct materials (7)
Direct materials costs (7)

Ethics (5)
Factory overhead (7)
Factory overhead costs (7)
Finished goods inventory (10)
Indirect costs (6)
Indirect labor (7)
Indirect materials (7)
Institute of Management Accountants (IMA) (5)
Internal control system (5)
ISO 9000 standards (16)
Just-in-time (JIT) manufacturing (16)
Lean business model (16)
Managerial accounting (3)
Period costs (8)
Planning (3)

Prime costs (7)
Product costs (8)
Raw materials inventory (10)
Raw materials inventory turnover (18)
Schedule of cost of goods manufactured (13)
Sustainability Accounting Standards Board (SASB) (17)
Total quality management (TQM) (16)
Triple bottom line (17)
Value chain (16)
Work in process inventory (10)

## Multiple Choice Quiz

1. Period costs
   a. Include direct materials and direct labor.
   b. Are capitalized as inventory.
   c. Are expensed in the period incurred.
   d. Include factory overhead.
   e. Are included in total manufacturing costs.
2. Factory overhead
   a. Includes selling expenses.
   b. Includes indirect labor.
   c. Is a period cost.
   d. Includes general and administrative expenses.
   e. Is included in nonmanufacturing costs.
3. A manufacturer reports the following.

| | |
|---|---|
| Raw materials purchases | $81,200 |
| Raw materials inventory, ending | 12,000 |
| Raw materials inventory, beginning | 8,000 |

   Its cost of materials used is
   a. $81,200  c. $85,200  e. $101,200
   b. $77,200  d. $89,200

4. A manufacturer reports the following.

| | | | |
|---|---|---|---|
| Direct materials used | $22,650 | Factory utilities | 800 |
| Selling expenses | 800 | Direct labor | 8,720 |
| Finished goods inventory, ending | 4,000 | Indirect labor | 4,000 |

   Its total manufacturing costs equal
   a. $36,170  c. $32,970  e. $32,170
   b. $36,970  d. $40,970
5. A manufacturer reports the following.

| | |
|---|---|
| Finished goods inventory, beginning | $6,000 |
| Finished goods inventory, ending | 3,200 |
| Cost of goods sold | 7,500 |

   Its cost of goods manufactured is
   a. $1,500.  c. $7,500.  e. $4,700.
   b. $1,700.  d. $2,800.

### ANSWERS TO MULTIPLE CHOICE QUIZ

1. c
2. b
3. b; Beginning raw materials inventory + Raw materials purchases − Ending raw materials inventory = $8,000 + $81,200 − $12,000 = $77,200
4. a; Direct materials + Direct labor + Factory overhead = $22,650 + $8,720 + $800 + $4,000 = $36,170
5. e; Beginning finished goods + Cost of goods manufactured (COGM) − Ending finished goods = Cost of goods sold
   $6,000 + COGM − $3,200 = $7,500
   COGM = $4,700

*Select Quick Study and Exercise assignments feature Guided Example videos, called "Hints" in Connect. Hints use different numbers, and instructors can turn this feature on or off.*

## QUICK STUDY

**QS 1-1**

Managerial vs. financial accounting

**C1**

Identify whether each description most likely applies to managerial or financial accounting.

**1.** Its primary users are company managers.

**2.** Its information is often available only after an audit is complete.

**3.** Its primary focus is on the organization as a whole.

**4.** Its principles and practices are relatively flexible.

**5.** It focuses mainly on past results.

---

**QS 1-2**

Classifying direct and indirect costs

**C2**

Diez Company produces sporting equipment, including leather footballs. Assume that the cost object is a football. Classify each of the following costs as direct or indirect.

**1.** Electricity used in the production plant.

**2.** Labor used on the football production line.

**3.** Salary of manager who supervises the entire plant.

**4.** Depreciation on maintenance equipment used in the plant.

**5.** Leather used to produce footballs.

---

**QS 1-3**

Classifying direct materials, direct labor, and overhead

**C2**

A company manufactures tennis balls. Classify each of the following costs as either direct materials, direct labor, or factory overhead.

**1.** Rubber used to form the cores.

**2.** Factory maintenance.

**3.** Wages paid to assembly workers.

**4.** Glue used in binding rubber cores to felt covers.

**5.** Depreciation on factory equipment.

**6.** Cans to package the balls.

---

**QS 1-4**

Classifying product and period costs

**C2**

Classify each of the following costs as either a product cost or a period cost for a manufacturer.

**1.** Factory insurance.

**2.** Sales commissions.

**3.** Depreciation on factory equipment.

**4.** Depreciation on office equipment.

**5.** Rent on factory building.

**6.** Tax accountant salary.

**7.** Office manager salary.

**8.** Indirect labor in making goods.

---

**QS 1-5**

Identifying prime and conversion costs

**C2**

A company manufactures guitars. Identify each of the following costs as either a prime cost, a conversion cost, or both.

**1.** Wood used to build the guitar body.

**2.** Glue used to bind the guitar wood.

**3.** Wages paid to assembly workers.

**4.** Depreciation on factory equipment.

**5.** Rent on factory building.

**6.** Wood to build the guitar bridge.

---

**QS 1-6**

Computing ending work in process inventory

**P1**

Compute ending work in process inventory for a manufacturer using the following information.

| | | | |
|---|---|---|---|
| Raw materials purchased | $124,000 | Factory overhead | $ 95,000 |
| Direct materials used | 74,000 | Work in process inventory, beginning | 26,000 |
| Direct labor used | 55,000 | Cost of goods manufactured | 220,000 |

---

**QS 1-7**

Computing cost of goods sold for a manufacturer

**P1**

Compute cost of goods sold using the following information.

| | | | |
|---|---|---|---|
| Finished goods inventory, beginning | $ 500 | Finished goods inventory, ending | $700 |
| Cost of goods manufactured | 4,000 | | |

---

**QS 1-8**

Computing cost of goods sold for a manufacturer

**P1**

Compute cost of goods sold using the following information.

| | | | |
|---|---|---|---|
| Finished goods inventory, beginning | $345,000 | Cost of goods manufactured | $918,000 |
| Work in process inventory, beginning | 83,000 | Finished goods inventory, ending | 283,000 |
| Work in process inventory, ending | 72,000 | | |

Compute cost of goods sold using the following information.

| | | | |
|---|---|---|---|
| Merchandise inventory, beginning ..... | $12,000 | Merchandise inventory, ending ......... | $18,000 |
| Cost of merchandise purchased ....... | 85,000 | | |

**QS 1-9**
Computing cost of goods sold for a merchandiser
**P1**

Determine the missing amount for each separate situation involving inventory cost flows.

| | (1) | (2) | (3) |
|---|---|---|---|
| Cost of merchandise purchased | $  ? | $140,000 | $289,000 |
| Merchandise inventory, beginning | 106,000 | ? | 28,000 |
| Merchandise inventory, ending | 82,000 | 33,000 | ? |
| Cost of goods sold | 205,000 | 128,000 | 267,000 |

**QS 1-10**
Determining merchandiser cost flows
**P1**

Prepare an income statement for Rex Manufacturing for the year ended December 31 using the following information. *Hint:* Not all information given is needed for the solution.

| | | | |
|---|---|---|---|
| Finished goods inventory, ending ...... | $16,000 | Selling expenses ..................... | $12,000 |
| General and administrative expenses... | 14,000 | Cash............................... | 55,000 |
| Accounts receivable ................. | 18,000 | Land............................... | 28,000 |
| Finished goods inventory, beginning. ... | 19,000 | Sales.............................. | 92,000 |
| Cost of goods manufactured .......... | 40,000 | Equipment ......................... | 1,000 |

**QS 1-11**
Preparing an income statement
**P1**

Prepare the current assets section of the balance sheet at December 31 for Bin Manufacturing using the following information. *Hint:* Not all information given is needed for the solution.

| | | | |
|---|---|---|---|
| Cash.............................. | $22,000 | Selling expenses ..................... | $12,000 |
| Accounts payable ................... | 2,000 | Finished goods inventory .............. | 22,000 |
| Raw materials inventory.............. | 8,000 | Work in process inventory ............ | 18,000 |
| General and administrative expenses... | 42,000 | Prepaid insurance ................... | 4,000 |
| Accounts receivable, net ............. | 12,000 | Cost of goods sold .................. | 33,000 |

**QS 1-12**
Preparing a balance sheet
**P1**

Garcia Company reports beginning raw materials inventory of $855 and ending raw materials inventory of $717. If the company purchased $3,646 of raw materials during the month, what is the amount of materials used during the month? *Note:* Assume all raw materials were used as direct materials.

**QS 1-13**
Computing direct materials used  **P2**

Determine the missing amount for each separate situation involving manufacturing costs.

| | (1) | (2) | (3) |
|---|---|---|---|
| Direct materials used | $8,000 | $14,000 | $  ? |
| Direct labor used | 4,000 | ? | 18,000 |
| Factory overhead | 5,000 | 23,000 | 22,000 |
| Total manufacturing costs | ? | 50,000 | 72,000 |

**QS 1-14**
Computing total manufacturing costs
**P2**

Prepare the schedule of cost of goods manufactured for Barton Company using the following information for the year ended December 31.

| | | | |
|---|---|---|---|
| Direct materials used ... | $190,000 | Work in process inventory, beginning.... | $157,000 |
| Direct labor........... | 63,000 | Work in process inventory, ending ...... | 142,000 |
| Factory overhead ...... | 24,000 | | |

**QS 1-15**
Preparing a schedule of cost of goods manufactured
**P2**

**QS 1-16**

Computing direct
materials used

**P2**

Use the following information to compute the cost of direct materials used for the current year. *Note*: Assume all raw materials were used as direct materials.

| Inventories | Beginning of Year | End of Year | | Activity during current year | |
|---|---|---|---|---|---|
| Raw materials inventory .... | $ 6,000 | $7,000 | | Raw materials purchased ... | $123,000 |
| Work in process inventory ... | 12,000 | 9,000 | | Direct labor............... | 94,000 |
| Finished goods inventory ... | 8,000 | 5,000 | | Factory overhead.......... | 39,000 |

**QS 1-17**

Schedule of cost of goods
manufactured

**P2**

Refer to the data in Quick Study 1-16. Factory overhead of $39,000 consists of Indirect labor of $20,000, Depreciation expense—Factory of $15,000, and Factory utilities of $4,000.

**a.** Compute total manufacturing costs.
**b.** Prepare a schedule of cost of goods manufactured.

**QS 1-18**

Determining components
of cost of goods
manufactured

**P2**

Determine the missing amount for each separate situation involving work in process cost flows.

| | (1) | (2) | (3) |
|---|---|---|---|
| Total manufacturing costs | $    ? | $150,000 | $217,000 |
| Work in process inventory, beginning | 105,000 | ? | 32,000 |
| Work in process inventory, ending | 84,000 | 22,000 | ? |
| Cost of goods manufactured | 200,000 | 138,000 | 237,000 |

**QS 1-19**

Computing average
manufacturing cost
per unit   **P2**

A company reports cost of goods manufactured of $918,700 and cost of goods sold of $955,448. Compute the average manufacturing cost per unit assuming 18,374 units were produced.

**QS 1-20**

Trends in managerial
accounting

**C4**

Match each concept with its best description.

**1.** Just-in-time manufacturing
**2.** Continuous improvement
**3.** Customer orientation
**4.** Total quality management
**5.** Triple bottom line

**A.** Focuses on quality throughout the production process.
**B.** Flexible product designs can be modified to accommodate customer choices.
**C.** Managers and employees constantly look to improve operations.
**D.** Reports on financial, social, and environmental performance.
**E.** Inventory is acquired or produced only as needed.

**QS 1-21**

Computing inventory ratios

**A1**

Sims Company reports beginning raw materials inventory of $900 and ending raw materials inventory of $1,100. Assume the company purchased $5,200 of raw materials and used $5,000 of raw materials during the year. Compute raw materials inventory turnover (round to one decimal) and the number of days' sales in raw materials inventory (round to the nearest day).

## EXERCISES

**Exercise 1-1**

Managerial vs. financial
accounting

**C1**

Indicate whether each decision is most likely to be made using managerial accounting information or financial accounting information.

| Business Decision | Primary Information Source |
|---|---|
| 1. Determine whether to lend to a company.............. | _____ |
| 2. Evaluate a purchasing department's performance....... | _____ |
| 3. Report financial performance to shareholders .......... | _____ |
| 4. Estimate product cost for a new line of shoes........... | _____ |
| 5. Plan the manufacturing budget for next quarter......... | _____ |
| 6. Measure profitability of an individual store............. | _____ |
| 7. Prepare financial reports according to GAAP .......... | _____ |
| 8. Determine location and size for a new plant............ | _____ |

Listed here are product costs for production of soccer balls. Classify each cost as either direct or indirect.

**Exercise 1-2**
Classifying direct and indirect costs
C2

| Product Cost | Direct or Indirect | Product Cost | Direct or Indirect |
|---|---|---|---|
| 1. Leather covers for soccer balls ......... | _____ | 6. Taxes on factory .................. | _____ |
| 2. Annual flat fee paid for factory security... | _____ | 7. Machinery depreciation (straight-line) . | _____ |
| 3. Coolants for machinery ............... | _____ | 8. Rubber bladder interior for balls ..... | _____ |
| 4. Wages of product assembly workers..... | _____ | 9. Ink for labeling soccer balls......... | _____ |
| 5. Factory supervisor salary .............. | _____ | 10. Factory building rent .............. | _____ |

TechPro offers instructional courses in website design. The company holds classes in a building that it owns. The cost object is an individual class. Classify each of TechPro's costs below as direct or indirect.

**Exercise 1-3**
Classifying direct and indirect costs for a service company
C2

**1.** Depreciation on classroom building

**5.** Depreciation on computers used for classes

**2.** Monthly Internet connection cost

**6.** Instructor wage (per class)

**3.** Instructional manuals for students

**7.** Classroom cleaning fees

**4.** Classroom building utilities cost

**8.** Snacks for the class

Listed below are costs of services provided by an airline company. Consider the cost object to be a flight. Flight attendants and pilots are paid based on hours of flight time. Classify each cost as direct, indirect, selling, or general and administrative.

**Exercise 1-4**
Classifying costs for a service company
C2

| Cost | Classification | Cost | Classification |
|---|---|---|---|
| 1. Advertising........................... | _____ | 5. Fuel used for plane flight............ | _____ |
| 2. Beverages served on plane .............. | _____ | 6. Flight attendant wages for flight...... | _____ |
| 3. Accounting manager salary .............. | _____ | 7. Pilot wages for flight ............... | _____ |
| 4. Depreciation (straight-line) on plane ....... | _____ | 8. Aircraft maintenance manager salary.. | _____ |

Selected costs related to **Apple**'s iPhone are listed below. Classify each cost as either direct materials, direct labor, factory overhead, selling expenses, or general and administrative expenses.

**Exercise 1-5**
Classifying costs
C2

**1.** Display screen

**5.** Glue to hold iPhone cases together

**2.** Assembly-line supervisor salary

**6.** Uniforms provided for each factory worker

**3.** Wages for assembly workers

**7.** Wages for retail store salesperson

**4.** Salary of chief executive officer

**8.** Depreciation (straight-line) on robotic equipment used in assembly

A car manufacturer incurs the following costs. Classify each cost as either a product or period cost. If a product cost, classify it as direct materials, direct labor, or factory overhead. If a period cost, classify it as a selling expense or a general and administrative expense. Place an "X" in the correct column for each cost.

**Exercise 1-6**
Classifying product and period costs  C2

| | Product Costs | | | Period Costs | |
|---|---|---|---|---|---|
| Cost | Direct Materials | Direct Labor | Factory Overhead | Selling Expense | General and Administrative Expense |
| 1. Factory electricity ...................... | _____ | _____ | _____ | _____ | _____ |
| 2. Advertising............................ | _____ | _____ | _____ | _____ | _____ |
| 3. Depreciation on factory machine........... | _____ | _____ | _____ | _____ | _____ |
| 4. Batteries for electric cars ................. | _____ | _____ | _____ | _____ | _____ |
| 5. Office supplies used .................... | _____ | _____ | _____ | _____ | _____ |
| 6. Wages to assembly workers............... | _____ | _____ | _____ | _____ | _____ |
| 7. Salesperson commissions ................ | _____ | _____ | _____ | _____ | _____ |
| 8. Steel for cars .......................... | _____ | _____ | _____ | _____ | _____ |
| 9. Depreciation on office equipment .......... | _____ | _____ | _____ | _____ | _____ |
| 10. Leather for car seats..................... | _____ | _____ | _____ | _____ | _____ |

**Exercise 1-7**
Computing cost of goods manufactured and cost of goods sold

**P1**  **P2**

Using the following data from both Garcon Company and Pepper Company for the year ended December 31 to compute (1) the cost of goods manufactured and (2) the cost of goods sold for each company. *Hint:* Not all information is needed for the solution.

| | Garcon Co. | Pepper Co. |
|---|---|---|
| Finished goods inventory, beginning....... | $ 12,000 | $ 16,450 |
| Work in process inventory, beginning...... | 14,500 | 19,950 |
| Raw materials inventory, beginning........ | 7,250 | 9,000 |
| Rental cost on factory equipment......... | 27,000 | 22,750 |
| Direct labor........................... | 19,000 | 35,000 |
| Finished goods inventory, ending......... | 17,650 | 13,300 |
| Work in process inventory, ending......... | 22,000 | 16,000 |
| Raw materials inventory, ending.......... | 5,300 | 7,200 |
| Factory utilities....................... | 9,000 | 12,000 |
| General and administrative expenses..... | 21,000 | 43,000 |
| Indirect labor......................... | 9,450 | 10,860 |
| Repairs—Factory equipment............. | 4,780 | 1,500 |
| Raw materials purchases .............. | 33,000 | 52,000 |
| Selling expenses ..................... | 50,000 | 46,000 |
| Sales ............................... | 195,030 | 290,010 |
| Cash................................ | 20,000 | 15,700 |
| Accounts receivable, net ............... | 13,200 | 19,450 |

**Exercise 1-8**
Preparing financial statements for a manufacturer  **P1**

Refer to the data in Exercise 1-7. For each company, prepare (1) an income statement and (2) the current assets section of the balance sheet.

**Exercise 1-9**
Computing prime and conversion costs  **C2**

Refer to the data in Exercise 1-7. For each company, compute the total (1) prime costs and (2) conversion costs.

**Exercise 1-10**
Cost of goods sold computation for a merchandiser and manufacturer

**P1**

Compute cost of goods sold for each of these two companies.

| | A | B | C |
|---|---|---|---|
| 1 | | **Unimart** | **Bare Manufacturing** |
| 2 | Beginning inventory | | |
| 3 |   Merchandise | $275,000 | |
| 4 |   Finished goods | | $450,000 |
| 5 | Cost of merchandise purchased | 500,000 | |
| 6 | Cost of goods manufactured | | 900,000 |
| 7 | Ending inventory | | |
| 8 |   Merchandise | 115,000 | |
| 9 |   Finished goods | | 375,000 |

**Check**  Unimart COGS, $660,000

**Exercise 1-11**
Balance sheet identification and preparation

**P1**

End-of-year current assets for two different companies follow. One is a manufacturer, Rayzer Skis Mfg., and the other, Sunrise Foods, is a merchandiser.

1. Identify which set of numbers relates to the manufacturer and which to the merchandiser.

2. Prepare the current asset section of the balance sheet at December 31 for each company.

| Account | Company 1 | Company 2 |
|---|---|---|
| Cash ..................... | $ 7,000 | $ 5,000 |
| Merchandise inventory ....... | 45,000 | — |
| Raw materials inventory ...... | — | 42,000 |
| Work in process inventory ..... | — | 30,000 |
| Finished goods inventory ..... | — | 50,000 |
| Accounts receivable, net ...... | 62,000 | 75,000 |
| Prepaid expenses .......... | 1,500 | 900 |

For each of the following accounts for a manufacturing company, place a ✓ in the column indicating that it is included in selling expenses, general and administrative expenses, or the calculation of cost of goods manufactured. An account can only be included in one column.

**Exercise 1-12**
Components of accounting reports
**P2**

| | A | B | C | D |
|---|---|---|---|---|
| **1** | **Account** | **Selling Expenses** | **General & Admin. Expenses** | **Cost of Goods Manufactured** |
| 2 | Advertising | | | |
| 3 | Work in process inventory, beginning | | | |
| 4 | Computer supplies used in office | | | |
| 5 | Depreciation expense—Factory | | | |
| 6 | Depreciation expense—Office | | | |
| 7 | Wages for assembly workers | | | |
| 8 | Office employee wages | | | |
| 9 | Factory maintenance wages | | | |
| 10 | Property taxes on factory | | | |
| 11 | Raw materials purchases | | | |
| 12 | Sales commissions | | | |

Use the following selected account balances of Delray Mfg. to prepare its schedule of cost of goods manufactured for the year ended December 31.

**Exercise 1-13**
Preparing schedule of cost of goods manufactured
**P2**

| | | | |
|---|---|---|---|
| Sales | $1,250,000 | Repairs—Factory equipment | $ 23,000 |
| Raw materials inventory, beginning | 37,000 | Rent cost of factory building | 57,000 |
| Work in process inventory, beginning | 53,900 | Selling expenses | 94,000 |
| Finished goods inventory, beginning | 62,700 | General and administrative expenses | 129,300 |
| Raw materials purchases | 175,600 | Raw materials inventory, ending | 42,700 |
| Direct labor | 225,000 | Work in process inventory, ending | 41,500 |
| Indirect labor | 47,000 | Finished goods inventory, ending | 67,300 |

**Check**   Direct materials used, $169,900

Refer to the information in Exercise 1-13 to prepare an income statement for Delray Mfg. (a manufacturer). Assume that its cost of goods manufactured is $534,300.

**Exercise 1-14**
Income statement preparation   **P1**

Beck Manufacturing reports the following information in T-accounts for the current year.

1. Prepare the schedule of cost of goods manufactured for the year.
2. Compute cost of goods sold for the year.

**Exercise 1-15**
Schedule of cost of goods manufactured and cost of goods sold   **P2**

| Raw Materials Inventory | | | |
|---|---|---|---|
| Beginning | 10,000 | | |
| Purchases | 45,000 | | |
| Avail. for use | 55,000 | | |
| | | DM* used | 46,500 |
| Ending | 8,500 | | |

| Work in Process Inventory | | | |
|---|---|---|---|
| Beginning | 14,000 | | |
| DM used | 46,500 | | |
| Direct labor | 27,500 | | |
| Overhead | 55,000 | | |
| | 143,000 | | |
| | | Cost of goods manuf. | 131,000 |
| Ending | 12,000 | | |

| Finished Goods Inventory | | | |
|---|---|---|---|
| Beginning | 16,000 | | |
| Cost of goods manuf. | 131,000 | | |
| Avail. for sale | 147,000 | | |
| | | Cost of goods sold | 129,000 |
| Ending | 18,000 | | |

*DM = Direct materials

The following chart shows how costs flow through a business as a product is manufactured. All boxes in the chart show cost amounts. Compute the cost amounts for the boxes that contain question marks.

**Exercise 1-16**
Cost flows in manufacturing—visualization
**C3**

[continued on next page]

[continued from previous page]

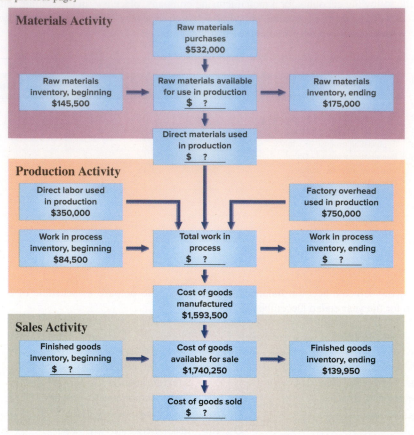

---

**Exercise 1-17**

Determining cost flows for manufacturers

P2

Determine the missing amount for each separate situation involving manufacturing cost flows.

|                                       | (1)         | (2)      | (3)      |
|---------------------------------------|-------------|----------|----------|
| Direct materials used                 | $    (a)    | $150,480 | $33,890  |
| Direct labor used                     | 75,000      | (d)      | 45,720   |
| Factory overhead                      | 122,000     | 32,840   | 60,275   |
| Total manufacturing costs             | 243,500     | 238,700  | (g)      |
| Work in process inventory, beginning  | (b)         | 56,920   | 8,245    |
| Total cost of work in process         | 289,325     | (e)      | (h)      |
| Work in process inventory, ending     | (c)         | 22,545   | 11,250   |
| Cost of goods manufactured            | 265,420     | (f)      | (i)      |

---

**Exercise 1-18**

Lean business practices

C4

Many fast-food restaurants compete on lean business practices. Identify which lean business practice *a, b,* or *c,* is being implemented with each of the following activities.

1. Courteous employees
2. Food produced to order
3. Clean tables and floors
4. Orders filled within three minutes
5. Standardized food-making processes
6. New product development

a. Just-in-time (JIT)
b. Continuous improvement (CI)
c. Total quality management (TQM)

---

**Exercise 1-19**

Triple bottom line

C4

In a recent annual report and related *Global Responsibility Report,* **Starbucks** provides information on company performance on several dimensions. Indicate whether the following items best fit into the financial (label your answer "Profit"), social (label your answer "People"), or environmental (label your answer "Planet") aspects of triple bottom line reporting.

1. Sales revenue totaled $22.4 billion.
2. 99% of coffee was purchased from suppliers certified for paying fair wages.

[continued on next page]

**3.** Company reported reduced water consumption.

**4.** Net income totaled $2.9 billion.

**5.** Increased purchases of energy from renewable sources.

**6.** Stopped working with factories that had poor working conditions.

Listed here are the costs associated with the production of 1,000 drum sets manufactured by TrueBeat.

| Costs | Product | Period |
|---|---|---|
| 1. Plastic for casing—$17,000 | $17,000 | —— |
| 2. Wages of assembly workers—$82,000 | —— | —— |
| 3. Property taxes on factory—$5,000 | —— | —— |
| 4. Office accounting salaries—$35,000 | —— | —— |
| 5. Drum stands—$26,000 | —— | —— |
| 6. Rent cost of office for accountants—$10,000 | —— | —— |
| 7. Office management salaries—$125,000 | —— | —— |
| 8. Annual fee for factory maintenance—$10,000 | —— | —— |
| 9. Sales commissions—$15,000 | —— | —— |
| 10. Factory machinery depreciation, straight-line—$40,000 | —— | —— |

**PROBLEM SET A**

**Problem 1-1A**
Classifying costs and computing cost per unit

**C2    P2**

**Required**

**1.** Classify each cost and its amount as either product or period. The first cost is completed as an example.

**2.** Compute the average manufacturing cost per drum set.

The following year-end information is taken from the December 31 adjusted trial balance and other records of Leone Company.

| | | | |
|---|---|---|---|
| Advertising expense | $ 28,750 | Direct labor | $675,480 |
| Depreciation expense—Office equipment | 7,250 | Indirect labor | 159,475 |
| Depreciation expense—Selling equipment | 8,600 | Office salaries expense | 63,000 |
| Depreciation expense—Factory equipment | 49,325 | Rent expense—Office space | 22,000 |
| Raw materials purchases (all direct materials) | 925,000 | Rent expense—Selling space | 26,100 |
| Maintenance expense—Factory equipment | 35,400 | Rent expense—Factory building | 76,800 |
| Factory utilities | 33,000 | Sales salaries expense | 392,560 |

**Problem 1-2A**
Classifying costs

**C2**

**Required**

Identify each cost as either a product cost or a period cost. If a product cost, classify it as direct materials, direct labor, or factory overhead. If a period cost, classify it as a selling expense or a general and administrative expense.

Using the data from Problem 1-2A and the following additional information for Leone Company, complete the requirements below.

| | | | |
|---|---|---|---|
| Raw materials inventory, beginning | $ 166,850 | Work in process inventory, ending | $ 19,380 |
| Raw materials inventory, ending | 182,000 | Finished goods inventory, beginning | 167,350 |
| Work in process inventory, beginning | 15,700 | Finished goods inventory, ending | 136,490 |
| Sales | 4,462,500 | | |

**Problem 1-3A**
Schedule of cost of goods manufactured and income statement

**P1    P2**

**Required**

**1.** Prepare the schedule of cost of goods manufactured for the current year.

**2.** Prepare the current year income statement.

**Check**    (1) Cost of goods manufactured, $1,935,650

**Problem 1-4A**
Reporting cost of goods sold
**P1**

Shown here are annual financial data for a merchandising company and a manufacturing company.

|  | Music World Retail | Wave-Board Manufacturing |
|---|---|---|
| Beginning inventory |  |  |
|    Merchandise | $200,000 |  |
|    Finished goods |  | $500,000 |
| Cost of merchandise purchased | 300,000 |  |
| Cost of goods manufactured |  | 875,000 |
| Ending inventory |  |  |
|    Merchandise | 175,000 |  |
|    Finished goods |  | 225,000 |

**Required**

Prepare the cost of goods sold section of the income statement for each company.

**Problem 1-5A**
Raw materials inventory turnover
**A1**

A manufacturing company reports the following information.

|  | Current Year | 1 Year Ago | 2 Years Ago |
|---|---|---|---|
| Raw materials inventory, ending | $ 169,500 | $ 190,500 | $ 197,500 |
| Raw materials used | 2,160,000 | 2,522,000 | 2,765,000 |

**Required**

1. Compute raw materials inventory turnover for the most recent two years.
2. Is the current year change in raw materials inventory turnover ratio favorable or unfavorable?
3. Compute days' sales in raw materials inventory for the current year.

## PROBLEM SET B

**Problem 1-1B**
Classifying costs and computing cost per unit
**C2    P2**

Listed here are the costs associated with the production of 18,000 Blu-ray discs (BDs) manufactured by Maxwell.

| Costs | Product | Period |
|---|---|---|
| 1.  Plastic for BDs—$1,500 | $1,500 | —— |
| 2.  Wages of assembly workers—$30,000 | —— | —— |
| 3.  Factory rent—$6,750 | —— | —— |
| 4.  Human resources staff salaries—$15,000 | —— | —— |
| 5.  BD labeling—$3,750 | —— | —— |
| 6.  Office equipment rent—$1,050 | —— | —— |
| 7.  Office management salaries—$120,000 | —— | —— |
| 8.  Annual fee for factory maintenance—$21,000 | —— | —— |
| 9.  Advertising—$7,200 | —— | —— |
| 10. Factory machinery depreciation, straight-line—$18,000 | —— | —— |

**Required**

1. Classify each cost and its amount as either product or period. The first cost is completed as an example.
2. Compute the average manufacturing cost per BD.

**Problem 1-2B**
Classifying costs
**C2**

The following year-end information is taken from the December 31 adjusted trial balance and other records of Best Bikes.

| | | | |
|---|---|---|---|
| Advertising expense | $ 20,250 | Direct labor | $562,500 |
| Depreciation expense—Office equipment | 8,440 | Indirect labor | 180,500 |
| Depreciation expense—Selling equipment | 10,125 | Office salaries expense | 70,875 |
| Depreciation expense—Factory equipment | 49,900 | Rent expense—Office space | 23,625 |
| Raw materials purchases (all direct materials) | 894,375 | Rent expense—Selling space | 27,000 |
| Maintenance expense—Factory equipment | 30,375 | Rent expense—Factory building | 93,500 |
| Factory utilities | 37,500 | Sales salaries expense | 295,300 |

**Required**

Identify each cost as either a product cost or a period cost. If a product cost, classify it as direct materials, direct labor, or factory overhead. If a period cost, classify it as a selling expense or a general and administrative expense.

Using the information from Problem 1-2B and the following additional information for Best Bikes, complete the requirements below.

**Problem 1-3B**
Schedule of cost of goods manufactured and income statement

**P1   P2**

| | | | |
|---|---|---|---|
| Raw materials inventory, beginning .......... | $  40,375 | Work in process inventory, ending........... | $ 14,100 |
| Raw materials inventory, ending ............. | 70,430 | Finished goods inventory, beginning......... | 177,200 |
| Work in process inventory, beginning......... | 12,500 | Finished goods inventory, ending ........... | 141,750 |
| Sales .................................... | 4,942,625 | | |

**Required**

1. Prepare the schedule of cost of goods manufactured for the year.
2. Prepare the current year income statement.

**Check**   (1) Cost of goods manufactured, $1,816,995

Shown here are annual financial data for a merchandising company and a manufacturing company.

**Problem 1-4B**
Reporting cost of goods sold

**P1**

| | TeeMart Retailing | Aim Labs Manufacturing |
|---|---|---|
| Beginning inventory | | |
| Merchandise ................. | $100,000 | |
| Finished goods .............. | | $300,000 |
| Cost of merchandise purchased .... | 250,000 | |
| Cost of goods manufactured ....... | | 586,000 |
| Ending inventory | | |
| Merchandise ................. | 150,000 | |
| Finished goods .............. | | 200,000 |

**Required**

1. Prepare the cost of goods sold section of the income statement for each company.
2. Write a half-page memorandum to your instructor (*a*) identifying the inventory accounts and (*b*) identifying where each is reported on the income statement and/or balance sheet for both companies.

A manufacturing company reports the following information.

**Problem 1-5B**
Raw materials inventory turnover

**A1**

| | Current Year | 1 Year Ago | 2 Years Ago |
|---|---|---|---|
| Raw materials inventory, ending | $ 270,225 | $ 259,775 | $ 230,225 |
| Raw materials used | 2,385,000 | 2,695,000 | 2,700,000 |

**Required**

1. Compute raw materials inventory turnover for the most recent two years.
2. Is the current year change in raw materials inventory turnover ratio favorable or unfavorable?
3. Compute days' sales in raw materials inventory for the current year.

*Serial Problem starts here and follows the same company throughout the text. It is available in Connect.*

## SERIAL PROBLEM
Business Solutions

C4  P1  P2

Alexander Image/Shutterstock

**SP 1**  Santana Rey, owner of **Business Solutions**, diversifies her business by also manufacturing computer workstation furniture.

**Required**

**1.** Classify the following manufacturing costs of Business Solutions as either direct (D) or indirect (I).

| Manufacturing Costs | Direct or Indirect |
|---|---|
| 1. Monthly fee to clean workshop .............. | _____ |
| 2. Laminate coverings for desktops.............. | _____ |
| 3. Taxes on assembly workshop ................. | _____ |
| 4. Glue to assemble workstation components ...... | _____ |
| 5. Wages of desk assembler ................... | _____ |
| 6. Electricity for workshop .................... | _____ |
| 7. Depreciation on manufacturing tools .......... | _____ |

**2.** Prepare a schedule of cost of goods manufactured for Business Solutions for the month ended January 31, 2022. Assume the following manufacturing costs.

| | | | |
|---|---|---|---|
| Work in process inventory, beginning ... | $ 0 | Direct materials used .... | $2,200 |
| Work in process inventory, ending ...... | 540 | Direct labor ............ | 900 |
| Finished goods inventory, beginning .... | 0 | Factory overhead ....... | 490 |
| Finished goods inventory, ending ....... | 350 | | |

**3.** Refer to the data in part 2 and prepare the cost of goods sold section of a partial income statement for Business Solutions for the month ended January 31, 2022.

## TABLEAU DASHBOARD ACTIVITIES

**Tableau Dashboard Activities** expose students to accounting analytics using visual displays. These assignments run in **Connect**. All are auto-gradable.

**Tableau DA 1-1 Quick Study**, Computing direct materials used, **C2**—similar to QS 1-13.
**Tableau DA 1-2 Exercise**, Cost classification and current assets section of balance sheet, **P1**, **C2**—similar to Exercises 1-8 & 1-9.
**Tableau DA 1-3 Mini-case**, Schedule of cost of goods manufactured and income statement preparation, **C2**—similar to Exercise 1-7.

## Accounting Analysis

### COMPANY ANALYSIS

A1

**AA 1-1**  For **Apple**'s current annual report, assume it reports the following for raw materials.

| $ millions | Current Year | 1 Year Ago | 2 Years Ago |
|---|---|---|---|
| Raw materials inventory, ending ... | $ 2,100 | $ 1,900 | $ 2,500 |
| Raw materials used.............. | 72,000 | 74,800 | 79,200 |

**Required**

**1.** Compute Apple's raw materials inventory turnover ratio for the most recent two years.
**2.** Is the current year change in Apple's raw materials inventory turnover ratio favorable or unfavorable?

**AA 1-2**    For the current annual reports of **Apple** and **Google**, assume they report the following.

| $ millions | Apple | | | Google | | |
|---|---|---|---|---|---|---|
| | Current Year | 1 Year Ago | 2 Years Ago | Current Year | 1 Year Ago | 2 Years Ago |
| Raw materials inventory, ending ... | $ 2,100 | $ 1,900 | $ 2,500 | $ 500 | $ 700 | $ 300 |
| Raw materials used............. | 72,000 | 74,800 | 79,200 | 42,000 | 30,000 | 27,000 |

**Required**

1. Compute the recent two years' raw materials inventory turnover ratio for (*a*) Apple and (*b*) Google.

2. Is the current year change in Apple's raw materials inventory turnover ratio favorable or unfavorable? Is the current year change in Google's raw materials inventory turnover ratio favorable or unfavorable?

3. For the current year, does raw materials inventory turnover outperform or underperform the industry (assumed) average of 40 for (*a*) Apple and (*b*) Google?

---

**AA 1-3**    For the current annual reports of **Samsung** and **Apple**, assume they report the following.

| $ millions | Samsung | | Apple | |
|---|---|---|---|---|
| | Current Year | Prior Year | Current Year | Prior Year |
| Raw materials inventory, ending ... | $11,500 | $12,400 | $ 2,100 | $ 1,900 |
| Raw materials used............. | 63,598 | 56,575 | 72,000 | 74,800 |

**Required**

1. Compute the recent two years' days' sales in raw materials inventory for (*a*) Samsung and (*b*) Apple.

2. Is the current year change in Samsung's days' sales in raw materials inventory favorable or unfavorable? Is the current year change in Apple's days' sales in raw materials inventory favorable or unfavorable?

3. For the current year, is Samsung's days' sales in raw materials inventory better or worse than Apple's? (Assume all production needs can be met for both companies.)

## Discussion Questions

1. Describe the managerial accountant's role in business planning, control, and decision making.

2. Distinguish between managerial and financial accounting on the following information attributes.
   a. Users.          d. Time dimension.
   b. Purpose.        e. Focus.
   c. Flexibility of reporting.    f. Nature.

3. Identify the usual changes that a company must make when it adopts a customer orientation.

4. Distinguish between direct labor and indirect labor.

5. Distinguish between (*a*) factory overhead and (*b*) selling, general, and administrative expenses.

6. Distinguish between direct materials and indirect materials.

7. What product cost is both a prime cost and a conversion cost?

8. Assume that we tour **Apple**'s factory where it makes iPhones. List three direct costs and three indirect costs that we are likely to see.

9. List several examples of nonmanufacturing costs.

10. Should we evaluate a production manager's performance on the basis of general and administrative expenses? Why?

11. Explain why product costs are capitalized but period costs are expensed in the current accounting period.

12. Explain how business activities and inventories for a manufacturing company, a merchandising company, and a service company differ.

13. Why does managerial accounting often involve working with numerous predictions and estimates?

14. How do an income statement and a balance sheet for a manufacturing company and a merchandising company differ?

15. Besides inventories, what other assets often appear on manufacturers' balance sheets but not on merchandisers' balance sheets?

16. Why does a manufacturing company require three different inventory categories?

**17.** What are the goals of the lean business model?

**18.** What are the three categories of manufacturing costs?

**19.** List several examples of factory overhead.

**20.** List the four components of a schedule of cost of goods manufactured and provide specific examples of each for **Apple**.

**21.** Prepare a proper title for the annual schedule of cost of goods manufactured of **Google**. Does the date match the balance sheet or income statement? Why?

**22.** How does the cost of goods manufactured schedule relate to the income statement?

**23.** Define and describe two measures to assess raw materials inventory management.

**24.** The triple bottom line includes what three main dimensions?

**25.** Read the *Statement of Ethical Professional Practice* posted at **IMAnet.org**. (Under "Career Resources," select "Ethics Center," and then select "IMA Statement of Ethical Professional Practice.") What four overarching ethical principles underlie the IMA's statement? Describe the courses of action the IMA recommends in resolving ethical conflicts.

## Beyond the Numbers

**ETHICS CHALLENGE**

**C3**

**BTN 1-1** You are the managerial accountant at Infostore, a manufacturer of hard drives. Its reporting year-end is December 31. The chief financial officer is concerned about having enough cash to pay the expected income tax bill because of poor cash flow management. On November 15, the purchasing department purchased excess inventory of raw materials in anticipation of rapid sales growth beginning in January. The chief financial officer tells you to record the purchase of raw materials as an expense in the current year; this would decrease the company's tax liability by increasing expenses and reducing income.

**Required**

**1.** In which account should the purchase of raw materials be recorded?

**2.** How should you respond to this request by the chief financial officer?

**COMMUNICATING IN PRACTICE**

**C1**

**BTN 1-2** Write a one-page memorandum to a prospective college student about salary expectations for graduates in business. Compare and contrast the expected salaries for accounting (including different subfields such as public, corporate, tax, audit, and so forth), marketing, management, and finance majors. Prepare a graph showing average starting salaries (and those for experienced professionals in those fields if available). To get this information, stop by your school's career services office; libraries also have this information. The website **JobStar.org** (click on "Salary Info") also can get you started.

**TEAMWORK IN ACTION**

**P1  P2**

**BTN 1-3** The following calendar-year information is taken from the adjusted trial balance and other records of Dahlia Company.

| | | | | |
|---|---:|---|---:|---|
| Advertising expense | $ 19,125 | Direct labor | $ 650,750 |
| Depreciation expense—Office equipment | 8,750 | Indirect labor | 182,500 |
| Depreciation expense—Selling equipment | 10,000 | Office salaries expense | 100,875 |
| Depreciation expense—Factory equipment | 32,500 | Raw materials purchases | 872,500 |
| Inventories | | Rent expense—Office space | 21,125 |
|    Raw materials, beginning | 177,500 | Rent expense—Selling space | 25,750 |
|    Raw materials, ending | 168,125 | Rent expense—Factory building | 79,750 |
|    Work in process, beginning | 15,875 | Maintenance expense—Factory equipment | 27,875 |
|    Work in process, ending | 14,000 | Sales | 3,217,500 |
|    Finished goods, beginning | 164,375 | Sales salaries expense | 286,250 |
|    Finished goods, ending | 129,000 | Factory utilities | 60,500 |

**Required**

1. *Each* team member is to be responsible for computing **one** of the following amounts. Do not duplicate your teammates' work. Get any necessary amounts from teammates. Each member is to explain the computation to the team in preparation for reporting to class.
   - **a.** Direct materials used
   - **b.** Factory overhead
   - **c.** Total manufacturing costs
   - **d.** Total cost of work in process
   - **e.** Cost of goods manufactured

2. Check your cost of goods manufactured amount with the instructor. If it is correct, proceed to part 3.

3. *Each* team member is to be responsible for computing **one** of the following amounts. Do not duplicate your teammates' work. Get any necessary amounts from teammates. Each member is to explain the computation to the team in preparation for reporting to class.
   - **a.** Cost of goods sold
   - **b.** Gross profit
   - **c.** Total selling expenses
   - **d.** Total general and administrative expenses
   - **e.** Net income

---

**BTN 1-4**  Teanna Bass of **Sweet Tea Cosmetics** understands and controls merchandising costs.

**ENTREPRENEURIAL DECISION**

P1   C4

**Required**

1. How does a merchandiser such as Sweet Tea Cosmetics compute cost of goods sold? Provide examples of costs Teanna must monitor and control.

2. What are four goals of a total quality management process? *Hint:* The goals are listed in a "Point." Assume Sweet Tea Cosmetics decides to manufacture its own makeup. How could the company use TQM to improve its business activities?

# 2 Job Order Costing and Analysis

## Chapter Preview

### JOB ORDER COSTING

**C1** Job order production

Job order vs. process operations

Production activities

Cost flows

Job cost sheet

**NTK 2-1**

### MATERIALS AND LABOR COSTS

**P1** Materials cost flows and documents

**P2** Labor cost flows and documents

Linking job cost sheets with accounts

**NTK 2-2, 2-3**

### OVERHEAD COSTS

**P3** Predetermined overhead rate

Applied overhead

Actual overhead

Summary of cost flows

Reporting costs

**NTK 2-4, 2-5**

### CLOSING OVERHEAD AND SERVICE USES

**P4** Overhead account

Underapplied or overapplied overhead

Job order costing for services

**A1** Pricing services

**NTK 2-6**

## Learning Objectives

### CONCEPTUAL

**C1** Explain job order costing and job cost sheets.

### ANALYTICAL

**A1** Apply job order costing in pricing services.

### PROCEDURAL

**P1** Describe and record the flow of materials costs in job order costing.

**P2** Describe and record the flow of labor costs in job order costing.

**P3** Describe and record the flow of overhead costs in job order costing.

**P4** Close overapplied and underapplied factory overhead.

# Chip Off the Old Block

*"Preserve history with craftsmanship"*
—**MARK WALLACE**

ClarenceTabb Jr./Detroit News/AP Images

DETROIT—Touring a warehouse of salvaged materials, Mark Wallace said that it "would be cool to build a guitar from old wood." After learning how to use a router, Mark built a prototype and founded his company, **Wallace Detroit Guitars** (**WallaceDetroitGuitars.com**).

Most of the reclaimed wood Mark uses is over 100 years old and bears unique scars and stains. "We take something that was once great but cast aside and turn it into something new and vital," says Mark. Each guitar takes about three months to build. "Every guitar we make is truly unique," explains Mark. "All are hand-made to precise customer specifications."

Businesses like Mark's that produce goods to customer order use job order costing to determine the cost of each order. Understanding what customers want, and the costs required, enables Mark to properly price orders. "Prices depend on the rarity of wood and the components our customers want," admits Mark. Job order costing enables Mark to control costs that are often the downfall of startups.

Social media has spurred momentum for Mark's venture. "The **Instagram** photo of my first guitar went viral." Through analytics, Mark saw that followers enjoy "photos of artisans crafting old wood into new guitars." His posts help drive sales, currently topping $100,000 and 50 guitars per year. Mark lives by the motto: "Go for it!"

Sources: *Wallace Detroit Guitars website*, January 2021; *CNN Business*, August 2018; *Entrepreneur*, November 2017

# JOB ORDER COSTING

A **cost accounting system** accumulates production costs and assigns them to products and services. Managers use this information to control costs and set selling prices. Two basic types of cost accounting systems are *job order costing* and *process costing*. We describe job order costing in this chapter and process costing in the next chapter.

**C1**

Explain job order costing and job cost sheets.

## Job Order Production

Many companies produce customized products for specific customers. Each customized product is manufactured separately, and its production is called **job order production,** or *job order manufacturing*. Examples of job order production include a custom home, a factory building, custom jewelry, wedding invitations, tattoos, and audits by an accounting firm.

Production activities for a customized product represent a **job.** A key feature of job order production is the diversity of the products produced. Each customer order is unique. For example, **Disney** produces movies according to unique scripts, actors, and set locations.

When a job involves producing more than one unit of a custom product, it is called a **job lot.** Examples of products produced as job lots include T-shirts for a 10K race and advertising signs for a chain of stores. The volume of production is typically low such as 200 T-shirts or 100 signs.

## Job Order vs. Process Operations

**Process operations,** also called *process manufacturing* or *process production,* is the mass production of large quantities of similar products in a continuous flow of steps. For example, **Penn** uses process operations to make millions of tennis balls and **The Hershey Company** uses it to produce over a billion pounds of chocolate. Exhibit 2.1 lists key features of job order and process operations.

| Job Order Operations | Process Operations |
| --- | --- |
| • Custom orders | • Repetitive procedures |
| • Diverse products and services | • Similar products and services |
| • Low production volume | • High production volume |
| • High product flexibility | • Low product flexibility |
| • Low standardization | • High standardization |

**EXHIBIT 2.1**

Comparing Job Order and Process Operations

## Production Activities in Job Order Costing

An overview of job order production activity and cost flows is shown in Exhibit 2.2. This exhibit shows the March production activity of Road Warriors, which customizes vehicles with paint, speakers, amplifiers, video systems, alarms, and reinforced exteriors.

Job order production requires materials, labor, and overhead costs.

- *Direct materials* are key parts of a finished product and are clearly identified with one job.
- *Direct labor* is employee effort to directly convert materials to finished product on one job.
- *Overhead,* or *factory overhead,* includes manufacturing costs that indirectly support production of more than one job.

Common overhead items are depreciation on factory buildings and equipment, indirect materials, supervision and maintenance (indirect labor), factory insurance and property taxes, factory cleaning, and factory utilities.

Exhibit 2.2 shows that direct materials, direct labor, and overhead are added to three jobs started during March. Alarm systems and paint jobs are added to Jobs B15, B16, and B17. Job B16 also receives a high-end audio system. The company completed Job B15 in March and delivered it to the customer. At the end of March, Job B16 is in finished goods inventory and Job B17 is in work in process inventory.

**EXHIBIT 2.2**

Job Order Production
Activities and Cost Flows

## Cost Flows

Manufacturing costs flow through Raw Materials Inventory, Work in Process Inventory, and Finished Goods Inventory until the related goods are sold. While a job is being produced, its costs are recorded in **Work in Process Inventory.** When a job is finished, its total costs are transferred from Work in Process Inventory to **Finished Goods Inventory.** When a finished job is delivered to a customer, its total costs are transferred from Finished Goods Inventory to **Cost of Goods Sold.**

These **general ledger** inventory accounts do not provide enough cost detail for managers to plan and control production activities. Managers need to know the costs of each individual job or job lot. **Subsidiary records** are created to store job-specific cost data and are described next.

## Job Cost Sheet

A **job order costing system** is used to determine the cost of producing each job or job lot. A **job cost sheet** is a cost record maintained for each job. Exhibit 2.3 shows a job cost sheet for Road Warriors. This job cost sheet identifies the customer, the job number, the costs, and key dates. Only product costs are on job cost sheets. Direct materials and direct labor costs incurred on the job are on this sheet. For Job B15, the direct materials and direct labor costs total $700 and $1,000. *Estimated* overhead costs are included on job cost sheets using a process we explain later in the chapter. For Job B15, estimated overhead costs are $1,600. When each job is complete, the supervisor enters the completion date and signs the sheet. Managers use job cost sheets to monitor costs incurred and to predict costs for each job.

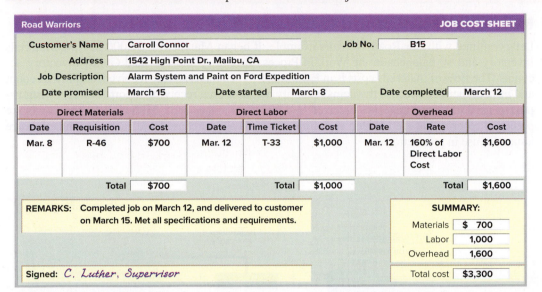

**EXHIBIT 2.3**

Job Cost Sheet

Direct Materials
+ Direct Labor
+ Overhead (estimated)
= Total job cost

**Linking Job Cost Sheets with Accounts**   Balances in the accounts equal the sums of costs on job cost sheets as defined in the table below.

| Account | Balance equals costs on job cost sheets for |
| --- | --- |
| Work in Process Inventory . . . . . . . . . . . | All jobs not yet done |
| Finished Goods Inventory . . . . . . . . . . . | All jobs complete but not yet sold |
| Cost of Goods Sold . . . . . . . . . . . . . . . . | All jobs sold in that period |

■ **Decision Insight**

**Target Costing**   Many producers determine a **target cost** for their jobs. Target cost is determined as follows: Expected selling price − Desired profit = Target cost. If the projected target cost of the job as determined by job costing is too high, the producer can apply *value engineering,* which is a method of determining ways to reduce job cost until the target cost is met. ■

A manufacturer has the following costs for Job No. 501 that requires printing 200 custom T-shirts for a bikers' reunion.

**NEED-TO-KNOW** 2-1

Job Cost Sheet

C1

| | |
| --- | --- |
| Direct materials, from requisition R-22 . . . . . . . . . . | $1,150 |
| Direct labor, from time ticket T-31 . . . . . . . . . . . . . | $ 250 |
| Estimated overhead . . . . . . . . . . . . . . . . . . . . . . . . | $ 400 |

1. Complete a (partial) job cost sheet and compute the total cost of this job lot.
2. Compute the cost per unit (T-shirt) for this job lot.

*Solution*

1.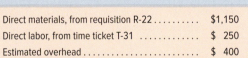

2. Cost per unit = Total cost/ Total number of units in job lot
   = $1,800/200 units
   = $9 per T-shirt

Do More: QS 2-3, QS 2-4, QS 2-5, E 2-2, E 2-4

## MATERIALS AND LABOR COSTS

### Materials Cost Flows and Documents

**P1**

Describe and record the flow of materials costs in job order costing.

Let's continue with our Road Warriors example. It began March with $1,000 in Raw Materials Inventory and $0 balances in the Work in Process Inventory and Finished Goods Inventory accounts. The flow of materials costs is in Exhibit 2.4. When materials are received, employees count and inspect them and record the items' quantity and cost on a receiving report. The **receiving report** is used to record materials received in a materials ledger card. **Materials ledger cards** are perpetual records that are updated each time materials are purchased and each time materials are issued for use in production.

**EXHIBIT 2.4**

Materials Cost Flows

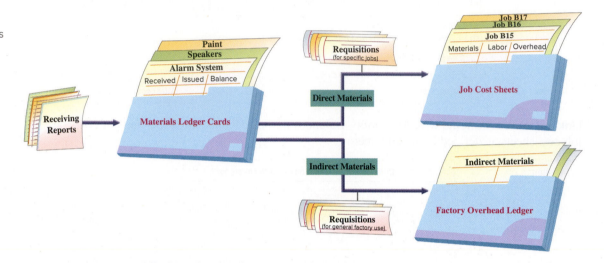

**Materials Purchases**     Road Warriors purchases $2,750 of materials on credit on March 4. These raw materials include both direct and indirect materials. This purchase is recorded below. Each materials ledger card is updated for the purchased materials.

| Mar. 4 | Raw Materials Inventory . . . . . . . . . . . . . . . . . . . . . . . . . | 2,750 | |
|---|---|---|---|
| | Accounts Payable . . . . . . . . . . . . . . . . . . . . . . . . | | 2,750 |
| | *Purchase materials for production.* | | |

**Materials Use (Requisitions)**     Exhibit 2.4 shows that materials are commonly requisitioned, or requested, to be used on a specific job (direct materials) or as overhead (indirect materials). Direct materials are costs that *can* be cost-effectively traced to individual jobs, such as alarm systems. Indirect materials are costs that *cannot* be cost-effectively traced to individual jobs, such as the cost of electrical tape and glue.

Direct materials costs flow to job cost sheets. Indirect materials costs flow to the Factory Overhead general ledger account. The Factory Overhead account is a clearing (temporary) account consisting of indirect costs.

Exhibit 2.5 shows a materials ledger card for an alarm system. The card shows the stock number, location in the storeroom, maximum and minimum quantities available, and the reorder quantity. For example, two alarm systems were purchased on March 4 as recorded in receiving report C-71. After this purchase, the company has three alarm systems in inventory.

**EXHIBIT 2.5**

Materials Ledger Card

**MATERIALS LEDGER CARD**

Road Warriors
Los Angeles, California

| Item | Alarm system | | Stock No. | M–3 | | Location in Storeroom | | Bin 7 |
| Maximum quantity | 5 units | | Minimum quantity | 1 unit | | Quantity to reorder | | 2 units |

| | Received | | | | Issued | | | | Balance | | |
|---|---|---|---|---|---|---|---|---|---|---|---|
| Date | Receiving Report Number | Units | Unit Price | Total Price | Requisition Number | Units | Unit Price | Total Price | Units | Unit Price | Total Price |
| Mar. 4 | C-71 | 2 | $600 | $1,200 | | | | | 1 | $600 | $  600 |
| | | | | | | | | | 3 | 600 | 1,800 |
| Mar. 8 | | | | | R–46 | 1 | $600 | $600 | 2 | 600 | 1,200 |

When materials are needed in production, a production manager prepares a **materials requisition** and sends it to the materials manager. For direct materials, the requisition shows the job number, the types of materials, and the quantities needed. On March 8, one alarm system was issued and recorded in requisition R-46.

Exhibit 2.6 shows the materials requisitions for Job B15, Job B16, and Job B17. For requisitions of indirect materials, the "Job No." line might read "For General Factory Use."

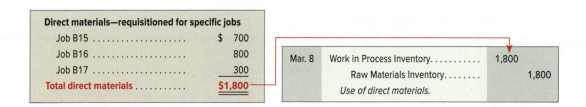

**EXHIBIT 2.6**

Materials Requisition

**MATERIALS REQUISITION  No. R–48**

Road Warriors

B17

By *C. Luther*

| | Total Cost |
|---|---|
| | $  75 |
| | 225 |
| | $300 |

**MATERIALS REQUISITION  No. R–47**

Road Warriors

B16

By *C. Luther*

| | Total Cost |
|---|---|
| | $600 |
| | 100 |
| | 100 |
| | $800 |

**MATERIALS REQUISITION  No. R–46**

Road Warriors

| Date | Mar. 8 | Job No. | B15 |
| Filled By | *M. Bateman* | Requested By | *C. Luther* |

| Part No. | Description | Units | Unit Cost | Total Cost |
|---|---|---|---|---|
| M–3 | Alarm system | 1 | $600 | $600 |
| P–2 | Paint | 4 | 25 | 100 |
| | | | | $700 |

Requisitions often are accumulated by job and recorded in one journal entry. Road Warriors records its materials requisitions as follows.

| Direct materials—requisitioned for specific jobs | |
|---|---|
| Job B15 ................... | $  700 |
| Job B16 ................... | 800 |
| Job B17 ................... | 300 |
| **Total direct materials** ......... | **$1,800** |

| Mar. 8 | Work in Process Inventory .......... | 1,800 | |
| | Raw Materials Inventory ....... | | 1,800 |
| | *Use of direct materials.* | | |

Exhibit 2.7 shows the postings to Work in Process Inventory and Raw Materials Inventory general ledger accounts. The exhibit shows summary job cost sheets for all three jobs, and it shows a detailed partial job cost sheet for Job B15.

**EXHIBIT 2.7**

Posting Direct Materials
Used to Accounts and
Job Cost Sheet

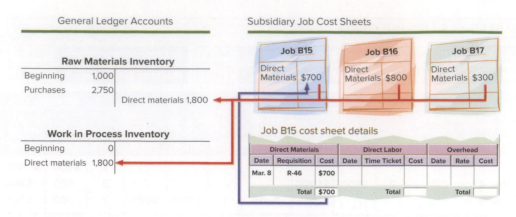

The Raw Materials Inventory account began the month with $1,000 of beginning inventory; it was increased for purchases of $2,750. The $1,800 cost of direct materials used reduces Raw Materials Inventory and increases Work in Process Inventory. The total amount of direct materials used so far ($1,800) is reflected in the job cost sheets. Later we show the accounting for indirect materials. At this point, know that requisitions of indirect materials are not separately recorded on job cost sheets.

 **NEED-TO-KNOW  2-2**

Recording Direct
Materials

**P1**

Prepare journal entries to record the following transactions of a manufacturing company.

**1.** Purchased $1,200 of materials on credit for use in production.

**2.** Used $200 of direct materials on Job 1 and $300 of direct materials on Job 2.

**3.** Compute the ending balance of Raw Materials Inventory. Its beginning balance was $200.

**Solution**

Do More: QS 2-6, E 2-13

**1.**

| Raw Materials Inventory. . . . . . . . . . . . . | 1,200 | |
| Accounts Payable . . . . . . . . . . . . . | | 1,200 |
| *Purchase of materials on credit.* | | |

**2.**

| Work in Process Inventory . . . . . . . . . . . | 500 | |
| Raw Materials Inventory . . . . . . . . | | 500 |
| *Use of direct materials.* | | |

**3.** Ending raw materials inventory = Beginning raw materials inventory + Raw materials purchases − Direct materials used
= $200 + $1,200 − $500 = $900

**P2** _____

Describe and record the
flow of labor costs in job
order costing.

# Labor Cost Flows and Documents

Exhibit 2.8 shows that labor costs are classified as either direct or indirect. Direct labor costs flow to job cost sheets. To assign direct labor costs to individual jobs, companies use **time tickets** to track how much time employees spend on each job. This process is often automated. Employees swipe identification badges and a computer system assigns employees' hours worked to individual jobs.

**EXHIBIT 2.8**

Labor Cost Flows

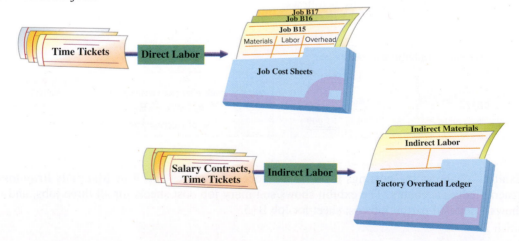

Indirect labor includes factory costs like supervisor salaries and maintenance worker wages. These costs are not assigned directly to individual jobs. Instead, indirect labor costs flow to the Factory Overhead ledger account.

Exhibit 2.9 shows time tickets for Jobs B15, B16, and B17.

**EXHIBIT 2.9**

Time Ticket

Time tickets are often accumulated and recorded in one journal entry. For March, Road Warriors's direct labor costs total $4,200.

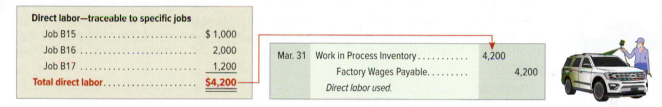

The entry for direct labor is posted to the Work in Process Inventory and Factory Wages Payable (or Cash) accounts. Exhibit 2.10 shows these postings. The exhibit also shows summary job cost sheets for all three jobs, and it shows a partial job cost sheet for Job B15.

**EXHIBIT 2.10**

Posting Direct Labor to Accounts and Job Cost Sheet

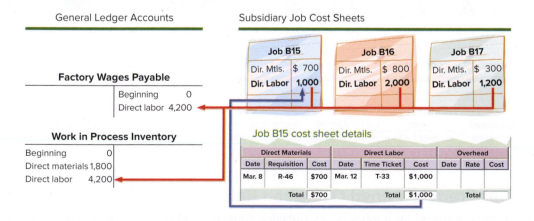

Time tickets are used to determine direct labor cost ($4,200) to assign to specific jobs. This total is the amount of direct labor posted to the Work in Process Inventory account. After this entry is posted, the balance in Work in Process Inventory is $6,000, consisting of $1,800 of direct materials and $4,200 of direct labor. Later we show the accounting for indirect labor, which is not separately recorded on job cost sheets.

**NEED-TO-KNOW** 2-3

Recording Direct Labor

**P2** ▶

A company started two jobs in June, Job A1 and Job A2.  Time tickets for June report 270 direct labor hours worked at a rate of $20 per direct labor hour.  Job A1 used 150 direct labor hours and Job A2 used 120 direct labor hours.

**1.** What is cost of direct labor on Job A1's cost sheet and on Job A2's cost sheet?

**2.** Prepare the journal entry to record direct labor used.

*Solution*

**1.** Job A1's cost of direct labor is $3,000 (150 DLH × $20).

   Job A2's cost of direct labor is $2,400 (120 DLH × $20).

**2.**

| | | |
|---|---|---|
| Work in Process Inventory . . . . . . . . . . | 5,400 | |
|     Factory Wages Payable . . . . . . . . | | 5,400 |
| *Direct labor used.* | | |

Do More: QS 2-7, E 2-14

---

# OVERHEAD COSTS

**P3** _____

Describe and record the flow of overhead costs in job order costing.

Unlike direct materials and direct labor, actual overhead costs *cannot* be cost-effectively traced to individual jobs. Still, each job's total cost must include *estimated* overhead costs.

**Overhead Process**   Accounting for overhead costs follows the four-step process shown in Exhibit 2.11. Overhead accounting requires managers to first estimate what total overhead costs will be for the coming period and how to apply those costs to jobs. Managers cannot wait until the end of a period to allocate actual overhead to jobs because they need it in setting prices and monitoring job profitability. At the end of each period, the company closes its overhead account.

**EXHIBIT 2.11**

Four-Step Process for Overhead

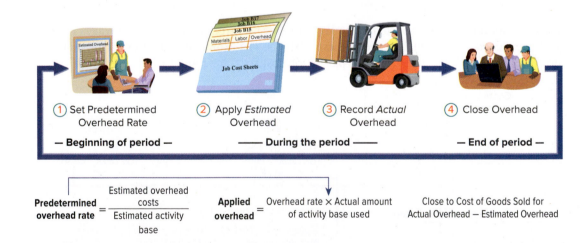

$$\text{Predetermined overhead rate} = \frac{\text{Estimated overhead costs}}{\text{Estimated activity base}}$$

$$\text{Applied overhead} = \text{Overhead rate} \times \text{Actual amount of activity base used}$$

Close to Cost of Goods Sold for Actual Overhead − Estimated Overhead

## ① Set Predetermined Overhead Rate

Estimating overhead for a job requires a **predetermined overhead rate,** also called *predetermined overhead allocation* (or *application*) *rate*. This in turn requires an estimate of total overhead cost and an estimated activity base *before* the start of the period. Exhibit 2.12 shows how to compute a predetermined overhead rate. This rate is used during the period to apply estimated overhead to jobs, based on each job's *actual* usage of the activity.

**EXHIBIT 2.12**

Predetermined Overhead Rate

$$\text{Predetermined overhead rate} = \frac{\text{Estimated overhead costs}}{\text{Estimated activity base}}$$

**Estimated Activity Base**   The *activity* (or *allocation*) *base* is a measure of production, such as direct labor or machine hours. The activity base should relate to the use of overhead costs. The choice of which activity base to use affects the accuracy of job costs, which likely impacts prices set and other key decisions.

**Computing Predetermined Overhead Rate**   Let's return to Road Warriors and compute its predetermined overhead rate. At the start of the year, Road Warriors estimated total direct labor costs of $125,000 and total overhead costs of $200,000. Its predetermined overhead rate follows.

Diego Cervo/Shutterstock

$$\frac{\$200,000}{\$125,000} = 160\% \text{ (or 1.6 times) of direct labor costs}$$

## ② Apply Estimated Overhead to Jobs

Overhead is applied to each job based on the actual activity base used for that job.

**Applied overhead = Predetermined overhead rate × Actual activity base used**

Activity base is direct labor cost for Road Warriors. Exhibit 2.13 shows overhead applied for its March production activity. Overhead costs for each job are often accumulated and recorded in one entry, as shown. Applied overhead is credited to Factory Overhead.

**Point:** Factory Overhead is a clearing (temporary) account that is closed to zero at each period-end.

**EXHIBIT 2.13**

Overhead Applied to Jobs

| Job | Direct Labor Cost | Predetermined Overhead Rate | Applied Overhead |
|-----|------|------|------|
| B15 | $1,000 | 1.6 | $1,600 |
| B16 | 2,000 | 1.6 | 3,200 |
| B17 | 1,200 | 1.6 | 1,920 |
| Total | $4,200 | | $6,720 |

| | | | |
|---|---|---|---|
| Mar. 31 | Work in Process Inventory . . . . . . . . . . . | 6,720 | |
| | Factory Overhead . . . . . . . . . . . . | | 6,720 |
| | *Apply overhead at 160% direct labor.* | | |

This entry is posted to the Work in Process Inventory and the Factory Overhead accounts. Exhibit 2.14 shows these postings. The exhibit shows summary job cost sheets for all three jobs, and it shows a partial job cost sheet for Job B15.

**EXHIBIT 2.14**

Posting Overhead to Accounts and Job Cost Sheet

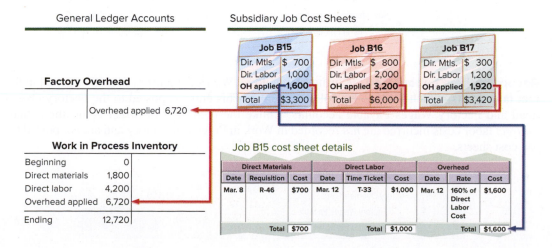

| General Ledger Accounts | | Subsidiary Job Cost Sheets |
|---|---|---|

**Job B15**

| Dir. Mtls. | $ 700 |
| Dir. Labor | 1,000 |
| OH applied | 1,600 |
| Total | $3,300 |

**Job B16**

| Dir. Mtls. | $ 800 |
| Dir. Labor | 2,000 |
| OH applied | 3,200 |
| Total | $6,000 |

**Job B17**

| Dir. Mtls. | $ 300 |
| Dir. Labor | 1,200 |
| OH applied | 1,920 |
| Total | $3,420 |

**Factory Overhead**

| | |
|---|---|
| | Overhead applied 6,720 |

**Work in Process Inventory**

| Beginning | 0 |
| Direct materials | 1,800 |
| Direct labor | 4,200 |
| Overhead applied | 6,720 |
| Ending | 12,720 |

**Job B15 cost sheet details**

| | Direct Materials | | | Direct Labor | | | Overhead | | |
|------|------|------|------|------|------|------|------|------|------|
| Date | Requisition | Cost | Date | Time Ticket | Cost | Date | Rate | Cost |
| Mar. 8 | R-46 | $700 | Mar. 12 | T-33 | $1,000 | Mar. 12 | 160% of Direct Labor Cost | $1,600 |
| | Total | $700 | | Total | $1,000 | | Total | $1,600 |

At this point, $6,720 of applied overhead has been posted to Work in Process Inventory and Factory Overhead accounts. The ending balance of $12,720 in the Work in Process Inventory account equals the sum of the ending balances in the job cost sheets.

---

**NEED-TO-KNOW** **2-4**

Recording Applied Overhead

**P3**

Do More: QS 2-8, QS 2-9, QS 2-10, QS 2-11, E 2-17

At the beginning of the year, a manufacturing company estimates it will incur $240,000 of overhead costs. The company applies overhead using machine hours and estimates it will use 1,600 machine hours for the year. During June, the company used 80 machine hours on Job 1 and 70 machine hours on Job 2.

1. Compute the predetermined overhead rate.
2. Determine overhead applied in June to (*a*) Job 1 and (*b*) Job 2.
3. Prepare the journal entry to record overhead applied for June.

*Solution*

1. $240,000/1,600 = $150 per machine hour.
2. (*a*) 80 × $150 = $12,000 applied to Job 1.
   (*b*) 70 × $150 = $10,500 applied to Job 2.

3.

| Work in Process Inventory . . . . . . | 22,500 | |
|---|---|---|
| Factory Overhead . . . . . . . . | | 22,500 |
| *Applied overhead.* | | |

---

### ③ Record Actual Overhead

We showed how applied (estimated) overhead costs are recorded on job cost sheets and in journal entries. We now show how *actual* overhead costs are accounted for, and that they are *not* recorded on job cost sheets.

Factory overhead includes indirect materials, indirect labor, and other overhead costs. These costs are recorded from materials requisition forms for indirect materials, and from salary contracts or time tickets for indirect labor. Other sources of actual overhead costs include vouchers authorizing payment for factory items such as supplies and utilities, and journal entries for costs such as depreciation on factory assets. Actual overhead costs are recorded with debits to the Factory Overhead account. We show these entries next.

**Point:** Nonmanufacturing costs such as advertising and sales commissions are not overhead, but instead are period costs and reported on the income statement.

**Raw Materials Inventory**

| Beginning | 1,000 | | |
|---|---|---|---|
| Purchases | 2,750 | | |
| | | Direct materials | 1,800 |
| | | Indirect materials | 550 |
| Ending | 1,400 | | |

**Record Indirect Materials Used**   During March, Road Warriors incurred $550 of actual indirect materials costs, which leads to the following entry. This entry is posted to the Factory Overhead and Raw Materials Inventory accounts. Unlike the recording of *direct* materials, the actual *indirect* materials costs incurred are *not* recorded in Work in Process Inventory and are *not* posted to job cost sheets.

| Mar. 31 | Factory Overhead. . . . . . . . . . . . . . . . . . . . . . . . . . . . . | 550 | |
|---|---|---|---|
| | Raw Materials Inventory . . . . . . . . . . . . . . . . . . . . | | 550 |
| | *Record indirect materials used.* | | |

**Record Indirect Labor Used**   During March, Road Warriors incurred $1,100 of actual indirect labor costs, which leads to the following entry. This entry is posted to the Factory Overhead and Factory Wages Payable accounts. Unlike the recording of *direct* labor, the actual *indirect* labor costs incurred are *not* recorded in Work in Process Inventory and are *not* posted to job cost sheets.

| Mar. 31 | Factory Overhead. . . . . . . . . . . . . . . . . . . . . . . . . . . . | 1,100 | |
|---|---|---|---|
| | Factory Wages Payable. . . . . . . . . . . . . . . . . . . . . | | 1,100 |
| | *Record indirect labor used.* | | |

**Record Other Overhead Costs**   During March, Road Warriors incurred $5,270 of actual other overhead costs. These costs often include items such as depreciation on factory equipment, factory building rent, factory utilities, expired factory insurance, and other costs indirectly related to production. These costs are recorded with a debit to Factory Overhead and credits to other accounts such as Cash, Accounts Payable, Utilities Payable, and Accumulated Depreciation. The entry to record Road Warriors's actual other overhead costs for March follows.

| Mar. 31 | Factory Overhead......................................... | 5,270 | |
| | Accumulated Depreciation—Factory Equipment....... | | 2,400 |
| | Rent Payable................................... | | 1,620 |
| | Utilities Payable................................ | | 250 |
| | Prepaid Insurance.............................. | | 1,000 |
| | *Actual other overhead costs.* | | |

This entry is posted to the Factory Overhead account. These actual overhead costs are *not* recorded in Work in Process Inventory and are *not* posted to job cost sheets. Only applied overhead is recorded in Work in Process Inventory and posted to job cost sheets.

| Factory Overhead | | | |
|---|---|---|---|
| Indirect materials | 550 | 6,720 | Overhead |
| Indirect labor | 1,100 | | applied |
| Other overhead | 5,270 | | |

A manufacturing company used $400 of indirect materials and $2,000 of indirect labor during the period. The company also incurred $1,200 for depreciation on factory equipment and $300 for factory utilities. Prepare the journal entry to record actual overhead costs.

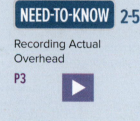

**NEED-TO-KNOW** **2-5**

Recording Actual
Overhead

**P3**

**Solution**

| Factory Overhead................................. | 3,900 | |
| | Raw Materials Inventory....................... | | 400 |
| | Factory Wages Payable........................ | | 2,000 |
| | Accumulated Depreciation—Factory Equipment.... | | 1,200 |
| | Utilities Payable............................. | | 300 |
| | *Actual other overhead costs.* | | |

Do More: E 2-13, E 2-18

# Cost Flows to Financial Statements

Exhibit 2.15 shows how costs for a manufacturing company flow to financial statements. We see that costs of direct materials used, direct labor used, and overhead applied flow through the Work in Process Inventory and Finished Goods Inventory balance sheet accounts. The cost of goods manufactured (COGM) is computed on the schedule of cost of goods manufactured. When goods are sold, their costs are transferred from Finished Goods Inventory on the balance sheet to the income statement as cost of goods sold.

**EXHIBIT 2.15**

Cost Flows and Reports

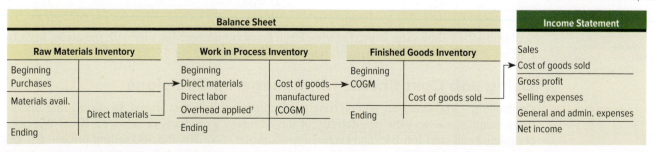

† Predetermined overhead rate × Actual activity base used.

**Point:** Sales revenue is also recorded for Job B15 (see Exhibit 2.17).

For Road Warriors, the entries to record the flow of costs from Work in Process Inventory to Finished Goods Inventory (for Jobs B15 and B16), and from Finished Goods Inventory to Cost of Goods Sold (for Job B15), follow.

| Mar. 31 | Finished Goods Inventory . . . . . . . . . . . . . . . . . . . . . . . | 9,300 | |
| | Work in Process Inventory . . . . . . . . . . . . . . . . . . | | 9,300 |
| | *Transfer cost of goods manufactured for Jobs B15 & B16.* | | |

| Mar. 31 | Cost of Goods Sold. . . . . . . . . . . . . . . . . . . . . . . . . . | 3,300 | |
| | Finished Goods Inventory. . . . . . . . . . . . . . . . . . | | 3,300 |
| | *Record cost of goods sold for Job B15.* | | |

Period costs (selling expenses and general and administrative expenses) do not impact inventory accounts. As a result, they do not impact cost of goods sold, and they are not reported on the schedule of cost of goods manufactured. They are reported on the income statement as operating expenses.

**Accounting for Cost Flows**   The upper part of Exhibit 2.16 shows the flow of direct materials, direct labor, and overhead costs through the inventory accounts and eventually cost of goods sold. Each numbered cost flow reflects journal entries.

The lower part of Exhibit 2.16 shows job cost sheets at the period-end. The costs assigned to the job in process (Job B17) equal the $3,420 balance in Work in Process Inventory. Costs assigned to the completed Job B16 equal the $6,000 balance in Finished Goods Inventory. The balances in Raw Materials Inventory, Work in Process Inventory, and Finished Goods Inventory are reported on the end-of-period balance sheet. The costs assigned to the sold Job B15 equals the $3,300 balance in Cost of Goods Sold. This is reported on the income statement for the period.

**EXHIBIT 2.16**

Job Order Cost Flows and Ending Job Cost Sheets

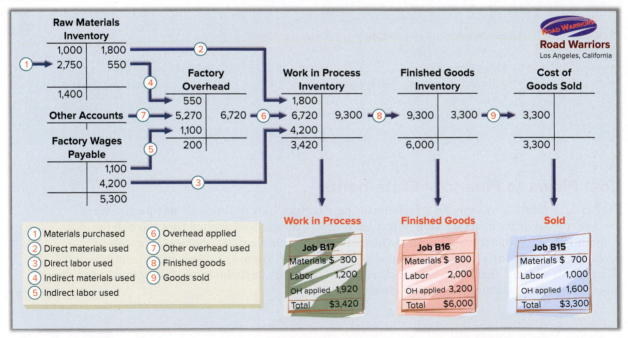

**Point:** *Actual* overhead is debited to Factory Overhead. *Applied* overhead is credited to Factory Overhead.

Exhibit 2.17 shows the journal entries. Each entry is numbered to link with the arrow lines in Exhibit 2.16. Exhibit 2.17 concludes with the sale of Job B15 for $5,500.

# Using Job Cost Sheets for Managerial Decisions

**Controlling**   Managers depend on timely information in job cost sheets. In *controlling* operations, managers assess the profitability of the company's products or services. Road Warriors completed and sold Job B15 and earned a gross profit of $2,200 ($5,500 selling price − $3,300 cost of goods sold). If this gross profit is higher than expected, managers will try to determine if

| ① | Raw Materials Inventory | 2,750 | |
|---|---|---|---|
| | Accounts Payable | | 2,750 |
| | *Acquired raw materials.* | | |

| ② | Work in Process Inventory | 1,800 | |
|---|---|---|---|
| | Raw Materials Inventory | | 1,800 |
| | *Direct materials used.* | | |

| ③ | Work in Process Inventory | 4,200 | |
|---|---|---|---|
| | Factory Wages Payable | | 4,200 |
| | *Direct labor used.* | | |

| ④ | Factory Overhead | 550 | |
|---|---|---|---|
| | Raw Materials Inventory | | 550 |
| | *Indirect materials used.* | | |

| ⑤ | Factory Overhead | 1,100 | |
|---|---|---|---|
| | Factory Wages Payable | | 1,100 |
| | *Indirect labor used.* | | |

| ⑥ | Work in Process Inventory | 6,720 | |
|---|---|---|---|
| | Factory Overhead | | 6,720 |
| | *Apply overhead at 160% of direct labor.* | | |

| ⑦ | Factory Overhead | 5,270 | |
|---|---|---|---|
| | Accumulated Depreciation—Factory Equipment | | 2,400 |
| | Rent Payable | | 1,620 |
| | Utilities Payable | | 250 |
| | Prepaid Insurance | | 1,000 |
| | *Actual overhead costs.* | | |

| ⑧ | Finished Goods Inventory | 9,300 | |
|---|---|---|---|
| | Work in Process Inventory | | 9,300 |
| | *Record completion of Jobs B15 and B16.* | | |

| ⑨ | Cost of Goods Sold | 3,300 | |
|---|---|---|---|
| | Finished Goods Inventory | | 3,300 |
| | *Record cost of goods sold for Job B15.* | | |

| ⑩ | Accounts Receivable | 5,500 | |
|---|---|---|---|
| | Sales | | 5,500 |
| | *Record sale of Job B15.* | | |

**EXHIBIT 2.17**

Entries for Job Order Costing

there are production efficiencies that can be applied to future jobs. For example, has the business found a way to reduce the amount of direct labor? If gross profit is low, managers will determine if costs are too high. In this case, can cheaper raw materials be used without sacrificing product quality? Is the company using costly overtime to complete jobs? Managers can also evaluate costs to date for in-process jobs (B17) to determine whether costs are as planned.

**Planning**   In *planning* future production, managers consider selling prices. Can the company raise selling prices without losing business? Can the company match competitors' price cuts and earn profit? Managers can use information in job cost sheets to focus efforts toward more profitable types of jobs. The detailed and timely information in job cost sheets helps managers make better decisions for each job and for the business as a whole.

**Bidding**   Job costs can be used in *bidding* on new custom jobs. Some companies use **cost-plus pricing,** where a markup is added to cost to yield a target price. For example, if the estimated production costs for a potential job are $1,000 and Road Warriors wants a markup of 30% of production costs, it could bid a price of $1,300 (computed as $1,000 + [$1,000 × 30%]).

## Schedule of Cost of Goods Manufactured

Road Warriors' schedule of cost of goods manufactured is in Exhibit 2.18. This schedule is similar to that in the previous chapter, with one key difference: *Total manufacturing costs include overhead applied, not actual overhead costs.*

**ROAD WARRIORS**
**Schedule of Cost of Goods Manufactured**
**For Month Ended March 31**

| | |
|---|---|
| Direct materials used | $ 1,800 |
| Direct labor | 4,200 |
| Factory overhead applied | 6,720 |
| Total manufacturing costs | 12,720 |
| Add work in process inventory, beginning | 0 |
| Total cost of work in process | 12,720 |
| Less work in process inventory, ending | 3,420 |
| Cost of goods manufactured | $ 9,300 |

**EXHIBIT 2.18**

Schedule of Cost of Goods Manufactured

## Financial Statements

Road Warriors' income statement for March and a partial balance sheet as of March 31 follow. The income statement reports sales and cost of goods sold information from Exhibit 2.17. Selling expenses of $400 and general and administrative expenses of $1,200 are provided by management. The partial balance sheet reports inventory account balances from Exhibit 2.16.

| ROAD WARRIORS Income Statement For Month Ended March 31 | |
|---|---|
| Sales . . . . . . . . . . . . . . . . . . . . . . . . . | $5,500 |
| Cost of goods sold . . . . . . . . . . . . . . . . | 3,300 |
| Gross profit . . . . . . . . . . . . . . . . . . . . . | 2,200 |
| Selling expenses. . . . . . . . . . . . . . . . . . | 400 |
| General and administrative expenses . . . | 1,200 |
| Net income . . . . . . . . . . . . . . . . . . . . . . | $  600 |

| ROAD WARRIORS Inventory Balances on Balance Sheet March 31 | |
|---|---|
| Current assets | |
| Raw materials inventory . . . . | $ 1,400 |
| Work in process inventory . . . | 3,420 |
| Finished goods inventory . . . | 6,000 |
| Total inventory . . . . . . . . . . . | $10,820 |

# CLOSING OVERHEAD

**P4**

Close overapplied and underapplied factory overhead.

Refer to the debits in the Factory Overhead account in Exhibit 2.16 or Exhibit 2.17. The total cost of *actual* factory overhead during March is $6,920 ($550 + $5,270 + $1,100). The $6,920 actual overhead costs do not equal the $6,720 overhead *applied* to work in process inventory (see ⑥ in Exhibit 2.17). This leaves a debit balance of $200 in the Factory Overhead account. Because it is hard to precisely estimate future costs, actual overhead rarely equals applied overhead. Companies wait until the end of the period to close the Factory Overhead account for differences between actual and applied overhead. We show how this is done.

## Factory Overhead Account

**EXHIBIT 2.19**

Factory Overhead T-account

| Factory Overhead | |
|---|---|
| Actual overhead costs | Applied overhead costs |
| Underapplied overhead    or | Overapplied overhead |

Exhibit 2.19 shows the Factory Overhead account. The company applies overhead (credits the Factory Overhead account) using a predetermined rate estimated at the beginning of the period. During the period, the company records actual overhead costs with debits to the Factory Overhead account. At period-end, we determine whether actual overhead is more or less than applied overhead.

- When actual overhead is *more* than applied overhead, the remaining debit balance in the Factory Overhead account is **underapplied overhead.**
- When actual overhead is *less* than applied overhead, the resulting credit balance in the Factory Overhead account is **overapplied overhead.**

When overhead is underapplied, jobs have not been charged enough overhead during the period, and cost of goods sold is undercosted. When overhead is overapplied, jobs have been charged too much overhead during the period, and cost of goods sold is overcosted. In both cases, we close Factory Overhead to Cost of Goods Sold with a journal entry, see Exhibit 2.20.

**EXHIBIT 2.20**

Closing Factory Overhead

| Overhead Costs | Overhead Balance | Overhead Is | Jobs Are | Journal Entry Required | |
|---|---|---|---|---|---|
| Actual > Applied | Debit | Underapplied | Undercosted | Cost of Goods Sold . . . . .    # | |
| | | | | Factory Overhead . . . . | # |
| Actual < Applied | Credit | Overapplied | Overcosted | Factory Overhead . . . . . .    # | |
| | | | | Cost of Goods Sold . . .    | # |

## ④ **Close Underapplied or Overapplied Overhead**

Road Warriors applied $6,720 of overhead to jobs during March, but it incurred actual overhead of $6,920 during March. This means the Factory Overhead account has a debit balance of $200, see the following T-account.

| Factory Overhead | | | |
|---|---|---|---|
| Indirect materials | 550 | 6,720 | Overhead applied |
| Indirect labor | 1,100 | | |
| Other overhead | 5,270 | | |
| Underapplied overhead | 200 | | |

The $200 debit balance is *underapplied overhead*. This means the balances in Work in Process Inventory, Finished Goods Inventory, and Cost of Goods Sold understate the manufacturing costs incurred. Assuming this difference is immaterial, it is closed to Cost of Goods Sold with the following entry.

**Point:** When underapplied or overapplied overhead is material, the amount can be divided among Cost of Goods Sold, Finished Goods Inventory, and Work in Process Inventory accounts. This is covered in advanced courses.

| Mar. 31 | Cost of Goods Sold............................. | 200 | |
|---|---|---|---|
| | Factory Overhead .......................... | | 200 |
| | *Close underapplied overhead costs.* | | |

The $200 debit (increase) to Cost of Goods Sold reduces net income by $200. After this entry, the Factory Overhead account has a zero balance (is closed). Cost of Goods Sold now reflects actual overhead costs for the period. The entry to close Factory Overhead at period-end does not impact any job cost sheets. *Note:* If instead we had overapplied overhead at the end of the period, we would debit Factory Overhead and credit Cost of Goods Sold for the amount.

A manufacturing company applied $300,000 of overhead to its jobs during the period. Prepare the journal entry to close over- or underapplied overhead to Cost of Goods Sold for each of the following two separate cases.

**1.** Actual overhead costs equal $305,000.

**2.** Actual overhead costs equal $298,500.

**NEED-TO-KNOW 2-6**

Closing Factory Overhead

**P4**

Do More: QS 2-18, QS 2-19, QS 2-20, QS 2-21, E 2-25, E 2-26, E 2-27

*Solution*

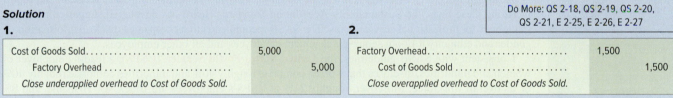

**1.**

| Cost of Goods Sold............................. | 5,000 | |
|---|---|---|
| Factory Overhead .......................... | | 5,000 |
| *Close underapplied overhead to Cost of Goods Sold.* | | |

**2.**

| Factory Overhead............................. | 1,500 | |
|---|---|---|
| Cost of Goods Sold ........................ | | 1,500 |
| *Close overapplied overhead to Cost of Goods Sold.* | | |

## **Job Order Costing of Services**

Job order costing also applies to service companies. Service companies often perform custom services for specific customers. Examples include an accountant auditing a client's financial statements, an interior designer remodeling an office, a wedding consultant planning and supervising a reception, and a lawyer defending a client.

Job order costing has some important differences for service firms.

- Most service firms do not have raw materials inventory nor finished goods inventory. However, they do have inventories of supplies, and they can have services in process inventory. Often these supplies are immaterial and are considered overhead costs.
- Direct labor is often used to apply overhead because service firms do not use direct materials.
- Service firms typically use different account titles, for example **Services in Process Inventory** and **Services Overhead.** When service jobs are completed, costs are transferred from Services in Process Inventory to **Cost of Services Provided.**

| Service Cost | |
|---|---|
| Traced to service → Direct labor ............... | $ |
| Applied to service → Overhead ................... | $ |
| Total cost of service | $ |

Exhibit 2.21 shows the flow of costs for a service firm called AdWorld, a developer of advertising materials. During the month, AdWorld worked on custom advertising campaigns for clients that wanted ads for three different platforms: mobile devices, television, and radio. In this chapter's Decision Analysis section, we show an example of using job order costing to price advertising services for AdWorld.

**EXHIBIT 2.21**

Flow of Costs for Service Firm

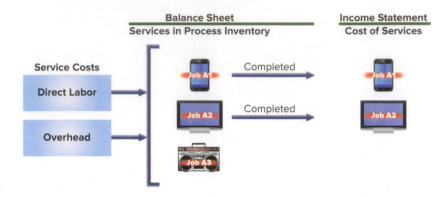

###  Analytics **Insight**

**Picture of Health**   Health care providers use electronic records and data analytics to reduce costs and improve patient care. *Risk scores,* which combine data from lab tests, biometrics, health insurance claims, and health surveys, enable doctors to customize individual patient treatment and prevention plans. By analyzing patterns in historical patient data, doctors can better diagnose issues, plan better care, and reduce costs. ■

## CORPORATE SOCIAL RESPONSIBILITY

Jesse David Green

Professional service firms in accounting, consulting, law, and financial services compete for highly talented employees with strong technical skills. In addition, a more diverse workforce is likely to lead to different points of view that arguably can produce even better services and ultimately more profit for the company. Enhancing workforce diversity can also help attract and retain talented people.

Although workforce diversity is not recorded on job cost sheets, many companies measure and report it. Along these lines, the Sustainability Accounting Standards Board has developed suggested reporting guidelines for professional service firms. The SASB recommends that companies disclose information on gender and ethnicity for both senior management employees and all other employees.

Consistent with SASB guidelines, the **United States Postal Service (USPS)**, a leading employer of women and minorities, discloses that women comprise roughly 40% and minorities comprise roughly 40% of its overall workforce. Moreover, roughly 21% of USPS's employees are Black, 8% Hispanic, and 8% Asian.

**Wallace Detroit Guitars**, the focus of this chapter's opening feature, uses reclaimed wood as direct materials in making electric guitars. Founder Mark Wallace requires his wood to be "responsibly harvested, and never from a property that could be renovated." He also sources his wood through local nonprofit organizations that train and employ local residents. "It's exciting," says Mark, "we are revitalizing Detroit."

**Decision Analysis**  **Pricing for Services**

## A1

Apply job order costing in pricing services.

The chapter describes job order costing mainly within a manufacturing setting. However, service providers also use job order costing. Consider AdWorld, a service company that prepares advertisements. Each customer has unique requirements, so costs for each individual job are tracked separately.

AdWorld uses two types of direct labor: designers ($65 per hour) and staff ($50 per hour). It applies overhead costs using a predetermined overhead rate of $108 per direct labor hour. For each job, AdWorld estimates the number of designer and staff hours needed. Then, total costs of each job are determined using job order costing.

To demonstrate, a manufacturer requests a quote from AdWorld for an advertising engagement. AdWorld estimates that the job will require 43 designer hours and 61 staff hours. Total estimated cost for this job follows.

| Estimated Job Cost—Advertising Services | |
|---|---|
| **Direct Labor** | |
| Designers (43 hours × $65)........ | $ 2,795 |
| Staff (61 hours × $50) ............ | 3,050 |
| Total direct labor................. | 5,845 |
| **Overhead** | |
| Total overhead (104 hours × $108) . | 11,232 |
| Total estimated job cost........... | $17,077 |

AdWorld can use this cost information to help determine the price quote for the job. If AdWorld's normal pricing policy is to apply a markup of 18% on total costs, it would compute a quoted price as follows. *Hint:* An 18% markup on cost is the same as saying price is 118% of total cost.

Price Quote = 118% × $17,077 = $20,151.

AdWorld must also consider the market, that is, how much competitors will quote for this job. Competitor information is often unavailable. Therefore, AdWorld's managers must use estimates based on their assessment of the competitive environment.

| Price Quote | |
|---|---|
| Job cost | $17,077 |
| Markup (18%) | 3,074 |
| Price | $20,151 |

Service companies can use the *gross profit ratio,* also called *gross margin* ratio, computed as follows.

$$\text{Gross profit ratio} = \frac{\text{Service revenue} - \text{Cost of services}}{\text{Service revenue}}$$

A higher gross profit ratio indicates a company is more able to submit a lower price quote. This ability increases when a company increases its gross profit ratio. This also applies when comparing companies: the company with the higher gross profit ratio has more ability to bid a lower price for a job.

## ■ Decision Maker

**Sales Manager**   As AdWorld's sales manager, you are planning to quote a price of $20,151 (computed above) for the advertising job. However, you learn that three other agencies are likely to bid for the same job, and that their quotes will range from $16,500 to $22,000. What price should you quote? What factors other than cost must you consider? ■   *Answer:* One option is to apply normal pricing policy and quote a price of $20,151. It is, however, useful to assess competitor pricing, especially in terms of service quality and other benefits. Although price is important, factors such as quality and timeliness (responsiveness) of suppliers are also important. Thus, another option is to highlight these factors.

Miller Company reports the following for its job order production activities for May.

| | | | |
|---|---|---|---|
| Raw materials purchases............. | $16,000 | Indirect materials................. | $5,000 |
| Direct materials used ............... | 8,450 | Indirect labor .................... | 3,500 |
| Direct labor........................ | 11,900 | Other factory overhead ........... | 9,500 |

**NEED-TO-KNOW** 2-7

**COMPREHENSIVE**

Job Costs, Journal Entries, and Schedule of Cost of Goods Manufactured

Miller's predetermined overhead rate is 150% of direct labor cost. Job cost sheet information for the three jobs worked on during May follows.

| | Job 401 | Job 402 | Job 403 |
|---|---|---|---|
| Work in process inventory, April 30 | | | |
| Direct materials used (in April) .... | $3,600 | | |
| Direct labor used (in April)........ | 1,700 | | |
| Overhead applied (April) ......... | 2,550 | | |
| Costs incurred in May | | | |
| Direct materials used............. | 3,550 | $3,500 | $1,400 |
| Direct labor used ............... | 5,100 | 6,000 | 800 |
| Overhead applied .............. | ? | ? | ? |
| Status on May 31 ................ | **Finished (sold)** | **Finished (unsold)** | **In process** |

[continued on next page]

[continued from previous page]

**Required**

1. Determine the cost for factory overhead, both actual and applied, during May. Compute the amount of any over- or underapplied overhead on May 31.
2. Compute the total cost of (*a*) each job as of May 31, (*b*) the May 31 inventories for both Work in Process and Finished Goods, and (*c*) the cost of goods sold for May.
3. Prepare journal entries for the month to record each part *a* through *f*.
   a. Materials purchases (on credit), direct materials used, direct labor used, and overhead applied.
   b. Actual overhead costs, consisting of indirect materials, indirect labor, and other overhead costs paid in cash.
   c. Transfer of each completed job to the Finished Goods Inventory account.
   d. Record cost of goods sold.
   e. Record sale (on credit) of Job 401 for $35,000.
   f. Close any underapplied or overapplied overhead in Factory Overhead to Cost of Goods Sold.
4. Prepare a schedule of cost of goods manufactured for May.

## SOLUTION

1. Actual and applied factory overhead, and under- or overapplied.

| Actual overhead | |
|---|---:|
| Indirect materials . . . . . . . . . . . . . . . . . . . . . . . . . . . | $  5,000 |
| Indirect labor . . . . . . . . . . . . . . . . . . . . . . . . . . . | 3,500 |
| Other factory overhead . . . . . . . . . . . . . . . . . . . . . . | 9,500 |
| Total actual overhead . . . . . . . . . . . . . . . . . . . . . . . . | 18,000 |
| Overhead applied (150% × $11,900) . . . . . . . . . . . . | 17,850 |
| Underapplied overhead . . . . . . . . . . . . . . . . . . . . . . . | $   150 |

2. a. Total cost of each job.

| | 401 | 402 | 403 |
|---|---:|---:|---:|
| Work in process, April 30 | | | |
| Direct materials used (in April) . . . . . . . . | $  3,600 | | |
| Direct labor used (in April) . . . . . . . . . . . | 1,700 | | |
| Overhead applied (April) . . . . . . . . . . . . | 2,550 | | |
| Costs incurred in May | | | |
| Direct materials used . . . . . . . . . . . . . . . | 3,550 | $  3,500 | $1,400 |
| Direct labor used . . . . . . . . . . . . . . . . . | 5,100 | 6,000 | 800 |
| Overhead applied (150% of direct labor) | 7,650 | 9,000 | 1,200 |
| Total cost of each job . . . . . . . . . . . . . . . | $24,150 | $18,500 | $3,400 |

   b. Work in Process Inventory (Job 403) = $3,400
      Finished Goods Inventory (Job 402) = $18,500
   c. Cost of goods sold for May (Job 401) = $24,150

3. Journal entries.
   a. Record raw materials purchases, direct materials used, direct labor used, and overhead applied.

| Raw Materials Inventory . . . . . . . . . | 16,000 | |
|---|---:|---:|
| Accounts Payable . . . . . . . . . . | | 16,000 |
| *Record materials purchases.* | | |
| Work in Process Inventory . . . . . . . . | 8,450 | |
| Raw Materials Inventory . . . . . | | 8,450 |
| *Direct materials used.* | | |

| Work in Process Inventory . . . . . . . . | 11,900 | |
|---|---:|---:|
| Factory Wages Payable . . . . . . | | 11,900 |
| *Direct labor used.* | | |
| Work in Process Inventory . . . . . . . . | 17,850 | |
| Factory Overhead . . . . . . . . . | | 17,850 |
| *Overhead applied to jobs.* | | |

**b.** Record actual overhead costs.

| Factory Overhead.................. | 5,000 | |
| Raw Materials Inventory........ | | 5,000 |
| *Indirect materials used.* | | |

| Factory Overhead.................. | 3,500 | |
| Factory Wages Payable......... | | 3,500 |
| *Indirect labor used.* | | |

| Factory Overhead.................. | 9,500 | |
| Cash........................ | | 9,500 |
| *Record actual other overhead.* | | |

**c.** Transfer cost of completed jobs to Finished Goods Inventory.

| Finished Goods Inventory ........... | 42,650 | |
| Work in Process Inventory........ | | 42,650 |
| *Record completion of jobs.* | | |
| *$24,150 Job 401 + $18,500 Job 402.* | | |

**d.** Record cost of job sold.

| Cost of Goods Sold................ | 24,150 | |
| Finished Goods Inventory........ | | 24,150 |
| *Record costs for sale of Job 401.* | | |

**e.** Record sales for job sold.

| Accounts Receivable .............. | 35,000 | |
| Sales........................ | | 35,000 |
| *Record sale of Job 401.* | | |

**f.** Close underapplied overhead to cost of goods sold.

| Cost of Goods Sold................ | 150 | |
| Factory Overhead ............ | | 150 |
| *Close underapplied overhead.* | | |

**4.**

| MILLER COMPANY | |
| --- | --- |
| Schedule of Cost of Goods Manufactured | |
| For Month Ended May 31 | |
| Direct materials used .......................... | $ 8,450 |
| Direct labor .................................. | 11,900 |
| Factory overhead applied ..................... | 17,850 |
| Total manufacturing costs ...................... | 38,200 |
| Add: work in process inventory, beginning......... | 7,850 |
| Total cost of work in process ................... | 46,050 |
| Less: work in process inventory, ending .......... | 3,400 |
| Cost of goods manufactured ................... | $42,650 |

## Summary: Cheat Sheet

### JOB ORDER COSTING

**Job:** Production of a custom product.
**Job lot:** Producing more than one unit of a custom product.
**Job cost sheet:** Cost record kept for each job or job lot.

**Direct materials** used in manufacturing and clearly identified with one job.
**Direct labor** is employee effort on one specific job.
**Overhead** costs support production of more than one job.

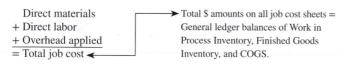

Direct materials
+ Direct labor
+ Overhead applied
= Total job cost → Total $ amounts on all job cost sheets = General ledger balances of Work in Process Inventory, Finished Goods Inventory, and COGS.

### Flow of Manufacturing Costs

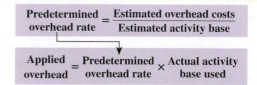

| Raw Materials Inventory | Work in Process Inventory | Finished Goods Inventory |
| --- | --- | --- |
| Beg. bal. | Beg. bal. | Beg. bal. |
| Purchases | DM used | COGM |
| DM Used | DL used | COGS |
| End. bal. | FOH used  COGM | End. bal. |
| | End. bal. | |

DM = direct materials; DL = direct labor; FOH = factory overhead applied; COGM = cost of goods manufactured; COGS = cost of goods sold

### MATERIALS AND LABOR COSTS

**Acquire raw materials**

| Raw Materials Inventory.......................... | 2,750 | |
| Accounts Payable .......................... | | 2,750 |

**Record *direct* materials used**

| Work in Process Inventory ....................... | 1,800 | |
| Raw Materials Inventory ..................... | | 1,800 |

**Record *direct* labor used**

| Work in Process Inventory ....................... | 4,200 | |
| Factory Wages Payable...................... | | 4,200 |

### OVERHEAD COSTS

$$\frac{\text{Predetermined}}{\text{overhead rate}} = \frac{\text{Estimated overhead costs}}{\text{Estimated activity base}}$$

$$\frac{\text{Applied}}{\text{overhead}} = \frac{\text{Predetermined}}{\text{overhead rate}} \times \frac{\text{Actual activity}}{\text{base used}}$$

**Record *indirect* materials used**

| | | |
|---|---|---|
| Factory Overhead............................ | 550 | |
|    Raw Materials Inventory...................... | | 550 |

**Record *indirect* labor used**

| | | |
|---|---|---|
| Factory Overhead............................... | 1,100 | |
|    Factory Wages Payable....................... | | 1,100 |

**Apply overhead using predetermined rate**

| | | |
|---|---|---|
| Work in Process Inventory...................... | 6,720 | |
|    Factory Overhead .......................... | | 6,720 |

**Record *actual* overhead costs**

| | | |
|---|---|---|
| Factory Overhead............................... | 5,270 | |
|    Accumulated Depreciation—Factory Equipment ... | | 2,400 |
|    Rent Payable .......................... | | 1,620 |
|    Utilities Payable........................... | | 250 |
|    Prepaid Insurance.......................... | | 1,000 |

**Record completion of jobs**

| | | |
|---|---|---|
| Finished Goods Inventory ......................... | 9,300 | |
|    Work in Process Inventory.................... | | 9,300 |

**Record cost of goods sold for sold jobs**

| | | |
|---|---|---|
| Cost of Goods Sold............................... | 3,300 | |
|    Finished Goods Inventory.................... | | 3,300 |

**Record sales for sold jobs**

| | | |
|---|---|---|
| Accounts Receivable ........................... | 5,500 | |
|    Sales..................................... | | 5,500 |

## CLOSING OVERHEAD

| Factory Overhead | |
|---|---|
| Actual overhead costs | Applied overhead costs |
| Underapplied overhead   or | Overapplied overhead |

**Close overhead and COGS at period-end**

| Overhead Costs | Overhead Balance | Overhead Is | Journal Entry Required |
|---|---|---|---|
| Actual > Applied | Debit | Underapplied | Cost of Goods Sold......... # |
| | | |    Factory Overhead ....... # |
| Actual < Applied | Credit | Overapplied | Factory Overhead.......... # |
| | | |    Cost of Goods Sold ..... # |

**ROAD WARRIORS**
**Schedule of Cost of Goods Manufactured**
**For Month Ended March 31**

| | |
|---|---|
| Direct materials used ..................... | $ 1,800 |
| Direct labor ............................. | 4,200 |
| Factory overhead applied ................ | 6,720 |
| Total manufacturing costs ................ | 12,720 |
| Add work in process inventory, beginning ... | 0 |
| Total cost of work in process .............. | 12,720 |
| Less work in process inventory, ending ..... | 3,420 |
| Cost of goods manufactured ............. | $ 9,300 |

## Multiple Choice Quiz

**1.** A company's predetermined overhead rate is 150% of its direct labor costs. How much overhead is applied to a job that used total direct labor costs of $30,000?

  **a.** $15,000      **c.** $45,000      **e.** $75,000
  **b.** $30,000      **d.** $60,000

**2.** A company uses direct labor costs to apply overhead. Its costs for the period are direct materials, $45,000; direct labor, $35,000; and overhead applied, $38,500. What is its predetermined overhead rate?

  **a.** 10%      **c.** 86%      **e.** 117%
  **b.** 110%      **d.** 91%

**3.** A company's ending inventory of finished goods has a total cost of $10,000 and consists of 500 units. If the overhead applied to these goods is $4,000 and the predetermined overhead rate is 80% of direct labor costs, how much direct materials cost was incurred in producing these 500 units?

  **a.** $10,000      **c.** $4,000      **e.** $1,000
  **b.** $6,000      **d.** $5,000

**4.** A company's Work in Process Inventory T-account follows.

| Work in Process Inventory | | | |
|---|---|---|---|
| Beginning | 9,000 | | |
| Direct materials | 94,200 | | |
| Direct labor | 59,200 | Cost of goods | |
| Overhead applied | 31,600 | manufactured | ? |
| Ending | 17,800 | | |

The cost of goods manufactured is

**a.** $193,000.          **c.** $185,000.          **e.** $176,200.

**b.** $211,800.          **d.** $144,600.

**5.** At the end of its current period, a company's overhead was underapplied by $1,500. This amount is not material. The company should

   **a.** credit the $1,500 to Finished Goods Inventory.

   **b.** credit the $1,500 to Cost of Goods Sold.

   **c.** debit the $1,500 to Cost of Goods Sold.

   **d.** do nothing as overhead is likely to be overapplied by a similar amount next period.

   **e.** report the $1,500 on the income statement as "Other Expense."

### ANSWERS TO MULTIPLE CHOICE QUIZ

**1.** c; $30,000 × 150% = $45,000

**2.** b; $38,500/$35,000 = 110%

**3.** e; Direct materials + Direct labor + Overhead = Total cost;
Direct materials + ($4,000/0.80) + $4,000 = $10,000
Direct materials = $1,000

**4.** e; $9,000 + $94,200 + $59,200 + $31,600 − Cost of goods manufactured = $17,800.
Thus, cost of goods manufactured = $176,200

**5.** c

---

*Select Quick Study and Exercise assignments feature Guided Example videos, called "Hints" in Connect. Hints use different numbers, and instructors can turn this feature on or off.*

---

Indicate which of the following are most likely to be considered as a job and which as a job lot.

**1.** 200 hats imprinted with company logo

**2.** 80 Little League trophies

**3.** Unique handcrafted table

**4.** A 90-foot custom yacht

**5.** 50 advertisements for a chain of stores

**6.** A custom-designed home

**QUICK STUDY**

**QS 2-1**
Distinguishing jobs and job lots   C1

---

Indicate whether each item *a* through *e* is a feature of a job order or process operation.

**a.** Diverse products and services

**b.** Routine, repetitive procedures

**c.** Low product flexibility

**d.** Low production volume

**e.** Low product standardization

**QS 2-2**
Comparing process and job order operations

C1

---

Auto Safe's job cost sheet for Job A40 shows that the total cost to add security features to a car was $10,500. The car was delivered to the customer, who paid $14,900 cash for this job.
   Prepare the journal entries for Job A40 to record (*a*) its completion and (*b*) its sale.

**QS 2-3**
Recording job completion and sale   C1

---

EcoSkate makes skateboards from recycled plastic. For a recent job lot of 100 skateboards, the company incurred direct materials costs of $600 and direct labor costs of $200. Factory overhead applied to this job is $900. (1) What is the total manufacturing cost of this job lot? (2) What is the cost per skateboard?

**QS 2-4**
Computing total cost and cost per unit   C1

---

The following partial job cost sheet is for a job lot of 2,500 units completed.

**QS 2-5**
Job cost sheet

C1

| JOB COST SHEET | | | | | | | |
|---|---|---|---|---|---|---|---|
| Customer's Name | Huddits Company | | Quantity | 2,500 | Job No. | 202 | |
| | Direct Materials | | Direct Labor | | | Overhead | |
| Date | Requisition | Cost | Time Ticket | Cost | Date | Rate | Cost |
| Mar. 8 | #55 | $43,750 | #1–10 | $60,000 | Mar. 8 | 160% of Direct Labor Cost | $96,000 |
| Mar. 11 | #56 | 25,250 | | | | | |

**1.** What is the total cost of this job lot?

**2.** What is the total cost per unit completed?

**QS 2-6**

Recording
materials   **P1    P3**

A company that uses job order costing purchases $50,000 in raw materials for cash. It then uses $12,000 of raw materials as indirect materials and uses $32,000 of raw materials as direct materials.

Prepare journal entries to record the (*a*) purchase of raw materials, (*b*) use of indirect materials, and (*c*) use of direct materials.

**QS 2-7**

Recording labor   **P2    P3**

A company that uses job order costing incurred a monthly factory payroll of $180,000. Of this amount, $30,000 is indirect labor and $150,000 is direct labor.

Prepare journal entries to record the (*a*) use of direct labor and (*b*) use of indirect labor.

**QS 2-8**

Computing predetermined
overhead rates   **P3**

A company estimates the following manufacturing costs at the beginning of the period: direct labor, $468,000; direct materials, $390,000; and factory overhead, $117,000. Compute its predetermined overhead rate as a percent of (1) direct labor and (2) direct materials. Express answers as percents.

**QS 2-9**

Applying overhead   **P3**

At the beginning of the year, a company estimates total overhead costs of $560,000. The company applies overhead using machine hours and estimates it will use 1,400 machine hours during the year.

What amount of overhead should be applied to Job 65A if that job uses 13 machine hours that year?

**QS 2-10**

Computing predetermined
overhead rate   **P3**

At the beginning of the year, a company estimates total direct materials costs of $900,000 and total overhead costs of $1,170,000. If the company uses direct materials costs as its activity base to apply overhead, what is the predetermined overhead rate it should use during the year?

**QS 2-11**

Applying overhead

**P3**

On March 1, a dressmaker starts work on three different custom-designed wedding dresses. The company uses job order costing and applies overhead to each job (dress) at the rate of 40% of direct materials costs. During the month, the jobs used direct materials as shown below. Compute the amount of overhead applied to each of the three jobs.

|                          | Job 1  | Job 2  | Job 3  |
|--------------------------|--------|--------|--------|
| Direct materials used .......... | $5,000 | $7,000 | $1,500 |

**QS 2-12**

Computing overhead
applied; service company

**P3**

Ace Patios applies overhead using direct labor hours as its activity base. At the beginning of the year, the company estimates total direct labor hours of 20,000 and total overhead costs of $600,000 for the year.

**1.** Determine the company's predetermined overhead rate.

**2.** Job A2 used 50 direct labor hours. What is the total of overhead costs applied to this job?

**QS 2-13**

Recording actual overhead
costs   **P3**

A manufacturer incurred the following actual factory overhead costs: indirect materials, $6,200; indirect labor (factory wages payable), $9,000; depreciation on factory equipment, $12,000; factory utilities (utilities payable), $800; and factory insurance expired, $500. Prepare journal entries to record (*a*) indirect materials, (*b*) indirect labor, and (*c*) other actual overhead costs.

**QS 2-14**

Recording job completion
and sale   **P3**

A custom manufacturer completed Jobs 103 and 104. Job 103 cost $12,000 and was sold (on credit) for $20,000. Job 104 cost $15,000. Prepare journal entries to record (*a*) the completion of both jobs, (*b*) the sale of Job 103, and (*c*) cost of goods sold for Job 103.

**QS 2-15**

Computing overhead cost
flows   **P4**

Built-Tite uses job order costing. The T-account below summarizes Factory Overhead activity for the current year.

| Factory Overhead | |
|---|---|
| 16,000 | 105,800 |
| 25,000 | |
| 60,000 | |
| | |

**1.** Compute total *applied* overhead cost.

**2.** Compute total *actual* overhead cost.

**3.** Compute the underapplied or overapplied overhead.

A company that uses job order costing reports the costs incurred below. Overhead is applied at the rate of 60% of direct materials cost. The company has no beginning Work in Process or Finished Goods inventories. Jobs 1 and 3 are not finished by the end of the month, and Job 2 is finished but not sold by month-end.

|  | Job 1 | Job 2 | Job 3 |
|---|---|---|---|
| Direct materials used . . . . . . . . . . . | $5,000 | $7,000 | $1,500 |
| Direct labor used. . . . . . . . . . . . . . | $9,000 | $4,000 | $3,000 |

**1.** Prepare job cost sheets that have direct materials, direct labor, and overhead applied for *each of the three jobs* for the month.
**2.** Determine the total dollar amount of Work in Process Inventory at the end of the month.
**3.** Determine the total dollar amount of Finished Goods Inventory at the end of the month.

**QS 2-16**
Preparing and interpreting job cost sheet
**P1  P2  P3**

---

Shen Co. reports the costs incurred below for the month ended May 31. The company has no beginning Work in Process Inventory. Overhead is applied using a predetermined overhead rate of 120% of direct materials costs. Job 4 was completed and Job 5 is still in process at month-end. Prepare a schedule of cost of goods manufactured for the month.

|  | Job 4 | Job 5 |
|---|---|---|
| Direct materials used . . . . . . . . . . . | $1,500 | $1,000 |
| Direct labor used. . . . . . . . . . . . . . | 2,100 | 200 |

**QS 2-17**
Preparing a schedule of cost of goods manufactured
**P3**

---

A company applies overhead at a rate of 150% of direct labor cost. Actual overhead cost for the current period is $950,000, and direct labor cost is $600,000.

**1.** Compute the under- or overapplied overhead.
**2.** Prepare the journal entry to close over- or underapplied overhead to Cost of Goods Sold.

**QS 2-18**
Computing and recording over- or underapplied overhead  **P4**

---

A company's Factory Overhead account shows total debits of $624,000 and total credits of $646,000 at the end of the year.

**1.** Compute the under- or overapplied overhead.
**2.** Prepare the journal entry to close the balance in the Factory Overhead account to Cost of Goods Sold.

**QS 2-19**
Computing and recording over- or underapplied overhead  **P4**

---

Rize Co. reports the following (partial) T-account activity at the end of its first year of operations.

| Factory Overhead | |
|---|---|
| 80,500 | 404,000 |
| 125,100 | |
| 194,400 | |

**1.** Compute the under- or overapplied overhead for the year.
**2.** Prepare the journal entry to close Factory Overhead to Cost of Goods Sold.

**QS 2-20**
Computing and recording under- or overapplied overhead  **P4**

---

Custom Co. reports the following (partial) T-account activity at the end of its first year of operations.

| Factory Overhead | |
|---|---|
| 80,400 | 390,000 |
| 130,000 | |
| 184,600 | |

**1.** Compute the under- or overapplied overhead for the year.
**2.** Prepare the journal entry to close Factory Overhead to Cost of Goods Sold.

**QS 2-21**
Computing and recording under- or overapplied overhead  **P4**

**QS 2-22**
Job order costing
of services   **A1**

An advertising agency is estimating costs for promoting a music festival. The job will require 200 direct labor hours at a cost of $50 per hour. Overhead costs are applied at a rate of $65 per direct labor hour.

**1.** What is the total estimated cost for this job?

**2.** If the company applies a markup of 20% of total costs (price quote is 120% of total costs), what price should it quote for this job?

---

**QS 2-23**
Job order costing
of services   **A1**

A marketing agency used 60 hours of direct labor in creating advertising for a film festival. Direct labor costs $50 per hour. The agency applies overhead at a rate of $40 per direct labor hour.

**1.** What is the total estimated cost for this job?

**2.** If the company applies a markup of 10% of total costs (price quote is 110% of total costs), what price should it quote for this job?

---

**QS 2-24**
Gross profit ratio   **A1**

A manufacturer reports sales of $80,000 and cost of goods sold of $60,000.

**1.** Compute its gross profit ratio.

**2.** If competitors average a 10% gross profit ratio, does this manufacturer compare favorably or unfavorably to its peers?

---

# EXERCISES

**Exercise 2-1**
Defining production
activities   **C1**

Match each of the terms with the best definition *a* through *d*.

**1.** Cost accounting system
**2.** Target cost
**3.** Job
**4.** Process operation

**a.** Production activities for a custom product.
**b.** Mass production in a continuous flow of steps.
**c.** A system that records manufacturing costs.
**d.** The expected selling price of a job minus its desired profit.

---

**Exercise 2-2**
Preparing job cost sheet
and computing costs

**C1**

The following information is from the materials requisitions and time tickets for Job 9 completed by Great Bay Boats. Materials requisitions are identified by code numbers starting with the letter M, and the time tickets start with T. Estimated (applied) overhead for Job 9 is $1,400. Prepare a job cost sheet for Job 9, which includes costs for direct materials, direct labor, overhead, and total cost.

| Date | Document | Amount |
|---|---|---|
| July 1....... | M-46 | $1,250 |
| July 1....... | T-33 | 600 |
| July 5....... | M-47 | 1,000 |
| July 5....... | T-34 | 450 |
| July 10...... | T-35 | 300 |

---

**Exercise 2-3**
Interpreting job cost sheets

**C1**

Following are simplified job cost sheets for three custom jobs at the end of June for Custom Patios.

| Job No. 102 | |
|---|---|
| Materials.......... | $15,000 |
| Labor.............. | 8,000 |
| Overhead ......... | 4,000 |

| Job No. 103 | |
|---|---|
| Materials.......... | $33,000 |
| Labor.............. | 14,200 |
| Overhead ......... | 7,100 |

| Job No. 104 | |
|---|---|
| Materials.......... | $27,000 |
| Labor.............. | 21,000 |
| Overhead ......... | 10,500 |

All jobs were started in June. Overhead is applied with a predetermined rate based on direct labor cost. Jobs 102 and 103 were finished in June, and Job 104 will be finished in July.

**1.** What was the total cost of direct materials requisitioned in June?

**2.** How much total direct labor cost was incurred in June?

**3.** How much total cost is transferred to Finished Goods Inventory in June?

---

**Exercise 2-4**
Computing cost per unit

**C1**

Bell Co. produces stainless steel drink tumblers, its only product. These tumblers are stamped with company logos and used as promotional items. Following are simplified job cost sheets for two separate recently completed job lots. Job 1 was for 250 units and Job 2 was for 260 units.

| Job No. 1 | 250 units | | Job No. 2 | 260 units |
|---|---|---|---|---|
| Materials........... | $425 | | Materials........... | $403 |
| Labor............. | 750 | | Labor............. | 780 |
| Overhead ......... | 900 | | Overhead ......... | 936 |

**1.** Compute total cost per unit for Job 1 and for Job 2. Which job has a higher total cost per unit?

**2.** Compute direct materials cost per unit for each job. Which job has a higher direct materials cost per unit?

---

A manufacturer's Raw Materials Inventory account appears as follows.

**Exercise 2-5**
Record materials purchase and use   **P1  P3**

| Raw Materials Inventory | | | |
|---|---|---|---|
| Beginning | 25,000 | | |
| Purchases | 100,000 | | |
| | | 80,000 | Direct materials used |
| | | 15,000 | Indirect materials used |
| Ending | 30,000 | | |

All raw materials purchases are made on credit. Prepare journal entries to record the:

**1.** Purchase of raw materials.

**2.** Direct materials used.

**3.** Indirect materials used.

---

Information on Kwon Mfg.'s activities for its first month of operations follows.

**Exercise 2-6**
Computing job costs and gross profit   **P1  P2  P3**

**a.** Purchased $100,000 of raw materials on credit.

**b.** Materials requisitions show the following materials used for the month.

| | |
|---|---|
| Job 201 | $48,200 |
| Job 202 | 23,600 |
| Total direct materials | 71,800 |
| Indirect materials | 8,620 |
| Total materials used | $80,420 |

**c.** Time tickets show the following labor used for the month.

| | |
|---|---|
| Job 201 | $39,200 |
| Job 202 | 12,600 |
| Total direct labor | 51,800 |
| Indirect labor | 24,200 |
| Total labor used | $76,000 |

**d.** Applied overhead to Job 201 and to Job 202 using a predetermined overhead rate of 80% of direct materials cost.

**e.** Transferred Job 201 to Finished Goods Inventory.

**f.** (1) Sold Job 201 for $163,760 on credit. (2) Record cost of goods sold for Job 201.

**g.** Incurred the following actual other overhead costs for the month.

| | |
|---|---|
| Depreciation of factory equipment | $32,000 |
| Rent on factory building (payable) | 500 |
| Factory utilities (payable) | 800 |
| Expired factory insurance | 3,000 |
| Total other factory overhead costs | $36,300 |

**1.** Prepare a job cost sheet for Job 201 and for Job 202 for the month. Use the following simplified form.

| Job No. _____ | |
|---|---|
| Materials........... | $ |
| Labor............. | |
| Overhead ......... | |
| Total cost ......... | $ |

**2.** Compute gross profit on the sale of Job 201.

**Exercise 2-7**
Recording materials, labor, overhead, and sales
P1   P2   P3

Refer to information in Exercise 2-6. Prepare journal entries to record the transactions reflected in items *a* through *g*.

**Exercise 2-8**
T-accounts for manufacturing activities
P1   P2   P3

Refer to information in Exercises 2-6 and 2-7. Set up T-accounts for each of the following accounts, each of which started the month with a zero balance: Raw Materials Inventory, Work in Process Inventory, Finished Goods Inventory, Factory Overhead, Cost of Goods Sold. Then post entries for transactions *a* through *g* to the T-accounts and determine the balance of each account.

**Exercise 2-9**
Recording materials, labor, and overhead
P1   P2   P3

Starr Company shows the following information for the month.

| | | | |
|---|---|---|---|
| Raw materials purchased on credit...... | $76,200 | Direct labor used ................. | $15,350 |
| Direct materials used ................. | $48,000 | Overhead rate.................... | 120% of direct labor cost |

Prepare journal entries to record the following.

**1.** Raw materials purchased.      **3.** Direct labor used.

**2.** Direct materials used.       **4.** Applied overhead.

**Exercise 2-10**
Recording materials, labor, overhead, and sales; computing inventory cost
P1   P2   P3

Custom Cabinetry has one job in process (Job 120) as of June 30; at that time, its job cost sheet reports direct materials of $6,000, direct labor of $2,800, and applied overhead of $2,240. Custom Cabinetry applies overhead at the rate of 80% of direct labor cost. During July, Job 120 is sold (on credit) for $22,000, Job 121 is started and completed, and Job 122 is started and still in process at the end of July. Custom Cabinetry incurs the following costs during July.

| | Job 120 | Job 121 | Job 122 |
|---|---|---|---|
| Direct materials used ........ | $1,000 | $6,000 | $2,500 |
| Direct labor used ........... | 2,200 | 3,700 | 2,100 |

**1.** Prepare journal entries for the following July transactions and events *a* through *e*.

     **a.** Direct materials used.       **d.** Sale of Job 120.

     **b.** Direct labor used.         **e.** Cost of goods sold for Job 120. *Hint*: Job 120 has costs from June and July.

     **c.** Overhead applied.

**2.** Compute the July 31 balances of the Work in Process Inventory and the Finished Goods Inventory accounts. (There were no jobs in Finished Goods Inventory at June 30.)

**Exercise 2-11**
Computing inventory balances and over- or underapplied overhead
P1   P2   P3   P4

The following information is available for a custom manufacturer.

| Inventories | | Costs incurred for the period | |
|---|---|---|---|
| Raw materials, beginning .............. | $ 38,000 | Raw materials purchases .............. | $18,460 |
| Work in process, beginning ............ | 12,400 | Direct materials used ................. | 43,250 |
| Finished goods, beginning............. | 8,750 | Direct labor used .................... | 22,800 |
| Cost of goods manufactured ............. | 95,290 | Factory overhead (actual) | |
| Cost of goods sold (not considering over- or | |    Indirect materials used ............. | 9,300 |
|    underapplied overhead)............... | 83,200 |    Indirect labor used ................. | 16,400 |
| Sales...................... | 100,000 |    Other overhead costs............... | 4,300 |
| Predetermined overhead rate based on | | | |
|    direct materials used ................. | 80% | | |

**1.** Compute the ending balances of Raw Materials Inventory, Work in Process Inventory, and Finished Goods Inventory. *Hint:* Set up T-accounts for each of these three inventory accounts.

**2.** Compute overapplied or underapplied overhead.

The following information is available for ADT Company, which produces special-order security products and uses a job order costing system. Overhead is applied using a predetermined overhead rate of 70% of direct labor cost.

**Exercise 2-12**
Computing materials, labor, overhead, and cost of goods manufactured

P1  P2  P3  P4

| Inventories | Beginning of Period | End of Period |
|---|---|---|
| Raw materials.... | $43,000 | $52,000 |
| Work in process .. | 10,200 | 21,300 |
| Finished goods... | 63,000 | 35,600 |

| Costs incurred for the period | |
|---|---|
| Raw materials purchases........ | $210,000 |
| Factory payroll ................ | 345,000 |
| Factory overhead (actual) | |
| Indirect materials used ....... | 15,000 |
| Indirect labor used........... | 80,000 |
| Other overhead costs......... | 120,000 |

1. Set up a Raw Materials Inventory T-account and insert amounts for beginning and ending balances along with purchases and indirect materials used. Solve for direct materials used in the period.
2. Compute the cost of direct labor used for the period.
3. Set up a Work in Process Inventory T-account and insert amounts for beginning and ending balances along with direct materials used (from part 1), direct labor used (from part 2), and applied overhead. Solve for cost of goods manufactured in the period.
4. Set up a Finished Goods Inventory T-account and insert amounts for beginning and ending balances along with cost of goods manufactured (from part 3). Solve for cost of goods sold in the period (do not consider any under- or overapplied overhead).
5. Set up a Factory Overhead T-account and insert amounts for indirect materials used, indirect labor used, other overhead costs, and applied overhead. Solve for underapplied or overapplied overhead.

Use information in Exercise 2-12 to prepare journal entries for the following events for the period.
1. Raw materials purchases for cash.      3. Indirect materials used.
2. Direct materials used.

**Exercise 2-13**
Recording materials; direct and indirect  P1  P3

Use information in Exercise 2-12 to prepare journal entries for the following events for the period.
1. Direct labor used (recorded as factory wages payable).
2. Indirect labor used (recorded as factory wages payable).

**Exercise 2-14**
Recording direct and indirect labor  P2  P3

Use information in Exercise 2-12 to prepare journal entries for the following events for the period.
1. Incurred other actual overhead costs (all paid in Cash).
2. Applied overhead to work in process.

**Exercise 2-15**
Recording actual and applied overhead  P3

Telstar uses job order costing. The T-accounts below summarize its production activity for the year.

**Exercise 2-16**
Manufacturing cost flows

P1  P2  P3

| Raw Materials Inventory | | Factory Wages Payable | | Factory Overhead | | Work in Process Inventory | | Finished Goods Inventory | |
|---|---|---|---|---|---|---|---|---|---|
| 45,000 | 24,250 | 126,000 | 85,750 | 8,000 | 102,684 | 24,250 | 170,320 | 170,320 | 153,290 |
| 8,000 | | | 40,250 | 40,250 | | 85,750 | | | |
| | | | | 61,370 | | 102,684 | | | |

1. Compute the amount for each of the following.
   a. Direct materials used     d. Indirect labor used        f. Cost of goods sold (before closing
   b. Indirect materials used   e. Cost of goods manufactured      over- or underapplied overhead)
   c. Direct labor used
2. Compute the amount that overhead is overapplied or underapplied.

**Exercise 2-17**
Overhead rate; costs assigned to jobs

P3

Shire Company's predetermined overhead rate is based on direct labor cost. Management estimates the company will incur $747,500 of overhead costs and $575,000 of direct labor cost for the period. During March, Shire began and completed Job 56.

1. What is the predetermined overhead rate for this period?
2. Use the information on the following job cost sheet to determine the total cost of Job 56.

**JOB COST SHEET**

Customer's Name          Keiser Co.                              Job No.     56

Job Description                 3 customized systems

| | Direct Materials | | | Direct Labor | | Overhead | |
|---|---|---|---|---|---|---|---|
| Date | Requisition No. | Cost | | Time-Ticket No. | Cost | Rate | Cost |
| Mar. 8 | M-129 | $5,000 | | T-306 | $ 700 | | |
| Mar. 11 | M-142 | 7,000 | | T-432 | 1,250 | | |
| Mar. 18 | M-167 | 3,640 | | T-456 | 1,250 | | |
| Totals | | | | | | | |

**Exercise 2-18**
Recording transactions in job order costing

P1   P2   P3   P4

Prepare journal entries to record transactions *a* through *h*.

a. Raw materials purchased on credit, $90,000.
b. Direct materials used, $36,500. Indirect materials used, $19,200.
c. Direct labor used, $38,000. Indirect labor used, $12,000. (Record using Factory Wages Payable.)
d. Paid cash for other actual overhead costs, $11,475.
e. Applied overhead at the rate of 125% of direct labor cost.
f. Transferred cost of jobs completed to finished goods, $56,800.
g. Sales of jobs on credit was $82,000.
h. Cost of jobs sold was $56,800.

**Exercise 2-19**
Analyzing costs assigned to work in process

P3

Lorenzo Company applies overhead to jobs on the basis of direct materials cost. At year-end, the Work in Process Inventory account shows the following.

| Work in Process Inventory | | | |
|---|---|---|---|
| Beginning | 0 | | |
| Direct materials used | 1,500,000 | | |
| Direct labor used | 300,000 | | |
| Overhead applied | 600,000 | | |
| | | 2,350,000 | Cost of goods manufactured |
| Ending | 50,000 | | |

1. Determine the predetermined overhead rate used (based on direct materials cost).
2. Only one job remains in work in process inventory at year-end. Its direct materials cost is $30,000. How much direct labor cost and applied overhead are assigned to this job?

**Exercise 2-20**
Computing overhead rate and direct materials

P3

Tasty Bakery applies overhead based on direct labor costs. The company reports the following costs for the year: direct materials, $650,000; direct labor, $3,000,000; and overhead applied, $1,800,000.

1. Determine the company's predetermined overhead rate for the year.
2. The ending balance of its Work in Process Inventory account was $71,000, which included $20,000 of direct labor costs. Determine the direct materials costs in ending Work in Process Inventory.

Tyler Corp. reports the following results for its first month of operations ended December 31. Overhead is applied using a predetermined overhead rate of 80% of direct materials cost.

**Exercise 2-21**
Preparing an income statement and determining inventory balances
P3

| | | | |
|---|---|---|---|
| Raw materials purchased ....... | $18,400 | Sales ............................ | $36,000 |
| Direct materials used .......... | 12,000 | Cost of goods sold ................... | 28,400 |
| Direct labor used ............. | 18,400 | Selling expenses ..................... | 2,100 |
| Cost of goods manufactured .... | 32,000 | General and administrative expenses .... | 3,200 |

1. Prepare an income statement for the month ended December 31.
2. Determine the December 31 ending inventory balances for Raw Materials, Work in Process, and Finished Goods. *Hint:* Because Tyler is in its first month of operations, each account begins with a $0 balance; also, there were no indirect materials used this month.

A manufacturer began operations on April 1 and reports the information below. All jobs are sold for 20% above cost.

**Exercise 2-22**
Computing inventory balances and gross profit
P3

| | Manufacturing Costs | | |
|---|---|---|---|
| Job number | April | May | Job Status at May 31 |
| 1 | $ 800 | $2,120 | Completed and sold during May |
| 2 | 650 | 1,840 | In process |
| 3 | 1,200 | 2,630 | Completed but not sold |
| 4 | 475 | 400 | Completed and sold during May |
| 5 | | 3,600 | In process |

1. Compute the May 31 balance in (*a*) Work in Process Inventory and (*b*) Finished Goods Inventory.
2. Compute gross profit for May.

A manufacturer reports the following information at **June 30**.

**Exercise 2-23**
Computing inventory balances and cost of goods sold   P3

| Job number | Started | Completed | Sold | Cost at June 30 |
|---|---|---|---|---|
| 46 | April 5 | May 25 | June 1 | $1,775 |
| 47 | May 2 | May 30 | June 2 | 625 |
| 48 | May 21 | July 1 | July 2 | 640 |
| 49 | June 8 | June 29 | July 6 | 585 |
| 50 | June 19 | July 5 | July 10 | 960 |

1. Compute Work in Process Inventory at June 30.
2. Compute Finished Goods Inventory at June 30.
3. Compute cost of goods sold for June.

A manufacturing company reports the following for the period.

**Exercise 2-24**
Preparing a cost of goods manufactured schedule
P3

| Inventories | Beginning | Ending | | Activities for the period | |
|---|---|---|---|---|---|
| Raw materials........ | $18,020 | $12,000 | | Raw materials purchases..... | $ 8,100 |
| Work in process ...... | 9,400 | 11,200 | | Direct materials used ........ | 14,120 |
| Finished goods....... | 12,460 | 8,630 | | Direct labor used ........... | 9,200 |
| | | | | Overhead applied........... | 11,040 |
| | | | | Sales .................... | 40,000 |

1. Prepare a schedule of cost of goods manufactured.
2. Compute gross profit.

**Exercise 2-25**
Closing over- or underapplied overhead
P4

Prepare the journal entry to close over- or underapplied overhead to Cost of Goods Sold for each of the two companies below.

|  | Star Promotions | Valle Builders |
|---|---|---|
| Indirect materials . . . . . . . . . . . . | $22,000 | $ 12,500 |
| Indirect labor. . . . . . . . . . . . . . . | 46,000 | 46,500 |
| Other overhead. . . . . . . . . . . . . | 17,000 | 47,000 |
| Overhead applied. . . . . . . . . . . | 88,000 | 105,000 |

**Exercise 2-26**
Computing applied overhead and closing over- or underapplied overhead
P4

At the beginning of the year, Custom Mfg. set its predetermined overhead rate using the following estimates: overhead costs, $750,000, and direct materials costs, $625,000. At year-end, the company reports that actual overhead costs for the year are $758,000.

**1.** Determine the predetermined overhead rate using estimated direct materials costs.

**2.** Set up a T-account for Factory Overhead and enter the actual overhead costs incurred *and* the amount of overhead cost applied to jobs during the year using the predetermined overhead rate. Determine whether overhead is over- or underapplied (and the amount) for the year.

**3.** Prepare the entry to close any over- or underapplied overhead to Cost of Goods Sold.

**Exercise 2-27**
Computing applied overhead and closing over- or underapplied overhead
P4

At the beginning of the year, Mirmax set its predetermined overhead rate for movies produced during the year by using the following estimates: overhead costs, $1,680,000, and direct labor costs, $480,000. At year-end, the company's actual overhead costs for the year are $1,670,000.

**1.** Determine the predetermined overhead rate using estimated direct labor costs.

**2.** Set up a T-account for Factory Overhead and enter the actual overhead costs incurred *and* the amount of overhead cost applied to movies during the year using the predetermined overhead rate. Determine whether overhead is over- or underapplied (and the amount) for the year.

**3.** Prepare the entry to close any over- or underapplied overhead to Cost of Goods Sold.

**Exercise 2-28**
Computing overhead rate; setting price quote—service company
A1

Sofía Gomez runs a mobile pet grooming service. She charges $35 direct labor per grooming hour. She applies overhead to jobs on the basis of grooming hours. She predicts 800 grooming hours for the year. Her estimated overhead costs for the year follow.

| Van depreciation . . . . . . . . | $5,500 | Van insurance expense . . . | $1,000 | Tool depreciation . . . . . . . . . | $350 |
|---|---|---|---|---|---|
| Van maintenance . . . . . . . . | 1,200 | Indirect materials . . . . . . . | 600 | Other overhead . . . . . . . . . . | 950 |

**1.** Compute the predetermined overhead rate using estimated grooming hours.

**2.** Sofía has been asked to groom three large dogs. She expects this job to require a total of 12 direct labor grooming hours. Compute her total cost (direct labor plus applied overhead) for this job.

**3.** If Sofía targets a markup of 25% on the total cost for each job, what price should she quote for the job in part 2?

**Exercise 2-29**
Pricing services using job order costing
A1

Hansel Company has requested bids from several architects to design its new corporate headquarters. Frey Architects is bidding on the job. Frey estimates that the job will require the following direct labor.

| Direct Labor | Estimated Hours | Hourly Rate |
|---|---|---|
| Architects | 150 | $300 |
| Staff | 300 | 75 |
| Clerical | 500 | 20 |

Frey applies overhead to jobs at 175% of direct labor cost. Frey wants to earn at least $80,000 profit on the architectural job. Based on past experience and market research, it estimates that the competition will bid between $285,000 and $350,000 for the job.

1. What is Frey's estimated cost of the architectural job?

2. If Frey bids a price of $285,000, what is its expected profit? Will it earn its target profit of $80,000?

3. What bid price would earn the desired $80,000 target profit?

**Check**   (1) $213,125

---

Diaz and Associates incurred the following direct labor costs in completing tax services job for a client. Diaz applies overhead at 50% of direct labor cost.

**Exercise 2-30**
Determining cost and price for services
**A1**

| Direct Labor on Tax Job | Hours Used | Hourly Rate |
|---|---|---|
| Partner.................... | 5 | $500 |
| Senior manager ............ | 12 | 200 |
| Staff accountants .......... | 100 | 50 |

1. Determine the total cost of this tax services job.

2. If Diaz charged $20,000 for this tax services job, what is the gross profit for the job?

---

Rolex Company reports the following information.

**Exercise 2-31**
Gross profit ratio
**A1**

| | Current Year | Prior Year |
|---|---|---|
| Sales ................... | $220,000 | $180,000 |
| Cost of goods sold ........ | 132,000 | 135,000 |

1. Compute the gross profit ratio for each of the two years reported.

2. Did the company outperform or underperform the industry average gross profit ratio of 30% in the current year?

3. Did the gross profit ratio improve or decline in the current year?

---

Mc Graw Hill **connect**

At the end of June, the job cost sheets at Ace Roofers show the following costs accumulated on three jobs.

**PROBLEM SET A**

**Problem 2-1A**
Computing job costs and overhead rate; assigning costs to inventory

**C1  P3**

| At June 30 | Job 5 | Job 6 | Job 7 |
|---|---|---|---|
| Direct materials ......... | $15,000 | $33,000 | $27,000 |
| Direct labor ............ | 8,000 | 14,200 | 21,000 |
| Overhead applied ....... | 4,000 | 7,100 | 10,500 |

**Additional information**

a. Job 5 was started in May, and the following costs were assigned to it in May: direct materials, $6,000; direct labor, $1,800; and applied overhead, $900. Job 5 was finished in June.

b. Job 6 and Job 7 were started in June; Job 6 was finished in June, and Job 7 is to be completed in July.

c. Overhead cost is applied with a predetermined rate based on direct labor cost. The predetermined overhead rate did not change across these months.

[continued on next page]

[continued from previous page]

**Required**

1. What is the total cost of direct materials requisitioned in June?
2. What is the total cost of direct labor used in June?
3. What is the predetermined overhead rate?
4. What is the total cost transferred to Finished Goods Inventory in June?

---

**Problem 2-2A**

Computing and recording job costs; preparing schedule of cost of goods manufactured

**P1  P2  P3  P4**

Marco Company shows the following costs for three jobs worked on in April.

| | Job 306 | Job 307 | Job 308 |
|---|---|---|---|
| **Balances on March 31** | | | |
| Direct materials used (in March) . | $ 29,000 | $ 35,000 | |
| Direct labor used (in March) . . . . | 20,000 | 18,000 | |
| Overhead applied (March). . . . . . | 10,000 | 9,000 | |
| **Costs during April** | | | |
| Direct materials used. . . . . . . . . | 135,000 | 220,000 | $100,000 |
| Direct labor used . . . . . . . . . . . . | 85,000 | 150,000 | 105,000 |
| Overhead applied. . . . . . . . . . . . | ? | ? | ? |
| Status on April 30 . . . . . . . . . . . . . | Finished (sold) | Finished (unsold) | In process |

**Additional Information**

a. Raw Materials Inventory has a March 31 balance of $80,000.
b. Raw materials purchases in April are $500,000, and total factory payroll cost in April is $363,000.
c. Actual overhead costs incurred in April are indirect materials, $50,000; indirect labor, $23,000; factory rent, $32,000; factory utilities, $19,000; and factory equipment depreciation, $51,000.
d. Predetermined overhead rate is 50% of direct labor cost.
e. Job 306 is sold for $635,000 cash in April.

**Required**

1. Determine the amount of overhead applied to each job in April.
2. Determine the total cost assigned to each job as of April 30 (including the balances from March 31).
3. Prepare journal entries for the month of April to record the following.
   a. Materials purchases (on credit).
   b. Direct materials used.
   c. Direct labor used (and paid in cash) and assigned to Work in Process Inventory.
   d. Indirect materials used and assigned to Factory Overhead.
   e. Indirect labor used (and paid in cash) and assigned to Factory Overhead.
   f. Overhead costs applied to Work in Process Inventory.
   g. Actual other overhead costs incurred. (Factory rent and utilities are paid in cash.)
   h. Transfer of Jobs 306 and 307 to Finished Goods Inventory.
   i. Cost of goods sold for Job 306.
   j. Revenue from the sale of Job 306 received in cash.
   k. Close underapplied or overapplied overhead to the Cost of Goods Sold account.

**Check**  (4) Cost of goods manufactured, $828,500

4. Prepare a schedule of cost of goods manufactured.
5. Compute gross profit for April. Show how the three inventory accounts are reported on the April 30 balance sheet.

---

**Problem 2-3A**

Computing and recording job costs; preparing income statement and balance sheet  **P1  P2  P3  P4**

Bergo Bay's accounting system generated the following account balances on December 31. The company's manager knows something is wrong with this list of balances because it does not show any balance for Work in Process Inventory, and the accrued factory payroll (Factory Wages Payable) has not been recorded.

| | Debit | Credit |
|---|---|---|
| Cash ............................... | $170,000 | |
| Accounts receivable ................. | 75,000 | |
| Raw materials inventory............... | 80,000 | |
| Work in process inventory ............. | 0 | |
| Finished goods inventory ............. | 15,000 | |
| Prepaid rent ........................ | 3,000 | |
| Accounts payable ................... | | $ 17,000 |
| Notes payable....................... | | 25,000 |
| Common stock ...................... | | 50,000 |
| Retained earnings (prior year) .......... | | 271,000 |
| Sales .............................. | | 373,000 |
| Cost of goods sold ................... | 218,000 | |
| Factory overhead .................... | 115,000 | |
| General and administrative expenses .... | 60,000 | |
| Totals ............................ | $736,000 | $736,000 |

These six documents must be processed to bring the accounting records up to date.

| | |
|---|---|
| Materials requisition 10: $10,200 direct materials to Job 402 | Labor time ticket 52: $36,000 direct labor to Job 402 |
| Materials requisition 11: $18,600 direct materials to Job 404 | Labor time ticket 53: $23,800 direct labor to Job 404 |
| Materials requisition 12: $5,600 indirect materials | Labor time ticket 54: $8,200 indirect labor |

Jobs 402 and 404 are the only jobs in process at year-end. The predetermined overhead rate is 200% of direct labor cost.

**Required**

1. Use the document information above to prepare journal entries for the following costs.

   **a.** Direct materials.        **d.** Indirect materials.
   **b.** Direct labor.            **e.** Indirect labor.
   **c.** Overhead applied.

2. Set up a Factory Overhead T-account and enter amounts from part 1 related to factory overhead. Determine the amount of over- or underapplied overhead. Prepare the entry to close any over- or underapplied overhead to Cost of Goods Sold.

3. Prepare a revised list of account balances as of December 31. *Hint:* Use the prior year's Retained Earnings balance of $271,000 in this list.

4. Prepare an income statement for the year and a balance sheet as of December 31. *Hint:* Retained earnings is $356,800 at the end of the current year.

5. Assume that the $5,600 on materials requisition 12 should have been direct materials charged to Job 404. Does this error result in overstatement or understatement of total assets on the balance sheet at December 31?

**Check**  (4) Total assets, $516,800

---

Watercraft's predetermined overhead rate is 200% of direct labor. Information on the company's production activities during May follows.

**a.** Purchased raw materials on credit, $200,000.
**b.** Materials requisitions record use of the following materials for the month.

| | |
|---|---|
| Job 136.......................... | $ 48,000 |
| Job 137.......................... | 32,000 |
| Job 138.......................... | 19,200 |
| Job 139.......................... | 22,400 |
| Job 140.......................... | 6,400 |
| Total direct materials .............. | 128,000 |
| Indirect materials ................. | 19,500 |
| Total materials requisitions ......... | $147,500 |

**Problem 2-4A**
Preparing job cost sheets, recording costs, preparing inventory ledger accounts

**P1**  **P2**  **P3**

[continued on next page]

[continued from previous page]

**c.** Time tickets record use of the following labor for the month. These wages were paid in cash.

| | |
|---|---:|
| Job 136 | $ 12,000 |
| Job 137 | 10,500 |
| Job 138 | 37,500 |
| Job 139 | 39,000 |
| Job 140 | 3,000 |
| Total direct labor | 102,000 |
| Indirect labor | 24,000 |
| Total labor cost | $126,000 |

**d.** Applied overhead to Jobs 136, 138, and 139.
**e.** Transferred Jobs 136, 138, and 139 to Finished Goods Inventory.
**f.** Sold Jobs 136 and 138 on credit at a total price of $525,000.
**g.** Recorded the cost of goods sold for Jobs 136 and 138.
**h.** Incurred the following actual other overhead costs during the month.

| | | | |
|---|---:|---|---:|
| Depreciation of factory building | $68,000 | Expired factory insurance | $10,000 |
| Depreciation of factory equipment | 36,500 | Accrued property taxes payable | 35,000 |

**i.** Applied overhead at month-end to the Work in Process Inventory account (for Job 137 and Job 140) using the predetermined overhead rate of 200% of direct labor cost.

**Required**

**1.** Prepare a job cost sheet for each job worked on during the month. Use the following simplified form.

| Job No. _____ |
|---|
| Materials.......... $_____ |
| Labor............. _____ |
| Overhead ......... _____ |
| Total cost ........ $_____ |

**Check**   (2d) Cr. Factory Overhead, $177,000

**2.** Prepare journal entries to record the events and transactions *a* through *i*.
**3.** Set up T-accounts for each of the following accounts, each of which started the month with a zero balance: Raw Materials Inventory, Work in Process Inventory, Finished Goods Inventory, Factory Overhead, Cost of Goods Sold. Post the journal entries to these T-accounts and determine the ending balance of each account.

(4) Finished Goods Inventory, $139,400

**4.** (a) Compute the total cost of each job in process and prove that the sum of their costs equals the Work in Process Inventory account balance. (b) Compute the total cost of each job finished but not sold, and prove that the sum of their costs equals the Finished Goods Inventory balance. (c) Compute the total cost of each job sold, and prove that the sum of their costs equals the Cost of Goods Sold balance.

---

**Problem 2-5A**

Computing and applying overhead to jobs; recording under- or overapplied overhead

**P3   P4**

At the beginning of the year, Learer Company's manager estimated total direct labor cost to be $2,500,000. The manager also estimated the following overhead costs for the year.

| | |
|---|---:|
| Indirect labor | $ 559,200 |
| Rent on factory building | 140,000 |
| Factory utilities | 156,000 |
| Depreciation—Factory equipment | 480,000 |
| Repairs expense—Factory equipment | 60,000 |
| Indirect materials | 104,800 |
| Total estimated overhead costs | $1,500,000 |

For the year, the company incurred $1,520,000 of actual overhead costs. It completed and sold five jobs with the following direct labor costs: Job 201, $604,000; Job 202, $563,000; Job 203, $298,000; Job 204, $716,000; and Job 205, $314,000. In addition, Job 206 is in process at the end of the year and had been charged $17,000 for direct labor. No jobs were in process at the beginning of the year. The company's predetermined overhead rate is based on a percent of direct labor cost.

**Required**

1. Determine the following.
   a. Predetermined overhead rate for the year.
   b. Overhead applied to each of the six jobs during the year.
   c. Over- or underapplied overhead at year-end.
2. Prepare the entry to close any over- or underapplied overhead to Cost of Goods Sold at year-end.

---

Sager Company builds custom retaining walls for large commercial customers. On May 1, the company had no inventories of work in process or finished goods but held the following raw materials.

**Problem 2-6A**

Preparing job cost sheets and materials ledger cards; computing inventory

**P1   P2   P3   P4**

| | | |
|---|---|---|
| Cinder block . . . . . . . . . . . . . . . . . . . | 200 units @ $250 = | $50,000 |
| Boulders . . . . . . . . . . . . . . . . . . . . . . | 95 units @   180 = | 17,100 |
| Stain (indirect materials). . . . . . . . . . | 55 units @     75 = | 4,125 |
| Total. . . . . . . . . . . . . . . . . . . . . . . . . | | $71,225 |

On May 4, the company began work on Job 102 for Woz Company and Job 103 for Reuben Company.

**Required**

1. Prepare job cost sheets for Jobs 102 and 103 using the layout in Exhibit 2.3, and prepare three materials ledger cards for cinder blocks, boulders, and stain using the layout in Exhibit 2.5. Enter the beginning raw materials inventory amounts from above for each of these materials on their ledger cards. Then, follow the instructions in this list of activities to complete the job cost sheets and the materials ledger cards.

   a. Purchased raw materials on credit and recorded the following information from receiving reports.

   > Receiving Report No. 426, cinder blocks, 250 units at $250 each.   Receiving Report No. 427, boulders, 90 units at $180 each.

   *Instructions:* Enter the receiving report information on the materials ledger cards.
   b. Requisitioned the following raw materials for production.

   > Requisition No. 35, for Job 102, 135 units of cinder blocks.   Requisition No. 38, for Job 103, 38 units of boulders.
   > Requisition No. 36, for Job 102, 72 units of boulders.   Requisition No. 39, for 15 units of stain.
   > Requisition No. 37, for Job 103, 70 units of cinder blocks.

   *Instructions:* Enter amounts for direct materials requisitions on the materials ledger cards and the job cost sheets. Enter the indirect materials amount on the materials ledger card.
   c. Received the following employee time tickets for work in May.

   > Time tickets Nos. 1 to 10 for direct labor on Job 102, $90,000.
   > Time tickets Nos. 11 to 30 for direct labor on Job 103, $65,000.
   > Time tickets Nos. 31 to 36 for indirect labor, $19,250.

   *Instructions:* Record direct labor from the time tickets on the job cost sheets.
   d. Finished Job 102. The company applies overhead to each job with a predetermined overhead rate of 80% of direct labor cost.

   *Instructions:* Enter the applied overhead on the cost sheet for Job 102, fill in the cost summary section of the cost sheet, and then mark the cost sheet "Finished."
   e. Applied overhead cost to Job 103 based on the job's direct labor used to date.

   *Instructions:* Enter applied overhead on the job cost sheet for Job 103.
2. Job 102 was sold on credit for $400,000. Compute gross profit for the month.
3. Determine the balances reported on the month-end balance sheet for Raw Materials Inventory and Work in Process Inventory.

## PROBLEM SET B

### Problem 2-1B

Computing job costs and overhead rate; assigning costs to inventory

C1    P3

At the end of May, the job cost sheets at Cool Pool show the following costs accumulated on three jobs.

| At May 31 | Job 8 | Job 9 | Job 10 |
|---|---|---|---|
| Direct materials...... | $25,000 | $23,240 | $26,800 |
| Direct labor......... | 10,000 | 8,600 | 9,500 |
| Overhead applied.... | 6,000 | 5,160 | 5,700 |

**Additional information**

a. Job 8 was started in April, and the following costs were assigned to it in April: direct materials, $8,000; direct labor, $2,000; and applied overhead, $1,200. Job 8 was finished in May.

b. Job 9 and Job 10 were started in May; Job 9 was finished in May, and Job 10 is to be completed in June.

c. Overhead cost is applied with a predetermined rate based on direct labor cost. The predetermined overhead rate did not change across these months.

**Required**

1. What is the total cost of direct materials requisitioned in May?

2. What is the total cost of direct labor used in May?

3. What is the predetermined overhead rate?

4. What is the total cost transferred to Finished Goods Inventory in May?

---

### Problem 2-2B

Computing and recording job costs; preparing schedule of cost of goods manufactured

P1    P2    P3    P4

Perez Company shows the following costs for three jobs worked on in September.

| | Job 114 | Job 115 | Job 116 |
|---|---|---|---|
| **Balances on August 31** | | | |
| Direct materials used (in August) ... | $ 14,000 | $ 18,000 | |
| Direct labor used (in August)....... | 18,000 | 16,000 | |
| Overhead applied (August) ........ | 9,000 | 8,000 | |
| **Costs during September** | | | |
| Direct materials used............. | 100,000 | 170,000 | $ 80,000 |
| Direct labor used ................ | 30,000 | 68,000 | 120,000 |
| Overhead applied................. | ? | ? | ? |
| Status on September 30 ............ | Finished (sold) | Finished (unsold) | In process |

**Additional Information**

a. Raw Materials Inventory has an August 31 balance of $150,000.

b. Raw materials purchases in September are $400,000, and total factory payroll cost in September is $232,000.

c. Actual overhead costs incurred in September are indirect materials, $30,000; indirect labor, $14,000; factory rent, $20,000; factory utilities, $12,000; and factory equipment depreciation, $30,000.

d. Predetermined overhead rate is 50% of direct labor cost.

e. Job 114 is sold for $380,000 cash in September.

**Required**

1. Determine the amount of overhead applied to each job in September.

2. Determine the total cost assigned to each job as of September 30 (including the balances from August 31).

3. Prepare journal entries for the month of September to record the following.

   a. Materials purchases (on credit).

   b. Direct materials used.

   c. Direct labor used (and paid in cash) and assigned to Work in Process Inventory.

   d. Indirect materials used and assigned to Factory Overhead.

   e. Indirect labor used (and paid in cash) and assigned to Factory Overhead.

   f. Overhead costs applied to Work in Process Inventory.

   g. Actual other overhead costs incurred. (Factory rent and utilities are paid in cash.)

   h. Transfer of Jobs 114 and 115 to the Finished Goods Inventory.

   i. Cost of Job 114 in the Cost of Goods Sold account.

   j. Revenue from the sale of Job 114 received in cash.

   k. Close underapplied or overapplied overhead to the Cost of Goods Sold account.

**4.** Prepare a schedule of cost of goods manufactured.

**5.** Compute gross profit for September. Show how the three inventory accounts are reported on the September 30 balance sheet.

**6.** Over- or underapplied overhead is closed to Cost of Goods Sold but not posted to job cost sheets. For this period, is gross profit at the job level understated or overstated?

**Check**  (4) Cost of goods manufactured, $500,000

---

Cavallo Mfg.'s computer system generated the following account balances on December 31. The company's manager knows that this list of balances is wrong because it does not show any balance for Work in Process Inventory, and the accrued factory payroll (Factory Wages Payable) has not been recorded.

**Problem 2-3B**
Computing and recording job costs; preparing income statement and balance sheet

**P1  P2  P3  P4**

|  | Debit | Credit |
|---|---|---|
| Cash............................. | $ 64,000 | |
| Accounts receivable ................... | 42,000 | |
| Raw materials inventory................ | 26,000 | |
| Work in process inventory ............. | 0 | |
| Finished goods inventory ............. | 9,000 | |
| Prepaid rent ........................ | 3,000 | |
| Accounts payable .................... | | $ 10,500 |
| Notes payable....................... | | 13,500 |
| Common stock ...................... | | 30,000 |
| Retained earnings (prior year) ........... | | 87,000 |
| Sales ............................. | | 180,000 |
| Cost of goods sold ................... | 105,000 | |
| Factory overhead .................... | 27,000 | |
| General and administrative expenses .... | 45,000 | |
| Totals............................. | $321,000 | $321,000 |

These six documents must be processed to bring the accounting records up to date.

| | |
|---|---|
| Materials requisition 31: $4,600 direct materials to Job 603 | Labor time ticket 65: $5,000 direct labor to Job 603 |
| Materials requisition 32: $7,600 direct materials to Job 604 | Labor time ticket 66: $8,000 direct labor to Job 604 |
| Materials requisition 33: $2,100 indirect materials | Labor time ticket 77: $3,000 indirect labor |

Jobs 603 and 604 are the only jobs in process at year-end. The predetermined overhead rate is 200% of direct labor cost.

**Required**

**1.** Use the document information above to prepare journal entries for the following costs.
   **a.** Direct materials.      **d.** Indirect materials.
   **b.** Direct labor.           **e.** Indirect labor.
   **c.** Overhead applied.

**2.** Set up a Factory Overhead T-account and enter amounts from part 1 related to factory overhead. Determine the amount of over- or underapplied overhead. Prepare the entry to close any over- or underapplied overhead to Cost of Goods Sold.

**3.** Prepare a revised list of account balances as of December 31. *Hint:* Use the prior year's Retained Earnings balance of $87,000.

**4.** Prepare an income statement for the year and a balance sheet as of December 31. *Hint:* Retained earnings is $110,900 at the end of the current year.

**5.** Assume that the $2,100 indirect materials on materials requisition 33 should have been direct materials charged to Job 604. Does this error result in overstatement or understatement of total assets on the balance sheet at December 31?

**Check**  (4) Net income, $23,900

**Problem 2-4B**

Preparing job cost sheets, recording costs, preparing inventory ledger accounts

P1    P2    P3

Starr Mfg.'s predetermined overhead rate is 200% of direct labor. Information on the company's production activities during September follows.

**a.** Purchased raw materials on credit, $125,000.

**b.** Materials requisitions record use of the following materials for the month.

| | |
|---|---|
| Job 487.................... | $30,000 |
| Job 488.................... | 20,000 |
| Job 489.................... | 12,000 |
| Job 490.................... | 14,000 |
| Job 491.................... | 4,000 |
| Total direct materials ........... | 80,000 |
| Indirect materials ............. | 12,000 |
| Total materials requisitions ....... | $92,000 |

**c.** Time tickets record use of the following labor for the month. These wages are paid in cash.

| | |
|---|---|
| Job 487.................... | $ 8,000 |
| Job 488.................... | 7,000 |
| Job 489.................... | 25,000 |
| Job 490.................... | 26,000 |
| Job 491.................... | 2,000 |
| Total direct labor............. | 68,000 |
| Indirect labor.................. | 16,000 |
| Total labor cost............... | $84,000 |

**d.** Applied overhead to Jobs 487, 489, and 490.

**e.** Transferred Jobs 487, 489, and 490 to Finished Goods Inventory.

**f.** Sold Jobs 487 and 489 on credit for a total price of $340,000.

**g.** Recorded the cost of goods sold for Jobs 487 and 489.

**h.** Incurred the following actual other overhead costs during the month.

| | | | |
|---|---|---|---|
| Depreciation of factory building ........ | $37,000 | Expired factory insurance............. | $ 7,000 |
| Depreciation of factory equipment ...... | 21,000 | Accrued property taxes payable ........ | 31,000 |

**i.** Applied overhead at month-end to the Work in Process Inventory account (for Job 488 and Job 491) using the predetermined overhead rate of 200% of direct labor cost.

**Required**

**1.** Prepare a job cost sheet for each job worked on in the month. Use the following simplified form.

| Job No. _____ |  |
|---|---|
| Materials........... | $_____ |
| Labor............. | _____ |
| Overhead ......... | _____ |
| Total cost .......... | $_____ |

**Check**   (2d) Cr. Factory Overhead, $118,000
(3) Finished Goods Inventory, $92,000 bal.

**2.** Prepare journal entries to record the events and transactions *a* through *i*.

**3.** Set up T-accounts for each of the following accounts, each of which started the month with a zero balance: Raw Materials Inventory, Work in Process Inventory, Finished Goods Inventory, Factory Overhead, Cost of Goods Sold. Post the journal entries to these T-accounts and determine the ending balance of each account.

**4.** (a) Compute the total cost of each job in process and prove that the sum of their costs equals the Work in Process Inventory account balance. (b) Compute the total cost of each job finished but not sold, and prove that the sum of their costs equals the Finished Goods Inventory balance. (c) Compute the total cost of each job sold, and prove that the sum of their costs equals the Cost of Goods Sold balance.

At the beginning of the year, Pavelka Company's manager estimated total direct labor cost to be $1,500,000. The manager also estimated the following overhead costs for the year.

**Problem 2-5B**
Computing and applying overhead to jobs; recording under- or overapplied overhead
**P3   P4**

| | |
|---|---:|
| Indirect labor . . . . . . . . . . . . . . . . . . . . . . . . . . . . . . . . . | $279,600 |
| Rent on factory building . . . . . . . . . . . . . . . . . . . . . . . | 70,000 |
| Factory utilities . . . . . . . . . . . . . . . . . . . . . . . . . . . . . | 78,000 |
| Depreciation—Factory equipment . . . . . . . . . . . . . . . . | 240,000 |
| Repairs expense—Factory equipment . . . . . . . . . . . . . | 30,000 |
| Indirect materials. . . . . . . . . . . . . . . . . . . . . . . . . . . . | 52,400 |
| Total estimated overhead costs . . . . . . . . . . . . . . . . . | $750,000 |

For the year, the company incurred $725,000 of actual overhead costs. It completed and sold five jobs with the following direct labor costs: Job 625, $354,000; Job 626, $330,000; Job 627, $175,000; Job 628, $420,000; and Job 629, $184,000. In addition, Job 630 is in process at the end of the year and had been charged $10,000 for direct labor. No jobs were in process at the beginning of the year. The company's predetermined overhead rate is based on a percent of direct labor cost.

**Required**

1. Determine the following.
   a. Predetermined overhead rate for the year.
   b. Overhead applied to each of the six jobs during the year.
   c. Over- or underapplied overhead at year-end.
2. Prepare the entry to close any over- or underapplied overhead to Cost of Goods Sold at year-end.

King Company builds custom order fulfillment centers for large e-commerce companies. On June 1, the company had no inventories of work in process or finished goods but held the following raw materials.

**Problem 2-6B**
Preparing job cost sheets and materials ledger cards; computing inventory
**P1   P2   P3   P4**

| | | |
|---|---|---:|
| Steel . . . . . . . . . . . . . . . . . . . . . . . . . . . | 120 units @ $200 = | $24,000 |
| Wood. . . . . . . . . . . . . . . . . . . . . . . . . . . | 80 units @   160 = | 12,800 |
| Paint (indirect materials). . . . . . . . . . . . | 44 units @   72 = | 3,168 |
| Total . . . . . . . . . . . . . . . . . . . . . . . . . . . | | $39,968 |

On June 3, the company began work on Job 450 for Encinita Company and Job 451 for Fargo Inc.

**Required**

1. Prepare job cost sheets for Jobs 450 and 451 using the layout in Exhibit 2.3, and prepare three materials ledger cards for steel, wood, and paint using the layout in Exhibit 2.5. Enter the beginning raw materials inventory amounts from above for each of these materials on their ledger cards. Then, follow instructions in this list of activities to complete the job cost sheets and the materials ledger cards.
   a. Purchased raw materials on credit and recorded the following information from receiving reports.

| | |
|---|---|
| Receiving Report No. 20, steel, 150 units at $200 each. | Receiving Report No. 21, wood, 70 units at $160 each. |

   *Instructions:* Enter the receiving report information on the materials ledger cards.
   b. Requisitioned the following raw materials for production.

| | |
|---|---|
| Requisition No. 223, for Job 450, 80 units of steel. | Requisition No. 226, for Job 451, 30 units of wood. |
| Requisition No. 224, for Job 450, 60 units of wood. | Requisition No. 227, for 12 units of paint. |
| Requisition No. 225, for Job 451, 40 units of steel. | |

*Instructions:* Enter amounts for direct materials requisitions on the materials ledger cards and the job cost sheets. Enter the indirect materials amount on the materials ledger card.

c. Received the following employee time tickets for work in June.

> Time tickets Nos. 1 to 10 for direct labor on Job 450, $40,000.
>
> Time tickets Nos. 11 to 20 for direct labor on Job 451, $32,000.
>
> Time tickets Nos. 21 to 24 for indirect labor, $12,000.

*Instructions:* Record direct labor from the time tickets on the job cost sheets.

d. Finished Job 450. The company applies overhead to each job with a predetermined overhead rate equal to 70% of direct labor cost.

*Instructions:* Enter the applied overhead on the cost sheet for Job 450, fill in the cost summary section of the cost sheet, and then mark the cost sheet "Finished."

e. Applied overhead cost to Job 451 based on the job's direct labor used to date.

*Instructions:* Enter applied overhead on the job cost sheet for Job 451.

**2.** Job 450 was sold on credit for $290,000. Compute gross profit for the month.

**3.** Determine the balances reported on the month-end balance sheet for Raw Materials Inventory and Work in Process Inventory.

## SERIAL PROBLEM
Business Solutions

**P1   P2   P3**

Alexander Image/Shutterstock

**Check**   (1) Total direct materials, $6,900

*Serial problem began in Chapter 1. If previous chapter segments were not completed, the serial problem can begin at this point. It is available in **Connect** with an algorithmic option.*

**SP 2**   The computer workstation furniture manufacturing that Santana Rey started is progressing well. As of the end of June, **Business Solutions**'s job cost sheets show the following total costs accumulated on three furniture jobs.

|  | Job 602 | Job 603 | Job 604 |
|---|---|---|---|
| Direct materials. . . . . . . . . . . | $1,500 | $3,300 | $2,700 |
| Direct labor . . . . . . . . . . . . . . | 800 | 1,420 | 2,100 |
| Overhead applied. . . . . . . . . | 400 | 710 | 1,050 |

Job 602 was started in May, and the following costs were assigned to it in May: direct materials, $600; direct labor, $180; and overhead, $90. Jobs 603 and 604 were started in June. Overhead cost is applied with a predetermined rate as a percent of direct labor costs. Jobs 602 and 603 are finished in June, and Job 604 is expected to be finished in July. The company's predetermined overhead rate did not change over these months.

### Required

**1.** What is the cost of direct materials used in June for each of the three jobs and in total?

**2.** What is the cost of direct labor used in June for each of the three jobs and in total?

**3.** What predetermined overhead rate is used in June?

**4.** How much cost is transferred to Finished Goods Inventory in June?

## TABLEAU DASHBOARD ACTIVITIES

**Tableau Dashboard Activities** expose students to accounting analytics using visual displays. These assignments (1) do not require instructors to know Tableau, (2) are accessible to introductory students, (3) do not require Tableau software, and (4) run in **Connect**. All are auto-gradable.

**Tableau DA 2-1 Quick Study**, Computing cost of direct materials used, **P1**—similar to Exercise 2-12.
**Tableau DA 2-2 Exercise**, Computing cost of goods sold, **P1, P2, P3**—similar to Exercise 2-12.
**Tableau DA 2-3 Mini-case**, Computing gross profit and overapplied or underapplied overhead, **P1, P2, P3, P4**—similar to Exercise 2-12 and Exercise 2-20.

**General Ledger (GL) Assignments** expose students to general ledger software similar to that in practice. **GL** is part of **Connect**, and **GL** assignments are auto-gradable and have algorithmic options. For the following **GL** assignment, prepare summary journal entries to record the transactions. Calculate the total cost of each job worked on. Then prepare a schedule of cost of goods manufactured and compute gross profit.

**GENERAL LEDGER PROBLEM**

**GL 2-1**   Based on Problem 2-2A

---

## Accounting Analysis

**AA 2-1**   **Apple** provides device support services to large business clients. These services use direct labor and overhead costs. Assume Apple uses two types of direct labor: phone support staff, paid $12 per hour, and technical specialists, paid $25 per hour. Overhead is applied using a rate of $18 per direct labor hour (for both types of labor). A potential client requests a price quote for services that Apple estimates will use 1,800 phone support hours and 2,200 technical specialist hours.

**COMPANY ANALYSIS**
**A1**

**APPLE**

**Required**

**1.** What is this job's total estimated cost?
**2.** If Apple applies a markup of 40% on total estimated cost of these services, what price will it quote?

---

**AA 2-2**   **Apple** and **Google** report the following income statement data (some are assumed). Use the companies' service revenue and cost data to answer the requirements.

**COMPARATIVE ANALYSIS**
**A1**

**APPLE**
**GOOGLE**

| $ millions | Apple | | Google | |
| --- | --- | --- | --- | --- |
| | Current Year | Prior Year | Current Year | Prior Year |
| Service revenue ................ | $46,291 | $39,748 | $134,811 | $116,461 |
| Cost of services ................ | 16,786 | 15,592 | 59,856 | 50,661 |

**Required**

**1.** Compute the gross profit ratio for each of the two years shown for each company.
**2.** Is the change in Apple's current year gross profit ratio on its services favorable or unfavorable?
**3.** Is the change in Google's current year gross profit ratio on its services favorable or unfavorable?
**4.** Does Google's current year gross profit ratio underperform or outperform the industry (assumed) average of 60%?

---

**AA 2-3**   Assume **Samsung** and **Apple** are bidding on a large device support service job for a U.S.-based business. Samsung estimates direct labor for this service job to include 800 phone support hours and 1,200 technical specialist hours. Samsung pays phone support staff $11 per hour and technical specialists $22 per hour. Overhead is applied using a rate of $24 per direct labor hour (for both types of labor).

**EXTENDED ANALYSIS**
**A1**

**APPLE**
**Samsung**

**Required**

**1.** For Samsung, what is this job's estimated total cost?
**2.** Samsung believes that the customer will choose the company that offers the lower price. If Samsung applies a markup of 30% on total cost, will its quoted price be lower than Apple's expected quoted price of $105,000?

## Discussion Questions

1. Why must a company estimate the amount of factory overhead applied to individual jobs or job lots?

2. Many companies use direct labor cost to apply factory overhead to jobs. Identify another activity base a company might use to apply overhead costs.

3. What information is recorded on a job cost sheet? How do management and employees use job cost sheets?

4. How do the balances in the Work in Process Inventory, Finished Goods Inventory, and Cost of Goods Sold general ledger accounts link to job cost sheets?

5. What journal entry is recorded when a materials manager receives a materials requisition and then issues direct materials for use in the factory? What journal entry is recorded for requisitions of indirect materials?

6. Distinguish between a receiving report and a materials requisition.

7. **Google** uses an electronic "time ticket" for some employees. How are time tickets used **GOOGLE** in job order costing?

8. What events cause debits to be recorded in the Factory Overhead account? What events cause credits to be recorded in the Factory Overhead account?

9. **Google** applies overhead to product costs. What account is used to close the Factory **GOOGLE** Overhead account, assuming the amount is not material?

10. Assume that **Apple** produces a batch of 1,000 iPhones. Does it account for this as 1,000 indi- **APPLE** vidual jobs or as a job lot? Explain (consider costs and benefits).

11. Why must a company use predetermined overhead rates when using job order costing?

12. How would a hospital apply job order costing? Explain.

13. **Harley-Davidson** manufactures 30 custom-made, luxury-model motorcycles. Each is unique. Does it account for these motorcycles as 30 individual jobs or as a job lot? Explain.

14. Assume **Verizon** will install and service a server to link all of a customer's employees' smartphones to a centralized cloud server for an up-front flat price. How can Verizon use a job order costing system?

15. What is cost-plus pricing?

## Beyond the Numbers

**ETHICS CHALLENGE**

P3

**BTN 2-1** Assume that your company sells portable housing to both general contractors and the government. It sells jobs to contractors on a bid basis. A contractor asks for three bids from different manufacturers. The combination of low bid and high quality wins the job. However, jobs sold to the government are bid on a cost-plus basis. This means price is determined by adding all costs plus a profit based on cost at a specified percent, such as 10%. You observe that the amount of overhead applied to government jobs is much higher than that applied to similar contract jobs. This concerns you.

**Point:** Students could compare responses and discuss differences in concerns with allocating overhead.

**Required**

Write a half-page memo to your company's chief financial officer outlining your concerns with overhead application.

**COMMUNICATING IN PRACTICE**

P3

**BTN 2-2** Assume you are preparing for a class presentation on the accounting for factory overhead. Prepare a set of notes to guide a presentation that addresses the questions below.

**Point:** Have a student make the presentation in class, with another student acting as the instructor.

**Required**

1. Describe the four-step overhead process.
2. How are applied and actual factory overhead costs recorded in general ledger accounts?
3. Explain how underapplied or overapplied factory overhead impacts cost of goods sold.

**TEAMWORK IN ACTION**

C1

**BTN 2-3** Consider the activities of a medical clinic in your area.

**Required**

1. Is a job order costing system appropriate for the clinic? Explain.
2. Identify as many factors as possible to lead you to conclude that the clinic uses a job order system.

ENTREPRENEURIAL
DECISION

C1

**BTN 2-4**   Refer to the chapter opener regarding Mark Wallace and his company, **Wallace Detroit Guitars**. All successful businesses track their costs, and it is especially important for start-up businesses to monitor and control costs.

**Required**

1. Assume that Mark uses a job order costing system. For the basic cost category of direct materials, explain how Mark's job cost sheet would differ from a job cost sheet for a service company.

2. For the basic cost categories of direct materials, direct labor, and overhead, provide examples of the types of costs that would fall into each category for Wallace Detroit Guitars.

# 3 Process Costing and Analysis

## Chapter Preview

### PROCESS OPERATIONS

**C1** Organization of process operations

Comparing process and job order systems

**NTK 3-1**

### PROCESS COSTING DEMONSTRATION

**P1** Physical flow of units

Equivalent units of production (EUP)

Cost per EUP

Cost assignment

**P2** Production cost report

**NTK 3-2, 3-3**

### ACCOUNTING FOR COSTS AND TRANSFERS

**P3** Accounting for production costs

**P4** Accounting for transfers

**A1** Hybrid costing

**C2** *Appendix:* FIFO

**NTK 3-4**

## Learning Objectives

### CONCEPTUAL

**C1** Explain process costing and contrast it with job order costing.

**C2** *Appendix*—Compute process activity costs and prepare a production cost report using FIFO.

### ANALYTICAL

**A1** Illustrate a hybrid costing system and analyze process system yield.

### PROCEDURAL

**P1** Compute process activity costs using weighted average.

**P2** Prepare a production cost report using weighted average.

**P3** Record the flow of production costs in process costing.

**P4** Record the transfer of goods across departments, to Finished Goods Inventory, and to Cost of Goods Sold.

# ¡Todos Gritamos por Helado!

*"Always room for ice cream"* —**SUZY BATLLE**

MIAMI—Suzy Batlle was new to running a business when she started **Azucar Ice Cream Company** (**azucaricecream.com**). But Suzy knew ice cream, having grown up in a family that ate it nearly every night. "We Cuban people love ice cream," exclaims Suzy from her shop in the Little Havana section of Miami. Suzy took classes to learn the ice cream–making process and mastered the permitting process to open her store.

Suzy's recipes use tropical fruits found throughout Central and South America—ruby-red guava, mamey, papaya, and plantains, for example—and stem from an adventurous streak passed down through her family.

"My grandmother traveled extensively," explains Suzy, "and always made ice cream with the new exotic fruits she found. We have Cuban-inspired flavors you won't see anywhere else."

Ice cream is made in a process operation and produced in large volumes. "I'll buy 1,000 pounds of mamey at a time" says Suzy. These perishable raw materials enter a continuous production process that also uses direct labor (Suzy has 14 employees) and overhead (depreciation on processing machines, for example).

©Azucar Ice Cream Company

Each production run yields many gallons of ice cream. Suzy uses a process costing system to determine her production costs per gallon. Suzy credits courses from nearby Miami Dade College with improving her management and accounting skills.

Azucar is flourishing, and Suzy opened a new store in Dallas. Suzy advises, "Work hard and love what you do!"

Sources: *Azucar Ice Cream Company website,* January 2021; *Saveur,* July 7, 2016; *Miami Today,* February 2, 2016; *Mic.com,* November 28, 2016

## PROCESS OPERATIONS

**C1**_____

Explain process costing and contrast it with job order costing.

**Process operations** involve the mass production of similar products in a continuous flow of sequential processes. Process operations use a standardized process to make large volumes of similar products; job order operations use a customized process to make unique products.

**Kraft Heinz** makes trail mix in a process operation at its Planters division. Ingredients are often roasted, then blended and carefully mixed, in a standardized process that can produce large quantities of trail mix to exact specifications. Process operations also extend to services, such as mail sorting in large post offices and order processing in retailers like **Amazon**. Other companies using process operations follow.

| Company | Product | Company | Product |
|---|---|---|---|
| **General Mills** | Cereals | **PepsiCo** | Beverages |
| **Pfizer** | Pharmaceuticals | **Kar's** | Trail mix |
| **Procter & Gamble** | Household products | **Hershey** | Chocolate |
| **Coca-Cola** | Soft drinks | **Suja** | Organic juice |

## Organization of Process Operations

Each of the above products is made in a series of repetitive *processes,* or steps. Understanding such processes is crucial for measuring product costs. Increasingly, process operations use machines and automation to control product quality and reduce manufacturing costs.

In a process operation, each process is a separate *production department* or *workstation.* Each process applies direct labor, overhead, and often direct materials to move the product toward completion. The final process or department in the series finishes the goods and makes them ready for sale.

Exhibit 3.1 shows the production of FitMix, an organic trail mix by GenX Company. FitMix is manufactured in a continuous, two-process operation: Roasting and Blending.

**EXHIBIT 3.1**

GenX Process Operations:
Making Trail Mix

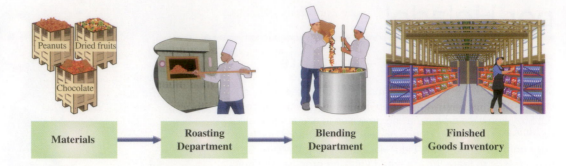

| Materials | Roasting Department | Blending Department | Finished Goods Inventory |

In the first process (Roasting department), the company roasts with oils, salts, and organic peanuts. The roasted peanuts are then passed to the Blending department, the second process. In the Blending department, workers blend organic chocolate pieces and organic dried fruits with the peanuts from the first process. The blended mix is then inspected and packaged for sale.

## Comparing Process and Job Order Costing Systems

Exhibit 3.2 shows similarities and differences in job order and process systems.

**EXHIBIT 3.2**

Comparing Process and
Job Order Costing

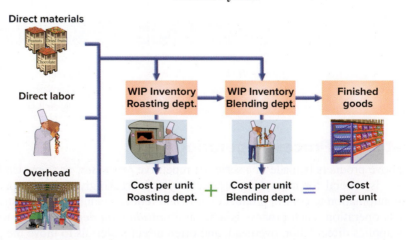

Job order and process operations share these features.

- Both use materials, labor, and overhead costs.
- Both aim to compute the cost per unit of product (or service).

Job order and process operations have important differences.

| | |
|---|---|
| **Cost object** | Job order system: cost object is a job or job lot.<br>Process system: cost object is the process or department. |
| **Cost per unit** | Job order system: measures cost per unit after completion of a job.<br>Process system: measures unit costs at the end of a period<br>(such as a month) by combining costs per unit from each process. |
| **Internal reporting** | Job order system: job cost sheets.<br>Process system: production cost report. |
| **Work in process inventory** | Job order system: one Work in Process Inventory account.<br>Process system: one Work in Process Inventory account *per process*. |

Complete the table with either a *yes* or *no* regarding the attributes of job order and process costing systems.

| | Job Order | Process |
|---|---|---|
| Uses direct materials, direct labor, and overhead costs . . . . . . . | a. _____ | e. _____ |
| Uses job cost sheets to accumulate costs . . . . . . . . . . . . . . . . . | b. _____ | f. _____ |
| Typically uses several Work in Process Inventory accounts . . . . . | c. _____ | g. _____ |
| Yields a cost per unit of product . . . . . . . . . . . . . . . . . . . . . . . . . | d. _____ | h. _____ |

*Solution*

**a.** yes **b.** yes **c.** no **d.** yes **e.** yes **f.** no **g.** yes **h.** yes

**NEED-TO-KNOW** 3-1

Job Order vs. Process Costing Systems

C1

Do More: QS 3-1, QS 3-2, QS 3-3, E 3-1, E 3-2

# PROCESS COSTING DEMONSTRATION

We provide a step-by-step demonstration of process costing for GenX's production of FitMix, an organic trail mix. FitMix is manufactured in a continuous, two-process operation: Roasting and Blending. We focus on the first process, Roasting. Accounting for each process or department in a process operation follows four steps.

**P1**

Compute process activity costs using weighted average.

1. **Determine the physical flow of units.**
2. **Compute equivalent units of production.**
3. **Compute cost per equivalent unit of production.**
4. **Assign and reconcile costs.**

> The following sections on process costing use the *weighted average method*. The *FIFO method* is in Appendix 3A. These methods make different assumptions about cost flows.
>
> - **Weighted average method** combines units and costs across two periods in computing equivalent units and cost per equivalent unit.
>
> - **FIFO method** computes equivalent units and cost per equivalent unit based only on production activity in the current period.
>
> The objectives, concepts, and journal entries (but not dollar amounts) are the same under both methods; the computation of equivalent units differs. Both methods are used in practice, but weighted average requires fewer calculations. Differences between the two methods are often small. With a just-in-time inventory system, those differences are even less because inventories are immaterial.

## Step 1: Determine Physical Flow of Units

Step 1 is to determine the number of units to account for and units accounted for. For FitMix, a unit is a cup of trail mix.

Exhibit 3.3 shows production data in units for the first process: Roasting department. On the left we compute the 120,000 *units to account for,* which are the 30,000 units in beginning work in process inventory plus 90,000 units started this period. On the right we reconcile (match) with the 120,000 *units accounted for,* which are the 100,000 units completed and transferred out plus 20,000 units in ending work in process inventory.

**EXHIBIT 3.3**

Production Data (in units) for Roasting Department

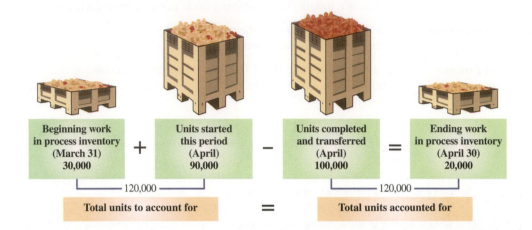

| Beginning work in process inventory (March 31) 30,000 | **+** | Units started this period (April) 90,000 | **−** | Units completed and transferred (April) 100,000 | **=** | Ending work in process inventory (April 30) 20,000 |
|---|---|---|---|---|---|---|
| └─── 120,000 ───┘ | | | | └─── 120,000 ───┘ | | |
| **Total units to account for** | | | **=** | **Total units accounted for** | | |

A *physical unit flow reconciliation* proves that (1) beginning units in process plus those started in the period equals the (2) ending units in process plus those completed and transferred out in the period. A physical unit flow reconciliation for the Roasting department for April is in Exhibit 3.4.

**EXHIBIT 3.4**

Physical Unit Flow Reconciliation

| WIP–Roasting (in units) | | | |
|---|---|---|---|
| Beginning | 30,000 | | |
| Started | 90,000 | | |
| To account for | 120,000 | | |
| | | 100,000 | Transferred out |
| Ending | 20,000 | | |

| Roasting Department | | | |
|---|---|---|---|
| **Units to Account For** | | **Units Accounted For** | |
| Beginning work in process........ | 30,000 units | Units completed and transferred out.... | 100,000 units |
| Units started this period.......... | 90,000 units | Ending work in process .............. | 20,000 units |
| Total units to account for ........ | **120,000 units** | Total units accounted for.............. | **120,000 units** |

reconciled

## Step 2: Compute Equivalent Units of Production

Step 2 is to compute *equivalent units of production.* **Equivalent units of production (EUP)** is the number of whole units that *could have been* started and completed given the costs incurred in the period. The reason we use equivalent units of production is that some units are not finished at the end of a period but still need to be assigned costs.

**Point: Whole units** is the number of physical units in production in a period.

To demonstrate, 10 cups of trail mix 60% through the production process is *equivalent to* 6 (10 × 60%) cups of completed trail mix. This means that the cost of 10 units that are 60% complete is *equivalent to* the cost of 6 completed units.

Exhibit 3.5 shows *percent complete* data for direct materials and conversion for the Roasting department. Those percents are needed to compute equivalent units of production. In both Roasting and Blending, direct materials enter production at the beginning of the process, while conversion costs occur throughout each department's processing. **Conversion costs** consist of direct labor and applied overhead. They are called conversion costs because they are the costs of converting raw materials into finished goods.

**Point:** Units transferred out are always 100% complete for direct materials and conversion.

We see that beginning work in process inventory is 100% complete for direct materials but only 65% complete for conversion. Ending work in process inventory is 100% complete for direct materials but only 25% complete for conversion. Units completed and transferred to the Blending department are 100% complete for both direct materials and conversion.

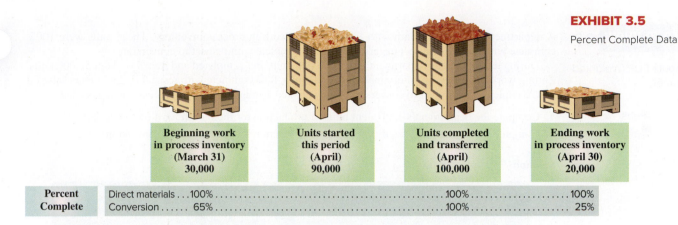

**EXHIBIT 3.5**

Percent Complete Data

| | | Beginning work in process inventory (March 31) 30,000 | Units started this period (April) 90,000 | Units completed and transferred (April) 100,000 | Ending work in process inventory (April 30) 20,000 |
|---|---|---|---|---|---|
| **Percent Complete** | Direct materials . . .100% | | | 100% | 100% |
| | Conversion . . . . . . 65% | | | 100% | 25% |

We separately compute equivalent units of production for direct materials and conversion costs. This is because direct materials and conversion costs typically enter processes at different rates. We see this for FitMix in Exhibit 3.5 where there are different percents of completion for direct materials and conversion costs for both beginning and ending work in process inventories.

Exhibit 3.6 shows the formula to compute equivalent units of production under the weighted average method for both direct materials and conversion costs.

$$\text{Equivalent units of production (EUP)} = \text{Equivalent units completed and transferred out} + \text{Equivalent units in ending work in process}$$

**EXHIBIT 3.6**

Computing EUP—Weighted Average Method

We compute the equivalent units of production (EUP) for both direct materials and conversion in Exhibit 3.7. We start with the 120,000 units accounted for from Step 1 and convert them to EUP. Units completed and transferred out are *always* 100% complete for both materials and conversion. This means the Roasting department completed and transferred 100,000 EUP for both materials and conversion.

**EXHIBIT 3.7**

Equivalent Units of Production—Weighted Average

| Roasting Department | | Direct Materials | | Conversion | |
|---|---|---|---|---|---|
| | Units | Percent Complete | Equivalent Units of Production | Percent Complete | Equivalent Units of Production |
| Completed and transferred out | 100,000 | 100% | 100,000 | 100% | 100,000 |
| Ending work in process | 20,000 | 100% | 20,000 | 25% | 5,000 |
| | | | 120,000 EUP | | 105,000 EUP |

Units Accounted For (Step 1)

Ending work in process inventory has 20,000 partially complete units. Direct materials is 100% complete. This means it has 20,000 EUP (20,000 units × 100%). Conversion is 25% complete. This means it has 5,000 EUP (20,000 units × 25%).

Total equivalent units of production equals 120,000 for direct materials (100,000 + 20,000) and 105,000 for conversion (100,000 + 5,000). The amount of inputs used to produce 100,000 completed units and to start 20,000 additional units is equivalent to the amount of direct materials in 120,000 whole units and the amount of conversion in 105,000 whole units.

**NEED-TO-KNOW** 3-2

Compute EUP (Weighted Average)

P1

A department began the month with 8,000 units in work in process inventory. These units were 100% complete with respect to direct materials and 40% complete with respect to conversion.

During the month, the department started 56,000 units and completed and transferred out 58,000 units. Ending work in process inventory includes 6,000 units, 80% complete with respect to direct materials and 70% complete with respect to conversion. The weighted average method of process costing is used.

1. Compute the department's equivalent units of production for the month for direct materials.
2. Compute the department's equivalent units of production for the month for conversion.

**Solution**

| | | Direct Materials | | Conversion | |
|---|---|---|---|---|---|
| | Units | Percent Complete | Equivalent Units of Production | Percent Complete | Equivalent Units of Production |
| Completed and transferred out .. | 58,000 | 100% | 58,000 | 100% | 58,000 |
| Ending work in process ....... | 6,000 | 80% | 4,800 | 70% | 4,200 |
| | | | 62,800 EUP | | 62,200 EUP |

Do More: QS 3-5, QS 3-10, E 3-4, E 3-8

## Step 3: Compute Cost per Equivalent Unit

Step 3 uses equivalent units of production from step 2, along with cost data, to compute cost per equivalent unit. Production cost data for the Roasting department are in Exhibit 3.8. *Recall:* Conversion costs equal direct labor costs plus overhead costs applied.

**EXHIBIT 3.8**

Roasting Department Production Cost Data

| Roasting Department: Production Cost Data (April) | | |
|---|---|---|
| Beginning work in process inventory | | |
|     Direct materials ..................... | $ 81,000 | |
|     Conversion ......................... | 108,900 | $ 189,900 |
| Costs added this period | | |
|     Direct materials ..................... | 279,000 | |
|     Conversion ......................... | 376,200 | 655,200 |
|     Total production costs ............... | | **$845,100** |

To compute **cost per equivalent unit,** we add costs for beginning work in process to costs added this period, and then divide by equivalent units of production from step 2. Exhibit 3.9 shows this separately for direct materials and for conversion. The cost for direct materials is $3.00 per EUP, and for conversion is $4.62 per EUP.

**EXHIBIT 3.9**

Cost per Equivalent Unit of Production—Weighted Average

$$\text{Cost per EUP} = \frac{\text{Total costs}}{\text{EUP}}$$

| Roasting Department | | |
|---|---|---|
| Cost per Equivalent Unit of Production | Direct Materials | Conversion |
| Costs of beginning work in process............... | $ 81,000 | $108,900 |
| Costs added this period ........................ | 279,000 | 376,200 |
| Total costs ................................... | $360,000 | $485,100 |
| ÷ Equivalent units of production (from step 2) ........ | 120,000 EUP | 105,000 EUP |
| = Cost per equivalent unit of production............. | $3.00 per EUP | $4.62 per EUP |

## Step 4: Assign and Reconcile Costs

Step 4 uses the EUP from step 2 and the cost per EUP from step 3 to assign costs to the 100,000 units completed and transferred out and to the 20,000 units in ending work in process. Those costs are accounted for in Exhibit 3.10.

From Step 2    From Step 3

| Roasting Department | | | |
|---|---|---|---|
| | **EUP** | **Cost per EUP** | **Total Cost** |
| **Completed and transferred out** | | | |
| Direct materials . . . . . . . . . . . | 100,000 | $3.00 | $300,000 |
| Conversion . . . . . . . . . . . . . . . | 100,000 | $4.62 | 462,000 |
| | | | $762,000 |
| **Ending work in process** | | | |
| Direct materials . . . . . . . . . . . | 20,000 | $3.00 | $ 60,000 |
| Conversion . . . . . . . . . . . . . . . | 5,000 | $4.62 | 23,100 |
| | | | 83,100 |
| **Total costs accounted for.** . . . . | | | **$845,100** |

**EXHIBIT 3.10**

Cost Assignment—Weighted Average

**Point:** See that 'Total costs accounted for' equals 'Total production costs' to account for from Exhibit 3.8.

**Cost of Units Completed and Transferred Out**    The 100,000 units completed and transferred out used 100,000 EUP of direct materials and 100,000 EUP of conversion. We assign $300,000 (100,000 EUP × $3.00 per EUP) of direct materials cost and $462,000 (100,000 EUP × $4.62 per EUP) of conversion cost to those units. Total cost of the 100,000 units completed and transferred out is $762,000 ($300,000 + $462,000).

**Cost of Units in Ending Work in Process Inventory**    There are 20,000 units in work in process inventory at period-end. For direct materials, those units have 20,000 EUP (from step 2) at a cost of $3.00 per EUP (from step 3), which results in direct materials cost of work in process inventory of $60,000 (20,000 EUP × $3.00 per EUP). For conversion, we use the 5,000 EUP (from step 2) and the $4.62 conversion cost per EUP (from step 3) to compute conversion costs for work in process inventory of $23,100 (5,000 EUP × $4.62 per EUP). Total cost of work in process inventory at period-end is $83,100 ($60,000 + $23,100).

**Reconciliation**    Management verifies that total costs assigned to units completed and transferred out plus the costs of units in ending work in process (from Exhibit 3.10) equal the costs incurred by production. Exhibit 3.10 shows total costs accounted for of $845,100 equals total production costs of $845,100 from Exhibit 3.8.

## Using Process Cost Information    Process cost information is used to:

- **Control costs**—The department's equivalent costs per unit can be compared with prior months. If materials and/or conversion costs have changed a lot, managers should determine why and take corrective action.
- **Evaluate performance**—Top management can evaluate department managers based on their control of costs. Costs per equivalent unit are often compared to budgeted amounts.
- **Evaluate process improvements**—Organizations strive to improve processes. The success of process improvements can be evaluated by examining how costs per equivalent unit change after process improvements.
- **Prepare financial statements**—Cost of goods sold and ending inventory amounts computed from process cost data are reported on the income statement and balance sheet, respectively.

CDL Creative Studio/Shutterstock

**NEED-TO-KNOW** 3-3

Cost per EUP and Cost
Assignment

A department reports the following equivalent units of production and production cost data for the month. The weighted-average method is used.

| | Direct Materials EUP | Conversion EUP |
|---|---|---|
| Completed and transferred out .. | 58,000 | 58,000 |
| Ending work in process ........ | 4,800 | 4,200 |
| | 62,800 EUP | 62,200 EUP |

| Beginning work in process | | |
|---|---|---|
| Direct materials ....... | $ 26,960 | |
| Conversion .......... | 25,700 | $ 52,660 |
| Costs added this period | | |
| Direct materials ....... | 98,640 | |
| Conversion .......... | 129,800 | 228,440 |
| Total production costs .... | | **$281,100** |

1. Compute the department's cost per equivalent unit for direct materials and conversion for the month.

2. Assign costs to units completed and transferred out and to ending work in process inventory.

**Solution**

1.

| Cost per Equivalent Unit of Production | Direct Materials | Conversion |
|---|---|---|
| Costs of beginning work in process ..... | $ 26,960 | $ 25,700 |
| Costs added this period .............. | 98,640 | 129,800 |
| Total costs ........................ | $125,600 | $155,500 |
| ÷ Equivalent units of production ......... | 62,800 EUP | 62,200 EUP |
| = Cost per equivalent unit of production .... | $2.00 per EUP | $2.50 per EUP |

2.

| | EUP | Cost per EUP | Total Cost |
|---|---|---|---|
| **Completed and transferred out** | | | |
| Direct materials ........... | 58,000 | $2.00 | $116,000 |
| Conversion .............. | 58,000 | $2.50 | 145,000 |
| | | | $261,000 |
| **Ending work in process** | | | |
| Direct materials ........... | 4,800 | $2.00 | $ 9,600 |
| Conversion .............. | 4,200 | $2.50 | 10,500 |
| | | | 20,100 |
| **Total costs accounted for.....** | | | **$281,100** |

Do More: QS 3-11, E 3-6

## Production Cost Report

**P2**

Prepare a production cost report using weighted average.

The **production cost report,** or *process cost summary,* summarizes the four-step process. It shows the results of Exhibits 3.4, 3.7, 3.9, and 3.10 in one report. The production cost report for the Roasting department is in Exhibit 3.11.

1. Physical flow of units. This reconciles the beginning units in process and those started in a period with the ending units in process and those completed and transferred out.
2. Equivalent units of production for direct materials and for conversion.
3. Costs per equivalent unit of production for direct materials and for conversion.
4. Assignment of total costs among units worked on in the period.

The $762,000 is the total cost of the 100,000 units transferred out of the Roasting department to the Blending department. The $83,100 is the cost of the 20,000 partially completed units in ending work in process inventory in the Roasting department. The assigned costs are then added to show that the total $845,100 cost charged to the Roasting department is now assigned to the units.

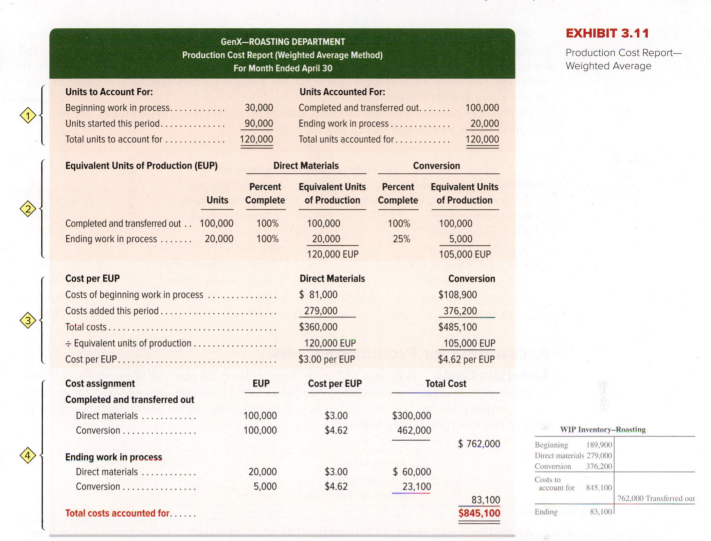

**EXHIBIT 3.11**

Production Cost Report—Weighted Average

### GenX—ROASTING DEPARTMENT
### Production Cost Report (Weighted Average Method)
### For Month Ended April 30

**Units to Account For:**

| | | | | |
|---|---|---|---|---|
| Beginning work in process............. | 30,000 | | Completed and transferred out....... | 100,000 |
| Units started this period.............. | 90,000 | | Ending work in process............. | 20,000 |
| Total units to account for ............. | 120,000 | | Total units accounted for........... | 120,000 |

**Equivalent Units of Production (EUP)**

| | Units | Percent Complete (Direct Materials) | Equivalent Units of Production (Direct Materials) | Percent Complete (Conversion) | Equivalent Units of Production (Conversion) |
|---|---|---|---|---|---|
| Completed and transferred out .. | 100,000 | 100% | 100,000 | 100% | 100,000 |
| Ending work in process ....... | 20,000 | 100% | 20,000 | 25% | 5,000 |
| | | | 120,000 EUP | | 105,000 EUP |

**Cost per EUP**

| | Direct Materials | Conversion |
|---|---|---|
| Costs of beginning work in process ............... | $ 81,000 | $108,900 |
| Costs added this period ........................ | 279,000 | 376,200 |
| Total costs.................................... | $360,000 | $485,100 |
| ÷ Equivalent units of production ................. | 120,000 EUP | 105,000 EUP |
| Cost per EUP.................................. | $3.00 per EUP | $4.62 per EUP |

**Cost assignment**

| | EUP | Cost per EUP | Total Cost |
|---|---|---|---|
| **Completed and transferred out** | | | |
| Direct materials ............ | 100,000 | $3.00 | $300,000 |
| Conversion ................ | 100,000 | $4.62 | 462,000 |
| | | | $ 762,000 |
| **Ending work in process** | | | |
| Direct materials ............ | 20,000 | $3.00 | $ 60,000 |
| Conversion ................ | 5,000 | $4.62 | 23,100 |
| | | | 83,100 |
| **Total costs accounted for**...... | | | **$845,100** |

**WIP Inventory–Roasting**

| | | | |
|---|---|---|---|
| Beginning | 189,900 | | |
| Direct materials | 279,000 | | |
| Conversion | 376,200 | | |
| Costs to account for | 845,100 | | |
| | | 762,000 | Transferred out |
| Ending | 83,100 | | |

## ACCOUNTING FOR PROCESS COSTING

Exhibit 3.12 shows the flow of materials, labor, and overhead costs through the manufacturing processes. There are separate Work in Process Inventory accounts for the Roasting and Blending departments; when goods are packaged and ready for sale, their costs are transferred to the Finished Goods Inventory account. When goods are sold, their costs are transferred to Cost of Goods Sold.

**P3**

Record the flow of production costs in process costing.

**EXHIBIT 3.12**

Process Manufacturing Operations and Costs: GenX

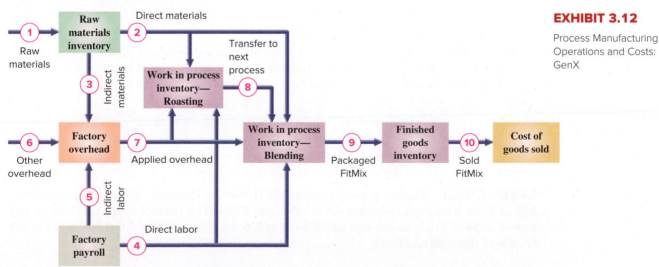

While many companies combine direct labor and overhead into conversion costs when computing costs per equivalent unit (as we showed), direct labor and overhead costs are accounted for separately in general ledger accounts. Because overhead costs typically cannot be tied to individual processes, most process operations use a single Factory Overhead account to accumulate actual and applied overhead costs.

Exhibit 3.13 presents cost data for GenX's Roasting and Blending departments. We use these data to show the journal entries in a process costing system.

**EXHIBIT 3.13**

Cost Data—GenX
(Weighted Average)

| GenX—Cost Data for Month Ending April 30 | | | |
|---|---|---|---|
| Raw materials inventory (March 31) . . . . . . . . . . . | $100,000 | Factory payroll for April | |
| Beginning work in process inventories (March 31) | | Direct labor—Roasting . . . . . . . . . . . . . . . . . . | $171,000 |
| Work in process—Roasting . . . . . . . . . . . . . . . . | $189,900 | Direct labor—Blending . . . . . . . . . . . . . . . . . . | 183,160 |
| Work in process—Blending . . . . . . . . . . . . . . . . | 151,688 | Indirect labor . . . . . . . . . . . . . . . . . . . . . . . . . | 78,350 |
| Materials purchased (on credit) . . . . . . . . . . . . . . | $400,000 | Other overhead costs added in April | |
| Materials requisitions during April | | Insurance expense—Factory . . . . . . . . . . . . . . | $ 11,930 |
| Direct materials—Roasting . . . . . . . . . . . . . . . | $279,000 | Utilities expense—Factory . . . . . . . . . . . . . . . | 7,945 |
| Direct materials—Blending . . . . . . . . . . . . . . . | 102,000 | Depreciation expense—Factory equipment . . . | 220,650 |
| Indirect materials . . . . . . . . . . . . . . . . . . . . . . | 71,250 | Other (paid in cash) . . . . . . . . . . . . . . . . . . . . | 34,867 |

## Accounting for Production Costs

**Materials Costs**    In Exhibit 3.12, arrow line ① reflects the purchase of raw materials. These materials include organic peanuts, chocolate pieces, dried fruits, oil, salt, and packaging. GenX uses a perpetual inventory system and makes all purchases on credit. The summary entry for receipt of raw materials in April follows.

Assets  = Liabilities + Equity
+400,000    +400,000

| ① | Raw Materials Inventory . . . . . . . . . . . . . . . . . . . . . . . . . | 400,000 | |
|---|---|---|---|
| | Accounts Payable . . . . . . . . . . . . . . . . . . . . . . . . . | | 400,000 |
| | *Purchased materials on credit for factory use.* | | |

Arrow line ② in Exhibit 3.12 shows the flow of *direct* materials to production in the Roasting and Blending departments. The manager of a process usually obtains materials by submitting a *materials requisition* to the materials storeroom manager. The entry to record the use of direct materials follows. These direct materials costs flow into each department's separate Work in Process Inventory account.

Assets  =  Liabilities  +  Equity
+279,000
+102,000
−381,000

| ② | Work in Process Inventory—Roasting . . . . . . . . . . . . . . | 279,000 | |
|---|---|---|---|
| | Work in Process Inventory—Blending . . . . . . . . . . . . . . | 102,000 | |
| | Raw Materials Inventory . . . . . . . . . . . . . . . . . . . . | | 381,000 |
| | *Record direct materials used.* | | |

Arrow line ③ reflects the flow of *indirect* materials to factory overhead. These materials cannot be cost-effectively traced to any specific production process or department but are used in production. These costs are recorded in the single Factory Overhead account with this entry.

| ③ | Factory Overhead . . . . . . . . . . . . . . . . . . . . . . . . . . . . . | 71,250 | |
|---|---|---|---|
| | Raw Materials Inventory . . . . . . . . . . . . . . . . . . . . | | 71,250 |
| | *Record indirect materials used.* | | |

**Labor Costs**    Factory payroll costs are $171,000 for Roasting department direct labor, $183,160 for Blending department direct labor, and $78,350 for indirect labor. This total factory payroll of $432,510 is assigned to either Work in Process Inventory (for direct labor) or Factory Overhead (for indirect labor).

Arrow line ④ shows use of *direct* labor. The following entry records direct labor used. Direct labor costs flow into each department's separate Work in Process Inventory account.

| ④ | Work in Process Inventory—Roasting............... | 171,000 | |
|---|---|---|---|
| | Work in Process Inventory—Blending.............. | 183,160 | |
| |     Factory Wages Payable .................... | | 354,160 |
| | *Record direct labor used.* | | |

Assets  =  Liabilities + Equity<br>+171,000    +354,160<br>+183,160

Arrow line ⑤ reflects *indirect* labor costs. This is labor that supports or supervises production in both the Roasting and Blending departments. For example, they order materials and deliver them to the factory floor, repair equipment, program computers used in production, clean up, and move goods across departments. The following entry records indirect labor costs.

| ⑤ | Factory Overhead ............................. | 78,350 | |
|---|---|---|---|
| |     Factory Wages Payable .................... | | 78,350 |
| | *Record indirect labor used.* | | |

## Other Factory Overhead Costs

Overhead costs other than indirect materials and indirect labor are reflected by arrow line ⑥. Other overhead items include costs of insuring production assets, renting the factory building, using factory utilities, and depreciating factory equipment not directly related to a specific process. The following entry records these other overhead costs.

| ⑥ | Factory Overhead ............................. | 275,392 | |
|---|---|---|---|
| |     Prepaid Insurance......................... | | 11,930 |
| |     Utilities Payable ......................... | | 7,945 |
| |     Cash..................................... | | 34,867 |
| |     Accumulated Depreciation—Factory Equipment . | | 220,650 |
| | *Record other overhead costs incurred.* | | |

## Applying Overhead to Work in Process

Companies use *predetermined overhead rates* to apply overhead. These rates are estimated at the beginning of a period and used to apply overhead during the period. This is important for process costing, where goods are transferred across departments before the entire production process is complete. Factory overhead is applied to processes using activity bases such as direct labor or machine hours.

Arrow line ⑦ in Exhibit 3.12 shows factory overhead applied to the two production departments. GenX applies overhead using a predetermined rate of 120% of direct labor cost in Exhibit 3.14.

| Production Department | Direct Labor Cost | Predetermined Rate | Overhead Applied |
|---|---|---|---|
| Roasting .......... | $171,000 | 120% | $205,200 |
| Blending .......... | 183,160 | 120 | 219,792 |
| Total ............. | | | $424,992 |

**EXHIBIT 3.14**

Applying Factory Overhead

GenX records applied overhead with this entry.

| ⑦ | Work in Process Inventory—Roasting............... | 205,200 | |
|---|---|---|---|
| | Work in Process Inventory—Blending.............. | 219,792 | |
| |     Factory Overhead......................... | | 424,992 |
| | *Applied overhead at 120% of direct labor.* | | |

**Point:** GenX's applied and actual overhead both equal $424,992, so no period-end closing entry for factory overhead is recorded. If actual overhead > applied overhead, we debit cost of goods sold and credit factory overhead for the difference. If applied overhead < actual overhead, we debit factory overhead and credit cost of goods sold for the difference.

**NEED-TO-KNOW** 3-4

Overhead Rate and Costs

P3

Tower Mfg. applies overhead based on machine hours. Tower estimates it will incur $200,000 of total overhead costs and use 10,000 machine hours this year. During February, the Fabricating department used 425 machine hours and the Assembly department used 375 machine hours. In addition, Tower incurred actual overhead costs as follows during February: indirect materials, $1,800; indirect labor, $5,700; depreciation on factory equipment, $8,000; and utilities payable, $500.

1. Compute the predetermined overhead rate.
2. Prepare journal entries to record (a) overhead applied for the Fabricating department and the Assembly department for February and (b) actual overhead costs incurred during February for indirect materials, indirect labor, and other overhead.

*Solution*

1. Predetermined overhead rate = Estimated overhead costs ÷ Estimated activity base
   = $200,000/10,000 machine hours = $20 per machine hour

**2a.**

| | | |
|---|---|---|
| Work in Process Inventory—Fabricating........ | 8,500 | |
| Work in Process Inventory—Assembly ......... | 7,500 | |
| Factory Overhead ..................... | | 16,000 |
| *Applied overhead at $20 per machine hour.* | | |

Do More: QS 3-25, E 3-20, E 3-21

**2b.**

| | | |
|---|---|---|
| Factory Overhead ............................. | 1,800 | |
| Raw Materials Inventory.................... | | 1,800 |
| *Record indirect materials used.* | | |
| Factory Overhead ............................. | 5,700 | |
| Factory Wages Payable..................... | | 5,700 |
| *Record indirect labor used.* | | |
| Factory Overhead ............................. | 8,500 | |
| Accumulated Depreciation—Factory Equipment .. | | 8,000 |
| Utilities Payable.......................... | | 500 |
| *Record other actual overhead used.* | | |

**P4** _____

Record the transfer of goods across departments, to Finished Goods Inventory, and to Cost of Goods Sold.

# Accounting for Transfers

## Transfers across Departments
Arrow line ⑧ in Exhibit 3.12 shows the transfer of partially completed units from Roasting to Blending. The production cost report for the Roasting department (Exhibit 3.11) shows that the 100,000 units transferred to the Blending department are assigned a cost of $762,000. The entry to record this transfer follows.

Assets = Liabilities + Equity
+762,000
−762,000

| ⑧ | Work in Process Inventory—Blending............... | 762,000 | |
|---|---|---|---|
| | Work in Process Inventory—Roasting .......... | | 762,000 |
| | *Transfer units from Roasting to Blending.* | | |

Units and costs *transferred out* of the Roasting department are *transferred into* the Blending department. Exhibit 3.15 shows this transfer using T-accounts for the separate Work in Process Inventory accounts (first in units and then in dollars).

| WIP Inventory—Roasting (Units) | | |
|---|---|---|
| Beginning   30,000 units | | |
| Started   90,000 units | | |
| Subtotal   120,000 units | | |
| | **100,000 units transferred to Blending** | |
| Ending   20,000 units | | |

| WIP Inventory—Blending (Units) | | |
|---|---|---|
| Beginning   12,000 units | | |
| → **Transferred from Roasting   100,000 units** | | |
| Subtotal   112,000 units | 97,000 units transferred to Finished Goods Inventory | |
| Ending   15,000 units | | |

| WIP Inventory—Roasting ($) | | |
|---|---|---|
| Beginning*   189,900 | | |
| Direct materials   279,000 | | |
| Conversion   376,200 | | |
| Subtotal   845,100 | | |
| | **762,000 Transferred to Blending** | |
| Ending   83,100 | | |

| WIP Inventory—Blending ($) | | |
|---|---|---|
| Beginning   151,688 | | |
| → **Transferred from Roasting   762,000** | | |
| Direct materials   102,000 | | |
| Conversion   402,952 | 1,262,940 Transferred to Finished Goods | |
| Subtotal   1,418,640 | | |
| Ending   155,700 | | |

*$81,000 direct materials + $108,900 conversion

**EXHIBIT 3.15**

Transfers using T-accounts

We see that the Blending department began the month with 12,000 units in beginning inventory with a cost of $151,688. Then 100,000 units and costs of $762,000 are transferred to the Blending department from the Roasting department. The Blending department adds direct materials costs of $102,000 and conversion costs of $402,952 during the month.

### Transfer to Finished Goods

Arrow line ⑨ in Exhibit 3.12 shows the transfer of units and costs from the Blending department to finished goods inventory. The Blending department transferred 97,000 completed units along with costs of $1,262,940 to finished goods. The entry to record this transfer follows.

Industryview/Getty Images

| ⑨ | Finished Goods Inventory . . . . . . . . . . . . . . . . . . . . . . . | 1,262,940 | |
|---|---|---|---|
| | Work in Process Inventory—Blending . . . . . . . . . | | 1,262,940 |
| | *Record transfer of completed goods.* | | |

Assets = Liabilities + Equity
+1,262,940
−1,262,940

### Computing Cost of Goods Sold

Arrow line ⑩ shows the sale of finished goods. Assume that GenX sold 103,000 units of FitMix this period, and that its beginning finished goods inventory was 26,000 units with a cost of $338,520. Also assume that its ending finished goods inventory consists of 20,000 units at a cost of $260,400. Using this information, cost of goods sold is computed in Exhibit 3.16.

| Finished Goods Inventory | | |
|---|---|---|
| Beginning   338,520 | | |
| COGM   1,262,940 | | |
| Available   1,601,460 | | |
| | | COGS   1,341,060 |
| Ending   260,400 | | |

**EXHIBIT 3.16**

Cost of Goods Sold

| GenX—Cost of Goods Sold | |
|---|---|
| Beginning finished goods inventory . . . . . . . . | $  338,520 |
| + Cost of goods manufactured . . . . . . . . . . . . . . | 1,262,940 |
| = Cost of goods available for sale . . . . . . . . . . . | 1,601,460 |
| − Ending finished goods inventory . . . . . . . . . . | 260,400 |
| = Cost of goods sold . . . . . . . . . . . . . . . . . . . . . . | $1,341,060 |

### Sales and the Transfer to Cost of Goods Sold

GenX's selling price for FitMix is $18.60 per unit. The entry to record sales of 103,000 units (on credit) for this period follows (103,000 units × $18.60 price per unit = $1,915,800).

| ⑩ | Accounts Receivable . . . . . . . . . . . . . . . . . . . . . . . . . . . | 1,915,800 | |
|---|---|---|---|
| | Sales . . . . . . . . . . . . . . . . . . . . . . . . . . . . . . . . . . | | 1,915,800 |
| | *Record sales for April.* | | |

Assets = Liabilities + Equity
+1,915,800              +1,915,800

The entry to record cost of goods sold for this period follows. This entry moves production costs from the balance sheet to the income statement.

Assets = Liabilities + Equity
−1,341,060          −1,341,060

| ⑩ | Cost of Goods Sold ........................... | 1,341,060 | |
|---|---|---|---|
| | Finished Goods Inventory ................... | | 1,341,060 |
| | *Record cost of goods sold for April.* | | |

### Financial Statement Reporting

GenX prepares monthly financial statements. It reports the following on its April income statement (partial) and April 30 balance sheet (partial).

| GenX Income Statement (partial) For Month Ended April 30 | |
|---|---|
| Sales......................... | $1,915,800 |
| Cost of goods sold............. | 1,341,060 |
| Gross profit ................... | $ 574,740 |

| GenX Balance Sheet (partial) April 30 | |
|---|---|
| Inventories | |
| Raw materials* .............. | $ 47,750 |
| Work in process† ............ | 238,800 |
| Finished goods‡ ............. | 260,400 |
| Total ...................... | $546,950 |

*Beginning raw materials inventory + Raw materials purchased − Materials requisitioned (from Exhibit 3.13)
  = $100,000 + $400,000 − $279,000 − $102,000 − $71,250 = $47,750.

†Work in Process Inventory Roasting + Work in Process Inventory Blending (from Exhibit 3.15) = $83,100 + $155,700 = $238,800.

‡From Exhibit 3.16.

### Cost per Completed Unit

In making pricing decisions, managers often use the cost per completed unit. This computation for FitMix follows.

$$\text{Cost per completed unit} = \frac{\text{Cost of goods manufactured this period}}{\text{Number of units transferred to finished goods}} = \frac{\$1,262,940}{97,000} = \$13.02$$

The cost of goods manufactured for a process manufacturer equals the costs transferred from the last production process to finished goods inventory. GenX must set the price of FitMix high enough to cover its cost of completed units, plus its selling and general and administrative costs, to be profitable.

## Trends in Process Operations

### Process Design

Concerns with production efficiency can lead companies to reorganize production processes. For example, instead of producing different types of computers in a series of departments, a separate work center for each computer type can be set up in one department. The process cost system is then changed to account for each work center's costs.

### Just-in-Time Production

With a just-in-time production system, inventory levels can be minimal. If raw materials are not ordered or received until needed, a Raw Materials Inventory account might be unnecessary. Instead, direct materials cost is immediately debited to Work in Process Inventory. Similarly, a Finished Goods Inventory account may not be needed. Instead, cost of goods manufactured might be immediately debited to Cost of Goods Sold.

### Robotics and Automation

Many production processes are automated. This results in reduced direct labor costs. Machine learning can lead to process improvements that reduce costs and increase efficiency.

PopTika/Shutterstock

### Continuous Processing

In some companies, like **Pepsi Bottling**, materials move continuously through the manufacturing process. In these cases, a **materials consumption report** summarizes the materials used and replaces materials requisitions.

**Services**    Service-based businesses are common. For standardized services like oil changes and simple tax returns, computing costs based on the process is simpler and more useful than a cost per individual job. More complex service companies use process departments to perform specific tasks for consumers. Hospitals, for example, have radiology and physical therapy facilities, each with special equipment and trained employees. When patients need services, they are processed through departments to receive prescribed care.

**Customer Orientation**    Focus on customer orientation leads to improved processes. A manufacturer of control devices improved quality and reduced production time by forming teams to study processes and suggest improvements. An ice cream maker studied customer tastes to develop a more pleasing ice cream texture.

 **CORPORATE SOCIAL RESPONSIBILITY**

Food processor **General Mills** needs a steady supply of high-quality corn, oats, and sugarcane. These agricultural inputs face risks due to water scarcity and climate change that could disrupt General Mills's process operations and hurt profits.

Buying from suppliers that follow sustainable principles reduces risk of reputational damage. The Sustainability Accounting Standards Board (SASB) recommends that food processors disclose information on *priority food ingredients* (those that are essential to the company's products), including details on the company's strategies to address strategic risks.

Consistent with SASB guidelines, General Mills disclosed the following in its recent *Global Responsibility Report*.

| General Mills Performance Dashboard (partial) | | |
|---|---|---|
| Ingredient | Target* | Progress |
| Vanilla | 100% | 32% |
| Oats | 100 | 90 |
| Sugarcane | 100 | 70 |
| Palm oil | 100 | 100 |

*Target and progress amounts are the percent of the ingredient sourced sustainably.
Source: General Mills, *Global Sustainability Report,* 2019.

Emily Michot/TNS/Newscom

In addition to making continuous process improvements to reduce materials waste and increase yield, Suzy Batlle, founder of **Azucar Ice Cream Company**, seeks high-quality fresh ingredients. For Suzy, buying from local suppliers provides a sustainable supply chain that benefits her business and the local community.

---

**Hybrid Costing System**  **Decision Analysis**

A **hybrid costing system** contains features of both process and job order operations and is also called an **operation costing system**. To illustrate, consider a car manufacturer's assembly line. The line resembles a process operation in that the assembly steps for each car are nearly identical. But the specifications of most cars have several important differences. Each car assembled can be different from the previous car and the next car. This means that the costs of direct materials (subassemblies or components) for each car can differ. While the conversion costs can be accounted for using a process costing system, direct materials are accounted for using a job order system (separately for each car or type of car).

A hybrid system of processes requires a *hybrid costing system* to properly cost products or services. Assembly costs per car are computed using process costing. The costs of additional custom components

**A1**

Illustrate a hybrid costing system and analyze process system yield.

StudioByTheSea/Shutterstock

are computed using job order costing. The costs of custom choices are then added to the assembly process costs to determine each car's total cost. To illustrate, consider the following information for a daily assembly process.

| Hybrid Costs | Per Car |
|---|---|
| Direct materials (excluding wheels and sound system) . . . | $10,600 |
| Conversion . . . . . . . . . . . . . . . . . . . . . . . . . . . . . . . . . . . . . . | 12,000 |
| Assembly process costs . . . . . . . . . . . . . . . . . . . . . . . . . . . | $22,600 |
| Customer choices: Wheel types. . . . . . . . . . . . . . . . . . . . . | $240; $330; $480 |
| Customer choices: Sound system types . . . . . . . . . . . . . . | $620; $840; $1,360 |

The assembly process costs $22,600 per car. Depending on the type of wheels and sound system the customer requests, the cost of a car can range from $23,460 to $24,440. If the company's target markup is 20% above cost, its selling prices would range from $28,152 ($23,460 × 120%) to $29,328 ($24,440 × 120%).

**Yield,** which is a measure of *output* divided by *input*, can be used to measure the efficiency of process operations. If **Ford** entered enough direct materials into production to produce 10,000 Mustangs, but only 9,900 nondefective cars were produced, yield is computed as follows.

$$\text{Yield} = \frac{\text{Nondefective units produced}}{\text{Units that could have been produced}} = \frac{9,900}{10,000} = 99\%$$

If a trail mix manufacturer started 10,000 pounds of peanuts in production and ended with processed peanuts of 9,650 pounds, its yield is 96.5% (9,650/10,000). Yield might be less than expected due to inferior direct materials or issues with the production process. When yields are lower than expected, managers ask why and take corrective action.

## ▉ Analytics **Insight**

**Right-Sized**   Using machine learning and data analytics, **Hershey** discovered that making candy in smaller sizes enables it to better control cooking temperatures and produce Twizzlers licorice in more precise weights. The company estimates savings of about $500,000 per batch from this process improvement. ▪

---

## NEED-TO-KNOW 3-5

**COMPREHENSIVE 1**

Weighted Average Method

Mortar Company produces a product that passes through two processes: Grinding and Mixing. Information related to its Grinding department manufacturing activities for July follows. The company uses the weighted average method of process costing.

| Cost Data | | |
|---|---|---|
| Beginning work in process | | |
|    Direct materials . . . . . . . | $ 20,000 | |
|    Conversion . . . . . . . . . . | 28,747 | $ 48,747 |
| Costs added this period | | |
|    Direct materials . . . . . . . | $190,000 | |
|    Conversion . . . . . . . . . . | 166,553 | 356,553 |
| Total production costs . . . . | | $405,300 |

| Units Data | |
|---|---|
| Beginning work in process. . . . . . . . . . | 5,000 units |
|    Percent Complete: Direct materials. . | 100% |
|    Percent Complete: Conversion . . . . . | 70% |
| Units started this period. . . . . . . . . . . . | 20,000 units |
| Units completed and transferred out. . . | 17,000 units |
| Ending work in process . . . . . . . . . . . . | 8,000 units |
|    Percent Complete: Direct materials. . | 100% |
|    Percent Complete: Conversion . . . . . | 20% |

**Required**

Complete the requirements below for the Grinding department.

**1.** Prepare a physical unit flow reconciliation for July.

**2.** Compute the equivalent units of production in July for direct materials and conversion.

**3.** Compute the costs per equivalent unit of production in July for direct materials and conversion.

**4.** Assign costs to units completed and transferred out and to units in ending work in process inventory.

*Solution*

**1.** Physical unit flow reconciliation.

| Units to Account For | | Units Accounted For | |
|---|---|---|---|
| Beginning work in process... | 5,000 units | Units completed and transferred out .. | 17,000 units |
| Units started this period..... | 20,000 units | Ending work in process............. | 8,000 units |
| Total units to account for .... | **25,000 units** | Total units accounted for........... | **25,000 units** |

reconciled

**2.** Equivalent units of production (weighted average).

| | Units | Direct Materials | | Conversion | |
|---|---|---|---|---|---|
| | | Percent Complete | Equivalent Units of Production | Percent Complete | Equivalent Units of Production |
| Completed and transferred out ... | 17,000 | 100% | 17,000 | 100% | 17,000 |
| Ending work in process ........ | 8,000 | 100% | 8,000 | 20% | 1,600 |
| | | | 25,000 EUP | | 18,600 EUP |

**3.** Costs per equivalent unit of production (weighted average).

| Costs per Equivalent Unit of Production | Direct Materials | Conversion |
|---|---|---|
| Costs of beginning work in process................. | $  20,000 | $   28,747 |
| Costs added this period.......................... | 190,000 | 166,553 |
| Total costs...................................... | $ 210,000 | $   195,300 |
| ÷ Equivalent units of production (from part 2).......... | 25,000 EUP | 18,600 EUP |
| = Costs per equivalent unit of production ............. | $8.40 per EUP | $10.50 per EUP |

**4.** Assign and reconcile costs (weighted average).

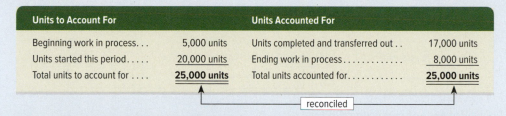

| | EUP | Cost per EUP | Total Cost |
|---|---|---|---|
| **Completed and transferred out** | | | |
| Direct materials ........... | 17,000 | $ 8.40 | $142,800 |
| Conversion ............... | 17,000 | $10.50 | 178,500 |
| | | | $ 321,300 |
| **Ending work in process** | | | |
| Direct materials ........... | 8,000 | $ 8.40 | $ 67,200 |
| Conversion ............... | 1,600 | $10.50 | 16,800 |
| | | | 84,000 |
| **Total costs accounted for.....** | | | **$405,300** |

| Cost Data (given) | | |
|---|---|---|
| **Beginning work in process** | | |
| Direct materials ....... | $ 20,000 | |
| Conversion .......... | 28,747 | $ 48,747 |
| **Costs added this period** | | |
| Direct materials ....... | $190,000 | |
| Conversion .......... | 166,553 | 356,553 |
| **Total production costs ...** | | **$405,300** |

reconciled

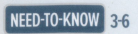

**NEED-TO-KNOW 3-6**

**COMPREHENSIVE 2**

FIFO Method
(Appendix 3A)

Refer to the information in Need-To-Know 3-5. For the Grinding department, complete requirements 1 through 4 using the **FIFO** method. (Round the cost per equivalent unit of conversion to two decimal places.)

## SOLUTION

**1.** Physical unit flow reconciliation (FIFO).

Units started and completed = Units completed and transferred − Units in beginning work in process

$$\underline{12{,}000 \text{ units}} = 17{,}000 \text{ units} − 5{,}000 \text{ units}$$

| Units to Account For | | Units Accounted For | |
|---|---|---|---|
| Beginning work in process . . . . | 5,000 units | Beginning work in process . . . . . . . . | 5,000 units |
| Units started . . . . . . . . . . . . . . | 20,000 units | Units started and completed . . . . . . . | 12,000 units |
| | | Ending work in process . . . . . . . . . . | 8,000 units |
| Total units to account for . . . . . | 25,000 units | Total units accounted for . . . . . . . . . | 25,000 units |

reconciled

**2.** Equivalent units of production (FIFO).

| | Units | Direct Materials | | Conversion | |
|---|---|---|---|---|---|
| | | Percent Added | Equivalent Units of Production | Percent Added | Equivalent Units of Production |
| Beginning work in process. . . . | 5,000 | 0% | 0 | 30% | 1,500 |
| Started and completed. . . . . . . | 12,000 | 100% | 12,000 | 100% | 12,000 |
| Ending work in process . . . . . . | 8,000 | 100% | 8,000 | 20% | 1,600 |
| | | | 20,000 EUP | | 15,100 EUP |

**3.** Costs per equivalent unit of production (FIFO).

| Costs per Equivalent Unit of Production | Direct Materials | Conversion |
|---|---|---|
| Costs added this period. . . . . . . . . . . . . . . . . . . . . . | $190,000 | $ 166,553 |
| ÷ Equivalent units of production (from part 2) . . . . . . . | 20,000 EUP | 15,100 EUP |
| = Costs per equivalent unit of production . . . . . . . . . : | $9.50 per EUP | $11.03 per EUP |

**4.** Assign and reconcile costs (FIFO).

| | EUP | Cost per EUP | Total Cost |
|---|---|---|---|
| Beginning work in process. . . . . . . . . . . | | | $  48,747 |
| **To complete beginning work in process** | | | |
| Direct materials . . . . . . . . . . . . . . . . . . | 0 | $ 9.50 | $        0 |
| Conversion . . . . . . . . . . . . . . . . . . . . . . | 1,500 | $11.03 | 16,545 |
| | | | 16,545 |
| **Started and completed** | | | |
| Direct materials . . . . . . . . . . . . . . . . . . | 12,000 | $ 9.50 | 114,000 |
| Conversion . . . . . . . . . . . . . . . . . . . . . . | 12,000 | $11.03 | 132,360 |
| | | | 246,360 |
| Completed and transferred out. . . . . . | | | 311,652 |
| **Ending work in process** | | | |
| Direct materials . . . . . . . . . . . . . . . . . . | 8,000 | $ 9.50 | 76,000 |
| Conversion . . . . . . . . . . . . . . . . . . . . . . | 1,600 | $11.03 | 17,648 |
| | | | 93,648 |
| **Total costs accounted for**. . . . . . . . . . . | | | **$405,300** |

| Cost Data | | |
|---|---|---|
| **Beginning work in process inventory** | | |
| Direct materials . . . . . . . . . . . . . . . | $ 20,000 | |
| Conversion . . . . . . . . . . . . . . . . . . . | 28,747 | $ 48,747 |
| **Costs added this period** | | |
| Direct materials . . . . . . . . . . . . . . . | 190,000 | |
| Conversion . . . . . . . . . . . . . . . . . . . | 166,553 | 356,553 |
| **Total costs to account for**. . . . . . . . . | | **$405,300** |

reconciled

Garcia Manufacturing produces a product that passes through a molding process and then through an assembly process. Partial information related to its manufacturing activities for July follows.

NEED-TO-KNOW 3-7

**COMPREHENSIVE 3**

Journal Entries for Process Costing

| Direct materials | | Factory Overhead Applied | |
|---|---|---|---|
| Raw materials purchased on credit .. | $400,000 | Molding (150% of direct labor)........ | $ 63,000 |
| Direct materials used—Molding ..... | 190,000 | Assembly (200% of direct labor) ...... | 110,750 |
| Direct materials used—Assembly.... | 88,600 | Total factory overhead applied........ | $173,750 |
| **Direct Labor** | | **Cost Transfers** | |
| Direct labor—Molding............. | $ 42,000 | From Molding to Assembly........... | $277,200 |
| Direct labor—Assembly............ | 55,375 | From Assembly to finished goods ..... | 578,400 |
| **Factory Overhead (Actual costs)** | | From finished goods to cost | |
| Indirect materials used ............ | $ 51,400 | of goods sold ................... | 506,100 |
| Indirect labor used ............... | 50,625 | Sales................................ | $900,000 |
| Other overhead costs ............. | 71,725 | | |
| Total factory overhead incurred ..... | $173,750 | | |

### Required

Prepare journal entries to record the transactions and events of July for (a) raw materials purchases, (b) direct materials usage, (c) indirect materials usage, (d) direct labor usage, (e) indirect labor usage, (f) other overhead costs (paid in cash), (g) application of overhead to the two departments, (h) transfer of partially completed goods from Molding to Assembly, (i) transfer of finished goods out of Assembly, (j) sales on credit, and (k) cost of goods sold.

### Solution

Journal entries for the transactions and events in July.

| | | | | | | | | |
|---|---|---|---|---|---|---|---|---|
| **a.** | Raw Materials Inventory................ | 400,000 | | **f.** | Factory Overhead .................... | 71,725 | |
| | Accounts Payable................ | | 400,000 | | Cash .......................... | | 71,725 |
| | *Record raw materials purchases.* | | | | *Record other overhead costs.* | | |
| **b.** | Work in Process Inventory—Molding ..... | 190,000 | | **g.** | Work in Process Inventory—Molding ..... | 63,000 | |
| | Work in Process Inventory—Assembly.... | 88,600 | | | Work in Process Inventory—Assembly.... | 110,750 | |
| | Raw Materials Inventory .......... | | 278,600 | | Factory Overhead................ | | 173,750 |
| | *Record direct materials used.* | | | | *Record applied overhead.* | | |
| **c.** | Factory Overhead .................... | 51,400 | | **h.** | Work in Process Inventory—Assembly.... | 277,200 | |
| | Raw Materials Inventory .......... | | 51,400 | | Work in Process Inventory—Molding | | 277,200 |
| | *Record indirect materials used.* | | | | *Transfer from Molding to Assembly.* | | |
| **d.** | Work in Process Inventory—Molding ..... | 42,000 | | **i.** | Finished Goods Inventory.............. | 578,400 | |
| | Work in Process Inventory—Assembly.... | 55,375 | | | Work in Process Inventory—Assembly | | 578,400 |
| | Factory Wages Payable ........... | | 97,375 | | *Transfer to finished goods.* | | |
| | *Record direct labor used.* | | | **j.** | Accounts Receivable.................. | 900,000 | |
| **e.** | Factory Overhead .................... | 50,625 | | | Sales.......................... | | 900,000 |
| | Factory Wages Payable ........... | | 50,625 | | *Record sales for July.* | | |
| | *Record indirect labor used.* | | | **k.** | Cost of Goods Sold .................. | 506,100 | |
| | | | | | Finished Goods Inventory ......... | | 506,100 |
| | | | | | *Record cost of goods sold.* | | |

**APPENDIX**

# FIFO Method of Process Costing

**3A**

C2

Compute process activity costs and prepare a production cost report using FIFO.

We provide a step-by-step demonstration of process costing for GenX's production of FitMix, an organic trail mix. FitMix is manufactured in a continuous, two-process operation: Roasting and Blending. We focus on the first process, Roasting. Accounting for each process or department in a process operation follows four steps.

1. **Determine the physical flow of units.**
2. **Compute equivalent units of production.**

3. **Compute cost per equivalent unit of production.**
4. **Assign and reconcile costs.**

In each step, we demonstrate process costing using the first-in, first-out (FIFO) method. FIFO assigns costs to units assuming a first-in, first-out flow of product. We explain how this affects process costing in each step.

---

The following sections on process costing use the *first-in, first out (FIFO) method*. The *weighted average method* is in the chapter under learning objectives P1 and P2. These methods make different assumptions about cost flows.

- Weighted average method combines units and costs across two periods in computing equivalent units and cost per equivalent unit.

- FIFO method computes equivalent units and cost per equivalent unit based only on production activity in the current period.

The objectives, concepts, and journal entries (but not dollar amounts) are the same under both methods; the computation of equivalent units differs. Both methods are used in practice, but weighted average requires fewer calculations. Differences between the two methods are often small. With a just-in-time inventory system, those differences are even less because inventories are immaterial.

---

## Step 1: Determine Physical Flow of Units

Step 1 is to determine the number of units to account for and units accounted for. For FitMix, a unit is a cup of trail mix.

Exhibit 3.A1 shows production data in units for the first process: Roasting.

**EXHIBIT 3.A1**

Unit Data—Roasting Department

| | | | |
|---|---|---|---|
| Beginning work in process inventory . . . . | 30,000 units | Units completed and transferred out. . . . . | 100,000 units |
| Units started this period . . . . . . . . . . . . . . | 90,000 units | Ending work in process inventory . . . . . . . | 20,000 units |

### Units to Account For

Units to account for is computed for FitMix as follows.

$$\text{Units to account for} = \text{Beginning work in process inventory} + \text{Units started this period}$$
$$= 30,000 \text{ units} + 90,000 \text{ units}$$
$$= 120,000 \text{ units}$$

### Units Accounted For

Using FIFO, we look at three groups of units when determining units accounted for:

- Beginning work in process inventory.
- Units started and completed this period.
- Ending work in process inventory.

Beginning work in process inventory for Roasting is 30,000 units, and its ending work in process inventory is 20,000 units (from Exhibit 3A.1). To get the number of units started and completed this period we apply the following procedure.

**Units Started and Completed**    FIFO assumes that the units in beginning work in process inventory are the first units completed in the period. For FitMix, this means that of the 100,000 units completed and transferred out this period, we assume 30,000 are from beginning work in process inventory. This implies that 70,000 (100,000 − 30,000) units were started and completed this period. The computation follows.

**Point:** Units Started and Completed is also computed as: Units started – Ending work in process.

For FitMix, **90,000** units started − **20,000** units in ending work in process = **70,000** units started and completed.

$$\text{Units started and completed} = \text{Completed and transferred out} - \text{Beginning work in process inventory}$$
$$= 100,000 \text{ units} - 30,000 \text{ units}$$
$$= 70,000 \text{ units}$$

Exhibit 3A.2 shows the three groups of units for determining units accounted for.

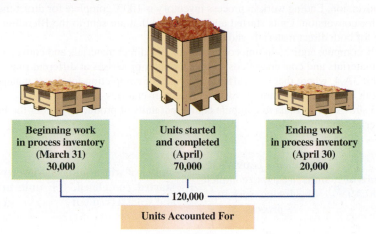

| Beginning work in process inventory (March 31) 30,000 | Units started and completed (April) 70,000 | Ending work in process inventory (April 30) 20,000 |

120,000

Units Accounted For

**Determine Flow of Units**   A *physical unit flow reconciliation* proves that (1) beginning units in process plus units started in the period equals the (2) beginning units in process plus units started and completed plus units in ending work in process. A physical unit flow reconciliation for the Roasting department for April is in Exhibit 3A.3.

| Roasting Department | | | |
|---|---|---|---|
| **Units to Account For** | | **Units Accounted For** | |
| Beginning work in process.... | 30,000 units | Beginning work in process ........ | 30,000 units |
| Units started .............. | 90,000 units | Units started and completed...... | 70,000 units |
| | | Ending work in process .......... | 20,000 units |
| Total units to account for ..... | 120,000 units | Total units accounted for......... | 120,000 units |

reconciled

**Step 2: Compute Equivalent Units of Production**   Step 2 is to compute *equivalent units of production*. **Equivalent units of production (EUP)** is the number of whole units that *could have been* started and completed given the costs incurred in the period. The reason we use equivalent units of production is that some units are not finished in beginning and ending work in process inventory but still need to be assigned costs.

To demonstrate, 10 cups of trail mix 60% through the production process is *equivalent to* 6 (10 × 60%) cups of completed trail mix. This means that the cost of 10 units that are 60% complete is *equivalent to* the cost of 6 completed units.

Exhibit 3A.4 shows *percent complete* data for direct materials and conversion for the Roasting department. The percents are needed to compute equivalent units of production. In both Roasting and Blending, direct materials enter production at the beginning of the process, while conversion costs occur throughout each department's processing. **Conversion costs** consist of direct labor and overhead. They are called conversion costs because they are the costs of *converting* raw materials into finished goods.

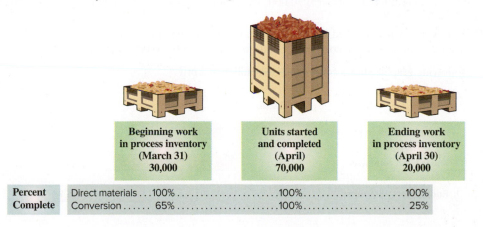

| | Beginning work in process inventory (March 31) 30,000 | Units started and completed (April) 70,000 | Ending work in process inventory (April 30) 20,000 |
|---|---|---|---|
| **Percent Complete** | Direct materials . . . 100% | 100% | 100% |
| | Conversion . . . . . . 65% | 100% | 25% |

**Point:** Units started and completed are always 100% complete for direct materials and conversion.

We see that beginning work in process inventory is 100% complete for direct materials but only 65% complete for conversion. Ending work in process inventory is 100% complete for direct materials but only 25% complete for conversion. Units started and completed that are sent to the Blending department are 100% complete for both direct materials and conversion.

We separately compute equivalent units of production for direct materials and conversion costs. This is because direct materials and conversion costs typically enter processes at different rates. We see this for FitMix in Exhibit 3A.4, where there are different percents of completion for direct materials and conversion costs for both beginning and ending work in process inventories.

Exhibit 3A.5 shows the formula to compute equivalent units of production under the FIFO method for both direct materials and conversion.

**EXHIBIT 3A.5**

Computing EUP—FIFO

$$\begin{array}{c}\text{Equivalent units of}\\\text{production (EUP)}\end{array} = \begin{array}{c}\text{Number of equivalent}\\\text{units needed to complete}\\\text{beginning work in}\\\text{process}\end{array} + \begin{array}{c}\text{Number of whole units}\\\text{started, completed,}\\\text{and transferred out}\end{array} + \begin{array}{c}\text{Number of equivalent}\\\text{units in ending work}\\\text{in process}\end{array}$$

We compute the equivalent units of production (EUP) for both direct materials and conversion in Exhibit 3A.6.

**EXHIBIT 3A.6**

Equivalent Units of Production—FIFO

| | | Roasting Department | | | |
| --- | --- | --- | --- | --- | --- |
| | | Direct Materials | | Conversion | |
| | Units | Percent Added | Equivalent Units of Production | Percent Added | Equivalent Units of Production |
| Beginning work in process.... | 30,000 | 0% | 0 | 35% | 10,500 |
| Started and completed....... | 70,000 | 100% | 70,000 | 100% | 70,000 |
| Ending work in process ...... | 20,000 | 100% | 20,000 | 25% | 5,000 |
| | | | 90,000 EUP | | 85,500 EUP |

**Direct Materials**   Total equivalent units of production is 90,000 for direct materials (0 + 70,000 + 20,000).

- **Beginning work in process** had 30,000 units that were 100% complete with respect to direct materials. EUP is 0 as no additional direct materials were added to complete these units.
- **Started and completed** units were 70,000. These units received 100% of direct materials during the month, so EUP is 70,000.
- **Ending work in process** had 20,000 units started but not completed during the month. These units received 100% of its direct materials this period, so EUP is 20,000.

**Conversion**   Total equivalent units of production is 85,500 for conversion (10,500 + 70,000 + 5,000).

- **Beginning work in process** had 30,000 units that were 65% complete for conversion. These units needed another 35% (100% − 65%) of conversion costs to complete them, so EUP is 10,500 (30,000 × 35%).
- **Started and completed** units were 70,000. These units received 100% of conversion costs during the month, so EUP is 70,000.
- **Ending work in process** had 20,000 units started but not completed during the month. These units received 25% of conversion costs this period, so EUP is 5,000 (20,000 × 25%).

The following graphic shows conversion costs added in April.

**Point:** FIFO focuses on production activity in the current period only.

A department began the month with 8,000 units in work in process inventory. These units were 100% complete for direct materials and 40% complete for conversion.

NEED-TO-KNOW 3-8

Compute EUP (FIFO)

C2

During the month, the department started 56,000 units and completed and transferred out 58,000 units. Ending work in process inventory is 6,000 units, 80% complete for direct materials and 70% complete for conversion. The FIFO method of process costing is used.

1. Compute units started and completed this month.
2. Compute the department's equivalent units of production for the month for direct materials and for conversion.

**Solution**

1. **Units started and completed** = Completed and transferred out − Beginning work in process inventory

$$= 58,000 \text{ units} - 8,000 \text{ units}$$
$$= 50,000 \text{ units}$$

**Point:** Or **56,000** units started − **6,000** units in ending work in process = **50,000** units started and completed.

2.

|  | Units | Direct Materials | | Conversion | |
|---|---|---|---|---|---|
|  |  | Percent Added | Equivalent Units of Production | Percent Added | Equivalent Units of Production |
| Beginning work in process.... | 8,000 | 0% | 0 | 60% | 4,800 |
| Started and completed....... | 50,000 | 100% | 50,000 | 100% | 50,000 |
| Ending work in process ...... | 6,000 | 80% | 4,800 | 70% | 4,200 |
|  |  |  | 54,800 EUP |  | 59,000 EUP |

Do More: QS 3-14, QS 3-15, E 3-5, E 3-10

## Step 3: Compute Cost per Equivalent Unit

Step 3 uses equivalent units of production from step 2, along with cost data, to compute cost per equivalent unit. FIFO computes the cost per equivalent unit based solely on this period's costs (unlike the weighted average method, which includes costs of beginning work in process inventory). Production cost data for the Roasting department are in Exhibit 3A.7. *Recall:* Conversion costs equal direct labor costs plus overhead costs applied.

| Roasting Department: Production Cost Data (April) | | |
|---|---|---|
| Beginning work in process inventory | | |
| Direct materials ................... | $ 81,000 | |
| Conversion ...................... | 108,900 | $ 189,900 |
| Costs added this period | | |
| Direct materials ................... | 279,000 | |
| Conversion ...................... | 376,200 | 655,200 |
| Total production costs ............. | | **$845,100** |

**EXHIBIT 3A.7**

Roasting Department Production Cost Data

To compute cost per equivalent unit, we take only the direct materials and conversion costs *added this period* and then divide by equivalent units of production from step 2. Exhibit 3A.8 shows this separately for direct materials and for conversion. The cost for direct materials is $3.10 per EUP, and for conversion is $4.40 per EUP.

| Roasting Department | | |
|---|---|---|
| Cost per Equivalent Unit of Production | Direct Materials | Conversion |
| Costs added this period .................... | $ 279,000 | $ 376,200 |
| ÷ Equivalent units of production (from step 2) ..... | 90,000 EUP | 85,500 EUP |
| Cost per equivalent unit of production......... | $3.10 per EUP | $4.40 per EUP |

**EXHIBIT 3A.8**

Cost per Equivalent Unit of Production—FIFO

## Step 4: Assign and Reconcile Costs

The EUP from step 2 and the cost per EUP from step 3 are used in step 4 to assign costs to (a) units that the Roasting department completed and transferred out to the Blending department and (b) units that remain in process in the Roasting department. This is shown in Exhibit 3A.9.

**EXHIBIT 3A.9**

Cost Assignment—FIFO

| Roasting Department | | | |
|---|---|---|---|
| | EUP | Cost per EUP | Total Cost |
| Beginning work in process............. | | | $ 189,900 |
| **To complete beginning work in process** | | | |
|    Direct materials .................... | 0 | $3.10 | $        0 |
|    Conversion ...................... | 10,500 | $4.40 | 46,200      46,200 |
| **Started and completed** | | | |
|    Direct materials .................... | 70,000 | $3.10 | 217,000 |
|    Conversion ...................... | 70,000 | $4.40 | 308,000 |
| | | | 525,000 |
| Completed and transferred out....... | | | 761,100 |
| **Ending work in process** | | | |
|    Direct materials .................... | 20,000 | $3.10 | 62,000 |
|    Conversion ...................... | 5,000 | $4.40 | 22,000      84,000 |
| **Total costs accounted for............** | | | **$845,100** |

**Beginning Work in Process Inventory**  The cost of beginning work in process is $189,900 (from Exhibit 3A.7). These costs were carried over from the prior period for work already completed on the 30,000 units in beginning work in process inventory.

**To Complete Beginning Work in Process Inventory**  The cost to complete beginning work in process inventory is $46,200. We assign $0 of direct materials as there were 0 equivalent units. Recall, EUP is 0 because beginning inventory was already 100% complete for direct materials. We assign $46,200 (10,500 EUP × $4.40 per EUP) of conversion cost. This is the remaining conversion costs required on beginning work in process inventory to complete it for the next department.

**Started and Completed**  The 70,000 units started and completed this month used 70,000 EUP of direct materials and 70,000 EUP of conversion. We assign $217,000 (70,000 EUP × $3.10 per EUP) of direct materials cost and $308,000 (70,000 EUP × $4.40 per EUP) of conversion cost to these units.

    Completed and transferred-out costs total $761,100 ($189,900 + $46,200 + $525,000). This consists of the cost of beginning work in process, the costs to complete beginning work in process, and the cost of started and completed units. These units and costs move on to Blending.

**Ending Work in Process Inventory**  There are 20,000 units in work in process inventory at period-end. We assign $62,000 (20,000 EUP × $3.10 per EUP) of direct materials cost and $22,000 (5,000 EUP × $4.40 per EUP) of conversion cost to these units. Total cost of work in process inventory at period-end is $84,000 ($62,000 + $22,000).

**Reconciliation**  Management verifies that total costs assigned to units completed and transferred out plus the costs of units in ending work in process equal total production costs. Exhibit 3A.9 shows total costs accounted for of $845,100, which equals total production costs of $845,100 from Exhibit 3A.7.

---

**NEED-TO-KNOW** 3-9

Cost per EUP and Cost Assignment

C2

A department reports the following equivalent units of production along with production cost data for the month. It uses the FIFO method.

| | Direct Materials | Conversion |
|---|---|---|
| | EUP | EUP |
| Beginning work in process...... | 0 | 4,800 |
| Started and completed......... | 50,000 | 50,000 |
| Ending work in process ........ | 4,800 | 4,200 |
| | 54,800 EUP | 59,000 EUP |

| Beginning work in process | | |
|---|---|---|
|    Direct materials ....... | $ 26,960 | |
|    Conversion ........... | 25,700 | $ 52,660 |
| Costs added this period | | |
|    Direct materials ....... | 98,640 | |
|    Conversion ........... | 129,800 | 228,440 |
| Total production costs .... | | **$281,100** |

**1.** Compute the department's cost per equivalent unit for direct materials and conversion.

**2.** Assign costs to units completed and transferred out to ending work in process inventory.

*Solution*

1.

| Cost per Equivalent Unit of Production | Direct Materials | Conversion |
|---|---|---|
| Costs added this period . . . . . . . . . . . . . . | $ 98,640 | $129,800 |
| ÷ Equivalent units of production . . . . . . . . . | 54,800 EUP | 59,000 EUP |
| = Cost per equivalent unit of production . . | $1.80 per EUP | $2.20 per EUP |

2.

| | EUP | Cost per EUP | Total Cost |
|---|---|---|---|
| Beginning work in process. . . . . . . . . . . | | | $  52,660 |
| **To complete beginning work in process** | | | |
| Direct materials . . . . . . . . . . . . . . . . . | 0 | $1.80 | $         0 |
| Conversion . . . . . . . . . . . . . . . . . . . . . | 4,800 | $2.20 | 10,560 |
| | | | 10,560 |
| **Started and completed** | | | |
| Direct materials . . . . . . . . . . . . . . . . . | 50,000 | $1.80 | 90,000 |
| Conversion . . . . . . . . . . . . . . . . . . . . . | 50,000 | $2.20 | 110,000 |
| | | | 200,000 |
| Completed and transferred out. . . . . . | | | 263,220 |
| **Ending work in process** | | | |
| Direct materials . . . . . . . . . . . . . . . . . | 4,800 | $1.80 | 8,640 |
| Conversion . . . . . . . . . . . . . . . . . . . . . | 4,200 | $2.20 | 9,240 |
| | | | 17,880 |
| **Total costs accounted for**. . . . . . . . . . | | | **$281,100** |

Do More: QS 3-15, QS 3-16, E 3-7

## Production Cost Report

**Production Cost Report**    The **production cost report,** or *process cost summary,* summarizes the four-step process. It shows the results of Exhibits 3A.3, 3A.6, 3A.8, and 3A.9 in one report. The production cost report for the Roasting department is in Exhibit 3A.10.

⟨1⟩ Physical flow of units. This reconciles the units started with the units completed and in-process at period-end.

⟨2⟩ Equivalent units of production for direct materials and for conversion.

⟨3⟩ Costs per equivalent unit of production for direct materials and for conversion.

⟨4⟩ Assignment of total costs among units worked on in the period.

The $761,100 is the total cost of the 100,000 units transferred out of the Roasting department to the Blending department. The $84,000 is the cost of the 20,000 partially completed units in ending work in process inventory in the Roasting department. The assigned costs are then added to show that the total $845,100 production cost charged to the Roasting department is now assigned to the units.

## ■ Decision Maker

**Cost Manager**    As cost manager for an electronics manufacturer, you apply a process costing system using FIFO. Your company plans to adopt a just-in-time system and eliminate inventories. What is the impact of using FIFO (versus the weighted average method) given these plans? ■    *Answer:* Differences between the FIFO and weighted average methods are greatest when large work in process inventories exist and when costs fluctuate. The method used if inventories are eliminated does not matter; both produce identical costs.

**EXHIBIT 3A.10**

Production Cost Report—
FIFO

### GenX—ROASTING DEPARTMENT
### Production Cost Report (FIFO Method)
### For Month Ended April 30

| Units to Account For: | | Units Accounted For: | |
|---|---|---|---|
| Beginning work in process...... | 30,000 units | Beginning work in process ...... | 30,000 units |
| Units started ................. | 90,000 units | Units started and completed..... | 70,000 units |
| | | Ending work in process ......... | 20,000 units |
| Total units to account for ....... | 120,000 units | Total units accounted for ........ | 120,000 units |

| Equivalent Units of Production (EUP) | | Direct Materials | | Conversion | |
|---|---|---|---|---|---|
| | Units | Percent Added | Equivalent Units of Production | Percent Added | Equivalent Units of Production |
| Beginning work in process... | 30,000 | 0% | 0 | 35% | 10,500 |
| Started and completed...... | 70,000 | 100% | 70,000 | 100% | 70,000 |
| Ending work in process ..... | 20,000 | 100% | 20,000 | 25% | 5,000 |
| | | | 90,000 EUP | | 85,500 EUP |

| Cost per EUP | Direct Materials | Conversion |
|---|---|---|
| Costs added this period ......................... | $279,000 | $376,200 |
| ÷ Equivalent units of production .................... | 90,000 EUP | 85,500 EUP |
| Cost per equivalent unit of production ................ | $3.10 per EUP | $4.40 per EUP |

| Cost Assignment | EUP | Cost per EUP | Total Cost | |
|---|---|---|---|---|
| Beginning work in process............. | | | | $ 189,900 |
| **To complete beginning work in process** | | | | |
| Direct materials .................... | 0 | $3.10 | $      0 | |
| Conversion ...................... | 10,500 | $4.40 | 46,200 | |
| | | | | 46,200 |
| **Started and completed** | | | | |
| Direct materials .................. | 70,000 | $3.10 | 217,000 | |
| Conversion ...................... | 70,000 | $4.40 | 308,000 | |
| | | | | 525,000 |
| Completed and transferred out....... | | | | 761,100 |
| **Ending work in process** | | | | |
| Direct materials .................... | 20,000 | $3.10 | 62,000 | |
| Conversion ...................... | 5,000 | $4.40 | 22,000 | |
| | | | | 84,000 |
| **Total costs accounted for** ............. | | | | **$845,100** |

| WIP Inventory–Roasting | | | |
|---|---|---|---|
| Beginning | 189,900 | | |
| Direct materials | 279,000 | | |
| Conversion | 376,200 | | |
| Costs to account for | 845,100 | | |
| | | 761,100 | Transferred out |
| Ending | 84,000 | | |

---

## Summary: Cheat Sheet

### PROCESS OPERATIONS

**Process operation:** Mass production of similar products in a flow of sequential processes.

**Process costing system:** Measures costs per equivalent unit at period-end. Each process has a separate Work in Process Inventory account.

**Conversion costs:** Direct labor + Applied factory overhead.

**Equivalent units** is the number of whole units that could have been started and completed given the costs incurred. Compute separately for direct materials and conversion costs.

### PROCESS COSTING

**Equivalent Units of Production (EUP)**

**Weighted average:** Combines units and costs across *two periods* in computing EUP.

**Weighted average (WA) computations:**

$$\text{Equivalent units of production (EUP)} = \text{Equivalent units completed and transferred out} + \text{Equivalent units in ending work in process}$$

$$\text{Cost per EUP (WA)} = \frac{\text{Costs of beginning WIP} + \text{Costs added this period}}{\text{Equivalent units of production}}$$

**Production Cost Report (Weighted Average)**

| GenX—ROASTING DEPARTMENT<br>Production Cost Report (Weighted Average Method)<br>For Month Ended April 30 | | | | |
|---|---|---|---|---|
| **Units to account for:** | | **Units accounted for:** | | |
| Beginning work in process............. | 30,000 | Completed and transferred out....... | 100,000 | |
| Units started this period.............. | 90,000 | Ending work in process............. | 20,000 | |
| Total units to account for ............. | 120,000 | Total units accounted for............ | 120,000 | |

| **Equivalent Units of Production (EUP)** | | **Direct Materials** | | **Conversion** | |
|---|---|---|---|---|---|
| | **Units** | **Percent Complete** | **Equivalent Units of Production** | **Percent Complete** | **Equivalent Units of Production** |
| Completed and transferred out .. | 100,000 | 100% | 100,000 | 100% | 100,000 |
| Ending work in process ....... | 20,000 | 100% | 20,000 | 25% | 5,000 |
| | | | 120,000 EUP | | 105,000 EUP |

| **Cost per EUP** | | **Direct Materials** | | **Conversion** |
|---|---|---|---|---|
| Costs of beginning work in process ............... | | $ 81,000 | | $108,900 |
| Costs added this period ........................ | | 279,000 | | 376,200 |
| Total costs................................. | | $360,000 | | $485,100 |
| ÷ Equivalent units of production .................. | | 120,000 EUP | | 105,000 EUP |
| Cost per EUP............................... | | $3.00 per EUP | | $4.62 per EUP |

| **Cost assignment** | **EUP** | **Cost per EUP** | **Total Cost** | |
|---|---|---|---|---|
| **Completed and transferred out** | | | | |
| Direct materials ............ | 100,000 | $3.00 | $300,000 | |
| Conversion ................ | 100,000 | $4.62 | 462,000 | |
| | | | | $ 762,000 |
| **Ending work in process** | | | | |
| Direct materials ............ | 20,000 | $3.00 | $ 60,000 | |
| Conversion ................ | 5,000 | $4.62 | 23,100 | |
| | | | | 83,100 |
| **Total costs accounted for......** | | | | **$845,100** |

## ACCOUNTING FOR COSTS AND TRANSFERS

**Acquire raw materials:**

| Raw Materials Inventory......................... | 16,000 | |
|---|---|---|
| Accounts Payable............................. | | 16,000 |

**Record *direct* materials used:**

| Work in Process Inventory—Process 1 ............... | 279,000 | |
|---|---|---|
| Work in Process Inventory—Process 2 .............. | 102,000 | |
| Raw Materials Inventory ...................... | | 381,000 |

**Record *indirect* materials used:**

| Factory Overhead.............................. | 71,250 | |
|---|---|---|
| Raw Materials Inventory ...................... | | 71,250 |

**Record *direct* labor used:**

| Work in Process Inventory—Process 1 .............. | 171,000 | |
|---|---|---|
| Work in Process Inventory—Process 2 .............. | 183,160 | |
| Factory Wages Payable........................ | | 354,160 |

**Record *indirect* labor used:**

| Factory Overhead.............................. | 78,350 | |
|---|---|---|
| Factory Wages Payable ......................... | | 78,350 |

**Record *actual* other overhead costs such as insurance, rent, utilities, and depreciation on factory assets:**

| Factory Overhead.............................. | 275,392 | |
|---|---|---|
| Prepaid Insurance ......................... | | 11,930 |
| Utilities Payable............................ | | 7,945 |
| Cash ..................................... | | 34,867 |
| Accumulated Depreciation—Factory Equipment .... | | 220,650 |

***Apply* overhead using predetermined rate:**

| Work in Process Inventory—Process 1 .............. | 205,200 | |
|---|---|---|
| Work in Process Inventory—Process 2 .............. | 219,792 | |
| Factory Overhead ......................... | | 424,992 |

**Record transfer of costs to next department:**

| Work in Process Inventory—Process 2 .............. | 762,000 | |
|---|---|---|
| Work in Process Inventory—Process 1 ............ | | 762,000 |

**Record transfer of costs to finished goods (cost of goods manufactured):**

| Finished Goods Inventory ......................... | 1,262,940 | |
|---|---|---|
| Work in Process Inventory—Process 2............ | | 1,262,940 |

**Record sales:**

| Accounts Receivable ........................... | 1,915,800 | |
|---|---|---|
| Sales..................................... | | 1,915,800 |

**Record cost of goods sold:**

| Cost of Goods Sold............................. | 1,341,060 | |
|---|---|---|
| Finished Goods Inventory ...................... | | 1,341,060 |

## FIFO—APPENDIX

**FIFO:** Based on *current-period* production activity.
**FIFO computations:**

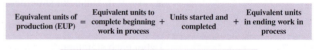

$$\text{Equivalent units of production (EUP)} = \text{Equivalent units to complete beginning work in process} + \text{Units started and completed} + \text{Equivalent units in ending work in process}$$

$$\text{Cost per EUP (FIFO)} = \frac{\text{Costs added this period}}{\text{Equivalent units of production}}$$

---

## Key Terms

Conversion cost (84)

Cost per equivalent unit (86)

Equivalent units of production (EUP) (84)

FIFO method (83)

Hybrid costing system (95)

Materials consumption report (94)

Operation costing system (95)

Process operations (81)

Production cost report (88)

Weighted average method (83)

Whole units (84)

Yield (96)

## Multiple Choice Quiz

1. Equivalent units of production are equal to
   a. Units that were completed this period from all effort being applied to them.
   b. The number of units introduced to the process this period.
   c. The number of finished units completed this period.
   d. The number of units that could have been started and completed given the cost incurred.
   e. The number of units in the process at period-end.

2. Recording the cost of raw materials purchased for use in a process costing system includes a
   a. Credit to Raw Materials Inventory.
   b. Debit to Work in Process Inventory.
   c. Debit to Factory Overhead.
   d. Credit to Factory Overhead.
   e. Debit to Raw Materials Inventory.

3. The Cutting department started the month with a beginning work in process inventory of $20,000. During the month, it was assigned the following costs: direct materials, $152,000; direct labor, $45,000; and overhead applied at the rate of 40% of direct labor cost. Inventory with a cost of

$218,000 was transferred to the next department. The ending balance of Work in Process Inventory—Cutting is
   a. $330,000.    c. $220,000.    e. $118,000.
   b. $17,000.     d. $112,000.

4. A process's beginning work in process inventory consists of 10,000 units that are 20% complete with respect to conversion costs. A total of 40,000 units are completed this period. There are 15,000 units in ending work in process, one-third complete for conversion. The equivalent units of production (EUP) with respect to conversion at period-end, assuming the weighted average method, are
   a. 45,000 EUP.    c. 5,000 EUP.    e. 43,000 EUP.
   b. 40,000 EUP.    d. 37,000 EUP.

5. Assume the same information as in question 4. Also assume that beginning work in process had $6,000 in conversion cost and that $84,000 in conversion is added during this period. What is the cost per EUP for conversion?
   a. $0.50 per EUP    c. $2.00 per EUP    e. $2.25 per EUP
   b. $1.87 per EUP    d. $2.10 per EUP

### ANSWERS TO MULTIPLE CHOICE QUIZ

1. d
2. e
3. b; $20,000 + $152,000 + $45,000 + $18,000 − $218,000 = $17,000

4. a; 40,000 + (15,000 × 1/3) = 45,000 EUP
5. c; ($6,000 + $84,000) ÷ 45,000 EUP = $2 per EUP

---

*Superscript letter A denotes assignments based on Appendix 3A.*

 *Select Quick Study and Exercise assignments feature Guided Example videos, called "Hints" in Connect. Hints use different numbers, and instructors can turn this feature on or off.*

---

**QUICK STUDY**

**QS 3-1**
Process vs. job order operations **C1**

For each of the following products and services, indicate whether it is more likely produced in a process operation or in a job order operation.

1. Tennis courts
2. Organic juice
3. Audit of financial statements
4. Luxury yachts
5. Ice cream
6. Tennis balls
7. House painting
8. Granola bars
9. Backpacks

---

**QS 3-2**
Process vs. job order costing

**C1**

Label each statement below as either true or false.

1. Cost per unit is computed by combining costs per unit across separate processes.
2. Service companies cannot use process costing.
3. Costs per job are computed in both job order and process costing systems.
4. Both job order and process operations combine materials, labor, and overhead in producing products.

---

**QS 3-3**
Process vs. job order operations

**C1**

For each of the following products and services, indicate whether it is more likely produced in a process operation or a job order operation.

1. Beach toys
2. Custom swimming pool
3. Smartphones
4. Wedding reception
5. Custom suits
6. Juice
7. Tattoos
8. Guitar picks
9. Solar panels

Prepare a physical unit flow reconciliation with the following information.

| Blending Process | Units of Product |
|---|---|
| Beginning work in process inventory . . . . . | 150,000 |
| Units started this period. . . . . . . . . . . . . . . | 310,000 |
| Units completed and transferred out . . . . . | 340,000 |
| Ending work in process inventory . . . . . . . . | 120,000 |

**QS 3-4**
**Weighted average:**
Physical unit flow
reconciliation
**P1**

A process manufacturer reports the following. Compute the total equivalent units of production for conversion. The company uses the weighted average method.

| | Units | Conversion Percent Complete |
|---|---|---|
| Beginning work in process inventory . . . . . | 150,000 | 80% |
| Units started this period. . . . . . . . . . . . . . . | 310,000 | |
| Units completed and transferred out . . . . . | 340,000 | |
| Ending work in process inventory . . . . . . . . | 120,000 | 25% |

**QS 3-5**
**Weighted average:**
Computing equivalent
units of production  **P1**

Refer to the information in QS 3-5. (*a*) Compute the number of units started and completed this period. (*b*) Compute the total equivalent units of production for conversion. The company uses the FIFO method.

**QS 3-6**[A]
**FIFO:** Computing
equivalent units  **C2**

A production department reports the following conversion costs. Equivalent units of production for conversion total 450,000 units this period. Calculate the cost per equivalent unit of production for conversion. The company uses the weighted average method.

| Costs of beginning work in process . . . . . | $200,000 |
|---|---|
| Costs added this period . . . . . . . . . . . . . . | 700,000 |

**QS 3-7**
**Weighted average:**
Cost per EUP  **P1**

An ice cream maker reports the following. Compute the total equivalent units of production for conversion. The company uses the weighted average method.

| | Units | Conversion Percent Complete |
|---|---|---|
| Beginning work in process inventory . . . . . | 320,000 | 25% |
| Units started this period. . . . . . . . . . . . . . . | 620,000 | |
| Units completed and transferred out . . . . . | 680,000 | |
| Ending work in process inventory . . . . . . . . | 260,000 | 60% |

**QS 3-8**
**Weighted average:**
Computing equivalent units
of production  **P1**

Refer to the information in QS 3-8. (*a*) Compute the number of units started and completed this period. (*b*) Compute the total equivalent units of production for conversion. The company uses the FIFO method.

**QS 3-9**[A]
**FIFO:** Computing
equivalent units  **C2**

**The following information applies to QS 3-10 through QS 3-17.**

Carlberg Company has two manufacturing departments, Assembly and Painting. The Assembly department started 10,000 units during November. The following production activity in both units and costs refers to the Assembly department's November activities.

**QS 3-10**
**Weighted average:**
Equivalent units of
production  **P1**

| Assembly Department | Units | Percent Complete for Direct Materials | Percent Complete for Conversion |
|---|---|---|---|
| Beginning work in process inventory . . | 2,000 | 60% | 40% |
| Units started this period . . . . . . . . . . . . | 10,000 | | |
| Units completed and transferred out . . | 9,000 | | |
| Ending work in process inventory . . . . . | 3,000 | 80% | 30% |

| Cost of beginning work in process | | |
|---|---|---|
| Direct materials. . . . . . . . . . . . | $ 996 | |
| Conversion . . . . . . . . . . . . . . . | 585 | $ 1,581 |
| Costs added this month | | |
| Direct materials . . . . . . . . . . . | 10,404 | |
| Conversion . . . . . . . . . . . . . . . | 12,285 | 22,689 |

[continued on next page]

[continued from previous page]

**Required**

Calculate the Assembly department's equivalent units of production for materials and for conversion for November. Use the weighted average method.

---

**QS 3-11**
**Weighted average:**
Cost per EUP   **P1**

Refer to the information in QS 3-10. Calculate the Assembly department's cost per equivalent unit of production for materials and for conversion for November. Use the weighted average method.

---

**QS 3-12**
**Weighted average:**
Assigning costs to output
**P1**

Refer to the information in QS 3-10. Assign costs to the Assembly department's output—specifically, the units transferred out to the Painting department and the units that remain in process in the Assembly department at month-end. Use the weighted average method.

---

**QS 3-13**
**Weighted average:** Entry
to transfer costs   **P4**

Refer to the information in QS 3-10. Prepare the November 30 journal entry to record the transfer of costs from the Assembly department to the Painting department. Use the weighted average method.

---

**QS 3-14ᴬ**
**FIFO:** Equivalent units
of production   **C2**

Refer to the information in QS 3-10. For the Assembly department: (*a*) Compute the number of units started and completed this period. (*b*) Compute the equivalent units of production for materials and for conversion for November. Use the FIFO method.

---

**QS 3-15ᴬ**
**FIFO:** Cost per EUP   **C2**

Refer to the information in QS 3-10. Calculate the Assembly department's cost per equivalent unit of production for materials and for conversion for November. Use the FIFO method.

---

**QS 3-16ᴬ**
**FIFO:** Assigning costs
to output   **C2**

Refer to the information in QS 3-10. Assign costs to the Assembly department's output—specifically, the units transferred out to the Painting department and the units that remain in work in process in the Assembly department at month-end. Use the FIFO method.

---

**QS 3-17ᴬ**
**FIFO:** Journal entry to
transfer costs   **P4**

Refer to the information in QS 3-10. Prepare the November 30 journal entry to record the transfer of costs from the Assembly department to the Painting department. Use the FIFO method.

---

**QS 3-18**
**Weighted average:**
Computing equivalent
units and cost per EUP
(direct materials)
**P1**

Zia Co. makes flowerpots from recycled plastic in two departments, Molding and Packaging. Zia uses the weighted average method, and units completed in the Molding department are transferred to the Packaging department. Production unit information for the Molding department follows.

| Molding—Direct Materials | Units | Percent Complete |
|---|---|---|
| Beginning work in process inventory . . . . | 2,000 | 70% |
| Units started this period. . . . . . . . . . . . . . | 18,000 | |
| Ending work in process inventory . . . . . . . | 3,000 | 80% |

Production cost information for the Molding department for the same period follows.

| | |
|---|---|
| Beginning work in process inventory (direct materials) . . . | $ 1,200 |
| Direct materials added this period . . . . . . . . . . . . . . . . . . | 27,900 |

Compute the Molding department's (*a*) units completed and transferred out, (*b*) equivalent units of production for direct materials, and (*c*) cost per equivalent unit of production for direct materials.

Refer to information in QS 3-18. Using the weighted average method, assign direct materials costs to the Molding department's output—specifically, the units transferred out to the Packaging department and the units that remain in work in process in the Molding department at month-end.

**QS 3-19**
**Weighted average:**
Assigning costs to output
**P1**

Azule Co. manufactures in two sequential processes, Cutting and Binding. The two processes report the information below for a recent month. Determine the ending balances in the Work in Process Inventory accounts for Cutting and for Binding. *Hint:* Set up T-accounts for Work in Process Inventory for both Cutting and for Binding.

**QS 3-20**
Transfer of costs; ending WIP balances **P4**

|  | Cutting | Binding |
|---|---|---|
| Beginning work in process inventory... | $ 3,445 | $ 6,426 |
| Costs added this period |  |  |
| Direct materials ................. | 8,240 | 6,356 |
| Conversion ..................... | 11,100 | 18,575 |

| | |
|---|---|
| Transferred from Cutting to Binding...... | $15,685 |
| Transferred from Binding to finished goods.. | 30,000 |

BOGO Inc. has two sequential processing departments, Roasting and Mixing. BOGO uses the FIFO method. Production unit information for the Roasting department follows.

**QS 3-21**[A]
**FIFO:** Computing equivalent units and cost per EUP
**C2**

| Roasting—Direct Materials | Units | Percent Complete |
|---|---|---|
| Beginning work in process inventory .... | 2,000 | 70% |
| Units started and completed ........... | 15,000 |  |
| Ending work in process inventory ....... | 3,000 | 80% |

Production cost information for the Roasting department for the same period follows.

| | |
|---|---|
| Beginning work in process inventory (direct materials) ... | $ 2,170 |
| Direct materials added this period ................... | 27,900 |

Compute the Roasting department's (a) equivalent units of production for direct materials and (b) cost per equivalent unit of production for direct materials.

Refer to the information in QS 3-21. Using the FIFO method, assign direct materials costs to the Roasting department's output—specifically, to the units completed and transferred out to the Mixing department *and* to the units that remain in work in process in the Roasting department at month-end.

**QS 3-22**[A]
**FIFO:** Assigning costs to output **C2**

Hotwax makes surfboard wax in two sequential processes. This period, Hotwax purchased $62,000 of raw materials on credit. Its Mixing department requisitioned $50,000 of direct materials for use in production. Prepare journal entries to record the (a) purchase of raw materials and (b) requisition of direct materials.

**QS 3-23**
Recording costs of materials **P3**

Prepare journal entries to record the following production activities for Hotwax.

**a.** Incurred $75,000 of direct labor in its Mixing department and $50,000 of direct labor in its Shaping department. *Hint:* Credit Factory Wages Payable.

**b.** Incurred indirect labor of $10,000. *Hint:* Credit Factory Wages Payable.

**QS 3-24**
Recording costs of labor
**P3**

Prepare journal entries to record the following production activities for Hotwax.

**a.** Requisitioned $9,000 of indirect materials for use in production of surfboard wax.

**b.** Incurred $156,000 in actual other overhead costs (paid in cash).

**c.** Applied overhead at the rate of 140% of direct labor costs. Direct labor costs were $75,000 in the Mixing department and $50,000 in the Shaping department.

**QS 3-25**
Recording costs of factory overhead
**P3**

**QS 3-26**
Recording transfer of costs
to finished goods   **P4**

Hotwax completed the production of goods costing $275,000 and transferred them to finished goods. Prepare the journal entry to record the transfer of units from the Shaping department to Finished Goods Inventory.

**QS 3-27**
Computing cost per unit
and gross profit   **P4**

Cool Scoops makes ice cream in two processes, Mixing and Packaging. During April, its first month of business, the packaging department transferred 50,000 units and $175,000 of production costs to finished goods. The company completed and sold 48,000 units at a price of $5 per unit in April.

**a.** What is the cost to produce one unit of ice cream during April?

**b.** What is the total gross profit on ice cream sales for April?

**QS 3-28**
Hybrid costing

**A1**

Trident Bikes uses a hybrid costing system and reports the following for its motorcycle assembly process.

| | Per Bike |
|---|---|
| Direct materials..................... | $12,000 |
| Conversion ........................ | 8,000 |
| Assembly process costs ............. | $20,000 |
| Customer choices—Option packages | |
| Mega; Ultra...................... | $4,000; $6,000 |

**a.** Compute the cost per unit for the Mega option.

**b.** If the company has a target markup of 20% above cost, compute the selling price per unit for the Mega option.

**QS 3-29**
Process yield

**A1**

For the current period, an ice cream producer added raw materials to production that should have produced 50,000 gallons of ice cream. Actual production was 47,000 gallons of (nondefective) ice cream. Compute the yield for this production process. Express the answer in percent.

## EXERCISES

**Exercise 3-1**
Process vs. job order
operations   **C1**

For each of the following products and services, indicate whether it is more likely produced in a process operation or in a job order operation.

**1.** Beach towels
**2.** Bolts and nuts
**3.** Lawn chairs

**4.** Headphones
**5.** Custom patio
**6.** Door hardware

**7.** Financial statement analysis
**8.** Paint cans
**9.** Custom home

**Exercise 3-2**
Process vs. job order
operations

**C1**

Identify each of the following production features as applying more to job order operations, to process operations, or to *both* job order and process operations.

**1.** Cost object is a process.
**2.** Measures unit costs at period-end.
**3.** Transfers costs between multiple Work in Process Inventory accounts.

**4.** Uses indirect costs.
**5.** Uses only one Work in Process Inventory account.
**6.** Uses materials, labor, and overhead costs.

**Exercise 3-3**
Terminology in process
costing

**C1**

Match each of the following items *A* through *G* with the best numbered description of its purpose.

**A.** Factory Overhead account
**B.** Production cost report
**C.** Equivalent units of production
**D.** Work in Process Inventory accounts

**E.** Raw Materials Inventory account
**F.** Materials requisition
**G.** Finished Goods Inventory account

**1.** Notifies the materials manager to send materials to a production department.
**2.** Holds indirect costs until assigned to production.
**3.** Holds production costs until products are transferred from production to finished goods (or another department).
**4.** Standardizes partially completed units into equivalent completed units.
**5.** Holds costs of finished products until sold to customers.
**6.** Describes the activity and output of a production department for a period.
**7.** Holds costs of materials until they are used in production or as factory overhead.

The first production department in a process manufacturing system reports the following unit data.

**Exercise 3-4**
**Weighted average:**
Computing equivalent units
**P1**

| | |
|---|---|
| Beginning work in process inventory . . . | 24,000 units |
| Units started and completed . . . . . . . . . . | 56,000 units |
| Units completed and transferred out . . . | 80,000 units |
| Ending work in process inventory . . . . . . | 16,000 units |

Compute this production department's equivalent units of production for direct materials under each of the following three separate assumptions using the weighted average method.

**a.** All direct materials are added to products when processing begins.

**b.** Beginning inventory is 40% complete as to direct materials costs. Ending inventory is 75% complete as to direct materials costs.

**c.** Beginning inventory is 60% complete as to direct materials costs. Ending inventory is 30% complete as to direct materials costs.

Refer to the information in Exercise 3-4 and compute the department's equivalent units of production for direct materials for each of the three separate assumptions *a, b,* and *c* using the FIFO method.

**Exercise 3-5**[A]
**FIFO:** Computing equivalent units   **C2**

Fields Company has two manufacturing departments, Forming and Painting. The company uses the weighted average method and it reports the following unit data for the Forming department. Units completed in the Forming department are transferred to the Painting department.

**Exercise 3-6**
**Weighted average:**
Cost per EUP and costs assigned to output
**P1**

| | | Direct Materials | Conversion |
|---|---|---|---|
| | Units | Percent Complete | Percent Complete |
| Beginning work in process inventory . . . | 25,000 | 60% | 40% |
| Units started this period . . . . . . . . . . . . . . | 300,000 | | |
| Completed and transferred out . . . . . . . . | 295,000 | | |
| Ending work in process inventory . . . . . . | 30,000 | 80% | 30% |

Production cost information for the Forming department follows.

| | | |
|---|---|---|
| Beginning work in process | | |
| Direct materials . . . . . . . . . . | $  44,800 | |
| Conversion . . . . . . . . . . . . . | 15,300 | $  60,100 |
| Costs added this period | | |
| Direct materials . . . . . . . . . . | 1,231,200 | |
| Conversion . . . . . . . . . . . . . | 896,700 | 2,127,900 |
| Total costs to account for . . . . . | | $2,188,000 |

**a.** Calculate the equivalent units of production for both direct materials and conversion for the Forming department.

**b.** Calculate the costs per equivalent unit of production for both direct materials and conversion for the Forming department.

**c.** Using the weighted average method, assign costs to the Forming department's output—specifically, its units transferred to Painting and its ending work in process inventory.

Refer to the information in Exercise 3-6. Assume that Fields uses the FIFO method of process costing.

**Exercise 3-7**[A]
**FIFO:** Cost per EUP
**C2**

**a.** Calculate the number of units started and completed this period for the Forming department.

**b.** Calculate the equivalent units of production for both direct materials and conversion for the Forming department.

**c.** Calculate the costs per equivalent unit of production for both direct materials and conversion for the Forming department.

**Exercise 3-8**
**Weighted average:**
Computing equivalent units of production
**P1**

The first production department of Stone Inc. reports the following for April. Compute the number of equivalent units of production for both direct materials and conversion for April using the weighted average method.

| | Units | Direct Materials Percent Complete | Conversion Percent Complete |
|---|---|---|---|
| Beginning work in process inventory . . . | 60,000 | 60% | 40% |
| Units started this period. . . . . . . . . . . . | 322,000 | | |
| Completed and transferred out . . . . . . . | 300,000 | | |
| Ending work in process inventory . . . . . . | 82,000 | 80% | 30% |

**Exercise 3-9**
**Weighted average:**
Cost per equivalent unit; costs assigned to output and inventory
**P1**

The production department described in Exercise 3-8 reports the cost information below.

| Beginning work in process inventory | | |
|---|---|---|
| Direct materials . . . . . . . . . . | $118,472 | |
| Conversion . . . . . . . . . . . . . | 48,594 | $ 167,066 |
| Costs added this period | | |
| Direct materials . . . . . . . . . . | 850,368 | |
| Conversion . . . . . . . . . . . . . | 649,296 | 1,499,664 |
| Total costs to account for. . . . . | | $1,666,730 |

a. Compute cost per equivalent unit for both direct materials and conversion.

b. Using the weighted average method, assign April's costs to the department's output—specifically, its units transferred to the next department *and* its ending work in process inventory.

**Exercise 3-10ᴬ**
**FIFO:** Computing equivalent units of production   **C2**

Refer to the information in Exercise 3-8. (*a*) Compute the number of units started and completed this period for the first production department. (*b*) Compute the number of equivalent units of production for both direct materials and conversion for the first production department for April using the FIFO method.

**Exercise 3-11ᴬ**
**FIFO:** Costs assigned to output   **C2**

Refer to the information in Exercise 3-9. (*a*) Calculate the costs per equivalent unit of production for both direct materials and conversion for the department. (*b*) Assign costs to the department's output—specifically, to the units transferred out and to the units that remain in work in process at period-end. Use the FIFO method.

**Exercise 3-12**
**Weighted average:** Cost per equivalent unit; costs assigned to products   **P1**

Hi-T Company uses the weighted average method of process costing. Information for the company's first production process follows. All direct materials are added at the beginning of this process, and conversion costs are added uniformly throughout the process.

| | Units | Direct Materials Percent Complete | Conversion Percent Complete |
|---|---|---|---|
| Beginning work in process inventory . . . | 2,000 | 100% | 80% |
| Completed and transferred out . . . . . . . | 23,000 | | |
| Ending work in process inventory . . . . . . | 7,000 | 100% | 40% |

| Beginning work in process | | |
|---|---|---|
| Direct materials . . . . . . . | $ 45,000 | |
| Conversion . . . . . . . . . . | 56,320 | $101,320 |
| Costs added this period | | |
| Direct materials . . . . . . . | 375,000 | |
| Conversion . . . . . . . . . . | 341,000 | 716,000 |
| Total costs to account for. . | | $817,320 |

a. Compute the equivalent units of production for both direct materials and conversion.

b. Compute the cost per equivalent unit for both direct materials and conversion.

c. Assign costs to the department's output—specifically, to the units transferred out *and* to the units in ending work in process inventory.

Midway Metal produces wire baskets in two departments, Bending and Painting. Information for the Bending department follows. The 2,000 units in beginning work in process inventory had direct materials costs of $2,400 and conversion costs of $1,600. The weighted-average method is used.

**Exercise 3-13**
**Weighted average:**
Costs assigned to
output   **P1**

| Bending Department | Units | Direct Materials Percent Complete | Conversion Percent Complete |
|---|---|---|---|
| Beginning work in process inventory ... | 2,000 | 100% | 20% |
| Units started this period.............. | 6,000 | | |
| Completed and transferred out ........ | 7,000 | | |
| Ending work in process inventory ...... | 1,000 | 100% | 60% |

| Work in Process Inventory—Bending ($) | | | |
|---|---|---|---|
| Beginning | 4,000 | ? | Transferred out |
| Direct materials | 7,200 | | |
| Conversion | 17,400 | | |
| Ending | ? | | |

a. Compute equivalent units of production for both direct materials and conversion.
b. Compute cost per equivalent unit of production for both direct materials and conversion.
c. Assign costs to the department's output—specifically, to the units transferred out *and* to the units in ending work in process inventory.

The following data reports on the July production activities of the Molding department at Ash Company. Prepare the Molding department's production cost report using the weighted average method.

**Exercise 3-14**
**Weighted average:**
Production cost report   **P2**

| Beginning work in process | | |
|---|---|---|
| Direct materials. ....... | $ 18,550 | |
| Conversion ........... | 2,280 | $ 20,830 |
| Costs added this period | | |
| Direct materials ....... | 357,500 | |
| Conversion ........... | 188,670 | 546,170 |
| Total costs to account for .. | | $567,000 |

| | Units | Direct Materials Percent Complete | Conversion Percent Complete |
|---|---|---|---|
| Beginning work in process inventory ... | 2,000 | 100% | 20% |
| Units started this period.............. | 32,500 | | |
| Completed and transferred out ........ | 32,000 | | |
| Ending work in process inventory ...... | 2,500 | 100% | 60% |

Refer to the information in Exercise 3-14. Prepare a production cost report using the FIFO method.

**Exercise 3-15ᴬ**
**FIFO:** Production cost
report   **C2**

Elliott Company produces large quantities of a standardized product. The following information is available for its first production department for March. Prepare a production cost report for this department using the weighted average method.

**Exercise 3-16**
**Weighted average:**
Production cost report   **P2**

| | Units | Direct Materials Percent Complete | Conversion Percent Complete |
|---|---|---|---|
| Beginning work in process inventory . | 2,000 | | |
| Units started this period............ | 20,000 | | |
| Completed and transferred out ...... | 17,000 | | |
| Ending work in process inventory .... | 5,000 | 100% | 35% |

| Beginning work in process inventory | | |
|---|---|---|
| Direct materials ............. | $ 2,500 | |
| Conversion ................. | 6,360 | $ 8,860 |
| Costs added this period | | |
| Direct materials ............. | 168,000 | |
| Conversion ................. | 479,640 | 647,640 |
| Total costs to account for ........ | | $656,500 |

**Check**   Cost per equivalent
unit: conversion, $25.92

**Exercise 3-17**
**Weighted average:**
Production cost report **P2**

Oslo Company produces large quantities of a standardized product. The following information is available for the first production department for May. Prepare a production cost report for this process using the weighted average method.

| | Units | Direct Materials<br>Percent Complete | Conversion<br>Percent Complete |
|---|---|---|---|
| Beginning work in process inventory . . . | 4,000 | | |
| Units started this period. . . . . . . . . . . . . . | 12,000 | | |
| Completed and transferred out . . . . . . . . | 13,000 | | |
| Ending work in process inventory . . . . . . | 3,000 | 100% | 25% |

| | | |
|---|---|---|
| Beginning work in process inventory | | |
|    Direct materials . . . . . . . . . . . . | $ 2,880 | |
|    Conversion . . . . . . . . . . . . . . . . | 5,358 | $ 8,238 |
| Costs added this period | | |
|    Direct materials . . . . . . . . . . . . | 197,120 | |
|    Conversion . . . . . . . . . . . . . . . . | 234,992 | 432,112 |
| Total costs to account for . . . . . . . | | $440,350 |

**Check**   Cost per equivalent
unit: materials, $12.50

---

**Exercise 3-18**
Recording costs
of materials

**P3**

Prepare journal entries to record the following production activities.

**1.** Purchased $80,000 of raw materials on credit.
**2.** Used $42,000 of direct materials in the Roasting department.
**3.** Used $22,500 of indirect materials in production.

---

**Exercise 3-19**
Recording costs of labor

**P3**

Prepare journal entries to record the following production activities.

**1.** Incurred $42,000 of direct labor in the Roasting department and $33,000 of direct labor in the Blending department. Credit Factory Wages Payable.
**2.** Incurred $20,000 of indirect labor in production. Credit Factory Wages Payable.

---

**Exercise 3-20**
Recording overhead costs

**P3**

Prepare journal entries to record the following production activities.

**1.** Paid other actual overhead costs of $40,000 in cash.
**2.** Applied overhead at 110% of direct labor costs. Direct labor costs were $42,000 in the Roasting department and $33,000 in the Blending department.

---

**Exercise 3-21**
Computing and applying
predetermined overhead
rate   **P3**

Blue Sky Soda estimates total factory overhead costs of $4,200,000 and total direct labor costs of $2,800,000 for its first year of operations. During January, the company used $80,000 of direct labor cost in its Blending department and $60,000 of direct labor cost in its Bottling department.

**1.** Compute the predetermined overhead rate as a percentage of direct labor cost.
**2.** Prepare the journal entry to apply factory overhead to the Blending and Bottling departments.

---

**Exercise 3-22**
Recording production costs

**P3**   **P4**

Sharpe Co. makes organic salsa in two production departments, Cooking and Bottling. Direct materials costs are added at the beginning of each process, and conversion costs are added evenly throughout each process. The company reports the following for a recent month.

| | Cooking | Bottling |
|---|---|---|
| Beginning work in process inventory . . | $ 0 | $5,500 |
| Activity during the month | | |
|    Direct materials . . . . . . . . . . . . . . . . | $18,000 | $8,200 |
|    Direct labor. . . . . . . . . . . . . . . . . . . . | 12,000 | 6,800 |
|    Overhead applied . . . . . . . . . . . . . . | 15,000 | 8,500 |

| | |
|---|---|
| Costs transferred from Cooking to Bottling . . . . . . . . | $42,000 |
| Costs transferred from Bottling to finished goods . . . | 67,000 |

1. Prepare journal entries to record (*a*) direct materials used, (*b*) direct labor, and (*c*) overhead applied.
2. Prepare journal entries to record the costs transferred from (*a*) Cooking to Bottling and (*b*) Bottling to Finished Goods.
3. Use T-accounts to compute (*a*) the ending balance of Work in Process Inventory—Cooking and (*b*) the ending balance of Work in Process Inventory—Bottling.

---

Re-Tire produces bagged mulch from recycled tires. Production involves shredding tires and packaging the pieces in the Bagging department. All direct materials enter in the Shredding process. A predetermined overhead rate of 175% of direct labor costs is used in both departments. The following describes production operations for October.

**Exercise 3-23**
Recording production costs
**P3   P4**

| | |
|---|---|
| Direct materials used (Shredding) | $ 522,000 |
| Direct labor used (Shredding) | 26,000 |
| Direct labor used (Bagging) | 104,000 |
| Costs transferred from Shredding to Bagging | 595,000 |
| Costs transferred from Bagging to Finished Goods | 580,000 |

Sales (on credit) for the month total $950,000 and cost of goods sold for the month is $540,000. Prepare journal entries dated October 31 to record October production activities for (1) direct materials usage, (2) direct labor usage, (3) overhead applied, (4) costs transfer from Shredding to Bagging, (5) costs transfer from Bagging to finished goods, (6) credit sales, and (7) cost of goods sold.

**Check** (3) Cr. Factory Overhead, $227,500

---

Pro-Weave manufactures stadium blankets by passing the products through a Weaving department and then a Sewing department. The following information is available regarding its June inventories.

**Exercise 3-24**
Entries for transfer of goods across departments

**P4**

| | Beginning Inventory | Ending Inventory |
|---|---|---|
| Raw materials inventory............ | $ 120,000 | $ 185,000 |
| Work in process inventory—Weaving .. | 300,000 | 330,000 |
| Work in process inventory—Sewing ... | 570,000 | 700,000 |
| Finished goods inventory........... | 1,266,000 | 1,206,000 |

The following additional information describes the company's manufacturing activities for June.

| | | | |
|---|---|---|---|
| Raw materials purchases (on credit)....... | $500,000 | Labor used | |
| Other actual overhead cost (paid in cash)... | 156,000 | Direct—Weaving.................... | $1,200,000 |
| Materials used | | Direct—Sewing.................... | 360,000 |
| Direct—Weaving..................... | $240,000 | Indirect .......................... | 1,224,000 |
| Direct—Sewing..................... | 75,000 | Overhead rates as a percent of direct labor | |
| Indirect ........................... | 120,000 | Weaving .......................... | 80% |
| | | Sewing ........................... | 150% |
| | | Sales (on credit) ..................... | $4,000,000 |

**Required**

1. Compute the (*a*) cost of products transferred from Weaving to Sewing, (*b*) cost of products transferred from Sewing to finished goods, and (*c*) cost of goods sold. *Hint:* Compute the total production costs in each department and then subtract the ending inventory to get the amount transferred out of each department.
2. Prepare journal entries dated June 30 to record (*a*) goods transferred from Weaving to Sewing, (*b*) goods transferred from Sewing to finished goods, (*c*) sale of finished goods, and (*d*) cost of goods sold.

**Check** (1c) Cost of goods sold, $3,275,000

---

Refer to the information in Exercise 3-24. Prepare journal entries dated June 30 to record (*a*) raw materials purchases, (*b*) direct materials used, (*c*) indirect materials used, (*d*) direct labor used, (*e*) indirect labor used, (*f*) other actual overhead costs, and (*g*) overhead applied.

**Exercise 3-25**
Recording product costs
**P3**

**Exercise 3-26**
Production cost flows
**P3    P4**

The flowchart below shows the August production activity of the Punching and Bending departments of Wire Box Company. Use the amounts shown on the flowchart to compute the missing numbers identified by question marks.

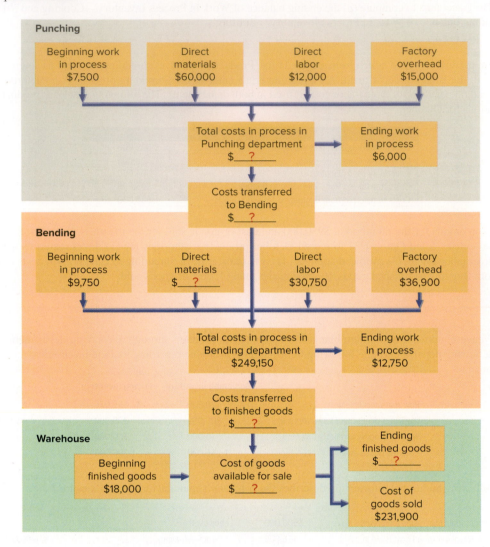

---

**Exercise 3-27**
Recording cost of
completed goods
**P4**

Prepare journal entries to record the following production activities.

**1.** Transferred completed goods from the Assembly department to finished goods inventory. The goods cost $135,600.

**2.** Sold $315,000 of goods on credit. Their cost is $175,000.

---

**Exercise 3-28**
Computing and analyzing
cost per unit
**P4**

Pro Power makes a protein powder in several processes. Packaging, the last department in the company's production process, reports the following.

|                                         | Current month | Prior month |
|-----------------------------------------|---------------|-------------|
| Costs transferred to finished goods ....... | $168,000      | $165,750    |
| Units transferred to finished goods........  | 21,000        | 19,500      |
| Units sold ..........................        | 20,000        | 19,200      |

**1.** Compute the cost per completed unit for both the current month and the prior month.

**2.** Does the change in the cost per completed unit indicate better or worse control of costs in the current month?

RSTN Co. produces its product in two sequential processing departments. During October, the first process finished and transferred 150,000 units of its product to the second process. Of these units, 30,000 were in process at the beginning of the month and 120,000 were started and completed during the month. At month-end, 20,000 units were in process.

Compute the number of equivalent units of production for direct materials for the first process for October under each of the following three separate assumptions using the FIFO method.

**1.** All direct materials are added to products when processing begins.

**2.** Beginning work in process inventory is 30% complete for direct materials cost. Ending inventory is 80% complete for direct materials cost.

**3.** Beginning work in process inventory is 60% complete for direct materials cost. Ending inventory is 20% complete for direct materials cost.

**Exercise 3-29**[A]
**FIFO:** Computing equivalent units
**C2**

College Life produces sweatshirts for college organizations and uses hybrid costing. It reports the following for its fabrication process. Customers choose screen-printed or embroidered logos.

**Exercise 3-30**
Hybrid costing and yield
**A1**

|  | Per Unit |
| --- | --- |
| Direct materials.................. | $12 |
| Conversion ..................... | 6 |
| Fabrication process costs.......... | $18 |
| Customer choices—Logo types |  |
| Screen-printed; Embroidered .... | $2; $10 |

**a.** Compute the cost per unit for both the screen-printed and embroidered sweatshirts.

**b.** If the company has a target markup of 30% above cost, compute the selling price for each type of sweatshirt.

**c.** For the current period, the company added direct materials into production that should have produced 5,000 sweatshirts. Actual production was 4,900 (nondefective) sweatshirts. Compute the yield for this period. Express the answer in percent.

**connect**

Victory Company uses weighted average process costing. The company has two production processes. Conversion cost is added evenly throughout each process. Direct materials are added at the beginning of the first process. Additional information for the first process follows.

**PROBLEM SET A**

**Problem 3-1A**
**Weighted average:** Cost per equivalent unit; costs assigned to products **P1**

|  | Units | Direct Materials Percent Complete | Conversion Percent Complete |
| --- | --- | --- | --- |
| Beginning work in process inventory... | 60,000 | 100% | 80% |
| Units started this period............ | 820,000 |  |  |
| Units completed and transferred out... | 700,000 |  |  |
| Ending work in process inventory .... | 180,000 | 100% | 30% |

| Beginning work in process inventory |  |  |
| --- | --- | --- |
| Direct materials .......... | $ 420,000 |  |
| Conversion ............. | 139,000 | $ 559,000 |
| Costs added this period |  |  |
| Direct materials .......... | 2,220,000 |  |
| Conversion ............. | 3,254,000 | 5,474,000 |
| Total costs to account for..... |  | $6,033,000 |

**Required**

**1.** Compute equivalent units of production for both direct materials and conversion.

**2.** Compute cost per equivalent unit of production for both direct materials and conversion.

**3.** Assign costs to the department's output—specifically, to the units transferred out and to the units in ending work in process inventory.

**Check** (2) Conversion cost per equivalent unit, $4.50

## Problem 3-2A
**Weighted average:**
Production cost report

**P2   P4**

Fast Co. produces its product through two processing departments: Cutting and Assembly. Information for the Cutting department follows.

| | Units | Direct Materials Percent Complete | Conversion Percent Complete |
|---|---|---|---|
| Beginning work in process inventory... | 30,000 | | |
| Units started this period............ | 140,000 | | |
| Units completed and transferred out... | 150,000 | | |
| Ending work in process inventory .... | 20,000 | 100% | 80% |

| Beginning work in process inventory | | |
|---|---|---|
| Direct materials ........... | $ 17,100 | |
| Conversion ............... | 67,200 | $ 84,300 |
| Costs added this period | | |
| Direct materials ........... | 144,400 | |
| Conversion ............... | 862,400 | 1,006,800 |
| Total costs to account for...... | | $1,091,100 |

**Required**

**Check** (1) Costs transferred out, $982,500

**1.** Prepare the Cutting department's production cost report for October using the weighted average method.

**2.** Prepare the October 31 journal entry to transfer the cost of completed units from Cutting to Assembly.

## Problem 3-3A
**Weighted average:**
Production cost report

**P2   P4**

Tamar Co. manufactures a single product in two departments: Forming and Assembly. Information for the Forming process for May follows.

| | Units | Direct Materials Percent Complete | Conversion Percent Complete |
|---|---|---|---|
| Beginning work in process inventory... | 3,000 | 100% | 40% |
| Units started this period............ | 21,600 | | |
| Units completed and transferred out... | 22,200 | | |
| Ending work in process inventory .... | 2,400 | 100% | 80% |

| Beginning work in process inventory | | |
|---|---|---|
| Direct materials ......... | $ 19,800 | |
| Conversion ............. | 221,940 | $ 241,740 |
| Costs added this period | | |
| Direct materials ......... | 496,800 | |
| Conversion ............. | 2,165,940 | 2,662,740 |
| Total costs to account for.... | | $2,904,480 |

**Required**

**1.** Prepare the Forming department's production cost report for May using the weighted average method.

**2.** Prepare the May 31 journal entry to transfer the cost of units from Forming to Assembly.

## Problem 3-4A[A]
**FIFO:** Production cost report

**C2   P4**

Refer to the data in Problem 3-3A. Assume that Tamar uses the FIFO method of process costing. The units started and completed for May total 19,200.

**Required**

**1.** Prepare the Forming department's production cost report for May using FIFO.

**2.** Prepare the May 31 journal entry to transfer the cost of units from Forming to Assembly.

## Problem 3-5A
Production cost flow and measurement; journal entries

**P3   P4**

Sierra Company manufactures soccer balls in two sequential processes: Cutting and Stitching. All direct materials enter production at the beginning of the cutting process. The following information is available regarding its May inventories.

| | Beginning Inventory | Ending Inventory |
|---|---|---|
| Raw materials inventory............ | $ 6,000 | $ 3,250 |
| Work in process inventory—Cutting ... | 43,500 | 51,500 |
| Work in process inventory—Stitching .. | 63,300 | 60,500 |
| Finished goods inventory........... | 20,100 | 8,250 |

The following additional information describes the company's production activities for May.

| Direct Materials | | Factory Overhead (actual costs) | |
|---|---|---|---|
| Raw materials purchased on credit..... | $25,000 | Indirect materials used ........ | $ 6,000 |
| Direct materials used—Cutting ........ | 21,750 | Indirect labor used............ | 55,000 |
| Direct materials used—Stitching ....... | 0 | Other overhead costs ......... | 46,505 |
| **Direct Labor** | | **Factory Overhead Rates** | |
| Direct labor—Cutting ................ | $15,600 | Cutting .................... | 150% of direct materials used |
| Direct labor—Stitching .............. | 62,400 | Stitching .................. | 120% of direct labor used |
| | | Sales........................ | $256,000 |

**Required**

1. Compute the amount of (*a*) production costs transferred from Cutting to Stitching, (*b*) production costs transferred from Stitching to finished goods, and (*c*) cost of goods sold. *Hint:* Compute the total production costs in each department and then subtract the ending inventory to get the amount transferred out of each department.

2. Prepare May 31 journal entries to record the following May activities.

   a. Raw materials purchases
   b. Direct materials used
   c. Indirect materials used
   d. Direct labor used
   e. Indirect labor used

   f. Other overhead costs (paid in cash)
   g. Overhead applied
   h. Goods transferred from Cutting to Stitching

   i. Goods transferred from Stitching to finished goods
   j. Sales
   k. Cost of goods sold

**Check** (1c) Cost of goods sold, $213,905

---

QualCo manufactures a single product in two departments: Cutting and Assembly. Information for the Cutting department for May follows.

**Problem 3-6A**[A]
**FIFO:** Cost per equivalent unit; costs assigned to products **C2**

| | | Direct Materials | Conversion |
|---|---|---|---|
| | **Units** | **Percent Complete** | **Percent Complete** |
| Beginning work in process inventory .. | 37,500 | 60% | 40% |
| Units started and completed ........ | 150,000 | | |
| Units completed and transferred out... | 187,500 | | |
| Ending work in process inventory .... | 51,250 | 60% | 20% |

| Beginning work in process | | |
|---|---|---|
| Direct materials ....... | $ 74,250 | |
| Conversion ........... | 28,500 | $ 102,750 |
| Costs added this period | | |
| Direct materials ....... | 505,035 | |
| Conversion ........... | 398,395 | 903,430 |
| Total costs to account for ... | | $1,006,180 |

1. Compute equivalent units of production for both direct materials and conversion.
2. Compute cost per equivalent unit of production for both direct materials and conversion.
3. Assign costs to the department's output—specifically, to the units transferred out and to the units that remain in work in process at period-end.

**Check** (1) EUP for materials, 195,750

---

Dengo Co. makes a trail mix in two departments: Roasting and Blending. Direct materials are added at the beginning of each process, and conversion costs are added evenly throughout each process. The company uses the FIFO method of process costing. October data for the Roasting department follow.

**Problem 3-7A**[A]
**FIFO:** Cost per equivalent unit; costs assigned to products **C2**

| | | Direct Materials | Conversion |
|---|---|---|---|
| | **Units** | **Percent Complete** | **Percent Complete** |
| Beginning work in process inventory .. | 3,000 | 100% | 40% |
| Units started and completed ........ | 19,200 | | |
| Units completed and transferred out... | 22,200 | | |
| Ending work in process inventory .... | 2,400 | 100% | 80% |

| Beginning work in process .. | | $ 120,870 |
|---|---|---|
| Costs added this period | | |
| Direct materials ........ | $ 248,400 | |
| Conversion ........... | 1,082,970 | 1,331,370 |
| Total costs to account for ... | | $1,452,240 |

[continued on next page]

[continued from previous page]

**Required**

1. Compute equivalent units of production for both direct materials and conversion.
2. Compute cost per equivalent unit of production for both direct materials and conversion.
3. Assign costs to the department's output—specifically, to the units transferred out and to the units that remain in work in process at period-end.

## PROBLEM SET B

**Problem 3-1B**

**Weighted average:** Cost per equivalent unit; costs assigned to products **P1**

Abraham Company uses weighted average process costing to account for its production costs. The company has two production processes. Conversion is added evenly throughout each process. Direct materials are added at the beginning of the first process. Additional information for the first process follows.

| | Units | Direct Materials Percent Complete | Conversion Percent Complete |
|---|---|---|---|
| Beginning work in process inventory... | 2,000 | 100% | 85% |
| Units started this period............ | 86,000 | | |
| Units completed and transferred out... | 80,000 | | |
| Ending work in process inventory .... | 8,000 | 100% | 25% |

| | | | |
|---|---|---|---|
| Beginning work in process inventory | | | |
| Direct materials .......... | $ | 58,000 | |
| Conversion ............. | | 86,400 | $ 144,400 |
| Costs added this period | | | |
| Direct materials .......... | | 712,000 | |
| Conversion ............. | | 1,980,000 | 2,692,000 |
| Total costs to account for..... | | | $2,836,400 |

**Required**

1. Compute the equivalent units of production for both direct materials and conversion.
2. Compute cost per equivalent unit of production for both direct materials and conversion.
3. Assign costs to the department's output—specifically, to the units transferred out and to the units in ending work in process inventory.

**Check** (2) Conversion cost per equivalent unit, $25.20

*Analysis Component*

4. Assume that an error is made in determining the percent complete for units in ending inventory in the first process. Instead of being 25% complete for conversion, they are actually 75% complete. Write a one-half-page memo to the plant manager describing how this error affects this period's financial statements.

**Problem 3-2B**

**Weighted average:** Production cost report

**P2　P4**

Brun Company produces its product through two processing departments: Mixing and Baking. Information for the Mixing department follows.

| | Units | Direct Materials Percent Complete | Conversion Percent Complete |
|---|---|---|---|
| Beginning work in process inventory... | 7,500 | | |
| Units started this period............ | 104,500 | | |
| Units completed and transferred out... | 100,000 | | |
| Ending work in process inventory .... | 12,000 | 100% | 25% |

| | | | |
|---|---|---|---|
| Beginning work in process inventory | | | |
| Direct materials .......... | $ | 6,800 | |
| Conversion ............. | | 14,500 | $ 21,300 |
| Costs added this period | | | |
| Direct materials .......... | | 116,400 | |
| Conversion ............. | | 1,067,000 | 1,183,400 |
| Total costs to account for..... | | | $1,204,700 |

**Required**

1. Prepare the Mixing department's production cost report for November using the weighted average method.
2. Prepare the November 30 journal entry to transfer the cost of completed units from Mixing to Baking.

**Check** (1) Cost transferred out, $1,160,000

Switch Co. manufactures a single product in two departments: Cutting and Assembly. Information for the Cutting process for January follows.

**Problem 3-3B**
**Weighted average:**
Production cost report
**P2   P4**

| | Units | Direct Materials Percent Complete | Conversion Percent Complete |
|---|---|---|---|
| Beginning work in process inventory .. | 10,000 | 75% | 60% |
| Units started this period............ | 250,000 | | |
| Units completed and transferred out... | 220,000 | | |
| Ending work in process inventory.... | 40,000 | 50% | 30% |

| Beginning work in process inventory | | |
|---|---|---|
| Direct materials ............ | $ 7,500 | |
| Conversion ................ | 49,840 | $ 57,340 |
| Costs added this period | | |
| Direct materials ............ | 112,500 | |
| Conversion ................ | 616,000 | 728,500 |
| Total costs to account for....... | | $785,840 |

**Required**

**1.** Prepare the Cutting department's production cost report for January using the weighted average method.
**2.** Prepare the January 31 journal entry to transfer the cost of units from Cutting to Assembly.

**Check**   (2) Cost transferred out, $741,400

Refer to the information in Problem 3-3B. Assume that Switch uses the FIFO method of process costing. The units started and completed for January total 210,000.

**Problem 3-4B**[A]
**FIFO:** Production cost report
**C2   P4**

**Required**

**1.** Prepare the Cutting department's production cost report for January using FIFO. Round cost per EUP to three decimals.
**2.** Prepare the January 31 journal entry to transfer the cost of units from Cutting to Assembly.

**Check**   (2) Cost transferred out, $743,554

Ho Chee makes ice cream in two sequential processes: Mixing and Blending. Direct materials enter production at the beginning of each process. The following information is available regarding its March inventories.

**Problem 3-5B**
Production cost flow and measurement; journal entries
**P3   P4**

| | Beginning Inventory | Ending Inventory |
|---|---|---|
| Raw materials inventory............. | $ 72,000 | $ 24,800 |
| Work in process inventory—Mixing.... | 156,000 | 250,000 |
| Work in process inventory—Blending .. | 160,000 | 198,000 |
| Finished goods inventory............ | 80,200 | 60,250 |

The following additional information describes the company's production activities for March.

| Direct Materials | | Factory Overhead (actual costs) | |
|---|---|---|---|
| Raw materials purchased on credit...... | $212,000 | Indirect materials used......... | $41,200 |
| Direct materials used—Mixing.......... | 174,000 | Indirect labor used ........... | 69,500 |
| Direct materials used—Blending........ | 44,000 | Other overhead costs.......... | 64,608 |
| **Direct Labor** | | **Factory Overhead Rates** | |
| Direct labor—Mixing.................. | $ 52,500 | Mixing .................... | 75% of direct materials used |
| Direct labor—Blending................ | 74,680 | Blending .................. | 60% of direct labor used |
| | | Sales...................... | $490,000 |

**Required**

**1.** Compute the amount of (a) production costs transferred from Mixing to Blending, (b) production costs transferred from Blending to finished goods, and (c) cost of goods sold. *Hint:* Compute the total production costs in each department and then subtract the ending inventory to get the amount transferred out of each department.

**Check**   (1c) Cost of goods sold, $408,438

**2.** Prepare March 31 journal entries to record the following March activities.

  **a.** Raw materials purchases
  **b.** Direct materials used
  **c.** Indirect materials used
  **d.** Direct labor used
  **e.** Indirect labor used

  **f.** Other overhead costs (paid in cash)
  **g.** Overhead applied
  **h.** Goods transferred from Mixing to Blending

  **i.** Goods transferred from Blending to finished goods
  **j.** Sales
  **k.** Cost of goods sold

**Problem 3-6B**[A]

**FIFO:** Cost per equivalent unit; costs assigned to products **C2**

Harson Co. manufactures a single product in two departments: Forming and Assembly. Information for the Forming department for May follows.

| | Units | Direct Materials Percent Complete | Conversion Percent Complete |
|---|---|---|---|
| Beginning work in process inventory... | 62,500 | 40% | 80% |
| Units started and completed........ | 175,000 | | |
| Units completed and transferred out... | 237,500 | | |
| Ending work in process inventory.... | 76,250 | 80% | 20% |

| Beginning work in process | | |
|---|---|---|
| Direct materials ........ | $ 60,000 | |
| Conversion ............ | 112,500 | $ 172,500 |
| Costs added this period | | |
| Direct materials ........ | 683,750 | |
| Conversion ............ | 446,050 | 1,129,800 |
| Total costs to account for... | | $1,302,300 |

**Check**   (1) EUP for materials, 273,500

1. Compute equivalent units of production for both direct materials and conversion.
2. Compute cost per equivalent unit of production for both direct materials and conversion.
3. Assign costs to the department's output—specifically, to the units transferred out and to the units that remain in work in process at period-end.

**Problem 3-7B**[A]

**FIFO:** Cost per equivalent unit; costs assigned to products **C2**

Belda Co. makes organic juice in two departments: Cutting and Blending. Direct materials are added at the beginning of each process, and conversion costs are added evenly throughout each process. The company uses the FIFO method of process costing. Data for March for the Cutting department follows.

| | Units | Direct Materials Percent Complete | Conversion Percent Complete |
|---|---|---|---|
| Beginning work in process inventory... | 10,000 | 75% | 60% |
| Units started and completed........ | 210,000 | | |
| Units completed and transferred out... | 220,000 | | |
| Ending work in process inventory.... | 40,000 | 50% | 30% |

| Beginning work in process.. | | $ 114,520 |
|---|---|---|
| Costs added this period | | |
| Direct materials ........ | $ 223,200 | |
| Conversion ............ | 1,233,960 | 1,457,160 |
| Total costs to account for... | | $1,571,680 |

**Required**

1. Compute equivalent units of production for both direct materials and conversion.
2. Compute cost per equivalent unit of production for both direct materials and conversion.
3. Assign costs to the department's output—specifically, to the units transferred out and to the units that remain in work in process at period-end.

**SERIAL PROBLEM**
Business Solutions **P1**

Alexander Image/Shutterstock

*This serial problem began in Chapter 1 and continues through most of the book. If previous chapter segments were not completed, the serial problem can begin at this point.*

**SP 3**   Based on customer interest in February, Santana expands her computer workstation furniture business to include mass production of standardized desks and chairs. She uses the weighted average method of process costing for these products. Desks are made in three processes: Cutting, Finishing, and Packaging. Information below is for the Cutting process for desks for February.

| Cutting process—Desks | Units |
|---|---|
| Beginning work in process inventory ....................... | 0 |
| Units started this period................................. | 60 |
| Units completed and transferred to Finishing................ | 40 |
| Ending work in process inventory (100% complete for direct materials, 80% complete for conversion).................. | 20 |
| **Costs added this month** | **Cost** |
| Direct materials ..................................... | $24,000 |
| Conversion ......................................... | 4,200 |

**Required**

1. Compute equivalent units of production for both direct materials and conversion for February.
2. Compute cost per equivalent unit for both direct materials and conversion for February.
3. Assign costs to units transferred out to Finishing and to units in ending work in process inventory.

**CP 3**  **Major League Bat Company** manufactures baseball bats. In addition to its work in process inventories, the company maintains inventories of raw materials and finished goods. It uses raw materials as direct materials in production and as indirect materials. Its factory payroll costs include direct labor for production and indirect labor. All materials are added at the beginning of the process, and conversion costs are applied uniformly throughout the production process.

**COMPREHENSIVE PROBLEM**

**Major League Bat Company**
Weighted average:
Review of Chapters 1 and 3

**Required**

You are to maintain records and produce measures of inventories to reflect the July events of this company. Set up the following general ledger accounts and enter the June 30 balances: Raw Materials Inventory, $25,000; Work in Process Inventory, $8,135 ($2,660 of direct materials and $5,475 of conversion); Finished Goods Inventory, $110,000; Sales, $0; Cost of Goods Sold, $0; Factory Wages Payable, $0; and Factory Overhead, $0.

1. Prepare journal entries to record the following July transactions and events.
   a. Purchased raw materials for $125,000 cash.
   b. Used raw materials as follows: direct materials, $52,440, and indirect materials, $10,000.
   c. Recorded factory wages payable costs as follows: direct labor, $202,250, and indirect labor, $25,000.
   d. Incurred other actual factory overhead costs of $66,125 paid in cash.
   e. Applied factory overhead to production at 50% of direct labor costs.
2. Information about the July work in process (WIP) inventory follows. Use this information with that from part 1 to prepare a production cost report, assuming the weighted average method is used.

**Check** (1e) Cr. Factory Overhead, $101,125
(2) EUP for conversion, 14,200

| Units | | Beginning WIP inventory | | Ending WIP inventory | |
|---|---|---|---|---|---|
| Beginning WIP inventory .. | 5,000 units | Direct materials—Percent complete .. | 100% | Direct materials—Percent complete .. | 100% |
| Started ............... | 14,000 units | Conversion—Percent complete..... | 75% | Conversion—Percent complete..... | 40% |
| Units transferred out ..... | 11,000 units | | | | |
| Ending WIP inventory..... | 8,000 units | | | | |

3. Using the results from part 2 and the available information, make computations and prepare journal entries to record the following:
   f. Total costs transferred to finished goods for July.
   g. Sale of finished goods costing $265,700 for $625,000 in cash.
4. Post entries from parts 1 and 3 to the ledger accounts set up at the beginning of the problem.
5. Compute the amount of gross profit from the sales in July.

(3f) $271,150

**Tableau Dashboard Activities** expose students to accounting analytics using visual displays. These assignments run in **Connect**. All are auto-gradable.

**TABLEAU DASHBOARD ACTIVITIES**

**Tableau DA 3-1 Quick Study**, Computing equivalent units, **P1**—similar to QS 3-5 & QS 3-8.
**Tableau DA 3-2 Exercise**, Computing cost per equivalent unit and assigning costs to output, **P1**—similar to Exercise 3-6.
**Tableau DA 3-3 Mini-case**, Preparing and using a production cost report, **P2**—similar to Exercise 3-16 & Exercise 3-17.

**General Ledger (GL) Assignments** expose students to general ledger software similar to that in practice. **GL** is part of **Connect**, and **GL** assignments are auto-gradable and have algorithmic options. For the following **GL** assignment, prepare summary journal entries to record transactions. Compute cost of goods sold and gross profit.

**GENERAL LEDGER**

**GL 3-1**  Based on Problem 3-5A

## Accounting Analysis

**COMPANY ANALYSIS**

A1

**APPLE**

**AA 3-1   Apple** allows customers to select different cases for the watches it produces and sells. Assume the following data for the newest Apple Watch.

| | Cost per Watch |
|---|---|
| **Assembly process costs** | |
| Direct materials, excluding case . . . . . . . | $ 85 |
| Conversion . . . . . . . . . . . . . . . . . . . . . . . | 165 |

| | Cost per Watch |
|---|---|
| **Custom choices** | |
| Aluminum case . . . . . . . | $ 50 |
| Titanium case . . . . . . . . | 200 |

1. Compute cost per unit for an Apple watch with either an (*a*) aluminum case or (*b*) titanium case.
2. In setting price, assume Apple marks up total cost per unit by 30%. Compute the selling price per unit for an Apple watch with either an (*a*) aluminum case or (*b*) titanium case.

---

**COMPARATIVE ANALYSIS**

A1

**GOOGLE**

**AA 3-2   Google**'s Fitbit division makes fitness trackers. Assume the following data from Google.

| | Cost per Tracker |
|---|---|
| **Assembly process costs** | |
| Direct materials . . . . . . . . . . . . . . . . . . . | $80 |
| Conversion . . . . . . . . . . . . . . . . . . . . . . . | 60 |

| | Cost per Tracker |
|---|---|
| **Custom option** | |
| Company logo . . . . . . . | $30 |

1. Compute cost per unit for (*a*) a noncustom (standard) fitness tracker and (*b*) a custom tracker with a company logo.
2. Assume Google marks up its fitness trackers by 40%. Compute the selling price per unit for each type of fitness tracker.
3. Assume Google wants its standard fitness tracker to compete with the entry level **Apple** Watch. Assume the entry level Apple Watch sells for $200 per unit. Is Google's selling price for its noncustom (standard) fitness tracker lower than $200 per unit for the Apple Watch?

---

**EXTENDED ANALYSIS**

A1

**Samsung**

**APPLE**

**AA 3-3   Apple** and **Samsung** make smartwatches. Assume the following data for each company for a recent week.

| | Apple Current week | Samsung Current week | Samsung Prior week |
|---|---|---|---|
| Number of nondefective watches actually made . . . | 396,000 | 29,400 | 27,160 |
| Number of watches that could have been made from direct materials put into production . . . . . . . . | 400,000 | 30,000 | 28,000 |

1. Compute yield for the current week for both Apple and Samsung. Which company's process manufacturing system is more efficient?
2. Compute yield for the prior week for Samsung. Did Samsung's process manufacturing system become more efficient or less efficient for the current week?

## Discussion Questions

1. What is the main factor for a company in choosing between job order costing and process costing systems? For each type of costing system, list two types of companies that would likely use that system.
2. The focus in a job order costing system is the job or batch. Identify the main focus in process costing.
3. Can services be provided through process operations? Support your answer with an example.
4. Which costing system, job order or process, typically uses more Work in Process Inventory accounts?
5. Identify the control document for materials flow when a materials requisition slip is not used.
6. Define equivalent units of production (EUP). Why is it necessary to use EUP in process costing?
7. What are the two main inventory methods used in computing equivalent units of production? Which method combines production activity across two periods in computing equivalent units? Which is generally considered more precise?
8. List four ways managers can use process cost information.

9. Explain how labor costs flow through a company's process cost system.

10. Do process costing systems use multiple Factory Overhead accounts?

11. Is it possible to have under- or overapplied overhead costs in a process costing system? Explain.

12. Explain why equivalent units of production for conversion can be the same as, and why they can be different from, equivalent units for direct materials.

13. List the four steps in accounting for production activity in a reporting period (for process operations).

14. How does a process manufacturer compute the cost of a completed unit?

15. Are there situations where **Google** can use process costing? Identify at least one and explain it.

16. **Samsung** produces digital televisions with a multiple-process production line. Identify and list some of its likely production processing steps and departments.

17. **General Mills** needs a steady supply of ingredients for processing. What are some risks the company faces regarding its ingredients?

18. How could a production cost report be used to determine if a program to reduce water usage is successful?

19. Explain a hybrid costing system. Identify a product or service operation that might be suited to a hybrid costing system.

## Beyond the Numbers

**BTN 3-1**   Many accounting professionals are skilled in financial analysis, but less are skilled in manufacturing. This is especially true for process manufacturing environments. To provide professional accounting and financial services, one must understand the industry, product, and processes. We have an ethical responsibility to develop this understanding before offering services to clients in these areas.

**ETHICS CHALLENGE**

C1

**Required**

Write a one-half-page action plan, in memorandum format, discussing how we would obtain an understanding of key business processes of a company that hires us to provide financial services. The memorandum should specify an industry, a product, and one selected process and should draw on at least one reference, such as a professional journal or industry magazine.

**BTN 3-2**   Many companies use technology to help them improve processes. One example of such a tool is robotic process automation. Access https://www2.deloitte.com/us/en/pages/operations/articles/a-guide-to-robotic-process-automation-and-intelligent-automation.html and read the information displayed.

**COMMUNICATING IN PRACTICE**

C1

**Required**

What processes are robotic process automation (RPA) tools most useful for? Explain how RPA tools work and list their proposed benefits.

**BTN 3-3**   The purpose of this team activity is to ensure that each team member understands process operations and the related accounting entries. Find the activities and flows identified in Exhibit 3.12 with numbers ① through ⑩. Pick a member of the team to start by describing activity number ① in this exhibit, then verbalizing the related journal entry, and describing how the amounts in the entry are computed. The other members of the team are to agree or disagree; discussion is to continue until all members express understanding. Rotate to the next numbered activity and next team member until all activities and entries have been discussed. If at any point a team member is uncertain about an answer, the team member may pass and get back in the rotation when he or she can contribute to the team's discussion.

**TEAMWORK IN ACTION**

C1   P3   P4

**BTN 3-4**   This chapter's opener featured Suzy Batlle and her company **Azucar Ice Cream Company**.

**ENTREPRENEURIAL DECISION**

A1

**Required**

1. Suzy tries to buy raw materials just-in-time for their use in production. How does holding raw materials inventories increase costs? If the items are not used in production, how can they impact profits? Explain.

2. How can companies like Suzy's use *yield* to improve their production processes?

3. Suppose Azucar Ice Cream decides to allow customers to make their own unique ice cream flavors. Why might the company then use a hybrid costing system?

# 4 Activity-Based Costing and Analysis

## Chapter Preview

| PLANTWIDE RATE METHOD | DEPARTMENTAL RATE METHOD | ACTIVITY-BASED COSTING (ABC) | ABC FOR SERVICES AND CUSTOMER ANALYSIS |
|---|---|---|---|
| **P1** Applying plantwide method | **P2** Applying departmental method | **P3** Applying activity-based costing | **P4** Activities for service providers |
| Overhead allocated | Overhead allocated | **C1** Types of activities | Applying ABC to services |
| | | | **A1** Customer profitability |
| **NTK 4-1** | **NTK 4-2** | **NTK 4-3** | **NTK 4-4** |

## Learning Objectives

### CONCEPTUAL

**C1** Describe the four types of activities that cause overhead costs.

### ANALYTICAL

**A1** Allocate selling, general and administrative expenses to products and assess profitability.

### PROCEDURAL

**P1** Allocate overhead costs using the plantwide overhead rate method.

**P2** Allocate overhead costs using the departmental overhead rate method.

**P3** Allocate overhead costs using activity-based costing.

**P4** Allocate overhead costs to service companies using activity-based costing.

# Brewing Profits

*"Follow your interests"*—**JOE GRIMM**

BROOKLYN, NY—Captivated by a college class on fermentation, Joe and Lauren Grimm began making beer in their basement. "Initially, it was just an outlet for our creativity," recalls Lauren. Soon however, the duo immersed themselves in learning about different beers and launched their company, **Grimm Artisanal Ales (GrimmAles.com)**.

Joe and Lauren began as *contract brewers,* renting production equipment from existing breweries. Soon they bought their own production facility. With it came increased overhead costs for things like brewery maintenance, supervision, and cleanup.

"It's pretty crazy," explains Joe, "suddenly there is a lot more to handle. We now have employees and infrastructure." Joe and Lauren know that how they control and allocate overhead costs are crucial for product pricing and product mix decisions.

When they first began and had few product lines, a *single plantwide rate* was sufficient. Unlike many brewers who focus on a flagship beer, Joe and Lauren prefer to experiment with many different varieties. As their business grew to offer more diverse product lines, more detailed overhead costing techniques were required.

*Activity-based costing* can be useful when different product lines use different amounts of the activities that drive overhead costs. "We constantly refine and improve our processes," admits Lauren. Their focus on improving activities leads to a focus on activity-based costing to control costs.

BRIAN HARKIN/The New York Times/Redux Pictures

Having already produced over 80 different beers, the Grimms keep experimenting. Satisfied customers and a *Young Entrepreneurs of the Year* award from the U.S. Small Business Administration are witness to their success. "Believe!" insists Lauren. "When we started, only Joe and I believed."

Sources: *Grimm Artisanal Ales website,* January 2021; *Brooklyn Paper,* May 2018; *BKBeerReview.com blog,* August 2018; *GrubStreet.com,* June 2018

## Overhead Cost Allocation Methods

Manager decisions involving product pricing, product mix, and cost control depend on accurate product cost information. Because direct materials and direct labor can often be reliably traced to units of output, allocating these costs to products is clear. Overhead costs, however, cannot be traced to units of product. Overhead costs are allocated to products using one of three methods: (1) the plantwide overhead rate method, (2) the departmental overhead rate method, or (3) the activity-based costing method.

Exhibit 4.1 summarizes key features of the three overhead allocation methods.

- *Plantwide overhead rate method* and *Departmental overhead rate method* use volume-based measures like direct labor hours or machine hours to allocate overhead costs. The plantwide method uses a single rate for allocating overhead costs, and the departmental rate method uses at least two rates.

- *Activity-based costing* focuses on activities and their costs. Activity-based costing typically uses more overhead allocation rates than the plantwide and departmental methods.

| Allocation Method | Number of Overhead Rates | Overhead Allocation Rates Based on |
|---|---|---|
| Plantwide rate.......... | One rate | Volume-based measures like direct labor hours or machine hours |
| Departmental rate ...... | Two or more rates | Volume-based measures like direct labor hours or machine hours |
| Activity-based costing ... | Many rates | Activities that drive costs, like number of batches of product produced |

**EXHIBIT 4.1**

Overhead Cost Allocation Methods

# PLANTWIDE OVERHEAD RATE METHOD

**P1**

Allocate overhead costs using the plantwide overhead rate method.

The *plantwide overhead rate method* uses one overhead rate to allocate overhead costs. The target of the cost assignment, or **cost object,** is the unit of product—see Exhibit 4.2. The rate is determined using a volume-related measure such as direct labor hours or machine hours.

**EXHIBIT 4.2**

Plantwide Overhead Rate Method

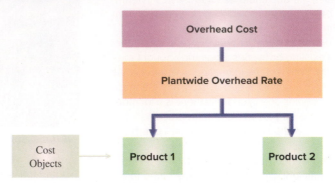

## Applying Plantwide Overhead Rate Method

Sergey Ryzhov/123RF

Under the plantwide overhead rate method, total budgeted overhead costs are divided by the allocation base, such as total budgeted direct labor hours, to get the plantwide overhead rate. This rate is used to allocate overhead costs to *products* based on the actual amount of allocation base used.

To illustrate, consider data from KartCo, a go-kart manufacturer that produces both standard and custom go-karts for amusement parks. The standard go-kart is a basic model sold primarily to amusement parks that service county and state fairs. Custom go-karts are produced for theme parks that need unique go-karts to fit their themes. KartCo allocates overhead using direct labor hours and reports the following **budgeted** overhead cost and direct labor hours for this year.

| | |
|---|---|
| Budgeted overhead cost . . . . . . . . . . . . . . . . . | $4,800,000 |
| Budgeted direct labor hours . . . . . . . . . . . . . . | 100,000 hours |

**Actual Usage**    The actual direct labor hours used for the two go-kart models are in Exhibit 4.3.

**EXHIBIT 4.3**

Actual Direct Labor Hours

| Model | Number of Units | Direct Labor Hours per Unit | Direct Labor Hours |
|---|---|---|---|
| Standard go-kart. . . . . | 5,000 | 15 | 75,000 |
| Custom go-kart. . . . . . | 1,000 | 25 | 25,000 |
| Total. . . . . . . . . . . . . | | | 100,000 |

**Plantwide Overhead Rate**    The single plantwide overhead rate is computed as follows.

$$\frac{\text{Plant wide}}{\text{overhead rate}} = \frac{\text{Budgeted overhead cost}}{\text{Budgeted allocation base}} = \frac{\$4,800,000}{100,000 \text{ DLH}} = \$48 \text{ per DLH}$$

**Overhead Allocated**    This plantwide rate is then used to allocate overhead cost based on the actual direct labor hours used to produce each unit as follows.

$$\text{Overhead allocated} = \text{Plantwide overhead rate} \times \text{DLH used}$$

For KartCo, overhead cost is allocated to its two models as follows (on a per unit basis).

| Model | Plantwide Overhead Rate | Direct Labor Hours per Unit | Overhead Allocated |
|---|---|---|---|
| Standard go-kart . . . . . . . . . . | $48 per DLH | × 15 DLH per unit = | **$720 per unit** |
| Custom go-kart . . . . . . . . . . . | $48 per DLH | × 25 DLH per unit = | **$1,200 per unit** |

Exhibit 4.4 summarizes overhead allocation for KartCo using the plantwide method.

**Overhead Cost $4,800,000**

**Plantwide Overhead Rate**
$4,800,000/100,000 DLH = **$48 per DLH**

**Standard Go-Karts Overhead Allocated**
$48 per DLH × 15 DLH = **$720 per unit**

**Custom Go-Karts Overhead Allocated**
$48 per DLH × 25 DLH = **$1,200 per unit**

**EXHIBIT 4.4**

Plantwide Method—KartCo

**Product Cost**  We use the per unit overhead cost to compute the product cost per unit as follows. Direct materials and direct labor costs per unit are taken from cost records.

| Product Cost per Unit using the Plantwide Rate Method | | | | | | | | |
|---|---|---|---|---|---|---|---|---|
| Model | Direct Materials | + | Direct Labor | + | Overhead | = | Product Cost per Unit |
| Standard go-kart..... | $400 | + | $350 | + | $ 720 | = | $1,470 |
| Custom go-kart...... | 600 | + | 500 | + | 1,200 | = | 2,300 |

A manufacturer budgets $900,000 of overhead cost and 25,000 direct labor hours.

**1.** What is the plantwide overhead rate based on direct labor hours?

**2.** Using the plantwide overhead rate, how much overhead is allocated to a job that uses 10 direct labor hours?

*Solution*

**1.** Plantwide overhead rate $= \dfrac{\$900,000}{25,000 \text{ DLH}} = \$36$ per direct labor hour

**2.** Overhead allocated to job $= 10 \text{ DLH} \times \$36$ per DLH $= \$360$

**NEED-TO-KNOW** **4-1**

Plantwide Rate Method

**P1**

Do More: QS 4-1, QS 4-2, QS 4-3, QS 4-4, E 4-1, E 4-2, E 4-3

# DEPARTMENTAL OVERHEAD RATE METHOD

Many companies have several departments that use different amounts of overhead. Multiple overhead rates can result in better overhead cost allocations and improve management decisions.

The *departmental overhead rate method* uses a different overhead rate for each department. We use a three-step process (see Exhibit 4.5 showing two departments and two products).

**①** Assign budgeted overhead cost to department *cost pools*.

**②** Select an allocation base and compute an overhead allocation rate for each department.

**③** Allocate overhead costs to cost objects.

**P2**

Allocate overhead costs using the departmental overhead rate method.

**EXHIBIT 4.5**

Departmental Overhead Rate Method

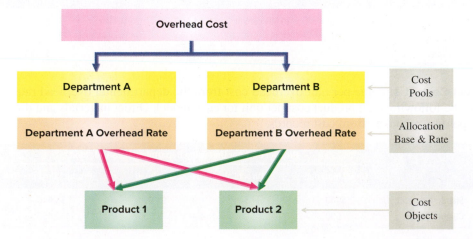

**Overhead Cost**

**Department A**          **Department B**          Cost Pools

**Department A Overhead Rate**    **Department B Overhead Rate**    Allocation Base & Rate

**Product 1**          **Product 2**          Cost Objects

**Point:** A cost pool is a grouping of costs, usually grouped by department or activity.

Overhead Cost $4,800,000

Machining $4,200,000　　Assembly $600,000

Each department has its own overhead rate and its own allocation base. An Assembly department might use direct labor hours to allocate its overhead cost, and a Machining department might use machine hours.

## Applying Departmental Overhead Rate Method　KartCo has two production departments: Machining and Assembly.

**1** KartCo assigns its $4,800,000 budgeted overhead cost to its two production departments: $4,200,000 of overhead is traceable to Machining and $600,000 is traceable to Assembly.

**2** Each department determines an allocation base. Machining uses machine hours (MH) and Assembly uses direct labor hours (DLH). Machining budgets 70,000 MH and Assembly budgets 100,000 DLH. Actual production information for Machining and Assembly follows.

| | Number of Units | Machining Department | | Assembly Department | |
|---|---|---|---|---|---|
| | | Hours per Unit | Total Hours | Hours per Unit | Total Hours |
| Standard go-kart . . . | 5,000 | 10 MH per unit | 50,000 MH | 15 DLH per unit | 75,000 DLH |
| Custom go-kart . . . . | 1,000 | 20 MH per unit | 20,000 MH | 25 DLH per unit | 25,000 DLH |
| Totals . . . . . . . . . . . . | | | 70,000 MH | | 100,000 DLH |

**Departmental Overhead Rate**　Each department computes an overhead rate as follows.

$$\text{Departmental overhead rate} = \frac{\text{Budgeted departmental overhead cost}}{\text{Budgeted departmental allocation base}}$$

KartCo's departmental overhead rates are computed as follows.

$$\text{Machining department overhead rate} = \frac{\$4,200,000}{70,000 \text{ MH}} = \$60 \text{ per MH}$$

$$\text{Assembly department overhead rate} = \frac{\$600,000}{100,000 \text{ DLH}} = \$6 \text{ per DLH}$$

**3 Overhead Allocated**　Step three allocates overhead cost to each product using departmental overhead rates along with the actual allocation bases used. Because each standard go-kart uses 10 MH from the Machining department and 15 DLH from the Assembly department, the overhead cost allocated to each standard go-kart is $600 from the Machining department (10 MH × $60 per MH) and $90 from the Assembly department (15 DLH × $6 per DLH). The same procedure is applied for its custom go-kart. Exhibit 4.6 summarizes KartCo's overhead allocation per go-kart using the departmental method.

**EXHIBIT 4.6**

Overhead Allocation Using Departmental Overhead Rates

| Department | Departmental Overhead Rate | Standard Go-Kart | | Custom Go-Kart | |
|---|---|---|---|---|---|
| | | Hours per Unit | Overhead Allocated | Hours per Unit | Overhead Allocated |
| Machining . . . | $60 per MH | 10 MH per unit | $ 600 | 20 MH per unit | $ 1,200 |
| Assembly . . . . | $6 per DLH | 15 DLH per unit | 90 | 25 DLH per unit | 150 |
| Totals . . . . . . . | | | $690 | | $1,350 |

**Product Cost**　Using the per unit overhead cost from the departmental overhead rate method yields the following total product cost per unit for each model. Direct materials and direct labor costs per unit are taken from cost records.

| | Product Cost per Unit using Departmental Rate Method | | | | | | |
|---|---|---|---|---|---|---|---|
| | Direct Materials | + | Direct Labor | + | Overhead | = | Product Cost per Unit |
| Standard go-kart . . . | $400 | + | $350 | + | $ 690 | = | $1,440 |
| Custom go-kart . . . | 600 | + | 500 | + | 1,350 | = | 2,450 |

**Plantwide versus Departmental Overhead Rate Methods**    Exhibit 4.7 compares the allocated overhead costs per unit for standard and custom go-karts under the plantwide overhead rate and the departmental overhead rate methods.

The overhead cost allocated to each standard go-kart *decreased* from $720 under the plantwide overhead rate method to $690 under the departmental overhead rate method, whereas overhead cost allocated to each custom go-kart *increased* from $1,200 to $1,350. These differences occur because the custom go-kart requires more hours in the Machining department (20 MH) than the standard go-kart requires (10 MH). Compared to the plantwide overhead rate method, the departmental overhead rate method arguably results in more accurate overhead allocations.

| | Overhead Cost per Unit | |
|---|---|---|
| Overhead Allocation Method | Standard Go-Kart | Custom Go-Kart |
| Plantwide rate method......... | $720 | $1,200 |
| Departmental rate method...... | 690 | 1,350 |

**EXHIBIT 4.7**

Overhead Cost per Unit for Plantwide vs Departmental Rates

**Assessing Plantwide and Departmental Overhead Rate Methods**    Both the plantwide and departmental overhead rate methods have three strengths: (1) They use readily available information like direct labor hours or machine hours. (2) They are easy to implement. (3) They comply with GAAP and can be used for external reporting. Both have a weakness: Overhead cost is often too complex to be explained by factors like direct labor hours or machine hours.

**Plantwide Overhead Rate Method**    The usefulness of the single plantwide overhead rate depends on two assumptions: (1) overhead costs change with the allocation base and (2) all products use overhead cost in the same proportions. For companies with many different products or those with products that use overhead cost in different ways, the assumptions of the single plantwide rate are not reasonable. When overhead cost bears little relation to the allocation base, allocating overhead cost using a single plantwide overhead rate can distort product cost and lead to poor managerial decisions.

Carl Lyttle/The Image Bank/ Getty Images

**Departmental Overhead Rate Method**    The departmental overhead rate method assumes that (1) different products are similar in volume, complexity, and batch size, and (2) departmental overhead costs are proportional to the department allocation base. When products differ in batch size and complexity, they usually consume different amounts of overhead cost. This can distort product costs. Because the departmental overhead rate method allocates overhead cost based on measures closely related to production volume, it fails to accurately assign many overhead costs, like warehouse depreciation or factory insurance, that are not driven by production volume.

■ **Decision Ethics** ━━━━━━━━━━━━━━━━━━

**Department Manager**    Three department managers hire a consulting firm for advice on increasing departmental performance. The consulting firm spends 50% of its efforts on department A and 25% on each of the other two departments. The manager for department A suggests that the three departments equally share the consulting fee. As a manager of one of the other two departments, do you believe equal sharing is fair? ■    *Answer:* If one department consumes more services than another, we attempt to share the bill in proportion to consumption. Equally dividing the bill among the number of departments is fair if each consumed equal services. This same notion applies in allocating costs to products and services.

---

A manufacturer reports the following budgeted data for its two production departments.

Departmental Rate Method

P2

| Budgeted Data | Machining | Assembly |
|---|---|---|
| Overhead costs......... | $600,000 | $300,000 |
| Machine hours (MH)...... | 20,000 | 0 |
| Direct labor hours (DLH)... | 10,000 | 5,000 |

**1.** What are the departmental overhead rates if the Machining department allocates overhead based on machine hours and the Assembly department allocates overhead based on direct labor hours?

**2.** Using the departmental overhead rates, how much overhead should be allocated to a job that uses 16 machine hours in the Machining department and 5 direct labor hours in the Assembly department?

**Solution**

1. Machining department rate $= \dfrac{\$600,000}{20,000 \text{ MH}} = \$30$ per machine hour

   Assembly department rate $= \dfrac{\$300,000}{5,000 \text{ DLH}} = \$60$ per direct labor hour

2. Overhead allocated to job

| Department | Departmental Overhead Rate | Hours Used | Overhead Allocated |
|---|---|---|---|
| Machining . . . . . | $30 per machine hour | 16 MH | $480 |
| Assembly . . . . . . | $60 per direct labor hour | 5 DLH | $300 |
| Total . . . . . . . . . | | | $780 |

> Do More: QS 4-7, QS 4-8, E 4-6, E 4-7

# ACTIVITY-BASED COSTING

**P3**

Allocate overhead costs using activity-based costing.

**Activity-based costing (ABC)** assigns overhead cost by focusing on *activities*. Unlike the plant-wide rate method, ABC uses more than a single rate, and unlike the departmental rate method, ABC focuses on activities rather than departments.

The basic principle underlying activity-based costing is that an **activity,** which is a task, operation, or procedure, is what causes overhead cost to be incurred. Examples of activities are production setups, machine usage, fabrication, design, assembly, and inspections. Instead of allocating overhead to departments, ABC allocates overhead to activities.

Activity-based costing follows three steps—see Exhibit 4.8.

1. Identify activities and assign budgeted costs to activity cost pools.
2. Compute an overhead activity rate for each activity cost pool.
3. Allocate overhead costs to cost objects (products).

**EXHIBIT 4.8**

Activity-Based Costing

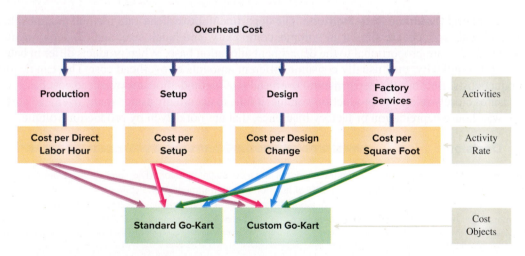

## Applying Activity-Based Costing

### Step 1: Identify Activities and Their Budgeted Overhead Cost
Step 1 identifies individual activities, which are grouped into *cost pools*. An **activity cost pool** is a group of costs that are related to the same activity. An **activity cost driver,** or *cost driver,* is a factor that causes the cost of an activity to go up or down. For example, factory maintenance, cleaning, and utilities can be grouped into a "factory services" activity cost pool because they are related to square feet of space.

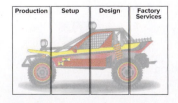

KartCo budgets total overhead cost of $4,800,000. Management assigns its overhead cost to four activity cost pools: production, setup, design, and factory services. To assign costs to activity cost pools, management looks for costs that are caused by similar activities.

The table below shows that $600,000 of overhead cost is assigned to the production cost pool; $2,000,000 to the setup cost pool; $1,200,000 to the design cost pool; and $1,000,000 to the factory services cost pool.

| Activity | Budgeted Cost | Activity Cost Driver | Budgeted Activity Usage |
|---|---|---|---|
| Production.......... | $ 600,000 | Direct labor hours | 100,000 direct labor hours |
| Setup.............. | 2,000,000 | Setups | 200 setups |
| Design............. | 1,200,000 | Design changes | 10 changes |
| Factory services ..... | 1,000,000 | Square feet | 20,000 square feet |
| Total.............. | $4,800,000 | | |

**Step 2: Compute Overhead Activity Rate for Each Activity**  Step 2 computes an **activity rate** for each cost pool.

**Overhead Activity Rate**  Each activity rate is computed as follows.

$$\text{Activity rate} = \frac{\text{Budgeted activity cost}}{\text{Budgeted activity usage}}$$

Activity rates for KartCo are computed and shown in Exhibit 4.9.

| Activity | Budgeted Cost | ÷ Budgeted Activity Usage | = Activity Rate |
|---|---|---|---|
| Production.............. | $ 600,000 | ÷ 100,000 direct labor hours | = $6 per direct labor hour |
| Setup.................. | 2,000,000 | ÷ 200 setups | = $10,000 per setup |
| Design................. | 1,200,000 | ÷ 10 design changes | = $120,000 per change |
| Factory services.......... | 1,000,000 | ÷ 20,000 square feet | = $50 per square foot |

**EXHIBIT 4.9**

Computing Activity Rates

**Step 3: Allocate Overhead Cost to Cost Objects**  Step 3 allocates overhead cost to products. KartCo collects the following information for this purpose.

| Activity Cost Driver | Actual Activity Usage Standard Model | Custom Model | Total |
|---|---|---|---|
| Direct labor hours...... | 75,000 | 25,000 | 100,000 |
| Setups.............. | 40 | 160 | 200 |
| Design changes ....... | 0 | 10 | 10 |
| Square feet........... | 12,000 | 8,000 | 20,000 |

We multiply a product's actual activity usage by the activity rate as follows to get the overhead cost allocated to each activity.

$$\text{Allocated cost} = \text{Actual activity usage} \times \text{Activity rate}$$

**Overhead Allocated**  For each product, the allocated costs are added together and divided by the number of units to compute the overhead cost per unit as shown in Exhibit 4.10. The company produced 5,000 standard go-karts and 1,000 custom go-karts.

Standard go-karts used 75,000 direct labor hours, so we allocate $450,000 (75,000 × $6 per DLH) of production costs to that product. Custom go-karts used 25,000 direct labor hours, so we allocate $150,000 (25,000 DLH × $6 per DLH) of production costs to that product.

We similarly allocate setup, design, and factory services costs to each model of go-kart. KartCo assigned no design costs to standard go-karts because standard go-karts are sold with no design changes.

The result is $1,450,000 of overhead cost allocated to standard go-karts and $3,350,000 allocated to custom go-karts. While the total cost allocated of $4,800,000 is the same as under the other methods, the amounts allocated to the two product lines differ.

**EXHIBIT 4.10**

Overhead Cost Allocation Using Activity-Based Costing

| Activity | Standard Go-Kart | | | Custom Go-Kart | | |
|---|---|---|---|---|---|---|
| | Activity Usage × | Activity Rate | = Allocated Cost | Activity Usage × | Activity Rate | = Allocated Cost |
| Production............. | 75,000 DLH | × $6 per DLH | = $ 450,000 | 25,000 DLH | × $6 per DLH | = $ 150,000 |
| Setup................. | 40 setups | × $10,000 per setup | = 400,000 | 160 setups | × $10,000 per setup | = 1,600,000 |
| Design................ | 0 changes | × $120,000 per change | = 0 | 10 changes | × $120,000 per change | = 1,200,000 |
| Factory services......... | 12,000 sq. ft. | × $50 per square foot | = 600,000 | 8,000 sq. ft. | × $50 per square foot | = 400,000 |
| Total allocated cost....... | | | $1,450,000 | | | $3,350,000 |
| Units produced.......... | | | ÷ 5,000 | | | ÷ 1,000 |
| Overhead cost per unit.... | | | = $290 | | | = $3,350 |

Overhead cost per unit is computed by dividing total overhead cost allocated to each product by the number of units produced. KartCo's overhead cost per unit is $290 for its standard go-kart and $3,350 for its custom go-kart.

**Product Cost**   The total product cost per unit for KartCo follows. Direct materials and direct labor cost per unit are taken from its cost records.

| | Product Cost per Unit using Activity-Based Costing | | | | |
|---|---|---|---|---|---|
| | Direct Materials + | Direct Labor + | Overhead = | Product Cost per Unit |
| Standard go-kart..... | $400 | + $350 | + $ 290 = | $1,040 |
| Custom go-kart...... | 600 | + 500 | + 3,350 = | 4,450 |

Exhibit 4.11 summarizes overhead cost allocations using activity-based costing.

**EXHIBIT 4.11**

Overhead Allocated to Go-Karts Summary

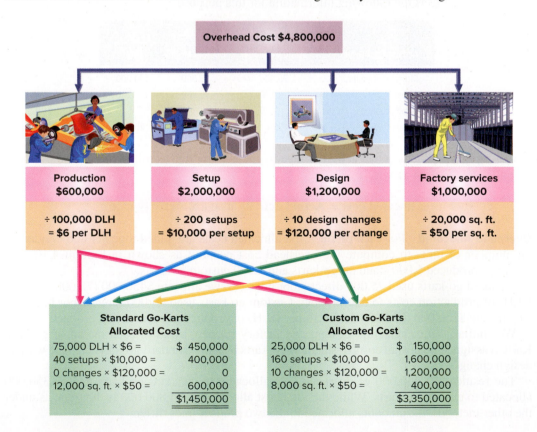

**Comparing Overhead Cost Allocation Methods**   Exhibit 4.12 summarizes KartCo's overhead allocation per go-kart under the three different methods. Overhead cost allocated to custom go-karts is much higher under ABC than under the other methods. This is because the custom model uses more of the activities that drive overhead costs. ABC emphasizes *activities* and their costs, and arguably better reflects how overhead cost is used in making products. The plantwide and departmental methods do not capture the products' different use of activities, and can distort overhead cost allocations. *With the plantwide and departmental methods, low-volume complex products are often undercosted, and high-volume simpler products are often overcosted.*

| | Overhead Cost per Go-Kart | |
|---|---|---|
| **Allocation Method** | **Standard Go-Kart** | **Custom Go-Kart** |
| Plantwide rate method . . . . . . . | $720 | $1,200 |
| Departmental rate method  . . . | 690 | 1,350 |
| Activity-based costing  . . . . . . . | 290 | 3,350 |

**EXHIBIT 4.12**

Comparison of Overhead Cost per Unit by Allocation Method

**Comparing Overhead Allocation Methods for Business Decisions**   Following are *total product costs per unit* for standard and custom go-karts for the three different overhead allocation methods. As we would expect, product cost per unit is lower for the standard go-kart compared with the custom go-kart. The cost difference between standard and custom go-karts is largest using activity-based costing. More accurate overhead allocation leads to better product pricing and product mix decisions.

| | Product Cost per Unit | |
|---|---|---|
| **Allocation Method** | **Standard Go-Kart** | **Custom Go-Kart** |
| Plantwide rate method . . . . . . . | $1,470 | $2,300 |
| Departmental rate method  . . . | 1,440 | 2,450 |
| Activity-based costing  . . . . . . . | 1,040 | 4,450 |

**Standard Go-Karts**   What are the implications if standard go-karts sell for $1,200 per unit? Using the plantwide or departmental methods, KartCo would not make standard go-karts as their product cost per unit ($1,470 or $1,440) would exceed the selling price. Using activity-based costing, however, the standard go-kart's $1,040 product cost per unit is below the $1,200 price per unit.

**Custom Go-Karts**   If the selling price of custom go-karts is $3,500 per unit, the plantwide and departmental methods both show that it exceeds the product cost per unit. Using activity-based costing, however, its $4,450 product cost per unit exceeds the price.

   The table below shows *gross profit per unit* (selling price – product price) for the plantwide and ABC methods.

**Point:** For this analysis and assignments assume the number of units produced equals the number of units sold.

| | Plantwide Rate Method | | | Activity-Based Costing | | |
|---|---|---|---|---|---|---|
| **Per Unit** | **Selling Price** | **Product Cost** | **Gross Profit** | **Selling Price** | **Product Cost** | **Gross Profit** |
| Standard go-kart . . . | $1,200 | $1,470 | $(270) | $1,200 | $1,040 | $160 |
| Custom go-kart . . . . | 3,500 | 2,300 | 1,200 | 3,500 | 4,450 | (950) |

**NEED-TO-KNOW** 4-3

Activity-Based Costing

**P3**

A manufacturer makes two types of snowmobiles, Basic and Deluxe, and reports the following data. The company budgets production of 6,000 Basic snowmobiles and 2,000 Deluxe snowmobiles.

| Activity | Budgeted Cost | Activity Cost Driver | Budgeted Activity Usage | Activity Usage Basic | Deluxe |
|---|---|---|---|---|---|
| Machine setup ....... | $ 150,000 | Setups | 500 setups | 200 setups | 300 setups |
| Materials handling .... | 250,000 | Parts | 100,000 parts | 60,000 parts | 40,000 parts |
| Machine depreciation .. | 720,000 | Machine hours (MH) | 9,000 MH | 6,000 MH | 3,000 MH |
| Total................ | $1,120,000 | | | | |

**1.** Compute an overhead activity rate for each activity using activity-based costing (ABC).

**2.** Compute the overhead cost per unit for each of the two product lines using ABC.

**Solution**

**1.**

| Activity | Budgeted Cost | ÷ Budgeted Activity Usage | = Activity Rate |
|---|---|---|---|
| Machine setup............. | $150,000 | ÷ 500 setups | = $300 per setup |
| Materials handling.......... | 250,000 | ÷ 100,000 parts | = $2.50 per part |
| Machine depreciation....... | 720,000 | ÷ 9,000 machine hours | = $80 per machine hour |

Do More: QS 4-11, QS 4-12,
QS 4-13, E 4-13, E 4-14,
E 4-15

**2.**

| | Basic Snowmobile | | | Deluxe Snowmobile | | |
|---|---|---|---|---|---|---|
| Activity | Activity Usage × | Activity Rate | = Allocated Cost | Activity Usage × | Activity Rate | = Allocated Cost |
| Machine setup.......... | 200 setups | × $300 per setup | = | $ 60,000 | 300 setups | × $300 per setup | = | $ 90,000 |
| Materials handling....... | 60,000 parts | × $2.50 per part | = | 150,000 | 40,000 parts | × $2.50 per part | = | 100,000 |
| Machine depreciation.... | 6,000 MH | × $80 per machine hour | = | 480,000 | 3,000 MH | × $80 per machine hour | = | 240,000 |
| Total allocated cost...... | | | | $690,000 | | | | $430,000 |
| Units produced ......... | | | | ÷ 6,000 | | | | ÷ 2,000 |
| Overhead cost per unit ... | | | | = $115 | | | | = $215 |

## C1 _____

Describe the four types of activities that cause overhead costs.

# Activity Levels and Cost Management

Activities causing overhead cost can be separated into four levels: (1) **unit level activities,** (2) **batch level activities,** (3) **product level activities,** and (4) **facility level activities.** These four activities are described as follows.

## Activity Levels

**Unit level activities** are performed on each unit. For example, the Production department needs electricity to power the machinery to produce each unit. Unit level costs tend to change with the number of units produced.

**Production**

**Batch level activities** are performed only on each batch of units. For example, machine setup is needed only for each batch regardless of the number of units in that batch. Batch level costs do not vary with the number of units, but instead vary with the number of batches.

**Setup**

**Design**

**Product level activities** are performed on each product line and are not affected by either the numbers of units or batches. For example, product design is needed only for each product line. Product level costs do not vary with the number of units or batches produced.

**Factory Services**

**Facility level activities** sustain facility capacity as a whole and are not caused by any specific product. For example, rent and factory maintenance costs are incurred no matter what is being produced. Facility level costs do not vary with the number of units, batches, or product lines produced.

For KartCo, the production pool reflects unit level costs, the setup pool reflects batch level costs, the design pool reflects product level costs, and factory services reflect facility level costs. Exhibit 4.13 shows additional examples of activities and activity drivers commonly found with each of the four activity levels.

Understanding the four levels of overhead cost can help control costs. **Activity-based management (ABM)** is an outgrowth of ABC that uses the link between activities and costs for better management. Activity-based management can help distinguish **value-added activities,** which add value to a product, from *non-value-added activities,* which do not. KartCo's value-added activities are production and design changes. Its non-value-added activities are setups and factory services. ABM aids cost control by reducing how much of an activity is performed.

**EXHIBIT 4.13**

Examples of Activities by Activity Level

| Activity Level | Examples of Activity | Activity Driver |
|---|---|---|
| Unit level | Cutting parts | Machine hours |
|  | Assembling components | Direct labor hours |
| Batch level | Setting up machines | Number of setups |
|  | Receiving shipments | Number of shipments |
|  | Sampling product quality | Number of batches |
|  | Recycling hazardous waste | Tons recycled |
| Product level | Design | Change requests |
|  | Controlling inventory | Parts per product |
| Facility level | Cleaning factory | Square feet |
|  | Providing electricity | Kilowatt hours |
|  | Reducing greenhouse gas emissions | Tons of $CO_2$ |

# Assessing Activity-Based Costing

## Advantages of Activity-Based Costing

**More Effective Overhead Cost Control**   ABC can be used to identify activities that can benefit from process improvement by focusing on activities. For KartCo, identifying large design costs allows managers to work to improve this process.

**Better Production and Pricing Decisions**   ABC can provide more accurate overhead cost allocation. More accurate costs allow managers to focus production activities on more profitable products and to more accurately set selling prices.

Paul Gilham/Getty Images

## Disadvantages of Activity-Based Costing

**Costly to Implement and Maintain**   ABC systems are costly. ABC requires a thorough analysis of cost activities and cost drivers, which can be expensive.

**Product Cost Distortion**   Even with ABC, product costs can be distorted. Two sources of cost distortion are (1) when costs cannot be readily classified into activity cost pools and (2) when cost drivers do not have a strong cause–effect relation with costs.

**Not Compliant with GAAP**   Activity-based costing cannot be used for external financial reporting purposes under GAAP.

---

■ **Decision Insight**

**ABCs of Decisions**   Business managers must make long-term strategic decisions, day-to-day operating decisions, and decisions on the type of financing the business needs. Survey evidence suggests that managers find ABC more useful in making strategic, operating, and financing decisions than non-ABC methods. Managers using ABC also felt better able to apply activity-based management. ■   *Source:* Stratton, W. O., Denis Desroches, R. A. Lawson and T. Hatch. *"Activity-Based Costing: Is It Still Relevant?"* Management Accounting Quarterly 10, no 3. Institute of Management Accountants.

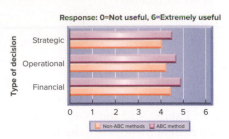

Response: 0=Not useful, 6=Extremely useful

---

# ABC FOR SERVICE PROVIDERS

## Activities for Service Providers

**P4**

Allocate overhead costs to service companies using activity-based costing.

ABC applies to service providers. Shipping companies like **FedEx** and **UPS** use ABC to track activities and costs involved with delivering packages. **Southwest Airlines** uses ABC to allocate costs to its passenger and ticketing cost pools. Laboratories performing medical tests, accounting and law offices, and advertising agencies are other examples of service firms that benefit from ABC.

In applying ABC, service companies classify costs by activity levels. Exhibit 4.14 shows typical activities within the four activity levels (unit, batch, service, and facility) for three service providers.

**EXHIBIT 4.14**

Examples of Activities for Service Providers

| Activity Level | Sports Arena | Hotel | Online Education |
|---|---|---|---|
| Unit Level | Sell a ticket to a fan | Check in a guest | Register a student |
| Batch Level | Hire vendors and security for a game | Prepare buffet, receive supply shipments | Deliver an online course |
| Service Level | Schedule a season of games | Schedule personnel | Create a new course |
| Facility Level | Clean the arena, provide utilities, update the website | Clean rooms, maintain pool | Maintain course sites, control course data |

Gallo Images/Getty Images; Jade LLC/Blend Images LLC; Prasit Rodphan/Shutterstock

## Applying Activity-Based Costing to a Service Provider

We apply activity-based costing to Garcia Company, a forensic accounting firm that provides two types of services: litigation support for lawsuits alleging financial statement fraud, and fraud investigations of local government entities. Garcia follows the three-step ABC process to allocate overhead costs to these service lines.

**Step 1: Identify Activities and Their Budgeted Overhead Cost**    The following activities, budgeted costs, activity cost drivers, and budgeted activity usage were identified.

| Activity | Budgeted Cost | Activity Cost Driver | Budgeted Activity Usage |
|---|---|---|---|
| Clerical support . . . . . . . | $90,000 | Documents prepared | 300 documents |
| Facility services . . . . . . . | 48,000 | Billable hours | 2,400 billable hours |
| Client consultations. . . . | 36,000 | Court dates | 12 court dates |

**Step 2: Compute Overhead Activity Rate for Each Activity**    For each activity, the following activity rate is computed for each activity cost pool.

| Activity | Budgeted Cost ÷ | Budgeted Activity Usage = | Activity Rate |
|---|---|---|---|
| Clerical support . . . . . . . . | $90,000 | ÷ 300 documents | = $300 per document |
| Facility services . . . . . . . . | 48,000 | ÷ 2,400 billable hours | = $20 per billable hour |
| Client consultations. . . . . | 36,000 | ÷ 12 court dates | = $3,000 per court date |

**Step 3: Allocate Overhead Cost to Cost Objects**    We use information on activity usage to allocated overhead cost. The company's activity usage on 39 litigation cases and 95 fraud cases follows.

| | Activity Usage | | |
|---|---|---|---|
| Activity Cost Driver | Litigation Support | Fraud Investigation | Total |
| Documents. . . . . . . | 225 | 75 | 300 |
| Billable hours. . . . . | 975 | 1,425 | 2,400 |
| Court dates . . . . . . | 10 | 2 | 12 |

We then allocate overhead cost to each service line, and compute overhead cost per case, as follows.

| Activity | Litigation Support Activity Usage × Activity Rate | = Allocated Cost | Fraud Investigation Activity Usage × Activity Rate | = Allocated Cost |
|---|---|---|---|---|
| Clerical support . . . . . . . . . . | 225 documents × $300 per document = | $67,500 | 75 documents × $300 per document = | $ 22,500 |
| Facility services . . . . . . . . . . | 975 billable hrs × $20 per billable hour = | 19,500 | 1,425 billable hrs × $20 per billable hour = | 28,500 |
| Client consultations. . . . . . . | 10 court dates × $3,000 per court date = | 30,000 | 2 court dates × $3,000 per court date = | 6,000 |
| **Total allocated cost. . . . . . .** | | **$117,000** | | **$57,000** |
| Units produced (cases) . . . . | | ÷ 39 | | ÷ 95 |
| **Overhead cost per case . . .** | | **= $3,000** | | **= $600** |

### ■ Analytics Insight

**Global Costing**    For many years, delivery company **DHL Express** used different cost allocation methods across the over 200 countries in which it operates. The resulting cost information was not useful and did not reconcile to the company's financial results. The company re-focused on collecting and analyzing good-quality data, and developed one worldwide cost allocation method. Today, DHL can compute accurate cost and profit per shipment. ■

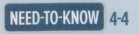 **4-4**

ABC for Service Providers

**P4**

Data Pro provides accounting services. The company reports the information below. The forensic accounting department has 8 employees, occupies 1,000 square feet of office space, and completed 20 jobs. (1) Compute the activity rate for each activity. (2) Allocate overhead to each activity and compute cost per unit (job) for the forensic accounting department.

| Activity | Budgeted Cost | Budgeted Activity Usage |
|---|---|---|
| Clerical support.......... | $ 50,000 | 20 employees |
| Building ................ | 100,000 | 2,500 square feet |
| Supplies ............... | 20,000 | 50 completed jobs |

**Solution**

**1.**

| Activity | Budgeted Cost | ÷ Budgeted Activity Usage | = Activity Rate |
|---|---|---|---|
| Clerical support.......... | $ 50,000 | ÷ 20 employees | = $2,500 per employee |
| Building ................ | 100,000 | ÷ 2,500 square feet | = $40 per square foot |
| Supplies ............... | 20,000 | ÷ 50 completed jobs | = $400 per completed job |

**2.**

| | Forensic Accounting Department | | |
|---|---|---|---|
| Activity | Activity Usage | × Activity Rate | = Allocated Cost |
| Clerical support............... | 8 employees | × $2,500 per employee | = $ 20,000 |
| Building ..................... | 1,000 square feet | × $40 per square foot | = 40,000 |
| Supplies ..................... | 20 completed jobs | × $400 per completed job | = 8,000 |
| Total allocated cost............. | | | $68,000 |
| Units produced (jobs) .......... | | | ÷ 20 |
| **Overhead cost per unit (job) ....** | | | **$ 3,400** |

Do More: QS 4-17, QS 4-18, E 4-22, E 4-23, E 4-24

---

 **CORPORATE SOCIAL RESPONSIBILITY**

BRIAN HARKIN/The New York Times/Redux Pictures

Analyzing activities leads many companies to **supply chain management,** which involves the coordination and control of goods, services, and information as they move from suppliers to consumers. **Accenture** estimates that supply chains account for 50%–70% of total expenses and greenhouse gas emissions for most manufacturing companies. More effective supply chains can benefit the bottom line and the environment.

**Walmart**, in conjunction with The Sustainability Consortium™, developed an index to assess its suppliers' policies and programs related to sustainability. Companies with high scores on the index are identified as Sustainability Leaders on Walmart's website, enabling customers to readily identify and perhaps buy from companies committed to sustainable practices. Walmart, in conjunction with its suppliers, is meeting its goal of eliminating greenhouse gases from its supply chain.

Joe and Lauren Grimm, owners of **Grimm Artisanal Ales**, this chapter's feature company, try to buy local ingredients whenever possible and focus special attention on byproduct disposal. "We have to think about how we dispose of grain," explains Joe, recognizing the environmental impact of beer production. The company also impacts the people aspect of the triple bottom line by keeping production local and hiring from the Brooklyn area.

**Customer Profitability**  **Decision Analysis**

Activity-based costing can be used to allocate selling, general, and administrative costs to products and determine the profitability of individual customers. As an example, let's return to KartCo and assume that costs of providing customer support (such as delivery, installation, and warranty work) are related to the distance a technician must travel to provide services. Assume that, as a result of applying activity-based costing, KartCo plans to sell its standard go-kart for $1,200 per unit. KartCo budgets $250,000 per year for customer support. It allocates customer support costs based on 100,000 budgeted miles traveled by customer support technicians. The customer support activity rate follows.

**A1**

Allocate selling, general, and administrative expenses to products and assess profitability.

$$\text{Customer support activity rate} = \frac{\text{Budgeted customer support cost}}{\text{Budgeted technician miles}} = \frac{\$250,000}{100,000 \text{ miles}} = \$2.50 \text{ per mile}$$

KartCo can add the costs of customer support to the costs of goods sold for an order to get the order's income. A **customer profitability report** for one of its customers, Six Flags, follows. KartCo sold 10 standard go-karts to Six Flags and a technician drove 200 miles to provide customer support.

| Customer Profitability Report—Six Flags | | |
|---|---:|---:|
| Sales (10 go-karts × $1,200) | | $12,000 |
| Cost of goods sold | | |
| Direct materials (10 go-karts × $400 per go-kart) | $4,000 | |
| Direct labor (10 go-karts × $350 per go-kart) | 3,500 | |
| Overhead (10 go-karts × $290 per go-kart, Exhibit 4.10) | 2,900 | 10,400 |
| Gross profit | | 1,600 |
| Customer service costs (200 miles × $2.50 per mile) | | 500 |
| Customer income | | $ 1,100 |

Income of $1,100 is generated from Six Flags. ABC encourages management to consider all resources used to serve a customer, not just manufacturing costs that are the focus of traditional costing methods. Customer support costs can also be allocated to product lines, for example to KartCo's standard and custom models, to determine their profitability.

VesPro manufactures motorized scooters in both standard and custom models. The standard scooter is a basic model with no custom options. The custom model is produced for college towns that want scooters with unique logos and color schemes. VesPro budgets $300,000 of overhead cost and 4,000 machine hours (MH) for the year. VesPro reports the following actual production information.

**NEED-TO-KNOW 4-4**

**COMPREHENSIVE**

Overhead Allocation

| | Number of Units | Machine Hours per Unit | Total Machine Hours |
|---|---:|---|---:|
| Standard scooter | 1,000 | 3 MH per unit | 3,000 MH |
| Custom scooter | 250 | 4 MH per unit | 1,000 MH |
| Total | | | 4,000 MH |

VesPro is considering the departmental rate method and traces $240,000 of overhead cost to its Assembly department and $60,000 to its Finishing department. The company budgets 4,000 machine hours in the Assembly department and budgets 1,250 direct labor hours (DLH) in the Finishing department. Actual production information for the two departments follows.

| | | Assembly Department | | Finishing Department | |
|---|---:|---|---:|---|---:|
| | Number of Units | Hours per Unit | Total Hours | Hours per Unit | Total Hours |
| Standard scooter | 1,000 | 3 MH per unit | 3,000 MH | 0.5 DLH per unit | 500 DLH |
| Custom scooter | 250 | 4 MH per unit | 1,000 MH | 3.0 DLH per unit | 750 DLH |
| Total | | | 4,000 MH | | 1,250 DLH |

VesPro is also considering activity-based costing and collects information in the following two tables.

| Activity | Budgeted Cost | Activity Cost Driver | Budgeted Activity Usage |
|---|---|---|---|
| Factory services.... | $260,000 | Square feet | 20,000 square feet |
| Setup ............ | 16,000 | Setups | 20 setups |
| Design .......... | 24,000 | Design changes | 10 design changes |

| | Actual Activity Usage | | |
|---|---|---|---|
| Activity Cost Driver | Standard | Custom | Total |
| Square feet ....... | 12,000 | 8,000 | 20,000 |
| Setups ........... | 5 | 15 | 20 |
| Design changes.... | 0 | 10 | 10 |

### Required

1. Compute overhead cost per unit for each type of scooter using a plantwide overhead rate based on machine hours.
2. Compute overhead cost per unit for each type of scooter using departmental overhead rates based on machine hours for the Assembly department and direct labor hours for the Finishing department.
3. Compute overhead cost per unit for each type of scooter using activity-based costing.
4. Prepare a summary table that reports the overhead cost per unit for both scooter types under each alternative allocation method from parts 1, 2, and 3.
5. VesPro reports the following additional information. Assuming the company uses activity-based costing, (a) compute product cost per unit and (b) compute gross profit per unit (selling price per unit minus product cost per unit).

| | Standard Scooter | Custom Scooter |
|---|---|---|
| Selling price per unit................. | $3,300 | $3,700 |
| Direct materials cost per unit .......... | 2,000 | 2,200 |
| Direct labor cost per unit ............. | 1,000 | 1,200 |

## SOLUTION

### 1. Plantwide rate method

$$\text{Plantwide overhead rate} = \frac{\text{Budgeted overhead cost}}{\text{Budgeted machine hours}} = \frac{\$300,000}{4,000 \text{ MH}} = \underline{\$75} \text{ per machine hour}$$

**Overhead Cost per Unit Allocation**

Standard scooter: $75 per machine hour × 3 machine hours per unit = **$225 per unit**
Custom scooter:   $75 per machine hour × 4 machine hours per unit = **$300 per unit**

### 2. Departmental method

$$\text{Assembly department overhead rate} = \frac{\$240,000}{4,000 \text{ MH}} = \underline{\$60} \text{ per machine hour}$$

$$\text{Finishing department overhead rate} = \frac{\$60,000}{1,250 \text{ DLH}} = \underline{\$48} \text{ per direct labor hour}$$

Overhead cost per unit allocation to the two products.

| Department | Departmental Overhead Rate | Standard Scooter Hours per Unit | Standard Scooter Overhead Allocated | Custom Scooter Hours per Unit | Custom Scooter Overhead Allocated |
|---|---|---|---|---|---|
| Assembly . . . . . . . . . . . . | $60 per MH | 3 MH per unit | $180 | 4 MH per unit | $240 |
| Finishing. . . . . . . . . . . . | $48 per DLH | 0.5 DLH per unit | 24 | 3 DLH per unit | 144 |
| Totals . . . . . . . . . . . . . . | | | $204 | | $384 |

**3. Activity-based costing**

| Activity | Budgeted Cost | Budgeted Activity Usage | Activity Rate |
|---|---|---|---|
| Factory services. . . . . . . . . | $260,000 | 20,000 square feet | $13 per square foot |
| Setup . . . . . . . . . . . . . . . . | 16,000 | 20 setups | $800 per setup |
| Design . . . . . . . . . . . . . . | 24,000 | 10 design changes | $2,400 per design change |

| Activity | Standard Scooter Activity Usage | Standard Scooter Activity Rate | Standard Scooter Allocated Cost | Custom Scooter Activity Usage | Custom Scooter Activity Rate | Custom Scooter Allocated Cost |
|---|---|---|---|---|---|---|
| Factory services. . . . . . . . | 12,000 sq. ft. | $13 per square foot | $156,000 | 8,000 square feet | $13 per square foot | $104,000 |
| Setup . . . . . . . . . . . . . . | 5 setups | $800 per setup | 4,000 | 15 setups | $800 per setup | 12,000 |
| Design . . . . . . . . . . . . . . | 0 changes | $2,400 per design change | 0 | 10 changes | $2,400 per design change | 24,000 |
| Total allocated cost . . . . . | | | $160,000 | | | $140,000 |
| Units produced . . . . . . . . | | | ÷ 1,000 | | | ÷ 250 |
| Overhead cost per unit . . | | | = $160 | | | = $560 |

**4. Comparing overhead cost per unit by allocation method**   We see that ABC shifts overhead cost from the high-volume standard model to the low-volume custom model. This is because the custom model uses more of the activities that drive overhead cost. The plantwide and departmental rate methods overcosted the standard model and undercosted the custom model.

| Allocation Method | Overhead Cost per Scooter Standard Scooter | Overhead Cost per Scooter Custom Scooter |
|---|---|---|
| Plantwide rate method . . . . . . . . | $225 | $300 |
| Departmental rate method . . . . . | 204 | 384 |
| Activity-based costing. . . . . . . . . | 160 | 560 |

**5.** Product cost per unit for each model using activity-based costing.

| Per Unit | Direct Materials | + | Direct Labor | + | Overhead | = | Product Cost per Unit |
|---|---|---|---|---|---|---|---|
| Standard scooter. . . . | $2,000 | + | $1,000 | + | $160 | = | $3,160 |
| Custom scooter . . . . . | 2,200 | + | 1,200 | + | 560 | = | 3,960 |

Gross profit per unit for each model.

| Per Unit | Selling Price | − | Product Cost | = | Gross Profit |
|---|---|---|---|---|---|
| Standard scooter. . . . . . . . . | $3,300 | − | $3,160 | = | $140 |
| Custom scooter . . . . . . . . . | 3,700 | − | 3,960 | = | (260) |

## Summary: Cheat Sheet

### PLANTWIDE RATE METHOD

**Plantwide rate method:** Uses one overhead rate.

**Computing plantwide overhead rate:**

$$\text{Plantwide overhead rate} = \frac{\text{Budgeted overhead cost}}{\text{Budgeted allocation base}} = \frac{\$4,800,000}{100,000 \text{ DLH}} = \frac{\$48 \text{ per}}{\text{DLH}}$$

**Allocating overhead using plantwide rate:**

**Allocated cost per unit = Plantwide overhead rate × DLH used**

| Allocated Overhead Cost |
| --- |
| Standard go-kart: $48 per DLH × 15 DLH per unit = **$720 per unit** |
| Custom go-kart:  $48 per DLH × 25 DLH per unit = **$1,200 per unit** |

### DEPARTMENTAL RATE METHOD

**Departmental rate method:** Uses a different overhead rate for each department.

**Computing departmental overhead rate:**

$$\frac{\text{Departmental}}{\text{overhead rate}} = \frac{\text{Budgeted departmental overhead cost}}{\text{Budgeted departmental allocation base}}$$

$$\text{Machining department overhead rate} = \frac{\$4,200,000}{70,000 \text{ MH}} = \$60 \text{ per MH}$$

$$\text{Assembly department overhead rate} = \frac{\$600,000}{100,000 \text{ DLH}} = \$6 \text{ per DLH}$$

**Allocating overhead using departmental rate:**

| Department | Departmental Overhead Rate | Standard Go-Kart | | Custom Go-Kart | |
| --- | --- | --- | --- | --- | --- |
| | | Hours per Unit | Overhead Allocated | Hours per Unit | Overhead Allocated |
| Machining ... | $60 per MH | 10 MH per unit | $600 | 20 MH per unit | $1,200 |
| Assembly.... | $6 per DLH | 15 DLH per unit | 90 | 25 DLH per unit | 150 |
| Totals....... | | | $690 | | $1,350 |

### ACTIVITY-BASED COSTING

**Activity cost pool:** Group of costs related to same activity.

**Activity cost driver:** Activity that causes costs to go up or down.

**Three Steps to Activity-Based Costing:**

❶ Identify activities and their budgeted overhead cost.
❷ Compute an overhead activity rate for each activity.

$$\text{Activity rate} = \frac{\text{Budgeted activity cost}}{\text{Budgeted activity usage}}$$

| Activity | Budgeted Cost | ÷ Budgeted Activity Usage | = Activity Rate |
| --- | --- | --- | --- |
| Production ............. | $ 600,000 | ÷ 100,000 direct labor hours | = $6 per direct labor hour |
| Setup ................. | 2,000,000 | ÷ 200 setups | = $10,000 per setup |
| Design ................ | 1,200,000 | ÷ 10 design changes | = $120,000 per change |
| Factory services.......... | 1,000,000 | ÷ 20,000 square feet | = $50 per square foot |

❸ Allocate overhead cost to cost objects (products).

**Allocated cost = Actual activity usage × Activity rate**

| Activity | Standard Go-Kart | | | Custom Go-Kart | | |
| --- | --- | --- | --- | --- | --- | --- |
| | Activity Usage × | Activity Rate | = Allocated Cost | Activity Usage × | Activity Rate | = Allocated Cost |
| Production ............. | 75,000 DLH | × $6 per DLH | = $ 450,000 | 25,000 DLH | × $6 per DLH | = $ 150,000 |
| Setup ................. | 40 setups | × $10,000 per setup | = 400,000 | 160 setups | × $10,000 per setup | = 1,600,000 |
| Design ............... | 0 changes | × $120,000 per change | = 0 | 10 changes | × $120,000 per change | = 1,200,000 |
| Factory services.......... | 12,000 sq. ft. | × $50 per square foot | = 600,000 | 8,000 sq. ft. | × $50 per square foot | = 400,000 |
| Total allocated cost........ | | | $1,450,000 | | | $3,350,000 |
| Units produced ........... | | | ÷ 5,000 | | | ÷ 1,000 |
| Overhead cost per unit ..... | | | = $290 | | | = $3,350 |

---

## Key Terms

---

## Multiple Choice Quiz

1. A company makes two products: A and B. It uses activity-based costing and prepares the following analysis showing budgeted overhead cost and activity usage for each of its three activities.

| Activity (cost driver) | Budgeted Overhead | Budgeted Activity Usage |
| --- | --- | --- |
| Assembly (MH) | $ 80,000 | 1,000 MH |
| Finishing (DLH) | 58,400 | 1,600 DLH |
| Factory services (sq. ft.) | 360,000 | 6,000 sq. ft. |

The company used 800 machine hours, 600 direct labor hours, and 5,400 square feet to produce 16,396 units of Product B. The overhead cost per unit of Product B using activity-based costing is

   **a.** $2.02.          **c.** $25.00.
   **b.** $5.00.          **d.** $22.40.

**2.** A company uses activity-based costing. Budgeted overhead cost and activity usage follows.

| Activity | Budgeted Overhead | Budgeted Activity Usage |
|---|---|---|
| Activity 1 | $19,800 | 1,100 DLH |
| Activity 2 | 16,000 | 40 setups |
| Activity 3 | 14,000 | 700 MH |

The overhead activity rate for Activity 3 is

   **a.** $4.00 per MH.          **c.** $18.00 per MH.
   **b.** $8.59 per MH.          **d.** $20.00 per MH.

**3.** Compared to the plantwide rate method, activity-based costing usually shifts costs from

   **a.** Low-volume to high-volume products.
   **b.** High-volume to low-volume products.
   **c.** Complex to simple products.
   **d.** Customized to standardized products.

**4.** Which of the following statements is true?

   **a.** An activity-based costing system is generally easy to implement and maintain.
   **b.** Activity-based management eliminates waste by allocating costs to products that waste resources.
   **c.** Activity-based costing uses a single rate to allocate overhead.
   **d.** Activity rates in activity-based costing are computed by dividing budgeted costs by the activity measure for each activity.

**5.** All of the following are examples of batch level activities except

   **a.** Sampling product quality.
   **b.** Setting up machines.
   **c.** Receiving shipments.
   **d.** Employee recreational facilities.

## ANSWERS TO MULTIPLE CHOICE QUIZ

**1.** c; The activity rate for each activity follows.

| Activity | Budgeted Cost | Budgeted Activity Usage | Activity Rate |
|---|---|---|---|
| Assembly . . . . . . . . . . | $ 80,000 | 1,000 MH | $80.00 per MH |
| Finishing. . . . . . . . . . | 58,400 | 1,600 DLH | $36.50 per DLH |
| Factory services. . . . . | 360,000 | 6,000 sq. ft. | $60.00 per sq. ft. |

Product B's overhead cost per unit follows.

| Activity | Activity Usage | × | Activity Rate | = | Allocated Cost |
|---|---|---|---|---|---|
| Assembly . . . . . . . . . . . . | 800 MH | × | $80.00 per MH | = | $ 64,000 |
| Finishing. . . . . . . . . . . . . | 600 DLH | × | $36.50 per DLH | = | 21,900 |
| Factory services. . . . . . . . | 5,400 sq. ft. | × | $60.00 per sq. ft. | = | 324,000 |
| Total allocated cost . . . . . | | | | | $409,900 |
| Units produced . . . . . . . . | | | | | ÷ 16,396 |
| Overhead cost per unit . . | | | | | = **$25** |

**2.** d; The activity rate for Activity 3 follows.

   Budgeted cost ÷ Budgeted activity = Activity rate
   $14,000   ÷     700 MH      = $20 per MH

**3.** b; Under the plantwide rate method, overhead is allocated using a volume-based measure like direct labor hours. This often results in more overhead cost allocated to high-volume products. Activity-based costing allocates overhead based on use of activities that drive overhead cost. This results in more overhead allocated to lower-volume, more complex products that use more activities.

**4.** d;

**5.** d; Batch level activities are activities that are performed each time a batch of goods is handled or processed, regardless of how many units are in a batch. Employee recreational facilities relate to the organization as a whole rather than to specific batches and, as such, are not considered to be batch level. The other activities are performed each time a batch of goods is handled or processed, and, as such, are batch level activities.

*Select Quick Study and Exercise assignments feature Guided Example videos, called "Hints" in Connect. Hints use different numbers, and instructors can turn this feature on or off.*

Shaw Co. budgets total overhead cost of $1,800,000. The company allocates overhead cost based on 100,000 budgeted direct labor hours. Compute the single plantwide overhead rate.

**QUICK STUDY**

**QS 4-1**
Computing plantwide overhead rate   **P1**

Neal Co. allocates overhead cost using a single plantwide overhead rate of $20 per direct labor hour. Each product unit uses three direct labor hours. Compute the overhead cost per unit.

**QS 4-2**
Allocating overhead—plantwide rate   **P1**

**QS 4-3**
Allocating overhead—plantwide rate

**P1**

A manufacturer uses machine hours to allocate overhead cost to products. Budgeted information for the current year follows. (*a*) Compute the plantwide overhead rate based on machine hours. (*b*) How much overhead cost is allocated to Job A2, which uses 4 machine hours?

| | |
|---|---|
| Budgeted overhead cost................. | $54,400 |
| Budgeted machine hours ................ | 640 machine hours |

**QS 4-4**
Computing plantwide overhead rate

**P1**

Chan Company identified the following budgeted data for this year. The company manufactures two types of scooters: standard and fast.

| Activity | Budgeted Overhead Cost | Budgeted Activity |
|---|---|---|
| Handling materials . . . . . | $625,000 | 100,000 parts |
| Quality inspection. . . . . . | 90,000 | 1,500 inspections |
| Purchasing . . . . . . . . . . . | 25,000 | 1,000 orders |
| Total. . . . . . . . . . . . . . . | $740,000 | |

1. Compute a single plantwide overhead rate assuming that the company allocates overhead cost based on 10,000 budgeted direct labor hours.
2. The standard model uses 5 direct labor hours per unit, and the fast model uses 10 direct labor hours per unit. Compute overhead cost per unit for each model.

**QS 4-5**
Computing overhead rates using ABC  **P3**

Refer to the information in QS 4-4. Compute an overhead activity rate for each activity assuming the company uses activity-based costing.

**QS 4-6**
Computing plantwide overhead rate

**P1**

Rafner Manufacturing has the following budgeted data for its two production departments.

| Budgeted Data | Assembly | Finishing |
|---|---|---|
| Overhead cost. . . . . . . . . . . . . . | $1,200,000 | $800,000 |
| Direct labor hours. . . . . . . . . . . | 12,000 direct labor hours | 20,000 direct labor hours |
| Machine hours . . . . . . . . . . . . . | 4,000 machine hours | 16,000 machine hours |

1. What is the company's single plantwide overhead rate based on direct labor hours?
2. What is the company's single plantwide overhead rate based on machine hours?

**QS 4-7**
Computing departmental overhead rates  **P2**

Refer to the information in QS 4-6. What is the Assembly department overhead rate using direct labor hours? What is the Finishing department overhead rate using machine hours?

**QS 4-8**
Allocating overhead with departmental rates  **P2**

Refer to the information in QS 4-6 and QS 4-7. Allocate overhead to a job that uses 80 direct labor hours in the Assembly department and uses 30 machine hours in the Finishing department.

**QS 4-9**
Cost drivers for activity-based costing  **P3**

A manufacturer reports two activities: cutting for production and product shipments. Determine whether each of the following cost drivers relates to the cutting activity or to the shipment activity.

1. Shipment orders
2. Direct labor hours for cutting

3. Cutting machine hours
4. Shipments received

A company sells two types of products: standard and deluxe. It prepares the following analysis showing budgeted cost and cost driver activity for each of its three activities. Compute an activity rate for each activity using activity-based costing.

| Activity | Budgeted Cost | Activity Cost Driver | Budgeted Activity Usage | | |
|---|---|---|---|---|---|
| | | | Standard | Deluxe | Total |
| Factory services .... | $87,000 | Square feet | 3,000 | 2,800 | 5,800 |
| Setup............. | 10,000 | Setups | 300 | 200 | 500 |
| Quality control...... | 93,000 | Units inspected | 2,500 | 5,250 | 7,750 |

A manufacturer uses activity-based costing to assign overhead cost to products. Budgeted cost information for its activities follows. Compute an activity rate for each activity.

| Activity | Budgeted Cost | Activity Cost Driver | Budgeted Activity Usage |
|---|---|---|---|
| Purchasing .......... | $135,000 | Purchase orders | 4,500 purchase orders |
| Factory services ...... | 32,000 | Square feet | 5,000 square feet |
| Setup............. | 65,000 | Setups | 50 setups |

Rand Co. computed the following activity rates using activity-based costing.

| Activity | Activity Rate |
|---|---|
| Setup................ | $1,000 per setup |
| Materials handling ..... | $50 per materials requisition |
| Inspection ........... | $2 per unit inspected |

The company's deluxe model used the following activities to produce 1,000 units. Compute the overhead cost per unit for the deluxe model using activity-based costing.

| Activity | Actual Activity Usage |
|---|---|
| Setup................ | 3 setups |
| Materials handling ..... | 25 materials requisitions |
| Inspection ........... | 1,000 units inspected |

Chen Co. uses activity-based costing. It budgets $825,000 of overhead cost to sustainably dispose of 3,300 tons of hazardous waste.

**a.** Compute the activity rate for hazardous waste disposal based on tons of hazardous waste.

**b.** The company disposed of 5 tons of hazardous waste in completing Job 125. Allocate overhead cost to hazardous waste disposal as part of Job 125 using activity-based costing.

Mia Co. uses activity-based costing and reports the following for this year. (*a*) Compute an activity rate for each activity using activity-based costing. (*b*) Allocate overhead costs to a job that uses 20 machine hours and 15 direct labor hours.

| Activity | Budgeted Cost | Activity Cost Driver | Budgeted Activity Usage |
|---|---|---|---|
| Cutting........ | $14,000 | Machine hours (MH) | 2,000 machine hours |
| Assembly..... | 60,000 | Direct labor hours (DLH) | 6,000 direct labor hours |
| Total......... | $74,000 | | |

**QS 4-15**

Classify activities

C1

Classify each of the following activities as unit level, batch level, product level, or facility level for a manufacturer of organic juices.

1. Cutting fruit
2. Developing new types of juice
3. Blending fruit into juice
4. Receiving fruit shipments
5. Cleaning blending machines
6. Water usage

---

**QS 4-16**

Classify activities

C1

Classify each of the following activities as unit level, batch level, product level, or facility level for a manufacturer of trail mix.

1. Roasting peanuts
2. Cleaning roasting machines
3. Sampling product quality
4. Providing utilities for factory
5. Calibrating mixing machines
6. Electricity usage

---

**QS 4-17**

Activity-based costing for services

P4

Data Insights provides accounting services. The company computed the following activity rates using activity-based costing. The forensic accounting department has 10 employees, occupies 1,500 square feet, and completed 40 jobs. Compute overhead cost per job for the forensic accounting department.

| Activity | Activity Rate |
|---|---|
| Clerical support........................ | $600 per employee |
| Building............................. | $50 per sq. foot |
| Supplies ............................. | $80 per job |

---

**QS 4-18**

Allocating costs using ABC for a service company

P4

Qinto Company sells two types of products: basic and deluxe. The company provides technical support for its products at a budgeted overhead cost of $250,000 per year. The company allocates technical support cost based on 10,000 budgeted technical support calls per year.

1. Compute the activity rate for technical support using activity-based costing.
2. During January, Qinto received 650 calls on its deluxe model and 150 calls on its basic model. Allocate technical support costs to each model.

---

**QS 4-19**

Customer profitability report

A1

Prepare a customer profitability report using the information below.

| | | | |
|---|---|---|---|
| Sales........................ | $10,000 | Overhead..................... | $2,600 |
| Direct materials ................ | 4,100 | Customer support costs .......... | 500 |
| Direct labor.................... | 1,300 | | |

---

Mc Graw Hill **connect**

**EXERCISES**

**Exercise 4-1**

Using plantwide overhead rate to allocate overhead

P1

Shakti Co. budgets overhead cost of $72,000 for the year. The company reports the following for its standard and deluxe models.

| Cost per Unit | Standard | Deluxe |
|---|---|---|
| Direct materials...... | $12 | $23 |
| Direct labor........ | 18 | 27 |

1. Compute a single plantwide overhead rate assuming the company allocates overhead cost based on 6,000 direct labor hours.
2. The standard model uses 2 direct labor hours per unit and the deluxe model uses 3 direct labor hours per unit. Compute overhead cost per unit for each model.
3. Compute the total product cost per unit for both models.

Hydro Sports budgets overhead cost of $420,000 for the year. The company manufactures two types of jet skis: standard and deluxe. Budgeted direct labor hours per unit are 8 for the standard model and 12 for the deluxe model. The company budgets production of 100 units of the standard model and 100 units of the deluxe model for the year.

**1.** Compute the total number of budgeted direct labor hours for the year.

**2.** Compute the plantwide overhead rate using budgeted direct labor hours.

**3.** Compute overhead cost per unit for each model using the plantwide overhead rate. Actual direct labor hours per unit are 8 for the standard model and 12 for the deluxe model.

**Exercise 4-2**
Computing plantwide overhead rate
**P1**

---

Dade Metals manufactures patio furniture. The company budgets overhead cost of $400,000 for the year. It also budgets 20,000 machine hours and 5,000 direct labor hours.

**1.** Compute the plantwide overhead rate, assuming the company allocates overhead based on (a) machine hours and (b) direct labor hours.

**2.** Job 121 uses 100 machine hours and 50 direct labor hours. Allocate overhead to Job 121 assuming overhead is allocated based on (a) machine hours—use answer from part 1a, and (b) direct labor hours—use answer from part 1b.

**Exercise 4-3**
Computing plantwide overhead rate
**P1**

---

Health Co-op is an outpatient surgical clinic. It budgets $540,000 of overhead cost for the year. The two main surgical units and their data follow.

**Exercise 4-4**
Plantwide rate for a service
**P1**

| Service | Budgeted Surgeries |
|---|---|
| General surgery ................ | 400 |
| Orthopedic surgery............. | 200 |

**1.** Compute a single plantwide rate, assuming the company allocates overhead cost based on 600 budgeted surgeries.

**2.** In May of this year, the company performed 20 general surgeries and 14 orthopedic surgeries. Allocate overhead to each of the two types of surgeries for May using the single plantwide overhead rate.

---

Wess Co. has limited capacity and can produce either its standard product or its deluxe product. Additional information follows.

**Exercise 4-5**
Product mix and plantwide rate versus activity-based costing
**P1    P3**

| Per Unit | Standard | Deluxe |
|---|---|---|
| Selling price............. | $60 | $90 |
| Direct materials.......... | 30 | 35 |
| Direct labor ............. | 20 | 25 |

**1.** Using a single plantwide rate, the company computes overhead cost per unit of $15 for the standard model and $20 for the deluxe model. Which model should the company produce? *Hint:* Compute product cost per unit and compare that with selling price to get gross profit per unit.

**2.** Using activity-based costing, the company computes overhead cost per unit of $5 for the standard model and $40 for the deluxe model. Which model should the company produce? *Hint:* Compute product cost per unit and compare that with selling price per unit to get gross profit per unit.

---

Hydro Sports budgets overhead cost of $420,000 for the year; of this amount, $240,000 is traceable to the Assembly department and $180,000 is traceable to the Finishing department. The company manufactures two types of jet skis: standard and deluxe. Budgeted direct labor hours for the standard model are 7 in Assembly and 1 in Finishing. Budgeted direct labor hours for the deluxe model are 9 in Assembly and 3 in Finishing. The company budgets production of 100 units of the standard model and 100 units of the deluxe model for the year.

**1.** Compute each department's total number of budgeted direct labor hours for the year.

**2.** Compute departmental overhead rates for each department using direct labor hours for that department.

**3.** Compute overhead cost per unit for each model using departmental overhead rates. Actual direct labor hours for the standard model are 7 in Assembly and 1 in Finishing. Actual direct labor hours for the deluxe model are 9 in Assembly and 3 in Finishing.

**Exercise 4-6**
Computing departmental overhead rates
**P2**

**Exercise 4-7**
Plantwide overhead rate
P1

Textra produces parts for a machine manufacturer. Parts go through two departments, Molding and Trimming. The company budgets overhead cost of $240,000 in the Molding department and $200,000 in the Trimming department. The company budgets 16,000 machine hours (MH) in Molding and 25,000 direct labor hours (DLH) in Trimming. Actual production information follows.

| | | Molding Department | | Trimming Department | |
|---|---|---|---|---|---|
| | Number of Units | Hours per Unit | Total Hours | Hours per Unit | Total Hours |
| Part Z . . . . . . . . . . | 3,000 | 2.0 MH per unit | 6,000 MH | 3 DLH per unit | 9,000 DLH |
| Part X . . . . . . . . . . | 4,000 | 2.5 MH per unit | 10,000 MH | 4 DLH per unit | 16,000 DLH |
| Totals . . . . . . . . . . | | | 16,000 MH | | 25,000 DLH |

**Required**

1. Compute the plantwide overhead rate using direct labor hours as the allocation base.
2. Determine the overhead cost per unit for each part using the plantwide rate.

**Exercise 4-8**
Departmental overhead rates
P2

Refer to the information in Exercise 4-7.

**Required**

1. Compute a departmental overhead rate for the Molding department based on machine hours and a departmental overhead rate for the Trimming department based on direct labor hours.
2. Determine the overhead cost per unit for each part using the departmental rates.

**Exercise 4-9**
Allocating overhead using plantwide rate and departmental rates
P1    P2

Laval produces lighting fixtures. Budgeted information for its two production departments follows. The departments use machine hours (MH) and direct labor hours (DLH).

| | Fabricating | Assembly |
|---|---|---|
| Overhead cost . . . . . . . . . . . . . | $300,000 | $200,000 |
| Direct labor hours . . . . . . . . . . | 75,000 DLH | 125,000 DLH |
| Machine hours . . . . . . . . . . . . . | 80,000 MH | 62,500 MH |

Laval reports the following for one of its products, a desk lamp.

| | | Fabricating Department | | Assembly Department | |
|---|---|---|---|---|---|
| | Number of Units | Direct Labor Hours per Unit | Machine Hours per Unit | Direct Labor Hours per Unit | Machine Hours per Unit |
| Desk lamp . . . | 4,000 | 4 DLH per unit | 3 MH per unit | 2 DLH per unit | 0.5 MH per unit |

**Required**

1. Determine the plantwide overhead rate using 200,000 direct labor hours as the allocation base.
2. Determine the overhead cost per unit for the desk lamp using the plantwide overhead rate.
3. Compute departmental overhead rates based on machine hours in the Fabricating department and direct labor hours in the Assembly department.
4. Determine the overhead cost per unit for the desk lamp using the departmental overhead rates.

**Exercise 4-10**
Using departmental overhead rates and computing gross profit
P2

Real Cool produces air conditioners in two departments: Assembly and Finishing. Budgeted information follows.

| Department | Budgeted Cost | Allocation Base | Budgeted Usage |
|---|---|---|---|
| Assembly . . . . . . . . . . . | $300,000 | Machine hours | 6,000 machine hours |
| Finishing. . . . . . . . . . . . | 21,000 | Direct labor hours | 3,000 direct labor hours |

Additional production information for two models of its air conditioners follows.

| Per unit | Model A | Model T |
|---|---|---|
| Selling price...... | $400 | $420 |
| Direct materials... | 100 | 90 |
| Direct labor ...... | 150 | 160 |

| | Model A | Model T |
|---|---|---|
| Units produced ................... | 400 | 500 |
| Assembly machine hours per unit .... | 2 MH | 3.5 MH |
| Finishing direct labor hours per unit .. | 3 DLH | 4 DLH |

1. Compute departmental overhead rates and determine overhead cost per unit for each model. Use machine hours to allocate budgeted Assembly costs and use direct labor hours to allocate budgeted Finishing costs.
2. Compute the total product cost per unit for each model.
3. For each model, compute the gross profit per unit (selling price per unit minus product cost per unit).

Consider the following data for two products of Vigano Manufacturing.

**Exercise 4-11**
Computing product cost per unit using plantwide method and activity-based costing

P1   P3

| Activity | Budgeted Cost | Activity Driver |
|---|---|---|
| Machine setup........... | $ 10,000 | 20 machine setups |
| Parts handling ........... | 8,000 | 16,000 parts |
| Quality inspections ....... | 12,000 | 100 inspections |
| Total budgeted overhead .. | $ 30,000 | |

| Unit Information | Product A | Product B |
|---|---|---|
| Units produced ....... | 1,000 units | 200 units |
| Direct materials cost ... | $20 per unit | $30 per unit |
| Direct labor cost ...... | $40 per unit | $50 per unit |
| Direct labor hours ..... | 2.0 per unit | 2.5 per unit |

1. Using a plantwide overhead rate based on 2,500 direct labor hours, compute the total product cost per unit for each product.
2. Consider the following additional information about these two products. If activity-based costing is used to allocate overhead cost, (*a*) compute overhead activity rates, (*b*) allocate overhead cost to Product A and Product B and compute overhead cost per unit for each, and (*c*) compute product cost per unit for each.

| Actual Activity Usage | Product A | Product B |
|---|---|---|
| Setups.................. | 8 setups | 12 setups |
| Parts ................... | 10,000 parts | 6,000 parts |
| Inspections .............. | 40 inspections | 60 inspections |

A manufacturer reports three activities: assembling components into products; product design; and sales order processing. Determine whether each of the following cost drivers relates to assembly, design, or order processing.

**Exercise 4-12**
Cost drivers for activity-based costing

P3

1. Number of sales orders processed
2. Direct labor hours to assemble components
3. Number of design changes
4. Number of components assembled
5. Number of design hours
6. Number of shipments made

Snow Cat manufactures snowmobiles and uses activity-based costing to allocate overhead cost. To produce snowmobiles, the company uses four activities. It sets up machines to produce batches of components. Assembly line employees assemble products. Completed snowmobiles are inspected for quality. Maintenance workers clean the factory after production finishes at the end of each day.

**Exercise 4-13**
Cost drivers for activity-based costing

P3

1. If $30,000 of Setup is used as an activity cost pool, which of the following would be used as a cost driver?
   **a.** Square feet  **b.** Number of setups  **c.** Design modifications  **d.** Number of employees hired
2. If $200,000 of Assembly is used as an activity cost pool, which of the following would be used as a cost driver?
   **a.** Direct labor hours  **b.** Square feet  **c.** Design modifications  **d.** Number of inspections
3. If $40,000 of Inspection is used as an activity cost pool, which of the following would be used as a cost driver?
   **a.** Engineering hours  **b.** Tons recycled  **c.** Number of orders  **d.** Number of inspections
4. If $10,000 of Maintenance is used as an activity cost pool, which of the following would be used as a cost driver?
   **a.** Engineering hours  **b.** Design modifications  **c.** Square feet  **d.** Number of orders

**Exercise 4-14**
Allocating overhead cost to jobs using activity-based costing

**P3**

Pro-Craft Co. computed the following activity rates to allocate overhead cost for the year.

| Activity | Activity Rate |
|---|---|
| Materials handling . . . . . | $50 per materials requisition |
| Quality inspection. . . . . . | $40 per inspection |
| Utilities . . . . . . . . . . . . . | $5 per machine hour |

During January, the company produced the following two jobs. Allocate overhead cost to each job using the activity rates.

| Activity Cost Driver | Activity Usage | |
|---|---|---|
| | Job A | Job B |
| Materials requisitions. . . . . | 5 | 3 |
| Inspections . . . . . . . . . . . . | 8 | 4 |
| Machine hours . . . . . . . . . . | 300 | 200 |

**Exercise 4-15**
Computing activity rates, overhead allocation, and cost per unit

**P3**

Lucern Co. reports the following for its overhead cost for the year.

| Activity | Budgeted Cost | Budgeted Activity Usage |
|---|---|---|
| Engineering support. . . . . | $24,500 | 70 design changes |
| Electricity. . . . . . . . . . . . . | 34,000 | 3,400 machine hours |
| Setup. . . . . . . . . . . . . . . . | 52,500 | 350 setups |

1. Compute the activity rate for each activity using activity-based costing.
2. The company's Pro model used these activities to produce 1,200 units during the year: 2 design changes, 140 machine hours, and 12 setups. Allocate overhead cost to the Pro model and compute its overhead cost per unit using activity-based costing.

**Exercise 4-16**
Allocating overhead costs and computing overhead cost per unit using activity-based costing

**P3**

Trax Co. manufactures 75 stationary bikes and 100 rowing machines with three activities. Activity rates to produce these products follow.

| Activity | Activity Rate |
|---|---|
| Assembly. . . . . . . | $20 per direct labor hour |
| Purchasing . . . . . | $10 per purchase order |
| Inspection . . . . . . | $25 per inspection |

Activity usage for each product follows. Compute the overhead cost per unit for the stationary bikes and the rowing machines.

| Activity Cost Driver | Activity Usage | |
|---|---|---|
| | Stationary Bikes | Rowing Machines |
| Direct labor hours. . . . . . . . . . . | 300 | 500 |
| Purchase orders . . . . . . . . . . . . | 12 | 18 |
| Inspections . . . . . . . . . . . . . . . | 15 | 20 |

Ice Cool produces two different models of air conditioners. The activities, costs, and cost drivers associated with the production processes follow.

| Process | Activity | Budgeted Cost | Activity Cost Driver | Budgeted Activity Usage |
|---------|----------|---------------|----------------------|-------------------------|
| **Assembly** | Machining | $279,000 | Machine hours (MH) | 6,000 |
| | Setups | 24,000 | Setups | 120 |
| | | $303,000 | | |
| **Finishing** | Inspection | $210,000 | Inspections | 700 |
| **Support** | Purchasing | $135,000 | Purchase orders | 450 |

**Exercise 4-17**

Using activity-based costing to allocate overhead, compute product cost and gross profit

**P3**

Additional production information concerning its two models follows.

| Units and Activities | Model X | Model Z |
|----------------------|---------|---------|
| Units produced . . . . . . . | 1,724 | 3,463 |
| Machine hours . . . . . . . | 1,800 | 4,200 |
| Setups  . . . . . . . . . . . . | 40 | 80 |
| Inspections . . . . . . . . . | 400 | 300 |
| Purchase orders . . . . . . | 300 | 150 |

| Per Unit | Model X | Model Z |
|----------|---------|---------|
| Selling price per unit. . . . . . . . . | $420 | $400 |
| Direct materials cost per unit . . . | 100 | 90 |
| Direct labor cost per unit . . . . . | 150 | 160 |

1. Compute the activity rate for each activity using activity-based costing.
2. Using activity-based costing, compute the overhead cost per unit for each model.
3. Compute the total product cost per unit for each model.
4. For each model, compute the gross profit per unit (selling price per unit minus product cost per unit).

A manufacturer identified the following activities, costs, and activity drivers. Compute the activity rate for each activity using activity-based costing.

**Exercise 4-18**

Computing overhead rates using activity-based costing

**P3**

| Activity | Budgeted Costs | Budgeted Activity Usage |
|----------|----------------|-------------------------|
| Handling materials . . | $625,000 | 100,000 parts |
| Inspecting product . . | 900,000 | 1,500 inspections |
| Processing orders. . . | 105,000 | 700 orders |
| Paying suppliers . . . . | 175,000 | 5,000 invoices |
| Insuring factory. . . . . | 300,000 | 40,000 square feet |

Northwest Company produces two types of glass shelving: rounded edge and squared edge. The company reports the following cost data.

**Exercise 4-19**

Activity-based costing to compute activity rates, overhead cost per unit, and product cost per unit

**P3**

| | Rounded Edge | Squared Edge | Total |
|---|---|---|---|
| Direct materials . . . . . . . . . . . . . . . . . | $31,200 | $ 44,800 | $ 76,000 |
| Direct labor . . . . . . . . . . . . . . . . . . . . | 12,200 | 23,800 | 36,000 |
| Overhead (using plantwide rate) . . . . . | 36,600 | 71,400 | 108,000 |
| Total product cost . . . . . . . . . . . . . . . | $80,000 | $140,000 | $220,000 |
| Units produced  . . . . . . . . . . . . . . . . | 10,000 | 14,000 | |
| Product cost per unit. . . . . . . . . . . . . | $    8 | $    10 | |

Northwest's controller wants to apply activity-based costing to allocate the $108,000 of overhead cost to the two products to see whether product cost per unit would change markedly from that above. The company's budgeted activity usage equals its actual activity usage for the period. The following additional information is collected.

| Activity | Budgeted Cost | Activity Cost Driver | Activity Usage Rounded Edge | Activity Usage Squared Edge | Activity Usage Total |
|---|---|---|---|---|---|
| Purchasing .............. | $ 5,400 | Purchase orders | 109 orders | 431 orders | 540 orders |
| Depreciation of machinery... | 56,600 | Machine hours | 500 hours | 1,500 hours | 2,000 hours |
| Setup.................. | 46,000 | Setups | 40 setups | 210 setups | 250 setups |
| Total.................. | $108,000 | | | | |

**Required**

1. Compute the activity rate for each activity using activity-based costing.
2. Compute overhead cost per unit for each of the two products using activity-based costing.
3. Determine product cost per unit for each of the two products using activity-based costing.

---

**Exercise 4-20**

Activity-based costing for overhead cost allocation

**P3**

Craft Co. reports the following partial activity-based costing information for its Deluxe model. Complete the table by entering amounts for the missing items *a* through *e*.

| Activity | Activity Usage | Activity Rate | Allocated Cost |
|---|---|---|---|
| Assembly ............. | 1,200 direct labor hours | $10 per direct labor hour | $ _c_ |
| Factory services........ | 1,000 square feet | $ _b_ per square foot | 14,000 |
| Setup ............... | _a_ setups | $200 per setup | 4,000 |
| Total allocated cost ..... | | | $ _d_ |
| Units produced ........ | | | 3,000 |
| Overhead cost per unit .. | | | $ _e_ |

---

**Exercise 4-21**

Classifying activities

**C1**

Classify each of the following activities as unit level, batch level, product level, or facility level to indicate how each is incurred with respect to production.

1. Paying real estate taxes on the factory building
2. Attaching labels to collars of shirts
3. Redesigning a bicycle seat
4. Cleaning the Assembly department
5. Polishing gold wedding rings
6. Mixing bread dough in a commercial bakery
7. Sampling cookies to determine quality
8. Recycling hazardous waste
9. Reducing greenhouse gas emissions

---

**Exercise 4-22**

Classifying activities for a service provider

**P4**

Following are activities in providing medical services at Healthsmart Clinic. Classify each activity as unit level, batch level, service level, or facility level.

1. Registering patients
2. Cleaning beds
3. Stocking examination rooms
4. Washing linens
5. Ordering medical equipment
6. Heating the clinic
7. Providing security services
8. Filling prescriptions

Singh and Danzin is an architectural firm that provides services for residential construction projects. The following overhead cost data are from the current period.

**Exercise 4-23**
Activity-based costing for a service provider
**P4**

| Activity | Budgeted Costs | Budgeted Activity Usage |
|---|---|---|
| Client consultation .... | $270,000 | 1,500 contact hours |
| Drawings............ | 115,000 | 2,000 design hours |

**1.** Compute an activity rate for each activity using activity-based costing.
**2.** Allocate overhead cost to a job that requires 45 contact hours and 340 design hours.

Silver Law Firm provides litigation and mediation services. The company reports the following overhead cost data for the year. It worked on 70 litigation cases and 80 mediation cases during this period.

**Exercise 4-24**
Activity-based costing for a service provider
**P4**

| Activity | Budgeted Cost | Budgeted Activity Usage |
|---|---|---|
| Clerical support............. | $63,000 | 360 documents |
| Facility services............. | 18,600 | 2,400 billable hours |
| Client consultations......... | 90,000 | 36 court dates |

Activity usage for each service follows.

| Activity Cost Driver | Activity Usage | | |
|---|---|---|---|
| | Litigation | Mediation | Total |
| Documents.................. | 192 | 168 | 360 |
| Billable hours............... | 800 | 1,600 | 2,400 |
| Court dates ................ | 30 | 6 | 36 |

**Required**

**1.** Compute an activity rate for each activity using activity-based costing.
**2.** Compute overhead cost per unit (case) for both litigation and mediation using activity-based costing.

Janix Company reports the following information for two large customers for the year.

**Exercise 4-25**
Allocating cost and customer profitability
**A1**

| | Western College | Eastern Technical |
|---|---|---|
| Sales..................... | $100,000 | $80,000 |
| Cost of goods sold......... | 70,000 | 55,000 |
| Gross profit .............. | $ 30,000 | $25,000 |

Using activity-based costing, the company computes a customer service activity rate of $125 per customer service call. For the year, the company reports 80 customer service calls for Western College and 20 customer service calls for Eastern Technical.

**Required**

**1.** Allocate customer service call costs to each customer and compute income for each customer.
**2.** After including customer service costs, which customer produces the highest income?

**Exercise 4-26**

Activity-based costing and customer profitability

**A1**

Neal Co. manufactures computer workstations. The company's three activities and their overhead cost drivers follow.

| Activity | Budgeted Cost | Activity Cost Driver | Budgeted Activity Usage |
|---|---|---|---|
| Fabrication.......... | $80,000 | Machine hours | 1,600 machine hours |
| Assembly ........... | 96,000 | Direct labor hours | 2,000 direct labor hours |
| Inspection .......... | 72,000 | Units inspected | 6,000 units |

Job 101's actual activity usage along with a partial customer profitability report follow.

| | Machine Hours | Direct Labor Hours | Units |
|---|---|---|---|
| Job 101 ... | 25 MH | 30 DLH | 10 |

| Profitability Report—Job 101 | | |
|---|---|---|
| Sales.................. | | $8,500 |
| Cost of goods sold | | |
| Direct materials...... | $1,940 | |
| Direct labor ......... | 750 | |
| Overhead........... | ? | ? |
| Gross profit ........... | | ? |
| Customer service costs.. | | 500 |
| Customer income ...... | | ? |

**Required**

1. Compute activity rates using activity-based costing.
2. Use the results from part 1 to allocate overhead cost to Job 101.
3. Complete the profitability report for Job 101.

**PROBLEM SET A**

**Problem 4-1A**

Comparing plantwide rate method and activity-based costing

**P1    P3**

Craftmore Machining reports the following budgeted overhead cost and related data for this year.

| Activity | Budgeted Cost | Activity Cost Driver | Budgeted Activity Usage |
|---|---|---|---|
| Assembly.......... | $390,000 | Direct labor hours (DLH) | 13,000 |
| Product design ..... | 60,000 | Engineering hours (EH) | 1,000 |
| Electricity.......... | 20,000 | Machine hours (MH) | 10,000 |
| Setup............. | 50,000 | Setups | 400 |
| Total............. | $520,000 | | |

**Required**

1. Compute a single plantwide overhead rate assuming the company allocates overhead cost based on 13,000 direct labor hours.
2. Job 31 used 200 direct labor hours and Job 42 used 480 direct labor hours. Allocate overhead cost to each job using the single plantwide overhead rate from part 1.
3. Compute an activity rate for each activity using activity-based costing.
4. Allocate overhead costs to the following jobs using activity-based costing.

| | Activity Usage | |
|---|---|---|
| Activity Cost Driver | Job 31 | Job 42 |
| Direct labor hours (DLH)... | 200 | 480 |
| Engineering hours (EH).... | 26 | 32 |
| Machine hours (MH) ...... | 50 | 60 |
| Setups ............... | 4 | 6 |

Tent Master produces Pup tents and Pop-up tents. The company budgets $252,000 of overhead cost and 42,000 direct labor hours. Additional information follows.

| Per Unit | Selling Price | Direct Materials | Direct Labor |
|---|---|---|---|
| Pup tent . . . . . . . | $78 | $20 | $45 |
| Pop-up tent . . . . . | 73 | 25 | 30 |

**Problem 4-2A**
Using plantwide overhead rate to allocate overhead cost, and compute overhead cost per unit and gross profit per unit
**P1**

**Required**

1. Compute a single plantwide overhead rate assuming the company allocates overhead cost based on 42,000 direct labor hours.
2. Pup tents use 3 direct labor hours (DLH) per unit and Pop-up tents use 2 direct labor hours per unit. Compute the overhead cost per unit for each product.
3. Compute the product cost per unit for each product.
4. For each product, compute the gross profit per unit (selling price per unit minus the product cost per unit).

Refer to the information in Problem 4-2A. Additional information on overhead cost follows.

| Activity | Budgeted Cost | Activity Cost Driver | Budgeted Activity Usage |
|---|---|---|---|
| Assembly. . . . . . . . . . . . . . | $168,000 | Direct labor hours (DLH) | 42,000 |
| Electricity. . . . . . . . . . . . . . | 24,000 | Machine hours (MH) | 10,000 |
| Materials purchasing . . . . . | 60,000 | Purchase orders (PO) | 400 |
| Total. . . . . . . . . . . . . . . . . . | $252,000 | | |

**Problem 4-3A**
Using activity-based costing to allocate overhead cost, and compute overhead cost per unit and gross profit per unit
**P3**

**Required**

1. Compute an activity rate for each activity using activity-based costing.
2. The following actual activity usage produced 10,000 Pup tents and 6,000 Pop-up tents. Allocate overhead cost to Pup tents and to Pop-up tents and compute overhead cost per unit for each product.

| | Activity Usage | |
|---|---|---|
| Activity Cost Driver | Pup tents | Pop-up tents |
| Direct labor hours (DLH). . . . | 30,000 | 12,000 |
| Machine hours (MH) . . . . . . . | 4,000 | 6,000 |
| Purchase orders (PO) . . . . . . | 150 | 250 |

3. Compute product cost per unit for Pup tents and for Pop-up tents.
4. For each product, compute the gross profit per unit (selling price per unit minus the product cost per unit).

Bike-O-Rama produces two bike models: Voltage and EasyRider. Departmental overhead data follow.

| Department | Budgeted Cost | Allocation Base | Budgeted Usage |
|---|---|---|---|
| Fabricating. . . . . . . . . . . | $100,000 | Machine hours (MH) | 8,000 MH |
| Assembly . . . . . . . . . . . | 75,000 | Direct labor hours (DLH) | 1,500 DLH |

**Problem 4-4A**
Using departmental overhead rate method to compute overhead cost per unit, product cost per unit, and gross profit per unit
**P2**

**Required**

1. Compute departmental overhead rates using (a) machine hours to allocate budgeted Fabricating costs and (b) direct labor hours to allocate budgeted Assembly costs.
2. The company reports the following actual production usage data. Compute the overhead cost per unit for each model.

|  | Voltage | EasyRider |
|---|---|---|
| Machine hours per unit............. | 2.0 MH | 3.0 MH |
| Direct labor hours per unit .......... | 1.5 DLH | 0.5 DLH |

3. The company reports additional information below. For each model, compute the product cost per unit.

| Per Unit | Selling Price | Direct Materials | Direct Labor |
|---|---|---|---|
| Voltage............. | $260 | $90 | $45 |
| EasyRider........... | 150 | 80 | 15 |

4. For each model, compute gross profit per unit (selling price per unit minus product cost per unit).

---

**Problem 4-5A**
Activity-based costing for a service company

**P4**

Optimal Health is an outpatient surgical clinic. The clinic's three activities, their overhead cost, and their cost drivers follow.

| Activity | Budgeted Cost | Activity Cost Driver | Budgeted Activity Usage |
|---|---|---|---|
| Supplies.............. | $200,000 | Surgical hours (SH) | 1,000 |
| Patient services....... | 37,500 | Number of patients | 500 |
| Building cost ........ | 300,000 | Square feet | 2,000 |

The two main surgical units and their actual activity usage follow.

| Service | Actual Activity Usage | | |
|---|---|---|---|
|  | Surgical Hours | Patients | Square Feet |
| General surgery ....... | 250 | 400 | 720 |
| Orthopedic surgery..... | 750 | 100 | 1,280 |

**Required**

1. Compute activity rates using activity-based costing.
2. Allocate overhead cost to the general surgery and to the orthopedic surgery units. Compute overhead cost per patient for each surgery unit.

---

**PROBLEM SET B**

BuiltRite Machining reports the following budgeted overhead cost and related data for the year.

**Problem 4-1B**
Comparing plantwide rate method and activity-based costing

**P1    P3**

| Activity | Budgeted Cost | Activity Cost Driver | Budgeted Activity Usage |
|---|---|---|---|
| Assembly .............. | $500,000 | Machine hours (MH) | 12,500 |
| Product design .......... | 30,000 | Engineering hours (EH) | 600 |
| Factory services ........ | 20,000 | Direct labor hours (DLH) | 1,250 |
| Inspection ............. | 50,000 | Inspections | 500 |
| Total ................. | $600,000 | | |

**Required**

1. Compute a single plantwide overhead rate assuming the company allocates overhead cost based on 12,500 machine hours.
2. Job 55 used 150 machine hours and Job 66 used 220 machine hours. Allocate overhead cost to each job using the single plantwide overhead rate from part 1.
3. Compute an activity overhead rate for each activity using activity-based costing.
4. Allocate overhead costs to the following jobs using activity-based costing.

| Activity Cost Driver | Activity Usage | |
|---|---|---|
| | Job 55 | Job 66 |
| Machine hours (MH) .......... | 150 | 220 |
| Engineering hours (EH) ........ | 15 | 8 |
| Direct labor hours (DLH) ....... | 12 | 24 |
| Inspections. ................ | 8 | 8 |

Sara's Salsa produces salsa in two types: Extra Fine for restaurants and Family Style for home use. The company budgets $280,000 of overhead cost and 40,000 direct labor hours. Additional information follows.

| Per Unit (case) | Selling Price | Direct Materials | Direct Labor |
|---|---|---|---|
| Extra Fine.............. | $64 | $18 | $30 |
| Family Style ............ | 53 | 16 | 25 |

**Problem 4-2B**

Using plantwide overhead rate to allocate overhead cost, and compute overhead cost per unit and gross profit per unit

**P1**

**Required**

1. Compute a single plantwide overhead rate assuming the company allocates overhead cost based on 40,000 direct labor hours.
2. Extra Fine uses 2 direct labor hours per unit and Family Style uses 1.5 direct labor hours per unit. Compute the overhead cost per unit for each product.
3. Compute the product cost per unit for each product.
4. For each product, compute the gross profit per unit (selling price per unit minus the product cost per unit).

Refer to the information in Problem 4-2B. Additional information on overhead cost follows.

| Activity | Budgeted Cost | Activity Cost Driver | Budgeted Activity Usage |
|---|---|---|---|
| Mixing. ............ | $160,000 | Direct labor hours (DLH) | 40,000 |
| Electricity .......... | 22,000 | Machine hours (MH) | 10,000 |
| Inspection ......... | 98,000 | Inspections | 490 |
| Total ............. | $280,000 | | |

**Problem 4-3B**

Using activity-based costing to allocate overhead cost, and compute overhead cost per unit and gross profit per unit

**P3**

**Required**

1. Compute an activity rate for each activity using activity-based costing.
2. The following actual activity usage produced 12,000 units of Extra Fine and 8,000 units of Family Style. Allocate overhead cost to Extra Fine and to Family Style and compute overhead cost per unit for each product using activity-based costing.

| Activity Cost Driver | Activity Usage | |
|---|---|---|
| | Extra Fine | Family Style |
| Direct labor hours (DLH) ...... | 28,000 | 12,000 |
| Machine hours (MH) ......... | 6,000 | 4,000 |
| Inspections. ................ | 274 | 216 |

3. Compute product cost per unit for Extra Fine and for Family Style.
4. For each product, compute the gross profit per unit (selling price per unit minus the product cost per unit).

**Problem 4-4B**
Using departmental overhead rate method to compute overhead cost per unit, product cost per unit, and gross profit per unit
**P2**

Del Sol produces two workout machines: ProPower and Crunch. Departmental overhead data follow.

| Department | Budgeted Cost | Allocation Base | Budgeted Usage |
|---|---|---|---|
| Fabricating... | $120,000 | Machine hours (MH) | 4,000 MH |
| Assembly .... | 72,000 | Direct labor hours (DLH) | 6,000 DLH |

**Required**

1. Compute departmental overhead rates using (a) machine hours to allocate budgeted Fabricating costs and (b) direct labor hours to allocate budgeted Assembly costs.
2. The company reports the following actual production usage data. Compute the overhead cost per unit for each model.

| | ProPower | Crunch |
|---|---|---|
| Machine hours per unit............. | 3.0 MH | 2.0 MH |
| Direct labor hours per unit .......... | 1.5 DLH | 1.0 DLH |

3. The company reports additional information below. For each product, compute the product cost per unit.

| Per Unit | Selling Price | Direct Materials | Direct Labor |
|---|---|---|---|
| ProPower.......... | $160 | $25 | $30 |
| Crunch ............ | 150 | 35 | 20 |

4. For each product, compute gross profit per unit (selling price per unit minus product cost per unit).

**Problem 4-5B**
Activity-based costing for a service company
**P4**

Perez Co. provides forensic accounting services. The company's three activities, their overhead cost, and their cost drivers follow.

| Activity | Budgeted Cost | Activity Cost Driver | Budgeted Activity Usage |
|---|---|---|---|
| Clerical support ... | $80,000 | Documents prepared | 2,000 documents |
| Facility services ... | 64,000 | Cases | 200 cases |
| Building cost ..... | 96,000 | Square feet | 6,000 square feet |

The company's two service lines and their actual activity usage follow.

| | Actual Activity Usage | | |
|---|---|---|---|
| Service | Documents | Cases | Square Feet |
| Litigation support ........... | 1,500 | 120 | 4,275 |
| Fraud investigation .......... | 500 | 80 | 1,725 |

**Required**

1. Compute activity rates using activity-based costing.
2. Allocate overhead cost to Litigation support and Fraud investigation. Compute overhead cost per case for each service line.

---

*This serial problem began in Chapter 1 and continues through most of the book. If previous chapter segments were not completed, the serial problem can begin at this point.*

**SP 4**   After reading an article about activity-based costing in a trade journal for the furniture industry, Santana Rey decides to analyze overhead cost at **Business Solutions**. In a recent month, Santana found that setup costs, inspection costs, and utility costs made up most of the company's overhead. Additional information about overhead follows.

| Activity | Budgeted Cost | Budgeted Activity Usage |
|---|---|---|
| Setup . . . . . . . . . . . . | $20,000 | 25 setups |
| Inspection . . . . . . . . | 7,500 | 5,000 parts inspected |
| Utilities. . . . . . . . . . . | 10,000 | 5,000 machine hours (MH) |
| Total . . . . . . . . . . . . . | $37,500 | |

Alexander Image/Shutterstock

The following data pertain to Job 615.

| Direct materials . . . . . . . . . | $2,500 | Setups . . . . . . . . . . . . . . | 2 setups |
|---|---|---|---|
| Direct labor . . . . . . . . . . . . | $3,500 | Parts inspected . . . . . . . | 400 parts inspected |
| Overhead. . . . . . . . . . . . . . | $ ____ | Machine hours. . . . . . . . | 600 machine hours |

**Required**

1. Classify each of the three overhead activities as unit level, batch level, product level, or facility level.
2. Assume Business Solutions allocates overhead cost using a plantwide rate based on 5,000 machine hours. Compute total product cost of Job 615.
3. Assume Business Solutions uses activity-based costing. (*a*) Compute overhead activity rates. (*b*) Allocate overhead cost to Job 615. (*c*) Compute total product cost of Job 615.

## Accounting Analysis

**AA 4-1**   Assume **Apple** uses activity-based costing to allocate customer support costs to products. For a MacBook Pro model, assume Apple budgets annual customer support costs of $850,000. Also assume Apple budgets 10,000 customer support calls per year for that model. Assumed product cost data for the MacBook Pro model follow.

| Product Cost | Per unit |
|---|---|
| Direct materials . . . . . . . . . . . | $490 |
| Direct labor . . . . . . . . . . . . . . | 60 |
| Overhead. . . . . . . . . . . . . . . . | 265 |
| Total product cost . . . . . . . . . | $815 |

**Required**

1. Compute the activity rate for the customer support cost.
2. Prepare a customer profitability report for an order from a local college for 500 MacBook Pros. Each unit sells for $1,199. Apple budgets 500 support calls for this order.

**COMPARATIVE ANALYSIS**

**A1**

**APPLE**

**GOOGLE**

**AA 4-2**   Assume Google and Apple use activity-based costing to allocate customer support costs to products. For a similar laptop model, assume the companies report the following information.

| Product Cost per Unit | Apple | Google |
|---|---|---|
| Direct materials........... | $490 | $470 |
| Direct labor .............. | 60 | 50 |
| Overhead................. | 265 | 260 |
| Total product cost ......... | $815 | $780 |

| Customer Support | Apple | Google |
|---|---|---|
| Annual costs .............. | $850,000 | $1,400,000 |
| Annual number of calls ...... | 10,000 | 10,000 |

**Required**

1. Compute the activity rate for the customer support cost for both Apple and Google.

2. Prepare a customer profitability report for both Apple and Google for an order from a local college for 500 laptops. Each unit sells for $1,199. Both companies budget 500 support calls for this order.

3. Which company, Apple or Google, would earn the most income from this customer?

**EXTENDED ANALYSIS**

**A1**

**Samsung**

**AA 4-3**   Assume Samsung uses activity-based costing to allocate customer support costs to products. For two of its laptop models, assume the company reports the data below. The Galaxy Book S sells for $1,000 per unit and the Galaxy Book Flex sells for $900 per unit.

| Product Cost per Unit | Galaxy Book S | Galaxy Book Flex |
|---|---|---|
| Direct materials............ | $520 | $390 |
| Direct labor ............... | 60 | 50 |
| Overhead................. | 120 | 140 |
| Total product cost .......... | $700 | $580 |

| Customer Support | Galaxy Book S | Galaxy Book Flex |
|---|---|---|
| Annual costs .............. | $650,000 | $950,000 |
| Annual number of calls ...... | 10,000 | 10,000 |

**Required**

1. Compute the activity rate for the customer support cost for each laptop model.

2. Prepare a customer profitability report for each laptop model for (a) an order for 500 S models from a local college and (b) an order for 500 Flex models from a local hospital. The company budgets 500 support calls for both orders.

3. Which order, for Galaxy Book S or Galaxy Book Flex, earns the most income?

## Discussion Questions

1. Why are overhead costs allocated to products and not traced to products as direct materials and direct labor are?

2. What are three common methods of assigning overhead costs to a product?

3. Why are direct labor hours and machine hours commonly used as the bases for overhead allocation?

4. What are the advantages of using a plantwide overhead rate?

5. How are overhead costs allocated to products with the plantwide rate method?

6. What is a cost object?

7. Explain why a plantwide overhead rate can distort the cost of a particular product.

8. Why are departmental overhead rates more accurate for product costing than a plantwide overhead rate?

9. Which overhead allocation methods can be used for external reporting?

10. Why is overhead allocation under ABC usually more accurate than either the plantwide rate method or the departmental rate method?

11. What is an activity cost driver?

12. What is the first step in applying activity-based costing?

13. What are the four activity levels associated with activity-based costing? Define each.

14. What are value-added activities?

15. "Activity-based costing is only useful for manufacturing companies." Is this a true statement? Explain.

## Beyond the Numbers

**BTN 4-1**  In conducting interviews and observing factory operations to implement an activity-based costing system, you determine that several activities are unnecessary. For example, warehouse personnel were inspecting purchased components as they were received at the loading dock. Later that day, the components were inspected again on the shop floor before being installed in the final product. Both of these activities caused costs to be incurred but were not adding value to the product. If you include this observation in your report, one or more employees who perform inspections will likely lose their jobs.

**ETHICS CHALLENGE**
C1

**Required**

1. As a plant employee, what is your responsibility to report your findings to superiors?
2. What is your responsibility to the employees whose jobs will likely be lost because of your report?
3. What facts should you consider before making your decision to report or not?

---

**BTN 4-2**  The chief executive officer (CEO) of your company recently returned from a meeting where activity-based costing was discussed. Though her background is not in accounting, she has worked for the company for 15 years and is thoroughly familiar with its operations. Her impression of ABC was that it was just another way of dividing up total overhead cost and that the total would still be the same "no matter how you sliced it."

**COMMUNICATING IN PRACTICE**
P3

**Required**

Write a memorandum to the CEO, no more than one page, explaining how ABC is different from traditional volume-based costing methods. Also identify its advantages and disadvantages vis-à-vis traditional methods. Be sure it is written to be understandable to someone who is not an accountant.

---

**BTN 4-3**  Observe the operations at your favorite fast-food restaurant.

**TEAMWORK IN ACTION**
C1

**Required**

1. How many people does it take to fill a typical order of a sandwich, beverage, and one side order?
2. Describe the activities involved in its food service process.
3. What costs are related to each activity identified in requirement 2?

---

**BTN 4-4**  **Grimm Artisanal Ales** brews many varieties of beer. Company founders Joe and Lauren Grimm know that financial success depends on cost control as well as revenue generation.

**ENTREPRENEURIAL DECISION**
C1

**Required**

1. If Grimm Artisanal Ales wanted to expand its product line to include whiskey, what activities would it need to perform that are not required for its current product lines?
2. Related to part 1, should the additional overhead costs related to new product lines be shared by existing product lines? Explain your reasoning.

# 5 Cost Behavior and Cost-Volume-Profit Analysis

## Chapter Preview

### IDENTIFYING COST BEHAVIOR

**C1** Fixed costs

Variable costs

Mixed costs

Step-wise costs

**NTK 5-1**

### MEASURING COST BEHAVIOR

**P1** Scatter diagrams

High-low method

Regression

Comparing cost estimation methods

**NTK 5-2**

### CONTRIBUTION MARGIN AND BREAK-EVEN

**A1** Contribution margin

**P2** Break-even

Cost-volume-profit chart

Changing estimates

**NTK 5-3**

### APPLYING COST-VOLUME-PROFIT ANALYSIS

**C2** Margin of safety

Expected income

Target income

Strategizing

**P3** Sales mix

**A2** Operating leverage

**NTK 5-4, 5-5**

## Learning Objectives

**CONCEPTUAL**

**C1** Describe different types of cost behavior in relation to production and sales volume.

**C2** Describe several applications of cost-volume-profit analysis.

**ANALYTICAL**

**A1** Compute the contribution margin and describe what it reveals about a company's cost structure.

**A2** Analyze changes in sales using the degree of operating leverage.

**PROCEDURAL**

**P1** Estimate costs using the scatter diagram, high-low method, and regression.

**P2** Compute the break-even point for a single-product company.

**P3** Compute the break-even point for a multiproduct company.

**P4** Appendix 5B—Compute unit cost and income under both absorption and variable costing.

# Sweet Success

*"Kick sugar, keep candy"*—**TARA BOSCH**

VANCOUVER, CA—Concerned with the health effects of sugar, Tara Bosch set out to make a sugar-free version of her favorite candy, gummy worms. "Gummy candy is 99% sugar," explains Tara. "So I had to start from scratch." Armed with a heavy-duty gummy bear mold and a strong belief she would succeed, Tara started her business, **SmartSweets** (**SmartSweets.com**).

"I had no idea what I was doing," Tara admits. "I spent months researching and trying recipes." After over 200 iterations, Tara developed a tasty prototype and obtained debt financing for her first manufacturing run. She won over her first retail customer through "cold-calling and persistence."

In addition to product development, financing, and distribution, Tara had to measure and control the costs of using high-quality ingredients and a specialized manufacturing process. Understanding fixed and variable costs, and how to control them, to achieve break-even and make profits were critical for her start-up.

Tara focused on analyzing the relations between costs, volume, and profit—called *CVP analysis*. Tara also uses data analytics in assessing the effectiveness of her company's digital marketing programs. "We track key metrics like AOV (average order value) and net new subscribers," exclaims Tara.

SmartSweets

SmartSweets continues to show enormous growth. Tara's vision is "to be the global leader in innovative candy products that kick sugar."

Sources: *SmartSweets website*, January 2021; *CNBC.com*, August 8, 2019; *Forbes.com*, May 29, 2017

## IDENTIFYING COST BEHAVIOR

Planning a company's future activities is crucial to successful management. Managers use **cost-volume-profit (CVP) analysis** to predict how changes in costs and sales levels affect profit. CVP analysis looks at how income (profit) is affected by the following four factors.

**C1**

Describe different types of cost behavior in relation to production and sales volume.

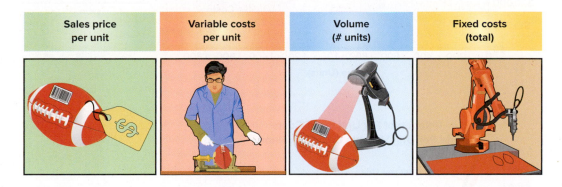

| Sales price per unit | Variable costs per unit | Volume (# units) | Fixed costs (total) |

Managers work with these four factors to answer questions such as:

- How many units must we sell to break even?
- What sales volume is needed to earn a target income?
- How much will income change if we buy a new machine to reduce labor costs?
- What is the change in income if selling prices decline and sales volume increases?
- How will income change if we change the sales mix of our products or services?

This chapter explains CVP analysis. We first review cost classifications and then show methods for measuring and analyzing costs.

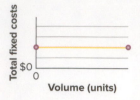

## Fixed Costs

*Fixed costs* do not change when the volume of activity changes (within a relevant range). For example, $32,000 in monthly rent paid for a factory building remains the same whether the factory operates eight hours or twenty-four hours per day. This means that rent cost is the same each month at any level of output from zero to the plant's monthly productive capacity.

Though the *total* amount of fixed cost does not change as volume changes, fixed cost *per unit* of output decreases as volume increases. If 200 units are produced when monthly rent is $32,000, the average rent cost per unit is $160 ($32,000/200 units). When production increases to 1,000 units per month, the average rent cost per unit decreases to $32 ($32,000/1,000 units).

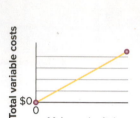

## Variable Costs

*Variable costs* change in proportion to changes in volume of activity. Direct materials cost is one example of a variable cost. If each unit produced uses $20 of direct materials, then when 10 units are made, the total direct materials costs are $200 ($20 × 10). While the *total* amount of variable cost changes with the level of production, variable cost *per unit* stays the same as volume changes.

## Graphing Fixed and Variable Costs

The upper graph in Exhibit 5.1 shows the relation between total fixed costs and volume, and the relation between total variable costs and volume. Total fixed costs of $32,000 remain the same

**EXHIBIT 5.1**

Relations of Total and Per Unit Costs to Volume

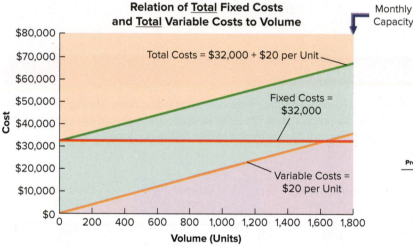

| Units Produced | Total Fixed Costs | Total Variable Costs |
|---|---|---|
| 0 | $32,000 | $    0 |
| 200 | 32,000 | 4,000 |
| 400 | 32,000 | 8,000 |
| ⋮ | ⋮ | ⋮ |
| 1,800 | 32,000 | 36,000 |

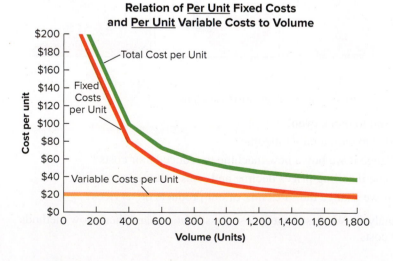

| Units Produced | Per Unit Fixed Costs | Per Unit Variable Costs |
|---|---|---|
| 1 | $32,000 | $20 |
| 200 | 160 | 20 |
| 400 | 80 | 20 |
| ⋮ | ⋮ | ⋮ |
| 1,800 | 17.78 | 20 |

at all production levels up to the company's monthly capacity of 1,800 units. Total variable costs increase by $20 per unit for each additional unit produced.

The lower graph in Exhibit 5.1 shows that fixed costs *per unit* decrease as production increases. This drop in per unit costs as production increases is called *economies of scale*. This lower graph also shows that variable costs per unit stay the same as production levels change.

## Mixed Costs

**Mixed costs** include both fixed and variable cost components. For example, compensation for sales representatives often includes a fixed monthly salary and a variable commission based on sales. Utilities costs such as electricity, water, and natural gas include a fixed service fee plus an amount that varies with usage. Like a fixed cost, a mixed cost is greater than zero when volume is zero; like a variable cost, it increases steadily in proportion to increases in volume.

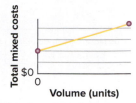

**Graphing Mixed Costs**   The green total cost line in the top graph in Exhibit 5.1 starts on the vertical axis at the $32,000 fixed cost point. At the zero volume level, total cost equals the fixed costs. As the volume of activity increases, the total cost line increases at an amount equal to the variable cost per unit. This total cost line is a "mixed cost."

## Step-wise Costs

A **step-wise cost,** or *stair-step cost*, has a step pattern in costs. Salaries of production supervisors are fixed within a *relevant range* of the current production volume. The **relevant range of operations** is the normal operating range for a business. For Rydell, a football manufacturer, this is one production shift, which can produce up to 1,800 units per month. However, if production volume greatly increases such as with the addition of another shift, more supervisors must be hired. This means that total cost for supervisor salaries steps up by a lump sum.

**Graphing Step-Wise Costs**   Step-wise behavior is graphed in Exhibit 5.2. For Rydell, each shift can produce up to 1,800 units, and requires one supervisor at a salary of $10,000 per month. Each added shift can produce up to 1,800 units and requires additional supervisor help at $10,000 per month. See how the step-wise cost line is flat within each relevant range.

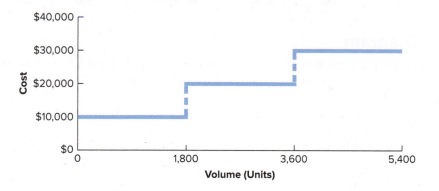

**EXHIBIT 5.2**

Step-wise Costs

**Examples of Costs**   Exhibit 5.3 lists examples of fixed, variable, mixed, and step-wise costs for a manufacturer of footballs.

| Fixed Costs | Variable Costs | Mixed Costs | Step-wise Costs |
|---|---|---|---|
| • Rent | • Direct materials | • Sales rep (salary plus commission) | • Add or drop a shift of workers |
| • Property taxes | • Direct labor | • Natural gas | • Add or drop a production line |
| • Insurance | • Packaging | • Maintenance | • Add or drop a warehouse |
| • Office salaries | • Shipping | • Electricity | • Add or drop a sales region |
| • Depreciation* | • Indirect materials | • Water | |

*Except for units-of-production.

**EXHIBIT 5.3**

Cost Examples

Determine whether each of the following is best described as a fixed, variable, mixed, or step-wise cost as the number of product units changes.

**a.** Rubber used to manufacture tennis balls
**b.** Depreciation (straight-line method)
**c.** Salesperson pay
**d.** Supervisory salaries—an additional supervisor is added as another shift is added
**e.** Packaging materials

***Solution***

**a.** Variable   **b.** Fixed   **c.** Mixed   **d.** Step-wise   **e.** Variable

# MEASURING COST BEHAVIOR

**P1**

Estimate costs using the scatter diagram, high-low method, and regression.

Cost-volume-profit analysis identifies and measures costs using their fixed and variable components. Managers do this by collecting cost data at various levels of activity. We then identify and measure the fixed and variable cost components. Three methods are commonly used to estimate fixed and variable costs.

- **Scatter Diagram**
- **High-Low Method**
- **Regression**

Each method is explained using the unit and cost data shown in Exhibit 5.4, which are from a start-up company that uses units produced as the activity base in estimating cost behavior.

**EXHIBIT 5.4**

Data for Estimating Cost Behavior

| Month | Units Produced | Total Cost | Month | Units Produced | Total Cost |
|---|---|---|---|---|---|
| January . . . | 27,500 | $21,500 | July . . . . . . . | 30,000 | $23,500 |
| February . . | 22,500 | 20,500 | August . . . . . | 52,500 | 28,500 |
| March . . . . | 25,000 | 25,000 | September . | 37,500 | 26,000 |
| April . . . . . . | 35,000 | 21,500 | October . . . . | 62,500 | 29,000 |
| May . . . . . . | 47,500 | 25,500 | November . . | 67,500 | 31,000 |
| June . . . . . . | 17,500 | 18,500 | December . . | 57,500 | 26,000 |

## Scatter Diagram

A **scatter diagram** is a graph of unit volume and cost data. In Exhibit 5.5, each point reflects total costs and units produced during each of the last 12 months. For example, March shows units produced of 25,000 and costs of $25,000.

The **estimated line of cost behavior** is drawn on a scatter diagram to show the relation between cost and unit volume. This line best visually "fits" the points in a scatter diagram. Fitting this line is sometimes done with spreadsheet software. The line in Exhibit 5.5 shows a

**EXHIBIT 5.5**

Scatter Diagram

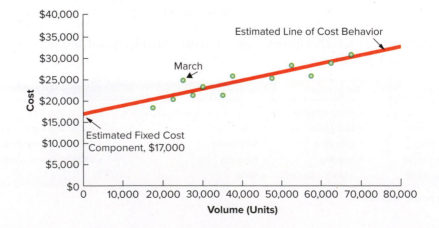

mixed cost. The total cost is greater than zero even when no units are produced, and it increases in proportion to increases in units produced. We discuss two approaches to estimating the fixed and variable cost components of this mixed cost.

## High-Low Method

The **high-low method** uses just two points to estimate the cost equation: the highest and lowest *volume* levels. The high-low method follows three steps.

**Step 1:** Identify the highest and lowest volume; these might not be the highest or lowest *costs*.

**Step 2:** Compute the slope (variable cost per unit) using the high and low volume.

**Step 3:** Compute total fixed costs by computing total variable cost at either the high or low volume, and then subtracting that amount from the total cost at that volume.

### High-Low Method Example

**Step 1:** In Exhibit 5.4, the lowest number of units produced is 17,500 and the highest is 67,500. The costs corresponding to these unit volumes are $18,500 and $31,000.

**Step 2:** The variable cost per unit is calculated as: change in cost divided by change in units. Using data from the highest and lowest unit volumes, this results in a *slope,* or estimated variable cost per unit of $0.25, as computed in Exhibit 5.6.

**EXHIBIT 5.6**

Variable Cost per Unit—High-Low Method

$$\frac{\text{Variable cost}}{\text{per unit}} = \frac{\text{Cost at highest volume} - \text{Cost at lowest volume}}{\text{Highest volume} - \text{Lowest volume}} = \frac{\$31{,}000 - \$18{,}500}{67{,}500 - 17{,}500} = \frac{\$12{,}500}{50{,}000} = \$0.25 \text{ per unit}$$

**Step 3:** To estimate fixed cost for the high-low method, we know that total cost equals fixed cost plus variable cost per unit times the number of units. Then we pick either the highest or lowest volume to compute fixed cost. This is shown in Exhibit 5.7—where we use either the highest volume (67,500 units) or the lowest volume (17,500 units) in determining the fixed cost of $14,125. The cost equation from the high-low method is **$14,125 + ($0.25 × Units produced).**

**EXHIBIT 5.7**

Determining Fixed Costs—High-Low Method

**Using data at highest volume**

| |
|---|
| **Total cost = Fixed cost + (Variable cost per unit × Units)** |
| $31,000 = Fixed cost + ($0.25 per unit × 67,500 units) |
| $31,000 = Fixed cost + $16,875 |
| $14,125 = Fixed cost |

**Using data at lowest volume**

| |
|---|
| **Total cost = Fixed cost + (Variable cost per unit × Units)** |
| $18,500 = Fixed cost + ($0.25 per unit × 17,500 units) |
| $18,500 = Fixed cost + $4,375 |
| $14,125 = Fixed cost |

## Regression

**Least-squares regression,** or simply *regression,* is a statistical method for identifying cost behavior. Excel has functions to determine the fixed cost (= Intercept) and the variable cost (= slope) components of a 'best fit' line for the cost data. This is shown in Appendix 5A. Using regression, the cost equation for the data in Exhibit 5.4 is **$16,688 + ($0.20 × Units produced).** This means the fixed cost is estimated as $16,688 and the variable cost at $0.20 per unit.

## Comparing Cost Estimation Methods

Different cost estimation methods usually result in different estimates of fixed and variable costs, as summarized in Exhibit 5.8. Regression uses more data and therefore should be more accurate than the high-low method. However, the high-low method is easier to apply and often useful for quick cost estimates.

**EXHIBIT 5.8**

Comparison of Cost Estimation Methods

| Estimation Method | Fixed Cost | Variable Cost |
|---|---|---|
| High-low ......... | $14,125 | $0.25 per unit |
| Regression ....... | 16,688 | 0.20 per unit |

**NEED-TO-KNOW** 5-2

High-Low Method

**P1**

Using the information below, apply the high-low method to determine the *cost equation* (total fixed costs plus variable costs per unit).

| Period | Units Produced | Total Costs |
|--------|---------------|-------------|
| 1........ | 2,400 | $11,800 |
| 2........ | 1,600 | 9,800 |
| 3........ | 3,200 | 15,200 |
| 4........ | 4,000 | 17,000 |

**Solution**

*Step 1:* Lowest number of units produced is 1,600 and the highest is 4,000. Costs at these volume levels are $9,800 and $17,000.

*Step 2:* Compute variable cost per unit.

$$\frac{\text{Cost at highest volume} - \text{Cost at lowest volume}}{\text{Highest volume} - \text{Lowest volume}} = \frac{\$17,000 - \$9,800}{4,000 - 1,600} = \frac{\$7,200}{2,400} = \$3 \text{ per unit}$$

Do More: QS 5-4, E 5-5

*Step 3:* Fixed costs are computed in one of two ways.

Using data at lowest volume:
Total cost = Fixed cost + (Variable cost per unit × Units)
$9,800 = Fixed cost + ($3 per unit × 1,600 units)
$9,800 = Fixed cost + $4,800
$5,000 = Fixed cost

Using data at highest volume:
Total cost = Fixed cost + (Variable cost per unit × Units)
$17,000 = Fixed cost + ($3 per unit × 4,000 units)
$17,000 = Fixed cost + $12,000
$ 5,000 = Fixed cost

# CONTRIBUTION MARGIN AND BREAK-EVEN ANALYSIS

## Contribution Margin

**A1**

Compute the contribution margin and describe what it reveals about a company's cost structure.

After classifying costs as fixed or variable, we can compute **contribution margin.**

**Contribution margin = Sales − Variable costs**

Contribution margin goes to cover fixed costs, and any excess is income. Managers use contribution margin and contribution margin per unit for many key managerial decisions.

**Contribution margin per unit** is the amount by which a product's unit selling price exceeds its variable costs per unit. Exhibit 5.9 shows the formula for contribution margin per unit.

**EXHIBIT 5.9**

Contribution Margin per Unit

$$\text{Contribution margin per unit} = \text{Selling price per unit} - \text{Variable costs per unit}$$

**Contribution margin ratio** is the percent of each sales dollar that remains after deducting the unit variable cost. Exhibit 5.10 shows the formula for contribution margin ratio.

**EXHIBIT 5.10**

Contribution Margin Ratio

$$\text{Contribution margin ratio} = \frac{\text{Contribution margin per unit}}{\text{Selling price per unit}} \text{ or } \frac{\text{Contribution margin}}{\text{Sales}}$$

As an example, Rydell sells footballs for $100 each and has variable costs of $70 per football. Its fixed costs are $24,000 per month with monthly capacity of 1,800 units (footballs). Rydell's contribution margin per unit is $30, and its contribution ratio is 30%, computed as follows.

| | | | |
|---|---|---|---|
| Selling price per unit......... | $100 | | |
| Variable costs per unit ........ | 70 | | |
| Contribution margin per unit ... | $ 30 | Contribution margin ratio ($30/$100) ... | 30% |

At a selling price of $100 per football, Rydell covers its per unit variable costs and makes $30 per unit to contribute to fixed costs and profit. Its contribution margin ratio is 30%, computed as $30/$100. A contribution margin ratio of 30% means that for each $1 in sales, we get 30 cents to cover fixed costs and produce income.

## Break-Even Point

The **break-even point**, or *break-even sales,* is the sales level at which total sales equal total costs, resulting in zero income. The break-even point can be stated in either units or dollars of sales. To illustrate, Rydell sells footballs for $100 per unit and has $70 of variable costs per football sold. Its fixed costs are $24,000 per month. We show three different methods to find the break-even point.

- **Formula method**
- **Contribution margin income statement**
- **Cost-volume-profit chart**

**P2**

Compute the break-even point for a single-product company.

**Formula Method**   We compute the break-even point (in units) using the formula in Exhibit 5.11. This formula uses the contribution margin per unit, which for Rydell is $30 ($100 − $70). The break-even sales in units follows.

$$\text{Break-even point in units} = \frac{\text{Fixed costs}}{\text{Contribution margin per unit}} = \frac{\$24,000}{\$30} = 800 \text{ units}$$

**EXHIBIT 5.11**

Break-Even Point in Units

If Rydell sells 800 units this month, its income will be zero. Income increases or decreases by $30 for each unit sold above or below 800 units. For example, if Rydell sells 801 units, income equals $30. If Rydell sells 802 units, income equals $60 (2 × $30).

We can calculate the break-even point in dollars. This uses the contribution margin ratio (30%, or 0.30) to determine the required sales dollars to break even. Exhibit 5.12 shows the formula and Rydell's break-even point in dollars.

$$\text{Break-even point in dollars} = \frac{\text{Fixed costs}}{\text{Contribution margin ratio}} = \frac{\$24,000}{30\% \text{ or } 0.30} = \$80,000 \text{ sales}$$

**EXHIBIT 5.12**

Break-Even Point in Dollars

**Contribution Margin Income Statement Method**   The left side of Exhibit 5.13 shows the format of a *contribution margin income statement*. It is an important tool for internal decision making, but it is not a replacement for a traditional income statement for external reporting. A contribution margin income statement separately classifies costs as variable or fixed, and it reports contribution margin.

| Contribution Margin Income Statement Format | Contribution Margin Income Statement (at Break-Even) For Month Ended January 31 | |
|---|---|---|
| Sales | Sales (800 units at $100 each) . . . . . . . . . . . . . . | $80,000 |
| − Variable costs | Variable costs (800 units at $70 each) . . . . . . . . . | 56,000 |
| Contribution margin | **Contribution margin (800 units at $30 each)** . . . | 24,000 |
| − Fixed costs | Fixed costs . . . . . . . . . . . . . . . . . . . . . . . . . . . . | 24,000 |
| Income | **Income** . . . . . . . . . . . . . . . . . . . . . . . . . . . . . . | $   0 |

**EXHIBIT 5.13**

Contribution Margin Income Statement

**Point:** At break-even, income=$0.

The right side of Exhibit 5.13 shows the contribution margin income statement at the break-even point for Rydell. We set income to zero and set contribution margin equal to fixed costs ($24,000). For Rydell's contribution margin to equal $24,000, it must sell 800 units ($24,000/$30). The resulting contribution margin income statement shows that sales of $80,000, or 800 units, is needed to cover the variable ($56,000) and fixed ($24,000) costs.

Dmitry Kalinovsky/Shutterstock

■ **Decision Maker**

**Sales Manager**    You can accept only one of two customer orders due to limited capacity. The first order is for 100 units with a contribution margin of $600 per unit. The second order is for 500 units with a contribution margin of $160 per unit. Which order do you accept? ■ *Answer:* Total contribution margin is $60,000 ($600 per unit × 100 units) or $80,000 ($160 per unit × 500 units) for the two orders. The second order provides the larger contribution margin and is the order you would accept. Another factor to consider is the potential for a long-term relationship with these customers, including repeat sales and growth.

**Cost-Volume-Profit Chart**    A third way to find the break-even point is to use a **cost-volume-profit (CVP) chart** (*break-even chart*). Exhibit 5.14 shows Rydell's CVP chart. Two key lines in the chart show sales and costs at different output levels.

① **Total costs.** This line starts at the $24,000 fixed costs level on the vertical axis. The slope of this line is the $70 variable cost per unit. This line ends at Rydell's capacity level of 1,800 units. Total costs at that point are $150,000: $24,000 fixed costs + ($70 per unit variable costs × 1,800 units).

② **Total sales.** This line starts at zero on the vertical axis (zero units and zero dollars of sales). The slope of this line equals the $100 selling price per unit. This line ends at Rydell's maximum capacity level of 1,800 units. Total sales at that point are $180,000: $100 sales price per unit × 1,800 units.

**EXHIBIT 5.14**

Cost-Volume-Profit Chart

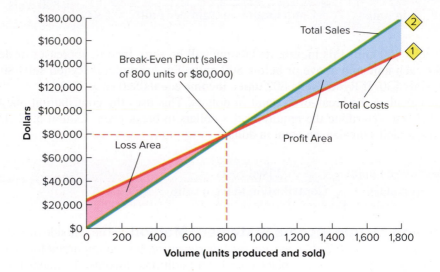

The CVP chart provides some key observations.

- **Break-even point,** where the total cost line and total sales line intersect—at 800 units, or $80,000.
- **Income or loss,** measured as the vertical distance between the sales line and the total cost line at any level of units sold (a loss is to the left of the break-even point; a profit is to the right). As the number of units sold increases, the loss area decreases or the profit area increases.
- **Maximum productive capacity,** which is 1,800 units (the largest unit number on the CVP chart). At this point, we expect sales of $180,000 and its largest income of $30,000.

## Changes in Estimates

CVP analysis uses past data for estimates of the future to make managerial decisions. We can change those estimates if we believe another set of estimates is more likely to occur or if we wish to see how sensitive the results are to a change in estimates. Exhibit 5.15 shows two different sets of estimates, most likely estimates and pessimistic estimates, and how they impact break-even points.

| | Selling Price per Unit | Variable Cost per Unit | Contribution Margin per Unit | Total Fixed Costs | Break-Even in Units |
|---|---|---|---|---|---|
| Most likely.... | $100 | $70 | $30 | $24,000 | 800 |
| Pessimistic ... | 96 | 72 | 24 | 27,000 | 1,125 |

**EXHIBIT 5.15**

Alternative Estimates for Break-Even Analysis

Using the pessimistic estimates, the contribution margin per unit is $24 ($96 − $72), and the revised break-even in units is in Exhibit 5.16.

$$\text{Revised break-even point in units} = \frac{\$27,000}{\$24} = 1,125 \text{ units}$$

**EXHIBIT 5.16**

Revised Break-Even in Units

Exhibit 5.17 summarizes the effects of changes in CVP inputs on break-even. If the sales price per unit increases, then break-even decreases. If the sales price per unit decreases, then break-even increases. If either variable cost per unit or total fixed cost increases, then break-even increases. If either variable cost per unit or total fixed cost decreases, then break-even decreases.

**EXHIBIT 5.17**

Break-Even for Alternative CVP Inputs

| Sales Price per Unit | Break-Even |
|---|---|
| Increases | Decreases |
| Decreases | Increases |

| Variable Cost per Unit | Break-Even |
|---|---|
| Increases | Increases |
| Decreases | Decreases |

| Fixed Costs in Total | Break-Even |
|---|---|
| Increases | Increases |
| Decreases | Decreases |

 **Decision Ethics**

**Supervisor** Your team is conducting a CVP analysis for a new product. Different sales projections have different incomes. One member suggests picking numbers yielding favorable income because any estimate is "as good as any other." Another member suggests dropping unfavorable data points for cost estimation. What do you do? ■ *Answer:* Your dilemma is whether to go along with the suggestions to "adjust" the numbers to make the project look like it will achieve sufficient profits. You should not follow these suggestions. People will be affected negatively if you adjust the numbers and the project is unprofitable. Moreover, if it does fail, an investigation would likely reveal that data in the proposal were adjusted to make the project look good.

Kadmy/iStock/Getty Images

Hudson Co. has annual fixed costs of $400,000. Its one product sells for $170 per unit, and it has variable costs of $150 per unit.

1. Compute the contribution margin per unit.
2. Compute the break-even point (in units) using the formula method.
3. Prepare a contribution margin income statement at the break-even point.

**NEED-TO-KNOW 5-3**

Contribution Margin and Break-Even Point

**A1    P2**

*Solution*

1. Contribution margin per unit
   = $170 − $150 = $20

2. Break-even point
   = $400,000/$20 = 20,000 units

3.

| Contribution Margin Income Statement (at Break-Even) For Year Ended December 31 | |
|---|---|
| Sales (20,000 units at $170 each)............. | $3,400,000 |
| Variable costs (20,000 units at $150 each) .... | 3,000,000 |
| Contribution margin (20,000 units at $20 each) .. | 400,000 |
| Fixed costs ............................. | 400,000 |
| Income................................. | $        0 |

Do More: QS 5-6, QS 5-8, QS 5-9, QS 5-10, E 5-7, E 5-9, E 5-11

# APPLYING COST-VOLUME-PROFIT ANALYSIS

Cost-volume-profit analysis is useful in evaluating the effects of different business strategies.

**C2**
_____

Describe several applications of cost-volume-profit analysis.

## Margin of Safety

All companies want to do better than break-even. A company's **margin of safety** follows.

$$\textbf{Margin of safety = Expected (or actual) sales} - \textbf{Break-even sales}$$

Margin of safety is the amount that sales can decline before the company incurs a loss. Margin of safety is expressed in dollars or as a percent of expected sales.

To demonstrate, Rydell's break-even point in dollars is $80,000. If its expected sales are $100,000, the margin of safety is $20,000 ($100,000 − $80,000). As a percent, the margin of safety is 20% of expected sales, as shown in Exhibit 5.18. Management decides whether the margin of safety is adequate given factors such as sales variability, competition, consumer tastes, and economic conditions.

**EXHIBIT 5.18**

Margin of Safety (in Percent)

$$\frac{\textbf{Margin of safety}}{\textbf{(in percent)}} = \frac{\textbf{Expected sales} - \textbf{Break-even sales}}{\textbf{Expected sales}} = \frac{\$100,000 - \$80,000}{\$100,000} = 20\%$$

## Computing Income from Expected Sales and Costs

Managers can use contribution margin income statements to forecast future sales and income. To demonstrate, assume Rydell's management expects to sell 1,500 units in January. What is the expected income if this sales level is achieved? We compute Rydell's expected income in Exhibit 5.19.

**Point:** 1,500 units of sales is 700 units above Rydell's break-even. Income can be computed as 700 units × $30 contribution per unit.

**EXHIBIT 5.19**

Computing Expected Income from Expected Sales

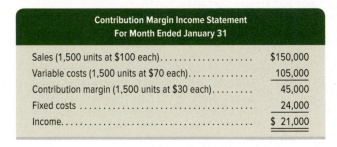

| Contribution Margin Income Statement<br>For Month Ended January 31 | |
|---|---:|
| Sales (1,500 units at $100 each)..................... | $150,000 |
| Variable costs (1,500 units at $70 each)............. | 105,000 |
| Contribution margin (1,500 units at $30 each)......... | 45,000 |
| Fixed costs ..................................... | 24,000 |
| Income........................................ | $ 21,000 |

"How many units must we sell to earn $12,000?"

## Computing Sales for a Target Income

Evaluating target income is a key application of CVP analysis. CVP analysis helps to determine the sales level needed to achieve the target income.

To demonstrate, Rydell has monthly fixed costs of $24,000 and a 30% (0.30) contribution margin ratio. Assume it sets a target income of $12,000. Using the formula in Exhibit 5.20, Rydell needs $120,000 of sales to get a $12,000 target income.

**EXHIBIT 5.20**

Computing Sales (Dollars) for a Target Income

$$\frac{\textbf{Dollar sales at}}{\textbf{target income}} = \frac{\textbf{Fixed costs} + \textbf{Target income}}{\textbf{Contribution margin ratio}} = \frac{\$24,000 + \$12,000}{30\% \text{ or } 0.30} = \$120,000$$

Alternatively, we can compute _unit sales_ needed to achieve a target income. To do this, use _contribution margin per unit_. Exhibit 5.21 shows this for Rydell.

**EXHIBIT 5.21**

Computing Sales (Units) for a Target Income

$$\frac{\textbf{Unit sales at}}{\textbf{target income}} = \frac{\textbf{Fixed costs} + \textbf{Target income}}{\textbf{Contribution margin per unit}} = \frac{\$24,000 + \$12,000}{\$30} = 1{,}200 \text{ units}$$

We can use the contribution margin income statement approach to compute sales for a target income in two steps.

**Step 1: Calculate contribution margin at target income.** Working backwards, we begin at the bottom and insert the $24,000 fixed costs and the $12,000 target income, as shown in Exhibit 5.22. This means contribution margin is $36,000 ($24,000 + $12,000).

**Step 2: Calculate Sales.** Divide the $36,000 contribution margin by the 30% contribution margin ratio to solve for sales of $120,000, or 1,200 units at $100 each. This also means variable costs are 70% of sales, or $84,000.

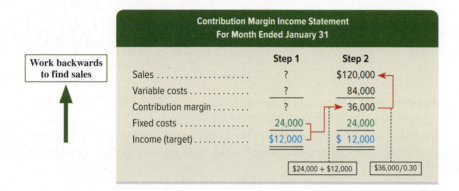

**EXHIBIT 5.22**

Using Contribution Margin Income Statement to Find Target Sales

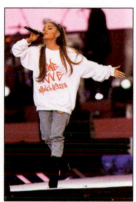

Dave Hogan/Getty Images

### Decision Insight

**Mic Drop**   Concert promotion is a risky and low-margin business. A recent **Ariana Grande** tour grossed over $100 million in ticket revenue. How much went to the promoters? After paying the costs of each venue (staff, electricity, security, insurance) and Ariana's share of ticket revenues, the promoters might have about $15 million to apply against their own costs. **Live Nation**, Ariana's promoters, recently posted a small profit after several successive years of not breaking even. ■

A manufacturer predicts fixed costs of $502,000. Its product sells for $180 per unit, and it incurs variable costs of $126 per unit. Its target income is $200,000.

**NEED-TO-KNOW 5-4**

Contribution Margin, Target Income, and Margin of Safety

**A1   C2**

1. Compute the contribution margin ratio.
2. Compute the dollar sales needed to achieve the target income.
3. Compute the unit sales needed to achieve the target income.
4. Break-even sales is 9,296 units. Compute the margin of safety (in dollars) if the company expects to sell 10,000 units.

**Solution**

1. Contribution margin ratio $= \dfrac{\$180 - \$126}{\$180} = 30\%$, or 0.30

2. Dollar sales at target income $= \dfrac{\$502,000 + \$200,000}{0.30} = \$2,340,000$

3. Unit sales at target income $= \dfrac{\$502,000 + \$200,000}{\$180 - \$126} = 13,000$ units

4. Margin of safety $= (10,000 \times \$180) - (9,296 \times \$180) = \$126,720$

Do More: QS 5-17, QS 5-18, QS 5-19, E 5-12, E 5-13

## Evaluating Business Strategies

We can use CVP to analyze the effects of alternative business strategies on break-even, income, and margin of safety. For example, we might want to know what happens to income if we automate a manual process or if we increase advertising. We provide two examples.

**Capital Expenditure—New Machinery**   Assume a new machine increases monthly fixed costs from $24,000 to $30,000 and decreases variable costs by $10 per unit (from $70 per unit to $60 per unit). Rydell's break-even point in dollars is currently $80,000. How would the new machine affect the break-even point in dollars? If Rydell maintains its selling price of $100 per unit, its contribution margin per unit increases to $40—computed as $100 per unit minus the (new) variable costs of $60 per unit. With this new machine, the revised contribution margin ratio per unit is 40% (computed as $40/$100). The revised break-even point in dollars is $75,000, as computed in Exhibit 5.23. The new machine would lower Rydell's break-even point by $5,000, or 50 units, per month.

**EXHIBIT 5.23**

Revised Break-Even

$$\text{Revised break-even point in dollars} = \frac{\text{Revised fixed costs}}{\text{Revised contribution margin ratio}} = \frac{\$30,000}{40\%} = \$75,000$$

**Spending—Advertising**   A manager proposes that an increase of $3,000 in monthly advertising will increase sales by $25,000 per month (at a selling price of $100 per unit). Fixed costs before the advertising increase are $24,000. The contribution margin ratio will continue to be 30%. With the advertising increase, the revised break-even point in dollars is $90,000, as computed in Exhibit 5.24.

**EXHIBIT 5.24**

Revised Break-Even

$$\text{Revised break-even point in dollars} = \frac{\text{Revised fixed costs}}{\text{Contribution margin ratio}} = \frac{\$27,000}{30\%} = \$90,000$$

Exhibit 5.18 showed Rydell's margin of safety was 20% when expected sales was $100,000. Rydell expects sales of $125,000 ($100,000 + $25,000) after the advertising increase. The revised margin of safety is computed in Exhibit 5.25. The advertising campaign would increase its margin of safety from 20% to 28%.

**EXHIBIT 5.25**

Revised Margin of Safety

$$\text{Revised margin of safety (in percent)} = \frac{\text{Expected sales} - \text{Break-even sales}}{\text{Expected sales}} = \frac{\$125,000 - \$90,000}{\$125,000} = 28\%$$

## Sales Mix and Break-Even

**P3**

Compute the break-even point for a multiproduct company.

For companies that sell more than one type of product, **sales mix** is the proportion of sales volume for each product. For example, if a company normally sells 1,200 footballs and 800 basketballs each period (2,000 units total), its sales mix is 60% footballs (1,200/2,000) and 40% basketballs (800/2,000). This sales mix is expressed as 6:4.

When a mix of products is sold, break-even can be computed with a **weighted-average contribution margin per unit.** This measure combines the per unit contribution margins of each product by their weights in the sales mix. To demonstrate, assume Rydell expands its product line to include basketballs. It adds another production shift, increasing its fixed costs to $48,000. Information for the two products is in Exhibit 5.26.

**EXHIBIT 5.26**

Sales Mix Data

| | Footballs | Basketballs |
|---|---|---|
| Sales price per unit. . . . . . . . . . | $100 | $120 |
| Variable costs per unit . . . . . . . . | 70 | 85 |
| Contribution margin per unit . . . | $ 30 | $ 35 |
| Sales mix percent . . . . . . . . . . . | 60% | 40% |

Using the data in Exhibit 5.26, the weighted-average contribution margin is computed in Exhibit 5.27

$$\begin{array}{c}\textbf{Weighted-average}\\ \textbf{contribution margin} =\\ \textbf{per unit}\end{array}\begin{array}{c}\textbf{Contribution}\\ \textbf{margin per unit} \times\\ \textbf{for each product}\end{array}\begin{array}{c}\textbf{Sales mix}\\ \textbf{percent for}\\ \textbf{each product}\end{array} = (\$30 \times 60\%) + (\$35 \times 40\%)\\ = \$32 \text{ per unit}$$

**EXHIBIT 5.27**

Weighted-Average Contribution Margin per Unit

The break-even point in unit sales is computed with the formula from Exhibit 5.11, but using the weighted-average contribution margin per unit, as shown in Exhibit 5.28.

$$\begin{array}{c}\textbf{Break-even point}\\ \textbf{in units}\end{array} = \frac{\textbf{Fixed costs}}{\textbf{Weighted-average contribution margin per unit}} = \frac{\$48,000}{\$32} = 1,500 \text{ units}$$

**EXHIBIT 5.28**

Weighted-Average Break-Even in Units

The number of units of each product type is then computed by multiplying the break-even point in units (1,500) by the sales mix percent, as shown in the second column of Exhibit 5.29. The right three columns compute contribution margin at break-even. We multiply unit sales by the contribution margin per unit to get contribution margin for each product. The $48,000 total contribution margin exactly equals the $48,000 fixed costs, resulting in zero income at break-even.

| Product | Break-Even Units × Sales Mix | Unit Sales | Contribution Margin per Unit | Contribution Margin |
|---|---|---|---|---|
| Footballs....... | 1,500 × 60% | 900 | $30 | $27,000 |
| Basketballs..... | 1,500 × 40% | 600 | 35 | 21,000 |
| Total.......... | | 1,500 | | $48,000 |

**EXHIBIT 5.29**

Unit Sales by Product Type at Break-Even

■ **Analytics Insight**

**For Our Eyes Only**   Retail businesses use big data to understand shopping behavior and attract new customers. **Amazon**'s "recommendation engine" tailors recommendations based on customers' browsing and buying habits. A consulting firm estimates that 35% of Amazon's revenue is generated from its recommendations. ■

A manufacturer of two models of soccer balls, Practice and Pro, shows the information below. The company has annual fixed costs of $700,000.

**NEED-TO-KNOW 5-5**

Contribution Margin and Break-Even Point for Two Products

**P3**

| | Practice | Pro |
|---|---|---|
| Sales price per unit........ | $20 | $60 |
| Variable costs per unit..... | 10 | 20 |
| Sales mix percent......... | 75% | 25% |

1. What is the weighted-average contribution margin per unit?

2. What is the break-even point in units?

3. How many units of each model is sold at the break-even point?

*Solution*

Do More: QS 5-21, E 5-22, E 5-23

1. Weighted-average contribution margin per unit = ($10 × 75%) + ($40 × 25%) = $17.50

2. Break-even point in units = $\frac{\$700,000}{\$17.50}$ = 40,000 units

3. Unit sales of each model at break-even point (table at right).

| Model | Break-Even Units × Sales Mix | Unit Sales |
|---|---|---|
| Practice ... | 40,000 × 75% = | 30,000 |
| Pro....... | 40,000 × 25% = | 10,000 |

## Assumptions in Cost-Volume-Profit Analysis

CVP analysis relies on several assumptions:

- Costs can be classified as variable or fixed.
- Costs are linear within the relevant range.
- Units produced are sold (inventory is constant).
- Sales mix is constant.

If costs and sales differ from these assumptions, the results of CVP analysis can be less useful. Managers understand that CVP analysis gives approximate answers to questions and enables them to make rough estimates about the future.

# CORPORATE SOCIAL RESPONSIBILITY

Manufacturers try to increase the sustainability of their materials and packaging. **Nike** recently reengineered its shoeboxes to use 30% less material. These lighter shoeboxes can be shipped in cartons that are 20% lighter. Nike also now uses recycled polyester in much of its clothing. The company estimates it has reused the equivalent of over 2 billion plastic bottles in recent years.

These and other sustainability initiatives impact both variable and fixed costs and CVP analysis. Consider Rydell, the football manufacturer illustrated in this chapter. Rydell expects to sell 1,500 footballs per month, at a price of $100 per unit. Variable costs are $70 per unit and monthly fixed costs are $24,000. Rydell is considering using recycled materials. This would add $1,160 in fixed costs per month and reduce variable costs by $4 per unit. Management wants to know the impact for break-even point, margin of safety, and forecasted income. Analysis is in Exhibit 5.30.

| Before Initiative | |
|---|---|
| Break-even | 800 units |
| Margin of safety | 20% |
| Forecasted income | $21,000 |

**EXHIBIT 5.30**

Revised Break-Even, Margin of Safety, and Income

$$\text{Revised break-even point in units} = \frac{\text{Revised fixed costs}}{\text{Revised contribution margin}} = \frac{\$25,160}{\$34} = 740 \text{ units}$$

$$\text{Revised margin of safety} = \frac{\text{Expected sales} - \text{Break-even sales}}{\text{Expected sales}} = \frac{\$150,000 - \$74,000}{\$150,000} = 50.7\%$$

$$\text{Revised forecasted income} = (\text{Units sold} \times \text{Contribution margin per unit}) - \text{Fixed costs}$$
$$= (1,500 \times \$34) - \$25,160 = \$25,840$$

SmartSweets

Tara Bosch, founder of this chapter's feature company, **SmartSweets**, is on a mission for people to "kick sugar and keep candy." SmartSweet customers "kick" out over 1 billion grams of sugar per year.

---

**Decision Analysis**  **Degree of Operating Leverage**

## A2

Analyze changes in sales using the degree of operating leverage.

CVP analysis is especially useful when management wishes to predict income from alternative strategies. These strategies can involve changes in selling prices, fixed costs, variable costs, sales volume, and product mix. Managers are interested in seeing the effects of changes in some or all of these factors. *Contribution margin per unit* is one way to predict income effects; for every additional unit sold, income increases by contribution margin per unit.

A useful measure to assess the effect of changes in the level of sales on income is the **degree of operating leverage (DOL),** as shown in Exhibit 5.31.

**EXHIBIT 5.31**

Degree of Operating Leverage

$$\text{Degree of operating leverage} = \frac{\text{Contribution margin}}{\text{Income}}$$

To demonstrate, assume Rydell Company sells 1,200 footballs. At this sales level, its contribution margin and income are computed as

| Rydell Company | |
|---|---:|
| Sales (1,200 × $100)........... | $120,000 |
| Variable costs (1,200 × $70).... | 84,000 |
| **Contribution margin**.......... | **36,000** |
| Fixed costs ................. | 24,000 |
| **Income** ..................... | **$ 12,000** |

Rydell's degree of operating leverage (DOL) is computed in Exhibit 5.32.

$$\text{Degree of operating leverage} = \frac{\text{Contribution margin}}{\text{Income}} = \frac{\$36,000}{\$12,000} = 3.0$$

**EXHIBIT 5.32**

Rydell's Degree of Operating Leverage

We then use DOL to predict the change in income from a change in sales. For example, if Rydell expects sales to either increase or decrease by 10%, and these changes are within Rydell's relevant range, we can compute the change in income using DOL in Exhibit 5.33.

$$\textbf{Change in income (\%) = DOL} \times \textbf{Change in sales (\%)}$$
$$= 3.0 \times 10\% = 30\%$$

**EXHIBIT 5.33**

Impact of Change in Sales on Income

If Rydell's sales *increase* by 10%, its income will increase by $3,600 (computed as $12,000 × 30%), to $15,600. If, instead, Rydell's sales decrease by 10%, its income will decrease by $3,600, to $8,400. We can prove these results with contribution margin income statements, as shown below. Companies with a higher degree of operating leverage have larger income effects from changes in unit sales. For example, a company with DOL of 3 will expect a larger income increase from a 10% change in sales than would a company with a DOL of 2.

| | Current | Sales Increase by 10% | Sales Decrease by 10% |
|---|---:|---:|---:|
| Sales.................. | $120,000 | $132,000 | $108,000 |
| Variable costs ........... | 84,000 | 92,400 | 75,600 |
| Contribution margin ...... | 36,000 | 39,600 | 32,400 |
| Fixed costs............. | 24,000 | 24,000 | 24,000 |
| Income................ | $ 12,000 | $ 15,600 | $ 8,400 |

Sport Caps manufactures and sells caps. Fixed costs are $150,000 per month, and variable costs are $5 per cap. The caps are sold for $8 each. Production capacity is 100,000 caps per month.

**NEED-TO-KNOW 5-6**

**COMPREHENSIVE**

Break-Even and Sales for Target Income

**Required**

1. Compute the following.
   a. Contribution margin per cap.
   b. Break-even point in number of caps sold.
   c. Income at 30,000 caps sold.
   d. Income at 85,000 caps sold.
   e. Number of caps sold to get $60,000 of income.
2. Compute the following.
   a. Contribution margin ratio.
   b. Break-even point in sales dollars.
   c. Income at $250,000 of sales.
   d. Income at $600,000 of sales.
   e. Dollars of sales to achieve $60,000 of income.

## SOLUTION

**1. a.** Contribution margin per cap = Selling price per unit − Variable cost per unit
= $8 − $5 = $3

**b.** Break-even point in caps $= \dfrac{\text{Fixed costs}}{\text{Contribution margin per cap}} = \dfrac{\$150,000}{\$3} = 50,000 \text{ caps}$

**c.** Income at 30,000 caps sold = (Units × Contribution margin per unit) − Fixed costs

= (30,000 × $3) − $150,000 = $(60,000) loss

**d.** Income at 85,000 caps sold = (Units × Contribution margin per unit) − Fixed costs

= (85,000 × $3) − $150,000 = $105,000 profit

**e.** Unit sales for $60,000 income $= \dfrac{\text{Fixed costs} + \text{Target income}}{\text{Contribution margin per cap}}$

$= \dfrac{\$150,000 + \$60,000}{\$3} = \underline{70,000 \text{ caps}}$

**2. a.** Contribution margin ratio $= \dfrac{\text{Contribution margin per unit}}{\text{Selling price per unit}} = \dfrac{\$3}{\$8} = \underline{0.375 \text{ or } 37.5\%}$

**b.** Break-even point in dollars $= \dfrac{\text{Fixed costs}}{\text{Contribution margin ratio}} = \dfrac{\$150,000}{37.5\%} = \underline{\$400,000}$

**c.** Income at sales of $250,000 = (Sales × Contribution margin ratio) − Fixed costs

= ($250,000 × 37.5%) − $150,000 = $(56,250) loss

**d.** Income at sales of $600,000 = (Sales × Contribution margin ratio) − Fixed costs

= ($600,000 × 37.5%) − $150,000 = $75,000 income

**e.** Dollars of sales to achieve $60,000 income $= \dfrac{\text{Fixed costs} + \text{Target income}}{\text{Contribution margin ratio}}$

$= \dfrac{\$150,000 + \$60,000}{37.5\%} = \underline{\$560,000}$

---

**APPENDIX**

# 5A    Using Excel for Cost Estimation

Microsoft Excel® and other spreadsheet software can be used to perform least-squares regressions to identify cost behavior. In Excel, the INTERCEPT and SLOPE functions are used. The following screen shot reports the data from Exhibit 5.4 in cells A1 through C13 and shows the cell contents to find the intercept (cell B15) and slope (cell B16). Cell B15 uses Excel to find the intercept from a least-squares regression of total cost (shown as C2:C13 in cell B15) on units produced (shown as B2:B13 in cell B15). Spreadsheet software is useful in understanding cost behavior when many data points (such as monthly total costs and units produced) are available.

Excel can also be used to create scatter diagrams such as that in Exhibit 5.5. To draw a scatter diagram with a line of fit, follow these steps:

1. Highlight the data cells we wish to diagram; in this example, start from cell C13 and highlight through cell B2.

2. Then select "Insert" and "Scatter" (X,Y) from the drop-down menus. Selecting the chart type in the upper left corner of the choices under "Scatter" will produce a diagram that looks like that in Exhibit 5.5, without a line of fit.

3. To add a line of fit (also called a trend line), select "Design," "Add Chart Element," "Trendline," and "Linear" from the drop-down menus. This will produce a diagram that looks like that in Exhibit 5.5, including the line of fit but without the formatting.

4. To have the trend line intersect the y-axis, add one more row to the data for zero units produced (0) and the fixed cost from the Excel slope function ($16,688.24 in this example).

**Point:** The intercept function solves for total fixed costs. The slope function solves for the variable cost per unit.

| | A | B | C |
|---|---|---|---|
| 1 | **Month** | **Units Produced** | **Total Cost** |
| 2 | January | 27,500 | $21,500 |
| 3 | February | 22,500 | 20,500 |
| 4 | March | 25,000 | 25,000 |
| 5 | April | 35,000 | 21,500 |
| 6 | May | 47,500 | 25,500 |
| 7 | June | 17,500 | 18,500 |
| 8 | July | 30,000 | 23,500 |
| 9 | August | 52,500 | 28,500 |
| 10 | September | 37,500 | 26,000 |
| 11 | October | 62,500 | 29,000 |
| 12 | November | 67,500 | 31,000 |
| 13 | December | 57,500 | 26,000 |
| 14 | | | **Result** |
| 15 | **Intercept** | =INTERCEPT(C2:C13, B2:B13) | $16,688.24 |
| 16 | **Slope** | =SLOPE(C2:C13, B2:B13) | $   0.1995 |

# Variable Costing and Performance Reporting

# 5B

This chapter showed the usefulness of *contribution margin,* or selling price minus variable costs, in CVP analysis. The contribution margin income statement introduced in this chapter is also known as a **variable costing income statement.** In **variable costing,** only variable costs relating to production are included in product costs. These costs include direct materials, direct labor, and *variable* overhead costs. Thus, under variable costing, *fixed* overhead costs are excluded from product costs and instead are expensed in the period incurred. Variable costing can be useful in many managerial analyses and decisions.

**P4**

Compute unit cost and income under both absorption and variable costing.

   The variable costing method is not allowed, however, for external financial reporting. Instead, GAAP requires **absorption costing.** Under absorption costing, product costs include direct materials, direct labor, *and all overhead,* both variable and fixed. Thus, under absorption costing, fixed overhead costs are expensed when the goods are sold. Managers can still use variable costing information for internal decision making, but they must use absorption costing for external reporting purposes.

## Computing Unit Cost

To illustrate the difference between absorption costing and variable costing, let's consider the product cost data in Exhibit 5B.1 from IceAge, a skate manufacturer.

| | | | |
|---|---|---|---|
| Direct materials. . . . . . . . . . . . | $4 per unit | Variable overhead . . . . . . | $3 per unit |
| Direct labor . . . . . . . . . . . . . . . | $8 per unit | Fixed overhead . . . . . . . . | $600,000 per year |
| Expected units produced per year | 60,000 units | | |

**EXHIBIT 5B.1**

Summary Product Cost Data

Using the product cost data, Exhibit 5B.2 shows the product cost per unit for both absorption and variable costing.

   For absorption costing, the product cost per unit is $25, which consists of $4 in direct materials, $8 in direct labor, $3 in variable overhead and $10 in fixed overhead ($600,000/60,000 units).

   For variable costing, the product cost per unit is $15, which consists of $4 in direct materials, $8 in direct labor, and $3 in variable overhead. Fixed overhead costs of $600,000 are treated as a period cost and are recorded as expense in the period incurred. *The difference between the two costing methods is the exclusion of fixed overhead from product costs for variable costing.*

**EXHIBIT 5B.2**

Unit Cost Computation

| Product Cost per Unit | Absorption Costing | Variable Costing |
|---|---|---|
| Direct materials. . . . . . . . . . . | $ 4 | $ 4 |
| Direct labor . . . . . . . . . . . . . . | 8 | 8 |
| Overhead | | |
|    Variable overhead . . . . . . . | 3 | 3 |
|    **Fixed overhead** . . . . . . . . | **10** | — |
| Total product cost per unit . . . | $25 | $15 |

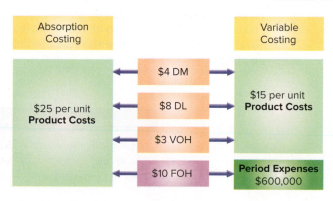

## Income Reporting

The prior section showed how different treatment of fixed overhead costs leads to different product costs per unit under absorption and variable costing. This section shows the effects for income reporting.

Let's return to IceAge Company. Below are the manufacturing cost data for IceAge as well as additional data on selling and administrative expenses. Assume that IceAge began the year with no units in inventory. During the year, IceAge produced 60,000 units and sold 40,000 units at $40 each, leaving 20,000 units in ending inventory.

Let's prepare income statements for IceAge both under absorption costing and under variable costing. Under variable costing, expenses are grouped according to cost behavior—variable or fixed, and production or nonproduction. Under absorption costing, expenses are grouped by function but not separated into variable and fixed components.

**Units Produced Exceed Units Sold**    Exhibit 5B.3 shows absorption costing and variable costing income statements. During the year, 60,000 units were produced, but only 40,000 units were sold, which means 20,000 units remain in ending inventory.

**EXHIBIT 5B.3**

Income under Absorption and Variable Costing

| ICEAGE COMPANY | |
|---|---|
| Income Statement (Absorption Costing) | |
| For Year Ended December 31 | |
| Sales (40,000 × $40) . . . . . . . . . . . . . . . . . | $1,600,000 |
| Cost of goods sold (40,000 × $25[†]) . . . . . . . | 1,000,000 |
| Gross profit . . . . . . . . . . . . . . . . . . . . . . . | 600,000 |
| Selling and administrative expenses | |
| [$200,000 + (40,000 × $2)] . . . . . . . . . | 280,000 |
| Income . . . . . . . . . . . . . . . . . . . . . . . . . | $  320,000 |

[†]$4 DM + $8 DL + $3 VOH + $10 FOH.
[‡]$4 DM + $8 DL + $3 VOH.

| ICEAGE COMPANY | | |
|---|---|---|
| Income Statement (Variable Costing) | | |
| For Year Ended December 31 | | |
| Sales (40,000 × $40) . . . . . . . . . . . . . . . . . . . . . . | | $1,600,000 |
| Variable expenses | | |
| Variable cost of goods sold (40,000 × $15[‡]) . . . | $600,000 | |
| Variable selling and | | |
| administrative expenses (40,000 × $2) . . . . . | 80,000 | 680,000 |
| Contribution margin . . . . . . . . . . . . . . . . . . . . . . . . | | 920,000 |
| Fixed expenses | | |
| Fixed overhead . . . . . . . . . . . . . . . . . . . . . . . . . | 600,000 | |
| Fixed selling and administrative expenses . . . . . | 200,000 | 800,000 |
| Income . . . . . . . . . . . . . . . . . . . . . . . . . . . . . . . | | $  120,000 |

Income is $320,000 under absorption costing. Under variable costing, income is $120,000. This $200,000 difference is due to the treatment of fixed overhead. Because the variable costing method expenses fixed overhead (FOH) as a period cost of $600,000, and the absorption costing method expenses FOH based on the number of units sold (40,000 × $10), income is lower under variable costing by $200,000 (20,000 units × $10).

When production exceeds sales by 20,000 units (60,000 versus 40,000), the $200,000 ($10 × 20,000 units) of fixed overhead cost allocated to these 20,000 units is included in the cost of ending inventory. This means that $200,000 of fixed overhead cost incurred in 2021 is not expensed until future years under absorption costing, when it is reported in cost of goods sold as those products are sold. Consequently, income for the current year under absorption costing is $200,000 higher than income under variable costing. Even though sales (of 40,000 units) and the number of units produced (totaling 60,000) are the same under both costing methods, income differs greatly due to the treatment of fixed overhead. We can generalize this result to link units produced and sold to income under absorption costing versus variable costing.

Toshifumi Kitamura/AFP/Getty Images

| Units produced are: | Income under absorption costing is: |
|---|---|
| Equal to units sold . . . . . . . . . | Equal to Income under variable costing |
| Greater than units sold . . . . . . | Greater than income under variable costing |
| Less than units sold . . . . . . . . | Less than income under variable costing |

**Converting Income under Variable Costing to Income under Absorption Costing**    In the current year, IceAge produced 20,000 more units than it sold. Those 20,000 units remaining in ending inventory will be sold in future years. When those units are sold, the $200,000 of fixed overhead costs attached to them will be expensed, resulting in lower income under the absorption costing method. This leads to a simple way to convert income under variable costing to income under absorption costing.

$$\text{Income under absorption costing} = \text{Income under variable costing} + \text{Fixed overhead cost in ending inventory*} - \text{Fixed overhead cost in beginning inventory*}$$

*Under absorption costing

For example, if IceAge produces 60,000 units and sells 80,000 units next year, it reports income under variable costing of $1,040,000. Income under absorption costing is then computed as

$$\text{Income under absorption costing} = \$1,040,000 + \$0 - \$200,000 = \$840,000$$

Differences in income between variable and absorption costing are summarized below.

**Current Year**

| Production | | Sales | | Income |
|---|---|---|---|---|
| 60,000 pairs | > | 40,000 pairs | | Absorption costing > Variable costing $320,000 > $120,000 |

**Next Year**

| Production | | Sales | | Income |
|---|---|---|---|---|
| 60,000 pairs | < | 80,000 pairs | | Absorption costing < Variable costing $840,000 < $1,040,000 |

A manufacturer reports the following data.

| Direct materials | $6 per unit | Variable overhead | $11 per unit |
|---|---|---|---|
| Direct labor | $14 per unit | Fixed overhead | $680,000 per year |
| Units produced | 20,000 units | | |

**NEED-TO-KNOW 5-7**

Computing Product Cost per Unit

**P4** ▶

1. Compute total product cost per unit under absorption costing.
2. Compute total product cost per unit under variable costing.

**Solution**

| Per Unit Costs | (1) Absorption Costing | (2) Variable Costing |
|---|---|---|
| Direct materials | $ 6 | $ 6 |
| Direct labor | 14 | 14 |
| Variable overhead | 11 | 11 |
| Fixed overhead ($680,000/20,000) | 34 | — |
| Total product cost per unit | $65 | $31 |

Do More: QS 5-23, QS 5-24, QS 5-25, QS 5-26, E 5-26

## Summary: Cheat Sheet

### IDENTIFYING COST BEHAVIOR

**Fixed costs:** Costs that do not change in total as volume changes.

**Variable costs:** Costs that change proportionately with volume.

**Mixed costs:** Costs that include both fixed and variable components.

**Step-wise costs:** Costs with step pattern, but fixed in each relevant range.

**Relevant range:** Normal operating range; neither near zero nor maximum capacity.

### MEASURING COST BEHAVIOR

**Cost equation:** Fixed costs + (Variable cost per unit × Units produced)

**High-Low:** Estimates cost equation using highest and lowest volumes.

$$\frac{\text{Variable cost per unit}} = \frac{\text{Cost at highest volume} - \text{Cost at lowest volume}}{\text{Highest volume} - \text{Lowest volume}}$$

Total costs = Fixed cost + (Variable cost per unit × # of units)

**Regression:** Statistical method using all data. Likely more accurate.

## CONTRIBUTION MARGIN AND BREAK-EVEN

$$\text{Contribution margin per unit} = \text{Selling price per unit} - \text{Variable costs per unit}$$

$$\text{Contribution margin ratio} = \frac{\text{Contribution margin per unit}}{\text{Selling price per unit}}$$

| Contribution Margin Income Statement Format | Contribution Margin Income Statement (at Break-Even) For Month Ended January 31 | |
|---|---|---|
| Sales | Sales (800 units at $100 each) ............... | $80,000 |
| − Variable costs | Variable costs (800 units at $70 each) .......... | 56,000 |
| Contribution margin | Contribution margin (800 units at $30 each) ... | 24,000 |
| − Fixed costs | Fixed costs ............................... | 24,000 |
| Income | Income .................................. | $ 0 |

### Break-even point in units and in dollars

$$\text{Break-even point in units} = \frac{\text{Fixed costs}}{\text{Contribution margin per unit}}$$

$$\text{Break-even point in dollars} = \frac{\text{Fixed costs}}{\text{Contribution margin ratio}}$$

## APPLYING COST-VOLUME-PROFIT ANALYSIS

**Margin of safety:** Amount that sales can drop before company incurs a loss.

$$\text{Margin of safety (in percent)} = \frac{\text{Expected sales} - \text{Break-even sales}}{\text{Expected sales}}$$

### Dollar sales for a target income

$$\frac{\text{Dollar sales at}}{\text{target income}} = \frac{\text{Fixed costs} + \text{Target income}}{\text{Contribution margin ratio}}$$

### Unit sales for a target income

$$\frac{\text{Unit sales at}}{\text{target income}} = \frac{\text{Fixed costs} + \text{Target income}}{\text{Contribution margin per unit}}$$

### Business strategy and break-even

$$\frac{\text{Revised break-even}}{\text{point in dollars}} = \frac{\text{Revised fixed costs}}{\text{Revised contribution margin ratio}}$$

## SALES MIX AND BREAK-EVEN

**Sales mix:** Proportion of sales volumes for various products or services.

**Weighted-average contribution margin:**

$$\begin{aligned} &\text{Contribution margin per unit product 1} \times \% \text{ sales product 1} \\ &+ \text{Contribution margin per unit product 2} \times \% \text{ sales product 2} \\ &= \text{Weighted-average contribution margin per unit} \end{aligned}$$

$$\text{Break-even sales in units} = \frac{\text{Fixed costs}}{\text{Weighted-average contribution margin per unit}}$$

$$\frac{\text{Units of each product}}{\text{to sell at break-even}} \left[ \begin{array}{l} \text{Break-even units} \times \% \text{ sales product 1} \\ \text{Break-even units} \times \% \text{ sales product 2} \end{array} \right.$$

### Degree of operating leverage (DOL)

$$\text{DOL} = \text{Contribution margin} / \text{Income}$$

### Using DOL to predict Income from Sales

$$\text{Change in income (\%)} = \text{DOL} \times \text{Change in sales (\%)}$$

---

## Key Terms

Absorption costing (183)

Break-even point (173)

Contribution margin (172)

Contribution margin per unit (172)

Contribution margin ratio (172)

Cost-volume-profit (CVP) analysis (167)

Cost-volume-profit (CVP) chart (174)

Degree of operating leverage (DOL) (180)

Estimated line of cost behavior (170)

High-low method (171)

Least-squares regression (171)

Margin of safety (176)

Mixed cost (169)

Relevant range of operations (169)

Sales mix (178)

Scatter diagram (170)

Step-wise cost (169)

Variable costing (183)

Variable costing income statement (183)

Weighted-average contribution margin per unit (178)

---

## Multiple Choice Quiz

**1.** A company's only product sells for $150 per unit. Its variable costs per unit are $100, and its fixed costs total $75,000. What is its contribution margin per unit?

   **a.** $50      **c.** $100      **e.** $25

   **b.** $250      **d.** $150

**2.** Using information from question 1, what is the company's contribution margin ratio?

   **a.** 66⅔%      **c.** 50%      **e.** 33⅓%

   **b.** 100%      **d.** 0%

**3.** Using information from question 1, what is the company's break-even point in units?

   **a.** 500 units      **c.** 1,500 units      **e.** 1,000 units

   **b.** 750 units      **d.** 3,000 units

**4.** A company's estimated sales are $300,000 and its sales at break-even are $180,000. Its margin of safety in dollars is

   **a.** $180,000.      **c.** $480,000.      **e.** $300,000.

   **b.** $120,000.      **d.** $60,000.

**5.** A product sells for $400 per unit and its variable costs per unit are $260. The company's fixed costs are $840,000. If the company desires $70,000 income, what is the required dollar sales?

| a. $2,400,000 | c. $2,600,000 | e. $1,400,000 |
| b. $200,000 | d. $2,275,000 | |

**ANSWERS TO MULTIPLE CHOICE QUIZ**

**1.** a; $150 − $100 = $50

**2.** e; ($150 − $100)/$150 = 33⅓%

**3.** c; $75,000/$50 CM per unit = 1,500 units

**4.** b; $300,000 − $180,000 = $120,000

**5.** c; Contribution margin ratio = ($400 − $260)/$400 = 0.35
     Targeted sales = ($840,000 + $70,000)/0.35 = $2,600,000

---

*Superscript letter A or B denotes assignments based on Appendix 5A or 5B.*

*Select Quick Study and Exercise assignments feature Guided Example videos, called "Hints" in Connect. Hints use different numbers, and instructors can turn this feature on or off.*

**Mc Graw Hill** connect

Listed here are three separate series of costs measured at various volume levels. Examine each series and identify whether it is best described as a fixed, variable, or step-wise cost. *Hint:* It can help to graph each cost series.

| Volume (Units) | Series 1 | Series 2 | Series 3 |
|---|---|---|---|
| 0 . . . . . . . . . . . | $    0 | $450 | $  800 |
| 100 . . . . . . . . . . . | 800 | 450 | 800 |
| 200 . . . . . . . . . . . | 1,600 | 450 | 800 |
| 300 . . . . . . . . . . . | 2,400 | 450 | 1,600 |
| 400 . . . . . . . . . . . | 3,200 | 450 | 1,600 |
| 500 . . . . . . . . . . . | 4,000 | 450 | 2,400 |
| 600 . . . . . . . . . . . | 4,800 | 450 | 2,400 |

**QUICK STUDY**

**QS 5-1**
Identifying cost type
**C1**

Excel:
Enter data
Select:
Insert
Charts
All Charts
Line

---

Determine whether each of the following is best described as a fixed, variable, or mixed cost with respect to product units.

**1.** Rubber used to manufacture athletic shoes.

**2.** Salesperson salary plus commission.

**3.** Packaging expense.

**4.** Depreciation expense of warehouse.

**5.** Factory rent.

**6.** Taxes on factory building.

**7.** Hourly wages of assembly-line worker.

**QS 5-2**
Identifying cost type
**C1**

---

Following are costs for eight different items. Costs are shown for three different levels of units produced and sold. Classify each of the eight cost items as either variable, fixed, or mixed.

| Costs for Different Levels of Units Produced and Sold | At 0 units | At 2,000 units | At 4,000 units |
|---|---|---|---|
| Direct labor . . . . . . . . . . . . . . . . . . . . . . . . . . . . . . . | $     0 | $10,000 | $20,000 |
| Depreciation on factory equipment . . . . . . . . . . . . . . . . . | 3,000 | 3,000 | 3,000 |
| Direct materials . . . . . . . . . . . . . . . . . . . . . . . . . . . | 0 | 6,000 | 12,000 |
| Rent on factory building . . . . . . . . . . . . . . . . . . . . . . . | 1,000 | 1,000 | 1,000 |
| Salesperson compensation . . . . . . . . . . . . . . . . . . . . . | 3,000 | 3,000 | 4,000 |
| Factory supervisor salary . . . . . . . . . . . . . . . . . . . . . . | 4,000 | 4,000 | 4,000 |
| Factory utilities . . . . . . . . . . . . . . . . . . . . . . . . . . . | 100 | 500 | 700 |
| Insurance on factory building . . . . . . . . . . . . . . . . . . . | 800 | 800 | 800 |

**QS 5-3**
Classifying costs
**C1**

---

The following information is available for a company's maintenance cost over the last seven months. Using the high-low method, estimate both the fixed and variable components of its maintenance cost.

| Month | Units Produced | Maintenance Cost |
|---|---|---|
| June . . . . . . . . . . . . . . | 90 | $5,450 |
| July . . . . . . . . . . . . . . | 180 | 6,900 |
| August . . . . . . . . . . . . | 120 | 5,100 |
| September . . . . . . . . . | 150 | 6,000 |
| October . . . . . . . . . . . . | 210 | 6,900 |
| November . . . . . . . . . . | 240 | 8,100 |
| December . . . . . . . . . . | 60 | 3,600 |

**QS 5-4**
Measuring costs using high-low method   **P1**

**QS 5-5**

Interpreting a scatter diagram

**P1**

This scatter diagram shows past units produced and their corresponding maintenance costs.

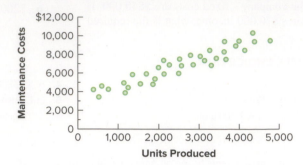

1. Review the scatter diagram and classify maintenance costs as either fixed, variable, or mixed.
2. If 3,000 units are produced, are maintenance costs expected to be greater than $5,000?

**QS 5-6**

Contribution margin ratio **A1**

Compute the contribution margin ratio and fixed costs using the following data.

| Sales . . . . . . | $5,000 | Variable costs . . . . . . . | $3,000 | Income. . . . . | $400 |

**QS 5-7**

Determining contribution margin components **A1**

Solve for the missing amounts *a* through *f* for the following separate cases.

| Case | Sales price per unit | Variable costs per unit | Contribution margin per unit | Contribution margin ratio |
|------|------|------|------|------|
| 1 | $20 | $16 | (a) | (b) |
| 2 | (c) | 30 | $10 | (d) |
| 3 | (e) | (f) | 50 | 20% |

**QS 5-8**

Contribution margin per unit and break-even units **P2**

Viva sells its waterproof phone case for $90 per unit. Fixed costs total $162,000, and variable costs are $36 per unit. Determine the (1) contribution margin per unit and (2) break-even point in units.

**QS 5-9**

Contribution margin ratio and break-even dollars **P2**

Viva sells its waterproof phone case for $90 per unit. Fixed costs total $162,000, and variable costs are $36 per unit. Determine the (1) contribution margin ratio and (2) break-even point in dollars.

**QS 5-10**

Computing break-even **P2**

Zhao Co. has fixed costs of $354,000. Its single product sells for $175 per unit, and variable costs are $116 per unit. Determine the break-even point in units.

**QS 5-11**

Preparing a contribution margin income statement **P2**

Zhao Co. has fixed costs of $354,000. Its single product sells for $175 per unit, and variable costs are $116 per unit. The company reports sales of 10,000 units. Prepare a contribution margin income statement for the year ended December 31.

**QS 5-12**

Determining break-even components **P2**

Solve for the missing amounts *a* through *d* for the following separate cases.

| Case | Sales price per unit | Variable costs per unit | Total Fixed costs | Break-even in units |
|------|------|------|------|------|
| 1 | $20 | $16 | $40,000 | (a) |
| 2 | 25 | 5 | (b) | 5,000 |
| 3 | 30 | (c) | 81,000 | 9,000 |
| 4 | (d) | 4 | 48,000 | 8,000 |

**QS 5-13**

Break-even and margin of safety **P2**

Coors Company expects sales of $340,000 (4,000 units at $85 per unit). The company's total fixed costs are $175,000 and its variable costs are $35 per unit. Compute (a) break-even in units and (b) the margin of safety in dollars.

Match the descriptions 1 through 5 with labels *a* through *e* on the CVP chart.

**1.** Break-even point   **2.** Total sales line   **3.** Loss area   **4.** Profit area   **5.** Total costs line

**QS 5-14**

Interpreting a CVP chart

**P2**

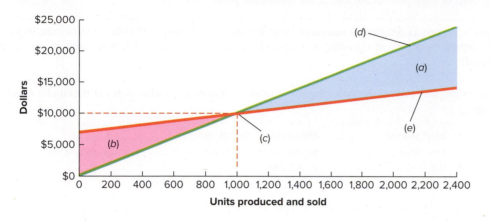

Refer to the CVP chart in QS 5-14 and solve for each of the items below.

**1.** Units produced at break-even point

**2.** Dollar sales at break-even point

**3.** Capacity in units

**4.** Are fixed costs greater than $10,000?

**5.** If 1,400 units are produced and sold, is there a profit or a loss?

**QS 5-15**

Interpreting a CVP chart

**P2**

Zulu sells its waterproof phone case for $90 per unit. Fixed costs total $200,000, and variable costs are $40 per unit. (*a*) Compute its break-even in units. (*b*) Will the break-even point in units increase or decrease in response to each of the following independent changes?

**QS 5-16**

Analyzing changes to break-even point

**C2**

| Change | Break-Even in Units will: | Change | Break-Even in Units will: |
|---|---|---|---|
| 1. Fixed costs increase to $225,000 ......... | _____ | 4. Variable costs increase to $58 per unit .... | _____ |
| 2. Variable costs decrease to $26 per unit .... | _____ | 5. Fixed costs decrease to $150,000 ........ | _____ |
| 3. Selling price per unit decreases to $80 ..... | _____ | 6. Selling price per unit increases to $120 ... | _____ |

Zulu sells its waterproof phone case for $90 per unit. Fixed costs total $200,000, and variable costs are $40 per unit. Compute the units that must be sold to get a target income of $216,000.

**QS 5-17**

Computing unit sales to get target income  **C2**

Zhao Co. has fixed costs of $354,000. Its single product sells for $175 per unit, and variable costs are $116 per unit. If the company expects sales of 10,000 units, compute its margin of safety (*a*) in dollars and (*b*) as a percent of expected sales.

**QS 5-18**

Margin of safety in dollars and as a percent of sales  **C2**

Zhao Co. has fixed costs of $354,000. Its single product sells for $175 per unit, and variable costs are $116 per unit. Compute the units that must be sold to achieve a target income of $118,000.

**QS 5-19**

Target income  **C2**

A manufacturer's contribution margin income statement for the year follows. Prepare a contribution margin income statement if the number of units sold (*a*) increases by 200 units and (*b*) decreases by 200 units.

**QS 5-20**

Computing income from unit sales changes

**C2**

| | |
|---|---:|
| Sales ($10 per unit × 10,000 units).. | $100,000 |
| Variable costs .................... | 60,000 |
| Contribution margin ............. | 40,000 |
| Fixed costs ..................... | 30,000 |
| Income....................... | $ 10,000 |

**QS 5-21**
Sales mix and break-even **P3**

US-Mobile manufactures and sells two products, tablet computers (60% of sales) and smartphones (40% of sales). Fixed costs are $500,000, and the weighted-average contribution margin per unit is $125. How many units of each product are sold at the break-even point?

**QS 5-22**
Computing and analyzing operating leverage **A2**

Singh Co. reports a contribution margin of $960,000 and fixed costs of $720,000. (1) Compute its income. (2) Compute its degree of operating leverage. (3) If sales increase by 15%, what amount of income is expected?

**QS 5-23**[B]
Computing unit cost under absorption costing **P4**

Vintage Company reports the following information. Compute its product cost per unit under absorption costing.

| | | | |
|---|---|---|---|
| Direct materials.......... | $10 per unit | Variable overhead ........ | $10 per unit |
| Direct labor............. | $20 per unit | Fixed overhead........... | $160,000 per year |
| Units produced........... | 20,000 units | | |

**QS 5-24**[B]
Computing unit cost under variable costing **P4**

Refer to QS 5-23. Compute its product cost per unit under variable costing.

**QS 5-25**[B]
Variable costing income statement **P4**

Aces Inc., a manufacturer of tennis rackets, began operations this year. The company produced 6,000 rackets and sold 4,900. Each racket was sold at a price of $90. Fixed overhead costs are $78,000 for the year, and fixed selling and administrative costs are $65,200 for the year. The company also reports the following per unit variable costs for the year. Prepare an income statement under variable costing.

| | |
|---|---|
| Direct materials.................................... | $12 |
| Direct labor......................................... | 8 |
| Variable overhead ................................. | 5 |
| Variable selling and administrative expenses............ | 2 |

**QS 5-26**[B]
Absorption costing income statement **P4**

Aces Inc., a manufacturer of tennis rackets, began operations this year. The company produced 6,000 rackets and sold 4,900. Each racket was sold at a price of $90. Fixed overhead costs are $78,000 for the year, and fixed selling and administrative costs are $65,200 for the year. The company also reports the following per unit variable costs for the year. Prepare an income statement under absorption costing.

| | |
|---|---|
| Direct materials.................................... | $12 |
| Direct labor......................................... | 8 |
| Variable overhead ................................. | 5 |
| Variable selling and administrative expenses............ | 2 |

Mc Graw Hill **connect**

# EXERCISES

**Exercise 5-1**
Identifying cost type
**C1**

Following are four graphs representing various cost behaviors.
1. Identify whether the cost behavior in each graph is mixed, step-wise, fixed, or variable.
2. Identify the graph (I, II, III, or IV) that best illustrates the cost behavior for each of the following: (a) Factory policy requires one supervisor for every 10,000 units produced; (b) real estate taxes on factory; (c) electricity charge that includes the standard monthly charge plus a charge for each kilowatt hour; and (d) leather used in making shoes.

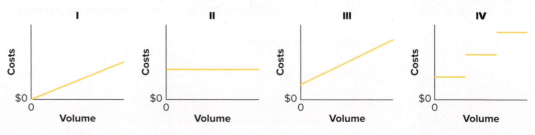

Match each of the cost classifications *a* through *e* with its definition.

a.  Total cost
b.  Mixed cost
c.  Variable cost
d.  Step-wise cost
e.  Fixed cost

1.  The combined amount of all costs.
2.  Remains constant over a relevant range of volume; when it reaches the end of its relevant range, it changes by a lump sum and remains at that level until it exceeds that relevant range.
3.  Has a component that remains the same over all volume levels and another component that increases in direct proportion to increases in volume.
4.  Remains constant over all volume levels within the relevant range.
5.  Increases in direct proportion to increases in volume; its amount is constant for each unit produced.

**Exercise 5-2**
Defining cost types

**C1**

Following are four series of costs measured at various volume levels. Identify each series as either fixed, variable, mixed, or step-wise. *Hint:* It can help to graph each cost series.

**Exercise 5-3**
Identifying cost type

**C1**

|   | A | B | C | D | E |
|---|---|---|---|---|---|
|   | Volume (Units) | Series A | Series B | Series C | Series D |
| 1 | 0 | $   0 | $2,500 | $1,000 | $5,000 |
| 2 | 400 | 3,600 | 3,100 | 1,000 | 5,000 |
| 3 | 800 | 7,200 | 3,700 | 2,000 | 5,000 |
| 4 | 1,200 | 10,800 | 4,300 | 2,000 | 5,000 |
| 5 | 1,600 | 14,400 | 4,900 | 3,000 | 5,000 |
| 6 | 2,000 | 18,000 | 5,500 | 3,000 | 5,000 |
| 7 | 2,400 | 21,600 | 6,100 | 4,000 | 5,000 |

Excel:
Enter data
Select:
Insert
Charts
All Charts
Line

Classify each of the following costs as either variable, fixed, or mixed. Costs are from a manufacturer of portable basketball hoops.

1.  Factory supervisor salary, $4,000 per month
2.  Utilities, $50 per month plus $0.05 per unit produced
3.  Assembly worker hourly wages
4.  Factory equipment depreciation, $2,000 per month
5.  Salesperson pay, $2,000 per month plus 5% of dollar sales

6.  Factory insurance, $1,500 per month
7.  Screws to assemble hoops
8.  Factory rent, $3,000 per month
9.  Metal for rims
10.  Glass for backboards
11.  Office salaries, $3,000 per month
12.  Plastic for hoop bases

**Exercise 5-4**
Classifying costs

**C1**

Felix & Co. reports the following information. (1) Use the high-low method to estimate the fixed and variable components of total costs. (2) Estimate total costs if 3,000 units are produced.

**Exercise 5-5**
Measuring costs using high-low method

**P1**

| Period | Units Produced | Total Costs | Period | Units Produced | Total Costs |
|---|---|---|---|---|---|
| 1 ....... | 0 | $2,500 | 6 ...... | 2,000 | $5,500 |
| 2 ...... | 400 | 3,100 | 7 ...... | 2,400 | 6,100 |
| 3 ...... | 800 | 3,700 | 8 ...... | 2,800 | 6,700 |
| 4 ...... | 1,200 | 4,300 | 9 ...... | 3,200 | 7,300 |
| 5 ...... | 1,600 | 4,900 | 10 ...... | 3,600 | 7,900 |

Refer to the information from Exercise 5-5. Use spreadsheet software to use ordinary least-squares regression to estimate the cost equation, including fixed and variable cost amounts.

**Exercise 5-6ᴬ**
**Appendix:** Measuring costs using regression   **P1**

A jeans maker is designing a new line of jeans called Slams. Slams will sell for $205 per unit and cost $164 per unit in variable costs to make. Fixed costs total $60,000.

1.  Compute the contribution margin per unit.
2.  Compute the contribution margin ratio.
3.  Compute income if 5,000 units are produced and sold.

**Exercise 5-7**
Contribution margin

**A1**

**Exercise 5-8**
Computing missing
amounts in contribution
margin income statements
**A1**

Compute the missing amounts *a* through *j* for the contribution margin income statements below.

| | Company A | | Company B | |
|---|---|---|---|---|
| Number of units sold . . . . . | *a* | | 1,975 | |
| | **Total** | **Per unit** | **Total** | **Per unit** |
| Sales . . . . . . . . . . . . . . . . . | $208,000 | $65 | *f* | *g* |
| Variable costs . . . . . . . . . . . | 150,400 | *b* | $39,500 | *h* |
| Contribution margin . . . . . . | *c* | *d* | 43,450 | *i* |
| Fixed costs . . . . . . . . . . . . . | *e* | | 19,750 | |
| Income. . . . . . . . . . . . . . . . | $ 46,400 | | *j* | |

**Exercise 5-9**
Contribution margin and
break-even   **P2**

Sunn Co. manufactures a single product that sells for $180 per unit and whose variable costs are $135 per unit. The company's annual fixed costs are $562,500. Compute (*a*) contribution margin per unit, (*b*) contribution margin ratio, (*c*) break-even point in units, and (*d*) break-even point in dollars of sales.

**Exercise 5-10**
Income reporting and
break-even analysis
**P2**

Sunn Co. manufactures a single product that sells for $180 per unit and whose variable costs are $135 per unit. The company's annual fixed costs are $562,500.

1. Prepare a contribution margin income statement at the break-even point.
2. If the company's fixed costs increase by $135,000, what amount of sales (in dollars) is needed to break even?

**Exercise 5-11**
Computing break-even
units and sales   **P2**

Hudson Co. reports the following contribution margin income statement. Compute (1) break-even point in units and (2) break-even point in sales dollars.

| Contribution Margin Income Statement | |
|---|---|
| **For Year Ended December 31** | |
| Sales (9,600 units at $225 each). . . . . . . . . . . . | $2,160,000 |
| Variable costs (9,600 units at $180 each). . . . . . | 1,728,000 |
| Contribution margin . . . . . . . . . . . . . . . . . . . . . | 432,000 |
| Fixed costs . . . . . . . . . . . . . . . . . . . . . . . . . . . . | 324,000 |
| Income. . . . . . . . . . . . . . . . . . . . . . . . . . . . . . . | $ 108,000 |

**Exercise 5-12**
Target income and margin
of safety   **C2**

Refer to the information in Exercise 5-11.

1. Assume Hudson has a target income of $162,000. What amount of sales dollars is needed to produce this target income?
2. If Hudson achieves its target income, what is its margin of safety (in percent)?

**Exercise 5-13**
Computing sales to achieve
target income   **C2**

Sunn Co. manufactures a single product that sells for $180 per unit and whose variable costs are $135 per unit. The company's annual fixed costs are $562,500. Management targets an annual income of $1,012,500. Compute the (1) unit sales to earn the target income and (2) dollar sales to earn the target income.

**Exercise 5-14**
Contribution margin
income statement
**C2**

Sunn Co. manufactures a single product that sells for $180 per unit and whose variable costs are $135 per unit. The company's annual fixed costs are $562,500. The sales manager predicts that next year's annual sales of the company's product will be 40,000 units at a price of $200 per unit. Variable costs are predicted to increase to $140 per unit, but fixed costs will remain at $562,500. What amount of income can the company expect to earn under these predicted changes? *Hint:* Prepare a contribution margin income statement as in Exhibit 5.19 for the next year.

**Exercise 5-15**
Predicting sales and
variable costs using
contribution margin   **C2**

Bloom Company predicts it will incur fixed costs of $160,000 and earn income of $164,000 in the next period. Its expected contribution margin ratio is 25%. Compute the amounts of expected (1) total dollar sales and (2) total variable costs.

Harrison Co. expects to sell 200,000 units of its product next year, which would generate total sales of $17,000,000. Management predicts that income for next year will be $1,250,000 and that the contribution margin per unit will be $25. Use this information to compute next year's expected (*a*) variable costs and (*b*) fixed costs.

**Exercise 5-16**
Computing variable and fixed costs  **C2**

Refer to the information in Exercise 5-11. The marketing manager believes that increasing advertising costs by $81,000 will increase the company's sales volume to 11,000 units. Prepare a contribution margin income statement for the next year assuming the company incurs the additional advertising costs.

**Exercise 5-17**
Evaluating strategies–advertising  **C2**

Refer to the information in Exercise 5-11. If the company raises its selling price to $240 per unit, compute its (1) contribution margin per unit, (2) contribution margin ratio, (3) break-even point in units, and (4) break-even point in sales dollars.

**Exercise 5-18**
Evaluating strategies–price increase  **C2**

Refer to the information in Exercise 5-11. The company is considering buying a new machine that will increase its fixed costs by $40,500 per year and decrease its variable costs by $9 per unit. Prepare a contribution margin income statement for the next year assuming the company purchases this machine.

**Exercise 5-19**
Evaluating strategies–new machine  **C2**

A manufacturer's contribution margin income statement for the year follows. Prepare contribution margin income statements for each of the three separate cases below.

**Exercise 5-20**
Computing income effects of different business strategies  **C2**

| Contribution Margin Income Statement | |
|---|---:|
| Sales (10,000 units × $10 per unit). . . . . . . . . . . . . | $100,000 |
| Variable costs (10,000 units × $6 per unit). . . . . . . . | 60,000 |
| Contribution margin (10,000 units × $4 per unit) . . | 40,000 |
| Fixed costs . . . . . . . . . . . . . . . . . . . . . . . . . . . . . . . | 30,000 |
| Income . . . . . . . . . . . . . . . . . . . . . . . . . . . . . . . . . . | $ 10,000 |

**1.** The 10,000 units produced and sold increases to 10,400 units and fixed costs increase by $5,000.

**2.** Unit selling price decreases by 5% and units produced and sold increase by 8%. *Hint:* A unit increase has both a sales and costs impact.

**3.** Fixed costs increase by $20,000, variable costs per unit decrease by $2, and units produced and sold increase by 500.

Nombre Company management predicts $390,000 of variable costs, $430,000 of fixed costs, and income of $155,000 in the next period. Management also predicts that the contribution margin per unit will be $9. Compute the (1) total expected dollar sales for next period and (2) number of units expected to be produced and sold next period.

**Exercise 5-21**
Predicting unit and dollar sales using contribution margin  **C2**

Handy Home sells windows (80% of sales) and doors (20% of sales). The selling price of each window is $200 and of each door is $500. The variable cost of each window is $125 and of each door is $350. Fixed costs are $720,000. Compute (1) weighted-average contribution margin, (2) break-even point in units using the weighted-average contribution margin, and (3) number of units of each product that will be sold at the break-even point.

**Exercise 5-22**
CVP analysis with two products  **P3**

R&R Tax Service offers tax and consulting services to individuals and small businesses. Data for fees and costs for three types of tax returns follow. Fixed costs total $18,000. Use this information to determine the (1) weighted-average contribution margin, (2) break-even point in units using the weighted-average contribution margin, and (3) number of units of each product that will be sold at the break-even point.

**Exercise 5-23**
CVP analysis with three products  **P3**

| Type of Return | Sales Mix | Fee Charged | Variable Cost per Return |
|---|---|---|---|
| Easy. . . . . . . . . | 50% | $ 50 | $ 30 |
| Moderate. . . . . | 30% | 125 | 75 |
| Business . . . . . | 20% | 275 | 100 |

**Exercise 5-24**
Computing and comparing operating leverage
**A2**

Information for two companies follows. (1) Compute the degree of operating leverage (DOL) for each company. (2) Which company is expected to produce a greater percent increase in income from a 20% increase in sales?

|  | Skittles Co. | Starburst Co. |
|---|---|---|
| Sales . . . . . . . . . . . . . | $6,000,000 | $4,500,000 |
| Contribution margin . . | 3,600,000 | 1,125,000 |
| Fixed costs . . . . . . . . . | 2,600,000 | 375,000 |

---

**Exercise 5-25**
Computing and analyzing operating leverage
**A2**

Refer to the information in Exercise 5-11.
1. Compute the company's degree of operating leverage.
2. If sales decrease by 5% in the next year, what will be the company's income?
3. Prepare a contribution margin income statement for the next year assuming sales decrease by 5%.

---

**Exercise 5-26**[B]
Computing absorption costing income    **P4**

A manufacturer reports the information below for three recent years. Compute income for each of the three years using absorption costing.

|  | Year 1 | Year 2 | Year 3 |
|---|---|---|---|
| Variable costing income . . . . . . . . . . . . . . . . . . . . . . . | $110,000 | $114,400 | $118,950 |
| Beginning finished goods inventory (units) . . . . . . . . . | 0 | 1,200 | 700 |
| Ending finished goods inventory (units) . . . . . . . . . . . . | 1,200 | 700 | 800 |
| Fixed overhead per unit . . . . . . . . . . . . . . . . . . . . . . . . | $2.50 | $2.50 | $2.50 |

---

**PROBLEM SET A**

**Problem 5-1A**
Measuring costs using high-low method    **P1**

Alden Co.'s monthly data for the past year follow. Management wants to use these data to predict future variable and fixed costs.

| Month | Units Sold | Total Cost | Month | Units Sold | Total Cost |
|---|---|---|---|---|---|
| 1 . . . . | 320,000 | $160,000 | 7 . . . . . . | 340,000 | $220,000 |
| 2 . . . . | 160,000 | 100,000 | 8 . . . . . . | 280,000 | 160,000 |
| 3 . . . . | 280,000 | 220,000 | 9 . . . . . . | 80,000 | 64,000 |
| 4 . . . . | 200,000 | 100,000 | 10 . . . . . . | 160,000 | 140,000 |
| 5 . . . . | 300,000 | 230,000 | 11 . . . . . . | 100,000 | 100,000 |
| 6 . . . . | 200,000 | 120,000 | 12 . . . . . . | 110,000 | 80,000 |

**Required**
1. Estimate both the variable costs per unit and the total monthly fixed costs using the high-low method.
2. Use the answers for variable and fixed costs from part 1 to predict future total costs when sales volume is (*a*) 220,000 units and (*b*) 240,000 units.

---

**Problem 5-2A**
Contribution margin income statement and contribution margin ratio
**A1**

The following costs result from the production and sale of 1,000 drum sets manufactured by Tight Drums Company for the year ended December 31. The drum sets sell for $500 each.

| Variable costs | | Fixed costs | |
|---|---|---|---|
| Plastic for casing . . . . . . . . . . . | $17,000 | Taxes on factory . . . . . . . . . . . . . . . . | $ 5,000 |
| Wages of assembly workers . . | 82,000 | Factory maintenance . . . . . . . . . . . . | 10,000 |
| Drum stands . . . . . . . . . . . . . . . | 26,000 | Factory machinery depreciation . . . | 40,000 |
| Sales commissions . . . . . . . . . . | 15,000 | Lease of equipment for sales staff . . | 10,000 |
| | | Accounting staff salaries . . . . . . . . . | 35,000 |
| | | Administrative salaries . . . . . . . . . . . | 125,000 |

**Required**

1. Prepare a contribution margin income statement for the year.
2. Compute contribution margin per unit and contribution margin ratio.

*Analysis Component*

3. For each dollar of sales, how much is left to cover fixed costs and contribute to income?

---

Astro Co. sold 20,000 units of its only product and reported income of $25,000 for the current year. During a planning session for next year's activities, the production manager notes that variable costs can be reduced 40% by installing a machine that automates several operations. To obtain these savings, the company must increase its annual fixed costs by $241,000. The selling price per unit will not change.

**Problem 5-3A**
Break-even analysis; income targeting and strategy

**C2   A1   P2**

| Contribution Margin Income Statement For Year Ended December 31 | |
|---|---:|
| Sales ($50 per unit). . . . . . . . . . | $1,000,000 |
| Variable costs ($40 per unit) . . . | 800,000 |
| Contribution margin . . . . . . . . . . | 200,000 |
| Fixed costs . . . . . . . . . . . . . . . . | 175,000 |
| Income. . . . . . . . . . . . . . . . . . . | $   25,000 |

**Required**

1. Compute the break-even point in dollar sales for next year assuming the machine is installed.
2. Prepare a contribution margin income statement for next year that shows the expected results with the machine installed. Assume sales are $1,000,000.
3. Compute the sales level required in both dollars and units to earn $208,000 of target income for next year with the machine installed.

**Check**   (2) Income, $104,000

---

Henna Co. produces and sells two products, Carvings and Mementos. It manufactures these products in separate factories and markets them through different channels. They have no shared costs. This year, the company sold 50,000 units of each product. Income statements for each product follow.

**Problem 5-4A**
Break-even analysis, different cost structures, and income calculations

**C2   A1   P2**

|  | Carvings | Mementos |
|---|---:|---:|
| Sales . . . . . . . . . . . . . | $2,000,000 | $2,000,000 |
| Variable costs . . . . . . . | 1,600,000 | 250,000 |
| Contribution margin . . | 400,000 | 1,750,000 |
| Fixed costs . . . . . . . . . | 125,000 | 1,475,000 |
| Income. . . . . . . . . . . . | $ 275,000 | $ 275,000 |

**Required**

1. Compute the break-even point in dollar sales for each product.
2. Assume that the company expects sales of each product to decline to 30,000 units next year with no change in unit selling price. Prepare a contribution margin income statement for the next year (as shown above with columns for each of the two products).
3. Assume that the company expects sales of each product to increase to 60,000 units next year with no change in unit selling price. Prepare a contribution margin income statement for the next year (as shown above with columns for each of the two products).

**Check**   (3) Income: Carvings, $355,000; Mementos, $625,000

*Analysis Component*

4. If sales of each product decrease to 30,000 units, which product would experience a greater decrease in income?

---

Burchard Company sold 40,000 units of its only product for $25 per unit this year. Manufacturing and selling the product required $525,000 of fixed costs. Its per unit variable costs follow.

**Problem 5-5A**
Contribution margin; income effects of alternative strategies

**C2   A1   P2**

| Direct materials. . . . . | $8.00 | Variable overhead costs. . . . . . . . . . . . . . . . | $1.00 |
|---|---|---|---|
| Direct labor . . . . . . . . | 5.00 | Variable selling and administrative costs . . . . | 0.50 |

For the next year, management will use a new material, which will reduce direct materials costs to $4.50 per unit and reduce direct labor costs to $2 per unit. Sales, total fixed costs, variable overhead costs per unit, and variable selling and administrative costs per unit will not change. Management is also considering raising its selling price to $30 per unit, which would decrease unit sales volume to 36,000 units.

**Required**

1. Compute the contribution margin per unit from (*a*) using the new material and (*b*) using the new material *and* increasing the selling price.

2. Prepare a contribution margin income statement for next year with two columns showing the expected results of (*a*) using the new material and (*b*) using the new material *and* increasing the selling price.

*Analysis Component*

3. Using answers to part 2, should management raise the selling price?

---

**Problem 5-6A**

Break-even analysis

**P2**

Praveen Co. manufactures and markets a number of rope products. Management is considering the future of Product XT, a special rope for hang gliding that has not been as profitable as planned. Because Product XT is manufactured and marketed independently of the other products, its total costs can be precisely measured. Next year's plans call for a $200 selling price per unit. Its fixed costs for the year are expected to be $270,000. Variable costs for the year are expected to be $140 per unit.

**Required**

**Check** (1*a*) Break-even sales, 4,500 units

1. Estimate Product XT's break-even point in terms of (*a*) sales units and (*b*) sales dollars.

2. Prepare a contribution margin income statement for Product XT at the break-even point.

---

**Problem 5-7A**

Break-even analysis with two products **P3**

Patriot Co. manufactures flags in two sizes, small and large. The company has total fixed costs of $240,000 per year. Additional data follow.

| | Small | Large |
|---|---|---|
| Sales price per unit...... | $20 | $30 |
| Variable costs per unit ... | $13 | $18 |
| Sales mix percent....... | 80% | 20% |

The company is considering buying new equipment that would increase total fixed costs by $48,000 per year *and* reduce the variable costs of each type of flag by $1 per unit.

**Required**

1. Compute the weighted-average contribution margin *without* the new equipment.

2. Assume the new equipment is *not* purchased. Determine the break-even point in total sales units and the break-even point in units for *each* product.

3. Assume the new equipment is purchased. Compute the break-even point in total sales units and the number of units to sell for *each* product.

---

**PROBLEM SET B**

**Problem 5-1B**

Cost estimation using high-low method **P1**

Sun Co.'s monthly data for the past year follow. Management wants to use these data to predict future variable and fixed costs.

| Month | Units Sold | Total Cost | Month | Units Sold | Total Cost |
|---|---|---|---|---|---|
| 1 .... | 195,000 | $ 97,000 | 7 ... | 145,000 | $ 93,000 |
| 2 .... | 125,000 | 87,000 | 8 ... | 185,000 | 105,000 |
| 3 .... | 105,000 | 73,000 | 9 ... | 135,000 | 85,000 |
| 4 .... | 155,000 | 89,000 | 10 ... | 85,000 | 58,000 |
| 5 .... | 95,000 | 81,000 | 11 ... | 175,000 | 95,000 |
| 6 .... | 215,000 | 110,000 | 12 ... | 115,000 | 79,000 |

**Required**

1. Estimate both the variable costs per unit and the total monthly fixed costs using the high-low method.

2. Use the answers for variable and fixed costs from part 1 to predict future total costs when sales volume is (*a*) 100,000 units and (*b*) 170,000 units.

*Analysis Component*

**3.** Use these data to prepare a scatter diagram. Draw an estimated line of cost behavior and determine whether the cost appears to be variable, fixed, or mixed.

---

The following costs result from the production and sale of 12,000 LEGO sets manufactured by LEGO Company for the year ended December 31. The LEGO sets sell for $20 each.

| Variable costs | | Fixed costs | |
|---|---|---|---|
| Plastic for LEGO sets . . . . . . . . . . | $ 3,000 | Rent on factory . . . . . . . . . . . . . . . . . | $ 6,750 |
| Wages of assembly workers . . . . | 30,000 | Factory cleaning service. . . . . . . . . . | 4,520 |
| Labeling . . . . . . . . . . . . . . . . . . . | 3,000 | Factory machinery depreciation . . . | 20,000 |
| Sales commissions. . . . . . . . . . . | 6,000 | Lease of office equipment . . . . . . . . | 1,050 |
| | | Office staff salaries . . . . . . . . . . . . . | 15,000 |
| | | Administrative salaries . . . . . . . . . . | 120,000 |

**Problem 5-2B**
Contribution margin income statement and contribution margin ratio

**A1**

**Required**

**1.** Prepare a contribution margin income statement for the year.

**2.** Compute contribution margin per unit and contribution margin ratio.

*Analysis Component*

**3.** For each dollar of sales, how much is left to cover fixed costs and contribute to income?

---

Rivera Co. sold 20,000 units of its only product and reported income of $20,000 for the current year. During a planning session for next year's activities, the production manager notes that variable costs can be reduced 25% by installing a machine that automates several operations. To obtain these savings, the company must increase its annual fixed costs by $113,000. The selling price will not change.

**Contribution Margin Income Statement**
**For Year Ended December 31**

| | |
|---|---|
| Sales (20,000 × $37.50 per unit) . . . . . . . . . . . | $750,000 |
| Variable costs (20,000 × $30 per unit) . . . . . . . | 600,000 |
| Contribution margin . . . . . . . . . . . . . . . . . . . . . | 150,000 |
| Fixed costs . . . . . . . . . . . . . . . . . . . . . . . . . . . | 130,000 |
| Income. . . . . . . . . . . . . . . . . . . . . . . . . . . . . . . | $ 20,000 |

**Problem 5-3B**
Break-even analysis; income targeting and strategy

**C2   A1   P2**

**Required**

**1.** Compute the break-even point in dollar sales for next year assuming the machine is installed.

**2.** Prepare a contribution margin income statement for next year that shows the expected results with the machine installed. Assume sales are $750,000.

**Check**  (2) Income, $57,000

**3.** Compute the sales level required in both dollars and units to earn $87,000 of target income for next year with the machine installed.

---

Stam Co. produces and sells two products, BB and TT. It manufactures these products in separate factories and markets them through different channels. They have no shared costs. This year, the company sold 50,000 units of each product. Income statements for each product follow.

| | Product BB | Product TT |
|---|---|---|
| Sales . . . . . . . . . . . . . . . . . | $800,000 | $800,000 |
| Variable costs . . . . . . . . . . . | 560,000 | 100,000 |
| Contribution margin . . . . . . | 240,000 | 700,000 |
| Fixed costs . . . . . . . . . . . . . | 100,000 | 560,000 |
| Income. . . . . . . . . . . . . . . . | $140,000 | $140,000 |

**Problem 5-4B**
Break-even analysis, different cost structures, and income calculations

**C2   A1   P2**

**Required**

1. Compute the break-even point in dollar sales for each product.

2. Assume that the company expects sales of each product to decline to 33,000 units next year with no change in the unit selling price. Prepare a contribution margin income statement for the next year (as shown above with columns for each of the two products).

3. Assume that the company expects sales of each product to increase to 64,000 units next year with no change in the unit selling prices. Prepare a contribution margin income statement for the next year (as shown above with columns for each of the two products).

**Analysis Component**

4. If sales of each product increase to 64,000 units, which product would experience a greater increase in income? Explain.

---

**Problem 5-5B**

Contribution margin; income effects of alternative strategies

C2   A1   P2

Connor Company sold 30,000 units of its only product for $28 per unit this year. Manufacturing and selling the product required $225,000 of fixed costs. Its per unit variable costs follow.

| | | | |
|---|---|---|---|
| Direct materials. . . . . | $10 | Variable overhead costs. . . . . . . . . . . . . . . . . | $2 |
| Direct labor . . . . . . . . | 6 | Variable selling and administrative costs . . . . | 1 |

For the next year, management will use a new material, which will reduce direct materials costs to $8 per unit and reduce direct labor costs to $5 per unit. Sales, total fixed costs, variable overhead costs per unit, and variable selling and administrative costs per unit will not change. Management is also considering raising its selling price to $30 per unit, which would decrease unit sales volume to 25,000 units.

**Required**

1. Compute the contribution margin per unit from (a) using the new material and (b) using the new material *and* increasing the selling price.

2. Prepare a contribution margin income statement for next year with two columns showing the expected results of (a) using the new material and (b) using the new material *and* increasing the selling price.

**Analysis Component**

3. Using answers to part 2, should management raise the selling price?

---

**Problem 5-6B**

Break-even analysis

P2   P3

Hip-Hop Co. manufactures and markets several products. Management is considering the future of one product, electronic keyboards, that has not been as profitable as planned. Because this product is manufactured and marketed independently of the other products, its total costs can be precisely measured. Next year's plans call for a $350 selling price per unit. Fixed costs for the year are expected to be $42,000. Variable costs for the year are expected to be $210 per unit.

**Required**

1. Estimate the keyboards' break-even point in terms of (a) sales units and (b) sales dollars.

2. Prepare a contribution margin income statement for keyboards at the break-even point.

3. Prepare a CVP chart for keyboards like that in Exhibit 5.14. Use 700 keyboards as the maximum number of sales units on the horizontal axis of the graph and $250,000 as the maximum dollar amount on the vertical axis.

---

**Problem 5-7B**

Break-even analysis with two products

P3

Milano Co. manufactures backpacks in two sizes, small and large. The company has total fixed costs of $520,000 per year. Additional data follow.

| | Small | Large |
|---|---|---|
| Sales price per unit. . . . . . | $60 | $80 |
| Variable costs per unit . . . | $30 | $60 |
| Sales mix percent . . . . . . . | 60% | 40% |

The company is considering buying new equipment that would increase total fixed costs by $50,000 per year *and* reduce the variable costs of each type of backpack by $4 per unit.

**Required**

1. Compute the weighted-average contribution margin *without* the new equipment.
2. Assume the new equipment is *not* purchased. Determine the break-even point in total sales units and the break-even point in units for *each* product.
3. Assume the new equipment is purchased. Compute the break-even point in total sales units and the number of units to sell for each product.

---

*This serial problem began in Chapter 1 and continues through most of the book. If previous chapter segments were not completed, the serial problem can begin at this point.*

**SP 5**   **Business Solutions** sells upscale modular desk units (60% of sales) and office chairs (40% of sales). Selling prices are $1,250 per desk unit and $500 per chair. Variable costs are $750 per desk unit and $250 per chair. Fixed costs are $120,000.

**Required**

1. Compute the weighted-average contribution margin.
2. Compute the break-even point in units.
3. Compute the number of units of each product that would be sold at the break-even point.

**SERIAL PROBLEM**
Business Solutions   **P3**

Alexander Image/Shutterstock

**Tableau Dashboard Activities** expose students to accounting analytics using visual displays. These assignments run in **Connect**. All are auto-gradable.

**TABLEAU DASHBOARD ACTIVITIES**

**Tableau DA 5-1 Quick Study**, Computing contribution margin and break-even, **A1**, **P1**—similar to QS 5-8 and QS 5-9.

**Tableau DA 5-2 Exercise**, Computing break-even, target income, and margin of safety, **C2**—similar to Exercise 5-11, Exercise 5-12, and Exercise 5-13.

**Tableau DA 5-3 Mini-case**, Evaluating strategies, **C2**—similar to Exercise 5-17, Exercise 5-19, and Exercise 5-20.

---

## Accounting Analysis

**AA 5-1**   **Apple** offers extended service contracts that provide repair coverage for its products. Assume its repair division reports the following annual results.

**COMPANY ANALYSIS**

**A2**

**APPLE**

| | |
|---|---:|
| Sales (60,000,000 units × $72 per unit).......... | $4,320,000,000 |
| Variable costs (60,000,000 units × $32 per unit) .. | 1,920,000,000 |
| Contribution margin ......................... | 2,400,000,000 |
| Fixed costs ............................... | 2,000,000,000 |
| Income.................................... | $  400,000,000 |

**Required**

1. Compute the repair division's degree of operating leverage.
2. Compute the amount of repair division income if unit sales increase by 8%.

---

**AA 5-2**   Both **Apple** and **Google** sell electronic devices, and each of these companies has a different product mix. Assume the following data are available for both companies.

**COMPARATIVE ANALYSIS**

**A2**

**APPLE**

**GOOGLE**

| $ millions | Apple | Google |
|---|---:|---:|
| Sales ............ | $260,174 | $161,857 |
| Variable costs ..... | 122,034 | 86,302 |
| Fixed costs ....... | 82,884 | 41,212 |

**Required**

1. Compute income for each company.
2. Compute the degree of operating leverage for each company.
3. If unit sales decline, which company would experience the larger decline in income?

EXTENDED
ANALYSIS
A2

**AA 5-3**   Assumed data for **Samsung** and **Apple** follow.

| $ millions | Samsung | Apple |
|---|---|---|
| Contribution margin ......... | $74,612 | $138,140 |
| Income.................... | 18,653 | 55,256 |

**Required**

1. Compute the degree of operating leverage for each company.
2. Based on the degree of operating leverage, which company's income will increase more from an increase in unit sales?

## Discussion Questions

1. What is a variable cost? Identify two variable costs.
2. When output volume increases, do variable costs per unit increase, decrease, or stay the same within the relevant range of activity? Explain.
3. When output volume increases, do fixed costs per unit increase, decrease, or stay the same within the relevant range of activity? Explain.
4. What four inputs are needed in cost-volume-profit analysis?
5. What is a mixed cost? Provide an example.
6. Define and describe *contribution margin per unit*.
7. Define and explain the *contribution margin ratio*.
8. Identify two ways in which a contribution margin income statement differs in format from a traditional income statement.
9. In performing CVP analysis for a manufacturing company, what simplifying assumption is usually made about the volume of production and the volume of sales?
10. What is margin of safety?
11. What is the relevant range of operations? How is it important in CVP analysis?
12. List three methods to measure cost behavior.
13. How is a scatter diagram used to identify and measure the behavior of a company's costs?

14. In cost-volume-profit analysis, what is the estimated income at the break-even point?
15. CVP analysis relies on what four assumptions?
16. Why are fixed costs shown as a horizontal line on a CVP chart?
17. What important assumption underlies *multiproduct* CVP analysis?
18. What is the degree of operating leverage? How is it computed?
19. **Apple** produces tablet computers. Identify some of the variable and fixed product costs associated with that production. *Hint:* Limit costs to product costs.   **APPLE**
20. Should **Apple** use single-product or multiproduct break-even analysis? Explain.   **APPLE**
21. **Samsung** is thinking of expanding sales of its most popular smartphone model by 65%. Should we expect its variable and fixed costs for this model to stay within the relevant range? Explain.   **Samsung**
22.B **Google** uses variable costing for several business decisions. How can variable costing income be converted to absorption costing income?   **GOOGLE**

## Beyond the Numbers

ETHICS
CHALLENGE
C1

**BTN 5-1**   Labor costs of an auto repair mechanic are seldom based on actual hours worked. Instead, this labor cost is based on an industry average of time estimated to complete a repair job. This means a customer can pay, for example, $120 for two hours of work on a car when the actual time worked was only one hour. Many experienced mechanics can complete repair jobs faster than the industry average. Assume that you are asked to complete a survey on time spent to complete common repair jobs for a repair center. The survey calls for objective input, and many questions require detailed cost data and analysis. The mechanics and owners know you have the survey and encourage you to complete it in a way that increases the average billable hours for repair work.

**Required**

Write a one-page memorandum to the mechanics and owners that describes the direct labor analysis you will undertake in completing this survey.

---

**BTN 5-2**   Several important assumptions underlie CVP analysis. Assumptions often help simplify and focus our analysis of sales and costs. A common application of CVP analysis is as a tool to forecast sales, costs, and income.

**Required**

Assume that you are actively searching for a job. Prepare a half-page report identifying (1) three assumptions relating to your expected revenue (salary) and (2) three assumptions relating to your expected costs for the first year of your new job. Be prepared to discuss your assumptions in class.

**COMMUNICATING IN PRACTICE**

C2

---

**BTN 5-3**   A local movie theater owner explains to you that ticket sales on weekends and evenings are strong, but attendance during the weekdays, Monday through Thursday, is poor. The owner proposes to offer a contract to the local grade school to show educational materials at the theater for a set charge per student during school hours. The owner asks your help to prepare a CVP analysis listing the cost and sales projections for the proposal. The owner must propose to the school's administration a charge per child. At a minimum, the charge per child needs to be sufficient for the theater to break even.

**Required**

Your team is to prepare two separate lists of questions that enable you to complete a reliable CVP analysis of this situation. One list is to be answered by the school's administration, the other by the owner of the movie theater.

**TEAMWORK IN ACTION**

C2

---

**BTN 5-4**   **SmartSweets**, launched by entrepreneur Tara Bosch as described in this chapter's opener, makes gummy candy without sugar and from all-natural ingredients.

**Required**

1. Identify at least two fixed costs that do not change regardless of how much candy Tara's company sells.
2. SmartSweets is growing. How could overly optimistic sales estimates hurt Tara's business?
3. Explain how cost-volume-profit analysis can help Tara manage her company.

**ENTREPRENEURIAL DECISION**

C1   A1

---

# 6 Variable Costing and Analysis

## Chapter Preview

### VARIABLE COSTING AND ABSORPTION COSTING

**P1** Variable costing

Absorption costing

Computing unit cost

**NTK 6-1**

### INCOME REPORTING

**P2** Production = sales

Production > sales

Production < sales

Reporting summary

**NTK 6-2**

### PRODUCTION AND PRICING

**C1** Planning production

**P3** Setting target prices and analyzing special orders

Variable costing for services

**A1** Contribution margin ratio

**A2** *Appendix:* Converting income

**NTK 6-3**

## Learning Objectives

### CONCEPTUAL

**C1** Describe how absorption costing can result in overproduction.

### ANALYTICAL

**A1** Apply contribution margin ratio for business decisions.

**A2** *Appendix 6A*—Convert income under variable costing to income under absorption costing.

### PROCEDURAL

**P1** Compute unit cost under both absorption and variable costing.

**P2** Prepare and analyze an income statement using absorption costing and using variable costing.

**P3** Determine product selling price and analyze special orders.

# Da Bomb!

*"Make it more fun!"*—CAROLINE AND ISABEL BERCAW

EDINA, MN—Sisters Caroline and Isabel Bercaw were bored. So, they made *bath bombs.* "We wanted ours to be more fun," recalls Caroline. Their creation was bath bombs that reveal a surprise after dissolving—charms, jewelry, and toys.

Consumers noticed. "We sold out on our first day," says Isabel. "We made more and those sold out the next day." Their idea turned into their company, **Da Bomb (DaBombFizzers.com)**.

"We use only a few ingredients, and we handmake everything in our own production facility," explains Caroline. They control product quality, packaging, and distribution. They also set up an accounting system to measure and track costs and income.

The sisters now produce about 700,000 bath bombs per month. To get there, they had to answer questions such as: "Should we take an order five-times our normal volume?" They also moved production out of their basement into a large manufacturing facility. This increased fixed costs. The sisters explain that understanding variable and fixed costs is key to know how income changes with production and sales changes.

Renee Jones Schneider/Minneapolis Star Tribune/ZUMA Wire/Alamy Live News

With Mom, Dad, and brother Harry pitching in, Da Bomb is flying high. "Our family makes a great team," says Isabel. Adds Caroline, "You are never too young, or too old, to accomplish something."

Sources: *Da Bomb website,* January 2021; *Business News Daily,* November 2017; *Edina Magazine,* May 2018; *UPS Longitudes,* May 2019

## INTRODUCING VARIABLE COSTING AND ABSORPTION COSTING

This chapter illustrates and compares two costing methods.

- **Variable costing** adds together direct materials, direct labor, and *variable* overhead costs in product costs. This method is useful for many managerial decisions, but it cannot be used for external financial reporting.

- **Absorption costing** adds together direct materials, direct labor, and both *variable* and *fixed* overhead costs in product costs. This method is required for external financial reporting under GAAP, but it can result in misleading product cost information and poor managerial decisions.

Exhibit 6.1 compares the absorption and variable costing methods. Both methods include direct materials, direct labor, and variable overhead in product costs. The key difference is their reporting of *fixed* overhead costs. Fixed overhead costs are included in product costs under absorption costing but included in period expenses under variable costing. Product costs are included in inventory until the goods are sold, at which time they are included in cost of goods sold. Period expenses are reported as expenses immediately in the period in which they are incurred.

**P1**

Compute unit cost under both absorption and variable costing.

**Point:** Under variable costing, fixed overhead is expensed when units are produced. Under absorption costing, fixed overhead is expensed when units are sold (as part of cost of goods sold).

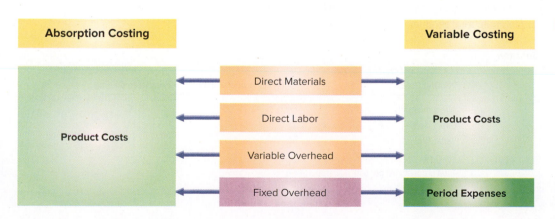

**EXHIBIT 6.1**

Absorption Costing versus Variable Costing

# Computing Unit Product Cost

To demonstrate the difference between absorption costing and variable costing, consider the product cost data in Exhibit 6.2 from IceAge, a skate manufacturer.

**EXHIBIT 6.2**

Product Cost Data

| | | | |
|---|---|---|---|
| Direct materials . . . . . . . . . . . . . . | $4 per unit | Variable overhead . . . . . | $3 per unit |
| Direct labor . . . . . . . . . . . . . . . . | $8 per unit | Fixed overhead . . . . . . . | $600,000 per year |
| Units produced (per year) . . . . . . | 60,000 units | | |

Using the product cost data, Exhibit 6.3 shows the product cost per unit computations for both absorption and variable costing.

- For absorption costing, product cost per unit is $25. This consists of $4 in direct materials, $8 in direct labor, $3 in variable overhead, and $10 in fixed overhead ($600,000/60,000 units).
- For variable costing, product cost per unit is $15, which consists of $4 in direct materials, $8 in direct labor, and $3 in variable overhead. Fixed overhead costs of $600,000 are treated as a period cost and expensed in the period incurred. **The difference between the costing methods is fixed overhead is included in product costs for absorption costing.**

**EXHIBIT 6.3**

Unit Cost Computation

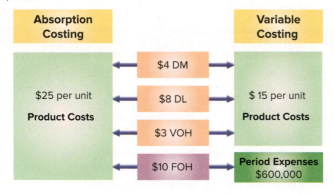

| Product Cost per Unit | Absorption Costing | Variable Costing |
|---|---|---|
| Direct materials . . . . . . . . . . . | $ 4 | $ 4 |
| Direct labor . . . . . . . . . . . . . . | 8 | 8 |
| Overhead costs | | |
| Variable . . . . . . . . . . . . . . | 3 | 3 |
| **Fixed** . . . . . . . . . . . . . . . | 10 | — |
| Total product cost per unit . . . . | $25 | $15 |

**NEED-TO-KNOW** 6-1

A manufacturer reports the following data.

Computing Product
Cost per Unit

P1

| | | | |
|---|---|---|---|
| Direct materials . . . . . | $6 per unit | Variable overhead . . . . | $11 per unit |
| Direct labor . . . . . . . . . | $14 per unit | Fixed overhead . . . . . . . | $680,000 per year |
| Units produced . . . . . | 20,000 units | | |

1. Compute total product cost per unit under absorption costing.
2. Compute total product cost per unit under variable costing.

**Solution**

| Per Unit Costs | (1) Absorption Costing | (2) Variable Costing |
|---|---|---|
| Direct materials . . . . . . . . . . . . . . . . . . | $ 6 | $ 6 |
| Direct labor . . . . . . . . . . . . . . . . . . . . | 14 | 14 |
| Variable overhead . . . . . . . . . . . . . . . . | 11 | 11 |
| Fixed overhead ($680,000/20,000). . . | 34 | — |
| Total product cost per unit . . . . . . . . . | $65 | $31 |

Do More: QS 6-1, QS 6-2,
QS 6-3, E 6-1, E 6-2

# INCOME REPORTING

The different treatment of fixed overhead costs leads to different product costs per unit under absorption and variable costing. This also impacts income reporting.

Below are data for IceAge Company. Assume its variable costs per unit, annual fixed costs, and sales price do not change.

**P2**

Prepare and analyze an income statement using absorption costing and using variable costing.

| Product Costs | | Selling and Administrative Expenses | |
|---|---|---|---|
| Direct materials........ | $4 per unit | Variable ........ | $2 per unit |
| Direct labor ........... | $8 per unit | Fixed........... | $200,000 per year |
| Variable overhead...... | $3 per unit | **Sales** | |
| Fixed overhead ........ | $600,000 per year | Sales price ...... | $40 per unit |

Sales and production information for IceAge follows. Units produced equal those sold for Year 1, but units produced exceed those sold for Year 2. Units produced are less than those sold for Year 3. IceAge began Year 1 with no units in beginning inventory.

| | Units Produced | Units Sold | Units in Ending Inventory |
|---|---|---|---|
| Year 1...... | 60,000 | 60,000 | 0 |
| Year 2...... | 60,000 | 40,000 | 20,000 |
| Year 3...... | 60,000 | 80,000 | 0 |

We prepare income statements for IceAge under absorption costing and under variable costing for each of these 3 years. We consider three cases: when units produced are equal to units sold; when units produced exceed units sold; when units produced are less than units sold. **Income differs between the costing methods when inventory levels change.** Inventory levels change when units produced do not equal units sold.

## Units Produced Equal Units Sold

Exhibit 6.4 presents the Year 1 income statement for both costing methods. The income statement under variable costing (on right) is a **contribution margin income statement. Contribution margin** is sales minus variable costs. **Variable cost of goods sold** is the direct

| Production | = | Sales | Income under |
|---|---|---|---|
| 60,000 pairs | = | 60,000 pairs | Absorption costing = Variable costing $580,000 = $580,000 |

Year 1

**EXHIBIT 6.4**

Income when Units Produced Equal Units Sold

**ICEAGE COMPANY**
**Income Statement (Absorption Costing)**
**For Year Ended December 31, Year 1**

| | |
|---|---|
| Sales (60,000 × $40).............. | $2,400,000 |
| Cost of goods sold (60,000 × $25†) ... | 1,500,000 |
| Gross profit ...................... | 900,000 |
| Selling and administrative expenses [$200,000 + (60,000 × $2)]...... | 320,000 |
| **Income** ....................... | **$ 580,000** |

†$4 DM + $8 DL + $3 VOH + $10 FOH
‡$4 DM + $8 DL + $3 VOH

**ICEAGE COMPANY**
**Income Statement (Variable Costing)**
**For Year Ended December 31, Year 1**

| | | |
|---|---|---|
| Sales (60,000 × $40) ..................................... | | $2,400,000 |
| Variable expenses | | |
| Variable cost of goods sold (60,000 × $15‡) .............. | $900,000 | |
| Variable selling and administrative expenses (60,000 × $2)... | 120,000 | 1,020,000 |
| Contribution margin...................................... | | 1,380,000 |
| Fixed expenses | | |
| Fixed overhead ......................................... | 600,000 | |
| Fixed selling and administrative expenses ................ | 200,000 | 800,000 |
| **Income** ................................................... | | **$ 580,000** |

materials, direct labor, and variable overhead costs for units sold. The absorption costing income statement (on left) does not separate expenses into variable and fixed components.

Exhibit 6.4 shows that **income is identical under absorption costing and variable costing when the units produced equal the units sold.** This is because the $600,000 fixed overhead (FOH) that is expensed under variable costing is equal to the $600,000 (60,000 units × $10 FOH per unit) that is included in cost of goods sold under absorption costing when units produced equal units sold.

**Point:** Contribution margin (Sales − Variable expenses) is different from gross profit (Sales − Cost of sales).

## Units Produced Exceed Units Sold

| Production | > | Sales |
|---|---|---|
| 60,000 pairs | > | 40,000 pairs |

**Income under**
Absorption costing > Variable costing
$320,000 > $120,000

**Year 2**

Exhibit 6.5 shows absorption costing and variable costing income statements for Year 2 when 60,000 units were produced, but only 40,000 units were sold. This means 20,000 units remain in ending inventory.

For Year 2, income is $320,000 under absorption costing. Under variable costing, income is $120,000. The cause of this $200,000 income difference is the different treatment of fixed overhead. The $600,000 of fixed overhead (FOH) is expensed under variable costing as a period cost, but under absorption costing the FOH is expensed based on the number of units sold (40,000 units × $10 FOH per unit). This means income is lower under variable costing by $200,000 (20,000 units × $10).

**EXHIBIT 6.5**

Income when Units Produced Exceed Units Sold

| ICEAGE COMPANY Income Statement (Absorption Costing) For Year Ended December 31, Year 2 | |
|---|---|
| Sales (40,000 × $40)............. | $1,600,000 |
| Cost of goods sold (40,000 × $25[†]) ... | 1,000,000 |
| Gross profit...................... | 600,000 |
| Selling and administrative expenses [$200,000 + (40,000 × $2)]...... | 280,000 |
| **Income** ....................... | **$ 320,000** |

[†]$4 DM + $8 DL + $3 VOH + $10 FOH
[‡]$4 DM + $8 DL + $3 VOH

| ICEAGE COMPANY Income Statement (Variable Costing) For Year Ended December 31, Year 2 | | |
|---|---|---|
| Sales (40,000 × $40) ..................................... | | $1,600,000 |
| Variable expenses | | |
| Variable cost of goods sold (40,000 × $15[‡]) .............. | $600,000 | |
| Variable selling and administrative expenses (40,000 × $2)... | 80,000 | 680,000 |
| Contribution margin...................................... | | 920,000 |
| Fixed expenses | | |
| Fixed overhead ....................................... | 600,000 | |
| Fixed selling and administrative expenses ................ | 200,000 | 800,000 |
| **Income**.................................................. | | **$ 120,000** |

When the number of units produced differs from the number of units sold, inventory levels change. The dollar amount for finished goods inventory reported on the balance sheet will also differ between absorption and variable costing. From Exhibit 6.3, product costs per unit are $25 under absorption costing and $15 per unit for variable costing. With 20,000 units in ending finished goods inventory (60,000 units produced − 40,000 units sold), the Year 2 inventory balances under each costing method follow. The $200,000 difference between the two methods is due to fixed overhead costs being included in finished goods inventory under absorption costing but not under variable costing. This $200,000 of fixed overhead cost is included in cost of goods sold under absorption costing only when that inventory is sold.

| Year 2 | Finished Goods Inventory |
|---|---|
| Absorption Costing (20,000 inventory units × $25 product cost) ....... | $500,000 |
| Variable Costing (20,000 inventory units × $15 product cost) ......... | $300,000 |

# Units Produced Are Less Than Units Sold

Exhibit 6.6 shows absorption costing and variable costing income statements for Year 3 when IceAge produced 60,000 units and sold 80,000 units. This means IceAge sold all that it produced in Year 3, and it sold the 20,000 units in beginning finished goods inventory. Its income is $840,000 using absorption costing, but it is $1,040,000 using variable costing.

| Production | < | Sales |
|---|---|---|
| 60,000 pairs | < | 80,000 pairs |

**Income under**

Absorption costing < Variable costing
$840,000 < $1,040,000

Year 3

## EXHIBIT 6.6

Income when Units Produced Are Less Than Units Sold

**ICEAGE COMPANY**
**Income Statement (Absorption Costing)**
**For Year Ended December 31, Year 3**

| | |
|---|---|
| Sales (80,000 × $40)............. | $3,200,000 |
| Cost of goods sold (80,000 × $25†) ... | 2,000,000 |
| Gross profit...................... | 1,200,000 |
| Selling and administrative expenses [$200,000 + (80,000 × $2)]...... | 360,000 |
| **Income** ........................ | **$ 840,000** |

†$4 DM + $8 DL + $3 VOH + $10 FOH
‡$4 DM + $8 DL + $3 VOH

**ICEAGE COMPANY**
**Income Statement (Variable Costing)**
**For Year Ended December 31, Year 3**

| | | |
|---|---|---|
| Sales (80,000 × $40) ...................................... | | $3,200,000 |
| Variable expenses | | |
| Variable cost of goods sold (80,000 × $15‡) ............... | $1,200,000 | |
| Variable selling and administrative expenses (80,000 × $2)... | 160,000 | 1,360,000 |
| Contribution margin....................................... | | 1,840,000 |
| Fixed expenses | | |
| Fixed overhead ......................................... | 600,000 | |
| Fixed selling and administrative expenses ................ | 200,000 | 800,000 |
| **Income** .................................................. | | **$1,040,000** |

The $200,000 income difference is due to fixed overhead (FOH). Beginning inventory in Year 3 under absorption costing includes $200,000 of fixed overhead cost incurred in Year 2, which is included in cost of goods sold in Year 3 under absorption costing when the units are sold. When 80,000 units are sold in Year 3, total cost of goods sold under absorption costing is $2,000,000 (80,000 units × $25). Of this amount, $800,000 is FOH (80,000 units × $10), which consists of $600,000 from the current year and $200,000 from the prior year. However, variable costing reports $600,000 in FOH expenses as it has for all 3 years.

## Summarizing Income Reporting

IceAge's income reported under both variable costing and absorption costing for Year 1 through Year 3 is summarized in Exhibit 6.7. Total income is $1,740,000 for this time period for *both* methods. **Income under absorption costing and income under variable costing differ whenever the units produced differ from units sold.** These differences in income are due to the different timing with which fixed overhead costs are reported in income under the two methods. *Income under absorption costing is higher when more units are produced than sold and is lower when less units are produced than sold.*

| Units | Income Effect |
|---|---|
| Production = Sales | Absorption = Variable |
| Production > Sales | Absorption > Variable |
| Production < Sales | Absorption < Variable |

**EXHIBIT 6.7**

Summary of Income
Reporting

| | Units Produced | Units Sold | Income under Absorption Costing | Income under Variable Costing |
|---|---|---|---|---|
| Year 1 ......... | 60,000 | 60,000 | $ 580,000 | $ 580,000 |
| Year 2 ......... | 60,000 | 40,000 | 320,000 | 120,000 |
| Year 3 ......... | 60,000 | 80,000 | 840,000 | 1,040,000 |
| Totals ......... | 180,000 | 180,000 | $1,740,000 | $1,740,000 |

For IceAge, the 180,000 total units produced over the three-year period exactly equal the 180,000 units sold over that period. This means that the difference between *total* absorption costing income and *total* variable costing income for the three-year period is zero. In reality, production and sales quantities rarely exactly equal each other over a short period of time. We normally see differences in income for these two methods extending over several years.

---

**NEED-TO-KNOW** 6-2

Computing Income under Absorption and Variable Costing

**P2**

ZBest Mfg. began operations and reported the following for its year ended December 31.

| | | | |
|---|---|---|---|
| Direct materials ........... | $6 per unit | Units produced ........................... | 20,000 units |
| Direct labor............... | $11 per unit | Units sold ................................. | 14,000 units |
| Variable overhead ......... | $3 per unit | Variable selling and administrative expenses ..... | $2 per unit |
| Fixed overhead ........... | $680,000 per year | Fixed selling and administrative expenses....... | $112,000 per year |
| Sales price................ | $80 per unit | | |

1. Prepare an income statement under absorption costing for the year ended December 31.
2. Prepare an income statement under variable costing for the year ended December 31.

**Solution**

**ZBEST MFG.**
**Income Statement (Absorption Costing)**
**For Year Ended December 31**

| | |
|---|---|
| Sales (14,000 × $80)................ | $1,120,000 |
| Cost of goods sold (14,000 × $54*).... | 756,000 |
| Gross profit ....................... | 364,000 |
| Selling and administrative expenses [$112,000 + (14,000 × $2)]........ | 140,000 |
| Income .......................... | $ 224,000 |

*$6 DM + $11 DL + $3 VOH + $34 FOH ($680,000/20,000)
†$6 DM + $11 DL + $3 VOH

Do More: QS 6-4 through QS 6-9,
E 6-7 through E 6-13

**ZBEST MFG.**
**Income Statement (Variable Costing)**
**For Year Ended December 31**

| | | |
|---|---|---|
| Sales (14,000 × $80)................................ | | $1,120,000 |
| Variable expenses | | |
| Variable cost of goods sold (14,000 × $20†) ........... | $280,000 | |
| Variable selling and admin. expenses (14,000 × $2)..... | 28,000 | 308,000 |
| Contribution margin................................ | | 812,000 |
| Fixed expenses | | |
| Fixed overhead ................................... | 680,000 | |
| Fixed selling and administrative expenses ............. | 112,000 | 792,000 |
| Income .......................................... | | $ 20,000 |

The $204,000 difference in income between the two methods is due to units produced exceeding units sold.

---

## PRODUCTION AND PRICING

This section examines absorption and variable costing in the following business decisions.

- **Planning production**
- **Setting target prices**
- **Analyzing special orders**
- **Assessing costs for services**

**C1**

Describe how absorption costing can result in overproduction.

### Planning Production

Many companies link manager bonuses to income computed under absorption costing because this is how income is reported to shareholders (per GAAP). This can lead some managers to overproduce and create excess inventory.

To illustrate how a bonus system can lead to overproduction under absorption costing, let's use IceAge's Year 1 data with one change: its manager decides to produce 100,000 units instead 60,000. Because only 60,000 units are sold, the 40,000 units of excess production will be in ending finished goods inventory.

The left side of Exhibit 6.8 shows the $25 product cost per unit under absorption costing when 60,000 units are produced (same as Exhibit 6.3). The right side shows the $21 product cost per unit when 100,000 units are produced.

Total product cost per unit is $4 less when 100,000 units are produced. This is because the company is spreading the $600,000 fixed overhead cost over 40,000 more units when 100,000 units are produced than when 60,000 units are produced.

| Absorption Costing 60,000 Units Produced | | Per Unit |
|---|---|---|
| Direct materials | | $ 4 |
| Direct labor | | 8 |
| Variable overhead | | 3 |
| Fixed overhead ($600,000/**60,000** units) | | 10 |
| **Total product cost per unit** | | **$25** |

| Absorption Costing 100,000 Units Produced | | Per Unit |
|---|---|---|
| Direct materials | | $ 4 |
| Direct labor | | 8 |
| Variable overhead | | 3 |
| Fixed overhead ($600,000/**100,000** units) | | 6 |
| **Total product cost per unit** | | **$21** |

**EXHIBIT 6.8**

Unit Cost under Absorption Costing for Different Production Levels

The $4 per unit difference in product cost impacts income. Exhibit 6.9 shows the Year 1 income statement under absorption costing for the two production levels.

| ICEAGE COMPANY Income Statement (Absorption Costing) For Year Ended December 31, Year 1 [60,000 Units Produced; 60,000 Units Sold] | |
|---|---|
| Sales (60,000 × $40) | $2,400,000 |
| Cost of goods sold (60,000 × **$25**) | 1,500,000 |
| Gross profit | 900,000 |
| Selling and administrative expenses | |
| [$200,000 + (60,000 × $2)] | 320,000 |
| **Income** | **$ 580,000** |

| ICEAGE COMPANY Income Statement (Absorption Costing) For Year Ended December 31, Year 1 [100,000 Units Produced; 60,000 Units Sold] | |
|---|---|
| Sales (60,000 × $40) | $2,400,000 |
| Cost of goods sold (60,000 × **$21**) | 1,260,000 |
| Gross profit | 1,140,000 |
| Selling and administrative expenses | |
| [$200,000 + (60,000 × $2)] | 320,000 |
| **Income** | **$ 820,000** |

**EXHIBIT 6.9**

Income under Absorption Costing for Different Production Levels

Common sense suggests that overproducing and creating excess inventory should not increase income. Yet, income under absorption costing is $240,000 greater if IceAge produces 40,000 more units than it sells. The reason is that $240,000 of fixed overhead (40,000 units × $6) is included in ending inventory instead of being expensed as cost of goods sold in Year 1. This shows that under absorption costing, a manager can increase current year income just by producing more and disregarding whether the excess units can be sold or not. This incentive problem encourages inventory buildup, which leads to increased costs in storage and obsolescence.

This manager incentive problem is avoided when income is measured using variable costing. To illustrate, Exhibit 6.10 reports income under variable costing for the same production levels used in Exhibit 6.9. Under variable costing, managers cannot increase income by merely increasing production without increasing sales. Income under variable costing is not affected by production level changes because *all* fixed overhead costs are expensed in the year when incurred. Under variable costing, companies increase income by selling more units, not by producing excess inventory.

Karl Weatherly/The Image Bank Unreleased/Getty Images

**EXHIBIT 6.10**

Income under Variable Costing for Different Production Levels

| ICEAGE COMPANY Income Statement (Variable Costing) For Year Ended December 31, Year 1 [60,000 Units Produced; 60,000 Units Sold] | | |
|---|---|---|
| Sales (60,000 × $40) | | $2,400,000 |
| Variable expenses | | |
| Variable cost of goods sold (60,000 × $15) | $900,000 | |
| Variable selling and administrative expenses (60,000 × $2) | 120,000 | 1,020,000 |
| Contribution margin | | 1,380,000 |
| Fixed expenses | | |
| Fixed overhead | 600,000 | |
| Fixed selling and administrative expenses | 200,000 | 800,000 |
| Income | | $ 580,000 |

| ICEAGE COMPANY Income Statement (Variable Costing) For Year Ended December 31, Year 1 [100,000 Units Produced; 60,000 Units Sold] | | |
|---|---|---|
| Sales (60,000 × $40) | | $2,400,000 |
| Variable expenses | | |
| Variable cost of goods sold (60,000 × $15) | $900,000 | |
| Variable selling and administrative expenses (60,000 × $2) | 120,000 | 1,020,000 |
| Contribution margin | | 1,380,000 |
| Fixed expenses | | |
| Fixed overhead | 600,000 | |
| Fixed selling and administrative expenses | 200,000 | 800,000 |
| Income | | $ 580,000 |

## ■ Decision **Ethics**

**Production Manager**   Due to competition, your company projects unit sales to be 35% less than last year. The CEO is concerned that top executives won't receive bonuses. The controller suggests that if the company produces as many units as last year, reported income might be high enough for bonuses to be paid. Should your company produce excess inventory to maintain income? ■   *Answer:* Under absorption costing, fixed overhead costs are spread over all units produced. Thus, fixed cost for each unit will be lower if more units are produced. This means the company can increase income by producing excess units even if sales remain constant. But excess inventory leads to increased storage cost and obsolescence. Also, producing excess inventory to meet income levels for bonuses harms owners and is unethical.

## Setting Target Price

**P3**

Determine product selling price and analyze special orders.

Over the long run, a product selling price must be high enough to cover all costs and provide an acceptable return to owners. For this purpose, *absorption* cost is useful because it reflects the full costs that a selling price must exceed for the company to be profitable. We use a three-step process to determine product selling price.

*Step 1:* Determine the product cost per unit using absorption costing.

*Step 2:* Determine the target *markup* on product cost per unit.

*Step 3:* Add the target markup to the product cost to find the target selling price.

To illustrate, under absorption costing, IceAge's product cost is $25 per unit (from Exhibit 6.3). IceAge's management determines a target **markup**, an amount added to cost, to cover selling and administrative expenses. IceAge targets a markup of 60% of absorption cost and computes a $40 target selling price in Exhibit 6.11.

**EXHIBIT 6.11**

Target Selling Price with Absorption Costing

| Step 1 | Absorption cost per unit (from Exhibit 6.3) | $25 |
|---|---|---|
| Step 2 | Target markup per unit ($25 × 60%) | 15 |
| Step 3 | Target selling price per unit | $40 |

## Analyzing Special Orders

Over the long run, a selling price must cover all fixed and variable costs. Over the short run, fixed costs do not change with changes in production levels. This means that managers should accept special orders *if the special-order price exceeds variable cost*.

Steve Mason/Photodisc/Getty Images

To illustrate, let's return to IceAge. Its variable cost of goods sold per unit is $15 and its variable selling and administrative expenses are $2 per unit. Assume that it receives a special order for 1,000 pairs of skates at an offer price of $22 per pair from a foreign skating school. This special order will not affect IceAge's regular sales and it has excess capacity to fill the order.

Using absorption costing, the product cost of $25 per unit is more than the special-order price of $22 per unit. This might suggest that management should reject the order. Closer analysis shows this order should be accepted. The $22 special-order price exceeds the $17 *variable* cost ($15 + $2) of the product. Specifically, Exhibit 6.12 reveals that contribution margin (and income) would increase by $5,000 from accepting the order. The reason for accepting the special order is in the different behavior of variable and fixed costs. If the order is rejected, only variable costs are saved. Fixed costs do not change in the short run regardless of rejecting or accepting this order. Because sales exceed variable costs for this order, accepting the special order increases contribution margin.

**Point:** Fixed overhead does not increase from this special order because IceAge has excess capacity.

| Special Order Analysis | |
|---|---|
| Sales (1,000 × $22) . . . . . . . . . . . . . . . . . . . . . . . . | $22,000 |
| Variable costs (1,000 × $17) . . . . . . . . . . . . . . . . | 17,000 |
| Contribution margin . . . . . . . . . . . . . . . . . . . . . . . | $ 5,000 |

**EXHIBIT 6.12**

Contribution Margin for a Special Order

### Decision Maker

**Internal Auditor** Your company uses absorption costing. Management is disappointed because its external auditors are requiring it to write off an inventory amount because it exceeds what the company could reasonably sell in the foreseeable future. Why would management produce more than it sells? ■ *Answer:* If bonuses are tied to income, managers have incentives to increase income for personal gain. If absorption costing is used, management can reduce current-period expenses (and raise income) with overproduction, which shifts fixed production costs to future periods. This decision fails to consider whether there is a viable market for all units produced. An auditor can conclude that the inventory does not have "future economic value" and pressure management to write it off. Such a write-off reduces income by the cost of excess inventory.

## Variable Costing for Services

Variable costing also applies to service companies. Because service companies do not produce inventory, differences in income from absorption and variable costing do not apply. Still, a focus on variable costs can be useful in managerial decisions for service firms.

For service firms, variable costs change as the volume of services provided change. Fixed costs do not change as the volume of services provided change. One example is a hotel receiving an offer to reserve a large block of rooms at a discounted price. Another example is "special-order" pricing for airlines when they sell tickets shortly before a flight at a deeply discounted price. If the discounted price exceeds variable costs, such sales increase contribution margin and income.

To illustrate, BlueSky provides charter airline services. Its variable costing income statement for the year is in Exhibit 6.13.

**EXHIBIT 6.13**

Variable Costing Income Statement for Service Provider

| Income Statement (Variable Costing) For Year Ended December 31 | | |
|---|---:|---:|
| Revenue (120 flights × $50,000 per flight)..... | | $6,000,000 |
| Variable expenses | | |
| Wages, salaries, and benefits............. | $1,920,000 | |
| Fuel and oil........................... | 1,080,000 | |
| Food and beverages ................... | 600,000 | 3,600,000 |
| Contribution margin ...................... | | 2,400,000 |
| Fixed expenses | | |
| Depreciation.......................... | 300,000 | |
| Rent................................ | 420,000 | 720,000 |
| Income................................. | | $1,680,000 |

Based on an activity level of 120 flights (60% of its capacity), variable cost per flight is $30,000, computed as $3,600,000/120. BlueSky's normal price is $50,000 per flight. A group has offered BlueSky $35,000 to fly its members to Washington, D.C. In making its decision, BlueSky should *ignore fixed costs and focus on variable costs*. The company's expected contribution margin from the special offer follows. BlueSky should accept the special offer as it provides a contribution margin of $5,000. An incorrect analysis based on absorption costing might lead management to reject the offer.

**Point:** In a later chapter we look at special offers with incremental fixed costs. This chapter assumes no incremental fixed costs for special offers.

| Special Offer Analysis | |
|---|---:|
| Revenue................................. | $35,000 |
| Variable costs ......................... | 30,000 |
| Contribution margin ..................... | $ 5,000 |

---

**NEED-TO-KNOW 6-3**

Setting Target Prices and Analyzing a Special Offer

**P3**

Do More: QS 6-20, E 6-14

**Part 1.** A manufacturer's absorption cost per unit is $60. Compute the target selling price per unit if a 30% markup is targeted.

**Solution**

| | |
|---|---:|
| Absorption cost per unit ................... | $60 |
| Target markup per unit ($60 × 30%) ......... | 18 |
| Target selling price per unit .............. | $78 |

**Part 2.** A hotel normally rents its 200 luxury suites at a rate of $500 per night per suite. The hotel's cost per night per suite is $400, shown below.

| | |
|---|---:|
| Variable costs ............................ | $160 |
| Fixed costs ............................. | 240 |
| Total cost per night per suite .............. | $400 |

The hotel's manager has received an offer to reserve a block of 40 suites for $250 per suite for one night during the hotel's off-season, when it has many available suites. Should the offer be accepted or rejected? What is the contribution margin from accepting the offer?

*Solution*

Contribution margin from accepting the offer is $3,600. The offer should be accepted.

| Special Offer Analysis | |
| --- | --- |
| Revenue (40 suites × $250) . . . . . . . . . . . . | $10,000 |
| Variable costs (40 suites × $160) . . . . . . . . | 6,400 |
| Contribution margin . . . . . . . . . . . . . . . . . . . | $ 3,600 |

Do More: QS 6-20, QS 6-21, E 6-17, E 6-18, E 6-19

 **CORPORATE SOCIAL RESPONSIBILITY**

This chapter showed alternative ways to compute income. When businesses consider the effects of their operations on the environment, more ways to measure income emerge.

For example, **PUMA**, a maker of athletic shoes and apparel, developed an **environmental profit and loss (EP&L) report,** or *EP&L report.* This report lists the impact on human welfare from PUMA's business activities in monetary terms. Profit is the monetary value of activities that benefit the environment, and loss is the monetary value of activities that harm the environment. While many companies measure and attempt to reduce their water usage, carbon emissions, and waste, PUMA takes the next step by putting environmental impacts into monetary terms.

Exhibit 6.14 shows one form of an EP&L report for PUMA. In this year, PUMA reported no profits from activities that benefited the environment, but it did report losses (costs) of several activities that harmed the environment.

| Environmental Profit and Loss ($ millions) | | |
| --- | --- | --- |
| Environmental profits . . . . . . . . . . . | | $  0 |
| Environmental losses | | |
| Water use. . . . . . . . . . . . . . . . . . | $47 | |
| Carbon emissions . . . . . . . . . . . | 47 | |
| Land use . . . . . . . . . . . . . . . . . . | 37 | |
| Air pollution . . . . . . . . . . . . . . . . | 11 | |
| Waste . . . . . . . . . . . . . . . . . . . . . | 3 | 145 |
| Net environmental loss . . . . . . . . . . | | $(145) |

**EXHIBIT 6.14**

Environmental Profit and Loss Report

Putting environmental impacts into monetary terms enables companies to better grasp the effects of their activities. PUMA's net environmental loss from Exhibit 6.14, although not included in computing GAAP net income, was over 70% of income for that year. In addition, over 85% of the company's environmental costs are from suppliers and processors at early stages of the company's supply chain, and roughly 66% of its environmental costs are from its footwear division. The EP&L report enables managers to develop strategies that are likely to have the greatest impact in reducing environmental costs.

**Da Bomb**, this chapter's opening company, is also concerned with the environment. Proceeds from the sale of its "Earth Bomb" go to organizations that help clean up oceans. Da Bomb has also created over 150 jobs in Caroline and Isabel's community.

Renee Jones Schneider/ Minneapolis Star Tribune/ZUMA Wire/Alamy Live News

---

Contribution Margin Ratio  **Decision Analysis**

Variable costing is useful in analyzing performance of business divisions such as sales territories and product lines. From the variable costing income statement, we compute the following **contribution margin ratio** for analysis purposes. Recall: Contribution margin = Sales − Variable expenses.

**A1**

Apply contribution margin ratio for business decisions.

$$\text{Contribution margin ratio} = \frac{\text{Contribution margin}}{\text{Sales}}$$

Contribution margin ratio is the percent of sales that remains after subtracting variable expenses. For example, if contribution margin is $200,000 and sales are $500,000, the contribution margin ratio is 0.40 ($200,000/$500,000), or 40%. This means 40% of each sales dollar remains to cover fixed costs and contribute to income. A higher contribution margin ratio is better.

**Contribution Margin Analysis by Territory**   We return to Year 1 of our IceAge example to show the use of contribution margin ratio in analyzing sales territories. IceAge has two sales territories, Western and Eastern, and each sells 30,000 units. A selling price of $40 per unit and a variable costs of goods sold of $15 per unit are the same in each territory. Variable selling and administrative expenses differ for the territories. Contribution margin ratio for each territory is in Exhibit 6.15.

**EXHIBIT 6.15**

Contribution Margin Ratio by Territory

| | Western Territory | | Eastern Territory | |
|---|---|---|---|---|
| Sales (30,000 × $40) | | $1,200,000 | | $1,200,000 |
| Variable expenses | | | | |
| Variable cost of goods sold (30,000 × $15) | $450,000 | | $450,000 | |
| Variable selling and admin. expenses (30,000 × $2.60; 30,000 × $1.40) | 78,000 | 528,000 | 42,000 | 492,000 |
| Contribution margin | | $ 672,000 | | $ 708,000 |
| **Contribution margin ratio** | | **56%** | | **59%** |

Although sales and variable cost of goods sold are the same for the two territories, the contribution margin ratio is higher for the Eastern territory of 59% ($708,000/$1,200,000) than for the Western territory of 56%. This difference in contribution margin ratio is from higher variable selling and administrative expenses in the Western territory. Analysis of contribution margin ratio by sales territory can impact IceAge's business decisions such as:

- Reducing variable selling and administrative expenses in the Western territory.
- Increasing sales efforts in the Eastern territory.

**Contribution Margin Analysis by Product Line**   We can also apply this analysis to IceAge's two product lines: hockey skates and figure skates. Units sold, selling prices per unit, and variable selling and administrative expenses per unit are the same for each product line, but variable cost of goods sold per unit is higher for figure skates. With this information we compute the contribution margin ratio by product line in Exhibit 6.16. Contribution margin ratio for hockey skates of 60% ($720,000/$1,200,000) is higher than that for figure skates of 55%. The difference in contribution margin ratio is due to higher variable cost of goods sold per unit for figure skates. Analysis of contribution margin ratio by product line can impact managerial decisions such as:

- Increasing the selling price per unit for figure skates.
- Decreasing the variable cost of goods sold per unit for figure skates.
- Increasing sales efforts for hockey skates.

**EXHIBIT 6.16**

Contribution Margin Ratio by Product Line

| | Hockey Skates | | Figure Skates | |
|---|---|---|---|---|
| Sales (30,000 × $40) | | $1,200,000 | | $1,200,000 |
| Variable expenses | | | | |
| Variable cost of goods sold (30,000 × $14; 30,000 × $16) | $420,000 | | $480,000 | |
| Variable selling and administrative expenses (30,000 × $2) | 60,000 | 480,000 | 60,000 | 540,000 |
| Contribution margin | | $ 720,000 | | $ 660,000 |
| **Contribution margin ratio** | | **60%** | | **55%** |

Navarro Company began operations on January 1, Year 1. Cost and sales data for its first two years of operations are shown below.

NEED-TO-KNOW 6-4

**COMPREHENSIVE**

Product Cost per Unit and Income Reporting under Variable and Absorption Costing

| Manufacturing costs | | Production and sales | |
|---|---|---|---|
| Direct materials.................. | $80 per unit | Units produced, Year 1............. | 2,000 units |
| Direct labor ...................... | $120 per unit | Units sold, Year 1 ................ | 1,900 units |
| Overhead costs | | Units in ending inventory, Year 1..... | 100 units |
| Variable...................... | $30 per unit | | |
| Fixed ........................ | $140,000 per year | Units produced, Year 2............. | 2,000 units |
| | | Units sold, Year 2 ................ | 2,100 units |
| Selling and administrative expenses | | Units in ending inventory, Year 2..... | 0 units |
| Variable....................... | $10 per unit | | |
| Fixed .......................... | $81,000 per year | Sales price per unit............... | $500 per unit |

**Required**

1. Compute product cost per unit under absorption costing and under variable costing.
2. Prepare an income statement for Year 1 under absorption costing and variable costing.
3. Prepare an income statement for Year 2 under absorption costing and variable costing.

## SOLUTION

**1.**

| Product Cost per Unit | Absorption Costing | Variable Costing |
|---|---|---|
| Direct materials........................ | $ 80 | $ 80 |
| Direct labor ........................... | 120 | 120 |
| Overhead | | |
| Variable........................... | 30 | 30 |
| Fixed ($140,000 ÷ 2,000 units)......... | 70 | — |
| Total product cost per unit ............... | $300 | $230 |

**2.** Absorption costing income statement for Year 1.

| Income Statement (Absorption Costing) | |
|---|---|
| For Year Ended December 31, Year 1 | |
| Sales (1,900 × $500) ........................................... | $950,000 |
| Cost of goods sold (1,900 × $300)................................. | 570,000 |
| Gross profit .................................................... | 380,000 |
| Selling and administrative expenses [$81,000 + (1,900 × $10)] ........... | 100,000 |
| Income ...................................................... | $280,000 |

Variable costing income statement for Year 1.

| Income Statement (Variable Costing) | | |
|---|---|---|
| For Year Ended December 31, Year 1 | | |
| Sales (1,900 × $500) ...................................... | | $950,000 |
| Variable expenses | | |
| Variable cost of goods sold (1,900 × $230)................. | $437,000 | |
| Variable selling and administrative expenses (1,900 × $10).... | 19,000 | 456,000 |
| Contribution margin ....................................... | | 494,000 |
| Fixed expenses | | |
| Fixed overhead......................................... | 140,000 | |
| Fixed selling and administrative expenses ................. | 81,000 | 221,000 |
| Income.................................................. | | $273,000 |

**3.** Absorption costing income statement for Year 2.

| Income Statement (Absorption Costing) For Year Ended December 31, Year 2 | |
|---|---|
| Sales (2,100 × $500) . . . . . . . . . . . . . . . . . . . . . . . . . . . . . . . . . . . . . . . | $1,050,000 |
| Cost of goods sold (2,100 × $300) . . . . . . . . . . . . . . . . . . . . . . . . . . . . . | 630,000 |
| Gross profit . . . . . . . . . . . . . . . . . . . . . . . . . . . . . . . . . . . . . . . . . . . . . | 420,000 |
| Selling and administrative expenses [$81,000 + (2,100 × $10)] . . . . . . . . . . . . | 102,000 |
| Income . . . . . . . . . . . . . . . . . . . . . . . . . . . . . . . . . . . . . . . . . . . . . . . . | $  318,000 |

Variable costing income statement for Year 2.

| Income Statement (Variable Costing) For Year Ended December 31, Year 2 | | |
|---|---|---|
| Sales (2,100 × $500) . . . . . . . . . . . . . . . . . . . . . . . . . . . . . . . . . . | | $1,050,000 |
| Variable expenses | | |
| Variable costs of goods sold (2,100 × $230) . . . . . . . . . . . . . . . | $483,000 | |
| Variable selling and administrative expenses (2,100 × $10). . . . | 21,000 | 504,000 |
| Contribution margin . . . . . . . . . . . . . . . . . . . . . . . . . . . . . . . . . . | | 546,000 |
| Fixed expenses | | |
| Fixed overhead. . . . . . . . . . . . . . . . . . . . . . . . . . . . . . . . . . . . . . . | 140,000 | |
| Fixed selling and administrative expenses . . . . . . . . . . . . . . . . . . | 81,000 | 221,000 |
| Income. . . . . . . . . . . . . . . . . . . . . . . . . . . . . . . . . . . . . . . . . . . . . | | $325,000 |

# Converting Income from Variable Costing to Absorption Costing

## 6A

**A2**

Convert income under variable costing to income under absorption costing.

Companies can use variable costing for *internal* reporting and business decisions, but they must use absorption costing for *external* reporting and tax reporting. For companies concerned about maintaining two costing systems, we can readily convert income under variable costing to income under absorption costing.

Income under variable costing is converted to income under absorption costing by adding the fixed overhead cost in ending finished goods (FG) inventory and subtracting the fixed overhead cost in beginning finished goods (FG) inventory. Exhibit 6A.1 shows this calculation.

**EXHIBIT 6A.1**

Formula to Convert Variable Costing Income to Absorption Costing

| Income under absorption costing | = | Income under variable costing | + | Fixed overhead in ending FG inventory* | − | Fixed overhead in beginning FG inventory* |
|---|---|---|---|---|---|---|

*Under absorption costing.

Exhibit 6A.2 shows the computations for IceAge. To convert variable costing income to absorption costing income for Year 2, add the fixed overhead in ending FG inventory. To restate variable costing income to absorption costing income for Year 3, subtract the fixed overhead in beginning FG inventory, which was incurred in Year 2 but expensed in the Year 3 cost of goods sold when the inventory was sold.

**EXHIBIT 6A.2**

Converting Variable Costing Income to Absorption Costing Income

|  | Year 1 | Year 2 | Year 3 |
|---|---|---|---|
| Variable costing income (from Exhibit 6.7) . . . . . . . . . . . . . . . . . . . | $580,000 | $120,000 | $1,040,000 |
| Add: Fixed overhead in ending FG inventory (Yr 2: 20,000 × $10). | 0 | 200,000 | 0 |
| Less: Fixed overhead in beginning FG inventory (Yr 3: 20,000 × $10) | 0 | 0 | (200,000) |
| Absorption costing income . . . . . . . . . . . . . . . . . . . . . . . . . . . . . | $580,000 | $320,000 | $ 840,000 |

Differences between absorption costing income and variable costing income are smaller when

- Fixed overhead is a small percentage of total manufacturing costs.
- Inventory levels are low, as with just-in-time systems.
- Inventory turnover is rapid. The more quickly inventory turns over, the greater proportion of product costs are included in cost of goods sold relative to that remaining in ending inventory.
- Period of analysis is long. Income differences between absorption costing and variable costing decrease as income is compared over longer periods.

## Summary: Cheat Sheet

### VARIABLE AND ABSORPTION COSTING

**Absorption costing:** Fixed overhead is in product costs.
**Variable costing:** Fixed overhead is in period expenses.

| Product Cost per Unit | Absorption Costing | Variable Costing |
|---|---|---|
| Direct materials. . . . . . . . . . . . | $ 4 | $ 4 |
| Direct labor. . . . . . . . . . . . . . . | 8 | 8 |
| Overhead costs | | |
| Variable . . . . . . . . . . . . . . . | 3 | 3 |
| **Fixed** . . . . . . . . . . . . . . . . . | 10 | — |
| Total product cost per unit. . . . | $25 | $15 |

### INCOME REPORTING

**General rule:** When inventory levels *change:* Absorption costing income ≠ Variable costing income.

| Units | Income Effect |
|---|---|
| Production = Sales | Absorption = Variable |
| Production > Sales | Absorption > Variable |
| Production < Sales | Absorption < Variable |

### Income Statement Formats:

**Income Statement (Absorption Costing)**

| | |
|---|---|
| Sales. . . . . . . . . . . . . . . . . . . . . . . . . . . . | $# |
| Cost of goods sold . . . . . . . . . . . . . . . . . . | # |
| Gross profit . . . . . . . . . . . . . . . . . . . . . . . | # |
| Selling and administrative expenses. . . . . | # |
| **Income** . . . . . . . . . . . . . . . . . . . . . . . . . | $# |

**Income Statement (Variable Costing)**

| | | |
|---|---|---|
| Sales. . . . . . . . . . . . . . . . . . . . . . . . . . . | | $# |
| Variable expenses | | |
| Variable cost of goods sold . . . . . . . . . . | $# | |
| Variable selling and admin. expenses. . . | # | # |
| Contribution margin . . . . . . . . . . . . . . . . . | | # |
| Fixed expenses | | |
| Fixed overhead . . . . . . . . . . . . . . . . . . . | # | |
| Fixed selling and admin. expenses . . . . | # | # |
| **Income**. . . . . . . . . . . . . . . . . . . . . . . . . | | $# |

### PRODUCTION AND PRICING

**Setting target price:**

| Step 1 | Absorption cost per unit (from Exhibit 6.3) . . . . | $25 |
|---|---|---|
| Step 2 | Target markup per unit ($25 × 60%) . . . . . . . . . | 15 |
| Step 3 | Target selling price per unit . . . . . . . . . . . . . . . | $40 |

**Analyzing special orders:**

Accept if: Price > Variable costs.

*Example* (per unit amounts): $22 special offer price for 1,000 units, $25 absorption cost; $17 variable cost.

**Special Order Analysis**

| | |
|---|---|
| Sales (1,000 × $22) . . . . . . . . . . . . . . . . . . . . . . . | $22,000 |
| Variable costs (1,000 × $17) . . . . . . . . . . . . . . . . | 17,000 |
| Contribution margin . . . . . . . . . . . . . . . . . . . . . . . | $ 5,000 |

**Contribution margin ratio:**

$$\text{Contribution margin ratio} = \frac{\text{Contribution margin}}{\text{Sales}}$$

**Convert income: Variable to Absorption costing**

$$\begin{array}{c} \text{Income under} \\ \text{absorption costing} \end{array} = \begin{array}{c} \text{Income under} \\ \text{variable costing} \end{array} + \begin{array}{c} \text{Fixed overhead in} \\ \text{ending FG inventory*} \end{array} - \begin{array}{c} \text{Fixed overhead in} \\ \text{beginning FG inventory*} \end{array}$$

*Under absorption costing.

## Key Terms

Absorption costing (also called **full costing**) (203)

Contribution margin (205)

Contribution margin income statement (205)

Contribution margin per unit (206)

Contribution margin ratio (213)

Environmental profit and loss (EP&L) report (213)

Markup (210)

Special order (211)

Variable costing (also called **direct** or **marginal costing**) (203)

Variable cost of goods sold (205)

## Multiple Choice Quiz

Answer questions 1 and 2 using the following data.

| Units produced | 1,000 |
|---|---|
| Variable costs | |
| Direct materials | $3 per unit |
| Direct labor | $5 per unit |
| Variable overhead | $3 per unit |
| Variable selling and administrative | $1 per unit |
| Fixed overhead | $3,000 total |
| Fixed selling and administrative | $1,000 total |

1. Product cost per unit under absorption costing is
   **a.** $11.    **c.** $14.    **e.** $16.
   **b.** $12.    **d.** $15.

2. Product cost per unit under variable costing is
   **a.** $11.    **c.** $14.    **e.** $16.
   **b.** $12.    **d.** $15.

3. Under variable costing, which costs are included in product cost?
   **a.** All variable product costs, including direct materials, direct labor, and variable overhead.

**b.** All variable and fixed product costs, including direct materials, direct labor, and both variable and fixed overhead.

**c.** All variable product costs except for variable overhead.

**d.** All variable and product costs, except for both variable and fixed overhead.

4. The difference between product cost per unit under absorption costing as compared to that under variable costing is
   **a.** Direct materials and direct labor.
   **b.** Fixed and variable portions of overhead.
   **c.** Fixed overhead only.
   **d.** Variable overhead only.

5. When production exceeds sales, which of the following is true?
   **a.** No change occurs to inventories for either absorption costing or variable costing methods.
   **b.** Use of absorption costing produces a higher income than the use of variable costing.
   **c.** Use of absorption costing produces a lower income than the use of variable costing.
   **d.** Use of absorption costing causes inventory value to decrease more than it would through the use of variable costing.

### ANSWERS TO MULTIPLE CHOICE QUIZ

1. c; $14, computed as $3 + $5 + $3 + ($3,000/1,000 units).
2. a; $11, computed as $3 + $5 + $3 (consisting of all variable product costs).

3. a
4. c
5. b

---

[A] *Superscript letter A denotes assignments based on Appendix 6A.*

 *Select Quick Study and Exercise assignments feature Guided Example videos, called "Hints" in Connect. Hints use different numbers, and instructors can turn this feature on or off.*

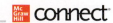

## QUICK STUDY

### QS 6-1
Computing unit cost under absorption costing

**P1**

Vintage Company reports the following information. Compute product cost per unit under absorption costing.

| Direct materials | $10 per unit | Variable overhead | $10 per unit |
|---|---|---|---|
| Direct labor | $20 per unit | Fixed overhead | $160,000 per year |
| Units produced per year | 20,000 units | | |

Refer to information in QS 6-1. Compute product cost per unit under variable costing.

**QS 6-2**
Computing unit cost under
variable costing    **P1**

Classify each of the costs below as either a product cost or a period cost under (*a*) absorption costing and (*b*) variable costing.

**QS 6-3**
Classifying product and
period costs

**P1**

| Cost | Amount | Absorption Costing | Variable Costing |
|---|---|---|---|
| Direct materials.............................. | $3 per unit | | |
| Direct labor ................................. | $5 per unit | | |
| Variable overhead........................... | $2 per unit | | |
| Fixed overhead ............................. | $200,000 per year | | |
| Variable selling and administrative expenses ...... | $0.50 per unit | | |
| Fixed selling and administrative expenses ........ | $100,000 per year | | |

Aces Inc., a manufacturer of tennis rackets, began operations this year. The company produced 6,000 rackets and sold 4,900. Each racket was sold at a price of $90. Fixed overhead costs are $78,000 per year, and fixed selling and administrative costs are $65,200 per year. The company also reports the following per unit variable costs for the year. Prepare an income statement under variable costing.

**QS 6-4**
Variable costing income
statement

**P2**

| | |
|---|---|
| Direct materials............................. | $12 |
| Direct labor ................................. | 8 |
| Variable overhead ........................... | 5 |
| Variable selling and administrative expenses...... | 2 |

Refer to information in QS 6-4. Compute the cost of ending finished goods inventory reported on the balance sheet using variable costing.

**QS 6-5**
Reporting inventory using
variable costing

**P2**

Aces Inc., a manufacturer of tennis rackets, began operations this year. The company produced 6,000 rackets and sold 4,900. Each racket was sold at a price of $90. Fixed overhead costs are $78,000 per year, and fixed selling and administrative costs are $65,200 per year. The company also reports the following per unit variable costs for the year. Prepare an income statement under absorption costing.

**QS 6-6**
Absorption costing income
statement

**P2**

| | |
|---|---|
| Direct materials............................. | $12 |
| Direct labor ................................. | 8 |
| Variable overhead ........................... | 5 |
| Variable selling and administrative expenses...... | 2 |

Refer to the information in QS 6-6. Compute the cost of ending finished goods inventory reported on the balance sheet using absorption costing.

**QS 6-7**
Reporting inventory using
absorption costing

**P2**

A manufacturer has 100 units in finished goods inventory at the end of the year. Using the per unit information below, compute the cost of finished goods inventory reported on the balance sheet under (*a*) absorption costing and (*b*) variable costing.

**QS 6-8**
Computing inventory
under absorption and
variable costing

**P2**

| | | | |
|---|---|---|---|
| Direct materials ..... | $20 per unit | Variable overhead..... | $8 per unit |
| Direct labor ........ | $12 per unit | Fixed overhead ....... | $10 per unit |

**QS 6-9**
Computing gross profit under absorption costing
**P2**

Ramort Company reports the following for its single product. Ramort produced and sold 20,000 units this year. Compute gross profit under absorption costing.

| | | | |
|---|---|---|---|
| Direct materials.............. | $10 per unit | Variable selling and administrative expenses ... | $2 per unit |
| Direct labor ................. | $12 per unit | Fixed selling and administrative expenses ..... | $65,200 per year |
| Variable overhead............ | $3 per unit | Sales price .............................. | $60 per unit |
| Fixed overhead .............. | $40,000 per year | | |

**QS 6-10**
Absorption costing and overproduction   **C1**

Refer to information in QS 6-9. Ramort doubles its production from 20,000 to 40,000 units while sales remain at the current 20,000 unit level. (*a*) Compute gross profit when production is 40,000 units under absorption costing. (*b*) What is the change in gross profit by increasing production from 20,000 units to 40,000 units under absorption costing?

**QS 6-11**
Computing contribution margin under variable costing   **P2**

Refer to information in QS 6-9. Compute contribution margin for the company under variable costing.

**QS 6-12**
Variable costing and overproduction   **C1**

Refer to information in QS 6-9. Ramort doubles its production from 20,000 to 40,000 units while sales remain at the current 20,000 unit level. (*a*) Compute contribution margin when production is 40,000 units under variable costing. (*b*) What is the change in contribution margin by increasing production from 20,000 units to 40,000 units under variable costing?

**QS 6-13**
Absorption costing and overproduction
**C1**

Under absorption costing, a company had the following per unit costs when 10,000 units were produced.

| | |
|---|---|
| Direct materials ..................... | $ 3 |
| Direct labor ........................ | 2 |
| Variable overhead.................... | 4 |
| Fixed overhead ($50,000/10,000 units) ... | 5 |
| Total product cost per unit ............. | $14 |

1. Compute total product cost per unit under absorption costing if instead 12,500 units are produced. Total fixed overhead remains at $50,000.
2. If units produced is greater than units sold, will cost of goods sold under absorption costing *increase* or *decrease*?

**QS 6-14**
Computing gross profit
**P2**

D'Souza Company sold 10,000 units of its product for $80 per unit. Cost of goods sold is $55 per unit. Variable selling and administrative expenses are $10 per unit. Compute gross profit under absorption costing.

**QS 6-15**
Computing contribution margin   **P2**

D'Souza Company sold 10,000 units of its product for $80 per unit. Each unit had $40 in variable cost of goods sold and $10 in variable selling and administrative expenses. Compute contribution margin.

**QS 6-16**
Compute contribution margin   **P2**

A manufacturer reports the following. Compute contribution margin.

| | | | |
|---|---|---|---|
| Sales..................... | $600,000 | Variable selling and administrative expenses ... | $70,000 |
| Variable cost of goods sold... | 200,000 | Fixed selling and administrative expenses ..... | 50,000 |
| Fixed overhead ............ | 160,000 | | |

**QS 6-17**
Compute contribution margin ratio   **A1**

Refer to information in QS 6-16 and compute the contribution margin ratio.

For each of the three independent cases below, determine whether absorption costing income will be greater than, less than, or equal to variable costing income.

QS 6-18
Comparing variable and absorption costing income **P2**

| | Case 1 | Case 2 | Case 3 |
|---|---|---|---|
| Beginning inventory units...... | 0 | 0 | 300 |
| Units produced ............. | 1,000 | 1,400 | 1,300 |
| Units sold.................. | 1,000 | 1,100 | 1,600 |

Diaz Company reports the following variable costing income statement for its only product. Sales total 50,000 units, but production was 80,000 units. Diaz had no beginning finished goods inventory. Prepare an absorption costing income statement.

QS 6-19
Prepare absorption costing income statement **P2**

| Income Statement (Variable Costing) | | |
|---|---|---|
| Sales (50,000 units × $60 per unit)..................................... | | $3,000,000 |
| Variable expenses | | |
| Variable cost of goods sold (50,000 units × $28 per unit)............... | $1,400,000 | |
| Variable selling and administrative expenses (50,000 units × $5 per unit).. | 250,000 | 1,650,000 |
| Contribution margin ................................................. | | 1,350,000 |
| Fixed expenses | | |
| Fixed overhead....................................................... | 320,000 | |
| Fixed selling and administrative expenses ............................ | 160,000 | 480,000 |
| Income...................................................... | | $ 870,000 |

A manufacturer reports the following information. Compute the (a) total product cost per unit under absorption costing and (b) target selling price per unit under absorption costing.

QS 6-20
Target pricing
P3

| | | | |
|---|---|---|---|
| Direct materials ........ | $50 per unit | Fixed overhead......... | $2 per unit |
| Direct labor ........... | $12 per unit | Target markup ......... | 40% |
| Variable overhead ...... | $6 per unit | | |

Li Company produces a product that sells for $84 per unit. The product cost per unit using absorption costing is $70. A customer contacts Li and offers to purchase 2,000 units of this product for $68 per unit. Variable costs of goods sold with this order would be $30 per unit, and variable selling and administrative costs would be $18 per unit. This special order would not require any additional fixed costs and Li has sufficient capacity to produce this special order without affecting regular sales.

(a) Compute contribution margin for this special order. (b) Should Li accept this special order?

QS 6-21
Analyze special order
P3

Dane Co. reports the information below. (a) Compute the contribution margin ratio for each sales territory. (b) Which sales territory performed better based on contribution margin ratio?

QS 6-22
Contribution margin ratio by sales territory **A1**

| | Northern Territory | Southern Territory |
|---|---|---|
| Sales................... | $1,000,000 | $1,200,000 |
| Contribution margin ...... | 400,000 | 540,000 |

Ming Company had income of $772,200 based on variable costing. Beginning and ending finished goods inventories were 7,800 units and 5,200 units, respectively. Assume the fixed overhead per unit was $3 for both the beginning and ending finished goods inventory. What is income under absorption costing?

QS 6-23[A]
Converting variable costing income to absorption costing income **A2**

**QS 6-24ᴬ**
Converting variable costing income to absorption costing income **A2**

Mortech had income of $250,000 based on variable costing. Beginning and ending finished goods inventories were 50,000 units and 48,000 units, respectively. Assume the fixed overhead per unit was $0.75 for both the beginning and ending finished goods inventory. What is income under absorption costing?

**QS 6-25ᴬ**
Converting variable costing income to absorption costing income **A2**

Hong Co. had income of $386,100 under variable costing. Beginning and ending finished goods inventories were 2,600 units and zero units, respectively. Fixed overhead cost was $4 per unit for the beginning finished goods inventory. What is income under absorption costing?

**QS 6-26ᴬ**
Converting variable costing income to absorption costing income **A2**

E-Com had income of $130,000 under variable costing. Beginning and ending finished goods inventories were zero units and 4,900 units, respectively. Fixed overhead cost was $2.50 per unit for the ending finished goods inventory. What is income under absorption costing?

**QS 6-27ᴬ**
Variable and absorption costing income **A2**

Alex Co. reports variable manufacturing costs of $120 per unit and fixed overhead of $10 per unit. The company produced 20,000 units and sold 18,000 units. The company had no beginning finished goods inventory. (*a*) Determine whether absorption costing income is greater than or less than variable costing income. (*b*) Compute the difference in income between absorption costing income and variable costing income.

**QS 6-28ᴬ**
Variable and absorption costing income **A2**

Zarne Co. reports variable manufacturing costs of $60 per unit and fixed overhead of $20 per unit. Beginning finished goods inventory under absorption costing is 500 units. The company produced 7,500 units and sold 8,000 units. (*a*) Determine whether absorption costing income is greater than or less than variable costing income. (*b*) Compute the difference in income between absorption costing income and variable costing income.

---

Mc Graw Hill **connect**

## EXERCISES

**Exercise 6-1**
Computing unit and inventory costs under absorption costing
**P1**

Trio Company reports the following information for its first year of operations.

| Direct materials | $15 per unit | Units produced | 20,000 units |
|---|---|---|---|
| Direct labor | $16 per unit | Units sold | 14,000 units |
| Variable overhead | $ 4 per unit | Ending finished goods inventory | 6,000 units |
| Fixed overhead | $160,000 per year | | |

1. Compute the product cost per unit using absorption costing.
2. Determine the cost of ending finished goods inventory using absorption costing.
3. Determine the cost of goods sold using absorption costing.

**Exercise 6-2**
Computing unit and inventory costs under variable costing **P1**

Refer to information in Exercise 6-1. Assume instead the company uses variable costing.
1. Compute the product cost per unit using variable costing.
2. Determine the cost of ending finished goods inventory using variable costing.
3. Determine the cost of goods sold using variable costing.

**Exercise 6-3**
Income statement under absorption costing and variable costing
**P1**   **P2**

Cool Sky reports the following for its first year of operations. The company produced 44,000 units and sold 36,000 units at a price of $140 per unit.

| Direct materials | $60 per unit | Variable selling and administrative expenses | $11 per unit |
|---|---|---|---|
| Direct labor | $22 per unit | Fixed selling and administrative expenses | $105,000 per year |
| Variable overhead | $8 per unit | | |
| Fixed overhead | $528,000 per year | | |

1. Assume the company uses absorption costing.
   a. Determine its total product cost per unit.
   b. Prepare its income statement for the year under absorption costing.
2. Assume the company uses variable costing.
   a. Determine its total product cost per unit.
   b. Prepare its income statement for the year under variable costing.

**Check**   (1a) Absorption cost per unit, $102

---

Barnes Co. reports the following for its product for its first year of operations. Compute total product cost per unit using absorption costing for the following production levels: (a) 2,000 units, (b) 2,400 units, and (c) 3,000 units.

**Exercise 6-4**
Computing cost per unit at different production levels

**P1   P2**

| Direct materials........ | $35 per unit | Fixed overhead ......................... | $48,000 per year |
| Direct labor ........... | $25 per unit | Variable selling and administrative expenses ... | $3 per unit |
| Variable overhead...... | $10 per unit | Fixed selling and administrative expenses ..... | $20,000 per year |

---

Refer to information in Exercise 6-4. The company sells its product for $150 per unit. Compute gross profit using absorption costing assuming the company (a) produces and sells 2,000 units and (b) produces 2,400 units and sells 2,000 units.

**Exercise 6-5**
Computing gross profit at different production levels

**P2**

---

Refer to information in Exercise 6-4. The company sells its product for $150 per unit. Compute contribution margin using variable costing assuming the company (a) produces and sells 2,000 units and (b) produces 2,400 units and sells 2,000 units.

**Exercise 6-6**
Computing contribution margin at different production levels   **P2**

---

Sims Company began operations on January 1. Its cost and sales information for this year follow.

**Exercise 6-7**
Income reporting under absorption costing and variable costing

**P2**

| Direct materials........ | $40 per unit | Variable selling and administrative expenses ... | $11 per unit |
| Direct labor ........... | $60 per unit | Fixed selling and administrative expenses ..... | $4,250,000 per year |
| Variable overhead...... | $30 per unit | | |
| Fixed overhead ........ | $7,000,000 per year | Units produced ......................... | 100,000 units |
| | | Units sold............................. | 70,000 units |
| | | Sales price............................ | $350 per unit |

1. Prepare an income statement for the year using variable costing.
2. Prepare an income statement for the year using absorption costing.

---

Kenzi, a manufacturer of kayaks, began operations this year. During this year, the company produced 1,050 kayaks and sold 800 at a price of $1,100 each. At year-end, the company reported the following income statement information using absorption costing.

**Exercise 6-8**
Variable costing income statement

**P2**

| Sales (800 × $1,100).................... | $880,000 |
| Cost of goods sold (800 × $500) ......... | 400,000 |
| Gross profit.......................... | 480,000 |
| Selling and administrative expenses ...... | 230,000 |
| Income ............................. | $250,000 |

**Additional Information**

a. Product cost per kayak under absorption costing totals $500, which consists of $400 in direct materials, direct labor, and variable overhead costs and $100 in fixed overhead cost. Fixed overhead of $100 per unit is based on $105,000 of fixed overhead per year divided by 1,050 kayaks produced.
b. The $230,000 in selling and administrative expenses consists of $75,000 that is variable and $155,000 that is fixed.

Prepare an income statement for the current year under variable costing.

**Exercise 6-9**
Absorption costing and variable costing income statements
P2

Rey Company's only product sells for $216 per unit. Data for its first year of operations follow. Prepare an income statement for the year assuming (a) absorption costing and (b) variable costing.

| | | | |
|---|---|---|---|
| Direct materials........... | $20 per unit | Variable selling and administrative expenses .. | $18 per unit |
| Direct labor .............. | $28 per unit | Fixed selling and administrative expenses ..... | $200,000 per year |
| Variable overhead......... | $ 6 per unit | Units produced and sold.................... | 20,000 units |
| Fixed overhead ........... | $160,000 per year | | |

**Exercise 6-10**
Absorption costing income statement
P2

Hayek Bikes prepares the income statement under variable costing for its managerial reports, and it prepares the income statement under absorption costing for external reporting. For its first month of operations, 375 bikes were produced and 225 were sold. Income statement information under variable costing follows.

| | |
|---|---:|
| Sales (225 × $1,600) .............................. | $360,000 |
| Variable cost of goods sold (225 × $625) .............. | 140,625 |
| Variable selling and administrative expenses (225 × $65) ... | 14,625 |
| Contribution margin ..................... | 204,750 |
| Fixed overhead ...................... | 56,250 |
| Fixed selling and administrative expenses ............. | 75,000 |
| Income .......................... | $ 73,500 |

Prepare the company's income statement under absorption costing.

**Exercise 6-11**
Absorption costing and variable costing income statements    P2

Oak Mart, a producer of solid oak tables, reports the following data from its first year of business.

| | | | |
|---|---|---|---|
| Sales price per unit ..................... | $320 per unit | Direct materials ............. | $40 per unit |
| Units produced this year ................. | 117,000 units | Direct labor................. | $62 per unit |
| Units sold this year..................... | 117,000 units | Variable overhead ........... | $28 per unit |
| Variable selling and administrative expenses .. | $12 per unit | Fixed overhead.............. | $7,020,000 per year |
| Fixed selling and administrative expenses.... | $4,600,000 per year | | |

1. Prepare the current year income statement using variable costing.
2. Prepare the current year income statement using absorption costing.

**Exercise 6-12**
Prepare variable costing income statement    P2

Dion Co. reports the absorption costing income statement below for May. The company began the month with no finished goods inventory. Dion produced 20,000 units, and 2,000 units remain in ending finished goods inventory for May. Fixed overhead was $50,000. Variable selling and administration expenses were $30,000 and fixed selling and administrative expenses were $10,000. Prepare an income statement using variable costing.

| | |
|---|---:|
| Sales (18,000 units) ................... | $360,000 |
| Cost of goods sold ................... | 300,000 |
| Gross profit ......................... | 60,000 |
| Selling and administrative expenses ...... | 40,000 |
| Income............................ | $ 20,000 |

**Exercise 6-13**
Prepare absorption costing income statement    P2

Trevor Co. reports the variable costing income statement below for June. The company began the month with no finished goods inventory. It produced 10,000 units in June, and 2,000 units remain in ending finished goods inventory. Prepare an income statement using absorption costing.

| Sales (8,000 units)................................ | | $320,000 |
|---|---|---|
| Variable expenses | | |
| Variable cost of goods sold .................... | $225,000 | |
| Variable selling and administrative expenses...... | 35,000 | 260,000 |
| Contribution margin ........................... | | 60,000 |
| Fixed expenses | | |
| Fixed overhead............................. | 8,000 | |
| Fixed selling and administrative expenses........ | 12,000 | 20,000 |
| Income....................................... | | $ 40,000 |

Jax Inc. reports the following data for its only product. The company had no beginning finished goods inventory and it uses absorption costing.

| Sales price ................... | $56.00 per unit | Direct labor .................... | $6.50 per unit |
|---|---|---|---|
| Direct materials ............... | $9.00 per unit | Variable overhead ............. | $11.00 per unit |
| | | Fixed overhead ................ | $720,000 per year |

**Exercise 6-14**
Absorption costing and overproduction

C1

1. Compute gross profit assuming (*a*) 60,000 units are produced and 60,000 units are sold and (*b*) 80,000 units are produced and 60,000 units are sold.
2. By how much would the company's gross profit increase or decrease from producing 20,000 more units than it sells?

A manufacturer reports direct materials of $5 per unit, direct labor of $2 per unit, and variable overhead of $3 per unit. Fixed overhead is $120,000 per year, and the company estimates sales of 12,000 units at a sales price of $25 per unit for the year. The company has no beginning finished goods inventory.

1. If the company uses absorption costing, compute gross profit assuming (*a*) 12,000 units are produced and 12,000 units are sold and (*b*) 15,000 units are produced and 12,000 units are sold.
2. If the company uses variable costing, how much would gross profit differ if the company produced 15,000 units instead of producing 12,000? Assume the company sells 12,000 units. *Hint:* Calculations are not required.

**Exercise 6-15**
Absorption costing and overproduction

C1

Huds Inc. reports the information below on its product. The company uses absorption costing and has a target markup of 40% of absorption cost per unit. Compute the target selling price per unit under absorption costing.

| Direct materials ........ | $100 per unit | Variable selling and administrative expenses .. | $3 per unit |
|---|---|---|---|
| Direct labor ........... | $30 per unit | Fixed selling and administrative expenses..... | $120,000 per year |
| Variable overhead ...... | $8 per unit | Units produced.......................... | 50,000 units per year |
| Fixed overhead......... | $600,000 per year | Units sold .............................. | 50,000 units per year |

**Exercise 6-16**
Target pricing    P3

Grand Garden is a hotel with 150 suites. Its regular suite price is $250 per night per suite. The hotel's total cost per night is $140 per suite and consists of the following.

| Variable cost................... | $110 |
|---|---|
| Fixed cost.................... | 30 |
| Total cost per night per suite...... | $140 |

**Exercise 6-17**
Analyzing a special offer for a service company

P3

The hotel manager receives an offer to hold the local Bikers' Club meeting at the hotel in March, which is the hotel's slow season with a low occupancy rate per night. The Bikers' Club would reserve 150 suites for one night if the hotel accepts a price of $125 per night. (*a*) What is the contribution margin from this special offer? (*b*) Should the Bikers' Club offer be accepted or rejected?

**Exercise 6-18**

Analyzing a special offer for a service company

P3

Empire Airlines reports the following cost data for the year. The company flew 100 private flights during the year. A group has offered Empire $11,000 for a private flight to Chicago for its members. (*a*) What is the contribution margin from accepting the offer? (*b*) Should the offer be accepted or rejected?

| | | | |
|---|---|---|---|
| Revenue..................... | $20,000 per flight | Food and beverages............. | $500 per flight |
| Wages, salaries, and benefits...... | $7,000 per flight | Depreciation .................. | $300,000 per year |
| Fuel and oil .................... | $4,500 per flight | Rent .......................... | $250,000 per year |

**Exercise 6-19**

Analyzing a special offer for a service company

P3

MidCoast Airlines provides charter airplane services. In October, when the company is operating at 60% of its capacity, it receives a bid from the local college. The college is organizing a trip for a student group. The college budgeted only $30,000 for round-trip airfare. MidCoast Airlines normally charges between $50,000 and $60,000 for such service. MidCoast determines its total cost for the round-trip flight to Washington to be $45,000, which consists of the following.

| | |
|---|---|
| Variable cost.... | $25,000 |
| Fixed cost ...... | 20,000 |
| Total cost....... | $45,000 |

Although the manager at MidCoast supports the college's educational efforts, she is struggling to justify accepting only $30,000. (*a*) What is the contribution margin from accepting the offer? (*b*) Should the airline accept the $30,000 offer from the college?

**Exercise 6-20**

Contribution margin ratio by sales territory

A1

Big Bikes manufactures and sells mountain bikes in two sales territories, West Coast and East Coast. Information for the year follows. The company sold 500 bikes in each territory.

| Per unit | West Coast | East Coast |
|---|---|---|
| Sales price................................. | $1,000 | $960 |
| Variable cost of goods sold .................... | 540 | 540 |
| Variable selling and administrative expenses...... | 120 | 60 |

a.  Compute contribution margin (in dollars) for each sales territory.

b.  Compute contribution margin ratio for each sales territory. Which sales territory has the better contribution margin ratio?

**Exercise 6-21**

Contribution margin ratio by product line

A1

Pro Bike manufactures and sells two types of bikes: road bikes and mountain bikes. The company sold 600 units of each type of bike during the year.

| Per unit | Road bikes | Mountain bikes |
|---|---|---|
| Sales price................................. | $1,200 | $800 |
| Variable cost of goods sold .................... | 840 | 480 |
| Variable selling and administrative expenses...... | 60 | 64 |

a.  Compute contribution margin (in dollars) for each product.

b.  Compute contribution margin ratio for each product. Which product has the better contribution margin ratio?

**Exercise 6-22**[A]

Converting variable costing income to absorption costing income

A2

A manufacturer reports the following information for the past three years. Compute income for each of the three years using absorption costing. *Hint:* Fixed overhead in inventory equals the FOH per unit x Units in inventory.

| | Year 1 | Year 2 | Year 3 |
|---|---|---|---|
| Variable costing income......................... | $110,000 | $114,400 | $118,950 |
| Beginning finished goods inventory (units).......... | 0 | 1,200 | 700 |
| Ending finished goods inventory (units) ........... | 1,200 | 700 | 800 |
| Fixed overhead (FOH) per unit.................... | $2.50 | $2.50 | $2.50 |

 connect

Dowell Company produces a single product. Its income statements under absorption costing for its first two years of operation follow.

| Income Statements (Absorption Costing) | Year 1 | Year 2 |
|---|---|---|
| Sales ($46 per unit) ................. | $920,000 | $1,840,000 |
| Cost of goods sold ($31 per unit) ...... | 620,000 | 1,240,000 |
| Gross profit......................... | 300,000 | 600,000 |
| Selling and administrative expenses ... | 170,000 | 220,000 |
| Income ........................... | $130,000 | $ 380,000 |

**PROBLEM SET A**

**Problem 6-1A**
Variable costing income statement for two consecutive years

**P2**

**Additional Information**

a. Sales and production data for these first two years follow.

| Units | Year 1 | Year 2 |
|---|---|---|
| Units produced...... | 30,000 | 30,000 |
| Units sold........... | 20,000 | 40,000 |

b. Variable costs per unit and fixed costs per year are unchanged during these years. The company's $31 per unit product cost using absorption costing consists of the following.

| | |
|---|---|
| Direct materials ........................... | $ 5 |
| Direct labor............................... | 9 |
| Variable overhead ........................ | 7 |
| Fixed overhead ($300,000/30,000 units) ...... | 10 |
| Total product cost per unit.................. | $31 |

c. Selling and administrative expenses consist of the following.

| Selling and Administrative Expenses | Year 1 | Year 2 |
|---|---|---|
| Variable selling and administrative ($2.50 per unit sold)...... | $ 50,000 | $100,000 |
| Fixed selling and administrative ......................... | 120,000 | 120,000 |
| Total ...................................... | $170,000 | $220,000 |

**Required**

Prepare income statements for each of these two years under variable costing.

---

Trez Company began operations this year. During this year, the company produced 100,000 units and sold 80,000 units. The absorption costing income statement for this year follows.

| Income Statement (Absorption Costing) | |
|---|---|
| Sales (80,000 units × $50 per unit) ....... | $4,000,000 |
| Cost of goods sold .................... | 2,400,000 |
| Gross profit......................... | 1,600,000 |
| Selling and administrative expenses ...... | 530,000 |
| Income ........................... | $1,070,000 |

**Problem 6-2A**
Variable costing income statement

**P2**

**Additional Information**

a. Selling and administrative expenses consist of $350,000 in annual fixed expenses and $2.25 per unit in variable selling and administrative expenses.

b. The company's product cost of $30 per unit consists of the following.

| | | | |
|---|---|---|---|
| Direct materials ..... | $5 per unit | Variable overhead......................... | $2 per unit |
| Direct labor......... | $14 per unit | Fixed overhead ($900,000/100,000 units) ..... | $9 per unit |

**Required**

Prepare an income statement for the company under variable costing.

**Problem 6-3A**

Income reporting, absorption costing, and managerial ethics

**C1**

Blazer Chemical produces and sells an ice-melting granular used on roadways and sidewalks in winter. It annually produces and sells 20,000 tons of its granular. Because of this year's mild winter, projected demand for its product is only 15,000 tons. Based on projected production and sales of 15,000 tons, the company estimates the following income using absorption costing.

| | |
|---|---|
| Sales (15,000 tons at $80 per ton) ................. | $1,200,000 |
| Cost of goods sold (15,000 tons at $60 per ton) ...... | 900,000 |
| Gross profit..................................... | 300,000 |
| Selling and administrative expenses .............. | 300,000 |
| Income .................................... | $        0 |

Its product cost per ton follows and consists mainly of fixed overhead because its automated production process uses expensive equipment.

| | | | |
|---|---|---|---|
| Direct materials................. | $13 per ton | Variable overhead...................... | $3 per ton |
| Direct labor .................... | $4 per ton | Fixed overhead ($600,000/15,000 tons).... | $40 per ton |

Selling and administrative expenses consist of variable selling and administrative expenses of $6 per ton and fixed selling and administrative expenses of $210,000 per year. The company's president will not earn a bonus unless a positive income is reported. The controller mentions that because the company has large storage capacity, it can report a positive income by setting production at the usual 20,000 ton level even though it expects to sell only 15,000 tons. The president is surprised that the company can report income by producing more without increasing sales.

**Required**

1. (*a*) Prepare an income statement using absorption costing based on production of 20,000 tons and sales of 15,000 tons. (*b*) Can the company report a positive income by increasing production to 20,000 tons and storing the 5,000 tons of excess production in inventory?

2. By how much does income increase by when producing 20,000 tons and storing 5,000 tons in inventory compared to only producing 15,000 tons?

**Problem 6-4A**[A]

Converting variable costing income to absorption costing income

**A2**

Dowell Company produces a single product. Its income under variable costing for its first two years of operation follow.

| Variable Costing Income | Year 1 | Year 2 |
|---|---|---|
| Income ........................... | $30,000 | $480,000 |

**Additional Information**

**a.** Sales and production data for these first two years follow.

| Units | Year 1 | Year 2 |
|---|---|---|
| Units produced...... | 30,000 | 30,000 |
| Units sold.......... | 20,000 | 40,000 |

**b.** The company's $31 per unit product cost (for both years) using absorption costing consists of the following.

| | |
|---|---|
| Direct materials ......................... | $ 5 |
| Direct labor............................. | 9 |
| Variable overhead ....................... | 7 |
| Fixed overhead ($300,000/30,000 units) ...... | 10 |
| Total product cost per unit................. | $31 |

**Required**

Prepare a table as in Exhibit 6A.2 to convert variable costing income to absorption costing income for both years.

**PROBLEM SET B**

Zule Company produces a single product. Its income statements under absorption costing for its first two years of operation follow.

**Problem 6-1B**
Variable costing income statement for two consecutive years

**P2**

| Income Statements (Absorption Costing) | Year 1 | Year 2 |
|---|---|---|
| Sales ($35 per unit) ................... | $1,925,000 | $2,275,000 |
| Cost of goods sold ($26 per unit) ........ | 1,430,000 | 1,690,000 |
| Gross profit............................ | 495,000 | 585,000 |
| Selling and administrative expenses ...... | 365,000 | 395,000 |
| Income ............................... | $ 130,000 | $ 190,000 |

**Additional Information**

**a.** Sales and production data for these first two years follow.

| Units | Year 1 | Year 2 |
|---|---|---|
| Units produced...... | 60,000 | 60,000 |
| Units sold........... | 55,000 | 65,000 |

**b.** Its variable costs per unit and fixed costs per year are unchanged during these years. Its $26 per unit product cost using absorption costing consists of the following.

| | |
|---|---|
| Direct materials ......................... | $ 4 |
| Direct labor.............................. | 6 |
| Variable overhead ....................... | 8 |
| Fixed overhead ($480,000/60,000 units) ...... | 8 |
| Total product cost per unit................. | $26 |

**c.** Its selling and administrative expenses consist of the following.

| Selling and Administrative Expenses | Year 1 | Year 2 |
|---|---|---|
| Variable selling and administrative ($3 per unit sold) ... | $165,000 | $195,000 |
| Fixed selling and administrative .................... | 200,000 | 200,000 |
| Total ........................................ | $365,000 | $395,000 |

**Required**

Prepare income statements under variable costing for each of these two years.

Lonte Company began operations this year. During this year, the company produced 300,000 units and sold 250,000 units. Its income statement under absorption costing for this year follows.

**Problem 6-2B**
Variable costing income statement

**P2**

| Income Statement (Absorption Costing) | |
|---|---|
| Sales (250,000 units × $18 per unit) ...... | $4,500,000 |
| Cost of goods sold .................... | 1,875,000 |
| Gross profit......................... | 2,625,000 |
| Selling and administrative expenses ...... | 2,200,000 |
| Income ............................. | $ 425,000 |

**Additional Information**

**a.** Selling and administrative expenses consist of $1,200,000 in annual fixed expenses and $4 per unit in variable selling and administrative expenses.

**b.** The company's product cost of $7.50 per unit consists of the following.

| | | | |
|---|---|---|---|
| Direct materials ..... | $2.00 per unit | Variable overhead.......................... | $1.60 per unit |
| Direct labor......... | $2.40 per unit | Fixed overhead ($450,000/300,000 units) ..... | $1.50 per unit |

**Required**

Prepare the company's income statement under variable costing.

---

**Problem 6-3B**

Income reporting, absorption costing, and managerial ethics

C1

Pool Pro produces and sells liquid chlorine for swimming pools. The company annually produces and sells 300,000 gallons of its chlorine. Because of this year's cool summer, projected demand for its product is only 250,000 gallons. Based on projected production and sales of 250,000 gallons, the company estimates the following income using absorption costing.

| | |
|---|---|
| Sales (250,000 gallons at $8 per gallon) ............... | $2,000,000 |
| Cost of goods sold (250,000 gallons at $6.80 per gallon) .. | 1,700,000 |
| Gross profit ........................................ | 300,000 |
| Selling and administrative expenses ................... | 300,000 |
| Income ........................................... | $        0 |

Its product cost per gallon follows and consists mainly of fixed overhead because its automated production process uses expensive equipment.

| | | | |
|---|---|---|---|
| Direct materials ..... | $1.00 per gallon | Variable overhead.......................... | $0.40 per gallon |
| Direct labor......... | $0.60 per gallon | Fixed overhead ($1,200,000/250,000 gallons) ... | $4.80 per gallon |

Selling and administrative expenses consist of variable selling and administrative expenses of $0.80 per gallon and fixed selling and administrative expenses of $100,000 per year. The company's president will not earn a bonus unless a positive income is reported. The controller suggests that because the company has large storage capacity, it can report a positive income by setting its production at the usual 300,000 gallon level even though it expects to sell only 250,000 gallons. The president is surprised that the company can report income by producing more without increasing sales.

**Required**

**1.** (*a*) Prepare an income statement using absorption costing based on production of 300,000 gallons and sales of 250,000 gallons. (*b*) Can the company report positive income by increasing production to 300,000 gallons and storing the 50,000 gallons of excess production in inventory?

**2.** Should the company produce 300,000 gallons given that projected demand is 250,000 gallons? Explain, and refer to any ethical implications of such a managerial decision for income reporting.

---

**Problem 6-4B**[A]

Converting variable costing income to absorption costing income

A2

Zule Company produces a single product. Its income under variable costing for its first two years of operation follow.

| Variable Costing Income | Year 1 | Year 2 |
|---|---|---|
| Income ......................... | $7,000 | $113,000 |

**Additional Information**

**a.** Sales and production data for these first two years follow.

| Units | Year 1 | Year 2 |
|---|---|---|
| Units produced...... | 60,000 | 60,000 |
| Units sold.......... | 56,000 | 64,000 |

**b.** The company's $26 per unit product cost (for both years) using absorption costing consists of the following.

| | |
|---|---|
| Direct materials ........................... | $ 4 |
| Direct labor............................... | 6 |
| Variable overhead ........................ | 8 |
| Fixed overhead ($480,000/60,000 units) ...... | 8 |
| Total product cost per unit................. | $26 |

**Required**

Prepare a table as in Exhibit 6A.2 to convert variable costing income to absorption costing income for both years.

---

**SERIAL PROBLEM**
Business Solutions
**P2**

*This serial problem began in Chapter 1 and continues through most of the book. If previous chapter segments were not completed, the serial problem can begin at this point.*

**SP 6**  Santana Rey expects sales of **Business Solutions'** line of computer workstation furniture to equal 300 workstations (at a sales price of $3,000 each) for 2021. The workstations' manufacturing costs include the following.

| | | | |
|---|---|---|---|
| Direct materials ..... | $800 per unit | Variable overhead...... | $100 per unit |
| Direct labor......... | $400 per unit | Fixed overhead ........ | $24,000 per year |

Selling and administrative expenses for these workstations follow.

| | | | |
|---|---|---|---|
| Variable........ | $50 per unit | Fixed .......... | $4,000 per year |

Santana is considering how many workstations to produce in 2021. She is confident that she will be able to sell any workstations in her 2021 ending inventory during 2022. However, Santana does not want to overproduce as she does not have sufficient storage space for many more workstations.

Alexander Image/Shutterstock

**Required**

1. Compute its income statement under absorption costing assuming
   **a.** 300 workstations are produced, and 300 workstations are sold.
   **b.** 320 workstations are produced, and 300 workstations are sold.
2. Compute its income statement under variable costing assuming
   **a.** 300 workstations are produced, and 300 workstations are sold.
   **b.** 320 workstations are produced, and 300 workstations are sold.
3. Reviewing results from parts 1 and 2, which costing method, absorption or variable, yields the higher income when 320 workstations are produced and 300 are sold?

---

**Tableau Dashboard Activities** expose students to accounting analytics using visual displays. These assignments run in **Connect**. All are auto-gradable.

**TABLEAU DASHBOARD ACTIVITIES**

**Tableau DA 6-1 Quick Study**, Computing unit and inventory costs under absorption costing, **P1**—similar to QS 6-1 and Exercise 6-1.

**Tableau DA 6-2 Exercise**, Computing unit and inventory costs under variable costing, **P1**—similar to QS 6-2 and Exercise 6-2.

**Tableau DA 6-3 Mini-Case**, Income reporting under absorption and variable costing, **P1, P2**—similar to QS 6-4, QS 6-6, and Exercise 6-9.

## Accounting Analysis

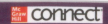

### COMPANY ANALYSIS
A1

**AA 6-1** **Apple** has the following product line information for the current year. Some data are assumed.

| $ millions | iPhone | Services |
|---|---|---|
| Sales................... | $142,381 | $46,291 |
| Contribution margin ...... | 68,343 | 33,330 |

**Required**

1. Compute the contribution margin ratio for both product lines for the current year.
2. Which product line performed better based on contribution margin ratio?

### COMPARATIVE ANALYSIS
A1

**APPLE**
**GOOGLE**

**AA 6-2** **Google** and **Apple** compete for smartphone sales. The companies show the following information for their smartphone product lines for the current year. Some data are assumed.

| $ millions | Apple | Google |
|---|---|---|
| Sales................... | $142,381 | $17,104 |
| Contribution margin ...... | 68,343 | 6,500 |

**Required**

1. Compute the contribution margin ratio for each company's smartphone product line for the current year.
2. Which company's smartphone product line performed better based on contribution margin ratio?

### EXTENDED ANALYSIS
A1

**AA 6-3** **Samsung** and **Apple** compete for smartphone sales. The companies show the following information for their smartphone product lines for the current year. Some data are assumed.

| $ millions | Apple | Samsung |
|---|---|---|
| Sales................... | $142,381 | $38,402 |
| Contribution margin ...... | 68,343 | 17,665 |

**Required**

1. Compute the contribution margin ratio for each company's smartphone product line for the current year.
2. Which company's smartphone product line performed better based on contribution margin ratio?

## Discussion Questions

1. What costs are included in product costs under variable costing?

2. What costs are included in product costs under absorption costing?

3. When units produced exceed units sold for a reporting period, would income under variable costing be greater than, equal to, or less than income under absorption costing? Explain.

4. Describe how the following items are computed: (*a*) gross profit and (*b*) contribution margin.

5. How can absorption costing lead to incorrect special offer decisions?

6. Describe how use of absorption costing in determining income can lead to overproduction and a buildup of inventory. Explain how variable costing can avoid this same problem.

7. Assume that **Apple** has received a special order from a retailer for 1,000 specially out-fitted iPads. This is a one-time order, which will not require any additional capacity or fixed costs. What should Apple consider when determining a selling price for these iPads? **APPLE**

8. How is the contribution margin ratio computed?

9. How can the contribution margin ratio be used in performance evaluation?

10. How can variable costing income be converted to absorption costing income?

## Beyond the Numbers

**BTN 6-1**   FDP Company produces a variety of home security products. Gary Price, the company's president, is concerned with the fourth-quarter market demand for the company's products. Unless something is done in the last two months of the year, the company is likely to miss its earnings expectation of Wall Street analysts. Price still remembers when FDP's earnings were below analysts' expectation by two cents a share three years ago and the company's share price fell 19% the day earnings were announced. In a recent meeting, Price told his top management that something must be done quickly. One proposal by the marketing vice president was to give a deep discount to the company's major customers to increase the company's sales in the fourth quarter. The company controller pointed out that while the discount could increase sales, it may not help the bottom line; to the contrary, it could lower income. The controller said, "Since we have enough storage capacity, we might simply increase our production in the fourth quarter to increase our reported income."

**ETHICS CHALLENGE**

C1

**Required**

1. Gary Price is not sure how the increase in production without a corresponding increase in sales could help boost the company's income. Explain to Price how reported income varies with respect to production level.
2. Is there an ethical concern in this situation? If so, which parties are affected? Explain.

---

**BTN 6-2**   Mertz Chemical has three divisions. Its consumer product division faces strong competition from companies overseas. During its recent teleconference, Ryan Peterson, the consumer product division manager, reported that his division's sales for the current year were below its break-even point. However, when the division's annual reports were received, Billie Mertz, the company president, was surprised that the consumer product division actually reported income of $264,000. How could this be possible?

**COMMUNICATING IN PRACTICE**

C1

**Required**

Assume that you work in the corporate controller's office. Write a half-page memorandum to the president explaining how the division can report income even if its sales are below the break-even point.

---

**BTN 6-3**   This chapter identified several decision contexts in which managers use product cost information.

**TEAMWORK IN ACTION**

P3

**Required**

Break into teams and identify at least one specific decision context in which absorption costing information is more relevant than variable costing information and at least one decision context in which variable costing information is more relevant than absorption costing. Be prepared to discuss your answers in class.

---

**BTN 6-4**   Da Bomb, co-founded by sisters Caroline and Isabel Bercaw, makes bath bombs.

**ENTREPRENEURIAL DECISION**

P2

**Required**

Isabel and Caroline use variable costing to make business decisions. If the sisters used absorption costing, would we expect the company's income to be more than, less than, or about the same as its income measured under variable costing? Explain.

# 7 Master Budgets and Performance Planning

## Learning Objectives

### CONCEPTUAL

**C1** Describe the benefits of budgeting.

### ANALYTICAL

**A1** Prepare a direct labor budget for a service firm and analyze revenue per employee.

### PROCEDURAL

**P1** Prepare the operating budgets of a master budget for a manufacturing company.

**P2** Prepare a cash budget for a manufacturing company.

**P3** Prepare budgeted financial statements.

**P4** *Appendix 7A—*Prepare each component of a master budget for a merchandising company.

# Bottled Bliss

*"Sell it, don't tell it"*—NAILAH ELLIS-BROWN

©Ellis Infinity, LLC

Detroit—Nailah Ellis-Brown's great-grandfather immigrated to the U.S. from Jamaica with a prized family recipe for hibiscus tea. Nailah recalls her great-grandfather's instruction: "This recipe is to be sold, not told." This is what her company, **Ellis Island Tropical Tea** (**Ellisislandtea.com**) does today.

Nailah started small, making tea in her mother's basement and selling it out of the trunk of her car. "Everything from day one has been trial and error," Nailah explains.

In addition to production, packaging, and distribution, Nailah budgets for and controls her costs. Managing direct materials, direct labor, and overhead costs is critical to survival.

Consumer tastes make sales forecasting hard, but Nailah knows that a good sales forecast is the cornerstone of a good budget. "Because our sales volume was low," explains Nailah, "we set our price too high to cover costs." She quickly adjusted the pricing.

As sales grew, Nailah expanded her production facility. Because production budgets are based on the level of sales, she had to update many of her budgets. This new facility increased her overhead costs, which also required changes to overhead budgets. Businesses revise budgets frequently.

Nailah proclaims: "Ours is the only Jamaican sweet tea on the market . . . quitting is not an option."

Sources: *Ellisislandtea* website, January 2021. *Blackenterprise.com,* January 2016; *ModelDmedia.com,* October 2016; *MSNBC.com* video interview, June 2017. *Youtube* interview on WXYZ in Detroit, April 2016; *Forbes,* June 2018

## BUDGET PROCESS AND ADMINISTRATION

### Budgeting Process

Managers must ensure that activities of employees and departments contribute to meeting the company's overall goals. This requires **budgeting,** the process of planning future business actions and expressing them as formal plans.

A **budget** is a formal statement of a company's plans in dollars. Unlike long-term *strategic plans,* budgets typically cover shorter periods such as a month, quarter, or year. The **budgetary control** process, shown in Exhibit 7.1, refers to management's use of budgets to see that planned objectives are met.

**C1**

Describe the benefits of budgeting.

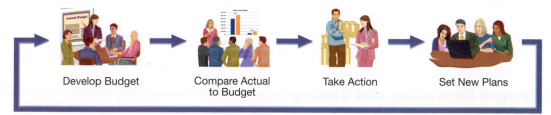

Develop Budget → Compare Actual to Budget → Take Action → Set New Plans

**EXHIBIT 7.1**

Process of Budgetary Control

The budgetary control process involves four steps: (1) develop the budget from planned objectives, (2) compare actual results to budgeted amounts and analyze differences, (3) take corrective and strategic actions, and (4) establish new objectives and a new budget.

This chapter focuses on the first step in the budgetary control process, developing a budget. The next chapter shows how managers compare budgeted and actual amounts to guide corrective actions and make new plans.

## Benefits of Budgeting

Budgets benefit the key managerial functions of planning and controlling.

- **Plan**    A budget focuses on future opportunities and threats to the organization. This focus on the future is important because the daily pressures of operating an organization can divert management's attention from planning. Budgeting forces managers to *plan* for the future.
- **Control**    The *control* function requires management to evaluate (benchmark) operations against some norm. Because budgeted performance considers important company, industry, and economic factors, a comparison of actual to budgeted performance provides an effective monitoring and control system. This comparison helps management identify problems and take corrective actions if necessary.
- **Coordinate**    Budgeting helps to *coordinate* activities so that all employees and departments understand and work toward the company's overall goals.
- **Communicate**    Written budgets effectively *communicate* management's specific action plans to all employees. When plans are not written down, conversations can lead to uncertainty and confusion among employees.
- **Motivate**    Budgets can be used to *motivate* employees. Budgeted performance levels can provide goals for employees to attain or even exceed. Many companies provide incentives, like cash bonuses, for employee performance that meets or exceeds budget goals.

■ **Decision Insight** ━━━━━━━━━━━━━━━━━━━━━━━━

**Budget Bonus**    Budgets are important in determining managers' pay. A recent survey shows that 82% of large companies tie managers' bonus payments to beating budget goals. For these companies, bonus payments are frequently more than 20% of total manager pay. ■

## Budgeting and Human Behavior

Budgeting can be a positive motivating force when three important guidelines are followed.

1. Goals reflected in a budget should be challenging but attainable.
2. Employees affected by a budget should help prepare it (*participatory budgeting*).
3. Evaluations offer opportunities to explain differences between actual and budgeted amounts.

**Potential Negative Outcomes**    Managers must be aware of potential negative outcomes of budgeting. Pressure to meet budgeted results can cause employees to engage in unethical behavior or commit fraud. Under participatory budgeting, some employees might understate sales budgets and overstate expense budgets to allow themselves a cushion, or *budgetary slack,* to aid in meeting targets. Employees might also spend their budgeted amounts, even on unnecessary items, to ensure their budgets aren't reduced for the next period.

**Example:** Assume a company's sales force receives a bonus when sales exceed the budgeted amount. How would this arrangement affect the participatory sales forecasts? *Answer:* Sales reps may understate their budgeted sales.

## Budget Reporting and Timing

The budget period usually is tied to the company's fiscal year. To help control operations, the annual budget can be separated into quarterly or monthly budgets. These short-term budgets allow management to periodically evaluate performance and take timely corrective action.

Many companies apply **continuous budgeting** by preparing **rolling budgets.** In continuous budgeting, a company continually revises its budgets as time passes. In a rolling budget, a company revises its entire set of budgets by adding a new quarterly budget to replace the quarter that just elapsed. Thus, at any point in time, monthly or quarterly budgets are available for the next 12 months or four quarters.

## Decision Insight

**Prove It**  Some companies use **zero-based budgeting,** which requires all expenses to be justified for each new budget. Rather than using last period's budgeted or actual amounts to determine this period's budgets, managers instead analyze each activity in the organization to see if it is necessary. Managers then budget for only necessary activities. Zero-based budgets can help identify waste and reduce costs. ∎

Shutterstock

Label each item as a positive outcome of budgeting or as a negative outcome of budgeting.

**NEED-TO-KNOW** 7-1

Budgeting Benefits

C1

1. Budgets provide goals for employees to work toward.
2. Written budgets help communicate plans to all employees.
3. Some employees might understate sales targets in budgets.
4. Budgets force managers to spend time planning for the future.
5. Some employees might always spend budgeted amounts.
6. With rolling budgets, managers can continuously plan ahead.

**Solution**

1. Positive  2. Positive  3. Negative  4. Positive  5. Negative  6. Positive

Do More: QS 7-1, QS 7-2

# OPERATING BUDGETS

## Master Budget Components

A **master budget** is a formal, comprehensive plan that contains several interconnected budgets. Exhibit 7.2 summarizes the master budgeting process. The master budgeting process begins with the sales budget. The master budget includes individual budgets for sales, production (or merchandise purchases), expenses, capital expenditures, and cash. The process ends with preparation of budgeted financial statements.

**P1**

Prepare the operating budgets of a master budget for a manufacturing company.

**EXHIBIT 7.2**

Master Budget Process for a Manufacturer

```
                        Sales
                          │
                          ▼
                      Production
              ┌───────────┼───────────┐
              ▼           ▼           ▼
      Direct materials  Direct labor  Factory overhead
              │           │           │
              ▼           ▼           ▼
  Capital expenditures → Cash ← Selling expenses
                              General & admin expenses
              └─── Budgeted financial statements ───┘
```

☐ Operating budgets
☐ Investing budgets
☐ Financing budgets

This chapter explains how **Toronto Sticks Company (TSC),** a manufacturer of hockey sticks, prepares its budgets. Its master budget includes operating, capital expenditures, and cash budgets for each month in each quarter. It also includes a budgeted income statement for each quarter and a budgeted balance sheet as of the last day of each quarter. We show how TSC prepares budgets for October, November, and December. Exhibit 7.3 presents TSC's balance sheet at the start of this budgeting period, which we refer to in preparing the component budgets.

**EXHIBIT 7.3**

Balance Sheet

| TORONTO STICKS COMPANY | | | | |
|---|---|---|---|---|
| Balance Sheet | | | | |
| September 30 | | | | |
| **Assets** | | | **Liabilities and Equity** | |
| Cash ..................................... | | $ 20,000 | Liabilities | |
| Accounts receivable ...................... | | 25,200 | Accounts payable ................. | $  7,060 |
| Raw materials inventory (178 pounds @ $20) ... | | 3,560 | Income taxes payable (due Oct. 31) .. | 20,000 |
| Finished goods inventory (1,010 units @ $17) .. | | 17,170 | Loan payable .................... | 10,000  $ 37,060 |
| Equipment* .............................. | $200,000 | | Equity | |
| Less: Accumulated depreciation ............. | 36,000 | 164,000 | Common stock ................... | 150,000 |
| | | | Retained earnings ............... | 42,870   192,870 |
| Total assets ............................. | | $229,930 | Total liabilities and equity ............ | $229,930 |

*Equipment is depreciated on a straight-line basis over 10 years (salvage value is $20,000).

## Sales Budget

The first step in preparing the master budget is the **sales budget,** which shows the planned sales units and the budgeted dollars from these sales. The sales budget is the starting point in the budgeting process because many costs, such as variable costs, change with sales. The sales budget comes from analysis of forecasted economic and market conditions, business capacity, and advertising plans.

TSC sold 700 hockey sticks at $60 per unit in September. After considering sales predictions and market conditions, TSC prepares its sales budget for the next three months and the three-month total. The sales budget in Exhibit 7.4 includes forecasts of both unit sales and unit prices.

**EXHIBIT 7.4**

Sales Budget

| TORONTO STICKS COMPANY | | | | |
|---|---|---|---|---|
| Sales Budget | | | | |
| | October | November | December | Totals |
| Budgeted sales units | 1,000 | 800 | 1,400 | 3,200 |
| Selling price per unit | × $    60 | × $    60 | × $    60 | × $    60 |
| Total budgeted sales | $60,000 | $48,000 | $84,000 | $192,000 |

## Production Budget

A manufacturer prepares a **production budget,** which shows the units to produce each period to meet budgeted sales and a desired inventory level. Manufacturers often set a **safety stock,** a quantity of inventory that helps protect against lost sales caused by unfulfilled demands from customers or delays in shipments from suppliers. Exhibit 7.5 shows how to compute units to produce for a period. **A production budget does not show costs; it is always expressed in <u>units</u> of product.**

**EXHIBIT 7.5**

Computing Units to Produce

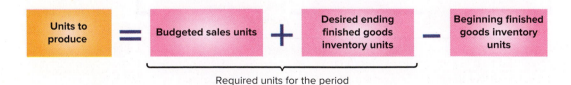

Required units for the period

Starting in October, TSC decides that the number of units in its finished goods inventory at each month-end should equal 90% of next month's budgeted sales. For example, inventory at the end of October should equal 90% of budgeted November sales, and so on. We can now prepare the production budget in Exhibit 7.6.

The production budget can be viewed in two parts.

1. **Total required units.** Budgeted sales units + Desired ending inventory units.
2. **Units to produce.** Total required units − Beginning inventory units.

This budget reports units to produce each period. Units to produce is the basis of the *manufacturing budgets* for direct materials, direct labor, and overhead.

**EXHIBIT 7.6**

Production Budget

| TORONTO STICKS COMPANY Production Budget | | | |
|---|---|---|---|
| | October | November | December |
| Budgeted sales units* | 1,000 | 800 | 1,400 |
| **Add:** Desired ending inventory | | | |
| Next period budgeted sales units* | 800 | 1,400 | 900 |
| Ratio of inventory to future sales | × 90% | × 90% | × 90% |
| Desired ending inventory units | 720 | 1,260 | 810 |
| Total required units | 1,720 | 2,060 | 2,210 |
| **Less:** Beginning inventory units | 1,010 | 720 | 1,260 |
| Units to produce | 710 | 1,340 | 950 |

1. Total required units
2. Units to produce

*From sales budget in Exhibit 7.4; assume January budgeted sales is 900 units.

---

■ **Decision Insight**

**Just-in-Time**   Managers of *just-in-time* (JIT) inventory systems use sales budgets for short periods (often as few as one or two days) to order just enough merchandise or materials to meet the immediate sales demand. This keeps inventory to a minimum (or zero in an ideal situation). A JIT system minimizes the costs of maintaining inventory, but it is practical only if customers can order in advance or if managers can accurately determine short-term sales demand. Suppliers must be able and willing to ship small quantities regularly and quickly. ■

Juanmonino/E+/Getty Images

---

A manufacturing company predicts sales of 220 units for May and 250 units for June. The company wants each month's ending inventory to equal 30% of next month's predicted unit sales. Beginning inventory for May is 66 units. Prepare the company's production budget for May.

**NEED-TO-KNOW 7-2**

Production Budget

**P1**

*Solution*

| Production Budget | May |
|---|---|
| Budgeted sales units | 220 |
| **Add:** Desired ending inventory | |
| Next period budgeted sales units | 250 |
| Ratio of inventory to future sales | × 30% |
| Desired ending inventory units | 75 |
| Total required units | 295 |
| **Less:** Beginning inventory units | 66 |
| Units to produce | 229 |

Do More: QS 7-6, QS 7-7, QS 7-8, E 7-3, E 7-4, E 7-5

---

## Direct Materials Budget

The **direct materials budget** shows the budgeted costs for direct materials that must be purchased to meet the budgeted production. Whereas the production budget shows *units* to produce, the direct materials budget translates the units to produce into budgeted *costs*.

Layout of the direct material budget follows.

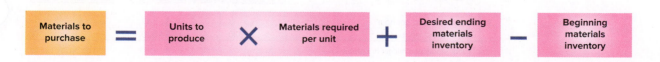

| Materials to purchase | = | Units to produce | × | Materials required per unit | + | Desired ending materials inventory | − | Beginning materials inventory |

Exhibit 7.7 shows the direct materials budget for TSC, which has 5 steps to prepare it.

① **Enter units to produce from the production budget.**
② **Enter materials required per unit.** For TSC, this is 0.5 pound of wood required per unit. We then compute materials needed for production: for October, we take the 710 units to produce and multiply it by 0.5 pound to get 355 lbs.
③ **Add desired ending materials inventory.** For TSC, its policy (starting in October) is to have ending materials equal to 50% of next period's materials needed. This is 335 lbs. for October (50% of 670).
④ **Subtract beginning materials inventory.** For TSC, this is 178 lbs. for October from Exhibit 7.3. We then compute materials to purchase, which is 512 lbs. (690 − 178).
⑤ **Enter materials cost.** Materials cost is $20 per pound. We then compute cost of direct materials purchases as $10,240 for October ($20 × 512 pounds).

**EXHIBIT 7.7**

Direct Materials Budget

| | TORONTO STICKS COMPANY Direct Materials Budget | October | November | December |
|---|---|---|---|---|
| ① | Units to produce* | 710 | 1,340 | 950 |
| ② | Materials required per unit (pounds) | × 0.5 | × 0.5 | × 0.5 |
| | Materials needed for production (pounds) | 355 | ×50% 670 | ×50% 475 |
| ③ | **Add:** Desired ending materials inventory (pounds) | 335 | 237.5 | 247.5[†] |
| | Total materials required (pounds) | 690 | 907.5 | 722.5 |
| ④ | **Less:** Beginning materials inventory (pounds) | 178 | 335 | 237.5 |
| | Materials to purchase (pounds) | 512 | 572.5 | 485.0 |
| | | | | |
| ⑤ | Materials cost per pound | $ 20 | $ 20 | $ 20 |
| | Cost of direct materials purchases | $10,240 | $11,450 | $9,700 |

*From production budget in Exhibit 7.6.  [†]Computed from January production requirements.

Labels at left: Materials needed for production (① ②); Materials to purchase (③ ④); Cost of materials purchases (⑤)

## Direct Labor Budget

The **direct labor budget** shows the budgeted costs for direct labor needed for the budgeted production for the period. Layout of the direct labor budget follows.

| Cost of direct labor | = | Units to produce | × | Direct labor hours required per unit | × | Direct labor cost per hour |

Exhibit 7.8 shows the direct labor budget for TSC, which has 3 steps to prepare it.

① **Enter units to produce from the production budget.**
② **Enter direct labor hours required per unit.** For TSC, this is 0.25 hour. We then compute direct labor hours needed. We multiply the 710 units to produce in October by 0.25 hour to get 177.5 direct hours needed.
③ **Enter direct labor cost per hour.** For TSC, direct labor cost is $12 per hour. We then compute cost of direct labor as $2,130 for October (177.5 hours × $12).

**Point:** Quarter of an hour can be expressed as 0.25 hour (15 min./60 min.).

**EXHIBIT 7.8**

Direct Labor Budget

| | TORONTO STICKS COMPANY Direct Labor Budget | October | November | December |
|---|---|---|---|---|
| ① | Units to produce* | 710 | 1,340 | 950 |
| ② | Direct labor hours required per unit | × 0.25 | × 0.25 | × 0.25 |
| | Direct labor hours needed | 177.5 | 335 | 237.5 |
| | | | | |
| ③ | Direct labor cost per hour | $ 12 | $ 12 | $ 12 |
| | Cost of direct labor | $2,130 | $4,020 | $2,850 |

Labels at left: Direct labor hours needed (① ②); Cost of direct labor (③)

*From production budget in Exhibit 7.6.

A manufacturing company budgets production of 800 units during June and 900 units during July. Each unit of finished goods requires 2 pounds of direct materials, at a cost of $8 per pound. The company maintains an inventory of direct materials equal to 10% of next month's budgeted production. Beginning direct materials inventory for June is 160 pounds. Each finished unit requires 1 hour of direct labor at the cost of $14 per hour. Prepare the company's (a) direct materials budget for June and (b) direct labor budget for June.

**NEED-TO-KNOW** 7-3

Direct Materials and Direct Labor Budgets

**P1**

*Solution*

**a.**

| Direct Materials Budget | June |
|---|---|
| Units to produce | 800 |
| Materials required per unit (lbs.) | × 2 |
| Materials needed for production (lbs.) | 1,600 |
| **Add:** Desired ending materials inventory (lbs.) | 180* |
| Total materials required (lbs.) | 1,780 |
| **Less:** Beginning materials inventory (lbs.) | 160 |
| Materials to purchase (lbs.) | 1,620 |
| Materials cost per pound | $    8 |
| Cost of direct materials purchases | $12,960 |

*900 units × 2 lbs. per unit × 10% = 180 lbs.

**b.**

| Direct Labor Budget | June |
|---|---|
| Units to produce | 800 |
| Direct labor hours required per unit | × 1 |
| Direct labor hours needed | 800 |
| Direct labor cost per hour | $    14 |
| Cost of direct labor | $11,200 |

Do More: QS 7-9, QS 7-10, QS 7-12, QS 7-13, E 7-8, E 7-9, E 7-10, E 7-11, E 7-12

## Factory Overhead Budget

The **factory overhead budget** shows the budgeted costs for factory overhead needed to complete the budgeted production for the period. Factory overhead budgets separate variable and fixed overhead costs. This is so that companies better estimate changes in overhead costs as production volume varies.

Exhibit 7.9 shows the factory overhead budget for TSC, which has 3 parts.

①  Compute **budgeted** *variable* **overhead**. This is direct labor hours from Exhibit 7.8 multiplied by the variable overhead rate per direct labor hour, or 177.5 × $10 for October.

②  Compute **budgeted** *fixed* **overhead**. For TSC, *fixed overhead* consists entirely of depreciation on manufacturing equipment. From Exhibit 7.3, this is $18,000 per year [($200,000 − $20,000)/10 years], or $1,500 per month ($18,000/12 months).

③  Compute **budgeted** *total* **overhead** as the total of parts 1 and 2.

| | | | |
|---|---|---|---|
| **TORONTO STICKS COMPANY** | | | |
| **Factory Overhead Budget** | | | |
| | **October** | **November** | **December** |
| Direct labor hours needed* | 177.5 | 335 | 237.5 |
| Variable overhead rate per direct labor hour | × $    10 | × $    10 | × $    10 |
| Budgeted variable overhead | 1,775 | 3,350 | 2,375 |
| Budgeted fixed overhead | 1,500 | 1,500 | 1,500 |
| Budgeted total factory overhead | $3,275 | $4,850 | $3,875 |

1. Variable overhead
2. Fixed overhead
3. Total overhead

*From direct labor budget in Exhibit 7.8.

**EXHIBIT 7.9**

Factory Overhead Budget

The budget in Exhibit 7.9 is condensed in that we do not list the individual line items making up variable overhead and fixed overhead. Variable cost line items commonly include indirect materials, indirect labor, factory utilities, and maintenance of manufacturing equipment. Fixed cost line items commonly include factory supervisor salaries, factory depreciation, and factory property taxes. We cover overhead budgets in detail in the next chapter.

## Budgeted Cost of Goods Sold

Once we have the three manufacturing budgets (direct materials, direct labor, and factory overhead), we can compute the **budgeted product cost per unit** and prepare a **cost of goods sold budget.** Exhibit 7.10 summarizes the product cost per unit calculation for TSC. The cost of direct materials is from Exhibit 7.7 and cost of direct labor is from Exhibit 7.8. The predetermined variable overhead rate is from Exhibit 7.9. To compute product cost per unit for fixed overhead, see that TSC expects to produce on average 1,000 units per month, which means its fixed overhead per unit is $1.50 ($1,500/1,000 units). Total product cost per unit is $17.00.

**EXHIBIT 7.10**

Budgeted Product Cost per Unit

| Budgeted Product Cost | Per Unit |
|---|---|
| Direct materials (0.5 pound of materials × $20 per pound of materials—Exhibit 7.7) . . . | $10.00 |
| Direct labor (0.25 hour of direct labor × $12 per hour of direct labor—Exhibit 7.8) . . . . | 3.00 |
| Variable overhead (0.25 direct labor hour × $10 variable overhead rate per direct labor hour—Exhibit 7.9) . . . . . . . . . . . . . . . . . . . . . . . . . . | 2.50 |
| Fixed overhead ($1,500 total fixed overhead per month/1,000 units of expected production per month) . . . . . . . . . . . . . . . . . . . . | 1.50 |
| Total product cost per unit  . . . . . . . . . . . . . . . . . . . . . . . . . . . . . . . . . . . . . . . . . . . | $17.00 |

| Cost of Goods Sold Budget | |
|---|---|
| Budgeted sales units | # |
| × Product cost per unit | $ |
| = Budgeted COGS | $ |

We then prepare the cost of goods sold budget as follows. We use the budgeted sales units from Exhibit 7.4 multiplied by the budgeted cost per unit from Exhibit 7.10.

| TORONTO STICKS COMPANY Cost of Goods Sold Budget | | | | |
|---|---|---|---|---|
| | October | November | December | Totals |
| Budgeted sales units* | 1,000 | 800 | 1,400 | 3,200 |
| Budgeted cost per unit | $ 17 | $ 17 | $ 17 | $ 17 |
| Budgeted cost of goods sold | $17,000 | $13,600 | $23,800 | $54,400 |

*From sales budget in Exhibit 7.4.

## Selling Expense Budget

The **selling expense budget** shows the types and amounts of selling expenses expected during the budget period. TSC's selling expense budget is in Exhibit 7.11. Its selling expenses consist of commissions of 10% of total sales paid to sales personnel and a $2,000 monthly salary paid to the sales manager. Sales commissions vary with sales volume, but the sales manager's salary is fixed. Other common selling expenses include advertising and delivery expenses.

**EXHIBIT 7.11**

Selling Expense Budget

| TORONTO STICKS COMPANY Selling Expense Budget | | | | |
|---|---|---|---|---|
| | October | November | December | Totals |
| Budgeted sales* | $60,000 | $48,000 | $84,000 | $192,000 |
| Sales commission of 10% | × 10% | × 10% | × 10% | × 10% |
| Sales commissions | 6,000 | 4,800 | 8,400 | 19,200 |
| Salary for sales manager | 2,000 | 2,000 | 2,000 | 6,000 |
| Total selling expenses | $ 8,000 | $ 6,800 | $10,400 | $ 25,200 |

*From sales budget in Exhibit 7.4.

## General and Administrative Expense Budget

The **general and administrative expense budget** reports those expenses expected during the budget period. Exhibit 7.12 shows TSC's general and administrative expense budget. It reports administrative salaries of $4,500 per month. Other common examples of general and administrative expenses include property taxes, office expenses, and insurance and depreciation on nonmanufacturing assets.

**EXHIBIT 7.12**

General and Administrative Expense Budget

| TORONTO STICKS COMPANY General and Administrative Expense Budget | | | | |
|---|---|---|---|---|
| | October | November | December | Totals |
| Administrative salaries | $4,500 | $4,500 | $4,500 | $13,500 |
| Total general and administrative expenses | $4,500 | $4,500 | $4,500 | $13,500 |

A manufacturing company budgets sales of $70,000 during July. It pays sales commissions of 5% of sales and also pays the sales manager salary of $3,000 per month. Other monthly costs include depreciation on office equipment ($500), office insurance expense ($200), advertising ($1,000), and an office manager salary of $2,500 per month. Prepare the company's (a) selling expense budget for July and (b) general and administrative expense budget for July.

**NEED-TO-KNOW 7-4**

Selling and General and Administrative Expense Budgets

**P1**

**Solution**

**a.**

| Selling Expense Budget | July |
|---|---|
| Budgeted sales | $70,000 |
| Sales commission of 5% | ×    5% |
| Sales commissions | 3,500 |
| Salary for sales manager | 3,000 |
| Advertising | 1,000 |
| Total selling expenses | $ 7,500 |

**b.**

| General and Administrative Expense Budget | July |
|---|---|
| Office manager salary | $2,500 |
| Depreciation on office equipment | 500 |
| Insurance on office | 200 |
| Total general and administrative expenses | $3,200 |

Do More: QS 7-15, QS 7-16

---

# INVESTING AND FINANCING BUDGETS

## Capital Expenditures Budget (Investing Budget)

The **capital expenditures budget** reports expected cash receipts and cash payments related to the sale and purchase of plant assets. The capital expenditures budget is usually prepared after the operating budgets. The process of preparing operating budgets can reveal that the company requires more (or less) plant assets. Following is the capital expenditures budget for TSC. TSC does not plan to dispose of any plant assets through December, but it does plan to buy equipment for $25,000 cash in December.

**P2** _____

Prepare a cash budget for a manufacturing company.

| TORONTO STICKS COMPANY Capital Expenditures Budget | | | |
|---|---|---|---|
| | October | November | December |
| Purchase of equipment | $0 | $0 | $25,000 |
| Total capital expenditures | $0 | $0 | $25,000 |

## Cash Budget (Financing Budget)

A **cash budget** shows budgeted cash receipts and cash payments during the budget period. Managing cash flows is vital, and a cash budget helps with that task. Most companies set a minimum cash balance to have available. If the cash budget indicates cash is below this minimum, the company can arrange loans. If the cash budget indicates cash is above the minimum, the company can plan to pay off loans. Exhibit 7.13 shows the layout for the cash budget. When preparing a cash budget, add budgeted cash receipts to the beginning cash balance and subtract budgeted cash payments.

**EXHIBIT 7.13**

Cash Budget Layout

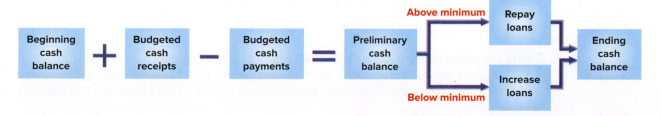

### Cash Receipts from Sales

**Cash Receipts from Sales**    Managers use the sales budget and knowledge about how frequently customers pay on credit sales to budget monthly cash receipts. Exhibit 7.14 presents TSC's schedule of budgeted cash receipts. We begin with budgeted sales. Analysis of past sales for TSC indicates that 40% of sales are for cash. The remaining 60% are credit sales; these customers are expected to pay in full in the month following the sales. For example, October's budgeted cash receipts consist of $24,000 from October cash sales ($60,000 × 40%) plus the anticipated collection of $25,200 ($42,000 × 60%) from September credit sales.

**EXHIBIT 7.14**

Schedule of Cash Receipts from Sales

| TORONTO STICKS COMPANY | | | | |
|---|---|---|---|---|
| Schedule of Cash Receipts from Sales | | | | |
| | September | October | November | December |
| Sales* | $42,000 | $60,000 | $48,000 | $84,000 |
| Cash receipts from: | | | | |
| Cash sales (40% of current sales) | | $24,000† | $19,200 | $33,600 |
| Collections of prior period sales (60%) | | 25,200‡ | 36,000 | 28,800 |
| Total cash receipts | | $49,200 | $55,200 | $62,400 |

*From sales budget in Exhibit 7.4.    †$24,000 = 40% × $60,000    ‡$25,200 = 60% × $42,000

**Collection of Credit Sales over Several Periods**    When credit sales take several periods to collect, the collections from prior periods reflect the multi-period collection pattern. For example, if TSC collects credit sales over two months such as 80% of credit sales in the first month after sale and 20% of credit sales in the second month after sale, and cash sales remain at 40% of current sales, then budgeted cash receipts for December follow.

| TORONTO STICKS COMPANY | | | |
|---|---|---|---|
| Schedule of Cash Receipts from Sales | | | |
| | October | November | December |
| Sales | $60,000 | $48,000 | $84,000 |
| Cash receipts from: | | | |
| Cash sales (40% of current sales) | | | $33,600* |
| Collections of 1 period ago sales (60% × $48,000 × 80%) | | | 23,040 |
| Collections of 2 period ago sales (60% × $60,000 × 20%) | | | 7,200 |
| Total cash receipts | | | $63,840 |

*$33,600 = 40% × $84,000

**Uncollectible Accounts**    Let's consider uncollectible accounts and assume that 5% of *credit sales* are uncollectible. For the remaining 95% that are collectible, assume TSC collects 80% of credit sales in the first month after sale and collects 15% of credit sales in the second month after sale. The schedule of cash receipts for December follows.

| TORONTO STICKS COMPANY | | | |
|---|---|---|---|
| Schedule of Cash Receipts from Sales | | | |
| | October | November | December |
| Sales | $60,000 | $48,000 | $84,000 |
| Cash receipts from: | | | |
| Cash sales (40% of current sales) | | | $33,600* |
| Collections of 1 period ago sales (60% × $48,000 × 80%) | | | 23,040 |
| Collections of 2 period ago sales (60% × $60,000 × 15%) | | | 5,400 |
| Total cash receipts | | | $62,040 |

*$33,600 = 40% × $84,000

### Cash Payments for Direct Materials

**Cash Payments for Direct Materials**    Managers prepare a schedule of cash payments for direct materials. To do this, managers must know how direct materials are purchased (with cash or on credit) and, if on credit, when payment is made. TSC's materials purchases are entirely on credit. It makes full payment in the month following purchases. Using this information, the schedule of cash payments for direct materials is in Exhibit 7.15.

| TORONTO STICKS COMPANY | | | | |
|---|---|---|---|---|
| Schedule of Cash Payments for Direct Materials | | | | |
| | September | October | November | December |
| Materials purchases* | $7,060 | $10,240 | $11,450 | $9,700 |
| Cash payments for: | | | | |
| Current period purchases (0%) | | $ 0 | $ 0 | $ 0 |
| Prior period purchases (100%) | | 7,060 | 10,240 | 11,450 |
| Total cash payments | | $ 7,060 | $10,240 | $11,450 |

*From direct materials budget in Exhibit 7.7.

**EXHIBIT 7.15**

Schedule of Cash Payments for Direct Materials

**Payment of Materials over Several Periods**   When payment for materials occurs over several periods, the payments for those prior periods reflect the multi-period payment pattern. For example, if TSC pays for 20% of purchases in the month of purchase and pays for 80% of purchases in the month after purchase, then its schedule of cash payments for direct materials follows.

| TORONTO STICKS COMPANY | | | | |
|---|---|---|---|---|
| Schedule of Cash Payments for Direct Materials | | | | |
| | September | October | November | December |
| Materials purchases* | $7,060 | $10,240 | $11,450 | $ 9,700 |
| Cash payments for: | | | | |
| Current period purchases (20%) | | $ 2,048 | $ 2,290 | $ 1,940† |
| Prior period purchases (80%) | | 5,648 | 8,192 | 9,160‡ |
| Total cash payments | | $ 7,696 | $10,482 | $11,100 |

*From direct materials budget in Exhibit 7.7.   †$1,940 = 20% × $9,700   ‡$9,160 = 80% × $11,450

**Preparing Cash Budget**   To prepare the cash budget, managers use the cash receipts and cash payments from several budgets and schedules. Exhibit 7.16 shows the cash budget for

| TORONTO STICKS COMPANY | | | |
|---|---|---|---|
| Cash Budget | | | |
| | October | November | December |
| **Beginning cash balance** | $20,000 | $20,000 | $ 38,881 |
| **Add:** Cash receipts from sales (Exhibit 7.14) | 49,200 | 55,200 | 62,400 |
| Total cash available | 69,200 | 75,200 | 101,281 |
| **Less:** Cash payments for | | | |
| Direct materials (Exhibit 7.15) | 7,060 | 10,240 | 11,450 |
| Direct labor (Exhibit 7.8) | 2,130 | 4,020 | 2,850 |
| Variable overhead (Exhibit 7.9) | 1,775 | 3,350 | 2,375 |
| Sales commissions (Exhibit 7.11) | 6,000 | 4,800 | 8,400 |
| Sales salaries (Exhibit 7.11) | 2,000 | 2,000 | 2,000 |
| Administrative salaries (Exhibit 7.12) | 4,500 | 4,500 | 4,500 |
| Income taxes (Exhibit 7.3) | 20,000 | 0 | 0 |
| Dividends | 0 | 3,000 | 0 |
| Interest on loan | | | |
| October ($10,000 × 1%)* | 100 | 0 | 0 |
| November ($4,365 × 1%)† | 0 | 44 | 0 |
| Purchase of equipment | 0 | 0 | 25,000 |
| Total cash payments | 43,565 | 31,954 | 56,575 |
| Preliminary cash balance | $25,635 | $43,246 | $ 44,706 |
| **Loan activity** | | | |
| Additional loan | $ 0 | $ 0 | $ 0 |
| Repayment of loan | 5,635 | 4,365 | 0 |
| **Ending cash balance** | $20,000 | $38,881 | $ 44,706 |
| Loan balance, end of month‡ | $ 4,365 | $ 0 | $ 0 |

*Beginning loan payable balance from Exhibit 7.3.        †Rounded to the dollar.

‡Beginning loan balance + New loans − Loan repayments. For October: $10,000 + $0 − $5,635 = $4,365.

**EXHIBIT 7.16**

Cash Budget

| Cash | | | |
|---|---|---|---|
| Oct. 1 | 20,000 | | |
| Receipts | 49,200 | | |
| | | 43,565 | Payments |
| Prelim. bal. | 25,635 | | |
| | | 5,635 | Repay loan |
| Oct. 31 | 20,000 | | |

TSC. The company begins October with $20,000 in cash (see Exhibit 7.3). We add $49,200 in cash receipts from customers. We then subtract $43,565 in cash payments for direct materials, direct labor, overhead, selling expenses, general and administrative expenses, and income taxes due and paid in October. A few additional points about TSC's cash budget:

- *Fixed overhead* from depreciation in the factory overhead budget (Exhibit 7.9) does not require a cash payment. Therefore, it is not in the cash budget. Other fixed overhead—such as payments for factory property taxes and insurance—*are* included if they require cash payments.
- It announces plans to pay $3,000 of cash dividends in November.
- It sets a minimum cash balance of $20,000 at each month-end. If TSC borrows cash, it must pay interest at 1% per month.

**Interest on Loan and Loan Activity**   If the cash balance exceeds $20,000 at month-end, TSC uses the excess to repay loans. If the cash balance is below $20,000 at month-end, TSC takes out a loan for the shortage. Interest on loans is computed as:

**Cash paid for interest = Interest rate (%) × Beginning loan balance**

Using TSC's interest rate of 1% per month, budgeted cash payments for interest follow and are reported in Exhibit 7.16.

| Budgeted cash payments for interest | Interest Rate | Beginning Loan Balance | Interest Cost |
|---|---|---|---|
| October | 1% | $10,000 | $100 |
| November | 1 | 4,365 | 44 |
| December | 1 | 0 | 0 |

The October 31 preliminary cash balance is $25,635 (before any loan activity). This amount is more than the $20,000 minimum. TSC uses the excess cash of $5,635 ($25,635 – $20,000) to pay off a portion of its loan. Looking at November, TSC's preliminary cash balance is $43,246, and its $23,246 excess is sufficient to pay off its entire loan balance.

Had TSC's preliminary cash balance been below the $20,000 minimum in any month, TSC would have borrowed an amount to bring its cash balance up to $20,000. We show an example of this situation in **Need-to-Know 7-7**.

Loan Payable

| | | 10,000 | Sep. 30 |
| Repay | 5,635 | | |
| | | 4,365 | Oct. 31 |
| Repay | 4,365 | | |
| | | 0 | Nov. 30 |

### ■ Decision Insight

**Cash Cushion**   Why do some companies maintain a minimum cash balance even when the budget shows extra cash is not needed? For example, **Apple**'s cash and short-term investments balance is over $60 billion. According to Apple's CEO, Tim Cook, the cushion provides "flexibility and security," important in navigating uncertain economic times. A cash cushion enables companies to jump on new ventures or acquisitions that may present themselves. The **Boston Red Sox** keep a cash cushion for its trades involving players with "cash considerations." ■

Adam Glanzman/Getty Images

**NEED-TO-KNOW 7-5**

Schedule of Cash Receipts; Cash Budget

P2

**Part 1**

Diaz Co. budgets sales of $80,000 for January and $90,000 for February. Seventy percent of Diaz's sales are for cash, and the remaining 30% are credit sales. All credit sales are collected in the month after sale. December's total sales are $66,667. Prepare the schedule of cash receipts from sales for January and February.

*Solution*

| Schedule of Cash Receipts from Sales | January | February |
|---|---|---|
| Sales | $80,000 | $90,000 |
| Cash receipts from: | | |
| Cash sales (70% of current sales) | 56,000 | 63,000 |
| Collections of prior period sales (30%) | 20,000 | 24,000 |
| Total cash receipts | $76,000 | $87,000 |

Do More: QS 7-17, QS 7-18, QS 7-19, E 7-18

**Part 2**

Use the following information to prepare a cash budget for the month ended January 31 for Garcia Company. The company requires a minimum $30,000 cash balance at the end of each month. Any preliminary cash balance above $30,000 is used to repay loans (if any). Garcia has a $2,000 loan outstanding at the beginning of January.

a. January 1 cash balance, $30,000

b. Cash receipts from sales, $132,000

c. Cash payments for direct materials, $63,500

d. Cash payments for direct labor, $33,400

e. Cash paid for interest on loan, $20

f. Cash repayment of loan, $2,000
   (1% of beginning loan balance of $2,000)

g. Cash paid for overhead, $8,180

**Solution**

| Cash Budget For Month Ended January 31 | |
|---|---|
| Beginning cash balance | $ 30,000 |
| **Add:** Cash receipts from sales | 132,000 |
| Total cash available | 162,000 |
| **Less:** Cash payments for | |
| Direct materials | 63,500 |
| Direct labor | 33,400 |
| Overhead | 8,180 |
| Interest on loan ($2,000 × 1%) | 20 |
| Total cash payments | 105,100 |
| Preliminary cash balance | $ 56,900 |
| **Loan activity** | |
| Repayment of loan | 2,000 |
| Ending cash balance | $ 54,900 |
| Loan balance, end of month | $       0 |

Do More: QS 7-24, E 7-17, E 7-20, E 7-21, E 7-22, E 7-23

# BUDGETED FINANCIAL STATEMENTS

## Budgeted Income Statement

The **budgeted income statement** shows budgeted sales and expenses for the budget period. TSC's budgeted income statement is in Exhibit 7.17. All information is taken from budgets in this chapter. We predict income tax expense as 40% of the budgeted income before income taxes. These taxes are not payable until next year and are not included on this quarter's cash budget.

**P3**

Prepare budgeted financial statements.

**Point:** Lenders often require potential borrowers to provide cash budgets, budgeted income statements, and budgeted balance sheets.

**EXHIBIT 7.17**

Budgeted Income Statement

| TORONTO STICKS COMPANY Budgeted Income Statement For Three Months Ended December 31 | | |
|---|---|---|
| Sales (Exhibit 7.4, 3,200 units @ $60) . . . . . . . | | $192,000 |
| Cost of goods sold (3,200 units @ $17)* . . . . . | | 54,400 |
| Gross profit . . . . . . . . . . . . . . . . . . . . . . . . . . . | | 137,600 |
| Selling, general, and administrative expenses | | |
| Sales commissions (Exhibit 7.11) . . . . . . . . | $19,200 | |
| Sales salaries (Exhibit 7.11) . . . . . . . . . . . . | 6,000 | |
| Administrative salaries (Exhibit 7.12) . . . . . | 13,500 | |
| Interest expense (Exhibit 7.16) . . . . . . . . . . | 144 | 38,844 |
| Income before income taxes . . . . . . . . . . . . . . | | 98,756 |
| Income tax expense ($98,756 × 40%)† . . . . . | | 39,502 |
| Net income . . . . . . . . . . . . . . . . . . . . . . . . . . . | | $ 59,254 |

*$17 product cost per unit from Exhibit 7.10.    †Rounded to the dollar.

# Budgeted Balance Sheet

The **budgeted balance sheet** shows budgeted amounts for assets, liabilities, and equity as of the end of the budget period. TSC's budgeted balance sheet in Exhibit 7.18 is prepared using information from other budgets. Sources of amounts are in notes to the budgeted balance sheet.

**EXHIBIT 7.18**

Budgeted Balance Sheet

| TORONTO STICKS COMPANY | | | | | |
|---|---|---|---|---|---|
| **Budgeted Balance Sheet** | | | | | |
| **December 31** | | | | | |
| **Assets** | | | **Liabilities and Equity** | | |
| Cash[a] ........................ | | $ 44,706 | Liabilities | | |
| Accounts receivable[b] ............ | | 50,400 | Accounts payable[g] ....... | $  9,700 | |
| Raw materials inventory[c] ........ | | 4,950 | Income taxes payable[h] ... | 39,502 | $ 49,202 |
| Finished goods inventory[d] ........ | | 13,770 | Equity | | |
| Equipment[e] ................... | $225,000 | | Common stock[i] .......... | 150,000 | |
| Less: Accumulated depreciation[f] ... | 40,500 | 184,500 | Retained earnings[j] ....... | 99,124 | 249,124 |
| Total assets ................... | | $298,326 | Total liabilities and equity.... | | $298,326 |

| Retained Earnings | | | |
|---|---|---|---|
| | | 42,870 | Sep. 30 |
| | | 59,254 | Net income |
| Dividends | 3,000 | | |
| | | 99,124 | Dec. 31 |

[a] Ending balance for December from the cash budget in Exhibit 7.16.
[b] 60% of $84,000 sales budgeted for December from the sales budget in Exhibit 7.4.
[c] 247.5 pounds of materials in ending inventory at $20 per pound from direct materials budget in Exhibit 7.7.
[d] 810 units in budgeted finished goods inventory in Exhibit 7.6 at $17 per unit from Exhibit 7.10.
[e] September 30 balance of $200,000 from the beginning balance sheet in Exhibit 7.3 plus $25,000 of new equipment from the cash budget in Exhibit 7.16.
[f] September 30 balance of $36,000 from the beginning balance sheet in Exhibit 7.3 plus $4,500 depreciation expense from the factory overhead budget in Exhibit 7.9.
[g] Budgeted cost of materials purchases for December from Exhibit 7.7, to be paid in January.
[h] Income tax expense from the budgeted income statement for the fourth quarter in Exhibit 7.17, to be paid in January.
[i] Unchanged from the beginning balance sheet in Exhibit 7.3.
[j] September 30 balance of $42,870 from the beginning balance sheet in Exhibit 7.3 plus budgeted net income of $59,254 from the budgeted income statement in Exhibit 7.17 minus budgeted cash dividends of $3,000 from Exhibit 7.16.

**Point:** A budgeted retained earnings statement is prepared in NTK 7-6.

**Using the Master Budget**   Managers use the master budget in several ways.

- *Sensitivity analysis*—Technologies like Excel and enterprise resource planning (ERP) systems enable managers to quickly compute alternative master budgets under different assumptions, allowing them to better plan for and adapt to changing conditions.

- *Planning*—Any stage in the master budgeting process might show results that require new plans. For example, an early version of the cash budget might show too little cash unless payments are reduced. A budgeted income statement might show income below its target, or a budgeted balance sheet might show too much debt from planned equipment purchases. Management can change its plans to aim for better results.

- *Controlling*—Managers compare actual results to budgeted results. Differences between actual and budgeted results are called *variances*. Managers examine variances to identify areas to improve and take corrective action.

**Budgeting for Service Companies**   Service providers also use master budgets; however, because they do not manufacture goods and hold no inventory, they typically need fewer operating budgets than manufacturers do. Exhibit 7.19 shows the master budget process for a service provider.

**EXHIBIT 7.19**

Master Budget Process for a Service Company

Service providers *do not prepare production, direct materials, or factory overhead budgets.* In addition, because many services such as accounting, banking, and landscaping are labor-intensive, the direct labor budget is especially important. We illustrate a direct labor budget for a service firm in this chapter's Decision Analysis.

### Analytics Insight

**Data Pop**    Online-first brands, which are companies without permanent storefronts, often use data analytics on customer ZIP codes and purchases to determine where and for how long to open their pop-up stores. Pop-up stores stay open only as long as they are profitable, sometimes just weeks or even days. A consulting firm estimates that about 4% of all online sales comes from online-first brands. ■

## CORPORATE SOCIAL RESPONSIBILITY

Budgets translate strategic goals into dollars. When setting strategic goals, managers must consider their effects on budgets. **Johnson & Johnson**, a manufacturer of pharmaceuticals, medical devices, and consumer health products, sets goals for both profits and sustainable practices. A recent company report discusses several sustainability goals and strategies, including those in Exhibit 7.20.

**EXHIBIT 7.20**

Sustainability Goals and Strategies

| Sustainability Goal | Strategy to Achieve Goal |
| --- | --- |
| Reduce waste by 10%. . . . . . . . . . . | Purchase pulping machine to grind and recycle packaging. |
| Reduce $CO_2$ emissions by 20%. . . . . | Purchase hybrid vehicles. |
| Reduce water usage by 10%. . . . . . . | Update plumbing, install water recovery systems, employee training. |

©Ellis Infinity, LLC

Several strategies involve asset purchases that will impact the capital expenditures budget. Additional employee training will impact the overhead budget. By reducing waste, increasing recycling, and reducing water usage, the company hopes to reduce some of the costs reflected in the direct materials and overhead budgets. Managers evaluate performance with respect to these goals and make adjustments to budgets.

Nailah Ellis-Brown, founder of this chapter's feature company, **Ellis Island Tropical Tea**, focuses on the "people" aspect of the triple bottom line. For her, that means doing what she can to help the people of Detroit. "My passion is for [Michigan] natives," explains Nailah, "many of whom happen to be Black."

---

**Direct Labor Budget and Revenue per Employee**    **Decision Analysis**

**Direct Labor Budget**    A direct labor budget is the key budget for a service firm. If an accounting firm underestimates the direct labor hours needed to complete an audit, it might charge too low a price. If the accounting firm overestimates the direct labor hours needed, it might bid too high a price (and lose jobs). Either way, income suffers if direct labor budgets are inaccurate.

The direct labor cost for employees follows.

**A1**

Prepare a direct labor budget for a service firm and analyze revenue per employee.

| Budgeted direct labor cost | = | Budgeted direct labor hours | × | Direct labor cost per hour |
| --- | --- | --- | --- | --- |

Exhibit 7.21 shows a direct labor budget for a services job. This firm would use the $6,200 total direct labor cost in determining a price to bid for the job.

**EXHIBIT 7.21**

Direct Labor Budget for a Services Firm

| Direct Labor Budget | | | |
| --- | --- | --- | --- |
| | Direct Labor Hours | Direct Labor Cost per Hour | Direct Labor Cost |
| Data mining and analysis | 40 | $30 | $1,200 |
| Staff investigative analyst | 100 | 40 | 4,000 |
| Senior forensic accountant | 20 | 50 | 1,000 |
| Cost of direct labor | | | $6,200 |

**Revenue per Employee**   Services and other types of businesses can assess effectiveness of their workforce using **revenue per employee,** a ratio that measures the revenue generated per employee and is computed as follows:

$$\text{Revenue per employee} = \frac{\text{Total revenue}}{\text{Total employees}}$$

Revenue per employee is shown below for **Microsoft** and **Hewlett Packard**. Microsoft's revenue per employee increased during the current year, suggesting the company's workforce became more effective in generating revenue. However, current year revenue per employee is higher for its competitor Hewlett Packard.

| | Microsoft, Prior Year | Microsoft, Current Year | Hewlett Packard, Current Year |
|---|---|---|---|
| Total revenue........... | $110,360,000,000 | $125,843,000,000 | $57,756,000,000 |
| Total employees ........ | 131,000 | 144,000 | 56,000 |
| Revenue per employee .. | $    842,443 | $    873,910 | $   1,031,357 |

### ■ Decision **Maker**

**Environmental Manager**   You hold the new position of sustainability manager for a chemical company. You are asked to develop a budget for your job and identify job responsibilities. How do you proceed? ■  *Answer:* You are unlikely to have data on this new position to use in preparing your budget. Instead, apply *zero-based budgeting.* Develop a list of this job's necessary activities, then determine the resources needed and their costs. Be sure the listed activities are necessary and the resources are required.

---

**NEED-TO-KNOW** **7-6**

**COMPREHENSIVE 1**

Master Budget—
Manufacturer

Payne Company's management requests that we prepare its master budget. The budget is to cover the months of April, May, and June. Its balance sheet at March 31 follows.

| **PAYNE COMPANY** Balance Sheet March 31 | | | | |
|---|---|---|---|---|
| **Assets** | | | **Liabilities and Equity** | |
| Cash ..................................... | | $ 50,000 | Liabilities | |
| Accounts receivable ....................... | | 175,000 | Accounts payable ....... $ 63,315 | |
| Raw materials inventory (2,425 lbs. @ $12.60)... | | 30,555 | Loan payable ........... 12,000 | |
| Finished goods inventory (8,400 units @ $11.45) .. | | 96,180 | Long-term note payable .. 200,000 $275,315 | |
| Equipment ................................ $480,000 | | | Equity | |
| Less: Accumulated depreciation .............. 90,000 | | 390,000 | Common stock .......... 435,000 | |
| | | | Retained earnings ....... 31,420 466,420 | |
| Total assets ................................ | | $741,735 | Total liabilities and equity ... $741,735 | |

**Additional Information**

a. Sales for March were 10,000 units. Budgeted sales units are 10,500 for April, 9,500 for May, 10,000 for June, and 10,500 for July. The product's selling price is $25 per unit.
b. Company policy calls for month-end finished goods inventory to equal 80% of next month's budgeted unit sales. The March 31 finished goods inventory of 8,400 units complies with the policy.

   Company policy also calls for month-end materials inventory to equal 50% of next month's budgeted direct materials needed for production. The March 31 ending materials inventory of 2,425 units complies with the policy. The company expects to have 2,100 units of materials inventory on June 30. Product cost information follows.

| Product Cost | Per Unit |
|---|---|
| Direct materials (0.5 pound of materials × $12.60 per pound of materials)..................... | $ 6.30 |
| Direct labor (0.25 direct labor hour × $15 per direct labor hour) ............................ | 3.75 |
| Variable overhead (0.25 direct labor hour × $3.60 variable overhead per direct labor hour)....... | 0.90 |
| Fixed overhead ($5,000 total fixed overhead per month/10,000 expected units of production)*.... | 0.50 |
| Total product cost per unit ........................................................ | $11.45 |

*Fixed overhead consists entirely of $5,000 of depreciation expense. In determining fixed overhead per unit, the company expects production to normally be 10,000 units per month.

c. Sales commissions of 12% of sales are paid in the month of the sales. The sales manager's monthly salary will be $3,500 in April and $4,000 per month thereafter.

d. Monthly general and administrative expenses include $8,000 for administrative salaries and 0.9% monthly interest on the long-term note payable.

e. The company expects 30% of sales to be for cash and the remaining 70% on credit. Credit sales are collected in full in the month following the sale (none are collected in the month of sale).

f. All direct materials purchases are on credit, and no payables arise from any other transactions. All credit purchases (recorded in accounts payable) are paid in the month following the purchase. Materials cost $12.60 per pound.

g. The minimum ending cash balance for all months is $50,000. If necessary, the company borrows enough cash using a loan to reach the minimum. Loans require an interest payment of 1% at each month-end (before any repayment). If the ending cash balance exceeds the minimum, the excess will be used to repay any loans.

h. Dividends of $100,000 are to be declared and paid in May.

i. No cash payments for income taxes are to be made during the second calendar quarter. Income taxes are budgeted at 35% in the quarter.

j. Equipment purchases for cash of $55,000 are budgeted for June.

k. Fixed overhead consists only of $5,000 per month of depreciation expense on factory equipment.

**Required**

Prepare the following budgets and schedules for each month of April, May, and June. In addition, compute the three-month total for parts 1, 6 and 7 for use in preparing financial statements.

1. Sales budget.
2. Production budget.
3. Direct materials budget. Round costs of materials purchases to the nearest dollar.
4. Direct labor budget.
5. Factory overhead budget.
6. Selling expense budget.

7. General and administrative expense budget.
8. Schedule of cash receipts from sales.
9. Schedule of cash payments for direct materials.
10. Cash budget.
11. Budgeted income statement, budgeted statement of retained earnings, and budgeted balance sheet.

## SOLUTION

**1.**

| Sales Budget | April | May | June | Quarter |
|---|---|---|---|---|
| Budgeted sales units | 10,500 | 9,500 | 10,000 | 30,000 |
| Selling price per unit | × $ 25 | × $ 25 | × $ 25 | × $ 25 |
| Total budgeted sales | $262,500 | $237,500 | $250,000 | $750,000 |

**2.**

| Production Budget | April | May | June |
|---|---|---|---|
| Budgeted sales units | 10,500 | 9,500 | 10,000 |
| **Add:** Desired ending inventory | | | |
| Next period budgeted sales units | 9,500 | 10,000 | 10,500* |
| Ratio of inventory to future sales | × 80% | × 80% | × 80% |
| Desired ending inventory units | 7,600 | 8,000 | 8,400 |
| Total required units | 18,100 | 17,500 | 18,400 |
| **Less:** Beginning inventory units | 8,400 | 7,600 | 8,000 |
| Units to produce | 9,700 | 9,900 | 10,400 |

*Budgeted sales for July (from part *a* of additional information).

**3.**

| Direct Materials Budget | April | May | June |
|---|---|---|---|
| Units to produce (from part 2) | 9,700 | 9,900 | 10,400 |
| Materials required per unit (pounds) | × 0.5 | × 0.5 | × 0.5 |
| Materials needed for production (pounds) | 4,850 | ×50% 4,950 | ×50% 5,200 |
| Add: Desired ending materials inventory (pounds) | 2,475 | 2,600 | 2,100* |
| Total materials required (pounds) | 7,325 | 7,550 | 7,300 |
| Less: Beginning materials inventory (pounds) | 2,425* | 2,475 | 2,600 |
| Materials to purchase (pounds) | 4,900 | 5,075 | 4,700 |
| | | | |
| Materials cost per pound | $ 12.60 | $ 12.60 | $ 12.60 |
| Cost of direct materials purchases | $61,740 | $63,945 | $59,220 |

*From part *b* of additional information.

**4.**

| Direct Labor Budget | April | May | June |
|---|---|---|---|
| Units to produce (from part 2) | 9,700 | 9,900 | 10,400 |
| Direct labor hours required per unit | × 0.25 | × 0.25 | × 0.25 |
| Direct labor hours needed | 2,425 | 2,475 | 2,600 |
| | | | |
| Direct labor cost per hour | $ 15 | $ 15 | $ 15 |
| Cost of direct labor | $36,375 | $37,125 | $39,000 |

**5.**

| Factory Overhead Budget | April | May | June |
|---|---|---|---|
| Direct labor hours needed (from part 4) | 2,425 | 2,475 | 2,600 |
| Variable overhead rate per direct labor hour* | × $ 3.60 | × $ 3.60 | × $ 3.60 |
| Budgeted variable overhead | 8,730 | 8,910 | 9,360 |
| Budgeted fixed overhead† | 5,000 | 5,000 | 5,000 |
| Budgeted total factory overhead | $13,730 | $13,910 | $14,360 |

*From parts *b* and *k* of additional information.   †From part *k* of additional information.

**6.**

| Selling Expense Budget | April | May | June | Quarter |
|---|---|---|---|---|
| Budgeted sales (from part 1) | $262,500 | $237,500 | $250,000 | $750,000 |
| Sales commissions of 12% | × 12% | × 12% | × 12% | × 12% |
| Sales commissions | 31,500 | 28,500 | 30,000 | 90,000 |
| Salary for sales manager | 3,500 | 4,000 | 4,000 | 11,500 |
| Total selling expenses | $ 35,000 | $ 32,500 | $ 34,000 | $101,500 |

**7.**

| General and Administrative Expense Budget | April | May | June | Quarter |
|---|---|---|---|---|
| Administrative salaries | $8,000 | $8,000 | $8,000 | $24,000 |
| Interest on long-term note payable (0.9% × $200,000) | 1,800 | 1,800 | 1,800 | 5,400 |
| Total general and administrative expenses | $9,800 | $9,800 | $9,800 | $29,400 |

**8.**

| Schedule of Cash Receipts from Sales | April | May | June |
|---|---|---|---|
| Sales (from part 1) | $262,500 | $237,500 | $250,000 |
| Cash receipts from: | | | |
| Cash sales (30% of current sales) | $ 78,750 | $ 71,250 | $ 75,000 |
| Collections of prior period sales (70%) | 175,000* | 183,750 | 166,250 |
| Total cash receipts | $253,750 | $255,000 | $ 241,250 |

*Credit sales from March (10,000 units × $25 price × 70% on credit).

**9.**

| Schedule of Cash Payments for Direct Materials | April | May | June |
|---|---|---|---|
| Materials purchases (from part 3) | $61,740 | $63,945 | $59,220 |
| Cash payments for: | | | |
| Current period purchases (0%) | $ 0 | $ 0 | $ 0 |
| Prior period purchases (100%) | 63,315* | 61,740 | 63,945 |
| Total cash payments | $63,315 | $ 61,740 | $63,945 |

*100% of prior period purchases equals Accounts Payable balance from March 31 balance sheet (see part *f*).

**10.**

| Cash Budget | April | May | June |
|---|---|---|---|
| Beginning cash balance | $ 50,000 | $138,410 | $ 143,335 |
| Add: Cash receipts from sales (part 8) | 253,750 | 255,000 | 241,250 |
| Total cash available | 303,750 | 393,410 | 384,585 |
| Less: Cash payments for | | | |
| Direct materials (part 9) | 63,315 | 61,740 | 63,945 |
| Direct labor (part 4) | 36,375 | 37,125 | 39,000 |
| Variable overhead (part 5) | 8,730 | 8,910 | 9,360 |
| Sales commissions (part 6) | 31,500 | 28,500 | 30,000 |
| Sales salaries (part 6) | 3,500 | 4,000 | 4,000 |
| Administrative salaries (part 7) | 8,000 | 8,000 | 8,000 |
| Dividends | 0 | 100,000 | 0 |
| Interest on long-term note (part 7) | 1,800 | 1,800 | 1,800 |
| Interest on loan | | | |
| April ($12,000 × 1%) | 120 | 0 | 0 |
| Purchase of equipment | 0 | 0 | 55,000 |
| Total cash payments | 153,340 | 250,075 | 211,105 |
| Preliminary cash balance | 150,410 | 143,335 | 173,480 |
| Loan activity | | | |
| Additional loan | $ 0 | $ 0 | $ 0 |
| Repayment of loan | 12,000 | 0 | 0 |
| Ending cash balance | $138,410 | $143,335 | $ 173,480 |
| Loan balance, end of month | $ 0 | $ 0 | $ 0 |

**11.**

### PAYNE COMPANY
### Budgeted Income Statement
### For Quarter Ended June 30

| | | |
|---|---|---|
| Sales (part 1) | | $750,000 |
| Cost of goods sold (30,000 units @ $11.45) | | 343,500 |
| Gross profit | | 406,500 |
| Selling, general, and administrative expenses | | |
| Sales commissions (part 6) | $90,000 | |
| Sales salaries (part 6) | 11,500 | |
| Administrative salaries (part 7) | 24,000 | |
| Interest on long-term note (part 7) | 5,400 | |
| Interest on loan (part 10) | 120 | 131,020 |
| Income before income taxes | | 275,480 |
| Income taxes (275,480 × 35%) | | 96,418 |
| Net income | | 179,062 |

### PAYNE COMPANY
### Budgeted Statement of Retained Earnings
### For Quarter Ended June 30

| | |
|---|---|
| Retained earnings, March 31 | $ 31,420 |
| Net income | 179,062 |
| | 210,482 |
| Less: Cash dividends (part 10) | 100,000 |
| Retained earnings, June 30 | $110,482 |

### PAYNE COMPANY
### Budgeted Balance Sheet
### June 30

| Assets | | | Liabilities and Equity | | |
|---|---|---|---|---|---|
| Cash (part 10) | | $173,480 | Liabilities | | |
| Accounts receivable (70% × $250,000; see part 8) | | 175,000 | Accounts payable (part 9) | $ 59,220 | |
| Raw materials inventory (2,100 pounds* @ $12.60) | | 26,460 | Income taxes payable | 96,418 | |
| Finished goods inventory (8,400 units @ $11.45) | | 96,180 | Long-term note payable (Mar. 31 bal.) | 200,000 | $355,638 |
| Equipment (Mar. 31 bal. plus purchase) | $535,000 | | Equity | | |
| Less: Accumulated depreciation | | | Common stock | 435,000 | |
| (Mar. 31 bal. plus depreciation expense) | 105,000 | 430,000 | Retained earnings | 110,482 | 545,482 |
| Total assets | | $901,120 | Total liabilities and equity | | $901,120 |

*2,100 pounds is from part 3.

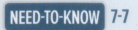

**COMPREHENSIVE 2**

Appendix:
Master
Budget—
Merchandiser

Wild Wood Company's management prepares its master budget using the following information. The budget covers the months of April, May, and June. Wild Wood is a merchandiser.

| WILD WOOD COMPANY | | | | |
|---|---|---|---|---|
| Balance Sheet | | | | |
| March 31 | | | | |
| **Assets** | | | **Liabilities and Equity** | |
| Cash ................................. | | $ 50,000 | Liabilities | |
| Accounts receivable ..................... | | 175,000 | Accounts payable ........ $162,000 | |
| Merchandise inventory (8,800 units × $15) .. | | 132,000 | Loan payable............ 12,000 | |
| Equipment ............................. | $480,000 | | Long-term note payable .. 200,000 | $374,000 |
| Less: Accumulated depreciation........... | 90,000 | 390,000 | Equity | |
| | | | Common stock .......... 235,000 | |
| | | | Retained earnings ....... 138,000 | 373,000 |
| Total assets ............................ | | $747,000 | Total liabilities and equity ... | $747,000 |

**Additional Information**

a. Sales for March were 10,000 units. Each month's sales units are expected to exceed the prior month's sales units by 10%. The product's selling price is $25 per unit.

b. Company policy calls for a given month's ending merchandise inventory to equal 80% of next month's budgeted unit sales. The March 31 merchandise inventory of 8,800 units complies with the policy. The purchase price is $15 per unit.

c. Sales commissions of 12% of sales are paid in the month of the sales. The sales manager's monthly salary will be $3,500 in April and $4,000 per month thereafter.

d. Monthly general and administrative expenses include $8,000 of administrative salaries, $5,000 of depreciation, and 0.9% monthly interest on the long-term note payable.

e. The company expects 30% of sales to be for cash and the remaining 70% on credit. Credit sales are collected in full in the month following the sale (none are collected in the month of the sale).

f. All merchandise purchases are on credit, and no payables arise from any other transactions. All credit purchases (recorded in accounts payable) are paid in the month following the purchase.

g. The minimum ending cash balance for all months is $50,000. If necessary, the company borrows enough cash using a loan to reach the minimum. Loans require an interest payment of 1% at each month-end (before any repayment). If the ending cash balance exceeds the minimum, the excess will be used to repay any loans.

h. Dividends of $80,000 are to be declared and paid in May.

i. Income taxes are budgeted at 30% in the quarter. No cash payments for income taxes are to be made during the second calendar quarter.

j. Equipment purchases for cash of $55,000 are scheduled for June.

**Required**

Prepare the following budgets and schedules for each month of April, May, and June. In addition, compute the three-month total for parts 1, 3, and 4 for use in preparing financial statements.

1. Sales budget, including budgeted sales for July.
2. Merchandise purchases budget.
3. Selling expense budget.
4. General and administrative expense budget.
5. Schedule of cash receipts from sales.
6. Schedule of cash payments for merchandise purchases.
7. Cash budget.
8. Budgeted income statement, budgeted statement of retained earnings, and budgeted balance sheet.

## SOLUTION

**1.**

| Calculation of Unit Sales | April | May | June | July |
|---|---|---|---|---|
| Prior period unit sales | 10,000 | 11,000 | 12,100 | 13,310 |
| Plus 10% growth | 1,000 | 1,100 | 1,210 | 1,331 |
| Budgeted sales units | 11,000 | 12,100 | 13,310 | 14,641 |

| Sales Budget | April | May | June | Quarter |
|---|---|---|---|---|
| Budgeted sales units | 11,000 | 12,100 | 13,310 | 36,410 |
| Selling price per unit | ×$   25 | ×$   25 | ×$   25 | ×$   25 |
| Total budgeted sales | $275,000 | $302,500 | $332,750 | $910,250 |

**2.**

| Merchandise Purchases Budget | April | May | June |
|---|---|---|---|
| Budgeted sales units | 11,000 | 12,100 | 13,310 |
| **Add:** Desired ending inventory | | | |
|     Next period budgeted sales units | 12,100 | 13,310 | 14,641 |
|     Ratio of inventory to future sales | ×   80% | ×   80% | ×   80% |
|     Desired ending inventory units | 9,680 | 10,648 | 11,713 |
| Total required units | 20,680 | 22,748 | 25,023 |
| **Less:** Beginning inventory units | 8,800 | 9,680 | 10,648 |
| Units to purchase | 11,880 | 13,068 | 14,375 |
| Cost per unit | $   15 | $   15 | $   15 |
| Cost of merchandise purchases | $178,200 | $196,020 | $215,625 |

**3.**

| Selling Expense Budget | April | May | June | Quarter |
|---|---|---|---|---|
| Budgeted sales (part 1) | $275,000 | $302,500 | $332,750 | $910,250 |
| Sales commissions of 12% | ×   12% | ×   12% | ×   12% | ×   12% |
| Sales commissions | 33,000 | 36,300 | 39,930 | 109,230 |
| Salary for sales manager | 3,500 | 4,000 | 4,000 | 11,500 |
| Total selling expenses | $ 36,500 | $ 40,300 | $ 43,930 | $120,730 |

**4.**

| General and Administrative Expense Budget | April | May | June | Quarter |
|---|---|---|---|---|
| Administrative salaries | $ 8,000 | $ 8,000 | $ 8,000 | $24,000 |
| Depreciation expense | 5,000 | 5,000 | 5,000 | 15,000 |
| Interest on long-term note payable (0.9% × $200,000) | 1,800 | 1,800 | 1,800 | 5,400 |
| Total general and administrative expenses | $14,800 | $14,800 | $14,800 | $44,400 |

**5.**

| Schedule of Cash Receipts from Sales | April | May | June |
|---|---|---|---|
| Sales (part 1) | $275,000 | $302,500 | $332,750 |
| Cash receipts from: | | | |
|     Cash sales (30% of current sales) | $ 82,500 | $ 90,750 | $ 99,825 |
|     Collections of prior period sales (70%) | 175,000* | 192,500 | 211,750 |
| Total cash receipts | $257,500 | $283,250 | $311,575 |

*70% of credit sales from March (10,000 units × $25 price × 70% on credit).

**6.**

| Schedule of Cash Payments for Merchandise Purchases | April | May | June |
|---|---|---|---|
| Merchandise purchases (part 2) | $178,200 | $196,020 | $ 215,625 |
| Cash payments for: | | | |
|     Current period purchases (0%) | $     0 | $     0 | $     0 |
|     Prior period purchases (100%) | 162,000* | 178,200 | 196,020 |
| Total cash payments | $162,000 | $178,200 | $196,020 |

*100% of prior-period purchases equals Accounts Payable balance from March 31 balance sheet (see part *f*).

**7.**

| Cash Budget | April | May | June |
|---|---|---|---|
| **Beginning cash balance** | $ 50,000 | $ 87,080 | $ 62,030 |
| **Add:** Cash receipts from sales (part 5) | 257,500 | 283,250 | 311,575 |
| Total cash available | 307,500 | 370,330 | 373,605 |
| **Less:** Cash payments for | | | |
|    Merchandise purchases (part 6) | 162,000 | 178,200 | 196,020 |
|    Sales commissions (part 3) | 33,000 | 36,300 | 39,930 |
|    Sales salaries (part 3) | 3,500 | 4,000 | 4,000 |
|    Administrative salaries (part 4) | 8,000 | 8,000 | 8,000 |
|    Interest on long-term note (part 4) | 1,800 | 1,800 | 1,800 |
|    Dividends | 0 | 80,000 | 0 |
|    Purchase of equipment | 0 | 0 | 55,000 |
|    Interest on loan | | | |
|      April ($12,000 × 1%) | 120 | 0 | 0 |
|    Total cash payments | 208,420 | 308,300 | 304,750 |
| Preliminary cash balance | 99,080 | 62,030 | 68,855 |
| **Loan activity** | | | |
|    Additional loan | $ 0 | $ 0 | $ 0 |
|    Repayment of loan | 12,000 | 0 | 0 |
| **Ending cash balance** | $ 87,080 | $ 62,030 | $ 68,855 |
| Loan balance, end of month | $ 0 | $ 0 | $ 0 |

**8.**

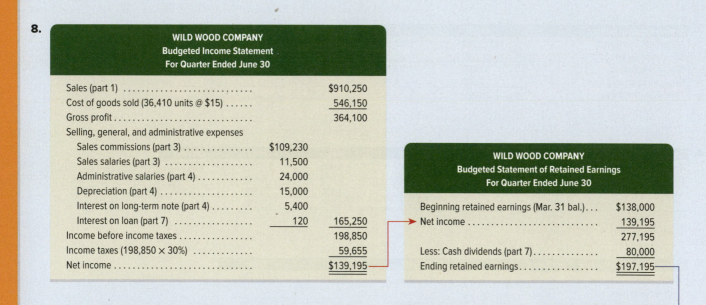

**WILD WOOD COMPANY**
**Budgeted Income Statement**
**For Quarter Ended June 30**

| | | |
|---|---|---|
| Sales (part 1) ............................. | | $910,250 |
| Cost of goods sold (36,410 units @ $15) ...... | | 546,150 |
| Gross profit ............................. | | 364,100 |
| Selling, general, and administrative expenses | | |
|    Sales commissions (part 3) .............. | $109,230 | |
|    Sales salaries (part 3) .................. | 11,500 | |
|    Administrative salaries (part 4) ............ | 24,000 | |
|    Depreciation (part 4) .................... | 15,000 | |
|    Interest on long-term note (part 4) ......... | 5,400 | |
|    Interest on loan (part 7) ................ | 120 | 165,250 |
| Income before income taxes ................ | | 198,850 |
| Income taxes (198,850 × 30%) ............. | | 59,655 |
| Net income .............................. | | $139,195 |

**WILD WOOD COMPANY**
**Budgeted Statement of Retained Earnings**
**For Quarter Ended June 30**

| | |
|---|---|
| Beginning retained earnings (Mar. 31 bal.)... | $138,000 |
| Net income ........................... | 139,195 |
| | 277,195 |
| Less: Cash dividends (part 7).............. | 80,000 |
| Ending retained earnings................. | $197,195 |

**WILD WOOD COMPANY**
**Budgeted Balance Sheet**
**June 30**

**Assets**

| | | |
|---|---|---|
| Cash (part 7) ............................ | | $ 68,855 |
| Accounts receivable (70% of June Sales) ..... | | 232,925 |
| Inventory (11,713 units @ $15 each) ........ | | 175,695 |
| | | |
| Equipment (Mar. 31 bal. plus purchase) ...... | $535,000 | |
| Less: Accumulated depreciation | | |
|    (Mar. 31 bal. plus depreciation expense) ... | 105,000 | 430,000 |
| Total assets ............................. | | $907,475 |

**Liabilities and Equity**

| | | |
|---|---|---|
| Liabilities | | |
|    Accounts payable (part 6) ........... | $215,625 | |
|    Income taxes payable .............. | 59,655 | |
|    Long-term note payable (Mar. 31 bal.) | 200,000 | $475,280 |
| Equity | | |
|    Common stock (Mar. 31 bal.) ........ | 235,000 | |
|    Retained earnings ................. | 197,195 | 432,195 |
| Total liabilities and equity ............. | | 907,475 |

# Merchandise Purchases Budget

## 7A

**P4**

Prepare each component of a master budget for a merchandising company.

Exhibit 7A.1 shows the master budget process for a merchandiser. Unlike a manufacturing company, a merchandiser prepares a merchandise purchases budget rather than a production budget. In addition, a merchandiser does not prepare direct materials, direct labor, or factory overhead budgets. We show the merchandise purchases budget for Hockey Den (HD), a retailer of hockey sticks.

**EXHIBIT 7A.1**

Master Budget Sequence—Merchandiser

### Preparing the Merchandise Purchases Budget

A merchandiser usually expresses a **merchandise purchases budget** in both units and dollars. Exhibit 7A.2 shows the layout for this budget. If only one product is involved, we can compute the number of dollars of inventory to be purchased for the budget by multiplying the units to be purchased by the cost per unit.

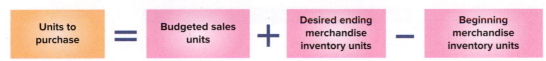

**EXHIBIT 7A.2**

Computing Units to Purchase

A merchandise purchases budget for HD is in Exhibit 7A.3, which consists of 3 parts.

1. **Budgeted sales units.** HD predicts unit sales as follows: October, 1,000; November, 800; December, 1,400; and January, 900.
2. **Desired ending inventory units.** Starting with October, HD set a policy that ending inventory units should equal 90% of next month's budgeted sales. For example, inventory units at the end of October should equal 90% of November's budgeted sales units.
3. **Cost of merchandise purchases.** HD expects the per unit purchase cost of $60 to remain unchanged through the budgeting period. Given 1,010 units are in inventory at September 30, HD can prepare the merchandise purchases budget shown in Exhibit 7A.3.

**EXHIBIT 7A.3**

Merchandise Purchases Budget

| HOCKEY DEN<br>Merchandise Purchases Budget | | | |
|---|---|---|---|
| | October | November | December |
| 1 Budgeted sales units | 1,000 | 800 | 1,400 |
| **Add:** Desired ending inventory | | | |
|     Next period budgeted sales units | 800 | 1,400 | 900 |
|     Ratio of inventory to future sales | × 90% | × 90% | × 90% |
| 2   Desired ending inventory units | 720 | 1,260 | 810 |
| Total required units | 1,720 | 2,060 | 2,210 |
| **Less:** Beginning inventory units | 1,010 | 720 | 1,260 |
| Units to purchase | 710 | 1,340 | 950 |
| | | | |
| Cost per unit | $ 60 | $ 60 | $ 60 |
| 3 Cost of merchandise purchases | $42,600 | $80,400 | $57,000 |

### Schedule of Cash Payments for Merchandise Purchases

Using the budgeted cost of merchandise purchases from Exhibit 7A.3, and given September purchases of $50,000, Hockey Den's schedule of cash payments for merchandise is in Exhibit 7A.4. HD pays 40% of a month's purchases in the month of purchase, and the remaining 60% is paid in the month after purchase.

**EXHIBIT 7A.4**

Schedule of Cash Payments for Merchandise Purchases

| HOCKEY DEN Schedule of Cash Payments for Merchandise Purchases | | | |
|---|---|---|---|
| | October | November | December |
| Merchandise purchases (from Exhibit 7A.3) | $42,600 | $80,400 | $57,000 |
| Cash payments for: | | | |
|   Current period purchases (40%) | $17,040 | $32,160 | $22,800 |
|   Prior period purchases (60%) | 30,000* | 25,560 | 48,240 |
|   Total cash payments for merchandise purchases | $47,040 | $57,720 | $71,040 |

*60% of prior period purchases equals the prior period Accounts Payable balance for this company.

## Other Master Budget Differences—Merchandiser vs. Manufacturer

In addition to preparing a merchandise purchases budget instead of production, direct materials, direct labor, and overhead budgets, other key differences in master budgets for merchandisers include:

- All depreciation expense is included in the general and administrative expense budget of the merchandiser. For the manufacturer, depreciation on manufacturing assets is included in the factory overhead budget and treated as a product cost; depreciation on nonmanufacturing assets is included in the general and administrative expense budget.

- The budgeted balance sheet for the merchandiser will report only one asset for inventory. The balance sheet for the manufacturer will typically report three inventory assets: raw materials, work in process, and finished goods.

See **Need-to-Know 7-7** for illustration of a complete master budget, including budgeted financial statements, for a merchandising company.

---

**NEED-TO-KNOW 7-8**

Merchandise Purchases Budget

P4

In preparing monthly budgets, a merchandiser budgeted sales of 120 units for July and 140 units for August. Management wants each month's ending inventory in units to be 60% of next month's sales units. The June 30 inventory consists of 72 units. The merchandise cost per unit is $50. Prepare the merchandise purchases budget for July.

**Solution**

| Merchandise Purchases Budget | July |
|---|---|
| Budgeted sales units | 120 |
| **Add:** Desired ending inventory | |
|   Next period budgeted sales units | 140 |
|   Ratio of inventory to future sales | × 60% |
|   Desired ending inventory units | 84 |
| Total required units | 204 |
| **Less:** Beginning inventory units | 72 |
| Units to purchase | 132 |
| | |
| Cost per unit | $ 50 |
| Cost of merchandise purchases | $6,600 |

Do More: QS 7-28, QS 7-29, QS 7-30, E 7-25

---

## Summary: Cheat Sheet

### BUDGET PROCESS

**Budget:** Formal statement of plans expressed in dollars and/or units.
**Budgeting benefits:** Plan, control, coordinate, communicate, and motivate.
**Budgeting guidelines:**
1. Employees affected should help prepare (*participatory budgeting*).
2. Goals should be challenging but attainable.
3. Chance to explain differences between actual and budgeted amounts.

### OPERATING BUDGETS

**Master Budget Components**

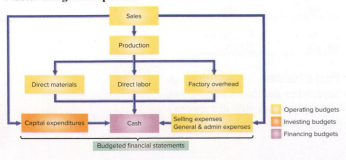

**Sales budget**
Budgeted sales $ = Budgeted sales units × Selling price per unit

| Sales Budget | October |
|---|---|
| Budgeted sales units | 1,000 |
| Selling price per unit | × $ 60 |
| Total budgeted sales | $60,000 |

**Production Budget**

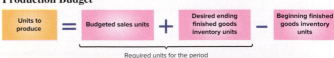

| Production Budget | October |
|---|---|
| Budgeted sales units | 1,000 |
| **Add:** Desired ending inventory | |
|   Next period budgeted sales units | 800 |
|   Ratio of inventory to future sales | × 90% |
|   Desired ending inventory units | 720 |
| Total required units | 1,720 |
| **Less:** Beginning inventory units | 1,010 |
| Units to produce | 710 |

## Direct Materials Budget

| Direct Materials Budget | October |
|---|---|
| Units to produce | 710 |
| Materials required per unit (pounds) | × 0.5 |
| Materials needed for production (pounds) | 355 |
| **Add:** Desired ending materials inventory (pounds) | 335 |
| Total materials required (pounds) | 690 |
| **Less:** Beginning materials inventory (pounds) | 178 |
| Materials to purchase (pounds) | 512 |
| | |
| Materials cost per pound | $   20 |
| Cost of direct materials purchases | $10,240 |

## Direct Labor Budget

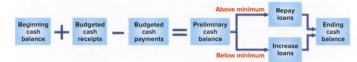

| Direct Labor Budget | October |
|---|---|
| Units to produce | 710 |
| Direct labor hours required per unit | × 0.25 |
| Direct labor hours needed | 177.5 |
| | |
| Direct labor cost per hour | $   12 |
| Cost of direct labor | $2,130 |

## Overhead Budget

| Factory Overhead Budget | October |
|---|---|
| Direct labor hours needed | 177.5 |
| Variable overhead rate per direct labor hour | ×$   10 |
| Budgeted variable overhead | 1,775 |
| Budgeted fixed overhead | 1,500 |
| Budgeted total factory overhead | $3,275 |

## Cost of Goods Sold Budget

| Cost of Goods Sold Budget | October |
|---|---|
| Budgeted sales units | 1,000 |
| Budgeted cost per unit | $   17 |
| Budgeted cost of goods sold | $17,000 |

## Selling Expense Budget

| Selling Expense Budget | October |
|---|---|
| Budgeted sales | $60,000 |
| Sales commission of 10% | ×   10% |
| Sales commissions | 6,000 |
| Salary for sales manager | 2,000 |
| Total selling expenses | $ 8,000 |

## General and Administrative Expense Budget

| General and Administrative Expense Budget | October |
|---|---|
| Administrative salaries | $4,500 |
| Total general and administrative expenses | $4,500 |

# INVESTING AND FINANCING BUDGETS

## Capital Expenditures Budget

| Capital Expenditures Budget | October | November | December |
|---|---|---|---|
| Purchase of equipment | $0 | $0 | $25,000 |
| Total capital expenditures | $0 | $0 | $25,000 |

## Cash Budget Layout

Beginning cash balance + Budgeted cash receipts − Budgeted cash payments = Preliminary cash balance → Above minimum → Repay loans → Ending cash balance; Below minimum → Increase loans → Ending cash balance

## Schedule of Cash Receipts from Sales

| Schedule of Cash Receipts from Sales | September | October |
|---|---|---|
| Sales | $42,000 | $60,000 |
| Cash receipts from: | | |
| Cash sales (40% of current sales) | | $24,000 |
| Collections of prior period sales (60%) | | 25,200 |
| Total cash receipts | | $49,200 |

## Schedule of Cash Payments for Direct Materials

| Schedule of Cash Payments for Direct Materials | September | October |
|---|---|---|
| Materials purchases | $7,060 | $10,240 |
| Cash payments for: | | |
| Current period purchases (0%) | | $    0 |
| Prior period purchases (100%) | | 7,060 |
| Total cash payments | | $ 7,060 |

## Cash Budget

| Cash Budget | October |
|---|---|
| Beginning cash balance | $20,000 |
| **Add:** Cash receipts from sales (Exhibit 7.14) | 49,200 |
| Total cash available | 69,200 |
| **Less:** Cash payments for | |
| Direct materials (Exhibit 7.15) | 7,060 |
| Direct labor (Exhibit 7.8) | 2,130 |
| Variable overhead (Exhibit 7.9) | 1,775 |
| Sales commissions (Exhibit 7.11) | 6,000 |
| Sales salaries (Exhibit 7.11) | 2,000 |
| Administrative salaries (Exhibit 7.12) | 4,500 |
| Income taxes (Exhibit 7.3) | 20,000 |
| Dividends | 0 |
| Interest on loan | |
| October ($10,000 × 1%) | 100 |
| Purchase of equipment | 0 |
| Total cash payments | 43,565 |
| Preliminary cash balance | $25,635 |
| **Loan activity** | |
| Additional loan | $    0 |
| Repayment of loan | 5,635 |
| Ending cash balance | $20,000 |
| Loan balance, end of month | $ 4,365 |

# BUDGETED FINANCIAL STATEMENTS

## Budgeted income statement

| Budgeted Income Statement | | |
|---|---:|---:|
| Sales (Exhibit 7.4, 3,200 units @ $60) | | $192,000 |
| Cost of goods sold (3,200 units @ $17) | | 54,400 |
| Gross profit | | 137,600 |
| Selling, general, and administrative expenses | | |
| Sales commissions (Exhibit 7.11) | $19,200 | |
| Sales salaries (Exhibit 7.11) | 6,000 | |
| Administrative salaries (Exhibit 7.12) | 13,500 | |
| Interest expense (Exhibit 7.16) | 144 | 38,844 |
| Income before income taxes | | 98,756 |
| Income tax expense ($98,756 × 40%) | | 39,502 |
| Net income | | $ 59,254 |

## Budgeted balance sheet

| Budgeted Balance Sheet | | | | | |
|---|---|---:|---|---|---:|
| **Assets** | | | **Liabilities and Equity** | | |
| Cash | | $ 44,706 | Liabilities | | |
| Accounts receivable | | 50,400 | Accounts payable | | $ 9,700 |
| Raw materials inventory | | 4,950 | Income taxes payable | | 39,502 $ 49,202 |
| Finished goods inventory | | 13,770 | Equity | | |
| Equipment | $225,000 | | Common stock | 150,000 | |
| Less: Accumulated depreciation | 40,500 | 184,500 | Retained earnings | 99,124 | 249,124 |
| Total assets | | $298,326 | Total liabilities and equity | | $298,326 |

# Key Terms

Budget (235)

Budgetary control (235)

Budgeted balance sheet (248)

Budgeted income statement (247)

Budgeting (235)

Capital expenditures budget (243)

Cash budget (243)

Continuous budgeting (236)

Cost of goods sold budget (241)

Direct labor budget (240)

Direct materials budget (239)

Factory overhead budget (241)

General and administrative expense budget (242)

Master budget (237)

Merchandise purchases budget (257)

Production budget (238)

Revenue per employee (250)

Rolling budget (236)

Safety stock (238)

Sales budget (238)

Selling expense budget (242)

Zero-based budgeting (237)

# Multiple Choice Quiz

**1.** A plan that reports the units to produce by a manufacturing company during the budget period is called a
- **a.** Sales budget.
- **b.** Cash budget.
- **c.** Production budget.
- **d.** Manufacturing budget.
- **e.** Capital expenditures budget.

**2.** The following sales are budgeted for the next four months.

| | April | May | June | July |
|---|---|---|---|---|
| Budgeted sales units . . . | 480 | 560 | 600 | 480 |

Each month's ending inventory of finished goods should be 30% of the next month's sales. The budgeted production for May is
- **a.** 572 units.
- **b.** 560 units.
- **c.** 548 units.
- **d.** 600 units.
- **e.** 180 units.

**3.** A store has the following budgeted sales for the next three months.

| | July | August | September |
|---|---|---|---|
| Budgeted sales . . . . . . . . | $180,000 | $220,000 | $240,000 |

Cash sales are 25% of total sales and all credit sales are expected to be collected in the month following the sale. The total amount of cash expected to be received from customers in September is
- **a.** $240,000.
- **b.** $225,000.
- **c.** $60,000.
- **d.** $165,000.
- **e.** $220,000.

**4.** A plan that shows the expected cash inflows and cash outflows during the budget period, including receipts from loans needed to maintain a minimum cash balance or repayments of such loans, is called
- **a.** A rolling budget.
- **b.** An income statement.
- **c.** A balance sheet.
- **d.** A cash budget.
- **e.** An operating budget.

**5.^A** A hardware store has budgeted cost of sales of $36,000 for its power tool department in July. Management wants to have $7,000 in tool inventory at the end of July. Its beginning inventory of tools is budgeted to be $6,000. What is the budgeted dollar amount of merchandise purchases?
- **a.** $36,000
- **b.** $43,000
- **c.** $42,000
- **d.** $35,000
- **e.** $37,000

## ANSWERS TO MULTIPLE CHOICE QUIZ

**1.** c

**2.** a; 560 units + (0.30 × 600 units) − (0.30 × 560 units) = 572 units

**3.** b; Cash collected = 25% of Sept sales + 75% of August sales
= (0.25 × $240,000) + (0.75 × $220,000) = $225,000

**4.** d

**5.** e; Budgeted purchases = $36,000 + $7,000 − $6,000 = $37,000

*Superscript letter A denotes assignments based on Appendix 7A.*

For each of the following indicate *yes* if the item is an important budgeting guideline or *no* if it is not.

1. Employees should have the opportunity to explain differences from budgeted amounts.
2. Budgets should include budgetary slack.
3. Employees impacted by a budget should be consulted when it is prepared.
4. Goals in a budget should be set low so targets can always be reached.
5. Budgetary goals should be attainable.

**QUICK STUDY**

**QS 7-1**

Budget motivation

**C1**

---

For each of the following indicate *yes* if it describes a potential benefit of budgeting or *no* if it describes a potential negative outcome of budgeting.

1. Budgets help coordinate activities across departments.
2. A budget forces managers to spend time planning for the future.
3. Some employees might overstate expenses in budgets.
4. Budgets can lead to excessive pressure to meet budgeted results.
5. Budgets can provide incentives for good performance.

**QS 7-2**

Budgeting benefits

**C1**

---

Grace manufactures and sells miniature digital cameras for $250 each. Sales in May were 1,000 units, and management forecasts 4% growth in unit sales each month. (*a*) Determine the budgeted sales units of cameras for June. (*b*) Prepare the sales budget for June.

**QS 7-3**

Sales budget    **P1**

---

Scora Inc. sells a single product for $50 per unit. Budgeted sales units for the next three months follow. Prepare a sales budget for the months of January, February, and March.

**QS 7-4**

Sales budget

**P1**

|  | January | February | March |
|---|---|---|---|
| Budgeted sales units . . . . | 1,200 | 2,000 | 1,600 |

---

Zahn Co. budgets sales of 220 units in May and 240 units in June. Each month's ending inventory should be 25% of the next month's sales. The April 30 ending finished goods inventory is 55 units. Prepare the production budget for May.

**QS 7-5**

Production budget    **P1**

---

Champ Inc. budgets the following sales in units for the coming two months. Each month's ending inventory of finished units should be 60% of the next month's sales. The April 30 finished goods inventory is 108 units. Prepare the production budget for May.

**QS 7-6**

**Manufacturing:**
Production budget

**P1**

|  | May | June |
|---|---|---|
| Budgeted sales units . . . . . . . | 180 | 200 |

---

Atlantic Surf manufactures surfboards. The company's budgeted sales units for the next three months is shown below. Company policy is to maintain finished goods inventory equal (in units) to 40% of the next month's unit sales. As of June 30, the company has 1,600 finished surfboards in inventory. Prepare the production budget for the months of July and August.

**QS 7-7**

**Manufacturing:**
Production budget

**P1**

|  | July | August | September |
|---|---|---|---|
| Budgeted sales units . . . . | 4,000 | 6,500 | 3,500 |

---

Forrest Company manufactures phone chargers and has a policy that ending inventory should equal 10% of the next month's budgeted unit sales. October's ending inventory equals 40,000 units. November and December sales are budgeted to be 400,000 units and 350,000 units, respectively. Prepare the production budget for November.

**QS 7-8**

**Manufacturing:**
Production budget

**P1**

**QS 7-9**
**Manufacturing:**
Direct materials budget
**P1**

Miami Solar manufactures solar panels for industrial use. The company budgets production of 5,000 units (solar panels) in July and 5,300 units in August. Each unit requires 3 pounds of direct materials, which cost $6 per pound. The company's policy is to maintain direct materials inventory equal to 30% of the next month's direct materials requirement. As of June 30, the company has 4,500 pounds of direct materials in inventory. Prepare the direct materials budget for July.

**QS 7-10**
**Manufacturing:**
Direct labor budget   **P1**

Miami Solar budgets production of 5,000 solar panels in July. Each unit requires 4 hours of direct labor at a rate of $16 per hour. Prepare a direct labor budget for July.

**QS 7-11**
**Manufacturing:** Factory
overhead budget   **P1**

Miami Solar budgets production of 5,300 solar panels for August. Each unit requires 4 hours of direct labor at a rate of $16 per hour. The company applies variable overhead at the rate of $12 per direct labor hour. Budgeted fixed factory overhead is $180,000 per month. Prepare a factory overhead budget for August.

**QS 7-12**
**Manufacturing:** Direct
materials budget   **P1**

Zortek Corp. budgets production of 400 units in January and 200 units in February. Each finished unit requires five pounds of material Z, which costs $2 per pound. Each month's ending inventory of material Z should be 40% of the following month's budgeted production. The January 1 inventory has 800 pounds of material Z. Prepare a direct materials budget for January.

**QS 7-13**
**Manufacturing:**
Direct labor budget   **P1**

Tora Co. plans to produce 1,020 units in July. Each unit requires two hours of direct labor. The direct labor rate is $20 per hour. Prepare a direct labor budget for July.

**QS 7-14**
**Manufacturing:** Factory
overhead budget   **P1**

Hockey Pro budgets 320 hours of direct labor during May. The company applies variable overhead at the rate of $18 per direct labor hour. Budgeted fixed overhead equals $46,000 per month. Prepare a factory overhead budget for May.

**QS 7-15**
Selling expense budget   **P1**

Zilly Co. budgets sales of $400,000 for June. Zilly pays a sales manager a monthly salary of $6,000 and a commission of 8% of that month's sales dollars. Prepare a selling expense budget for June.

**QS 7-16**
Selling expense budget
**P1**

X-Tel budgets sales of $60,000 for April, $100,000 for May, and $80,000 for June. Sales commissions are 10% of sales dollars and the company pays a sales manager a salary of $6,000 per month. Sales commissions and salaries are paid in the month incurred. Prepare a selling expense budget for April, May, and June.

**QS 7-17**
Schedule of cash
receipts   **P2**

Liza's budgets sales of $40,000 for May and $52,000 for June. Assume 60% of Liza's sales are for cash. The remaining 40% are credit sales; credit customers pay the entire amount owed in the month following the sale. Prepare the schedule of cash receipts from sales for June.

**QS 7-18**
Schedule of cash
receipts   **P2**

X-Tel budgets sales of $60,000 for April, $100,000 for May, and $80,000 for June. Sales are 40% cash and 60% on credit. All credit sales are collected in the month following the sale. Total sales for March were $25,000. Prepare a schedule of cash receipts from sales for April, May, and June.

**QS 7-19**
Schedule of cash
receipts   **P2**

Music World reports the following budgeted sales: August, $150,000; and September, $170,000. Cash sales are 40% of total sales, and all credit sales are collected in the month following the sale. Prepare a schedule of cash receipts from sales for September.

**QS 7-20**
Schedule of cash receipts
with uncollectibles
**P2**

The Guitar Shoppe reports the following budgeted sales: August, $150,000; and September, $170,000. For its total sales, 40% are immediately collected in cash, 55% are credit sales and collected in the month following sale, and the remaining 5% are written off as uncollectible. Prepare a schedule of cash receipts from sales for September.

**QS 7-21**
Schedule of cash receipts
with uncollectibles
**P2**

Wells Company reports the following budgeted sales: September, $55,000; October, $66,000; and November, $80,000. All sales are on credit, and 5% of those credit sales are budgeted as uncollectible. Collection of the remaining 95% of credit sales are budgeted as follows: 60% in the first month after sale and 35% in the second month after sale. Prepare a schedule of cash receipts from sales for November.

Kingston budgets total sales for June and July of $420,000 and $398,000, respectively. Cash sales are 60% of total sales. Of the credit sales, 20% are collected in the month of sale, 70% are collected during the first month after the sale, and the remaining 10% are collected in the second month after the sale. Determine the amount of accounts receivable reported on the company's budgeted balance sheet as of July 31. *Hint:* Determine the percent of June and July sales that are uncollected at July 31.

**QS 7-22**
Computing budgeted accounts receivable
**P2**

Santos Co. is preparing a cash budget for February. The company has $20,000 cash at the beginning of February and budgets $75,000 in cash receipts from sales and $100,250 in cash payments during February. Prepare the cash budget for February assuming the company maintains a $5,000 minimum cash balance and will take a loan if necessary to maintain this balance. The company has no loans outstanding on February 1.

**QS 7-23**
Cash budget
**P2**

Use the following information to prepare a cash budget for March for Gado Company.

**QS 7-24**
**Manufacturing:**
Cash budget
**P2**

a. Beginning cash balance on March 1, $72,000.
b. Cash receipts from sales, $300,000.
c. Cash payments for direct materials, $140,000.
d. Cash payments for direct labor, $80,000.
e. Cash payments for overhead, $45,000.

f. Cash payments for sales commissions, $7,000.
g. Cash payments for interest, $200 (1% of beginning loan balance of $20,000).
h. Cash repayment of loan, $20,000.

Following are selected accounts for a manufacturing company. For each account, indicate whether it will appear on a budgeted income statement or a budgeted balance sheet. If an item will not appear on either budgeted financial statement, label it neither.

**QS 7-25**
Budgeted financial statements
**P3**

| | | | |
|---|---|---|---|
| Sales . . . . . . . . . . . . . . . . . . . . . . | _____ | Interest expense on loan . . . . . . . . . . . | _____ |
| Office salaries expense . . . . . . . . | _____ | Cash dividends paid . . . . . . . . . . . . . . | _____ |
| Accumulated depreciation . . . . . . | _____ | Accounts payable . . . . . . . . . . . . . . . . | _____ |
| Sales commissions expense . . . . | _____ | Cost of goods sold . . . . . . . . . . . . . . . | _____ |

Garda purchased $600,000 of merchandise in August and budgets merchandise purchases of $720,000 in September. Merchandise purchases are paid as follows: 25% in the month of purchase and 75% in the month after the purchase. Prepare a schedule of cash payments for merchandise purchases for September.

**QS 7-26**[A]
**Merchandising:** Schedule of cash payments  **P4**

Torres Co. budgets merchandise purchases of $15,800 in January, $18,600 in February, and $20,200 in March. For those purchases, 40% of purchases are paid in the month of purchase and 60% are paid in the month after the purchase. The company purchased $25,000 of merchandise in December. Prepare a schedule of cash payments for merchandise for the months of January, February, and March.

**QS 7-27**[A]
**Merchandising:** Schedule of cash payments
**P4**

Raider-X Company budgets sales of 18,000 units for April and 20,000 units for May. Beginning inventory on April 1 is 3,600 units, and the company wants to have 20% of next month's unit sales in inventory at the end of each month. The merchandise cost per unit is $2. Prepare a merchandise purchases budget for the month of April.

**QS 7-28**[A]
**Merchandising:**
Merchandise purchases budget  **P4**

Lexi Company budgets unit sales of 1,040,000 in April, 1,220,000 in May, 980,000 in June, and 1,020,000 in July. Beginning inventory on April 1 is 312,000 units, and the company wants to have 30% of next month's unit sales in inventory at the end of each month. The merchandise cost per unit is $0.50. Prepare a merchandise purchases budget for the months of April, May, and June.

**QS 7-29**[A]
**Merchandising:**
Merchandise purchases budget  **P4**

Montel Company's July sales budget shows sales of $600,000. The company budgets beginning merchandise inventory of $50,000 and ending merchandise inventory of $40,000 for July. Cost of goods sold is 60% of sales. Determine the budgeted cost of merchandise purchases for July. *Hint:* Use the relation (Beg. Inventory + Purchases − Cost of Goods Sold = End. Inventory) to solve for purchases.

**QS 7-30**[A]
**Merchandising:** Computing merchandise purchases
**P4**

**Mc Graw Hill connect**

Match the definitions 1 through 6 with the phrase *a* through *f*.

**EXERCISES**

a. Participatory budgeting
b. Cash budget
c. Master budget

d. Budgetary slack
e. Sales budget
f. Budgeted income statement

**Exercise 7-1**
Budget language
**C1**

[continued on next page]

[continued from previous page]

1. Helps determine financing needs.
2. The usual starting point in the master budget process.
3. A report that shows predicted revenues and expenses for a budgeting period.
4. A budgetary cushion used to meet performance targets.
5. A comprehensive plan that consists of several budgets that are linked.
6. Employees affected by a budget help in preparing it.

---

**Exercise 7-2**
Revising budgeted
sales   P1

MM Co. budgets sales of $30,000 for May. MM's production manager discovered a way to use more sustainable packaging. As a result, MM's product will receive better placement on store shelves and May sales are predicted to increase by 8%. Compute budgeted sales for May assuming MM switches to this more sustainable packaging.

---

**Exercise 7-3**
**Manufacturing:**
Production budget

P1

Ruiz Co. provides the following budgeted sales for the next four months. The company wants to end each month with ending finished goods inventory equal to 25% of next month's budgeted unit sales. Finished goods inventory on April 1 is 125 units. Prepare a production budget for the months of April, May, and June.

|  | April | May | June | July |
|---|---|---|---|---|
| Budgeted sales units . . . | 500 | 580 | 540 | 620 |

---

**Exercise 7-4**
**Manufacturing:**
Production budget   P1

Blue Wave Co. budgets the following unit sales for the next four months: September, 4,000 units; October, 5,000 units; November, 7,000 units; and December, 7,600 units. The company's policy is to maintain finished goods inventory equal to 60% of the next month's unit sales. At the end of August, the company had 2,400 finished units in inventory. Prepare a production budget for each of the months of September, October, and November.

---

**Exercise 7-5**
**Manufacturing:**
Production budget

P1

Tyler Co. budgets the following unit sales for the next four months: April, 3,000 units; May, 4,000 units; June, 6,000 units; and July, 2,000 units. The company's policy is to maintain finished goods inventory equal to 30% of the next month's unit sales. At the end of March, the company had 900 finished units in inventory. Prepare a production budget for each of the months of April, May, and June.

---

**Exercise 7-6**
**Manufacturing:** Production
budget

P1

Electro Company manufactures transmissions for electric cars. Management reports ending finished goods inventory for the first quarter at 90,000 units. The following unit sales are budgeted during the rest of the year: second quarter, 450,000 units; third quarter, 525,000 units; and fourth quarter, 475,000 units. Company policy calls for the ending finished goods inventory of a quarter to equal 20% of the next quarter's budgeted unit sales. Prepare a production budget for both the second and third quarters that shows the number of transmissions to manufacture.

---

**Exercise 7-7**
**Manufacturing:** Direct
materials budget

P1

Rida Inc. is preparing its direct materials budget for the second quarter. It budgets production of 240,000 units in the second quarter and 52,500 units in the third quarter. Each unit requires 0.60 pound of direct material, priced at $175 per pound. The company plans to end each quarter with an ending inventory of this material equal to 30% of next quarter's budgeted direct materials required. Raw material inventory is 43,200 pounds at the beginning of the second quarter. Prepare a direct materials budget for the second quarter.

---

**Exercise 7-8**
**Manufacturing:** Direct
materials budget

P1

Zira Co. reports the following production budget for the next four months. Each finished unit requires five pounds of direct materials, and the company wants to end each month with direct materials inventory equal to 30% of next month's production needs. Beginning direct materials inventory for April was 683 pounds. Direct materials cost $4 per pound. Prepare a direct materials budget for April, May, and June.

|  | April | May | June | July |
|---|---|---|---|---|
| Units to produce . . . . . . . | 455 | 570 | 560 | 540 |

Ramos Co. provides the following budgeted production for the next four months.

| | April | May | June | July |
|---|---|---|---|---|
| Units to produce...................... | 442 | 570 | 544 | 540 |

Each finished unit requires 5 pounds of direct materials. The company wants to end each month with direct materials inventory equal to 30% of next month's production needs. Beginning direct materials inventory for April was 663 pounds. Direct materials cost $2 per pound. Prepare a direct materials budget for April, May, and June.

**Exercise 7-9**
**Manufacturing:** Direct materials budget
**P1**

Electro Company budgets production of 450,000 electric panels in the second quarter and 520,000 electric panels in the third quarter. Each panel requires 0.80 pound of direct material at a cost of $1.70 per pound. The company aims to end each quarter with an ending inventory of this material equal to 20% of next quarter's budgeted materials requirements. Beginning inventory of this material is 72,000 pounds. Prepare a direct materials budget for the second quarter.

**Exercise 7-10**
**Manufacturing:** Direct materials budget   **P1**

The production budget for Manner Company shows units to produce as follows: July, 620; August, 680; and September, 540. Each unit produced requires two hours of direct labor. The direct labor rate is budgeted at $20 per hour in July and August, but is budgeted to be $21 per hour in September. Prepare a direct labor budget for the months July, August, and September.

**Exercise 7-11**
**Manufacturing:** Direct labor budget   **P1**

Branson Belts makes handcrafted belts. The company budgets production of 4,500 belts during the second quarter. Each belt requires 4 direct labor hours, at a cost of $17 per hour. Prepare a direct labor budget for the second quarter.

**Exercise 7-12**
**Manufacturing:** Direct labor budget   **P1**

Addison Co. budgets production of 2,400 units during the second quarter. Information on its direct labor and its variable and fixed overhead is shown below. For the second quarter, prepare (1) a direct labor budget and (2) a factory overhead budget.

| Direct labor... | Each finished unit requires 4 direct labor hours, at a cost of $20 per hour. | Variable overhead.. | Budgeted at the rate of $11 per direct labor hour. |
|---|---|---|---|
| | | Fixed overhead .... | Budgeted at $450,000 per quarter. |

**Exercise 7-13**
**Manufacturing:** Direct labor and factory overhead budgets   **P1**

Ramos Co. provides the following (partial) production budget for the next three months. Each finished unit requires 0.50 hour of direct labor at the rate of $16 per hour. The company budgets variable overhead at the rate of $20 per direct labor hour and budgets fixed overhead of $8,000 per month. Prepare (1) a direct labor budget and (2) a factory overhead budget for April, May, and June.

| **Production Budget** | April | May | June |
|---|---|---|---|
| Units to produce................. | 442 | 570 | 544 |

**Exercise 7-14**
**Manufacturing:**
Direct labor and factory overhead budgets   **P1**

MCO Leather manufactures leather purses. Each purse requires 2 pounds of direct materials at a cost of $4 per pound and 0.8 direct labor hour at a rate of $16 per hour. Variable overhead is budgeted at a rate of $2 per direct labor hour. Budgeted fixed overhead is $10,000 per month. The company's policy is to end each month with direct materials inventory equal to 40% of the next month's direct materials requirement. At the end of August the company had 3,680 pounds of direct materials in inventory. The company's production budget reports the following. Prepare budgets for September and October for (1) direct materials, (2) direct labor, and (3) factory overhead.

| **Production Budget** | September | October | November |
|---|---|---|---|
| Units to produce................. | 4,600 | 6,200 | 5,800 |

**Exercise 7-15**
**Manufacturing:** Direct materials, direct labor, and overhead budgets
**P1**

**Exercise 7-16**

**Manufacturing:** Direct materials, direct labor, and overhead budgets

**P1**

Garden Yeti manufactures garden sculptures. Each sculpture requires 8 pounds of direct materials at a cost of $3 per pound and 0.5 direct labor hour at a rate of $18 per hour. Variable overhead is budgeted at a rate of $3 per direct labor hour. Budgeted fixed overhead is $4,000 per month. The company's policy is to maintain direct materials inventory equal to 20% of the next month's direct materials requirement. At the end of February the company had 5,280 pounds of direct materials in inventory. The company's production budget reports the following. Prepare budgets for March and April for (1) direct materials, (2) direct labor, and (3) factory overhead.

| Production Budget | March | April | May |
|---|---|---|---|
| Units to produce. . . . . . . . . . . . . . . . | 3,300 | 4,600 | 4,800 |

**Exercise 7-17**

Preparation of cash budgets (for three periods)

**P2**

Kayak Co. budgeted the following cash receipts (excluding cash receipts from loans received) and cash payments (excluding cash payments for loan principal and interest payments) for the first three months of next year.

| | Cash Receipts | Cash Payments |
|---|---|---|
| January . . . . . . . . . . . | $525,000 | $475,000 |
| February . . . . . . . . . . | 400,000 | 350,000 |
| March . . . . . . . . . . . . | 450,000 | 525,000 |

Kayak requires a minimum cash balance of $30,000 at each month-end. Loans taken to meet this requirement charge 1% interest per month, paid at each month-end. The interest is computed based on the beginning balance of the loan for the month. Any preliminary cash balance above $30,000 is used to repay loans at month-end. The company has a cash balance of $30,000 and a loan balance of $60,000 at January 1. Prepare monthly cash budgets for January, February, and March.

**Exercise 7-18**

Schedule of cash receipts

**P2**

Jasper Company has 70% of its sales on credit and 30% for cash. All credit sales are collected in full in the first month following the sale. The company budgets sales of $525,000 for April, $535,000 for May, and $560,000 for June. Total sales for March are $500,000. Prepare a schedule of cash receipts from sales for April, May, and June.

**Exercise 7-19**

Schedule of cash payments

**P2**

Zisk Co. purchases direct materials on credit. Budgeted purchases are April, $80,000; May, $110,000; and June, $120,000. Cash payments for purchases are: 70% in the month of purchase and 30% in the first month after purchase. Purchases for March are $70,000. Prepare a schedule of cash payments for direct materials for April, May, and June.

**Exercise 7-20**

Cash budget

**P2**

Karim Corp. requires a minimum $8,000 cash balance. Loans taken to meet this requirement cost 1% interest per month (paid at the end of each month). Any preliminary cash balance above $8,000 is used to repay loans at month-end. The cash balance on July 1 is $8,400, and the company has no outstanding loans. Budgeted cash receipts (other than for loans received) and budgeted cash payments (other than for loan or interest payments) follow. Prepare a cash budget for July, August, and September. Round interest payments to the nearest dollar.

| | July | August | September |
|---|---|---|---|
| Cash receipts . . . . . . . . . . . . . . | $20,000 | $26,000 | $40,000 |
| Cash payments. . . . . . . . . . . . . . | 28,000 | 30,000 | 22,000 |

**Exercise 7-21**

Cash budget

**P2**

Foyert Corp. requires a minimum $30,000 cash balance. Loans taken to meet this requirement cost 1% interest per month (paid at the end of each month). Any preliminary cash balance above $30,000 is used to repay loans at month-end. The cash balance on October 1 is $30,000, and the company has an outstanding loan of $10,000. Budgeted cash receipts (other than for loans received) and budgeted cash payments (other than for loan or interest payments) follow. Prepare a cash budget for October, November, and December. Round interest payments to the nearest dollar.

| | October | November | December |
|---|---|---|---|
| Cash receipts . . . . . . . . . . . . . . | $110,000 | $80,000 | $100,000 |
| Cash payments. . . . . . . . . . . . . . | 120,000 | 75,000 | 80,000 |

Use the following information to prepare the September cash budget for PTO Co. Ignore the "Loan activity" section of the budget.

a. Beginning cash balance, September 1, $40,000.

b. Budgeted cash receipts from September sales, $255,000.

c. Direct materials are purchased on credit. Purchase amounts are August (actual), $80,000; and September (budgeted), $110,000. Payments for direct materials follow: 65% in the month of purchase and 35% in the first month after purchase.

d. Budgeted cash payments for direct labor in September, $40,000.

e. Budgeted depreciation expense for September, $4,000.

f. Budgeted cash payment for dividends in September, $20,000.

g. Budgeted cash payment for income taxes in September, $10,000.

h. Budgeted cash payment for loan interest in September, $1,000.

**Exercise 7-22**
**Manufacturing:** Cash budget  **P2**

---

Motors Corp. manufactures motors for dirt bikes. The company requires a minimum $30,000 cash balance at each month-end. If necessary, the company borrows to meet this requirement at a cost of 2% interest per month (paid at the end of each month). Any preliminary cash balance above $30,000 at month-end is used to repay loans. The cash balance on July 1 is $34,000, and the company has no outstanding loans. Budgeted cash receipts and budgeted cash payments (other than for interest on the loan and loan activity) follow. Prepare a cash budget for July, August, and September.

**Exercise 7-23**
**Manufacturing:** Cash budget  **P2**

| | July | August | September |
|---|---|---|---|
| Cash receipts . . . . . . . . . . . . . . | $ 85,000 | $111,000 | $150,000 |
| Cash payments . . . . . . . . . . . . . . | 113,000 | 99,900 | 127,400 |

---

Fortune Inc. is preparing its master budget for the first quarter. The company sells a single product at a price of $25 per unit. Sales (in units) are budgeted at 150,000 for the first quarter. Cost of goods sold is $14 per unit. Other expense information for the first quarter follows. Prepare a budgeted income statement for the first quarter ended March 31. Round expense amounts to the dollar.

**Exercise 7-24**
Budgeted income statement  **P3**

| | | | |
|---|---|---|---|
| Sales commissions  . . . | 8% of sales dollars | Rent . . . . . . . . . . . . . . . | $  42,000 per quarter |
| Advertising . . . . . . . . . | $562,500 per quarter | Office salaries . . . . . . . . | $ 225,000 per quarter |
| Interest . . . . . . . . . . . . | 1.25% quarterly on $250,000 note payable | Depreciation. . . . . . . . . | $120,000 per quarter |
| Tax rate . . . . . . . . . . . . . | 30% | | |

---

Walker Company prepares monthly budgets. Company policy is to end each month with merchandise inventory equal to 15% of budgeted unit sales for the following month. Budgeted sales and merchandise purchases for the next three months follow. Beginning inventory on July 1 is 27,000 units. The company budgets sales of 200,000 units in October. The merchandise cost per unit is $2. Prepare the merchandise purchases budgets for the months of July, August, and September.

**Exercise 7-25ᴬ**
**Merchandising:**
Merchandise purchases budgets
**P4**

| | July | August | September |
|---|---|---|---|
| Budgeted sales units . . . . . . . . . . | 180,000 | 315,000 | 270,000 |

---

Ahmed Company purchases all merchandise on credit. It recently budgeted the month-end accounts payable balances below. Cash payments on accounts payable during each month are expected to be June, $1,490,000; July, $1,425,000; and August, $1,495,000. Use the information to compute the budgeted merchandise purchases for June, July, and August. *Hint:* Use the relation (Beg. Accounts Payable + Purchases on Credit − Payments on Accounts Payable = End. Accounts Payable) to solve for budgeted purchases.

**Exercise 7-26ᴬ**
**Merchandising:** Computing budgeted merchandise purchases from accounts payable  **P4**

| | May 31 | June 30 | July 31 | August 31 |
|---|---|---|---|---|
| Accounts payable  . . . . . . . . . . . . . . . . . . . | $150,000 | $200,000 | $235,000 | $195,000 |

**Check**   June purchases, $1,540,000

**Exercise 7-27^A**

**Merchandising:**
Preparing a cash budget

**P4**

Use the following information to prepare the July cash budget for Acco Co. Ignore the "Loan activity" section of the budget.

a. Beginning cash balance on July 1: $50,000.

b. Budgeted cash receipts from sales: 30% is collected in the month of sale, 50% in the next month, and 20% in the second month after sale. Sales amounts are May (actual), $1,720,000; June (actual), $1,200,000; and July (budgeted), $1,400,000.

c. Budgeted cash payments on merchandise purchases: 60% in the month of purchase and 40% in the month following purchase. Purchase amounts are June (actual), $700,000; and July (budgeted), $750,000.

d. Budgeted cash payments for salaries in July: $275,000.

e. Budgeted cash payments for sales commissions for July: $200,000.

f. Budgeted cash payment for income taxes in July: $80,000.

g. Budgeted cash payment for loan interest in July: $6,600.

---

**Exercise 7-28^A**

**Merchandising:** Preparing a budgeted income statement

**P4**

Lamonte Co. reports the following budgeted December 31 adjusted trial balance. Prepare the budgeted income statement for the current year ended December 31. Ignore income taxes.

|  | Debit | Credit |
|---|---|---|
| Cash | $ 50,000 | |
| Accounts receivable | 120,000 | |
| Merchandise inventory | 64,000 | |
| Equipment | 125,000 | |
| Accumulated depreciation—Equipment | | $ 25,000 |
| Accounts payable | | 34,000 |
| Loan payable | | 22,000 |
| Common stock | | 200,000 |
| Retained earnings (beginning year balance) | | 58,000 |
| Sales | | 520,000 |
| Cost of goods sold | 360,000 | |
| Loan interest expense | 8,000 | |
| Depreciation expense | 10,000 | |
| Salaries expense | 122,000 | |
| Totals | $859,000 | $859,000 |

---

**Exercise 7-29^A**

**Merchandising:** Preparing a budgeted balance sheet

**P4**

Use the budgeted information in Exercise 7-28, and the ending year balance of Retained Earnings of $78,000 on December 31, to prepare Lamonte Co.'s budgeted balance sheet as of December 31.

---

**Exercise 7-30^A**

**Merchandising:** Schedule of cash payments for merchandise purchases

**P4**

Hardy Co. reports budgeted merchandise purchases below. For those purchases, 40% of a month's purchases is paid in the month of purchase, and 60% is paid in the first month after purchase. Prepare the schedule of cash payments for merchandise purchases for September and October.

|  | August | September | October |
|---|---|---|---|
| Budgeted merchandise purchases .... | $194,400 | $183,600 | $157,200 |

---

**Exercise 7-31^A**

**Merchandising:** Cash budget and schedule of cash receipts

**P4**

Castor Inc. is preparing its master budget. Budgeted sales and cash payments for merchandise purchases for the next three months follow.

| Budgeted | April | May | June |
|---|---|---|---|
| Sales | $32,000 | $40,000 | $24,000 |
| Cash payments for merchandise purchases.... | 20,200 | 16,800 | 17,200 |

Sales are 50% cash and 50% on credit. Sales in March were $24,000. All credit sales are collected in the month following the sale. The March 31 balance sheet includes balances of $12,000 in cash and $2,000 in loans payable. A minimum cash balance of $12,000 is required. Loans are obtained at the end of any month when the preliminary cash balance is below $12,000. Interest is 1% per month based on the beginning-of-the-month loan balance and is paid at each month-end. If a preliminary cash balance above $12,000 at month-end exists, loans are repaid from the excess. Expenses are paid in the month incurred and include sales commissions (10% of sales), shipping (2% of sales), office salaries ($5,000 per month), and rent ($3,000 per month). (*a*) Prepare a schedule of cash receipts from sales for April, May, and June. (*b*) Prepare a cash budget for each of April, May, and June (round interest payments to the nearest dollar).

**Exercise 7-32A**
**Merchandising:** Cash budget and schedule of cash receipts
**P4**

Kelsey is preparing its master budget. Budgeted sales and cash payments for merchandise purchases for the next three months follow.

| Budgeted | July | August | September |
|---|---|---|---|
| Sales | $64,000 | $80,000 | $48,000 |
| Cash payments for merchandise purchases | 40,400 | 33,600 | 34,400 |

Sales are 20% cash and 80% on credit. Sales in June were $56,250. All credit sales are collected in the month following the sale. The June 30 balance sheet includes balances of $15,000 in cash and $5,000 in loans payable. A minimum cash balance of $15,000 is required. Loans are obtained at the end of any month when the preliminary cash balance is below $15,000. Interest is 1% per month based on the beginning-of-the-month loan balance and is paid at each month-end. If a preliminary cash balance above $15,000 at month-end exists, loans are repaid from the excess. Expenses are paid in the month incurred and consist of sales commissions (10% of sales), office salaries ($4,000 per month), and rent ($6,500 per month). (1) Prepare a schedule of cash receipts from sales for July, August, and September. (2) Prepare a cash budget for July, August, and September. (Round interest payments to the nearest dollar.)

**Exercise 7-33A**
**Merchandising:** Budgeted balance sheet
**P4**

Prepare a budgeted balance sheet at March 31 using the following information from Zimmer Company.

**a.** The cash budget for March shows an ending loan balance of $10,000 and an ending cash balance of $50,000.

**b.** The sales budget for March shows sales of $140,000. Accounts receivable at the end of March are budgeted to be 70% of March sales.

**c.** The merchandise purchases budget shows that $89,000 in merchandise will be purchased on credit in March. Purchases on credit are paid 100% in the month following the purchase.

**d.** Ending merchandise inventory for March is budgeted to be 600 units at a cost of $35 each.

**e.** Income taxes payable of $26,000 are budgeted at the end of March.

**f.** Accounting records at the end of March show budgeted equipment of $84,000 with accumulated depreciation of $47,000.

**g.** Common stock of $25,000 and retained earnings of $56,000 are budgeted at the end of March.

**Exercise 7-34**
Direct labor budget for a service company
**A1**

Render CPA is preparing direct labor budgets for the current year. The partners budget billable hours for the year as follows:

| | | | |
|---|---|---|---|
| Data entry | 2,200 hours | Tax | 4,300 hours |
| Auditing | 4,800 hours | Consulting | 750 hours |

The company budgets $15 per hour to data-entry clerks, $30 per hour to audit personnel, $40 per hour to tax personnel, and $50 per hour to consulting personnel. Prepare a direct labor budget for this service company for the year.

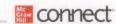

## PROBLEM SET A

### Problem 7-1A
**Manufacturing:** Preparing production, materials, labor, and overhead budgets

**P1**

**Check** (1) Units to produce, 148,500

Black Diamond Company produces snowboards. Each snowboard requires 2 pounds of carbon fiber. Management reports that 5,000 snowboards and 6,000 pounds of carbon fiber are in inventory at the beginning of the third quarter, and that 150,000 snowboards are budgeted to be sold during the third quarter. Management wants to end the third quarter with 3,500 snowboards and 4,000 pounds of carbon fiber in inventory. Carbon fiber costs $15 per pound. Each snowboard requires 0.5 hour of direct labor at $20 per hour. Variable overhead is budgeted at the rate of $8 per direct labor hour. The company budgets fixed overhead of $1,782,000 for the quarter.

**Required**

1. Prepare the production budget for the third quarter. *Hint:* Desired ending inventory units are given.
2. Prepare the direct materials budget for the third quarter.
3. Prepare the direct labor budget for the third quarter.
4. Prepare the factory overhead budget for the third quarter.

### Problem 7-2A
**Manufacturing:**
Cash budget and schedule of cash payments

**P2**

Built-Tight is preparing its master budget. Budgeted sales and cash payments follow.

| | July | August | September |
|---|---|---|---|
| Budgeted sales | $64,000 | $80,000 | $48,000 |
| Budgeted cash payments for | | | |
| Direct materials | 16,160 | 13,440 | 13,760 |
| Direct labor | 4,040 | 3,360 | 3,440 |
| Overhead | 20,200 | 16,800 | 17,200 |

Sales to customers are 20% cash and 80% on credit. Sales in June were $56,250. All credit sales are collected in the month following the sale. The June 30 balance sheet includes balances of $15,000 in cash and $5,000 in loans payable. A minimum cash balance of $15,000 is required. Loans are obtained at the end of any month when the preliminary cash balance is below $15,000. Interest is 1% per month based on the beginning-of-the-month loan balance and is paid at each month-end. Any preliminary cash balance above $15,000 is used to repay loans at month-end. Expenses are paid in the month incurred and consist of sales commissions (10% of sales), office salaries ($4,000 per month), and rent ($6,500 per month).

1. Prepare a schedule of cash receipts for the months of July, August, and September.
2. Prepare a cash budget for the months of July, August, and September. Round interest payments to the dollar.

### Problem 7-3A
**Manufacturing:**
Preparation and analysis of budgeted income statements

**P3**

Merline Manufacturing makes its product for $75 per unit and sells it for $150 per unit. The sales staff receives a commission of 10% of sales. Its December income statement follows.

**MERLINE MANUFACTURING**
**Income Statement**
**For Month Ended December 31**

| | | |
|---|---|---|
| Sales | | $2,250,000 |
| Cost of goods sold | | 1,125,000 |
| Gross profit | | 1,125,000 |
| Selling, general, and administrative expenses | | |
| Sales commissions (10%) | $225,000 | |
| Advertising | 250,000 | |
| Office rent | 30,000 | |
| Administrative salaries | 45,000 | |
| Depreciation—Office equipment | 50,000 | |
| Office insurance | 10,000 | 610,000 |
| Net income | | $ 515,000 |

Management expects December's results to be repeated in January, February, and March without any changes in strategy. Management, however, has an alternative plan. It believes that if the unit selling price is reduced to $125 per unit and advertising is increased to $287,500 per month, sales units will be 16,500 for January, 18,150 for February, and 19,965 for March. The cost of its product will remain at $75 per unit, the sales staff will continue to earn a 10% commission, and the remaining expenses will stay the same.

**Required**

**1.** Prepare budgeted income statements for each of the months of January, February, and March that show results from implementing the proposed plan. Use a three-column format, with one column for each month. Ignore income taxes.

*Analysis Component*

**2.** For the proposed plan, is income in March budgeted to be higher than income in December?

---

The management of Zigby Manufacturing prepared the following balance sheet for March 31.

**Problem 7-4A**
**Manufacturing:**
Preparation of a complete master budget

**P1    P2    P3**

### ZIGBY MANUFACTURING
### Balance Sheet
### March 31

| Assets | | | Liabilities and Equity | | |
|---|---|---|---|---|---|
| Cash. . . . . . . . . . . . . . . . . . . . . . . | | $    40,000 | Liabilities | | |
| Accounts receivable . . . . . . . . . . . | | 344,400 | Accounts payable. . . . . . . . | $201,000 | |
| Raw materials inventory. . . . . . . . . | | 98,500 | Loan payable . . . . . . . . . . . | 12,000 | |
| Finished goods inventory. . . . . . . . . | | 325,540 | Long-term note payable . . | 500,000 | $  713,000 |
| Equipment. . . . . . . . . . . . . . . . . . . | $ 600,000 | | Equity | | |
| Less: Accumulated depreciation . . | 150,000 | 450,000 | Common stock . . . . . . . . . . | 335,000 | |
| | | | Retained earnings . . . . . . . | 210,440 | 545,440 |
| Total assets . . . . . . . . . . . . . . . . . . | | $1,258,440 | Total liabilities and equity. . . . | | $1,258,440 |

To prepare a master budget for April, May, and June, management gathers the following information.

**a.** Sales for March total 20,500 units. Budgeted sales in units follow: April, 20,500; May, 19,500; June, 20,000; and July, 20,500. The product's selling price is $24.00 per unit and its total product cost is $19.85 per unit.

**b.** Raw materials inventory consists solely of direct materials that cost $20 per pound. Company policy calls for a given month's ending materials inventory to equal 50% of the next month's direct materials requirements. The March 31 raw materials inventory is 4,925 pounds. The budgeted June 30 ending raw materials inventory is 4,000 pounds. Each finished unit requires 0.50 pound of direct materials.

**c.** Company policy calls for a given month's ending finished goods inventory to equal 80% of the next month's budgeted unit sales. The March 31 finished goods inventory is 16,400 units.

**d.** Each finished unit requires 0.50 hour of direct labor at a rate of $15 per hour.

**e.** The predetermined variable overhead rate is $2.70 per direct labor hour. Depreciation of $20,000 per month is the only fixed factory overhead item.

**f.** Sales commissions of 8% of sales are paid in the month of the sales. The sales manager's monthly salary is $3,000.

**g.** Monthly general and administrative expenses include $12,000 for administrative salaries and 0.9% monthly interest on the long-term note payable.

**h.** The company budgets 30% of sales to be for cash and the remaining 70% on credit. Credit sales are collected in full in the month following the sale (no credit sales are collected in the month of sale).

[continued on next page]

[continued from previous page]

**i.** All raw materials purchases are on credit, and accounts payable are solely tied to raw materials purchases. Raw materials purchases are fully paid in the next month (none are paid in the month of purchase).

**j.** The minimum ending cash balance for all months is $40,000. If necessary, the company borrows enough cash using a loan to reach the minimum. Loans require an interest payment of 1% at each month-end (before any repayment). If the month-end preliminary cash balance exceeds the minimum, the excess will be used to repay any loans.

**k.** Dividends of $10,000 are budgeted to be declared and paid in May.

**l.** No cash payments for income taxes are budgeted in the second calendar quarter. Income tax will be assessed at 35% in the quarter and budgeted to be paid in the third calendar quarter.

**m.** Equipment purchases of $100,000 are budgeted for the last day of June.

**Required**

Prepare the following budgets for the months of April, May, and June, except as noted below.

<table>
<tr><td>**1.** Sales budget.</td><td>**8.** Schedule of cash receipts.</td></tr>
<tr><td>**2.** Production budget.</td><td>**9.** Schedule of cash payments for direct materials.</td></tr>
<tr><td>**3.** Direct materials budget.</td><td>**10.** Cash budget.</td></tr>
<tr><td>**4.** Direct labor budget.</td><td>**11.** Budgeted income statement for second quarter (not monthly).</td></tr>
<tr><td>**5.** Factory overhead budget.</td><td></td></tr>
<tr><td>**6.** Selling expense budget.</td><td>**12.** Budgeted balance sheet at June 30.</td></tr>
<tr><td>**7.** General and administrative expense budget.</td><td></td></tr>
</table>

**Check**  (2) Units to produce:
April, 19,700; May, 19,900
(3) Cost of direct materials
purchases: April, $198,000
(10) Ending cash balance: April,
$85,675; May, $129,420
(12) Budgeted total assets:
June 30, $1,292,620

---

**Problem 7-5A^A**

**Merchandising:**
Preparation of merchandise purchases budgets for three products

**P4**

Keggler's Supply is a merchandiser of three different products. Beginning inventories for March are footwear, 20,000 units; sports gear, 80,000 units; and apparel, 50,000 units. Management believes each of these inventories is too high and begins a new policy that ending inventory in any month should equal 30% of the budgeted sales units for the following month. Budgeted sales units for March, April, May, and June follow.

| Budgeted Sales Units | March | April | May | June |
|---|---|---|---|---|
| Footwear.................. | 15,000 | 25,000 | 32,000 | 35,000 |
| Sports gear ............... | 70,000 | 90,000 | 95,000 | 90,000 |
| Apparel .................. | 40,000 | 38,000 | 37,000 | 25,000 |

**Check**  March budgeted
purchases: Footwear, 2,500;
Sports gear, 17,000; Apparel,
1,400

**Required**

Prepare a merchandise purchases budget (in units only) for *each product* for the months of March, April, and May.

---

**Problem 7-6A^A**

**Merchandising:**
Preparation of cash budgets for three periods

**P4**

Oneida Company's operations began in August. August sales were $215,000 and purchases were $125,000. The beginning cash balance for September is $5,000. Oneida's owner approaches the bank for a $100,000 loan to be made on September 2 and repaid on November 30. The bank's loan officer asks the owner to prepare monthly cash budgets. Its budgeted sales, merchandise purchases, and cash payments for other expenses for the next three months follow.

| Budgeted | September | October | November |
|---|---|---|---|
| Sales | $250,000 | $375,000 | $400,000 |
| Merchandise purchases | 240,000 | 225,000 | 200,000 |
| Cash payments | | | |
| Salaries | 30,000 | 30,000 | 30,000 |
| Rent | 10,000 | 10,000 | 10,000 |
| Insurance | 4,000 | 4,000 | 4,000 |
| Repayment of loan | | | 100,000 |
| Interest on loan | 1,000 | 1,000 | 1,000 |

All sales are on credit where 70% of credit sales are collected in the month following the sale, and the remaining 30% collected in the second month following the sale. All merchandise is purchased on credit; 80% of the balance is paid in the month following a purchase, and the remaining 20% is paid in the second month.

**Required**

Prepare the following for the months of September, October, and November.

**1.** Schedule of cash receipts from sales.
**2.** Schedule of cash payments for direct materials.
**3.** Cash budget.

---

Aztec Company sells its product for $180 per unit. Its actual and budgeted sales follow.

| | May (Actual) | June (Budget) | July (Budget) | August (Budget) |
|---|---|---|---|---|
| Sales units | 2,000 | 6,000 | 5,000 | 3,800 |
| Sales dollars | $360,000 | $1,080,000 | $900,000 | $684,000 |

All sales are on credit. Collections are as follows: 30% is collected in the month of the sale, and the remaining 70% is collected in the month following the sale. Merchandise purchases cost $110 per unit. For those purchases, 60% is paid in the month of purchase and the other 40% is paid in the month following purchase. The company has a policy to maintain an ending monthly inventory of 20% of the next month's unit sales. The May 31 actual inventory level of 1,200 units is consistent with this policy. Selling and administrative expenses of $110,000 per month are paid in cash. The company's minimum cash balance at month-end is $100,000. Loans are obtained at the end of any month when the preliminary cash balance is below $100,000. Any preliminary cash balance above $100,000 is used to repay loans at month-end. This loan has a 1% monthly interest rate. On May 31, the loan balance is $25,000, and the company's cash balance is $100,000. Round amounts to the nearest dollar.

**Required**

**1.** Prepare a schedule of cash receipts from sales for each of the months of June and July.
**2.** Prepare the merchandise purchases budget for June and July.
**3.** Prepare a schedule of cash payments for merchandise purchases for June and July. Assume May's budgeted merchandise purchases is $308,000.
**4.** Prepare a cash budget for June and July, including any loan activity and interest expense. Compute the loan balance at the end of each month.

**Problem 7-7A<sup>A</sup>**
**Merchandising:** Preparation of cash budgets with supporting purchases budgets
**P4**

**Check** (1) Cash receipts: June, $576,000

(4) Budgeted ending loan balance: June, $65,250; July, $0

---

Dimsdale Sports, a merchandising company, reports the following balance sheet at December 31.

**Problem 7-8A<sup>A</sup>**
**Merchandising:** Preparation of a complete master budget  **P4**

| DIMSDALE SPORTS COMPANY | | | | |
|---|---|---|---|---|
| **Balance Sheet** | | | | |
| **December 31** | | | | |
| **Assets** | | | **Liabilities and Equity** | |
| Cash ......................... | | $ 36,000 | Liabilities | |
| Accounts receivable ............ | | 525,000 | Accounts payable ........... $360,000 | |
| Inventory .................... | | 150,000 | Loan payable .............. 15,000 | |
| | | | Taxes payable (due March 15) .. 90,000 | $ 465,000 |
| Equipment ................... | $540,000 | | Equity | |
| Less: Accumulated depreciation ... | 67,500 | 472,500 | Common stock ............ 472,500 | |
| | | | Retained earnings .......... 246,000 | 718,500 |
| Total assets ................. | | $1,183,500 | Total liabilities and equity ....... | $1,183,500 |

[continued on next page]

[continued from previous page]

To prepare a master budget for January, February, and March, use the following information.

a. The company's single product is purchased for $30 per unit and resold for $55 per unit. The inventory level of 5,000 units on December 31 is more than management's desired level, which is 20% of the next month's budgeted sales units. Budgeted sales are January, 7,000 units; February, 9,000 units; March, 11,000 units; and April, 10,000 units. All sales are on credit.

b. Cash receipts from sales are budgeted as follows: January, $221,250; February, $697,000; March, $489,500.

c. Cash payments for merchandise purchases are budgeted as follows: January, $80,000; February, $302,800; March, $147,600.

d. Sales commissions equal to 20% of sales dollars are paid each month. Sales salaries (excluding commissions) are $5,000 per month.

e. General and administrative salaries are $12,000 per month. Maintenance expense equals $2,000 per month and is paid in cash.

f. New equipment purchases are budgeted as follows: January, $36,000; February, $96,000; and March, $28,800. Budgeted depreciation expense is January, $6,000; February, $7,000; and March, $7,300.

g. The company budgets a land purchase at the end of March at a cost of $150,000, which will be paid with cash on the last day of the month.

h. The company has an agreement with its bank to obtain additional loans as needed. The interest rate is 1% per month and interest is paid at each month-end based on the beginning-month balance. Partial or full payments on these loans are made on the last day of the month. The company maintains a minimum ending cash balance of $25,000 at the end of each month.

i. The income tax rate for the company is 40%. Income taxes on the first quarter's income will not be paid until April 15.

**Required**

Prepare a master budget for the months of January, February, and March that has the following budgets (round amounts to the nearest dollar).

1. Sales budgets.
2. Merchandise purchases budgets.
3. Selling expense budgets.
4. General and administrative expense budgets. *Hint:* Depreciation is included in the general and administrative budget for merchandisers.
5. Capital expenditures budgets.
6. Cash budgets.
7. Budgeted income statement for entire quarter (not monthly) ended March 31.
8. Budgeted balance sheet as of March 31.

**Check**   (2) Budgeted purchases: Jan., $114,000; Feb., $282,000

(6) Ending cash bal.: Jan., $30,100; Feb., $210,300

(8) Budgeted total assets at March 31, $1,568,650

---

## PROBLEM SET B

### Problem 7-1B
**Manufacturing:**
Preparing production, materials, labor, and overhead budgets

**P1**

**Check**   (1) Units to produce, 248,000

NSA Company produces baseball bats. Each bat requires 3 pounds of aluminum alloy. Management reports that 8,000 bats and 15,000 pounds of aluminum alloy are in inventory at the beginning of the second quarter, and that 250,000 bats are budgeted to be sold during the second quarter. Management wants to end the second quarter with 6,000 finished bats and 12,000 pounds of aluminum alloy in inventory. Aluminum alloy costs $4 per pound. Each bat requires 0.5 hour of direct labor at $18 per hour. Variable overhead is budgeted at the rate of $12 per direct labor hour. The company budgets fixed overhead of $1,776,000 for the quarter.

**Required**

1. Prepare the production budget for the second quarter. *Hint:* Desired ending inventory units are given.
2. Prepare the direct materials budget for the second quarter.
3. Prepare the direct labor budget for the second quarter.
4. Prepare the factory overhead budget for the second quarter.

A1 Manufacturing is preparing its master budget. Budgeted sales and cash payments follow.

**Problem 7-2B**

**Manufacturing:**

Cash budget and schedule of cash payments

**P2**

| | July | August | September |
|---|---|---|---|
| Budgeted sales | $63,400 | $80,600 | $48,600 |
| Budgeted cash payments for | | | |
| Direct materials | 12,480 | 9,900 | 10,140 |
| Direct labor | 10,400 | 8,250 | 8,450 |
| Overhead | 18,720 | 14,850 | 15,210 |

Sales to customers are 20% cash and 80% on credit. Sales in June were $58,750. All credit sales are collected in the month following the sale. The June 30 balance sheet includes balances of $12,900 in cash and $2,600 in loans payable. A minimum cash balance of $12,900 is required. Loans are obtained at the end of any month when the preliminary cash balance is below $12,900. Interest is 1% per month based on the beginning-of-the-month loan balance and is paid at each month-end. Any preliminary cash balance above $12,900 is used to repay loans at month-end. Expenses are paid in the month incurred and consist of sales commissions (10% of sales), office salaries ($4,600 per month), and rent ($7,100 per month).

1. Prepare a schedule of cash receipts for the months of July, August, and September.
2. Prepare a cash budget for the months of July, August, and September. Round interest payments to the dollar.

HOG Company makes its product for $60 per unit and sells it for $130 per unit. The sales staff receives a commission of 10% of sales. Its June income statement follows.

**Problem 7-3B**

**Manufacturing:**

Preparation and analysis of budgeted income statements

**P3**

**HOG Company**
**Income Statement**
**For Month Ended June 30**

| | | |
|---|---|---|
| Sales | | $1,300,000 |
| Cost of goods sold | | 600,000 |
| Gross profit | | 700,000 |
| Selling, general, and administrative expenses | | |
| Sales commissions (10%) | $130,000 | |
| Advertising | 200,000 | |
| Office rent | 24,000 | |
| Administrative salaries | 40,000 | |
| Depreciation—Office equipment | 50,000 | |
| Office insurance | 12,000 | 456,000 |
| Net income | | $ 244,000 |

Management expects June's results to be repeated in July, August, and September without any changes in strategy. Management, however, has another plan. It believes that if the unit selling price is reduced to $115 per unit and advertising is increased to $250,000 per month, sales units will be 11,000 for July, 12,100 for August, and 13,310 for September. The cost of its product will remain at $60 per unit, the sales staff will continue to earn a 10% commission, and the remaining expenses will stay the same.

**Required**

1. Prepare budgeted income statements for each of the months of July, August, and September that show results from implementing the proposed plan. Use a three-column format, with one column for each month. Ignore income taxes.

**Check**    Budgeted net income: July, $102,500

*Analysis Component*

2. For the proposed plan, is income in September budgeted to be higher than income in June?

**Problem 7-4B**

**Manufacturing:**

Preparation of a complete master budget

**P1  P2  P3**

The management of Nabar Manufacturing prepared the following balance sheet for June 30.

| NABAR MANUFACTURING |||||
| --- |
| Balance Sheet |||||
| June 30 |||||

| Assets | | | Liabilities and Equity | | |
| --- | --- | --- | --- | --- | --- |
| Cash | | $ 40,000 | Liabilities | | |
| Accounts receivable | | 248,920 | Accounts payable | $ 51,400 | |
| Raw materials inventory | | 35,000 | Income taxes payable | 10,000 | |
| Finished goods inventory | | 241,080 | Loan payable | 24,000 | |
| | | | Long-term note payable | 300,000 | $ 385,400 |
| Equipment | $720,000 | | Equity | | |
| Less: Accumulated depreciation | 240,000 | 480,000 | Common stock | 600,000 | |
| | | | Retained earnings | 59,600 | 659,600 |
| Total assets | | $1,045,000 | Total liabilities and equity | | $1,045,000 |

To prepare a master budget for July, August, and September, use the following information.

**a.** Sales were 20,000 units in June. Budgeted sales in units follow: July, 21,000; August, 19,000; September, 20,000; and October, 24,000. The product's selling price is $17 per unit and its total product cost is $14.35 per unit.

**b.** Company policy calls for a given month's ending finished goods inventory to equal 70% of the next month's budgeted unit sales. The June 30 finished goods inventory is 16,800 units.

**c.** Raw materials inventory consists solely of direct materials that cost $8 per pound. Company policy calls for a given month's ending materials inventory to equal 20% of the next month's direct materials requirements. The June 30 raw materials inventory is 4,375 pounds. The budgeted September 30 ending raw materials inventory is 1,980 pounds. Each finished unit requires 0.50 pound of direct materials.

**d.** Each finished unit requires 0.50 hour of direct labor at a rate of $16 per hour.

**e.** The predetermined variable overhead rate is $2.70 per direct labor hour. Depreciation of $20,000 per month is the only fixed factory overhead item.

**f.** Monthly general and administrative expenses include $9,000 administrative salaries and 0.9% monthly interest on the long-term note payable.

**g.** Sales commissions of 10% of sales are paid in the month of the sales. The sales manager's monthly salary is $3,500.

**h.** The company budgets 30% of sales to be for cash and the remaining 70% on credit. Credit sales are collected in full in the month following the sale (no credit sales are collected in the month of sale).

**i.** All raw materials purchases are on credit, and accounts payable are solely tied to raw materials purchases. Raw materials purchases are fully paid in the next month (none are paid in the month of purchase).

**j.** Dividends of $20,000 are budgeted to be declared and paid in August.

**k.** Income Taxes Payable at June 30 are budgeted to be paid in July. Income tax expense will be assessed at 35% in the quarter and budgeted to be paid in October.

**l.** Equipment purchases of $100,000 are budgeted for the last day of September.

**m.** The minimum ending cash balance for all months is $40,000. If necessary, the company borrows enough cash using a loan to reach the minimum. Loans require an interest payment of 1% at each month-end (before any repayment). If the month-end preliminary cash balance exceeds the minimum, the excess will be used to repay any loans.

**Required**

Prepare the following budgets for the months of July, August, and September, except as noted below.

1. Sales budget.
2. Production budget.
3. Direct materials budget.
4. Direct labor budget.
5. Factory overhead budget.
6. Selling expense budget.
7. General and administrative expense budget.
8. Schedule of cash receipts from sales.
9. Schedule of cash payments for direct materials.
10. Cash budget.
11. Budgeted income statement for entire quarter (not monthly).
12. Budgeted balance sheet at September 30.

**Check**   (2) Units to produce: July, 17,500; August, 19,700

(3) Cost of direct materials purchases: July, $50,760

(10) Ending cash balance: July, $95,855; August, $140,200

(12) Budgeted total assets: Sep. 30, $1,054,920

H20 Sports is a merchandiser of three different products. Beginning inventories for April are water skis, 40,000 units; tow ropes, 90,000 units; and life jackets, 150,000 units. Management believes inventory levels are too high for all three products and begins a new policy that ending inventory in any month should equal 10% of the budgeted sales units for the following month. Budgeted sales units for April, May, June, and July follow.

| Budgeted Sales Units | April | May | June | July |
|---|---|---|---|---|
| Water skis . . . . . . . . . . . . | 70,000 | 90,000 | 130,000 | 100,000 |
| Tow ropes . . . . . . . . . . . . | 100,000 | 90,000 | 110,000 | 100,000 |
| Life jackets . . . . . . . . . . | 160,000 | 190,000 | 200,000 | 120,000 |

**Required**

Prepare a merchandise purchases budget (in units only) for *each product* for the months of April, May, and June.

**Problem 7-5B**[A]
**Merchandising:**
Preparation of merchandise purchases budgets for three products
**P4**

**Check**   April budgeted purchases: Water skis, 39,000; Tow ropes, 19,000; Life jackets, 29,000

---

Sony Stereo began operations in March. March sales were $180,000 and purchases were $100,000. The beginning cash balance for April is $3,000. Sony's owner approaches the bank for an $80,000 loan to be made on April 2 and repaid on June 30. The bank's loan officer asks the owner to prepare monthly cash budgets. Its budgeted sales, merchandise purchases, and cash payments for other expenses for the next three months follow.

| Budgeted | April | May | June |
|---|---|---|---|
| Sales | $220,000 | $300,000 | $380,000 |
| Merchandise purchases | 210,000 | 180,000 | 220,000 |
| Cash payments | | | |
| Salaries | 16,000 | 17,000 | 18,000 |
| Rent | 36,000 | 36,000 | 36,000 |
| Insurance | 2,000 | 2,000 | 2,000 |
| Repayment of loan | | | 80,000 |
| Interest on loan | 800 | 800 | 800 |

All sales are on credit where 90% of credit sales are collected in the month following the sale, and the remaining 10% is collected in the second month following the sale. All merchandise is purchased on credit; 80% of the balance is paid in the month following a purchase, and the remaining 20% is paid in the second month.

**Required**

Prepare the following for the months of April, May, and June.
1. Schedule of cash receipts from sales.
2. Schedule of cash payments for direct materials.
3. Cash budget.

**Problem 7-6B**[A]
**Merchandising:**
Preparation of cash budgets for three periods
**P4**

---

Connick Company sells its product for $22 per unit. Its actual and budgeted sales follow.

| | February (Actual) | March (Budget) | April (Budget) | May (Budget) |
|---|---|---|---|---|
| Sales units. . . . . . . . . . . . | 22,500 | 19,000 | 18,750 | 21,000 |
| Sales dollars . . . . . . . . . . | $495,000 | $418,000 | $412,500 | $462,000 |

All sales are on credit where 40% is collected in the month of the sale, and the remaining 60% is collected in the month following the sale. Merchandise purchases cost $12 per unit. For those purchases, 30% is paid in the month of purchase and the other 70% is paid in the month following purchase. The company has a policy to maintain an ending monthly inventory of 20% of the next month's unit sales. The February 28 actual inventory level of 3,800 units is consistent with this policy. Selling and administrative expenses of $160,000 per month are paid in cash. The company's minimum cash balance for month-end is $50,000. Loans are obtained at the end of any month when the preliminary cash balance is below $50,000. Any preliminary cash balance above $50,000 is used to repay loans at month-end. This loan has a 1% monthly interest rate. At February 28, the loan balance is $12,000, and the company's cash balance is $50,000.

**Required**

1. Prepare a schedule of cash receipts from sales for each of the months of March and April.

[continued on next page]

**Problem 7-7B**[A]
**Merchandising:**
Preparation of cash budgets with supporting purchases budgets
**P4**

**Check**   (1) Cash receipts: March, $464,200.

[continued from previous page]

**2.** Prepare the merchandise purchases budget for March and April.

**3.** Prepare a schedule of cash payments for merchandise purchases for March and April. Assume budgeted merchandise purchases of $261,600 for February.

(4) Ending cash balance: March, $90,740.

**4.** Prepare a cash budget for March and April, including any loan activity and interest expense. Compute the loan balance at the end of each month.

**Problem 7-8B**[A]

**Merchandising:**

Preparation of a complete master budget

**P4**

Isle Corp., a merchandising company, reports the following balance sheet at December 31.

### ISLE CORPORATION
### Balance Sheet
### December 31

| Assets | | | Liabilities and Equity | | |
|---|---|---|---|---|---|
| Cash ........................ | | $  36,000 | Liabilities | | |
| Accounts receivable ............. | | 525,000 | Accounts payable ................ | $360,000 | |
| Inventory ..................... | | 150,000 | Loan payable ................... | 15,000 | |
| | | | Taxes payable (due March 15) ...... | 90,000 | $  465,000 |
| Equipment ..................... | $540,000 | | Equity | | |
| Less: Accumulated depreciation .... | 67,500 | 472,500 | Common stock ................. | 472,500 | |
| | | | Retained earnings .............. | 246,000 | 718,500 |
| Total assets ................... | | $1,183,500 | Total liabilities and equity .......... | | $1,183,500 |

To prepare a master budget for January, February, and March, use the following information.

**a.** The company's single product is purchased for $30 per unit and resold for $45 per unit. The inventory level of 5,000 units on December 31 is more than management's desired level, which is 25% of the next month's budgeted sales units. Budgeted sales are January, 6,000 units; February, 8,000 units; March, 10,000 units; and April, 9,000 units. All sales are on credit.

**b.** Cash receipts from sales are budgeted as follows: January, $382,500; February, $421,500; March, $355,500.

**c.** Cash payments for merchandise purchases are budgeted as follows: January, $72,000; February, $306,000; March, $123,000.

**d.** Sales commissions equal to 20% of sales dollars are paid each month. Sales salaries (excluding commissions) are $7,500 per month.

**e.** General and administrative salaries are $12,000 per month. Maintenance expense equals $3,000 per month and is paid in cash.

**f.** New equipment purchases are budgeted as follows: January, $72,000; February, $96,000; and March, $28,800. Budgeted depreciation expense is January, $6,375; February, $7,375; and March, $7,675.

**g.** The company budgets a land purchase at the end of March at a cost of $150,000, which will be paid with cash on March 31.

**h.** The company has a contract with its bank to obtain additional loans as needed. The interest rate is 1% per month, and interest is paid at each month-end based on the beginning-month balance. Partial or full payments on these loans are made on the last day of the month. The company maintains a minimum ending cash balance of $36,000 at the end of each month.

**i.** The income tax rate for the company is 40%. Income taxes on the first quarter's income will not be paid until April 15.

**Required**

Prepare a master budget for the months of January, February, and March that has the following budgets (round amounts to the nearest dollar).

**1.** Sales budgets.

**2.** Merchandise purchases budgets.

**3.** Selling expense budgets.

**4.** General and administrative expense budgets. *Hint:* Depreciation is included in the general and administrative budget for merchandisers.

**5.** Capital expenditures budgets.

**6.** Cash budgets.

**7.** Budgeted income statement for entire quarter (not monthly) ended March 31.

**8.** Budgeted balance sheet as of March 31.

**Check**   (2) Budgeted purchases: Jan., $90,000; Feb., $255,000<br>(6) Ending cash bal.: Jan., $182,850; Feb., $107,850<br>(8) Budgeted total assets at March 31, $1,346,875

*This serial problem began in Chapter 1 and continues through most of the book. If previous chapter segments were not completed, the serial problem can begin at this point.*

**SERIAL PROBLEM**
Business Solutions
**P3**

**SP 7** Santana Rey expects second quarter 2022 net income of **Business Solutions**'s line of computer furniture to be the same as the first quarter's net income (reported below) without any changes in strategy. Sales were 120 desk units (sales price of $1,250) and 60 chairs (sales price of $500).

| BUSINESS SOLUTIONS—Computer Furniture Segment Segment Income Statement* For Quarter Ended March 31, 2022 | | |
|---|---|---|
| Sales[†] | | $180,000 |
| Cost of goods sold[‡] | | 105,000 |
| Gross profit | | 75,000 |
| Selling, general, and administrative expenses | | |
| Sales commissions (10%) | $18,000 | |
| Advertising expenses | 9,000 | |
| General and administrative expenses | 18,000 | 45,000 |
| Net income | | $ 30,000 |

*Reflects activity only related to the computer furniture segment.
[†] Sales: (120 desks × $1,250) + (60 chairs × $500) = $180,000.
[‡] Cost of goods sold: (120 desks × $750) + (60 chairs × $250) = $105,000.

Alexander Image/Shutterstock

Santana believes that sales will total 156 desks and 105 chairs for the next quarter *if* selling prices are reduced to $1,150 for desks and $450 for chairs and advertising expenses are increased to $12,000 for the quarter. Product costs per unit and amounts of all other expenses will not change.

**Required**

1. Prepare a budgeted income statement for the computer furniture segment for the quarter ended June 30, 2022, that shows the results from implementing the proposed changes.
2. Do the proposed changes increase or decrease budgeted net income for the quarter?

**Tableau Dashboard Activities** expose students to accounting analytics using visual displays. These assignments (1) do not require instructors to know Tableau, (2) are accessible to introductory students, (3) do not require Tableau software, and (4) run in **Connect**. All are auto-gradable.

**TABLEAU DASHBOARD ACTIVITIES**

**Tableau DA 7-1 Quick Study**, Prepare direct materials budget, **P1**—similar to QS 7-12.
**Tableau DA 7-2 Exercise**, Prepare direct materials budget, **P1**—similar to Exercise 7-8.
**Tableau DA 7-3 Mini-case**, Prepare direct labor and factory overhead budgets and analyze strategies, **P1**—similar to Exercise 7-13.

## Accounting Analysis

**AA 7-1** **Apple** provides customer service and device repair through its AppleCare program. In preparing its monthly master budget, assume Apple's AppleCare division reports the data below.

**COMPANY ANALYSIS**
**A1**

| | Total Employees | Direct Labor Rate per Hour |
|---|---|---|
| Support specialists | 5,000 | $20 |
| Customer relations specialists | 3,200 | 24 |
| Repair technicians | 1,400 | 28 |

**Required**

Prepare a direct labor budget for the AppleCare division for the month. Assume each employee works 150 hours per month.

**COMPARATIVE ANALYSIS**

**A1**

**AA 7-2**    Data below are from recent annual reports for **Apple** and **Google**.

| | Apple | | Google | |
| --- | --- | --- | --- | --- |
| | Current Year | Prior Year | Current Year | Prior Year |
| Total revenue............... | $260,174,000,000 | $265,595,000,000 | $161,857,000,000 | $136,819,000,000 |
| Total employees ............. | 137,000 | 132,000 | 118,899 | 99,000 |

**Required**

1. Compute revenue per employee for both Apple and Google for the current year. Round answers to the nearest dollar.
2. Using revenue per employee from part 1, which company's workforce was more effective at generating revenues in the current year?
3. Was its workforce more effective at generating revenues in the current year versus the prior year for (*a*) Apple and (*b*) Google?

**EXTENDED ANALYSIS**

**A1**

**AA 7-3**    Data below are from recent annual reports for **Samsung**, **Apple**, and **Google**.

| | Samsung | | Apple | Google |
| --- | --- | --- | --- | --- |
| | Current Year | Prior Year | Current Year | Current Year |
| Total revenue............... | $197,690,938,000 | $209,163,262,000 | $260,174,000,000 | $161,857,000,000 |
| Total employees ............. | 98,753 | 101,546 | 137,000 | 118,899 |

**Required**

1. Compute revenue per employee for Samsung for the current year and the prior year.
2. Using revenue per employee, did Samsung's workforce become more effective in generating revenues in the current year versus the prior year?
3. Which company, Apple, Google, or Samsung, was most effective at generating revenue in the current year based on revenue per employee?

## Discussion Questions

1. Identify at least three benefits of budgeting in helping managers plan and control a business.
2. How does a budget benefit management in its control function?
3. What is the benefit of continuous budgeting?
4. Identify three common time horizons for short-term planning and budgets.
5. Why should each department participate in preparing its own budget?
6. How does budgeting help management coordinate and plan business activities?
7. Why is the sales budget so important to the budgeting process?
8. What is a selling expense budget? What is a capital expenditures budget?
9. Identify at least two potential negative outcomes of budgeting.
10. **Google** prepares cash budgets. What is a **GOOGLE** cash budget? Why must operating budgets and the capital expenditures budget be prepared before the cash budget?

11. **Apple** regularly uses budgets. What is the difference between a production budget and a manufacturing budget? **APPLE**
12. How can managers use the master budget in controlling operations?
13. Explain how the budgeting process for service companies differs from that for manufacturers.
14. Certified Management Accountants must understand budgeting. Access the **Institute of Management Accountants** website (**imanet.org**), click on the "CMA Certification" tab, and select "Taking the Exam." Scroll down and select "Review the Most Recent Content Specifications Outline." Search for "budgeting methodologies." (*a*) List the budgeting methodologies that are covered on the CMA exam. Search for "annual profit plan." (*b*) List the types of budgets covered on the CMA exam.
15. **Coca-Cola** redesigned its bottle to reduce its use of glass, thus lowering its bottle's weight and $CO_2$ emissions. Which budgets in the company's master budget will this redesign impact?

## Beyond the Numbers

**BTN 7-1**   The budget process and budgets themselves can impact management actions, both positively and negatively. For instance, a common practice among not-for-profit organizations and government agencies is for management to spend any amounts remaining in a budget at the end of the budget period, a practice often called "use it or lose it." The view is that if a department manager does not spend the budgeted amount, top management will reduce next year's budget by the amount not spent. To avoid losing budget dollars, department managers often spend all budgeted amounts regardless of the value added to products or services. All of us pay for the costs associated with this budget system.

**ETHICS CHALLENGE**

C1

**Required**

Write a half-page report to a local not-for-profit organization or government agency offering a solution to the "use it or lose it" budgeting problem.

---

**BTN 7-2**   The sales budget is usually the first and most crucial of the component budgets in a master budget because all other budgets usually rely on it for planning purposes.

**COMMUNICATING IN PRACTICE**

C1

**Required**

Assume that your company's sales staff provides information on expected sales and selling prices for items making up the sales budget. Prepare a one-page memorandum to your supervisor outlining concerns with the sales staff's input in the sales budget when its compensation is at least partly tied to these budgets. More generally, explain the importance of assessing any potential bias in information provided to the budget process.

---

**BTN 7-3**   Your team is to prepare a budget report outlining the costs of attending college (full-time) for the next two semesters (30 hours) or three quarters (45 hours). This budget's focus is solely on attending college; do not include personal items in the team's budget. Your budget must include tuition, books, supplies, club fees, food, housing, and all costs associated with travel to and from college. Include a list of any assumptions you use in completing the budget. Be prepared to present your budget in class.

**TEAMWORK IN ACTION**

A1

---

**BTN 7-4**   **Ellis Island Tropical Tea** manufactures and sells tea. Founder Nailah Ellis-Brown stresses the importance of planning and budgeting for business success.

**ENTREPRENEURIAL DECISION**

C1

**Required**

1. How can budgeting help Nailah efficiently develop and operate her business?
2. Nailah hopes to further expand her business. How is a master budget useful in expanding a business's operations?

# 8 Flexible Budgets and Standard Costs

## Learning Objectives

### CONCEPTUAL

**C1** Define *standard costs* and explain how standard cost information is useful.

### ANALYTICAL

**A1** Analyze changes in sales from expected amounts.

### PROCEDURAL

**P1** Prepare a flexible budget and interpret a flexible budget performance report.

**P2** Compute the total cost variance.

**P3** Compute direct materials and direct labor variances.

**P4** Compute overhead controllable and volume variances.

**P5** *Appendix 8A*—Compute overhead spending and efficiency variances.

**P6** *Appendix 8A*—Prepare journal entries for standard costs and account for price and quantity variances.

# Have a Fit

Courtesy of True Fit

*"Let your belief drive opportunity"*—**Jessica Murphy**

BOSTON—Shoppers know there are no standard clothing sizes, a source of frustration to them and of sales returns to retailers. "Sizing is poorly defined and not standardized," argues Christopher Moore, chief analytics officer at **True Fit**, a retail software company. True Fit co-founders Jessica Murphy, Romney Evans, and Bill Adler are determined to solve this problem with data.

True Fit combines customer orders and personal preferences with manufacturers' data on clothing style, fit, and size. The resulting "Fashion Genome" includes data from over 170 million users, 250 retailers, and 17,000 brands.

"We apply machine-learning algorithms to crunch tons of data from billions of transactions and generate customer recommendations," explains Romney. As a result, customers buy more and return less.

Beyond personalized recommendations, True Fit determines standards for how much its activities should cost. Growing rapidly—sales increased by nearly 75% this past year—company managers must budget and control direct labor and overhead costs. *Flexible budgets,* which reflect budgeted costs at multiple sales levels, are used to analyze differences, or *variances,* between actual and budgeted costs.

"Believe . . . and persevere," implores Jessica. "From day one I was determined to solve this."

Sources: *True Fit website*, January 2021; *Forbes*, June 2018; *True Fit* blog, February 2019, March 2019; *PR Newswire*, March 2019; *Datainnovation.org*, October 2014

# FIXED AND FLEXIBLE BUDGETS

Managers use budgets to control operations and see that planned objectives are met. **Budget reports** compare budgeted results to actual results. These reports can be prepared at any time and for any period. Three common periods for a budget report are a month, quarter, and year.

From the previous chapter, a *master budget* is based on a predicted level of activity, such as sales volume, for the budget period. There are two options in preparing a master budget: *fixed budgeting* or *flexible budgeting.*

- **Fixed budget,** also called a *static budget,* is based on one predicted amount of sales or other activity measure.
- **Flexible budget,** also called a *variable budget,* is based on more than one amount of sales or other activity measure.

Exhibit 8.1 shows fixed and flexible budgets, prepared in a contribution margin format, for a guitar manufacturer.

**P1**

Prepare a flexible budget and interpret a flexible budget performance report.

| Fixed Budget (one activity level) | |
|---|---|
| Sales (in units) . . . . . . . . . . . . . . | **100** |
| Sales ($800 per unit) . . . . . . . . | $80,000 |
| Variable costs ($360 per unit) . . | 36,000 |
| Contribution margin . . . . . . . . . | 44,000 |
| Fixed costs . . . . . . . . . . . . . . . | 20,000 |
| Income. . . . . . . . . . . . . . . . . . . | $24,000 |

| Flexible Budget (three activity levels) | | | |
|---|---|---|---|
| Sales (in units) . . . . . . . . . . . . . | **100** | **120** | **140** |
| Sales ($800 per unit) . . . . . . . . . | $80,000 | $96,000 | $112,000 |
| Variable costs ($360 per unit) . . | 36,000 | 43,200 | 50,400 |
| Contribution margin . . . . . . . . . . | 44,000 | 52,800 | 61,600 |
| Fixed costs . . . . . . . . . . . . . . . . | 20,000 | 20,000 | 20,000 |
| Income . . . . . . . . . . . . . . . . . . . | $24,000 | $32,800 | $ 41,600 |

**EXHIBIT 8.1**

Fixed versus Flexible Budgets (condensed)

Exhibit 8.1 shows that the company budgets $24,000 of income if it produces and sells 100 guitars. The fixed budget is useful in evaluating how well the company controlled costs only in the case when exactly 100 guitars are sold. A flexible budget is useful for any sales level (three examples are shown in Exhibit 8.1). A fixed budget is less useful the more the actual activity level differs from the fixed budget activity level.

## Fixed Budget Performance Report

One use of a budget is to compare actual results with planned activities. A *performance report* shows budgeted amounts, actual amounts, and variances. A **variance** is the difference between budgeted and actual amounts.

Exhibit 8.2 shows a **fixed budget performance report,** a report that compares actual results with the results expected under a fixed budget. January's fixed budget for the guitar maker is based on 100 units, but 140 units were actually sold. The far-right column shows the variances between the budgeted and actual dollar amounts for each budget item. We use the letters *F* and *U* to identify variances.

**F = Favorable variance**    A favorable variance is when actual income is *higher* than budgeted income. It is also when actual revenue is higher than budgeted revenue, or when actual cost is lower than budgeted cost.

**U = Unfavorable variance**    An unfavorable variance is when actual income is *lower* than budgeted income. It is also when actual revenue is lower than budgeted revenue, or when actual cost is higher than budgeted cost.

**EXHIBIT 8.2**

Fixed Budget Performance Report

| Fixed Budget Performance Report | | | |
|---|---|---|---|
| **For Month Ended January 31** | **Fixed Budget** | **Actual Results** | **Variances*** |
| Sales (in units) . . . . . . . . . . . . . . . . . . | **100** | **140** | |
| Sales (in dollars) . . . . . . . . . . . . . . . . | $80,000 | $105,000 | $25,000 F |
| Variable costs . . . . . . . . . . . . . . . . . . | 36,000 | 54,600 | 18,600 U |
| Contribution margin . . . . . . . . . . . . . | $44,000 | 50,400 | 6,400 F |
| Fixed costs . . . . . . . . . . . . . . . . . . . . | 20,000 | 20,400 | 400 U |
| Income . . . . . . . . . . . . . . . . . . . . . . . | $24,000 | $ 30,000 | $ 6,000 F |

**Budget Reports for Evaluation**    Managers use budget reports to monitor and control operations. A fixed budget report is limited because it is not an *apples-to-apples* comparison based on similar levels of activity. In Exhibit 8.2 the budgeted amounts use 100 units of activity, but 140 units were actually sold.

## Flexible Budget Reports

Management uses a flexible budget both before and after the period's activities are complete.

### Purpose of Flexible Budgets

- A flexible budget prepared **before** the period begins is often based on several levels of activity. Budgets for different levels provide a "what-if" analysis that often includes best-case and worst-case activity levels. This allows management to make adjustments to increase profits or decrease losses.
- A flexible budget prepared **after** the period ends helps evaluate performance. It is an apples-to-apples comparison because *budgeted activity level equals actual activity level.* Comparisons of actual results with budgeted performance at the same activity level are more likely to reveal the real causes of any variances. Managers then focus attention on problems resulting in unfavorable variances and opportunities resulting in favorable variances.

**Preparation of Flexible Budgets**    To prepare a flexible budget we follow three steps, as explained here and applied in Exhibit 8.3.

1. **Identify activity levels.** Management often uses units sold as the activity driver. For SolCel, all units produced are sold. Management prepares flexible budgets at three unit sales levels: 10,000, 12,000 and 14,000.

**2** **Identify costs and classify them as fixed or variable.** SolCel's management classifies four costs as variable and three as fixed. Variable and fixed cost items are *not* the same for every company.

**3** **Compute budgeted sales.** Sales price per unit × Units of activity.

**Compute budgeted variable costs.** Variable costs per unit × Units of activity.

**Compute budgeted fixed costs.** Fixed costs are constant at each activity level.

**Compute budgeted income.** Sales − Variable costs − Fixed costs.

The flexible budgets in Exhibit 8.3 show that sales and total variable costs increase as the activity level increases, but total fixed costs stay unchanged.

### SOLCEL — Flexible Budgets

| For Month Ended January 31 | Variable Amount per Unit | Total Fixed Cost | Flexible Budget for Unit Sales of 10,000 | 12,000 | 14,000 |
|---|---|---|---|---|---|
| Sales | $10.00 | | $100,000 | $120,000 | $140,000 |
| **Variable costs** | | | | | |
| Direct materials | 1.00 | | 10,000 | 12,000 | 14,000 |
| Direct labor | 1.50 | | 15,000 | 18,000 | 21,000 |
| Indirect materials | 0.20 | | 2,000 | 2,400 | 2,800 |
| Sales commissions | 2.10 | | 21,000 | 25,200 | 29,400 |
| Total variable costs | 4.80 | | 48,000 | 57,600 | 67,200 |
| Contribution margin | $ 5.20 | | $ 52,000 | $ 62,400 | $ 72,800 |
| **Fixed costs** | | | | | |
| Depreciation—Machinery | | $28,000 | 28,000 | 28,000 | 28,000 |
| Supervisory salaries | | 11,000 | 11,000 | 11,000 | 11,000 |
| Insurance | | 1,000 | 1,000 | 1,000 | 1,000 |
| Total fixed costs | | $40,000 | 40,000 | 40,000 | 40,000 |
| Income | | | $ 12,000 | $ 22,400 | $ 32,800 |

Variable: Amounts equal Budgeted unit sales × Variable amount per unit

Fixed: Amounts constant at all sales levels

**EXHIBIT 8.3**

Flexible Budgets (prepared before period begins)

**Flexible Budget Equation for Total Budgeted Costs**   Flexible budgets can be prepared at any activity level. To compute total budgeted costs we use the **flexible budget equation**.

**Total budgeted costs = Total fixed costs + (Total variable cost per unit × Units of activity)**

Using this equation, management can quickly compare actual costs to budgeted costs at any activity level. For example, if 12,000 units are produced and sold, then:

Total budgeted costs = $40,000 total fixed costs + ($4.80 total variable cost per unit × 12,000 units of activity)
Total budgeted costs = $97,600

### Flexible Budget Performance Report   SolCel's actual sales volume for January was 12,000 units. A **flexible budget performance report** compares actual performance and budgeted performance *based on actual activity level*. This report directs management's attention to actual amounts that differ greatly from budgeted amounts. Exhibit 8.4 shows SolCel's flexible budget performance report based on 12,000 units produced and sold for January.

**Analyzing Variances**   Management uses the flexible budget performance report to investigate variances and evaluate performance. Management often focuses on large variances. Exhibit 8.4 shows a $5,000 favorable variance in dollar sales. Because actual and budgeted sales volumes are both 12,000 units, the $5,000 favorable sales variance must have resulted from a higher-than-expected selling price. Management would like to determine if the conditions that resulted in higher selling prices will continue.

**EXHIBIT 8.4**

Flexible Budget
Performance Report
(prepared after period ends)

| SOLCEL Flexible Budget Performance Report | | | |
|---|---|---|---|
| For Month Ended January 31 | Flexible Budget (12,000 units) | Actual Results (12,000 units) | Variances |
| Sales.................. | $120,000 | $125,000 | $5,000 F |
| **Variable costs** | | | |
| Direct materials.................. | 12,000 | 13,000 | 1,000 U |
| Direct labor...................... | 18,000 | 20,000 | 2,000 U |
| Indirect materials ................ | 2,400 | 2,100 | 300 F |
| Sales commissions ............... | 25,200 | 24,300 | 900 F |
| Total variable costs .............. | 57,600 | 59,400 | 1,800 U |
| Contribution margin................ | 62,400 | 65,600 | 3,200 F |
| **Fixed costs** | | | |
| Depreciation—Machinery .......... | 28,000 | 28,000 | 0 |
| Supervisory salaries ............. | 11,000 | 11,000 | 0 |
| Insurance....................... | 1,000 | 1,200 | 200 U |
| Total fixed costs................. | 40,000 | 40,200 | 200 U |
| Income ......................... | $ 22,400 | $ 25,400 | $3,000 F |

Both the direct materials ($1,000 U) and direct labor ($2,000 U) variances are relatively large and unfavorable. On the other hand, a relatively large favorable variance is observed for sales commissions ($900 F). Management will try to determine the causes for these variances, both favorable and unfavorable, and make changes to operations if needed.

### ■ Decision Maker

**Manager**   The head of the consulting division of your financial services firm complains about the unfavorable variances on the division's performance reports. "We worked on more consulting assignments than planned. It's not surprising our costs are higher than expected. This report characterizes our work as *poor*!" How do you respond? ■

*Answer:* Comparing actual results with a fixed budget is not useful in determining whether the division was more or less efficient. If the division worked on more assignments than expected, some costs will certainly increase. You should prepare a flexible budget using the actual number of consulting assignments and then compare actual performance to the flexible budget.

---

**NEED-TO-KNOW** **8-1**

Flexible Budget
Performance Report

**P1**

*Part A.* A manufacturing company reports the following fixed budget and actual results for the past year. The fixed budget uses a selling price of $40 per unit and variable costs of $8 per unit. Prepare a flexible budget performance report for the past year. Label variances as favorable (F) or unfavorable (U).

| | Fixed Budget (20,000 units) | Actual Results (24,000 units) |
|---|---|---|
| Sales ............. | $800,000 | $972,000 |
| Variable costs ...... | 160,000 | 240,000 |
| Fixed costs ........ | 500,000 | 490,000 |

**Solution**

| Flexible Budget Performance Report | | | |
|---|---|---|---|
| For Year Ended December 31 | Flexible Budget (24,000 units) | Actual Results (24,000 units) | Variances |
| Sales.................... | $960,000* | $972,000 | $12,000 F |
| Variable costs ............ | 192,000† | 240,000 | 48,000 U |
| Contribution margin ....... | 768,000 | 732,000 | 36,000 U |
| Fixed costs .............. | 500,000 | 490,000 | 10,000 F |
| Income.................. | $268,000 | $242,000 | $26,000 U |

*24,000 × $40       †24,000 × $8

***Part B.*** A manufacturer reports the following for May when it produced and sold 8,000 units. Prepare a flexible budget performance report at the activity level of 8,000 units. Compute variances and label them as favorable (F) or unfavorable (U).

|  | Flexible Budget | | |
|---|---|---|---|
|  | Variable Amount per Unit | Total Fixed Cost | Actual Results |
| Sales . . . . . . . . . . . . . . . . . . . . . . . . | $12.00 |  | $93,750 |
| Direct materials. . . . . . . . . . . . . . . . | 4.00 |  | 27,250 |
| Direct labor . . . . . . . . . . . . . . . . . . . | 2.50 |  | 21,125 |
| Indirect materials . . . . . . . . . . . . . . . | 0.30 |  | 2,150 |
| Utilities . . . . . . . . . . . . . . . . . . . . . . | 0.20 |  | 2,125 |
| Depreciation—Machinery. . . . . . . . . |  | $6,000 | 6,000 |
| Supervisory salaries . . . . . . . . . . . . . |  | 8,000 | 8,300 |

*Solution*

| Flexible Budget Performance Report | | | |
|---|---|---|---|
| For Month Ended May 31 | Flexible Budget (8,000 Units) | Actual Results (8,000 Units) | Variances |
| Sales . . . . . . . . . . . . . . . . . . . . | $96,000 | $93,750 | $ 2,250 U |
| **Variable costs** | | | |
| Direct materials . . . . . . . . . . | 32,000 | 27,250 | 4,750 F |
| Direct labor. . . . . . . . . . . . . . | 20,000 | 21,125 | 1,125 U |
| Indirect materials . . . . . . . . . | 2,400 | 2,150 | 250 F |
| Utilities . . . . . . . . . . . . . . . . | 1,600 | 2,125 | 525 U |
| Total variable costs . . . . . . . | 56,000 | 52,650 | 3,350 F |
| Contribution margin . . . . . . . . . | 40,000 | 41,100 | 1,100 F |
| **Fixed costs** | | | |
| Depreciation—Machinery . . | 6,000 | 6,000 | 0 |
| Supervisory salaries. . . . . . . | 8,000 | 8,300 | 300 U |
| Total fixed costs . . . . . . . . . | 14,000 | 14,300 | 300 U |
| Income. . . . . . . . . . . . . . . . . . | $26,000 | $26,800 | $ 800 F |

Do More: QS 8-1, QS 8-2, QS 8-3, QS 8-4, E 8-3, E 8-4, E 8-5, E 8-6

# STANDARD COSTING

We next show how *standard costs* can be used in a flexible budgeting system to enable management to better understand the reasons for variances.

 **C1**

Define *standard costs* and explain how standard cost information is useful.

## Standard Costs

**Standard costs** are preset costs for delivering a product or service under normal conditions. Manufacturing companies commonly use standard costing for direct materials, direct labor, and overhead costs. Production managers and engineers often determine the production requirements for one unit of product, and accountants put those requirements into dollars.

When actual costs vary from standard costs, management identifies the reason and takes corrective actions. **Management by exception** means that managers focus attention on the most significant differences between actual costs and standard costs.

Budgets are prepared using standard costs. If the standard direct materials cost is $2 per unit and expected production is 50,000 units, the total budgeted direct materials cost is $100,000.

Service companies also use standard costs. For example, while quality medical service is crucial, efficiency in providing that service is key to controlling medical costs. The use of budgeting and standard costing is effective in controlling costs, especially overhead.

## Setting Standard Costs

Standards for direct labor are set by *time and motion* studies that show the direct labor hours required under normal operations. Standards for direct materials are set by studying the quantity, grade, and cost of each material used. Overhead standards are set by studying the resources needed to support production activities. Standards should be challenging but attainable and should acknowledge machine breakdowns, material waste, and idle time.

**Illustration of Setting Standard Costs**   Let's look at wooden baseball bats manufactured by ProBat. Its engineers have determined that manufacturing each finished bat requires 2 pounds of high-grade wood. They also expect some loss of material in the process because of inefficiencies and waste. This results in adding an *allowance* of 0.2 pound, making the standard requirement 2.2 pounds of wood for each bat.

The 2 pound portion is called an *ideal standard;* it is the quantity of direct material required if the process is 100% efficient without any loss or waste. The standard of 2.2 pounds is known as the *practical standard,* the quantity of direct material required under normal operations. The standard direct labor rate should include allowances for employee breaks, cleanup, and machine downtime. Most companies use practical rather than ideal standards.

ProBat must develop standard quantities and standard prices. For overhead, ProBat must consider the activities that drive overhead costs. ProBat's standard costs follow.

**Direct materials**   The purchasing department sets a standard price of $10 per pound for high-grade wood. The purchasing department considers the quality of materials, economic conditions, supply factors (shortages and excesses), and discounts.

**Direct labor**   Two hours of direct labor are required to manufacture a bat. The direct labor rate is $15 per hour. This rate includes wages, taxes, and benefits.

**Overhead**   ProBat applies overhead at the rate of $5 per direct labor hour (DLH).

The standard costs of direct materials, direct labor, and overhead for one bat are shown in Exhibit 8.5 in a *standard cost card.*

**EXHIBIT 8.5**

Standard Cost Card

| STANDARD COST CARD | | | |
|---|---|---|---|
| Inputs | Standard Quantity or Hours | Standard Price or Rate | Standard Cost per Unit |
| Direct materials | 2.2 pounds | $10 per pound | $22 |
| Direct labor | 2.0 DLH | $15 per DLH | 30 |
| Overhead | 2.0 DLH | $5 per DLH | 10 |
| **Total** | | | **$62** |

## Cost Variance Analysis

**P2**

Compute the total cost variance.

A **cost variance,** or simply *variance,* is the difference between actual and standard cost. A cost variance can be favorable (F) or unfavorable (U).

- If actual cost is less than standard cost, the variance is favorable (F).
- If actual cost is greater than standard cost, the variance is unfavorable (U).

Exhibit 8.6 shows the flow of events in **variance analysis:** (1) preparing a standard cost performance report, (2) computing and analyzing variances, (3) identifying questions and their answers, and (4) taking corrective and strategic actions.

**EXHIBIT 8.6**

Variance Analysis

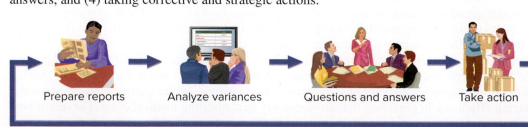

Prepare reports     Analyze variances     Questions and answers     Take action

## Cost Variance Computation
Exhibit 8.7 shows a general formula for computing a cost variance (CV).

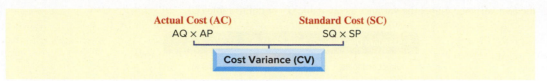

| Actual Cost (AC) | Standard Cost (SC) |
|---|---|
| AQ × AP | SQ × SP |

**Cost Variance (CV)**

*AQ is actual quantity; AP is actual price; SQ is standard quantity allowed for actual output; SP is standard price.

**EXHIBIT 8.7**

Cost Variance Formula*

*Actual quantity* (AQ) is the actual direct material or direct labor used (input) to manufacture the actual quantity of output for the period. *Standard quantity* (SQ) is the standard input expected for the actual quantity of output. *Actual price* (AP) is the actual amount paid to acquire the actual direct material or direct labor used for the period. SP is the *standard price* of direct material or direct labor.

**Illustration Applying Standard Costs**   Let's compute the total cost variance for G-Max, a manufacturer of golf equipment and accessories. G-Max set the following standard cost per unit for one of its clubheads.

| Inputs | Standard Quantity | Standard Price | Standard Cost per Unit |
|---|---|---|---|
| Direct materials | 0.5 lb. | $20 per lb. | $10 |
| Direct labor | 0.5 DLH | $32 per DLH | 16 |
| Overhead | 0.5 DLH | $10 per DLH | 5 |
| Total | | | $31 |

G-Max produced and sold 3,500 clubheads in May. Budgeted cost, which equals the standard cost per unit multiplied by the number of units produced, is $108,500, computed as $31 standard cost per unit × 3,500 units. Using the cost card above, we compute the amounts for all three inputs for the 3,500 units as follows:

**Budgeted Cost (3,500 units)**

| | |
|---|---|
| Direct materials (0.5 lb. × $20 per lb. × 3,500 units) . . . | $  35,000 |
| Direct labor (0.5 DLH × $32 per DLH × 3,500 units) . . . | 56,000 |
| Overhead (0.5 DLH × $10 per DLH × 3,500 units) . . . . | 17,500 |
| **Budgeted standard cost** . . . . . . . . . . . . . . . . . . . . . . . | **$108,500** |

Management reports the actual cost to produce these 3,500 units in May is $112,050. This is more than the $108,500 budgeted cost. The $3,550 cost variance is unfavorable.

| | |
|---|---|
| Actual cost. . . . . . . . . . . . . . . . . . . . . . . . . . . | $112,050 |
| Budgeted (standard) cost. . . . . . . . . . . . . . . | 108,500 |
| **Cost variance**. . . . . . . . . . . . . . . . . . . . . . . | **$  3,550 U** |

**■ Decision Insight**

**Measuring Up**   In the spirit of continuous improvement, competitors compare their processes and performance standards against benchmarks established by industry leaders. Service companies that use **benchmarking** include **Jiffy Lube**, **All Tune and Lube**, and **SpeeDee Oil Change and Auto Service**. ■

**NEED-TO-KNOW** 8-2

Cost Variances

P2 ▶

A manufacturer reports the following standards. The company produces 1,200 units and incurs actual total costs of $135,000 this period. Prepare the standard cost card, and then compute the budgeted standard cost and the cost variance. Label the variance as favorable (F) or unfavorable (U).

| Standard Quantity and Price per Unit | |
|---|---|
| Direct materials............ | 2.0 lbs. × $25 per lb. |
| Direct labor .............. | 1.5 DLH × $18 per DLH |
| Overhead ................ | 1.5 DLH × $22 per DLH |

**Solution**

| Inputs | Standard Quantity | Standard Price | Standard Cost per Unit |
|---|---|---|---|
| Direct materials | 2.0 lbs. | $25 per lb. | $ 50 |
| Direct labor | 1.5 DLH | $18 per DLH | 27 |
| Overhead | 1.5 DLH | $22 per DLH | 33 |
| Total | | | $110 |

| Budgeted Cost (1,200 units) | |
|---|---|
| Direct materials (2 lbs. × $25 per lb. × 1,200 units) ... | $ 60,000 |
| Direct labor (1.5 DLH × $18 per DLH × 1,200 units)... | 32,400 |
| Overhead (1.5 DLH × $22 per DLH × 1,200 units) .... | 39,600 |
| **Budgeted standard cost** ...................... | **$132,000** |

| Total Cost Variance | |
|---|---|
| Actual cost................. | $135,000 |
| Budgeted (standard) cost† .... | 132,000 |
| Cost variance ............. | $ 3,000 U |

†1,200 units × $110 standard cost.

Do More: QS 8-6, E 8-8

---

# DIRECT MATERIALS AND DIRECT LABOR VARIANCES

**P3**

Compute direct materials and direct labor variances.

Two factors explain direct materials and direct labor variances.

1. **Price variance.** Difference between actual *price* per unit of input and standard price per unit of input results in a **price** (or rate) **variance.**
2. **Quantity variance.** Difference between actual *quantity* of input used and standard quantity of input that should have been used results in a **quantity** (or efficiency) **variance.**

Formulas for the price variance and quantity variance are in Exhibit 8.8.

**EXHIBIT 8.8**

Price Variance and Quantity Variance Formulas*

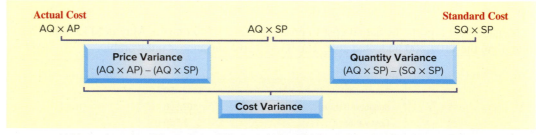

*AQ is actual quantity; AP is actual price; SP is standard price; SQ is standard quantity allowed for actual output.

Managers sometimes find it useful to use alternative formulas for price and quantity variances, as in Exhibit 8.9. Results from applying the formulas in Exhibits 8.8 and 8.9 are identical.

**EXHIBIT 8.9**

Alternative Price Variance and Quantity Variance Formulas

Price Variance (PV) = [**Actual Price (AP)** − **Standard Price (SP)**] × **Actual Quantity (AQ)**

Quantity Variance (QV) = [**Actual Quantity (AQ)** − **Standard Quantity (SQ)**] × **Standard Price (SP)**

# Direct Materials Variances

G-Max produced and sold 3,500 units in May and it used 1,800 pounds of direct materials (titanium) at a cost of $21 per pound. Actual cost of its direct materials is $37,800; see top row in table below.

Its materials standard shows that it should have used 1,750 pounds of direct materials to produce 3,500 units (0.5 lb. per unit). Using the standard cost of $20 per lb., we get the standard cost of $35,000 for 3,500 units; see second row in table below. Its direct materials variance is $2,800 U.

Kristjan Maack//Nordic Photos/ Getty Images

| Direct Materials | Quantity | | Price per Unit | | Cost |
|---|---|---|---|---|---|
| Actual quantity and price . . . . . . . . . . | 1,800 lbs. | × | $21 per lb. | = | $37,800 |
| Standard quantity and price. . . . . . . . . | 1,750 lbs. | × | $20 per lb. | = | 35,000 |
| **Direct materials variance**. . . . . . . . . . | | | | = | **$ 2,800 U** |

To identify the causes of this $2,800 U variance, we drill down into the materials price and quantity variances in Exhibit 8.10. The $1,800 unfavorable *price* variance results from paying $1 more per pound than the standard price, then multiplied by the actual 1,800 lbs. purchased and used. The $1,000 unfavorable *quantity* variance results from using 50 pounds more of material than the standard quantity, then multiplied by the $20 per lb. standard cost.

**EXHIBIT 8.10**

Direct Materials Price and Quantity Variances*

| Actual Cost | AQ × SP | Standard Cost |
|---|---|---|
| **AQ × AP** | | **SQ × SP** |
| 1,800 lbs. × $21 | 1,800 lbs. × $20 | 1,750 lbs. × $20 |
| $37,800 | $36,000 | $35,000 |

$1,800 U — **Price Variance** $37,800 − $36,000

$1,000 U — **Quantity Variance** $36,000 − $35,000

$2,800 U — **Direct Materials Variance** $1,800 U and $1,000 U $37,800 − $35,000

*AQ is actual quantity; AP is actual price; SP is standard price; SQ is standard quantity allowed for actual output.

**Point:** Direct materials price variance is also computed as ($21 − $20) × 1,800 = $1,800. Direct materials quantity variance is also computed as (1,800 − 1,750) × $20 = $1,000.

**Evaluating Direct Materials Variances**   The *purchasing department* is responsible for the price paid for materials. The purchasing manager might have negotiated poor prices, or purchased higher-quality materials.

The *production department* is responsible for the quantity of direct material used. The production department might have used more than the standard amount of material because low-quality material caused excessive waste. In this case, the purchasing manager must explain why inferior materials were acquired. However, if that waste was due to inefficiencies, not poor-quality materials, the production manager must explain why. In sum, variance analysis along with corrective action can improve future performance.

A manufacturing company reports the following for one of its products. Compute the direct materials (a) price variance and (b) quantity variance, and identify each as favorable or unfavorable.

 8-3

Direct Materials Price and Quantity Variances

P3

| | |
|---|---|
| Standard direct materials quantity and price per unit . . . . . | 8 pounds @ $6 per pound |
| Actual direct materials quantity and price. . . . . . . . . . . . . . | 83,000 pounds @ $5.80 per pound |
| Actual units produced and sold . . . . . . . . . . . . . . . . . . . . . . | 10,000 units |

*Solution*

Do More: QS 8-8, E 8-9,
E 8-13

**a.** Price variance    = (Actual quantity × Actual price) − (Actual quantity × Standard price)

= (83,000 × $5.80) − (83,000 × $6) = **$16,600 F**

**b.** Quantity variance = (Actual quantity × Standard price) − (Standard quantity* × Standard price)

= (83,000 × $6) − (80,000 × $6) = **$18,000 U**

*Standard quantity = 10,000 units × 8 standard pounds per unit = 80,000 pounds.

# Direct Labor Variances

G-Max used 1,700 direct labor hours at a cost of $33 per hour in May. Actual cost of its direct labor is $56,100; see top row in table below.

G-Max should have used 1,750 direct labor hours to produce 3,500 units (0.5 DLH per unit). Using the standard cost of $32 per DLH, we get the standard cost of $56,000 for 3,500 units; see second row in table below. Its direct labor variance is $100 U.

| Direct Labor | Quantity | Rate per Hour | Cost |
|---|---|---|---|
| Actual quantity and rate........... | 1,700 hrs. × | $33 per DLH | = $56,100 |
| Standard quantity and rate ........ | 1,750 hrs.* × | $32 per DLH | = 56,000 |
| **Direct labor variance** ............ | | | = **$   100 U** |

*Standard quantity = 3,500 units × 0.5 standard DLH per unit.

Actual direct labor cost is $100 over the standard, which might suggest no concern. A closer look reveals a problem. The direct labor variance can be divided into price and quantity variances, called *rate* and *efficiency* variances. Exhibit 8.11 shows the $100 total unfavorable labor variance results from a $1,600 favorable efficiency variance and a $1,700 unfavorable rate variance.

**EXHIBIT 8.11**

Direct Labor Rate and Efficiency Variances*

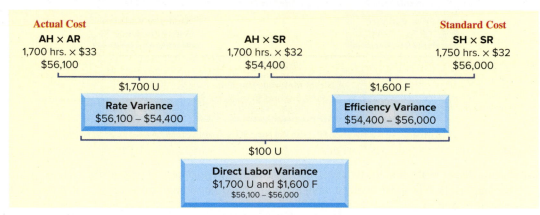

**Point:** Direct labor efficiency variance is also computed as (1,700 − 1,750) × $32 = $1,600. Direct labor rate variance is also computed as ($33 − $32) × 1,700 = $1,700.

*We use hours (H) for quantity (Q) and the wage rate (R) for price (P). Thus: AH is actual direct labor hours; AR is actual wage rate; SH is standard direct labor hours allowed for actual output; SR is standard wage rate.

**Evaluating Direct Labor Variances**   To produce 3,500 units, G-Max should use 1,750 direct labor hours (3,500 units × 0.5 standard DLH per unit). The $1,600 F *efficiency variance* results from using 50 fewer direct labor hours (1,700 actual DLH − 1,750 standard DLH) than standard for the units produced. The 50 fewer hours at $32 per hour, result in the $1,600 favorable efficiency variance. The production manager should explain how direct labor hours were reduced. If this efficiency can be repeated and transferred to other departments, more savings are possible.

The $1,700 U *rate variance* results from paying a rate that is $1 per hour higher than the standard ($33 actual rate − $32 standard rate). Each of the 1,700 actual direct labor hours used cost $1 more, resulting in the $1,700 unfavorable rate variance. Human resources or the production manager needs to explain why the wage rate is higher than the standard.

One possible explanation of direct labor rate and efficiency variances is the use of workers with different skill levels. Higher-skilled workers might finish the same units in fewer hours but have a higher wage rate. A higher-than-standard labor cost might require an adjustment of the standard, or the use of more lower-skilled workers. Other explanations for direct labor variances are possible. Lower-quality materials, poor employee training, little supervision, equipment breakdowns, and idle workers due to reduced product demand can lead to unfavorable direct labor efficiency variances.

## ■ Analytics **Insight**

**Data Tracking**  Manufacturers aim to keep their manufacturing processes running smoothly. Sensors placed in machines can be used to track usage and schedule maintenance. A consulting firm estimates such *predictive analytics* can reduce machine breakdowns and downtime by about 25%. **Tesla** uses predictive analytics to solve issues with its production process. ■

Jenson/Shutterstock

The following information is available for a manufacturer. Compute the (a) rate variance and (b) efficiency variance, and label each as favorable (F) or unfavorable (U).

| | | | |
|---|---|---|---|
| Standard direct labor hours per unit . . . | 2 hours | Actual direct labor cost (6,250 hours @ $13.10 per hour) . . . | $81,875 |
| Standard direct labor rate per hour . . . . | $13.00 | Actual units produced and sold . . . . . . . . . . . . . . . . . . . . . . . | 3,000 units |

**Solution**

**a.** Rate variance      = (Actual hours × Actual rate) − (Actual hours × Standard rate)
                            = (6,250 × $13.10) − (6,250 × $13.00) = **$625 U**

**b.** Efficiency variance = (Actual hours × Standard rate) − (Standard hours × Standard rate)
                            = (6,250 × $13.00) − (6,000* × $13.00) = **$3,250 U**
                            *Standard hours = 3,000 units × 2 DLH per unit.

**NEED-TO-KNOW** 8-4

Direct Labor Rate and Efficiency Variances

**P3**

Do More: QS 8-11, E 8-10, E 8-16

# OVERHEAD STANDARDS AND VARIANCES

In a standard cost system, managers apply overhead costs to products and services using a *standard overhead rate*. The resulting *standard overhead costs* are the overhead amounts budgeted to occur at a specific activity level. Managers set standards and budgets before each period in a desire to better control, monitor, and assign costs to products and services.

**P4** _____

Compute overhead controllable and volume variances.

## Flexible Overhead Budgets

We begin by showing how to use standard costs to develop flexible overhead budgets. The left two number columns of Exhibit 8.12 show the budgeted variable costs per unit and fixed costs for May. With these variable and fixed overhead costs, G-Max can prepare flexible overhead budgets at different capacity levels (see four rightmost number columns). At its maximum capacity of 100%, G-Max can produce 5,000 clubheads. At 100% capacity, total variable overhead costs are budgeted at $10,000 (5,000 × $2). At 70% of capacity, G-Max can produce 3,500 clubheads (5,000 × 70%). At 70% capacity, total variable overhead costs are budgeted at $7,000 (3,500 × $2). At all capacity levels within the relevant range, fixed overhead costs are budgeted at $12,000 per month.

## Standard Overhead Rate

To compute the standard overhead rate, we use a three-step process.

**Step 1: Determine an Allocation Base**  The allocation base is a measure of input related to overhead costs. Examples include direct labor hours or machine hours. G-Max uses direct labor hours as an allocation base and has a standard of 0.5 direct labor hour per unit.

**Point:** With increased automation, machine hours are increasingly used in applying overhead instead of labor hours.

**Step 2: Predict an Activity Level** The predicted activity level is not set at 100% of capacity. Difficulties in scheduling work, equipment breakdowns, and low product demand typically cause the activity level to be less than full capacity. G-Max managers predict an 80% activity level for May, or a production volume of 4,000 clubheads. We assume all units produced are sold.

**EXHIBIT 8.12**

Flexible Overhead Budgets

| G-MAX Flexible Overhead Budgets | | | | | | |
|---|---|---|---|---|---|---|
| | Variable Amount per Unit | Total Fixed Cost | Flexible Budget at Capacity Level of | | | |
| For Month Ended May 31 | | | 70% | 80% | 90% | 100% |
| Production (in units) .............. | 1 unit | | 3,500 | 4,000 | 4,500 | 5,000 |
| Factory overhead | | | | | | |
| Variable costs | | | | | | |
| Indirect labor ................. | $0.80/unit | | $ 2,800 | $ 3,200 | $ 3,600 | $ 4,000 |
| Indirect materials............. | 0.60/unit | | 2,100 | 2,400 | 2,700 | 3,000 |
| Power and lights ............. | 0.40/unit | | 1,400 | 1,600 | 1,800 | 2,000 |
| Maintenance ................. | 0.20/unit | | 700 | 800 | 900 | 1,000 |
| Total variable overhead costs.... | $2.00/unit | | 7,000 | 8,000 | 9,000 | 10,000 |
| Fixed costs (per month) | | | | | | |
| Building rent................. | | $ 2,000 | $ 2,000 | $ 2,000 | $ 2,000 | $ 2,000 |
| Depreciation—Machinery ....... | | 4,000 | 4,000 | 4,000 | 4,000 | 4,000 |
| Supervisory salaries ........... | | 6,000 | 6,000 | 6,000 | 6,000 | 6,000 |
| Total fixed overhead costs ...... | | $12,000 | 12,000 | 12,000 | 12,000 | 12,000 |
| Total overhead ................. | | | $19,000 | $20,000 | $21,000 | $22,000 |

Fuse/Getty Images

**Step 3: Compute the Standard Overhead Rate** At the predicted activity level of 4,000 units, the flexible budget in Exhibit 8.12 shows total overhead of $20,000. To make 4,000 units, the standard direct labor hours required are 2,000 DLH, computed as 4,000 units × 0.5 DLH per unit. The standard overhead rate follows and is used to compute overhead cost variances. Standard overhead rate depends on the predicted activity level. We can compute this rate separately for both variable costs and fixed costs (Appendix 8A).

$$\text{Standard overhead rate} = \frac{\text{Budgeted overhead at predicted activity level}}{\text{Standard allocation base at predicted activity level}}$$

$$= \frac{\$20,000}{2,000 \text{ DLH}} = \$10 \text{ per DLH}$$

## Computing Overhead Variances

**Standard overhead applied** is defined in Exhibit 8.13.

**EXHIBIT 8.13**

Standard Overhead Applied

$$\begin{matrix} \text{Standard overhead} \\ \text{applied} \end{matrix} = \begin{matrix} \text{Actual} \\ \text{production} \end{matrix} \times \begin{matrix} \text{Standard amount} \\ \text{of allocation base} \end{matrix} \times \text{Standard overhead rate}$$

**Standard amount of allocation base** is the overhead that *should have been used,* based on actual production. Recall that G-Max actually produced 3,500 units, which differs from its predicted activity of 4,000 units. The 3,500 units produced in May *should have used* 1,750 direct labor hours, computed as 3,500 actual units × 0.5 standard DLH per unit. Standard overhead applied is based on actual units produced and equals $17,500 as computed here.

**Point:** Direct labor hour is abbreviated DLH.

Standard overhead applied = 3,500 units × 0.5 DLH per unit × $10 per DLH = $17,500

### Overhead Variance

Actual overhead often differs from the standard overhead applied. The difference between the actual total overhead and the standard overhead applied is the **overhead variance** in Exhibit 8.14.

**EXHIBIT 8.14**

Total Overhead Variance

> **Overhead variance = Actual total overhead − Standard overhead applied**

Management reports that actual total overhead in May is $18,150 (given). Using the formula in Exhibit 8.14, total overhead variance is $650, computed as follows. This variance is unfavorable because actual overhead is higher than the standard.

| | |
|---|---:|
| Actual total overhead (given) | $18,150 |
| Standard overhead applied (from above) | 17,500 |
| **Overhead variance** | **$    650 U** |

### Controllable Variance and Volume Variance

To understand the factors driving the overhead variance, managers compute *controllable variance* and *volume variance* as in Exhibit 8.15.

**EXHIBIT 8.15**

Controllable and Volume Variances for Overhead

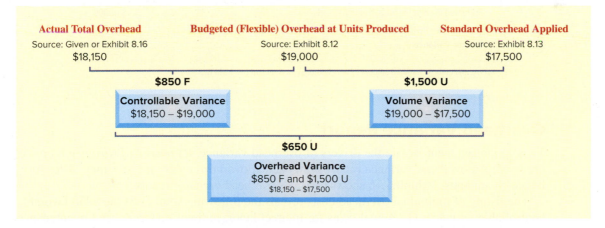

**Controllable Variance**    **Controllable variance** is computed as follows:

> **Controllable variance = Actual total overhead − Budgeted (flexible) total overhead at *actual* units produced**

Controllable variance is the part of overhead variance under the production manager's control. Actual total overhead is $18,150 (given). Flexible budget total overhead at 3,500 units is

$19,000 as shown in Exhibit 8.12. Controllable variance follows, and it is favorable because actual overhead is less than budgeted overhead.

| Controllable Variance | |
| --- | --- |
| Actual total overhead (given) . . . . . . . . . . . . . . . . . . . . . . . . . . . . . . . . . . . . . . | $18,150 |
| Budgeted (flexible) overhead at units produced . . . . . . . . . . . . . . . . . . . . . | 19,000 |
| **Controllable variance** . . . . . . . . . . . . . . . . . . . . . . . . . . . . . . . . . . . . . . . . . | **$ 850 F** |

**Volume Variance**    A **volume variance** is the difference between budgeted overhead and the standard overhead applied at the actual units produced. It occurs when the company operates at a different capacity level than was predicted. G-Max expected to manufacture 4,000 units, but it only manufactured 3,500 units. The volume variance is usually considered outside the control of the production manager, which is why it's also titled *noncontrollable variance*. Volume variance is computed as follows:

$$\text{Volume variance} = \text{Budgeted overhead} - \text{Standard overhead applied}$$

     G-Max's budgeted overhead is $19,000 at 3,500 units in Exhibit 8.12. Its standard overhead applied at 3,500 units is $17,500. This results in the following $1,500 volume variance. The volume variance is unfavorable because G-Max made 500 fewer units than predicted.

**Point:** Volume variance is also computed as:
Budgeted FOH . . . . . . . . . . $12,000
Standard FOH applied . . . . 10,500
Volume variance . . . . . . . . $ 1,500 U

| Volume Variance | |
| --- | --- |
| Budgeted (flexible) overhead at units produced . . . . . . . . . . . . . . . . . . . . . . . . . . . . . . . | $19,000 |
| Standard overhead applied (3,500 units × 0.5 DLH per unit × $10 per DLH)[†] . . . . . . . . . | 17,500 |
| **Volume variance** . . . . . . . . . . . . . . . . . . . . . . . . . . . . . . . . . . . . . . . . . . . . . . . . . . . . . | **$ 1,500 U** |

[†]Actual units × Standard amount of allocation base × Standard overhead rate.

## Overhead Variance Report

To help management isolate the drivers of overhead variance, an *overhead variance report* is prepared. An overhead variance report shows actual overhead costs and how they differ from budgeted amounts. Exhibit 8.16 shows G-Max's overhead variance report.

     The listing of individual overhead costs reveals the following sources of the $850 favorable controllable variance: (1) Actual costs for indirect labor, indirect materials, and maintenance were lower than budgeted. (2) Actual costs for power and lights were higher than budgeted. (3) Fixed supervisory salaries were lower than budgeted. Management uses the overhead variance report to identify controllable overhead costs to investigate.

     The $1,500 unfavorable volume variance means the company did not reach its predicted activity level. While 80% of manufacturing capacity was budgeted, only 70% was used. Management needs to know why the actual level of production differs from the predicted level. The reasons for failing to meet the predicted production level are often due to factors such as customer demand that are beyond the production manager's control. The bottom line for this report is the $650 U total overhead variance.

**Appendix 8A describes an expanded analysis of overhead variances.**

**EXHIBIT 8.16**

Overhead Variance Report

| G-MAX Overhead Variance Report For Month Ended May 31 | | | |
|---|---|---|---|
| **Production Level** | | | |
| Expected.............................. | 80% of capacity (4,000 units) | | |
| Actual ............................... | 70% of capacity (3,500 units) | | |
| **Controllable Variance** | **Flexible Budget** | **Actual Results** | **Variances** |
| Variable overhead costs | | | |
| Indirect labor ............................ | $ 2,800 | $ 2,375 | $   425 F |
| Indirect materials......................... | 2,100 | 1,925 | 175 F |
| Power and lights .......................... | 1,400 | 1,450 | 50 U |
| Maintenance ............................. | 700 | 600 | 100 F |
| Total variable overhead costs................ | 7,000 | 6,350 | 650 F |
| Fixed overhead costs | | | |
| Building rent ............................ | 2,000 | 2,000 | 0 |
| Depreciation—Machinery ................... | 4,000 | 4,000 | 0 |
| Supervisory salaries ...................... | 6,000 | 5,800 | 200 F |
| Total fixed overhead costs ................. | 12,000 | 11,800 | 200 F |
| Total overhead costs ....................... | $19,000 | $18,150 | $   850 F |
| **Volume Variance** | | | |
| Budgeted (flexible) overhead ................ | | | $19,000 |
| Standard overhead applied................... | | | 17,500 |
| Volume variance........................... | | | $ 1,500 U |
| **Total overhead variance** ($850 F and $1,500 U) ... | | | $   650 U |

**Point:** Both the flexible budget and actual results are based on 3,500 units produced.

A manufacturing company uses standard costs and reports the information below for January. The company uses machine hours (MH) to apply overhead, and the standard is 2 MH per unit, with a standard overhead rate of $4.50 per MH. Compute the total overhead variance, controllable variance, and volume variance for January. Indicate whether each variance is favorable or unfavorable.

**NEED-TO-KNOW 8-5**

Overhead Variances

**P4**

| Predicted activity level............... | 1,500 units |
|---|---|
| Budgeted variable overhead rate ...... | $5 per unit (or $2.50 per MH) |
| Budgeted fixed overhead ............ | $6,000 per month |
| Actual activity level.................. | 1,800 units |
| Actual total overhead................ | $15,800 |

*Solution*

| Overhead variance | |
|---|---|
| Actual total overhead (given)......................................... | $15,800 |
| Standard overhead applied (1,800 units × 2 MH per unit × $4.50 per MH) .. | 16,200 |
| Overhead variance ................................................ | $   400 F |

Do More: QS 8-13, QS 8-14, QS 8-15, E 8-17, E 8-19, E 8-20

| Controllable variance | |
|---|---|
| Actual total overhead (given)............................. | $15,800 |
| Budgeted (flexible) overhead (1,800 units × $5 per unit) + $6,000 .. | 15,000 |
| Controllable variance.................................... | $   800 U |

| Volume variance | |
|---|---|
| Budgeted (flexible) overhead ..................................... | $15,000 |
| Standard overhead applied (1,800 units × 2 MH per unit × $4.50 per MH) .. | 16,200 |
| Volume variance........................................... | $1,200 F |

**Summary of Variances**    Exhibit 8.17 summarizes manufacturing variances. The total cost variance equals the difference between budgeted (standard) costs and actual costs for the three manufacturing costs. Direct materials, direct labor, and overhead variances are each the sum of detailed variances.

**EXHIBIT 8.17**

Variance Summary

| Product Cost Variance | | | | | |
| --- | --- | --- | --- | --- | --- |

| Direct Materials Variance | | Direct Labor Variance | | Overhead Variance | |
| --- | --- | --- | --- | --- | --- |
| Direct Materials Price Variance (AQ × AP) − (AQ × SP) | Direct Materials Quantity Variance (AQ × SP) − (SQ × SP) | Direct Labor Rate Variance (AH × AR) − (AH × SR) | Direct Labor Efficiency Variance (AH × SR) − (SH × SR) | Controllable Variance Actual overhead − Budgeted (flexible) overhead | Volume Variance Budgeted (flexible) overhead − Applied overhead |

**Standard Costing—Management Considerations** Companies consider many factors, both positive and negative, in deciding whether and how to use standard costing. Below we summarize some factors.

| Standard Costing Considerations | |
| --- | --- |
| **Positives** | **Negatives** |
| Provides benchmarks for management by exception. | Standards are costly to develop and keep up-to-date. |
| Motivates employees to work toward goals. | Variances are not timely for adapting to rapidly changing business conditions. |
| Useful in the budgeting process. | |
| Isolates reasons for good or bad performance. | Employees might not try for continuous improvement. |

 ## CORPORATE SOCIAL RESPONSIBILITY

The **International Integrated Reporting Council** (IIRC) is a global group of regulators, investors, and accountants that develops methods for integrated reporting. **Integrated reporting** is designed to concisely report how an organization's strategy, performance, sustainability efforts, and governance lead to value creation.

**Intel**, a maker of computer chips, follows many of the IIRC's recommendations. In its integrated report, Intel links executive pay, in part, to corporate responsibility metrics. For example, 50% of top management's annual cash bonus is based on meeting operating performance targets, including those for corporate responsibility and environmental sustainability. By linking executive pay to sustainability targets, Intel motivates managers to integrate sustainability initiatives with their efforts to make financial profits and increase firm value.

**True Fit**, this chapter's feature company, uses data and machine-learning to improve the online clothes-shopping experience. According to the company, 40% of online apparel and footwear purchases are returned, as many customers resort to size sampling when buying online. As a result, the supply chain produces considerable unnecessary cardboard and packaging waste and carbon emissions. By reducing customer returns, True Fit increases income and decreases environmental harm.

## Decision Analysis  Sales Variances

**A1**

Analyze changes in sales from expected amounts.

Variance analysis also applies to sales. The budgeted amount of unit sales is the predicted activity level, and the budgeted selling price is treated as a "standard" price. To illustrate, consider the following sales data from G-Max for two of its products, Excel golf balls and Big Bert drivers.

| | Budgeted | Actual |
| --- | --- | --- |
| Sales of Excel golf balls (units)............... | 1,000 units | 1,100 units |
| Sales price per Excel golf ball ............... | $10 | $10.50 |
| Sales of Big Bert drivers (units) ............. | 150 units | 140 units |
| Sales price per Big Bert driver.............. | $200 | $190 |

The *sales price variance* and the *sales volume variance* are in Exhibit 8.18. The sales price variance measures the impact of the actual sales price differing from the expected price. The sales volume variance measures the impact of operating at a different capacity level than predicted by the fixed budget. The total sales price variance is $850 unfavorable, and the total sales volume variance is $1,000 unfavorable. Further analysis of these variances reveals that both the sales price and sales volume variances for Excel golf balls are favorable, while both variances are unfavorable for the Big Bert driver.

**EXHIBIT 8.18**

Computing Sales Variances*

*AS = actual sales units; AP = actual sales price; BP = budgeted sales price; BS = budgeted sales units (fixed budget).

   Managers use sales variances for planning and control. G-Max sold 90 combined total units (both balls and drivers) more than budgeted, yet its total sales price and sales volume variances are unfavorable. The unfavorable sales price variance is due mainly to a decrease in the selling price of Big Bert drivers by $10 per unit. Management must assess whether this price decrease should continue. The unfavorable sales volume variance is due to G-Max selling fewer Big Bert drivers (140) than were budgeted (150). Management must assess whether this decreased demand for Big Bert drivers will persist.

   Sales variance analysis depends on management's future sales estimates. Companies often use historical sales growth rates to estimate future sales. To illustrate, **Callaway Golf** reports the following sales data.

| Sales ($ millions) | Current year | Prior year |
|---|---|---|
| Golf balls . . . . . . . . . . . . . . | $195.6 | $162.5 |
| Woods . . . . . . . . . . . . . . . . | 304.4 | 307.9 |

Sales growth rates can be expressed in percents as shown below for Callaway Golf ($ millions).

$$\text{Sales growth rate} = \frac{\text{Analysis period sales} - \text{Base period sales}}{\text{Base period sales}}$$

$$\text{Sales growth rate, Golf balls} = \frac{\$195.6 - \$162.5}{\$162.5} = 20.4\% \text{ (rounded)}$$

$$\text{Sales growth rate, Woods} = \frac{\$304.4 - \$307.9}{\$307.9} = -1.1\% \text{ (rounded)}$$

Sales growth is over 20% for golf balls but declining by −1.1% for woods. Callaway managers might predict golf ball sales to grow at a 20.4% rate. If they do, estimated golf ball sales in the next year are $235.5 million, computed as $195.6 million × 1.204.

## ■ Decision Maker

**Sales Manager**   The current performance report reveals a large favorable sales volume variance but an unfavorable sales price variance. You did not expect a large increase in sales volume. What steps do you take to analyze this situation? ■   *Answer:* The unfavorable sales price variance suggests that actual prices were lower than budgeted prices. As the sales manager, you want to know the reasons for a lower-than-expected price. Perhaps your salespeople lowered the price of certain products by offering quantity discounts. You then might want to know what prompted them to offer the quantity discounts (perhaps competitors were offering discounts). You want to determine if the increased sales volume is due mainly to discounted prices or other factors (such as advertising).

**NEED-TO-KNOW** **8-6**

**COMPREHENSIVE**

Flexible Budgets and
Variance Analysis

**Point:** 0.125 DLH equals
7.5 minutes.

Pacific Company provides the following information about its standard costs per unit along with its budgeted and actual results for June. Although the budgeted June volume was 25,000 units produced and
sold, the company actually produced and sold 27,000 units.

| Standard Quantity and Cost | |
|---|---|
| Direct materials........ | 4 ounces per unit @ $0.31 per ounce |
| Direct labor........... | 0.125 DLH per unit @ $32 per DLH |
| Overhead ............ | $21.20 per DLH ($6 variable, $15.20 fixed) |

| Flexible Budget and Actual Results | Budget (25,000 units) | Actual (27,000 units) |
|---|---|---|
| Selling price ...................... | $10.00 per unit | $282,420 |
| **Variable costs (per unit)** | | |
| Direct materials ................... | 1.24 per unit | $ 30,800 |
| Direct labor...................... | 4.00 per unit | 99,900 |
| Indirect materials* ................ | 0.25 per unit | 9,990 |
| Utilities* ........................ | 0.50 per unit | 16,200 |
| Shipping ........................ | 0.40 per unit | 9,180 |
| **Fixed costs (per month)** | | |
| Depreciation—Machinery*........... | $47,500 | $ 47,500 |
| Insurance ....................... | 1,200 | 1,290 |
| Administrative salaries............. | 10,000 | 10,060 |

*Indicates overhead item.

| Actual quantity and cost to produce 27,000 units | Actual Cost |
|---|---|
| Direct materials (110,000 oz. @ $0.28 per oz.)............ | $30,800 |
| Direct labor (2,700 DLH @ $37.00 per DLH).............. | 99,900 |
| Overhead ($9,990 + $16,200 + $47,500) .............. | 73,690 |

**Required**

1. Prepare June's flexible budgets showing budgeted sales, costs, and income assuming 20,000, 25,000, 27,000, and 30,000 units produced and sold.
2. Prepare a flexible budget performance report for the actual volume of 27,000 units.
3. Apply variance analysis for direct materials and direct labor.
4. Compute the overhead variance and the controllable and volume variances.

**SOLUTION**

1.

| | | | Flexible Budgets | | | |
|---|---|---|---|---|---|---|
| | Variable | Total | | Flexible Budget for Unit Sales of | | |
| For Month Ended June 30 | Amount per Unit | Fixed Cost | 20,000 | 25,000 | 27,000 | 30,000 |
| Sales ..................... | $10.00 | | $200,000 | $250,000 | $270,000 | $300,000 |
| **Variable costs** | | | | | | |
| Direct materials .......... | 1.24 | | 24,800 | 31,000 | 33,480 | 37,200 |
| Direct labor.............. | 4.00 | | 80,000 | 100,000 | 108,000 | 120,000 |
| Indirect materials ........ | 0.25 | | 5,000 | 6,250 | 6,750 | 7,500 |
| Utilities ................. | 0.50 | | 10,000 | 12,500 | 13,500 | 15,000 |
| Shipping ............... | 0.40 | | 8,000 | 10,000 | 10,800 | 12,000 |
| Total variable costs ....... | 6.39 | | 127,800 | 159,750 | 172,530 | 191,700 |
| Contribution margin ......... | $ 3.61 | | 72,200 | 90,250 | 97,470 | 108,300 |
| **Fixed costs** | | | | | | |
| Depreciation—Machinery .. | | $47,500 | 47,500 | 47,500 | 47,500 | 47,500 |
| Insurance .............. | | 1,200 | 1,200 | 1,200 | 1,200 | 1,200 |
| Administrative salaries..... | | 10,000 | 10,000 | 10,000 | 10,000 | 10,000 |
| Total fixed costs .......... | | $58,700 | 58,700 | 58,700 | 58,700 | 58,700 |
| Income.................. | | | $ 13,500 | $ 31,550 | $ 38,770 | $ 49,600 |

**2.**

| Flexible Budget Performance Report | | | |
|---|---|---|---|
| For Month Ended June 30 | Flexible Budget (27,000 units) | Actual Results (27,000 units) | Variance |
| Sales (27,000 units) . . . . . . . . . . . | $270,000 | $282,420 | **$12,420 F** |
| **Variable costs** | | | |
| Direct materials . . . . . . . . . . . . . | 33,480 | 30,800 | **2,680 F** |
| Direct labor. . . . . . . . . . . . . . . . | 108,000 | 99,900 | **8,100 F** |
| Indirect materials . . . . . . . . . . . | 6,750 | 9,990 | **3,240 U** |
| Utilities . . . . . . . . . . . . . . . . . . . | 13,500 | 16,200 | **2,700 U** |
| Shipping . . . . . . . . . . . . . . . . . . | 10,800 | 9,180 | **1,620 F** |
| Total variable costs . . . . . . . . . | 172,530 | 166,070 | **6,460 F** |
| Contribution margin . . . . . . . . . . . | 97,470 | 116,350 | **18,880 F** |
| **Fixed costs** | | | |
| Depreciation—Machinery . . . . . | 47,500 | 47,500 | **0** |
| Insurance . . . . . . . . . . . . . . . . . . | 1,200 | 1,290 | **90 U** |
| Administrative salaries. . . . . . . . | 10,000 | 10,060 | **60 U** |
| Total fixed costs . . . . . . . . . . . . | 58,700 | 58,850 | **150 U** |
| Income. . . . . . . . . . . . . . . . . . . . . | $ 38,770 | $ 57,500 | **$18,730 F** |

**3.** Variance analysis of direct materials and direct labor costs.

**Direct materials variances**

| | Quantity | Price per Unit | Cost |
|---|---|---|---|
| Actual quantity and actual price . . . . . . . . . . | 110,000 oz. × | $0.28 per oz. = | $30,800 |
| Standard quantity and standard price . . . . . | 108,000 oz.* × | $0.31 per oz. = | 33,480 |
| Direct materials variance . . . . . . . . . . . . . . . | | = | **$ 2,680 F** |

Price and quantity variances (based on formulas in Exhibit 8.10):

**Actual Cost**                                                          **Standard Cost**
AQ × AP              AQ × SP              SQ* × SP
110,000 oz. × $0.28      110,000 oz. × $0.31      108,000 oz. × $0.31
$30,800              $34,100              $33,480

$3,300 F              $620 U

**Price Variance**          **Quantity Variance**

$2,680 F

**Direct Materials Variance**

*SQ = 27,000 actual units of output × 4 oz. standard quantity per unit.

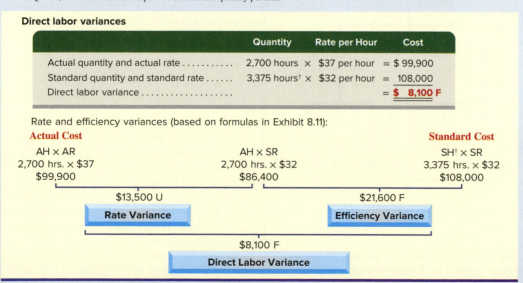

**Direct labor variances**

| | Quantity | Rate per Hour | Cost |
|---|---|---|---|
| Actual quantity and actual rate . . . . . . . . . . . | 2,700 hours × | $37 per hour | = $ 99,900 |
| Standard quantity and standard rate . . . . . . | 3,375 hours† × | $32 per hour | = 108,000 |
| Direct labor variance . . . . . . . . . . . . . . . . . . | | | = **$  8,100 F** |

Rate and efficiency variances (based on formulas in Exhibit 8.11):

**Actual Cost**                                                          **Standard Cost**
AH × AR              AH × SR              SH† × SR
2,700 hrs. × $37      2,700 hrs. × $32      3,375 hrs. × $32
$99,900              $86,400              $108,000

$13,500 U              $21,600 F

**Rate Variance**          **Efficiency Variance**

$8,100 F

**Direct Labor Variance**

†SH = 27,000 actual units of output × 0.125 standard DLH per unit.

**4.** Overhead variance and the controllable and volume variances.

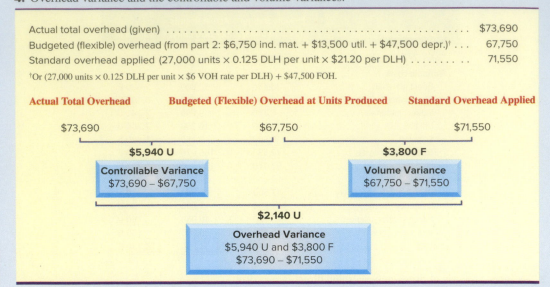

| | | |
|---|---|---|
| Actual total overhead (given) . . . . . . . . . . . . . . . . . . . . . . . . . . . . . . . . . | | $73,690 |
| Budgeted (flexible) overhead (from part 2: $6,750 ind. mat. + $13,500 util. + $47,500 depr.)[†] . . . | | 67,750 |
| Standard overhead applied (27,000 units × 0.125 DLH per unit × $21.20 per DLH) . . . . . . . . | | 71,550 |

[†]Or (27,000 units × 0.125 DLH per unit × $6 VOH rate per DLH) + $47,500 FOH.

**Actual Total Overhead**       **Budgeted (Flexible) Overhead at Units Produced**       **Standard Overhead Applied**

$73,690                                     $67,750                                     $71,550

**$5,940 U**                                                              **$3,800 F**

**Controllable Variance**                                              **Volume Variance**
$73,690 – $67,750                                                        $67,750 – $71,550

**$2,140 U**

**Overhead Variance**
$5,940 U and $3,800 F
$73,690 – $71,550

Do More: QS 8-19, QS 8-20, E 8-27, E 8-28

# Expanded Overhead Variances and Standard Cost Accounting System

## 8A

**P5**

Compute overhead spending and efficiency variances.

## Expanded Overhead Variances

Exhibit 8A.1 shows an expanded framework for analyzing overhead variances consisting of a spending variance and an efficiency variance. This exhibit also shows that controllable variance is the total of the variable overhead spending variance, the fixed overhead spending variance, and the variable overhead efficiency variance.

**EXHIBIT 8A.1**

Expanded Framework for Total Overhead Variance

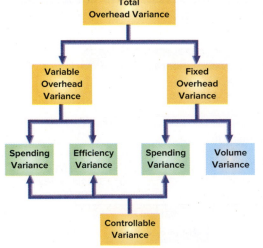

A **spending variance** occurs when management pays an amount different from the standard price to acquire an overhead item. For instance, the actual wage rate paid to indirect labor might be higher than the standard rate. Similarly, actual supervisory salaries might be different than expected.

An **efficiency variance** occurs when standard direct labor hours (the allocation base) expected for actual production differ from the actual direct labor hours used.

### Computing Variable and Fixed Overhead Variances

Recall the G-Max illustration in the chapter. G-Max produced 3,500 units when 4,000 units were budgeted. Additional data (from Exhibit 8.16) show that actual overhead incurred is $18,150 (the variable portion is $6,350 and the fixed portion is $11,800). Each unit requires 0.5 hour of direct labor.

We can separate the overhead rate into two rates: one for variable overhead (VOH) and one for fixed overhead (FOH). Both rates are computed using numbers in the 80% column from Exhibit 8.12. With this information, we compute overhead variances for both variable overhead and fixed overhead as follows:

$$\text{Variable overhead rate} = \frac{\text{VARIABLE overhead budgeted at predicted activity level}}{\text{Standard allocation base at predicted activity level}} = \frac{\$8,000 \text{ VOH}}{2,000 \text{ DLH}} = \$4 \text{ per DLH}$$

$$\text{Fixed overhead rate} = \frac{\text{FIXED overhead budgeted at predicted activity level}}{\text{Standard allocation base at predicted activity level}} = \frac{\$12,000 \text{ FOH}}{2,000 \text{ DLH}} = \$6 \text{ per DLH}$$

| Variable Overhead Variance | |
|---|---|
| Actual variable overhead (given in Exhibit 8.16)............................. | $6,350 |
| Standard variable overhead applied (3,500 units × 0.5 standard DLH × $4 VOH rate per DLH).... | 7,000 |
| **Variable overhead variance**................................. | **$   650 F** |

| Fixed Overhead Variance | |
|---|---|
| Actual fixed overhead (given in Exhibit 8.16)............................. | $11,800 |
| Standard fixed overhead applied (3,500 units × 0.5 standard DLH × $6 FOH rate per DLH) .... | 10,500 |
| **Fixed overhead variance** ................................. | **$ 1,300 U** |

## Expanded Overhead Variance Formulas

Exhibit 8A.2 shows formulas to use in computing detailed overhead variances.

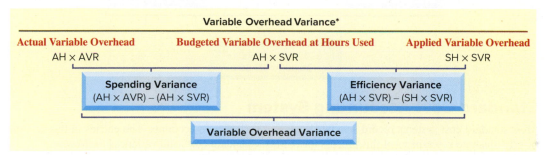

**EXHIBIT 8A.2**

Spending and Efficiency Variances for Overhead

*AH = actual direct labor hours; AVR = actual variable overhead rate; SH = standard direct labor hours; SVR = standard variable overhead rate.

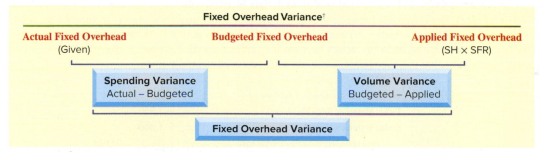

†SH = standard direct labor hours; SFR = standard fixed overhead rate.

## Variable Overhead Variances

Using these formulas, Exhibit 8A.3 shows the detailed analysis of G-Max's $650 favorable variable overhead variance. G-Max applies overhead based on direct labor hours. It actually used 1,700 direct labor hours to produce 3,500 units. This compares favorably to the standard requirement of 1,750 direct labor hours at 0.5 labor hour per unit. At a standard variable overhead rate of $4.00 per direct labor hour, this should have resulted in variable overhead costs of $6,800 (middle column of Exhibit 8A.3).

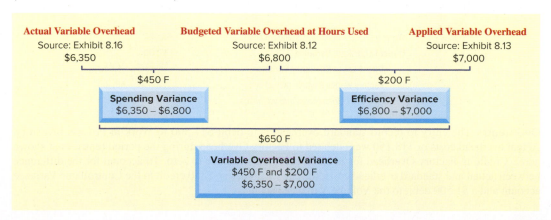

**EXHIBIT 8A.3**

Variable Overhead Spending and Efficiency Variances

G-Max reports actual variable overhead of $6,350, or $450 less than budgeted. This means it has a favorable variable overhead spending variance of $450 ($6,350 – $6,800). G-Max also used 50 fewer direct labor hours than budgeted to make 3,500 units. Thus, G-Max has a favorable variable overhead efficiency variance of $200 ($6,800 – $7,000).

**Fixed Overhead Variances**    Exhibit 8A.4 provides insight into the causes of G-Max's $1,300 unfavorable fixed overhead variance. G-Max incurred $11,800 in actual fixed overhead; this amount is $200 less than the $12,000 budgeted fixed overhead at the expected production level of 4,000 units (see Exhibit 8.12). This $200 favorable fixed overhead spending variance suggests good control of fixed overhead costs. We showed how to compute the $1,500 unfavorable volume variance in the chapter, and its calculation is repeated in Exhibit 8A.4.

**EXHIBIT 8A.4**

Fixed Overhead Spending and Volume Variances

| Actual Fixed Overhead | Budgeted Fixed Overhead | Applied Fixed Overhead |
|---|---|---|
| Source: Exhibit 8.16 | Source: Exhibit 8.12 | Source: Exhibit 8.13 |
| $11,800 | $12,000 | $10,500 |

$200 F

Spending Variance
$11,800 – $12,000

$1,500 U

Volume Variance
$12,000 – $10,500

$1,300 U

Fixed Overhead Variance
$200 F and $1,500 U
$11,800 – $10,500

## Standard Cost Accounting System

**P6**

Prepare journal entries for standard costs and account for price and quantity variances.

Most standard cost systems record standard costs and variances in accounts. The entries in this section briefly illustrate key aspects of this process for G-Max's standard costs and variances for May.

**Direct Materials**    The first entry records standard direct materials cost of $35,000 in the Work in Process Inventory account. This entry credits Raw Materials Inventory for the actual cost of direct materials used of $37,800. The difference between standard and actual direct materials costs is recorded with debits to two separate direct materials variance accounts (recall Exhibit 8.10). Both direct materials price and quantity variances are recorded as debits because they reflect additional costs *higher* than the standard cost (if actual costs are less than the standard, they are recorded as credits).

| May 31 | Work in Process Inventory (standard cost) . . . . . . . . . . . | 35,000 | |
|---|---|---|---|
| | **Direct Materials Price Variance*** . . . . . . . . . . . . . . . . . | **1,800** | |
| | **Direct Materials Quantity Variance** . . . . . . . . . . . . . . | **1,000** | |
| | Raw Materials Inventory (actual cost) . . . . . . . . . . | | 37,800 |
| | *Record direct materials costs and variances.* | | |

*Many companies record the materials price variance when materials are purchased. For simplicity, we record both the materials price and quantity variances when materials are issued to production.

**Direct Labor**    The second entry increases Work in Process Inventory for the standard direct labor cost of $56,000. Actual direct labor cost of $56,100 is credited to Factory Wages Payable. The difference between standard and actual labor costs is explained by two variances (see Exhibit 8.11). The direct labor rate variance is unfavorable and is debited. The direct labor efficiency variance is favorable and is credited. The direct labor efficiency variance is favorable because it represents a lower cost.

| May 31 | Work in Process Inventory (standard cost) . . . . . . . . . . . | 56,000 | |
|---|---|---|---|
| | **Direct Labor Rate Variance** . . . . . . . . . . . . . . . . . . . . . | **1,700** | |
| | **Direct Labor Efficiency Variance** . . . . . . . . . . . . . | | 1,600 |
| | Factory Wages Payable (actual cost) . . . . . . . . . . | | 56,100 |
| | *Record direct labor costs and variances.* | | |

**Overhead**    The entry to record standard overhead is to debit $17,500 to Work in Process Inventory. Actual overhead costs of $18,150 were debited to Factory Overhead during the period (entries not shown here). Crediting Factory Overhead for $18,150 reduces its balance to zero. To account for the difference between actual and standard overhead costs, the entry includes an $850 credit to the Controllable Variance account and a $1,500 debit to the Volume Variance account.

| May 31 | Work in Process Inventory (standard cost) ........... | 17,500 | |
|---|---|---|---|
| | **Volume Variance.............................** | **1,500** | |
| | Controllable Variance ..................... | | 850 |
| | Factory Overhead ......................... | | 18,150 |
| | *Apply overhead at standard rate of $10 per standard direct labor hour (1,750 hours) and record overhead variances.* | | |

The balances of these different variance accounts accumulate until the end of the accounting period. As a result, the unfavorable variances of some months can offset the favorable variances of other months.

These ending variance account balances, which reflect results of the period's various transactions and events, are closed at period-end. If the amounts are *immaterial,* they are added to or subtracted from the balance of the Cost of Goods Sold account. This process is similar to that shown in the job order costing chapter for eliminating an underapplied or overapplied balance in the Factory Overhead account.

## Standard Costing Income Statement

In addition to budget reports, management can use a standard costing income statement to summarize company performance for a period. A **standard costing income statement** reports sales and cost of goods sold at their *standard* amounts, and then lists individual sales and cost variances to compute gross profit at *actual* cost. Unfavorable cost variances are *added* to cost of goods sold at standard cost; favorable cost variances are *subtracted* from cost of goods sold at standard cost.

**NEED-TO-KNOW 8-7**

Part A: Expanded Overhead Variances

**P5**

**Part A:** Refer to the information in Need-to-Know 8-6 to answer the requirements.

**Required**

1. Compute the variable overhead spending variance and the variable overhead efficiency variance.
2. Compute the fixed overhead spending variance and the fixed overhead volume variance.

*Solution*

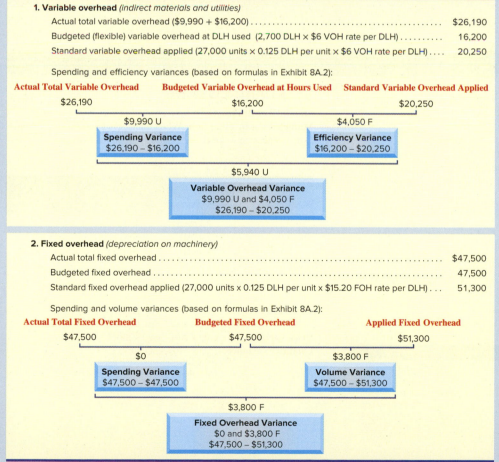

**1. Variable overhead** *(indirect materials and utilities)*

| | |
|---|---|
| Actual total variable overhead ($9,990 + $16,200) ........................................ | $26,190 |
| Budgeted (flexible) variable overhead at DLH used (2,700 DLH × $6 VOH rate per DLH) ......... | 16,200 |
| Standard variable overhead applied (27,000 units × 0.125 DLH per unit × $6 VOH rate per DLH) .... | 20,250 |

Spending and efficiency variances (based on formulas in Exhibit 8A.2):

| Actual Total Variable Overhead | Budgeted Variable Overhead at Hours Used | Standard Variable Overhead Applied |
|---|---|---|
| $26,190 | $16,200 | $20,250 |

$9,990 U

$4,050 F

**Spending Variance** $26,190 – $16,200

**Efficiency Variance** $16,200 – $20,250

$5,940 U

**Variable Overhead Variance** $9,990 U and $4,050 F $26,190 – $20,250

**2. Fixed overhead** *(depreciation on machinery)*

| | |
|---|---|
| Actual total fixed overhead ................................................. | $47,500 |
| Budgeted fixed overhead ................................................... | 47,500 |
| Standard fixed overhead applied (27,000 units x 0.125 DLH per unit x $15.20 FOH rate per DLH) ... | 51,300 |

Spending and volume variances (based on formulas in Exhibit 8A.2):

| Actual Total Fixed Overhead | Budgeted Fixed Overhead | Applied Fixed Overhead |
|---|---|---|
| $47,500 | $47,500 | $51,300 |

$0

$3,800 F

**Spending Variance** $47,500 – $47,500

**Volume Variance** $47,500 – $51,300

$3,800 F

**Fixed Overhead Variance** $0 and $3,800 F $47,500 – $51,300

We can also compute:

Controllable variance:   $5,940 U (add both spending variances plus efficiency variance)

Volume variance:     3,800 F (identified above)

Part B: Recording
Variances under
Standard Costing

**P6**

**Part B:** Prepare journal entries to record direct materials, direct labor, and overhead variances under *standard costing.*

| Direct Materials | | Direct Labor | | Overhead | |
|---|---|---|---|---|---|
| Actual cost ......... | $73,200 | Actual cost........... | $38,000 | Actual cost ............ | $60,000 |
| Standard cost ....... | 75,700 | Standard cost ......... | 40,000 | Standard cost .......... | 64,000 |
| Quantity variance .... | 3,800 F | Efficiency variance .... | 1,000 U | Volume variance........ | 1,500 F |
| Price variance ....... | 1,300 U | Rate variance......... | 3,000 F | Controllable variance .... | 2,500 F |

*Solution*

| Work in Process Inventory ............. | 75,700 | |
|---|---|---|
| Direct Materials Price Variance ........ | 1,300 | |
|    Direct Materials Quantity Variance. | | 3,800 |
|    Raw Materials Inventory ......... | | 73,200 |
| *Record direct materials and variances.* | | |

| Work in Process Inventory ............ | 64,000 | |
|---|---|---|
|    Volume Variance .............. | | 1,500 |
|    Controllable Variance .......... | | 2,500 |
|    Factory Overhead .............. | | 60,000 |
| *Record overhead variances.* | | |

| Work in Process Inventory ............ | 40,000 | |
|---|---|---|
| Direct Labor Efficiency Variance ....... | 1,000 | |
|    Direct Labor Rate Variance ...... | | 3,000 |
|    Factory Wages Payable ......... | | 38,000 |
| *Record direct labor and variances.* | | |

Do More: QS 8-18, E 8-14

---

## Summary: Cheat Sheet

### FIXED AND FLEXIBLE BUDGETS

**Fixed budget:** Based on a single activity level.
**Flexible budget:** Based on several activity levels.
**Variance:** Difference between budgeted and actual amounts is:
      Favorable → Leads to higher income.
      Unfavorable → Leads to lower income.

Total budgeted costs = Total fixed costs + (Total variable cost per unit × Units of activity level)

| Fixed Budget (one activity level) | |
|---|---|
| Sales (in units)............. | 100 |
| Sales ($800 per unit) ........ | $80,000 |
| Variable costs ($360 per unit) .. | 36,000 |
| Contribution margin ......... | 44,000 |
| Fixed costs ................. | 20,000 |
| Income.................... | $24,000 |

| Flexible Budget (three activity levels) | | | |
|---|---|---|---|
| Sales (in units)............... | 100 | 120 | 140 |
| Sales ($800 per unit) ......... | $80,000 | $96,000 | $112,000 |
| Variable costs ($360 per unit) .. | 36,000 | 43,200 | 50,400 |
| Contribution margin .......... | 44,000 | 52,800 | 61,600 |
| Fixed costs ................. | 20,000 | 20,000 | 20,000 |
| Income..................... | $24,000 | $32,800 | $ 41,600 |

### STANDARD COSTING

**Standard cost:** Preset cost for a product or service.
**Management by exception:** When managers focus on significant differences between actual costs and standard costs.

| STANDARD COST CARD | | | |
|---|---|---|---|
| Inputs | Standard Quantity or Hours | Standard Price or Rate | Standard Cost per Unit |
| Direct materials | 2.2 pounds | $10 per pound | $22 |
| Direct labor | 2.0 DLH | $15 per DLH | 30 |
| Overhead | 2.0 DLH | $5 per DLH | 10 |
| Total | | | $62 |

**Cost variance:**     Actual cost < Standard cost → Favorable
                      Actual cost > Standard cost → Unfavorable
**Price variance:**     $(AQ \times AP) - (AQ \times SP)$
**Quantity variance:**  $(AQ \times SP) - (SQ \times SP)$
                  AQ = actual quantity, AP = actual price
                  SQ = standard quantity, SP = standard price

# MATERIALS AND LABOR VARIANCES

**Materials Variances**

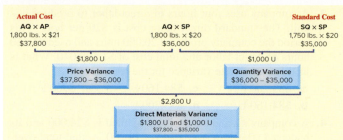

**Labor Variances**

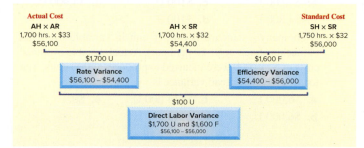

# OVERHEAD STANDARDS AND VARIANCES

| G-MAX Flexible Overhead Budgets | | | | | | |
|---|---|---|---|---|---|---|
| For Month Ended May 31 | Variable Amount per Unit | Total Fixed Cost | Flexible Budget at Capacity Level of | | | |
| | | | 70% | 80% | 90% | 100% |
| Production (in units) ............... | 1 unit | | 3,500 | 4,000 | 4,500 | 5,000 |
| Factory overhead | | | | | | |
| Variable costs | | | | | | |
| Indirect labor ................. | $0.80/unit | | $ 2,800 | $ 3,200 | $ 3,600 | $ 4,000 |
| Indirect materials.............. | 0.60/unit | | 2,100 | 2,400 | 2,700 | 3,000 |
| Power and lights ............... | 0.40/unit | | 1,400 | 1,600 | 1,800 | 2,000 |
| Maintenance ................... | 0.20/unit | | 700 | 800 | 900 | 1,000 |
| Total variable overhead costs .... | $2.00/unit | | 7,000 | 8,000 | 9,000 | 10,000 |
| Fixed costs (per month) | | | | | | |
| Building rent................. | | $ 2,000 | $ 2,000 | $ 2,000 | $ 2,000 | $ 2,000 |
| Depreciation—Machinery ........ | | 4,000 | 4,000 | 4,000 | 4,000 | 4,000 |
| Supervisory salaries ........... | | 6,000 | 6,000 | 6,000 | 6,000 | 6,000 |
| Total fixed overhead costs....... | | $12,000 | 12,000 | 12,000 | 12,000 | 12,000 |
| Total overhead ................. | | | $19,000 | $20,000 | $21,000 | $22,000 |

## Total Overhead Variance

$$\text{Overhead variance} = \text{Actual total overhead} - \text{Standard overhead applied}$$

## Standard Overhead Applied

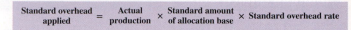

$$\text{Standard overhead applied} = \text{Actual production} \times \text{Standard amount of allocation base} \times \text{Standard overhead rate}$$

## Volume Variance and Controllable Variance

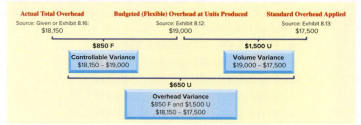

$$\text{Volume variance} = \text{Budgeted overhead} - \text{Standard overhead applied}$$

$$\text{Controllable variance} = \text{Actual total overhead} - \text{Budgeted (flexible) overhead at units produced}$$

### Sales Variances

$$\boxed{\text{Sales price variance}} = [AS \times AP] - [AS \times BP]$$

$$\boxed{\text{Sales volume variance}} = [AS \times BP] - [BS \times BP]$$

where AS = Actual Sales units; AP = Actual sales Price;
BP = Budgeted sales Price; BS = Budgeted Sales units (fixed budget).

### Detailed Overhead Variances (Appendix 8A)

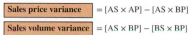

$$\boxed{\text{Variable overhead spending variance}} = [AH \times AVR] - [AH \times SVR]$$

$$\boxed{\text{Variable overhead efficiency variance}} = [AH \times SVR] - [SH \times SVR]$$

$$\boxed{\text{Fixed overhead spending variance}} = \text{Actual fixed overhead} - \text{Budgeted fixed overhead}$$

where AVR is Actual Variable Rate of overhead; SQ is Standard Quantity of materials;
SP is Standard Price of materials; SH is Standard Hours of labor;
SR is Standard Rate of wages; SVR is Standard Variable Rate of overhead.

---

## Key Terms

Benchmarking (289)

Budget report (283)

Controllable variance (295)

Cost variance (288)

Efficiency variance (302)

Favorable variance (284)

Fixed budget (283)

Fixed budget performance report (284)

Flexible budget (283)

Flexible budget performance report (285)

Integrated reporting (298)

International Integrated Reporting
    Council (298)

Management by exception (287)

Overhead variance (295)

Price variance (290)

Quantity variance (290)

Spending variance (302)

Standard costing income statement (305)

Standard costs (287)

Unfavorable variance (284)

Variance (284)

Variance analysis (288)

Volume variance (296)

## Multiple Choice Quiz

1. A company predicts its production and sales will be 24,000 units. At that level, its fixed costs are budgeted at $300,000, and its variable costs are budgeted at $246,000. If its activity level declines to 20,000 units, what will be its budgeted fixed and variable costs?

    a. Fixed, $300,000; variable, $246,000
    b. Fixed, $250,000; variable, $205,000
    c. Fixed, $300,000; variable, $205,000
    d. Fixed, $250,000; variable, $246,000
    e. Fixed, $300,000; variable, $300,000

2. Using the following information, compute the total actual cost of direct materials used.
    - Direct materials standard cost: 5 lbs. × $2 per lb. = $10.
    - Total direct materials variance: $15,000 unfavorable.
    - Actual direct materials used: 300,000 lbs.
    - Actual units produced: 60,000 units.

    a. $585,000     c. $300,000     e. $615,000
    b. $600,000     d. $315,000

3. A company uses four hours of direct labor to produce one unit. The standard direct labor cost is $20 per hour. This period the company produced 20,000 units and used 84,160 hours of direct labor at a total cost of $1,599,040. What is its direct labor rate variance for the period?

    a. $83,200 F     c. $84,160 F     e. $960 F
    b. $84,160 U     d. $83,200 U

4. A company's standard overhead applied is $24,000 and its budgeted (flexible) overhead is $19,200. Actual total overhead is $24,100. The volume variance is

    a. $4,800 U.     c. $100 U.     e. $4,900 U.
    b. $4,800 F.     d. $100 F.

5.[A] A company's standard is $6 per unit in variable overhead (4 machine hours × $1.50 per hour). Actual variable overhead costs of $150,000 were incurred to produce 24,000 units. The total variable overhead variance is

    a. $6,000 F.     c. $114,000 U.     e. $0.
    b. $6,000 U.     d. $114,000 F.

### ANSWERS TO MULTIPLE CHOICE QUIZ

1. c; Fixed costs remain at $300,000; Variable costs = ($246,000/24,000 units) × 20,000 units = $205,000

2. e; Budgeted direct materials + Unfavorable variance = Actual cost of direct materials used; or 60,000 units × $10 per unit = $600,000 + $15,000 U = $615,000

3. c; (AH × AR) − (AH × SR) = $1,599,040 − (84,160 hours × $20 per hour) = $84,160 F

4. a; Budgeted (flexible) overhead − Standard overhead applied = Volume variance; or $24,000 − $19,200 = $4,800 U

5. b; Actual variable overhead − Variable overhead applied = Variable overhead cost variance; or $150,000 − (24,000 hours × 4 MH × $1.50 per hour) = $6,000 U

*Superscript letter A denotes assignments based on Appendix 8A.*

*Select Quick Study and Exercise assignments feature Guided Example videos, called "Hints" in Connect. Hints use different numbers, and instructors can turn this feature on or off.*

### QUICK STUDY

**QS 8-1**

Flexible budget performance report   **P1**

Beech Company produced and sold 105,000 units in May. For the level of production in May, budgeted amounts were sales, $1,300,000; variable costs, $750,000; and fixed costs, $300,000. The following actual results are available for May. Prepare a flexible budget performance report for May. Indicate whether each variance is favorable or unfavorable.

|  | Actual Results |
|---|---|
| Sales (105,000 units) . . . . | $1,275,000 |
| Variable costs . . . . . . . . . . | 712,500 |
| Fixed costs . . . . . . . . . . . . | 300,000 |

**QS 8-2**

Flexible budget cost calculations   **P1**

Based on predicted production of 24,000 units, a company budgets $300,000 of fixed costs and $246,000 of variable costs. If the company actually produces 20,000 units, what are the flexible budget amounts of fixed and variable costs?

**QS 8-3**

Flexible budget income calculation   **P1**

The fixed budget for 20,000 units of production shows sales of $400,000; variable costs of $80,000; and fixed costs of $150,000. If the company actually produces and sells 26,000 units, calculate the flexible budget income.

**QS 8-4**

Flexible budget performance report   **P1**

The fixed budget for 20,000 units of production shows sales of $400,000; variable costs of $80,000; and fixed costs of $150,000. The company's actual sales were 26,000 units at $480,000. Actual variable costs were $112,000 and actual fixed costs were $145,000. Prepare a flexible budget performance report. Indicate whether each variance is favorable or unfavorable.

BatCo makes baseball bats. Each bat requires 2 pounds of wood at $18 per pound and 0.25 direct labor hour at $20 per hour. Overhead is applied at the rate of $40 per direct labor hour. Prepare a standard cost card for a baseball bat for BatCo.

**QS 8-5**
Standard cost card  **P2**

---

Refer to information in QS 8-5. Assume the actual cost to manufacture 100 bats is $5,400. Compute the total cost variance and identify it as favorable or unfavorable.

**QS 8-6**
Total cost variance  **P2**

---

A company reports the following for one of its products. Compute the total direct materials variance and identify it as favorable or unfavorable.

| | |
|---|---|
| Direct materials standard (4 lbs. @ $2 per lb.) ............ | $8 per unit |
| Actual units produced................................ | 60,000 units |
| Actual cost of direct materials used .................... | $540,000 |

**QS 8-7**
Direct materials variance

**P3**

---

A company reports the following for one of its products. Compute the direct materials price and quantity variances and identify each as favorable or unfavorable.

| | | | |
|---|---|---|---|
| Direct materials standard (4 lbs. @ $2 per lb.) ... | $8 per unit | Actual units produced.............. | 60,000 units |
| Actual direct materials used ................ | 300,000 lbs. | Actual cost of direct materials used... | $540,000 |

**QS 8-8**
Direct materials price and quantity variances

**P3**

---

For the current period, Kay Company's manufacturing operations show a $4,000 unfavorable direct materials price variance. The actual price per pound of material is $78; the standard price is $77.50 per pound. How many pounds of material were used in the current period?

**QS 8-9**
Direct materials price variance  **P3**

---

For the current period, Juan Company's standard cost of direct materials is $150,000. The direct materials variances consist of a $12,000 favorable price variance and a $2,000 favorable quantity variance. What is the actual cost of direct materials?

**QS 8-10**
Direct materials price and quantity variances  **P3**

---

A company reports the following for its direct labor. Compute the direct labor rate and efficiency variances and identify each as favorable or unfavorable.

| | | | |
|---|---|---|---|
| Actual hours of direct labor used.......... | 65,000 | Standard rate of direct labor per hour............. | $14 |
| Actual rate of direct labor per hour........ | $15 | Standard hours of direct labor for units produced ... | 67,000 |

**QS 8-11**
Direct labor rate and efficiency variances

**P3**

---

A company shows a $20,000 unfavorable direct labor rate variance and a $10,000 unfavorable direct labor efficiency variance. The company's standard cost of direct labor is $400,000. What is the actual cost of direct labor?

**QS 8-12**
Direct labor rate and efficiency variances  **P3**

---

Derr Co. reports the following. Compute (a) controllable variance, (b) volume variance, and (c) total overhead variance.

| | |
|---|---|
| Actual total overhead......................................... | $980 |
| Budgeted (flexible) overhead at units produced................... | 800 |
| Standard overhead applied .................................... | 900 |

**QS 8-13**
Overhead variances: total, controllable, and volume

**P4**

---

Fogel Co. expects to produce and sell 116,000 units for the period. The company's flexible budget for 116,000 units shows variable overhead costs of $162,400 and fixed overhead costs of $124,000. The company incurred actual total overhead costs of $262,800 while producing 110,000 units.
　　(a) Compute the total variable overhead costs for the flexible budget when producing 110,000 units. (b) Compute the budgeted (flexible) total overhead when producing 110,000 units. (c) Compute the controllable variance and identify it as favorable or unfavorable.

**QS 8-14**
Total overhead and controllable variances  **P4**

**QS 8-15**

Total overhead and controllable variances

**P4**

AirPro Corp. reports the following for this period. Compute the (*a*) total overhead variance and (*b*) controllable variance and identify each variance as favorable or unfavorable.

| | |
|---|---|
| Actual total overhead . . . . . . . . . . . . . . . . . . . . . . . . . . . . . . . . . . . . . . | $28,175 |
| Standard overhead applied . . . . . . . . . . . . . . . . . . . . . . . . . . . . . . . . . | $40,180 |
|    Budgeted (flexible) variable overhead rate . . . . . . . . . . . . . . . . . . . . | $3.10 per unit |
|    Budgeted fixed overhead . . . . . . . . . . . . . . . . . . . . . . . . . . . . . . . . . | $12,000 |
| Predicted activity level . . . . . . . . . . . . . . . . . . . . . . . . . . . . . . . . . . . . . | 12,000 units |
| Actual activity level . . . . . . . . . . . . . . . . . . . . . . . . . . . . . . . . . . . . . . . . | 9,800 units |

**QS 8-16**

Volume variance   **P4**

Refer to the information in QS 8-15. Compute the volume variance and identify it as favorable or unfavorable.

**QS 8-17**

Components of overhead variance   **P4**

Alvarez Company for the current period shows a $20,000 favorable volume variance and a $60,400 unfavorable controllable variance. Standard overhead applied for the period is $225,000. (*a*) What is the actual total overhead for the period? (*b*) What is the total overhead variance and is it favorable or unfavorable?

**QS 8-18ᴬ**

Preparing overhead entries

**P6**

Refer to the information in QS 8-17. Alvarez records standard costs in its accounts. Prepare the journal entry to charge overhead costs to the Work in Process Inventory account and to record any variances.

**QS 8-19ᴬ**

Variable overhead variance

**P5**

Mosaic Company applies overhead using machine hours and shows the following information. Compute the variable overhead variance and identify it as favorable or unfavorable.

| | |
|---|---|
| Actual hours of machine use . . . . . . . . . . . . . . . . . . . . . . . . . . . . . . . . . | 4,700 hours |
| Standard hours of machine use (for actual production) . . . . . . . . . . . . . | 5,000 hours |
| Actual variable overhead rate per machine hour . . . . . . . . . . . . . . . . . | $4.15 |
| Standard variable overhead rate per machine hour . . . . . . . . . . . . . . . | $4.00 |

**QS 8-20ᴬ**

Overhead spending and efficiency variances   **P5**

Refer to the information in QS 8-19. Compute the variable overhead spending variance and the variable overhead efficiency variance and identify each as favorable or unfavorable.

**QS 8-21**

Sales variances   **A1**

Farad Inc. sells used trucks. During the month, Farad sold 50 trucks at a price of $9,000 each. The budget for the month was to sell 45 trucks at a price of $9,500 each. Compute the sales price variance and sales volume variance for the month and identify each variance as favorable or unfavorable.

**QS 8-22**

Sales variances   **A1**

In a recent year a car manufacturer sold 182,158 cars. The company budgeted to sell 191,158 cars during the year. The budgeted sales price for each car was $30,000 and the actual sales price for each car was $30,200. Compute the sales price variance and the sales volume variance and identify each variance as favorable or unfavorable.

**QS 8-23**

Materials rate change

**P3**

Management believes it has found a more efficient way to package its products and use less cardboard. This new approach will reduce shipping costs from $10.00 per shipment to $9.25 per shipment. (1) If the company budgets 1,200 shipments this year, what amount of total direct materials costs would appear on the shipping department's flexible budget? (2) How much is this sustainability improvement predicted to save in direct materials costs for this coming year?

**QS 8-24**

Overhead rate change

**P4**

A company's returns department incurs annual overhead costs of $72,000 and budgets 2,000 returns per year. Management believes it has found a better way to package its products. As a result, the company expects to reduce the number of shipments that are returned due to damage by 5%. This is expected to reduce the department's annual overhead by $12,000.

   Compute the department's standard overhead rate per return (*a*) before the sustainability improvement and (*b*) after the sustainability improvement.

Match *a* through *d* with their definition 1 through 4.

**QS 8-25**
Standard costs terminology
**C1**

**a.** Standard cost card

**b.** Management by exception

**c.** Standard cost

**d.** Ideal standard

_____ **1.** Quantity of input required if a production process is 100% efficient.

_____ **2.** Managing by focusing on large differences from standard costs.

_____ **3.** Record that accumulates standard cost information.

_____ **4.** Preset cost for delivering a product or service under normal conditions.

![Mc Graw Hill] connect

Resset Co. had the following results for April's operations: *F* indicates favorable and *U* indicates unfavorable. In applying management by exception, the company investigates all variances of $400 or more. Which variances will the company investigate?

**EXERCISES**

**Exercise 8-1**
Management by exception
**C1**

| | | | |
|---|---|---|---|
| Direct materials price variance | $  300 F | Direct labor efficiency variance | $2,200 F |
| Direct materials quantity variance | 3,000 U | Overhead controllable variance | 400 U |
| Direct labor rate variance | 100 U | Overhead volume variance | 500 F |

JPAK manufactures and sells mountain bikes. Classify each of the following costs as fixed or variable with respect to the number of bikes made.

**Exercise 8-2**
Classifying costs as fixed or variable
**P1**

**a.** Bike frames

**b.** Screws for assembly

**c.** Assembly worker wages

**d.** Property taxes

**e.** Bike tires

**f.** Bike paint

**g.** Accountant salary

**h.** Depreciation on office

**i.** Supervisor salaries

Tempo Company's fixed budget (based on sales of 7,000 units) follows.

**Exercise 8-3**
Preparing flexible budgets
**P1**

| Fixed Budget | |
|---|---|
| Sales (7,000 units × $400 per unit) | $2,800,000 |
| Costs | |
| Direct materials | 280,000 |
| Direct labor | 490,000 |
| Indirect materials | 175,000 |
| Supervisor salary | 65,000 |
| Sales commissions | 140,000 |
| Shipping | 154,000 |
| Administrative salaries | 210,000 |
| Depreciation—Office equip. | 35,000 |
| Insurance | 20,000 |
| Office rent | 36,000 |
| Income | $1,195,000 |

**1.** Compute total variable cost per unit.

**2.** Compute total fixed costs.

**3.** Prepare a flexible budget at activity levels of 6,000 units and 8,000 units. Follow format in Exhibit 8.3.

Complete the following partial flexible budget performance report, and indicate whether each variance is favorable or unfavorable. The company budgets a selling price of $80 per unit and variable costs of $35 per unit.

**Exercise 8-4**
Preparing flexible budget performance report    **P1**

| Flexible Budget Performance Report | | | |
|---|---|---|---|
| For Month Ended June 30 | Flexible Budget (10,800 units) | Actual Results (10,800 units) | Variances |
| Sales | $      ? | $      ? | $21,000 F |
| Variable costs | ? | 351,000 | ? |
| Contribution margin | 486,000 | ? | ? |
| Fixed costs | 270,000 | 285,000 | ? |
| Income | $      ? | $      ? | $      ? |

**Exercise 8-5**

Preparing flexible budget performance report

**P1**

Nina Co. prepared the following fixed budget for July using 7,500 units for budgeted sales. Actual sales were 7,200 units and actual costs are shown below. Prepare a flexible budget performance report for July that shows variances between budgeted and actual amounts. Indicate whether each variance is favorable or unfavorable.

| For Month Ended July 31 | Fixed Budget Variable Amount per Unit | Total Fixed Cost | Fixed Budget (7,500 units) | Actual Results (7,200 units) |
|---|---|---|---|---|
| Sales................................ | $100 | | $750,000 | $737,000 |
| **Variable costs** | | | | |
| Direct materials.................. | 35 | | 262,500 | 266,800 |
| Direct labor ..................... | 15 | | 112,500 | 109,600 |
| Indirect materials................ | 4 | | 30,000 | 28,200 |
| Sales commissions .............. | 11 | | 82,500 | 78,400 |
| Total variable costs ............. | 65 | | 487,500 | 483,000 |
| Contribution margin............... | $ 35 | | $262,500 | $254,000 |
| **Fixed costs** | | | | |
| Depreciation—Machinery......... | | $ 68,200 | 68,200 | 68,200 |
| Supervisory salaries ............ | | 40,500 | 40,500 | 41,600 |
| Insurance...................... | | 10,000 | 10,000 | 10,000 |
| Depreciation—Office equipment ... | | 7,400 | 7,400 | 7,400 |
| Administrative salaries ........... | | 33,900 | 33,900 | 29,800 |
| Total fixed costs................. | | $160,000 | 160,000 | 157,000 |
| Income ......................... | | | $102,500 | $ 97,000 |

**Exercise 8-6**

Preparing flexible budget performance report

**P1**

Lewis Co. reports the following fixed budget and actual results for May. Prepare a flexible budget performance report showing variances between budgeted and actual results, and indicate whether each variance is favorable or unfavorable.

| | Fixed Budget | Actual Results |
|---|---|---|
| Sales (units produced and sold)..... | 1,200 | 1,400 |
| Sales (in dollars)................. | $300 per unit | $435,000 |
| Variable costs................... | $120 per unit | $172,000 |
| Fixed costs .................... | $125,000 | $122,000 |

**Exercise 8-7**

Standard cost per unit, total budgeted cost, and total cost variance

**P2**

A manufactured product has the following information for August. (1) Prepare the standard cost card showing standard cost per unit. (2) Compute total budgeted cost for production in August. (3) Compute total cost variance for August, and indicate whether the variance is favorable or unfavorable.

| | Standard Quantity and Cost | Actual Results |
|---|---|---|
| Direct materials ............. | 2 lbs. per unit @ $2.50 per lb. | |
| Direct labor................. | 0.5 hour per unit @ $16 per DLH | |
| Overhead .................. | $12 per DLH | |
| Units manufactured .......... | | 12,000 units |
| Total manufacturing costs ..... | | $225,400 |

**Exercise 8-8**

Standard cost per unit, total budgeted and actual costs, and total cost variance   **P2**

A manufactured product has the following information for June. (1) Prepare the standard cost card showing standard cost per unit. (2) Compute total budgeted cost for June production. (3) Compute total actual cost for June production. (4) Compute total cost variance for June, and indicate whether the variance is favorable or unfavorable.

| | Standard Quantity and Cost | Actual Results |
|---|---|---|
| Direct materials......... | 6 lbs. @ $8 per lb. | 48,500 lbs. @ $8.10 per lb. |
| Direct labor............ | 2 DLH @ $16 per DLH | 15,700 hrs. @ $16.50 per hr. |
| Units manufactured ..... | | 8,000 units |

---

Refer to the information in Exercise 8-8 and compute the (1) direct materials price variance and (2) direct materials quantity variance. Indicate whether each variance is favorable or unfavorable.

**Exercise 8-9**
Direct materials
variances **P3**

---

Refer to the information in Exercise 8-8 and compute the (1) direct labor rate variance and (2) direct labor efficiency variance. Indicate whether each variance is favorable or unfavorable.

**Exercise 8-10**
Direct labor variances **P3**

---

Lucia Company has set the following standard cost per unit for direct materials and direct labor.

| Direct materials (15 lbs. @ $4 per lb.) ........... | $60 | Direct labor (3 hrs. @ $15 per hr.) .............. | $45 |
|---|---|---|---|

During May the company incurred the following actual costs to produce 9,000 units.

| Direct materials (138,000 lbs. @ $3.75 per lb.).. | $517,500 | Direct labor (31,000 hrs. @ $15.10 per hr.) ... | $468,100 |
|---|---|---|---|

Compute the (1) direct materials price and quantity variances and (2) direct labor rate and efficiency variances. Indicate whether each variance is favorable or unfavorable.

**Exercise 8-11**
Direct materials and direct labor variances

**P3**

---

Camila Company has set the following standard cost per unit for direct materials and direct labor.

| Direct materials (10 lbs. @ $3 per lb.) .......... | $30 | Direct labor (2 hrs. @ $12 per hr.)............... | $24 |
|---|---|---|---|

During June the company incurred the following actual costs to produce 9,000 units.

| Direct materials (92,000 lbs. @ $2.95 per lb.)... | $271,400 | Direct labor (18,800 hrs. @ $12.05 per hr.) ... | $226,540 |
|---|---|---|---|

Compute the (1) direct materials price and quantity variances and (2) direct labor rate and efficiency variances. Indicate whether each variance is favorable or unfavorable.

**Exercise 8-12**
Direct materials and direct labor variances

**P3**

---

Hart Company made 3,000 shelves using 22,000 pounds of wood costing $266,200. The company's direct materials standards for one shelf are 8 pounds of wood at $12 per pound.

**1.** Compute the direct materials price and quantity variances along with the total direct materials variance and identify each as favorable or unfavorable.

**2.** Hart applies management by exception by investigating direct materials variances of more than 5% of actual direct materials costs. Which direct materials variances will Hart investigate further?

**Exercise 8-13**
Computing and analyzing materials variances **P3**

---

Refer to Exercise 8-13. Hart Company uses a standard costing system. Prepare the journal entry to charge direct materials costs to Work in Process Inventory and record the direct materials variances.

**Exercise 8-14ᴬ**
Recording materials variances **P6**

---

The following information relates to production activities of Mercer Manufacturing for the year.

| | |
|---|---|
| Actual direct materials used ......................... | 16,000 lbs. at $4.05 per lb. |
| Actual direct labor used ............................. | 16,635 hours at $19 per hour |
| Actual units produced ............................. | 30,000 |
| Standard quantity and price per unit for direct materials.... | 0.5 lb. at $4.00 per lb. |
| Standard quantity and rate per unit for direct labor........ | 0.5 hour at $20 per hour |

**Exercise 8-15**
Direct materials and direct labor variances

**P3**

**1.** Compute the direct materials price and quantity variances and identify each as favorable or unfavorable.

**2.** Compute the direct labor rate and efficiency variances and identify each as favorable or unfavorable.

**Exercise 8-16**
Computing and analyzing direct labor variances  **P3**

Javon Co. set standards of 3 hours of direct labor per unit at a rate of $15 per hour. During October, the company actually uses 16,250 hours of direct labor at a $247,000 total cost to produce 5,600 units. In November, the company uses 22,000 hours of direct labor at a $335,500 total cost to produce 6,000 units of product.

1. Compute the direct labor rate variance, the direct labor efficiency variance, and the total direct labor variance for each of these two months. Identify each variance as favorable or unfavorable.

2. Javon investigates variances of more than 5% of actual direct labor cost. Which direct labor variances will the company investigate further?

---

**Exercise 8-17**
Computing standard overhead rate and total overhead variance

**P4**

Manuel Company predicts it will operate at 80% of its capacity. Its overhead allocation base is DLH and its standard amount per allocation base is 0.5 DLH per unit. The company reports the following for this period.

|  | Fixed Budget at 80% Capacity | Actual Results |
|---|---|---|
| Production (in units) . . . . . . . . . | 50,000 | 44,000 |
| Overhead |  |  |
| Variable overhead . . . . . . . . | $275,000 |  |
| Fixed overhead. . . . . . . . . . | 50,000 |  |
| Total overhead . . . . . . . . . . | $325,000 | $305,000 |

1. Compute the standard overhead rate. *Hint:* Standard allocation base at 80% capacity is 25,000 DLH, computed as 50,000 units × 0.5 DLH per unit.

2. Compute the standard overhead applied.

3. Compute the total overhead variance.

---

**Exercise 8-18**
Volume and controllable variances  **P4**

Refer to the information from Exercise 8-17. Compute the overhead (1) volume variance and (2) controllable variance, and identify each as favorable or unfavorable. *Hint:* Compute total budgeted (flexible) overhead for 44,000 units.

---

**Exercise 8-19**
Overhead controllable and volume variances

**P4**

Blaze Corp. applies overhead on the basis of DLH and the standard amount per allocation base is 4 DLH per unit. For March, the company planned production of 8,000 units (80% of its capacity of 10,000 units) and prepared the following budget. The company actually operated at 90% capacity (9,000 units) in March and incurred actual total overhead costs of $81,700.

| Overhead Budget | 80% Capacity Level |
|---|---|
| Production (in units) . . . . . . . . . . . . . . . . . . | 8,000 |
| Budgeted variable overhead . . . . . . . . . . . | $32,000 |
| Budgeted fixed overhead. . . . . . . . . . . . . . | 48,000 |

1. Compute the standard overhead rate. *Hint:* Standard allocation base at 80% capacity is 32,000 DLH, computed as 8,000 units × 4 DLH per unit.

2. Compute the total overhead variance.

3. Compute the overhead controllable variance.

4. Compute the overhead volume variance.

---

**Exercise 8-20**
Controllable variance  **P4**

Kenshaw Company's flexible overhead budget at an actual activity level of 1,000 units shows $10,000 in variable overhead costs and $5,000 in fixed overhead costs. Actual total overhead is $13,000. Compute the controllable variance.

---

**Exercise 8-21**
Volume variance  **P4**

Shaw Co. produced 680 units. Its overhead allocation base is DLH and its standard amount per allocation base is 8 DLH per unit. Its standard overhead rate is $10 per DLH. The flexible overhead budget at an activity level of 680 units shows $26,000 in variable overhead costs and $30,000 in fixed overhead costs. Compute the volume variance.

Compute total overhead variance using the following information.

| | |
|---|---|
| Actual overhead for 10,000 units produced ........ | $44,000 |
| Standard overhead rate ...................... | $9 per DLH |
| Standard amount per allocation base (DLH) ........ | 0.5 DLH per unit |

**Exercise 8-22**
Total overhead variance
P4

Shawke Company's partially completed flexible overhead budget for the current period follows. This budget is based on its predicted activity of 50% of capacity. Complete its flexible overhead budgets for the current period using 1,000, 2,000, and 3,000 units of capacity.

**Exercise 8-23**
Flexible overhead budget
P1

| Flexible Overhead Budgets | | | | | |
|---|---|---|---|---|---|
| | Variable Amount per Unit | Total Fixed Cost | Flexible Budget at Capacity Level of | | |
| For Year Ended December 31 | | | 25% | 50% | 75% |
| Production (in units) ...................... | 1 unit | | 1,000 | 2,000 | 3,000 |
| Overhead | | | | | |
| Total variable overhead costs ............. | $12/unit | | | | |
| Total fixed overhead costs ............... | | $16,000 | | | |
| Total overhead ........................... | | | | | |

Shaw Inc. began this period with a budget for 1,000 units of predicted production. The budgeted overhead at this predicted activity follows. At period-end, total actual overhead was $92,000, and actual units produced were 900. The company applies overhead with a standard of 3 DLH per unit and a standard overhead rate of $30 per DLH.

**Exercise 8-24**
Controllable and volume variances
P4

| | |
|---|---|
| Variable overhead ..... | $50,000 |
| Fixed overhead ....... | 40,000 |
| Total overhead ........ | $90,000 |

**a.** Compute controllable variance.
**b.** Compute volume variance.

For May, Mariana Company planned production of 8,000 units (80% of its capacity of 10,000 units) and prepared the following overhead budget. The company applies overhead with a standard of 3 DLH per unit and a standard overhead rate of $3.85 per DLH.

**Exercise 8-25**
Overhead controllable and volume variances; overhead variance report
P4

| Overhead Budget | 80% Capacity Level |
|---|---|
| Production (in units) .............. | 8,000 |
| Budgeted overhead | |
| Variable overhead costs | |
| Indirect materials............. | $15,000 |
| Indirect labor ................ | 24,000 |
| Power...................... | 6,000 |
| Maintenance ................. | 3,000 |
| Total variable overhead costs .. | 48,000 |
| Fixed overhead costs | |
| Rent of building .............. | 15,000 |
| Depreciation—Machinery ...... | 10,000 |
| Supervisory salaries ......... | 19,400 |
| Total fixed overhead costs ..... | 44,400 |
| Total overhead ................ | $92,400 |

It actually operated at 90% capacity (9,000 units) in May and incurred the following actual overhead.

| Actual Overhead | 90% Capacity Level |
|---|---|
| Indirect materials . . . . . . . . . . . . . . . . . . . . . | $15,000 |
| Indirect labor . . . . . . . . . . . . . . . . . . . . . . . | 26,500 |
| Power . . . . . . . . . . . . . . . . . . . . . . . . . . . . | 6,750 |
| Maintenance . . . . . . . . . . . . . . . . . . . | 4,000 |
| Rent of building . . . . . . . . . . . . . . . . . . | 15,000 |
| Depreciation—Machinery . . . . . . . . . . . . . . | 10,000 |
| Supervisory salaries . . . . . . . . . . . . . . . . . . | 22,000 |
| Actual total overhead . . . . . . . . . . . . . . . . | $99,250 |

**1.** Compute the overhead controllable variance and identify it as favorable or unfavorable.

**2.** Compute the overhead volume variance and identify it as favorable or unfavorable.

**3.** Prepare an overhead variance report at the actual activity level of 9,000 units.

---

**Exercise 8-26**
Computing sales variances
**A1**

Mia Wiz sells computers. During May, it sold 350 computers at a $1,200 per unit price. The fixed budget for May predicted sales of 365 computers at a per unit price of $1,100.

**1.** Compute the sales price variance and identify it as favorable or unfavorable.

**2.** Compute the sales volume variance and identify it as favorable or unfavorable.

---

**Exercise 8-27ᴬ**
Computing total variable and fixed overhead variances
**P5**

Sedona Company set the following standard costs for one unit of its product for this year.

| | |
|---|---|
| Direct material (20 lbs. @ $2.50 per lb.) . . . . . . . . . . | $ 50 |
| Direct labor (10 hrs. @ $22.00 per DLH) . . . . . . . . . . | 220 |
| Variable overhead (10 hrs. @ $4.00 per DLH) . . . . . | 40 |
| Fixed overhead (10 hrs. @ $1.60 per DLH) . . . . . . . | 16 |
| Standard cost per unit . . . . . . . . . . . . . . . . . . . . . . | $326 |

The $5.60 ($4.00 + $1.60) total overhead rate per direct labor hour (DLH) is based on a predicted activity level of 37,500 units, which is 75% of the factory's capacity of 50,000 units per month. The following monthly flexible budget information is available.

| Flexible Budget | Flexible Budget at Capacity Level of | | |
|---|---|---|---|
| | 70% | 75% | 80% |
| Budgeted production (units) . . . . . . . . . . . | 35,000 | 37,500 | 40,000 |
| Budgeted direct labor (standard hours) . . . | 350,000 | 375,000 | 400,000 |
| Budgeted overhead | | | |
| Variable overhead . . . . . . . . . . . . . . . . . | $1,400,000 | $1,500,000 | $1,600,000 |
| Fixed overhead . . . . . . . . . . . . . . . . . . . | 600,000 | 600,000 | 600,000 |
| Total overhead . . . . . . . . . . . . . . . . . . . . | $2,000,000 | $2,100,000 | $2,200,000 |

During the current month, the company operated at 70% of capacity, direct labor of 340,000 hours were used, and the following actual overhead costs were incurred.

| Actual overhead | 70% of Capacity |
|---|---|
| Variable overhead . . . . . . . | $1,375,000 |
| Fixed overhead . . . . . . . . . | 628,600 |
| Total overhead . . . . . . . . . | $2,003,600 |

**1.** Compute the total variable overhead variance, and identify it as favorable or unfavorable.

**2.** Compute the total fixed overhead variance, and identify it as favorable or unfavorable.

Refer to the information from Exercise 8-27. Compute the following.

1. Variable overhead spending and efficiency variances.
2. Fixed overhead spending and volume variances.
3. Controllable variance.

**Exercise 8-28<sup>A</sup>**
Detailed overhead
variances  **P5**
**Check**  (1) Variable overhead:
Spending, $15,000 U

**connect**

Phoenix Company reports the following fixed budget. It is based on an expected production and sales volume of 15,000 units.

**PROBLEM SET A**

**Problem 8-1A**
Preparing and analyzing
a flexible budget

**P1**

| Fixed Budget For Year Ended December 31 | |
|---|---|
| Sales | $3,000,000 |
| Costs | |
| Direct materials | 975,000 |
| Direct labor | 225,000 |
| Sales staff commissions | 60,000 |
| Depreciation—Machinery | 300,000 |
| Supervisory salaries | 200,000 |
| Shipping | 225,000 |
| Sales staff salaries (fixed annual amount) | 250,000 |
| Administrative salaries | 411,000 |
| Depreciation—Office equipment | 195,000 |
| Income | $ 159,000 |

**Required**

1. Classify all items listed in the fixed budget as variable or fixed. For variable costs, determine their amounts per unit. For fixed costs, determine their amounts for the year.
2. Prepare flexible budgets (see Exhibit 8.3) at sales volumes of 14,000 and 16,000 units.
3. The company's business conditions are improving. One possible result is a sales volume of 18,000 units. Prepare a simple budgeted income statement (as in Exhibit 8.1) if 18,000 units are sold.

**Check**  (2) Budgeted income at 16,000 units, $260,000

Refer to the information in Problem 8-1A. Phoenix Company reports the following actual results. Actual sales were 18,000 units.

**Problem 8-2A**
Preparing a flexible budget
performance report

**P1**

| | |
|---|---|
| Sales (18,000 units) | $3,648,000 |
| Costs | |
| Direct materials | 1,185,000 |
| Direct labor | 278,000 |
| Sales staff commissions | 63,000 |
| Depreciation—Machinery | 300,000 |
| Supervisory salaries | 210,000 |
| Shipping | 261,500 |
| Sales staff salaries (fixed annual amount) | 268,000 |
| Administrative salaries | 419,000 |
| Depreciation—Office equipment | 195,000 |
| Income | $ 468,500 |

**Required**

Prepare a flexible budget performance report for the year.

**Problem 8-3A**

Flexible overhead budget; materials, labor, and overhead variances; and overhead variance report

P1   P2   P3   P4

Antuan Company set the following standard costs per unit for its product.

| | |
|---|---|
| Direct materials (6 lbs. @ $5 per lb.) . . . . . . . . | $ 30 |
| Direct labor (2 hrs. @ $17 per hr.) . . . . . . . . . | 34 |
| Overhead (2 hrs. @ $18.50 per hr.) . . . . . . . . . | 37 |
| Standard cost per unit . . . . . . . . . . . . . . . . . . | $101 |

The standard overhead rate ($18.50 per direct labor hour) is based on a predicted activity level of 75% of the factory's capacity of 20,000 units per month. Following are the company's budgeted overhead costs per month at the 75% capacity level.

| Overhead Budget (75% Capacity) | |
|---|---|
| **Variable overhead costs** | |
| Indirect materials . . . . . . . . . . . . . . . . . | $ 45,000 |
| Indirect labor . . . . . . . . . . . . . . . . . . . . | 180,000 |
| Power . . . . . . . . . . . . . . . . . . . . . . . . . . | 45,000 |
| Maintenance . . . . . . . . . . . . . . . . . . . . . | 90,000 |
| Total variable overhead costs . . . . . . . . | 360,000 |
| **Fixed overhead costs** | |
| Depreciation—Building . . . . . . . . . . . . . | 24,000 |
| Depreciation—Machinery . . . . . . . . . . . | 80,000 |
| Taxes and insurance. . . . . . . . . . . . . . . | 12,000 |
| Supervisory salaries . . . . . . . . . . . . . . . | 79,000 |
| Total fixed overhead costs. . . . . . . . . . . | 195,000 |
| Total overhead costs. . . . . . . . . . . . . . . . | $555,000 |

The company incurred the following actual costs when it operated at 75% of capacity in October.

| | | |
|---|---|---|
| Direct materials (91,000 lbs. @ $5.10 per lb.) . . . | | $ 464,100 |
| Direct labor (30,500 hrs. @ $17.25 per hr.) . . . . . | | 526,125 |
| Overhead costs | | |
| Indirect materials . . . . . . . . . . . . . . . . . . . . . . . | $ 44,250 | |
| Indirect labor . . . . . . . . . . . . . . . . . . . . . . . . . . | 177,750 | |
| Power . . . . . . . . . . . . . . . . . . . . . . . . . . . . . . . . | 43,000 | |
| Maintenance . . . . . . . . . . . . . . . . . . . . . . . . . . | 96,000 | |
| Depreciation—Building . . . . . . . . . . . . . . . . . . . | 24,000 | |
| Depreciation—Machinery . . . . . . . . . . . . . . . . . | 75,000 | |
| Taxes and insurance. . . . . . . . . . . . . . . . . . . . . | 11,500 | |
| Supervisory salaries . . . . . . . . . . . . . . . . . . . . . | 89,000 | 560,500 |
| Total costs . . . . . . . . . . . . . . . . . . . . . . . . . . . | | $1,550,725 |

**Required**

**Check**   (1) Budgeted total overhead at 13,000 units, $507,000

1. Prepare flexible overhead budgets (as in Exhibit 8.12) for October showing amounts of each variable and fixed cost at the 65%, 75%, and 85% capacity levels.

2. Compute the direct materials variance, including its price and quantity variances.

3. Compute the direct labor variance, including its rate and efficiency variances.

4. Prepare a detailed overhead variance report (as in Exhibit 8.16) that shows the variances for individual items of overhead.

**Problem 8-4A**

Computing materials, labor, and overhead variances

P3   P4

Trini Company set the following standard costs per unit for its single product.

| | |
|---|---|
| Direct materials (30 lbs. @ $4 per lb.) . . . . . . . . . . | $120 |
| Direct labor (5 hrs. @ $14 per hr.) . . . . . . . . . . . . . | 70 |
| Variable overhead (5 hrs. @ $8 per hr.) . . . . . . . . . | 40 |
| Fixed overhead (5 hrs. @ $10 per hr.) . . . . . . . . . . | 50 |
| Standard cost per unit . . . . . . . . . . . . . . . . . . . . . | $280 |

Overhead is applied using direct labor hours. The standard overhead rate is based on a predicted activity level of 80% of the company's capacity of 60,000 units per quarter. The following additional information is available.

| | Capacity Level | | |
| --- | --- | --- | --- |
| | 70% | 80% | 90% |
| Production (in units) . . . . . . . . . . . . . . . . . . . . . | 42,000 units | 48,000 units | 54,000 units |
| Standard direct labor hours (5 DLH/unit) . . . . . | 210,000 hrs. | 240,000 hrs. | 270,000 hrs. |
| Budgeted overhead (flexible budget) | | | |
|    Fixed overhead . . . . . . . . . . . . . . . . . . . . . . . | $2,400,000 | $2,400,000 | $2,400,000 |
|    Variable overhead . . . . . . . . . . . . . . . . . . . . . | $1,680,000 | $1,920,000 | $2,160,000 |

During the current quarter, the company operated at 90% of capacity and produced 54,000 units; actual direct labor totaled 265,000 hours. Units produced were assigned the following standard costs.

| | |
| --- | --- |
| Direct materials (1,620,000 lbs. @ $4 per lb.) . . . . . . . . . . | $ 6,480,000 |
| Direct labor (270,000 hrs. @ $14 per hr.) . . . . . . . . . . . . . | 3,780,000 |
| Overhead (270,000 hrs. @ $18 per hr.). . . . . . . . . . . . . . . | 4,860,000 |
| Standard (budgeted) cost. . . . . . . . . . . . . . . . . . . . . . . . . | $15,120,000 |

Actual costs incurred during the current quarter follow.

| | |
| --- | --- |
| Direct materials (1,615,000 lbs. @ $4.10 per lb.) . . . . . . . | $ 6,621,500 |
| Direct labor (265,000 hrs. @ $13.75 per hr.) . . . . . . . . . . | 3,643,750 |
| Fixed overhead . . . . . . . . . . . . . . . . . . . . . . . . . . . . . . . . | 2,350,000 |
| Variable overhead . . . . . . . . . . . . . . . . . . . . . . . . . . . . . . | 2,200,000 |
| Actual cost . . . . . . . . . . . . . . . . . . . . . . . . . . . . . . . . . . . . | $14,815,250 |

**Required**

**1.** Compute the direct materials variance, including its price and quantity variances.
**2.** Compute the direct labor variance, including its rate and efficiency variances.
**3.** Compute the overhead controllable and volume variances.

---

Refer to the information in Problem 8-4A.

**Required**

Compute these variances: (*a*) variable overhead spending and efficiency, (*b*) fixed overhead spending and volume, and (*c*) overhead controllable.

**Problem 8-5A**[A]
Expanded overhead variances

**P5**

---

Amada Company's standard cost system reports this information from its December operations.

| | |
| --- | --- |
| Standard direct materials cost. . . . . . . . . . . . . . | $100,000 |
|    Direct materials quantity variance . . . . . . . . | 3,000 U |
|    Direct materials price variance . . . . . . . . . . . | 500 F |
| Actual direct labor cost. . . . . . . . . . . . . . . . . . . | 90,000 |
|    Direct labor efficiency variance . . . . . . . . . . | 7,000 F |
|    Direct labor rate variance . . . . . . . . . . . . . . | 1,200 U |
| Actual overhead cost . . . . . . . . . . . . . . . . . . . . . | 375,000 |
|    Volume variance . . . . . . . . . . . . . . . . . . . . . | 12,000 U |
|    Controllable variance . . . . . . . . . . . . . . . . . | 9,000 U |

**Problem 8-6A**[A]
Recording and analyzing materials, labor, and overhead variances

**P6**

**Required**

**1.** Prepare December 31 journal entries to record the company's costs and variances for the month for (a) direct materials, (b) direct labor, and (c) overhead. Ignore the journal entry to close the variances.

*Analysis Component*

**2.** If management investigates all variances above $5,000, which variances will management investigate?

**PROBLEM SET B**

**Problem 8-1B**
Preparing and analyzing a flexible budget
**P1**

Toho Company reports the following fixed budget. It is based on an expected production and sales volume of 20,000 units.

| Fixed Budget<br>For Year Ended December 31 | |
| --- | ---: |
| Sales ............................................... | $3,000,000 |
| Costs | |
|     Direct materials ......................... | 1,200,000 |
|     Direct labor............................. | 260,000 |
|     Sales staff commissions ................. | 57,000 |
|     Depreciation—Machinery ................. | 250,000 |
|     Supervisory salaries..................... | 140,000 |
|     Shipping ................................ | 246,000 |
|     Sales staff salaries (fixed annual amount)..... | 160,000 |
|     Administrative salaries ................. | 422,000 |
|     Depreciation—Office equipment ........... | 140,000 |
| Income..................................... | $  125,000 |

**Required**

**1.** Classify all items listed in the fixed budget as variable or fixed. For variable costs, determine their amounts per unit. For fixed costs, determine their amounts for the year.

**Check**   (2) Budgeted income at 24,000 units, $372,400

**2.** Prepare flexible budgets (see Exhibit 8.3) at sales volumes of 18,000 and 24,000 units.

**3.** The company's business conditions are improving. One possible result is a sales volume of 28,000 units. Prepare a simple budgeted income statement (as in Exhibit 8.1) if 28,000 units are sold.

**Problem 8-2B**
Preparing and analyzing a flexible budget performance report
**P1**

Refer to the information in Problem 8-1B. Toho Company reports actual amounts for the year below. Actual sales were 24,000 units.

| | |
| --- | ---: |
| Sales (24,000 units) ....................... | $3,648,000 |
| Costs | |
|     Direct materials ......................... | 1,400,000 |
|     Direct labor............................. | 360,000 |
|     Sales staff commissions ................. | 60,000 |
|     Depreciation—Machinery ................. | 250,000 |
|     Supervisory salaries..................... | 219,000 |
|     Shipping ................................ | 214,000 |
|     Sales staff salaries (fixed annual amount) ... | 162,000 |
|     Administrative salaries ................. | 450,000 |
|     Depreciation—Office equipment .......... | 140,000 |
| Income .................................... | $  393,000 |

**Required**

Prepare a flexible budget performance report for the year.

Suncoast Company set the following standard costs per unit for its product.

**Problem 8-3B**
Flexible overhead budget;
materials, labor, and
overhead variances; and
overhead variance report
P1   P2   P3   P4

| | |
|---|---|
| Direct materials (4.5 lbs. @ $6 per lb.) . . . . . . . . . . . . . . . . . . | $27 |
| Direct labor (1.5 hrs. @ $12 per hr.). . . . . . . . . . . . . . . . . . . | 18 |
| Overhead (1.5 hrs. @ $16 per hr.) . . . . . . . . . . . . . . . . . . . . . | 24 |
| Standard cost per unit . . . . . . . . . . . . . . . . . . . . . . . . . . . . | $69 |

The standard overhead rate ($16 per direct labor hour) is based on a predicted activity level of 75% of the factory's capacity of 20,000 units per month. Following are the company's budgeted overhead costs per month at the 75% capacity level.

**Overhead Budget (75% Capacity)**

| | |
|---|---|
| Variable overhead costs | |
| Indirect materials . . . . . . . . . . . . . . . . . | $ 22,500 |
| Indirect labor . . . . . . . . . . . . . . . . . . . . . | 90,000 |
| Power . . . . . . . . . . . . . . . . . . . . . . . . . . | 22,500 |
| Maintenance . . . . . . . . . . . . . . . . . . . . . | 45,000 |
| Total variable overhead costs . . . . . . . . | 180,000 |
| Fixed overhead costs | |
| Depreciation—Building . . . . . . . . . . . . . | 24,000 |
| Depreciation—Machinery . . . . . . . . . . . | 72,000 |
| Taxes and insurance . . . . . . . . . . . . . . | 18,000 |
| Supervisory salaries . . . . . . . . . . . . . . . | 66,000 |
| Total fixed overhead costs. . . . . . . . . . . | 180,000 |
| Total overhead costs. . . . . . . . . . . . . . . | $360,000 |

The company incurred the following actual costs when it operated at 75% of capacity in December.

| | | |
|---|---|---|
| Direct materials (69,000 lbs. @ $6.10 per lb.) . | | $ 420,900 |
| Direct labor (22,800 hrs. @ $12.30 per hr.) . . . | | 280,440 |
| Overhead costs | | |
| Indirect materials . . . . . . . . . . . . . . . . . . . . . | $21,600 | |
| Indirect labor . . . . . . . . . . . . . . . . . . . . . . . . | 82,260 | |
| Power . . . . . . . . . . . . . . . . . . . . . . . . . . . . . . | 23,100 | |
| Maintenance . . . . . . . . . . . . . . . . . . . . . . . . | 46,800 | |
| Depreciation—Building . . . . . . . . . . . . . . . . | 24,000 | |
| Depreciation—Machinery . . . . . . . . . . . . . . | 75,000 | |
| Taxes and insurance . . . . . . . . . . . . . . . . . | 16,500 | |
| Supervisory salaries . . . . . . . . . . . . . . . . . | 66,000 | 355,260 |
| Total costs . . . . . . . . . . . . . . . . . . . . . . . . | | $1,056,600 |

**Required**

1. Prepare flexible overhead budgets (as in Exhibit 8.12) for December showing amounts of each variable and fixed cost at the 65%, 75%, and 85% capacity levels.
2. Compute the direct materials variance, including its price and quantity variances.
3. Compute the direct labor variance, including its rate and efficiency variances.
4. Prepare a detailed overhead variance report (as in Exhibit 8.16) that shows the variances for individual items of overhead.

**Check**   (1) Budgeted total
overhead at 17,000 units,
$384,000

**Problem 8-4B**
Computing materials,
labor, and overhead
variances

**P3　P4**

Kryll Company set the following standard costs per unit for its single product.

| | |
|---|---:|
| Direct materials (25 lbs. @ $4 per lb.) . . . . . . . . . . . . | $100 |
| Direct labor (6 hrs. @ $8 per hr.) . . . . . . . . . . . . . . . | 48 |
| Variable overhead (6 hrs. @ $5 per hr.) . . . . . . . . . . . | 30 |
| Fixed overhead (6 hrs. @ $7 per hr.) . . . . . . . . . . . . . | 42 |
| Standard cost per unit . . . . . . . . . . . . . . . . . . . . . . . | $220 |

Overhead is applied using direct labor hours. The standard overhead rate is based on a predicted activity level of 80% of the company's capacity of 60,000 units per quarter. The following additional information is available.

| | Capacity Level | | |
|---|---|---|---|
| | **70%** | **80%** | **90%** |
| Production (in units) . . . . . . . . . . . . . . . . . . . | 42,000 units | 48,000 units | 54,000 units |
| Standard direct labor hours (6 DLH/unit) . . . | 252,000 hrs. | 288,000 hrs. | 324,000 hrs. |
| Budgeted overhead (flexible budget) | | | |
| Fixed overhead . . . . . . . . . . . . . . . . . . . | $2,016,000 | $2,016,000 | $2,016,000 |
| Variable overhead . . . . . . . . . . . . . . . . . | $1,260,000 | $1,440,000 | $1,620,000 |

During the current quarter, the company operated at 70% of capacity and produced 42,000 units; direct labor hours worked were 250,000. Units produced were assigned the following standard costs.

| | |
|---|---:|
| Direct materials (1,050,000 lbs. @ $4 per lb.) . . . . . . . . . . . . | $4,200,000 |
| Direct labor (252,000 hrs. @ $8 per hr.) . . . . . . . . . . . . . . . . . | 2,016,000 |
| Overhead (252,000 hrs. @ $12 per hr.). . . . . . . . . . . . . . . . . . | 3,024,000 |
| Standard (budgeted) cost . . . . . . . . . . . . . . . . . . . . . . . . . . . | $9,240,000 |

Actual costs incurred during the current quarter follow.

| | |
|---|---:|
| Direct materials (1,000,000 lbs. @ $4.25 per lb.). . . . . . . . . . | $4,250,000 |
| Direct labor (250,000 hrs. @ $7.75 per hr.) . . . . . . . . . . . . . . | 1,937,500 |
| Fixed overhead. . . . . . . . . . . . . . . . . . . . . . . . . . . . . . . . . . . | 1,960,000 |
| Variable overhead . . . . . . . . . . . . . . . . . . . . . . . . . . . . . . . . . | 1,200,000 |
| Actual cost . . . . . . . . . . . . . . . . . . . . . . . . . . . . . . . . . . . . . . | $9,347,500 |

**Required**

1. Compute the direct materials variance, including its price and quantity variances.
2. Compute the direct labor variance, including its rate and efficiency variances.
3. Compute the overhead controllable and volume variances.

**Problem 8-5B**[A]
Expanded overhead
variances

**P5**

Refer to the information in Problem 8-4B.

**Required**

Compute these variances: (*a*) variable overhead spending and efficiency, (*b*) fixed overhead spending and volume, and (*c*) overhead controllable.

Kenya Company's standard cost system reports this information from its June operations.

| | |
|---|---:|
| Standard direct materials cost................ | $130,000 |
| Direct materials quantity variance........... | 5,000 F |
| Direct materials price variance ............. | 1,500 F |
| Actual direct labor cost..................... | 65,000 |
| Direct labor efficiency variance ............ | 3,000 F |
| Direct labor rate variance ................. | 500 U |
| Actual overhead cost ....................... | 250,000 |
| Volume variance ........................ | 12,000 U |
| Controllable variance ................... | 8,000 U |

**Problem 8-6B**[A]

Recording and analyzing materials, labor, and overhead variances

**P6**

**Required**

**1.** Prepare journal entries dated June 30 to record the company's costs and variances for the month for (*a*) direct materials, (*b*) direct labor, and (*c*) overhead. Ignore the journal entry to close the variances.

*Analysis Component*

**2.** Identify the variances that would attract the attention of a manager who uses management by exception. Describe what action(s) the manager should consider.

---

*This serial problem began in Chapter 1 and continues through most of the book. If previous chapter segments were not completed, the serial problem can begin at this point.*

**SP 8   Business Solutions**'s second-quarter 2022 fixed budget performance report for its computer furniture operations follows. The $156,000 budgeted expenses include $108,000 in variable expenses for desks and $18,000 in variable expenses for chairs, as well as $30,000 of fixed expenses. Actual fixed expenses total $31,000. Prepare a flexible budget performance report that shows variances between budgeted results and actual results. List fixed and variable expenses separately.

| | Fixed Budget | Actual Results | Variances |
|---|---:|---:|---:|
| Desk sales (in units) ........ | 144 | 150 | |
| Chair sales (in units) ........ | 72 | 80 | |
| Desk sales............... | $180,000 | $186,000 | $6,000 F |
| Chair sales.............. | 36,000 | 41,200 | 5,200 F |
| Total expenses ........... | 156,000 | 163,880 | 7,880 U |
| Income................. | $ 60,000 | $ 63,320 | $3,320 F |

**SERIAL PROBLEM**

Business Solutions

**P1**

**Check**   Variances: Fixed expenses, $1,000 U

---

**Tableau Dashboard Activities** expose students to accounting analytics using visual displays. These assignments (1) do not require instructors to know Tableau, (2) are accessible to introductory students, (3) do not require Tableau software, and (4) run in **Connect**. All are auto-gradable.

**Tableau DA 8-1 Quick Study**, Compute standard unit cost and total cost variance, **P2**—similar to QS 8-5 and 8-6.

**Tableau DA 8-2 Exercise**, Compute direct materials variances, **P3**—similar to QS 8-8 and Exercise 8-9.

**Tableau DA 8-3 Mini-case**, Compute direct labor and overhead variances, **P3**, **P4**—similar to Exercise 8-10 and Exercise 8-17.

**TABLEAU DASHBOARD ACTIVITIES**

## Accounting Analysis

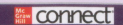

### COMPANY ANALYSIS
**A1**

**AA 8-1**  **Apple** offers sales price discounts to college students. Apple can use sales variance analysis to assess the effects of these sales discounts. Assumed data for a local college follow.

| MacBook Pro | Budgeted | Actual |
|---|---|---|
| Sales (units). . . . . . . . . . . . . . | 1,000 units | 1,150 units |
| Sales price per unit. . . . . . . . | $1,800 | $1,600 |

**Required**

1. Compute the sales price and sales volume variances and identify each as favorable or unfavorable.
2. Is the total sales variance favorable or unfavorable?

### COMPARATIVE ANALYSIS
**A1**

**AA 8-2**  **Apple** and **Google** use historical sales growth rates in estimating future sales. Data below are for one product segment for each company (Apple: iPhone; and Google: Apps, Hardware, and Cloud services).

| Sales ($ millions) | Apple, 1 Year Prior | Apple, 2 Years Prior | Sales ($ millions) | Google, 1 Year Prior | Google, 2 Years Prior |
|---|---|---|---|---|---|
| iPhone. . . . . . . . . | $164,688 | $149,337 | Apps, Hardware, and Cloud. . . | $19,906 | $15,503 |

**Required**

1. Compute the sales growth rate for each company's product segment. Which company's product segment grew at a faster rate?
2. Assume the sales growth rates computed in part 1 are expected to continue into the current year. Compute estimated sales for each company's product segment.

### EXTENDED ANALYSIS
**A1**

**AA 8-3**  **Samsung** offers sales price discounts on some products. Samsung can use sales variance analysis to assess the effects of these sales discounts. Assumed data for one model of a Samsung television follow.

| TV | Budgeted | Actual |
|---|---|---|
| Sales (units) . . . . . . . . . . . . . | 2,000 units | 3,000 units |
| Sales price per unit. . . . . . . . | $1,800 | $1,100 |

**Required**

1. Compute the sales price and sales volume variances and identify each as favorable or unfavorable.
2. Is the total sales variance favorable or unfavorable?

## Discussion Questions

1. What limits the usefulness of fixed budget performance reports for cost control?
2. Identify the two main purposes of a flexible budget.
3. What formula can be used to compute total budgeted costs at any activity level?
4. What type of analysis does a flexible budget performance report help management perform?
5. Describe the concept of *management by exception* and explain how standard costs help managers apply this concept to control costs.
6. What department is usually responsible for a direct labor rate variance? What department is usually responsible for a direct labor efficiency variance? Explain.
7. What is a price variance? What is a quantity variance?
8. What is the purpose of using standard costs?
9. In an analysis of fixed overhead cost variances, what is the volume variance?
10. In an analysis of overhead cost variances, what is the controllable variance and what causes it?
11. What is the standard overhead rate? How is it computed?

**12.** How are flexible budget reports useful in management by exception?

**13.** How can the manager of advertising sales at **Google** use flexible budgets to enhance performance?

**GOOGLE**

**14.** Can a retail store like **Apple** use variances in analyzing its operating performance? Explain.

**APPLE**

**15.** Assume that **Samsung** is budgeted to operate at 80% of capacity but actually operates at 75% of capacity. What effect will the 5% deviation have on controllable variance? Volume variance?

**Samsung**

**16.** List at least two positive and two negative features of standard costing systems.

---

## Beyond the Numbers

**BTN 8-1**   Setting standards is challenging. If standards are set too low, companies might purchase inferior products and employees might not work to their full potential. If standards are set too high, companies could be unable to offer a quality product at a profitable price and employees could be overworked. The ethical challenge is to set a high but reasonable standard. Assume that you are asked to set the standard materials price and quantity for a new warehouse robot, a technically advanced product. To properly set the price and quantity standards, you assemble a team of specialists to provide input.

**ETHICS CHALLENGE**

C1

**Required**

Identify three types of specialists that you would assemble to provide information to help set the materials price and quantity standards. Briefly explain why you chose each specialist.

---

**BTN 8-2**   The reason we use the words *favorable* and *unfavorable* when evaluating variances is made clear when we look at the closing of accounts. To see this, consider that (1) all variance accounts are closed at the end of each period (temporary accounts), (2) a favorable variance is always a credit balance, and (3) an unfavorable variance is always a debit balance. Write a half-page memorandum to your instructor with three parts that answer the following three requirements. (Assume that variance accounts are closed to Cost of Goods Sold.)

**COMMUNICATING IN PRACTICE**

P6

**Required**

**1.** Does Cost of Goods Sold increase or decrease when closing a favorable variance? Does income increase or decrease when a favorable variance is closed to Cost of Goods Sold? Explain.

**2.** Does Cost of Goods Sold increase or decrease when closing an unfavorable variance? Does income increase or decrease when an unfavorable variance is closed to Cost of Goods Sold? Explain.

**3.** Explain the meaning of a favorable variance and an unfavorable variance.

---

**BTN 8-3**   Many service industries link labor rate and time (quantity) standards with their processes. One example is the standard time to board an aircraft. The reason time plays such an important role in the service industry is that it is viewed as a competitive advantage: best service in the shortest amount of time. Although the labor rate component is difficult to observe, the time component of a service delivery standard is often readily apparent—for example, "Lunch will be served in less than five minutes, or it is free."

**TEAMWORK IN ACTION**

C1

**Required**

Break into teams and select two service industries for your analysis. Identify and describe all the time elements each industry uses to create a competitive advantage.

---

**BTN 8-4**   **True Fit**, as discussed in the chapter opener, uses a costing system with standard costs for direct labor and overhead costs. Two comments frequently are mentioned in relation to standard costing and variance analysis: "Variances are not explanations" and "Management's goal is not to minimize variances."

**ENTREPRENEURIAL DECISION**

C1

**Required**

Write a short memo (no more than one-half page) to Romney Evans, Jessica Murphy, and Bill Adler, cofounders of True Fit, interpreting these two comments in the context of their business.

---

Design Element: ©Danil Melekhin/Getty Images

# 9 Performance Measurement and Responsibility Accounting

## Chapter Preview

### RESPONSIBILITY ACCOUNTING

**P1** Performance evaluation

Controllable versus uncontrollable costs

Cost centers

**NTK 9-1**

### PROFIT CENTERS

**P2** Direct and indirect expense allocation

**P3** Departmental income statements

Departmental contribution to overhead

**NTK 9-2**

### INVESTMENT CENTERS

**A1** Return on investment

Residual income

**A2** Profit margin

Investment turnover

**NTK 9-3**

### SCORECARD AND TRANSFER PRICING

**A3** Balanced scorecard

**C1** Transfer pricing

**A4** Cash conversion cycle

**C2** *Appendix:* Joint costs

**NTK 9-4**

## Learning Objectives

### CONCEPTUAL

**C1** Explain transfer pricing and methods to set transfer prices.

**C2** *Appendix 9A*—Describe allocation of joint costs across products.

### ANALYTICAL

**A1** Analyze investment centers using return on investment and residual income.

**A2** Analyze investment centers using profit margin and investment turnover.

**A3** Analyze investment centers using the balanced scorecard.

**A4** Compute the number of days in the cash conversion cycle.

### PROCEDURAL

**P1** Prepare a responsibility accounting report using controllable costs.

**P2** Allocate indirect expenses to departments.

**P3** Prepare departmental income statements and contribution reports.

# Step by Step

*"Paso a paso . . . never stop going"*—
**SOFIA LUZ ECKRICH**

PASTORES, GUATEMALA—With a Mexican mother and American father, Sofia Luz Eckrich developed a passion for Mexican art and culture. This passion, combined with her college studies in sociology and international development, led Sofia to create **Teysha** (**Teysha.world**), a seller of shoes handcrafted by Latin American artisans. Sofia's goal: "share traditional arts and different cultures with the world in an ethical way."

"We don't follow a 'top-down' approach," declares Sofia. "We let local entrepreneurs create, using classic methods." Her business team offers advice on sales, quality control, and online presence. This decentralized structure encourages creativity and innovation.

Starting with just two shoe styles, Teysha now offers over 20 different styles and custom orders, and has expanded into home goods. This diverse product line requires Sofia to measure performance and allocate indirect expenses to control costs and grow her business.

Departmental income statements help Sofia analyze her shoe and home goods departments. She also looks at

Alyssa Greenberg

return on investment and residual income in making business decisions.

"Learn to love the numbers," Sofia asserts, "they hold the key to building a sustainable future!"

Sources: *Teysha website,* January 2021; *Hiplatina.com,* January 2018; *Fierce.com,* April 2018; *sofialuze.com,* January 2021

# RESPONSIBILITY ACCOUNTING

## Performance Evaluation

Many large companies are easier to manage if they are divided into smaller units, called *divisions, segments,* or *departments.* **Callaway Golf** uses two product lines, golf balls and golf clubs, while **Kraft Heinz** has both geographic and product lines. In these **decentralized organizations,** unit managers make decisions and top management then evaluates the performance of unit managers.

**Responsibility accounting** evaluates unit managers only on activities they can control. Methods of performance evaluation vary for cost centers, profit centers, and investment centers. Responsibility accounting divides a company into three types of *responsibility centers* and then measures their performances.

- **Cost center** incurs costs without generating revenues. The manufacturing departments of a manufacturer are cost centers. Kraft Heinz's Dover, Delaware, manufacturing plant is a cost center. Service departments such as office support and purchasing are also cost centers. *Cost center managers are evaluated on their success in controlling actual costs* compared to budgeted costs.

- **Profit center** generates revenues and incurs costs. Product lines are often evaluated as profit centers. Kraft Heinz's condiment product line is a profit center. *Profit center managers are evaluated on their success in generating income.* A profit center manager does not have the authority to make major investing decisions, such as the decision to build a new manufacturing plant.

- **Investment center** generates revenues and incurs costs, and its manager is responsible for major investing decisions. Kraft Heinz's chief operating officer for U.S. operations has the authority to make decisions such as building a new manufacturing plant. *Investment center managers are evaluated on their use of assets to generate income.*

**P1**

Prepare a responsibility accounting report using controllable costs.

## Controllable versus Uncontrollable Costs

Performance evaluations are best done using controllable costs.

- **Controllable costs** are costs a manager can determine or influence.
- **Uncontrollable costs** are costs not within the manager's control or influence.

For example, department managers rarely control their own salaries. However, they often control or influence items such as utilities and supplies used in their departments. Higher-level managers *can* control department manager salaries and other costs like rent and insurance.

A responsibility accounting system recognizes that control over costs is different for different levels of management as in the partial organization chart in Exhibit 9.1. The lines in this chart connecting the managerial levels reflect channels of authority. For example, the three department managers (Beverage, Food, and Service) are responsible for controllable costs incurred in their departments. These department managers report to the plant manager of the Western factory, who has overall control of department costs. The costs of the Western factory are reported to and controlled by the executive vice president (EVP) of U.S.A. operations, who reports to the president, who reports to the board of directors.

**EXHIBIT 9.1**

Responsibility Accounting Chart

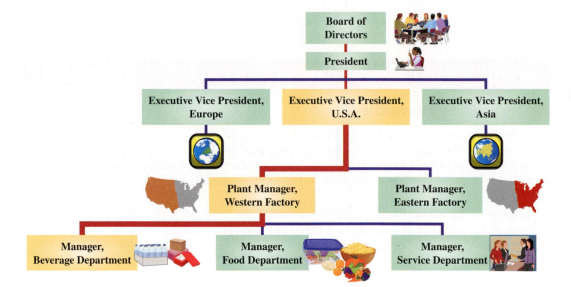

## Responsibility Accounting for Cost Centers

A **responsibility accounting performance report** lists actual costs that a manager is responsible for and their budgeted amounts. Analysis of differences between budgeted and actual amounts often results in corrective or strategic managerial actions.

Exhibit 9.2 shows performance reports for the three management levels identified in Exhibit 9.1. The Beverage department is a **cost center**. The Beverage department's total controllable costs are included in the controllable costs of the Plant Manager of the Western Factory. The controllable costs of this plant manager are included in the controllable costs of the Executive VP, U.S.A.

Lower-level managers have responsibility for more detailed costs. Higher-level managers are responsible for larger and broader costs. Reports to higher-level managers usually are less detailed because (1) lower-level managers are often responsible for detailed costs and (2) detailed reports can distract from key issues facing top managers.

**EXHIBIT 9.2**

Responsibility Accounting
Performance Reports

**Executive Vice President, U.S.A.**

| Controllable Costs | For July Budgeted | Actual | Over (Under) Budget |
|---|---|---|---|
| Salaries, plant managers ............... | $ 80,000 | $ 81,400 | $ 1,400 |
| Depreciation ........................... | 21,000 | 21,000 | 0 |
| Office costs ........................... | 29,500 | 28,800 | (700) |
| **Western factory** .................... | **276,700** | **279,500** | **2,800** ◄ |
| Eastern factory ....................... | 390,000 | 380,600 | (9,400) |
| Totals ................................. | $797,200 | $ 791,300 | $(5,900) |

**Plant Manager, Western Factory**

| Controllable Costs | For July Budgeted | Actual | Over (Under) Budget |
|---|---|---|---|
| Salaries, department managers .......... | $ 75,000 | $ 76,500 | $ 1,500 |
| Building rent ......................... | 10,600 | 10,600 | 0 |
| Insurance ............................. | 6,800 | 6,300 | (500) |
| **Beverage department** ................ | **79,600** | **79,900** | **300** |
| Food department ...................... | 61,500 | 64,200 | 2,700 |
| Service department ................... | 43,200 | 42,000 | (1,200) |
| **Totals** ............................. | **$276,700** | **$279,500** | **$ 2,800** |

**Manager, Beverage Department**

| Controllable Costs | For July Budgeted | Actual | Over (Under) Budget |
|---|---|---|---|
| Direct materials ...................... | $ 51,600 | $ 52,500 | $ 900 |
| Direct labor ......................... | 20,000 | 19,600 | (400) |
| Utilities ............................. | 8,000 | 7,800 | (200) |
| **Totals** ............................. | **$ 79,600** | **$ 79,900** | **$ 300** |

---

Following are Rios Co.'s annual budgeted and actual costs for the Western region's manufacturing plant. The plant has two departments: Motorcycle and ATV. The plant manager is responsible for all of the plant's costs (other than her own salary). Each department has a manager who is responsible for that department's direct materials, direct labor, and supplies used. Prepare responsibility accounting reports like those in Exhibit 9.2 for (1) each department manager and (2) the plant manager.

**NEED-TO-KNOW 9-1**

Responsibility Accounting

P1

| | Budgeted Amount | | Actual Amount | |
|---|---|---|---|---|
| | Motorcycle | ATV | Motorcycle | ATV |
| Direct materials.............. | $ 97,000 | $138,000 | $ 98,500 | $133,800 |
| Direct labor ................. | 52,000 | 105,000 | 56,100 | 101,300 |
| Department manager salaries.. | 60,000 | 56,000 | 60,000 | 56,000 |
| Rent........................ | 9,000 | 12,000 | 8,400 | 10,900 |
| Supplies used .............. | 5,000 | 11,000 | 7,000 | 8,000 |
| Totals...................... | $223,000 | $322,000 | $230,000 | $310,000 |

*Solution*  **1a.**

**Responsibility Accounting Performance Report**
**Department Manager, Motorcycle Department**

| | Budgeted | Actual | Over (Under) Budget |
|---|---|---|---|
| Direct materials............. | $ 97,000 | $ 98,500 | $1,500 |
| Direct labor ............... | 52,000 | 56,100 | 4,100 |
| Supplies used ............. | 5,000 | 7,000 | 2,000 |
| **Totals** ................... | **$154,000** | **$161,600** | **$7,600** |

**1b.**

| Responsibility Accounting Performance Report<br>Department Manager, ATV Department | | | |
|---|---|---|---|
| | **Budgeted** | **Actual** | **Over (Under) Budget** |
| Direct materials............ | $ 138,000 | $ 133,800 | $ (4,200) |
| Direct labor............... | 105,000 | 101,300 | (3,700) |
| Supplies used............. | 11,000 | 8,000 | (3,000) |
| **Totals** ................. | **$254,000** | **$243,100** | **$(10,900)** |

**2.**

| Responsibility Accounting Performance Report<br>Plant Manager, Western Region | | | |
|---|---|---|---|
| | **Budgeted** | **Actual** | **Over (Under) Budget** |
| Department manager salaries | $116,000 | $116,000 | $ 0 |
| Rent..................... | 21,000 | 19,300 | (1,700) |
| Motorcycle department ..... | **154,000** | **161,600** | 7,600 |
| ATV department ........... | **254,000** | **243,100** | (10,900) |
| Totals................... | $545,000 | $540,000 | $ (5,000) |

Do More: QS 9-3, QS 9-4,
E 9-1, E 9-2, P 9-1

# PROFIT CENTERS

When departments are organized as profit centers, responsibility accounting focuses on how well each department controlled costs *and* generated revenues. **Departmental income statements** are used to report profit center performance. When computing departmental income, we make two decisions for allocating expenses.

**P2**
_____

Allocate indirect expenses to departments.

1. How to allocate *indirect expenses* such as rent and utilities, which benefit several departments.
2. How to allocate *service department expenses* such as payroll and purchasing, which benefit several departments.

## Expenses

**Direct expenses** are costs readily traced to a department because they are incurred for that department's sole benefit. They are *not* allocated across departments. For example, the salary of an employee who works in only one department is a direct expense of that one department. Direct expenses are often, but not always, controllable costs.

   **Indirect expenses** are costs incurred for the joint benefit of more than one department; they cannot be readily traced to only one department. For example, if two or more departments share a single building, all enjoy the benefits of the expenses for rent, heat, and light.

   *Service department expenses* are costs that benefit more than one department; they cannot be readily traced to only one department. The *operating departments* that perform an organization's main functions, for example, manufacturing and selling, benefit from the work of *service departments*. Service departments do not generate revenues, but their support is crucial for operating department success.

## Expense Allocations

Indirect expenses and service department expenses are allocated to departments that benefit from them. Exhibit 9.3 shows a formula for cost allocation.

**EXHIBIT 9.3**

Cost Allocation Formula

> **Allocated cost = Total cost to allocate × Percentage of allocation base used**

**Allocating Indirect Expenses**    No standard rule for the "best" allocation base exists. Exhibit 9.4 shows commonly used bases for allocating indirect expenses.

| Indirect Expense | Common Allocation Bases |
|---|---|
| Supervisor salaries..... | Number of employees in department |
| Rent and utilities....... | Square feet of space occupied |
| Advertising .......... | Percentage of total sales |
| Insurance ............ | Value of insured assets |

## Allocating Service Department Expenses

Operating departments use service departments such as personnel, payroll, and purchasing. Exhibit 9.5 shows commonly used bases for allocating service department expenses.

| Service Department | Common Allocation Bases |
|---|---|
| Office................. | Number of employees or sales in department |
| Personnel and payroll ... | Number of employees in department |
| Purchasing ........... | Dollars of purchases or number of purchase orders processed |
| Maintenance .......... | Square feet of space occupied |

## Cost Allocation Demo

We demonstrate allocating costs by looking at cleaning services for a retail store (an indirect expense). An outside company cleans the retail store for a total cost of $800 per month. Management allocates this cost to the store's three departments based on the square feet that each department occupies. Exhibit 9.6 shows this allocation. The total cost to allocate is $800. Because the Jewelry department occupies 60% of the total floor space (2,400 square feet/4,000 square feet), it is allocated $480 (60% × $800) of the cleaning cost. Calculations are similar for other departments.

| Department | Department Square Feet | Percent of Total Square Feet | Cost Allocated to Department |
|---|---|---|---|
| Jewelry ........ | 2,400 | 60% (2,400/4,000) | $480 (60% × $800) |
| Repair ......... | 600 | 15  (600/4,000) | 120 (15% × $800) |
| Clothes ........ | 1,000 | 25  (1,000/4,000) | 200 (25% × $800) |
| Totals.......... | 4,000 | 100% | $800 |

Allocate a retailer's purchasing department's costs of $20,000 to its operating departments using each department's percentage of total purchase orders.

| Department | Number of Purchase Orders |
|---|---|
| Clothing................ | 250 |
| Health Care............. | 450 |
| Sporting Goods.......... | 300 |
| Total.................. | 1,000 |

*Solution*

| Department | Number of Purchase Orders | Percent of Total Purchase Orders | Cost Allocated to Department |
|---|---|---|---|
| Clothing......... | 250 | 25% (250/1,000) | $ 5,000 |
| Health Care...... | 450 | 45% (450/1,000) | 9,000 |
| Sporting Goods... | 300 | 30% (300/1,000) | 6,000 |
| Total............ | 1,000 | 100% | $20,000 |

Do More: QS 9-6, QS 9-7, QS 9-8, E-9-3, E-9-4, E-9-5

## Departmental Income Statements

Departmental income is computed using the formula in Exhibit 9.7.

**EXHIBIT 9.7**

Departmental Income

$$\begin{array}{c}\text{Departmental}\\\text{income}\end{array} = \begin{array}{c}\text{Department}\\\text{sales}\end{array} - \begin{array}{c}\text{Department direct}\\\text{expenses}\end{array} - \begin{array}{c}\text{Allocated indirect}\\\text{expenses}\end{array} - \begin{array}{c}\text{Allocated service}\\\text{department expenses}\end{array}$$

**P3**

Prepare departmental income statements and contribution reports.

We prepare departmental income statements using **Outdoor Gal** and its three departments. It has Purchasing, a service department, and two operating departments, Hiking and Camping.

Preparing departmental income statements involves three steps.

**Step** ①: Accumulate sales, direct expenses, and indirect expenses by department.

**Step** ②: Allocate indirect expenses to both service and operating departments.

**Step** ③: Allocate service department expenses to operating departments.

Exhibit 9.8 summarizes these steps in preparing departmental performance reports for cost centers and profit centers (links to the steps are coded with circled numbers *1* through *3*). The service department (Purchasing) is a **cost center**, so its performance is based on how well it controls direct department expenses. The operating departments (Hiking and Camping) are **profit centers**, and their performance is based on how well they generate departmental income.

**EXHIBIT 9.8**

Departmental Performance Reporting

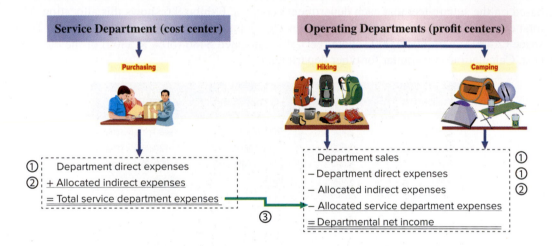

**Step 1:** We list sales, cost of goods sold, direct expenses, and indirect expenses for each department in Exhibit 9.9. The total for each expense is in the Expenses column.

**EXHIBIT 9.9**

Sales and Expenses Data

| OUTDOOR GAL<br>Sales and Expenses Data | | Service Department | Operating Departments | |
|---|---|---|---|---|
| **For Year Ended Dec. 31** | **Expenses** | **Purchasing** | **Hiking** | **Camping** |
| Sales | | $ 0 | $136,200 | $90,800 |
| Cost of goods sold | $148,000 | 0 | 78,000 | 70,000 |
| **Direct expenses** | | | | |
|   Salaries | 41,000 | 15,000 | 14,020 | 11,980 |
|   Depreciation—Equipment | 3,000 | 2,000 | 600 | 400 |
| **Indirect expenses** | | | | |
|   Rent | 12,000 | | | |
|   Advertising | 4,000 | | | |
| **Total expenses** | $208,000 | | | |

**Step 2:**    We allocate indirect expenses to all departments. We show this with the *departmental expense allocation spreadsheet* in Exhibit 9.10. Calculations follow for allocating Rent and Advertising. Direct expenses do not show an allocation base because they are not allocated.

**Allocating Rent**    Rent of $12,000 is allocated to all departments based on 9,000 square feet of space occupied.

| Department | Square Feet | Percent of Total | Allocated Cost |
|---|---|---|---|
| Purchasing . . . . | 1,800 | 20% (1,800/9,000) | $ 2,400 |
| Hiking . . . . . . . . | 2,700 | 30% (2,700/9,000) | 3,600 |
| Camping . . . . . . | 4,500 | 50% (4,500/9,000) | 6,000 |
| Total. . . . . . . . . | 9,000 | 100% | $12,000 |

**Allocating Advertising**    Advertising of $4,000 is allocated only to operating departments, based on sales. Service departments do not generate sales so they are not allocated advertising costs.

| Department | Sales* | Percent of Total | Allocated Cost |
|---|---|---|---|
| Hiking . . . . . . . . . . | $136,200 | 60% ($136,200/$227,000) | $2,400 |
| Camping . . . . . . . . | 90,800 | 40% ($90,800/$227,000) | 1,600 |
| Total. . . . . . . . . . . | $227,000 | 100% | $4,000 |

*Sales are from Exhibit 9.9.

**Step 3:**    We allocate service department expenses to operating departments. Service department expenses are not allocated to other service departments. The purchasing department has $19,400 of expenses to allocate to operating departments. This consists of $17,000 of direct expenses and $2,400 of indirect expenses (computed in step 2). Purchasing department expenses are allocated based on each operating department's number of purchase orders as follows.

| Department | Purchase Orders | Percent of Total | Allocated Cost |
|---|---|---|---|
| Hiking . . . . . . . . . . | 840 | 70% (840/1,200) | $13,580 |
| Camping . . . . . . . . | 360 | 30% (360/1,200) | 5,820 |
| Total. . . . . . . . . . . | 1,200 | 100% | $19,400 |

After service department costs are allocated, no expenses remain in the service department.

**EXHIBIT 9.10**

Departmental Expense Allocation Spreadsheet

| OUTDOOR GAL Departmental Expense Allocations | | | | | | |
|---|---|---|---|---|---|---|
| | | | | Allocation of Expenses to Departments | | |
| For Year Ended Dec. 31 | Allocation Base | Expenses | Purchasing | Hiking | Camping |
| **Direct expenses** (Exhibit 9.9) | | | | | |
| Salaries | | $41,000 | $15,000 | $14,020 | $11,980 |
| Depreciation—Equipment | | 3,000 | 2,000 | 600 | 400 |
| **Indirect expenses** (Step 2) | | | | | |
| Rent | Square feet of space | 12,000 | 2,400 | 3,600 | 6,000 |
| Advertising | Sales | 4,000 | 0 | 2,400 | 1,600 |
| Total department expenses | | 60,000 | 19,400 | 20,620 | 19,980 |
| **Service department expenses** (Step 3) | | | | | |
| Purchasing department | Purchase orders | | (19,400) | 13,580 | 5,820 |
| **Total expenses allocated to operating departments** | | $60,000 | $   0 | $34,200 | $25,800 |

**Prepare Income Statements:**    The departmental expense allocation spreadsheet is used to prepare departmental income statements. Exhibit 9.11 shows income statements for the two operating departments. This exhibit uses the spreadsheet in Exhibit 9.10 for expenses; information on sales and cost of goods sold comes from Exhibit 9.9. We do not prepare a departmental income statement for Purchasing because it is a service department and does not generate sales. After considering all costs, we see the Hiking department is most profitable.

**EXHIBIT 9.11**

Departmental Income Statements (operating departments)

| OUTDOOR GAL Departmental Income Statements | | | |
|---|---|---|---|
| For Year Ended December 31 | Hiking | Camping | Combined |
| Sales . . . . . . . . . . . . . . . . . . . . . . | $136,200 | $90,800 | $227,000 |
| Cost of goods sold . . . . . . . . . . | 78,000 | 70,000 | 148,000 |
| Gross profit . . . . . . . . . . . . . . . . | 58,200 | 20,800 | 79,000 |
| Expenses | | | |
|   Salaries . . . . . . . . . . . . . . . . | 14,020 | 11,980 | 26,000 |
|   Depreciation—Equipment . . . | 600 | 400 | 1,000 |
|   Rent . . . . . . . . . . . . . . . . . . . | 3,600 | 6,000 | 9,600 |
|   Advertising . . . . . . . . . . . . . . | 2,400 | 1,600 | 4,000 |
|   Share of purchasing expenses | 13,580 | 5,820 | 19,400 |
|   Total expenses . . . . . . . . . . . | 34,200 | 25,800 | 60,000 |
| **Income (loss)** . . . . . . . . . . . . . . | **$ 24,000** | **$(5,000)** | **$ 19,000** |

*Labels at left of exhibit:*
- Direct expenses — Salaries, Depreciation—Equipment
- Allocated indirect expenses — Rent, Advertising
- Allocated service department expenses — Share of purchasing expenses

## Departmental Contribution to Overhead

The Camping department shows a loss of $(5,000). Did its manager perform poorly? Should the Camping department be eliminated? To answer these questions, we compute **departmental contribution to overhead,** which is sales minus cost of goods sold and direct expenses. It is a performance measure based on *controllable* costs.

Exhibit 9.12 shows each department's contribution to overhead. For this purpose we use pre-allocation data from Exhibit 9.9. The Camping department's contribution to overhead is $8,420. Its manager performed better than its loss of $(5,000) would suggest. If the Camping department were eliminated, the company's income would decrease by $8,420. This is because the company's indirect expenses would not change and they would be allocated to the Hiking department. Based on contribution to overhead, the Camping department should not be eliminated.

**EXHIBIT 9.12**

Departmental Contribution to Overhead

| OUTDOOR GAL Departmental Contribution to Overhead | | | |
|---|---|---|---|
| For Year Ended December 31 | Hiking | Camping | Combined |
| Sales . . . . . . . . . . . . . . . . . . . . . . . . . . . . . | $136,200 | $90,800 | $227,000 |
| Cost of goods sold . . . . . . . . . . . . . . . . . . . . | 78,000 | 70,000 | 148,000 |
| Gross profit . . . . . . . . . . . . . . . . . . . . . . . . . | 58,200 | 20,800 | 79,000 |
| Direct expenses | | | |
|   Salaries . . . . . . . . . . . . . . . . . . . . . . . . . | 14,020 | 11,980 | 26,000 |
|   Depreciation—Equipment . . . . . . . . . . . . . . | 600 | 400 | 1,000 |
|   Total direct expenses . . . . . . . . . . . . . . . . | 14,620 | 12,380 | 27,000 |
| **Departmental contribution to overhead** . . . . | **$ 43,580** | **$ 8,420** | **$ 52,000** |

■ **Decision Insight**

**Performance Pay**    Bonuses are linked to performance measures that executives have some control over. Bonus plans are often based on exceeding a target return on investment or certain balanced scorecard indicators. The goal of bonus plans is to encourage executives to make decisions that increase company performance and value. ■

# INVESTMENT CENTERS

Investment center managers are responsible for revenues and costs, *and for investments in operating assets.* We describe financial and nonfinancial measures of investment center performance.

## Return on Investment and Residual Income

Assume a company operates two divisions as **investment centers**: LCD and Phone. The LCD division manufactures liquid crystal display (LCD) touch-screens and sells them for use in computers and smartphones. The Phone division sells smartphones. The table below shows current year income and average assets for the divisions.

**A1**_____

Analyze investment centers using return on investment and residual income.

| Division | LCD | Phone |
|---|---|---|
| Income . . . . . . . . . . . . . . . . . | $ 750,000 | $ 370,000 |
| Average assets . . . . . . . . . . . . | 2,500,000 | 1,850,000 |

**Return on Investment**    One measure to evaluate division performance is **return on investment (ROI),** also called *return on assets* (ROA). This measure is defined in Exhibit 9.13.

$$\text{Return on investment} = \frac{\text{Income}}{\text{Average assets}}$$

**EXHIBIT 9.13**

Return on Investment

Return on investment for the LCD division is 30%, computed as $750,000/$2,500,000. The Phone division's return on investment is 20%, computed as $370,000/$1,850,000. Management can use ROI as part of its performance evaluation. For example, actual ROI can be compared to target ROI or to the ROI for similar divisions.

**Residual Income**    Another way to evaluate division performance is to compute **residual income,** which equals income minus a target income (see Exhibit 9.14).

$$\text{Residual income} = \text{Income} - \text{Target income}$$

**EXHIBIT 9.14**

Residual Income

Assume management sets target income at 8% of average assets. (The target percentage is often the interest rate on financing.) Residual income for the LCD and Phone divisions follow. The LCD division earned more residual income than the Phone division.

| Division | LCD | Phone |
|---|---|---|
| Income . . . . . . . . . . . . . . . . . . . . . . . . . . . . . | $750,000 | $370,000 |
| Less target income: $2,500,000 × 8% . . . . | 200,000 | |
| $1,850,000 × 8% . . . . | | 148,000 |
| Residual income . . . . . . . . . . . . . . . . . . . . . | $550,000 | $222,000 |

Using residual income to evaluate division performance encourages division managers to accept opportunities that return more than the target income, thus increasing company value. For example, the Phone division might (mistakenly) not want to accept a new customer that will provide a 15% return on investment because that will reduce the Phone division's overall return on investment (20%, as shown above). However, the Phone division *should* accept this opportunity because the new customer would increase residual income by providing income above the target of 8% of assets.

### A2 _____

Analyze investment centers using profit margin and investment turnover.

## Profit Margin and Investment Turnover

We can further examine investment center (division) performance by splitting return on investment into two measures—profit margin and investment turnover—as in Exhibit 9.15.

**EXHIBIT 9.15**

Profit Margin and Investment Turnover

$$\text{Return on investment} = \text{Profit margin} \times \text{Investment turnover}$$

$$\text{Return on investment} = \frac{\text{Income}}{\text{Sales}} \times \frac{\text{Sales}}{\text{Average assets}}$$

- **Profit margin** measures the income per dollar of sales. It is shown as a percent. A higher profit margin indicates better performance.
- **Investment turnover** measures how efficiently an investment center generates sales from its assets. Higher investment turnover indicates better use of assets.

To demonstrate, the following table shows results from the LCD and Phone divisions.

|                   | LCD         | Phone       |
|-------------------|-------------|-------------|
| Sales ........... | $9,375,000  | $7,400,000  |
| Income.......... | 750,000     | 370,000     |
| Average assets ... | 2,500,000  | 1,850,000   |

Profit margin and investment turnover for these two divisions are computed in Exhibit 9.16. This means the LCD division makes 8 cents profit on each dollar of sales. The Phone division makes 5 cents profit on each dollar of sales. The Phone division (4.00 investment turnover) is more efficient in its use of assets than the LCD division (3.75 investment turnover). Management can use these measures to evaluate performance, determine strategy, and direct future investment.

**EXHIBIT 9.16**

Division Profit Margin and Investment Turnover

|                      |                               | LCD   | Phone |
|----------------------|-------------------------------|-------|-------|
| Profit margin:       | $750,000/$9,375,000 .....     | 8%    |       |
|                      | $370,000/$7,400,000 .....     |       | 5%    |
| Investment turnover: | $9,375,000/$2,500,000 ...     | 3.75  |       |
|                      | $7,400,000/$1,850,000 ...     |       | 4.00  |

Ariel Skelley/Blend Images LLC

### ■ Analytics Insight

**Customer ROI**   Marketing departments use data analytics to apply ROI at the customer level. *Customer lifetime value* (CLV) considers the costs of acquiring, retaining, and supporting customers. With this measure, companies can market to customers with a higher CLV, and thus increase ROI. **Amazon** used CLV to determine that its Prime members and Kindle owners spend more each year in comparison with other customers.

**Part A** The Media division of a company reports income of $600,000, average assets of $7,500,000, and a target income of 6% of average assets. Compute the division's (a) return on investment and (b) residual income.

*Solution*

**a.** $600,000/$7,500,000 = 8%     **b.** $600,000 − ($7,500,000 × 6%) = $150,000

**Part B** A division reports sales of $50,000, income of $2,000, and average assets of $10,000. Compute the division's (a) profit margin, (b) investment turnover, and (c) return on investment.

*Solution*

**a.** $2,000/$50,000 = 4%     **b.** $50,000/$10,000 = 5.0     **c.** $2,000/$10,000 = 20%

**NEED-TO-KNOW** 9-3

Return on Investment and Residual Income; Margin, Turnover, and Return on Investment

**A1**   **A2**

Do More: QS 9-12, QS 9-13, QS 9-15, E 9-9, E 9-10, E 9-11, E 9-12

## BALANCED SCORECARD AND TRANSFER PRICING

Evaluating performance solely on financial measures has limitations such as: (1) some managers might forgo profitable projects to keep their return on investment high, (2) residual income is less useful when comparing investment centers of different size, and (3) both return on investment and residual income can encourage managers to focus too heavily on short-term financial goals.

In response to such limitations, companies also use *nonfinancial* measures. **FedEx** tracks the percentage of on-time deliveries. **Penn** judges production managers on the percent of defective tennis balls manufactured. **Walmart**'s credit card screens often ask customers at checkout whether the cashier was friendly or the store was clean. **Coca-Cola** measures its water usage to enhance sustainability. This kind of information helps division managers run operations and helps top management evaluate division managers.

**A3**

Analyze investment centers using the balanced scorecard.

### Balanced Scorecard

The **balanced scorecard** is a system of performance measures, including nonfinancial measures, used to assess company and division manager performance. The balanced scorecard requires managers to think of their company from four perspectives.

1. **Customer:** What do customers think of us?
2. **Internal Processes:** Which operations are crucial to customers?
3. **Innovation/Learning:** How can we improve?
4. **Financial:** What do our owners think of us?

The balanced scorecard collects information on *key performance indicators* (KPIs) on each of the four perspectives. KPIs vary across companies. Exhibit 9.17 lists common KPIs on the balanced scorecard.

**Point:** A survey found that nearly 60% of global companies use some form of balanced scorecard.

**EXHIBIT 9.17**

Balanced Scorecard Performance Indicators

| Customer | Internal Processes | Innovation/Learning | Financial |
|---|---|---|---|
| • Customer satisfaction rating | • Defect rates | • Employee satisfaction | • Net income |
| • # of new customers | • Cycle time | • Employee turnover | • ROI |
| • % of on-time deliveries | • Product costs | • $ spent on training | • Sales growth |
| • % of sales from new products | • Labor hours per order | • # of new products | • Profit margin |
| • Time to fill orders | • Accident-free days | • # of patents | • Residual income |
| • % of sales returned | • Warranty claims | • $ spent on research | • Investment turnover |

After selecting KPIs, companies collect data on each indicator and compare actual amounts to target (goal) amounts. For example, a company might have a goal of filling 98% of customer orders within two hours. Results on this KPI help division managers in improving order fulfillment.

Exhibit 9.18 is an example of balanced scorecard reporting on the customer perspective for a retailer. This scorecard reports that 1.2% of all orders are returned. The color of the circles in the Signal column reveals whether the company is beating its goal (green), meeting its goal (gray), or not meeting its goal (red). The retailer is meeting or exceeding its goals on orders returned and customer satisfaction. However, the company received more customer complaints than was hoped for. A manager would combine this information with information from other performance indicators to improve customer service.

**EXHIBIT 9.18**

Balanced Scorecard
Reporting: Retailer

| KPI: Customer Perspective | Actual | Goal | Signal |
|---|---|---|---|
| Orders returned | 1.2% | 2% | 🟢 |
| Customer satisfaction rating | 9.5 of 10.0 | 9.5 | ⚪ |
| Number of customer complaints | 142 | 100 | 🔴 |

### ▪ Decision **Maker**

**CFO**    As CFO, your best division, based on ROI, reports a large decrease in employee satisfaction. Should you investigate reasons for employee dissatisfaction or ignore it because financial performance is superb? ▪    *Answer:* You should investigate. Lower employee satisfaction can lead to higher employee turnover and lower customer satisfaction, both of which can increase financial costs.

---

**NEED-TO-KNOW** 9-4

Balanced Scorecard

**A3**

Do More: QS 9-16, QS 9-17, E 9-17, E 9-18

Classify each of the performance measures below into the best balanced scorecard perspective to which it relates: customer (**C**), internal processes (**P**), innovation and learning (**I**), or financial (**F**).

**1.** On-time delivery rate
**2.** Accident-free days
**3.** Sustainability training workshops
**4.** Defective products made

**5.** Residual income
**6.** Patents applied for
**7.** Sales returns
**8.** Customer complaints

*Solution*

**1.** C    **2.** P    **3.** I    **4.** P    **5.** F    **6.** I    **7.** C    **8.** C

---

## Transfer Pricing

**C1** _____

Explain transfer pricing and methods to set transfer prices.

Divisions within a company sometimes do business with one another. For example, a separate division of **Harley-Davidson** manufactures the plastic and fiberglass parts used in its motorcycles. **Anheuser-Busch InBev**'s metal container division makes cans used in its brewing operations and also sells cans to soft-drink companies. A division of **Prince** produces strings used in tennis rackets made by Prince and other manufacturers.

The price used to record transfers of goods across divisions of the same company is called the **transfer price.** Transfer prices can be used in cost, profit, and investment centers.

Because these transfers are not with customers outside the company, the transfer price has no direct impact on *company income*. However, transfer prices can impact *division income* and, if set incorrectly, lead to bad decisions.

To illustrate the impact of alternative transfer prices on division income, consider a company who's LCD division makes touch-screens that are used in its Phone division or sold to outside customers. LCD's variable manufacturing cost is $30 per screen, and the market price is $80 per screen. There are two extremes for the transfer price.

- **Low Transfer Price** The *Phone division manager* wants to pay a *low* transfer price. The transfer price cannot be less than the $30 variable cost per screen, as any lower price would cause the LCD manager to lose money on each screen.
- **High Transfer Price** The *LCD division manager* wants to receive a *high* transfer price. The transfer price cannot be more than $80 per screen, as the Phone division manager will not pay more than the market price.

The transfer price must be between $30 and $80 per screen, and a negotiated price somewhere between these two extremes is reasonable—see the graphic below.

How do we determine the transfer price? The answer depends in part on whether the LCD division has excess capacity.

**No Excess Capacity**   If the LCD division can sell every screen it produces at a market price of $80 per screen, the LCD manager would not accept any transfer price less than $80. This is a **market-based transfer price**—one based on the market price of the good or service being transferred. Any transfer price less than $80 would cause the LCD manager to incur an unnecessary *opportunity cost* that would lower the division's income and hurt its manager's performance evaluation.

**Excess Capacity**   With excess capacity, LCD should accept any transfer price of $30 per unit or greater, and the Phone division would purchase screens from the LCD division. This would allow the LCD division to cover variable costs *and* some (or all) of its fixed costs and to increase company income. For example, if a transfer price of $50 per screen is used, the Phone manager will buy from LCD division because that price is below the $80 market price. For each screen transferred from LCD to Phone at $50, the LCD division receives a *contribution margin* of $20 (computed as $50 transfer price less $30 variable cost) to contribute toward recovering its fixed costs. This is called **cost-based transfer pricing.** Under this approach, the transfer price might be based on variable costs, total costs, or variable costs plus a markup.

**Transfer Pricing Used by Companies**

With excess capacity, division managers often negotiate a transfer price between variable cost per unit and market price per unit. The **negotiated transfer price** and resulting departmental performance reports reflect, in part, the negotiating skills of the respective division managers. This might not be best for overall company performance. Determining the transfer price under excess capacity is complex and is covered in advanced courses.

## CORPORATE SOCIAL RESPONSIBILITY

This chapter focused on performance measurement and reporting. Companies report on their sustainability performance in a variety of ways. One approach integrates sustainability metrics in the four balanced scorecard perspectives (customer, internal process, innovation and learning, and financial). Many key performance indicators address the internal process and innovation and learning perspectives. For example, **General Mills** reports on its environmental targets and progress in its annual corporate sustainability report. Exhibit 9.19 captures how this information might appear as part of a balanced scorecard report.

Some companies report the direct effects on income from a focus on sustainability. For example, **Target** recently started a *Made to Matter* department. To be sold in this department, brands must focus on consumer wellness and be committed to social responsibility. Target's *Made to Matter* department reported sales of over $1 billion in a recent year.

**Teysha**, this chapter's feature company, uses a labor-intensive production process. This provides jobs for local Latin Americans. "Every artisan we work with receives fair trade wages and consistent work," explains Sofia Luz Eckrich, owner. While focused on the "people" aspect of the triple bottom line, Teysha fills a niche by bringing unique products to market.

Alyssa Greenberg

**EXHIBIT 9.19**

Balanced Scorecard—
Sustainability

| KPI: Internal Process Perspective | Actual Reduction | Goal Reduction | Signal |
|---|---|---|---|
| Emissions | 23% | 20% | 🟢 |
| Energy usage | 10% | 20% | 🔴 |
| Solid waste | 38% | 50% | 🔴 |
| Fuel | 25% | 35% | 🔴 |

---

**Decision Analysis**  **Cash Conversion Cycle**

## A4

Compute the number of days in the cash conversion cycle.

Effectively managing working capital is important for businesses to survive and profit. For example, lean manufacturers try to reduce the time from paying for raw materials (cash outflow) to collecting on credit sales from customers (cash inflow). Measures based on accounts receivable, accounts payable, and inventory are used to evaluate performance on each of these separate dimensions. These measures can be combined to show how a company manages its working capital. The **cash conversion cycle,** or *cash-to-cash cycle,* measures the average time it takes to convert cash outflows into cash inflows. It is defined in Exhibit 9.20.

**EXHIBIT 9.20**

Cash Conversion Cycle

$$\text{Cash conversion cycle} = \frac{\text{Days' sales in}}{\text{accounts receivable}} + \frac{\text{Days' sales in}}{\text{inventory}} - \frac{\text{Days' payable}}{\text{outstanding}}$$

| Formulas for Components of Cash Conversion Cycle | |
|---|---|
| Days' sales in accounts receivable | $= \dfrac{\text{Accounts receivable, net}}{\text{Net sales}} \times 365$ |
| Days' sales in inventory | $= \dfrac{\text{Inventory}}{\text{Cost of goods sold}} \times 365$ |
| Days' payable outstanding (*Days' sales in accounts payable*) | $= \dfrac{\text{Accounts payable}}{\text{Cost of goods sold}} \times 365$ |

Exhibit 9.21 shows these calculations for **General Mills**, a food processor.

| $ millions | Current year | Prior year |
|---|---|---|
| Accounts receivable, net.................... | $ 1,430 | $ 1,361 |
| Net sales................................... | $15,620 | $16,563 |
| **①  Days' sales in accounts receivable** .......... | **33 days** | **30 days** |
| Inventory .................................. | $ 1,484 | $ 1,414 |
| Cost of goods sold.......................... | $10,056 | $10,734 |
| **②  Days' sales in inventory** ................... | **54 days** | **48 days** |
| Accounts payable........................... | $ 2,120 | $ 2,047 |
| Cost of goods sold.......................... | $10,056 | $10,734 |
| **③  Days' payable outstanding**.................. | **77 days** | **70 days** |
| **Cash conversion cycle** (1) + (2) − (3)......... | **10 days** | **8 days** |

**EXHIBIT 9.21**

Cash Conversion Cycle Applied

**Point:** Calculations rounded to the nearest day.

General Mills's cash conversion cycle is 10 days in the current year and 8 days in the prior year. This is a short period and indicates the company efficiently manages its cash. For comparison, the American Productivity and Quality Center (APQC) reports an average cash conversion cycle of 45 days. The most efficient companies report cash conversion cycles of 30 days or less, while the least efficient take over 80 days to convert cash outflows to cash inflows.

If the cash conversion cycle is too long, companies do not have use of that money and risk missing investment opportunities. To speed up the cash conversion cycle companies can:

- Offer customers fewer days to pay.
- Offer customers discounts for prompt payment.
- Adopt lean principles to reduce inventory.
- Negotiate longer times to pay suppliers.

Gamer's Haven is a computer store that has five departments. Three are operating departments (Hardware, Software, and Repairs) and two are service departments (Office and Purchasing).

**NEED-TO-KNOW 9-5**

**COMPREHENSIVE**

Departmental Cost Allocations and Income Statements

| | Office | Purchasing | Hardware | Software | Repairs |
|---|---|---|---|---|---|
| Sales ............... | — | — | $960,000 | $600,000 | $840,000 |
| Cost of goods sold .... | — | — | 500,000 | 300,000 | 200,000 |
| Direct expenses | | | | | |
| Salaries .......... | $60,000 | $45,000 | 80,000 | 25,000 | 325,000 |
| Depreciation ...... | 6,000 | 7,200 | 33,000 | 4,200 | 9,600 |
| Supplies used...... | 15,000 | 10,000 | 10,000 | 2,000 | 25,000 |

To prepare departmental income statements, indirect expenses must be allocated across five departments. Then service department expenses must be allocated to the three operating departments. Allocation information follows.

| | Total Cost | Allocation Basis |
|---|---|---|
| **Indirect expenses** | | |
| Rent................. | $150,000 | Square feet occupied |
| Utilities ............... | 50,000 | Square feet occupied |
| Advertising ........... | 125,000 | Dollars of sales |
| Insurance ............ | 30,000 | Value of insured assets |
| **Service department expenses** | | |
| Office ............... | ?* | Number of employees |
| Purchasing ........... | ? | Number of purchases |

*Equals service department direct expenses plus allocated indirect expenses (shown next).

The following additional information is obtained for indirect expense allocations.

| Department | Square Feet | Sales | Insured Assets | Employees | Number of Purchases |
|---|---|---|---|---|---|
| Office........... | 500 | | $ 60,000 | | |
| Purchasing ...... | 500 | | 72,000 | | |
| Hardware ....... | 4,000 | $ 960,000 | 330,000 | 5 | 2,000 |
| Software ........ | 3,000 | 600,000 | 42,000 | 5 | 1,200 |
| Repairs ......... | 2,000 | 840,000 | 96,000 | 10 | 800 |
| Totals........... | 10,000 | $2,400,000 | $600,000 | 20 | 4,000 |

### Required

**1.** Prepare a departmental expense allocation spreadsheet.
**2.** Prepare a departmental income statement for each operating department and for all operating departments combined. Refer to Exhibit 9.11.
**3.** Prepare a departmental contribution to overhead report. Refer to Exhibit 9.12.

### SOLUTION

**1.** Allocations of the four indirect expenses across the departments.

| Rent | Square Feet | Percent of Total | Allocated Cost |
|---|---|---|---|
| Office........... | 500 | 5% | $ 7,500 |
| Purchasing ...... | 500 | 5 | 7,500 |
| Hardware ....... | 4,000 | 40 | 60,000 |
| Software ........ | 3,000 | 30 | 45,000 |
| Repairs ......... | 2,000 | 20 | 30,000 |
| Totals........... | 10,000 | 100% | $150,000 |

| Utilities | Square Feet | Percent of Total | Allocated Cost |
|---|---|---|---|
| Office........... | 500 | 5% | $ 2,500 |
| Purchasing ...... | 500 | 5 | 2,500 |
| Hardware ....... | 4,000 | 40 | 20,000 |
| Software ........ | 3,000 | 30 | 15,000 |
| Repairs ......... | 2,000 | 20 | 10,000 |
| Totals........... | 10,000 | 100% | $50,000 |

| Advertising | Sales Dollars | Percent of Total | Allocated Cost |
|---|---|---|---|
| Hardware ..... | $ 960,000 | 40% | $ 50,000 |
| Software ...... | 600,000 | 25 | 31,250 |
| Repairs ....... | 840,000 | 35 | 43,750 |
| Totals......... | $2,400,000 | 100% | $125,000 |

| Insurance | Assets Insured | Percent of Total | Allocated Cost |
|---|---|---|---|
| Office............ | $ 60,000 | 10% | $ 3,000 |
| Purchasing ....... | 72,000 | 12 | 3,600 |
| Hardware ........ | 330,000 | 55 | 16,500 |
| Software ......... | 42,000 | 7 | 2,100 |
| Repairs .......... | 96,000 | 16 | 4,800 |
| Totals........... | $600,000 | 100% | $30,000 |

Allocations of service department expenses to the three operating departments.

| Office Allocations to | Employees | Percent of Total | Allocated Cost |
|---|---|---|---|
| Hardware . . . . . . | 5 | 25% | $23,500 |
| Software . . . . . . . | 5 | 25 | 23,500 |
| Repairs . . . . . . . . | 10 | 50 | 47,000 |
| Totals. . . . . . . . . | 20 | 100% | $94,000* |

| Purchasing Allocations to | Number of Purchases | Percent of Total | Allocated Cost |
|---|---|---|---|
| Hardware . . . . . . | 2,000 | 50% | $37,900 |
| Software . . . . . . . | 1,200 | 30 | 22,740 |
| Repairs . . . . . . . . | 800 | 20 | 15,160 |
| Totals. . . . . . . . . | 4,000 | 100% | $75,800** |

*$81,000 direct expenses + $7,500 rent + $2,500 utilities + $3,000 insurance

**$62,200 direct expenses + $7,500 rent + $2,500 utilities + $3,600 insurance

| Departmental Expense Allocations | | | | | | | |
|---|---|---|---|---|---|---|---|
| For Year Ended Dec. 31 | Allocation Base | Expenses | Office | Purchasing | Hardware | Software | Repairs |
| **Direct expenses** | | | | | | | |
| Salaries | | $ 535,000 | $60,000 | $45,000 | $ 80,000 | $ 25,000 | $325,000 |
| Depreciation | | 60,000 | 6,000 | 7,200 | 33,000 | 4,200 | 9,600 |
| Supplies used | | 62,000 | 15,000 | 10,000 | 10,000 | 2,000 | 25,000 |
| **Indirect expenses** | | | | | | | |
| Rent | Square ft. | 150,000 | 7,500 | 7,500 | 60,000 | 45,000 | 30,000 |
| Utilities | Square ft. | 50,000 | 2,500 | 2,500 | 20,000 | 15,000 | 10,000 |
| Advertising | Sales | 125,000 | | | 50,000 | 31,250 | 43,750 |
| Insurance | Assets | 30,000 | 3,000 | 3,600 | 16,500 | 2,100 | 4,800 |
| Total expenses | | 1,012,000 | 94,000 | 75,800 | 269,500 | 124,550 | 448,150 |
| **Service department expenses** | | | | | | | |
| Office department | Employees | | (94,000) | | 23,500 | 23,500 | 47,000 |
| Purchasing department | Purchases | | | (75,800) | 37,900 | 22,740 | 15,160 |
| **Total expenses allocated to operating departments** | | $1,012,000 | $      0 | $      0 | $330,900 | $170,790 | $510,310 |

**2.** Departmental income statements.

| Departmental Income Statements | | | | |
|---|---|---|---|---|
| For Year Ended December 31 | Hardware | Software | Repairs | Combined |
| Sales . . . . . . . . . . . . . . . . . . . . . . . . . . | $ 960,000 | $ 600,000 | $ 840,000 | $2,400,000 |
| Cost of goods sold . . . . . . . . . . . . . . . . | 500,000 | 300,000 | 200,000 | 1,000,000 |
| Gross profit . . . . . . . . . . . . . . . . . . . . . | 460,000 | 300,000 | 640,000 | 1,400,000 |
| Expenses | | | | |
| Salaries. . . . . . . . . . . . . . . . . . . . . . | 80,000 | 25,000 | 325,000 | 430,000 |
| Depreciation. . . . . . . . . . . . . . . . . . . | 33,000 | 4,200 | 9,600 | 46,800 |
| Supplies used. . . . . . . . . . . . . . . . . . | 10,000 | 2,000 | 25,000 | 37,000 |
| Rent. . . . . . . . . . . . . . . . . . . . . . . . . | 60,000 | 45,000 | 30,000 | 135,000 |
| Utilities . . . . . . . . . . . . . . . . . . . . . . | 20,000 | 15,000 | 10,000 | 45,000 |
| Advertising . . . . . . . . . . . . . . . . . . . | 50,000 | 31,250 | 43,750 | 125,000 |
| Insurance . . . . . . . . . . . . . . . . . . . . | 16,500 | 2,100 | 4,800 | 23,400 |
| Share of office expenses . . . . . . . . . . | 23,500 | 23,500 | 47,000 | 94,000 |
| Share of purchasing expenses . . . . . | 37,900 | 22,740 | 15,160 | 75,800 |
| Total expenses . . . . . . . . . . . . . . . . . | 330,900 | 170,790 | 510,310 | 1,012,000 |
| **Income** . . . . . . . . . . . . . . . . . . . . . . . | **$129,100** | **$129,210** | **$129,690** | **$ 388,000** |

**3.** Departmental contribution to overhead.

| Departmental Contribution to Overhead | | | | |
|---|---|---|---|---|
| For Year Ended December 31 | Hardware | Software | Repairs | Combined |
| Sales ..................................... | $ 960,000 | $ 600,000 | $ 840,000 | $2,400,000 |
| Cost of goods sold ......................... | 500,000 | 300,000 | 200,000 | 1,000,000 |
| Gross profit................................ | 460,000 | 300,000 | 640,000 | 1,400,000 |
| Direct expenses | | | | |
|   Salaries................................. | 80,000 | 25,000 | 325,000 | 430,000 |
|   Depreciation............................. | 33,000 | 4,200 | 9,600 | 46,800 |
|   Supplies used............................ | 10,000 | 2,000 | 25,000 | 37,000 |
|   Total direct expenses.................... | 123,000 | 31,200 | 359,600 | 513,800 |
| Departmental contribution to overhead ..... | $337,000 | $268,800 | $280,400 | $ 886,200 |

# 9A    Joint Costs and Their Allocation

**C2**

Describe allocation of joint costs across products.

Some manufacturing processes involve **joint costs,** which are costs incurred to produce or purchase two or more products at the same time. For example, a dairy company incurs joint costs when it processes raw milk, as shown in Exhibit 9A.1. The joint costs are the costs to process and pasteurize milk. After milk is pasteurized, any further processing costs are not joint costs.

When management wishes to estimate the costs of individual products, joint costs must be allocated to these joint products. Financial statements prepared according to GAAP also must assign joint costs to products. The preferred approach is the *value basis,* which allocates a joint cost in proportion to the sales value of the output produced by the process at the "split-off point"; see Exhibit 9A.1. The split-off point is the point at which separate products can be identified.

**Value Basis Allocation of Joint Costs**    Exhibit 9A.2 illustrates the value basis method of allocation. It determines the percents of the $30,000 total cost allocated to each product by the ratio of each product's sales value at the split-off point to the $50,000 total sales value. Whole milk receives 24% of the total cost ($12,000/$50,000). This means it is allocated $7,200 (24% × $30,000) of cost and earns $4,800 ($12,000 − $7,200) of gross profit.

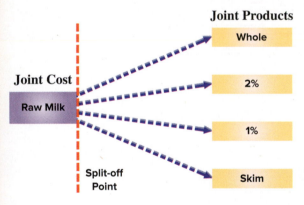

**EXHIBIT 9A.1**

Joint Products from Raw Milk

An outcome of value basis allocation is that *each* type of milk produces exactly the same 40% gross profit at the split-off point. This 40% rate equals the gross profit rate from selling all types of milk made from the raw milk for a combined price of $50,000. It is this closer matching of cost and revenues that makes the value basis allocation of joint costs a popular method of joint cost allocation.

**EXHIBIT 9A.2**

Allocating Joint Costs on a Value Basis

| Type of Milk | Sales Value | Percent of Total | Allocated Cost | Gross Profit |
|---|---|---|---|---|
| Whole ........ | $12,000 | 24% | $ 7,200 | $ 4,800 |
| 2% .......... | 18,000 | 36 | 10,800 | 7,200 |
| 1% .......... | 16,000 | 32 | 9,600 | 6,400 |
| Skim ........ | 4,000 | 8 | 2,400 | 1,600 |
| Totals........ | $50,000 | 100% | $30,000 | $20,000 |

## Summary: Cheat Sheet

## RESPONSIBILITY ACCOUNTING

**Cost center:** A center that incurs costs but generates no revenues.

**Profit center:** A center that incurs costs *and* generates revenues.

**Investment center:** A center that incurs costs *and* generates revenues, and where managers are responsible for center investments.

**Controllable costs:** Manager can control or influence these costs.

**Uncontrollable costs:** Costs not within manager's control or influence.

## PROFIT CENTERS

**Direct expenses:** Can be readily traced to departments; *not* allocated.

**Indirect expenses:** Incurred for joint benefit of more than one department; *must be* allocated.

### Cost allocation

$$\text{Allocated cost} = \text{Total cost to allocate} \times \text{Percentage of allocation base used}$$

**Indirect expenses.** Allocate to all departments. *Example:* $12,000 of rent allocated based on 9,000 square feet occupied.

| Department | Square Feet | Percent of Total | Allocated Cost |
|---|---|---|---|
| Purchasing .... | 1,800 | 20% (1,800/9,000) | $ 2,400 |
| Hiking ........ | 2,700 | 30% (2,700/9,000) | 3,600 |
| Camping ...... | 4,500 | 50% (4,500/9,000) | 6,000 |
| Total.......... | 9,000 | 100% | $12,000 |

**Service department expenses.** Allocate to operating departments. *Example:* $19,400 of purchasing expenses allocated to Operating departments.

| Department | Purchase Orders | Percent of Total | Allocated Cost |
|---|---|---|---|
| Hiking ........ | 840 | 70% (840/1,200) | $13,580 |
| Camping ...... | 360 | 30% (360/1,200) | 5,820 |
| Total.......... | 1,200 | 100% | $19,400 |

### Departmental income statement

$$\begin{array}{c} \text{Departmental} \\ \text{income} \end{array} = \begin{array}{c} \text{Department} \\ \text{sales} \end{array} - \begin{array}{c} \text{Department direct} \\ \text{expenses} \end{array} - \begin{array}{c} \text{Allocated indirect} \\ \text{expenses} \end{array} - \begin{array}{c} \text{Allocated service} \\ \text{department expenses} \end{array}$$

**OUTDOOR GAL**
**Departmental Income Statements**

| For Year Ended December 31 | Hiking | Camping | Combined |
|---|---|---|---|
| Sales ..................... | $136,200 | $90,800 | $227,000 |
| Cost of goods sold ........... | 78,000 | 70,000 | 148,000 |
| Gross profit ................. | 58,200 | 20,800 | 79,000 |
| Expenses | | | |
| Salaries ................ | 14,020 | 11,980 | 26,000 |
| Depreciation—Equipment ... | 600 | 400 | 1,000 |
| Rent .................... | 3,600 | 6,000 | 9,600 |
| Advertising .............. | 2,400 | 1,600 | 4,000 |
| Share of purchasing expenses | 13,580 | 5,820 | 19,400 |
| Total expenses ............. | 34,200 | 25,800 | 60,000 |
| Income (loss).............. | $ 24,000 | $(5,000) | $ 19,000 |

### Departmental contribution to overhead

**OUTDOOR GAL**
**Departmental Contribution to Overhead**

| For Year Ended December 31 | Hiking | Camping | Combined |
|---|---|---|---|
| Sales ..................................... | $136,200 | $90,800 | $227,000 |
| Cost of goods sold ...................... | 78,000 | 70,000 | 148,000 |
| Gross profit ............................ | 58,200 | 20,800 | 79,000 |
| Direct expenses | | | |
| Salaries............................ | 14,020 | 11,980 | 26,000 |
| Depreciation—Equipment .............. | 600 | 400 | 1,000 |
| Total direct expenses................. | 14,620 | 12,380 | 27,000 |
| Departmental contribution to overhead .... | $ 43,580 | $ 8,420 | $ 52,000 |

## INVESTMENT CENTERS

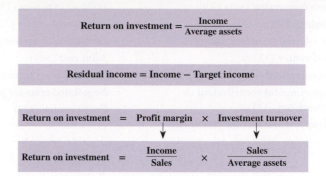

$$\text{Return on investment} = \frac{\text{Income}}{\text{Average assets}}$$

$$\text{Residual income} = \text{Income} - \text{Target income}$$

$$\text{Return on investment} = \text{Profit margin} \times \text{Investment turnover}$$

$$\text{Return on investment} = \frac{\text{Income}}{\text{Sales}} \times \frac{\text{Sales}}{\text{Average assets}}$$

## BALANCED SCORECARD & TRANSFER PRICING

**Balanced scorecard:** System of performance measures.

Customers: What do they think of us?

Internal processes: Which are crucial to customers?

Innovation/learning: How can we improve?

Financial: What do owners think of us?

**Transfer price:** Price set on transfers of goods across divisions.

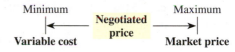

Minimum                                      Maximum

**Negotiated price**

**Variable cost**                            **Market price**

**Cash conversion cycle:** Efficiency measure of cash management.

$$\begin{array}{c} \text{Days' sales in} \\ \text{accounts receivable} \end{array} + \begin{array}{c} \text{Days' sales in} \\ \text{inventory} \end{array} - \begin{array}{c} \text{Days' payable} \\ \text{outstanding} \end{array}$$

$$\text{Days' sales in accounts receivable} = \frac{\text{Accounts receivable, net}}{\text{Net sales}} \times 365$$

$$\text{Days' sales in inventory} = \frac{\text{Inventory}}{\text{Cost of goods sold}} \times 365$$

$$\text{Days' payable outstanding} = \frac{\text{Accounts payable}}{\text{Cost of goods sold}} \times 365$$

## Key Terms

| | | |
|---|---|---|
| Balanced scorecard (337) | Direct expenses (330) | Profit margin (336) |
| Cash conversion cycle (340) | Indirect expenses (330) | Residual income (335) |
| Controllable costs (328) | Investment center (327) | Responsibility accounting (327) |
| Cost-based transfer pricing (339) | Investment turnover (336) | Responsibility accounting |
| Cost center (327) | Joint cost (344) | performance report (328) |
| Decentralized organization (327) | Market-based transfer price (339) | Return on investment (ROI) (335) |
| Departmental contribution to | Negotiated transfer price (340) | Transfer price (339) |
| overhead (334) | Profit center (327) | Uncontrollable costs (328) |
| Departmental income statements (330) | | |

## Multiple Choice Quiz

1. A retailer has three departments—Housewares, Appliances, and Clothing—and buys advertising that benefits all departments. Advertising expense is $150,000, and departmental sales follow: Housewares, $356,250; Appliances, $641,250; and Clothing, $427,500. How much advertising expense is allocated to Appliances if allocation is based on departmental sales?

   a. $37,500          c. $45,000          e. $641,250

   b. $67,500          d. $150,000

2. Indirect expenses

   a. Cannot be readily traced to one department.

   b. Are allocated to departments based on the relative benefit each department receives.

   c. Are the same as uncontrollable expenses.

   d. *a*, *b*, and *c* are true.

   e. *a* and *b* are true.

3. A division reports the information below. What is the division's return on investment?

   | | |
   |---|---|
   | Sales . . . . . . . . . . . . . . . . . . | $500,000 |
   | Income. . . . . . . . . . . . . . . . | 75,000 |
   | Average assets . . . . . . . . . . | 200,000 |

   a. 37.5%          c. 15%          e. 2.5%

   b. 30%            d. 40%

4. Using the data in question 3, the department's investment turnover is

   a. 37.5          c. 2.5          e. 4

   b. 15            d. 2.67

5. A company operates three retail departments X, Y, and Z as profit centers. Which department has the largest departmental contribution to overhead, and what is the amount contributed?

   | Department | Sales | Cost of Goods Sold | Direct Expenses | Allocated Indirect Expenses |
   |---|---|---|---|---|
   | X . . . . . | $500,000 | $350,000 | $50,000 | $40,000 |
   | Y . . . . . | 200,000 | 75,000 | 20,000 | 50,000 |
   | Z . . . . . | 350,000 | 150,000 | 75,000 | 10,000 |

   a. Department Y, $55,000          d. Department Z, $200,000

   b. Department Z, $125,000         e. Department X, $60,000

   c. Department X, $500,000

### ANSWERS TO MULTIPLE CHOICE QUIZ

1. b; [$641,250/($356,250 + $641,250 + $427,500)] × $150,000 = $67,500

2. d

3. a; $75,000/$200,000 = 37.5%

4. c; $500,000/200,000 = 2.5

5. b;

| | Dept. X | Dept. Y | Dept. Z |
|---|---|---|---|
| Sales. . . . . . . . . . . . . . . . . . . . . . . . . . . | $500,000 | $200,000 | $350,000 |
| Cost of goods sold. . . . . . . . . . . . . . . . . | 350,000 | 75,000 | 150,000 |
| Gross profit. . . . . . . . . . . . . . . . . . . . . . | 150,000 | 125,000 | 200,000 |
| Direct expenses . . . . . . . . . . . . . . . . . . . | 50,000 | 20,000 | 75,000 |
| Departmental contribution to overhead . . . | $100,000 | $105,000 | $125,000 |

*Superscript letter A denotes assignments based on Appendix 9A.*

**Mc Graw Hill** **connect**®    *Select Quick Study and Exercise assignments feature Guided Example videos, called "Hints" in Connect. Hints use different numbers, and instructors can turn this feature on or off.*

For each of the following, select its best description.

**QUICK STUDY**

**QS 9-1**
Allocation and measurement terms
P1

1. Cost center
2. Profit center
3. Responsibility accounting system
4. Operating department
5. Indirect expenses
6. Controllable costs

a. Incurs costs without directly yielding revenues.
b. Evaluates unit managers only on activities they can control.
c. Performs an organization's main functions, like manufacturing and selling.
d. Costs incurred for the joint benefit of more than one department.
e. Costs that a manager has the ability to affect.
f. Incurs costs and also generates revenues.

---

Jose Ruiz manages a construction firm's equipment repair department. His department is a cost center. Costs for a recent period follow. Jose cannot control his salary, rent, or insurance. Compute total controllable costs that would appear on a responsibility accounting report for the repair department.

**QS 9-2**
Responsibility accounting report—cost center
P1

| | | | |
|---|---|---|---|
| Cost of parts used.............. | $22,400 | Shop supplies used ............. | $1,200 |
| Mechanics' wages .............. | 14,300 | Rent........................... | 800 |
| Department manager's salary ...... | 8,000 | Insurance ..................... | 2,200 |

---

A partial responsibility accounting report for a cost center follows. Complete the report by determining the missing items *a*, *b*, and *c*.

**QS 9-3**
Responsibility accounting report—cost center
P1

| Controllable Costs | Budgeted | Actual | Over (Under) Budget |
|---|---|---|---|
| Direct materials.... | $52,800 | $    *a* | $(1,200) |
| Direct labor........ | 24,000 | 26,000 | *b* |
| Utilities .......... | 19,200 | *c* | (200) |
| Totals............ | $96,000 | $96,600 | $   600 |

---

The plant manager of the Ohio factory is responsible for two cost centers: Clothing and Shoes. Responsibility accounting reports for the Ohio factory (incomplete) and for the Shoes department (complete) follow. Finish the report for the Ohio factory by determining the missing items *a* through *e*.

**QS 9-4**
Responsibility accounting report
P1

| Plant Manager, Ohio Factory Controllable Costs | Budgeted | Actual | Over (Under) Budget |
|---|---|---|---|
| Salaries, department managers..... | $ 20,000 | $ 20,000 | $  0 |
| Rent......................... | 8,500 | 8,500 | 0 |
| Insurance .................... | 2,200 | 2,400 | *a* |
| Clothing department ........... | 40,000 | 38,900 | *b* |
| Shoes department ............. | *c* | *d* | *e* |
| Totals....................... | $127,700 | $128,420 | $720 |

| Manager, Shoes Department Controllable Costs | Budgeted | Actual | Over (Under) Budget |
|---|---|---|---|
| Direct materials................. | $32,400 | $31,100 | $(1,300) |
| Direct labor .................. | 16,400 | 17,200 | 800 |
| Supplies used ................. | 8,200 | 10,320 | 2,120 |
| Totals ...................... | $57,000 | $58,620 | $ 1,620 |

**QS 9-5**

Basis for cost allocation

**P2**

For each of the following expenses, select the best allocation basis.

1. Purchasing department expenses for the operating departments.
2. Office department expenses of the operating departments.
3. Advertising expenses of the operating departments.
4. Electric utility expenses of all departments.

   a. Relative number of employees.
   b. Proportion of total sales for each operating department.
   c. Proportion of floor space occupied by each department.
   d. Proportion of total purchase orders for each operating department.

---

**QS 9-6**

Allocating costs to departments

**P2**

Macee Store has three operating departments, and it conducts advertising that benefits all departments. Advertising costs are $100,000. Sales for its operating departments follow. How much advertising cost is allocated to each operating department if the allocation is based on departmental sales?

| Department | Sales |
|---|---|
| 1 ........... | $220,000 |
| 2 ........... | 400,000 |
| 3 ........... | 180,000 |

---

**QS 9-7**

Allocating costs to departments **P2**

SodaPop Company has two operating departments: Mixing and Bottling. Mixing has 300 employees and Bottling has 200 employees. Office costs of $160,000 are allocated to operating departments based on the number of employees. Determine the office costs allocated to each operating department.

---

**QS 9-8**

Allocating costs to departments **P2**

Sierra Company has two operating departments: Mixing and Bottling. Mixing occupies 22,000 square feet. Bottling occupies 18,000 square feet. Maintenance costs of $200,000 are allocated to operating departments based on square feet occupied. Determine the maintenance costs allocated to each operating department.

---

**QS 9-9**

Rent expense allocated to departments

**P2**

A retailer pays $130,000 rent each year for its two-story building. Space in this building is occupied by five departments as shown here.

| Department | Square feet occupied | Department | Square feet occupied |
|---|---|---|---|
| Jewelry .............. | 1,440 (first-floor) | Housewares ........... | 2,016 (second-floor) |
| Cosmetics ............ | 3,360 (first-floor) | Tools ................. | 960 (second-floor) |
| | | Shoes ................ | 1,824 (second-floor) |

**Check** Allocated to Jewelry, $25,350

The company allocates $84,500 of total rent expense to the first floor and $45,500 to the second floor. It then allocates rent expense for each floor to the departments on that floor based on square feet occupied. Determine the rent expense to be allocated to each department.

---

**QS 9-10**

Departmental contribution to overhead

**P3**

Use the following information to compute each department's contribution to overhead. Which department contributes the largest amount toward total overhead?

| | Dept. A | Dept. B | Dept. C |
|---|---|---|---|
| Sales ..................... | $53,000 | $180,000 | $84,000 |
| Cost of goods sold ......... | 34,185 | 103,700 | 49,560 |
| Gross profit ............... | 18,815 | 76,300 | 34,440 |
| Total direct expenses ........ | 3,660 | 37,060 | 7,386 |
| Contribution to overhead..... | $ _____ | $ _____ | $ _____ |

Use the information below to prepare (*a*) departmental income statements and (*b*) the departmental contribution to overhead. Salaries are direct expenses, and all other expenses are indirect expenses.

| | Food | Beverage |
|---|---|---|
| Sales .............................. | $120,000 | $80,000 |
| Cost of goods sold ................. | 72,000 | 44,000 |
| Gross profit ........................ | 48,000 | 36,000 |
| Expenses | | |
|    Salaries ........................ | 14,500 | 8,250 |
|    Rent............................ | 3,300 | 1,700 |
|    Utilities ......................... | 2,200 | 1,100 |
|    Share of office expenses........... | 4,250 | 5,100 |
|    Share of purchasing expenses ...... | 3,750 | 5,650 |

**QS 9-11**
Departmental income and contribution to overhead
**P3**

---

Compute return on investment for each investment center. Which center performed the best based on return on investment?

| Investment Center | Income | Average Assets | Return on Investment |
|---|---|---|---|
| Cameras ......... | $4,500,000 | $20,000,000 | _____% |
| Phones .......... | 1,500,000 | 12,500,000 | _____ |
| Computers........ | 800,000 | 10,000,000 | _____ |

**QS 9-12**
Computing return on investment
**A1**

---

Refer to the information in QS 9-12. Assume a target income of 12% of average assets. Compute residual income for each center.

**QS 9-13**
Computing residual income  **A1**

---

Fill in the blanks in the schedule below for two separate investment centers A and B.

| Investment Center | A | B |
|---|---|---|
| Sales .................... | $_____ | $10,400,000 |
| Income................... | $ 240,000 | $ _____ |
| Average assets ........... | $1,200,000 | $ _____ |
| Profit margin............. | 8.0% | _____% |
| Investment turnover....... | _____ | 2.0 |
| Return on investment...... | _____% | 12.0% |

**QS 9-14**
Components of performance measures
**A1   A2**

---

A company's division has sales of $2,000,000, income of $80,000, and average assets of $1,600,000. Compute the division's profit margin, return on investment, and investment turnover.

**QS 9-15**
Computing profit margin, ROI, and investment turnover  **A2**

---

Classify each of the performance measures below into the most likely of four balanced scorecard perspectives it relates to: Customer, Internal process, Innovation & learning, or Financial.

**1.** Customer wait time
**2.** Days of employee absences
**3.** Profit margin
**4.** Number of new products introduced

**5.** Employee sustainability sessions attended
**6.** Length of time raw materials are in inventory
**7.** Customer satisfaction index
**8.** Gallons of water reused

**QS 9-16**
Balanced scorecard measures
**A3**

---

A hotel reports the following for its two divisions. The company uses a balanced scorecard and sets a goal of 85% occupancy in its hotels.

| | U.S. | | International | |
|---|---|---|---|---|
| | Current Year | Prior Year | Current Year | Prior Year |
| Hotel occupancy rates ............ | 87% | 83% | 79% | 78% |

**QS 9-17**
Preparing a balanced scorecard
**A3**

[continued on next page]

[continued from previous page]

**1.** Which division(s) exceeded the occupancy goal for the current year?

**2.** Which division(s) improved its occupancy performance for the current year?

**3.** Prepare a balanced scorecard for the current year following the layout in Exhibit 9.18.

---

**QS 9-18**

Determining transfer prices without excess capacity

**C1**

The Windshield division of Jaguar Co. makes windshields for use in its Assembly division. The Windshield division incurs variable costs of $200 per windshield and has capacity to make 500,000 windshields per year. The market price is $450 per windshield. The Windshield division incurs total fixed costs of $3,000,000 per year. If the Windshield division *is operating at full capacity,* what transfer price should be used on transfers between the Windshield and Assembly divisions?

---

**QS 9-19**

Determining transfer prices with excess capacity

**C1**

The Windshield division of Jaguar Co. makes windshields for use in its Assembly division. The Windshield division incurs variable costs of $200 per windshield and has capacity to make 500,000 windshields per year. The market price is $450 per windshield. The Windshield division incurs total fixed costs of $3,000,000 per year. If the Windshield division *has excess capacity,* what is the range of possible transfer prices that could be used on transfers between the Windshield and Assembly divisions?

---

**QS 9-20**

Cash conversion cycle

**A4**

(1) Use the information below to compute the days in the cash conversion cycle for each company. (2) Which company is more effective at managing cash based on this measure?

|  | Sparta Co. | Athens Co. |
|---|---|---|
| Days' sales in accounts receivable . . . . . . . . . | 32 | 45 |
| Days' sales in inventory . . . . . . . . . . . . . . . . . | 20 | 24 |
| Days' payable outstanding . . . . . . . . . . . . . . | 27 | 32 |

---

**QS 9-21**[A]

Joint cost allocation

**C2**

A company purchases a 10,020-square-foot building for $375,000. The building has two separate rental units. Unit A, which has the desirable location on the corner and contains 3,340 square feet, will be rented for $1.00 per square foot. Unit B contains 6,680 square feet and will be rented for $0.75 per square foot. How much of the joint cost should be allocated to Unit A and to Unit B using the value basis of allocation?

---

**EXERCISES**

**Exercise 9-1**

Responsibility accounting performance report

**P1**

Arctica manufactures snowmobiles and ATVs. These products are made in different departments, and each department has its own manager. Each responsibility performance report includes only those costs that the department manager can control: direct materials, direct labor, supplies used, and utilities. Prepare a responsibility accounting performance report for the Snowmobile department.

|  | Budgeted | | Actual | |
|---|---|---|---|---|
| **For Year Ended December 31** | **Snowmobile** | **ATV** | **Snowmobile** | **ATV** |
| Direct materials | $19,500 | $27,500 | $19,420 | $28,820 |
| Direct labor | 10,400 | 20,500 | 10,660 | 21,240 |
| Department manager salaries | 4,300 | 5,200 | 4,400 | 4,400 |
| Supplies used | 3,300 | 900 | 3,170 | 920 |
| Utilities | 360 | 540 | 330 | 500 |
| Rent | 5,700 | 6,300 | 5,300 | 6,300 |
| **Totals** | **$43,560** | **$60,940** | **$43,280** | **$62,180** |

---

**Exercise 9-2**

Responsibility accounting performance report    **P1**

Refer to the information in Exercise 9-1 and prepare a responsibility accounting performance report for the ATV department.

Lucia Company has two service departments: Office and Purchasing. Total expenses for the Office is $24,000 and for Purchasing is $34,000. Expenses for the Office are allocated to operating departments based on sales. Expenses for Purchasing are allocated to operating departments based on purchase orders. Allocate the expenses from (*a*) the Office and (*b*) Purchasing to each of the company's three operating departments using the following information.

**Exercise 9-3**
Service department expenses allocated to operating departments
**P2**

| Department | Sales | Purchase Orders |
|---|---|---|
| Books . . . . . . . . . . . | $495,000 | 516 |
| Magazines . . . . . . . . | 198,000 | 360 |
| Newspapers . . . . . . | 207,000 | 324 |
| Totals . . . . . . . . . . . | $900,000 | 1,200 |

Mia works in both the Jewelry department and the Cosmetics department of a retail store. She assists customers in both departments and organizes merchandise in both departments. The store allocates her wages between the two departments based on the time worked in the two departments in each two-week pay period. Mia reports the following hours and activities spent in the two departments in the most recent two weeks. Allocate Mia's $1,200 of wages for two weeks to the two departments.

**Exercise 9-4**
Payroll expense allocated to departments
**P2**

| Activities | Hours |
|---|---|
| Selling in Jewelry department . . . . . . . . . . . . | 51 |
| Organizing in Jewelry department . . . . . . . . | 6 |
| Selling in Cosmetics department . . . . . . . . . | 12 |
| Organizing in Cosmetics department . . . . . . | 7 |
| Total . . . . . . . . . . . . . . . . . . . . . . . . . . . . . . . | 76 |

Renata Co. has four departments: Materials, Personnel, Manufacturing, and Packaging. Information follows.

**Exercise 9-5**
Departmental expense allocations
**P2**

| Department | Employees | Square Feet | Asset Values |
|---|---|---|---|
| Materials . . . . . . . . . | 27 | 25,000 | $ 6,000 |
| Personnel . . . . . . . . | 9 | 5,000 | 1,200 |
| Manufacturing . . . . . | 63 | 55,000 | 37,800 |
| Packaging . . . . . . . . | 51 | 15,000 | 15,000 |
| Totals . . . . . . . . . . . | 150 | 100,000 | $60,000 |

The four departments share the following indirect expenses for supervision, utilities, and insurance. Allocate each of the three indirect expenses to the four departments according to their allocation bases.

| Indirect Expense | Cost | Allocation Base |
|---|---|---|
| Supervision . . . . . | $ 82,500 | Number of employees |
| Utilities . . . . . . . . | 50,000 | Square feet occupied |
| Insurance . . . . . . | 22,500 | Asset values |
| Total . . . . . . . . . . | $155,000 | |

Gomez Company has two service departments (Personnel and Office) and two operating departments (Shoes and Clothing). Following are the direct expenses and square feet occupied by the four departments, and the total sales for the two operating departments.

**Exercise 9-6**
Departmental expense allocations
**P2**

| Department | Direct Expenses | Square Feet | Sales |
|---|---|---|---|
| Personnel . . . . . . . . | $ 18,000 | 1,120 | — |
| Office . . . . . . . . . . . | 25,000 | 1,400 | — |
| Shoes . . . . . . . . . . . | 103,000 | 7,140 | $273,000 |
| Clothing . . . . . . . . . | 15,000 | 4,340 | 77,000 |

The company also has $64,000 of utilities expense, which is an indirect expense to all departments and is allocated to the four departments based on square feet occupied.

The Shoes department has 9 employees and the Clothing department has 3 employees. Personnel expense is allocated to operating departments based on the number of employees. Office expense is allocated to operating departments based on sales.

1. Allocate utilities expense to the four departments.
2. Allocate personnel expense to the Shoes and Clothing departments.
3. Allocate office expense to the Shoes and Clothing departments.

---

**Exercise 9-7**
Departmental contribution to overhead
P3

Below are departmental income statements for a guitar manufacturer. The company classifies advertising, rent, and utilities as indirect expenses. The manufacturer is considering eliminating its Electric Guitar department because it shows a loss.

| Departmental Income Statements For Year Ended December 31 | Acoustic | Electric |
|---|---|---|
| Sales | $112,500 | $105,500 |
| Cost of goods sold | 55,675 | 66,750 |
| Gross profit | 56,825 | 38,750 |
| Expenses | | |
| Advertising | 8,075 | 6,250 |
| Depreciation—Equipment | 10,150 | 9,000 |
| Salaries | 17,300 | 13,500 |
| Supplies used | 2,030 | 1,700 |
| Rent | 6,105 | 5,950 |
| Utilities | 3,045 | 2,550 |
| Total expenses | 46,705 | 38,950 |
| Income (loss) | $ 10,120 | $ (200) |

1. Prepare a departmental contribution to overhead report (see Exhibit 9.12).
2. Based on contribution to overhead, should the Electric Guitar department be eliminated?

---

**Exercise 9-8**
Departmental income statement and contribution to overhead
P3

The Ski department reports sales of $605,000 and cost of goods sold of $425,000. Its expenses follow.

| Direct expenses | | Indirect expenses | | Service department expenses | |
|---|---|---|---|---|---|
| Salaries | $112,000 | Rent | $14,000 | Office | $20,000 |
| Depreciation | 42,000 | | | | |

For the Ski department only, prepare a (1) departmental income statement and (2) departmental contribution to overhead report. (3) Based on these two reports, should the Ski department be eliminated?

---

**Exercise 9-9**
Return on investment analysis
A1

A growing chain is trying to decide which store location to open. The West location requires a $1,000,000 investment in average assets and is expected to yield annual income of $160,000. The East location requires a $600,000 investment in average assets and is expected to yield annual income of $108,000. (1) Compute the expected return on investment for each location. (2) Using return on investment, which location (West or East) should the company open?

---

**Exercise 9-10**
Computing return on investment and residual income; investing decision
A1

Megamart provides the following information on its two investment centers.

| Investment Center | Sales | Income | Average Assets |
|---|---|---|---|
| Electronics | $40,000,000 | $2,880,000 | $16,000,000 |
| Sporting Goods | 20,000,000 | 2,040,000 | 12,000,000 |

1. Compute return on investment for each center. Using return on investment, which center is most efficient at using assets to generate income?
2. Assume a target income of 12% of average assets. Compute residual income for each center. Which center generated the most residual income?
3. Assume the Electronics center is presented with a new investment opportunity that will yield a 15% return on investment. Should the new investment opportunity be accepted? The target return is 12%.

Refer to information in Exercise 9-10. (1) Compute profit margin and investment turnover for each center. (2) Which center generates more income per dollar of sales? (3) Which center has the better investment turnover?

**Exercise 9-11**
Computing profit margin and investment turnover
**A2**

---

A manufacturer reports the following for two of its divisions for a recent month. For each division, compute (1) return on investment, (2) profit margin, and (3) investment turnover.

| | Beverage Division | Cheese Division |
|---|---|---|
| Average assets . . . . . | $5,000 | $10,000 |
| Sales . . . . . . . . . . . . | 3,000 | 5,000 |
| Income. . . . . . . . . . . | 600 | 800 |

**Exercise 9-12**
Computing ROI, profit margin, and investment turnover
**A1   A2**

---

Refer to the information in Exercise 9-12. Assume that each of the company's divisions has a target income at 7% of average assets. Compute residual income for each division.

**Exercise 9-13**
Residual income   **A1**

---

A company reports the following for the past year.

| Sales . . . . . . . | $5,000,000 | Income. . . . . . . . . . . . . | $1,000,000 | Average assets. . . . . . . . . . | $12,500,000 |
|---|---|---|---|---|---|

The company's CFO believes that income for next year will be $1,200,000. Average assets will be the same as the past year.

**1.** Compute return on investment for the past year.
**2.** If the CFO's forecast is correct, what will return on investment be for next year?

**Exercise 9-14**
Return on investment
**A1**

---

A retailer reports the following for its geographic divisions for the year.

| | Americas | Europe | China |
|---|---|---|---|
| Income. . . . . | $ 300,000 | $ 80,000 | $ 60,000 |
| Sales . . . . . . | 1,000,000 | 400,000 | 240,000 |

**1.** Compute profit margin for each division.
**2.** Based on profit margin, which division performed best?

**Exercise 9-15**
Profit margin
**A2**

---

The Food division of Garcia Company reports the following for the current year.

| | |
|---|---|
| Sales . . . . . . . . . . . . . . . . . . . . . . . . . . | $4,000,000 |
| Cost of goods sold . . . . . . . . . . . . . . . | 2,800,000 |
| Gross profit . . . . . . . . . . . . . . . . . . . . . | 1,200,000 |
| Expenses. . . . . . . . . . . . . . . . . . . . . . . | 1,000,000 |
| Income. . . . . . . . . . . . . . . . . . . . . . . . | $ 200,000 |

**Exercise 9-16**
Profit margin
**A2**

The Food division wants to make at least a 10% profit margin next year. Two alternative strategies are proposed.

**Strategy 1:** Increase advertising expenses by $225,000. The company expects this to increase sales by $600,000 due to a higher sales price for its products. Cost of goods sold will not change.

**Strategy 2:** Develop a more efficient manufacturing process. This will decrease cost of goods sold by $140,000.

**a.** For each strategy, compute the profit margin expected for next year.
**b.** Which strategy should Garcia choose based on expected profit margin?

**Exercise 9-17**
Performance measures—
balanced scorecard

**A3**

USA Airlines uses the following performance measures. Classify each performance measure into the most likely balanced scorecard perspective it relates to: customer, internal process, innovation and learning, or financial.

1. Cash flow from operations
2. Percentage of ground crew trained
3. Return on investment
4. Market value
5. Safety violations per mile flown
6. Customer complaints
7. Flight attendant training sessions attended
8. Time airplane is on ground between flights
9. Airplane miles per gallon of fuel
10. Revenue per seat
11. Cost of leasing airplanes

**Exercise 9-18**
Performance measures—
balanced scorecard

**A3**

Midwest Mfg. uses a balanced scorecard as part of its performance evaluation. The company wants to include information on its sustainability efforts in its balanced scorecard. For each performance measure below, indicate the most likely balanced scorecard perspective it relates to: customer, internal process, innovation and learning, or financial.

1. $CO_2$ emissions
2. Number of solar panels installed
3. Gallons of water used
4. Customer feedback on sustainability reputation
5. Pounds of recyclable packaging used
6. Pounds of trash diverted from landfill
7. Dollar sales of green products
8. Number of sustainability trainings held
9. Cubic feet of natural gas used
10. Patents for green products applied for

**Exercise 9-19**
Determining transfer prices

**C1**

The Trailer division of Baxter Bicycles makes bike trailers that attach to bicycles and can carry children or cargo. The trailers have a market price of $200 each. Each trailer incurs $80 of variable manufacturing costs. The Trailer division has capacity for 40,000 trailers per year and has fixed costs of $1,000,000 per year.

1. Assume the Assembly division of Baxter Bicycles wants to buy 15,000 trailers per year from the Trailer division. If the Trailer division can sell all of the trailers it manufactures to outside customers (and has no excess capacity), what price should be used on transfers between divisions?

2. Assume the Trailer division currently only sells 20,000 trailers to outside customers and has excess capacity. The Assembly division wants to buy 15,000 trailers per year from the Trailer division. What is the range of acceptable prices on transfers between divisions?

**Exercise 9-20**
Cash conversion cycle

**A4**

A manufacturer reports the data below. (1) Compute the number of days in the cash conversion cycle for each year. (2) Did the company manage cash more effectively in the current year?

|  | Current Year | Prior Year |
|---|---|---|
| Accounts payable . . . . . . . . . . . . . . . . . . . . . . . . . | $ 4,603 | $ 8,548 |
| Accounts receivable . . . . . . . . . . . . . . . . . . . . . . . | 18,685 | 15,726 |
| Inventory . . . . . . . . . . . . . . . . . . . . . . . . . . . . . . . . | 6,904 | 6,055 |
| Net sales . . . . . . . . . . . . . . . . . . . . . . . . . . . . . . . . | 220,186 | 205,000 |
| Cost of goods sold . . . . . . . . . . . . . . . . . . . . . . . | 139,998 | 130,000 |

**Exercise 9-21**
Cash conversion cycle

**A4**

A manufacturer reports the data below. (1) Compute the number of days in the cash conversion cycle. (2) Is the company more efficient at managing cash than its competitor who has a cash conversion cycle of 14 days?

| | | | |
|---|---|---|---|
| Accounts payable . . . . . . . . . . . . . . . . . . . . . | $ 9,049 | Net sales . . . . . . . . . . . . . . . . . . . . . . . | $233,007 |
| Accounts receivable . . . . . . . . . . . . . . . . . . . | 17,874 | Cost of goods sold . . . . . . . . . . . . . . . . | 137,600 |
| Inventory . . . . . . . . . . . . . . . . . . . . . . . . . . . . | 4,855 | | |

**Exercise 9-22[A]**
Assigning joint
costs **C2**

Home Properties is developing a subdivision that includes 600 home lots. The 450 lots in the Canyon section are below a ridge and do not have views of the neighboring canyons and hills; the 150 lots in the Hilltop section offer unobstructed views. The expected selling price for each Canyon lot is $55,000 and for each Hilltop lot is $110,000. The developer acquired the land for $4,000,000 and spent another $3,500,000 on street and utilities improvements. Assign the joint land and improvement costs of $7,500,000 to the Canyon section and the Hilltop section using the value basis of allocation.

A dairy company processed raw milk for $60,000. This raw milk can be converted into the following types of milk with listed sales values. Use the value basis to (1) allocate the total cost of the raw milk to each type of milk and (2) determine the gross profit for each type of milk.

**Exercise 9-23ᴬ**
Assigning joint product costs **C2**

| Joint Products | Sales Value |
|---|---|
| Whole milk . . . . . . | $ 25,000 |
| 2% milk . . . . . . . . . | 40,000 |
| Skim milk. . . . . . . . | 35,000 |
| Total. . . . . . . . . . . | $100,000 |

**Mc Graw Hill connect**

Ana Perez is the plant manager of Travel Free's Indiana plant. The Camper and Trailer operating departments manufacture products and have their own managers. The Office department, which Perez also manages, provides services equally to the two operating departments.

Each performance report includes only those costs that a particular operating department manager can control: direct materials, direct labor, supplies used, and utilities. The plant manager is responsible for the department managers' salaries, building rent, office salaries other than her own, and other office costs plus all costs controlled by the two operating department managers.

The annual departmental budgets and actual costs for the two operating departments follow.

**PROBLEM SET A**

**Problem 9-1A**
Responsibility accounting performance reports; controllable and budgeted costs

**P1**

| For Year Ended December 31 | Budgeted | | Actual | |
|---|---|---|---|---|
| | Campers | Trailers | Campers | Trailers |
| Direct materials. . . . . . . . . . . . . . . . . . . . . | $195,000 | $275,000 | $194,200 | $273,200 |
| Direct labor . . . . . . . . . . . . . . . . . . . . . . | 104,000 | 205,000 | 106,600 | 206,400 |
| Department manager salaries . . . . . . . . . | 43,000 | 52,000 | 44,000 | 53,500 |
| Supplies used . . . . . . . . . . . . . . . . . . . . . | 3,000 | 9,000 | 3,700 | 8,600 |
| Utilities . . . . . . . . . . . . . . . . . . . . . . . . . | 3,600 | 5,400 | 3,300 | 5,000 |
| Building rent . . . . . . . . . . . . . . . . . . . . . . | 5,700 | 9,300 | 5,300 | 8,700 |
| Office department costs. . . . . . . . . . . . . . | 68,750 | 68,750 | 67,550 | 67,550 |
| Totals. . . . . . . . . . . . . . . . . . . . . . . . . . | $423,050 | $624,450 | $424,650 | $622,950 |

The Office department's budgeted and actual costs follow.

| For Year Ended December 31 | Budgeted | Actual |
|---|---|---|
| Plant manager salary . . . . . . . . . . . | $ 80,000 | $ 82,000 |
| Other office salaries . . . . . . . . . . . | 32,500 | 30,100 |
| Other office costs . . . . . . . . . . . . . | 25,000 | 23,000 |
| Totals. . . . . . . . . . . . . . . . . . . . . | $137,500 | $135,100 |

**Required**

Prepare responsibility accounting performance reports like those in Exhibit 9.2 that list costs controlled by the following.

**1.** Manager of Camper department.

**2.** Manager of Trailer department.

**3.** Manager of Indiana plant.

**Problem 9-2A**
Allocation of indirect expenses to departments
**P2**

National Retail has two departments, Housewares and Sporting. Indirect expenses for the period follow.

| | |
|---|---|
| Rent................................. | $45,000 |
| Advertising ......................... | 25,000 |
| Insurance ......................... | 10,000 |
| Total............................... | $80,000 |

The company occupies 4,000 square feet of a rented building. In prior periods, the company divided the $80,000 of indirect expenses by 4,000 square feet to find an average cost of $20 per square foot, and then allocated indirect expenses to each department based on the square feet it occupied.

The company now wants to allocate indirect expenses using the allocation bases shown below.

| Department | Square Feet | Sales | Value of Insured Assets |
|---|---|---|---|
| Housewares ............. | 2,200 | $180,000 | $ 40,000 |
| Sporting................. | 1,800 | 320,000 | 60,000 |
| Total.................... | 4,000 | $500,000 | $100,000 |

**Required**

**Check**   (1) Total allocated to Housewares, $44,000
(2) Advertising allocated to Sporting, $16,000

1. Allocate indirect expenses to the two departments using the allocation method used in prior periods.
2. Allocate indirect expenses to the two departments. Rent expense is allocated based on square feet occupied. Advertising expense is allocated based on total sales. Insurance expense is allocated based on the value of insured assets.

---

**Problem 9-3A**
Departmental income statements
**P3**

Garcia Company has two operating departments (Phone and Earbuds) and one service department (Office). Its departmental income statements follow. Indirect expenses and service department expenses consist of rent, utilities, and office department expenses.

| Departmental Income Statements | | | |
|---|---|---|---|
| For Year Ended December 31 | Phone | Earbuds | Combined |
| Sales ................................ | $130,000 | $55,000 | $185,000 |
| Cost of goods sold .................... | 63,700 | 34,100 | 97,800 |
| Gross profit .......................... | 66,300 | 20,900 | 87,200 |
| Expenses | | | |
| Sales salaries ........................ | 21,200 | 7,500 | 28,700 |
| Supplies used........................ | 900 | 400 | 1,300 |
| Depreciation—Equipment .............. | 1,500 | 300 | 1,800 |
| Rent ............................... | 7,020 | 3,780 | 10,800 |
| Utilities ............................. | 2,600 | 1,400 | 4,000 |
| Share of office department expenses..... | 10,500 | 4,500 | 15,000 |
| Total expenses ....................... | 43,720 | 17,880 | 61,600 |
| Income.............................. | $ 22,580 | $ 3,020 | $ 25,600 |

**Required**

Prepare a departmental contribution to overhead report (see Exhibit 9.12).

Diaz Company is a retail store with two operating departments, Clothes and Shoes. Information follows.

**Problem 9-4A**
Departmental income

**P3**

| For Year Ended December 31 | Clothes | Shoes |
|---|---|---|
| Sales......................... | $800,000 | $450,000 |
| Cost of goods sold .............. | 497,000 | 291,000 |
| Direct expenses: Wages........... | 125,000 | 88,000 |
| Supplies used..... | 20,000 | 10,000 |
| Depreciation...... | 28,000 | 17,000 |

The company reports the following indirect expenses for the year.

| Indirect Expense | Amount | Allocation Base |
|---|---|---|
| Utilities............ | $ 6,000 | Square feet of space occupied |
| Supervisor salaries .. | 50,000 | Number of employees in department |

Additional information about the two departments follows.

| Department | Square Footage | Number of Employees |
|---|---|---|
| Clothes ...... | 28,000 | 75 |
| Shoes ....... | 12,000 | 50 |

**Required**

1. Allocate indirect expenses to the two operating departments.
2. Prepare departmental income statements.

**Check**   (2) Clothes income,
$95,800

California Orchards reports the following sales data for the year ended December 31.

**Problem 9-5A**[A]
Allocation of joint costs

**C2**

| Grade of Walnuts | Sales |
|---|---|
| No. 1 ........... | $450,000 |
| No. 2 ........... | 300,000 |
| No. 3 ........... | 187,500 |
| Total............ | $937,500 |

The company incurred the following joint costs for the year.

| | |
|---|---|
| Tree pruning and care................ | $405,000 |
| Pickup, sorting, and grading.......... | 202,500 |

**Required**

1. Use the value basis to allocate joint costs to the three grades of walnuts.
2. Compute gross profit for each of the three grades of walnuts.

Britney Brown is the plant manager of GT Co.'s Chicago plant. The Refrigerator and Dishwasher operating departments manufacture products and have their own managers. The Office department, which Brown also manages, provides services equally to the two operating departments.

Each performance report includes only those costs that a particular operating department manager can control: direct materials, direct labor, supplies used, and utilities. The plant manager is responsible for the department managers' salaries, building rent, office salaries other than her own, and other office costs plus all costs controlled by the two operating department managers.

**PROBLEM SET B**

**Problem 9-1B**
Responsibility accounting
performance reports;
controllable and budgeted
costs

**P1**

The April departmental budgets and actual costs for the two operating departments follow.

| | Budgeted | | Actual | |
| --- | --- | --- | --- | --- |
| **For Month Ended April 30** | **Refrigerators** | **Dishwashers** | **Refrigerators** | **Dishwashers** |
| Direct materials.................. | $400,000 | $200,000 | $385,000 | $202,000 |
| Direct labor...................... | 170,000 | 80,000 | 174,700 | 81,500 |
| Department manager salaries........ | 55,000 | 49,000 | 55,000 | 46,500 |
| Supplies used.................... | 15,000 | 9,000 | 14,000 | 9,700 |
| Utilities ........................ | 30,000 | 18,000 | 34,500 | 20,700 |
| Building rent.................... | 63,000 | 17,000 | 65,800 | 16,500 |
| Office department costs............ | 70,500 | 70,500 | 75,000 | 75,000 |
| Totals......................... | $803,500 | $443,500 | $804,000 | $451,900 |

The Office department's budgeted and actual costs follow.

| **For Month Ended April 30** | **Budgeted** | **Actual** |
| --- | --- | --- |
| Plant manager salary ........... | $ 80,000 | $ 85,000 |
| Other office salaries............ | 40,000 | 35,200 |
| Other office costs.............. | 21,000 | 29,800 |
| Totals....................... | $141,000 | $150,000 |

### Required

**Check**   (1a) $6,800 total under budget
(1c) Chicago plant controllable costs, $3,900 total over budget

1. Prepare responsibility accounting performance reports like those in Exhibit 9.2 that list costs controlled by the following.

    **a.** Manager of Refrigerator department.      **c.** Manager of Chicago plant.

    **b.** Manager of Dishwasher department.

### Analysis Component

2. Did the plant manager or one of the operating department managers best control costs?

---

**Problem 9-2B**

Allocation of indirect expenses to departments

**P2**

Harmon's has two operating departments, Clothing and Shoes. Indirect expenses for the period follow.

| | |
| --- | --- |
| Rent............................. | $50,000 |
| Advertising ......................... | 30,000 |
| Insurance ......................... | 12,000 |
| Total............................. | $92,000 |

The company occupies 4,000 square feet of a rented building. In prior periods, the company divided the $92,000 of indirect expenses by 4,000 square feet to find an average cost of $23 per square foot, and then allocated indirect expenses to each department based on the square feet it occupied.

    The company now wants to allocate indirect expenses using the allocation bases shown below.

| **Department** | **Square Feet** | **Sales** | **Value of Insured Assets** |
| --- | --- | --- | --- |
| Clothing................ | 2,400 | $240,000 | $ 36,000 |
| Shoes.................. | 1,600 | 360,000 | 84,000 |
| Total................... | 4,000 | $600,000 | $120,000 |

**Required**

1. Allocate indirect expenses to the two departments using the allocation method used in prior periods.
2. Allocate indirect expenses to the two departments. Rent expense is allocated based on square feet occupied. Advertising expense is allocated based on total sales. Insurance expense is allocated based on the value of insured assets.

**Check**   (1) Total allocated to Shoes, $36,800
(2) Insurance allocated to Clothing, $3,600

Bonanza has two operating departments (Movies and Video Games) and one service department (Office). Its departmental income statements follow. Indirect expenses and service department expenses consist of rent, utilities, and office department expenses.

**Problem 9-3B**
Departmental income statements
P3

| Departmental Income Statements | | | |
|---|---|---|---|
| For Year Ended December 31 | Movies | Video Games | Combined |
| Sales .............................. | $600,000 | $200,000 | $800,000 |
| Cost of goods sold .................... | 420,000 | 154,000 | 574,000 |
| Gross profit ......................... | 180,000 | 46,000 | 226,000 |
| Expenses | | | |
| Sales salaries ....................... | 49,500 | 21,000 | 70,500 |
| Supplies used........................ | 4,000 | 1,000 | 5,000 |
| Depreciation—Equipment .............. | 4,500 | 3,000 | 7,500 |
| Rent.................................. | 41,000 | 9,000 | 50,000 |
| Utilities ............................. | 7,380 | 1,620 | 9,000 |
| Share of office department expenses..... | 56,250 | 18,750 | 75,000 |
| Total expenses ...................... | 162,630 | 54,370 | 217,000 |
| Income (loss)......................... | $ 17,370 | $ (8,370) | $ 9,000 |

**Required**

1. Prepare a departmental contribution to overhead report (see Exhibit 9.12).
2. Should the video games department be eliminated? Explain.

Sadar Company is a store with two operating departments, Guitar and Piano. Information follows.

**Problem 9-4B**
Departmental income
P3

| For Year Ended December 31 | Guitar | Piano |
|---|---|---|
| Sales. ........................ | $370,500 | $279,500 |
| Cost of goods sold ............. | 320,000 | 175,000 |
| Direct expenses: Salaries......... | 35,000 | 25,000 |
| Depreciation...... | 12,000 | 10,000 |
| Supplies used.... | 4,200 | 3,700 |

The company reports the following indirect expenses for the year.

| Indirect Expense | Amount | Allocation Base |
|---|---|---|
| Advertising......... | $15,000 | Percentage of total sales |
| Rent .............. | 3,200 | Square feet of space occupied |

Additional information about the two operating departments follows.

| Department | Square Footage | Sales |
|---|---|---|
| Guitar........ | 5,000 | $370,500 |
| Piano........ | 3,000 | 279,500 |

**Required**

**Check**   (2) Piano dept.
income, $58,150

1. Allocate indirect expenses to the two operating departments.
2. Prepare departmental income statements.

---

**Problem 9-5B^A**
Allocation of joint costs

C2

Tampa Tomatoes reports the following sales data for the year ended December 31.

| Grade of Tomatoes | Sales |
|---|---|
| No. 1 ............ | $  600,000 |
| No. 2 ............ | 350,000 |
| No. 3 ........... | 50,000 |
| Total............ | $1,000,000 |

The company incurred the following joint costs for the year.

| | |
|---|---|
| Land preparation, seeding, and cultivating ..... | $700,000 |
| Harvesting, sorting, and grading ............. | 40,000 |

**Required**

1. Use the value basis to allocate joint costs to the three grades of tomatoes.
2. Compute gross profit for each of the three grades of tomatoes.

---

**SERIAL PROBLEM**
Business Solutions

A4

Alexander Image/Shutterstock

*This serial problem began in Chapter 1 and continues through most of the book. If previous chapter segments were not completed, the serial problem can begin at this point.*

**SP 9**   Santana Rey's two departments, Computer Consulting Services and Computer Workstation Furniture Manufacturing, have each been profitable for **Business Solutions**. Santana has heard of the cash conversion cycle and wants to use it as another performance measure for the workstation manufacturing department. Data below are for the most recent two quarters.

| | 1st Quarter | 2nd Quarter |
|---|---|---|
| Days' sales in accounts receivable ........... | 19 days | 21 days |
| Days' sales in inventory .................... | 25 days | 24 days |
| Days' payable outstanding.................. | 31 days | 28 days |

**Required**

1. Compute cash conversion cycle for the first quarter.
2. Compute cash conversion cycle for the second quarter.
3. Did cash conversion cycle improve or worsen from the first to the second quarter?

---

**TABLEAU
DASHBOARD
ACTIVITIES**

**Tableau Dashboard Activities** expose students to accounting analytics using visual displays. These assignments (1) do not require instructors to know Tableau, (2) are accessible to introductory students, (3) do not require Tableau software, and (4) run in **Connect.** All are auto-gradable.

**Tableau DA 9-1 Quick Study**, Allocate indirect expenses, **P2**—similar to QS 9-6, QS 9-7, and QS 9-8.

**Tableau DA 9-2 Exercise**, Allocate indirect expenses and prepare departmental income statements, **P2, P3**—similar to Exercise 9-5, Exercise 9-6, and Exercise 9-8.

**Tableau DA 9-3 Mini-case**, Prepare departmental contribution to overhead report and analyze strategies, **P3**—similar Exercise 9-8.

## Accounting Analysis

McGraw Hill **connect**

**AA 9-1**   Information for **Google** follows.

COMPANY
ANALYSIS

A4

| $ millions | Current Year | One Year Prior |
|---|---|---|
| Accounts receivable, net | $ 25,326 | $ 20,838 |
| Net sales | 161,857 | 136,819 |
| Inventory | 999 | 1,107 |
| Cost of goods sold | 71,896 | 59,549 |
| Accounts payable | 5,561 | 4,378 |

**Required**

1. Compute Google's cash conversion cycle for both the current and prior years.
2. Did Google become more effective at managing cash in the current year?

**AA 9-2**   Current year information for **Apple** and **Google** follows.

COMPARATIVE
ANALYSIS

A2

APPLE
GOOGLE

| $ millions | Apple | Google |
|---|---|---|
| Sales | $260,174 | $161,857 |
| Income | 55,256 | 34,343 |
| Average assets | 352,121 | 254,351 |

**Required**

1. Compute profit margin for each company.
2. Compute investment turnover for each company.
3. Refer to answers for parts 1 and 2. Which company performed better on investment turnover?

**AA 9-3**   Current year information for **Samsung** and **Google** follows.

EXTENDED
ANALYSIS

A4

Samsung
GOOGLE

| $ millions | Samsung | Google |
|---|---|---|
| Accounts receivable, net | $ 30,144 | $ 25,326 |
| Net sales | 197,691 | 161,857 |
| Inventory | 22,966 | 999 |
| Cost of goods sold | 126,336 | 71,896 |
| Accounts payable | 7,480 | 5,561 |

**Required**

1. Compute the cash conversion cycle for both Samsung and Google for the current year.
2. Which company, Samsung or Google, was more effective at managing cash in the current year?

## Discussion Questions

1. Why are many companies divided into departments?
2. What is the difference between operating departments and service departments?
3. What are controllable costs?
4. How is the performance of cost center managers evaluated?
5. In responsibility accounting, why are reports to higher-level managers usually less detailed?
6. How are decisions made in decentralized organizations?

**7.** How is the performance of profit center managers evaluated?

**8.** What is the difference between direct and indirect expenses?

**9.** Suggest a reasonable basis for allocating each of the following indirect expenses to departments: (*a*) salary of a supervisor who manages several departments, (*b*) rent, (*c*) heat, (*d*) advertising, and (*e*) property taxes on equipment.

**10.** How is a department's contribution to overhead measured?

**11.** Describe the four perspectives of the balanced scorecard.

**12.** What is a transfer price? What are the three main approaches to setting transfer prices?

**13.** Under what conditions is a market-based transfer price most likely to be used?

**14.**<sup>A</sup> What is a joint cost? How are joint costs usually allocated among the products produced from them?

**15.** Each **Apple** retail store has several departments. Why is it useful for its management to (*a*) collect accounting information about each department and (*b*) treat each department as a profit center?    **APPLE**

**16.** **Apple** delivers its products to locations around the world. List three controllable and three uncontrollable costs for its delivery department.    **APPLE**

**17.** Define and describe the *cash conversion cycle* and identify its three components.

**18.** Can management of a company such as **Samsung** use the cash conversion cycle as a useful measure of performance? Explain.    **Samsung**

## Beyond the Numbers

**ETHICS
CHALLENGE
P3**

**BTN 9-1**   Super Security Co. offers security services for athletes and entertainers. Each type of service is considered within a separate department. Marc Pincus, the overall manager, is compensated partly on the basis of departmental performance by staying within the quarterly cost budget. He often revises operations to make sure departments stay within budget. Says Pincus, "I will not go over budget even if it means slightly compromising the level and quality of service. These are minor compromises that don't significantly affect my clients, at least in the short term."

**Required**

**1.** Is there an ethical concern in this situation? If so, which parties are affected? Explain.

**2.** Can Pincus take action to eliminate or reduce any ethical concerns? Explain.

**3.** What is Super Security's ethical responsibility in offering professional services?

**COMMUNICATING
IN PRACTICE
P2**

**BTN 9-2**   Improvement Station is a national home improvement chain with more than 100 stores throughout the country. The manager of each store receives a salary plus a bonus equal to a percent of the store's income for the reporting period. The following income calculation is on the Denver store manager's performance report for the recent monthly period.

| | |
|---|---:|
| Sales . . . . . . . . . . . . . . . . . . . . . . . . . | $2,500,000 |
| Cost of goods sold . . . . . . . . . . . . . . . | 800,000 |
| Salaries expense. . . . . . . . . . . . . . . . . | 500,000 |
| Depreciation—Equipment . . . . . . . . . . | 200,000 |
| General office expense . . . . . . . . . . . . | 75,000 |
| Income. . . . . . . . . . . . . . . . . . . . . . . . | $ 925,000 |
| Manager's bonus (0.5%). . . . . . . . . . . | $ 4,625 |

In previous periods, the bonus had also been 0.5%, but the performance report had not included any charges for the general office expense, which is now allocated to each store as a percent of its sales.

**Required**

Assume that you are the national office manager. Write a half-page memorandum to your store managers explaining why general office expense is in the new performance report.

**BTN 9-3**   **Apple** and **Samsung** compete across the world in several markets.

**TEAMWORK IN ACTION**
P1
**APPLE**
**Samsung**

**Required**

1. Design a three-tier responsibility accounting organizational chart assuming that you have available internal information for both companies. Use Exhibit 9.1 as an example. The goal of this assignment is to design a reporting framework for the companies; numbers are not required. Limit your reporting framework to sales activity only.

2. Explain why it is important to have similar performance reports when comparing performance within a company (and across different companies). Be specific in your response.

---

**BTN 9-4**   Sofia Luz Eckrich's company **Teysha** makes hand-made boots, shoes, and home goods.

**ENTREPRENEURIAL DECISION**
P3

**Required**

1. How can Sofia use departmental (product line) income statements to assist in understanding and controlling operations?

2. Are departmental income statements always the best measure of a department's performance? Explain.

# 10 Relevant Costs for Managerial Decisions

## Chapter Preview

### DECISIONS AND INFORMATION

Managerial decisions

**C1** Relevant revenues and costs

**NTK 10-1**

### PRODUCTION DECISIONS

**P1** Make or buy

**P2** Sell or process
Scrap or rework

**P3** Sales mix

**NTK 10-2, 3, 4**

### CAPACITY DECISIONS

**P4** Segment elimination

**P5** Keep or replace

**NTK 10-5**

### PRICING DECISIONS

**P6** Normal pricing

**P7** Special pricing

**A1** Time and materials

**NTK 10-6**

## Learning Objectives

### CONCEPTUAL

**C1** Describe the use of relevant costs and benefits for short-term decisions.

### ANALYTICAL

**A1** Determine price of services using time and materials pricing.

### PROCEDURAL

**P1** Evaluate make or buy decisions.

**P2** Evaluate sell or process decisions.

**P3** Determine sales mix with constrained resources.

**P4** Evaluate segment elimination decisions.

**P5** Evaluate keep or replace decisions.

**P6** Determine product selling price.

**P7** Evaluate special offer decisions.

# Catch a Wave

*"Create something that makes people happy"*
—**MAX STEWART**

SYDNEY, AUSTRALIA—Working days for surfboard manufacturers and nights fixing shoes, Max Stewart saved enough money to finance his own start-up, **Eye Symmetry (EyeSymmetry.com)**. A one-man manufacturer, Max makes about 30 surfboards per month. "My goal is to create unique boards that surfers love," proclaims Max.

Each step of surfboard making is done by Max. "I have a unique way to laminate boards to make them lighter," explains Max. "I have a patented surfboard core." Unlike Max, many competitors outsource parts of board making, like fiberglass finishing and polishing. This "make or buy" decision depends on the costs of alternatives.

Max knows his costs. "My blanks cost about $85 to $110 each." Adding overhead costs like rent and utilities, Max estimates a cost of "about $500 per board, without paying myself anything." He tracks costs to help price his boards, which can sell for $850 per board or more.

Eye Symmetry recently expanded into other products, like clothing. Max tracks sales and costs for each business segment to ensure that it makes a positive contribution to covering costs

Eye Symmetry Pty Ltd.

and generating income. It is clear that Max is riding a wave of success. Says Max, "Go for it!"

Sources: *Eye Symmetry website*, January 2021; *Stabmag.com*, 2016; *Pacific Standard*, June 2017; www.youtube.com/watch?v=9Cbz43MKEgk

## DECISIONS AND INFORMATION

This chapter focuses on using accounting information to make managerial decisions. Many managerial tasks involve short-term decisions. This differs from longer-term managerial decisions described in the next chapter.

## Decision Making

Managerial decision making has five steps: (1) Define the decision, (2) identify alternatives, (3) collect relevant information and evaluate alternatives, (4) select the course of action, and (5) analyze and assess decisions made. These five steps are illustrated in Exhibit 10.1. Managers use *financial* information, like expected revenues and costs, for decision making. *Nonfinancial* information is also important and includes environmental and social data.

| Define decision | Identify alternative actions | Collect relevant information | Select course of action | Analyze and assess decision |

**EXHIBIT 10.1**

Managerial Decision Making

## Relevant Costs and Benefits

Managers must be able to distinguish between relevant and irrelevant costs and benefits. *Relevant costs and benefits* must be considered in managerial decisions. Relevant costs and benefits are future-oriented and focus on incremental effects from alternative managerial decisions. Those incremental, also called differential or avoidable, effects are important to define so that good managerial decisions are made.

- **Incremental revenues** are the additional revenues from selecting a certain course of action over another.

**C1**

Describe the use of relevant costs and benefits for short-term decisions.

"Sunk costs are not relevant to my decision."

"I must consider out-of-pocket and opportunity costs."

- **Incremental costs,** or *differential costs,* are the additional costs from selecting a certain course of action.
- **Incremental income** is incremental revenues minus incremental costs. A good rule is to choose the alternative that most increases incremental income.

Four types of costs are important in distinguishing relevant costs.

- *Sunk cost* arises from a past decision and cannot be avoided or changed; it is irrelevant to current and future decisions. An example is the $1,000 we *previously* paid for a smartphone. That sunk cost is not relevant to a decision to replace it if it breaks. Likewise, depreciation of the original cost of an asset is a sunk cost. Most of a company's allocated costs, including fixed overhead, are sunk costs.
- *Out-of-pocket cost* requires a future outlay of cash and is relevant for decisions. For instance, the cost of a *future* phone purchase is relevant to the decision of whether to replace a phone.
- *Opportunity cost* is the potential benefit lost by taking an action instead of an alternative action. An example is a student giving up wages from a job to attend summer school. The lost wages are part of the cost of attending summer school. Although opportunity costs are not entered in accounting records, they are relevant to many managerial decisions.
- *Avoidable cost* is a cost that can be eliminated by choosing one action versus another; an avoidable cost is always relevant. An example is worker pay that is avoidable if the work is automated.

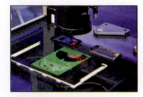

Zorazhuang/iStock/Getty Images Plus Collection/Getty Images

### ▪ Analytics **Insight**

**Sam-apple?** **Apple** buys its component parts from over 200 different suppliers, including competitors. For example, **Samsung** supplies screens for iPhones and iPads. Apple relies on data analytics to manage its vast supply chain and to analyze its incremental costs and revenues for production decisions. ▪

---

**NEED-TO-KNOW** 10-1

Relevant Costs

C1

Do More: QS 10-1, QS 10-3, QS 10-4

Georgia Co. produces and harvests peanuts at a cost of $20,000. The peanuts can be sold as is to a manufacturer for $35,000. Instead, Georgia can process the peanuts further into peanut butter. Processing further will cost an additional $25,000 and will result in total revenues of $55,000. Identify each revenue or cost as relevant or not relevant to Georgia's decision to sell as is or process further.

**Solution**

| Revenues and Costs | Relevant | Not Relevant |
|---|:---:|:---:|
| $20,000 cost to produce and harvest............ | | x |
| $55,000 revenue after further processing ....... | x | |
| $25,000 additional cost to process further....... | x | |
| $35,000 "as is" selling price ................. | x | |

---

## PRODUCTION DECISIONS

Analysis of incremental costs and benefits is useful in several short-term production decisions.

### Make or Buy

**P1** _____

Evaluate make or buy decisions.

Buying goods or services from an external supplier is called **outsourcing.** The decision to make or buy depends on the costs of each alternative. To illustrate, let's look at FasTrac, an exercise supplements and equipment manufacturer operating at 80% of capacity, and consider its production decisions.

FasTrac currently buys a key part for its main product for $1.20 per unit. With excess capacity, making this part would incur per unit variable costs of $0.35 for direct materials and $0.50 for direct labor. Management must also consider *incremental* overhead costs, which include power for operating machines, extra supplies, and added cleanup costs. Management estimates *incremental overhead* of $0.20 per unit if it makes the part. (A predetermined overhead rate is not relevant for this decision.) Our cost per unit analysis is in Exhibit 10.2. The cost to make this part is $1.05, which is less than the $1.20 to buy it. **Decision rule:** Select the action with the lower cost.

**EXHIBIT 10.2**

Make or Buy Analysis

| Make or Buy Analysis | Make | Buy |
|---|---|---|
| Direct materials . . . . . . . . . . . . . . . . . . . . . . . . . | $0.35 | — |
| Direct labor . . . . . . . . . . . . . . . . . . . . . . . . | 0.50 | — |
| Overhead (<u>incremental only</u>) . . . . . . . . . . . . . . . | 0.20 | — |
| Cost to buy. . . . . . . . . . . . . . . . . . . . . . . . . . . | — | $1.20 |
| Cost per unit . . . . . . . . . . . . . . . . . . . . . . . . . | $1.05 | $1.20 |
| **Decision: Cost savings to Make**. . . . . . . . . . . | | **$0.15** |

**Additional Factors**    While it is less costly to make the part in this case, the company also should consider nonfinancial factors. These include product quality, timeliness of delivery, reactions of suppliers, and employee morale and workload. When additional factors are considered, small cost per unit differences might not matter.

A company pays $5 per unit to buy a part for a product it manufactures. It can make the part for $1.50 per unit for direct materials and $3.50 per unit for direct labor. The company normally applies overhead costs at a predetermined rate of 50% of direct labor cost. Incremental overhead cost to make this part is $0.75 per unit. Should the company make or buy the part?

**NEED-TO-KNOW** 10-2

Make or Buy

**P1**

*Solution*

| Make or Buy Analysis | Make | Buy |
|---|---|---|
| Direct materials. . . . . . . . . . . . . . . . . | $1.50 | — |
| Direct labor . . . . . . . . . . . . . . . . . . . . | 3.50 | — |
| Overhead (incremental) . . . . . . . . . . | 0.75 | — |
| Cost to buy . . . . . . . . . . . . . . . . . . . . | — | $5.00 |
| Cost per unit . . . . . . . . . . . . . . . . . . | $5.75 | $5.00 |
| **Decision: Cost savings to Buy** . . . . | | **$0.75** |

The company should **buy the part** because the $5.75 cost to make it is more than the $5.00 cost to buy it. The predetermined overhead rate is not relevant, but incremental overhead cost is relevant.

Do More: QS 10-5, QS 10-6, E 10-1, E 10-2

# Sell or Process

Many companies must decide whether to sell partially completed products as is or to process them further into other products. For example, a peanut grower could sell its peanut harvest as is, or it could process peanuts further into other products such as peanut butter, peanut oil, and peanut lotion. The decision depends on the incremental costs and revenues of processing further.

**P2**

Evaluate sell or process decisions.

To illustrate, suppose a company has spent $30,000 to harvest peanuts. The company can sell the peanuts to another manufacturer as raw material for $50,000. Alternatively, it can process them further and produce a nutritional supplement. Processing further costs an additional $80,000 and will result in revenues of $150,000. The company must decide whether selling as is or processing further produces the higher income.

Exhibit 10.3 shows the sell or process analysis. The income of $70,000 from processing further is greater than the income of $50,000 from selling as is. The company should process further and earn $20,000 of incremental income ($70,000 − $50,000). The $30,000 of previously incurred harvest costs are excluded from the analysis. Those are sunk costs and are not relevant to the decision. **Decision rule:** Select the action with the higher income.

**EXHIBIT 10.3**

Sell or Process Analysis

| Sell or Process Analysis | Sell As Is | Process Further |
|---|---|---|
| Revenue . . . . . . . . . . . . . . . . . . . . . . . . . . | $50,000 | $150,000 |
| Cost. . . . . . . . . . . . . . . . . . . . . . . . . . . . . . . | — | 80,000 |
| Income. . . . . . . . . . . . . . . . . . . . . . . . . . . . | $50,000 | $ 70,000 |
| **Decision: Incremental income to Process Further. . . .** | | **$20,000** |

## Scrap or Rework

A variation of the sell or process further analysis is the scrap or rework analysis. Manufacturing processes sometimes yield defective products. Managers must decide whether to scrap or rework such products.

FasTrac has 1,000 defective units of a product that have already cost $10,000 to manufacture. These units can be sold as scrap for $4,000, or they can be reworked for $8,000 and then sold for $15,000. Should FasTrac sell the units as scrap or rework them?

The $10,000 manufacturing cost already incurred is a sunk cost and is irrelevant. The $4,000 revenue as scrap is the opportunity cost of reworking and is relevant. Analysis is in Exhibit 10.4. FasTrac should rework the units and obtain $3,000 ($7,000 − $4,000) of incremental income.

**EXHIBIT 10.4**

Scrap or Rework Analysis

| Scrap or Rework Analysis | Scrap | Rework |
|---|---|---|
| Revenue from scrapped/reworked units. . . . . | $ 4,000 | $15,000 |
| Cost of reworked units. . . . . . . . . . . . . . . . . . | | 8,000 |
| Income. . . . . . . . . . . . . . . . . . . . . . . . . . . . . | $ 4,000 | $ 7,000 |
| **Decision: Incremental income to Rework . . .** | | **$3,000** |

---

**NEED-TO-KNOW** 10-3

Sell or Process; and Scrap or Rework

**P2**

1. $20,000 of costs have been incurred to produce raw milk. The milk can be sold as is for $40,000 or processed further into ice cream. Processing further will cost $25,000, and the resulting ice cream can be sold for $60,000. Should the company sell the milk as is or process further?

2. $50,000 of costs have been incurred to produce a batch of defective handbags. The handbags can be sold as scrap for $15,000 or reworked into saleable handbags. Rework will cost $9,000, and the reworked handbags can be sold for $20,000. Should the company scrap or rework the handbags?

**Solution**

**1.**

| Sell or Process Further Analysis | Sell As Is | Process Further |
|---|---|---|
| Revenue . . . . . . . . . . . . . . . . . . . . . . . . . . . | $40,000 | $60,000 |
| Cost. . . . . . . . . . . . . . . . . . . . . . . . . . . . . . | — | 25,000 |
| Income. . . . . . . . . . . . . . . . . . . . . . . . . . . . | $40,000 | $35,000 |
| **Decision: Incremental income to Sell As Is . . .** | | **$5,000** |

**2.**

| Scrap or Rework Analysis | Scrap | Rework |
|---|---|---|
| Revenue from scrapped/reworked units . . | $15,000 | $20,000 |
| Cost of reworked units. . . . . . . . . . . . . . . | — | 9,000 |
| Income. . . . . . . . . . . . . . . . . . . . . . . . . . . . | $15,000 | $11,000 |
| **Decision: Incremental income to Scrap . . .** | | **$4,000** |

The milk should be **sold as is;** doing so will yield $5,000 ($40,000 − $35,000) of incremental income.

The handbags should be **scrapped;** doing so will yield $4,000 ($15,000 − $11,000) of incremental income.

Do More: QS 10-7, QS 10-8, E 10-3

---

## Sales Mix When Resources Constrained

**P3**_____

Determine sales mix with constrained resources.

When a company sells a mix of products, and its production facilities are operating at or near capacity, management looks for the most profitable *sales mix* of products. The *contribution margin per unit of constrained resource* is used to find the best sales mix.

To illustrate, let's look at a company that makes two models of scooters with selling prices and variable costs in Exhibit 10.5. The same machines are used to produce both models. The company has a capacity of 2,000 machine hours (MH) per year. Pro model uses 1 machine hour per unit while Max uses 2 machine hours per unit. **The company should produce the model that yields the highest contribution margin per machine hour, until market demand is satisfied.** Exhibit 10.5 shows the contribution margin per machine hour for both models. The Pro model has a higher contribution margin of $150 per *machine hour*. The company should produce as many units of Pro as possible, up to the market demand.

**EXHIBIT 10.5**

Product Contribution Margin per Machine Hour

| Product Contribution Margin | Pro | Max |
|---|---|---|
| Selling price per unit. . . . . . . . . . . . . . . . . . . . . . . . . | $500 | $750 |
| Variable costs per unit . . . . . . . . . . . . . . . . . . . . . . . | 350 | 550 |
| Contribution margin per unit . . . . . . . . . . . . . . . . . . | $150 | $200 |
| Machine hours per unit. . . . . . . . . . . . . . . . . . . . . . | 1 hr. | 2 hrs. |
| **Contribution margin per machine hour** . . . . . . . . . | **$150** ($150/1 hr.) | **$100** ($200/2 hrs.) |

**Point:** A machine hour producing Pro earns $150 versus only $100 from Max.

**Unlimited Demand**   If the market will buy all that the company can produce, the company should devote all 2,000 machine hours to produce the Pro model and none to the Max model. The 2,000 MH can produce 2,000 Pro scooters as each Pro requires 1 MH to make. This sales mix yields a contribution margin of $300,000, see Exhibit 10.6.

| Sales Mix with Unlimited Demand | Contribution Margin | Machine Hours Used |
|---|---|---|
| Pro (2,000 units × $150 per unit) . . . . . . . . | $300,000 | 2,000 |
| Max (0 units) . . . . . . . . . . . . . . . . . . . . . . . . | 0 | 0 |
| Total. . . . . . . . . . . . . . . . . . . . . . . . . . . . . . | $300,000 | 2,000 |

**EXHIBIT 10.6**

Contribution Margin from Sales Mix with **Unlimited** Demand

**Limited Demand**   If demand for the Pro model is limited to 1,200 units, the company will first produce 1,200 units of Pro using 1,200 machine hours required to make them. This leaves 800 machine hours to produce the Max model. The 800 MH result in 400 Max scooters as each Max requires 2 MH to make. This sales mix yields a $220,000 contribution margin in Exhibit 10.7.

| Sales Mix with Limited Demand | Contribution Margin | Machine Hours Used |
|---|---|---|
| Pro (1,200 units × $150 per unit) . . . . . . . . | $180,000 | 1,200 |
| Max (400 units × $100 per unit) . . . . . . . . . | 40,000 | 800 |
| Total. . . . . . . . . . . . . . . . . . . . . . . . . . . . . . | $220,000 | 2,000 |

**EXHIBIT 10.7**

Contribution Margin from Sales Mix with **Limited** Demand

**Decision rule:** Produce the product with the highest contribution margin per unit of scarce resource up to its total demand. Use remaining capacity to produce the product with the next highest contribution margin per unit of scarce resource.

 **Decision Insight** ━━━━━━━━━━━━━━━━━━━━━━━━━━

**Truckin'**   **Ford** sells over 2 million vehicles per year. With customers preferring larger vehicles, Ford's sales mix has shifted towards trucks and SUVs. Car sales are now less than 15% of Ford's total unit sales. ■

iqoncept/123RF

**NEED-TO-KNOW** 10-4

Sales Mix

P3

A company produces two products, Gamma and Omega. Gamma sells for $10 per unit and Omega sells for $12.50 per unit. Variable costs are $7 per unit for Gamma and $8 per unit for Omega. The company has a capacity of 5,000 machine hours per month. Gamma uses 1 machine hour per unit and Omega uses 3 machine hours per unit.

1. Compute the contribution margin per machine hour for each product.

2. Demand for Gamma is limited to 3,800 units per month. How many units of Gamma and Omega should the company produce, and what is the total contribution margin from this sales mix?

**Solution**

1.

| Product Contribution Margin | Gamma | Omega |
|---|---|---|
| Selling price per unit.......................... | $10.00 | $12.50 |
| Variable costs per unit ......................... | 7.00 | 8.00 |
| Contribution margin per unit .................... | $ 3.00 | $ 4.50 |
| Machine hours per unit......................... | 1 hr. | 3 hrs. |
| Contribution margin per machine hour......... | $ 3.00 | $ 1.50 |

2. Because Gamma has the higher contribution margin per machine hour, the company will begin by producing Gamma to meet the market demand of 3,800 units. That production level will use 3,800 machine hours, leaving 1,200 machine hours to produce Omega. With 1,200 machine hours, the company can produce 400 units (1,200 remaining machine hours/3 machine hours per unit) of Omega. Total contribution margin from this sales mix follows.

| Sales Mix with Limited Demand | Contribution Margin | Machine Hours Used |
|---|---|---|
| Gamma (3,800 units × $3.00 per unit) ...... | $11,400 | 3,800 |
| Omega (400 units × $4.50 per unit) ........ | 1,800 | 1,200 |
| Total.................................... | $13,200 | 5,000 |

Do More: QS 10-12, E 10-6, E 10-7

---

## CAPACITY DECISIONS

**P4**

Evaluate segment elimination decisions.

### Segment Elimination

When a segment of a business is performing poorly, management must consider eliminating it. Segments with contribution margin less than *avoidable fixed costs* are candidates for elimination.

- **Avoidable costs** are eliminated when the segment is eliminated; they include all variable costs and direct fixed costs such as rent on that segment's space and insurance on that segment's eliminated equipment.

- **Unavoidable costs** remain even if the segment is eliminated; these costs are allocated to remaining segments when a segment is eliminated.

FasTrac reports results for its three segments in Exhibit 10.8. Total income is $95,000. However, its Treadmill segment shows a $10,000 loss. Management is considering eliminating its Treadmill segment. We must be careful as some segment costs might be unavoidable even if the segment is eliminated.

**EXHIBIT 10.8**

Segment Income

| | Segment Income before Segment Elimination | | | |
|---|---|---|---|---|
| | Treadmill | Wellness | Fitness | Total |
| Sales | $ 40,000 | $200,000 | $100,000 | $340,000 |
| Variable costs | 35,000 | 110,000 | 55,000 | 200,000 |
| Contribution margin | 5,000 | 90,000 | 45,000 | 140,000 |
| Fixed costs | 15,000 | 20,000 | 10,000 | 45,000 |
| Income (loss) | $(10,000) | $ 70,000 | $ 35,000 | $ 95,000 |

Eliminating the Treadmill division would eliminate its sales, variable costs, and contribution margin. Its $15,000 in fixed costs consists of $4,000 in avoidable costs and $11,000 in unavoidable costs. The $11,000 in unavoidable costs would be reallocated to Wellness ($8,000) and Fitness ($3,000). Revised results are in Exhibit 10.9. We see that if the Treadmill

**Point:** Treadmill's $5,000 contribution margin in Exhibit 10.8 exceeded its $4,000 avoidable fixed costs.

segment is eliminated, total income decreases by $1,000, from $95,000 to $94,000. This means the *Treadmill segment should continue*.

| Segment Income after Segment Elimination | | | |
|---|---|---|---|
| | **Wellness** | **Fitness** | **Total** |
| Sales | $200,000 | $100,000 | $300,000 |
| Variable costs | 110,000 | 55,000 | 165,000 |
| Contribution margin | 90,000 | 45,000 | 135,000 |
| Fixed costs | **28,000** | **13,000** | 41,000 |
| Income (loss) | $ 62,000 | $ 32,000 | **$ 94,000** |

**EXHIBIT 10.9**

Segment Income after Segment Elimination

The same decision is made using the segment elimination analysis in Exhibit 10.10. The Continue column shows Treadmill results for the current period. The Eliminate column shows what items remain after the segment is eliminated. We see $0 for sales, variable costs, and contribution margin as they all disappear if the segment is eliminated. The Eliminate column does show $11,000 of fixed costs that are unavoidable even if the segment is eliminated.

The Income Increase (Decrease) column shows the $1,000 decreased income if the segment is eliminated. This indicates the segment should *not* be eliminated and is the same result from comparing Exhibit 10.8 to Exhibit 10.9. **Decision rule:** A segment should be eliminated if income increases from elimination; it should continue if income decreases from elimination.

**Point:** Segment should continue if its contribution margin exceeds its avoidable fixed costs.

| Segment Elimination Analysis | Continue | Eliminate | Income Increase (Decrease) |
|---|---|---|---|
| Sales | $ 40,000 | $      0 | |
| Variable costs | 35,000 | 0 | |
| Contribution margin | 5,000 | 0 | |
| Fixed costs | 15,000 | 11,000 | |
| Income (loss) | $(10,000) | $(11,000) | **$(1,000)** |

**EXHIBIT 10.10**

Segment Elimination Analysis

## Keep or Replace

Managers periodically must decide whether to keep using a plant asset such as equipment or to replace it. Advances in technology typically mean newer equipment can operate more efficiently and at lower cost.

The keep or replace analysis compares the revenues and costs of keeping the old asset versus replacing with the new asset. Relevant revenues and costs include any change in variable manufacturing costs with the new asset and the net cost of the new asset (computed as its purchase price minus any trade-in allowance or cash received from sale of the old asset).

To illustrate, FasTrac is considering replacing an existing machine with a new machine.

**P5**

Evaluate keep or replace decisions.

**Point:** Next chapter looks at time value of money in a keep or replace analysis.

| **Existing Machine** | |
|---|---|
| Book value . . . . . . . . . . . . . . . . . . . . . . . . | $20,000 |
| Variable manufacturing costs per year . . . | $50,000 |
| Salvage value . . . . . . . . . . . . . . . . . . . . . . | $    0 |
| Selling price currently. . . . . . . . . . . . . . . . | $25,000 |
| Remaining useful life . . . . . . . . . . . . . . . . | 5 years |

| **New Machine** | |
|---|---|
| Purchase price . . . . . . . . . . . . . . . . . . . . . | $100,000 |
| Variable manufacturing costs per year . . . | $ 36,000 |
| | |
| | |
| Useful life . . . . . . . . . . . . . . . . . . . . . . . . | 5 years |

The keep or replace analysis is in Exhibit 10.11. We should keep the existing machine because to replace it will decrease income by $5,000. The $20,000 book value of the old machine is not relevant as book value is a sunk cost and cannot be changed. **Decision rule:** Replace an asset if income increases (but keep the asset if income decreases) from the replacement.

**EXHIBIT 10.11**

Keep or Replace Analysis

| Keep or Replace Analysis | Keep | Replace | Income Increase (Decrease) |
|---|---|---|---|
| Revenues | | | |
|   Sale of existing machine | | $  25,000 | |
| Costs | | | |
|   Purchase of new machine | | (100,000) | |
|   Variable manufacturing costs | $(250,000)[†] | (180,000)[‡] | |
| Income (loss) | $(250,000) | $(255,000) | **$(5,000)** |

[†]$50,000 × 5 years    [‡]$36,000 × 5 years

 **10-5**

Segment Elimination

**P4**

A bike maker is considering eliminating its Tandem Bike division as it reports the following loss for the year. All $30,000 of its variable costs are avoidable, and $12,000 of its fixed costs are avoidable. Determine whether the division should be eliminated.

|  | Tandem Bike |
|---|---|
| Sales | $40,000 |
| Variable costs | 30,000 |
| Contribution margin | 10,000 |
| Fixed costs | 16,000 |
| Income (loss) | $ (6,000) |

**Solution**

| Segment Elimination Analysis | Continue | Eliminate | Income Increase (Decrease) |
|---|---|---|---|
| Sales | $40,000 | $    0 | |
| Variable costs | 30,000 | 0 | |
| Contribution margin | 10,000 | 0 | |
| Fixed costs | 16,000 | 4,000 | |
| Income (loss) | $ (6,000) | $(4,000) | **$2,000** |

Do More: QS 10-13, QS 10-14, E 10-8

Decision: Eliminate the division. Total income increases by $2,000 from eliminating the division. This is because the $10,000 in lost contribution margin from the Tandem bike division is exceeded by the $12,000 savings from eliminating avoidable fixed costs.

# PRICING DECISIONS

**P6**

Determine product selling price.

**Price-Setters**

- Weak competition
- Product is unique
- Product branded
- High barriers to entry
- → Cost-plus pricing

**Price-Takers**

- Strong competition
- Product not unique
- Product not branded
- Low barriers to entry
- → Target pricing

Eye Symmetry Pty Ltd.

## Normal Pricing

Pricing decisions are one of the more important decisions managers make. They are also one of the most difficult decisions. Managers must take concepts involving supply and demand and apply them to product or service pricing. It is important for managers to understand the setting in which they set prices.

Companies can be **price-takers** or **price-setters** or anywhere in between. The graphic to the side reflects this range and the characteristics of companies at the extremes. Price-setters have more control over setting prices, whereas price-takers have less control. Price-setters use more cost-plus pricing methods, and price-takers use more target pricing. Most companies lie in between. We describe three normal pricing methods.

**Total Cost Method**   *Cost-plus* methods are common when companies are price-setters. Management adds a **markup** to cost to get selling price: Selling price per unit = Cost per unit + Markup per unit. The **total cost method**, or *cost-plus pricing,* is a three-step process.

**1** Determine total cost per unit.

> **Total costs = Product costs + Selling, general, and administrative costs**

> **Total cost per unit = Total costs ÷ Total units expected to be produced and sold**

**2** Determine dollar markup per unit.

> **Markup per unit = Total cost per unit × Markup percentage**

**3** Determine selling price per unit.

> **Selling price per unit = Total cost per unit + Markup per unit**

To illustrate, a company produces headphones and it targets a 20% markup on total cost. It expects to produce and sell 10,000 headphones. The following additional information is available.

| Variable costs (per unit) | | Fixed costs (total) | |
|---|---|---|---|
| Direct materials | $20 | Overhead | $140,000 |
| Direct labor | 16 | Selling, general, and administrative | 60,000 |
| Overhead | 8 | | |
| Selling, general, and administrative | 6 | | |

We apply the three-step total cost method to determine selling price per unit.

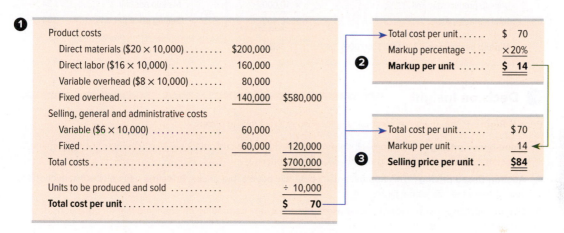

**Target Cost Method**   When competition is high, companies might be price-takers and have little control in setting prices. In such cases **target costing**, or *target pricing,* can be useful. Target cost is defined as

$$\text{Target cost} = \text{Expected selling price} - \text{Target profit}$$

If the target cost is too high, lean techniques can be used to determine whether the cost can be reduced enough that the target profit can be made. For example, if the expected selling price for headphones is $80 each and the company wants to make a profit of $14 per unit, it must find a way to reduce its target cost per unit to $66 ($80 price − $14 target profit).

**Variable Cost Method**   The **variable cost method** determines price by adding a markup to variable cost. The markup is set to cover fixed costs plus target profit on top of variable cost. Three steps are needed.

① Determine markup percentage.

$$\text{Markup percentage} = \frac{\text{Target profit} + \text{Total fixed costs}}{\text{Total variable cost}}$$

② Determine dollar markup per unit.

$$\text{Markup per unit} = \text{Variable cost per unit} \times \text{Markup percentage}$$

③ Determine selling price per unit.

$$\text{Selling price per unit} = \text{Variable cost per unit} + \text{Markup per unit}$$

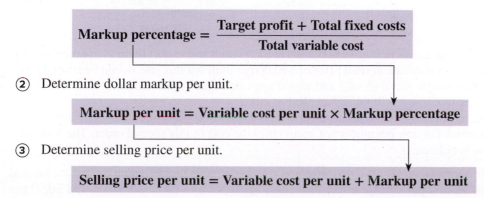

To illustrate, we apply these three steps to the 10,000 headphones from the total cost example above. Assume the target profit is $140,000. Following shows the selling price is $84 per unit.

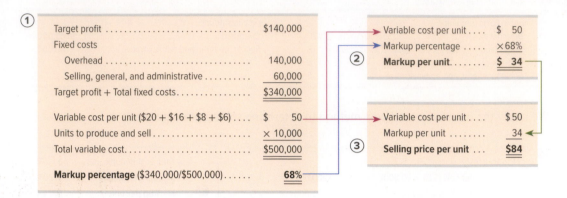

| ① | | | | | | | |
|---|---|---|---|---|---|---|---|
| Target profit | $140,000 | | | Variable cost per unit | $ 50 | | |
| Fixed costs | | | | Markup percentage | ×68% | | |
| Overhead | 140,000 | | ② | **Markup per unit** | **$ 34** | | |
| Selling, general, and administrative | 60,000 | | | | | | |
| Target profit + Total fixed costs | $340,000 | | | | | | |
| | | | | Variable cost per unit | $ 50 | | |
| Variable cost per unit ($20 + $16 + $8 + $6) | $ 50 | | | Markup per unit | 34 | | |
| Units to produce and sell | × 10,000 | | ③ | **Selling price per unit** | **$84** | | |
| Total variable cost | $500,000 | | | | | | |
| **Markup percentage ($340,000/$500,000)** | **68%** | | | | | | |

Kaspars Grinvalds/Shutterstock

### ■ Decision Insight

**Price is Right**    Companies use some very unique ways to set selling prices.

● **Value-based pricing**    This approach determines the maximum customers will pay without reducing demand. **Starbucks** uses data analytics in setting value-based prices.

● **Auction-based pricing**    This approach uses potential buyers' bid prices. **Priceline** uses electronic auctions to sell hotel rooms and airline flights.

● **Dynamic pricing** (*surge pricing*)    **Uber** uses prices that vary depending on changing market conditions or customer demand. ■

## P7

Evaluate special offer decisions.

## Special Pricing

Companies sometimes receive special offers at prices lower than their normal selling prices. We evaluate these special offers by computing their income effects. To illustrate, FasTrac produces and sells 100,000 units annually. Its per unit and annual sales and costs are in the contribution margin income statement in Exhibit 10.12. Its normal selling price is $10.00 per unit, and each unit sold generates $2.00 per unit of income.

**EXHIBIT 10.12**

Contribution Margin Income Statement

| Contribution Margin Income Statement | | |
|---|---|---|
| For Year Ended December 31 | Per Unit | Total |
| Sales (100,000 units) | $10.00 | $1,000,000 |
| Variable costs | | |
| Direct materials | 3.50 | 350,000 |
| Direct labor | 2.20 | 220,000 |
| Variable overhead | 0.90 | 90,000 |
| Contribution margin | 3.40 | 340,000 |
| Fixed costs | | |
| Fixed overhead | 0.60 | 60,000 |
| Fixed general and administrative | 0.80 | 80,000 |
| Income | $ 2.00 | $ 200,000 |

A new customer wants to buy 10,000 units at $8.50 each and export them to another country. The offer price is below the normal price of $10.00 per unit, but this sale would be several times larger than any single previous sale and would use idle capacity. Because the units will be exported, this new business will not affect current sales.

We focus on incremental costs to determine whether accepting the offer will increase income. The historical cost per unit is not necessarily the cost of this special order. The following information is collected.

● Variable manufacturing costs to produce this order will be the same as for its normal business—$3.50 per unit for direct materials, $2.20 per unit for direct labor, and $0.90 per unit for variable overhead.

- Fixed overhead costs will not change regardless of whether this order is accepted. Fixed overhead costs of $0.60 per unit on normal business are not relevant to this decision.
- This order will incur *incremental* fixed general and administrative costs of $1,000.

We prepare a contribution margin income statement covering only this special offer in Exhibit 10.13. It shows that accepting this special offer yields $18,000 of additional income. **Decision rule:** Accept the special offer if income increases (reject it if income decreases).

**EXHIBIT 10.13**

Special Offer Analysis

| Special Offer Analysis | Per Unit | Total |
|---|---|---|
| Sales (10,000 units) . . . . . . . . . . . . . . . . . . . | $8.50 | $85,000 |
| Variable costs | | |
| Direct materials . . . . . . . . . . . . . . . . . . . . | 3.50 | 35,000 |
| Direct labor. . . . . . . . . . . . . . . . . . . . . . . | 2.20 | 22,000 |
| Variable overhead . . . . . . . . . . . . . . . . . | 0.90 | 9,000 |
| Contribution margin . . . . . . . . . . . . . . . . . | 1.90 | 19,000 |
| Fixed costs | | |
| Fixed overhead. . . . . . . . . . . . . . . . . . . . | — | — |
| Fixed general and administrative . . . . . . . | 0.10 | 1,000 |
| **Income** . . . . . . . . . . . . . . . . . . . . . . . . . . | **$1.80** | **$18,000** |

A company produces a single product and operates at 80% of its capacity. Costs to produce its current monthly sales of 8,000 units follow. The normal selling price is $22 per unit. A potential new customer wants to buy 1,000 units for $18 per unit. These units would be exported and not affect domestic sales. This order would require $3,000 of incremental fixed overhead and $1,000 of incremental fixed general and administrative costs. Should management accept the special offer?

**NEED-TO-KNOW 10-6**

Special Pricing

**P7**

| Total Costs (at 8,000 units) | Per Unit | Total |
|---|---|---|
| Variable costs | | |
| Direct materials . . . . . . . . . . . . . . . . . . . . | $5.00 | $40,000 |
| Direct labor. . . . . . . . . . . . . . . . . . . . . . . | 8.00 | 64,000 |
| Variable overhead . . . . . . . . . . . . . . . . . | 2.20 | 17,600 |
| Fixed costs | | |
| Fixed overhead. . . . . . . . . . . . . . . . . . . . | 2.80 | 22,400 |
| Fixed general and administrative . . . . . . . . | 1.00 | 8,000 |
| Total costs . . . . . . . . . . . . . . . . . . . . . . . | $19.00 | $152,000 |

*Solution*

| Special Offer Analysis | Per Unit | Total |
|---|---|---|
| Sales (1,000 units) . . . . . . . . . . . . . . . . . . | $18.00 | $18,000 |
| Variable costs | | |
| Direct materials . . . . . . . . . . . . . . . . . . . . | 5.00 | 5,000 |
| Direct labor. . . . . . . . . . . . . . . . . . . . . . . | 8.00 | 8,000 |
| Variable overhead . . . . . . . . . . . . . . . . . | 2.20 | 2,200 |
| Contribution margin . . . . . . . . . . . . . . . . . | 2.80 | 2,800 |
| Fixed costs | | |
| Fixed overhead. . . . . . . . . . . . . . . . . . . . | 3.00 | 3,000 |
| Fixed general and administrative . . . . . . . . | 1.00 | 1,000 |
| **Income (loss)** . . . . . . . . . . . . . . . . . . . . . | **$(1.20)** | **$(1,200)** |

Do More: QS 10-20, E 10-13, E 10-14

**Special offer should be rejected.** The special offer would decrease income by $1,200.

## CORPORATE SOCIAL RESPONSIBILITY

Eye Symmetry Pty Ltd.

Managers consider social responsibility in many of the decisions in this chapter. Companies that buy rather than make components must consider the labor and safety practices of suppliers. **Apple** requires its suppliers to comply with its *Supplier Code of Conduct* (https://images.apple.com/supplier-responsibility/pdf/Apple-Supplier-Code-of-Conduct-January.pdf). This code details Apple's requirements with respect to antidiscrimination, antiharassment, prevention of involuntary labor and human trafficking, and other issues. In a recent report, Apple noted 97% compliance with its requirements.

Another responsible practice is to reduce waste. Poorly made surfboards that break usually end up in landfills. Max Stewart, founder of **Eye Symmetry**, uses carbon fiber "stringers" [middle pieces] in his boards. "Making the stringers by hand adds four hours to each surfboard," explains Max, "but it keeps the board from breaking in half." Max's focus on innovation is good for his customers and the environment.

---

**Decision Analysis**       **Time and Materials Pricing**

## A1

Determine price of services using time and materials pricing.

It is common to price services using **time and materials pricing.** With this method, companies set a price for direct labor and a price for direct materials, and each includes a charge for overhead costs and a target profit. Auto mechanics, construction companies, electricians, and accounting firms commonly use time and materials pricing. Time and materials pricing follows three steps.

1. Compute **time charge** (in $) per hour of direct labor. This includes a charge for non-materials-related overhead costs plus a target profit.

2. Compute **materials markup** (%), which includes overhead costs related to buying, storing, and handling materials, plus a target profit margin on materials' cost.

3. Estimate direct labor hours and costs, direct materials cost, and the markup to get price.

To illustrate, we use the following estimates for Erin Builders.

| | |
|---|---|
| Direct labor rate ........................................... | $40 per DLH |
| Non-materials-related overhead ............................. | $10 per DLH |
| Materials-related overhead ................................. | 3% of direct materials cost |
| Target profit margin (on both conversion and direct materials)..... | 22% |

**1** Time charge per hour of direct labor.

| | |
|---|---|
| Direct labor rate per hour................. | $40 |
| Non-materials-related overhead per hour.... | 10 |
| Total hourly conversion cost .............. | 50 |
| Target profit ($50 × 22%)................ | 11 |
| Time charge per hour of direct labor........ | $61 |

**2** Materials markup per dollar of materials cost.

| | |
|---|---|
| Materials-related overhead ........... | 3% |
| Target profit margin ................. | 22% |
| Materials markup .................... | 25% |

**3** Job is estimated to use 300 direct labor hours (DLH) and $14,000 of direct materials. Time and materials pricing yields a $35,800 price in Exhibit 10.14.

**EXHIBIT 10.14**

Time and Materials Pricing

| Time and Materials Price | |
|---|---|
| Direct labor (300 hours × $61 per DLH) ..... | $18,300 |
| Direct materials ........................ | 14,000 |
| Materials markup ($14,000 × 25%) ........ | 3,500 |
| **Time and materials price ...............** | **$35,800** |

---

**NEED-TO-KNOW 10-7**

**COMPREHENSIVE**

Manager Decisions

Determine the best decision in each of the following separate situations. For each decision, assume the company has sufficient excess capacity.

**Production Decisions**

1. **Make or Buy.**   Green Co. uses part JJ in manufacturing its products. It currently buys this part for $40 per unit. Making the part would require direct materials of $11 per unit and direct labor of $15 per unit (1 direct labor hour per unit). Green normally applies overhead using a predetermined overhead

rate of $30 per direct labor hour. Making the part would require incremental overhead of $17 per direct labor hour. Should Green make or buy the part?

**2. Sell or Process.**   Gold Co. makes a product that can be either sold as is or processed further. The company has already spent $75,000 to produce 10,000 units that can be sold as is for $100,000. Instead, the units can be processed further at a cost of $80,000, and then sold for $220,000.  Should Gold sell the 10,000 units as is or process them further?

**3. Scrap or Rework.**   Packer Co. has already spent $90,000 to produce 1,200 defective earbuds. A salvage company will buy the earbuds as is for $66,000. Instead, Packer can rework the earbuds for $30,000 and sell them for $120,000. Should Packer scrap or rework the earbuds?

**4. Sales Mix.**   Champ Co. can sell all units of both types of scooters it produces, but it has capacity of only 900 machine hours. The Edge model uses two machine hours per unit and the Razz model uses three machine hours per unit. Selling prices and variable costs per unit follow. Compute the contribution margin per machine hour for each product and then determine the best sales mix.

| Product Models | Edge | Razz |
|---|---|---|
| Selling price per unit...... | $150 | $180 |
| Variable costs per unit .... | 100 | 120 |

## Capacity Decisions

**5. Segment Elimination.**   Badger Co. is considering eliminating its snowboard division as it shows a $5,000 loss for the year (see below). All its variable costs are avoidable, and $25,000 of its fixed costs are avoidable. Compute the income increase or decrease from eliminating this segment. Should the division be eliminated?

| Segment Results | Snowboard |
|---|---|
| Sales | $98,000 |
| Variable costs | 75,000 |
| Contribution margin | 23,000 |
| Fixed costs | 28,000 |
| Income (loss) | $ (5,000) |

**6. Keep or Replace.**   Buckeye Inc. has an old machine with a book value of $95,000 and a remaining five-year useful life. Buckeye can sell this old machine today for $70,000. The old machine has variable manufacturing costs of $26,000 per year. A new machine can be purchased for $115,000. The new machine would reduce variable manufacturing costs by $16,000 per year over its five-year useful life. Should Buckeye keep or replace the old machine?

## Pricing Decisions

**7. Total Cost Pricing.**   LA Surf sells surfboards. Each surfboard requires direct materials of $55, direct labor of $35, variable overhead of $20, and variable selling, general, and administrative costs of $20. Fixed overhead costs are $90,000 per year and fixed selling, general, and administrative costs are $120,000 per year. The company plans to produce and sell 1,000 surfboards in the next year. Compute the selling price per unit if LA Surf uses a markup of 20% of total cost.

**8. Special Offer Pricing.**   Marlin Co. produces and sells fishing rods for $35 each. Per unit costs follow. A foreign company has offered to buy 10,000 units at $22 each. If Marlin accepts this special offer, it will incur $2,000 of incremental fixed overhead costs and $5,000 of incremental fixed general and administrative costs. Should Marlin accept the special offer?

| Total Costs | Per Unit |
|---|---|
| Variable costs | |
| Direct materials ....................... | $ 8.00 |
| Direct labor.......................... | 7.00 |
| Variable overhead ................... | 1.50 |
| Fixed costs | |
| Fixed overhead....................... | 2.00 |
| Fixed general and administrative ......... | 1.00 |
| Total costs.............................. | $19.50 |

## SOLUTION

### 1. Make or Buy Decision

| Make or Buy Analysis | Make | Buy |
|---|---|---|
| Direct materials. . . . . . . . . . . . . . . | $11 | — |
| Direct labor . . . . . . . . . . . . . . . . . . | 15 | — |
| Overhead (incremental) . . . . . . . . | 17 | — |
| Cost to buy . . . . . . . . . . . . . . . . . . | — | $40 |
| Cost per unit . . . . . . . . . . . . . . . . . | $43 | $40 |
| **Decision: Cost savings to Buy** . . . | | **$3** |

Buy the part as there is an incremental cost savings of $3 per unit.

### 2. Sell or Process Further Decision

| Sell or Process Analysis | Sell As Is | Process Further |
|---|---|---|
| Revenue . . . . . . . . . . . . . . . . . | $100,000 | $220,000 |
| Cost . . . . . . . . . . . . . . . . . . . . | — | 80,000 |
| Income . . . . . . . . . . . . . . . . . | $100,000 | $140,000 |
| **Decision: Incremental income to Process Further** . . . . . . . . . . . . . . . . | | **$40,000** |

Process further and earn incremental income of $40,000.

### 3. Scrap or Rework Decision

| Scrap or Rework Analysis | Scrap | Rework |
|---|---|---|
| Revenue from scrapped/reworked units . . . . . | $66,000 | $120,000 |
| Cost of reworked units . . . . . . . . . . . . . . . . | — | 30,000 |
| Income. . . . . . . . . . . . . . . . . . . . . . . . . . . | $66,000 | $ 90,000 |
| **Decision: Incremental income to Rework** . . . | | **$24,000** |

Rework the units and earn incremental income of $24,000.

### 4. Sales Mix Decision

| Product Contribution margin | Edge | Razz |
|---|---|---|
| Selling price per unit. . . . . . . . . . . . . . . . . . . . | $150 | $180 |
| Variable costs per unit . . . . . . . . . . . . . . . . . . | 100 | 120 |
| Contribution margin per unit . . . . . . . . . . . . . | $ 50 | $ 60 |
| Machine hours per unit. . . . . . . . . . . . . . . . . | 2 hrs. | 3 hrs. |
| **Contribution margin per machine hour** . . . . | **$ 25**<br>($50/2hrs.) | **$ 20**<br>($60/3 hrs.) |

With unlimited demand, only make the Edge.

Sales mix and resulting contribution margin follow.

| Sales Mix with<br>Unlimited Demand | Contribution<br>Margin | Machine<br>Hours Used |
|---|---|---|
| Edge (450 units × $50 per unit) . . . . | $22,500 | 900 |
| Razz (0 units). . . . . . . . . . . . . . . . . | 0 | 0 |
| Total. . . . . . . . . . . . . . . . . . . . . . . | $22,500 | 900 |

### 5. Segment Elimination Decision

| Segment Elimination Analysis | Continue | Eliminate | Income Increase (Decrease) |
|---|---|---|---|
| Sales | $98,000 | $ 0 | |
| Variable costs | 75,000 | 0 | |
| Contribution margin | 23,000 | 0 | |
| Fixed costs | 28,000 | 3,000 | |
| Income (loss) | $ (5,000) | $(3,000) | **$2,000** |

Eliminate the segment and increase income by $2,000.

### 6. Keep or Replace Decision

| Keep or Replace Analysis | Keep | Replace | Income Increase (Decrease) |
|---|---|---|---|
| Revenues | | | |
| Sale of existing machine | | $ 70,000 | |
| Costs | | | |
| Purchase of new machine | | (115,000) | |
| Variable manufacturing costs | $(130,000)[†] | (50,000)[‡] | |
| Income (loss) | $(130,000) | $ (95,000) | **$35,000** |

[†]$26,000 × 5 years    [‡]$10,000 × 5 years

Replace the machine and increase income by $35,000.

### 7. Total Cost Pricing Decision

①

| | | |
|---|---|---|
| Product costs | | |
| Direct materials ($55 × 1,000) . . . . . . . . . | $ 55,000 | |
| Direct labor ($35 × 1,000). . . . . . . . . . . . . | 35,000 | |
| Variable overhead ($20 × 1,000) . . . . . . . . | 20,000 | |
| Fixed overhead. . . . . . . . . . . . . . . . . . . . | 90,000 | $200,000 |
| Selling, general, and administrative costs | | |
| Variable ($20 × 1,000) . . . . . . . . . . . . . . . | 20,000 | |
| Fixed . . . . . . . . . . . . . . . . . . . . . . . . . . . | 120,000 | 140,000 |
| Total costs . . . . . . . . . . . . . . . . . . . . . . . . | | $340,000 |
| Units to be produced and sold . . . . . . . . . . | | ÷ 1,000 |
| Total cost per unit . . . . . . . . . . . . . . . . . . . | | $ 340 |

② 

| | |
|---|---|
| Total cost per unit . . . . | $ 340 |
| Markup percentage . . | × 20% |
| Markup per unit . . . . . | $ 68 |

③

| | |
|---|---|
| Total cost per unit . . . . . . . | $340 |
| Markup per unit . . . . . . . . | 68 |
| **Selling price per unit** . . . | **$408** |

Set the selling price at $408 per unit.

### 8. Special Offer Pricing Decision

| Special Offer Analysis | Per Unit | Total |
|---|---|---|
| Sales (10,000 units) . . . . . . . . . . . . . . . . . . | $22.00 | $220,000 |
| Variable costs | | |
| Direct materials . . . . . . . . . . . . . . . . . . . | 8.00 | 80,000 |
| Direct labor. . . . . . . . . . . . . . . . . . . . . . | 7.00 | 70,000 |
| Variable overhead . . . . . . . . . . . . . . . . . | 1.50 | 15,000 |
| Contribution margin . . . . . . . . . . . . . . . . . | 5.50 | 55,000 |
| Fixed costs | | |
| Fixed overhead. . . . . . . . . . . . . . . . . . . . | 0.20 | 2,000 |
| Fixed general and administrative . . . . . . | 0.50 | 5,000 |
| **Income** . . . . . . . . . . . . . . . . . . . . . . . . . . | **$ 4.80** | **$ 48,000** |

Accept the special offer as it increases income by $48,000.

## Summary: Cheat Sheet

### DECISIONS AND INFORMATION

| Revenues and Costs | Relevant? |
|---|---|
| **Incremental revenue:** Additional revenues from a decision. | Yes |
| **Incremental cost:** Additional costs from a decision. | Yes |
| **Incremental income:** Income difference across alternatives. | Yes |
| **Sunk cost:** From a past decision and cannot be changed. | No |
| **Out-of-pocket cost:** Future outlay of cash. | Yes |
| **Opportunity cost:** Potential benefit lost from taking an action when alternatives exist. | Yes |

### PRODUCTION DECISIONS

#### Make or Buy
Select action with lower cost.

| Make or Buy Analysis | Make | Buy |
|---|---|---|
| Direct materials | $0.35 | — |
| Direct labor | 0.50 | — |
| Overhead (incremental only) | 0.20 | — |
| Cost to buy | — | $1.20 |
| Cost per unit | $1.05 | $1.20 |
| **Decision: Cost savings to Make** | **$0.15** | |

#### Sell or Process
Select action with higher income.

| Sell or Process Analysis | Sell As Is | Process Further |
|---|---|---|
| Revenue | $50,000 | $150,000 |
| Cost | — | 80,000 |
| Income | $50,000 | $ 70,000 |
| **Decision: Incremental income to Process Further** | **$20,000** | |

#### Scrap or Rework
Select action with higher income.

| Scrap or Rework Analysis | Scrap | Rework |
|---|---|---|
| Revenue from scrapped/reworked units | $4,000 | $15,000 |
| Cost of reworked units | | 8,000 |
| Income | $4,000 | $ 7,000 |
| **Decision: Incremental income to Rework** | **$3,000** | |

#### Sales Mix

| Product Contribution Margin | Pro | Max |
|---|---|---|
| Selling price per unit | $500 | $750 |
| Variable costs per unit | 350 | 550 |
| Contribution margin per unit | $150 | $200 |
| Machine hours per unit | 1 hr. | 2 hrs. |
| **Contribution margin per machine hour** | **$150**<br>($150/1 hr.) | **$100**<br>($200/2 hrs.) |

**Unlimited Demand:** Produce product with highest contribution margin per unit of scarce resource.

| Sales Mix with Unlimited Demand | Contribution Margin | Machine Hours Used |
|---|---|---|
| Pro (2,000 units × $150 per unit) | $300,000 | 2,000 |
| Max (0 units) | 0 | 0 |
| Total | $300,000 | 2,000 |

**Limited Demand:** Produce product with highest contribution margin per unit of scarce resource up to its total demand. Then produce the product with next highest contribution margin, and so forth.

| Sales Mix with Limited Demand | Contribution Margin | Machine Hours Used |
|---|---|---|
| Pro (1,200 units × $150 per unit) | $180,000 | 1,200 |
| Max (400 units × $100 per unit) | 40,000 | 800 |
| Total | $220,000 | 2,000 |

### CAPACITY DECISIONS

#### Segment Elimination

Eliminate if total income increases; continue segment if total income decreases after segment elimination.

| Segment Elimination Analysis | Continue | Eliminate | Income Increase (Decrease) |
|---|---|---|---|
| Sales | $ 40,000 | $    0 | |
| Variable costs | 35,000 | 0 | |
| Contribution margin | 5,000 | 0 | |
| Fixed costs | 15,000 | 11,000 | |
| Income (loss) | $(10,000) | $(11,000) | **$(1,000)** |

#### Keep or Replace

Replace if income increases; keep asset if income decreases.

| Keep or Replace Analysis | Keep | Replace | Income Increase (Decrease) |
|---|---|---|---|
| Revenues | | | |
| Sale of existing machine | | $  25,000 | |
| Costs | | | |
| Purchase of new machine | | (100,000) | |
| Variable manufacturing costs | $(250,000)† | (180,000)‡ | |
| Income (loss) | $(250,000) | $(255,000) | **$(5,000)** |

†$50,000 × 5 years    ‡$36,000 × 5 years

### PRICING DECISIONS

**Normal Pricing**  Price must cover all costs plus provide a profit.
*Total cost*

$$\text{Price per unit} = \text{Total cost per unit} + \text{Markup per unit}$$

where Markup per unit = Total cost per unit × Markup percentage
*Target cost*

$$\text{Target cost} = \text{Expected selling price} - \text{Target profit}$$

*Variable cost*

$$\text{Price per unit} = \text{Variable cost per unit} + \text{Markup per unit}$$

where Markup per unit = Variable cost per unit × Markup percentage

**Special Offer Pricing**
  Accept special offer if its income is positive.

**Time and Materials Pricing**

$$\text{Price} = \text{Direct labor} + \text{Direct materials} + \text{Materials markup}$$

where Direct labor = DLH × Time charge per DLH;
      Materials markup = Direct materials × Materials markup %

## Key Terms

## Multiple Choice Quiz

**1.** A cost that cannot be changed because it arises from a past decision and is irrelevant to future decisions is

  **a.** An uncontrollable cost.

  **b.** An out-of-pocket cost.

  **c.** A sunk cost.

  **d.** An opportunity cost.

  **e.** An incremental cost.

**2.** The potential benefit of one alternative that is lost by choosing another is known as

  **a.** An alternative cost.

  **b.** A sunk cost.

  **c.** A differential cost.

  **d.** An opportunity cost.

  **e.** An out-of-pocket cost.

**3.** A company produced 3,000 defective music players. The players cost $12 each to produce. A recycler offers to purchase the defective players "as is" for $8 each. The defects can be reworked for $10 each and the players then sold at their regular market price of $19 each. The company should

  **a.** Rework the players and sell at the regular price.

  **b.** Sell the players to the recycler for $8 each.

  **c.** Sell 2,000 to the recycler and rework the rest.

  **d.** Sell 1,000 to the recycler and rework the rest.

  **e.** Throw the defective players away.

**4.** A company's productive capacity is 480,000 machine hours. Product X requires 10 machine hours to produce; Product Y requires 2 machine hours to produce. Product X

sells for $32 per unit and has variable costs of $12 per unit; Product Y sells for $24 per unit and has variable costs of $10 per unit. Assuming that the company can sell as many of either product as it produces, it should

  **a.** Produce 48,000 units of Product X.

  **b.** Produce X and Y in the ratio of 83% X and 17% Y.

  **c.** Produce two of Product X for every one of Product Y.

  **d.** Produce only Product X.

  **e.** Produce only Product Y.

**5.** A company receives a special one-time order for 3,000 units of its product at $15 per unit. The company has excess capacity and it currently produces and sells the units at $20 each to its regular customers. Production costs are $13.50 per unit, which includes $9 of variable costs. To produce the special order, the company must incur additional fixed costs of $5,000. Should the company accept the special order?

  **a.** Yes, as revenue exceeds costs.

  **b.** No, as costs exceed revenue.

  **c.** No, as the offer is $5 less than the regular price.

  **d.** Yes, as costs exceed revenue.

  **e.** No, because costs exceed $15 per unit when total costs are considered.

### ANSWERS TO MULTIPLE CHOICE QUIZ

**1.** c

**2.** d

**3.** a; Reworking provides revenue of $11 per unit ($19 − $8); it costs $10 to rework them. The company is better off by $1 per unit when it reworks and sells these players.

**4.** e; Product X has a $2 contribution margin per machine hour [($32 − $12)/10 MH]; Product Y has a $7 contribution margin

per machine hour [($24 − $10)/2 MH]. It should produce as much of Product Y as possible.

**5.** a; Revenue = 3,000 units × $15 per unit = $45,000;

    Costs = (3,000 units × $9 per unit) + $5,000 = $32,000.

    Income = $45,000 − $32,000 = $13,000. Accept order.

---

 *Select Quick Study and Exercise assignments feature Guided Example videos, called "Hints" in Connect. Hints use different numbers, and instructors can turn this feature on or off.*

**QUICK STUDY**

**QS 10-1**

Identifying relevant costs

**C1**

Helix Company is approached by a new customer to provide 2,000 units of its product at a special price of $6 per unit. The normal selling price of the product is $8 per unit. Helix is operating at 75% of its capacity of 10,000 units. No incremental fixed overhead will be incurred because of this order. Also, there will be no incremental fixed general and administrative costs because of this order. Identify whether each of the following is relevant or not relevant to accepting this order.

| Item | Relevant | Not Relevant |
|---|---|---|
| a. Special selling price of $6.00 per unit | _____ | _____ |
| b. Direct materials of $1.00 per unit | _____ | _____ |
| c. Direct labor of $2.00 per unit | _____ | _____ |
| d. Variable overhead of $1.50 per unit | _____ | _____ |
| e. Fixed overhead of $0.75 per unit | _____ | _____ |
| f. Fixed general and administrative costs of $0.60 per unit | _____ | _____ |

Refer to the information in QS 10-1. Based on income, should Helix accept this new customer order at the special price?

**QS 10-2**
Special offer   **P7**

Zycon has produced 10,000 units of raw milk at a $15,000 cost. These units can be sold as is to another manufacturer for $20,000. Instead, Zycon can process the units further and produce yogurt. Processing further will cost an additional $22,000 and will yield revenues of $35,000. Identify whether each of the following is relevant or not relevant to the sell or process further decision.

**QS 10-3**
Identifying relevant costs

**C1**

| Item | Relevant | Not Relevant |
|---|---|---|
| a. $15,000 cost already incurred to produce milk | _____ | _____ |
| b. $20,000 selling price for milk as is | _____ | _____ |
| c. $22,000 further processing costs | _____ | _____ |
| d. $35,000 revenue from further processing | _____ | _____ |

For these two separate cases, identify each item as a sunk cost, a relevant cost, or a relevant revenue.

**QS 10-4**
Identifying sunk and relevant costs

**C1**

1. A company is considering replacing an old machine. The old machine has a book value of $50,000 and a remaining five-year life. The old machine can be sold now for $55,000. The new machine can be purchased for $100,000.

| Item | Sunk cost | Relevant cost | Relevant revenue |
|---|---|---|---|
| $50,000 book value of old machine . . . . . . . . | _____ | _____ | _____ |
| $55,000 selling price of old machine . . . . . . . | _____ | _____ | _____ |
| $100,000 price of new machine . . . . . . . . . . . | _____ | _____ | _____ |

2. A company spent $2,000 to make shirts. Customer tastes have changed and the shirts cannot be sold for their normal price. The shirts can be sold as is to another manufacturer to make into rags for $1,000. Instead, the company can spend $6,000 to rework the shirts with different designs. The reworked shirts can be sold for $10,000.

| Item | Sunk cost | Relevant cost | Relevant revenue |
|---|---|---|---|
| $2,000 already spent to make shirts. . . . . . . . . . | _____ | _____ | _____ |
| $6,000 cost to rework shirts . . . . . . . . . . . . . . . | _____ | _____ | _____ |
| $10,000 selling price of reworked shirts . . . . . . . | _____ | _____ | _____ |

Kando Company currently pays $7 per unit to buy a part for a product it manufactures. Instead, Kando could make the part for per unit costs of $3 for direct materials, $2 for direct labor, and $1 for incremental overhead. Kando normally applies overhead costs using a predetermined rate of 200% of direct labor cost. (*a*) Prepare a make or buy analysis of costs for this part. (*b*) Should Kando make or buy the part?

**QS 10-5**
Make or buy

**P1**

Maya Co. currently buys a component part for $3 per unit. Maya estimates that making the part would require $2.25 per unit of direct materials and $1.00 per unit of direct labor. Maya normally applies overhead using a predetermined overhead rate of 125% of direct labor cost. Maya estimates incremental overhead of $0.75 per unit to make the part. (*a*) Prepare a make or buy analysis of costs for this part. (*b*) Should Maya make or buy the part?

**QS 10-6**
Make or buy

**P1**

Holmes Company has already spent $50,000 to harvest peanuts. Those peanuts can be sold as is for $67,500. Alternatively, Holmes can process further into peanut butter at an additional cost of $312,500. If Holmes processes further, the peanut butter can be sold for $468,750. (*a*) Prepare a sell as is or process further analysis of income effects. (*b*) Should Holmes sell as is or process further?

**QS 10-7**
Sell or process

**P2**

A company has already spent $5,000 to harvest tomatoes. The tomatoes can be sold as is for $90,000. Instead, the company could incur further processing costs of $48,000 and sell the resulting salsa for $126,000. (*a*) Prepare a sell as is or process further analysis of income effects. (*b*) Should the company sell as is or process further?

**QS 10-8**
Sell or process   **P2**

**QS 10-9**

Scrap or rework

P2

Garcia Company has 10,000 units of its product that were produced at a cost of $150,000. The units were damaged in a rainstorm. Garcia can sell the units as scrap for $20,000, or it can rework the units at a cost of $38,000 and then sell them for $50,000. (*a*) Prepare a scrap or rework analysis of income effects. (*b*) Should Garcia sell the units as scrap or rework them and then sell them?

**QS 10-10**

Scrap or rework

P2

Rosa Company produced 1,000 defective phones due to a production error. The phones had cost $60,000 to produce. A salvage company will buy the defective phones as scrap for $30,000. It would cost Rosa $80,000 to rework the phones. If the phones are reworked, Rosa could sell them for $120,000. (*a*) Prepare a scrap or rework analysis of income effects. (*b*) Should Rosa scrap or rework the phones?

**QS 10-11**

Product contribution margin analysis

P3

Estela Company produces skateboards and scooters. Their per unit selling prices and variable costs follow. Skateboards require 2 machine hours per unit. Scooters require 3 machine hours per unit. For each product, compute (*a*) contribution margin per unit and (*b*) contribution margin per machine hour.

| | Skateboards | Scooters |
|---|---|---|
| Selling price per unit......... | $200 | $400 |
| Variable costs per unit ....... | 120 | 310 |

**QS 10-12**

Sales mix analysis

P3

Surf Company can sell all of the two surfboard models it produces, but it has only 400 direct labor hours available. The Glide model requires 2 direct labor hours per unit. The Ultra model requires 4 direct labor hours per unit. Contribution margin per unit is $200 for Glide and $300 for Ultra. (*a*) Compute the contribution margin per direct labor hour for each product. (*b*) Determine the best sales mix and the resulting contribution margin.

**QS 10-13**

Segment elimination

P4

A manufacturer is considering eliminating a segment because it shows the following $6,000 loss. All $20,000 of its variable costs are avoidable, and $36,000 of its fixed costs are avoidable. (*a*) Compute the income increase or decrease from eliminating this segment. (*b*) Should the segment be eliminated?

| Segment Income (Loss) | |
|---|---|
| Sales ................. | $60,000 |
| Variable costs .......... | 20,000 |
| Contribution margin ..... | 40,000 |
| Fixed costs ........... | 46,000 |
| Income (loss).......... | $ (6,000) |

**QS 10-14**

Segment elimination

P4

A segment of a company reports the following loss for the year. All $140,000 of its variable costs are avoidable, and $75,000 of its fixed costs are avoidable. (*a*) Compute the income increase or decrease from eliminating this segment. (*b*) Should the segment be eliminated?

| Segment Income (Loss) | |
|---|---|
| Sales ................. | $200,000 |
| Variable costs .......... | 140,000 |
| Contribution margin ..... | 60,000 |
| Fixed costs ........... | 80,000 |
| Income (loss).......... | $ (20,000) |

**QS 10-15**

Keep or replace

P5

Rory Company has an old machine with a book value of $75,000 and a remaining five-year useful life. Rory is considering purchasing a new machine at a price of $90,000. Rory can sell its old machine now for $60,000. The old machine has variable manufacturing costs of $33,000 per year. The new machine will reduce variable manufacturing costs by $13,000 per year over its five-year useful life. (*a*) Prepare a keep or replace analysis of income effects for the machines. (*b*) Should the old machine be replaced?

Garcia Co. sells snowboards. Each snowboard requires direct materials of $100, direct labor of $30, variable overhead of $45, and variable selling, general, and administrative costs of $3. The company has fixed overhead costs of $635,000 and fixed selling, general, and administrative costs of $85,000. It expects to produce and sell 10,000 snowboards. What is the selling price per unit if Garcia uses a markup of 20% of total cost?

**QS 10-16**
Pricing using total cost   **P6**

José Ruiz starts a company that makes handcrafted birdhouses. Competitors sell a similar birdhouse for $245 each. José believes he can produce a birdhouse for a total cost of $200 per unit, and he plans a 25% markup on total cost. (*a*) Compute José's planned selling price. (*b*) Is José's price lower than competitors' price?

**QS 10-17**
Pricing using total cost   **P6**

GoSnow sells snowboards. Each snowboard requires direct materials of $110, direct labor of $35, variable overhead of $45, and variable selling, general, and administrative costs of $10. The company has fixed overhead costs of $265,000 and fixed selling, general, and administrative costs of $335,000. The company has a target profit of $200,000. It expects to produce and sell 10,000 snowboards. Compute the selling price per unit using the variable cost method.

**QS 10-18**
Pricing using variable cost   **P6**

Raju is in a competitive product market. The expected selling price is $80 per unit, and Raju's target profit is 20% of selling price. Using the target cost method, what is the highest Raju's cost per unit can be?

**QS 10-19**
Pricing using target cost   **P6**

Radar Company sells bikes for $300 each. The company currently sells 3,750 bikes per year and could make as many as 5,000 bikes per year. The bikes cost $225 each to make: $150 in variable costs per bike and $75 of fixed costs per bike. Radar receives an offer from a potential customer who wants to buy 750 bikes for $250 each. Incremental fixed costs to make this order are $60 per bike. No other costs will change if this order is accepted. (*a*) Compute the income for the special offer. (*b*) Should Radar accept this offer?

**QS 10-20**
Special offer pricing   **P7**

Meng uses time and materials pricing. Its time charge per hour of direct labor is $55. Its materials markup is 30%. What price should Meng quote for a job that will take 80 direct labor hours and use $3,800 of direct materials?

**QS 10-21**
Time and materials pricing   **A1**

Cheng Co. reports the following information. Determine its (*a*) time charge per hour of direct labor and (*b*) materials markup percentage.

**QS 10-22**
Time and materials pricing
**A1**

| | |
|---|---|
| Direct labor rate. . . . . . . . . . . . . . . . . . . . . . . . . . . . . . . . . . . . . . . . | $50 per DLH |
| Non-materials-related overhead . . . . . . . . . . . . . . . . . . . . . . . . . . . . | $30 per DLH |
| Materials-related overhead . . . . . . . . . . . . . . . . . . . . . . . . . . . . . | 7% of direct materials costs |
| Target profit margin (on both conversion and direct materials) . . . . | 30% |

![McGraw Hill Connect logo] connect

Beto Company pays $2.50 per unit to buy a part for one of the products it manufactures. With excess capacity, the company is considering making the part. Making the part would cost $1.20 per unit for direct materials and $1.00 per unit for direct labor. The company normally applies overhead at the predetermined rate of 200% of direct labor cost. Incremental overhead to make the part would be 80% of direct labor cost. (*a*) Prepare a make or buy analysis of costs for this part. (*b*) Should Gilberto make or buy the part?

**EXERCISES**

**Exercise 10-1**
Make or buy

**P1**

Gelb Co. currently makes a key part for its main product. Making this part incurs per unit variable costs of $1.20 for direct materials and $0.75 for direct labor. Incremental overhead to make this part is $1.40 per unit. The company can buy the part for $3.50 per unit. (*a*) Prepare a make or buy analysis of costs for this part. (*b*) Should Gelb make or buy the part?

**Exercise 10-2**
Make or buy

**P1**

**Exercise 10-3**

Sell or process

P2

Cobe Co. has manufactured 200 partially finished cabinets at a cost of $50,000. These can be sold as is for $60,000. Instead, the cabinets can be stained and fitted with hardware to make finished cabinets. Further processing costs would be $12,000, and the finished cabinets could be sold for $80,000. (*a*) Prepare a sell as is or process further analysis of income effects. (*b*) Should the cabinets be sold as is or processed further and then sold?

**Exercise 10-4**

Scrap or rework

P2

A company must decide between scrapping or reworking units that do not pass inspection. The company has 22,000 defective units that have already cost $132,000 to manufacture. The units can be sold as scrap for $78,000 or reworked for $99,000 and then sold for $187,000. (*a*) Prepare a scrap or rework analysis of income effects. (*b*) Should the company sell the units as scrap or rework them?

**Exercise 10-5**

Sell or process

P2

Varto Company has 7,000 units of its product in inventory that it produced last year at a cost of $154,000. This year's model is better than last year's, and the 7,000 units cannot be sold at last year's normal selling price of $35 each. Varto has two alternatives for these units: (1) They can be sold as is to a wholesaler for $56,000 or (2) they can be processed further at an additional cost of $125,000 and then sold for $175,000. (*a*) Prepare a sell as is or process further analysis of income effects. (*b*) Should Varto sell the products as is or process further and then sell them?

**Exercise 10-6**

Sales mix

P3

Colt Company produces two skateboard models. Machine time per unit for Hero is two hours and for Flip is one hour. The machine's capacity is 1,600 hours per year. Colt can sell up to 500 units of Hero and 900 units of Flip per year. Selling prices and variable costs follow. (*a*) Compute the contribution margin per machine hour for each product. (*b*) Determine the best sales mix of products. (*c*) Compute the total contribution margin for the best sales mix.

| | Hero | Flip |
|---|---|---|
| Selling price per unit ......... | $150 | $95 |
| Variable costs per unit ........ | 50 | 55 |

**Exercise 10-7**

Sales mix

P3

Chip Company produces three products, Kin, Ike, and Bix. Each product uses the same direct material. Kin uses 4 pounds of the material, Ike uses 3 pounds of the material, and Bix uses 6 pounds of the material. Selling price per unit and variable costs per unit of each product follow. (*a*) Compute contribution margin per pound of material for each product. (*b*) If demand is limited, list the three products in the order in which management should produce and meet demand.

| | Kin | Ike | Bix |
|---|---|---|---|
| Selling price per unit. .......... | $160 | $112 | $210 |
| Variable costs per unit ......... | 96 | 85 | 144 |

**Exercise 10-8**

Segment elimination

P4

Marin Company makes several products, including canoes. The company reports a loss from its canoe segment (see below). All its variable costs are avoidable, and $300,000 of its fixed costs are avoidable. (*a*) Compute the income increase or decrease from eliminating this segment. (*b*) Should the segment be eliminated?

| Segment Income (Loss) | |
|---|---|
| Sales ................. | $980,000 |
| Variable costs .......... | 700,000 |
| Contribution margin ..... | 280,000 |
| Fixed costs ........... | 340,000 |
| Income (loss)........... | $ (60,000) |

Suresh Co. reports the following segment (department) income results for the year.

**Exercise 10-9**
Segment elimination
P4

|  | Dept. M | Dept. N | Dept. O | Dept. P | Dept. T | Total |
|---|---|---|---|---|---|---|
| Sales | $63,000 | $ 35,000 | $56,000 | $42,000 | $ 28,000 | $224,000 |
| Expenses |  |  |  |  |  |  |
| Avoidable | 9,800 | 36,400 | 22,400 | 14,000 | 37,800 | 120,400 |
| Unavoidable | 51,800 | 12,600 | 4,200 | 29,400 | 9,800 | 107,800 |
| Total expenses | 61,600 | 49,000 | 26,600 | 43,400 | 47,600 | 228,200 |
| Income (loss) | $ 1,400 | $(14,000) | $29,400 | $ (1,400) | $(19,600) | $ (4,200) |

**a.** If the company plans to eliminate departments that have sales less than avoidable costs, which department(s) would be eliminated?

**b.** Compute the total increase in income if the departments with sales less than avoidable costs, as identified in part *a*, are eliminated.

Lopez Co. is considering replacing one of its old manufacturing machines. The old machine has a book value of $45,000 and a remaining useful life of five years. It can be sold now for $52,000. Variable manufacturing costs are $36,000 per year for this old machine. Information on two alternative replacement machines follows. The expected useful life of each replacement machine is five years. (*a*) Compute the income increase or decrease from replacing the old machine with Machine A. (*b*) Compute the income increase or decrease from replacing the old machine with Machine B. (*c*) Should Lopez keep or replace its old machine? (*d*) If the machine should be replaced, which new machine should Lopez purchase?

**Exercise 10-10**
Keep or replace
P5

|  | Machine A | Machine B |
|---|---|---|
| Purchase price | $115,000 | $125,000 |
| Variable manufacturing costs per year | 19,000 | 15,000 |

Skull Co. makes snowboards and uses the total cost method in setting product price. Its costs for producing 10,000 units follow. The company targets a 12.5% markup on total cost.

**Exercise 10-11**
Pricing using total costs
P6

| Variable Costs per Unit |  |
|---|---|
| Direct materials | $100 |
| Direct labor | 25 |
| Overhead | 20 |
| Selling, general and administrative | 5 |

| Fixed Costs (total) |  |
|---|---|
| Overhead | $470,000 |
| Selling, general and administrative | 430,000 |

**1.** Compute the total cost per unit if 10,000 units are produced.
**2.** Compute the dollar markup per unit.
**3.** Compute the selling price per unit.

Rios Co. makes drones and uses the variable cost method in setting product price. Its costs for producing 20,000 units follow. The company targets a profit of $300,000 on this product.

**Exercise 10-12**
Pricing using variable costs
P6

| Variable Costs per Unit |  |
|---|---|
| Direct materials | $70 |
| Direct labor | 40 |
| Overhead | 25 |
| Selling, general and administrative | 15 |

| Fixed Costs (total) |  |
|---|---|
| Overhead | $670,000 |
| Selling, general and administrative | 590,000 |

**1.** Compute the total variable cost and the markup percentage.
**2.** Compute the dollar markup per unit on variable cost.
**3.** Compute the selling price per unit.

**Exercise 10-13**

Special offer pricing

P7

Farrow Co. reports the following annual results. The company receives a special offer for 15,000 units at $12 per unit. The additional sales would not affect its normal sales. Variable costs per unit would be the same for the special offer as they are for the normal units. The special offer would require incremental fixed overhead of $60,000 and incremental fixed general and administrative costs of $4,500. (*a*) Compute the income for the special offer. (*b*) Should the company accept the special offer?

| Contribution Margin Income Statement | Per Unit | Annual Total |
|---|---|---|
| Sales (150,000 units) . . . . . . . . . . . . . . . . | $15.00 | $2,250,000 |
| Variable costs | | |
|     Direct materials . . . . . . . . . . . . . . . . . . . . | 2.00 | 300,000 |
|     Direct labor. . . . . . . . . . . . . . . . . . . . . . . | 4.00 | 600,000 |
|     Overhead . . . . . . . . . . . . . . . . . . . . . . . | 2.50 | 375,000 |
| Contribution margin . . . . . . . . . . . . . . . . . | 6.50 | 975,000 |
| Fixed costs | | |
|     Fixed overhead. . . . . . . . . . . . . . . . . . . | 2.00 | 300,000 |
|     Fixed general and administrative . . . . . | 1.50 | 225,000 |
| Income . . . . . . . . . . . . . . . . . . . . . . . . . | $ 3.00 | $ 450,000 |

**Exercise 10-14**

Special offer pricing

P7

Pardo Company produces a single product and has capacity to produce 120,000 units per month. Costs to produce its current monthly sales of 80,000 units follow. The normal selling price of the product is $100 per unit. A new customer offers to purchase 20,000 units for $75 per unit. If the special offer is accepted, there will be no additional fixed overhead and no additional fixed general and administrative costs. The special offer would not affect its normal sales. (*a*) Compute the income from the special offer. (*b*) Should the company accept the special offer?

| | Per Unit | Costs at 80,000 Units |
|---|---|---|
| Direct materials. . . . . . . . . . . . . . . . . . . . . . . . . | $12.50 | $1,000,000 |
| Direct labor . . . . . . . . . . . . . . . . . . . . . . . . . . . | 29.00 | 2,320,000 |
| Variable overhead . . . . . . . . . . . . . . . . . . . . . . | 10.00 | 800,000 |
| Fixed overhead . . . . . . . . . . . . . . . . . . . . . . . | 17.50 | 1,400,000 |
| Fixed general and administrative . . . . . . . . . . . | 13.00 | 1,040,000 |
| Totals. . . . . . . . . . . . . . . . . . . . . . . . . . . . . . . | $82.00 | $6,560,000 |

**Exercise 10-15**

Time and materials pricing

A1

HH Electric reports the following information.

| | |
|---|---|
| Direct labor rate . . . . . . . . . . . . . . . . . . . . . . . . . . . . . . . . . . . . . . . . | $30 per DLH |
| Non-materials-related overhead . . . . . . . . . . . . . . . . . . . . . . . . . . . . | $15 per DLH |
| Materials-related overhead . . . . . . . . . . . . . . . . . . . . . . . . . . . . . . . | 5% of direct materials cost |
| Target profit margin (on both conversion and direct materials). . . . . | 20% |

**a.** Compute the time charge per hour of direct labor.

**b.** Compute the materials markup percentage.

**c.** What price should the company quote for a job requiring four direct labor hours and $580 in materials?

**McGraw Hill connect**

Haver Company currently pays an outside supplier $15 per unit for a part for one of its products. Haver is considering two alternative methods of making the part. Method 1 for making the part would require direct materials of $5 per unit, direct labor of $8 per unit, and incremental overhead of $3 per unit. Method 2 for making the part would require direct materials of $5 per unit, direct labor of $2 per unit, and incremental overhead of $7 per unit.

**Required**

**1.** Compute the cost per unit for each alternative method of making the part.

**2.** Should Haver make or buy the part? If Haver makes the part, which production method should it use?

**PROBLEM SET A**

**Problem 10-1A**
Make or buy
**P1**

---

Hip Manufacturing produces denim clothing. This year it produced 3,000 denim jackets at a cost of $90,000. These jackets were damaged in the warehouse during storage. Management identified three alternatives for these jackets.

**1.** Jackets can be sold as scrap to a secondhand clothing shop for $18,000.

**2.** Jackets can be disassembled at a cost of $6,000 and sold to a recycler for $36,000.

**3.** Jackets can be reworked and turned into good jackets. The cost of reworking the jackets will be $102,000, and the jackets can then be sold for $135,000.

**Required**

(1) Compute the income for each alternative. (2) Which alternative should be chosen?

**Problem 10-2A**
Scrap or rework
**P2**

---

Edge Company produces two models of its product with the same machine. The machine has a capacity of 176 hours per month. The following information is available.

**Problem 10-3A**
Sales mix strategies
**P3**

|  | Standard | Deluxe |
|---|---|---|
| Selling price per unit . . . . . . . . . . . . | $120 | $160 |
| Variable costs per unit . . . . . . . . . . . | 40 | 90 |
| Contribution margin per unit . . . . . . | $ 80 | $ 70 |
| Machine hours per unit . . . . . . . . . . | 1 hour | 2 hours |
| Maximum unit sales per month . . . . | 600 units | 200 units |

**Required**

**1.** Determine the contribution margin per machine hour for each model.

**2.** How many units of each model should the company produce? How much total contribution margin does this mix produce per month?

**3.** Assume the maximum demand for the Standard model is 100 units (not 600 units). How many units of each model should the company produce? How much total contribution margin does this mix produce per month?

---

Techcom is designing a new smartphone. Each unit of this new phone will require $230 of direct materials; $10 of direct labor; $22 of variable overhead; $18 of variable selling, general, and administrative costs; $30 of fixed overhead costs; and $10 of fixed selling, general, and administrative costs.

**1.** Compute the selling price per unit if the company uses the total cost method and plans a markup of 180% of total costs.

**2.** The company is a price-taker and the expected selling price for this type of phone is $800 per unit. Compute the target cost per unit if the company's target profit is 60% of expected selling price.

**3.** Compute the selling price per unit if the company uses the variable cost method and plans a markup of 200% of variable costs.

**Problem 10-4A**
Pricing using total cost, target cost, and variable cost
**P6**

**Problem 10-5A**

Special offer pricing

**P7**

JART manufactures and sells underwater markers. Its contribution margin income statement follows.

| Contribution Margin Income Statement For Year Ended December 31 | Per Unit | Annual Total |
|---|---|---|
| Sales (400,000 units) . . . . . . . . . . . . . | $6.00 | $2,400,000 |
| Variable costs | | |
| Direct materials . . . . . . . . . . . . . . . | 1.44 | 576,000 |
| Direct labor. . . . . . . . . . . . . . . . . . | 0.36 | 144,000 |
| Variable overhead . . . . . . . . . . . . . | 0.60 | 240,000 |
| Contribution margin . . . . . . . . . . . . . | 3.60 | 1,440,000 |
| Fixed costs | | |
| Fixed overhead . . . . . . . . . . . . . . . | 0.20 | 80,000 |
| Fixed general and administrative . . . | 0.15 | 60,000 |
| Income . . . . . . . . . . . . . . . . . . . . . | $3.25 | $1,300,000 |

A potential customer offers to buy 50,000 units for $3.20 each. These sales would not affect the company's sales through its normal channels. Details about the special offer follow.
- Direct materials cost per unit and variable overhead cost per unit would not change.
- Direct labor cost per unit would be $0.54 because the offer would require overtime pay.
- Accepting the offer would require incremental fixed general and administrative costs of $5,000.
- Accepting the offer would require no incremental fixed overhead costs.

**Required**

1. Compute income from the special offer.
2. Should the company accept or reject the special offer?

**Problem 10-6A**

Special offer pricing

**P7**

FURY produces and sells skateboards. Its contribution margin income statement follows.

| Contribution Margin Income Statement For Year Ended December 31 | Per Unit | Annual Total |
|---|---|---|
| Sales (80,000 units) . . . . . . . . . . . . . | $50.00 | $4,000,000 |
| Variable costs | | |
| Direct materials . . . . . . . . . . . . . . . | 20.00 | 1,600,000 |
| Direct labor. . . . . . . . . . . . . . . . . . | 8.00 | 640,000 |
| Variable overhead . . . . . . . . . . . . . | 12.00 | 960,000 |
| Contribution margin . . . . . . . . . . . . . | 10.00 | 800,000 |
| Fixed costs | | |
| Fixed overhead . . . . . . . . . . . . . . . | 3.00 | 240,000 |
| Fixed general and administrative . . . | 2.00 | 160,000 |
| Income . . . . . . . . . . . . . . . . . . . . . | $ 5.00 | $ 400,000 |

A potential customer offers to buy 10,000 units for $42.00 each. These sales would not affect the company's sales through its normal channels. Details of the special offer follow.
- Variable costs per unit would not change.
- Accepting the offer would require incremental fixed overhead costs of $10,000.
- Accepting the offer would require incremental fixed general and administrative costs of $15,000.

**Required**

1. Compute income from the special offer.
2. Should the company accept or reject the special offer?

Alto Company currently pays an outside supplier $4.50 per unit for a part for one of its products. Alto is considering two alternative methods of making the part. Method 1 of making the part would require direct materials of $1.20 per unit, direct labor of $1.50 per unit, and incremental overhead of $2 per unit. Method 2 of making the part would require direct materials of $1.20 per unit, direct labor of $1 per unit, and incremental overhead of $2.75 per unit.

**Required**

1. Compute the cost per unit for each alternative method of making the part.
2. Should Alto make or buy the part? If Alto makes the part, which production method should it use?

**PROBLEM SET B**

**Problem 10-1B**
Make or buy
**P1**

---

Micron Manufacturing produces telescopes. This month it produced 50 telescopes at a cost of $9,000. These telescopes were damaged in storage. Management has identified three alternatives for these telescopes.

1. They can be sold as scrap to a wholesaler for $3,750.
2. They can be disassembled at a cost of $2,000 and the parts sold to a recycler for $6,500.
3. They can be reworked and turned into good units. The cost of reworking the units will be $3,600, after which the units can be sold for $25,000.

**Required**

(1) Compute the income for each alternative. (2) Which alternative should management select?

**Problem 10-2B**
Scrap or rework
**P2**

---

Sung Company produces two models of its product with the same machine. The machine has a capacity of 200 hours per month. The following information is available.

| | Standard | Pro |
|---|---|---|
| Selling price per unit . . . . . . . . . . . . | $60 | $80 |
| Variable costs per unit . . . . . . . . . . . | 20 | 30 |
| Contribution margin per unit . . . . . . | $40 | $50 |
| Machine hours per unit . . . . . . . . . . | 1 hour | 2 hours |
| Maximum unit sales per month . . . . | 550 units | 175 units |

**Required**

1. Determine the contribution margin per machine hour for each model.
2. How many units of each model should the company produce? How much total contribution margin does this mix produce per month?
3. Assume the maximum demand for the Standard model is 180 units (not 550 units). How many units of each model should the company produce? How much total contribution margin does this mix produce per month?

**Problem 10-3B**
Sales mix strategies
**P3**

---

ComPro is designing a new smartphone. Each unit of this new phone will require $285 of direct materials; $10 of direct labor; $30 of variable overhead; $5 of variable selling, general, and administrative costs; $14 of fixed overhead costs; and $16 of fixed selling, general, and administrative costs.

1. Compute the selling price per unit if the company uses the total cost method and plans a markup of 220% of total costs.
2. The company is a price-taker and the expected selling price for this type of phone is $1,000 per unit. Compute the target cost per unit if the company's target profit is 60% of expected selling price.
3. Compute the selling price per unit if the company uses the variable cost method and plans a markup of 250% of variable costs.

**Problem 10-4B**
Pricing using total cost, target cost, and variable cost   **P6**

**Problem 10-5B**
Special offer pricing
P7

Ace produces and sells energy drinks. Its contribution margin income statement follows.

| Contribution Margin Income Statement For Year Ended December 31 | Per Unit | Annual Total |
|---|---|---|
| Sales (300,000 units). . . . . . . . . . . . . | $4.00 | $1,200,000 |
| Variable costs | | |
|    Direct materials . . . . . . . . . . . . . . | 1.28 | 384,000 |
|    Direct labor. . . . . . . . . . . . . . . . . . | 0.32 | 96,000 |
|    Variable overhead . . . . . . . . . . . . | 0.74 | 222,000 |
| Contribution margin . . . . . . . . . . . . . | 1.66 | 498,000 |
| Fixed costs | | |
|    Fixed overhead. . . . . . . . . . . . . . | 0.24 | 72,000 |
|    Fixed general and administrative. . . | 0.30 | 90,000 |
| Income. . . . . . . . . . . . . . . . . . . . . . | $1.12 | $ 336,000 |

A potential customer offers to buy 50,000 units for $3.00 each. These sales would not affect the company's sales through its normal channels. Details of the special offer follow.
- Direct materials cost per unit and variable overhead cost per unit would not change.
- Direct labor cost per unit would be $0.48 because the offer would require overtime pay.
- Accepting the offer would require incremental fixed general and administrative costs of $5,000.
- Accepting the offer would require no incremental fixed overhead costs.

**Required**

1. Compute income from the special offer.
2. Should the company accept or reject the special offer?

**Problem 10-6B**
Special offer pricing
P7

MAX produces and sells power adapters. Its contribution margin income statement follows.

| Contribution Margin Income Statement For Year Ended December 31 | Per Unit | Annual Total |
|---|---|---|
| Sales (55,000 units) . . . . . . . . . . . . . . | $8.00 | $440,000 |
| Variable costs | | |
|    Direct materials . . . . . . . . . . . . . . | 1.50 | 82,500 |
|    Direct labor. . . . . . . . . . . . . . . . . . | 2.10 | 115,500 |
|    Variable overhead . . . . . . . . . . . . | 1.90 | 104,500 |
| Contribution margin . . . . . . . . . . . . . | 2.50 | $137,500 |
| Fixed costs | | |
|    Fixed overhead. . . . . . . . . . . . . . | 0.50 | 27,500 |
|    Fixed general and administrative. . . | 1.20 | 66,000 |
| Income. . . . . . . . . . . . . . . . . . . . . . | $0.80 | $ 44,000 |

A potential customer offers to buy 10,000 units for $5.80 each. These sales would not affect the company's sales through its normal channels. Details of the special offer follow.
- Variable costs per unit would not change.
- Accepting the offer would require incremental fixed overhead costs of $2,200.
- Accepting the offer would require incremental fixed general and administrative costs of $1,800.

**Required**

1. Compute income from the special offer.
2. Should the company accept or reject the special offer?

**SERIAL PROBLEM**
Business Solutions

**P3**

*This serial problem began in Chapter 1 and continues through most of the book. If previous chapter segments were not completed, the serial problem can begin at this point.*

**SP 10**    Santana Rey sees that **Business Solutions**'s line of computer desks and chairs is popular, and she is finding it hard to keep up with demand. Santana only has 1,015 direct labor hours available. She must determine the best sales mix given her limited hours. Information about the desks and chairs follows.

|  | Desks | Chairs |
|---|---|---|
| Selling price per unit............. | $1,125 | $375 |
| Variable costs per unit ............ | 500 | 200 |
| Contribution margin per unit ....... | $ 625 | $175 |
| Direct labor hours per unit ........ | 5 hours | 4 hours |
| Maximum demand per quarter ..... | 175 desks | 50 chairs |

**Required**

Determine the best sales mix and the contribution margin the business will earn at that sales mix.

Alexander Image/Shutterstock

**Tableau Dashboard Activities** expose students to accounting analytics using visual displays. These assignments (1) do not require instructors to know Tableau, (2) are accessible to introductory students, (3) do not require Tableau software, and (4) run in **Connect**. All are auto-gradable.

**Tableau DA 10-1 Quick Study**, Compute contribution margin, **P3**—similar to QS 10-11.
**Tableau DA 10-2 Exercise**, Sales mix selection, **P3**—similar to QS 10-12 and Exercise 10-6.
**Tableau DA 10-3 Mini-case**, Analyzing sales mix strategies, **P3**—similar to Problem 10-3A.

**TABLEAU
DASHBOARD
ACTIVITIES**

## Accounting Analysis

**AA 10-1**    **Apple** offers device service and repair through its AppleCare program. Assumed data follow.

| | |
|---|---|
| Direct labor rate ........................................... | $40 per direct labor hour |
| Non-materials-related overhead ............................. | $10 per direct labor hour |
| Materials-related overhead ................................. | 4% of direct materials cost |
| Target profit margin (on both conversion and direct materials) ..... | 40% |

**COMPANY
ANALYSIS**

**A1**

**APPLE**

**Required**

1. Compute time charge per hour of direct labor (in $).
2. Compute materials markup per dollar of direct material cost (in %).
3. Use time and materials pricing to compute the price for a local college. Apple estimates the obligation to this college will require 1,000 direct labor hours and $35,000 of direct materials cost.

**AA 10-2**    **Google** wants to develop a laptop to compete with **Apple**'s MacBook Pro. Google believes the price of this model must be no more than Apple's price of $1,199 per unit to be competitive. Google expects to sell 20,000 units of this laptop model and has a target markup percentage of 25%. Assumed data for Google follow. Google uses the total cost method in setting its laptop price.

**COMPARATIVE
ANALYSIS**

**P6**

**GOOGLE**

**APPLE**

| Variable costs | Per unit |
|---|---|
| Direct materials...................... | $490 |
| Direct labor........................ | 60 |
| Overhead .......................... | 140 |
| Selling, general, and administrative ..... | 10 |

| Fixed costs | Annual total |
|---|---|
| Overhead ...................... | $2,500,000 |
| Selling, general, and administrative .. | 1,500,000 |

**Required**

1.  Compute Google's total cost per unit if 20,000 units are produced.
2.  Determine Google's dollar markup per unit.
3.  Determine Google's selling price per unit.

---

**EXTENDED ANALYSIS**

**A1**

**Samsung**

**APPLE**

**AA 10-3**  **Samsung**'s service and repair program competes with **Apple**'s AppleCare. Assumed data follow.

| | Samsung | Apple |
|---|---|---|
| Direct labor rate . . . . . . . . . . . . . . . . . . . . . . . . . . . . . . . . . . . . . | $38 per direct labor hour | $40 per direct labor hour |
| Non-materials-related overhead . . . . . . . . . . . . . . . . . . . . . . . . . | $10 per direct labor hour | $10 per direct labor hour |
| Materials-related overhead . . . . . . . . . . . . . . . . . . . . . . . . . . . . | 6% of direct materials cost | 4% of direct materials cost |
| Target profit margin (on both conversion and direct materials). . . | 40% | 40% |

**Required**

1.  For both Samsung and Apple, compute time charge per hour of direct labor (in $).
2.  For both Samsung and Apple, compute materials markup per dollar of direct material cost (in %).
3.  For both Samsung and Apple, use time and materials pricing to compute the price quote for a local college. Both companies estimate the obligation to this college will require 1,000 direct labor hours and $35,000 of direct materials cost.

---

## Discussion Questions

1.  Identify the five steps involved in the managerial decision-making process.
2.  Is nonfinancial information ever useful in managerial decision making?
3.  What is a relevant cost? Identify the two types of relevant costs.
4.  What are incremental revenues?
5.  Identify some qualitative factors that should be considered when making managerial decisions.
6.  What is an out-of-pocket cost? What is an opportunity cost? Are opportunity costs recorded in the accounting records?
7.  Why are sunk costs irrelevant in deciding whether to sell a product as is or to make it into a new product through additional processing?

8.  Identify the incremental costs incurred by **Apple** for shipping one additional iPhone from a warehouse to a retail store along with the store's normal order of 75 iPhones.  **APPLE**
9.  **Apple** is considering eliminating one of its stores in a large U.S. city. What are some factors that it should consider in making this decision?  **APPLE**
10. A company's normal selling price is $100 per unit. Describe a situation in which the company would accept a special offer at a selling price of $80 per unit.
11. Explain how a price-setter differs from a price-taker.
12. What is time and materials pricing?

---

## Beyond the Numbers

**ETHICS CHALLENGE**

**P7**

**BTN 10-1**  Bert Asiago, a salesperson for Convertco, received an order from a potential new customer for 50,000 units of Convertco's single product at a price $25 below its regular selling price of $65. Asiago knows that Convertco has the capacity to produce this order without affecting regular sales. He has spoken to Convertco's controller, Bia Morgan, who has informed Asiago that at the $40 selling price, Convertco will not be covering its variable costs of $42 for the product, and she recommends the order not be accepted. Asiago knows that variable costs include his sales commission of $4 per unit. If he accepts a $2 per unit commission, the sale will produce a contribution margin of zero. Asiago is eager to get the new customer because he believes that this could lead to the new customer becoming a regular customer.

**Required**

1. Determine the contribution margin per unit on the order as determined by the controller.
2. Determine the contribution margin per unit on the order as determined by Asiago if he takes the lower commission.
3. Do you recommend Convertco accept the special order? What factors must management consider?

---

**BTN 10-2**   Assume that you work for Greeble's Sporting Goods, and your manager requests that you outline the pros and cons of discontinuing its Golf department. That department is generating losses, and your manager believes that discontinuing it will increase overall store profits.

**COMMUNICATING IN PRACTICE**
C1

**Required**

Prepare a memorandum to your manager outlining what management should consider when trying to decide whether to discontinue its Golf department.

---

**BTN 10-3**   Break into teams and identify costs that an airline such as **Delta Air Lines** would incur on a flight from Green Bay to Minneapolis. (1) Identify the individual costs as variable or fixed. (2) Assume that Delta is trying to decide whether to drop this flight because it seems to be unprofitable. Determine which costs are likely to be saved if the flight is dropped. Set up your answer in the following format.

**TEAMWORK IN ACTION**
C1

| Cost | Variable or Fixed | Cost Saved If Flight Is Dropped | Rationale |
|------|-------------------|--------------------------------|-----------|
|      |                   |                                |           |

---

**BTN 10-4**   **Eye Symmetry**'s founder Max Stewart makes surfboards in different lengths. He must decide on the best sales mix. Assume Max has a capacity of 240 hours of direct labor time available each month, and he makes two types of boards: Short and Long. Information on these products follows.

**ENTREPRENEURIAL DECISION**
P3

| Surfboards | Short | Long |
|------------|-------|------|
| Selling price per unit......................... | $700 | $900 |
| Variable costs per unit ...................... | 400 | 500 |
| Direct labor hours per unit .................. | 8 hours | 16 hours |

**Required**

1. Assume the markets for both types of surfboards are unlimited. How many Short boards and how many Long boards should Max make each month?
2. How much total contribution margin does the sales mix from part 1 produce each month?
3. Assume the market for Short boards is limited to 20 per month, with no market limit for Long boards. How many Short boards and how many Long boards should Max make each month? How much total contribution margin does this mix produce each month?

# 11 Capital Budgeting and Investment Analysis

## Learning Objectives

**ANALYTICAL**

**A1** Analyze a capital investment project using break-even time.

**PROCEDURAL**

**P1** Compute payback period and describe its use.

**P2** Compute accounting rate of return and explain its use.

**P3** Compute net present value and describe its use.

**P4** Compute internal rate of return and explain its use.

# Dream Machine

*"Solve a big problem"*—**JAKE LOOSARARIAN**

PITTSBURGH—As part of his college coursework, Jake Loosararian worked on a team project involving a local power plant. The focus was on making inspections of its plant assets safer, faster, and less costly. "The cost of shutting down the plant [for inspections] is $1 million per day," explains Jake. This experience led Jake to start **Gecko Robotics** (**GeckoRobotics.com**), a company devoted to robotic industrial inspections.

Jake's robots climb the walls of boilers, tanks, and scrubbers of power companies. The robots work 10 times faster than humans and reduce injuries. "They collect so much more data than humans," says Jake. With these data, companies identify areas of weakness and perform key repairs. This extends the lives of plant assets and impacts capital budgeting decisions.

"I practically lived at power plants to find out their needs," admits Jake. With that information, Jake explains how his robotic data aid management in key investment decisions on asset planning. "We wanted to make a great impact," says Jake. His customers agree, as his sales increased by over 500% in the past year and his employee numbers went from 10 to over 100.

Gecko Robotics

"Follow your customers' feedback," declares Jake. And "launch quickly!"

Sources: *Gecko Robotics website,* January 2021; *Entrepreneur's Handbook,* March 2019; *youtube.com/channel/UCxHRYDh6nW6vDs1Kn6zKgCg*

## PAYBACK PERIOD

**Capital budgeting** is the process of analyzing alternative long-term investments and deciding which assets to acquire or sell. Common examples of capital budgeting decisions include buying a machine or a building or acquiring an entire company. The objective for these decisions is to earn a satisfactory return on investment.

**Capital Budgeting Process**    Exhibit 11.1 summarizes the capital budgeting process.

**EXHIBIT 11.1**

Capital Budgeting Process

The process begins when a manager submits a proposal for a new investment in a plant asset. A capital budget committee evaluates the proposal and recommends approval or rejection. The board of directors, or managers, then approves the capital investments for the year.

Capital budgeting decisions are usually the most difficult and risky that managers make. These decisions are difficult because they require predicting events that will occur well into the future. A capital budgeting decision is risky because

- The outcome is uncertain.
- Large amounts of money are usually involved.
- The investment involves a long-term commitment.
- The decision could be difficult or impossible to reverse.

**Capital Investment Cash Flows** Managers use several methods to evaluate capital budgeting decisions. Most methods use expected future cash outflows and inflows. Exhibit 11.2 summarizes cash outflows (−) and cash inflows (+) over the life of a typical capital investment.

**EXHIBIT 11.2**

Capital Investment Cash Flows

An investment begins with an initial cash outflow to buy the asset. Over the asset's life, it generates cash inflows and cash outflows. Cash inflows are from sales. Cash outflows are for materials, labor, and overhead (except depreciation). At the end of their useful lives, some assets can be sold for salvage value, providing another cash inflow. *Salvage value* is an asset's estimated value at the end of its useful life. There are methods to help us choose among investments. Many use *net cash flows,* which is cash inflows minus cash outflows.

**P1**

Compute payback period and describe its use.

# Payback Period with Equal Cash Flows

**Payback period (PBP)** is a method used to evaluate investment decisions by measuring the expected amount of time to recover the initial investment amount. Managers prefer assets with shorter payback periods to reduce the risk of an unprofitable investment over the long run.

FasTrac, a manufacturer of exercise equipment and supplies, is considering investing in a machine to manufacture a new product. Management gathers the following data.

| | | | |
|---|---|---|---|
| Initial investment | $16,000 | Materials, labor, and overhead (except depreciation) | $16,500 |
| Useful life | 8 years | Depreciation—Machinery | $2,000 |
| Salvage value | $0 | Selling, general, and administrative expenses | $9,500 |
| Expected sales per year | 1,000 units | Selling price per unit | $30 |

Exhibit 11.3 shows the expected annual income and net cash flow from an investment in this machine during its useful life. We see its annual income is $2,000, but its net cash flow is $4,000. The difference is because the $2,000 of depreciation expense has no cash outflow.

**EXHIBIT 11.3**

Annual Results from Potential Investment

| Annual Results from Investment | Income | Cash Flow |
|---|---|---|
| Sales of new product (1,000 × $30) | $30,000 | $30,000 |
| Expenses | | |
|   Materials, labor, and overhead (except depreciation) | 16,500 | 16,500 |
|   Depreciation—Machinery [($16,000 − $0)/8 years] | 2,000 | — |
|   Selling, general and administrative expenses | 9,500 | 9,500 |
| Income | $ 2,000 | |
| Net cash flow | | $ 4,000 |

**Point:** Excel for payback.

| | A | B |
|---|---|---|
| 1 | Investment | $16,000 |
| 2 | Cash flow | $4,000 |
| 3 | Payback period | |

=B1/B2 = 4

The formula to compute the payback period of an investment that produces equal net cash flows per period is in Exhibit 11.4. The payback period is the amount of time for the investment to generate enough net cash flow to pay back the initial investment. The payback period for this machine is 4 years. (Payback period assumes cash flows occur evenly *within* each year.)

**EXHIBIT 11.4**

Payback Period Calculation with Equal Cash Flows

$$\text{Payback period} = \frac{\text{Initial investment}}{\text{Annual net cash flow}} = \frac{\$16,000}{\$4,000} = \underline{\underline{4 \text{ years}}}$$

## Payback Period with <u>Unequal</u> Cash Flows

If net cash flows are unequal, or not the same each period, the payback period is computed using the *cumulative net cash flows. Cumulative* refers to the addition of each period's net cash flows over time. To demonstrate, FasTrac is evaluating an investment in a machine that will generate unequal net cash flows over the next eight years. The data and payback period computation are in Exhibit 11.5.

**EXHIBIT 11.5**

Payback Period Calculation with Unequal Cash Flows

| Year | Net Cash Flows per Year | Cumulative Net Cash Flows | |
|---|---|---|---|
| Initial investment ......... | $(16,000) | $(16,000) | |
| Year 1.................... | 2,000 | (14,000) | |
| Year 2.................... | 4,000 | (10,000) | |
| Year 3.................... | 4,000 | (6,000) | |
| Year 4.................... | 4,000 | **(2,000)** | Payback occurs between Years 4 and 5. |
| Year 5................... | **4,000** | **2,000** | |

Payback period = 4 years + ($2,000/$4,000) or 0.5 of Year 5 = 4.5 years

At the beginning of Year 1, there is an initial $16,000 cash outflow to buy the machine. By the end of Year 1, the cumulative net cash flow is $(14,000), computed as the $(16,000) initial cash outflow plus Year 1's $2,000 cash inflow. This process continues over the asset's life.

The cumulative net cash flow changes from negative to positive in Year 5. We see at the end of Year 4, the cumulative net cash flow is $(2,000). When FasTrac receives $2,000 of the $4,000 net cash flow in Year 5, it has fully recovered the $16,000 initial investment. If we assume that cash flows are received evenly *within* each year, receipt of the $2,000 occurs halfway through the fifth year. This is computed as $2,000 divided by Year 5's total net cash flow of $4,000, or 0.5. This yields a payback period of 4.5 years, computed as 4 years plus 0.5 of Year 5.

**Evaluating Payback Period**    Payback period has the following strengths and weaknesses.

| Strengths | Weaknesses |
|---|---|
| • It uses cash flows. | • It ignores the time value of money. |
| • It is easy to compute. | • It ignores cash flows after payback period. |

Its weaknesses are serious. To illustrate cash timing, if FasTrac had another $16,000 investment with predicted net cash flows of $6,000, $5,000, $2,000, $1,000, and $4,000 over its five-year life, its payback period would also be 4.5 years. However, this alternative is preferred because it returns cash more quickly. To illustrate longer term cash flows, an investment with a 3-year payback period that stops producing cash after 4 years might not be as good as an alternative with a 5-year payback period that generates increasing net cash flows for 15 years.

🟦 **Decision Insight** ━━━━━━━━━━━━━━━━━━━━━━━━

**e-Payback**    Health care providers use electronic systems to improve their operations. With *e-charting,* doctors' orders and notes are saved electronically. Such systems allow for more personalized care plans, more efficient staffing, and reduced costs. Investments in such systems are evaluated on the basis of payback periods and other financial measures. ◾

Oxygen/Getty Images

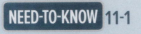 **11-1**

Payback Period

**P1**

A company is considering purchasing equipment costing $75,000. Expected annual net cash flows from this equipment are $30,000, $25,000, $18,000, $10,000, and $5,000. What is this investment's payback period?

**Solution**

| Year | Net Cash Flows per Year | Cumulative Net Cash Flows |
|---|---|---|
| Initial investment ......... | $(75,000) | $(75,000) |
| Year 1 ................. | 30,000 | (45,000) |
| Year 2 ................. | 25,000 | (20,000) |
| Year 3 ................. | 18,000 | (2,000) ⎱ |
| Year 4 ................. | 10,000 | 8,000 ⎰ |
| Year 5 ................. | 5,000 | 13,000 |

Payback occurs between Years 3 and 4.

**Payback period = 3.2 years**, computed as 3 years plus 0.2 of Year 4.

Do More: QS 11-1, QS 11-4, E 11-1, E 11-3, E 11-4

*Explanation:* Once cumulative net cash flow reaches $0 during Year 4, the initial investment is paid back. This occurs 0.2 of the way through Year 4 ($2,000/$10,000 = 0.2).

# ACCOUNTING RATE OF RETURN

**P2**

Compute accounting rate of return and explain its use.

**Accounting rate of return (ARR)** is an investment's annual income divided by the average investment in it. To illustrate, we return to FasTrac's $16,000 machine investment described in Exhibit 11.3.

We find the average investment by using the formula in Exhibit 11.6. For this machine, we take the initial investment at the start of the asset's life of $16,000 plus the salvage value at the end of the asset's life of $0, and then divide by 2. This gives an "average" investment over the asset's life of $8,000.

**EXHIBIT 11.6**

Average Investment Calculation

$$\text{Average investment} = \frac{\text{Initial investment} + \text{Salvage value}}{2} = \frac{\$16,000 + \$0}{2} = \$8,000$$

Using the $8,000 average investment and the annual income of $2,000 from Exhibit 11.3, FasTrac calculates accounting rate of return in Exhibit 11.7.

**EXHIBIT 11.7**

Accounting Rate of Return Calculation

$$\text{Accounting rate of return} = \frac{\text{Annual income}}{\text{Average investment}} = \frac{\$2,000}{\$8,000} = 25.0\%$$

**Point:** Excel for ARR.

| | A | B |
|---|---|---|
| 1 | Investment | $16,000 |
| 2 | Salvage value | $0 |
| 3 | Income | $2,000 |
| 4 | Acctg rate of return | ← |

=B3/((B1+B2)/2) = 25%

**ARR Decision Rule**   Management uses this 25% to compare with alternative investments. Managers prefer investments with a higher accounting rate of return, and they normally set a minimum required rate of return.

**Evaluating Accounting Rate of Return**   The accounting rate of return's strength is its easy computation. It does, however, have two weaknesses.

• It ignores the time value of money.
• It does not directly consider cash flows and their timing.

Compute accounting rate of return for the machine investment below.

| | |
|---|---|
| Initial investment ................... | $180,000 |
| Salvage value ...................... | 20,000 |
| Income (annual) .................... | 40,000 |

**Solution**

Average investment = ($180,000 + $20,000)/2 = $100,000
Accounting rate of return = $40,000/$100,000 = 40%

Do More: QS 11-5, QS 11-6, QS 11-7, E 11-5

# NET PRESENT VALUE (NPV)

Net present value analysis applies the "time value of money" to future cash inflows and cash outflows of a project to assess its desirability. Appendix B explains the present value concept, which is often summarized as: *A dollar tomorrow is worth less than a dollar today.* Assignments that use present value are solved using Appendix B tables, Excel, or a calculator.

**Net present value (NPV)** is the discounted future net cash flows from the investment at the required rate of return, then minus the initial investment. A company's required rate of return, often called its **hurdle rate,** or its **cost of capital,** is an average of the rate the company must pay to its lenders and investors.

**P3** _____

Compute net present value and describe its use.

**NPV Demo: Equal Cash Flows**    A company is considering a $20,000 investment in a machine that is expected to provide $10,000 annual net cash flows for the next three years. Assume net cash flows from this machine occur at each year-end and the company requires a 9% return. Net present value is computed in Exhibit 11.8. The initial investment occurs at the beginning of Year 1.

| | Net Cash Flows | Present Value of 1 at 9%[†] | Present Value of Net Cash Flows |
|---|---|---|---|
| Year 1................ | $10,000 | 0.9174 | $ 9,174 |
| Year 2................ | 10,000 | 0.8417 | 8,417 |
| Year 3................ | 10,000 | 0.7722 | 7,722 |
| Totals ............... | $30,000 | | 25,313 |
| Initial investment...... | | | (20,000) |
| Net present value ..... | | | $ 5,313 |

[†]Present value of 1 factors are taken from Table B.1 in Appendix B.

**EXHIBIT 11.8**

Net Present Value Calculation with Equal Cash Flows

Present value of net cash flows
− Initial investment
= Net present value

Exhibit 11.8 shows annual net cash flows and a column of present value of 1 factors, also called *discount factors,* taken from Table B.1 in Appendix B. *(To simplify present value computations and for all assignments, we assume that net cash flows occur at year-end.)* Annual net cash flows are multiplied by the discount factors to give present values of annual net cash flows in the far-right column. The present values are added to get total present value of net cash flows of $25,313.

The $20,000 initial investment is subtracted from the $25,313 total present value to get this asset's NPV of $5,313. We interpret this to mean the $25,313 present value of future net cash flows exceeds the initial $20,000 investment by $5,313. FasTrac should invest in this machine.

**Net Present Value Decision Rule**   The decision rule in applying NPV is:

- If an asset's future net cash flows yield a *positive* net present value, then invest.
- When comparing projects with similar initial investments and risk, invest in the one with the highest net present value.

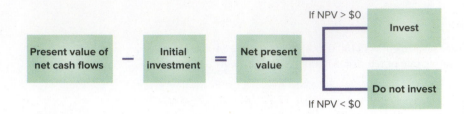

**Annuity Assumption**   NPV is simplified if annual net cash flows are equal. A series of cash flows of equal amount is called an **annuity.** Table B.3 in Appendix B gives the present value of an annuity of 1 to be received for different periods. To compute the present value of net cash flows in Exhibit 11.8 discounted at 9%, go down the 9% column of Table B.3 to the factor on the third line. This discount factor, also known as an *annuity* factor, is 2.5313. We compute the $25,313 present value as 2.5313 × $10,000. We visually show the calculations in Exhibit 11.8 as follows.

**Point: Excel for NPV.**

|   | A | B |
|---|---|---|
| 1 | Investment | $20,000 |
| 2 | Cash flow | $10,000 |
| 3 | Periods | 3 |
| 4 | Interest rate | 9% |
| 5 | NPV | |

=PV(B4,B3,−B2)−B1 = $5,313

**Point: NPV with calculator:**

N       3
I/Y     9
PMT   10000
CPT   PV
Multiply $−25,313 answer by −1 for money received, and subtract initial investment of $20,000 to get NPV of $5,313.

$(20,000)

$ 25,313   $10,000 × 2.5313
$  5,313   NPV

**Initial investment**   Net cash inflow, Years 1–3

$(20,000)

$0 salvage value

**Applying Annuity Assumption to Strategic Plans**   NPV analysis can be used to help assess the value of strategic plans such as whether to automate a production process. For example, an eye-wear manufacturer is considering investing in an $80,000 automated manufacturing system. If the investment is made, the company can reduce its labor costs by $15,000 per year of the 10-year useful life of the system. All other costs and revenues are unchanged. The NPV analysis, using a 10% discount rate and no salvage value, is in Exhibit 11.9. The $92,169 present value of the cash flows from reduced labor costs exceeds the $80,000 cost of the new system. The company should automate its production process.

**EXHIBIT 11.9**

Net Present Value Calculation Using Annuity Factor

|   | Net Cash Flows | Present Value of an Annuity at 10%[†] | Present Value of Net Cash Flows |
|---|---|---|---|
| Years 1–10 . . . . . . . . | $15,000 | 6.1446 | $ 92,169 |
| Initial investment . . . | | | (80,000) |
| Net present value . . : | | | $ 12,169 |

[†]6.1446 is the present value of an annuity of 1, where $n = 10$, $i = 10\%$ (from Table B.3).

**NPV Demo: Unequal Cash Flows**   Net present value analysis can be used when net cash flows are unequal. Assume a company can choose only one capital investment: Project A or Project B. Each project requires a $12,000 initial investment. Exhibit 11.10 shows Projects A and B have equal total net cash flows of $15,000. Project A is expected to produce equal amounts

**EXHIBIT 11.10**

Net Present Value
Calculation with Unequal
Cash Flows

| | Net Cash Flows | | Present Value of 1 at 10% | Present Value of Net Cash Flows | |
|---|---|---|---|---|---|
| | A | B | | A | B |
| Year 1 ............ | $ 5,000 | $ 8,000 | 0.9091 | $ 4,546 | $ 7,273 |
| Year 2 ............ | 5,000 | 5,000 | 0.8264 | 4,132 | 4,132 |
| Year 3 ............ | 5,000 | 2,000 | 0.7513 | 3,757 | 1,503 |
| Totals............. | $15,000 | $15,000 | | 12,435 | 12,908 |
| **Initial investment** .. | | | | (12,000) | (12,000) |
| **Net present value** .. | | | | $   435 | $   908 |

of $5,000 each year. Project B is expected to produce a larger amount in the first year and a smaller amount in the third year.

Exhibit 11.10 shows the present value of 1 factors from Table B.1 assuming a 10% required return. Computations in the two rightmost columns show that Project A has a $435 NPV, but Project B has a higher NPV of $908 because it has a larger cash flow in Year 1. Projects with higher cash flows in earlier years generally yield higher net present values. If only one project can be accepted, Project B is better because of its higher NPV.

**NPV: With Salvage Value**    Many assets have salvage values. If so, this amount is an additional net cash inflow at the end of the asset's life.

**Example**    To illustrate, an asset requires an initial investment of $80,000 and generates $15,000 of net cash flows for each of the next ten years. It has a salvage value of $10,000 at the end of its 10-year life. The net present value computation, using a 10% discount rate, follows.

**Point:** NPV of annuity with salvage value

| | A | B |
|---|---|---|
| 1 | Investment | $80,000 |
| 2 | Salvage value | $10,000 |
| 3 | Cash flow | $15,000 |
| 4 | Periods | 10 |
| 5 | Interest rate | 10% |
| 6 | PV annuity | |
| 7 | PV salvage | |
| 8 | NPV | |

=PV(B5,B4,−B3) = $92,169
=PV(B5,B4,0,−B2) = $3,855
=B6+B7−B1) = $16,024

| | Net Cash Flows | Present Value of Factor at 10%* | Present Value of Net Cash Flows |
|---|---|---|---|
| Years 1–10 ............. | $15,000 | 6.1446 | $ 92,169 |
| Salvage value at Year 10 .. | 10,000 | 0.3855 | 3,855 |
| Total................... | | | 96,024 |
| **Initial investment** ....... | | | (80,000) |
| **Net present value** ....... | | | $ 16,024 |

*6.1446 = Present value of an annuity of 1, where $n = 10$, $i = 10\%$ (from Table B.3).
 0.3855 = Present value of 1, where $n = 10$, $i = 10\%$ (from Table B.1).

**NPV: Comparing Projects**    When comparing projects of *similar* initial investments and risk levels, we can rank them on NPV. However, if the initial investments *differ* across projects, we need a different method. One way to compare projects, especially when a company cannot fund all positive net present value projects, is to use the **profitability index.**

**Example:** When is it appropriate to use different discount rates for different projects? *Answer:* When risk levels are different.

$$\text{Profitability index} = \frac{\text{Present value of net cash flows}}{\text{Initial investment}}$$

Exhibit 11.11 illustrates computation of the profitability index for three potential investments. A profitability index less than 1 indicates an investment with a *negative* net present value. This means we drop Project 3 from consideration. Both Projects 1 and 2 have profitability indexes greater than 1, meaning they have positive net present values. If forced to choose, we select the project with the higher profitability index. Project 2 returns $1.50 NPV per dollar invested, whereas Project 1 returns only $1.20 NPV per dollar invested. **Rule:** Invest in the project with the highest profitability index (must exceed 1.0).

**EXHIBIT 11.11**

Profitability Index Analysis

| Potential Projects | Project 1 | Project 2 | Project 3 |
|---|---|---|---|
| Present value of net cash flows . . . | $900,000 | $375,000 | $270,000 |
| Initial investment . . . . . . . . . . . . . . | 750,000 | 250,000 | 300,000 |
| Profitability index . . . . . . . . . . . . . | 1.2 | 1.5 | 0.9 |

---

**NEED-TO-KNOW 11-3**

Net Present Value

**P3**

A company is considering two potential projects. Each project requires a $20,000 initial investment and is expected to generate annual net cash flows as follows. Assuming a discount rate of 10%, compute the net present value of each project. If only one project can be selected, which is chosen?

| | Net Cash Flows | |
|---|---|---|
| Year | Project A | Project B |
| 1 . . . . . . . | $12,000 | $ 4,500 |
| 2 . . . . . . . | 8,500 | 8,500 |
| 3 . . . . . . . | 4,000 | 13,000 |

**Solution**

Net present values follow. Because the projects have the same initial investment and similar risk, we compare their net present values. Project A should be selected because of its higher positive NPV.

| | | Project A | | Project B | |
|---|---|---|---|---|---|
| Year | Present Value of 1 at 10%* | Net Cash Flows | Present Value of Net Cash Flows | Net Cash Flows | Present Value of Net Cash Flows |
| 1 | 0.9091 | $12,000 | $ 10,909 | $ 4,500 | $ 4,091 |
| 2 | 0.8264 | 8,500 | 7,024 | 8,500 | 7,024 |
| 3 | 0.7513 | 4,000 | 3,005 | 13,000 | 9,767 |
| Totals | | $24,500 | 20,938 | $26,000 | 20,882 |
| Initial investment | | | (20,000) | | (20,000) |
| Net present value | | | $    938 | | $    882 |

*Present value of 1 factors are taken from Table B.1 in Appendix B.

Do More: QS 11-10, QS 11-11, E 11-7, E 11-8

---

# INTERNAL RATE OF RETURN (IRR)

**P4**

Compute internal rate of return and explain its use.

Another way to evaluate investments is to use the **internal rate of return (IRR),** which is the discount rate that yields an NPV of zero.

**IRR: Equal Cash Flows**   Assume an asset requires a $12,009 initial investment and is expected to generate $5,000 net cash flows in each year of its 3-year life. Below is the two-step process for finding IRR with equal cash flows.

**Step 1:** Compute present value factor for investment.

Point: Excel for IRR.

| | A | B |
|---|---|---|
| 1 | Investment | –$12,009 |
| 2 | Cash flow Year 1 | 5,000 |
| 3 | Cash flow Year 2 | 5,000 |
| 4 | Cash flow Year 3 | 5,000 |
| 5 | Internal rate of return | ← |
| | =IRR(B1:B4) = 12% | |

$$\text{Present value factor} = \frac{\text{Initial investment}}{\text{Annual net cash flows}} = \frac{\$12,009}{\$5,000} = 2.4018$$

**Step 2:** Identify rate (IRR) yielding the present value factor.

Search Table B.3 (partially shown below) for a present value factor of 2.4018 in the 3-period row (the period is the 3-year project life). A present value factor of 2.4018 is in the 12% column. This means IRR is 12%.

| Present Value of an Annuity of 1 for Three Periods | | | | | |
|---|---|---|---|---|---|
| Discount Rate | | | | | |
| Periods | 1% | 5% | 10% | 12% | 15% |
| 3 . . . . | 2.9410 | 2.7232 | 2.4869 | **2.4018** | 2.2832 |

IRR with a financial calculator: Student steps are in Blue; what the calculator returns is in **Black**.

CF
CF$_0$ = 12009 +/- ENTER ▼
C01 = 5000            ENTER ▼
F01 = 3               ENTER ▼
C02
IRR CPT
IRR = 12.0

**IRR: Unedual Cash Flows**   If net cash flows are unequal, it is best to use a calculator or spreadsheet software to compute IRR. We show the use of Excel in this chapter's appendix.

**IRR Decision Rule**   To use IRR to evaluate a project, we compare it to a predetermined *hurdle rate,* which is a minimum acceptable rate of return. If the IRR is greater than the hurdle rate, invest in the project. If the IRR is less than the hurdle rate, do not invest.

**Rule:** If IRR > Hurdle rate, then invest.

| Internal rate of return | > | Hurdle rate | → | Invest |
|---|---|---|---|---|
| Internal rate of return | < | Hurdle rate | → | Do not invest |

**IRR: Comparing Projects**   Multiple projects are often ranked by the extent IRR exceeds the hurdle rate. IRR can be used to compare projects with different amounts invested because the IRR is expressed as a percent rather than as a dollar value as in NPV.

■ **Decision Insight**

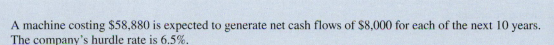

**Manager Bonus and IRR**   A survey reported that 41% of top managers would reject a project with an internal rate of return *above* the cost of capital *if* the project would cause the company to miss its earnings forecast. The roles of benchmarks and manager bonuses based on earnings must be considered in capital budgeting decisions. ■

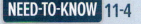
REJECTED

A machine costing $58,880 is expected to generate net cash flows of $8,000 for each of the next 10 years. The company's hurdle rate is 6.5%.

**1.** Find the machine's internal rate of return (IRR).

**2.** Using IRR, should the company purchase this machine?

*Solution*

**1.** PV factor = Initial investment/Annual net cash flows = $58,880/$8,000 = 7.36. Scanning the "Periods equal 10" row in Table B.3 for a present value factor near 7.36 indicates the IRR is 6%.

**2.** The machine should not be purchased because its IRR (6%) is less than the company's hurdle rate (6.5%).

**NEED-TO-KNOW 11-4**

Internal Rate of Return

**P4**

Do More: QS 11-21, QS 11-22, QS 11-23, E 11-15

## Comparing Capital Budgeting Methods

Exhibit 11.12 compares the four methods shown in this chapter.

**EXHIBIT 11.12**

Comparing Capital Budgeting Methods

| | Payback Period | Accounting Rate of Return | Net Present Value | Internal Rate of Return |
|---|---|---|---|---|
| **Focus** | • Cash flows | • Income | • Cash flows | • Cash flows |
| **Yields** | • Years | • Percent | • Dollars | • Percent |
| **Strengths** | • Easy to compute | • Easy to compute | • Reflects time value of money | • Reflects time value of money |
| | | | • Reflects changing risks over project's life | • Allows comparisons of projects |
| **Weaknesses** | • Ignores time value of money | • Ignores time value of money | • Difficult to compare projects | • Ignores changing risks over project's life |
| | • Ignores cash flows after payback period | • Ignores cash flows | | |

- Payback period is the simplest method.
- Accounting rate of return is simple but not commonly used in practice.
- Net present value considers all net cash flows from a project. It can be applied to equal and unequal cash flows and can reflect changes in the level of risk over a project's life. Because NPV is in dollars, comparing projects with different initial investment amounts is difficult. The profitability index can be used in this case.
- Internal rate of return considers all cash flows from a project. Because IRR is a percent, it can be used to compare projects with different investment amounts. However, IRR does not reflect changes in risk over a project's life.

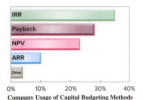

Company Usage of Capital Budgeting Methods

### Decision Insight

**And the Winner Is . . .** How do we choose among the methods for evaluating capital investments? Management surveys consistently show internal rate of return (IRR) as the most popular method, followed by payback period and net present value (NPV). Few companies use accounting rate of return (ARR), but nearly all use more than one method. ■

## CORPORATE SOCIAL RESPONSIBILITY

Net present value calculations extend to investments in sustainable energy. To illustrate, consider a potential investment of $11,000 in a solar panel system in Phoenix. The system is expected to last for 30 years and require $100 of maintenance costs per year. The typical home uses 14,000 kilowatt hours (kWh) of electricity per year, at a cost of $0.12 per kilowatt hour. According to the **National Renewable Energy Laboratory** (**pvwatts.nrel.gov**), a typical solar panel system in Phoenix could supply 8,642 kilowatt hours (kWh) of electricity per year. The net present value of a potential investment in a solar panel system, using a 6% discount rate, is computed in Exhibit 11.13. The NPV is $1,898, indicating the investment should be accepted.

**EXHIBIT 11.13**

NPV of Solar Investment

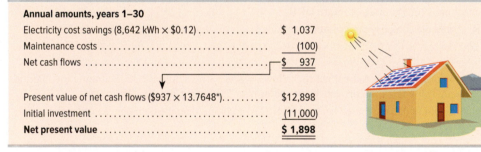

| Annual amounts, years 1–30 | |
| --- | --- |
| Electricity cost savings (8,642 kWh × $0.12) . . . . . . . . . . . . . . . | $ 1,037 |
| Maintenance costs . . . . . . . . . . . . . . . . . . . . . . . . . . . . . . . . . | (100) |
| Net cash flows . . . . . . . . . . . . . . . . . . . . . . . . . . . . . . . . . . . . | $ 937 |
| Present value of net cash flows ($937 × 13.7648*) . . . . . . . . . | $12,898 |
| Initial investment . . . . . . . . . . . . . . . . . . . . . . . . . . . . . . . . . . | (11,000) |
| **Net present value** . . . . . . . . . . . . . . . . . . . . . . . . . . . . . . . . | **$ 1,898** |

*From Table B.3: using 30 periods at 6%

Gecko Robotics

**Gecko Robotics**, this chapter's feature company, makes robots to inspect power plants. These robots enable human workers to perform safer and more interesting tasks, like data analysis. This investment increases profits *and* increases employee satisfaction, which can increase morale and decrease turnover.

## Decision Analysis      Break-Even Time (BET)

**A1**

Analyze a capital investment project using break-even time.

**Break-even time** is a measure of the expected time until the *present value* of the net cash flows from an investment equals the initial investment. It overcomes the payback period's limitation of ignoring the time value of money. It is computed like the payback period but uses discounted cash flows.

    To illustrate, we consider a $12,000 investment in machinery. The annual net cash flows from this investment are $4,100 for 5 years. Exhibit 11.14 shows the computation of break-even time for this investment using a 10% discount rate.

**EXHIBIT 11.14**

Break-Even Time Analysis

| Year | Net Cash Flows | Present Value of 1 at 10%* | Present Value of Net Cash Flows | Cumulative Present Value of Net Cash Flows |
|---|---|---|---|---|
| Initial investment .... | $(12,000) | 1.0000 | $(12,000) | $(12,000) |
| 1.................. | 4,100 | 0.9091 | 3,727 | (8,273) |
| 2.................. | 4,100 | 0.8264 | 3,388 | (4,885) |
| 3.................. | 4,100 | 0.7513 | 3,080 | (1,805) |
| 4.................. | 4,100 | 0.6830 | 2,800 | 995 |
| 5.................. | 4,100 | 0.6209 | 2,546 | **3,541** |

⟵ Break-even time

⟵ Net present value

*Present value of 1 factors from Table B.1 in Appendix B.

The rightmost column of this exhibit shows that break-even time is between 3 and 4 years, or about 3.64 years. This is computed as 3 years plus $1,805/$2,800 or 0.64 of year 4 (rounded). Cash flows earned after the break-even time contribute to a positive net present value that, in this case, eventually amounts to $3,541.

Break-even time is useful because it identifies the point in time when cash flows begin to yield net positive returns. The method allows managers to compare and rank alternative investments, giving the project with the shortest break-even time the highest rank.

West Company can invest in one of two projects, T1 or T2. Each project requires an initial investment of $101,250 and produces the following net cash flows.

**NEED-TO-KNOW 11-5**

**COMPREHENSIVE**

Evaluating Investments

| | Net Cash Flows | |
|---|---|---|
| Year | T1 | T2 |
| Year 1 ......... | $ 20,000 | $ 40,000 |
| Year 2 ......... | 30,000 | 40,000 |
| Year 3 ......... | 70,000 | 40,000 |
| Totals.......... | $120,000 | $120,000 |

**Required**

1. Compute the payback period for both projects. Which project has the shorter payback period?
2. The company requires a 10% return from its investments. Compute the net present value of each project. Determine which project, if any, should be chosen.
3. Compute the internal rate of return for Project T2. Based on its internal rate of return, should Project T2 be chosen?

**SOLUTION**

1. **T1:** Determining the payback period for a series of unequal cash flows (as in Project T1) requires us to compute the cumulative net cash flows from the project at the end of each year. The payback period calculation follows. The cumulative net cash flow for Project T1 changes from negative to positive in Year 3. When net cash flow of $51,250 is received during year 3, the initial investment is fully recovered. Assuming cash flows are received evenly within each year, this occurs about 0.73 ($51,250/$70,000) or 0.73 of the way through the third year. The payback period is then **2.73 years**, computed as 2 years plus 0.73 of year 3.

| Year | Net Cash Flows per Year | Cumulative Net Cash Flows |
|---|---|---|
| Initial investment....... | $(101,250) | $(101,250) |
| 1 .................... | 20,000 | (81,250) |
| 2 .................... | 30,000 | (51,250) |
| 3 .................... | 70,000 | 18,750 |

⟵ Break-even time

**T2:** The payback period for a project with a series of equal cash flows is computed as follows. The company expects to recover its investment in 2.53 years.

$$\text{Payback period} = \frac{\text{Initial investment}}{\text{Annual net cash flow}} = \frac{\$101,250}{\$40,000} = \underline{\underline{\textbf{2.53 years}}} \text{ (rounded)}$$

**2. T1:**

| Year | Net Cash Flows | Present Value of 1 at 10% | Present Value of Net Cash Flows |
|---|---|---|---|
| Year 1 ............. | $ 20,000 | 0.9091 | $ 18,182 |
| Year 2 ............. | 30,000 | 0.8264 | 24,792 |
| Year 3 ............. | 70,000 | 0.7513 | 52,591 |
| Totals.............. | $120,000 | | 95,565 |
| **Initial investment** ... | | | **(101,250)** |
| **Net present value** ... | | | **$ (5,685)** |

**T2:**

| Year | Net Cash Flows | Present Value of 1 at 10% | Present Value of Net Cash Flows |
|---|---|---|---|
| Year 1 ............. | $ 40,000 | 0.9091 | $ 36,364 |
| Year 2 ............. | 40,000 | 0.8264 | 33,056 |
| Year 3 ............. | 40,000 | 0.7513 | 30,052 |
| Totals.............. | $120,000 | | 99,472 |
| **Initial investment** ... | | | **(101,250)** |
| **Net present value** ... | | | **$ (1,778)** |

**Decision:** The company should not invest in either project. Both are expected to yield a negative net present value, and it should invest only in positive net present value projects.

**3.** To compute Project T2's internal rate of return, we first compute a present value factor as follows.

$$\text{Present value factor} = \frac{\text{Initial investment}}{\text{Net cash flow}} = \frac{\$101,250}{\$40,000} = 2.5313 \text{ (rounded)}$$

Then, we search Table B.3 for the discount rate that corresponds to the present value factor of 2.5313 for three periods. From Table B.3, this discount rate is 9%. Project T2's internal rate of return of **9%** is below this company's hurdle rate of 10%. Project T2 should *not* be chosen.

---

**APPENDIX**

# 11A

# Using Excel to Compute Internal Rate of Return

Internal rate of return calculations for unequal annual cash flows can be made easier by using Excel. To illustrate, a company is considering investing in a new machine with the expected cash flows shown in the following spreadsheet. Cash outflows are entered as negative numbers, and cash inflows are entered as positive numbers.

**IRR**    To compute the internal rate of return the following is entered into cell C11:

**=IRR(C1:C10)**

This instructs Excel to use its IRR function to compute the internal rate of return of the unequal cash flows in cells C1 through C10. The IRR equals 14.47%.

| | A | B | C |
|---|---|---|---|
| 1 | Initial investment | | −16000 |
| 2 | Annual cash flows received at year-end | | |
| 3 | | 1 | 3000 |
| 4 | | 2 | 4000 |
| 5 | | 3 | 4000 |
| 6 | | 4 | 4000 |
| 7 | | 5 | 5000 |
| 8 | | 6 | 3000 |
| 9 | | 7 | 2000 |
| 10 | | 8 | 2000 |
| 11 | | | =IRR(C1:C10) |

## Summary: Cheat Sheet

### PAYBACK PERIOD

**Payback period:** Expected time to recover initial investment.
**Payback period with equal cash flows:**

$$\text{Payback period} = \frac{\text{Initial investment}}{\text{Annual net cash flow}} = \frac{\$16,000}{\$4,000} = 4 \text{ years}$$

Excel for Payback.

|   | A | B |
|---|---|---|
| 1 | Investment | $16,000 |
| 2 | Cash flow | $4,000 |
| 3 | Payback period | ← |

=B1/B2 = 4

**Payback period with unequal cash flows:** Determine when cumulative net cash flows change from negative to positive.

| Year | Net Cash Flows per Year | Cumulative Net Cash Flows |
|---|---|---|
| Initial investment ......... | $(16,000) | $(16,000) |
| Year 1.................... | 2,000 | (14,000) |
| Year 2.................... | 4,000 | (10,000) |
| Year 3.................... | 4,000 | (6,000) |
| Year 4.................... | 4,000 | (2,000) |
| Year 5.................... | 4,000 | 2,000 |

Payback occurs between Years 4 and 5.

**Payback period = 4 years + ($2,000/$4,000) or 0.5 of Year 5 = 4.5 years**

### ACCOUNTING RATE OF RETURN

**Accounting rate of return (ARR):** Percentage accounting return on average investment.

$$\text{Average investment} = \frac{\text{Initial investment} + \text{Salvage value}}{2} = \frac{\$16,000 + \$0}{2} = \$8,000$$

$$\text{Accounting rate of return} = \frac{\text{Annual income}}{\text{Average investment}} = \frac{\$2,000}{\$8,000} = 25.0\%$$

Excel for ARR.

|   | A | B |
|---|---|---|
| 1 | Investment | $16,000 |
| 2 | Salvage value | $0 |
| 3 | Income | $2,000 |
| 4 | Acctg rate of return | ← |

=B3/((B1+B2)/2) = 25%

### NET PRESENT VALUE (NPV)

**Net present value (NPV):** Discounted net cash flows − Initial investment.
**Cost of capital** (*hurdle rate*): Required rate of return on a potential investment.
**Net present value decision rule:** If NPV > 0, then invest.
**Annuity:** Series of cash flows of equal dollar amounts.

**NPV with equal cash flows:**

|   | Net Cash Flows | Present Value of 1 at 9%[†] | Present Value of Net Cash Flows |
|---|---|---|---|
| Year 1................. | $10,000 | 0.9174 | $  9,174 |
| Year 2................. | 10,000 | 0.8417 | 8,417 |
| Year 3................. | 10,000 | 0.7722 | 7,722 |
| Totals ............... | $30,000 |  | 25,313 |
| Initial investment...... |  |  | (20,000) |
| Net present value ..... |  |  | $  5,313 |

[†]Present value of 1 factors are taken from Table B.1 in Appendix B.

Excel for NPV.

|   | A | B |
|---|---|---|
| 1 | Investment | $20,000 |
| 2 | Cash flow | $10,000 |
| 3 | Periods | 3 |
| 4 | Interest rate | 9% |
| 5 | Net present value | ← |

=PV(B4,B3,−B2)−B1 = $5,313

**NPV with unequal cash flows:**

|   | Net Cash Flows | | Present Value of 1 at 10% | Present Value of Net Cash Flows | |
|---|---|---|---|---|---|
|   | A | B |   | A | B |
| Year 1 ........... | $ 5,000 | $ 8,000 | 0.9091 | $ 4,546 | $ 7,273 |
| Year 2 ........... | 5,000 | 5,000 | 0.8264 | 4,132 | 4,132 |
| Year 3 ........... | 5,000 | 2,000 | 0.7513 | 3,757 | 1,503 |
| Totals............ | $15,000 | $15,000 |  | 12,435 | 12,908 |
| Initial investment .. |  |  |  | (12,000) | (12,000) |
| Net present value .. |  |  |  | $   435 | $   908 |

**NPV with salvage value:**

|   | Net Cash Flows | Present Value of Factor at 10%[*] | Present Value of Net Cash Flows |
|---|---|---|---|
| Years 1–10 ............. | $15,000 | 6.1446 | $ 92,169 |
| Salvage value at Year 10 .. | 10,000 | 0.3855 | 3,855 |
| Total................. |  |  | 96,024 |
| Initial investment ....... |  |  | (80,000) |
| Net present value ....... |  |  | $ 16,024 |

[*]6.1446 = Present value of an annuity of 1, where $n = 10$, $i = 10\%$ (from Table B.3).
0.3855 = Present value of 1, where $n = 10$, $i = 10\%$ (from Table B.1).

**NPV: Comparing projects with profitability index:**

$$\text{Profitability index} = \frac{\text{Present value of net cash flows}}{\text{Initial investment}}$$

**Rule:** Pick project with highest profitability index (must exceed 1.0).

## INTERNAL RATE OF RETURN (IRR)

**IRR:** Discount rate that yields NPV of zero for an investment.
**Internal rate of return decision rule:** If IRR > Hurdle rate, then invest.

$$\text{Present value factor} = \frac{\text{Initial investment}}{\text{Annual net cash flows}} = \frac{\$12,009}{\$5,000} = 2.4018$$

Search for 2.4018 in Table B.3, $n = 3$. IRR is 12.0%.

Excel for IRR.

| | A | B |
|---|---|---|
| 1 | Investment | –$12,009 |
| 2 | Cash flow Year 1 | 5,000 |
| 3 | Cash flow Year 2 | 5,000 |
| 4 | Cash flow Year 3 | 5,000 |
| 5 | Internal rate of return | |

=IRR(B1:B4) = 12%

## Key Terms

| | | |
|---|---|---|
| Accounting rate of return (ARR) (398) | Cost of capital (399) | Payback period (PBP) (396) |
| Annuity (400) | Hurdle rate (399) | Profitability index (401) |
| Break-even time (BET) (404) | Internal rate of return (IRR) (402) | |
| Capital budgeting (395) | Net present value (NPV) (399) | |

## Multiple Choice Quiz

1. A company is considering the purchase of equipment for $270,000. Projected annual net cash flow from this equipment is $61,200 per year. The payback period is
   a. 0.2 years.      c. 4.4 years.      e. 3.9 years.
   b. 5.0 years.      d. 2.3 years.

2. A disadvantage of using the payback period to compare investment alternatives is that it
   a. Ignores cash flows beyond the payback period.
   b. Cannot be used to compare alternatives with different initial investments.
   c. Cannot be used when cash flows are not uniform.
   d. Involves the time value of money.
   e. Cannot be used if a company records depreciation.

3. A company buys a machine for $180,000 that has an expected life of nine years and no salvage value. The company

   expects an annual income of $8,550. What is the accounting rate of return?
   a. 4.75%      c. 2.85%      e. 6.65%
   b. 42.75%     d. 9.50%

4. The minimum acceptable rate of return for an investment decision is called the
   a. Hurdle rate.                 d. Average rate of return.
   b. Payback rate.                e. Break-even rate of return.
   c. Internal rate of return.

5. A company is considering the purchase of a machine costing $90,000. The annual net cash flow from the machine is $33,600. Assume cash flows are received at each year-end, and the machine has a useful life of three years with zero salvage value. Management requires a 12% return on its investments. What is the net present value of this machine?
   a. $60,444      c. $(88,560)      e. $(9,300)
   b. $80,700      d. $90,000

### ANSWERS TO MULTIPLE CHOICE QUIZ

1. c; Payback = $270,000/$61,200 per year = 4.4 years
2. a
3. d; Accounting rate of return = $8,550/[($180,000 + $0)/2] = 9.5%
4. a

5. e;

| | Net Cash Flows | Present Value of an Annuity of 1 at 12% | Present Value of Net Cash Flows |
|---|---|---|---|
| Years 1–3 .......... | $33,600 | 2.4018 | $ 80,700 |
| Initial investment .... | | | (90,000) |
| Net present value ... | | | $ (9,300) |

*ASuperscript letter A denotes assignments based on Appendix 11A.*

*Select Quick Study and Exercise assignments feature Guided Example videos, called "Hints"
in Connect. Hints use different numbers, and instructors can turn this feature on or off.*

Park Co. is considering an investment of $27,000 that provides net cash flows of $9,000 annually for four years. What is the investment's payback period?

**QUICK STUDY**

**QS 11-1**
Payback period and equal
cash flows   **P1**

Project A requires a $280,000 initial investment for new machinery. Project A is expected to yield income of $20,000 per year and net cash flow of $70,000 per year for the next five years. Compute Project A's payback period.

**QS 11-2**
Payback period and equal
cash flows   **P1**

Howard Co. is considering two alternative investments. The payback period is 3.5 years for Investment A and 4 years for Investment B.

**a.** If management uses payback period, which investment is preferred?

**b.** Will an investment with a shorter payback period always be chosen over an investment with a longer payback period?

**QS 11-3**
Analyzing payback
periods

**P1**

Compute the payback period for an investment with the following net cash flows.

**QS 11-4**
Payback period and
unequal cash flows

**P1**

| Year | Net Cash Flows per Year | Cumulative Net Cash Flows |
|---|---|---|
| Initial investment .... | $(100,000) | $(100,000) |
| 1................. | 10,000 | (90,000) |
| 2................. | 20,000 | (70,000) |
| 3................. | 20,000 | (50,000) |
| 4................. | 30,000 | (20,000) |
| 5................. | 40,000 | 20,000 |
| 6................. | 40,000 | 60,000 |

A company is considering three alternative investment projects. Accounting rate of return computations are calculated using Excel and are shown below. If the company can choose only one project, which will it choose on the basis of accounting rate of return?

**QS 11-5**
Interpreting accounting
rate of return; no
calculations

**P2**

| Potential Projects | Project A | Project B | Project C |
|---|---|---|---|
| Average investment ........ | $16,000 | $90,000 | $60,000 |
| Annual income ............ | $ 4,000 | $18,000 | $13,200 |
| **Accounting rate of return...** | **25%** | **20%** | **22%** |

Project A requires a $280,000 initial investment for new machinery with a five-year life and a salvage value of $30,000. Project A is expected to yield annual income of $20,000 per year and net cash flow of $70,000 per year for the next five years. Compute Project A's accounting rate of return.

**QS 11-6**
Accounting rate of return

**P2**

Peng Company is considering buying a machine that will yield income of $1,950 and net cash flow of $14,950 per year for three years. The machine costs $45,000 and has an estimated $6,000 salvage value. Compute the accounting rate of return for this investment.

**QS 11-7**
Accounting
rate of return   **P2**

Net present values for three alternative investment projects follow. (*a*) If the company accepts all positive net present value investments, which of these projects will it accept? (*b*) If the company can choose only one project, which will it choose?

**QS 11-8**
Net present value analysis,
no calculations

**P3**

| Potential Projects | Project A | Project B | Project C |
|---|---|---|---|
| Net present value ....... | $12,000 | $20,000 | $(5,000) |

**QS 11-9**

Net present value analysis; no present value calculations

**P3**

A company is considering three alternative investment projects with different net cash flows. The present value of net cash flows is calculated using Excel and the results follow.

| Potential Projects | Project A | Project B | Project C |
|---|---|---|---|
| Present value of net cash flows.. (excluding initial investment) | $10,832 | $11,876 | $9,870 |
| Initial investment ............. | (10,000) | (10,000) | (10,000) |

**a.** Compute the net present value of each project.

**b.** If the company accepts all positive net present value projects, which of these will it accept?

**c.** If the company can choose only one project, which will it choose on the basis of net present value?

**QS 11-10**

Net present value of annuity (PV factors given)

**P3**

Ibez Co. is considering a project that requires an initial investment of $60,000 and will generate net cash flows of $16,000 per year for 6 years. Ibez requires a return of 9% on its investments. The present value factor of an annuity for 6 years at 9% is 4.4859.

**a.** Compute the net present value of the project.

**b.** Determine whether the project should be accepted on the basis of net present value.

**QS 11-11**

Net present value (PV factors given)

**P3**

Dax Co. is considering an investment with the following information.

| Year | Net Cash Flows | Present Value of 1 at 12% | Present Value of Net Cash Flows |
|---|---|---|---|
| 1................ | $ 8,000 | 0.8929 | $_____ |
| 2................ | 10,000 | 0.7972 | _____ |
| 3................ | 12,000 | 0.7118 | _____ |
| Totals............ | $30,000 | | _____ |
| Initial investment ... | | | (25,000) |
| Net present value... | | | $_____ |

**a.** Compute the net present value of the investment.

**b.** Determine whether the investment should be accepted on the basis of net present value.

**QS 11-12**

Net present value analysis with salvage value; no present value calculations

**P3**

A company is considering two alternative machines with different net cash flows and salvage values. Present value amounts are calculated using Excel and the results follow.

| Potential Machine Investments | A | B |
|---|---|---|
| Present value of net cash flows.................. (excluding initial investment and salvage) | $19,902 | $20,800 |
| Present value of net cash flow from salvage value .. | 2,100 | 552 |
| Initial investment ............................ | (20,000) | (20,000) |

**a.** Compute the net present value of each machine A and B.

**b.** If the company can choose only one machine, which will it choose on the basis of net present value?

**QS 11-13**

Profitability index analysis, no calculations

**P3**

The profitability indexes for three alternative investment projects follow. Each project has a five-year life. (*a*) Which project(s) will the company accept on the basis of profitability index? (*b*) If the company can choose only one project, which will it choose?

| Potential Projects | Project A | Project B | Project C |
|---|---|---|---|
| Profitability index | 0.80 | 1.40 | 1.20 |

Pena Co. is considering an investment of $27,000 that provides net cash flows of $9,000 annually for four years. (*a*) If Pena Co. requires a 10% return on its investments, what is the net present value of this investment? (*b*) Based on net present value, should Pena Co. make this investment?

**QS 11-14**
Net present value of an annuity   **P3**

A company is considering investing in a new machine that requires an initial investment of $47,947. The machine will generate annual net cash flows of $21,000 for the next three years. The company uses an 8% discount rate. Compute the net present value of this investment.

**QS 11-15**
Net present value of an annuity   **P3**

Quail Co. is considering buying a food truck that will yield net cash inflows of $10,000 per year for seven years. The truck costs $50,000 and has an estimated $6,000 salvage value at the end of the seventh year. What is the net present value of this investment assuming a required 10% return?

**QS 11-16**
Net present value of annuity and salvage value   **P3**

Pablo Company is considering buying a machine that will yield income of $1,950 and net cash flow of $14,950 per year for three years. The machine costs $45,000 and has an estimated $6,000 salvage value. Pablo requires a 15% return on its investments. Compute the net present value of this investment.

**QS 11-17**
Net present value of annuity and salvage value

**P3**

Yokam Company is considering two alternative projects. Project 1 requires an initial investment of $400,000 and has a present value of net cash flows of $1,100,000. Project 2 requires an initial investment of $4 million and has a present value of net cash flows of $6 million. (*a*) Compute the profitability index for each project. (*b*) Based on the profitability index, which project should the company select?

**QS 11-18**
Profitability index

**P3**

Following is information on an investment in a manufacturing machine. The machine has zero salvage value. The company requires a 12% return from its investments. Compute this machine's net present value.

| | |
|---|---|
| Initial investment . . . . . . | $(200,000) |
| Net cash flows: Year 1 . . | 100,000 |
| Year 2 . . | 90,000 |
| Year 3 . . | 75,000 |

**QS 11-19**
Net present value with unequal cash flows

**P3**

Refer to the information in QS 11-19 and instead assume the machine has a salvage value of $20,000 at the end of its three-year life. Compute the machine's net present value.

**QS 11-20**
Net present value with uneven cash flows and salvage value   **P3**

Internal rates of return for three alternative investment projects follow. Each project has a five-year life. The company requires a 12% rate of return on its investments. (*a*) Which project(s) will the company accept on the basis of internal rate of return? (*b*) If the company can choose only one project, which will it choose?

| Potential Projects | Project X | Project Y | Project Z |
|---|---|---|---|
| Internal rate of return | 13% | 11% | 15% |

**QS 11-21**
Internal rate of return analysis, no calculations

**P4**

A company is considering investing in a new machine that requires an initial investment of $47,947. The machine will generate annual net cash flows of $21,000 for the next three years. What is the internal rate of return of this machine?

**QS 11-22**
Internal rate of return   **P4**

**QS 11-23**
Internal rate of return **P4**

Perez Co. is considering an investment of $27,336 that provides net cash flows of $9,000 annually for four years. (*a*) What is the internal rate of return of this investment? (*b*) The hurdle rate is 10%. Should the company invest in this project on the basis of internal rate of return?

**QS 11-24**
Break-even time
**A1**

A $100,000 initial investment will generate the following present values of net cash flows. What is the break-even time for this investment?

| Year | Present Value of Net Cash Flows | Cumulative Present Value of Net Cash Flows |
|---|---|---|
| Initial investment ... | $(100,000) | $(100,000) |
| 1................ | 36,364 | (63,636) |
| 2................ | 33,056 | (30,580) |
| 3................ | 25,116 | (5,464) |
| 4................ | 27,320 | 21,856 |
| 5................ | 24,836 | 46,692 |

Mc Graw Hill **connect**

**EXERCISES**

**Exercise 11-1**
Payback period, equal cash flows, and depreciation adjustment
**P1**

Information for two alternative projects involving machinery investments follows. Project 1 requires an initial investment of $140,000. Project 2 requires an initial investment of $90,000. Compute (*a*) annual net cash flow and (*b*) payback period for each investment.

| Annual Amounts | Project 1 | Project 2 |
|---|---|---|
| Sales of new product ............................ | $100,000 | $80,000 |
| Expenses...................................... | | |
| Materials, labor, and overhead (except depreciation) .. | 64,000 | 35,000 |
| Depreciation—Machinery ......................... | 20,000 | 18,000 |
| Selling, general, and administrative expenses........ | 8,000 | 20,000 |
| Income........................................ | $ 8,000 | $ 7,000 |

**Exercise 11-2**
Payback period, equal cash flows, and depreciation adjustment **P1**

Quary Co. is considering an investment in machinery with the following information. Compute the investment's (*a*) annual income *and* annual net cash flow and (*b*) payback period.

| | | | |
|---|---|---|---|
| Initial investment .......... | $200,000 | Materials, labor, and overhead (except depreciation) ..... | $45,000 |
| Useful life ................ | 9 years | Depreciation—Machinery........................ | 20,000 |
| Salvage value ............. | $20,000 | Selling, general, and administrative expenses........... | 5,000 |
| Expected sales per year..... | 10,000 units | Selling price per unit ............................. | $10 |

**Exercise 11-3**
Payback period and unequal cash flows **P1**

Beyer Company is considering buying an asset for $180,000. It is expected to produce the following net cash flows. Compute the payback period for this investment.

| | Year 1 | Year 2 | Year 3 | Year 4 | Year 5 |
|---|---|---|---|---|---|
| Net cash flows ......... | $60,000 | $40,000 | $70,000 | $125,000 | $35,000 |

**Exercise 11-4**
Payback period, unequal cash flows, and depreciation adjustment
**P1**

A machine can be purchased for $150,000 and used for five years, yielding the following income. This income computation includes annual depreciation expense of $30,000. Compute the machine's payback period.

| | Year 1 | Year 2 | Year 3 | Year 4 | Year 5 |
|---|---|---|---|---|---|
| Income.............. | $10,000 | $25,000 | $50,000 | $37,500 | $100,000 |

Information for two alternative projects involving machinery investments follows.

|                       | Project 1   | Project 2  |
|-----------------------|-------------|------------|
| Initial investment .....  | $(120,000)  | $(90,000)  |
| Salvage value . . . . . . . .  | 0           | 10,000     |
| Annual income . . . . . . .  | 15,000      | 12,000     |

**Exercise 11-5**
Accounting rate of return
**P2**

**a.** Compute accounting rate of return for each project.
**b.** Based on accounting rate of return, which project is preferred?

B2B Co. is considering the purchase of equipment that would allow the company to add a new product to its line. The equipment costs $360,000 and has a 12-year life and no salvage value. The expected annual income for each year from this equipment follows. Compute the (*a*) annual net cash flow, (*b*) payback period, and (*c*) accounting rate of return for this equipment.

**Exercise 11-6**
Payback period, equal cash flows, and accounting rate of return
**P1   P2**

| Sales of new product . . . . . . . . . . . . . . . . . . . . . . . . . . . . . . . . . . . . . . . .  | $225,000   |
|-----------------------------------------------------------------|------------|
| Expenses                                                        |            |
| Materials, labor, and overhead (except depreciation) . . . . . . . . . . . . . .  | 120,000    |
| Depreciation—Equipment . . . . . . . . . . . . . . . . . . . . . . . . . . . . . . . . . .  | 30,000     |
| Selling, general, and administrative expenses. . . . . . . . . . . . . . . . . . .  | 38,250     |
| Income. . . . . . . . . . . . . . . . . . . . . . . . . . . . . . . . . . . . . . . . . . . . . . . . . .  | $ 36,750   |

Gomez is considering a $180,000 investment with the following net cash flows. Gomez requires a 10% return on its investments. (*a*) Compute the net present value of this investment. (*b*) Should Gomez accept the investment?

**Exercise 11-7**
Net present value and unequal cash flows   **P3**

|                      | Year 1   | Year 2   | Year 3   | Year 4    | Year 5   |
|----------------------|----------|----------|----------|-----------|----------|
| Net cash flows . . . . . . . . . . . | $60,000  | $40,000  | $70,000  | $125,000  | $35,000  |

A company is considering a $150,000 investment in machinery with the following net cash flows. The company requires a 10% return on its investments. (*a*) Compute the net present value of this investment. (*b*) Should the machinery be purchased?

**Exercise 11-8**
Net present value and unequal cash flows   **P3**

|                      | Year 1   | Year 2   | Year 3   | Year 4    | Year 5    |
|----------------------|----------|----------|----------|-----------|-----------|
| Net cash flows . . . . . . . . . . . | $10,000  | $25,000  | $50,000  | $37,500   | $100,000  |

Gonzalez Co. is considering two new projects with the following net cash flows. The company's required rate of return on investments is 10%.

**Exercise 11-9**
Payback period; net present value; unequal cash flows

**P1   P3**

|                       | Net Cash Flows |           |
|-----------------------|----------------|-----------|
| Year                  | Project 1      | Project 2 |
| Initial investment . . . . .  | $(60,000)      | $(60,000) |
| 1. . . . . . . . . . . . . . . . . . .  | 30,000         | 35,000    |
| 2. . . . . . . . . . . . . . . . . . .  | 30,000         | 20,000    |
| 3. . . . . . . . . . . . . . . . . . .  | 5,000          | 20,000    |

**a.** Compute payback period for each project. Based on payback period, which project is preferred?
**b.** Compute net present value for each project. Based on net present value, which project is preferred?

**Exercise 11-10**

Net present value, unequal cash flows, and profitability index

P3

Following is information on two alternative investment projects being considered by Tiger Co. The company requires a 4% return from its investments. Compute each project's (a) net present value and (b) profitability index. Round present value calculations to the nearest dollar and round the profitability index to two decimals. (c) If the company can choose only one project, which should it choose on the basis of profitability index?

| | Project X1 | Project X2 |
|---|---|---|
| Initial investment .............. | $(80,000) | $(120,000) |
| Net cash flows: Year 1 ........... | 25,000 | 60,000 |
| Year 2 ........... | 35,500 | 50,000 |
| Year 3 ........... | 60,500 | 40,000 |

**Exercise 11-11**

Net present value, unequal cash flows, and profitability index   P3

Refer to the information in Exercise 11-10. The company instead requires a 12% return on its investments. Compute each project's (a) net present value and (b) profitability index. Round present value calculations to the nearest dollar and round the profitability index to two decimals. (c) If the company can choose only one project, which should it choose on the basis of profitability index?

**Exercise 11-12**

Net present value, unequal cash flows, profitability index, and service company

P3

Following is information on two alternative investments. Beachside Resort is considering building a new pool or spa. The company requires a 10% return from its investments. For each investment project, compute (a) net present value and (b) profitability index. (c) If the company can only select one project, which should it choose on the basis of profitability index?

| | Pool | Spa |
|---|---|---|
| Initial investment ............... | $(160,000) | $(105,000) |
| Net cash flows: Year 1 ........... | 40,000 | 32,000 |
| Year 2 ........... | 56,000 | 50,000 |
| Year 3 ........... | 80,295 | 66,000 |
| Year 4 ........... | 90,400 | 72,000 |
| Year 5 ........... | 65,000 | 24,000 |

**Exercise 11-13**

Net present value of an annuity   P3

Refer to the information in Exercise 11-6. B2B Co. requires at least an 8% return on this investment. (a) Compute the net present value of this investment. (b) Should the investment be accepted on the basis of net present value?

**Exercise 11-14**

Net present value of an annuity   P3

Refer to the information in Exercise 11-1. Project 1 has a seven-year useful life, and Project 2 has a five-year useful life. Assume the company requires a 10% rate of return on its investments. Compute the net present value of each potential investment.

**Exercise 11-15**

Internal rate of return

P4

GTO Inc. is considering an investment costing $214,170 that results in net cash flows of $30,000 annually for 11 years. (a) What is the internal rate of return of this investment? (b) The hurdle rate is 9.5%. Should the company invest in this project on the basis of internal rate of return?

**Exercise 11-16**

Investment decisions; no calculations

P1   P3   P4

Lopez Co. is considering three alternative investment projects below. Which project is preferred if management makes its decision based on (a) payback period, (b) net present value, and (c) internal rate of return?

| | Project 1 | Project 2 | Project 3 |
|---|---|---|---|
| Payback period......... | 3.5 years | 4.0 years | 3.2 years |
| Net present value....... | $25,000 | $32,000 | $18,000 |
| Internal rate of return.... | 12.5% | 11.4% | 10.8% |

OptiLux is considering investing in an automated manufacturing system. The system requires an initial investment of $4 million, has a 20-year life, and will have zero salvage value. If the system is implemented, the company will save $500,000 per year in direct labor costs. The company requires a 10% return from its investments.

**a.** Compute the proposed investment's net present value.

**b.** Using the answer from part *a*, is the investment's internal rate of return higher or lower than 10%? *Hint:* It is not necessary to compute IRR to answer this question.

**Exercise 11-17**
NPV and IRR for strategic investment
**P3  P4**

---

Phoenix Company is considering investments in projects C1 and C2. Both require an initial investment of $228,000 and would yield the following annual net cash flows.

| Net cash flows | Project C1 | Project C2 |
|---|---|---|
| Year 1 ........ | $ 12,000 | $ 96,000 |
| Year 2 ........ | 108,000 | 96,000 |
| Year 3 ........ | 168,000 | 96,000 |
| Totals......... | $288,000 | $288,000 |

**a.** The company requires a 12% return from its investments. Compute net present values using factors from Table B.1 in Appendix B to determine which projects, if any, should be accepted.

**b.** Using the answer from part *a,* is the internal rate of return higher or lower than 12% for (i) Project C1 and (ii) Project C2? *Hint:* It is not necessary to compute IRR to answer this question.

**Exercise 11-18**
Net present value, unequal cash flows, and internal rate of return
**P3  P4**

---

Refer to the information in Exercise 11-2. The company's required rate of return is 12%.

**a.** Compute the investment's net present value.

**b.** Using the answer from part *a*, is the investment's internal rate of return higher or lower than 12%? *Hint:* It is not necessary to compute the IRR to answer this question.

**Exercise 11-19**
Net present value; internal rate of return; equal cash flows  **P3  P4**

---

Refer to the information in Exercise 11-17. Create an Excel spreadsheet to compute the internal rate of return for the proposed investment.

**Exercise 11-20ᴬ**
IRR for investment using Excel  **P4**

---

Refer to the information in Exercise 11-10. (*a*) Create an Excel spreadsheet to compute the internal rate of return for each of the projects. (*b*) Based on internal rate of return, determine whether the company should accept either of the two projects.

**Exercise 11-21ᴬ**
Internal rate of return using Excel  **P4**

---

Refer to the information in Exercise 11-12. Create an Excel spreadsheet to compute the internal rate of return for each of the projects.

**Exercise 11-22ᴬ**
Using Excel to compute IRR  **P4**

---

A shoe manufacturer is evaluating new equipment that would custom fit athletic shoes. The new equipment costs $90,000 and will generate $35,000 in net cash flows for five years. Determine the break-even time for this equipment.

**Exercise 11-23**
Break-even time
**A1**

| Year | Net Cash Flows | Present Value of 1 at 10% | Present Value of Net Cash Flows | Cumulative Present Value of Net Cash Flows |
|---|---|---|---|---|
| Initial investment | $(90,000) | 1.0000 | _____ | _____ |
| 1 | 35,000 | 0.9091 | _____ | _____ |
| 2 | 35,000 | 0.8264 | _____ | _____ |
| 3 | 35,000 | 0.7513 | _____ | _____ |
| 4 | 35,000 | 0.6830 | _____ | _____ |
| 5 | 35,000 | 0.6209 | _____ | _____ |

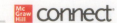

## PROBLEM SET A

### Problem 11-1A
Payback period, net present value, and net cash flow calculation

P1    P3

Factor Company is planning to add a new product to its line. To manufacture this product, the company needs to buy a new machine at a $480,000 cost with an expected four-year life and a $20,000 salvage value. Additional annual information for this new product line follows.

| | |
|---|---|
| Sales of new product . . . . . . . . . . . . . . . . . . . . . . . . . . . . . . . . . . | $1,840,000 |
| Expenses | |
| Materials, labor, and overhead (except depreciation) . . . . | 1,488,000 |
| Depreciation—Machinery . . . . . . . . . . . . . . . . . . . . . . . . . . . | 115,000 |
| Selling, general, and administrative expenses. . . . . . . . . | 183,100 |

**Required**

1. Determine income and net cash flow for each year of this machine's life.
2. Compute this machine's payback period, assuming that cash flows occur evenly throughout each year.
3. Compute net present value for this machine using a discount rate of 7%.

### Problem 11-2A
Payback period, accounting rate of return, net present value, and net cash flow calculation

P1    P2    P3

Project Y requires a $350,000 investment for new machinery with a four-year life and no salvage value. The project yields the following annual results. Cash flows occur evenly within each year.

| Annual Amounts | Project Y |
|---|---|
| Sales of new product . . . . . . . . . . . . . . . . . . . . . . . . . . . . . | $350,000 |
| Expenses | |
| Materials, labor, and overhead (except depreciation) . . | 157,500 |
| Depreciation—Machinery . . . . . . . . . . . . . . . . . . . . . . | 87,500 |
| Selling, general, and administrative expenses. . . . . . . . | 49,000 |
| Income. . . . . . . . . . . . . . . . . . . . . . . . . . . . . . . . . . . . . . . . | $ 56,000 |

**Required**

1. Compute Project Y's annual net cash flows.
2. Determine Project Y's payback period.
3. Compute Project Y's accounting rate of return.
4. Determine Project Y's net present value using 8% as the discount rate.

### Problem 11-3A
Applying payback period, accounting rate of return, and net present value

P1    P2    P3

Garcìa Co. can invest in one of two alternative projects. Project Y requires a $360,000 initial investment for new machinery with a four-year life and no salvage value. Project Z requires a $360,000 initial investment for new machinery with a three-year life and no salvage value. The two projects yield the following annual results. Cash flows occur evenly within each year.

| Annual Amounts | Project Y | Project Z |
|---|---|---|
| Sales of new product . . . . . . . . . . . . . . . . . . . . . . . . . . . . | $400,000 | $500,000 |
| Expenses | | |
| Materials, labor, and overhead (except depreciation) . . | 190,000 | 200,000 |
| Depreciation—Machinery . . . . . . . . . . . . . . . . . . . . . . | 90,000 | 120,000 |
| Selling, general, and administrative expenses. . . . . . . . | 50,000 | 50,000 |
| Income. . . . . . . . . . . . . . . . . . . . . . . . . . . . . . . . . . . . . . . | $ 70,000 | $130,000 |

**Required**

1. Compute each project's annual net cash flows.
2. Compute each project's payback period. If the company bases investment decisions solely on payback period, which project will it choose?

**3.** Compute each project's accounting rate of return. If the company bases investment decisions solely on accounting rate of return, which project will it choose?

**4.** Compute each project's net present value using 8% as the discount rate. If the company bases investment decisions solely on net present value, which project will it choose?

---

Rowan Co. is considering two alternative investment projects. Each requires a $250,000 initial investment. Project A is expected to generate net cash flows of $60,000 per year over the next six years. Project B is expected to generate net cash flows of $50,000 per year over the next seven years. Management requires an 8% rate of return on its investments.

**Problem 11-4A**
Applying net present value and profitability index
**P3**

**Required**

**1.** Compute each project's net present value.

**2.** Compute each project's profitability index.

**3.** If the company can choose only one project, which should it choose, based on profitability index?

---

Salsa Company is considering an investment in technology to improve its operations. The investment costs $250,000 and will yield the following net cash flows. Management requires a 10% return on investments.

**Problem 11-5A**
Payback period, break-even time, and net present value

**A1    P1    P3**

| | Year 1 | Year 2 | Year 3 | Year 4 | Year 5 |
|---|---|---|---|---|---|
| Net cash flows ......... | $47,000 | $52,000 | $75,000 | $94,000 | $125,000 |

**Required**

**1.** Determine the payback period for this investment.

**2.** Determine the break-even time for this investment.

**3.** Determine the net present value for this investment.

*Analysis Component*

**4.** Should management invest in this project based on net present value?

---

Interstate Manufacturing is considering either overhauling an old machine or replacing it with a new machine. Information about the two alternatives follows. Management requires a 10% rate of return on its investments.

**Problem 11-6A**
Net present value of alternate investments
**P3**

**Alternative 1:** Keep the old machine and have it overhauled. This requires an initial investment of $150,000 and results in $50,000 of net cash flows in each of the next five years. After five years, it can be sold for a $15,000 salvage value.

**Alternative 2:** Sell the old machine for $29,000 and buy a new one. The new machine requires an initial investment of $300,000 and can be sold for a $20,000 salvage value in five years. It would yield cost savings and higher sales, resulting in net cash flows of $65,000 in each of the next five years.

**Required**

**1.** Determine the net present value of alternative 1.

**2.** Determine the net present value of alternative 2.

**3.** Which alternative should management select based on net present value?

---

Cortino Company is planning to add a new product to its line. To manufacture this product, the company needs to buy a new machine at a $300,000 cost with an expected four-year life and a $20,000 salvage value. Additional annual information for this new product line follows.

**PROBLEM SET B**

**Problem 11-1B**
Payback period, net present value, and net cash flow calculation

**P1    P3**

| | |
|---|---|
| Sales of new product ............................... | $1,150,000 |
| Expenses | |
| Materials, labor, and overhead (except depreciation) .... | 930,000 |
| Depreciation—Machinery ......................... | 70,000 |
| Selling, general, and administrative expenses......... | 115,000 |

[continued on next page]

[continued from previous page]

**Required**

1. Determine income and net cash flow for each year of this machine's life.
2. Compute this machine's payback period, assuming that cash flows occur evenly throughout each year.
3. Compute net present value for this machine using a discount rate of 7%.

---

**Problem 11-2B**
Payback period, accounting rate of return, net present value, and net cash flow calculation

P1   P2   P3

Project A requires a $240,000 investment for new machinery with a four-year life and no salvage value. The project yields the following annual results. Cash flows occur evenly within each year.

| Annual Amounts | Project A |
|---|---|
| Sales of new product . . . . . . . . . . . . . . . . . . . . . . . . . . . . . . . . . . . . . . . . | $250,000 |
| Expenses | |
| Materials, labor, and overhead (except depreciation) . . . . . . . . . . . . | 115,000 |
| Depreciation—Machinery . . . . . . . . . . . . . . . . . . . . . . . . . . . . . . . . | 60,000 |
| Selling, general, and administrative expenses. . . . . . . . . . . . . . . . . | 35,100 |
| Income. . . . . . . . . . . . . . . . . . . . . . . . . . . . . . . . . . . . . . . . . . . . . . . | $ 39,900 |

**Required**

1. Compute Project A's annual net cash flows.
2. Determine Project A's payback period.
3. Compute Project A's accounting rate of return.
4. Determine Project A's net present value using 8% as the discount rate.

---

**Problem 11-3B**
Applying payback period, accounting rate of return, and net present value

P1   P2   P3

Lopez Co. can invest in one of two alternative projects. Project Y requires a $240,000 initial investment for new machinery with a four-year life and no salvage value. Project Z requires a $240,000 initial investment for new machinery with a three-year life and no salvage value. The two projects yield the following annual results. Cash flows occur evenly within each year.

| Annual Amounts | Project Y | Project Z |
|---|---|---|
| Sales of new product . . . . . . . . . . . . . . . . . . . . . . . . . . . . | $320,000 | $350,000 |
| Expenses | | |
| Materials, labor, and overhead (except depreciation) . . | 146,000 | 150,000 |
| Depreciation—Machinery . . . . . . . . . . . . . . . . . . . . . . . | 60,000 | 70,000 |
| Selling, general, and administrative expenses. . . . . . . . | 50,000 | 40,000 |
| Income. . . . . . . . . . . . . . . . . . . . . . . . . . . . . . . . . . . . . . | $ 64,000 | $ 90,000 |

**Required**

1. Compute each project's annual net cash flows.
2. Compute each project's payback period. If the company bases investment decisions solely on payback period, which project will it choose?
3. Compute each project's accounting rate of return. If the company bases investment decisions solely on accounting rate of return, which project will it choose?
4. Compute each project's net present value using 9% as the discount rate. If the company bases investment decisions solely on net present value, which project will it choose?

Milan Co. is considering two alternative investment projects. Each requires a $300,000 initial investment. Project A is expected to generate net cash flows of $90,000 per year over the next five years. Project B is expected to generate net cash flows of $80,000 per year over the next six years. Management requires an 8% rate of return on its investments.

**Problem 11-4B**

Applying net present value and profitability index

**P3**

**Required**

1. Compute each project's net present value.
2. Compute each project's profitability index.
3. If the company can choose only one project, which will it choose, based on profitability index?

Aster Company is considering an investment in technology to improve its operations. The investment costs $800,000 and yields the following net cash flows. Management requires a 10% return on its investments.

**Problem 11-5B**

Payback period, break-even time, and net present value

**A1    P1    P3**

|  | Year 1 | Year 2 | Year 3 | Year 4 |
|---|---|---|---|---|
| Net cash flows .. | $300,000 | $350,000 | $400,000 | $450,000 |

**Required**

1. Determine the payback period for this investment.
2. Determine the break-even time for this investment.
3. Determine the net present value for this investment.

*Analysis Component*

4. Should management invest in this project based on net present value?

Archer Foods is considering whether to overhaul an old freezer or replace it with a new freezer. Information about the two alternatives follows. Management requires a 10% rate of return on its investments.

**Problem 11-6B**

Net present value of alternate investments

**P3**

**Alternative 1:** Keep the old freezer and have it overhauled. This requires an initial investment of $50,000, resulting in $10,000 of net cash flows in each of the next eight years. After eight years, it can be sold for a $4,000 salvage value.

**Alternative 2:** Sell the old freezer for $5,000 and buy a new one. The new freezer requires an initial investment of $150,000 and can be sold for an $8,000 salvage value in eight years. The new freezer is larger, would increase sales, and would result in net cash flows of $40,000 in each of the next eight years.

**Required**

1. Determine the net present value of alternative 1.
2. Determine the net present value of alternative 2.
3. Which alternative should management select based on net present value?

*This serial problem began in Chapter 1 and continues through most of the book. If previous chapter segments were not completed, the serial problem can begin at this point.*

**SERIAL PROBLEM**

Business Solutions

**P1    P2    P4**

**SP 11**    Santana Rey is considering the purchase of equipment for **Business Solutions** that would allow the company to add a new product to its computer furniture line. The equipment is expected to cost $300,000 and to have a six-year life and no salvage value. The equipment is expected to generate income of $12,939 and net cash flow of $62,939 in each year of its six-year life. Santana requires an 8% return on all investments.

**Required**

1. Compute payback period, net present value, and internal rate of return for this equipment.
2. If Santana requires investments to have payback periods of four years or less, should she invest in this equipment?
3. If Santana requires investments to have at least an 8% internal rate of return, should she invest in this equipment?

Alexander Image/Shutterstock

## Accounting Analysis

**COMPANY ANALYSIS**

**A1**

**APPLE**

**AA 11-1**  **Apple** invested $10,495 in the current year to expand its manufacturing capacity. Assume that these assets have a 10-year life and generate net cash flows of $3,000 per year, and that Apple requires a 7% return on its investments. (Apple $s in millions.)

**Required**

1. Compute break-even time.
2. Compute the net present value of this investment.

---

**COMPARATIVE ANALYSIS**

**A1**

**GOOGLE**

**APPLE**

**AA 11-2**  Information on assumed capital investments in the current year for **Google** and **Apple** follow.

| $ millions | Google | Apple |
|---|---|---|
| Initial investment ........................ | $(23,548) | $(10,495) |
| Annual net cash flows, years 1–10 .......... | $4,000 | $3,000 |
| Required rate of return on investment ....... | 6% | 7% |

**Required**

1. Compute break-even time for both companies.
2. Based on break-even time, which company can expect its investment to more quickly yield positive net cash flows?

---

**EXTENDED ANALYSIS**

**A1**

**Samsung**

**AA 11-3**  **Samsung** invested $21,766 in the current year to expand its manufacturing capacity. Assume that these assets have an 8-year life and generate net cash flows of $4,000 per year, and that Samsung requires a 7% return on its investments. (Samsung $s in millions.)

**Required**

Compute break-even time.

## Discussion Questions

1. What is capital budgeting?
2. Identify four reasons that capital budgeting decisions are risky.
3. Describe the cash inflows and outflows that occur over the life of a typical capital expenditure.
4. Identify two weaknesses of the payback period method.
5. Why is an investment more attractive if it has a shorter payback period?

6. What is the average amount invested in a machine during its predicted five-year life if it costs $200,000 and has a $20,000 salvage value?
7. If the present value of the net cash flows from a machine, discounted at 10%, exceeds the initial investment, what can you say about the investment's internal rate of return? What can you say about the internal rate of return if the present value of the net cash flows, discounted at 10%, is less than the initial investment?

8. Why is the present value of $100 that you expect to receive one year from today worth less than $100 received today?

9. If a potential investment's internal rate of return is above the company's hurdle rate, should the investment be made?

10. **Samsung** is planning to invest in a new companywide computerized inventory tracking system. What makes this potential investment risky? **Samsung**

11. **Google** is planning to acquire new equipment to manufacture tablet computers. **GOOGLE**

What are some of the cash flows that would be included in Google's analysis?

12. **Apple** is considering expanding a store. Identify three methods management can use to evaluate whether to expand. **APPLE**

13. Discuss the advantage of break-even time over the payback period.

## Beyond the Numbers

**BTN 11-1** Management requires purchases above $5,000 to be submitted with cash flow projections for capital budget approval. As systems manager, you want to upgrade your computers at a $25,000 cost. You consider submitting several orders, each under $5,000 to avoid the approval process. You believe the computers will increase income and wish to avoid a delay.

**ETHICS CHALLENGE**

P3

**Required**

As systems manager, is your plan to submit several separate orders appropriate? What should you do?

---

**BTN 11-2** Payback period and net present value are common methods to evaluate capital investment opportunities. Assume that your manager asks you to explain why net present value is better than payback period for making investment choices. Present your response in memorandum format of less than one page.

**COMMUNICATING IN PRACTICE**

P1  P3

---

**BTN 11-3** Assume an airline is considering an investment in a new baggage handling system. Separate into teams and identify at least three *qualitative* factors that should be considered in this investment decision.

**TEAMWORK IN ACTION**

P1  P3

---

**BTN 11-4** Read the chapter opener about Jake Loosararian and his company, **Gecko Robotics**. Suppose Jake's business continues to grow, and he builds a massive new manufacturing facility and warehousing center to make the business more efficient and reduce costs.

**ENTREPRENEURIAL DECISION**

P1 P2 P3 P4

**Required**

1. What are some of the management tools that Jake can use to evaluate whether the new manufacturing facility and warehousing center will be a good investment?

2. What information does Jake need to use the tools that you identified in your answer to part 1?

3. What are some of the strengths and weaknesses of each tool identified in your answer to part 1?

# 12 Reporting Cash Flows

## Learning Objectives

### CONCEPTUAL

**C1** Distinguish between operating, investing, and financing activities, and describe how noncash investing and financing activities are disclosed.

### ANALYTICAL

**A1** Analyze the statement of cash flows and apply the cash flow on total assets ratio.

### PROCEDURAL

**P1** Prepare a statement of cash flows.

**P2** Compute cash flows from operating activities using the indirect method.

**P3** Determine cash flows from both investing and financing activities.

**P4** *Appendix 12A*—Illustrate use of a spreadsheet to prepare a statement of cash flows.

**P5** *Appendix 12B*—Compute cash flows from operating activities using the direct method.

# Show Your Colors

*"Follow your strengths"*—**Barbara Bradley**

FORT WAYNE, IN—"I never saw myself going into business," recalls Barbara Bradley. Until one day, "we were at the airport when we noticed no one was carrying anything colorful or fun. So we decided to start a company to make handbags and luggage," exclaims Barbara.

Barbara and her co-founder had no cash, so they borrowed $250 and started "cutting fabric out on a Ping-Pong table," explains Barbara. "We decided to name the company **Vera Bradley** (**VeraBradley.com**) after [my mother]."

As business grew, Barbara had to manage cash flows. "The first year, we did $10,000 in sales," proclaims Barbara. "Then things got chaotic." While cash flows from operations were good, the business had to expand to meet demand.

"We went to a bank, seeking a $5,000 loan," says Barbara. The loan was a welcome cash inflow that allowed the company to "build its own building!"

Barbara admits that she's "not a great finance [and accounting] person," but she insists that accounting and attention to cash flows are key to running a successful business. Mixing in Barbara's special talents, her company is reaching new heights.

Jason Kempin/Getty Images

Although cash may be king, Barbara insists that "business is all about forming relationships. My father always said, 'In business, you sell yourself first, your company second, and the product third,' and he was right."

Sources: *Vera Bradley website*, January 2021; *Vera Bradley Foundation*, January 2021; *Fortune*, October 2015; *Wane.com*, March 2019

# BASICS OF CASH FLOW REPORTING

## Purpose of the Statement of Cash Flows

The **statement of cash flows** reports cash receipts (inflows) and cash payments (outflows) for a period. Cash flows are separated into operating, investing, and financing activities. The details of sources and uses of cash make this statement useful. The statement of cash flows helps answer

- What explains the change in the cash balance?
- Where does a company spend its cash?
- How does a company receive its cash?
- Why do income and cash flows differ?

**C1** ___

Distinguish between operating, investing, and financing activities, and describe how noncash investing and financing activities are disclosed.

## Importance of Cash Flows

Information about cash flows influences decisions. Cash flows help users decide whether a company has enough cash to pay its debts. They also help evaluate a company's ability to pursue opportunities. Managers use cash flow information to plan day-to-day operations and make long-term investment decisions.

**W. T. Grant Co.** is a classic example of the importance of cash flows. Grant reported net income of more than $40 million per year for three consecutive years. At that same time, cash outflow was more than $90 million by the end of that three-year period. Grant soon went bankrupt. Users who relied only on Grant's income numbers were caught off guard.

## Measurement of Cash Flows

Cash flows include both *cash* and *cash equivalents*. The statement of cash flows explains the difference between the beginning and ending balances of cash and cash equivalents. We continue to use the phrases *cash flows* and the *statement of cash flows,* but remember that both phrases refer to cash *and* cash equivalents. Because cash and cash equivalents are combined, the statement of cash flows does not report transactions *between* cash and cash equivalents, such as cash paid to purchase cash equivalents and cash received from selling cash equivalents.

A cash equivalent has two criteria: (1) be readily convertible to a known amount of cash and (2) be sufficiently close to its maturity so its market value is unaffected by interest rate changes. **American Express** defines its cash equivalents as including "highly liquid investments with original maturities of 90 days or less."

## Classification of Cash Flows

Cash receipts and cash payments are classified in one of three categories: operating, investing, or financing activities. A net cash inflow (source) occurs when the receipts in a category exceed the payments. A net cash outflow (use) occurs when the payments in a category exceed the receipts.

### Operating Activities

**Operating activities** include transactions and events that affect net income. Examples are the production and purchase of inventory, the sale of goods and services to customers, and the expenditures to operate the business. Not all items in income, such as unusual gains and losses, are operating activities (we discuss these exceptions later). Exhibit 12.1 lists common cash inflows and outflows from operating activities.

**EXHIBIT 12.1**

Cash Flows from Operating Activities

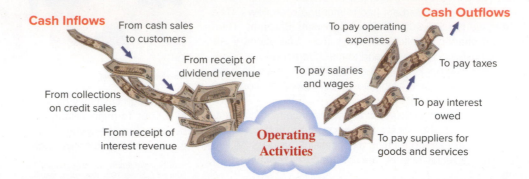

### Investing Activities

**Investing activities** include transactions and events that come from the purchase and sale of long-term assets. They also include (1) the purchase and sale of investments and (2) lending and collecting money for notes receivable. Exhibit 12.2 lists examples of cash flows from investing activities. Cash from collecting the principal on notes is an investing activity. However, collecting interest on notes is an operating activity; also, if a note results from sales to customers, it is an operating activity.

**Point:** For simplicity, we assume purchases and sales of equity and debt investments are investing activities.

**EXHIBIT 12.2**

Cash Flows from Investing Activities

### Financing Activities

**Financing activities** include transactions and events that affect long-term liabilities and equity. Examples are (1) getting cash from issuing debt and repaying debt and (2) receiving cash from or distributing cash to owners. Borrowing and repaying principal on long-term debt are financing activities. However, payments of interest are operating activities. Exhibit 12.3 lists examples of cash flows from financing activities.

**EXHIBIT 12.3**

Cash Flows from Financing Activities

**Link between Classification of Cash Flows and the Balance Sheet** Operating, investing, and financing activities are loosely linked to different parts of the balance sheet. Operating activities are affected by changes in current assets and current liabilities (and the income statement). Investing activities are affected by changes in long-term assets. Financing activities are affected by changes in long-term liabilities and equity. These links are shown in Exhibit 12.4. Exceptions to these links include (1) current assets *unrelated* to operations—such as short-term notes receivable from noncustomers and from investment securities, which are investing activities, and (2) current liabilities *unrelated* to operations—such as dividends payable, which are financing activities.

**EXHIBIT 12.4**

Linkage of Cash Flow Classifications to the Balance Sheet

# Noncash Investing and Financing

Some investing and financing activities do not affect cash flows. One example is the purchase of long-term assets using a long-term notes payable (loan). This transaction impacts both investing and financing activities but does not impact current-period cash. Such transactions are reported at the bottom of the statement of cash flows or in a note to the statement—Exhibit 12.5 has examples.

| |
|---|
| ● Retirement of debt by issuing equity stock.    ● Purchase of long-term assets by issuing a note or bond. |
| ● Conversion of preferred stock to common stock.    ● Exchange of noncash assets for other noncash assets. |
| ● Lease of assets in a long-term lease transaction.    ● Purchase of noncash assets by issuing equity or debt. |

**EXHIBIT 12.5**

Examples of Noncash Investing and Financing Activities

# Format of the Statement of Cash Flows

A statement of cash flows reports cash flows from three activities: operating, investing, and financing. Exhibit 12.6 shows the usual format. The statement shows the net increase or decrease from those activities and ties it into the cash balance. Any noncash investing and financing transactions are disclosed in a note or separate schedule.

**P1**

Prepare a statement of cash flows.

| COMPANY NAME<br>Statement of Cash Flows<br>For *period* Ended *date* | | |
|---|---|---|
| **Cash flows from operating activities** | | |
| [Compute operating cash flows using indirect or direct method] | | |
| Net cash provided (used) by operating activities . . . . . . . . . . . . . . . . . . . . . . . . . . | $ | # |
| **Cash flows from investing activities** | | |
| [List of individual inflows and outflows] | | |
| Net cash provided (used) by investing activities . . . . . . . . . . . . . . . . . . . . . . . . . . | | # |
| **Cash flows from financing activities** | | |
| [List of individual inflows and outflows] | | |
| Net cash provided (used) by financing activities . . . . . . . . . . . . . . . . . . . . . . . . . . | | # |
| **Net increase (decrease) in cash**. . . . . . . . . . . . . . . . . . . . . . . . . . . . . . . . . . . . . . . | $ | # |
| Cash (and equivalents) balance at prior period-end. . . . . . . . . . . . . . . . . . . . . . . . | | # |
| Cash (and equivalents) balance at current period-end . . . . . . . . . . . . . . . . . . . . . | $ | # |
| Separate schedule or note disclosure of any noncash investing and financing transactions is required. | | |

**EXHIBIT 12.6**

Format of the Statement of Cash Flows

**Point:** Positive cash flows for a section are titled net cash "provided by" or "from." Negative cash flows are labeled as net cash "used by" or "for."

# Preparing the Statement of Cash Flows

Preparing a statement of cash flows has five steps, shown in Exhibit 12.7. Computing the net increase or net decrease in cash is a simple but crucial computation. It equals the current period's cash balance minus the prior period's cash balance. This is the *bottom-line* figure for the statement of cash flows and is a check on accuracy.

**EXHIBIT 12.7**

Five Steps in Preparing the Statement of Cash Flows

1 Compute net increase or decrease in cash.

2 Compute net cash from or for operating activities.

3 Compute net cash from or for investing activities.

4 Compute net cash from or for financing activities.

5 Compute net cash from all sources; then *prove* it by adding it to beginning cash to get ending cash.

## Analyzing the Cash Account

A company's cash receipts and cash payments are recorded in its Cash account. The Cash account is one place to look for information about cash flows. The summarized Cash T-account of Genesis, Inc., is in Exhibit 12.8. Preparing a statement of cash flows requires classifying each cash inflow or outflow as an operating, investing, or financing activity.

**EXHIBIT 12.8**

Summarized Cash Account

| Cash | | | |
|---|---|---|---|
| Balance, Dec. 31, 2020 | 12,000 | | |
| Receipts from customers | 570,000 | Payments for inventory | 319,000 |
| Receipts from asset sales | 2,000 | Payments for operating exp. | 218,000 |
| Receipts from stock issuance | 15,000 | Payments for interest | 8,000 |
| | | Payments for taxes | 5,000 |
| | | Payments for notes retirement | 18,000 |
| | | Payments for dividends | 14,000 |
| Balance, Dec. 31, 2021 | 17,000 | | |

## Analyzing Noncash Accounts

A second approach to preparing the statement of cash flows analyzes noncash accounts and uses double-entry accounting. Exhibit 12.9 uses the accounting equation to show the relation between the Cash account and the noncash balance sheet accounts. We can explain changes in cash and prepare a statement of cash flows by analyzing changes in liability accounts, equity accounts, and noncash asset accounts (along with income statement accounts).

**EXHIBIT 12.9**

Relation between Cash and Noncash Accounts

$$\text{Cash} = \text{Liabilities} + \text{Equity} - \text{Noncash assets}$$

## Information to Prepare the Statement

Information to prepare the statement of cash flows comes from three sources: (1) comparative balance sheets, (2) the current income statement, and (3) additional information. Comparative balance sheets are used to compute changes in noncash accounts from the beginning to the end of the period. The current income statement is used to help compute cash flows from operating activities. Additional information includes details that help explain cash flows and noncash activities.

■ **Decision Maker**

Classify each of the following cash flows as operating, investing, or financing activities.

| | |
|---|---|
| **a.** Purchase equipment for cash | **g.** Cash paid for utilities |
| **b.** Cash payment of wages | **h.** Cash paid to acquire investments |
| **c.** Issuance of stock for cash | **i.** Cash paid to retire debt |
| **d.** Receipt of cash dividends from investments | **j.** Cash received as interest on investments |
| **e.** Cash collections from customers | **k.** Cash received from selling investments |
| **f.** Notes payable issued for cash | **l.** Cash received from a bank loan |

**NEED-TO-KNOW** **12-1**

Classifying Cash Flows

**C1   P1**

**Solution**

| | | | | | |
|---|---|---|---|---|---|
| **a.** Investing | **c.** Financing | **e.** Operating | **g.** Operating | **i.** Financing | **k.** Investing |
| **b.** Operating | **d.** Operating | **f.** Financing | **h.** Investing | **j.** Operating | **l.** Financing |

Do More: QS 12-1, QS 12-2, E 12-1

## CASH FLOWS FROM OPERATING

### Indirect and Direct Methods of Reporting

Cash flows provided (used) by operating activities are reported using the *direct method* or the *indirect method.* **These two different methods apply only to the operating activities section.**

**P2**

Compute cash flows from operating activities using the indirect method.

- The **direct method** separately lists operating cash receipts (such as cash received from customers) and operating cash payments (such as cash paid for inventory). The cash payments are then subtracted from cash receipts. The direct method is covered in Appendix 12B.
- The **indirect method** reports net income and then adjusts it for items that do not affect cash. It does *not* report individual items of cash inflows and cash outflows from operating activities.

**The net cash amount provided by operating activities is *identical* under both the direct and indirect methods.** The difference is with the computation and presentation. The indirect method is arguably easier. Nearly all companies report operating cash flows using the indirect method, including **Apple**, **Google**, and **Samsung** in Appendix A.

**Demonstration Data**   Exhibit 12.10 shows Genesis's income statement and balance sheets. We use this information to prepare a statement of cash flows that explains the $5,000 increase in cash.

### Applying the Indirect Method

Net income is computed using accrual accounting. Revenues and expenses rarely match the receipt and payment of cash. The indirect method adjusts net income to get the net cash provided or used by operating activities. We begin with Genesis's income of $38,000 and adjust it

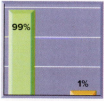

**Firms Using Indirect vs. Direct**

99%

1%

Indirect     Direct

| GENESIS Income Statement For Year Ended December 31, 2021 | | |
|---|---:|---:|
| Sales ........................... | | $590,000 |
| Cost of goods sold ............... | $300,000 | |
| Operating expenses (excluding depreciation) ......... | 216,000 | |
| Depreciation expense ............. | 24,000 | |
| Interest expense.................. | 7,000 | (547,000) |
| | | 43,000 |
| Other gains (losses) | | |
| Loss on sale of plant assets ...... | (6,000) | |
| Gain on retirement of notes ...... | 16,000 | 10,000 |
| Income before taxes............... | | 53,000 |
| Income taxes expense ............. | | (15,000) |
| Net income ...................... | | $ 38,000 |

**Additional information for 2021**

**a.** The accounts payable balances result from inventory purchases.

**b.** Purchased $60,000 in plant assets by issuing $60,000 of notes payable.

**c.** Sold plant assets with a book value of $8,000 (original cost of $20,000 and accumulated depreciation of $12,000) for $2,000 cash, yielding a $6,000 loss.

**d.** Received $15,000 cash from issuing 3,000 shares of common stock.

**e.** Paid $18,000 cash to retire notes with a $34,000 book value, yielding a $16,000 gain.

**f.** Declared and paid cash dividends of $14,000.

| GENESIS Balance Sheets | | | |
|---|---:|---:|---:|
| At December 31 | 2021 | 2020 | Change |
| **Assets** | | | |
| Current assets | | | |
| Cash ........................ | $ 17,000 | $ 12,000 | $ 5,000 Increase |
| Accounts receivable .......... | 60,000 | 40,000 | 20,000 Increase |
| Inventory ................... | 84,000 | 70,000 | 14,000 Increase |
| Prepaid expenses ............ | 6,000 | 4,000 | 2,000 Increase |
| Total current assets .......... | 167,000 | 126,000 | |
| Long-term assets | | | |
| Plant assets ................ | 250,000 | 210,000 | 40,000 Increase |
| Accumulated depreciation ..... | (60,000) | (48,000) | 12,000 Increase |
| Total assets.................. | $357,000 | $288,000 | |
| **Liabilities** | | | |
| Current liabilities | | | |
| Accounts payable............. | $ 35,000 | $ 40,000 | $ 5,000 Decrease |
| Interest payable.............. | 3,000 | 4,000 | 1,000 Decrease |
| Income taxes payable ......... | 22,000 | 12,000 | 10,000 Increase |
| Total current liabilities ........ | 60,000 | 56,000 | |
| Long-term notes payable......... | 90,000 | 64,000 | 26,000 Increase |
| Total liabilities................. | 150,000 | 120,000 | |
| **Equity** | | | |
| Common stock, $5 par........... | 95,000 | 80,000 | 15,000 Increase |
| Retained earnings ............. | 112,000 | 88,000 | 24,000 Increase |
| Total equity.................... | 207,000 | 168,000 | |
| Total liabilities and equity ........ | $357,000 | $288,000 | |

**EXHIBIT 12.10**

Financial Statements

to get cash provided by operating activities of $20,000—see Exhibit 12.11. There are two types of adjustments: ① Adjustments to income statement items that do not impact cash and ② Adjustments for changes in current assets and current liabilities (linked to operating activities). Nearly all companies group adjustments into these two types, including Apple, Google, and Samsung in Appendix A.

**EXHIBIT 12.11**

Operating Activities Section—Indirect Method

| GENESIS Statement of Cash Flows—Operating Section under Indirect Method For Year Ended December 31, 2021 | |
|---|---:|
| Cash flows from operating activities | |
| Net income...................................................... | $ 38,000 |
| Adjustments to reconcile net income to net cash provided by operating activities | |
| Income statement items not affecting cash | |
| ① Depreciation expense........................................ | 24,000 |
| Loss on sale of plant assets ................................. | 6,000 |
| Gain on retirement of notes ................................. | (16,000) |
| Changes in current assets and liabilities | |
| Increase in accounts receivable.............................. | (20,000) |
| Increase in inventory........................................ | (14,000) |
| ② Increase in prepaid expenses ............................... | (2,000) |
| Decrease in accounts payable ............................... | (5,000) |
| Decrease in interest payable ................................ | (1,000) |
| Increase in income taxes payable ............................ | 10,000 |
| **Net cash provided by operating activities** ................... | **$20,000** |

**①** **Adjustments for Income Statement Items Not Affecting Cash**    Some expenses and losses subtracted from net income are not cash outflows. Examples are depreciation, amortization, depletion, bad debts expense, loss from an asset sale, and loss from retirement of notes payable. The indirect method requires that

> **Expenses and losses with no cash outflows are added back to net income.**

These expenses and losses did *not* reduce cash, and adding them back cancels their deductions from net income. Any cash received or paid from a transaction that yields a loss, such as from an asset sale or payoff of a note, is reported under investing or financing activities.

When net income has revenues and gains that are not cash inflows, the indirect method requires that

> **Revenues and gains with no cash inflows are subtracted from net income.**

Section ① of Exhibit 12.11 shows three adjustments for items that did not impact cash for Genesis.

**Depreciation**    Depreciation expense is Genesis's only operating item in net income that had no effect on cash flows. We add back the $24,000 depreciation expense to net income because depreciation did not reduce cash.

**Loss on Sale of Plant Assets**    Genesis reported a $6,000 loss on sale of plant assets that reduced net income but did not affect cash flows. This $6,000 loss is added back to net income because it is not a cash outflow.

**Gain on Retirement of Debt**    A $16,000 gain on retirement of debt increased net income but did not affect cash flows. This $16,000 gain is subtracted from net income because it was not a cash inflow.

**②Adjustments for Changes in Current Assets and Current Liabilities**    This section covers adjustments for changes in current assets and current liabilities.

**Adjustments for Changes in Current Assets**

> **Decreases in current assets are added to net income.**
>
> **Increases in current assets are subtracted from net income.**

**Adjustments for Changes in Current Liabilities**

> **Increases in current liabilities are added to net income.**
>
> **Decreases in current liabilities are subtracted from net income.**

The lower section of Exhibit 12.11 shows adjustments to the three noncash current assets and three current liabilities for Genesis. We explain each adjustment next.

**Accounts Receivable**    The $20,000 increase in the current asset of accounts receivable is subtracted from income (showing less cash available). This increase means Genesis collects less cash than is reported in sales. To help see this, we use *account analysis*. This involves setting up a T-account, entering **in black** the balances and entries we know, and computing **in red** the cash receipts or payments. We see cash receipts are $20,000 less than sales, which is why we subtract $20,000 from income in computing the cash flow.

**Point:** An income statement reports revenues, gains, expenses, and losses on an accrual basis. The statement of cash flows reports cash received and cash paid for operating, financing, and investing activities.

**Point:** Section ② adjustments.

|  | Account Increases | Account Decreases |
|---|---|---|
| **Current assets** | Subtract from net income | Add to net income |
| **Current liabilities** | Add to net income | Subtract from net income |

Black numbers are from Exhibit 12.10. Red number → is computed.

| Accounts Receivable | | | |
|---|---|---|---|
| Bal., Dec. 31, 2020 | 40,000 | | |
| Sales | 590,000 | **Cash receipts = 570,000** ← 40,000 + 590,000 − 60,000 |
| Bal., Dec. 31, 2021 | 60,000 | | |

| Inventory | | | |
|---|---|---|---|
| Bal., Dec. 31, 2020 | 70,000 | | |
| **Purchases =** | **314,000** | Cost of goods sold | 300,000 |
| Bal., Dec. 31, 2021 | 84,000 | | |

**Inventory**  The $14,000 increase in inventory is subtracted from income. The T-account shows that purchases are $14,000 more than cost of goods sold. This means that cost of goods sold excludes $14,000 of inventory purchased this year, which is why we subtract $14,000 from income in computing cash flow.

| Prepaid Expenses | | | |
|---|---|---|---|
| Bal., Dec. 31, 2020 | 4,000 | | |
| **Cash payments =** | **218,000** | Operating expenses | 216,000 |
| Bal., Dec. 31, 2021 | 6,000 | | |

**Prepaid Expenses**  The $2,000 increase in prepaid expenses, which is related to operating expenses, is subtracted from income. The T-account shows that cash paid is $2,000 more than expenses recorded, which is why we subtract $2,000 from income in computing cash flow.

| Accounts Payable | | | |
|---|---|---|---|
| | | Bal., Dec. 31, 2020 | 40,000 |
| **Cash payments =** | **319,000** | Purchases | 314,000 |
| | | Bal., Dec. 31, 2021 | 35,000 |

**Accounts Payable**  The $5,000 decrease in accounts payable is subtracted from income. The T-account shows that cash paid is $5,000 more than purchases recorded, which is why we subtract $5,000 from income in computing cash flow.

| Interest Payable | | | |
|---|---|---|---|
| | | Bal., Dec. 31, 2020 | 4,000 |
| **Cash paid for interest = 8,000** | | Interest expense | 7,000 |
| | | Bal., Dec. 31, 2021 | 3,000 |

**Interest Payable**  The $1,000 decrease in interest payable is subtracted from income. The T-account shows that cash paid is $1,000 more than interest expense recorded, which is why we subtract $1,000 from income in computing cash flow.

| Income Taxes Payable | | | |
|---|---|---|---|
| | | Bal., Dec. 31, 2020 | 12,000 |
| **Cash paid for taxes = 5,000** | | Income taxes expense | 15,000 |
| | | Bal., Dec. 31, 2021 | 22,000 |

**Income Taxes Payable**  The $10,000 increase in income taxes payable is added to income. The T-account shows that cash paid is $10,000 less than tax expense recorded, which is why we add $10,000 to income in computing cash flow.

## Summary of Adjustments for Indirect Method

Exhibit 12.12 summarizes the adjustments to net income under the indirect method.

**EXHIBIT 12.12**

Summary of Adjustments for Operating Activities—Indirect Method

---

**Net Income (or Loss)**

① Adjustments for operating items not providing or using cash

   + Noncash expenses and losses

     *Examples:* Expenses for depreciation, depletion, and amortization; losses from disposal of long-term assets and from retirement of debt

   − Noncash revenues and gains

     *Examples:* Gains from disposal of long-term assets and from retirement of debt

② Adjustments for changes in current assets and current liabilities

   + Decrease in noncash current operating assets

   − Increase in noncash current operating assets

   + Increase in current operating liabilities

   − Decrease in current operating liabilities

**Net cash provided (used) by operating activities**

---

Mark Lenin/AP Images

### ■ Decision Insight

**One for the Road**  Even though **Tesla** reported net losses and large cash outflows, its market value tripled in five years. Tesla now rivals both **GM** and **Ford** as one of the most valued U.S. automakers. Investors are counting on Tesla's Model 3 and Model Y to create positive and sustainable operating cash flows. In the past, Tesla funded its operations with cash inflows from stock and debt issuances. ■

A company's current-year income statement and selected balance sheet data at December 31 of the current and prior years follow. Prepare the operating activities section of the statement of cash flows using the indirect method for the current year.

Reporting Operating
Cash Flows (Indirect)

**P2**

| Income Statement For Current Year Ended December 31 | |
|---|---|
| Sales revenue .................... | $120 |
| Expenses: Cost of goods sold........ | 50 |
| Depreciation expense..... | 30 |
| Salaries expense......... | 17 |
| Interest expense ......... | 3 |
| Net income...................... | $ 20 |

| Selected Balance Sheet Accounts At December 31 | Current Yr | Prior Yr |
|---|---|---|
| Accounts receivable .... | $12 | $10 |
| Inventory ............. | 6 | 9 |
| Accounts payable ...... | 7 | 11 |
| Salaries payable ....... | 8 | 3 |
| Interest payable........ | 1 | 0 |

*Solution*

| Cash Flows from Operating Activities—Indirect Method For Current Year Ended December 31 | | |
|---|---|---|
| **Cash flows from operating activities** | | |
| Net income......................................................... | | $20 |
| Adjustments to reconcile net income to net cash provided by operating activities | | |
| Income statement items not affecting cash | | |
| Depreciation expense ................................................ | $30 | |
| Changes in current assets and current liabilities | | |
| Increase in accounts receivable ......................................... | (2) | |
| Decrease in inventory .................................................. | 3 | |
| Decrease in accounts payable........................................... | (4) | |
| Increase in salaries payable ............................................ | 5 | |
| Increase in interest payable............................................. | 1 | 33 |
| Net cash provided by operating activities ................................. | | $53 |

Do More: QS 12-3 through
QS 12-7, and E 12-2
through E 12-7

---

# CASH FLOWS FROM INVESTING

To compute cash flows from investing activities, we analyze changes in (1) all long-term asset accounts and (2) any current accounts for notes receivable and investments in securities. **Reporting of investing activities is identical under the direct method and indirect method.**

## Three-Step Analysis

To determine cash provided or used by investing activities: (1) identify changes in investing-related accounts, (2) determine the cash effects using T-accounts and reconstructed entries, and (3) report the cash flow effects.

**P3** _____

Determine cash flows from both investing and financing activities.

## Analyzing Noncurrent Assets

Genesis both purchased and sold long-term assets during the period. These transactions are investing activities and are analyzed in this section.

## Plant Asset Transactions

**First Step**    Analyze Genesis's Plant Assets account and its Accumulated Depreciation account to identify changes in those accounts. Comparative balance sheets in Exhibit 12.10 show a $40,000 increase in plant assets from $210,000 to $250,000 and a $12,000 increase in accumulated depreciation from $48,000 to $60,000.

**Point:** Investing activities include (1) purchasing and selling long-term assets, (2) lending and collecting on notes receivable, and (3) purchasing and selling investments.

**Second Step**   Items *b* and *c* of the additional information in Exhibit 12.10 relate to plant assets. Recall that the Plant Assets account is impacted by both asset purchases and sales; its Accumulated Depreciation account is increased by depreciation and decreased by the removal of accumulated depreciation in asset sales. To explain changes in these accounts and to identify their cash flow effects, we prepare *reconstructed entries, which is our attempt to re-create actual entries previously made by the preparer.* Item *b* says Genesis purchased plant assets of $60,000 by issuing $60,000 in notes payable. The reconstructed entry is

| | | | |
|---|---|---|---|
| **Reconstruction** | Plant Assets . . . . . . . . . . . . . . . . . . . . . . . . . . . . . . . . . . . . . . . . . . . . . . . . . . | 60,000 | |
| | Notes Payable. . . . . . . . . . . . . . . . . . . . . . . . . . . . . . . . . . . . . | | 60,000 |

Item *c* says Genesis sold plant assets costing $20,000 (with $12,000 of accumulated depreciation) for $2,000 cash, resulting in a $6,000 loss. The reconstructed entry is

| | | | |
|---|---|---|---|
| **Reconstruction** | **Cash**. . . . . . . . . . . . . . . . . . . . . . . . . . . . . . . . . . . . . . . . . . . . . . . | **2,000** | |
| | Accumulated Depreciation . . . . . . . . . . . . . . . . . . . . . . . . . . . . . . . | 12,000 | |
| | Loss on Sale of Plant Assets . . . . . . . . . . . . . . . . . . . . . . . . . . . . | 6,000 | |
| | Plant Assets. . . . . . . . . . . . . . . . . . . . . . . . . . . . . . . . . . . . | | 20,000 |

We also reconstruct the entry for depreciation from the income statement, which does not impact cash.

| | | | |
|---|---|---|---|
| **Reconstruction** | Depreciation Expense . . . . . . . . . . . . . . . . . . . . . . . . . . . . . . . . . . . . . . | 24,000 | |
| | Accumulated Depreciation. . . . . . . . . . . . . . . . . . . . . . . . . . . . . | | 24,000 |

The three reconstructed entries are shown in the following T-accounts. This reconstruction analysis is complete in that changes in the long-term asset accounts are entirely explained.

| Plant Assets | | | | | Accumulated Depreciation—Plant Assets | | | |
|---|---|---|---|---|---|---|---|---|
| Bal., Dec. 31, 2020 | 210,000 | | | | | | Bal., Dec. 31, 2020 | 48,000 |
| **Purchase** | **60,000** | **Sale** | **20,000** | **Sale** | **12,000** | **Depr. expense** | | **24,000** |
| Bal., Dec. 31, 2021 | 250,000 | | | | | | Bal., Dec. 31, 2021 | 60,000 |

**Third Step**   Look at the reconstructed entries to identify cash flows. The identified cash flows are reported in the investing section of the statement.

| **Cash flows from investing activities** | |
|---|---|
| Cash received from sale of plant assets . . . . . . . . . . . | $2,000 |

**Example:** If a plant asset costing $40,000 with $37,000 of accumulated depreciation is sold at a $4,000 gain, what is the cash flow? *Answer:* +$7,000

The $60,000 purchase in item *b,* paid for by issuing notes, is a noncash investing and financing activity. It is reported in a note or in a separate schedule to the statement.

| **Noncash investing and financing activity** | |
|---|---|
| Purchased plant assets with issuance of notes. . . . . . | $60,000 |

### Additional Long-Term Assets   Genesis did not have any additional noncurrent assets (or nonoperating current assets). If such assets do exist, we analyze and report investing cash flows using the same three-step process.

### Ethical Risk

**Location, Location, Location**   Cash flows can be delayed or accelerated at period-end to improve or reduce current-period cash flows. Cash flows also can be misclassified. We know cash outflows under operating activities are viewed as expense payments. However, cash outflows under investing activities are viewed as a sign of growth potential. This requires investors to review where cash flows are reported. ■

Use the following information to determine this company's cash flows from investing activities.

**a.** Sold a factory (costing $800, with $700 of accumulated depreciation), at a loss of $10.

**b.** Paid $70 cash for new equipment.

**c.** Long-term stock investments were sold for $20 cash, yielding a loss of $4.

**d.** Sold land costing $175 for $160 cash, yielding a loss of $15.

NEED-TO-KNOW **12-3**

Reporting Investing
Cash Flows

**P3**

*Solution*

| Cash flows from investing activities | |
| --- | --- |
| Cash received from sale of factory (from *a*\*—also see margin entry) . . . . | $ 90 |
| Cash paid for new equipment (from *b*) . . . . . . . . . . . . . . . . . . . . . . . . . . | (70) |
| Cash received from sale of long-term investments (from *c*). . . . . . . . . . . | 20 |
| Cash received from sale of land (from *d*) . . . . . . . . . . . . . . . . . . . . . . . | 160 |
| Net cash provided by investing activities . . . . . . . . . . . . . . . . . . . . . . . . | $200 |

*\*Cash received from sale of factory = Cost − Accum. Depr. − Loss = $800 − $700 − $10 = $90.*

Reconstruction for part *a*.
Cash . . . . . . . . . . . . . .  **90**
Accum. Depreciation . . 700
Loss on asset sale . . . .  10
    Factory . . . . . . . . . .       800

Do More: QS 12-8 through
QS 12-13, E 12-9

# CASH FLOWS FROM FINANCING

To compute cash flows from financing activities, we analyze changes in all noncurrent liability accounts (including the current portion of any notes and bonds) and equity accounts. These accounts include long-term debt, notes payable, bonds payable, common stock, and retained earnings. **Reporting of financing activities is identical under the direct method and indirect method.**

## Three-Step Analysis

To determine cash provided or used by financing activities: (1) identify changes in financing-related accounts, (2) determine the cash effects using T-accounts and reconstructed entries, and (3) report the cash flow effects.

## Analyzing Noncurrent Liabilities

Genesis retired notes payable by paying cash. This is a change in noncurrent liabilities.

**Point:** Examples of financing activities are (1) receiving cash from issuing debt or repaying amounts borrowed and (2) receiving cash from or distributing cash to owners.

### Notes Payable Transactions

**First Step**  Review comparative balance sheets in Exhibit 12.10, which shows an increase in notes payable from $64,000 to $90,000.

**Second Step**  Item *e* of the additional information in Exhibit 12.10 reports that notes with a carrying value of $34,000 are retired for $18,000 cash, resulting in a $16,000 gain. The reconstructed entry is

| Reconstruction | Notes Payable . . . . . . . . . . . . . . . . . . . . . . . . . . . . . . . . . . . . | 34,000 | |
| --- | --- | --- | --- |
| | Gain on retirement of debt. . . . . . . . . . . . . . . . . . . . . . | | 16,000 |
| | **Cash** . . . . . . . . . . . . . . . . . . . . . . . . . . . . . . . . . . . . . . . | | **18,000** |

Item *b* of the additional information reports that Genesis purchased plant assets costing $60,000 by issuing $60,000 in notes payable. This $60,000 increase to notes payable is reported as a noncash investing and financing transaction. The Notes Payable account is explained by these reconstructed entries.

| Notes Payable | | | |
| --- | --- | --- | --- |
| | | Bal., Dec. 31, 2020 | 64,000 |
| Retired notes | 34,000 | **Issued notes** | **60,000** |
| | | Bal., Dec. 31, 2021 | 90,000 |

**Third Step**   Report cash paid for the notes retirement in the financing activities section.

| Cash flows from financing activities | |
|---|---|
| Cash paid to retire notes................ | $(18,000) |

## Analyzing Equity

Genesis had two equity transactions. The first is the issuance of common stock for cash. The second is the declaration and payment of cash dividends.

### Common Stock Transactions

**First Step**   Review the comparative balance sheets in Exhibit 12.10, which show an increase in common stock from $80,000 to $95,000.

**Second Step**   Item *d* of the additional information in Exhibit 12.10 reports that 3,000 shares of common stock are issued at par for $5 per share. The reconstructed entry and the complete Common Stock T-account follow.

Reconstruction   Cash............................................... 15,000
                   Common Stock ..................................         15,000

| Common Stock | | |
|---|---|---|
| | Bal., Dec. 31, 2020 | 80,000 |
| | Issued stock | 15,000 |
| | Bal., Dec. 31, 2021 | 95,000 |

**Third Step**   Report cash received from stock issuance in the financing activities section.

| Cash flows from financing activities | |
|---|---|
| Cash received from issuing stock......... | $15,000 |

### Retained Earnings Transactions

**First Step**   Review the comparative balance sheets in Exhibit 12.10, which show an increase in retained earnings from $88,000 to $112,000.

**Second Step**   Item *f* of the additional information in Exhibit 12.10 reports that cash dividends of $14,000 are declared and paid. The reconstructed entry follows.

Reconstruction   Retained Earnings .................................... 14,000
                   Cash ..........................................         14,000

Retained Earnings also is impacted by net income of $38,000. (Net income is covered in operating activities.) The reconstructed Retained Earnings account follows.

| Retained Earnings | | | |
|---|---|---|---|
| | | Bal., Dec. 31, 2020 | 88,000 |
| Cash dividend | 14,000 | Net income | 38,000 |
| | | Bal., Dec. 31, 2021 | 112,000 |

**Point:** Stock dividends and splits do not impact cash.

**Third Step**   Report cash paid for dividends in the financing activities section.

| Cash flows from financing activities | |
|---|---|
| Cash paid for dividends................ | $(14,000) |

## Proving Cash Balances

The final stage in preparing the statement is to report the beginning and ending cash balances and prove that the *net change in cash* is explained by operating, investing, and financing cash flows. The last three rows of Exhibit 12.13 show that the $5,000 net increase in cash, from $12,000 at the beginning of the period to $17,000 at the end, is reconciled by net cash flows from operating ($20,000 inflow), investing ($2,000 inflow), and financing ($17,000 outflow) activities.

**EXHIBIT 12.13**

Complete Statement
of Cash Flows—Indirect
Method

| GENESIS Statement of Cash Flows (Indirect Method) For Year Ended December 31, 2021 | | |
|---|---:|---:|
| **Cash flows from operating activities** | | |
| Net income | $ 38,000 | |
| Adjustments to reconcile net income to net cash provided by operating activities | | |
| Income statement items not affecting cash | | |
| Depreciation expense | 24,000 | |
| Loss on sale of plant assets | 6,000 | |
| Gain on retirement of notes | (16,000) | |
| Changes in current assets and liabilities | | |
| Increase in accounts receivable | (20,000) | |
| Increase in inventory | (14,000) | |
| Increase in prepaid expenses | (2,000) | |
| Decrease in accounts payable | (5,000) | |
| Decrease in interest payable | (1,000) | |
| Increase in income taxes payable | 10,000 | |
| Net cash provided by operating activities | | $ 20,000 |
| **Cash flows from investing activities** | | |
| Cash received from sale of plant assets | 2,000 | |
| Net cash provided by investing activities | | 2,000 |
| **Cash flows from financing activities** | | |
| Cash received from issuing stock | 15,000 | |
| Cash paid to retire notes | (18,000) | |
| Cash paid for dividends | (14,000) | |
| Net cash used in financing activities | | (17,000) |
| Net increase in cash | | $ 5,000 |
| Cash balance at prior year-end | | 12,000 |
| Cash balance at current year-end | | $ 17,000 |

## ◼ Decision **Maker**

**Reporter**  Management is in labor contract negotiations and grants you an interview. It highlights a total net cash outflow of $550,000 (which includes net cash outflows of $850,000 for investing activities and $350,000 for financing activities). What is your assessment of this company? ◼  *Answer:* An initial reaction from the $550,000 decrease in net cash is not positive. However, closer scrutiny shows a more positive picture. Cash flow from operations is $650,000, computed as [?] − $850,000 − $350,000 = $(550,000).

---

Use the following information to determine cash flows from financing activities.

**a.** Issued common stock for $40 cash.

**b.** Paid $70 cash to retire a notes payable at its $70 maturity value.

**c.** Paid cash dividend of $15.

**d.** Paid $5 cash to acquire its treasury stock.

*Solution*

| Cash flows from financing activities | |
|---|---:|
| Cash received from issuance of common stock (from *a*) | $ 40 |
| Cash paid to settle notes payable (from *b*) | (70) |
| Cash paid for dividend (from *c*) | (15) |
| Cash paid to acquire treasury stock (from *d*) | (5) |
| Net cash used by financing activities | $(50) |

 **NEED-TO-KNOW** 12-4

Reporting Financing
Cash Flows

**P3**

Do More: QS 12-14, QS 12-15,
QS 12-16, QS 12-17, E 12-10

## SUMMARY USING T-ACCOUNTS

Exhibit 12.14 uses T-accounts to summarize how changes in Genesis's noncash balance sheet accounts affect its cash inflows and outflows (dollar amounts in thousands). The top of the exhibit shows Genesis's Cash T-account, and the lower part shows T-accounts for its remaining balance sheet accounts. We see that the $20,000 net cash provided by operating activities and the $5,000 net increase in cash shown in the Cash T-account agree with the same figures in the statement of cash flows in Exhibit 12.13. We explain Exhibit 12.14 in five parts.

**a.** Entry **(1)** records $38 net income on the credit side of the Retained Earnings account and the debit side of the Cash account. This $38 net income in the Cash T-account is adjusted until it reflects the $5 net increase in cash.

**b.** Entries **(2)** through **(4)** add the $24 depreciation and $6 loss on asset sale to net income and subtract the $16 gain on retirement of notes.

**c.** Entries **(5)** through **(10)** adjust net income for changes in current asset and current liability accounts.

**EXHIBIT 12.14**

**d.** Entry **(11)** records the noncash investing and financing transaction involving a $60 purchase of assets by issuing $60 of notes.

Balance Sheet T-Accounts to Explain the Change in Cash ($ thousands)

**e.** Entries **(12)** and **(13)** record the $15 stock issuance and the $14 dividend.

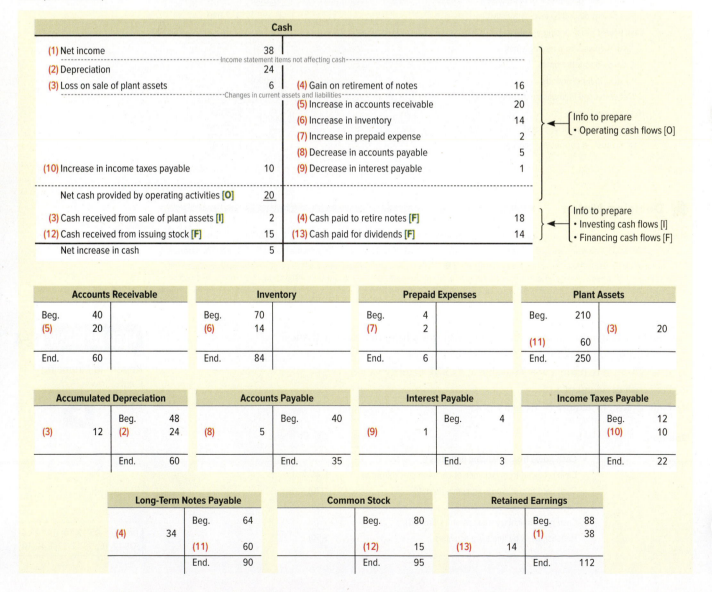

## Analyzing Cash Sources and Uses

Managers review cash flows for business decisions. Creditors evaluate a company's ability to generate enough cash to pay debt. Investors assess cash flows before buying and selling stock.

To effectively evaluate cash flows, we separately analyze investing, financing, and operating activities. Consider data from three different companies in Exhibit 12.15 that operate in the same industry and have been in business for several years. Each company has the same $15,000 net increase in cash, but its sources and uses of cash flows are different. BMX's operating activities provide net cash flows of $90,000, allowing it to purchase plant assets of $48,000 and repay $27,000 of its debt. ATV's operating activities provide $40,000 of cash flows, limiting its purchase of plant assets to $25,000. Trex's $15,000

**A1**

Analyze the statement of cash flows and apply the cash flow on total assets ratio.

**EXHIBIT 12.15**

Cash Flows of Competing Companies

| $ thousands | BMX | ATV | Trex |
|---|---|---|---|
| Cash provided (used) by operating activities . . . | $90,000 | $40,000 | $(24,000) |
| Cash provided (used) by investing activities | | | |
|   Proceeds from sale of plant assets. . . . . . . . | | | 26,000 |
|   Purchase of plant assets . . . . . . . . . . . . . . . : | (48,000) | (25,000) | |
| Cash provided (used) by financing activities | | | |
|   Proceeds from issuance of debt . . . . . . . . . . | | | 13,000 |
|   Repayment of debt . . . . . . . . . . . . . . . . . . . | (27,000) | | |
| Net increase (decrease) in cash . . . : . . . . . . . | $15,000 | $15,000 | $ 15,000 |

net cash increase is due to selling plant assets and incurring additional debt. Its operating activities yield a cash outflow of $24,000. Overall, analysis of cash flows reveals that BMX is more capable of generating future cash flows than is ATV or Trex.

### ■ Decision Insight

**Free Cash Flows** · Many investors use cash flows to value company stock. However, cash-based valuation models often yield different stock values due to differences in measurement of cash flows. Most models require cash flows that are "free" for distribution to shareholders. These *free cash flows* are defined as cash flows available to shareholders after operating asset reinvestments and debt payments. A company's growth and financial flexibility depend on adequate free cash flows. ■

**Point:** Cash flow from operations
 − Capital expenditures
 − Debt repayments
 = Free cash flows

## Cash Flow on Total Assets

Cash flow information can help measure a company's ability to meet its obligations, pay dividends, expand operations, and obtain financing. The **cash flow on total assets** ratio is in Exhibit 12.16. Average total assets is computed by adding beginning and ending assets for the period and dividing by 2.

$$\text{Cash flow on total assets} = \frac{\text{Cash flow from operations}}{\text{Average total assets}}$$

**EXHIBIT 12.16**

Cash Flow on Total Assets

This ratio measures actual cash flows and is not affected by accounting recognition and measurement. It can help estimate the amount and timing of cash flows from operating activities.

The cash flow on total assets ratios for competitors **Nike** and **Under Armour** are in Exhibit 12.17. In all years, Nike's cash flow on total assets ratio exceeded Under Armour's ratio. This means that Nike did a better job of generating operating cash flows given its assets. Also, Nike's cash flow on total assets increased each of the last two years, which is a positive result. At the same time, Under Armour's lower and uneven cash flow on total assets makes it difficult to predict the amount and timing of its cash flows.

**EXHIBIT 12.17**

Cash Flow on Total Assets for Two Competitors

| Company | Figure ($ millions) | Current Year | 1 Year Ago | 2 Years Ago |
|---|---|---|---|---|
| **Nike** | Operating cash flows . . . . . . . . . . . | $ 5,903 | $ 4,955 | $ 3,846 |
| | Average total assets . . . . . . . . . . . | $23,127 | $22,898 | $22,328 |
| | **Cash flow on total assets. . . . . . .** | **25.5%** | **21.6%** | **17.2%** |
| **Under Armour** | Operating cash flows . . . . . . . . . . . | $ 509 | $ 628 | $ 237 |
| | Average total assets . . . . . . . . . . . | $ 4,544 | $ 4,126 | $ 3,825 |
| | **Cash flow on total assets. . . . . . .** | **11.2%** | **15.2%** | **6.2%** |

**NEED-TO-KNOW 12-5**    Comparative balance sheets, an income statement, and additional information follow.

**COMPREHENSIVE**

Preparing Statement of
Cash Flows—Indirect
*and* Direct Methods

| UMA COMPANY Balance Sheets At December 31 | Current Yr | Prior Yr |
|---|---|---|
| **Assets** | | |
| Cash .......................... | $ 43,050 | $ 23,925 |
| Accounts receivable .............. | 34,125 | 39,825 |
| Inventory ...................... | 156,000 | 146,475 |
| Prepaid expenses ................ | 3,600 | 1,650 |
| Total current assets.............. | 236,775 | 211,875 |
| Equipment ..................... | 135,825 | 146,700 |
| Accum. depreciation—Equipment ... | (61,950) | (47,550) |
| Total assets .................... | $310,650 | $311,025 |
| **Liabilities** | | |
| Accounts payable ................ | $ 28,800 | $ 33,750 |
| Income taxes payable ............ | 5,100 | 4,425 |
| Dividends payable ............... | 0 | 4,500 |
| Total current liabilities............. | 33,900 | 42,675 |
| Bonds payable................... | 0 | 37,500 |
| Total liabilities ................. | 33,900 | 80,175 |
| **Equity** | | |
| Common stock, $10 par ........... | 168,750 | 168,750 |
| Retained earnings ............... | 108,000 | 62,100 |
| Total liabilities and equity ......... | $310,650 | $311,025 |

| UMA COMPANY Income Statement For Current Year Ended December 31 | | |
|---|---|---|
| Sales ....................... | | $446,100 |
| Cost of goods sold ............. | $222,300 | |
| Operating expenses (excluding depreciation) ...... | 120,300 | |
| Depreciation expense .......... | 25,500 | (368,100) |
| | | 78,000 |
| Other gains (losses) | | |
| Loss on sale of equipment .... | 3,300 | |
| Loss on retirement of bonds ... | 825 | (4,125) |
| Income before taxes ........... | | 73,875 |
| Income tax expense ........... | | (13,725) |
| Net income ................. | | $ 60,150 |

**Additional Information for the Current Year**

a. Equipment costing $21,375 with accumulated depreciation of $11,100 is sold for cash.

b. Equipment purchases are for cash.

c. Accumulated Depreciation is affected by depreciation expense and the sale of equipment.

d. The balance of Retained Earnings is affected by dividend declarations and net income.

e. All sales are made on credit.

f. All inventory purchases are on credit.

g. Accounts Payable balances result from inventory purchases.

h. Prepaid expenses relate to Operating Expenses.

**Required**

**1.** Prepare a statement of cash flows using the indirect method for the current year.

**2.**[B] Prepare a statement of cash flows using the direct method for the current year.

**SOLUTION**

Supporting computations for cash receipts and cash payments for the current year.

| | | |
|---|---|---|
| (1) | Cost of equipment sold* ........................... | $ 21,375 |
| | Accumulated depreciation of equipment sold .......... | (11,100) |
| | Book value of equipment sold....................... | 10,275 |
| | Loss on sale of equipment......................... | (3,300) |
| | Cash received from sale of equipment................ | **$ 6,975** |
| | Cost of equipment sold ........................... | $ 21,375 |
| | Less decrease in the Equipment account balance....... | (10,875) |
| | Cash paid for new equipment ...................... | **$10,500** |
| (2) | Loss on retirement of bonds ....................... | $   825 |
| | Carrying value of bonds retired..................... | 37,500 |
| | Cash paid to retire bonds ......................... | **$38,325** |

*Supporting T-account analysis for part 1 follows.

| Equipment | | | |
|---|---|---|---|
| Bal., Dec. 31, Prior Year | 146,700 | | |
| Cash purchase | 10,500 | Sale 21,375 | |
| Bal., Dec. 31, Current Year | 135,825 | | |

| Accumulated Depreciation—Equipment | | | |
|---|---|---|---|
| | | Bal., Dec. 31, Prior Year | 47,550 |
| Sale 11,100 | | Depr. expense | 25,500 |
| | | Bal., Dec. 31, Current Year | 61,950 |

(3) Beg. Ret. Earn. + Net Income − Div. Declared = End. Ret. Earn.
    $62,100           $60,150        **$14,250**      $108,000

Beg. Div. Pay. + Div. Declared − Div. Paid = End. Div. Pay.
    $4,500            $14,250        **$18,750**      $ 0

| | | |
|---|---|---|
| (4)[B] | Sales..................................... | $ 446,100 |
| | Add decrease in accounts receivable........... | 5,700 |
| | Cash received from customers ............... | **$451,800** |
| (5)[B] | Cost of goods sold ......................... | $ 222,300 |
| | Plus increase in inventory .................... | 9,525 |
| | Purchases................................. | 231,825 |
| | Plus decrease in accounts payable............. | 4,950 |
| | Cash paid for inventory ...................... | **$236,775** |
| (6)[B] | Operating expenses (excluding depreciation) .... | $ 120,300 |
| | Plus increase in prepaid expenses ............. | 1,950 |
| | Cash paid for operating expenses ............. | **$122,250** |
| (7)[B] | Income tax expense......................... | $ 13,725 |
| | Less increase in income taxes payable.......... | (675) |
| | Cash paid for income taxes................... | **$ 13,050** |

**1.** Indirect method.

| UMA COMPANY<br>Statement of Cash Flows (Indirect Method)<br>For Current Year Ended December 31 | | |
|---|---:|---:|
| Cash flows from operating activities | | |
| Net income..................................... | $ 60,150 | |
| Adjustments to reconcile net income to net<br>cash provided by operating activities | | |
| Income statement items not affecting cash | | |
| Depreciation expense ..................... | 25,500 | |
| Loss on sale of plant assets................. | 3,300 | |
| Loss on retirement of bonds ............... | 825 | |
| Changes in current assets and current liabilities | | |
| Decrease in accounts receivable............. | 5,700 | |
| Increase in inventory ...................... | (9,525) | |
| Increase in prepaid expenses ............... | (1,950) | |
| Decrease in accounts payable............... | (4,950) | |
| Increase in income taxes payable ............ | 675 | |
| Net cash provided by operating activities .......... | | $ 79,725 |
| Cash flows from investing activities | | |
| Cash received from sale of equipment............. | 6,975 | |
| Cash paid for equipment........................ | (10,500) | |
| Net cash used in investing activities .............. | | (3,525) |
| Cash flows from financing activities | | |
| Cash paid to retire bonds payable ................ | (38,325) | |
| Cash paid for dividends......................... | (18,750) | |
| Net cash used in financing activities .............. | | (57,075) |
| Net increase in cash............................ | | $ 19,125 |
| Cash balance at prior year-end.................... | | 23,925 |
| Cash balance at current year-end.................. | | $ 43,050 |

**2.**[B] Direct method (Appendix 12B).

| UMA COMPANY<br>Statement of Cash Flows (Direct Method)<br>For Current Year Ended December 31 | | |
|---|---:|---:|
| Cash flows from operating activities | | |
| Cash received from customers............. | $ 451,800 | |
| Cash paid for inventory .................. | (236,775) | |
| Cash paid for operating expenses.......... | (122,250) | |
| Cash paid for income taxes ............... | (13,050) | |
| Net cash provided by operating activities.... | | $ 79,725 |
| Cash flows from investing activities | | |
| Cash received from sale of equipment ...... | 6,975 | |
| Cash paid for equipment ................. | (10,500) | |
| Net cash used in investing activities ........ | | (3,525) |
| Cash flows from financing activities | | |
| Cash paid to retire bonds payable.......... | (38,325) | |
| Cash paid for dividends .................. | (18,750) | |
| Net cash used in financing activities ........ | | (57,075) |
| Net increase in cash ...................... | | $ 19,125 |
| Cash balance at prior year-end .............. | | 23,925 |
| Cash balance at current year-end ............ | | $ 43,050 |

**APPENDIX**

# Spreadsheet Preparation of the Statement of Cash Flows

# 12A

This appendix explains how to use a spreadsheet (work sheet) to prepare the statement of cash flows under the indirect method.

**P4**

Illustrate use of a spreadsheet to prepare a statement of cash flows.

### Preparing the Indirect Method Spreadsheet

A *spreadsheet,* also called *work sheet,* can help us prepare a statement of cash flows. To demonstrate, we return to the comparative balance sheets and income statement shown in Exhibit 12.10. We use letters *a* through *g* to code changes in accounts, and letters *h* through *m* for additional information, to prepare the statement of cash flows.

**a.** Net income is $38,000.

**b.** Accounts receivable increase by $20,000.

**c.** Inventory increases by $14,000.

**d.** Prepaid expenses increase by $2,000.

**e.** Accounts payable decrease by $5,000.

**f.** Interest payable decreases by $1,000.

**g.** Income taxes payable increase by $10,000.

**h.** Depreciation expense is $24,000.

**i.** Plant assets costing $20,000 with accumulated depreciation of $12,000 are sold for $2,000 cash. This yields a loss on sale of assets of $6,000.

**j.** Notes with a book value of $34,000 are retired with a cash payment of $18,000, yielding a $16,000 gain on retirement.

**k.** Plant assets costing $60,000 are purchased with an issuance of notes payable for $60,000.

**l.** Issued 3,000 shares of common stock for $15,000 cash.

**m.** Paid cash dividends of $14,000.

Exhibit 12A.1 shows the indirect method spreadsheet for Genesis. We enter both beginning and ending balance sheet amounts on the spreadsheet. We also enter information in the Analysis of Changes columns (keyed to the additional information items *a* through *m*) to explain changes in the accounts and determine the cash flows for operating, investing, and financing activities. Information about noncash investing and financing activities is reported near the bottom.

### Entering the Analysis of Changes on the Spreadsheet    The following steps are used to complete the spreadsheet after the beginning and ending balances of the balance sheet accounts are entered.

① Enter net income as the first item in the statement of cash flows section for computing operating cash inflow (debit) and as a credit to Retained Earnings. **(Entry *a*)**

**EXHIBIT 12A.1**

Spreadsheet for Preparing Statement of Cash Flows— Indirect Method

| GENESIS<br>Spreadsheet for Statement of Cash Flows—Indirect Method<br>For Year Ended December 31, 2021 | | | | | | | |
|---|---|---|---|---|---|---|---|
| | Dec. 31,<br>2020 | | Analysis of Changes | | | | Dec. 31,<br>2021 |
| | | | Debit | | Credit | | |
| **Balance Sheet—Debit Bal. Accounts** | | | | | | | |
| Cash | $ 12,000 | | | | | | $ 17,000 |
| Accounts receivable | 40,000 | (b) | $ 20,000 | | | | 60,000 |
| Inventory | 70,000 | (c) | 14,000 | | | | 84,000 |
| Prepaid expenses | 4,000 | (d) | 2,000 | | | | 6,000 |
| Plant assets | 210,000 | (k1) | 60,000 | (i) | $ 20,000 | | 250,000 |
| | $336,000 | | | | | | $417,000 |
| **Balance Sheet—Credit Bal. Accounts** | | | | | | | |
| Accumulated depreciation | $ 48,000 | (i) | 12,000 | (h) | 24,000 | | $ 60,000 |
| Accounts payable | 40,000 | (e) | 5,000 | | | | 35,000 |
| Interest payable | 4,000 | (f) | 1,000 | | | | 3,000 |
| Income taxes payable | 12,000 | | | (g) | 10,000 | | 22,000 |
| Notes payable | 64,000 | (j) | 34,000 | (k2) | 60,000 | | 90,000 |
| Common stock, $5 par value | 80,000 | | | (l) | 15,000 | | 95,000 |
| Retained earnings | 88,000 | (m) | 14,000 | (a) | 38,000 | | 112,000 |
| | $336,000 | | | | | | $417,000 |
| **Statement of Cash Flows** | | | | | | | |
| Operating activities | | | | | | | |
| Net income | | (a) | 38,000 | | | | |
| Increase in accounts receivable | | | | (b) | 20,000 | | |
| Increase in inventory | | | | (c) | 14,000 | | |
| Increase in prepaid expenses | | | | (d) | 2,000 | | |
| Decrease in accounts payable | | | | (e) | 5,000 | | |
| Decrease in interest payable | | | | (f) | 1,000 | | |
| Increase in income taxes payable | | (g) | 10,000 | | | | |
| Depreciation expense | | (h) | 24,000 | | | | |
| Loss on sale of plant assets | | (i) | 6,000 | | | | |
| Gain on retirement of notes | | | | (j) | 16,000 | | |
| Investing activities | | | | | | | |
| Receipts from sale of plant assets | | (i) | 2,000 | | | | |
| Financing activities | | | | | | | |
| Payment to retire notes | | | | (j) | 18,000 | | |
| Receipts from issuing stock | | (l) | 15,000 | | | | |
| Payment of cash dividends | | | | (m) | 14,000 | | |
| | | | | | | | |
| **Noncash Investing and Financing Activities** | | | | | | | |
| Purchase of plant assets with notes | | (k2) | 60,000 | (k1) | 60,000 | | |
| | | | $317,000 | | $317,000 | | |

② In the statement of cash flows section, adjustments to net income are entered as debits if they increase cash flows and as credits if they decrease cash flows. Applying this rule, adjust net income for the change in each noncash current asset and current liability account related to operating activities. For each adjustment to net income, the offsetting debit or credit must help reconcile the beginning and ending balances of a current asset or current liability account. **(Entries b through g)**

③ Enter adjustments to net income for income statement items not providing or using cash in the period. For each adjustment, the offsetting debit or credit must help reconcile a noncash balance sheet account. **(Entry h)**

④ Adjust net income to eliminate any gains or losses from investing and financing activities. Because the cash from a gain must be excluded from operating activities, the gain is entered as a credit in the operating activities section. Losses are entered as debits. For each adjustment, the related debit and/or credit must help reconcile balance sheet accounts and involve reconstructed entries to show the cash flow from investing or financing activities. **(Entries i and j)**

⑤ After reviewing any unreconciled balance sheet accounts and related information, enter the remaining reconciling entries for investing and financing activities. Examples are purchases of plant assets, issuances of long-term debt, stock issuances, and dividend payments. Some of these may require entries in the noncash investing and financing section of the spreadsheet. **(Entries k through m)**

⑥ Check accuracy by totaling the Analysis of Changes columns and by determining that the change in each balance sheet account has been explained (reconciled).

Because adjustments *i, j,* and *k* are more challenging, we show them in the following debit and credit format. These entries are for purposes of our understanding; they are *not* entries made in the journals when preparing the statement. Changes in the Cash account are identified as sources or uses of cash.

| | | | |
|---|---|---:|---:|
| *i.* | Cash—Receipt from sale of plant assets **(source of cash)** | 2,000 | |
| | Loss from sale of plant assets | 6,000 | |
| | Accumulated depreciation | 12,000 | |
| | Plant assets | | 20,000 |
| | *Describe sale of plant assets.* | | |
| *j.* | Notes payable | 34,000 | |
| | Cash—Payments to retire notes **(use of cash)** | | **18,000** |
| | Gain on retirement of notes | | 16,000 |
| | *Describe retirement of notes.* | | |
| *k1.* | Plant assets | 60,000 | |
| | Cash—Purchase of plant assets financed by notes | | **60,000** |
| | *Describe purchase of plant assets.* | | |
| *k2.* | Cash—Purchase of plant assets financed by notes | **60,000** | |
| | Notes payable | | 60,000 |
| | *Issue notes for purchase of assets.* | | |

**APPENDIX**

# Direct Method of Reporting Operating Cash Flows

## 12B

We compute operating cash flows under the direct method by adjusting accrual-based income statement items to the cash basis as follows.

**P5**

Compute cash flows from operating activities using the direct method.

| Revenue or expense | + or − | Adjustments for changes in related balance sheet accounts | = | Cash receipts or cash payments |
|---|---|---|---|---|

The framework for reporting cash receipts and cash payments for the operating section under the direct method is shown in Exhibit 12B.1.

## Operating Cash Receipts

The financial statements and additional information reported by Genesis in Exhibit 12.10 show one cash receipt: sales to customers. We start with sales to customers as reported on the income statement and then adjust it to get cash received from customers.

**Cash Received from Customers**   If all sales are for cash, cash received from customers equals the sales reported on the income statement. When some or all sales are on credit, we must adjust the amount of sales for the change in Accounts Receivable. To help us compute cash receipts, we use a T-account that includes accounts receivable balances for Genesis on December 31, 2020 and 2021. The beginning balance is $40,000 and the ending balance is $60,000. Next, the income statement shows sales of $590,000, which is put on the debit side. We now reconstruct the account to determine the cash receipts from customers are $570,000, computed as $40,000 + $590,000 − [?] = $60,000.

**Point:** An accounts receivable increase implies that cash received from customers is less than sales (the converse is also true).

**Reconstructed Entry**

| | | |
|---|---|---|
| Cash. . . . . . . . . | 570,000 | |
| Accts Recble. . . . | 20,000 | |
|    Sales . . . . . . . | | 590,000 |

| Accounts Receivable | | | |
|---|---|---|---|
| Bal., Dec. 31, 2020 | 40,000 | | |
| Sales | 590,000 | **Cash receipts =** | **570,000** |
| Bal., Dec. 31, 2021 | 60,000 | | |

Cash receipts also can be computed as sales of $590,000 minus a $20,000 increase in accounts receivable. This computation is in Exhibit 12B.2. Genesis reports the $570,000 cash received from customers as a cash inflow from operating activities.

Cash received from customers = Sales    **+ Decrease** in accounts receivable
       or
       **− Increase** in accounts receivable

**Other Cash Receipts**   Other common cash receipts involve rent, interest, and dividends. We compute cash received from these items by subtracting an increase in their receivable or adding a decrease. For example, if rent receivable increases in the period, cash received from renters is less than rent revenue reported on the income statement. If rent receivable decreases, cash received is more than reported rent revenue. The same applies to interest and dividends.

## Operating Cash Payments

The financial statements and additional information for Genesis in Exhibit 12.10 show four expenses (excluding depreciation): cost of goods sold; operating expenses; interest expense; and taxes expense. We analyze each expense to compute its cash impact.

**Cash Paid for Inventory**   We compute cash paid for inventory by analyzing both cost of goods sold and inventory. If all inventory purchases are for cash and the balance of Inventory is unchanged, the amount of cash paid for inventory equals cost of goods sold—an uncommon situation. Instead, there normally is some change in the Inventory balance. Also, some or all purchases are often made on credit, which changes the Accounts Payable balance. When the balances of both Inventory and Accounts Payable change, we must adjust the cost of goods sold for changes in both accounts to compute cash paid for inventory. This is a two-step adjustment.

    First, we use the change in the account balance of Inventory, along with the cost of goods sold amount, to compute cost of purchases for the period. An increase in inventory means that we bought more than we sold, and we add this inventory increase to cost of goods sold to compute cost of purchases. A decrease in inventory means that we bought less than we sold, and we subtract the inventory decrease from cost of goods sold to compute purchases. We show the *first step* by reconstructing the Inventory account. We determine purchases to be $314,000, computed as cost of goods sold of $300,000 plus the $14,000 increase in inventory.

| Inventory | | | |
|---|---|---|---|
| Bal., Dec. 31, 2020 | 70,000 | | |
| **Purchases =** | **314,000** | Cost of goods sold | 300,000 |
| Bal., Dec. 31, 2021 | 84,000 | | |

The second step uses the change in the balance of Accounts Payable, and the cost of purchases, to compute cash paid for inventory. A decrease in accounts payable means that we paid for more goods than we acquired this period, and we would add the accounts payable decrease to cost of purchases to compute cash paid for inventory. An increase in accounts payable means that we paid for less than the amount of goods acquired, and we would subtract the accounts payable increase from purchases to compute cash paid for inventory. The *second step* is applied to Genesis by reconstructing its Accounts Payable account to get cash paid of $319,000 (or $40,000 + $314,000 − [?] = $35,000).

| Accounts Payable | | | |
|---|---|---|---|
| | | Bal., Dec. 31, 2020 | 40,000 |
| **Cash payments =** | **319,000** | **Purchases** | **314,000** |
| | | Bal., Dec. 31, 2021 | 35,000 |

**Reconstructed Entry**
Cost of Goods Sold . . 300,000
Inventory . . . . . . . . .   14,000
Accounts Payable . .    5,000
    Cash. . . . . . . . . .          319,000

Alternatively, cash paid for inventory is equal to purchases of $314,000 plus the $5,000 decrease in accounts payable. The $319,000 cash paid for inventory is reported as a cash outflow under operating activities. This two-step adjustment to cost of goods sold to compute cash paid for inventory is in Exhibit 12B.3.

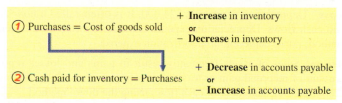

**EXHIBIT 12B.3**

Cash Paid for Inventory—
Direct Method

**Cash Paid for Operating Expenses (Excluding Depreciation)**   The Genesis income statement shows operating expenses of $216,000 (see Exhibit 12.10). To compute cash paid for operating expenses, we adjust for any changes in related balance sheet accounts. We begin by looking for any prepaid expenses and accrued liabilities in the balance sheets in Exhibit 12.10. The balance sheets show prepaid expenses but no accrued liabilities. Thus, the adjustment is only for the change in prepaid expenses. The adjustment is computed by assuming that all cash paid for operating expenses is initially debited to Prepaid Expenses. This assumption allows us to reconstruct the Prepaid Expenses account to get cash paid of $218,000.

**Point:** A decrease in prepaid expenses implies that reported expenses include an amount(s) that did not require a cash outflow in the period.

| Prepaid Expenses | | | |
|---|---|---|---|
| Bal., Dec. 31, 2020 | 4,000 | | |
| **Cash payments =** | **218,000** | Operating expenses | 216,000 |
| Bal., Dec. 31, 2021 | 6,000 | | |

**Reconstructed Entry**
Operating Expenses .  216,000
Prepaid Expenses . .    2,000
    Cash. . . . . . . . . .          218,000

Cash paid also can be calculated as reported expenses of $216,000 plus the $2,000 increase in prepaid expenses. Exhibit 12B.4 summarizes the adjustments to operating expenses.

$$\text{Cash paid for operating expenses} = \text{Operating expenses} \quad \begin{array}{l} \text{+ \textbf{Increase} in prepaid expenses} \\ \text{or} \\ \text{− \textbf{Decrease} in prepaid expenses} \end{array} \quad \begin{array}{l} \text{+ \textbf{Decrease} in accrued liabilities} \\ \text{or} \\ \text{− \textbf{Increase} in accrued liabilities} \end{array}$$

**EXHIBIT 12B.4**

Cash Paid for Operating
Expenses—Direct Method

**Cash Paid for Accrued Liabilities**   The Genesis balance sheet did not report accrued liabilities, but we include them in the formula to explain the adjustment to cash when they do exist. A decrease in accrued liabilities means that we paid cash for more goods or services than received this period, so cash paid is higher than the recorded expense. Alternatively, an increase in accrued liabilities implies that we paid less cash than what was received, so cash paid is less than the recorded expense.

**Cash Paid for Interest and Income Taxes**   Computing operating cash flows for interest and taxes requires adjustments for amounts reported on the income statement for changes in related balance sheet accounts.

The Genesis income statement shows interest expense of $7,000 and income taxes expense of $15,000. To compute the cash paid, we adjust interest expense for the change in interest payable and adjust income taxes expense for the change in income taxes payable. These computations involve reconstructing both liability accounts and show cash paid for interest of $8,000 and cash paid for income taxes of $5,000.

**Reconstructed Entry**
| | | |
|---|---|---|
| Interest Expense | 7,000 | |
| Interest Payable | 1,000 | |
|     Cash | | 8,000 |

**Reconstructed Entry**
| | | |
|---|---|---|
| Income Tax Expense | 15,000 | |
|     Income Tax Payable | | 10,000 |
|     Cash | | 5,000 |

| Interest Payable | | | |
|---|---|---|---|
| | Bal., Dec. 31, 2020 | 4,000 | |
| Cash paid for interest = 8,000 | Interest expense | 7,000 | |
| | Bal., Dec. 31, 2021 | 3,000 | |

| Income Taxes Payable | | | |
|---|---|---|---|
| | Bal., Dec. 31, 2020 | 12,000 | |
| Cash paid for taxes = 5,000 | Income taxes expense | 15,000 | |
| | Bal., Dec. 31, 2021 | 22,000 | |

The formulas to compute these amounts are in Exhibit 12B.5. Both of these cash payments are reported as operating cash outflows.

**EXHIBIT 12B.5**

Cash Paid for Both Interest and Taxes—Direct Method

$$\frac{\text{Cash paid}}{\text{for interest}} = \text{Interest expense} \quad \begin{array}{l} + \textbf{ Decrease} \text{ in interest payable} \\ \text{or} \\ - \textbf{ Increase} \text{ in interest payable} \end{array}$$

$$\frac{\text{Cash paid}}{\text{for taxes}} = \text{Income taxes expense} \quad \begin{array}{l} + \textbf{ Decrease} \text{ in income taxes payable} \\ \text{or} \\ - \textbf{ Increase} \text{ in income taxes payable} \end{array}$$

**Analyzing Additional Expenses, Gains, and Losses**   Genesis has three more items reported on its income statement: depreciation, loss on sale of assets, and gain on retirement of debt. We consider each for its potential cash effects.

**Depreciation Expense**   Depreciation expense is $24,000. It is often called a *noncash expense* because depreciation has no cash flows. Depreciation expense is *never* reported on a statement of cash flows using the direct method; nor is depletion or amortization expense.

**Loss on Sale of Assets**   Sales of assets frequently result in gains and losses reported as part of net income, but the amount of recorded gain or loss does *not* impact cash. Thus, the loss or gain on a sale of assets is *never* reported on a statement of cash flows using the direct method.

**Gain on Retirement of Debt**   Retirement of debt usually yields a gain or loss reported as part of net income, but that gain or loss does *not* impact cash. Thus, the loss or gain from retirement of debt is *never* reported on a statement of cash flows using the direct method.

**Point:** The FASB requires a reconciliation of net income to net cash provided (used) by operating activities when the direct method is used. This reconciliation follows the operating activities section using the indirect method.

## Summary of Adjustments for Direct Method   Exhibit 12B.6 summarizes common adjustments for net income to yield net cash provided (used) by operating activities under the direct method.

**EXHIBIT 12B.6**

Summary of Selected Adjustments for Direct Method

| Item | From Income Statement | Adjustments to Obtain Cash Flow Numbers | |
|---|---|---|---|
| **Receipts** | | | |
| From sales | Sales Revenue | + Decrease in Accounts Receivable<br>− Increase in Accounts Receivable | |
| From rent | Rent Revenue | + Decrease in Rent Receivable<br>− Increase in Rent Receivable | |
| From interest | Interest Revenue | + Decrease in Interest Receivable<br>− Increase in Interest Receivable | |
| From dividends | Dividend Revenue | + Decrease in Dividends Receivable<br>− Increase in Dividends Receivable | |
| **Payments** | | | |
| To suppliers | Cost of Goods Sold | + Increase in Inventory<br>− Decrease in Inventory | + Decrease in Accounts Payable<br>− Increase in Accounts Payable |
| For operations | Operating Expense | + Increase in Prepaids<br>− Decrease in Prepaids | + Decrease in Accrued Liabilities<br>− Increase in Accrued Liabilities |
| To employees | Wages (Salaries) Expense | + Decrease in Wages (Salaries) Payable<br>− Increase in Wages (Salaries) Payable | |
| For interest | Interest Expense | + Decrease in Interest Payable<br>− Increase in Interest Payable | |
| For taxes | Income Tax Expense | + Decrease in Income Tax Payable<br>− Increase in Income Tax Payable | |

## Direct Method Format of Operating Activities Section   Exhibit 12B.7 shows
the Genesis statement of cash flows using the direct method. Operating cash outflows are subtracted from operating cash inflows to get net cash provided (used) by operating activities.

| GENESIS | |
| --- | --- |
| **Statement of Cash Flows (Direct Method)** | |
| **For Year Ended December 31, 2021** | |
| Cash flows from operating activities | |
| Cash received from customers . . . . . . . . . . . . . . $ 570,000 | |
| Cash paid for inventory . . . . . . . . . . . . . . . . . . . . (319,000) | |
| Cash paid for operating expenses . . . . . . . . . . . (218,000) | |
| Cash paid for interest. . . . . . . . . . . . . . . . . . . . . . (8,000) | |
| Cash paid for taxes . . . . . . . . . . . . . . . . . . . . . . . (5,000) | |
| Net cash provided by operating activities . . . . . | $ 20,000 |
| Cash flows from investing activities | |
| Cash received from sale of plant assets. . . . . . . 2,000 | |
| Net cash provided by investing activities . . . . . . | 2,000 |
| Cash flows from financing activities | |
| Cash received from issuing stock . . . . . . . . . . . . 15,000 | |
| Cash paid to retire notes . . . . . . . . . . . . . . . . . . . (18,000) | |
| Cash paid for dividends. . . . . . . . . . . . . . . . . . . . (14,000) | |
| Net cash used in financing activities. . . . . . . . . . | (17,000) |
| Net increase in cash. . . . . . . . . . . . . . . . . . . . . . . . . . | $ 5,000 |
| Cash balance at prior year-end . . . . . . . . . . . . . . . . | 12,000 |
| Cash balance at current year-end . . . . . . . . . . . . . . | $ 17,000 |

**EXHIBIT 12B.7**

Statement of Cash Flows—Direct Method

---

A company's current-year income statement and selected balance sheet data at December 31 of the current and prior years follow. Prepare the operating activities section of the statement of cash flows using the direct method for the current year.

| Income Statement | |
| --- | --- |
| **For Current Year Ended December 31** | |
| Sales revenue . . . . . . . . . . . . . . . . . . . . $120 | |
| Expenses: Cost of goods sold. . . . . . . . 50 | |
| Depreciation expense. . . . . . 30 | |
| Salaries expense. . . . . . . . . 17 | |
| Interest expense . . . . . . . . . 3 | |
| Net income. . . . . . . . . . . . . . . . . . . . . . . $ 20 | |

| Selected Balance Sheet Accounts | | |
| --- | --- | --- |
| **At December 31** | **Current Yr** | **Prior Yr** |
| Accounts receivable . . . . | $12 | $10 |
| Inventory . . . . . . . . . . . . | 6 | 9 |
| Accounts payable . . . . . . | 7 | 11 |
| Salaries payable . . . . . . . | 8 | 3 |
| Interest payable. . . . . . . . | 1 | 0 |

**NEED-TO-KNOW 12-6**

Reporting Operating Cash Flows (Direct)

P5

**Solution**

| Cash Flows from Operating Activities—Direct Method | |
| --- | --- |
| **For Current Year Ended December 31** | |
| Cash flows from operating activities* | |
| Cash received from customers . . . . . . . . . . . . . . . . . . . . . $118 | |
| Cash paid for inventory . . . . . . . . . . . . . . . . . . . . . . . . . . . (51) | |
| Cash paid for salaries . . . . . . . . . . . . . . . . . . . . . . . . . . . . (12) | |
| Cash paid for interest. . . . . . . . . . . . . . . . . . . . . . . . . . . . . (2) | |
| Net cash provided by operating activities. . . . . . . . . . . . . . | $53 |

*Supporting computations:
Cash received from customers = Sales of $120 − Accounts Receivable increase of $2.
Cash paid for inventory = COGS of $50 − Inventory decrease of $3 + Accounts Payable decrease of $4.
Cash paid for salaries = Salaries Expense of $17 − Salaries Payable increase of $5.
Cash paid for interest = Interest Expense of $3 − Interest Payable increase of $1.

Do More: QS 12-22 through QS 12-28, E 12-17 through E 12-21

## Summary: Cheat Sheet

## BASICS OF CASH FLOW REPORTING

**Format for statement of cash flows:**

| COMPANY NAME<br>Statement of Cash Flows<br>For *period* Ended *date* | | |
|---|---|---|
| **Cash flows from operating activities** | | |
| [Compute operating cash flows using indirect or direct method] | | |
| Net cash provided (used) by operating activities | $ # | |
| **Cash flows from investing activities** | | |
| [List of individual inflows and outflows] | | |
| Net cash provided (used) by investing activities | # | |
| **Cash flows from financing activities** | | |
| [List of individual inflows and outflows] | | |
| Net cash provided (used) by financing activities | # | |
| **Net increase (decrease) in cash** | $ # | |
| **Cash (and equivalents) balance at prior period-end** | # | |
| **Cash (and equivalents) balance at current period-end** | $ # | |

Separate schedule or note disclosure of any noncash investing and financing transactions is required.

**Noncash investing and financing activities:** Some investing and financing activities do not affect cash flows, such as the purchase of long-term assets using a long-term notes payable (loan). Such transactions are reported at the bottom of the statement of cash flows or in a note to the statement.

## CASH FLOWS FROM OPERATING—INDIRECT

**Operating activities:** Generally include transactions and events that affect net income.

**Operating cash inflow examples:** Cash sales to customers, collections on credit sales, receipt of dividend revenue, receipt of interest revenue.

**Operating cash outflow examples:** Cash to pay operating expenses, including that to pay salaries and wages, pay suppliers for goods and services, pay for rent, pay interest owed, pay taxes.

**Indirect method:** Reports net income and then adjusts it for items that do not affect cash. Indirect method only affects the presentation of operating cash flows, not investing or financing sections.

**Summary of adjustments for *indirect* method:**

**Net Income (or Loss)**

① Adjustments for operating items not providing or using cash

   + Noncash expenses and losses

     *Examples:* Expenses for depreciation, depletion, and amortization; losses from disposal of long-term assets and from retirement of debt

   − Noncash revenues and gains

     *Examples:* Gains from disposal of long-term assets and from retirement of debt

② Adjustments for changes in current assets and current liabilities

   + Decrease in noncash current operating assets

   − Increase in noncash current operating assets

   + Increase in current operating liabilities

   − Decrease in current operating liabilities

**Net cash provided (used) by operating activities**

## CASH FLOWS FROM INVESTING

**Investing activities:** Generally include transactions and events that come from the purchase and sale of long-term assets.

**Investing cash inflow examples:** Cash from selling plant assets, selling intangible assets, selling investments, collecting principal (but *not* interest) on notes receivable.

**Investing cash outflow examples:** Cash to buy plant assets, buy intangible assets, buy investments, loan money in return for notes receivable.

**Example of investing section format:**

| Cash flows from investing activities | | |
|---|---|---|
| Cash received from sale of plant assets | $2,000 | |
| Net cash provided by investing activities | | $2,000 |

## CASH FLOWS FROM FINANCING

**Financing activities:** Generally include transactions and events that affect long-term liabilities and equity.

**Financing cash inflow examples:** Cash from issuing common and preferred stock, issuing long-term debt (notes payable and bonds payable), reissuing treasury stock.

**Financing cash outflow examples:** Cash to pay dividends to shareholders, pay off long-term debt (notes payable and bonds payable), purchase treasury stock.

**Example of financing section format:**

| Cash flows from financing activities | | |
|---|---|---|
| Cash received from issuing stock | $ 15,000 | |
| Cash paid to retire notes | (18,000) | |
| Cash paid for dividends | (14,000) | |
| Net cash used in financing activities | | $(17,000) |

## CASH FLOWS FROM OPERATING—DIRECT

**Direct method:** Separately lists operating cash receipts and operating cash payments. Cash payments are subtracted from cash receipts. Unlike the indirect method, it does not start with net income. This only affects the operating section of the statement of cash flows.

**Summary of adjustments for *direct* method:**

| Item | From Income Statement | Adjustments to Obtain Cash Flow Numbers | |
|---|---|---|---|
| **Receipts** | | | |
| From sales | Sales Revenue | + Decrease in Accounts Receivable<br>− Increase in Accounts Receivable | |
| From rent | Rent Revenue | + Decrease in Rent Receivable<br>− Increase in Rent Receivable | |
| From interest | Interest Revenue | + Decrease in Interest Receivable<br>− Increase in Interest Receivable | |
| From dividends | Dividend Revenue | + Decrease in Dividends Receivable<br>− Increase in Dividends Receivable | |
| **Payments** | | | |
| To suppliers | Cost of Goods Sold | + Increase in Inventory<br>− Decrease in Inventory | + Decrease in Accounts Payable<br>− Increase in Accounts Payable |
| For operations | Operating Expense | + Increase in Prepaids<br>− Decrease in Prepaids | + Decrease in Accrued Liabilities<br>− Increase in Accrued Liabilities |
| To employees | Wages (Salaries) Expense | + Decrease in Wages (Salaries) Payable<br>− Increase in Wages (Salaries) Payable | |
| For interest | Interest Expense | + Decrease in Interest Payable<br>− Increase in Interest Payable | |
| For taxes | Income Tax Expense | + Decrease in Income Tax Payable<br>− Increase in Income Tax Payable | |

## Key Terms

Cash flow on total assets (437)

Direct method (427)

Financing activities (424)

Indirect method (427)

Investing activities (424)

Operating activities (424)

Statement of cash flows (423)

## Multiple Choice Quiz

**1.** Use the following information to determine the net cash provided or used by operating activities under the indirect method.

| | |
|---|---|
| Net income | $15,200 |
| Depreciation expense | 10,000 |
| Cash payment on notes payable | 8,000 |
| Gain on sale of land | 3,000 |
| Increase in inventory | 1,500 |
| Increase in accounts payable | 2,850 |

   **a.** $23,550 used by operating activities
   **b.** $23,550 provided by operating activities
   **c.** $15,550 provided by operating activities
   **d.** $42,400 provided by operating activities
   **e.** $20,850 provided by operating activities

**2.** A machine with a cost of $175,000 and accumulated depreciation of $94,000 is sold for $87,000 cash. The amount reported as a source of cash under cash flows from investing activities is

   **a.** $81,000.    **d.** $0; this is a financing activity.
   **b.** $6,000.     **e.** $0; this is an operating activity.
   **c.** $87,000.

**3.** A company settles a long-term notes payable plus interest by paying $68,000 cash toward the principal amount and

$5,440 cash for interest. The amount reported as a use of cash under cash flows from financing activities is

   **a.** $73,440.    **d.** $0; this is an investing activity.
   **b.** $68,000.    **e.** $0; this is an operating activity.
   **c.** $5,440.

**4.** The following information is available regarding a company's annual salaries and wages. What amount of cash is paid for salaries and wages?

| | |
|---|---|
| Salaries and wages expense | $255,000 |
| Salaries and wages payable, prior year-end | 8,200 |
| Salaries and wages payable, current year-end | 10,900 |

   **a.** $252,300   **c.** $255,000   **e.** $235,900
   **b.** $257,700   **d.** $274,100

**5.** The following information is available for a company. What amount of cash is paid for inventory for the current year?

| | |
|---|---|
| Cost of goods sold | $545,000 |
| Inventory, prior year-end | 105,000 |
| Inventory, current year-end | 112,000 |
| Accounts payable, prior year-end | 98,500 |
| Accounts payable, current year-end | 101,300 |

   **a.** $545,000   **c.** $540,800   **e.** $549,200
   **b.** $554,800   **d.** $535,200

### ANSWERS TO MULTIPLE CHOICE QUIZ

**1.** b;

| | |
|---|---|
| Net income | $15,200 |
| Depreciation expense | 10,000 |
| Gain on sale of land | (3,000) |
| Increase in inventory | (1,500) |
| Increase in accounts payable | 2,850 |
| Net cash provided by operations | $23,550 |

**2.** c; Cash from sale of machine is reported as an investing activity.
**3.** b; FASB requires cash interest paid be reported under operating.
**4.** a; Cash paid for salaries and wages = $255,000 + $8,200 −
   $10,900 = $252,300
**5.** e; Increase in inventory = $112,000 − $105,000 = $7,000
   Increase in accounts payable = $101,300 − $98,500 = $2,800
   Cash paid for inventory = $545,000 + $7,000 − $2,800 = $549,200

*Superscript letter A or B denotes assignments based on Appendix 12A or 12B.*

*Select Quick Study and Exercise assignments feature Guided Example videos, called "Hints" in Connect. Hints use different numbers, and instructors can turn this feature on or off.*

Mc Graw Hill **connect**

Classify the following cash flows as either operating, investing, or financing activities.

**1.** Sold stock investments for cash.
**2.** Received cash payments from customers.
**3.** Paid cash for wages and salaries.
**4.** Purchased inventories with cash.
**5.** Paid cash dividends.

**6.** Issued common stock for cash.
**7.** Received cash interest on a note.
**8.** Paid cash interest on outstanding notes.
**9.** Received cash from sale of land.
**10.** Paid cash for property taxes on building.

**QUICK STUDY**

**QS 12-1**

Classifying transactions by activity

C1

**QS 12-2**

Statement of cash flows

**P1**

Label the following headings, line items, and notes with the numbers *1* through *13* according to their sequential order (from top to bottom) for presentation on the statement of cash flows.

_____ a. "Cash flows from investing activities" title

_____ b. "For *period* Ended *date*" heading

_____ c. "Cash flows from operating activities" title

_____ d. Company name

_____ e. Schedule or note disclosure of noncash investing and financing transactions

_____ f. "Statement of Cash Flows" heading

_____ g. Net increase (decrease) in cash . . . . . . . . . . . . . . . . . . . . . . . . . . . .  $

_____ h. Net cash provided (used) by operating activities . . . . . . . . . . . .  $

_____ i. Cash (and equivalents) balance at prior period-end . . . . . . . . . .  $

_____ j. Net cash provided (used) by financing activities . . . . . . . . . . . .  $

_____ k. "Cash flows from financing activities" title

_____ l. Net cash provided (used) by investing activities. . . . . . . . . . . .  $

_____ m. Cash (and equivalents) balance at current period-end . . . . . . . .  $

---

**QS 12-3**

**Indirect:** Computing cash flows from operations   **P2**

Bryant Co. reports net income of $20,000. For the year, depreciation expense is $7,000 and the company reports a gain of $3,000 from sale of machinery. It also had a $2,000 loss from retirement of notes. Compute cash flows from operations using the *indirect method*.

---

**QS 12-4**

**Indirect:** Computing cash flows from operations   **P2**

Cain Inc. reports net income of $15,000. Its comparative balance sheet shows the following changes: accounts receivable increased $6,000; inventory decreased $8,000; prepaid insurance decreased $1,000; accounts payable increased $3,000; and taxes payable decreased $2,000. Compute cash flows from operations using the *indirect method*.

---

**QS 12-5**

**Indirect:** Computing cash flows from operations

**P2**

For each separate company, compute cash flows from operations using the *indirect method*.

| | Twix | Dots | Skor |
|---|---|---|---|
| Net income . . . . . . . . . . . . . . . . . . . . . . . . . . . . | $ 4,000 | $100,000 | $72,000 |
| Depreciation expense . . . . . . . . . . . . . . . . . . . | 30,000 | 8,000 | 24,000 |
| Accounts receivable increase (decrease) . . . . . | 40,000 | 20,000 | (4,000) |
| Inventory increase (decrease) . . . . . . . . . . . . . . | (20,000) | (10,000) | 10,000 |
| Accounts payable increase (decrease) . . . . . . . | 24,000 | (22,000) | 14,000 |
| Accrued liabilities increase (decrease) . . . . . . . | (44,000) | 12,000 | (8,000) |

---

**QS 12-6**

**Indirect:** Computing cash from operations   **P2**

Use the following information to determine cash flows from operating activities using the *indirect method*.

**MOSS COMPANY**
**Income Statement**
**For Year Ended December 31, 2021**

| | |
|---|---|
| Sales . . . . . . . . . . . . . . . . . . . . . . | $515,000 |
| Cost of goods sold . . . . . . . . . . . | 331,600 |
| Gross profit . . . . . . . . . . . . . . . . . | 183,400 |
| Operating expenses (excluding depreciation) . . . . | 121,500 |
| Depreciation expense . . . . . . . . | 36,000 |
| Income before taxes. . . . . . . . . . | 25,900 |
| Income taxes expense . . . . . . . . | 7,700 |
| Net income . . . . . . . . . . . . . . . . | $ 18,200 |

**MOSS COMPANY**
**Selected Balance Sheet Information**

| At December 31 | 2021 | 2020 |
|---|---|---|
| Current assets | | |
|   Cash . . . . . . . . . . . . . . . . . | $84,650 | $26,800 |
|   Accounts receivable. . . . . | 25,000 | 32,000 |
|   Inventory. . . . . . . . . . . . . | 60,000 | 54,100 |
| Current liabilities | | |
|   Accounts payable. . . . . . . | 30,400 | 25,700 |
|   Income taxes payable . . . | 2,050 | 2,200 |

QS 12-7
**Indirect:** Computing cash from operations   P2

**CRUZ, INC.**
**Comparative Balance Sheets**

| At December 31 | 2021 | 2020 |
|---|---|---|
| **Assets** | | |
| Cash | $ 94,800 | $ 24,000 |
| Accounts receivable, net | 41,000 | 51,000 |
| Inventory | 85,800 | 95,800 |
| Prepaid expenses | 5,400 | 4,200 |
| Total current assets | 227,000 | 175,000 |
| Furniture | 109,000 | 119,000 |
| Accum. depreciation—Furniture | (17,000) | (9,000) |
| Total assets | $319,000 | $285,000 |
| **Liabilities and Equity** | | |
| Accounts payable | $ 15,000 | $ 21,000 |
| Wages payable | 9,000 | 5,000 |
| Income taxes payable | 1,400 | 2,600 |
| Total current liabilities | 25,400 | 28,600 |
| Notes payable (long-term) | 29,000 | 69,000 |
| Total liabilities | 54,400 | 97,600 |
| **Equity** | | |
| Common stock, $5 par value | 229,000 | 179,000 |
| Retained earnings | 35,600 | 8,400 |
| Total liabilities and equity | $319,000 | $285,000 |

**CRUZ, INC.**
**Income Statement**
**For Year Ended December 31, 2021**

| | |
|---|---|
| Sales | $488,000 |
| Cost of goods sold | 314,000 |
| Gross profit | 174,000 |
| Operating expenses (excluding depreciation) | 89,100 |
| Depreciation expense | 37,600 |
| Income before taxes | 47,300 |
| Income taxes expense | 17,300 |
| Net income | $ 30,000 |

**Required**

Use the *indirect method* to prepare the operating activities section of Cruz's statement of cash flows.

QS 12-8
Computing cash from asset sales
P3

The following information is from Ellerby Company's comparative balance sheets. The current-year income statement reports depreciation expense on furniture of $18,000. During the year, furniture costing $52,500 was sold for its book value. Compute cash received from the sale of furniture.

| At December 31 | Current Year | Prior Year |
|---|---|---|
| Furniture | $132,000 | $ 184,500 |
| Accumulated depreciation—Furniture | (88,700) | (110,700) |

QS 12-9
Computing investing cash flows
P3

Indicate the effect each separate transaction has on *investing* cash flows.

**a.** Sold a truck costing $40,000, with $22,000 of accumulated depreciation, for $8,000 cash. The sale results in a $10,000 loss.

**b.** Sold a machine costing $10,000, with $8,000 of accumulated depreciation, for $5,000 cash. The sale results in a $3,000 gain.

**c.** Purchased stock investments for $16,000 cash. The purchaser believes the stock is worth at least $30,000.

QS 12-10
Computing investing cash flows
P3

The plant assets section of the comparative balance sheets of Anders Company is reported below.

**ANDERS COMPANY**
**Comparative Year-End Balance Sheets**

| Plant assets | 2021 | 2020 |
|---|---|---|
| Equipment | $ 180,000 | $ 270,000 |
| Accumulated depreciation—Equipment | (100,000) | (210,000) |
| Equipment, net | $ 80,000 | $ 60,000 |
| Buildings | $ 380,000 | $ 400,000 |
| Accumulated depreciation—Buildings | (100,000) | (285,000) |
| Buildings, net | $ 280,000 | $ 115,000 |

Refer to the balance sheet data above from Anders Company. During 2021, equipment with a book value of $40,000 and an original cost of $210,000 was sold at a loss of $3,000.

1. How much cash did Anders receive from the sale of equipment?
2. How much depreciation expense was recorded on equipment during 2021?
3. What was the cost of new equipment purchased by Anders during 2021?

---

**QS 12-11**
Computing investing cash flows
**P3**

Refer to the balance sheet data in QS 12-10 from Anders Company. During 2021, a building with a book value of $70,000 and an original cost of $300,000 was sold at a gain of $60,000.

1. How much cash did Anders receive from the sale of the building?
2. How much depreciation expense was recorded on buildings during 2021?
3. What was the cost of buildings purchased by Anders during 2021?

---

**QS 12-12**
Computing cash flows from investing
**P3**

Compute cash flows from investing activities using the following company information.

| | | | |
|---|---|---|---|
| Sale of investments . . . . . . . . . . . . . . . . . | $ 6,000 | Cash purchase of used equipment . . . . . . | $5,000 |
| Cash collections from customers. . . . . . . | 16,000 | Depreciation expense . . . . . . . . . . . . . . | 2,000 |

---

**QS 12-13**
Computing cash from asset sales **P3**

Refer to the data in QS 12-7.

Furniture costing $55,000 is sold at its book value in 2021. Acquisitions of furniture total $45,000 cash, on which no depreciation is necessary because it is acquired at year-end. What is the cash inflow from the sale of furniture?

---

**QS 12-14**
Computing financing cash flows
**P3**

Indicate the effect, if any, that each separate transaction has on *financing* cash flows.

a. Long-term notes payable with a carrying value of $15,000 are retired for $16,000 cash, resulting in a $1,000 loss.
b. Paid cash dividends of $11,000 to common stockholders.
c. Acquired $20,000 worth of machinery in exchange for common stock.

---

**QS 12-15**
Computing financing cash flows
**P3**

The following information is from Princeton Company's comparative balance sheets.

| At December 31 | Current Year | Prior Year |
|---|---|---|
| Common stock, $10 par value. . . . . . . | $105,000 | $100,000 |
| Paid-in capital in excess of par . . . . . . | 567,000 | 342,000 |
| Retained earnings. . . . . . . . . . . . . . . . | 313,500 | 287,500 |

The company's net income for the current year ended December 31 was $48,000.

1. Compute the cash received from the sale of its common stock during the current year.
2. Compute the cash paid for dividends during the current year.

---

**QS 12-16**
Computing cash flows from financing
**P3**

Compute cash flows from financing activities using the following company information.

| | | | |
|---|---|---|---|
| Cash received from long-term notes payable. . . . . . | $20,000 | Cash dividends paid. . . . . . . . . . . . . . . . . | $16,000 |
| Purchase of investments . . . . . . . . . . . . . . . . . . | 5,000 | Interest paid . . . . . . . . . . . . . . . . . . . . . | 8,000 |

---

**QS 12-17**
Computing financing cash outflows **P3**

Refer to the data in QS 12-7.

1. Assume that all common stock is issued for cash. What amount of cash dividends is paid during 2021?
2. Assume that no additional notes payable are issued in 2021. What cash amount is paid to reduce the notes payable balance in 2021?

Use the following information for VPI Co. to prepare a statement of cash flows for the year ended December 31 using the *indirect method*.

| | | | |
|---|---|---|---|
| Cash balance at prior year-end............. | $40,000 | Gain on sale of machinery................. | $ 2,000 |
| Increase in inventory..................... | 5,000 | Cash received from sale of machinery....... | 9,500 |
| Depreciation expense .................... | 4,000 | Increase in accounts payable ............. | 1,500 |
| Cash received from issuing stock ........... | 8,000 | Net income............................ | 23,000 |
| Cash paid for dividends................... | 1,000 | Decrease in accounts receivable ........... | 3,000 |

**QS 12-18**
**Indirect:** Preparing statement of cash flows
**P2   P3**

---

Financial data from three competitors in the same industry follow.

1. Rank the three companies from high to low on cash from operating activities.
2. Which company has the largest cash outflow for investing activities?
3. Which company has the largest cash inflow from financing activities?
4. Which company has the highest cash flow on total assets ratio?

**QS 12-19**
Interpreting disclosures on sources and uses of cash
**A1**

| | Mancala | Yahtzee | Cluedo |
|---|---|---|---|
| Cash provided (used) by operating activities | $ 70,000 | $ 60,000 | $ (24,000) |
| Cash provided (used) by investing activities | (28,000) | (34,000) | 26,000 |
| Cash provided (used) by financing activities | (6,000) | 0 | 23,000 |
| Net increase (decrease) in cash | $ 36,000 | $ 26,000 | $ 25,000 |
| Average total assets | $790,000 | $625,000 | $300,000 |

---

Revo Co. reports average total assets of $200,000, revenue of $90,000, net income of $30,000, and cash flow from operations of $38,000.

1. Compute its cash flow on total assets.
2. Is Revo's cash flow on total assets better than the 8% for its competitor, Epix Co.?

**QS 12-20**
Computing and analyzing cash flow on total assets
**A1**

---

A company uses a spreadsheet to prepare its statement of cash flows. Indicate whether each of the following items would be recorded in the Debit column or Credit column of the spreadsheet's *statement of cash flows section*.

**a.** Decrease in accounts payable      **d.** Loss on sale of machinery
**b.** Payment of cash dividends      **e.** Net income
**c.** Increase in accounts receivable      **f.** Increase in interest payable

**QS 12-21**[A]
Recording entries in a spreadsheet
**P4**

---

Russell Co. reports sales revenue of $30,000 and interest revenue of $5,000. Its comparative balance sheet shows that accounts receivable decreased $4,000 and interest receivable increased $1,000. Compute cash provided by operating activities using the *direct method*.

**QS 12-22**[B]
**Direct:** Computing cash receipts from operations
**P5**

---

Bioware Co. reports cost of goods sold of $42,000. Its comparative balance sheet shows that inventory decreased $7,000 and accounts payable increased $5,000. Compute cash payments to suppliers using the *direct method*.

**QS 12-23**[B]
**Direct:** Computing cash payments to suppliers  **P5**

---

BTN Inc. reports operating expenses of $27,000. Its comparative balance sheet shows that accrued liabilities decreased $6,000 and prepaid expenses increased $2,000. Compute cash used in operating activities using the *direct method*.

**QS 12-24**[B]
**Direct:** Computing cash paid for operations  **P5**

---

For each separate case, compute the required cash flow information for BioClean.

**QS 12-25**[B]
**Direct:** Computing cash flows
**P5**

| Case A: Compute cash interest received | | Case B: Compute cash paid for wages | |
|---|---|---|---|
| Interest revenue......................... | $5,000 | Wages expense....................... | $9,000 |
| Interest receivable, beginning of year.......... | 600 | Wages payable, beginning of year........ | 2,200 |
| Interest receivable, end of year .............. | 1,700 | Wages payable, end of year............ | 1,000 |

**QS 12-26<sup>B</sup>**

**Direct:** Computing cash received from customers

**P5**

Refer to the data in QS 12-7.

1. How much cash is received from sales to customers for year 2021?
2. What is the net increase or decrease in the Cash account for year 2021?

---

**QS 12-27<sup>B</sup>**

**Direct:** Computing operating cash outflows

**P5**

Refer to the data in QS 12-7.

1. How much cash is paid to acquire inventory during year 2021?
2. How much cash is paid for operating expenses (excluding depreciation) during year 2021? *Hint:* Examine prepaid expenses and wages payable.

---

**QS 12-28<sup>B</sup>**

**Direct:** Computing cash from operations   **P5**

Refer to the data in QS 12-7.

Use the *direct method* to prepare the operating activities section of Cruz's statement of cash flows.

---

**EXERCISES**

**Exercise 12-1**

**Indirect:**

Classifying cash flows

**C1**

Indicate where each item would appear on a statement of cash flows using the *indirect method* by placing an *x* in the appropriate column.

| | Statement of Cash Flows | | | Noncash Investing and Financing Activities | Not Reported on Statement or in Notes |
|---|---|---|---|---|---|
| | Operating Activities | Investing Activities | Financing Activities | | |
| a. Declared and paid a cash dividend . . . . . . . . . . | ____ | ____ | ____ | ____ | ____ |
| b. Recorded depreciation expense . . . . . . . . . . . . | ____ | ____ | ____ | ____ | ____ |
| c. Paid cash to settle long-term notes payable  . . | ____ | ____ | ____ | ____ | ____ |
| d. Prepaid expenses increased in the year . . . . . . | ____ | ____ | ____ | ____ | ____ |
| e. Accounts receivable decreased in the year  . . . | ____ | ____ | ____ | ____ | ____ |
| f. Purchased land by issuing common stock  . . . . | ____ | ____ | ____ | ____ | ____ |
| g. Inventory increased in the year . . . . . . . . . . . . | ____ | ____ | ____ | ____ | ____ |
| h. Sold equipment for cash, yielding a loss . . . . . . | ____ | ____ | ____ | ____ | ____ |
| i. Accounts payable decreased in the year  . . . . . | ____ | ____ | ____ | ____ | ____ |
| j. Income taxes payable increased in the year . . . | ____ | ____ | ____ | ____ | ____ |

---

**Exercise 12-2**

**Indirect:** Reporting cash flows from operations

**P2**

Hampton Company reports the following information for its recent calendar year. Prepare the operating activities section of the statement of cash flows using the *indirect method*.

| Income Statement Data | | | Selected Year-End Balance Sheet Data | |
|---|---|---|---|---|
| Sales. . . . . . . . . . . . . . . . . . . . . . . . . . . . | $160,000 | | Accounts receivable increase. . . . . . . . . | $10,000 |
| Expenses: Cost of goods sold. . . . . . . . . . . | 100,000 | | Inventory decrease . . . . . . . . . . . . . . . . . | 16,000 |
| Salaries expense . . . . . . . . . . . . | 24,000 | | Salaries payable increase. . . . . . . . . . . . | 1,000 |
| Depreciation expense. . . . . . . . . | 12,000 | | | |
| Net income. . . . . . . . . . . . . . . . . . . . . . | $ 24,000 | | | |

---

**Exercise 12-3**

**Indirect:** Reporting cash flows from operations

**P2**

Arundel Company disclosed the following information for its recent calendar year. Prepare the operating activities section of the statement of cash flows using the *indirect method*.

| Income Statement Data | | | Selected Year-End Balance Sheet Data | |
|---|---|---|---|---|
| Revenues . . . . . . . . . . . . . . . . . . . . . . . . . | $100,000 | | Accounts receivable decrease . . . . . . . . . | $24,000 |
| Expenses: Salaries expense . . . . . . . . . . . . . . | 84,000 | | Purchased a machine for cash . . . . . . . . | 10,000 |
| Utilities expense . . . . . . . . . . . . . . | 14,000 | | Salaries payable increase. . . . . . . . . . . . | 18,000 |
| Depreciation expense . . . . . . . . . . | 14,600 | | Interest payable decrease . . . . . . . . . . . | 8,000 |
| Interest expense . . . . . . . . . . . . . . | 3,400 | | | |
| Net loss . . . . . . . . . . . . . . . . . . . . . . . . . . | $ (16,000) | | | |

Using the following income statement and additional year-end information, prepare the operating activities section of the statement of cash flows using the *indirect method*.

**SONAD COMPANY**
**Income Statement**
**For Year Ended December 31**

| | | |
|---|---:|---:|
| Sales .............................. | | $1,828,000 |
| Cost of goods sold ................. | | 991,000 |
| Gross profit ....................... | | 837,000 |
| Operating expenses | | |
| Salaries expense ................ | $245,535 | |
| Depreciation expense ........... | 44,200 | |
| Rent expense .................... | 49,600 | |
| Amortization expense—Patents .... | 4,200 | |
| Utilities expense................. | 18,125 | 361,660 |
| | | 475,340 |
| Gain on sale of equipment........... | | 6,200 |
| Net income ....................... | | $  481,540 |

| Selected Year-End Balance Sheet Data | |
|---|---|
| Accounts receivable .. | $30,500 increase |
| Inventory ........... | 25,000 increase |
| Accounts payable .... | 12,500 decrease |
| Salaries payable ..... | 3,500 decrease |

Fitz Company reports the following information. Use the *indirect method* to prepare the operating activities section of its statement of cash flows for the year ended December 31.

| Selected Annual Income Statement Data | |
|---|---:|
| Net income .......................... | $374,000 |
| Depreciation expense ................ | 44,000 |
| Amortization expense................. | 7,200 |
| Gain on sale of plant assets........... | 6,000 |

| Selected Year-End Balance Sheet Data | |
|---|---:|
| Accounts receivable decrease ............. | $17,100 |
| Inventory decrease ....................... | 42,000 |
| Prepaid expenses increase................. | 4,700 |
| Accounts payable decrease ................ | 8,200 |
| Salaries payable increase................. | 1,200 |

Salud Company reports the following information. Use the *indirect method* to prepare the operating activities section of its statement of cash flows for the year ended December 31.

| Selected Annual Income Statement Data | |
|---|---:|
| Net income .......................... | $400,000 |
| Depreciation expense ................ | 80,000 |
| Gain on sale of machinery ............. | 20,000 |

| Selected Year-End Balance Sheet Data | |
|---|---:|
| Accounts receivable increase............... | $40,000 |
| Prepaid expenses decrease................. | 12,000 |
| Accounts payable increase................. | 6,000 |
| Wages payable decrease .................. | 2,000 |

Prepare the operating activities section of the statement of cash flows for GreenGarden using the *indirect method*.

| Annual Income Statement Data | |
|---|---:|
| Sales ............................... | $50,000 |
| Expenses: Cost of goods sold........... | 30,000 |
| Wages expense.............. | 10,000 |
| Amortization expense........ | 1,500 |
| Net income ...................... | $  8,500 |

| Selected Year-End Balance Sheet Data | |
|---|---:|
| Wages payable decrease .................. | $3,000 |
| Inventory increase ...................... | 500 |
| Accounts payable decrease .............. | 1,000 |

Cain Co. reports net cash provided by operating activities of $30,000. It also reports the following information under "Adjustments to reconcile net income to net cash provided by operating activities" on its statement of cash flows (using the *indirect method*). Determine Cain's net income.

| | | | |
|---|---:|---|---:|
| Gain on sale of equipment................. | $8,000 | Decrease in inventory .................... | $4,000 |
| Increase in accounts receivable ............ | 3,000 | Increase in prepaid expenses.............. | 2,000 |
| Depreciation expense ................... | 5,000 | Decrease in wages payable .............. | 1,000 |

**Exercise 12-9**

Cash flows from investing activities

**P3**

Use the following information to determine cash flows from investing activities.

**a.** Equipment with a book value of $65,300 and an original cost of $133,000 was sold at a loss of $14,000.

**b.** Paid $89,000 cash for a new truck.

**c.** Sold land costing $154,000 for $198,000 cash, yielding a gain of $44,000.

**d.** Stock investments were sold for $60,800 cash, yielding a gain of $4,150.

**Exercise 12-10**

Cash flows from financing activities

**P3**

Use the following information to determine cash flows from financing activities.

**a.** Net income was $35,000.

**b.** Issued common stock for $64,000 cash.

**c.** Paid cash dividend of $14,600.

**d.** Paid $50,000 cash to settle a long-term notes payable at its $50,000 maturity value.

**e.** Paid $12,000 cash to acquire its treasury stock.

**f.** Purchased equipment for $39,000 cash.

**Exercise 12-11**

Reconstructed entries

**P3**

For each of the following separate transactions, (*a*) prepare the reconstructed journal entry and (*b*) identify the effect it has, if any, on the *investing section* or *financing section* of the statement of cash flows.

**1.** Sold a building costing $30,000, with $20,000 of accumulated depreciation, for $8,000 cash, resulting in a $2,000 loss.

**2.** Acquired machinery worth $10,000 by issuing $10,000 in notes payable.

**3.** Issued 1,000 shares of common stock at par for $2 per share.

**4.** Long-term notes payable with a carrying value of $40,000 were retired for $47,000 cash, resulting in a $7,000 loss.

**Exercise 12-12**

**Indirect:** Preparing statement of cash flows

**A1   P2   P3**

The following financial statements and additional information are reported. (1) Prepare a statement of cash flows using the *indirect method* for the year ended June 30, 2021. (2) Compute the company's cash flow on total assets ratio for fiscal year 2021.

| IKIBAN INC. Income Statement For Year Ended June 30, 2021 | |
|---|---|
| Sales . . . . . . . . . . . . . . . . . . . . . . . . . . . . . . . | $678,000 |
| Cost of goods sold . . . . . . . . . . . . . . . . . . . . . . | 411,000 |
| Gross profit . . . . . . . . . . . . . . . . . . . . . . . . . . . | 267,000 |
| Operating expenses (excluding depreciation) . . | 67,000 |
| Depreciation expense . . . . . . . . . . . . . . . . . . . | 58,600 |
| | 141,400 |
| Other gains (losses) | |
| Gain on sale of equipment. . . . . . . . . . . . . . | 2,000 |
| Income before taxes. . . . . . . . . . . . . . . . . . . . . | 143,400 |
| Income taxes expense . . . . . . . . . . . . . . . . . . . | 43,890 |
| Net income . . . . . . . . . . . . . . . . . . . . . . . . . . . | $ 99,510 |

| IKIBAN INC. Comparative Balance Sheets | | |
|---|---|---|
| **At June 30** | **2021** | **2020** |
| **Assets** | | |
| Cash. . . . . . . . . . . . . . . . . . . . . . . . . . | $ 87,500 | $ 44,000 |
| Accounts receivable, net . . . . . . . . . . | 65,000 | 51,000 |
| Inventory . . . . . . . . . . . . . . . . . . . . . . . | 63,800 | 86,500 |
| Prepaid expenses. . . . . . . . . . . . . . . . . | 4,400 | 5,400 |
| Total current assets . . . . . . . . . . . . . . | 220,700 | 186,900 |
| Equipment. . . . . . . . . . . . . . . . . . . . . . | 124,000 | 115,000 |
| Accum. depreciation—Equipment . . . | (27,000) | (9,000) |
| Total assets . . . . . . . . . . . . . . . . . . . . . | $317,700 | $292,900 |
| **Liabilities and Equity** | | |
| Accounts payable . . . . . . . . . . . . . . . . | $ 25,000 | $ 30,000 |
| Wages payable . . . . . . . . . . . . . . . . . . | 6,000 | 15,000 |
| Income taxes payable. . . . . . . . . . . . . | 3,400 | 3,800 |
| Total current liabilities . . . . . . . . . . . | 34,400 | 48,800 |
| Notes payable (long term) . . . . . . . . . | 30,000 | 60,000 |
| Total liabilities. . . . . . . . . . . . . . . . . . . | 64,400 | 108,800 |
| **Equity** | | |
| Common stock, $5 par value . . . . . . . | 220,000 | 160,000 |
| Retained earnings. . . . . . . . . . . . . . . . | 33,300 | 24,100 |
| Total liabilities and equity. . . . . . . . . . | $317,700 | $292,900 |

**Additional Information**

**a.** A $30,000 notes payable is retired at its $30,000 carrying (book) value in exchange for cash.

**b.** The only changes affecting retained earnings are net income and cash dividends paid.

**c.** New equipment is acquired for $57,600 cash.

**d.** Received cash for the sale of equipment that had cost $48,600, yielding a $2,000 gain.

**e.** Prepaid Expenses and Wages Payable relate to Operating Expenses on the income statement.

**f.** All purchases and sales of inventory are on credit.

**Check** (1*b*) Cash paid for dividends, $90,310
(1*d*) Cash received from equip. sale, $10,000

Use the following information to prepare a statement of cash flows for the current year using the *indirect method*.

**Exercise 12-13**

**Indirect:** Preparing statement of cash flows

**P2 P3**

| MONTGOMERY INC. Comparative Balance Sheets | | |
| --- | --- | --- |
| **At December 31** | **Current Year** | **Prior Year** |
| **Assets** | | |
| Cash.......................... | $ 30,400 | $ 30,550 |
| Accounts receivable, net .......... | 10,050 | 12,150 |
| Inventory...................... | 90,100 | 70,150 |
| Total current assets ............. | 130,550 | 112,850 |
| Equipment..................... | 49,900 | 41,500 |
| Accum. depreciation—Equipment ... | (22,500) | (15,300) |
| Total assets.................... | $157,950 | $139,050 |
| **Liabilities and Equity** | | |
| Accounts payable............... | $ 23,900 | $ 25,400 |
| Salaries payable................ | 500 | 600 |
| Total current liabilities ........... | 24,400 | 26,000 |
| **Equity** | | |
| Common stock, no par value ....... | 110,000 | 100,000 |
| Retained earnings............... | 23,550 | 13,050 |
| Total liabilities and equity......... | $157,950 | $139,050 |

| MONTGOMERY INC. Income Statement For Current Year Ended December 31 | |
| --- | --- |
| Sales ................... | $45,575 |
| Cost of goods sold ......... | (18,950) |
| Gross profit............... | 26,625 |
| Salaries expense .......... | 5,550 |
| Depreciation expense ...... | 7,200 |
| Income before taxes ....... | 13,875 |
| Income tax expense........ | 3,375 |
| Net income .............. | $10,500 |

**Additional Information on Current-Year Transactions**

a. No dividends are declared or paid.

b. Issued additional stock for $10,000 cash.

c. Purchased equipment for cash; no equipment was sold.

---

Use the following Cash account to determine (*a*) cash flows used by investing activities and (*b*) cash flows provided by financing activities.

**Exercise 12-14**

Using the Cash account to determine cash flows

**P3**

| Cash | | | |
| --- | --- | --- | --- |
| Balance, Dec. 31, prior year ................. | 10,000 | | |
| Receipts from customers ...................... | 60,000 | Payments for inventory ........................... | 31,000 |
| Receipts from equipment sale ............. | 26,000 | Payments for salaries ............................. | 20,000 |
| Receipts from issuing stock ................. | 40,000 | Payments for land ................................. | 50,000 |
| | | Payments for a copyright ....................... | 17,000 |
| | | Payments for dividends ......................... | 3,000 |
| Balance, Dec. 31, current year ................. | 15,000 | | |

---

A company reported average total assets of $1,240,000 in Year 1 and $1,510,000 in Year 2. Its net operating cash flow was $102,920 in Year 1 and $138,920 in Year 2. (1) Calculate its cash flow on total assets ratio for both years. (2) Did its cash flow on total assets improve in Year 2 versus Year 1?

**Exercise 12-15**

Analyzing cash flow on total assets **A1**

---

Complete the following spreadsheet in preparation of the statement of cash flows. (The statement of cash flows is not required.) Prepare the spreadsheet as in Exhibit 12A.1 under the *indirect method*. Identify the debits and credits in the Analysis of Changes columns with letters that correspond to the following transactions and events *a* through *h*.

**Exercise 12-16**[A]

**Indirect:** Cash flows spreadsheet

**P4**

a. Net income for the year was $100,000.

b. Dividends of $80,000 cash were declared and paid.

c. The only noncash expense was $70,000 of depreciation.

d. Purchased plant assets for $90,000 cash.

e. Notes payable of $20,000 were issued for $20,000 cash.

f. $50,000 increase in accounts receivable.

g. $30,000 decrease in inventory.

h. $10,000 decrease in accounts payable.

[continued on next page]

[continued from previous page]

| SCORETECK CORPORATION<br>Spreadsheet for Statement of Cash Flows—Indirect Method<br>For Year Ended December 31, 2021 | | | | |
|---|---|---|---|---|
| | | **Analysis of Changes** | | |
| | **Dec. 31, 2020** | **Debit** | **Credit** | **Dec. 31, 2021** |
| **Balance Sheet—Debit Bal. Accounts** | | | | |
| Cash | $ 80,000 | | | $ 70,000 |
| Accounts receivable | 120,000 | | | 170,000 |
| Inventory | 250,000 | | | 220,000 |
| Plant assets | 600,000 | | | 690,000 |
| | $1,050,000 | | | $1,150,000 |
| **Balance Sheet—Credit Bal. Accounts** | | | | |
| Accumulated depreciation | $ 100,000 | | | $ 170,000 |
| Accounts payable | 150,000 | | | 140,000 |
| Notes payable | 370,000 | | | 390,000 |
| Common stock | 200,000 | | | 200,000 |
| Retained earnings | 230,000 | | | 250,000 |
| | $1,050,000 | | | $1,150,000 |
| **Statement of Cash Flows** | | | | |
| Operating activities | | | | |
| Net income | | | | |
| Increase in accounts receivable | | | | |
| Decrease in inventory | | | | |
| Decrease in accounts payable | | | | |
| Depreciation expense | | | | |
| Investing activities | | | | |
| Cash paid to purchase plant assets | | | | |
| Financing activities | | | | |
| Cash paid for dividends | | | | |
| Cash from issuance of notes | | | | |

---

**Exercise 12-17ᴮ**

**Direct:** Classifying cash flows

**C1    P5**

Indicate where each item would appear on a statement of cash flows using the *direct method* by placing an *x* in the appropriate column.

| | Statement of Cash Flows | | | Noncash Investing and Financing Activities | Not Reported on Statement or in Notes |
|---|---|---|---|---|---|
| | **Operating Activities** | **Investing Activities** | **Financing Activities** | | |
| a. Retired long-term notes payable by issuing common stock . . . . . . . . . . . | ___ | ___ | ___ | ___ | ___ |
| b. Paid cash toward accounts payable . . . | ___ | ___ | ___ | ___ | ___ |
| c. Sold inventory for cash . . . . . . . . . . . . | ___ | ___ | ___ | ___ | ___ |
| d. Paid cash dividends . . . . . . . . . . . . . . . | ___ | ___ | ___ | ___ | ___ |
| e. Accepted note receivable in exchange for plant assets . . . . . . . . . . . . . . . . | ___ | ___ | ___ | ___ | ___ |
| f. Recorded depreciation expense . . . . . | ___ | ___ | ___ | ___ | ___ |
| g. Paid cash to acquire treasury stock . . . | ___ | ___ | ___ | ___ | ___ |
| h. Collected cash from sales . . . . . . . . . . | ___ | ___ | ___ | ___ | ___ |
| i. Borrowed cash from bank by signing a nine-year notes payable . . . . . . . . | ___ | ___ | ___ | ___ | ___ |
| j. Paid cash to purchase a patent . . . . . . | ___ | ___ | ___ | ___ | ___ |

---

**Exercise 12-18ᴮ**

**Direct:** Computing cash flows

**P5**

For each of the following separate cases, compute the required cash flow information.

**Case X:** Compute cash received from customers

| | |
|---|---|
| Sales. . . . . . . . . . . . . . . . . . . . . . . . . . . . . | $515,000 |
| Accounts receivable, Beginning balance. . . . | 27,200 |
| Accounts receivable, Ending balance . . . . . | 33,600 |

**Case Y:** Compute cash paid for rent

| | |
|---|---|
| Rent expense. . . . . . . . . . . . . . . . . . . . . . . | $139,800 |
| Rent payable, Beginning balance. . . . . . . . . | 7,800 |
| Rent payable, Ending balance . . . . . . . . . . | 6,200 |

**Case Z:** Compute cash paid for inventory

| | |
|---|---|
| Cost of goods sold . . . . . . . . . . . . . . . . . | $525,000 |
| Inventory, Beginning balance . . . . . . . . . | 158,600 |
| Accounts payable, Beginning balance . . . | 66,700 |
| Inventory, Ending balance . . . . . . . . . . . . | 130,400 |
| Accounts payable, Ending balance . . . . . | 82,000 |

---

**Exercise 12-19ᴮ**

**Direct:** Preparing statement of cash flows    **P5**

Refer to the information in Exercise 12-12. Using the *direct method,* prepare the statement of cash flows for the year ended June 30, 2021. *Hint:* Prepaid Expenses and Wages Payable relate to Operating Expenses on the income statement.

Refer to information in Exercise 12-4. Use the *direct method* to prepare the operating activities section of Sonad's statement of cash flows.

**Exercise 12-20ᴮ**
**Direct:** Cash flows from operating activities **P5**

Use the following information about Ferron Company to prepare a complete statement of cash flows (*direct method*) for the current year ended December 31. Use a note disclosure for any noncash investing and financing activities.

**Exercise 12-21ᴮ**
**Direct:** Preparing statement of cash flows and supporting note
**P5**

| | | | |
|---|---|---|---|
| Cash and cash equivalents, Dec. 31 prior year-end. | $ 40,000 | Cash received from sale of equipment | $ 60,250 |
| Cash and cash equivalents, Dec. 31 current year-end. | 148,000 | Land purchased by issuing long-term notes payable | 105,250 |
| | | Cash paid for store equipment | 24,750 |
| Cash received as interest. | 3,500 | Cash dividends paid | 10,000 |
| Cash paid for salaries. | 76,500 | Cash paid for other expenses. | 20,000 |
| Bonds payable retired by issuing common stock (no gain or loss on retirement) | 185,500 | Cash received from customers. | 495,000 |
| Cash paid to retire long-term notes payable | 65,000 | Cash paid for inventory. | 254,500 |

The following Cash T-account shows the total debits and total credits to the Cash account of Thomas Corporation for the current year.

1. Prepare a complete statement of cash flows for the current year using the *direct method.*
2. Refer to the statement of cash flows prepared for part 1 to answer the following questions. (*a*) Which section—operating, investing, or financing—shows the largest cash (i) inflow and (ii) outflow? (*b*) What is the largest individual item among the investing cash outflows? (*c*) Are the cash proceeds larger from issuing notes or issuing stock? (*d*) Does the company have a net cash inflow or outflow from borrowing activities?

**Exercise 12-22ᴮ**
**Direct:** Preparing statement of cash flows from Cash T-account
**P1 P3 P5**

| Cash | | | |
|---|---|---|---|
| Balance, Dec. 31, prior year | 333,000 | | |
| Receipts from customers | 5,000,000 | Payments for inventory | 2,590,000 |
| Receipts from dividends | 208,400 | Payments for wages | 550,000 |
| Receipts from land sale | 220,000 | Payments for rent | 320,000 |
| Receipts from machinery sale | 710,000 | Payments for interest | 218,000 |
| Receipts from issuing stock | 1,540,000 | Payments for taxes | 450,000 |
| Receipts from borrowing | 3,600,000 | Payments for machinery | 2,236,000 |
| | | Payments for stock investments | 1,260,000 |
| | | Payments for long-term notes payable | 386,000 |
| | | Payments for dividends | 500,000 |
| | | Payments for treasury stock | 218,000 |
| Balance, Dec. 31, current year | ? | | |

**MᶜGraw Hill connect**

Lansing Company's current-year income statement and selected balance sheet data at December 31 of the current and prior years follow.

**PROBLEM SET A**

**Problem 12-1A**
**Indirect:** Computing cash flows from operations
**P2**

| LANSING COMPANY Selected Balance Sheet Accounts | | |
|---|---|---|
| At December 31 | Current Year | Prior Year |
| Accounts receivable | $5,600 | $5,800 |
| Inventory | 1,980 | 1,540 |
| Accounts payable | 4,400 | 4,600 |
| Salaries payable | 880 | 700 |
| Utilities payable | 220 | 160 |
| Prepaid insurance | 260 | 280 |
| Prepaid rent | 220 | 180 |

| LANSING COMPANY Income Statement For Current Year Ended December 31 | |
|---|---|
| Sales revenue | $97,200 |
| Expenses | |
| Cost of goods sold | 42,000 |
| Depreciation expense | 12,000 |
| Salaries expense | 18,000 |
| Rent expense | 9,000 |
| Insurance expense | 3,800 |
| Interest expense | 3,600 |
| Utilities expense | 2,800 |
| Net income | $ 6,000 |

**Required**

Prepare the operating activities section of the statement of cash flows using the *indirect method* for the current year.

**Check** Cash from operating activities, $17,780

**Problem 12-2A**[B]

**Direct:** Computing cash flows from operations

**P5**

Refer to the information in Problem 12-1A.

**Required**

Prepare the operating activities section of the statement of cash flows using the *direct method* for the current year.

---

**Problem 12-3A**

**Indirect:** Statement of cash flows

**A1   P2   P3**

Forten Company's current-year income statement, comparative balance sheets, and additional information follow. For the year, (1) all sales are credit sales, (2) all credits to Accounts Receivable reflect cash receipts from customers, (3) all purchases of inventory are on credit, and (4) all debits to Accounts Payable reflect cash payments for inventory.

| FORTEN COMPANY<br>Income Statement<br>For Current Year Ended December 31 | | |
|---|---:|---:|
| Sales . . . . . . . . . . . . . . . . . . . . . . . . . . . . . . . . . . . | | $582,500 |
| Cost of goods sold . . . . . . . . . . . . . . . . . . . . . . . . | | 285,000 |
| Gross profit . . . . . . . . . . . . . . . . . . . . . . . . . . . . . . | | 297,500 |
| Operating expenses (excluding depreciation) . . | $132,400 | |
| Depreciation expense . . . . . . . . . . . . . . . . . . . . | 20,750 | 153,150 |
| Other gains (losses) | | |
|    Loss on sale of equipment. . . . . . . . . . . . . . | | (5,125) |
| Income before taxes. . . . . . . . . . . . . . . . . . . . . | | 139,225 |
| Income taxes expense . . . . . . . . . . . . . . . . . . . . | | 24,250 |
| Net income . . . . . . . . . . . . . . . . . . . . . . . . . . . . . | | $114,975 |

| FORTEN COMPANY<br>Comparative Balance Sheets | | |
|---|---:|---:|
| **At December 31** | **Current Year** | **Prior Year** |
| **Assets** | | |
| Cash. . . . . . . . . . . . . . . . . . . . . . . . . . . . . . . . . . | $ 49,800 | $ 73,500 |
| Accounts receivable . . . . . . . . . . . . . . . . . . . . | 65,810 | 50,625 |
| Inventory . . . . . . . . . . . . . . . . . . . . . . . . . . . . . | 275,656 | 251,800 |
| Prepaid expenses . . . . . . . . . . . . . . . . . . . . . . | 1,250 | 1,875 |
| Total current assets. . . . . . . . . . . . . . . . . . . . | 392,516 | 377,800 |
| Equipment . . . . . . . . . . . . . . . . . . . . . . . . . . . | 157,500 | 108,000 |
| Accum. depreciation—Equipment . . . . . . . . . . | (36,625) | (46,000) |
| Total assets . . . . . . . . . . . . . . . . . . . . . . . . . . | $513,391 | $439,800 |
| **Liabilities and Equity** | | |
| Accounts payable . . . . . . . . . . . . . . . . . . . . . . | $ 53,141 | $114,675 |
| Long-term notes payable . . . . . . . . . . . . . . . . | 75,000 | 54,750 |
| Total liabilities . . . . . . . . . . . . . . . . . . . . . . . | 128,141 | 169,425 |
| **Equity** | | |
| Common stock, $5 par value . . . . . . . . . . . . . . | 162,750 | 150,250 |
| Paid-in capital in excess of par, common stock . . . | 37,500 | 0 |
| Retained earnings . . . . . . . . . . . . . . . . . . . . . . | 185,000 | 120,125 |
| Total liabilities and equity . . . . . . . . . . . . . . . . | $513,391 | $439,800 |

**Additional Information on Current-Year Transactions**

a. The loss on the cash sale of equipment was $5,125 (details in *b*).

b. Sold equipment costing $46,875, with accumulated depreciation of $30,125, for $11,625 cash.

c. Purchased equipment costing $96,375 by paying $30,000 cash and signing a long-term notes payable for the balance.

d. Paid $46,125 cash to reduce the long-term notes payable.

e. Issued 2,500 shares of common stock for $20 cash per share.

f. Declared and paid cash dividends of $50,100.

**Check**  Cash from operating activities, $40,900

**Required**

**1.** Prepare a complete statement of cash flows using the *indirect method* for the current year. Disclose any noncash investing and financing activities in a note.

*Analysis Component*

**2.** Analyze and discuss the statement of cash flows prepared in part 1, giving special attention to the wisdom of the cash dividend payment.

---

**Problem 12-4A**[A]

**Indirect:** Cash flows spreadsheet

**P4**

Refer to the information reported about Forten Company in Problem 12-3A.

**Required**

Prepare a complete statement of cash flows using a spreadsheet as in Exhibit 12A.1 using the *indirect method*. Identify the debits and credits in the Analysis of Changes columns with letters that correspond to the following list of transactions and events.

a. Net income was $114,975.

b. Accounts receivable increased.

c. Inventory increased.

d. Prepaid expenses decreased.

e. Accounts payable decreased.

f. Depreciation expense was $20,750.

g. Sold equipment costing $46,875, with accumulated depreciation of $30,125, for $11,625 cash. This yielded a loss of $5,125.

h. Purchased equipment costing $96,375 by paying $30,000 cash and **(i.)** by signing a long-term notes payable for the balance.

j. Paid $46,125 cash to reduce the long-term notes payable.

k. Issued 2,500 shares of common stock for $20 cash per share.

l. Declared and paid cash dividends of $50,100.

Refer to Forten Company's financial statements and related information in Problem 12-3A.

**Required**

Prepare a complete statement of cash flows using the *direct method*. Disclose any noncash investing and financing activities in a note.

**Problem 12-5A**ᴮ

**Direct:** Statement of cash flows **P5**

**Check** Cash used in financing activities, $(46,225)

Golden Corp.'s current-year income statement, comparative balance sheets, and additional information follow. For the year, (1) all sales are credit sales, (2) all credits to Accounts Receivable reflect cash receipts from customers, (3) all purchases of inventory are on credit, (4) all debits to Accounts Payable reflect cash payments for inventory, and (5) any change in Income Taxes Payable reflects the accrual and cash payment of taxes.

**Problem 12-6A**

**Indirect:** Statement of cash flows

**P2   P3**

| GOLDEN CORPORATION Comparative Balance Sheets | | |
|---|---|---|
| At December 31 | Current Year | Prior Year |
| **Assets** | | |
| Cash.......................... | $ 164,000 | $107,000 |
| Accounts receivable ............. | 83,000 | 71,000 |
| Inventory ..................... | 601,000 | 526,000 |
| Total current assets.............. | 848,000 | 704,000 |
| Equipment..................... | 335,000 | 299,000 |
| Accum. depreciation—Equipment ... | (158,000) | (104,000) |
| Total assets ................... | $1,025,000 | $899,000 |
| **Liabilities and Equity** | | |
| Accounts payable ............... | $ 87,000 | $ 71,000 |
| Income taxes payable............ | 28,000 | 25,000 |
| Total current liabilities........... | 115,000 | 96,000 |
| **Equity** | | |
| Common stock, $2 par value ....... | 592,000 | 568,000 |
| Paid-in capital in excess of par value, common stock...... | 196,000 | 160,000 |
| Retained earnings............... | 122,000 | 75,000 |
| Total liabilities and equity ......... | $1,025,000 | $899,000 |

| GOLDEN CORPORATION Income Statement For Current Year Ended December 31 | |
|---|---|
| Sales ..................................... | $1,792,000 |
| Cost of goods sold ........................ | 1,086,000 |
| Gross profit............................... | 706,000 |
| Operating expenses (excluding depreciation) .... | 494,000 |
| Depreciation expense ...................... | 54,000 |
| Income before taxes........................ | 158,000 |
| Income taxes expense ...................... | 22,000 |
| Net income ............................... | $ 136,000 |

**Additional Information on Current-Year Transactions**

**a.** Purchased equipment for $36,000 cash.

**b.** Issued 12,000 shares of common stock for $5 cash per share.

**c.** Declared and paid $89,000 in cash dividends.

**Required**

Prepare a complete statement of cash flows using the *indirect method* for the current year.

**Check** Cash from operating activities, $122,000

Refer to the information reported about Golden Corporation in Problem 12-6A.

**Required**

Prepare a complete statement of cash flows using a spreadsheet as in Exhibit 12A.1 under the *indirect method*. Identify the debits and credits in the Analysis of Changes columns with letters that correspond to the following list of transactions and events.

**a.** Net income was $136,000.

**b.** Accounts receivable increased.

**c.** Inventory increased.

**d.** Accounts payable increased.

**e.** Income taxes payable increased.

**f.** Depreciation expense was $54,000.

**g.** Purchased equipment for $36,000 cash.

**h.** Issued 12,000 shares at $5 cash per share.

**i.** Declared and paid $89,000 of cash dividends.

**Problem 12-7A**ᴬ

**Indirect:** Cash flows spreadsheet

**P4**

**Check** Analysis of Changes column totals, $481,000

Refer to Golden Corporation's financial statements and related information in Problem 12-6A.

**Required**

Prepare a complete statement of cash flows using the *direct method* for the current year.

**Problem 12-8A**ᴮ

**Direct:** Statement of cash flows **P5**

**Check** Cash used in financing activities, $(29,000)

**PROBLEM SET B**

**Problem 12-1B**

**Indirect:** Computing cash flows from operations

**P2**

Salt Lake Company's current-year income statement and selected balance sheet data at December 31 of the current and prior years follow.

| SALT LAKE COMPANY Income Statement For Current Year Ended December 31 | | |
|---|---:|---:|
| Sales revenue . . . . . . . . . . . . . . . . . . . . | | $156,000 |
| Expenses | | |
| Cost of goods sold . . . . . . . . . . . . . . | 72,000 | |
| Depreciation expense. . . . . . . . . . . . | 32,000 | |
| Salaries expense. . . . . . . . . . . . . . . | 20,000 | |
| Rent expense . . . . . . . . . . . . . . . . . | 5,000 | |
| Insurance expense . . . . . . . . . . . . . | 2,600 | |
| Interest expense. . . . . . . . . . . . . . . | 2,400 | |
| Utilities expense . . . . . . . . . . . . . . | 2,000 | |
| Net income. . . . . . . . . . . . . . . . . . . | | $ 20,000 |

| SALT LAKE COMPANY Selected Balance Sheet Accounts | | |
|---|---:|---:|
| At December 31 | Current Year | Prior Year |
| Accounts receivable . . . | $3,600 | $3,000 |
| Inventory. . . . . . . . . . . . | 860 | 980 |
| Accounts payable . . . . . | 2,400 | 2,600 |
| Salaries payable . . . . . . | 900 | 600 |
| Utilities payable . . . . . . | 200 | 0 |
| Prepaid insurance. . . . . | 140 | 180 |
| Prepaid rent . . . . . . . . . | 100 | 200 |

**Required**

**Check**   Cash from operating activities, $51,960

Prepare the operating activities section of the statement of cash flows using the *indirect method* for the current year.

**Problem 12-2B**[B]

**Direct:** Computing cash flows from operations

**P5**

Refer to the information in Problem 12-1B.

**Required**

Prepare the operating activities section of the statement of cash flows using the *direct method* for the current year.

**Problem 12-3B**

**Indirect:** Statement of cash flows

**A1   P2   P3**

Gazelle Corporation's current-year income statement, comparative balance sheets, and additional information follow. For the year, (1) all sales are credit sales, (2) all credits to Accounts Receivable reflect cash receipts from customers, (3) all purchases of inventory are on credit, and (4) all debits to Accounts Payable reflect cash payments for inventory.

| GAZELLE CORPORATION Comparative Balance Sheets | | |
|---|---:|---:|
| At December 31 | Current Year | Prior Year |
| **Assets** | | |
| Cash. . . . . . . . . . . . . . . . . . . . . . . . | $123,450 | $ 61,550 |
| Accounts receivable . . . . . . . . . . . . . | 77,100 | 80,750 |
| Inventory . . . . . . . . . . . . . . . . . . . . | 240,600 | 250,700 |
| Prepaid expenses . . . . . . . . . . . . . . | 15,100 | 17,000 |
| Total current assets. . . . . . . . . . . . . | 456,250 | 410,000 |
| Equipment . . . . . . . . . . . . . . . . . . . | 262,250 | 200,000 |
| Accum. depreciation—Equipment . . . . | (110,750) | (95,000) |
| Total assets . . . . . . . . . . . . . . . . . . | $607,750 | $515,000 |
| **Liabilities and Equity** | | |
| Accounts payable . . . . . . . . . . . . . . | $ 17,750 | $102,000 |
| Long-term notes payable . . . . . . . . . | 115,000 | 87,500 |
| Total liabilities . . . . . . . . . . . . . . . . | 132,750 | 189,500 |
| **Equity** | | |
| Common stock, $5 par . . . . . . . . . . . | 215,000 | 200,000 |
| Paid-in capital in excess | | |
| of par, common stock . . . . . . . . . . | 30,000 | 0 |
| Retained earnings . . . . . . . . . . . . . . | 230,000 | 125,500 |
| Total liabilities and equity . . . . . . . . . | $607,750 | $515,000 |

| GAZELLE CORPORATION Income Statement For Current Year Ended December 31 | | |
|---|---:|---:|
| Sales . . . . . . . . . . . . . . . . . . . . . . . . . . . . . . . . | | $1,185,000 |
| Cost of goods sold . . . . . . . . . . . . . . . . . . . . . . | | 595,000 |
| Gross profit . . . . . . . . . . . . . . . . . . . . . . . . . . . | | 590,000 |
| Operating expenses (excluding depreciation) . . | | 362,850 |
| Depreciation expense . . . . . . . . . . . . . . . . . . . . | | 38,600 |
| | | 188,550 |
| Other gains (losses) | | |
| Loss on sale of equipment. . . . . . . . . . . . . . . | | (2,100) |
| Income before taxes. . . . . . . . . . . . . . . . . . . . | | 186,450 |
| Income taxes expense . . . . . . . . . . . . . . . . . . | | 28,350 |
| Net income . . . . . . . . . . . . . . . . . . . . . . . . . . . | | $ 158,100 |

**Additional Information on Current-Year Transactions**

a. The loss on the cash sale of equipment was $2,100 (details in b).

b. Sold equipment costing $51,000, with accumulated depreciation of $22,850, for $26,050 cash.

c. Purchased equipment costing $113,250 by paying $43,250 cash and signing a long-term notes payable for the balance.

d. Paid $42,500 cash to reduce the long-term notes payable.

e. Issued 3,000 shares of common stock for $15 cash per share.

f. Declared and paid cash dividends of $53,600.

**Required**

**1.** Prepare a complete statement of cash flows using the *indirect method* for the current year. Disclose any noncash investing and financing activities in a note.

**Check**   Cash from operating activities, $130,200

*Analysis Component*

**2.** Analyze and discuss the statement of cash flows prepared in part 1, giving special attention to the wisdom of the cash dividend payment.

---

Refer to the information reported about Gazelle Corporation in Problem 12-3B.

**Problem 12-4B**[A]
**Indirect:** Cash flows spreadsheet
**P4**

**Required**

Prepare a complete statement of cash flows using a spreadsheet as in Exhibit 12A.1 using the *indirect method.* Identify the debits and credits in the Analysis of Changes columns with letters that correspond to the following list of transactions and events.

**a.** Net income was $158,100.

**b.** Accounts receivable decreased.

**c.** Inventory decreased.

**d.** Prepaid expenses decreased.

**e.** Accounts payable decreased.

**f.** Depreciation expense was $38,600.

**g.** Sold equipment costing $51,000, with accumulated depreciation of $22,850, for $26,050 cash. This yielded a loss of $2,100.

**h.** Purchased equipment costing $113,250 by paying $43,250 cash and **(i.)** by signing a long-term notes payable for the balance.

**j.** Paid $42,500 cash to reduce the long-term notes payable.

**k.** Issued 3,000 shares of common stock for $15 cash per share.

**l.** Declared and paid cash dividends of $53,600.

---

Refer to Gazelle Corporation's financial statements and related information in Problem 12-3B.

**Problem 12-5B**[B]
**Direct:** Statement of cash flows   **P5**

**Required**

Prepare a complete statement of cash flows using the *direct method.* Disclose any noncash investing and financing activities in a note.

**Check**   Cash used in financing activities, $(51,100)

---

Satu Company's current-year income statement, comparative balance sheets, and additional information follow. For the year, (1) all sales are credit sales, (2) all credits to Accounts Receivable reflect cash receipts from customers, (3) all purchases of inventory are on credit, (4) all debits to Accounts Payable reflect cash payments for inventory, and (5) any change in Income Taxes Payable reflects the accrual and cash payment of taxes.

**Problem 12-6B**
**Indirect:** Statement of cash flows
**P2   P3**

| SATU COMPANY Comparative Balance Sheets | | |
|---|---|---|
| **At December 31** | **Current Year** | **Prior Year** |
| **Assets** | | |
| Cash.......................... | $ 58,750 | $ 28,400 |
| Accounts receivable ............... | 20,222 | 25,860 |
| Inventory ....................... | 165,667 | 140,320 |
| Total current assets................ | 244,639 | 194,580 |
| Equipment...................... | 107,750 | 77,500 |
| Accum. depreciation—Equipment .... | (46,700) | (31,000) |
| Total assets .................... | $305,689 | $241,080 |
| **Liabilities and Equity** | | |
| Accounts payable ................. | $ 20,372 | $157,530 |
| Income taxes payable.............. | 2,100 | 6,100 |
| Total current liabilities............. | 22,472 | 163,630 |
| **Equity** | | |
| Common stock, $5 par value ........ | 40,000 | 25,000 |
| Paid-in capital in excess of par, common stock............ | 68,000 | 20,000 |
| Retained earnings................. | 175,217 | 32,450 |
| Total liabilities and equity........... | $305,689 | $241,080 |

| SATU COMPANY Income Statement For Current Year Ended December 31 | |
|---|---|
| Sales ..................................... | $750,800 |
| Cost of goods sold ......................... | 269,200 |
| Gross profit................................ | 481,600 |
| Operating expenses (excluding depreciation) .. | 173,933 |
| Depreciation expense ...................... | 15,700 |
| Income before taxes........................ | 291,967 |
| Income taxes expense ...................... | 89,200 |
| Net income ............................... | $202,767 |

**Additional Information on Current-Year Transactions**

**a.** Purchased equipment for $30,250 cash.

**b.** Issued 3,000 shares of common stock for $21 cash per share.

**c.** Declared and paid $60,000 of cash dividends.

[continued on next page]

[continued from previous page]

**Required**

Prepare a complete statement of cash flows using the *indirect method* for the current year.

---

**Problem 12-7B**[A]

**Indirect:** Cash flows
spreadsheet

**P4**

Refer to the information reported about Satu Company in Problem 12-6B.

**Required**

Prepare a complete statement of cash flows using a spreadsheet as in Exhibit 12A.1 under the *indirect method*. Identify the debits and credits in the Analysis of Changes columns with letters that correspond to the following list of transactions and events.

a. Net income was $202,767.

b. Accounts receivable decreased.

c. Inventory increased.

d. Accounts payable decreased.

e. Income taxes payable decreased.

f. Depreciation expense was $15,700.

g. Purchased equipment for $30,250 cash.

h. Issued 3,000 shares at $21 cash per share.

i. Declared and paid $60,000 of cash dividends.

---

**Problem 12-8B**[B]

**Direct:** Statement of
cash flows   **P5**

Refer to Satu Company's financial statements and related information in Problem 12-6B.

**Required**

Prepare a complete statement of cash flows using the *direct method* for the current year.

---

**SERIAL PROBLEM**

Business Solutions **(Indirect)**

**P2   P3**

Alexander Image/Shutterstock

*Serial problem began in Chapter 1. If previous chapter segments were not completed, the serial problem can begin at this point. It is available in **Connect** with an algorithmic option.*

**SP 12**   Santana Rey, owner of **Business Solutions**, decides to prepare a statement of cash flows for her business. (Although the serial problem allowed for various ownership changes in earlier chapters, we will prepare the statement of cash flows using the following financial data.)

| BUSINESS SOLUTIONS Income Statement For Three Months Ended March 31, 2022 | | |
|---|---|---|
| Computer services revenue.. | | $25,307 |
| Net sales................. | | 18,693 |
| Total revenue ............. | | 44,000 |
| Cost of goods sold ......... | $14,052 | |
| Depreciation expense— | | |
| Office equipment ........ | 400 | |
| Depreciation expense— | | |
| Computer equipment..... | 1,250 | |
| Wages expense............ | 3,250 | |
| Insurance expense......... | 555 | |
| Rent expense ............. | 2,475 | |
| Computer supplies expense .. | 1,305 | |
| Advertising expense........ | 600 | |
| Mileage expense .......... | 320 | |
| Repairs expense—Computer.. | 960 | |
| Total expenses ............ | | 25,167 |
| Net income ............... | | $18,833 |

| BUSINESS SOLUTIONS Comparative Balance Sheets | Mar. 31, 2022 | Dec. 31, 2021 |
|---|---|---|
| **Assets** | | |
| Cash ..................... | $ 68,057 | $48,372 |
| Accounts receivable ......... | 22,867 | 5,668 |
| Inventory.................. | 704 | 0 |
| Computer supplies .......... | 2,005 | 580 |
| Prepaid insurance........... | 1,110 | 1,665 |
| Prepaid rent .............. | 825 | 825 |
| Total current assets ......... | 95,568 | 57,110 |
| Office equipment ........... | 8,000 | 8,000 |
| Accumulated depreciation— | | |
| Office equipment ......... | (800) | (400) |
| Computer equipment........ | 20,000 | 20,000 |
| Accumulated depreciation— | | |
| Computer equipment...... | (2,500) | (1,250) |
| Total assets ............... | $120,268 | $83,460 |
| **Liabilities and Equity** | | |
| Accounts payable ........... | $ 0 | $ 1,100 |
| Wages payable ............. | 875 | 500 |
| Unearned computer service | | |
| revenue................. | 0 | 1,500 |
| Total current liabilities ....... | 875 | 3,100 |
| **Equity** | | |
| Common stock ............. | 98,000 | 73,000 |
| Retained earnings........... | 21,393 | 7,360 |
| Total liabilities and equity..... | $120,268 | $83,460 |

**Required**

Prepare a statement of cash flows for Business Solutions using the *indirect method* for the three months ended March 31, 2022. Recall that owner Santana Rey contributed $25,000 to the business in exchange for additional stock in the first quarter of 2022 and has received $4,800 in cash dividends.

**Check**  Cash flows used by operations: $(515)

**Tableau Dashboard Activities** expose students to accounting analytics using visual displays. These assignments run in **Connect** and all are auto-gradable.

**Tableau DA 12-1 Quick Study**, Computing net increase (decrease) in cash, **C1**—similar to QS 12-1

**Tableau DA 12-2 Exercise**, Analyzing cash flows, **P2**, **P3**—similar to Exercise 12-1

**Tableau DA 12-3 Mini-Case**, Analyzing cash flows, **P2**, **P3**—similar to Exercise 12-12

**TABLEAU DASHBOARD ACTIVITIES**

**General Ledger (GL) Assignments** expose students to general ledger software similar to that in practice. **GL** is part of **Connect**, and **GL** assignments are auto-gradable and have algorithmic options.

**GL 12-1, GL 12-2, GL 12-3**  Prepare journal entries, general ledger, trial balance, and statement of cash flows (indirect & direct).

**GENERAL LEDGER**

## Accounting Analysis

**AA 12-1**  Use **Apple**'s financial statements in Appendix A to answer the following.

1. Is Apple's statement of cash flows prepared under the direct method or the indirect method?
2. For each fiscal year 2019, 2018, and 2017, identify the amount of cash provided by operating activities and cash paid for dividends.
3. In 2019, did Apple have sufficient cash flows from operations to pay dividends?
4. Did Apple spend more or less cash to repurchase common stock in 2019 versus 2018?

**COMPANY ANALYSIS**

**A1**

**AA 12-2**  Key figures for **Apple** and **Google** follow.

**COMPARATIVE ANALYSIS**

**A1**

| $ millions | Apple | | | Google | | |
|---|---|---|---|---|---|---|
| | Current Year | 1 Year Prior | 2 Years Prior | Current Year | 1 Year Prior | 2 Years Prior |
| Operating cash flows .......... | $ 69,391 | $ 77,434 | $ 64,225 | $ 54,520 | $ 47,971 | $ 37,091 |
| Total assets ................. | 338,516 | 365,725 | 375,319 | 275,909 | 232,792 | 197,295 |

**Required**

1. Compute the recent two years' cash flow on total assets ratios for Apple and Google.
2. For the current year, which company has the better cash flow on total assets ratio?
3. For the current year, does cash flow on total assets outperform or underperform the industry (assumed) average of 15% for (*a*) Apple and (*b*) Google?

**AA 12-3**  Key comparative information for **Samsung**, **Apple**, and **Google** follows.

**EXTENDED ANALYSIS**

**C1**

| $ millions | Samsung | | | Apple | | Google | |
|---|---|---|---|---|---|---|---|
| | Current Year | 1 Year Prior | 2 Years Prior | Current Year | 1 Year Prior | Current Year | 1 Year Prior |
| Operating cash flows ... | $ 38,940 | $ 57,515 | $ 56,500 | $ 69,391 | $ 77,434 | $ 54,520 | $ 47,971 |
| Total assets ........... | 302,511 | 291,179 | 274,268 | 338,516 | 365,725 | 275,909 | 232,792 |

**Required**

1. Compute the recent two years' cash flow on total assets ratio for Samsung.
2. Is the change in Samsung's cash flow on total assets ratio favorable or unfavorable?
3. For the current year, is Samsung's cash flow on total assets ratio better or worse than (*a*) Apple's and (*b*) Google's?

## Discussion Questions

1. What is the reporting purpose of the statement of cash flows? Identify at least two questions that this statement can answer.

2. What are some investing activities reported on the statement of cash flows?

3. What are some financing activities reported on the statement of cash flows?

4.[B] Describe the direct method of reporting cash flows from operating activities.

5.[B] When a statement of cash flows is prepared using the direct method, what are some of the operating cash flows?

6. Describe the indirect method of reporting cash flows from operating activities.

7. Where on the statement of cash flows is the payment of cash dividends reported?

8. Assume that a company purchases land for $1,000,000, paying $400,000 cash and borrowing the remainder with a long-term notes payable. How should this transaction be reported on a statement of cash flows?

9. On June 3, a company borrows $200,000 cash by giving its bank a 90-day, interest-bearing note. On the statement of cash flows, where should this be reported?

10. If a company reports positive net income for the year, can it also show a net cash outflow from operating activities? Explain.

11. Is depreciation a source of cash flow?

## Beyond the Numbers

**ETHICS CHALLENGE**

C1   A1

**BTN 12-1**   Katie Murphy is preparing for a meeting with her banker. Her business is finishing its fourth year of operations. In the first year, it had negative cash flows from operations. In the second and third years, cash flows from operations were positive. However, inventory costs rose significantly in Year 4, and cash flows from operations will probably be down 25%. Murphy wants to secure a line of credit from her banker as a financing buffer. From experience, she knows the banker will scrutinize operating cash flows for Years 1 through 4 and will want a projected number for Year 5. Murphy knows that a steady progression upward in operating cash flows for Years 1 through 4 will help her case. She decides to use her discretion as owner and considers several business actions that will turn her operating cash flow in Year 4 from a decrease to an increase.

**Required**

1. Identify two business actions Murphy might take to improve cash flows from operations.
2. Comment on the ethics and possible consequences of Murphy's decision to pursue these actions.

**COMMUNICATING IN PRACTICE**

C1

**BTN 12-2**   Your friend, Diana Wood, recently completed the second year of her business and just received annual financial statements from her accountant. Wood finds the income statement and balance sheet informative but does not understand the statement of cash flows. She says the first section is especially confusing because it contains a lot of additions and subtractions that do not make sense to her. Wood adds, "The income statement tells me the business is more profitable than last year and that's most important. If I want to know how cash changes, I can look at comparative balance sheets."

**Required**

Write a half-page memorandum to your friend explaining the purpose of the statement of cash flows. Speculate as to why the first section is so confusing and how it might be rectified.

**BTN 12-3**  Team members are to coordinate and independently answer one question within each of the following three sections. Team members should then report to the team and confirm or correct teammates' answers.

1. Answer *one* of the following questions about the statement of cash flows: (*a*) What are this statement's reporting objectives? (*b*) What two methods are used to prepare it? Identify similarities and differences between them. (*c*) What steps are followed to prepare the statement? (*d*) What types of analyses are often made from this statement's information?

2. Identify and explain the adjustment from net income to obtain cash flows from operating activities using the indirect method for *one* of the following items: (*a*) Noncash operating revenues and expenses. (*b*) Nonoperating gains and losses. (*c*) Increases and decreases in noncash current assets. (*d*) Increases and decreases in current liabilities.

3.ᴮ Identify and explain the formula for computing cash flows from operating activities using the direct method for *one* of the following items: (*a*) Cash receipts from sales to customers. (*b*) Cash paid for inventory. (*c*) Cash paid for wages and operating expenses. (*d*) Cash paid for interest and taxes.

**TEAMWORK IN ACTION**

C1   A1   P2   P5

**Note:** For teams of more than four, some pairing within teams is necessary. Use as an in-class activity or as an assignment. If used in class, specify a time limit on each part. Conclude with reports to the entire class, using team rotation. Each team can prepare responses on a transparency.

**BTN 12-4**  Review the chapter's opener involving **Vera Bradley** and its founder, Barbara Bradley.

**Required**

1. In a business such as Vera Bradley, monitoring cash flow is always a priority. Explain how cash flow can lag behind net income.

2. What are potential sources of financing for Vera Bradley's future expansion?

**ENTREPRENEURIAL DECISION**

C1   A1

**BTN 12-5**  Jenna and Matt Wilder are completing their second year operating Mountain High, a downhill ski area and resort. Mountain High reports a net loss of $(10,000) for its second year, which includes an $85,000 unusual loss from fire. This past year also involved major purchases of plant assets for renovation and expansion, yielding a year-end total asset amount of $800,000. Mountain High's net cash outflow for its second year is $(5,000); a summarized version of its statement of cash flows follows.

| | |
|---|---|
| Net cash flow provided by operating activities | $ 295,000 |
| Net cash flow used by investing activities | (310,000) |
| Net cash flow provided by financing activities | 10,000 |

**Required**

Write a one-page memorandum to the Wilders evaluating Mountain High's current performance and assessing its future. Give special emphasis to cash flow data and their interpretation.

**ENTREPRENEURIAL DECISION**

C1   A1

# 13 Analysis of Financial Statements

## Chapter Preview

### BASICS OF ANALYSIS

**C1** Analysis purpose

Building blocks

Standards for comparisons

Analysis tools

### HORIZONTAL ANALYSIS

**P1** Comparative balance sheets

Comparative income statements

Trend analysis

Data Visualizations

**NTK 13-1**

### VERTICAL ANALYSIS

**P2** Common-size balance sheet

Common-size income statement

Data Visualizations

**NTK 13-2**

### RATIO ANALYSIS AND REPORTING

**P3** Liquidity and efficiency

Solvency

Profitability

Market prospects

**A1** Analysis reports

**NTK 13-3**

## Learning Objectives

### CONCEPTUAL

**C1** Define the building blocks of analysis and the standards for comparisons.

### ANALYTICAL

**A1** Summarize and report results of analysis.

**A2** *Appendix 13A*—Explain the form and assess the content of a complete income statement.

### PROCEDURAL

**P1** Explain and apply methods of horizontal analysis.

**P2** Describe and apply methods of vertical analysis.

**P3** Define and apply ratio analysis.

# Accounting Analytics

*"Expect to win!"*—CARLA HARRIS

NEW YORK—"I grew up as an only child in a no-nonsense, no-excuses household," recalls Carla Harris. "My parents gave me the sense that I was supposed to do well." Fast-forward and Carla is now vice chair of **Morgan Stanley**'s (**MorganStanley.com**) prized Global Wealth Management division and past chair of the Morgan Stanley Foundation.

Carla Harris and her colleagues at Morgan Stanley analyze financial statements for profit. One of Morgan Stanley's key tools for analysis is *ModelWare*. ModelWare is a framework to analyze the nuts and bolts of companies' financial statements and then to compare those companies head-to-head.

Morgan Stanley uses the accounting numbers in financial statements to produce comparable metrics using techniques such as horizontal and vertical analysis. It also computes financial ratios for analysis and interpretation. Those ratios include return on equity, return on assets, asset turnover, profit margin, price-to-earnings, and many other accounting measures. The focus is to uncover the drivers of profitability and to predict future levels of those drivers.

Carla has experienced much success through analyzing financial statements. As Carla likes to say, "I'm tough and analytical!" She says that people do not take full advantage of information available in financial statements.

Marla Aufmuth/Getty Images

Carla plays by the rules and asserts that those with accounting skills earn profits from financial statement analysis and interpretation. Carla is proud of her success and adds: "Always start from a place of doing the right thing."

Sources: *Morgan Stanley website*, January 2021; *MorganStanleyIQ*, November 2007; *Alumni.HBS.edu/Stories*, September 2006; *Fortune*, August 2013 and March 2016

---

## BASICS OF ANALYSIS

**Financial statement analysis** applies analytical tools to financial statements and related data for making business decisions.

**C1** _____

Define the building blocks of analysis and the standards for comparisons.

### Purpose of Analysis

Internal users of accounting information manage and operate the company. They include managers, officers, and internal auditors. The purpose of financial statement analysis for internal users is to provide information to improve efficiency and effectiveness.

External users of accounting information are *not* directly involved in running the company. External users use financial statement analysis to pursue their own goals. Shareholders and creditors assess company performance to make investing and lending decisions. A board of directors analyzes financial statements to monitor management's performance. External auditors use financial statements to assess "fair presentation" of financial results.

The common goal of these users is to evaluate company performance and financial condition. This includes evaluating past and current performance, current financial position, and future performance and risk.

**Point:** Financial statement analysis is a topic on the CPA, CMA, CIA, and CFA exams.

### Building Blocks of Analysis

Financial statement analysis focuses on one or more of the four *building blocks* of financial statement analysis. The four building blocks cover different, but interrelated, aspects of financial condition or performance.

- **Liquidity** and **efficiency**—ability to meet short-term obligations and efficiently generate revenues.
- **Solvency**—ability to meet long-term obligations and generate future revenues.
- **Profitability**—ability to provide financial rewards to attract and retain financing.
- **Market prospects**—ability to generate positive market expectations.

## Information for Analysis

Financial analysis uses **general-purpose financial statements** that include the (1) income statement, (2) balance sheet, (3) statement of stockholders' equity (or statement of retained earnings), (4) statement of cash flows, and (5) notes to these statements.

**Financial reporting** is the communication of financial information useful for making investment, credit, and other business decisions. Financial reporting includes general-purpose financial statements, information from SEC 10-K and other filings, press releases, shareholders' meetings, forecasts, management letters, and auditors' reports.

Management's Discussion and Analysis (MD&A) is one example of useful information outside usual financial statements. **Apple**'s MD&A (available at **Investor.Apple.com**, see "Item 7" in the annual report) begins with an overview, followed by critical accounting policies and estimates. It then discusses operating results followed by financial condition (liquidity, capital resources, and cash flows). The final few parts discuss risks. The MD&A is an excellent starting point in understanding a company's business.

## Standards for Comparisons

When analyzing financial statements, we use the following standards (benchmarks) for comparisons. Benchmarks from a competitor or group of competitors are often best. Intracompany and industry measures are also good. Guidelines can be applied, but only if they seem reasonable given recent experience.

- *Intracompany*—The company's current performance is compared to its prior performance and its relations between financial items. Apple's current net income, for example, can be compared with its prior years' net income and in relation to its revenues or total assets.
- *Competitor*—Competitors provide standards for comparisons. **Coca-Cola**'s profit margin can be compared with **PepsiCo**'s profit margin.
- *Industry*—Industry statistics provide standards of comparisons. **Intel**'s profit margin can be compared with the industry's profit margin.
- *Guidelines (rules of thumb)*—Standards of comparison can develop from experience. Examples are the 2:1 level for the current ratio or 1:1 level for the acid-test ratio.

**Point:** Each chapter's Accounting Analysis assignments cover *intracompany* analysis. *Comparative Analysis* and *Extended Analysis* problems cover competitor analysis (**Apple** vs. **Google** vs. **Samsung**).

## Tools of Analysis

There are three common tools of financial statement analysis. This chapter describes these analysis tools and how to apply them.

1. **Horizontal analysis**—comparison of financial condition and performance across time.
2. **Vertical analysis**—comparison of financial condition and performance to a base amount.
3. **Ratio analysis**—measurement of key relations between financial statement items.

 **Decision Insight**

**Play the Market** *Blue chips* are stocks of big, established companies. The phrase comes from poker, where the most valuable chips are blue. *Brokers* execute orders to buy or sell stock. The term comes from wine retailers—individuals who broach (break) wine casks. ■

## HORIZONTAL ANALYSIS

**P1**
Explain and apply methods of horizontal analysis.

Horizontal analysis is the review of financial statement data *across time*. *Horizontal* comes from the left-to-right (or right-to-left) movement of our eyes as we review comparative financial statements across time.

### Comparative Statements

**Comparative financial statements** show financial amounts in side-by-side columns on a single statement, called a *comparative format*. Using **Apple**'s financial statements, this section explains how to compute dollar changes and percent changes for comparative statements.

## Dollar Changes and Percent Changes

Comparing financial statements is often done by analyzing dollar amount changes and percent changes in line items. Both analyses are relevant because small dollar changes can yield large percent changes inconsistent with their importance. A 50% change from a base figure of $100 is less important than a 50% change from a base amount of $100,000. We compute the *dollar change* for a financial statement item as follows.

$$\text{Dollar change} = \text{Analysis period amount} - \text{Base period amount}$$

*Analysis period* refers to the financial statements under analysis, and *base period* refers to the financial statements used for comparison. The prior year is commonly used as a base period. We compute the *percent change* as follows.

$$\text{Percent change (\%)} = \frac{\text{Analysis period amount} - \text{Base period amount}}{\text{Base period amount}} \times 100$$

We must know a few rules in working with percent changes. Let's look at four separate cases.

- **Cases A and B:** When a negative amount is in one period and a positive amount is in the other, we cannot compute a meaningful percent change.
- **Case C:** When no amount is in the base period, no percent change is computable.
- **Case D:** When a positive amount is in the base period and zero is in the analysis period, the decrease is 100%.

**Example:** When there is a value in the base period and zero in the analysis period, the decrease is 100%. Why isn't the reverse situation an increase of 100%? *Answer:* A 100% increase of zero is still zero.

| Case | Analysis Period | Base Period | Change Analysis Dollar | Change Analysis Percent |
|------|-----------------|-------------|--------|---------|
| A | $ 1,500 | $(4,500) | $ 6,000 | — |
| B | (1,000) | 2,000 | (3,000) | — |
| C | 8,000 | — | 8,000 | — |
| D | 0 | 10,000 | (10,000) | (100%) |

## Comparative Balance Sheets

Analysis of comparative financial statements begins by focusing on large dollar and percent changes. We then identify the reasons and implications for these changes. We also review small changes when we expected large changes.

Exhibit 13.1 shows comparative balance sheets for Apple Inc. (ticker: AAPL). A few items stand out on the asset side. Apple's long-term marketable securities decreased by $65,458 million, or 38.3%, in the current year. This substantial decrease is partially the result of many of these securities maturing or being sold. The substantial decrease also coincides with large increases in cash and cash equivalents and in short-term marketable securities. Cash and cash equivalents increased 88.5% and short-term marketable securities increased 28.0% in the current year. Looking at these changes, a user of accounting information could assume that Apple is shifting away from investing in long-term securities, and instead choosing to hold cash and cash equivalents or invest in short-term securities. This strategy has led to an increase in current assets of 24.0%, or $31,480 million, even while total assets decreased.

Looking at Apple's financing side, we see that total liabilities and equity declined by 7.4%, or $27,209 million. The 4.1% decrease in total liabilities is largely driven by a decrease in accounts payable, suggesting Apple made significant payments to suppliers in the current year or is potentially making fewer purchases on credit. The 15.5% reduction in equity is caused by a marked decrease in retained earnings, which results from Apple's share buyback and dividend plan. In reviewing Apple's financial statements in Appendix A, we see that dividends of $14,129 million and common stock repurchases of $67,101 million reduced retained earnings.

## Comparative Income Statements

Exhibit 13.2 shows Apple's comparative income statements. Apple reports a slight decrease in net sales of 2.0% and an 11.4% increase in total operating expenses, neither of which is favorable. The increase in operating expenses is mainly driven by the 13.9% increase in research and development costs, from which management

**EXHIBIT 13.1**

Comparative Balance Sheets

| APPLE INC. Comparative Year-End Balance Sheets | | | | |
|---|---|---|---|---|
| $ millions | Current Year | Prior Year | Dollar Change | Percent Change |
| **Assets** | | | | |
| Cash and cash equivalents . . . . . . . . . . . . . . . | $ 48,844 | $ 25,913 | $ 22,931 | 88.5% |
| Short-term marketable securities . . . . . . . . . . . | 51,713 | 40,388 | 11,325 | 28.0% |
| Accounts receivable, net . . . . . . . . . . . . . . . . . | 22,926 | 23,186 | (260) | (1.1)% |
| Inventories . . . . . . . . . . . . . . . . . . . . . . . . . . | 4,106 | 3,956 | 150 | 3.8% |
| Vendor nontrade receivables. . . . . . . . . . . . . . | 22,878 | 25,809 | (2,931) | (11.4)% |
| Other current assets. . . . . . . . . . . . . . . . . . . . | 12,352 | 12,087 | 265 | 2.2% |
| Total current assets . . . . . . . . . . . . . . . . . . | 162,819 | 131,339 | 31,480 | 24.0% |
| Long-term marketable securities. . . . . . . . . . . | 105,341 | 170,799 | (65,458) | (38.3)% |
| Property, plant and equipment, net. . . . . . . . . | 37,378 | 41,304 | (3,926) | (9.5)% |
| Other noncurrent assets. . . . . . . . . . . . . . . . . | 32,978 | 22,283 | 10,695 | 48.0% |
| Total assets. . . . . . . . . . . . . . . . . . . . . . . . . | $338,516 | $365,725 | $(27,209) | (7.4)% |
| **Liabilities** | | | | |
| Accounts payable . . . . . . . . . . . . . . . . . . . . . . | $ 46,236 | $ 55,888 | $ (9,652) | (17.3)% |
| Other current liabilities. . . . . . . . . . . . . . . . . . | 37,720 | 33,327 | 4,393 | 13.2% |
| Deferred revenue . . . . . . . . . . . . . . . . . . . . . . | 5,522 | 5,966 | (444) | (7.4)% |
| Commercial paper . . . . . . . . . . . . . . . . . . . . . | 5,980 | 11,964 | (5,984) | (50.0)% |
| Current portion of long-term debt . . . . . . . . . . | 10,260 | 8,784 | 1,476 | 16.8% |
| Total current liabilities . . . . . . . . . . . . . . . . | 105,718 | 115,929 | (10,211) | (8.8)% |
| Long-term debt. . . . . . . . . . . . . . . . . . . . . . . . | 91,807 | 93,735 | (1,928) | (2.1)% |
| Other noncurrent liabilities . . . . . . . . . . . . . . . | 50,503 | 48,914 | 1,589 | 3.2% |
| Total Liabilities . . . . . . . . . . . . . . . . . . . . . . | 248,028 | 258,578 | (10,550) | (4.1)% |
| **Stockholders' Equity** | | | | |
| Common stock . . . . . . . . . . . . . . . . . . . . . . . . | 45,174 | 40,201 | 4,973 | 12.4% |
| Retained earnings. . . . . . . . . . . . . . . . . . . . . . | 45,898 | 70,400 | (24,502) | (34.8)% |
| Accumulated other comprehensive income . . . . | (584) | (3,454) | 2,870 | — |
| Total stockholders' equity . . . . . . . . . . . . . . | 90,488 | 107,147 | (16,659) | (15.5)% |
| Total liabilities and stockholders' equity . . . . . . | $338,516 | $365,725 | $(27,209) | (7.4)% |

**EXHIBIT 13.2**

Comparative Income Statements

| APPLE INC. Comparative Income Statements | | | | |
|---|---|---|---|---|
| $ millions, except per share data | Current Year | Prior Year | Dollar Change | Percent Change |
| Net sales. . . . . . . . . . . . . . . . . . . . . . . . . . . . . | $260,174 | $265,595 | $(5,421) | (2.0)% |
| Cost of sales . . . . . . . . . . . . . . . . . . . . . . . . . . | 161,782 | 163,756 | (1,974) | (1.2)% |
| Gross margin. . . . . . . . . . . . . . . . . . . . . . . . . . | 98,392 | 101,839 | (3,447) | (3.4)% |
| Research and development . . . . . . . . . . . . . . . | 16,217 | 14,236 | 1,981 | 13.9% |
| Selling, general and administrative. . . . . . . . . . | 18,245 | 16,705 | 1,540 | 9.2% |
| Total operating expenses. . . . . . . . . . . . . . . . . | 34,462 | 30,941 | 3,521 | 11.4% |
| Operating income. . . . . . . . . . . . . . . . . . . . . . . | 63,930 | 70,898 | (6,968) | (9.8)% |
| Other income, net. . . . . . . . . . . . . . . . . . . . . . . | 1,807 | 2,005 | (198) | (9.9)% |
| Income before provision for income taxes . . . . . | 65,737 | 72,903 | (7,166) | (9.8)% |
| Provision for income taxes. . . . . . . . . . . . . . . . | 10,481 | 13,372 | (2,891) | (21.6)% |
| Net income . . . . . . . . . . . . . . . . . . . . . . . . . . . | $ 55,256 | $ 59,531 | (4,275) | (7.2)% |
| Basic earnings per share . . . . . . . . . . . . . . . . . | $ 11.97 | $ 12.01 | $ (0.04) | (0.3)% |
| Diluted earnings per share. . . . . . . . . . . . . . . . | $ 11.89 | $ 11.91 | $ (0.02) | (0.2)% |

**Point:** Percent change is also computed by dividing the current period by the prior period and then subtracting 1.0.

and investors hope to reap future income. We also see a decline in the provision for income taxes, which is the result of corporate tax decrease along with a lower income. Apple's net income decreased by 7.2%. However, its basic earnings per share only decreased 0.3%, mostly due to fewer shares outstanding because of Apple's share buyback policy.

## Trend Analysis

*Trend analysis* is computing trend percents that show patterns in data across periods. Trend percent is computed as follows.

$$\text{Trend percent (\%)} = \frac{\text{Analysis period amount}}{\text{Base period amount}} \times 100$$

Trend analysis is shown in Exhibit 13.3 using data from Apple's current and prior financial statements.

| $ millions | Current Yr | 1 Yr Ago | 2 Yrs Ago | 3 Yrs Ago | 4 Yrs Ago |
|---|---|---|---|---|---|
| Net sales | $260,174 | $265,595 | $229,234 | $215,639 | $233,715 |
| Cost of sales | 161,782 | 163,756 | 141,048 | 131,376 | 140,089 |
| Operating expenses | 34,462 | 30,941 | 26,842 | 24,239 | 22,396 |

**EXHIBIT 13.3**

Sales and Expenses

The trend percents—using data from Exhibit 13.3—are shown in Exhibit 13.4. The base period is the number reported four years ago, and the trend percent is computed for each year by dividing that year's amount by the base period amount. For example, the net sales trend percent for the current year is 111.3%, computed as $260,174/$233,715.

**Point:** Trend analysis expresses a percent of base, not a percent of change.

| In trend percent | Current Yr | 1 Yr Ago | 2 Yrs Ago | 3 Yrs Ago | 4 Yrs Ago |
|---|---|---|---|---|---|
| Net sales | 111.3% | 113.6% | 98.1% | 92.3% | 100.0% |
| Cost of sales | 115.5% | 116.9% | 100.7% | 93.8% | 100.0% |
| Operating expenses | 153.9% | 138.2% | 119.9% | 108.2% | 100.0% |

**EXHIBIT 13.4**

Trend Percents for Sales and Expenses

Exhibit 13.5 shows the trend percents from Exhibit 13.4 in a *line graph,* which helps us see trends and detect changes in direction or magnitude. It shows that the trend line for operating expenses exceeds net sales in each of the recent 3 years shown. This is not positive for Apple. Apple's net income will suffer if expenses rise faster than sales.

Exhibit 13.6 compares Apple's revenue trend line to those of **Google** and **Samsung**. Google was able to grow revenue in each year relative to the base year. Apple and Samsung were able to grow revenue overall in the last five years, but at a slower pace than Google.

Trend analysis can show relations between items on different

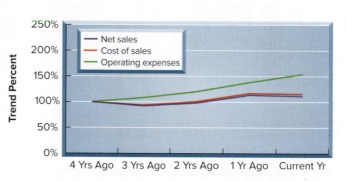

**EXHIBIT 13.5**

Trend Percent Lines for Sales and Expenses

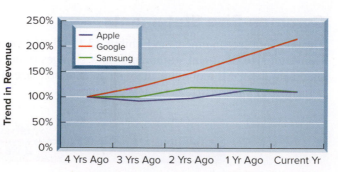

**EXHIBIT 13.6**

Revenue Trend Percent Lines

**EXHIBIT 13.7**

Sales and Asset Data

| $ millions | Current Yr | 4 Yrs Ago | Change |
|---|---|---|---|
| Net sales..... | $260,174 | $233,715 | 11.3% |
| Total assets... | 338,516 | 290,345 | 16.6% |

financial statements. Exhibit 13.7 compares Apple's net sales and total assets. The increase in total assets (16.6%) has exceeded the increase in net sales (11.3%). Is this result favorable or not? One interpretation is that Apple was *less* efficient in using its assets in the current year versus four years ago.

### Decision Maker

**Auditor**    Your tests reveal a 3% increase in sales from $200,000 to $206,000 and a 4% decrease in expenses from $190,000 to $182,400. Both changes are within your "reasonableness" criterion of ±5%, and thus you don't pursue additional tests. The audit partner in charge questions your lack of follow-up and mentions the *joint relation* between sales and expenses. What is the partner referring to? ■    *Answer:* Both *individual* accounts (sales and expenses) yield percent changes within the ±5% acceptable range. However, a *joint analysis* shows an increase in sales and a decrease in expenses producing a more than 5% increase in income. This client's profit margin is 11.46% (($206,000 − $182,400)/$206,000) for the current year compared with 5.0% (($200,000 − $190,000)/$200,000) for the prior year—a 129% increase!

---

**NEED-TO-KNOW 13-1**

Horizontal Analysis

**P1**

Compute trend percents for the following accounts using 3 Years Ago as the base year. Indicate whether the trend appears to be favorable or unfavorable for each account.

| $ millions | Current Yr | 1 Yr Ago | 2 Yrs Ago | 3 Yrs Ago |
|---|---|---|---|---|
| Sales ...................... | $500 | $350 | $250 | $200 |
| Cost of goods sold ........... | 400 | 175 | 100 | 50 |

*Solution*

| $ millions | Current Yr | 1 Yr Ago | 2 Yrs Ago | 3 Yrs Ago |
|---|---|---|---|---|
| Sales ...................... | 250% | 175% | 125% | 100% |
| | ($500/$200) | ($350/$200) | ($250/$200) | ($200/$200) |
| Cost of goods sold ........... | 800% | 350% | 200% | 100% |
| | ($400/$50) | ($175/$50) | ($100/$50) | ($50/$50) |

*Analysis:* The trend in sales is favorable; however, we need more information about economic conditions and competitors' performances to better assess it. Cost of goods sold also is rising (as expected with increasing sales). However, cost of goods sold is rising faster than the increase in sales, which is bad news.

Do More: QS 13-3, QS 13-4, QS 13-5, QS 13-6, E 13-3

---

## VERTICAL ANALYSIS

**P2**

Describe and apply methods of vertical analysis.

Vertical analysis, or *common-size analysis,* is used to evaluate individual financial statement items or a group of items. *Vertical* comes from the up-down [or down-up] movement of our eyes as we review common-size financial statements.

### Common-Size Statements

**Point:** Numerator and denominator in common-size percent are taken from the same financial statement and from the same period.

The comparative statements in Exhibits 13.1 and 13.2 show the change in each item over time. **Common-size financial statements** show changes in the relative importance of each financial statement item. All individual amounts in common-size statements are shown in common-size percents. A *common-size percent* is calculated as

$$\text{Common-size percent (\%)} = \frac{\text{Analysis amount}}{\text{Base amount}} \times 100$$

## Common-Size Balance Sheets

Common-size statements show each item as a percent of a *base amount,* which for a common-size balance sheet is total assets. The base amount is assigned a value of 100%. (Total liabilities plus equity also equals 100% because this amount equals total assets.) We then compute a common-size percent for each asset, liability, and equity item using total assets as the base amount.

Exhibit 13.8 shows common-size comparative balance sheets for **Apple**. Two results that stand out on both a magnitude and percentage basis include (1) an increase in cash and cash equivalents and in short-term marketable securities and (2) a decrease in long-term marketable securities. These changes may represent a shift in Apple strategy to keep excess funds in cash and cash equivalents and short-term securities, instead of long-term securities.

The common-size percents also reveal Apple's smaller retained earnings balance, which is the result of cash dividends and stock buybacks. Relatively minor changes across the rest of the balance sheet are common among mature companies such as Apple.

**Point:** Common-size statements often are used to compare companies in the same industry.

**EXHIBIT 13.8**

Common-Size Comparative Balance Sheets

| APPLE INC. Common-Size Comparative Balance Sheets | | | Common-Size Percents* | |
|---|---|---|---|---|
| $ millions | Current Year | Prior Year | Current Year | Prior Year |
| **Assets** | | | | |
| Cash and cash equivalents ............... | $ 48,844 | $ 25,913 | 14.4% | 7.1% |
| Short-term marketable securities .......... | 51,713 | 40,388 | 15.3% | 11.0% |
| Accounts receivable, net ................. | 22,926 | 23,186 | 6.8% | 6.3% |
| Inventories ........................... | 4,106 | 3,956 | 1.2% | 1.1% |
| Vendor nontrade receivables.............. | 22,878 | 25,809 | 6.8% | 7.1% |
| Other current assets..................... | 12,352 | 12,087 | 3.6% | 3.3% |
| Total current assets ................... | 162,819 | 131,339 | 48.1% | 35.9% |
| Long-term marketable securities........... | 105,341 | 170,799 | 31.1% | 46.7% |
| Property, plant and equipment, net......... | 37,378 | 41,304 | 11.0% | 11.3% |
| Other noncurrent assets.................. | 32,978 | 22,283 | 9.7% | 6.1% |
| Total assets........................... | $338,516 | $365,725 | 100.0% | 100.0% |
| **Liabilities** | | | | |
| Accounts payable........................ | $ 46,236 | $ 55,888 | 13.7% | 15.3% |
| Other current liabilities.................. | 37,720 | 33,327 | 11.1% | 9.1% |
| Deferred revenue ....................... | 5,522 | 5,966 | 1.6% | 1.6% |
| Commercial Paper ...................... | 5,980 | 11,964 | 1.8% | 3.3% |
| Current portion of long-term debt .......... | 10,260 | 8,784 | 3.0% | 2.4% |
| Total current liabilities ................ | 105,718 | 115,929 | 31.2% | 31.7% |
| Long-term debt......................... | 91,807 | 93,735 | 27.1% | 25.6% |
| Other noncurrent liabilities ............... | 50,503 | 48,914 | 14.9% | 13.4% |
| Total Liabilities ....................... | 248,028 | 258,578 | 73.3% | 70.7% |
| **Stockholders' Equity** | | | | |
| Common stock ......................... | 45,174 | 40,201 | 13.3% | 11.0% |
| Retained earnings....................... | 45,898 | 70,400 | 13.6% | 19.2% |
| Accumulated other comprehensive income .. | (584) | (3,454) | (0.2)% | (0.9)% |
| Total stockholders' equity ............... | 90,488 | 107,147 | 26.7% | 29.3% |
| Total liabilities and stockholders' equity ..... | $338,516 | $365,725 | 100.0% | 100.0% |

*Percents are rounded to tenths and thus may not exactly sum to totals and subtotals.

## Common-Size Income Statements

Analysis also involves the use of a common-size income statement. Revenue is the base amount, which is assigned a value of 100%. Each income statement item is shown as a percent of revenue. If we think of the 100% revenue amount as representing one sales dollar, the remaining items show how each revenue dollar is distributed among costs, expenses, and income.

**EXHIBIT 13.9**

Common-Size Comparative
Income Statements

| | APPLE INC. Common-Size Comparative Income Statements | | Common Size Percents* | |
|---|---|---|---|---|
| $ millions | Current Yr | Prior Yr | Current Yr | Prior Yr |
| Net sales | $260,174 | $265,595 | 100.0% | 100.0% |
| Cost of sales | 161,782 | 163,756 | 62.2% | 61.7% |
| Gross margin | 98,392 | 101,839 | 37.8% | 38.3% |
| Research and development | 16,217 | 14,236 | 6.2% | 5.4% |
| Selling, general and administrative | 18,245 | 16,705 | 7.0% | 6.3% |
| Total operating expenses | 34,462 | 30,941 | 13.2% | 11.6% |
| Operating income | 63,930 | 70,898 | 24.6% | 26.7% |
| Other income, net | 1,807 | 2,005 | 0.7% | 0.8% |
| Income before provision for income taxes | 65,737 | 72,903 | 25.3% | 27.4% |
| Provision for income taxes | 10,481 | 13,372 | 4.0% | 5.0% |
| Net income | $ 55,256 | $ 59,531 | 21.2% | 22.4% |

*Percents are rounded to tenths and thus may not exactly sum to totals and subtotals.

Exhibit 13.9 shows common-size comparative income statements for each dollar of Apple's net sales. The past two years' common-size numbers are similar with two exceptions. One is the increase of 0.8 cents in research and development costs, which can be a positive development if these costs lead to future revenues. Another is the decrease in provision for income taxes, which mainly results from a lower corporate tax rate.

**EXHIBIT 13.10**

Common-Size Graphic of
Income Statement

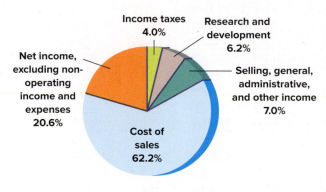

## Data Visualizations

Data visualizations reveal trends and insights not easily seen by looking at numbers. **Tableau Dashboard Activities** (available in **Connect**) have students practice interpreting graphics and making business decisions. Exhibit 13.10 is a graphic of Apple's current year common-size income statement. This pie chart shows the contribution of each cost component of net sales for net income.

Exhibit 13.11 takes data from Apple's *Segments* footnote. The exhibit shows the level of net sales for each of Apple's five operating segments. Its Americas segment generates $116.9 billion net sales, which is roughly 45% of its total sales ($116.9 bil./$260.174 bil.). Within each bar is that segment's operating income margin (Operating income/Segment net sales). The Americas segment has a 30% operating income margin. This type of graphic can raise questions about the profitability of each segment and lead to discussion of further expansions into more profitable segments. For example, the Japan segment has an operating margin of 44%. A natural question for management is what potential is there to expand sales into the Japan segment

**EXHIBIT 13.11**

Sales and Operating
Income Margin by Segment

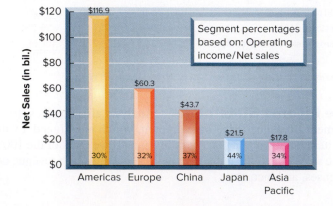

and maintain this operating margin? This type of analysis can help determine strategic plans.

Visualizations also are used to identify (1) sources of financing, including the distribution among current liabilities, noncurrent liabilities, and equity capital, and (2) types of investing activities, including the distribution among current and noncurrent assets. Exhibit 13.12 shows a visualization of Apple's assets, a high percentage of which are in securities, followed by property, plant and equipment.

Common-size financial statements are useful in comparing companies. Exhibit 13.13 shows visualizations of Apple, Google, and Samsung on financing sources. This graphic shows the larger percent of equity financing for Google and Samsung versus Apple. It also shows the larger noncurrent debt financing of Apple versus Google and Samsung. Comparison of a company's common-size statements with competitors' or industry common-size statistics alerts us to differences in the structure of its financing.

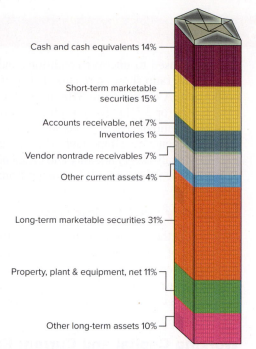

**EXHIBIT 13.12**

Data visualization of Asset Components

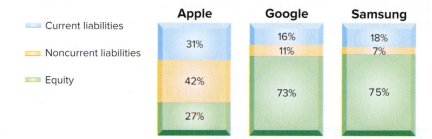

**EXHIBIT 13.13**

Data visualization of Financing Sources

### Ethical Risk

**To Tell The Truth** In a survey of nearly 200 CFOs of large companies, roughly 20% say that firms use accounting tools to report earnings that do not fully reflect the firms' underlying operations. One goal of financial analysis is to see through such ploys. The top reasons CFOs gave for this were to impact stock price, hit an earnings target, and influence executive pay (*Wall Street Journal*). ■

---

Express the following comparative income statements in common-size percents and assess whether this company's situation has improved in the current year.

**NEED-TO-KNOW** 13-2

Vertical Analysis

P2

| Comparative Income Statements | | |
|---|---|---|
| For Years Ended December 31 | Current Yr | Prior Yr |
| Sales ........................... | $800 | $500 |
| Total expenses .................... | 560 | 400 |
| Net income ...................... | $240 | $100 |

**Solution**

| | Current Yr | Prior Yr |
|---|---|---|
| Sales ........... | 100% ($800/$800) | 100% ($500/$500) |
| Total expenses .... | 70% ($560/$800) | 80% ($400/$500) |
| Net income ....... | 30% | 20% |

*Analysis:* This company's situation has improved. This is evident from its substantial increase in net income as a percent of sales for the current year (30%) relative to the prior year (20%). Further, the company's sales increased from $500 to $800 (while expenses declined as a percent of sales from 80% to 70%).

Do More: QS 13-7, QS 13-8, E 13-4, E 13-5, E 13-6

# RATIO ANALYSIS

**P3**
Define and apply ratio analysis.

Ratios are used to uncover conditions and trends difficult to detect by looking at individual amounts. A ratio shows a relation between two amounts. It can be shown as a percent, rate, or proportion. A change from $100 to $250 can be shown as (1) 150% increase, (2) 2.5 times, or (3) 2.5 to 1 (or 2.5:1). To be useful, a ratio must show an economically important relation. For example, a ratio of cost of goods sold to sales is useful, but a ratio of freight costs to patents is not.

This section covers important financial ratios organized into the four building blocks of financial statement analysis: (1) liquidity and efficiency, (2) solvency, (3) profitability, and (4) market prospects. We use four standards for comparison: intracompany, competitor, industry, and guidelines.

## Liquidity and Efficiency

*Liquidity* is the availability of resources to pay short-term cash requirements. It is affected by the timing of cash inflows and outflows along with prospects for future performance. A lack of liquidity often is linked to lower profitability. To creditors, lack of liquidity can cause delays in collecting payments. *Efficiency* is how productive a company is in using its assets. Inefficient use of assets can cause liquidity problems. This section covers key ratios used to assess liquidity and efficiency.

**Working Capital and Current Ratio**   The amount of current assets minus current liabilities is called **working capital,** or *net working capital.* A company that runs low on working capital is less likely to pay debts or to continue operating. When evaluating a company's working capital, we look at the dollar amount of current assets minus current liabilities *and* at their ratio. The *current ratio* is defined as follows.

$$\text{Current ratio} = \frac{\text{Current assets}}{\text{Current liabilities}}$$

**EXHIBIT 13.14**

Working Capital and Current Ratio

Current ratio
Google = 3.37
Samsung = 2.84
Industry = 2.5

| $ millions | Current Yr | Prior Yr |
|---|---|---|
| Current assets............. | $162,819 | $131,339 |
| Current liabilities........... | 105,718 | 115,929 |
| **Working capital**........... | **$ 57,101** | **$ 15,410** |
| **Current ratio** | | |
| $162,819/$105,718 = | **1.54 to 1** | |
| $131,339/$115,929 = | | **1.13 to 1** |

**Apple**'s working capital and current ratio are shown in Exhibit 13.14. Also, **Google**'s (3.37), **Samsung**'s (2.84), and the industry's (2.5) current ratios are shown in the margin. Although its ratio (1.54) is lower than competitors' ratios, Apple is not in danger of defaulting on loan payments. A high current ratio suggests a strong ability to meet current obligations. An excessively high current ratio can mean that the company has invested too much in current assets compared to current obligations. An excessive investment in current assets is not an efficient use of funds because current assets normally earn a low return on investment (compared with long-term assets).

Many analysts use a guideline of 2:1 (or 1.5:1) for the current ratio. A 2:1 or higher ratio is considered low risk in the short run. Analysis of the current ratio, and many other ratios, must consider type of business, composition of current assets, and turnover rate of current asset components.

- **Business Type**   A service company that grants little or no credit and carries few inventories can probably operate on a current ratio of less than 1:1 if its revenues generate enough cash to pay its current liabilities. On the other hand, a company selling high-priced clothing or furniture requires a higher ratio because of difficulties in judging customer demand and cash receipts.

- **Asset Composition**   The composition of assets is important to assess short-term liquidity. For instance, cash, cash equivalents, and short-term investments are more liquid than accounts and notes receivable. An excessive amount of receivables and inventory weakens a company's ability to pay current liabilities.

- **Turnover Rate**   Asset turnover measures efficiency in using assets. A measure of asset efficiency is revenue generated.

**Global:** Ratio analysis is unaffected by currency but is affected by differences in accounting principles.

### ■ Decision Maker

**Banker** A company requests a one-year, $200,000 loan for expansion. This company's current ratio is 4:1, with current assets of $160,000. Key competitors have a current ratio of 1.9:1. Using this information, do you approve the loan? ■ *Answer:* The loan application is likely approved for at least two reasons. First, the current ratio suggests an ability to meet short-term obligations. Second, current assets of $160,000 and a current ratio of 4:1 imply current liabilities of $40,000 (one-fourth of current assets) and a working capital excess of $120,000. The working capital is 60% of the loan.

## Acid-Test Ratio

Quick assets are cash, short-term investments, and current receivables. These are the most liquid types of current assets. The *acid-test ratio,* also called *quick ratio* evaluates a company's short-term liquidity.

$$\text{Acid-test ratio} = \frac{\text{Cash} + \text{Short-term investments} + \text{Current receivables}}{\text{Current liabilities}}$$

Apple's acid-test ratio is computed in Exhibit 13.15. Apple's acid-test ratio (1.17) is lower than those for Google (3.21) and Samsung (2.32), but it is higher than the 1:1 guideline for an acceptable acid-test ratio. As with analysis of the current ratio, we must consider other factors. How frequently a company converts its current assets into cash also affects its ability to pay current obligations. This means analysis of short-term liquidity should consider receivables and inventories, which we cover next.

**EXHIBIT 13.15**

Acid-Test Ratio

| $ millions | Current Yr | Prior Yr |
|---|---|---|
| Cash and equivalents............ | $ 48,844 | $ 25,913 |
| Short-term securities ............ | 51,713 | 40,388 |
| Current receivables ............. | 22,926 | 23,186 |
| Total quick assets .............. | $123,483 | $ 89,487 |
| Current liabilities............... | $105,718 | $115,929 |
| **Acid-test ratio** | | |
| $123,483/$105,718 = | **1.17 to 1** | |
| $89,487/$115,929 = | | **0.77 to 1** |

**Acid-test ratio**
Google = 3.21
Samsung = 2.32
Industry = 0.9

## Accounts Receivable Turnover

*Accounts receivable turnover* measures how frequently a company converts its receivables into cash. This ratio is defined as follows. Apple's accounts receivable turnover is computed next to the formula ($ millions). Apple's turnover of 11.3 exceeds Google's 7.0 and Samsung's 6.7 turnover. Accounts receivable turnover is high when accounts receivable are quickly collected. A high turnover is favorable because it means the company does not tie up assets in accounts receivable. However, accounts receivable turnover can be too high; this can occur when credit terms are so restrictive that they decrease sales.

**Accounts receivable turnover**
Google = 7.0
Samsung = 6.7
Industry = 5.0

$$\frac{\text{Accounts receivable}}{\text{turnover}} = \frac{\text{Net sales}}{\text{Average accounts receivable, net}} = \frac{\$260,174}{(\$23,186 + \$22,926)/2} = 11.3 \text{ times}$$

## Inventory Turnover

*Inventory turnover* measures how long a company holds inventory before selling it. It is defined as follows. Next to the formula we compute Apple's inventory turnover at 40.1. Apple's inventory turnover is higher than Samsung's 5.3 but lower than Google's 68.3. A company with a high turnover requires a smaller investment in inventory than one producing the same sales with a lower turnover. However, high inventory turnover can be bad if inventory is so low that stock-outs occur.

**Inventory turnover**
Google = 68.3
Samsung = 5.3
Industry = 7.0

$$\text{Inventory turnover} = \frac{\text{Cost of goods sold}}{\text{Average inventory}} = \frac{\$161,782}{(\$3,956 + \$4,106)/2} = 40.1 \text{ times}$$

## Days' Sales Uncollected

*Days' sales uncollected* measures how frequently a company collects accounts receivable and is defined as follows. Apple's days' sales uncollected of 32.2 days is shown next to the formula. Both Google's days' sales uncollected of 57.1 days and Samsung's 62.3 days are more than the 32.2 days for Apple. Days' sales uncollected is more meaningful if we know company credit terms. A rough guideline is that days' sales uncollected should not

exceed 1⅓ times the days in its (1) credit period, *if* discounts are not offered, or (2) discount period, *if* favorable discounts are offered.

$$\text{Days' sales uncollected} = \frac{\text{Accounts receivable, net}}{\text{Net sales}} \times 365 = \frac{\$22,926}{\$260,174} \times 365 = 32.2 \text{ days}$$

### Days' Sales in Inventory

*Days' sales in inventory* is used to evaluate inventory liquidity. We compute days' sales in inventory as follows. Apple's days' sales in inventory of 9.3 days is shown next to the formula. If the products in Apple's inventory are in demand by customers, this formula estimates that its inventory will be converted into receivables (or cash) in 9.3 days. If all of Apple's sales were credit sales, the conversion of inventory to receivables in 9.3 days *plus* the conversion of receivables to cash in 32.2 days implies that inventory will be converted to cash in about 41.5 days (9.3 + 32.2).

$$\text{Days' sales in inventory} = \frac{\text{Ending inventory}}{\text{Cost of goods sold}} \times 365 = \frac{\$4,106}{\$161,782} \times 365 = 9.3 \text{ days}$$

### Total Asset Turnover

*Total asset turnover* measures a company's ability to use its assets to generate sales and reflects on operating efficiency. The definition of this ratio follows. Apple's total asset turnover of 0.74 is shown next to the formula. Apple's turnover is greater than that for Google (0.64) and Samsung (0.67).

$$\text{Total asset turnover} = \frac{\text{Net sales}}{\text{Average total assets}} = \frac{\$260,174}{(\$338,516 + \$365,725)/2} = 0.74 \text{ times}$$

## Solvency

*Solvency* is a company's ability to meet long-term obligations and generate future revenues. Analysis of solvency is long term and uses broader measures than liquidity. An important part of solvency analysis is a company's capital structure. *Capital structure* is a company's makeup of equity and debt financing. Our analysis here focuses on a company's ability to both meet its obligations and provide security to its creditors *over the long run*.

### Debt Ratio and Equity Ratio

One part of solvency analysis is to assess a company's mix of debt and equity financing. The *debt ratio* shows total liabilities as a percent of total assets. The **equity ratio** shows total equity as a percent of total assets. Apple's debt and equity ratios follow. Apple's ratios reveal more debt than equity. A company is considered less risky if its capital structure (equity plus debt) has more equity. Debt is considered more risky because of its required payments for interest and principal. Stockholders cannot require payment from the company. However, debt can increase income for stockholders if the company earns a higher return than interest paid on the debt.

| Apple, $ millions | Current Year | Ratios | |
|---|---|---|---|
| Total liabilities . . . . . . . . . . . . . | $248,028 | 73.3% | [Debt ratio] |
| Total equity . . . . . . . . . . . . . . | 90,488 | 26.7% | [Equity ratio] |
| Total liabilities and equity. . . . . | $338,516 | 100.0% | |

### Debt-to-Equity Ratio

The *debt-to-equity* ratio is another measure of solvency. We compute the ratio as follows. Apple's debt-to-equity ratio of 2.74 is shown next to the formula. Apple's ratio is higher than those of Google (0.37) and Samsung (0.34), and greater than the industry ratio of 0.6. Apple's capital structure has more debt than equity. Debt must be repaid with interest, while equity does not. Debt payments can be burdensome when the industry and/or the economy experience a downturn.

$$\text{Debt-to-equity ratio} = \frac{\text{Total liabilities}}{\text{Total equity}} = \frac{\$248,028}{\$90,488} = 2.74$$

**Debt-to-equity**
**Google = 0.37**
**Samsung = 0.34**
**Industry = 0.6**

### Times Interest Earned

The amount of income before subtracting interest expense and income tax expense is the amount available to pay interest expense. The following *times interest earned* ratio measures a company's ability to pay interest.

$$\text{Times interest earned} = \frac{\text{Income before interest expense and income tax expense}}{\text{Interest expense}}$$

The larger this ratio is, the less risky the company is for creditors. One guideline says that creditors are reasonably safe if the company has a ratio of two or more. Apple's times interest earned ratio of 19.4 follows. It suggests that creditors have little risk of nonrepayment.

$$\frac{\$55,256 + \$3,576 + \$10,481}{\$3,576} = 19.4 \text{ times}$$

**Times interest earned**
**Google = 397.3**
**Samsung = 46.3**

## Profitability

*Profitability* is a company's ability to earn an adequate return. This section covers key profitability measures.

### Gross Margin Ratio

*Gross margin ratio* is a company's percent of gross margin in each dollar of net sales. Gross margin is net sales minus cost of goods sold. The gross margin ratio is the amount of each dollar left over to cover all other operating expenses and still yield a profit. Apple's gross margin ratio is 37.8%; see its calculation next to the formula. Apple's 37.8% profit margin is lower than Google's 55.6% but higher than Samsung's 36.1% and the industry's 30% margin.

$$\text{Gross margin ratio} = \frac{\text{Net sales} - \text{Cost of goods sold}}{\text{Net sales}} = \frac{\$260,174 - \$161,782}{\$260,174} = 37.8\%$$

**Gross margin**
**Google = 55.6%**
**Samsung = 36.1%**
**Industry = 30%**

### Profit Margin

*Profit margin* measures a company's ability to earn net income from sales. Apple's profit margin of 21.2% is shown next to the formula. To evaluate profit margin, we must consider the industry. For instance, an appliance company might require a profit margin of 15%, whereas a retail supermarket might require a profit margin of 2%. Apple's 21.2% profit margin is the same as Google's 21.2%, but higher than Samsung's 9.4% and the industry's 11% margin.

$$\text{Profit margin} = \frac{\text{Net income}}{\text{Net sales}} = \frac{\$55,256}{\$260,174} = 21.2\%$$

**Profit margin**
**Google = 21.2%**
**Samsung = 9.4%**
**Industry = 11%**

### Return on Total Assets

*Return on total assets* is defined as follows. Apple's return on total assets of 15.7% is shown next to the formula. Apple's 15.7% return on total assets is higher than Google's 13.5%, Samsung's 6.3%, and the industry's 8%. We also should evaluate any trend in the return.

$$\text{Return on total assets} = \frac{\text{Net income}}{\text{Average total assets}} = \frac{\$55,256}{(\$338,516 + \$365,725)/2} = 15.7\%$$

**Return on total assets**
**Google = 13.5%**
**Samsung = 6.3%**
**Industry = 8%**

The relation between profit margin, total asset turnover, and return on total assets follows.

$$\text{Profit margin} \times \text{Total asset turnover} = \text{Return on total assets}$$

$$\frac{\text{Net income}}{\text{Net sales}} \times \frac{\text{Net sales}}{\text{Average total assets}} = \frac{\text{Net income}}{\text{Average total assets}}$$

Both profit margin and total asset turnover affect operating efficiency, as measured by return on total assets. This formula is applied to Apple as follows. This analysis shows that Apple's superior return on assets versus that of Google is driven by its higher asset turnover.

Google = 21.2% × 0.64 ≃13.6%
Samsung = 9.4% × 0.67 ≃ 6.3%
(with rounding)

$$21.2\% \times 0.74 = 15.7\% \text{ (with rounding)}$$

### Return on Equity

An important goal in operating a company is to earn income for its owner(s). *Return on equity* measures a company's ability to earn income for its stockholders and is defined as follows.

$$\text{Return on equity} = \frac{\text{Net income}}{\text{Average total equity}}$$

Apple's return on equity is computed as follows. Apple's 55.9% return on equity is superior to Google's 18.1% and Samsung's 8.4%.

**Return on equity**
Google = 18.1%
Samsung = 8.4%
Industry = 15%

$$\frac{\$55,256}{(\$107,147 + \$90,488)/2} = 55.9\%$$

### ◼ Decision Insight

**Shiver Me Timbers**   *Wall Street* is synonymous with financial markets, but its name comes from the street location of the original New York Stock Exchange. The street's name comes from stockades built by early settlers to protect New York from pirate attacks. ◼

## Market Prospects

Market measures are useful for analyzing corporations with publicly traded stock. These market measures use stock price, which reflects the market's (public's) expectations for the company. This includes market expectations of both company return and risk.

### Price-Earnings Ratio

Computation of the *price-earnings ratio* follows. This ratio is used to measure market expectations for future growth. The market price of Apple's common stock at the start of the current fiscal year was $293.65. Using Apple's $11.97 basic earnings per share, we compute its price-earnings ratio as follows. Apple's price-earnings ratio is less than that for Google, but it is higher than that for Samsung and the industry.

**Point:** Low expectations = low PE. High expectations = high PE.

**PE (year-end)**
Google = 27.0
Samsung = 17.6
Industry = 11

$$\text{Price-earnings ratio} = \frac{\text{Market price per common share}}{\text{Earnings per share}} = \frac{\$293.65}{\$11.97} = 24.5$$

### Dividend Yield

*Dividend yield* is used to compare the dividend-paying performance of different companies. We compute dividend yield as follows. Apple's dividend yield of 1.0%, based on its fiscal year-end market price per share of $293.65 and its $3.00 cash dividends per share, is shown next to the formula. Some companies, such as Google, do not pay dividends because they reinvest the cash to grow their businesses in the hope of generating greater future earnings and dividends.

**Dividend yield**
Google = 0.0%
Samsung = 2.5%

$$\text{Dividend yield} = \frac{\text{Annual cash dividends per share}}{\text{Market price per share}} = \frac{\$3.00}{\$293.65} = 1.0\%$$

### ◼ Decision Insight

Reinhard Dachlauer/Amirphoto/ Panther Media GmbH/Alamy Stock Photo

**Bulls and Bears**   A *bear market* is a declining market. The phrase comes from bear-skin hunters who sold the skins before the bears were caught. The term *bear* was then used to describe investors who sold shares they did not own in anticipation of a price decline. A *bull market* is a rising market. This phrase comes from the once-popular sport of bear and bull baiting. The term *bull* means the opposite of *bear.* ◼

# Summary of Ratios

Exhibit 13.16 summarizes the ratios in this chapter and many of those in the book to this point.

**EXHIBIT 13.16**

Financial Statement Analysis Ratios

| Ratio | Formula | Measure of |
|---|---|---|
| **Liquidity and Efficiency** | | |
| Current ratio | $=\dfrac{\text{Current assets}}{\text{Current liabilities}}$ | Short-term debt-paying ability |
| Acid-test ratio | $=\dfrac{\text{Cash + Short-term investments + Current receivables}}{\text{Current liabilities}}$ | Immediate short-term debt-paying ability |
| Accounts receivable turnover | $=\dfrac{\text{Net sales}}{\text{Average accounts receivable, net}}$ | Efficiency of collection |
| Inventory turnover | $=\dfrac{\text{Cost of goods sold}}{\text{Average inventory}}$ | Efficiency of inventory management |
| Days' sales uncollected | $=\dfrac{\text{Accounts receivable, net}}{\text{Net sales}} \times 365$ | Liquidity of receivables |
| Days' sales in inventory | $=\dfrac{\text{Ending inventory}}{\text{Cost of goods sold}} \times 365$ | Liquidity of inventory |
| Total asset turnover | $=\dfrac{\text{Net sales}}{\text{Average total assets}}$ | Efficiency of assets in producing sales |
| **Solvency** | | |
| Debt ratio | $=\dfrac{\text{Total liabilities}}{\text{Total assets}}$ | Creditor financing and leverage |
| Equity ratio | $=\dfrac{\text{Total equity}}{\text{Total assets}}$ | Owner financing |
| Debt-to-equity ratio | $=\dfrac{\text{Total liabilities}}{\text{Total equity}}$ | Debt versus equity financing |
| Times interest earned | $=\dfrac{\text{Income before interest expense and income tax expense}}{\text{Interest expense}}$ | Protection in meeting interest payments |
| **Profitability** | | |
| Profit margin ratio | $=\dfrac{\text{Net income}}{\text{Net sales}}$ | Net income in each sales dollar |
| Gross margin ratio | $=\dfrac{\text{Net sales − Cost of goods sold}}{\text{Net sales}}$ | Gross margin in each sales dollar |
| Return on total assets | $=\dfrac{\text{Net income}}{\text{Average total assets}}$ | Overall profitability of assets |
| Return on equity | $=\dfrac{\text{Net income}}{\text{Average total equity}}$ | Profitability of owner investment |
| Basic earnings per share | $=\dfrac{\text{Net income − Preferred dividends}}{\text{Weighted-average common shares outstanding}}$ | Net income per common share |
| **Market Prospects** | | |
| Price-earnings ratio | $=\dfrac{\text{Market price per common share}}{\text{Earnings per share}}$ | Market value relative to earnings |
| Dividend yield | $=\dfrac{\text{Annual cash dividends per share}}{\text{Market price per share}}$ | Cash return per common share |

**NEED-TO-KNOW 13-3**

Ratio Analysis

**P3**

For each ratio listed, identify whether the change in ratio value from the prior year to the current year is favorable or unfavorable.

| Ratio | Current Yr | Prior Yr | Ratio | Current Yr | Prior Yr |
|---|---|---|---|---|---|
| 1. Profit margin ........... | 6% | 8% | 4. Accounts receivable turnover...... | 8.8 | 9.4 |
| 2. Debt ratio.............. | 50% | 70% | 5. Basic earnings per share ......... | $2.10 | $2.00 |
| 3. Gross margin ........... | 40% | 36% | 6. Inventory turnover............... | 3.6 | 4.0 |

**Solution**

| Ratio | Current Yr | Prior Yr | Change |
|---|---|---|---|
| 1. Profit margin ratio...................... | 6% | 8% | Unfavorable |
| 2. Debt ratio........................... | 50% | 70% | Favorable |
| 3. Gross margin ratio..................... | 40% | 36% | Favorable |
| 4. Accounts receivable turnover............. | 8.8 | 9.4 | Unfavorable |
| 5. Basic earnings per share ................ | $2.10 | $2.00 | Favorable |
| 6. Inventory turnover..................... | 3.6 | 4.0 | Unfavorable |

Do More: QS 13-9 through
QS 13-17, E 13-7 through
E 13-16

---

**Decision Analysis**      ■ ■ ■   Analysis Reporting

**A1**
_____

Summarize and report
results of analysis.

A *financial statement analysis report* usually consists of six sections.

1. **Executive summary**—brief analysis of results and conclusions.
2. **Analysis overview**—background on the company, its industry, and the economy.
3. **Evidential matter**—financial statements and information used in the analysis, including ratios, trends, comparisons, and all analytical measures used.
4. **Assumptions**—list of assumptions about a company's industry and economic environment, and other assumptions underlying estimates.
5. **Key factors**—list of favorable and unfavorable factors, both quantitative and qualitative, for company performance; usually organized by areas of analysis.
6. **Inferences**—forecasts, estimates, interpretations, and conclusions of the analysis report.

We must remember that the user dictates relevance, meaning that the analysis report should include a brief table of contents to help readers focus on those areas most relevant to their decisions. Finally, writing is important. Mistakes in grammar and errors of fact compromise the report's credibility.

■ **Decision Insight** ━━━━━━━━━━━━━━━━━━━━━━━━━━━

**Going Short**   *Short selling* refers to selling stock before you buy it. Here's an example: You borrow 100 shares of **Nike** stock, sell them at $55 each, and receive money from their sale. You then wait. You hope that Nike's stock price falls to, say, $50 each and you can replace the borrowed stock for less than you sold it, reaping a profit of $5 each less any transaction costs. ■

---

**NEED-TO-KNOW 13-4**

**COMPREHENSIVE**

Applying Horizontal,
Vertical, and Ratio
Analyses

Use the following financial statements of Precision Co. to complete these requirements.

1. Prepare comparative income statements showing the percent increase or decrease for the current year in comparison to the prior year.
2. Prepare common-size comparative balance sheets for both years.
3. Compute the following ratios for the current year and identify each one's building block category for financial statement analysis.

   a. Current ratio
   b. Acid-test ratio
   c. Accounts receivable turnover
   d. Days' sales uncollected
   e. Inventory turnover
   f. Debt ratio

   g. Debt-to-equity ratio
   h. Times interest earned
   i. Profit margin ratio
   j. Total asset turnover
   k. Return on total assets
   l. Return on equity

| PRECISION COMPANY Comparative Income Statements | | |
| --- | --- | --- |
| **For Years Ended December 31** | **Current Yr** | **Prior Yr** |
| Sales ...................... | $2,486,000 | $2,075,000 |
| Cost of goods sold ........... | 1,523,000 | 1,222,000 |
| Gross profit ................. | 963,000 | 853,000 |
| Operating expenses | | |
| Advertising expense......... | 145,000 | 100,000 |
| Sales salaries expense...... | 240,000 | 280,000 |
| Office salaries expense ..... | 165,000 | 200,000 |
| Insurance expense......... | 100,000 | 45,000 |
| Supplies expense........... | 26,000 | 35,000 |
| Depreciation expense ...... | 85,000 | 75,000 |
| Miscellaneous expenses .... | 17,000 | 15,000 |
| Total operating expenses ... | 778,000 | 750,000 |
| Operating income............ | 185,000 | 103,000 |
| Interest expense.............. | 44,000 | 46,000 |
| Income before taxes........... | 141,000 | 57,000 |
| Income tax expense........... | 47,000 | 19,000 |
| Net income ................. | $ 94,000 | $ 38,000 |
| Earnings per share ........... | $ 0.99 | $ 0.40 |

| PRECISION COMPANY Comparative Year-End Balance Sheets | | |
| --- | --- | --- |
| **At December 31** | **Current Yr** | **Prior Yr** |
| **Assets** | | |
| Current assets | | |
| Cash ..................... | $ 79,000 | $ 42,000 |
| Short-term investments ...... | 65,000 | 96,000 |
| Accounts receivable, net ..... | 120,000 | 100,000 |
| Merchandise inventory ...... | 250,000 | 265,000 |
| Total current assets ......... | 514,000 | 503,000 |
| Plant assets | | |
| Store equipment, net........ | 400,000 | 350,000 |
| Office equipment, net ....... | 45,000 | 50,000 |
| Buildings, net .............. | 625,000 | 675,000 |
| Land ..................... | 100,000 | 100,000 |
| Total plant assets ........... | 1,170,000 | 1,175,000 |
| Total assets ................. | $1,684,000 | $1,678,000 |
| **Liabilities** | | |
| Current liabilities | | |
| Accounts payable........... | $ 164,000 | $ 190,000 |
| Short-term notes payable .... | 75,000 | 90,000 |
| Taxes payable.............. | 26,000 | 12,000 |
| Total current liabilities ....... | 265,000 | 292,000 |
| Long-term liabilities | | |
| Notes payable ............. | 400,000 | 420,000 |
| Total liabilities................ | 665,000 | 712,000 |
| **Stockholders' Equity** | | |
| Common stock, $5 par value .... | 475,000 | 475,000 |
| Retained earnings............ | 544,000 | 491,000 |
| Total stockholders' equity ...... | 1,019,000 | 966,000 |
| Total liabilities and equity....... | $1,684,000 | $1,678,000 |

## SOLUTION

1.

| PRECISION COMPANY Comparative Income Statements | | | | |
| --- | --- | --- | --- | --- |
| **For Years Ended December 31** | **Current Yr** | **Prior Yr** | **Dollar Change** | **Percent Change** |
| Sales ...................... | $2,486,000 | $2,075,000 | **$411,000** | **19.8%** |
| Cost of goods sold ............ | 1,523,000 | 1,222,000 | **301,000** | **24.6** |
| Gross profit ................. | 963,000 | 853,000 | **110,000** | **12.9** |
| Operating expenses | | | | |
| Advertising expense......... | 145,000 | 100,000 | **45,000** | **45.0** |
| Sales salaries expense....... | 240,000 | 280,000 | **(40,000)** | **(14.3)** |
| Office salaries expense ...... | 165,000 | 200,000 | **(35,000)** | **(17.5)** |
| Insurance expense.......... | 100,000 | 45,000 | **55,000** | **122.2** |
| Supplies expense........... | 26,000 | 35,000 | **(9,000)** | **(25.7)** |
| Depreciation expense ....... | 85,000 | 75,000 | **10,000** | **13.3** |
| Miscellaneous expenses ..... | 17,000 | 15,000 | **2,000** | **13.3** |
| Total operating expenses .... | 778,000 | 750,000 | **28,000** | **3.7** |
| Operating income............. | 185,000 | 103,000 | **82,000** | **79.6** |
| Interest expense.............. | 44,000 | 46,000 | **(2,000)** | **(4.3)** |
| Income before taxes........... | 141,000 | 57,000 | **84,000** | **147.4** |
| Income tax expense .......... | 47,000 | 19,000 | **28,000** | **147.4** |
| Net income ................. | $ 94,000 | $ 38,000 | **$ 56,000** | **147.4** |
| Earnings per share ........... | $ 0.99 | $ 0.40 | **$ 0.59** | **147.5** |

[continued on next page]

[continued from previous page]

**2.**

| PRECISION COMPANY | | | | |
|---|---|---|---|---|
| Common-Size Comparative Year-End Balance Sheets | | | | |
| | | | Common-Size Percents | |
| At December 31 | Current Yr | Prior Yr | Current Yr* | Prior Yr* |
| **Assets** | | | | |
| Current assets | | | | |
| Cash...................... | $    79,000 | $    42,000 | 4.7% | 2.5% |
| Short-term investments ....... | 65,000 | 96,000 | 3.9 | 5.7 |
| Accounts receivable, net ...... | 120,000 | 100,000 | 7.1 | 6.0 |
| Merchandise inventory........ | 250,000 | 265,000 | 14.8 | 15.8 |
| Total current assets........... | 514,000 | 503,000 | 30.5 | 30.0 |
| Plant assets | | | | |
| Store equipment, net ......... | 400,000 | 350,000 | 23.8 | 20.9 |
| Office equipment, net......... | 45,000 | 50,000 | 2.7 | 3.0 |
| Buildings, net ............... | 625,000 | 675,000 | 37.1 | 40.2 |
| Land....................... | 100,000 | 100,000 | 5.9 | 6.0 |
| Total plant assets ............ | 1,170,000 | 1,175,000 | 69.5 | 70.0 |
| Total assets ................... | $1,684,000 | $1,678,000 | 100.0% | 100.0% |
| **Liabilities** | | | | |
| Current liabilities | | | | |
| Accounts payable ............ | $  164,000 | $  190,000 | 9.7% | 11.3% |
| Short-term notes payable...... | 75,000 | 90,000 | 4.5 | 5.4 |
| Taxes payable ............... | 26,000 | 12,000 | 1.5 | 0.7 |
| Total current liabilities......... | 265,000 | 292,000 | 15.7 | 17.4 |
| Long-term liabilities | | | | |
| Notes payable............... | 400,000 | 420,000 | 23.8 | 25.0 |
| Total liabilities ................ | 665,000 | 712,000 | 39.5 | 42.4 |
| **Stockholders' Equity** | | | | |
| Common stock, $5 par value ..... | 475,000 | 475,000 | 28.2 | 28.3 |
| Retained earnings.............. | 544,000 | 491,000 | 32.3 | 29.3 |
| Total stockholders' equity........ | 1,019,000 | 966,000 | 60.5 | 57.6 |
| Total liabilities and equity ........ | $1,684,000 | $1,678,000 | 100.0% | 100.0% |

*Columns do not always exactly add to 100 due to rounding.

**3. Ratios:**

**a.** Current ratio: $514,000/$265,000 = 1.9:1 (liquidity and efficiency)

**b.** Acid-test ratio: ($79,000 + $65,000 + $120,000)/$265,000 = 1.0:1 (liquidity and efficiency)

**c.** Average receivables: ($120,000 + $100,000)/2 = $110,000
Accounts receivable turnover: $2,486,000/$110,000 = 22.6 times (liquidity and efficiency)

**d.** Days' sales uncollected: ($120,000/$2,486,000) × 365 = 17.6 days (liquidity and efficiency)

**e.** Average inventory: ($250,000 + $265,000)/2 = $257,500
Inventory turnover: $1,523,000/$257,500 = 5.9 times (liquidity and efficiency)

**f.** Debt ratio: $665,000/$1,684,000 = 39.5% (solvency)

**g.** Debt-to-equity ratio: $665,000/$1,019,000 = 0.65 (solvency)

**h.** Times interest earned: $185,000/$44,000 = 4.2 times (solvency)

**i.** Profit margin ratio: $94,000/$2,486,000 = 3.8% (profitability)

**j.** Average total assets: ($1,684,000 + $1,678,000)/2 = $1,681,000
Total asset turnover: $2,486,000/$1,681,000 = 1.48 times (liquidity and efficiency)

**k.** Return on total assets: $94,000/$1,681,000 = 5.6% or 3.8% × 1.48 = 5.6% (profitability)

**l.** Average total equity: ($1,019,000 + $966,000)/2 = $992,500
Return on equity: $94,000/$992,500 = 9.5% (profitability)

# Sustainable Income

# 13A

**A2**

Explain the form and assess the content of a complete income statement.

When a company's activities include income-related events not part of its normal, continuing operations, it must disclose these events. To alert users to these activities, companies separate the income statement into continuing operations, discontinued segments, comprehensive income, and earnings per share. Exhibit 13A.1 shows such an income statement for ComUS. These separations help us measure *sustainable income,* which is the income level most likely to continue into the future. Sustainable income is commonly used in performance measures.

**EXHIBIT 13A.1**

Income Statement (all-inclusive) for a Corporation

| ComUS Income Statement For Year Ended December 31 | | |
|---|---:|---:|
| Net sales . . . . . . . . . . . . . . . . . . . . . . . . . . . . . . . . . . . . . . . . | | $8,478,000 |
| Operating expenses | | |
| Cost of goods sold . . . . . . . . . . . . . . . . . . . . . . . . . . . . . . . . | $5,950,000 | |
| Depreciation expense . . . . . . . . . . . . . . . . . . . . . . . . . . . . . | 35,000 | |
| Other selling, general, and administrative expenses . . . . . . . . . . | 515,000 | |
| Interest expense. . . . . . . . . . . . . . . . . . . . . . . . . . . . . . . . . . | 20,000 | |
| ① Total operating expenses. . . . . . . . . . . . . . . . . . . . . . . . . . . | | (6,520,000) |
| Other unusual and/or infrequent gains (losses) | | |
| Loss on plant relocation. . . . . . . . . . . . . . . . . . . . . . . . . . . . . | | (45,000) |
| Gain on sale of surplus land. . . . . . . . . . . . . . . . . . . . . . . . . . | | 72,000 |
| Income from continuing operations before taxes . . . . . . . . . . . . . . | | 1,985,000 |
| Income tax expense . . . . . . . . . . . . . . . . . . . . . . . . . . . . . . . . | | (595,500) |
| Income from continuing operations. . . . . . . . . . . . . . . . . . . . . . . | | 1,389,500 |
| **Discontinued segment** | | |
| ② Income from operating Division A (net of $180,000 taxes) . . . . . . . | 420,000 | |
| Loss on disposal of Division A (net of $66,000 tax benefit) . . . . . . . | (154,000) | 266,000 |
| Net income . . . . . . . . . . . . . . . . . . . . . . . . . . . . . . . . . . . . . . | | $ 1,655,500 |
| **Earnings per common share (200,000 outstanding shares)** | | |
| ③ Income from continuing operations . . . . . . . . . . . . . . . . . . . . . . | | $    6.95 |
| Discontinued operations . . . . . . . . . . . . . . . . . . . . . . . . . . . . . | | 1.33 |
| Net income (basic earnings per share) . . . . . . . . . . . . . . . . . . . . | | $    8.28 |

**① Continuing Operations**     Section ① shows revenues, expenses, and income from continuing operations. This information is used to predict future operations, and most view this section as the most important.

Gains and losses that are normal and frequent are reported as part of continuing operations. Gains and losses that are either unusual and/or infrequent are reported as part of continuing operations *but after* the normal revenues and expenses. Items considered unusual and/or infrequent include (1) property taken away by a foreign government, (2) condemning of property, (3) prohibiting use of an asset from a new law, (4) losses and gains from an unusual and infrequent calamity ("act of God"), and (5) financial effects of labor strikes.

**Point:** FASB no longer allows *extraordinary items.*

**② Discontinued Segments**     A **business segment** is a part of a company that is separated by its products/services or by geographic location. A segment has assets, liabilities, and financial results of operations that can be separated from those of other parts of the company. A gain or loss from selling or closing down a segment is separately reported. Section ② of Exhibit 13A.1 reports both (a) income from operating the discontinued segment before its disposal and (b) the loss from disposing of the segment's net assets. The income tax effects of each are reported separately from the income tax expense in section ①.

**③ Earnings per Share**     Section ③ of Exhibit 13A.1 reports earnings per share for both continuing operations and discontinued segments (when they both exist).

**Changes in Accounting Principles**     Changes in accounting principles require retrospective application to prior periods' financial statements. *Retrospective application* means applying a different accounting principle to prior periods as if that principle had always been used. Retrospective application enhances the consistency of financial information between periods, which improves the usefulness of information, especially with comparative analyses.

### ■ Decision Maker

**Small Business Owner** You own an orange grove near Jacksonville, Florida. A bad frost destroys about one-half of your oranges. You are currently preparing an income statement for a bank loan. Where on the income statement do you report the loss of oranges? ■ *Answer:* The frost loss is likely unusual, meaning it is reported in the nonrecurring section of continuing operations. Managers would highlight this loss apart from ongoing, normal results so that the bank views it separately from normal operations.

## Summary: Cheat Sheet

### BASICS OF ANALYSIS

**Liquidity and efficiency:** Ability to meet short-term obligations and efficiently generate revenues.

**Solvency:** Ability to meet long-term obligations and generate future revenues.

**Profitability:** Ability to provide financial rewards to attract and retain financing.

**Market prospects:** Ability to generate positive market expectations.

**General-purpose financial statements:** Include the (1) income statement, (2) balance sheet, (3) statement of stockholders' equity (or statement of retained earnings), (4) statement of cash flows, and (5) notes to these statements.

### HORIZONTAL ANALYSIS

**Comparative financial statements:** Show financial amounts in side-by-side columns on a single statement.

**Analysis period:** The financial statements under analysis.

**Base period:** The financial statements used for comparison. The prior year is commonly used as a base period.

**Dollar change formula:**

$$\text{Dollar change} = \text{Analysis period amount} - \text{Base period amount}$$

**Percent change formula:**

$$\text{Percent change (\%)} = \frac{\text{Analysis period amount} - \text{Base period amount}}{\text{Base period amount}} \times 100$$

**Apple comparative balance sheet:** The prior year is the base period and current year is the analysis period.

| $ millions | Current Yr | Prior Yr | Dollar Change | Percent Change |
|---|---|---|---|---|
| **Assets** | | | | |
| Cash and cash equivalents ............ | $48,844 | $25,913 | **$22,931** | **88.5%** |
| Short-term marketable securities ....... | 51,713 | 40,388 | **11,325** | **28.0%** |
| Accounts receivable, net .............. | 22,926 | 23,186 | **(260)** | **(1.1)%** |

**Trend analysis:** Computing trend percents that show patterns in data across periods.

$$\text{Trend percent (\%)} = \frac{\text{Analysis period amount}}{\text{Base period amount}} \times 100$$

**Apple trend analysis:** 4 years ago is the base period, and each subsequent year is the analysis period.

| In trend percent | Current Yr | 1 Yr Ago | 2 Yrs Ago | 3 Yrs Ago | 4 Yrs Ago |
|---|---|---|---|---|---|
| Net sales................. | 111.3% | 113.6% | 98.1% | 92.3% | 100.0% |
| Cost of sales............. | 115.5% | 116.9% | 100.7% | 93.8% | 100.0% |
| Operating expenses........ | 153.9% | 138.2% | 119.9% | 108.2% | 100.0% |

### VERTICAL ANALYSIS

**Common-size financial statements:** Show changes in the relative importance of each financial statement item. All individual amounts in common-size statements are shown in common-size percents.

**Common-size percent formula:**

$$\text{Common-size percent (\%)} = \frac{\text{Analysis amount}}{\text{Base amount}} \times 100$$

**Base amount:** Comparative balance sheets use total assets, and comparative income statements use net sales.

**Apple common-size balance sheet:**

| $ millions | Current Yr | Prior Yr | Common-Size Percents Current Yr | Common-Size Percents Prior Yr |
|---|---|---|---|---|
| Long-term marketable securities | 105,341 | 170,799 | **31.1%** | **46.7%** |
| Property, plant and equipment, net | 37,378 | 41,304 | **11.0%** | **11.3%** |
| Other noncurrent assets | 32,978 | 22,283 | **9.7%** | **6.1%** |
| Total assets | $338,516 | $365,725 | **100.0%** | **100.0%** |

**Apple common-size income statement:**

| $ millions | Current Yr | Prior Yr | Common-Size Percents Current Yr | Common-Size Percents Prior Yr |
|---|---|---|---|---|
| Net sales | $260,174 | $265,595 | **100.0%** | **100.0%** |
| Cost of sales | 161,782 | 163,756 | **62.2%** | **61.7%** |
| Gross margin | $ 98,392 | $101,839 | **37.8%** | **38.3%** |

### RATIO ANALYSIS AND REPORTING

| Ratio | Formula |
|---|---|
| **Liquidity and Efficiency** | |
| Current ratio | $= \dfrac{\text{Current assets}}{\text{Current liabilities}}$ |
| Acid-test ratio | $= \dfrac{\text{Cash} + \text{Short-term investments} + \text{Current receivables}}{\text{Current liabilities}}$ |
| Accounts receivable turnover | $= \dfrac{\text{Net sales}}{\text{Average accounts receivable, net}}$ |
| Inventory turnover | $= \dfrac{\text{Cost of goods sold}}{\text{Average inventory}}$ |
| Days' sales uncollected | $= \dfrac{\text{Accounts receivable, net}}{\text{Net sales}} \times 365$ |
| Days' sales in inventory | $= \dfrac{\text{Ending inventory}}{\text{Cost of goods sold}} \times 365$ |
| Total asset turnover | $= \dfrac{\text{Net sales}}{\text{Average total assets}}$ |
| **Solvency** | |
| Debt ratio | $= \dfrac{\text{Total liabilities}}{\text{Total assets}}$ |
| Equity ratio | $= \dfrac{\text{Total equity}}{\text{Total assets}}$ |
| Debt-to-equity ratio | $= \dfrac{\text{Total liabilities}}{\text{Total equity}}$ |
| Times interest earned | $= \dfrac{\text{Income before interest expense and income tax expense}}{\text{Interest expense}}$ |
| **Profitability** | |
| Profit margin ratio | $= \dfrac{\text{Net income}}{\text{Net sales}}$ |
| Gross margin ratio | $= \dfrac{\text{Net sales} - \text{Cost of goods sold}}{\text{Net sales}}$ |
| Return on total assets | $= \dfrac{\text{Net income}}{\text{Average total assets}}$ |
| Return on equity | $= \dfrac{\text{Net income}}{\text{Average total equity}}$ |
| Basic earnings per share | $= \dfrac{\text{Net income} - \text{Preferred dividends}}{\text{Weighted-average common shares outstanding}}$ |
| **Market Prospects** | |
| Price-earnings ratio | $= \dfrac{\text{Market price per common share}}{\text{Earnings per share}}$ |
| Dividend yield | $= \dfrac{\text{Annual cash dividends per share}}{\text{Market price per share}}$ |

## Key Terms

| | | |
|---|---|---|
| Business segment (485) | Financial statement analysis (467) | Profitability (467) |
| Common-size financial statement (472) | General-purpose financial | Ratio analysis (468) |
| Comparative financial statement (468) | statements (468) | Solvency (467) |
| Efficiency (467) | Horizontal analysis (468) | Vertical analysis (468) |
| Equity ratio (478) | Liquidity (467) | Working capital (476) |
| Financial reporting (468) | Market prospects (467) | |

## Multiple Choice Quiz

**1.** A company's sales in the prior year were $300,000 and in the current year were $351,000. Using the prior year as the base year, the sales trend percent for the current year is

   **a.** 17%.      **c.** 100%.      **e.** 48%.

   **b.** 85%.      **d.** 117%.

**Use the following information for questions 2 through 5.**

| ELLA COMPANY | | | |
|---|---|---|---|
| **Balance Sheet** | | | |
| **December 31** | | | |
| **Assets** | | **Liabilities** | |
| Cash .................. | $ 86,000 | Current liabilities ........ | $124,000 |
| Accounts receivable..... | 76,000 | Long-term liabilities ...... | 90,000 |
| Merchandise inventory .. | 122,000 | **Equity** | |
| Prepaid insurance ...... | 12,000 | Common stock .......... | 300,000 |
| Long-term investments .. | 98,000 | Retained earnings ....... | 316,000 |
| Plant assets, net........ | 436,000 | | |
| Total assets............ | $830,000 | Total liabilities and equity .. | $830,000 |

**2.** What is Ella Company's current ratio?

   **a.** 0.69           **d.** 6.69

   **b.** 1.31           **e.** 2.39

   **c.** 3.88

**3.** What is Ella Company's acid-test ratio?

   **a.** 2.39           **d.** 6.69

   **b.** 0.69           **e.** 3.88

   **c.** 1.31

**4.** What is Ella Company's debt ratio?

   **a.** 25.78%      **d.** 137.78%

   **b.** 100.00%    **e.** 34.74%

   **c.** 74.22%

**5.** What is Ella Company's equity ratio?

   **a.** 25.78%      **d.** 74.22%

   **b.** 100.00%    **e.** 137.78%

   **c.** 34.74%

### ANSWERS TO MULTIPLE CHOICE QUIZ

**1.** d; ($351,000/$300,000) × 100 = 117%

**2.** e; ($86,000 + $76,000 + $122,000 + $12,000)/$124,000 = 2.39

**3.** c; ($86,000 + $76,000)/$124,000 = 1.31

**4.** a; ($124,000 + $90,000)/$830,000 = 25.78%

**5.** d; ($300,000 + $316,000)/$830,000 = 74.22%

*Superscript letter A denotes assignments based on Appendix 13A.*

*Select Quick Study and Exercise assignments feature Guided Example videos, called "Hints" in Connect. Hints use different numbers, and instructors can turn this feature on or off.*

Identify whether each of the following items is included as part of general-purpose financial statements.

**a.** Income statement

**b.** Balance sheet

**c.** Shareholders' meetings

**d.** Financial statement notes

**e.** Company news releases

**f.** Statement of cash flows

**g.** Stock price information and investor analysis

**h.** Statement of shareholders' equity

**QUICK STUDY**

**QS 13-1**
Financial reporting
**C1**

Identify which standard of comparison, (*a*) intracompany, (*b*) competitor, (*c*) industry, or (*d*) guidelines, best describes each of the following examples.

**1.** Compare **Ford**'s return on assets to **GM**'s return on assets.

**2.** Compare a company's acid-test ratio to the 1:1 rule of thumb.

**3.** Compare **Netflix**'s current year sales to its prior year sales.

**4.** Compare **McDonald's** profit margin to the fast-food industry profit margin.

**QS 13-2**
Standard of comparison
**C1**

**QS 13-3**
Percent change   **P1**

In the current year, Aveeno reported net income of $50,400, which was a 12% increase over prior year net income. Compute prior year net income.

**QS 13-4**
Horizontal analysis
**P1**

Compute the annual dollar changes and percent changes for each of the following accounts.

| | Current Yr | Prior Yr |
|---|---|---|
| Short-term investments ............ | $374,634 | $234,000 |
| Accounts receivable ............... | 97,364 | 101,000 |
| Notes payable .................... | 0 | 88,000 |

**QS 13-5**
Horizontal analysis
**P1**

Compute the annual dollar changes and percent changes for each of the following items.

| | Current Yr | Prior Yr |
|---|---|---|
| Cash | $ 7,440 | $ 8,000 |
| Accounts receivable | 54,000 | 18,000 |
| Equipment, net | 44,000 | 40,000 |
| Land | 91,680 | 66,000 |
| Total assets | $197,120 | $132,000 |

**QS 13-6**
Vertical analysis   **P2**

Express the items from QS 13-5 in common-size percents.

**QS 13-7**
Trend percents
**P1**

Use the following information to determine the prior year and current year trend percents for net sales using the prior year as the base year.

| $ thousands | Current Yr | Prior Yr |
|---|---|---|
| Net sales ....................... | $801,810 | $453,000 |
| Cost of goods sold .............. | 392,887 | 134,088 |

**QS 13-8**
Common-size analysis   **P2**

Refer to the information in QS 13-7. Determine the prior year and current year common-size percents for cost of goods sold using net sales as the base.

**QS 13-9**
Computing current ratio and acid-test ratio   **P3**

Pritchett Co. reported the following year-end data: cash of $15,000; short-term investments of $5,000; accounts receivable (current) of $8,000; inventory of $20,000; prepaid (current) assets of $6,000; and total current liabilities of $20,000. Compute the (a) current ratio and (b) acid-test ratio. Round to one decimal.

**QS 13-10**
Analyzing effect of transactions on current ratio
**P3**

At its prior year-end, VPN Co. reported current assets of $60,000 and current liabilities of $55,000. Determine how each of the following transactions would increase, decrease, or have no effect on total current assets, total current liabilities, and the current ratio.

**1.** Acquired inventory for $200 cash.
**2.** Sold a long-term asset (equipment) for $4,000 cash.
**3.** Accrued wages payable of $1,500.

**QS 13-11**
Computing accounts receivable turnover and days' sales uncollected   **P3**

Mifflin Co. reported the following for the current year: net sales of $60,000; cost of goods sold of $38,000; beginning balance in accounts receivable of $14,000; and ending balance in accounts receivable of $6,000. Compute (a) accounts receivable turnover and (b) days' sales uncollected. Round to one decimal. *Hint:* Accounts receivable turnover uses average accounts receivable and days' sales uncollected uses the ending balance in accounts receivable.

**QS 13-12**
Computing inventory turnover and days' sales in inventory   **P3**

SCC Co. reported the following for the current year: net sales of $48,000; cost of goods sold of $40,000; beginning balance in inventory of $2,000; and ending balance in inventory of $8,000. Compute (a) inventory turnover and (b) days' sales in inventory. *Hint:* Inventory turnover uses average inventory and days' sales in inventory uses the ending balance in inventory.

Dundee Co. reported the following for the current year: net sales of $80,000; cost of goods sold of $60,000; beginning balance of total assets of $115,000; and ending balance of total assets of $85,000. Compute total asset turnover. Round to one decimal.

**QS 13-13**

Computing total asset turnover   **P3**

Paddy's Pub reported the following year-end data: income before interest expense and income tax expense of $30,000; cost of goods sold of $17,000; interest expense of $1,500; total assets of $70,000; total liabilities of $20,000; and total equity of $50,000. Compute the (a) debt-to-equity ratio and (b) times interest earned. Round to one decimal.

**QS 13-14**

Computing debt-to-equity ratio and times interest earned   **P3**

Edison Co. reported the following for the current year: net sales of $80,000; cost of goods sold of $56,000; net income of $16,000; beginning balance of total assets of $60,000; and ending balance of total assets of $68,000. Compute (a) profit margin and (b) return on total assets.

**QS 13-15**

Computing profit margin and return on total assets   **P3**

Franklin Co. reported the following year-end data: net income of $220,000; annual cash dividends per share of $3; market price per (common) share of $150; and earnings per share of $10. Compute the (a) price-earnings ratio and (b) dividend yield.

**QS 13-16**

Computing price-earnings ratio and dividend yield   **P3**

For each ratio listed, identify whether the change in ratio value from the prior year to the current year is usually regarded as favorable or unfavorable.

**QS 13-17**

Ratio interpretation

**P3**

| Ratio | Current Yr | Prior Yr | Ratio | Current Yr | Prior Yr |
|---|---|---|---|---|---|
| 1. Profit margin . . . . . . | 9% | 8% | 5. Accounts receivable turnover . . . . . . | 5.5 | 6.7 |
| 2. Debt ratio. . . . . . . . . | 47% | 42% | 6. Basic earnings per share . . . . . . . . . . | $1.25 | $1.10 |
| 3. Gross margin . . . . . . | 34% | 46% | 7. Inventory turnover . . . . . . . . . . . . . . | 3.6 | 3.4 |
| 4. Acid-test ratio . . . . . | 1.00 | 1.15 | 8. Dividend yield. . . . . . . . . . . . . . . . . . | 2.0% | 1.2% |

We are evaluating whether or not to make a loan to a company. Indicate whether each of the following separate trends would make us more or less likely to make the loan.

**a.** Current ratio is increasing, from 0.8 to 1.3.

**b.** Acid-test ratio is increasing, from 0.6 to 1.0.

**c.** Times interest earned is decreasing, from 9.0 to 6.2.

**d.** Total asset turnover is decreasing, from 0.5 to 0.3.

**QS 13-18**

Ratio analysis for lending decisions

**P3**

We are evaluating whether or not to invest in a company. Indicate whether each of the following separate trends would make us more or less likely to invest.

**a.** Return on equity is increasing, from 19% to 24%.

**b.** Days' sales in inventory is increasing, from 22 days to 38 days.

**c.** Profit margin is decreasing, from 25% to 19%.

**d.** Return on total assets is increasing, from 12% to 16%.

**QS 13-19**

Ratio analysis for investing decisions

**P3**

Following is information for Morgan Company and Parker Company, which are similar firms operating in the same industry.

**QS 13-20**

Analyzing short-term financial condition

**A1**

| | Morgan | Parker |
|---|---|---|
| Current ratio | 1.7 | 3.2 |
| Acid-test ratio | 1.0 | 2.8 |
| Accounts receivable turnover | 30.5 | 16.4 |
| Inventory turnover | 24.2 | 14.5 |

**1.** Based on current ratio and acid-test ratio, which company appears better positioned to pay current liabilities?

**2.** Based on accounts receivable turnover, which company converts its receivables into cash more frequently?

**3.** Based on inventory turnover, which company appears to hold inventory for the least amount of time?

**QS 13-21<sup>A</sup>**

**Identifying unusual and/or infrequent gains or losses**

**A2**

Which of the following gains or losses would Organic Foods account for as unusual and/or infrequent?

**a.** A hurricane destroys rainwater tanks that result in a loss for Organic Foods.

**b.** The used vehicle market is weak and Organic Foods is forced to sell its used delivery truck at a loss.

**c.** Organic Foods owns an organic farm in Venezuela that is seized by the government. The company records a loss.

---

**QS 13-22<sup>A</sup>**

**Reporting a discontinued segment**

**A2**

Wipfli Co. provides auditing services and consulting services. Wipfli sells the consulting services segment for a gain of $75,000 (net of tax). Income from consulting services during the year is $20,000 (net of tax). Wipfli reports income from continuing operations of $180,000. Prepare the discontinued segment portion of its income statement.

---

**McGraw Hill connect®**

## EXERCISES

**Exercise 13-1**

**Building blocks of analysis**

**C1**

Match the ratio to the building block of financial statement analysis to which it best relates.

**A.** Liquidity and efficiency    **B.** Solvency    **C.** Profitability    **D.** Market prospects

| | | |
|---|---|---|
| **1.** Equity ratio | **4.** Days' sales in inventory | **7.** Times interest earned |
| **2.** Return on total assets | **5.** Accounts receivable turnover | **8.** Gross margin ratio |
| **3.** Dividend yield | **6.** Debt-to-equity ratio | **9.** Acid-test ratio |

---

**Exercise 13-2**

**Identifying financial ratios**

**C1**

Identify which of the following six metrics *a* through *f* best completes questions 1 through 3.

**a.** Days' sales uncollected    **c.** Working capital    **e.** Total asset turnover

**b.** Accounts receivable turnover    **d.** Return on total assets    **f.** Profit margin

**1.** Which two ratios are key components in measuring a company's operating efficiency? _____ _____ Which ratio summarizes these two components? _____

**2.** What measure reflects the difference between current assets and current liabilities? _____

**3.** Which two short-term liquidity ratios measure how frequently a company collects its accounts? _____ _____

---

**Exercise 13-3**

**Computing and analyzing trend percents**

**P1**

Compute trend percents for the following accounts using 2017 as the base year. For each of the three accounts, state whether the situation as revealed by the trend percents appears to be favorable or unfavorable.

| | 2021 | 2020 | 2019 | 2018 | 2017 |
|---|---|---|---|---|---|
| Sales . . . . . . . . . . . . . . . . | $282,880 | $270,800 | $252,600 | $234,560 | $150,000 |
| Cost of goods sold . . . . . . | 128,200 | 122,080 | 115,280 | 106,440 | 67,000 |
| Accounts receivable . . . . . | 18,100 | 17,300 | 16,400 | 15,200 | 9,000 |

---

**Exercise 13-4**

**Computing and interpreting common-size percents**

**P2**

Compute common-size percents for the following comparative income statements (round percents to one decimal). Using the common-size percents, which item is most responsible for the decline in net income?

| GOMEZ CORPORATION | | |
|---|---|---|
| Comparative Income Statements | | |
| For Years Ended December 31 | Current Yr | Prior Yr |
| Sales . . . . . . . . . . . . . . . . . . . . . . | $740,000 | $625,000 |
| Cost of goods sold . . . . . . . . . . . . | 560,300 | 290,800 |
| Gross profit . . . . . . . . . . . . . . . . . | 179,700 | 334,200 |
| Operating expenses . . . . . . . . . . . | 128,200 | 218,500 |
| Net income . . . . . . . . . . . . . . . . . | $ 51,500 | $115,700 |

---

**Exercise 13-5**

**Determining income effects from common-size and trend percents    P1    P2**

Common-size and trend percents for Roxi Company's sales, cost of goods sold, and expenses follow. Determine whether net income increased, decreased, or remained unchanged in this three-year period.

| | Common-Size Percents | | | Trend Percents | | |
|---|---|---|---|---|---|---|
| | Current Yr | 1 Yr Ago | 2 Yrs Ago | Current Yr | 1 Yr Ago | 2 Yrs Ago |
| Sales................... | 100.0% | 100.0% | 100.0% | 105.4% | 104.2% | 100.0% |
| Cost of goods sold........ | 63.4 | 61.9 | 59.1 | 113.1 | 109.1 | 100.0 |
| Operating expenses....... | 15.3 | 14.8 | 15.1 | 106.8 | 102.1 | 100.0 |

Simon Company's year-end balance sheets follow. (1) Express the balance sheets in common-size percents. Round percents to one decimal. (2) Assuming annual sales have not changed in the last three years, is the change in accounts receivable as a percentage of total assets favorable or unfavorable? (3) Is the change in merchandise inventory as a percentage of total assets favorable or unfavorable?

**Exercise 13-6**
Common-size percents
**P2**

| At December 31 | Current Yr | 1 Yr Ago | 2 Yrs Ago |
|---|---|---|---|
| **Assets** | | | |
| Cash.......................... | $ 31,800 | $ 35,625 | $ 37,800 |
| Accounts receivable, net ........... | 89,500 | 62,500 | 50,200 |
| Merchandise inventory............. | 112,500 | 82,500 | 54,000 |
| Prepaid expenses................. | 10,700 | 9,375 | 5,000 |
| Plant assets, net ................. | 278,500 | 255,000 | 230,500 |
| Total assets ..................... | $523,000 | $445,000 | $377,500 |
| **Liabilities and Equity** | | | |
| Accounts payable ................. | $129,900 | $ 75,250 | $ 51,250 |
| Long-term notes payable........... | 98,500 | 101,500 | 83,500 |
| Common stock, $10 par value....... | 163,500 | 163,500 | 163,500 |
| Retained earnings................. | 131,100 | 104,750 | 79,250 |
| Total liabilities and equity........... | $523,000 | $445,000 | $377,500 |

Refer to Simon Company's balance sheets in Exercise 13-6. (1) Compute the current ratio for each of the three years. Did the current ratio improve or worsen over the three-year period? (2) Compute the acid-test ratio for each of the three years. Did the acid-test ratio improve or worsen over the three-year period? Round ratios to two decimals.

**Exercise 13-7**
Analyzing liquidity
**P3**

Refer to the Simon Company information in Exercise 13-6. The company's income statements for the current year and one year ago follow. Assume that all sales are on credit and then compute (1) days' sales uncollected, (2) accounts receivable turnover, (3) inventory turnover, and (4) days' sales in inventory. For each ratio, determine if it improved or worsened in the current year. Round to one decimal.

**Exercise 13-8**
Analyzing and interpreting liquidity
**P3**

| For Year Ended December 31 | Current Yr | | 1 Yr Ago | |
|---|---|---|---|---|
| Sales ..................... | | $673,500 | | $532,000 |
| Cost of goods sold .......... | $411,225 | | $345,500 | |
| Other operating expenses .... | 209,550 | | 134,980 | |
| Interest expense............ | 12,100 | | 13,300 | |
| Income tax expense......... | 9,525 | | 8,845 | |
| Total costs and expenses..... | | 642,400 | | 502,625 |
| Net income ................ | | $ 31,100 | | $ 29,375 |
| Earnings per share .......... | | $ 1.90 | | $ 1.80 |

Refer to the Simon Company information in Exercises 13-6 and 13-8. For both the current year and one year ago, compute the following ratios: (1) debt ratio and equity ratio—percent rounded to one decimal, (2) debt-to-equity ratio—rounded to two decimals; based on debt-to-equity ratio, does the company have more or less debt in the current year versus one year ago? and (3) times interest earned—rounded to one decimal. Based on times interest earned, is the company more or less risky for creditors in the current year versus one year ago?

**Exercise 13-9**
Analyzing risk and capital structure
**P3**

**Exercise 13-10**

Analyzing efficiency and profitability

**P3**

Refer to Simon Company's financial information in Exercises 13-6 and 13-8. For both the current year and one year ago, compute the following ratios: (1) profit margin ratio—percent rounded to one decimal; did profit margin improve or worsen in the current year versus one year ago? (2) total asset turnover—rounded to one decimal, and (3) return on total assets—percent rounded to one decimal. Based on return on total assets, did Simon's operating efficiency improve or worsen in the current year versus one year ago?

**Exercise 13-11**

Analyzing profitability

**P3**

Refer to Simon Company's financial information in Exercises 13-6 and 13-8. Additional information about the company follows. For both the current year and one year ago, compute the following ratios: (1) return on equity—percent rounded to one decimal, (2) dividend yield—percent rounded to one decimal, and (3) price-earnings ratio on December 31—rounded to one decimal. Assuming Simon's competitor has a price-earnings ratio of 10, which company has higher market expectations for future growth?

| | | | |
|---|---|---|---|
| Common stock market price, December 31, current year..... | $30.00 | Annual cash dividends per share in current year .... | $0.29 |
| Common stock market price, December 31, 1 year ago...... | 28.00 | Annual cash dividends per share 1 year ago........ | 0.24 |

**Exercise 13-12**

Analyzing effect of transactions on current ratio

**P3**

On January 1, 5G Co. reported current assets of $72,000 and current liabilities of $60,000. Compute total current assets, total current liabilities, and the current ratio at January 1 and after each of the following transactions.

Jan.   5    Purchased equipment to be used in operations for $18,000 cash.
Jan. 12    Paid $5,000 cash for accounts payable.
Jan. 18    Acquired a building in exchange for a $99,000 long-term note payable, first payment to occur in 3 years.
Jan. 22    Purchased $12,000 of merchandise on credit, terms n/45.
Jan. 31    Sold outdated machinery for $12,700 cash.

**Exercise 13-13**

Computing current ratio and profit margin

**P3**

Niantic reported the following financial information (amounts in millions). Compute the current ratio and profit margin.

| | | | |
|---|---|---|---|
| Current assets......... | $ 9,000 | Net sales........... | $4,400 |
| Total assets........... | 11,477 | Net income ......... | 176 |
| Current liabilities ...... | 900 | | |

**Exercise 13-14**

Analyzing efficiency and profitability

**P3**

Following are data for BioBeans and GreenKale, which sell organic produce and are of similar size.

**1.** Compute the profit margin and the return on total assets for both companies.
**2.** Based on analysis of these two measures, which company is the preferred investment?

| | BioBeans | GreenKale |
|---|---|---|
| Average total assets........... | $187,500 | $150,000 |
| Net sales.................... | 75,000 | 60,000 |
| Net income ................. | 15,000 | 9,000 |

**Exercise 13-15**

Reconstructing an income statement with ratios

**P3**

Following is an incomplete current year income statement.

| Income Statement | |
|---|---|
| Net sales ..................................... | $ (a) |
| Cost of goods sold ........................... | (b) |
| Selling, general, and administrative expenses.... | 7,000 |
| Income tax expense.......................... | 2,000 |
| Net income ................................. | (c) |

Determine amounts a, b, and c. Additional information follows:
- Return on total assets is 16% (average total assets is $68,750).
- Inventory turnover is 5 (average inventory is $6,000).
- Accounts receivable turnover is 8 (average accounts receivable is $6,250).

Roak Company and Clay Company are similar firms that operate in the same industry. Clay began operations two years ago and Roak started five years ago. In the current year, both companies pay 6% interest on their debt to creditors. The following additional information is available.

**Exercise 13-16**
Interpreting financial ratios
**A1    P3**

| | Roak Company | | | Clay Company | | |
|---|---|---|---|---|---|---|
| | Current Yr | 1 Yr Ago | 2 Yrs Ago | Current Yr | 1 Yr Ago | 2 Yrs Ago |
| Total asset turnover . . . . . . . | 3.1 | 2.8 | 3.0 | 1.7 | 1.5 | 1.1 |
| Return on total assets . . . . . | 7.4% | 7.0% | 6.9% | 4.8% | 4.5% | 3.2% |
| Profit margin ratio . . . . . . . . | 2.4% | 2.5% | 2.3% | 2.8% | 3.0% | 2.9% |
| Sales . . . . . . . . . . . . . . . . . . | $410,000 | $380,000 | $396,000 | $210,000 | $170,000 | $110,000 |

**1.** Which company has the better (a) profit margin, (b) asset turnover, and (c) return on assets?

**2.** Which company has the better rate of growth in sales?

**3.** Did the company successfully use financial leverage in the current year, as judged by return on assets exceeding its interest rate on debt, in the case of (a) Roak and (b) Clay?

In the current year, Randa Merchandising Inc. sold its interest in a chain of wholesale outlets, taking the company completely out of the wholesaling business. The company still operates its retail outlets. A listing of the major sections of an income statement follows.

**Exercise 13-17ᴬ**
Income statement
categories
**A2**

**A.** Net sales less operating expense section

**B.** Other unusual and/or infrequent gains (losses)

**C.** Taxes reported on income (loss) from continuing operations

**D.** Income (loss) from operating a discontinued segment, or gain (loss) from its disposal

Indicate where each of the following income-related items for this company appears on its current year income statement by writing the letter of the appropriate section in the blank beside each item.

| Section | Item | Debit | Credit |
|---|---|---|---|
| _____ | 1. Net sales. . . . . . . . . . . . . . . . . . . . . . . . . . . . . . . . . . . . . . . . . . . | | $2,900,000 |
| _____ | 2. Gain on state's condemnation of company property . . . . . . . . . . | | 230,000 |
| _____ | 3. Cost of goods sold . . . . . . . . . . . . . . . . . . . . . . . . . . . . . . . . . . . | $1,480,000 | |
| _____ | 4. Income tax expense . . . . . . . . . . . . . . . . . . . . . . . . . . . . . . . . . . | 217,000 | |
| _____ | 5. Depreciation expense . . . . . . . . . . . . . . . . . . . . . . . . . . . . . . . . | 232,000 | |
| _____ | 6. Gain on sale of wholesale business segment, net of tax . . . . . . . | | 775,000 |
| _____ | 7. Loss from operating wholesale business segment, net of tax . . . | 444,000 | |
| _____ | 8. Loss of assets from meteor strike . . . . . . . . . . . . . . . . . . . . . . . | 640,000 | |

Use the financial data for Randa Merchandising Inc. in Exercise 13-17ᴬ to prepare its December 31 year-end income statement. Ignore the earnings per share section.

**Exercise 13-18ᴬ**
Income statement
presentation  **A2**

 **connect**

Selected comparative financial statements of Haroun Company follow.

**PROBLEM SET A**

**Problem 13-1A**
Calculating and analyzing
trend percents

**P1**

| HAROUN COMPANY Comparative Income Statements For Years Ended December 31 | | | | | | | |
|---|---|---|---|---|---|---|---|
| $ thousands | 2021 | 2020 | 2019 | 2018 | 2017 | 2016 | 2015 |
| Sales . . . . . . . . . . . . . . . | $1,694 | $1,496 | $1,370 | $1,264 | $1,186 | $1,110 | $928 |
| Cost of goods sold . . . . | 1,246 | 1,032 | 902 | 802 | 752 | 710 | 586 |
| Gross profit . . . . . . . . . . | 448 | 464 | 468 | 462 | 434 | 400 | 342 |
| Operating expenses . . . | 330 | 256 | 234 | 170 | 146 | 144 | 118 |
| Net income . . . . . . . . . | $ 118 | $ 208 | $ 234 | $ 292 | $ 288 | $ 256 | $224 |

[continued on next page]

[continued from previous page]

| HAROUN COMPANY Comparative Year-End Balance Sheets | | | | | | | |
| --- | --- | --- | --- | --- | --- | --- | --- |
| At December 31, $ thousands | 2021 | 2020 | 2019 | 2018 | 2017 | 2016 | 2015 |
| **Assets** | | | | | | | |
| Cash. . . . . . . . . . . . . . . . . . | $ 58 | $ 78 | $ 82 | $ 84 | $ 88 | $ 86 | $ 89 |
| Accounts receivable, net . . . | 490 | 514 | 466 | 360 | 318 | 302 | 216 |
| Merchandise inventory. . . . . | 1,838 | 1,364 | 1,204 | 1,032 | 936 | 810 | 615 |
| Other current assets. . . . . . . | 36 | 32 | 14 | 34 | 28 | 28 | 9 |
| Long-term investments. . . . . | 0 | 0 | 0 | 146 | 146 | 146 | 146 |
| Plant assets, net . . . . . . . . . . | 2,020 | 2,014 | 1,752 | 944 | 978 | 860 | 725 |
| Total assets . . . . . . . . . . . . . | $4,442 | $4,002 | $3,518 | $2,600 | $2,494 | $2,232 | $1,800 |
| **Liabilities and Equity** | | | | | | | |
| Current liabilities. . . . . . . . . . | $1,220 | $1,042 | $ 718 | $ 614 | $ 546 | $ 522 | $ 282 |
| Long-term liabilities . . . . . . . | 1,294 | 1,140 | 1,112 | 570 | 580 | 620 | 400 |
| Common stock . . . . . . . . . . . | 1,000 | 1,000 | 1,000 | 850 | 850 | 650 | 650 |
| Other paid-in capital. . . . . . . | 250 | 250 | 250 | 170 | 170 | 150 | 150 |
| Retained earnings. . . . . . . . . | 678 | 570 | 438 | 396 | 348 | 290 | 318 |
| Total liabilities and equity. . . | $4,442 | $4,002 | $3,518 | $2,600 | $2,494 | $2,232 | $1,800 |

**Required**

**Check**   (1) 2021, Total
assets trend, 246.8%

**1.** Compute trend percents for all components of both statements using 2015 as the base year. Round percents to one decimal.

*Analysis Component*

**2.** Refer to the results from part 1. (*a*) Did sales grow steadily over this period? (*b*) Did net income as a percent of sales grow over the past four years? (*c*) Did inventory increase over this period?

---

**Problem 13-2A**

Ratios, common-size statements, and trend percents

**P1   P2   P3**

Selected comparative financial statements of Korbin Company follow.

| KORBIN COMPANY Comparative Income Statements | | | |
| --- | --- | --- | --- |
| For Years Ended December 31 | 2021 | 2020 | 2019 |
| Sales . . . . . . . . . . . . . . . . . . . . | $555,000 | $340,000 | $278,000 |
| Cost of goods sold . . . . . . . . . | 283,500 | 212,500 | 153,900 |
| Gross profit . . . . . . . . . . . . . . . | 271,500 | 127,500 | 124,100 |
| Selling expenses. . . . . . . . . . . | 102,900 | 46,920 | 50,800 |
| Administrative expenses . . . . . | 50,668 | 29,920 | 22,800 |
| Total expenses . . . . . . . . . . . . | 153,568 | 76,840 | 73,600 |
| Income before taxes. . . . . . . . | 117,932 | 50,660 | 50,500 |
| Income tax expense . . . . . . . . | 40,800 | 10,370 | 15,670 |
| Net income . . . . . . . . . . . . . . . | $ 77,132 | $ 40,290 | $ 34,830 |

| KORBIN COMPANY Comparative Balance Sheets | | | |
| --- | --- | --- | --- |
| At December 31 | 2021 | 2020 | 2019 |
| **Assets** | | | |
| Current assets. . . . . . . . . . . . | $ 52,390 | $ 37,924 | $ 51,748 |
| Long-term investments. . . . . . | 0 | 500 | 3,950 |
| Plant assets, net . . . . . . . . . . . | 100,000 | 96,000 | 60,000 |
| Total assets . . . . . . . . . . . . . . | $152,390 | $134,424 | $115,698 |
| **Liabilities and Equity** | | | |
| Current liabilities. . . . . . . . . . . | $ 22,800 | $ 19,960 | $ 20,300 |
| Common stock . . . . . . . . . . . . | 72,000 | 72,000 | 60,000 |
| Other paid-in capital. . . . . . . . | 9,000 | 9,000 | 6,000 |
| Retained earnings. . . . . . . . . . | 48,590 | 33,464 | 29,398 |
| Total liabilities and equity. . . . | $152,390 | $134,424 | $115,698 |

**Required**

**Check**   (3) 2021, Total
assets trend, 131.71%

**1.** Compute each year's current ratio. Round ratios to one decimal.

**2.** Express the income statement data in common-size percents. Round percents to two decimals.

**3.** Express the balance sheet data in trend percents with 2019 as base year. Round percents to two decimals.

### Analysis Component

**4.** Refer to the results from parts 1, 2, and 3. (*a*) Did cost of goods sold make up a greater portion of sales for the most recent year compared to the prior year? (*b*) Did income as a percent of sales improve in the most recent year compared to the prior year? (*c*) Did plant assets grow over this period?

---

Plum Corporation began the month of May with $700,000 of current assets, a current ratio of 2.50:1, and an acid-test ratio of 1.10:1. During the month, it completed the following transactions. The company uses a perpetual inventory system.

**Problem 13-3A**
Transactions, working capital, and liquidity ratios
**P3**

| | |
|---|---|
| May 2 | Purchased $50,000 of merchandise inventory on credit. |
| 8 | Sold merchandise inventory that cost $55,000 for $110,000 cash. |
| 10 | Collected $20,000 cash on an account receivable. |
| 15 | Paid $22,000 cash to settle an account payable. |
| 17 | Wrote off a $5,000 bad debt against the Allowance for Doubtful Accounts account. |
| 22 | Declared a $1 per share cash dividend on its 50,000 shares of outstanding common stock. |
| 26 | Paid the dividend declared on May 22. |
| 27 | Borrowed $100,000 cash by giving the bank a 30-day, 10% note. |
| 28 | Borrowed $80,000 cash by signing a long-term secured note. |
| 29 | Used the $180,000 cash proceeds from the notes to buy new machinery. |

**Check** May 22: Current ratio, 2.19; Acid-test ratio, 1.11

May 29: Current ratio, 1.80; Working capital, $325,000

**Required**

Prepare a table, similar to the following, showing Plum's (1) current ratio, (2) acid-test ratio, and (3) working capital after each transaction. Round ratios to two decimals.

| | A | B | C | D | E | F | G |
|---|---|---|---|---|---|---|---|
| 1 | | **Current Assets** | **Quick Assets** | **Current Liabilities** | **Current Ratio** | **Acid-Test Ratio** | **Working Capital** |
| 2 | **Transaction** | | | | | | |
| 3 | Beginning | $700,000 | — | — | 2.50 | 1.10 | — |

---

Selected current year-end financial statements of Cabot Corporation follow. All sales were on credit; selected balance sheet amounts at December 31 of the *prior year* were inventory, $48,900; total assets, $189,400; common stock, $90,000; and retained earnings, $33,748.

**Problem 13-4A**
Calculating financial statement ratios
**P3**

**CABOT CORPORATION**
**Balance Sheet**
**December 31 of Current Year**

| Assets | | Liabilities and Equity | |
|---|---|---|---|
| Cash. . . . . . . . . . . . . . . . . | $ 10,000 | Accounts payable. . . . . . . . . . . . . . . . | $ 17,500 |
| Short-term investments . . | 8,400 | Accrued wages payable. . . . . . . . . . . | 3,200 |
| Accounts receivable, net . | 33,700 | Income taxes payable . . . . . . . . . . . . | 3,300 |
| Merchandise inventory. . . | 32,150 | Long-term note payable, secured | |
| Prepaid expenses. . . . . . . | 2,650 | by mortgage on plant assets. . . . . . | 63,400 |
| Plant assets, net . . . . . . . . | 153,300 | Common stock . . . . . . . . . . . . . . . . . . | 90,000 |
| | | Retained earnings . . . . . . . . . . . . . . . | 62,800 |
| Total assets. . . . . . . . . . . | $240,200 | Total liabilities and equity . . . . . . . . | $240,200 |

**CABOT CORPORATION**
**Income Statement**
**For Current Year Ended December 31**

| | |
|---|---|
| Sales . . . . . . . . . . . . . . . . | $448,600 |
| Cost of goods sold . . . . . . | 297,250 |
| Gross profit . . . . . . . . . . . . | 151,350 |
| Operating expenses. . . . . . | 98,600 |
| Interest expense. . . . . . . . | 4,100 |
| Income before taxes. . . . . | 48,650 |
| Income tax expense . . . . . | 19,598 |
| Net income . . . . . . . . . . . . | $ 29,052 |

**Required**

Compute the following: (1) current ratio, (2) acid-test ratio, (3) days' sales uncollected, (4) inventory turnover, (5) days' sales in inventory, (6) debt-to-equity ratio, (7) times interest earned, (8) profit margin ratio, (9) total asset turnover, (10) return on total assets, and (11) return on equity. Round to one decimal place; for part 6, round to two decimals.

**Check** Acid-test ratio, 2.2 to 1; Inventory turnover, 7.3

**Problem 13-5A**
Comparative ratio analysis

**P3**

Summary information from the financial statements of two companies competing in the same industry follows.

| | Barco Company | Kyan Company | | Barco Company | Kyan Company |
|---|---|---|---|---|---|
| **Data from the current year-end balance sheets** | | | **Data from the current year's income statement** | | |
| **Assets** | | | Sales.................................. | $770,000 | $880,200 |
| Cash........................... | $ 19,500 | $ 34,000 | Cost of goods sold.................... | 585,100 | 632,500 |
| Accounts receivable, net .............. | 46,500 | 64,600 | Interest expense .................... | 7,900 | 13,000 |
| Merchandise inventory................ | 84,440 | 132,500 | Income tax expense ................. | 14,800 | 24,300 |
| Prepaid expenses.................... | 5,000 | 6,950 | Net income ........................ | 162,200 | 210,400 |
| Plant assets, net .................... | 290,000 | 304,400 | Basic earnings per share............. | 4.51 | 5.11 |
| Total assets........................ | $445,440 | $542,450 | Cash dividends per share ............ | 3.81 | 3.93 |
| **Liabilities and Equity** | | | **Beginning-of-year balance sheet data** | | |
| Current liabilities.................... | $ 61,340 | $ 93,300 | Accounts receivable, net.............. | $ 29,800 | $ 54,200 |
| Long-term notes payable.............. | 80,800 | 101,000 | Merchandise inventory .............. | 55,600 | 107,400 |
| Common stock, $5 par value.......... | 180,000 | 206,000 | Total assets ....................... | 398,000 | 382,500 |
| Retained earnings................... | 123,300 | 142,150 | Common stock, $5 par value .......... | 180,000 | 206,000 |
| Total liabilities and equity............. | $445,440 | $542,450 | Retained earnings................... | 98,300 | 93,600 |

**Required**

1. For both companies compute the (*a*) current ratio, (*b*) acid-test ratio, (*c*) accounts receivable turnover, (*d*) inventory turnover, (*e*) days' sales in inventory, and (*f*) days' sales uncollected. Round to one decimal place. Identify the company you consider to be the better short-term credit risk and explain why.

2. For both companies compute the (*a*) profit margin ratio, (*b*) total asset turnover, (*c*) return on total assets, and (*d*) return on equity. Assuming that each company's stock can be purchased at $75 per share, compute their (*e*) price-earnings ratios and (*f*) dividend yields. Round to one decimal place. Identify which company's stock you would recommend as the better investment and explain why.

**Problem 13-6A**[A]
Income statement
computations and format

**A2**

Selected account balances from the adjusted trial balance for Olinda Corporation as of its calendar year-end December 31 follow.

| | Debit | Credit |
|---|---|---|
| a. Interest revenue............................................ | | $ 14,000 |
| b. Depreciation expense—Equipment.......................... | $ 34,000 | |
| c. Loss on sale of equipment................................ | 25,850 | |
| d. Accounts payable......................................... | | 44,000 |
| e. Other operating expenses................................. | 106,400 | |
| f. Accumulated depreciation—Equipment ..................... | | 71,600 |
| g. Gain from settlement of lawsuit............................ | | 44,000 |
| h. Accumulated depreciation—Buildings ...................... | | 174,500 |
| i. Loss from operating a discontinued segment (pretax)........... | 18,250 | |
| j. Gain on insurance recovery of tornado damage .............. | | 20,000 |
| k. Net sales................................................ | | 998,000 |
| l. Depreciation expense—Buildings .......................... | 52,000 | |
| m. Correction of overstatement of prior year's sales (pretax)........ | 16,000 | |
| n. Gain on sale of discontinued segment's assets (pretax) ......... | | 34,000 |
| o. Loss from settlement of lawsuit............................ | 23,250 | |
| p. Income tax expense....................................... | ? | |
| q. Cost of goods sold ....................................... | 482,500 | |

**Required**

1. Assume that the company's income tax rate is 30% for all items. Identify the tax effects and after-tax amounts of the three items labeled pretax.

2. Compute the amount of income from continuing operations before income taxes. What is the amount of the income tax expense? What is the amount of income from continuing operations?

3. What is the total amount of after-tax income (loss) associated with the discontinued segment?

4. What is the amount of net income for the year?

**Check**  (3) $11,025

(4) $257,425

---

Selected comparative financial statements of Tripoly Company follow.

**PROBLEM SET B**

**Problem 13-1B**
Calculating and analyzing trend percents
**P1**

| | | | TRIPOLY COMPANY<br>Comparative Income Statements<br>For Years Ended December 31 | | | | |
|---|---|---|---|---|---|---|---|
| $ thousands | 2021 | 2020 | 2019 | 2018 | 2017 | 2016 | 2015 |
| Sales . . . . . . . . . . . . . . . . | $560 | $610 | $630 | $680 | $740 | $770 | $860 |
| Cost of goods sold . . . . . . | 276 | 290 | 294 | 314 | 340 | 350 | 380 |
| Gross profit . . . . . . . . . . . | 284 | 320 | 336 | 366 | 400 | 420 | 480 |
| Operating expenses . . . . . | 84 | 104 | 112 | 126 | 140 | 144 | 150 |
| Net income . . . . . . . . . . . | $200 | $216 | $224 | $240 | $260 | $276 | $330 |

| | | | TRIPOLY COMPANY<br>Comparative Year-End Balance Sheets | | | | |
|---|---|---|---|---|---|---|---|
| At December 31, $ thousands | 2021 | 2020 | 2019 | 2018 | 2017 | 2016 | 2015 |
| **Assets** | | | | | | | |
| Cash. . . . . . . . . . . . . . . . . . . . . | $ 44 | $ 46 | $ 52 | $ 54 | $ 60 | $ 62 | $ 68 |
| Accounts receivable, net . . . . . . | 130 | 136 | 140 | 144 | 150 | 154 | 160 |
| Merchandise inventory. . . . . . . . | 166 | 172 | 178 | 180 | 186 | 190 | 208 |
| Other current assets. . . . . . . . . | 34 | 34 | 36 | 38 | 38 | 40 | 40 |
| Long-term investments. . . . . . . | 36 | 30 | 26 | 110 | 110 | 110 | 110 |
| Plant assets, net . . . . . . . . . . . . | 510 | 514 | 520 | 412 | 420 | 428 | 454 |
| Total assets . . . . . . . . . . . . . . . | $920 | $932 | $952 | $938 | $964 | $984 | $1,040 |
| **Liabilities and Equity** | | | | | | | |
| Current liabilities. . . . . . . . . . . . | $148 | $156 | $186 | $190 | $210 | $260 | $ 280 |
| Long-term liabilities . . . . . . . . . | 92 | 120 | 142 | 148 | 194 | 214 | 260 |
| Common stock . . . . . . . . . . . . . | 160 | 160 | 160 | 160 | 160 | 160 | 160 |
| Other paid-in capital. . . . . . . . . | 70 | 70 | 70 | 70 | 70 | 70 | 70 |
| Retained earnings. . . . . . . . . . . | 450 | 426 | 394 | 370 | 330 | 280 | 270 |
| Total liabilities and equity. . . . . | $920 | $932 | $952 | $938 | $964 | $984 | $1,040 |

**Required**

1. Compute trend percents for all components of both statements using 2015 as the base year. Round percents to one decimal.

**Check**  (1) 2021, Total assets trend, 88.5%

*Analysis Component*

2. Analyze and comment on the financial statements and trend percents from part 1.

---

Selected comparative financial statement information of Bluegrass Corporation follows.

**Problem 13-2B**
Ratios, common-size statements, and trend percents  **P1  P2  P3**

[continued on next page]

[continued from previous page]

| BLUEGRASS CORPORATION Comparative Year-End Balance Sheets | | | |
|---|---|---|---|
| **At December 31** | **2021** | **2020** | **2019** |
| **Assets** | | | |
| Current assets............ | $ 54,860 | $ 32,660 | $ 36,300 |
| Long-term investments..... | 0 | 1,700 | 10,600 |
| Plant assets, net.......... | 112,810 | 113,660 | 79,000 |
| Total assets.............. | $167,670 | $148,020 | $125,900 |
| **Liabilities and Equity** | | | |
| Current liabilities.......... | $ 22,370 | $ 19,180 | $ 16,500 |
| Common stock ........... | 46,500 | 46,500 | 37,000 |
| Other paid-in capital....... | 13,850 | 13,850 | 11,300 |
| Retained earnings......... | 84,950 | 68,490 | 61,100 |
| Total liabilities and equity... | $167,670 | $148,020 | $125,900 |

| BLUEGRASS CORPORATION Comparative Income Statements | | | |
|---|---|---|---|
| **For Years Ended December 31** | **2021** | **2020** | **2019** |
| Sales ................. | $198,800 | $166,000 | $143,800 |
| Cost of goods sold ...... | 108,890 | 86,175 | 66,200 |
| Gross profit............ | 89,910 | 79,825 | 77,600 |
| Selling expenses........ | 22,680 | 19,790 | 18,000 |
| Administrative expenses . | 16,760 | 14,610 | 15,700 |
| Total expenses ......... | 39,440 | 34,400 | 33,700 |
| Income before taxes..... | 50,470 | 45,425 | 43,900 |
| Income tax expense ..... | 6,050 | 5,910 | 5,300 |
| Net income ............ | $ 44,420 | $ 39,515 | $ 38,600 |

**Required**

1. Compute each year's current ratio. Round ratios to one decimal.

2. Express the income statement data in common-size percents. Round percents to two decimals.

**Check** (3) 2021, Total assets trend, 133.18%

3. Express the balance sheet data in trend percents with 2019 as the base year. Round percents to two decimals.

*Analysis Component*

4. Comment on any significant relations revealed by the ratios and percents computed.

---

**Problem 13-3B**

Transactions, working capital, and liquidity ratios   **P3**

**Check** June 3: Current ratio, 2.88; Acid-test ratio, 2.40

June 30: Working capital, $(10,000); Current ratio, 0.97

Koto Corporation began the month of June with $300,000 of current assets, a current ratio of 2.5:1, and an acid-test ratio of 1.4:1. During the month, it completed the following transactions. The company uses a perpetual inventory system.

| June | 1 | Sold merchandise inventory that cost $75,000 for $120,000 cash. |
|---|---|---|
| | 3 | Collected $88,000 cash on an account receivable. |
| | 5 | Purchased $150,000 of merchandise inventory on credit. |
| | 7 | Borrowed $100,000 cash by giving the bank a 60-day, 10% note. |
| | 10 | Borrowed $120,000 cash by signing a long-term secured note. |
| | 12 | Purchased machinery for $275,000 cash. |
| | 15 | Declared a $1 per share cash dividend on its 80,000 shares of outstanding common stock. |
| | 19 | Wrote off a $5,000 bad debt against the Allowance for Doubtful Accounts account. |
| | 22 | Paid $12,000 cash to settle an account payable. |
| | 30 | Paid the dividend declared on June 15. |

**Required**

Prepare a table, similar to the following, showing the company's (1) current ratio, (2) acid-test ratio, and (3) working capital after each transaction. Round ratios to two decimals.

| | A | B | C | D | E | F | G |
|---|---|---|---|---|---|---|---|
| 1 | | **Current** | **Quick** | **Current** | **Current** | **Acid-Test** | **Working** |
| 2 | **Transaction** | **Assets** | **Assets** | **Liabilities** | **Ratio** | **Ratio** | **Capital** |
| 3 | Beginning | $300,000 | — | — | 2.50 | 1.40 | — |

---

**Problem 13-4B**

Calculating financial statement ratios

**P3**

Selected current year-end financial statements of Overton Corporation follow. (All sales were on credit; selected balance sheet amounts at December 31 of the *prior year* were inventory, $17,400; total assets, $94,900; common stock, $35,500; and retained earnings, $18,800.)

| OVERTON CORPORATION |  |
| --- | --- |
| **Income Statement** |  |
| **For Current Year Ended December 31** |  |
| Sales . . . . . . . . . . . . . . . . . | $315,500 |
| Cost of goods sold . . . . . . | 236,100 |
| Gross profit . . . . . . . . . . . | 79,400 |
| Operating expenses . . . . . | 49,200 |
| Interest expense . . . . . . . . | 2,200 |
| Income before taxes . . . . . | 28,000 |
| Income tax expense . . . . . | 4,200 |
| Net income . . . . . . . . . . . | $ 23,800 |

**OVERTON CORPORATION**
**Balance Sheet**
**December 31 of Current Year**

| Assets |  | Liabilities and Equity |  |
| --- | --- | --- | --- |
| Cash. . . . . . . . . . . . . . . . . . | $  6,100 | Accounts payable. . . . . . . . . . . . . . | $ 11,500 |
| Short-term investments . . . . | 6,900 | Accrued wages payable. . . . . . . . . . | 3,300 |
| Accounts receivable, net . . . | 15,100 | Income taxes payable . . . . . . . . . . . | 2,600 |
| Merchandise inventory. . . . . | 13,500 | Long-term note payable, secured |  |
| Prepaid expenses. . . . . . . . . | 2,000 |   by mortgage on plant assets. . . . | 30,000 |
| Plant assets, net . . . . . . . . . . | 73,900 | Common stock, $5 par value. . . . . . | 35,000 |
|  |  | Retained earnings . . . . . . . . . . . . . . | 35,100 |
| Total assets . . . . . . . . . . . . . | $117,500 | Total liabilities and equity . . . . . . . . | $117,500 |

**Required**

Compute the following: (1) current ratio, (2) acid-test ratio, (3) days' sales uncollected, (4) inventory turnover, (5) days' sales in inventory, (6) debt-to-equity ratio, (7) times interest earned, (8) profit margin ratio, (9) total asset turnover, (10) return on total assets, and (11) return on equity. Round to one decimal place; for part 6, round to two decimals.

**Check**  Acid-test ratio, 1.6 to 1; Inventory turnover, 15.3

Summary information from the financial statements of two companies competing in the same industry follows.

**Problem 13-5B**
Comparative ratio analysis  **P3**

|  | Fargo Company | Ball Company |  | Fargo Company | Ball Company |
| --- | --- | --- | --- | --- | --- |
| **Data from the current year-end balance sheets** |  |  | **Data from the current year's income statement** |  |  |
| **Assets** |  |  | Sales. . . . . . . . . . . . . . . . . . . . . . . . . . | $393,600 | $667,500 |
| Cash. . . . . . . . . . . . . . . . . . . . . . | $ 20,000 | $ 36,500 | Cost of goods sold. . . . . . . . . . . . . . . | 290,600 | 480,000 |
| Accounts receivable, net . . . . . . . . . . . . . | 88,700 | 79,500 | Interest expense . . . . . . . . . . . . . . . . . | 5,900 | 12,300 |
| Merchandise inventory. . . . . . . . . . . . . . . | 86,800 | 82,000 | Income tax expense . . . . . . . . . . . . . . | 5,700 | 12,300 |
| Prepaid expenses. . . . . . . . . . . . . . . . . . | 9,700 | 10,100 | Net income . . . . . . . . . . . . . . . . . . . . | 33,850 | 61,700 |
| Plant assets, net . . . . . . . . . . . . . . . . . . . | 176,900 | 252,300 | Basic earnings per share. . . . . . . . . . . . | 1.27 | 2.19 |
| Total assets . . . . . . . . . . . . . . . . . . . . . . | $382,100 | $460,400 |  |  |  |
| **Liabilities and Equity** |  |  | **Beginning-of-year balance sheet data** |  |  |
| Current liabilities. . . . . . . . . . . . . . . . . . . | $ 90,500 | $ 97,000 | Accounts receivable, net. . . . . . . . . . . . | $ 72,200 | $ 73,300 |
| Long-term notes payable. . . . . . . . . . . . . | 93,000 | 93,300 | Merchandise inventory . . . . . . . . . . . . . | 105,100 | 80,500 |
| Common stock, $5 par value . . . . . . . . . . | 133,000 | 141,000 | Total assets . . . . . . . . . . . . . . . . . . . . | 383,400 | 443,000 |
| Retained earnings. . . . . . . . . . . . . . . . . . | 65,600 | 129,100 | Common stock, $5 par value . . . . . . . . . | 133,000 | 141,000 |
| Total liabilities and equity. . . . . . . . . . . . . | $382,100 | $460,400 | Retained earnings . . . . . . . . . . . . . . . . | 49,100 | 109,700 |

**Required**

**1.** For both companies compute the (*a*) current ratio, (*b*) acid-test ratio, (*c*) accounts receivable turnover, (*d*) inventory turnover, (*e*) days' sales in inventory, and (*f*) days' sales uncollected. Round to one decimal place. Identify the company you consider to be the better short-term credit risk and explain why.

**2.** For both companies compute the (*a*) profit margin ratio, (*b*) total asset turnover, (*c*) return on total assets, and (*d*) return on equity. Assuming that each company paid cash dividends of $1.50 per share and each company's stock can be purchased at $25 per share, compute their (*e*) price-earnings ratios and (*f*) dividend yields. Round to one decimal place; for part *b*, round to two decimals. Identify which company's stock you would recommend as the better investment and explain why.

**Check**  (1) Fargo: Accounts receivable turnover, 4.9; Inventory turnover, 3.0

(2) Ball: Profit margin, 9.2%; PE, 11.4

**Problem 13-6B^A**
Income statement computations and format

A2

Selected account balances from the adjusted trial balance for Harbor Corp. as of its calendar year-end December 31 follow.

| | Debit | Credit |
|---|---|---|
| a. Accumulated depreciation—Buildings .......................... | | $ 400,000 |
| b. Interest revenue........................................ | | 20,000 |
| c. Net sales............................................... | | 2,640,000 |
| d. Income tax expense...................................... | $      ? | |
| e. Loss on hurricane damage ............................... | 48,000 | |
| f. Accumulated depreciation—Equipment...................... | | 220,000 |
| g. Other operating expenses................................ | 328,000 | |
| h. Depreciation expense—Equipment.......................... | 100,000 | |
| i. Loss from settlement of lawsuit ........................... | 36,000 | |
| j. Gain from settlement of lawsuit ............................ | | 68,000 |
| k. Loss on sale of equipment................................ | 24,000 | |
| l. Loss from operating a discontinued segment (pretax)............ | 120,000 | |
| m. Depreciation expense—Buildings........................... | 156,000 | |
| n. Correction of overstatement of prior year's expense (pretax)....... | | 48,000 |
| o. Cost of goods sold...................................... | 1,040,000 | |
| p. Loss on sale of discontinued segment's assets (pretax) ........... | 180,000 | |
| q. Accounts payable....................................... | | 132,000 |

**Required**

1. Assume that the company's income tax rate is 25% for all items. Identify the tax effects and after-tax amounts of the three items labeled pretax.

2. What is the amount of income from continuing operations before income taxes? What is the amount of income tax expense? What is the amount of income from continuing operations?

**Check**   (3) $(225,000)

(4) $522,000

3. What is the total amount of after-tax income (loss) associated with the discontinued segment?

4. What is the amount of net income for the year?

---

**SERIAL PROBLEM**
Business Solutions

P3

Alexander Image/Shutterstock

*Serial problem began in Chapter 1. If previous chapter segments were not completed, the serial problem can begin at this point. It is available in **Connect** with an algorithmic option.*

**SP 13**   Use the following selected data from **Business Solutions**'s income statement for the three months ended March 31, 2022, and from its March 31, 2022, balance sheet to complete the requirements.

| | | | | | | |
|---|---|---|---|---|---|---|
| Computer services revenue....... | $25,307 | Net income......... | $ 18,833 | Current liabilities ..... | $ | 875 |
| Net sales (of goods) ............. | 18,693 | Quick assets........ | 90,924 | Total liabilities ....... | | 875 |
| Total sales and revenue .......... | 44,000 | Current assets ...... | 95,568 | Total equity.......... | | 119,393 |
| Cost of goods sold ............. | 14,052 | Total assets ........ | 120,268 | | | |

**Required**

1. Compute the gross margin ratio (both with and without services revenue) and net profit margin ratio (round the percent to one decimal).

2. Compute the current ratio and acid-test ratio (round to one decimal).

3. Compute the debt ratio and equity ratio (round the percent to one decimal).

4. What percent of its assets are current? What percent are long term? Round percents to one decimal.

---

**TABLEAU DASHBOARD ACTIVITIES**

**Tableau Dashboard Activities** expose students to accounting analytics using visual displays. These assignments run in **Connect**. All are auto-gradable.

**Tableau DA 13-1 Quick Study**, Computing profit margin, **P3**—similar to QS 13-15, part *a*

**Tableau DA 13-2 Exercise**, Computing profit margin and return on assets, **P3**—similar to QS 13-15

**Tableau DA 13-3 Mini-Case**, Computing ratios and making business decisions, **P3**—similar to Exercise 13-10

## Accounting Analysis

**AA 13-1**  Use **Apple**'s financial statements in Appendix A to answer the following.

1. Using fiscal 2017 as the base year, compute trend percents for fiscal years 2017, 2018, and 2019 for total net sales, total cost of sales, operating income, other income (expense) net, provision for income taxes, and net income. Round percents to one decimal.

2. Compute common-size percents for fiscal years 2018 and 2019 for the following categories of assets: (*a*) total current assets; (*b*) property, plant and equipment, net; and (*c*) accounts receivable, net. Round percents to one decimal.

3. Using current assets as a percent of total assets to measure liquidity, did Apple's asset makeup become more liquid or less liquid in 2019?

**COMPANY ANALYSIS**

A1   P1   P2

---

**AA 13-2**  Key figures for **Apple** and **Google** follow.

**COMPARATIVE ANALYSIS**

C1   P2

| $ millions | Apple | Google | $ millions | Apple | Google |
|---|---|---|---|---|---|
| Cash and equivalents............. | $48,844 | $ 18,498 | Cost of sales .......... | $161,782 | $ 71,896 |
| Accounts receivable, net .......... | 22,926 | 25,326 | Revenues ............ | 260,174 | 161,857 |
| Inventories ..................... | 4,106 | 999 | Total assets........... | 338,516 | 275,909 |
| Retained earnings................ | 45,898 | 152,122 | | | |

**Required**

1. Compute common-size percents for each company using the data given. Round percents to one decimal.

2. If Google paid a dividend, would retained earnings as a percent of total assets increase or decrease?

3. Which company has the better gross margin ratio on sales?

---

**AA 13-3**  Key figures for **Samsung** follow (in $ millions).

**EXTENDED ANALYSIS**

A1

| | | | | |
|---|---|---|---|---|
| Cash and equivalents............... | $ 23,069 | Cost of sales ...................... | $126,336 | |
| Accounts receivable, net ............ | 30,144 | Revenues ........................ | 197,691 | |
| Inventories ...................... | 22,966 | Total assets...................... | 302,511 | |
| Retained earnings ................. | 218,440 | | | |

**Required**

1. Compute common-size percents for Samsung using the data given. Round percents to one decimal.

2. What is Samsung's gross margin ratio on sales?

3. Does Samsung's gross margin ratio outperform or underperform the industry average of 25%?

## Discussion Questions

1. Explain the difference between financial reporting and financial statements.

2. What is the difference between comparative financial statements and common-size comparative statements?

3. Which items are usually assigned a 100% value on (*a*) a common-size balance sheet and (*b*) a common-size income statement?

4. What three factors would influence your evaluation as to whether a company's current ratio is good or bad?

5. Suggest several reasons why a 2:1 current ratio might not be adequate for a particular company.

6. Why is working capital given special attention in the process of analyzing balance sheets?

7. What does the number of days' sales uncollected indicate?

8. What does a relatively high accounts receivable turnover indicate about a company's short-term liquidity?

9. Why is a company's capital structure, as measured by debt and equity ratios, important to financial statement analysts?

10. How does inventory turnover provide information about a company's short-term liquidity?

11. What ratios would you compute to evaluate management performance?

12. Why would a company's return on total assets be different from its return on equity?

13. Where on the income statement does a company report an unusual gain not expected to occur more often than once every two years or so?

## Beyond the Numbers

**ETHICS CHALLENGE**

A1

**BTN 13-1**   As Beacon Company controller, you are responsible for informing the board of directors about its financial activities. At the board meeting, you present the following information.

|  | 2021 | 2020 | 2019 |
|---|---|---|---|
| Sales trend percent | 147.0% | 135.0% | 100.0% |
| Selling expenses to sales | 10.1% | 14.0% | 15.6% |
| Sales to plant assets ratio | 3.8 to 1 | 3.6 to 1 | 3.3 to 1 |
| Current ratio | 2.9 to 1 | 2.7 to 1 | 2.4 to 1 |
| Acid-test ratio | 1.1 to 1 | 1.4 to 1 | 1.5 to 1 |
| Inventory turnover | 7.8 times | 9.0 times | 10.2 times |
| Accounts receivable turnover | 7.0 times | 7.7 times | 8.5 times |
| Total asset turnover | 2.9 times | 2.9 times | 3.3 times |
| Return on total assets | 10.4% | 11.0% | 13.2% |
| Return on equity | 10.7% | 11.5% | 14.1% |
| Profit margin ratio | 3.6% | 3.8% | 4.0% |

After the meeting, the company's CEO holds a press conference with analysts in which she mentions the following ratios.

|  | 2021 | 2020 | 2019 |
|---|---|---|---|
| Sales trend percent | 147.0% | 135.0% | 100.0% |
| Selling expenses to sales | 10.1% | 14.0% | 15.6% |
| Sales to plant assets ratio | 3.8 to 1 | 3.6 to 1 | 3.3 to 1 |
| Current ratio | 2.9 to 1 | 2.7 to 1 | 2.4 to 1 |

**Required**

1. Why do you think the CEO decided to report 4 ratios instead of the 11 prepared?
2. Comment on the possible consequences of the CEO's reporting of the ratios selected.

**COMMUNICATING IN PRACTICE**

A1    P3

**BTN 13-2**   Each team is to select a different industry, and each team member is to select a different company in that industry and acquire its financial statements. Use those statements to analyze the company, including at least one ratio from each of the four building blocks of analysis. When necessary, use the financial press to determine the market price of its stock. Communicate with teammates via a meeting, e-mail, or telephone to discuss how different companies compare to each other and to industry norms. The team is to prepare a single one-page memorandum reporting on its analysis and the conclusions reached.

**TAKING IT TO THE NET**

P3

**BTN 13-3**   Access the February 22, 2019, filing of the December 31, 2018, 10-K report of **The Hershey Company** (ticker: HSY) at **SEC.gov** and complete the following requirements.

**Required**

Compute or identify the following profitability ratios of Hershey for its years ending December 31, 2018, *and* December 31, 2017. Interpret its profitability using the results obtained for these two years.

1. Profit margin ratio (round the percent to one decimal).
2. Gross profit ratio (round the percent to one decimal).
3. Return on total assets (round the percent to one decimal). (Total assets at year-end 2016 were $5,524,333 in thousands.)
4. Return on equity (round the percent to one decimal). (Total shareholders' equity at year-end 2016 was $827,687 in thousands.)
5. Basic net income per common share (round to the nearest cent).

**BTN 13-4** A team approach to learning financial statement analysis is often useful.

**Required**

1. Each team should write a description of horizontal and vertical analysis that all team members agree with and understand. Illustrate each description with an example.

2. *Each* member of the team is to select *one* of the following categories of ratio analysis. Explain what the ratios in that category measure. Choose one ratio from the category selected, present its formula, and explain what it measures.

    **a.** Liquidity and efficiency     **c.** Profitability

    **b.** Solvency     **d.** Market prospects

3. Each team member is to present his or her notes from part 2 to teammates. Team members are to confirm or correct other teammates' presentations.

**TEAMWORK IN ACTION**
P1 P2 P3

**Hint:** Pairing within teams may be necessary for part 2. Use as an in-class activity or as an assignment. Consider presentations to the entire class using team rotation with slides.

---

**BTN 13-5** Assume that Carla Harris of **Morgan Stanley** (**MorganStanley.com**) has impressed you with the company's success and its commitment to ethical behavior. You learn of a staff opening at Morgan Stanley and decide to apply for it. Your resume is successfully screened from those received and you advance to the interview process. You learn that the interview consists of analyzing the following financial facts and answering analysis questions below. (The data are taken from a small merchandiser in outdoor recreational equipment.)

**ENTREPRENEURIAL DECISION**
A1 P1 P2 P3

| | 2021 | 2020 | 2019 |
|---|---|---|---|
| Sales trend percents. . . . . . . . . . . . . . | 137.0% | 125.0% | 100.0% |
| Selling expenses to sales. . . . . . . . . . | 9.8% | 13.7% | 15.3% |
| Sales to plant assets ratio . . . . . . . . . | 3.5 to 1 | 3.3 to 1 | 3.0 to 1 |
| Current ratio . . . . . . . . . . . . . . . . . . . . | 2.6 to 1 | 2.4 to 1 | 2.1 to 1 |
| Acid-test ratio . . . . . . . . . . . . . . . . . . . | 0.8 to 1 | 1.1 to 1 | 1.2 to 1 |
| Merchandise inventory turnover . . . . . | 7.5 times | 8.7 times | 9.9 times |
| Accounts receivable turnover . . . . . . . | 6.7 times | 7.4 times | 8.2 times |
| Total asset turnover . . . . . . . . . . . . . . | 2.6 times | 2.6 times | 3.0 times |
| Return on total assets. . . . . . . . . . . . . | 8.8% | 9.4% | 11.1% |
| Return on equity . . . . . . . . . . . . . . . . . | 9.75% | 11.50% | 12.25% |
| Profit margin ratio. . . . . . . . . . . . . . . . | 3.3% | 3.5% | 3.7% |

**Required**

1. Is it becoming easier for the company to meet its current liabilities on time and to take advantage of any available cash discounts? Explain.

2. Is the company collecting its accounts receivable more rapidly? Explain.

3. Is the company's investment in accounts receivable decreasing? Explain.

4. Is the company's investment in plant assets increasing? Explain.

5. Is the owner's investment becoming more profitable? Explain.

6. Did the dollar amount of selling expenses decrease during the three-year period? Explain.

# Financial Statement Information

This appendix includes financial information for (1) **Apple**, (2) **Google**, and (3) **Samsung**. Apple states that it designs, manufactures and markets smartphones, personal computers, tablets, wearables, and accessories, and sells a variety of related services. It competes with both Google and Samsung in the United States and globally. The information in this appendix is taken from annual 10-K reports (or annual report for Samsung) filed with the SEC or other regulatory agency. An **annual report** is a summary of a company's financial results for the year along with its current financial condition and future plans. This report is directed to external users of financial information, but it also affects the actions and decisions of internal users.

A company often uses an annual report to showcase itself and its products. Many annual reports include photos, diagrams, and illustrations related to the company. The primary objective of annual reports, however, is the financial section, which communicates much information about a company, with most data drawn from the accounting information system. The content of a typical annual report's financial section follows.

- Letter to Shareholders
- Financial History and Highlights
- Quantitative and Qualitative Disclosures about Risk Factors
- Management Discussion and Analysis
- Management's Report on Financial Statements and on Internal Controls
- Report of Independent Accountants (Auditor's Report) and on Internal Controls
- Financial Statements
- Notes to Financial Statements
- Directors, Officers, and Corporate Governance
- Executive Compensation
- Accounting Fees and Services

This appendix provides the financial statements for Apple (plus selected notes), Google, and Samsung. (*Note:* Google is part of **Alphabet**; we refer to Alphabet as "Google" because of its global familiarity and because Google makes up 99% of Alphabet's revenues.) The appendix is organized as follows:

- **Apple** **A-1** through **A-8**
- **Google** **A-9** through **A-12**
- **Samsung** **A-13** through **A-16**

Many assignments at the end of each chapter refer to information in this appendix. We encourage readers to spend time with these assignments; they are especially useful in showing the relevance and diversity of accounting and reporting.

---

*Special note:* The SEC maintains the EDGAR (**E**lectronic **D**ata **G**athering, **A**nalysis, and **R**etrieval) database at **SEC.gov** for U.S. filers. The **Form 10-K** is the annual report form for most companies. It provides electronically accessible information. The **Form 10-KSB** is the annual report form filed by small businesses. It requires slightly less information than the Form 10-K. One of these forms must be filed within 90 days after the company's fiscal year-end. (Forms 10-K405, 10-KT, 10-KT405, and 10-KSB405 are slight variations of the usual form due to certain regulations or rules.)

## Apple Inc.
## CONSOLIDATED BALANCE SHEETS
(In millions, except number of shares which are reflected in thousands and par value)

|  | September 28, 2019 | September 29, 2018 |
|---|---|---|
| **ASSETS** | | |
| Current assets | | |
| Cash and cash equivalents | $ 48,844 | $ 25,913 |
| Marketable securities | 51,713 | 40,388 |
| Accounts receivable, net | 22,926 | 23,186 |
| Inventories | 4,106 | 3,956 |
| Vendor non-trade receivables | 22,878 | 25,809 |
| Other current assets | 12,352 | 12,087 |
| Total current assets | 162,819 | 131,339 |
| Non-current assets | | |
| Marketable securities | 105,341 | 170,799 |
| Property, plant and equipment, net | 37,378 | 41,304 |
| Other non-current assets | 32,978 | 22,283 |
| Total non-current assets | 175,697 | 234,386 |
| Total assets | $ 338,516 | $ 365,725 |
| **LIABILITIES AND SHAREHOLDERS' EQUITY** | | |
| Current liabilities | | |
| Accounts payable | $ 46,236 | $ 55,888 |
| Other current liabilities | 37,720 | 33,327 |
| Deferred revenue | 5,522 | 5,966 |
| Commercial paper | 5,980 | 11,964 |
| Term debt | 10,260 | 8,784 |
| Total current liabilities | 105,718 | 115,929 |
| Non-current liabilities | | |
| Term debt | 91,807 | 93,735 |
| Other non-current liabilities | 50,503 | 48,914 |
| Total non-current liabilities | 142,310 | 142,649 |
| Total liabilities | 248,028 | 258,578 |
| Commitments and contingencies | | |
| Shareholders' equity | | |
| Common stock and additional paid-in capital, $0.00001 par value: 12,600,000 shares authorized; 4,443,236 and 4,754,986 shares issued and outstanding, respectively | 45,174 | 40,201 |
| Retained earnings | 45,898 | 70,400 |
| Accumulated other comprehensive income (loss) | (584) | (3,454) |
| Total shareholders' equity | 90,488 | 107,147 |
| Total liabilities and shareholders' equity | $ 338,516 | $ 365,725 |

See accompanying Notes to Consolidated Financial Statements.

**APPLE**

## Apple Inc.
### CONSOLIDATED STATEMENTS OF OPERATIONS
(In millions, except number of shares which are reflected in thousands and per share amounts)

| Years ended | September 28, 2019 | September 29, 2018 | September 30, 2017 |
|---|---|---|---|
| Net sales: | | | |
| Products | $ 213,883 | $ 225,847 | $ 196,534 |
| Services | 46,291 | 39,748 | 32,700 |
| Total net sales | 260,174 | 265,595 | 229,234 |
| Cost of sales: | | | |
| Products | 144,996 | 148,164 | 126,337 |
| Services | 16,786 | 15,592 | 14,711 |
| Total cost of sales | 161,782 | 163,756 | 141,048 |
| Gross margin | 98,392 | 101,839 | 88,186 |
| Operating expenses: | | | |
| Research and development | 16,217 | 14,236 | 11,581 |
| Selling, general and administrative | 18,245 | 16,705 | 15,261 |
| Total operating expenses | 34,462 | 30,941 | 26,842 |
| Operating income | 63,930 | 70,898 | 61,344 |
| Other income (expense), net | 1,807 | 2,005 | 2,745 |
| Income before provision for income taxes | 65,737 | 72,903 | 64,089 |
| Provision for income taxes | 10,481 | 13,372 | 15,738 |
| Net income | $ 55,256 | $ 59,531 | $ 48,351 |
| Earnings per share: | | | |
| Basic | $ 11.97 | $ 12.01 | $ 9.27 |
| Diluted | $ 11.89 | $ 11.91 | $ 9.21 |
| Shares used in computing earnings per share: | | | |
| Basic | 4,617,834 | 4,955,377 | 5,217,242 |
| Diluted | 4,648,913 | 5,000,109 | 5,251,692 |

See accompanying Notes to Consolidated Financial Statements.

## Apple Inc.
### CONSOLIDATED STATEMENTS OF COMPREHENSIVE INCOME
(In millions)

| Years ended | September 28, 2019 | September 29, 2018 | September 30, 2017 |
|---|---|---|---|
| Net income | $ 55,256 | $ 59,531 | $ 48,351 |
| Other comprehensive income (loss): | | | |
| Change in foreign currency translation, net of tax | (408) | (525) | 224 |
| Change in unrealized gains/losses on derivative instruments, net of tax: | | | |
| Change in fair value of derivatives | (661) | 523 | 1,315 |
| Adjustment for net (gains) losses realized and included in net income | 23 | 382 | (1,477) |
| Total change in unrealized gains/losses on derivative instruments | (638) | 905 | (162) |
| Change in unrealized gains/losses on marketable securities, net of tax: | | | |
| Change in fair value of marketable securities | 3,802 | (3,407) | (782) |
| Adjustment for net (gains) losses realized and included in net income | 25 | 1 | (64) |
| Total change in unrealized gains/losses on marketable securities | 3,827 | (3,406) | (846) |
| Total other comprehensive income (loss) | 2,781 | (3,026) | (784) |
| Total comprehensive income | $ 58,037 | $ 56,505 | $ 47,567 |

See accompanying Notes to Consolidated Financial Statements.

APPLE

## Apple Inc.
## CONSOLIDATED STATEMENTS OF SHAREHOLDERS' EQUITY
(In millions)

| Years ended | September 28, 2019 | September 29, 2018 | September 30, 2017 |
|---|---|---|---|
| Total shareholders' equity, beginning balances | $ 107,147 | $ 134,047 | $ 128,249 |
| **Common stock and additional paid-in capital** | | | |
| Beginning balances | 40,201 | 35,867 | 31,251 |
| Common stock issued | 781 | 669 | 555 |
| Common stock withheld related to net share settlement of equity awards | (2,002) | (1,778) | (1,468) |
| Share-based compensation | 6,194 | 5,443 | 4,909 |
| Tax benefit from equity awards, including transfer pricing adjustments | — | — | 620 |
| Ending balances | 45,174 | 40,201 | 35,867 |
| | | | |
| **Retained earnings** | | | |
| Beginning balances | 70,400 | 98,330 | 96,364 |
| Net income | 55,256 | 59,531 | 48,351 |
| Dividends and dividend equivalents declared | (14,129) | (13,735) | (12,803) |
| Common stock withheld related to net share settlement of equity awards | (1,029) | (948) | (581) |
| Common stock repurchased | (67,101) | (73,056) | (33,001) |
| Cumulative effects of changes in accounting principles | 2,501 | 278 | — |
| Ending balances | 45,898 | 70,400 | 98,330 |
| | | | |
| **Accumulated other comprehensive income (loss)** | | | |
| Beginning balances | (3,454) | (150) | 634 |
| Other comprehensive income (loss) | 2,781 | (3,026) | (784) |
| Cumulative effects of changes in accounting principles | 89 | (278) | — |
| Ending balances | (584) | (3,454) | (150) |
| Total shareholders' equity, ending balances | $ 90,488 | $ 107,147 | $ 134,047 |

See accompanying Notes to Consolidated Financial Statements.

APPLE

## Apple Inc.
### CONSOLIDATED STATEMENTS OF CASH FLOWS
(In millions)

| Years ended | September 28, 2019 | September 29, 2018 | September 30, 2017 |
|---|---|---|---|
| Cash, cash equivalents and restricted cash, beginning balances | $ 25,913 | $ 20,289 | $ 20,484 |
| **Operating activities** | | | |
| Net income | 55,256 | 59,531 | 48,351 |
| Adjustments to reconcile net income to cash generated by operating activities: | | | |
| Depreciation and amortization | 12,547 | 10,903 | 10,157 |
| Share-based compensation expense | 6,068 | 5,340 | 4,840 |
| Deferred income tax expense (benefit) | (340) | (32,590) | 5,966 |
| Other | (652) | (444) | (166) |
| Changes in operating assets and liabilities: | | | |
| Accounts receivable, net | 245 | (5,322) | (2,093) |
| Inventories | (289) | 828 | (2,723) |
| Vendor non-trade receivables | 2,931 | (8,010) | (4,254) |
| Other current and non-current assets | 873 | (423) | (5,318) |
| Accounts payable | (1,923) | 9,175 | 8,966 |
| Deferred revenue | (625) | (3) | (593) |
| Other current and non-current liabilities | (4,700) | 38,449 | 1,092 |
| Cash generated by operating activities | 69,391 | 77,434 | 64,225 |
| **Investing activities** | | | |
| Purchases of marketable securities | (39,630) | (71,356) | (159,486) |
| Proceeds from maturities of marketable securities | 40,102 | 55,881 | 31,775 |
| Proceeds from sales of marketable securities | 56,988 | 47,838 | 94,564 |
| Payments for acquisition of property, plant and equipment | (10,495) | (13,313) | (12,451) |
| Payments made in connection with business acquisitions, net | (624) | (721) | (329) |
| Purchases of non-marketable securities | (1,001) | (1,871) | (521) |
| Proceeds from non-marketable securities | 1,634 | 353 | 126 |
| Other | (1,078) | (745) | (124) |
| Cash generated by (used in) investing activities | 45,896 | 16,066 | (46,446) |
| **Financing activities** | | | |
| Proceeds from issuance of common stock | 781 | 669 | 555 |
| Payments for taxes related to net share settlement of equity awards | (2,817) | (2,527) | (1,874) |
| Payments for dividends and dividend equivalents | (14,119) | (13,712) | (12,769) |
| Repurchases of common stock | (66,897) | (72,738) | (32,900) |
| Proceeds from issuance of term debt, net | 6,963 | 6,969 | 28,662 |
| Repayments of term debt | (8,805) | (6,500) | (3,500) |
| Proceeds from (Repayments of) commercial paper, net | (5,977) | (37) | 3,852 |
| Other | (105) | — | — |
| Cash used in financing activities | (90,976) | (87,876) | (17,974) |
| Increase (decrease) in cash, cash equivalents and restricted cash | 24,311 | 5,624 | (195) |
| Cash, cash equivalents and restricted cash, ending balances | $ 50,224 | $ 25,913 | $ 20,289 |
| **Supplemental cash flow disclosure:** | | | |
| Cash paid for income taxes, net | $ 15,263 | $ 10,417 | $ 11,591 |
| Cash paid for interest | $ 3,423 | $ 3,022 | $ 2,092 |

See accompanying Notes to Consolidated Financial Statements.

## APPLE INC.
## SELECTED NOTES TO CONSOLIDATED FINANCIAL STATEMENTS

### Basis of Presentation and Preparation

In the opinion of the Company's management, the consolidated financial statements reflect all adjustments, which are normal and recurring in nature, necessary for fair financial statement presentation. The preparation of these consolidated financial statements and accompanying notes in conformity with U.S. generally accepted accounting principles requires management to make estimates and assumptions that affect the amounts reported.

The Company's fiscal year is the 52- or 53-week period that ends on the last Saturday of September. The Company's fiscal years 2019 and 2018 spanned 52 weeks each, whereas fiscal year 2017 included 53 weeks. A 14th week was included in the first fiscal quarter of 2017, as is done every five or six years, to realign the Company's fiscal quarters with calendar quarters. Unless otherwise stated, references to particular years, quarters, months and periods refer to the Company's fiscal years ended in September and the associated quarters, months and periods of those fiscal years.

### Revenue Recognition

Net sales consist of revenue from the sale of iPhone, Mac, iPad, Services and other products. The Company recognizes revenue at the amount to which it expects to be entitled when control of the products or services is transferred to its customers. Control is generally transferred when the Company has a present right to payment and title and the significant risks and rewards of ownership of products or services are transferred to its customers. For most of the Company's Products net sales, control transfers when products are shipped. For the Company's Services net sales, control transfers over time as services are delivered. Payment for Products and Services net sales is collected within a short period following transfer of control or commencement of delivery of services, as applicable.

The Company records reductions to Products net sales related to future product returns, price protection and other customer incentive programs based on the Company's expectations and historical experience.

For arrangements with multiple performance obligations, which represent promises within an arrangement that are capable of being distinct, the Company allocates revenue to all distinct performance obligations based on their relative stand-alone selling prices ("SSPs"). When available, the Company uses observable prices to determine SSPs. When observable prices are not available, SSPs are established that reflect the Company's best estimates of what the selling prices of the performance obligations would be if they were sold regularly on a stand-alone basis.

The Company has identified up to three performance obligations regularly included in arrangements involving the sale of iPhone, Mac, iPad and certain other products. The first performance obligation, which represents the substantial portion of the allocated sales price, is the hardware and bundled software delivered at the time of sale. The second performance obligation is the right to receive certain product-related bundled services, which include iCloud, Siri and Maps. The third performance obligation is the right to receive, on a when-and-if-available basis, future unspecified software upgrades relating to the software bundled with each device. The Company allocates revenue and any related discounts to these performance obligations based on their relative SSPs. Because the Company lacks observable prices for the undelivered performance obligations, the allocation of revenue is based on the Company's estimated SSPs. Revenue allocated to the delivered hardware and bundled software is recognized when control has transferred to the customer, which generally occurs when the product is shipped. Revenue allocated to the product-related bundled services and unspecified software upgrade rights is deferred and recognized on a straight-line basis over the estimated period they are expected to be provided. Cost of sales related to delivered hardware and bundled software, including estimated warranty costs, are recognized at the time of sale. Costs incurred to provide product-related bundled services and unspecified software upgrade rights are recognized as cost of sales as incurred.

For the sale of third-party products where the Company obtains control of the product before transferring it to the customer, the Company recognizes revenue based on the gross amount billed to customers. The Company considers multiple factors when determining whether it obtains control of third-party products including, but not limited to, evaluating if it can establish the price of the product, retains inventory risk for tangible products or has the responsibility for ensuring acceptability of the product. For third-party applications sold through the App Store, Mac App Store, TV App Store and Watch App Store and certain digital content sold through the Company's other digital content stores, the Company does not obtain control of the product before transferring it to the customer. Therefore, the Company accounts for such sales on a net basis by recognizing in Services net sales only the commission it retains.

The Company has elected to record revenue net of taxes collected from customers that are remitted to governmental authorities, with the collected taxes recorded within other current liabilities until remitted to the relevant government authority.

*Deferred Revenue*    As of September 28, 2019 and September 29, 2018, the Company had total deferred revenue of $8.1 billion and $8.8 billion, respectively. As of September 28, 2019, the Company expects 68% of total deferred revenue to be realized in less than a year, 25% within one-to-two years, 6% within two-to-three years and 1% in greater than three years.

### Advertising Costs

Advertising costs are expensed as incurred and included in selling, general and administrative expenses.

APPLE

## Apple Inc. Notes—continued

### Other Income and Expense

| $ millions | 2019 | 2018 | 2017 |
|---|---|---|---|
| Interest and dividend income | $ 4,961 | $ 5,686 | $ 5,201 |
| Interest expense | (3,576) | (3,240) | (2,323) |
| Other income (expense), net | 422 | (441) | (133) |
| Total other income (expense), net | $ 1,807 | $ 2,005 | $ 2,745 |

### Cash Equivalents and Marketable Securities

All highly liquid investments with maturities of three months or less at the date of purchase are classified as cash equivalents. The Company's investments in marketable debt securities have been classified and accounted for as available-for-sale. The Company classifies its marketable debt securities as either short-term or long-term based on each instrument's underlying contractual maturity date. Unrealized gains and losses on marketable debt securities classified as available-for-sale are recognized in other comprehensive income/(loss) ("OCI").

The Company's investments in marketable equity securities are classified based on the nature of the securities and their availability for use in current operations. The Company's marketable equity securities are measured at fair value with gains and losses recognized in other income/(expense), net ("OI&E"). The cost of securities sold is determined using the specific identification method.

### Restricted Cash and Restricted Marketable Securities

The Company considers cash and marketable securities to be restricted when withdrawal or general use is legally restricted. The Company records restricted cash as other assets in the Consolidated Balance Sheets, and determines current or non-current classification based on the expected duration of the restriction. The Company records restricted marketable securities as current or non-current marketable securities in the Consolidated Balance Sheets based on the classification of the underlying securities.

The Company's restricted cash primarily consisted of cash required to be on deposit under a contractual agreement with a bank to support the Company's iPhone Upgrade Program.

### Accounts Receivable (Trade Receivables)

The Company has considerable trade receivables outstanding with its third-party cellular network carriers, wholesalers, retailers, resellers, small and mid-sized businesses and education, enterprise and government customers.

As of September 28, 2019, the Company had no customers that individually represented 10% or more of total trade receivables. As of September 29, 2018, the Company had one customer that represented 10% or more of total trade receivables, which accounted for 10%. The Company's cellular network carriers accounted for 51% and 59% of total trade receivables as of September 28, 2019 and September 29, 2018, respectively.

### Inventories

Inventories are measured using the first-in, first-out method.

### Property, Plant and Equipment

Depreciation on property, plant and equipment is recognized on a straight-line basis over the estimated useful lives of the assets, which for buildings is the lesser of 30 years or the remaining life of the underlying building; between one and five years for machinery and equipment, including product tooling and manufacturing process equipment; and the shorter of lease term or useful life for leasehold improvements. Capitalized costs related to internal-use software are amortized on a straight-line basis over the estimated useful lives of the assets, which range from three to five years. Depreciation and amortization expense on property and equipment was $11.3 billion, $9.3 billion and $8.2 billion during 2019, 2018 and 2017, respectively.

| $ millions | 2019 | 2018 |
|---|---|---|
| Land and buildings | $17,085 | $16,216 |
| Machinery, equipment and internal-use software | 69,797 | 65,982 |
| Leasehold improvements | 9,075 | 8,205 |
| Gross property, plant and equipment | 95,957 | 90,403 |
| Accumulated depreciation and amortization | (58,579) | (49,099) |
| Total property, plant and equipment, net | $37,378 | $41,304 |

### Fair Value Measurements

The fair values of the Company's money market funds and certain marketable equity securities are based on quoted prices in active markets for identical assets. The valuation techniques used to measure the fair value of the Company's debt instruments and all other financial instruments, which generally have counterparties with high credit ratings, are based on quoted market prices or model-driven valuations using significant inputs derived from or corroborated by observable market data.

### Financial Instruments

The Company typically invests in highly rated securities, with the primary objective of minimizing the potential risk of principal loss. The Company's investment policy generally requires securities to be investment grade and limits the amount of credit exposure to any one issuer. Fair values were determined for each individual security in the investment portfolio.

### Accrued Warranty and Guarantees

The following table shows changes in the Company's accrued warranties and related costs for 2019 and 2018:

| $ millions | 2019 | 2018 |
|---|---|---|
| Beginning accrued warranty and related costs | $ 3,692 | $ 3,834 |
| Cost of warranty claims | (3,857) | (4,115) |
| Accruals for product warranty | 3,735 | 3,973 |
| Ending accrued warranty and related costs | $ 3,570 | $ 3,692 |

## Apple Inc. Notes—continued

### Other Non-Current Liabilities

| $ millions | 2019 | 2018 |
|---|---|---|
| Long-term taxes payable | $29,545 | $33,589 |
| Other non-current liabilities | 20,958 | 15,325 |
| Total other non-current liabilities | $50,503 | $48,914 |

### Term Debt

As of September 28, 2019, the Company had outstanding floating- and fixed-rate notes with varying maturities for an aggregate principal amount of $101.7 billion (collectively the "Notes"). The Notes are senior unsecured obligations and interest is payable in arrears.

The Company recognized $3.2 billion, $3.0 billion and $2.2 billion of interest cost on its term debt for 2019, 2018 and 2017, respectively.

The future principal payments for the Company's Notes as of September 28, 2019 are as follows (in millions):

| | |
|---|---|
| 2020 | $ 10,270 |
| 2021 | 8,750 |
| 2022 | 9,528 |
| 2023 | 9,290 |
| 2024 | 10,039 |
| Thereafter | 53,802 |
| Total term debt | $101,679 |

As of September 28, 2019 and September 29, 2018, the fair value of the Company's Notes, based on Level 2 inputs, was $107.5 billion and $103.2 billion, respectively.

### Share Repurchase Program

On April 30, 2019, the Company announced the Board of Directors increased the current share repurchase program authorization from $100 billion to $175 billion of the Company's common stock, of which $96.1 billion had been utilized as of September 28, 2019. During 2019, the Company repurchased 345.2 million shares of its common stock for $67.1 billion, including 62.0 million shares delivered under a $12.0 billion accelerated share repurchase arrangement dated February 2019, which settled in August 2019. The Company's share repurchase program does not obligate it to acquire any specific number of shares.

### Contingencies

The Company is subject to various legal proceedings and claims that have arisen in the ordinary course of business and that have not been fully resolved. The outcome of litigation is inherently uncertain. If one or more legal matters were resolved against the Company in a reporting period for amounts above management's expectations, the Company's financial condition and operating results for that reporting period could be materially adversely affected. In the opinion of management, there was not at least a reasonable possibility the Company may have incurred a material loss, or a material loss greater than a recorded accrual, concerning loss contingencies for asserted legal and other claims, except for the following matters:

- VirnetX
- Qualcomm
- iOS Performance Management Cases
- French Competition Authority

### Disaggregated Revenue by Significant Products and Services

| Net sales (mil.) | 2019 | 2018 | 2017 |
|---|---|---|---|
| iPhone | $142,381 | $164,888 | $139,337 |
| Mac | 25,740 | 25,198 | 25,569 |
| iPad | 21,280 | 18,380 | 18,802 |
| Wearables, Home and Accessories | 24,482 | 17,381 | 12,826 |
| Services | 46,291 | 39,748 | 32,700 |
| Total net sales | $260,174 | $265,595 | $229,234 |

| Reportable segment (mil.) | 2019 | 2018 | 2017 |
|---|---|---|---|
| **Americas:** | | | |
| Net sales | $116,914 | $112,093 | $96,600 |
| Operating income | $ 35,099 | $ 34,864 | $30,684 |
| **Europe:** | | | |
| Net sales | $ 60,288 | $ 62,420 | $54,938 |
| Operating income | $ 19,195 | $ 19,955 | $16,514 |
| **Greater China:** | | | |
| Net sales | $ 43,678 | $ 51,942 | $44,764 |
| Operating income | $ 16,232 | $ 19,742 | $17,032 |
| **Japan:** | | | |
| Net sales | $ 21,506 | $ 21,733 | $17,733 |
| Operating income | $ 9,369 | $ 9,500 | $ 8,097 |
| **Rest of Asia Pacific:** | | | |
| Net sales | $ 17,788 | $ 17,407 | $15,199 |
| Operating income | $ 6,055 | $ 6,181 | $ 5,304 |

A reconciliation of the Company's segment operating income to the Consolidated Statements of Operations for 2019, 2018 and 2017 is as follows:

| $ millions | 2019 | 2018 | 2017 |
|---|---|---|---|
| Segment operating income | $ 85,950 | $ 90,242 | $77,631 |
| Research and development expense | (16,217) | (14,236) | (11,581) |
| Other corporate expenses, net | (5,803) | (5,108) | (4,706) |
| Total operating income | $ 63,930 | $ 70,898 | $61,344 |

APPLE

## Apple Inc. Notes—continued

### Selected Financial Data

(in millions, except number of shares, which are reflected in thousands, and per share amounts).

| | 2019 | 2018 | 2017 | 2016 | 2015 |
|---|---|---|---|---|---|
| Total net sales | $ 260,174 | $ 265,595 | $ 229,234 | $ 215,639 | $ 233,715 |
| Net income | $ 55,256 | $ 59,531 | $ 48,351 | $ 45,687 | $ 53,394 |
| Earnings per share: | | | | | |
| Basic | $ 11.97 | $ 12.01 | $ 9.27 | $ 8.35 | $ 9.28 |
| Diluted | $ 11.89 | $ 11.91 | $ 9.21 | $ 8.31 | $ 9.22 |
| Cash dividends declared per share | $ 3.00 | $ 2.72 | $ 2.40 | $ 2.18 | $ 1.98 |
| Shares used in computing earnings per share: | | | | | |
| Basic | 4,617,834 | 4,955,377 | 5,217,242 | 5,470,820 | 5,753,421 |
| Diluted | 4,648,913 | 5,000,109 | 5,251,692 | 5,500,281 | 5,793,069 |
| Total cash, cash equivalents and marketable securities | $ 205,898 | $ 237,100 | $ 268,895 | $ 237,585 | $ 205,666 |
| Total assets | $ 338,516 | $ 365,725 | $ 375,319 | $ 321,686 | $ 290,345 |
| Non-current portion of term debt | $ 91,807 | $ 93,735 | $ 97,207 | $ 75,427 | $ 53,329 |
| Other non-current liabilities | $ 50,503 | $ 48,914 | $ 44,212 | $ 39,986 | $ 38,104 |

### Company Background

The Company designs, manufactures and markets smartphones, personal computers, tablets, wearables and accessories, and sells a variety of related services. The Company's fiscal year is the 52- or 53-week period that ends on the last Saturday of September. The Company is a California corporation established in 1977.

### Products

*iPhone*   iPhone® is the Company's line of smartphones based on its iOS operating system. In September 2019, the Company introduced three new iPhones: iPhone 11, iPhone 11 Pro and iPhone 11 Pro Max.

*Mac*   Mac® is the Company's line of personal computers based on its macOS® operating system. During 2019, the Company released a new version of MacBook Air® and a new Mac mini®, and introduced an updated Mac Pro®, which is expected to be available in the fall of 2019.

*iPad*   iPad® is the Company's line of multi-purpose tablets. iPad is based on the Company's iPadOS™ operating system, which was introduced during 2019. Also during 2019, the Company released two new versions of iPad Pro®, an iPad Air®, an updated iPad mini® and a new 10.2-inch iPad.

*Wearables, Home and Accessories*   Wearables, Home and Accessories includes AirPods®, Apple TV®, Apple Watch®, Beats® products, HomePod™, iPod touch® and other Apple-branded and third-party accessories. AirPods are the Company's wireless headphones that interact with Siri. In October 2019, the Company introduced AirPods Pro™. Apple Watch is a personal electronic device that combines the watchOS® user interface and other technologies created specifically for a smaller device. In September 2019, the Company introduced Apple Watch Series 5.

### Services

*Digital Content Stores and Streaming Services*   The Company operates various platforms that allow customers to discover and download applications and digital content, such as books, music, video, games and podcasts. These platforms include the App Store®, available for iPhone and iPad, the Mac App Store, the TV App Store and the Watch App Store.

The Company also offers subscription-based digital content streaming services, including Apple Music®, which offers users a curated listening experience with on-demand radio stations, and Apple TV+, which offers exclusive original content, and is expected to be available in November 2019.

*AppleCare*   AppleCare® includes AppleCare+ ("AC+") and the AppleCare Protection Plan, which are fee-based services that extend the coverage of phone support eligibility and hardware repairs. AC+ offers additional coverage for instances of accidental damage and is available in certain countries for certain products. Additionally, AC+ with theft and loss protection is available for iPhone in the U.S.

*iCloud*   iCloud® is the Company's cloud service, which stores music, photos, contacts, calendars, mail, documents and more, keeping them up-to-date and available across multiple Apple devices and Windows personal computers.

*Licensing*   The Company licenses the use of certain of its intellectual property, and provides other related services.

*Other Services*   The Company delivers a variety of other services available in certain countries, including Apple Arcade™, a game subscription service; Apple Card™, a co-branded credit card; Apple News+, a subscription news and magazine service; and Apple Pay, a cashless payment service.

### Markets and Distribution

The Company's customers are primarily in the consumer, small and mid-sized business, education, enterprise and government markets. The Company sells its products and resells third-party products in most of its major markets directly to consumers, small and mid-sized businesses, and education, enterprise and government customers through its retail and online stores and its direct sales force. The Company also employs a variety of indirect distribution channels, such as third-party cellular network carriers, wholesalers, retailers and resellers. During 2019, the Company's net sales through its direct and indirect distribution channels accounted for 31% and 69%, respectively, of total net sales.

### Employees

As of September 28, 2019, the Company had approximately 137,000 full-time equivalent employees.

**Google Inc. (Alphabet Inc.)[a]**
**CONSOLIDATED BALANCE SHEETS**
**(In millions, except share amounts which are reflected in thousands,**
**and par value per share amounts)**

| | December 31, 2018 | December 31, 2019 |
|---|---:|---:|
| **Assets** | | |
| Current assets | | |
| Cash and cash equivalents | $ 16,701 | $ 18,498 |
| Marketable securities | 92,439 | 101,177 |
| Total cash, cash equivalents, and marketable securities | 109,140 | 119,675 |
| Accounts receivable, net of allowance of $729 and $753 | 20,838 | 25,326 |
| Income taxes receivable, net | 355 | 2,166 |
| Inventory | 1,107 | 999 |
| Other current assets | 4,236 | 4,412 |
| Total current assets | 135,676 | 152,578 |
| Non-marketable investments | 13,859 | 13,078 |
| Deferred income taxes | 737 | 721 |
| Property and equipment, net | 59,719 | 73,646 |
| Operating lease assets | 0 | 10,941 |
| Intangible assets, net | 2,220 | 1,979 |
| Goodwill | 17,888 | 20,624 |
| Other non-current assets | 2,693 | 2,342 |
| Total assets | $ 232,792 | $ 275,909 |
| **Liabilities and Stockholders' Equity** | | |
| Current liabilities | | |
| Accounts payable | $ 4,378 | $ 5,561 |
| Accrued compensation and benefits | 6,839 | 8,495 |
| Accrued expenses and other current liabilities | 16,958 | 23,067 |
| Accrued revenue share | 4,592 | 5,916 |
| Deferred revenue | 1,784 | 1,908 |
| Income taxes payable, net | 69 | 274 |
| Total current liabilities | 34,620 | 45,221 |
| Long-term debt | 4,012 | 4,554 |
| Deferred revenue, non-current | 396 | 358 |
| Income taxes payable, non-current | 11,327 | 9,885 |
| Deferred income taxes | 1,264 | 1,701 |
| Operating lease liabilities | 0 | 10,214 |
| Other long-term liabilities | 3,545 | 2,534 |
| Total liabilities | 55,164 | 74,467 |
| Commitments and Contingencies | | |
| Stockholders' equity | | |
| Convertible preferred stock, $0.001 par value per share, 100,000 shares authorized; no shares issued and outstanding | 0 | 0 |
| Class A and Class B common stock, and Class C capital stock and additional paid-in capital, $0.001 par value per share: 15,000,000 shares authorized (Class A 9,000,000, Class B 3,000,000, Class C 3,000,000); 695,556 (Class A 299,242, Class B 46,636, Class C 349,678) and 688,335 (Class A 299,828, Class B 46,441, Class C 342,066) shares issued and outstanding | 45,049 | 50,552 |
| Accumulated other comprehensive loss | (2,306) | (1,232) |
| Retained earnings | 134,885 | 152,122 |
| Total stockholders' equity | 177,628 | 201,442 |
| Total liabilities and stockholders' equity | $ 232,792 | $ 275,909 |

[a]Google is part of Alphabet, but we loosely refer to Alphabet as "Google" because of its global familiarity and because Google provides 99% of Alphabet's $161,857 billion in revenues.

See accompanying notes.

### Google Inc. (Alphabet Inc.)[a]
### CONSOLIDATED STATEMENTS OF INCOME
### (In millions)

| Year Ended December 31 | 2017 | 2018 | 2019 |
|---|---|---|---|
| Revenues | $ 110,855 | $ 136,819 | $ 161,857 |
| Costs and expenses | | | |
| Cost of revenues | 45,583 | 59,549 | 71,896 |
| Research and development | 16,625 | 21,419 | 26,018 |
| Sales and marketing | 12,893 | 16,333 | 18,464 |
| General and administrative | 6,840 | 6,923 | 9,551 |
| European Commission fines | 2,736 | 5,071 | 1,697 |
| Total costs and expenses | 84,677 | 109,295 | 127,626 |
| Income from operations | 26,178 | 27,524 | 34,231 |
| Other income (expense), net | 1,015 | 7,389 | 5,394 |
| Income before income taxes | 27,193 | 34,913 | 39,625 |
| Provision for income taxes | 14,531 | 4,177 | 5,282 |
| Net income | $ 12,662 | $ 30,736 | $ 34,343 |

[a]Google is part of Alphabet, but we loosely refer to Alphabet as "Google" because of its
global familiarity and because Google provides 99% of Alphabet's $161,857 billion in revenues.

See accompanying notes.

### Google Inc. (Alphabet Inc.)[a]
### CONSOLIDATED STATEMENTS OF COMPREHENSIVE INCOME
### (In millions)

| Year Ended December 31 | 2017 | 2018 | 2019 |
|---|---|---|---|
| Net income | $ 12,662 | $ 30,736 | $ 34,343 |
| Other comprehensive income (loss): | | | |
| Change in foreign currency translation adjustment | 1,543 | (781) | (119) |
| Available-for-sale investments: | | | |
| Change in net unrealized gains (losses) | 307 | 88 | 1,611 |
| Less: reclassification adjustment for net (gains) losses included in net income | 105 | (911) | (111) |
| Net change (net of tax effect of $0, $156, and $221) | 412 | (823) | 1,500 |
| Cash flow hedges: | | | |
| Change in net unrealized gains (losses) | (638) | 290 | 22 |
| Less: reclassification adjustment for net (gains) losses included in net income | 93 | 98 | (299) |
| Net change (net of tax effect of $247, $103, and $42) | (545) | 388 | (277) |
| Other comprehensive income (loss) | 1,410 | (1,216) | 1,104 |
| Comprehensive income | $ 14,072 | $ 29,520 | $ 35,447 |

[a]Google is part of Alphabet, but we loosely refer to Alphabet as "Google" because of its
global familiarity and because Google provides 99% of Alphabet's $161,857 billion in revenues.

See accompanying notes.

GOOGLE

**Google Inc. (Alphabet Inc.)[a]**
**CONSOLIDATED STATEMENTS OF STOCKHOLDERS' EQUITY**
**(In millions, except share amounts which are reflected in thousands)**

| | Class A and Class B Common Stock, Class C Capital Stock and Additional Paid-In Capital | | Accumulated Other Comprehensive Income (Loss) | Retained Earnings | Total Stockholders' Equity |
|---|---|---|---|---|---|
| | Shares | Amount | | | |
| Balance as of December 31, 2016 | 691,293 $ | 36,307 $ | (2,402) $ | 105,131 $ | 139,036 |
| Cumulative effect of accounting change | 0 | 0 | 0 | (15) | (15) |
| Common and capital stock issued | 8,652 | 212 | 0 | 0 | 212 |
| Stock-based compensation expense | 0 | 7,694 | 0 | 0 | 7,694 |
| Tax withholding related to vesting of restricted stock units | 0 | (4,373) | 0 | 0 | (4,373) |
| Repurchases of capital stock | (5,162) | (315) | 0 | (4,531) | (4,846) |
| Sale of interest in consolidated entities | 0 | 722 | 0 | 0 | 722 |
| Net income | 0 | 0 | 0 | 12,662 | 12,662 |
| Other comprehensive income | 0 | 0 | 1,410 | 0 | 1,410 |
| Balance as of December 31, 2017 | 694,783 | 40,247 | (992) | 113,247 | 152,502 |
| Cumulative effect of accounting change | 0 | 0 | (98) | (599) | (697) |
| Common and capital stock issued | 8,975 | 148 | 0 | 0 | 148 |
| Stock-based compensation expense | 0 | 9,353 | 0 | 0 | 9,353 |
| Tax withholding related to vesting of restricted stock units and other | 0 | (4,782) | 0 | 0 | (4,782) |
| Repurchases of capital stock | (8,202) | (576) | 0 | (8,499) | (9,075) |
| Sale of interest in consolidated entities | 0 | 659 | 0 | 0 | 659 |
| Net income | 0 | 0 | 0 | 30,736 | 30,736 |
| Other comprehensive loss | 0 | 0 | (1,216) | 0 | (1,216) |
| Balance as of December 31, 2018 | 695,556 | 45,049 | (2,306) | 134,885 | 177,628 |
| Cumulative effect of accounting change | 0 | 0 | (30) | (4) | (34) |
| Common and capital stock issued | 8,120 | 202 | 0 | 0 | 202 |
| Stock-based compensation expense | 0 | 10,890 | 0 | 0 | 10,890 |
| Tax withholding related to vesting of restricted stock units and other | 0 | (4,455) | 0 | 0 | (4,455) |
| Repurchases of capital stock | (15,341) | (1,294) | 0 | (17,102) | (18,396) |
| Sale of interest in consolidated entities | 0 | 160 | 0 | 0 | 160 |
| Net income | 0 | 0 | 0 | 34,343 | 34,343 |
| Other comprehensive income (loss) | 0 | 0 | 1,104 | 0 | 1,104 |
| Balance as of December 31, 2019 | 688,335 $ | 50,552 $ | (1,232) $ | 152,122 $ | 201,442 |

[a]Google is part of Alphabet, but we loosely refer to Alphabet as "Google" because of its
global familiarity and because Google provides 99% of Alphabet's $161,857 billion in revenues.

See accompanying notes.

## Google Inc. (Alphabet Inc.)[a]
## CONSOLIDATED STATEMENTS OF CASH FLOWS
### (In millions)

| Year Ended December 31 | 2017 | 2018 | 2019 |
|---|---|---|---|
| **Operating activities** | | | |
| Net income | $ 12,662 | $ 30,736 | $ 34,343 |
| Adjustments: | | | |
| Depreciation and impairment of property and equipment | 6,103 | 8,164 | 10,856 |
| Amortization and impairment of intangible assets | 812 | 871 | 925 |
| Stock-based compensation expense | 7,679 | 9,353 | 10,794 |
| Deferred income taxes | 258 | 778 | 173 |
| (Gain) loss on debt and equity securities, net | 37 | (6,650) | (2,798) |
| Other | 294 | (189) | (592) |
| Changes in assets and liabilities, net of effects of acquisitions: | | | |
| Accounts receivable | (3,768) | (2,169) | (4,340) |
| Income taxes, net | 8,211 | (2,251) | (3,128) |
| Other assets | (2,164) | (1,207) | (621) |
| Accounts payable | 731 | 1,067 | 428 |
| Accrued expenses and other liabilities | 4,891 | 8,614 | 7,170 |
| Accrued revenue share | 955 | 483 | 1,273 |
| Deferred revenue | 390 | 371 | 37 |
| Net cash provided by operating activities | 37,091 | 47,971 | 54,520 |
| **Investing activities** | | | |
| Purchases of property and equipment | (13,184) | (25,139) | (23,548) |
| Purchases of marketable securities | (92,195) | (50,158) | (100,315) |
| Maturities and sales of marketable securities | 73,959 | 48,507 | 97,825 |
| Purchases of non-marketable investments | (1,745) | (2,073) | (1,932) |
| Maturities and sales of non-marketable investments | 533 | 1,752 | 405 |
| Acquisitions, net of cash acquired, and purchases of intangible assets | (287) | (1,491) | (2,515) |
| Proceeds from collection of notes receivable | 1,419 | 0 | 0 |
| Other investing activities | 99 | 98 | 589 |
| Net cash used in investing activities | (31,401) | (28,504) | (29,491) |
| **Financing activities** | | | |
| Net payments related to stock-based award activities | (4,166) | (4,993) | (4,765) |
| Repurchases of capital stock | (4,846) | (9,075) | (18,396) |
| Proceeds from issuance of debt, net of costs | 4,291 | 6,766 | 317 |
| Repayments of debt | (4,377) | (6,827) | (585) |
| Proceeds from sale of interest in consolidated entities | 800 | 950 | 220 |
| Net cash used in financing activities | (8,298) | (13,179) | (23,209) |
| Effect of exchange rate changes on cash and cash equivalents | 405 | (302) | (23) |
| **Net increase (decrease) in cash and cash equivalents** | (2,203) | 5,986 | 1,797 |
| Cash and cash equivalents at beginning of period | 12,918 | 10,715 | 16,701 |
| **Cash and cash equivalents at end of period** | $ 10,715 | $ 16,701 | $ 18,498 |
| **Supplemental disclosures of cash flow information** | | | |
| Cash paid for taxes, net of refunds | $ 6,191 | $ 5,671 | $ 8,203 |

[a]Google is part of Alphabet, but we loosely refer to Alphabet as "Google" because of its
global familiarity and because Google provides 99% of Alphabet's $161,857 billion in revenues.

See accompanying notes.

## Samsung Electronics Co., Ltd. and Subsidiaries
### CONSOLIDATED STATEMENTS OF FINANCIAL POSITION

| In thousands of US dollars | December 31, 2019 | December 31, 2018 |
|---|---|---|
| **Assets** | | |
| **Current assets** | | |
| Cash and cash equivalents | $ 23,069,002 | $ 26,033,073 |
| Short-term financial instruments | 65,426,571 | 56,538,875 |
| Short-term financial assets at amortized cost | 3,358,516 | 2,319,851 |
| Short-term financial assets at fair value through profit or loss | 1,482,192 | 1,717,732 |
| Trade receivables | 30,143,757 | 29,059,541 |
| Non-trade receivables | 3,585,812 | 2,643,362 |
| Advance payments | 1,224,266 | 1,168,472 |
| Prepaid expenses | 2,064,610 | 3,548,957 |
| Inventories | 22,966,437 | 24,869,754 |
| Other current assets | 2,312,887 | 1,996,067 |
| **Total current assets** | **155,634,050** | **149,895,684** |
| **Non-current assets** | | |
| Financial assets at amortized cost | — | 204,476 |
| Financial assets at fair value through other comprehensive income | 7,654,241 | 6,264,780 |
| Financial assets at fair value through profit or loss | 900,077 | 665,340 |
| Investment in associates and joint ventures | 6,513,833 | 6,274,952 |
| Property, plant and equipment | 102,813,888 | 99,031,047 |
| Intangible assets | 17,764,234 | 12,777,442 |
| Net defined benefit assets | 506,094 | 482,518 |
| Deferred income tax assets | 3,865,469 | 4,691,711 |
| Other non-current assets | 6,859,137 | 10,890,850 |
| **Total assets** | **$302,511,023** | **$291,178,800** |
| **Liabilities and Equity** | | |
| **Current liabilities** | | |
| Trade payables | $ 7,480,499 | $ 7,276,025 |
| Short-term borrowings | 12,350,032 | 11,657,766 |
| Other payables | 10,298,520 | 9,190,823 |
| Advances received | 919,862 | 703,812 |
| Withholdings | 769,958 | 816,205 |
| Accrued expenses | 16,611,144 | 17,452,068 |
| Current income tax liabilities | 1,190,751 | 7,482,067 |
| Current portion of long-term liabilities | 725,971 | 28,646 |
| Provisions | 3,491,005 | 3,761,637 |
| Other current liabilities | 889,802 | 904,980 |
| **Total current liabilities** | **54,727,544** | **59,274,029** |
| **Non-current liabilities** | | |
| Debentures | 836,835 | 825,401 |
| Long-term borrowings | 1,885,248 | 73,006 |
| Long-term other payables | 1,874,152 | 2,740,586 |
| Net defined benefit liabilities | 403,944 | 432,502 |
| Deferred income tax liabilities | 14,632,684 | 13,009,904 |
| Long-term provisions | 524,342 | 569,405 |
| Other non-current liabilities | 2,066,906 | 1,674,233 |
| **Total liabilities** | **76,951,655** | **78,599,066** |
| **Equity attributable to owners of the parent company** | | |
| Preference shares | 102,506 | 102,506 |
| Ordinary shares | 667,588 | 667,588 |
| Share premium | 3,778,674 | 3,778,674 |
| Retained earnings | 218,439,838 | 208,243,059 |
| Other components of equity | (4,263,406) | (6,805,356) |
| | **218,725,200** | **205,986,471** |
| **Non-controlling interests** | 6,834,168 | 6,593,263 |
| **Total equity** | **225,559,368** | **212,579,734** |
| **Total liabilities and equity** | **$302,511,023** | **$291,178,800** |

The above consolidated statement of financial position should be read in conjunction with the accompanying notes.

**Samsung Electronics Co., Ltd. and Subsidiaries**
**CONSOLIDATED STATEMENTS OF PROFIT OR LOSS**

| For the year ended December 31 | 2019 | 2018 |
|---|---|---|
| *In thousands of US dollars* | | |
| Revenue | $197,690,938 | $209,163,262 |
| Cost of sales | 126,335,995 | 113,598,417 |
| **Gross profit** | **71,354,943** | **95,564,845** |
| Selling and administrative expenses | 47,528,721 | 45,038,298 |
| **Operating profit** | **23,826,222** | **50,526,547** |
| Other non-operating income | 1,526,149 | 1,274,207 |
| Other non-operating expense | 1,213,861 | 979,886 |
| Share of net profit of associates and joint ventures | 354,332 | 463,203 |
| Financial income | 8,718,988 | 8,579,720 |
| Financial expense | 7,100,090 | 7,386,694 |
| **Profit before income tax** | **26,111,740** | **52,477,097** |
| Income tax expense | 7,459,135 | 14,427,866 |
| **Profit for the year** | **$ 18,652,605** | **$ 38,049,231** |
| Profit attributable to owners of the parent company | $ 18,451,988 | $ 37,659,703 |
| Profit attributable to non-controlling interests | $    200,617 | $    389,528 |
| Earnings per share (in US dollars) | | |
| —Basic | $       2.72 | $       5.54 |
| —Diluted | 2.72 | 5.54 |

The above consolidated statement of financial position should be read in conjunction with the accompanying notes.

**Samsung Electronics Co., Ltd. and Subsidiaries**
**CONSOLIDATED STATEMENTS OF COMPREHENSIVE INCOME**

| For the year ended December 31 | 2019 | 2018 |
|---|---|---|
| *In thousands of US dollars* | | |
| **Profit for the year** | **$18,652,605** | **$38,049,231** |
| **Other comprehensive income (loss)** | | |
| **Items that will not be reclassified to profit or loss subsequently:** | | |
| Gain (loss) on valuation of financial assets at fair value through other comprehensive income, net of tax | 983,817 | (202,380) |
| Share of other comprehensive loss of associates and joint ventures, net of tax | (14,497) | (9,122) |
| Remeasurement of net defined benefit liabilities (assets), net of tax | (1,012,877) | (351,922) |
| **Items that may be reclassified to profit or loss subsequently:** | | |
| Share of other comprehensive income of associates and joint ventures, net of tax | 41,742 | 5,739 |
| Foreign currency translation, net of tax | 2,588,248 | 506,786 |
| Gain on valuation of cash flow hedge derivatives | 1,553 | 40,395 |
| **Other comprehensive income (loss) for the year, net of tax** | **2,587,986** | **(10,504)** |
| **Total comprehensive income for the year** | **$21,240,591** | **$38,038,727** |
| **Comprehensive income attributable to:** | | |
| Owners of the parent company | $20,993,415 | $37,652,492 |
| Non-controlling interests | $   247,176 | $   386,235 |

The above consolidated statement of financial position should be read in conjunction with the accompanying notes.

## Samsung Electronics Co., Ltd. and Subsidiaries
## CONSOLIDATED STATEMENTS OF CHANGES IN EQUITY
*(In thousands of US dollars)*

| | Preference shares | Ordinary shares | Share premium | Retained earnings | Other components of equity | Equity attributable to owners of the parent company | Non-controlling interests | Total |
|---|---|---|---|---|---|---|---|---|
| **Balance as of January 1, 2018** | 102,506 | 667,588 | $3,778,674 | $185,172,550 | $(11,925,927) | $177,795,391 | $6,244,755 | $184,040,146 |
| Cumulative effect of changes in accounting policies | — | — | — | 211,529 | (224,576) | (13,047) | — | (13,047) |
| **Restated total equity at the beginning of the financial year** | 102,506 | 667,588 | 3,778,674 | 185,384,079 | (12,150,503) | 177,782,344 | 6,244,755 | 184,027,099 |
| Profit for the year | — | — | — | 37,659,703 | — | 37,659,703 | 389,528 | 38,049,231 |
| Gain (loss) on valuation of financial assets at fair value through other comprehensive income, net of tax | — | — | — | (2,581) | (202,789) | (205,370) | 2,990 | (202,380) |
| Share of other comprehensive income (loss) of associates and joint ventures, net of tax | — | — | — | — | (3,463) | (3,463) | 80 | (3,383) |
| Foreign currency translation, net of tax | — | — | — | — | 497,023 | 497,023 | 9,763 | 506,786 |
| Remeasurement of net defined benefit liabilities (assets), net of tax | — | — | — | — | (335,796) | (335,796) | (16,126) | (351,922) |
| Gain on valuation of cash flow hedge derivatives | — | — | — | — | 40,395 | 40,395 | — | 40,395 |
| **Total comprehensive income (loss)** | — | — | — | 37,657,122 | (4,630) | 37,652,492 | 386,235 | 38,038,727 |
| Dividends | — | — | — | (8,703,297) | — | (8,703,297) | (43,465) | (8,746,762) |
| Capital transaction under common control | — | — | — | — | 1,474 | 1,474 | 6,856 | 8,330 |
| Changes in consolidated entities | — | — | — | — | — | — | 35 | 35 |
| Acquisition of treasury shares | — | — | — | — | (750,872) | (750,872) | — | (750,872) |
| Retirement of treasury shares | — | — | — | (6,094,845) | 6,094,845 | — | — | — |
| Other | — | — | — | — | 4,330 | 4,330 | (1,153) | 3,177 |
| **Total transactions with owners** | — | — | — | (14,798,142) | 5,349,777 | (9,448,365) | (37,727) | (9,486,092) |
| **Balance as of December 31, 2018** | 102,506 | 667,588 | 3,778,674 | 208,243,059 | (6,805,356) | 205,986,471 | 6,593,263 | 212,579,734 |
| **Balance as of January 1, 2019** | 102,506 | 667,588 | 3,778,674 | 208,243,059 | (6,805,356) | 205,986,471 | 6,593,263 | 212,579,734 |
| Profit for the year | — | — | — | 18,451,988 | — | 18,451,988 | 200,617 | 18,652,605 |
| Gain (loss) on valuation of financial assets at fair value through other comprehensive income, net of tax | — | — | — | (1,085) | 953,498 | 952,413 | 31,404 | 983,817 |
| Share of other comprehensive income (loss) of associates and joint ventures, net of tax | — | — | — | (522) | 27,009 | 26,487 | 758 | 27,245 |
| Foreign currency translation, net of tax | — | — | — | — | 2,545,753 | 2,545,753 | 42,495 | 2,588,248 |
| Remeasurement of net defined benefit liabilities (assets), net of tax | — | — | — | — | (984,779) | (984,779) | (28,098) | (1,012,877) |
| Gain on valuation of cash flow hedge derivatives | — | — | — | — | 1,553 | 1,553 | — | 1,553 |
| **Total comprehensive income** | — | — | — | 18,450,381 | 2,543,034 | 20,993,415 | 247,176 | 21,240,591 |
| Dividends | — | — | — | (8,253,602) | — | (8,253,602) | (18,327) | (8,271,929) |
| Capital transaction under common control | — | — | — | — | (73) | (73) | 6,312 | 6,239 |
| Changes in consolidated entities | — | — | — | — | — | — | 4,917 | 4,917 |
| Other | — | — | — | — | (1,011) | (1,011) | 827 | (184) |
| **Total transactions with owners** | — | — | — | (8,253,602) | (1,084) | (8,254,686) | (6,271) | (8,260,957) |
| **Balance as of December 31, 2019** | 102,506 | 667,588 | $3,778,674 | $218,439,838 | $(4,263,406) | $218,725,200 | $6,834,168 | $225,559,368 |

The above consolidated statement of financial position should be read in conjunction with the accompanying notes.

**Samsung Electronics Co., Ltd. and Subsidiaries**
**CONSOLIDATED STATEMENTS OF CASH FLOWS**

| For the year ended December 31 | 2019 | 2018 |
|---|---|---|
| *In thousands of US dollars* | | |
| **Cash flows from operating activities** | | |
| Profit for the year | $18,652,605 | $38,049,231 |
| Adjustments | 32,126,956 | 37,414,045 |
| Changes in assets and liabilities arising from operating activities | (2,184,336) | (8,515,406) |
| **Cash generated from operations** | **48,595,225** | **66,947,870** |
| Interest received | 1,978,962 | 1,534,604 |
| Interest paid | (497,640) | (470,434) |
| Dividends received | 207,473 | 185,328 |
| Income tax paid | (11,344,104) | (10,681,998) |
| **Net cash inflow from operating activities** | **38,939,916** | **57,515,370** |
| **Cash flows from investing activities** | | |
| Net increase in short-term financial instruments | (1,742,585) | (10,612,375) |
| Net increase in short-term financial assets at amortized cost | (701,945) | (1,232,856) |
| Net decrease (increase) in short-term financial assets at fair value through profit or loss | 321,746 | (119,839) |
| Disposal of long-term financial instruments | 3,935,450 | 219,527 |
| Acquisition of long-term financial instruments | (10,918,835) | (6,588,518) |
| Disposal of financial assets at amortized cost | 595,974 | — |
| Acquisition of financial assets at amortized cost | (707,898) | (136,183) |
| Disposal of financial assets at fair value through other comprehensive income | 1,351 | 13,910 |
| Acquisition of financial assets at fair value through other comprehensive income | (54,719) | (391,377) |
| Disposal of financial assets at fair value through profit or loss | 55,189 | 68,761 |
| Acquisition of financial assets at fair value through profit or loss | (116,543) | (166,327) |
| Disposal of investment in associates and joint ventures | 10,424 | 127 |
| Acquisition of investment in associates and joint ventures | (10,964) | (43,953) |
| Disposal of property, plant and equipment | 440,397 | 477,900 |
| Acquisition of property, plant and equipment | (21,766,303) | (25,360,292) |
| Disposal of intangible assets | 6,213 | 10,241 |
| Acquisition of intangible assets | (2,788,525) | (875,635) |
| Cash outflow from business combinations | (874,680) | (85,038) |
| Cash inflow (outflow) from other investing activities | 39,512 | (1,965) |
| **Net cash outflow from investing activities** | **(34,276,741)** | **(44,823,892)** |
| **Cash flows from financing activities** | | |
| Net increase (decrease) in short-term borrowings | 742,876 | (1,755,933) |
| Acquisition of treasury shares | — | (750,872) |
| Proceeds from long-term borrowings | — | 3,072 |
| Repayment of debentures and long-term borrowings | (608,687) | (1,704,560) |
| Dividends paid | (8,270,727) | (8,746,499) |
| Net increase (decrease) in non-controlling interests | (1,459) | 6,924 |
| **Net cash outflow from financing activities** | **(8,137,997)** | **(12,947,868)** |
| Effect of exchange rate changes on cash and cash equivalents | 510,751 | 80,816 |
| **Net decrease in cash and cash equivalents** | **(2,964,071)** | **(175,574)** |
| **Cash and cash equivalents** | | |
| Beginning of the year | 26,033,073 | 26,208,647 |
| End of the year | $23,069,002 | $26,033,073 |

The above consolidated statements of cash flows should be read in conjunction with the accompanying notes.

# B Time Value of Money

## Appendix Preview

### PRESENT AND FUTURE VALUE CONCEPTS

C1 Time is money

Concept of interest

### VALUE OF A SINGLE AMOUNT

P1 Present value of a single amount

P2 Future value of a single amount

**NTK B-1, B-2**

### VALUE OF AN ANNUITY

P3 Present value of an annuity

P4 Future value of an annuity

**NTK B-3, B-4**

## Learning Objectives

### CONCEPTUAL

C1 Describe the earning of interest and the concepts of present and future values.

### PROCEDURAL

P1 Apply present value concepts to a single amount by using interest tables.

P2 Apply future value concepts to a single amount by using interest tables.

P3 Apply present value concepts to an annuity by using interest tables.

P4 Apply future value concepts to an annuity by using interest tables.

# PRESENT AND FUTURE VALUE CONCEPTS

## C1

Describe the earning of interest and the concepts of present and future values.

The old saying "Time is money" means that as time passes, the values of assets and liabilities change. This change is due to *interest,* which is a borrower's payment to the owner of an asset for its use. The most common example of interest is a savings account. Cash in the account earns interest paid by the financial institution. An example of a liability is a car loan. As we carry the balance of the loan, we accumulate interest costs on it. We must ultimately repay this loan with interest.

Present and future value computations enable us to measure or estimate the interest component of holding assets or liabilities over time. The present value computation is used to compute the value of future-day assets *today.* The future value computation is used to compute the value of present-day assets *at a future date.* The first section focuses on the present value of a single amount. The second section focuses on the future value of a single amount. Then both the present and future values of a series of amounts (called an *annuity*) are defined and explained.

### ◼ Decision Insight

**What's Five Million Worth?**   Robert Miles, a maintenance worker, purchased a scratch-off ticket that won him a $5 million jackpot. The $5 million payout was offered to Miles as a $250,000 annuity for 20 years **or** as a lump-sum payment of $3,210,000, which is about $2,124,378 after taxes. ◼

# PRESENT VALUE OF A SINGLE AMOUNT

**Graph of PV of a Single Amount**   We graphically express the present value, called *p*, of a single future amount, called *f*, that is received or paid at a future date in Exhibit B.1.

**EXHIBIT B.1**

Present Value of a Single Amount Diagram

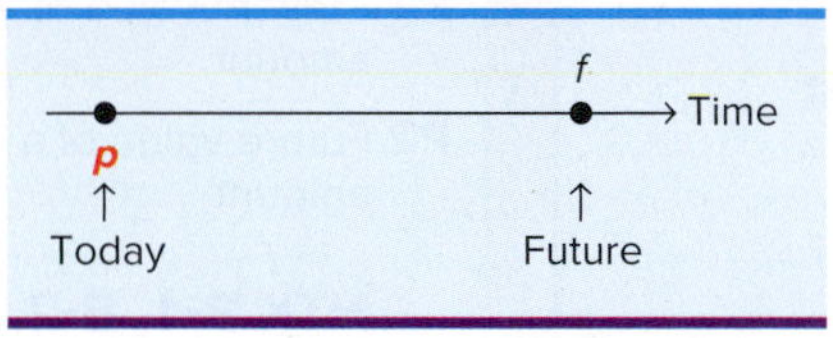

## P1

Apply present value concepts to a single amount by using interest tables.

**Formula of PV of a Single Amount**   The formula to compute the present value of a single amount is shown in Exhibit B.2, where *p* = present value (PV); *f* = future value (FV); *i* = rate of interest per period; and *n* = number of periods. (Interest is also called the *discount,* and interest rate is also called the *discount rate.*)

**EXHIBIT B.2**

Present Value of a Single Amount Formula

$$p = \frac{f}{(1 + i)^n}$$

**Illustration of PV of a Single Amount for One Period**   To illustrate present value concepts, assume that we need $220 one period from today. We want to know how much we must invest now, for one period, at an interest rate of 10% to provide for this $220. For this illustration, the *p*, or present value, is the unknown amount—the specifics are shown graphically as follows.

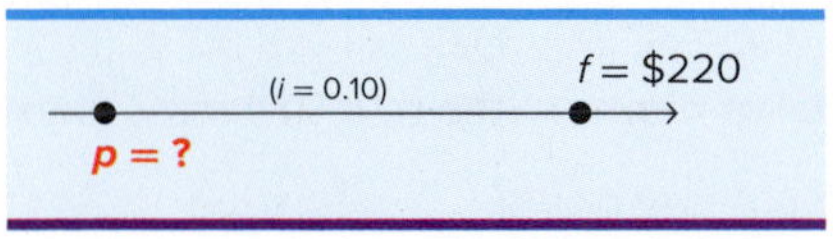

Conceptually, we know *p* must be less than $220. This is clear from the answer to: Would we rather have $220 today or $220 at some future date? If we had $220 today, we could invest it and see it grow to something more than $220 in the future. Therefore, we would prefer the $220 today. This means that if we were promised $220 in the future, we would take less than $220 today. But how much less? To answer that question, we compute an estimate of the present value of the $220 to be received one period from now using the formula in Exhibit B.2 as follows.

$$p = \frac{f}{(1+i)^n} = \frac{\$220}{(1+0.10)^1} = \$200$$

We interpret this result to say that given an interest rate of 10%, we are indifferent between $200 today or $220 at the end of one period.

### Illustration of PV of a Single Amount for Multiple Periods

We can use this formula to compute the present value for *any number of periods*. To illustrate, consider a payment of $242 at the end of two periods at 10% interest. The present value of this $242 to be received two periods from now is computed as follows.

$$p = \frac{f}{(1+i)^n} = \frac{\$242}{(1+0.10)^2} = \$200$$

Together, these results tell us we are indifferent between $200 today, or $220 one period from today, or $242 two periods from today given a 10% interest rate per period.

The number of periods (*n*) in the present value formula does not have to be expressed in years. Any period of time such as a day, a month, a quarter, or a year can be used. Whatever period is used, the interest rate (*i*) must be compounded for the same period. This means that if a situation expresses *n* in months and *i* equals 12% per year, then *i* is transformed into interest earned per month (or 1%). In this case, interest is said to be *compounded monthly*. For example, the present value of $1 when *n* is 12 months and *i* is 12% compounded monthly follows.

$$p = \frac{1}{(1+0.01)^{12}} = \$0.8874$$

**Point:** Excel for PV.

| | A | B |
|---|---|---|
| 1 | Future value | $242 |
| 2 | Periods | 2 |
| 3 | Period int. rate | 10% |
| 4 | Present value | |

=−PV(B3,B2,0,B1) = $200

I will pay your allowance at the end of the month. Do you want to wait or receive its present value today?

### Using Present Value Table to Compute PV of a Single Amount

A present value table helps us with present value computations. It gives us present values (factors) for a variety of both interest rates (*i*) and periods (*n*). Each present value in a present value table assumes that the future value (*f*) equals 1. When the future value (*f*) is different from 1, we simply multiply the present value (*p*) from the table by that future value to give us the estimate. The formula used to construct a table of present values for a single future amount of 1 is shown in Exhibit B.3.

$$p = \frac{1}{(1+i)^n}$$

**EXHIBIT B.3**

Present Value of 1 Formula

This formula is identical to that in Exhibit B.2 except that *f* equals 1. **Table B.1** at the end of this appendix is such a present value table. It is often called a **present value of 1 table**. A present value table has three factors: *p*, *i*, and *n*. Knowing two of these three factors allows us to compute the third. (A fourth is *f*, but, as already explained, we need only multiply the 1 used in the formula by *f*.) To illustrate the use of a present value table, consider three cases.

**Case 1**   **Solve for *p* when knowing *i* and *n*.** To show how we use a present value table, let's look again at how we estimate the present value of $220 (the *f* value) at the end of one period (*n* = 1) where the interest rate (*i*) is 10%. To solve this case, we go to the present value table (Table B.1) and look in the row for one period and in the column for 10% interest. Here we find a present value (*p*) of 0.9091 based on a future value of 1. This means, for instance, that $1 to be received one period from today at 10% interest is worth $0.9091 today. Because the future value in this case is not $1 but $220, we multiply the 0.9091 by $220 to get an answer of $200.

**Case 2**   **Solve for *n* when knowing *p* and *i*.** To illustrate, assume a $100,000 future value (*f*) that is worth $13,000 today (*p*) using an interest rate of 12% (*i*) but where *n* is unknown. In particular, we want to know how many periods (*n*) there are between the present value and the future value. To put this in context, it would fit a situation in which we want to retire with $100,000 but currently have only $13,000 that is earning a 12% return and we are unable to save additional money. How long will it be before we can retire? To answer this, we go to Table B.1

and look in the 12% interest column. Here we find a column of present values (*p*) based on a future value of 1. To use the present value table for this solution, we must divide $13,000 (*p*) by $100,000 (*f*), which equals 0.1300. This is necessary because *a present value table defines* f *equal to 1, and* p *as a fraction of 1.* We look for a value nearest to 0.1300 (*p*), which we find in the row for 18 periods (*n*). This means that the present value of $100,000 at the end of 18 periods at 12% interest is $13,000; alternatively stated, we must work 18 more years.

**Case 3**   **Solve for *i* when knowing *p* and *n*.** In this case, we have, say, a $120,000 future value (*f*) worth $60,000 today (*p*) when there are nine periods (*n*) between the present and future values, but the interest rate is unknown. As an example, suppose we want to retire with $120,000 in nine years, but we have only $60,000 and we are unable to save additional money. What interest rate must we earn to retire with $120,000 in nine years? To answer this, we go to the present value table (Table B.1) and look in the row for nine periods. To use the present value table, we must divide $60,000 (*p*) by $120,000 (*f*), which equals 0.5000. Recall that this step is necessary because a present value table defines *f* equal to 1 and *p* as a fraction of 1. We look for a value in the row for nine periods that is nearest to 0.5000 (*p*), which we find in the column for 8% interest (*i*). This means that the present value of $120,000 at the end of nine periods at 8% interest is $60,000 or, in our example, we must earn 8% annual interest to retire in nine years.

---

**NEED-TO-KNOW** **B-1**

Present Value of a Single Amount

**P1**

A company is considering an investment expected to yield $70,000 after six years. If this company demands an 8% return, how much is it willing to pay for this investment today?

*Solution*

Today's value = $70,000 × 0.6302 = $44,114 (using PV factor from Table B.1, *i* = 8%, *n* = 6)

---

# FUTURE VALUE OF A SINGLE AMOUNT

**P2**
_____

Apply future value concepts to a single amount by using interest tables.

**EXHIBIT B.4**

Future Value of a Single Amount Formula

**Formula of FV of a Single Amount**   We must modify the formula for the present value of a single amount to obtain the formula for the future value of a single amount. In particular, we multiply both sides of the equation in Exhibit B.2 by $(1 + i)^n$ to get the result shown in Exhibit B.4.

$$f = p \times (1 \times i)^n$$

**Illustration of FV of a Single Amount for One Period**   The future value (*f*) is defined in terms of *p*, *i*, and *n*. We can use this formula to determine that $200 (*p*) invested for one period (*n*) at an interest rate of 10% (*i*) yields a future value of $220 as follows.

$$f = p \times (1 + i)^n$$
$$= \$200 \times (1 + 0.10)^1$$
$$= \$220$$

**Point:** The FV factor in Table B.2 when *n* = 3 and *i* = 10% is 1.3310.

**Illustration of FV of a Single Amount for Multiple Periods**   This formula can be used to compute the future value of an amount for *any number of periods* into the future. To illustrate, assume that $200 is invested for three periods at 10%. The future value of this $200 is $266.20, computed as follows.

**Point:** Excel for FV.

| | A | B |
|---|---|---|
| 1 | Present value | $200 |
| 2 | Periods | 3 |
| 3 | Period int. rate | 10% |
| 4 | Future value | |

=−FV(B3,B2,0,B1) = $266.20

$$f = p \times (1 + i)^n$$
$$= \$200 \times (1 + 0.10)^3$$
$$= \$200 \times 1.3310$$
$$= \$266.20$$

**Using Future Value Table to Compute FV of a Single Amount**   A future value table makes it easier for us to compute future values (*f*) for many different combinations of interest rates (*i*) and time periods (*n*). Each future value in a future value table assumes the present value (*p*) is 1. If the future amount is something other than 1, we multiply our answer by that amount. The formula used to construct a table of future values (factors) for a single amount of 1 is in Exhibit B.5.

$$f = (1 + i)^n$$

**Table B.2** at the end of this appendix shows a table of future values for a current amount of 1. This type of table is called a **future value of 1 table**.

There are some important relations between Tables B.1 and B.2. In Table B.2, for the row where $n = 0$, the future value is 1 for each interest rate. This is because no interest is earned when time does not pass. We also see that Tables B.1 and B.2 report the same information but in a different manner. In particular, one table is simply the *reciprocal* of the other. To illustrate this inverse relation, let's say we invest $100 for a period of five years at 12% per year. How much do we expect to have after five years? We can answer this question using Table B.2 by finding the future value ($f$) of 1, for five periods from now, compounded at 12%. From that table we find $f = 1.7623$. If we start with $100, the amount it accumulates to after five years is $176.23 ($100 × 1.7623). We can alternatively use Table B.1. Here we find that the present value ($p$) of 1, discounted five periods at 12%, is 0.5674. Recall the inverse relation between present value and future value. This means that $p = 1/f$ (or equivalently, $f = 1/p$). We can compute the future value of $100 invested for five periods at 12% as follows: $f = \$100 × (1/0.5674) = \$176.24$ (which equals the $176.23 just computed, except for a 1 cent rounding difference).

**Point:**
1/PV factor = FV factor.
1/FV factor = PV factor.

A future value table has three factors: $f$, $i$, and $n$. Knowing two of these three factors allows us to compute the third. To illustrate, consider three possible cases.

**Point:** The FV factor when $n = 2$ and $i = 10\%$ is 1.2100. Its reciprocal, 0.8264, is the PV factor when $n = 2$ and $i = 10\%$.

**Case 1**    **Solve for $f$ when knowing $i$ and $n$.** Our preceding example fits this case. We found that $100 invested for five periods at 12% interest accumulates to $176.24.

**Case 2**    **Solve for $n$ when knowing $f$ and $i$.** In this case, we have, say, $2,000 ($p$) and we want to know how many periods ($n$) it will take to accumulate to $3,000 ($f$) at 7% interest ($i$). To answer this, we go to the future value table (Table B.2) and look in the 7% interest column. Here we find a column of future values ($f$) based on a present value of 1. To use a future value table, we must divide $3,000 ($f$) by $2,000 ($p$), which equals 1.500. This is necessary because *a future value table defines* p *equal to 1, and* f *as a multiple of 1.* We look for a value nearest to 1.50 ($f$), which we find in the row for six periods ($n$). This means that $2,000 invested for six periods at 7% interest accumulates to $3,000.

**Case 3**    **Solve for $i$ when knowing $f$ and $n$.** In this case, we have, say, $2,001 ($p$) today, and in nine years ($n$) we want to have $4,000 ($f$). What rate of interest must we earn to accomplish this? To answer that, we go to Table B.2 and search in the row for nine periods. To use a future value table, we must divide $4,000 ($f$) by $2,001 ($p$), which equals 1.9990. Recall that this is necessary because a future value table defines $p$ equal to 1 and $f$ as a multiple of 1. We look for a value nearest to 1.9990 ($f$), which we find in the column for 8% interest ($i$). This means that $2,001 invested for nine periods at 8% interest accumulates to $4,000.

■ **Decision Maker**

**Entrepreneur**    You are a retailer planning a sale on a security system that requires no payments for two years. At the end of two years, buyers must pay the full amount. The system's suggested retail price is $4,100, but you are willing to sell it today for $3,000 cash. What is your sale price if payment will not occur for two years and the market interest rate is 10%? ■ *Answer:* This is a present value question. The interest rate (10%) and present value ($3,000) are known, but the payment required two years later is unknown. The two-year-later price of $3,630 is computed as $3,000 × 1.10 × 1.10. The $3,630 two years from today is equivalent to $3,000 today.

Assume that you win a $150,000 cash sweepstakes today. You decide to deposit this cash in an account earning 8% annual interest, and you plan to quit your job when the account equals $555,000. How many years will it be before you can quit working?

**NEED-TO-KNOW** B-2

Future Value of a Single Amount

*Solution*

Future value factor = $555,000/$150,000 = 3.7000

Searching for 3.7 in the 8% column of Table B.2 shows you cannot quit working for <u>17 years</u> if your deposit earns 8% interest.

P2

## PRESENT VALUE OF AN ANNUITY

**P3**
_____

Apply present value concepts to an annuity by using interest tables.

**EXHIBIT B.6**

Present Value of an Ordinary Annuity Diagram

**Graph of PV of an Annuity**   An *annuity* is a series of equal payments occurring at equal intervals. One example is a series of three annual payments of $100 each. An *ordinary annuity* is defined as equal end-of-period payments at equal intervals. An ordinary annuity of $100 for three periods and its present value (*p*) are illustrated in Exhibit B.6.

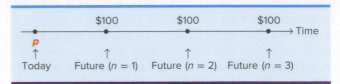

**Formula and Illustration of PV of an Annuity**   One way to compute the present value of an ordinary annuity is to find the present value of each payment using our present value formula from Exhibit B.3. We then add each of the three present values. To illustrate, let's look at three $100 payments at the end of each of the next three periods with an interest rate of 15%. Our present value computations are

$$p = \frac{\$100}{(1 + 0.15)^1} + \frac{\$100}{(1 + 0.15)^2} + \frac{\$100}{(1 + 0.15)^3} = \$228.32$$

**Using Present Value Table to Compute PV of an Annuity**   This computation is identical to computing the present value of each payment (from Table B.1) and taking their sum or, alternatively, adding the values from Table B.1 for each of the three payments and multiplying their sum by the $100 annuity payment.

A more direct way is to use a present value of annuity table. **Table B.3** at the end of this appendix is one such table. This table is called a **present value of an annuity of 1 table**. If we look at Table B.3 where $n = 3$ and $i = 15\%$, we see the present value is 2.2832. This means that the present value of an annuity of 1 for three periods, with a 15% interest rate, equals 2.2832.

A present value of an annuity formula is used to construct Table B.3. It also can be constructed by adding the amounts in a present value of 1 table. To illustrate, we use Tables B.1 and B.3 to confirm this relation for the prior example.

**Point:** Excel for PV annuity.

|   | A | B |
|---|---|---|
| 1 | Payment | $100 |
| 2 | Periods | 3 |
| 3 | Period int. rate | 15% |
| 4 | Present value |  |

=−PV(B3,B2,B1) = $228.32

| From Table B.1 | | From Table B.3 | |
|---|---|---|---|
| $i = 15\%, n = 1$ ......... | 0.8696 | | |
| $i = 15\%, n = 2$ ......... | 0.7561 | | |
| $i = 15\%, n = 3$ ......... | 0.6575 | | |
| Total................. | 2.2832 | $i = 15\%, n = 3$ .......... | 2.2832 |

We also can use business calculators or spreadsheet programs to find the present value of an annuity.

### ◼ Decision **Insight**

**Count Your Blessings**   "I don't have good luck—I'm blessed," proclaimed Andrew "Jack" Whittaker, a sewage treatment contractor, after winning the largest ever undivided jackpot in a U.S. lottery. Whittaker had to choose between $315 million in 30 annual installments or $170 million in one lump sum ($112 million after taxes). ◼

---

**NEED-TO-KNOW B-3**

Present Value of an Annuity

P3

A company is considering an investment that would produce payments of $10,000 every six months for three years. The first payment would be received in six months. If this company requires an 8% annual return, what is the maximum amount it is willing to pay for this investment today?

**Solution**

Maximum paid = $10,000 × 5.2421 = $52,421 (using PV of annuity factor from Table B.3, $i = 4\%, n = 6$)

# FUTURE VALUE OF AN ANNUITY

**P4**

Apply future value concepts to an annuity by using interest tables.

**Graph of FV of an Annuity**   The future value of an *ordinary annuity* is the accumulated value of each annuity payment with interest as of the date of the final payment. To illustrate, let's consider the earlier annuity of three annual payments of $100. Exhibit B.7 shows the point in time for the future value ($f$). The first payment is made two periods prior to the point when future value is determined, and the final payment occurs on the future value date.

**EXHIBIT B.7**

Future Value of an Ordinary Annuity Diagram

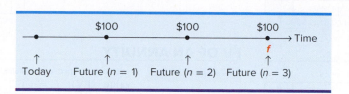

**Formula and Illustration of FV of an Annuity**   One way to compute the future value of an annuity is to use the formula to find the future value of *each* payment and add them. If we assume an interest rate of 15%, our calculation is

**Point:** An ordinary annuity is a series of equal cash flows, with the payment at the *end* of each period.

$$f = \$100 \times (1 + 0.15)^2 + \$100 \times (1 + 0.15)^1 + \$100 \times (1 + 0.15)^0 = \$347.25$$

This is identical to using Table B.2 and summing the future values of each payment, or adding the future values of the three payments of 1 and multiplying the sum by $100.

**Using Future Value Table to Compute FV of an Annuity**   A more direct way is to use a table showing future values of annuities. Such a table is called a **future value of an annuity of 1 table**. **Table B.4** at the end of this appendix is one such table. Note that in Table B.4 when $n = 1$, the future values equal 1 ($f = 1$) for all rates of interest. This is because such an annuity consists of only one payment, and the future value is determined on the date of that payment— no time passes between the payment and its future value. The future value of an annuity formula is used to construct Table B.4. We also can construct it by adding the amounts from a future value of 1 table. To illustrate, we use Tables B.2 and B.4 to confirm this relation for the prior example.

| From Table B.2 | | From Table B.4 | |
|---|---|---|---|
| $i = 15\%, n = 0$ .......... | 1.0000 | | |
| $i = 15\%, n = 1$ .......... | 1.1500 | | |
| $i = 15\%, n = 2$ .......... | 1.3225 | | |
| Total.................. | 3.4725 | $i = 15\%, n = 3$ .......... | 3.4725 |

**Point:** Excel for FV annuity.

| | A | B |
|---|---|---|
| 1 | Payment | $100 |
| 2 | Periods | 3 |
| 3 | Period int. rate | 15% |
| 4 | Future value | |

=−FV(B3,B2,B1) = $347.25

Note that the future value in Table B.2 is 1.0000 when $n = 0$, but the future value in Table B.4 is 1.0000 when $n = 1$. Is this a contradiction? No. When $n = 0$ in Table B.2, the future value is determined on the date when a single payment occurs. This means that no interest is earned because no time has passed, and the future value equals the payment. Table B.4 describes annuities with equal payments occurring at the end of each period. When $n = 1$, the annuity has one payment, and its future value equals 1 on the date of its final and only payment. Again, no time passes between the payment and its future value date.

---

A company invests $45,000 per year for five years at 12% annual interest. Compute the value of this annuity investment at the end of five years.

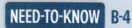
**NEED-TO-KNOW  B-4**

Future Value of an Annuity

**P4**

**Solution**

Future value = $45,000 × 6.3528 = $285,876 (using FV of annuity factor from Table B.4, $i = 12\%$, $n = 5$)

## Summary: Cheat Sheet

### PV OF A SINGLE AMOUNT

$$p = \frac{f}{(1+i)^n}$$ where $p$ = present value (PV); $f$ = future value (FV); $i$ = rate of interest per period; and $n$ = number of periods. Excel follows:

**Point:** Excel for PV.

|   | A | B |
|---|---|---|
| 1 | Future value | $242 |
| 2 | Periods | 2 |
| 3 | Period int. rate | 10% |
| 4 | Present value | |

=−PV(B3,B2,0,B1) = $200

### PV OF AN ANNUITY

$$p = f \times \left[1 - \frac{1}{(1+i)^n}\right]/i$$ where $p$ = present value (PV); $f$ = future value (FV); $i$ = rate of interest per period; and $n$ = number of periods. Excel follows:

**Point:** Excel for PV annuity.

|   | A | B |
|---|---|---|
| 1 | Payment | $100 |
| 2 | Periods | 3 |
| 3 | Period int. rate | 15% |
| 4 | Present value | |

=−PV(B3,B2,B1) = $228.32

### FV OF A SINGLE AMOUNT

$$f = p \times (1+i)^n$$ where $p$ = present value (PV); $f$ = future value (FV); $i$ = rate of interest per period; and $n$ = number of periods. Excel follows:

**Point:** Excel for FV.

|   | A | B |
|---|---|---|
| 1 | Present value | $200 |
| 2 | Periods | 3 |
| 3 | Period int. rate | 10% |
| 4 | Future value | |

=−FV(B3,B2,0,B1) = $266.20

### FV OF AN ANNUITY

$$f = p \times [(1+i)^n - 1]/i$$ where $p$ = present value (PV); $f$ = future value (FV); $i$ = rate of interest per period; and $n$ = number of periods. Excel follows:

**Point:** Excel for FV annuity.

|   | A | B |
|---|---|---|
| 1 | Payment | $100 |
| 2 | Periods | 3 |
| 3 | Period int. rate | 15% |
| 4 | Future value | |

=−FV(B3,B2,B1) = $347.25

*Select Quick Study and Exercise assignments feature Guided Example videos, called "Hints" in Connect. Hints use different numbers, and instructors can turn this feature on or off.*

---

## QUICK STUDY

**QS B-1**

Identifying interest rates in tables

**C1**

Assume that you must estimate what the future value will be two years from today using the *future value of 1 table* (Table B.2). Which interest rate column *and* number-of-periods row do you use when working with the following rates?

1. 12% annual rate, compounded annually
2. 6% annual rate, compounded semiannually
3. 8% annual rate, compounded quarterly
4. 12% annual rate, compounded monthly (the answer for number-of-periods in part 4 is not shown in Table B.2)

---

**QS B-2**

Interest rate on an investment  **P1**

Ken Francis is offered the possibility of investing $2,745 today; in return, he would receive $10,000 after 15 years. What is the annual rate of interest for this investment? (Use Table B.1.)

---

**QS B-3**

Number of periods of an investment  **P1**

Megan Brink is offered the possibility of investing $6,651 today at 6% interest per year in a desire to accumulate $10,000. How many years must Brink wait to accumulate $10,000? (Use Table B.1.)

---

**QS B-4**

Present value of an amount  **P1**

Flaherty is considering an investment that, if paid for immediately, is expected to return $140,000 five years from now. If Flaherty demands a 9% return, how much is she willing to pay for this investment?

---

**QS B-5**

Future value of an amount  **P2**

CII, Inc., invests $630,000 in a project expected to earn a 12% annual rate of return. The earnings will be reinvested in the project each year until the entire investment is liquidated 10 years later. What will the cash proceeds be when the project is liquidated?

---

**QS B-6**

Present value of an annuity  **P3**

Beene Distributing is considering a project that will return $150,000 annually at the end of each year for the next six years. If Beene demands an annual return of 7% and pays for the project immediately, how much is it willing to pay for the project?

---

**QS B-7**

Future value of an annuity  **P4**

Claire Fitch is planning to begin an individual retirement program in which she will invest $1,500 at the end of each year. Fitch plans to retire after making 30 annual investments in the program earning a return of 10%. What is the value of the program on the date of the last payment (30 years from the present)?

Mike Derr Company expects to earn 10% per year on an investment that will pay $606,773 six years from now. Use Table B.1 to compute the present value of this investment. (Round the amount to the nearest dollar.)

**Exercise B-1**
Present value of an amount  P1

On January 1, a company agrees to pay $20,000 in three years. If the annual interest rate is 10%, determine how much cash the company can borrow with this agreement.

**Exercise B-2**
Present value of an amount  P1

Tom Thompson expects to invest $10,000 at 12% and, at the end of a certain period, receive $96,463. How many years will it be before Thompson receives the payment? (Use Table B.2.)

**Exercise B-3**
Number of periods of an investment  P2

Bill Padley expects to invest $10,000 for 25 years, after which he wants to receive $108,347. What rate of interest must Padley earn? (Use Table B.2.)

**Exercise B-4**
Interest rate on an investment  P2

Mark Welsch deposits $7,200 in an account that earns interest at an annual rate of 8%, compounded quarterly. The $7,200 plus earned interest must remain in the account 10 years before it can be withdrawn. How much money will be in the account at the end of 10 years?

**Exercise B-5**
Future value of an amount  P2

Catten, Inc., invests $163,170 today earning 7% per year for nine years. Use Table B.2 to compute the future value of the investment nine years from now. (Round the amount to the nearest dollar.)

**Exercise B-6**
Future value of an amount  P2

Jones expects an immediate investment of $57,466 to return $10,000 annually for eight years, with the first payment to be received one year from now. What rate of interest must Jones earn? (Use Table B.3.)

**Exercise B-7**
Interest rate on an investment  P3

Keith Riggins expects an investment of $82,014 to return $10,000 annually for several years. If Riggins earns a return of 10%, how many annual payments will he receive? (Use Table B.3.)

**Exercise B-8**
Number of periods of an investment  P3

Dave Krug finances a new automobile by paying $6,500 cash and agreeing to make 40 monthly payments of $500 each, the first payment to be made one month after the purchase. The loan bears interest at an annual rate of 12%. What is the cost of the automobile?

**Exercise B-9**
Present value of an annuity  P3

C&H Ski Club recently borrowed money and agreed to pay it back with a series of six annual payments of $5,000 each. C&H subsequently borrows more money and agrees to pay it back with a series of four annual payments of $7,500 each. The annual interest rate for both loans is 6%.

1. Use Table B.1 to find the present value of these two separate annuities. (Round amounts to the nearest dollar.)
2. Use Table B.3 to find the present value of these two separate annuities. (Round amounts to the nearest dollar.)

**Exercise B-10**
Present values of annuities

P3

Otto Co. borrows money on January 1 and promises to pay it back in four semiannual payments of $13,000 each on June 30 and December 31 of both this year and next year.

1. How much money is Otto able to borrow if the interest rate is 8%, compounded semiannually?
2. How much money is Otto able to borrow if the interest rate is 12%, compounded semiannually?
3. How much money is Otto able to borrow if the interest rate is 16%, compounded semiannually?

**Exercise B-11**
Present value with semiannual compounding

C1    P3

Spiller Corp. plans to issue 10%, 15-year, $500,000 par value bonds payable that pay interest semiannually on June 30 and December 31. The bonds are dated January 1 of the current year and are issued on that date. If the market rate of interest for the bonds is 8% on the date of issue, what will be the total cash proceeds from the bond issue?

**Exercise B-12**
Present value of bonds

P1    P3

**Exercise B-13**

Present value of an amount and of an annuity

P1  P3

Compute the amount that can be borrowed under each of the following circumstances:

1. A promise to repay $90,000 seven years from now at an interest rate of 6%.

2. An agreement to make three separate annual payments of $20,000, with the first payment occurring 1 year from now. The annual interest rate is 10%.

---

**Exercise B-14**

Interest rate on an investment  P4

Algoe expects to invest $1,000 annually for 40 years to yield an accumulated value of $154,762 on the date of the last investment. For this to occur, what rate of interest must Algoe earn? (Use Table B.4.)

---

**Exercise B-15**

Number of periods of an investment  P4

Steffi Derr expects to invest $10,000 annually that will earn 8%. How many annual investments must Derr make to accumulate $303,243 on the date of the last investment? (Use Table B.4.)

---

**Exercise B-16**

Future value of an annuity  P4

Kelly Malone plans to have $50 withheld from her monthly paycheck and deposited in a savings account that earns 12% annually, compounded monthly. If Malone continues with her plan for two and one-half years, how much will be accumulated in the account on the date of the last deposit?

---

**Exercise B-17**

Future value of an amount plus an annuity

P2  P4

Starr Company decides to establish a fund that it will use 10 years from now to replace an aging production facility. The company will make a $100,000 initial contribution to the fund and plans to make quarterly contributions of $50,000 beginning in three months. The fund earns 12%, compounded quarterly. What will be the value of the fund 10 years from now?

---

**Exercise B-18**

Practical applications of the time value of money

P1  P2  P3  P4

a. How much would you have to deposit today if you wanted to have $60,000 in four years? Annual interest rate is 9%.

b. Assume that you are saving up for a trip around the world when you graduate in two years. If you can earn 8% on your investments, how much would you have to deposit today to have $15,000 when you graduate?

c. Would you rather have $463 now or $1,000 ten years from now? Assume that you can earn 9% on your investments.

d. Assume that a college parking sticker today costs $90. If the cost of parking is increasing at the rate of 5% per year, how much will the college parking sticker cost in eight years?

e. Assume that the average price of a new home is $158,500. If the cost of a new home is increasing at a rate of 10% per year, how much will a new home cost in eight years?

f. An investment will pay you $10,000 in 10 years *and* it also will pay you $400 at the end of *each* of the next 10 years (Years 1 through 10). If the annual interest rate is 6%, how much would you be willing to pay today for this type of investment?

g. A college student is reported in the newspaper as having won $10,000,000 in the Kansas State Lottery. However, as is often the custom with lotteries, she does *not* actually receive the entire $10 million now. Instead she will receive $500,000 at the end of the year for *each* of the next 20 years. If the annual interest rate is 6%, what is the present value (today's amount) that she won? (Ignore taxes.)

---

**Exercise B-19**

Using present and future value tables

C1  P1  P2  P3  P4

For each of the following situations, identify (1) the case as either (*a*) a present or a future value and (*b*) a single amount or an annuity, (2) the table you would use in your computations (but do not solve the problem), and (3) the interest rate and time periods you would use.

a. You need to accumulate $10,000 for a trip you wish to take in four years. You are able to earn 8% compounded semiannually on your savings. You plan to make only one deposit and let the money accumulate for four years. How would you determine the amount of the one-time deposit?

b. Assume the same facts as in part (*a*) except that you will make semiannual deposits to your savings account.

c. You want to retire after working 40 years with savings in excess of $1,000,000. You expect to save $4,000 a year for 40 years and earn an annual rate of interest of 8%. Will you be able to retire with more than $1,000,000 in 40 years? Explain.

d. A sweepstakes agency names you a grand prize winner. You can take $225,000 immediately or elect to receive annual installments of $30,000 for 20 years. You can earn 10% annually on any investments you make. Which prize do you choose to receive?

$$p = 1/(1+i)^n$$

**TABLE B.1\***

Present Value of 1

| Periods | 1% | 2% | 3% | 4% | 5% | 6% | 7% | 8% | 9% | 10% | 12% | 15% | Periods |
|---|---|---|---|---|---|---|---|---|---|---|---|---|---|
| | | | | | | Rate | | | | | | | |
| 1 | 0.9901 | 0.9804 | 0.9709 | 0.9615 | 0.9524 | 0.9434 | 0.9346 | 0.9259 | 0.9174 | 0.9091 | 0.8929 | 0.8696 | 1 |
| 2 | 0.9803 | 0.9612 | 0.9426 | 0.9246 | 0.9070 | 0.8900 | 0.8734 | 0.8573 | 0.8417 | 0.8264 | 0.7972 | 0.7561 | 2 |
| 3 | 0.9706 | 0.9423 | 0.9151 | 0.8890 | 0.8638 | 0.8396 | 0.8163 | 0.7938 | 0.7722 | 0.7513 | 0.7118 | 0.6575 | 3 |
| 4 | 0.9610 | 0.9238 | 0.8885 | 0.8548 | 0.8227 | 0.7921 | 0.7629 | 0.7350 | 0.7084 | 0.6830 | 0.6355 | 0.5718 | 4 |
| 5 | 0.9515 | 0.9057 | 0.8626 | 0.8219 | 0.7835 | 0.7473 | 0.7130 | 0.6806 | 0.6499 | 0.6209 | 0.5674 | 0.4972 | 5 |
| 6 | 0.9420 | 0.8880 | 0.8375 | 0.7903 | 0.7462 | 0.7050 | 0.6663 | 0.6302 | 0.5963 | 0.5645 | 0.5066 | 0.4323 | 6 |
| 7 | 0.9327 | 0.8706 | 0.8131 | 0.7599 | 0.7107 | 0.6651 | 0.6227 | 0.5835 | 0.5470 | 0.5132 | 0.4523 | 0.3759 | 7 |
| 8 | 0.9235 | 0.8535 | 0.7894 | 0.7307 | 0.6768 | 0.6274 | 0.5820 | 0.5403 | 0.5019 | 0.4665 | 0.4039 | 0.3269 | 8 |
| 9 | 0.9143 | 0.8368 | 0.7664 | 0.7026 | 0.6446 | 0.5919 | 0.5439 | 0.5002 | 0.4604 | 0.4241 | 0.3606 | 0.2843 | 9 |
| 10 | 0.9053 | 0.8203 | 0.7441 | 0.6756 | 0.6139 | 0.5584 | 0.5083 | 0.4632 | 0.4224 | 0.3855 | 0.3220 | 0.2472 | 10 |
| 11 | 0.8963 | 0.8043 | 0.7224 | 0.6496 | 0.5847 | 0.5268 | 0.4751 | 0.4289 | 0.3875 | 0.3505 | 0.2875 | 0.2149 | 11 |
| 12 | 0.8874 | 0.7885 | 0.7014 | 0.6246 | 0.5568 | 0.4970 | 0.4440 | 0.3971 | 0.3555 | 0.3186 | 0.2567 | 0.1869 | 12 |
| 13 | 0.8787 | 0.7730 | 0.6810 | 0.6006 | 0.5303 | 0.4688 | 0.4150 | 0.3677 | 0.3262 | 0.2897 | 0.2292 | 0.1625 | 13 |
| 14 | 0.8700 | 0.7579 | 0.6611 | 0.5775 | 0.5051 | 0.4423 | 0.3878 | 0.3405 | 0.2992 | 0.2633 | 0.2046 | 0.1413 | 14 |
| 15 | 0.8613 | 0.7430 | 0.6419 | 0.5553 | 0.4810 | 0.4173 | 0.3624 | 0.3152 | 0.2745 | 0.2394 | 0.1827 | 0.1229 | 15 |
| 16 | 0.8528 | 0.7284 | 0.6232 | 0.5339 | 0.4581 | 0.3936 | 0.3387 | 0.2919 | 0.2519 | 0.2176 | 0.1631 | 0.1069 | 16 |
| 17 | 0.8444 | 0.7142 | 0.6050 | 0.5134 | 0.4363 | 0.3714 | 0.3166 | 0.2703 | 0.2311 | 0.1978 | 0.1456 | 0.0929 | 17 |
| 18 | 0.8360 | 0.7002 | 0.5874 | 0.4936 | 0.4155 | 0.3503 | 0.2959 | 0.2502 | 0.2120 | 0.1799 | 0.1300 | 0.0808 | 18 |
| 19 | 0.8277 | 0.6864 | 0.5703 | 0.4746 | 0.3957 | 0.3305 | 0.2765 | 0.2317 | 0.1945 | 0.1635 | 0.1161 | 0.0703 | 19 |
| 20 | 0.8195 | 0.6730 | 0.5537 | 0.4564 | 0.3769 | 0.3118 | 0.2584 | 0.2145 | 0.1784 | 0.1486 | 0.1037 | 0.0611 | 20 |
| 25 | 0.7798 | 0.6095 | 0.4776 | 0.3751 | 0.2953 | 0.2330 | 0.1842 | 0.1460 | 0.1160 | 0.0923 | 0.0588 | 0.0304 | 25 |
| 30 | 0.7419 | 0.5521 | 0.4120 | 0.3083 | 0.2314 | 0.1741 | 0.1314 | 0.0994 | 0.0754 | 0.0573 | 0.0334 | 0.0151 | 30 |
| 35 | 0.7059 | 0.5000 | 0.3554 | 0.2534 | 0.1813 | 0.1301 | 0.0937 | 0.0676 | 0.0490 | 0.0356 | 0.0189 | 0.0075 | 35 |
| 40 | 0.6717 | 0.4529 | 0.3066 | 0.2083 | 0.1420 | 0.0972 | 0.0668 | 0.0460 | 0.0318 | 0.0221 | 0.0107 | 0.0037 | 40 |

\*Used to compute the present value of a known future amount. For example: How much would you need to invest today at 10% compounded semiannually to accumulate $5,000 in 6 years from today? Using the factors of $n = 12$ and $i = 5\%$ (12 semiannual periods and a semiannual rate of 5%), the factor is 0.5568. You would need to invest $2,784 today ($5,000 × 0.5568).

$$f = (1+i)^n$$

**TABLE B.2†**

Future Value of 1

| Periods | 1% | 2% | 3% | 4% | 5% | 6% | 7% | 8% | 9% | 10% | 12% | 15% | Periods |
|---|---|---|---|---|---|---|---|---|---|---|---|---|---|
| | | | | | | Rate | | | | | | | |
| 0 | 1.0000 | 1.0000 | 1.0000 | 1.0000 | 1.0000 | 1.0000 | 1.0000 | 1.0000 | 1.0000 | 1.0000 | 1.0000 | 1.0000 | 0 |
| 1 | 1.0100 | 1.0200 | 1.0300 | 1.0400 | 1.0500 | 1.0600 | 1.0700 | 1.0800 | 1.0900 | 1.1000 | 1.1200 | 1.1500 | 1 |
| 2 | 1.0201 | 1.0404 | 1.0609 | 1.0816 | 1.1025 | 1.1236 | 1.1449 | 1.1664 | 1.1881 | 1.2100 | 1.2544 | 1.3225 | 2 |
| 3 | 1.0303 | 1.0612 | 1.0927 | 1.1249 | 1.1576 | 1.1910 | 1.2250 | 1.2597 | 1.2950 | 1.3310 | 1.4049 | 1.5209 | 3 |
| 4 | 1.0406 | 1.0824 | 1.1255 | 1.1699 | 1.2155 | 1.2625 | 1.3108 | 1.3605 | 1.4116 | 1.4641 | 1.5735 | 1.7490 | 4 |
| 5 | 1.0510 | 1.1041 | 1.1593 | 1.2167 | 1.2763 | 1.3382 | 1.4026 | 1.4693 | 1.5386 | 1.6105 | 1.7623 | 2.0114 | 5 |
| 6 | 1.0615 | 1.1262 | 1.1941 | 1.2653 | 1.3401 | 1.4185 | 1.5007 | 1.5869 | 1.6771 | 1.7716 | 1.9738 | 2.3131 | 6 |
| 7 | 1.0721 | 1.1487 | 1.2299 | 1.3159 | 1.4071 | 1.5036 | 1.6058 | 1.7138 | 1.8280 | 1.9487 | 2.2107 | 2.6600 | 7 |
| 8 | 1.0829 | 1.1717 | 1.2668 | 1.3686 | 1.4775 | 1.5938 | 1.7182 | 1.8509 | 1.9926 | 2.1436 | 2.4760 | 3.0590 | 8 |
| 9 | 1.0937 | 1.1951 | 1.3048 | 1.4233 | 1.5513 | 1.6895 | 1.8385 | 1.9990 | 2.1719 | 2.3579 | 2.7731 | 3.5179 | 9 |
| 10 | 1.1046 | 1.2190 | 1.3439 | 1.4802 | 1.6289 | 1.7908 | 1.9672 | 2.1589 | 2.3674 | 2.5937 | 3.1058 | 4.0456 | 10 |
| 11 | 1.1157 | 1.2434 | 1.3842 | 1.5395 | 1.7103 | 1.8983 | 2.1049 | 2.3316 | 2.5804 | 2.8531 | 3.4785 | 4.6524 | 11 |
| 12 | 1.1268 | 1.2682 | 1.4258 | 1.6010 | 1.7959 | 2.0122 | 2.2522 | 2.5182 | 2.8127 | 3.1384 | 3.8960 | 5.3503 | 12 |
| 13 | 1.1381 | 1.2936 | 1.4685 | 1.6651 | 1.8856 | 2.1329 | 2.4098 | 2.7196 | 3.0658 | 3.4523 | 4.3635 | 6.1528 | 13 |
| 14 | 1.1495 | 1.3195 | 1.5126 | 1.7317 | 1.9799 | 2.2609 | 2.5785 | 2.9372 | 3.3417 | 3.7975 | 4.8871 | 7.0757 | 14 |
| 15 | 1.1610 | 1.3459 | 1.5580 | 1.8009 | 2.0789 | 2.3966 | 2.7590 | 3.1722 | 3.6425 | 4.1772 | 5.4736 | 8.1371 | 15 |
| 16 | 1.1726 | 1.3728 | 1.6047 | 1.8730 | 2.1829 | 2.5404 | 2.9522 | 3.4259 | 3.9703 | 4.5950 | 6.1304 | 9.3576 | 16 |
| 17 | 1.1843 | 1.4002 | 1.6528 | 1.9479 | 2.2920 | 2.6928 | 3.1588 | 3.7000 | 4.3276 | 5.0545 | 6.8660 | 10.7613 | 17 |
| 18 | 1.1961 | 1.4282 | 1.7024 | 2.0258 | 2.4066 | 2.8543 | 3.3799 | 3.9960 | 4.7171 | 5.5599 | 7.6900 | 12.3755 | 18 |
| 19 | 1.2081 | 1.4568 | 1.7535 | 2.1068 | 2.5270 | 3.0256 | 3.6165 | 4.3157 | 5.1417 | 6.1159 | 8.6128 | 14.2318 | 19 |
| 20 | 1.2202 | 1.4859 | 1.8061 | 2.1911 | 2.6533 | 3.2071 | 3.8697 | 4.6610 | 5.6044 | 6.7275 | 9.6463 | 16.3665 | 20 |
| 25 | 1.2824 | 1.6406 | 2.0938 | 2.6658 | 3.3864 | 4.2919 | 5.4274 | 6.8485 | 8.6231 | 10.8347 | 17.0001 | 32.9190 | 25 |
| 30 | 1.3478 | 1.8114 | 2.4273 | 3.2434 | 4.3219 | 5.7435 | 7.6123 | 10.0627 | 13.2677 | 17.4494 | 29.9599 | 66.2118 | 30 |
| 35 | 1.4166 | 1.9999 | 2.8139 | 3.9461 | 5.5160 | 7.6861 | 10.6766 | 14.7853 | 20.4140 | 28.1024 | 52.7996 | 133.1755 | 35 |
| 40 | 1.4889 | 2.2080 | 3.2620 | 4.8010 | 7.0400 | 10.2857 | 14.9745 | 21.7245 | 31.4094 | 45.2593 | 93.0510 | 267.8635 | 40 |

†Used to compute the future value of a known present amount. For example: What is the accumulated value of $3,000 invested today at 8% compounded quarterly for 5 years? Using the factors of $n = 20$ and $i = 2\%$ (20 quarterly periods and a quarterly interest rate of 2%), the factor is 1.4859. The accumulated value is $4,457.70 ($3,000 × 1.4859).

## TABLE B.3[‡]
Present Value of an Annuity of 1

$$p = \left[1 - \frac{1}{(1+i)^n}\right]/i$$

| Periods | | | | | | Rate | | | | | | | Periods |
|---|---|---|---|---|---|---|---|---|---|---|---|---|---|
| | 1% | 2% | 3% | 4% | 5% | 6% | 7% | 8% | 9% | 10% | 12% | 15% | |
| 1 | 0.9901 | 0.9804 | 0.9709 | 0.9615 | 0.9524 | 0.9434 | 0.9346 | 0.9259 | 0.9174 | 0.9091 | 0.8929 | 0.8696 | 1 |
| 2 | 1.9704 | 1.9416 | 1.9135 | 1.8861 | 1.8594 | 1.8334 | 1.8080 | 1.7833 | 1.7591 | 1.7355 | 1.6901 | 1.6257 | 2 |
| 3 | 2.9410 | 2.8839 | 2.8286 | 2.7751 | 2.7232 | 2.6730 | 2.6243 | 2.5771 | 2.5313 | 2.4869 | 2.4018 | 2.2832 | 3 |
| 4 | 3.9020 | 3.8077 | 3.7171 | 3.6299 | 3.5460 | 3.4651 | 3.3872 | 3.3121 | 3.2397 | 3.1699 | 3.0373 | 2.8550 | 4 |
| 5 | 4.8534 | 4.7135 | 4.5797 | 4.4518 | 4.3295 | 4.2124 | 4.1002 | 3.9927 | 3.8897 | 3.7908 | 3.6048 | 3.3522 | 5 |
| 6 | 5.7955 | 5.6014 | 5.4172 | 5.2421 | 5.0757 | 4.9173 | 4.7665 | 4.6229 | 4.4859 | 4.3553 | 4.1114 | 3.7845 | 6 |
| 7 | 6.7282 | 6.4720 | 6.2303 | 6.0021 | 5.7864 | 5.5824 | 5.3893 | 5.2064 | 5.0330 | 4.8684 | 4.5638 | 4.1604 | 7 |
| 8 | 7.6517 | 7.3255 | 7.0197 | 6.7327 | 6.4632 | 6.2098 | 5.9713 | 5.7466 | 5.5348 | 5.3349 | 4.9676 | 4.4873 | 8 |
| 9 | 8.5660 | 8.1622 | 7.7861 | 7.4353 | 7.1078 | 6.8017 | 6.5152 | 6.2469 | 5.9952 | 5.7590 | 5.3282 | 4.7716 | 9 |
| 10 | 9.4713 | 8.9826 | 8.5302 | 8.1109 | 7.7217 | 7.3601 | 7.0236 | 6.7101 | 6.4177 | 6.1446 | 5.6502 | 5.0188 | 10 |
| 11 | 10.3676 | 9.7868 | 9.2526 | 8.7605 | 8.3064 | 7.8869 | 7.4987 | 7.1390 | 6.8052 | 6.4951 | 5.9377 | 5.2337 | 11 |
| 12 | 11.2551 | 10.5753 | 9.9540 | 9.3851 | 8.8633 | 8.3838 | 7.9427 | 7.5361 | 7.1607 | 6.8137 | 6.1944 | 5.4206 | 12 |
| 13 | 12.1337 | 11.3484 | 10.6350 | 9.9856 | 9.3936 | 8.8527 | 8.3577 | 7.9038 | 7.4869 | 7.1034 | 6.4235 | 5.5831 | 13 |
| 14 | 13.0037 | 12.1062 | 11.2961 | 10.5631 | 9.8986 | 9.2950 | 8.7455 | 8.2442 | 7.7862 | 7.3667 | 6.6282 | 5.7245 | 14 |
| 15 | 13.8651 | 12.8493 | 11.9379 | 11.1184 | 10.3797 | 9.7122 | 9.1079 | 8.5595 | 8.0607 | 7.6061 | 6.8109 | 5.8474 | 15 |
| 16 | 14.7179 | 13.5777 | 12.5611 | 11.6523 | 10.8378 | 10.1059 | 9.4466 | 8.8514 | 8.3126 | 7.8237 | 6.9740 | 5.9542 | 16 |
| 17 | 15.5623 | 14.2919 | 13.1661 | 12.1657 | 11.2741 | 10.4773 | 9.7632 | 9.1216 | 8.5436 | 8.0216 | 7.1196 | 6.0472 | 17 |
| 18 | 16.3983 | 14.9920 | 13.7535 | 12.6593 | 11.6896 | 10.8276 | 10.0591 | 9.3719 | 8.7556 | 8.2014 | 7.2497 | 6.1280 | 18 |
| 19 | 17.2260 | 15.6785 | 14.3238 | 13.1339 | 12.0853 | 11.1581 | 10.3356 | 9.6036 | 8.9501 | 8.3649 | 7.3658 | 6.1982 | 19 |
| 20 | 18.0456 | 16.3514 | 14.8775 | 13.5903 | 12.4622 | 11.4699 | 10.5940 | 9.8181 | 9.1285 | 8.5136 | 7.4694 | 6.2593 | 20 |
| 25 | 22.0232 | 19.5235 | 17.4131 | 15.6221 | 14.0939 | 12.7834 | 11.6536 | 10.6748 | 9.8226 | 9.0770 | 7.8431 | 6.4641 | 25 |
| 30 | 25.8077 | 22.3965 | 19.6004 | 17.2920 | 15.3725 | 13.7648 | 12.4090 | 11.2578 | 10.2737 | 9.4269 | 8.0552 | 6.5660 | 30 |
| 35 | 29.4086 | 24.9986 | 21.4872 | 18.6646 | 16.3742 | 14.4982 | 12.9477 | 11.6546 | 10.5668 | 9.6442 | 8.1755 | 6.6166 | 35 |
| 40 | 32.8347 | 27.3555 | 23.1148 | 19.7928 | 17.1591 | 15.0463 | 13.3317 | 11.9246 | 10.7574 | 9.7791 | 8.2438 | 6.6418 | 40 |

[‡]Used to calculate the present value of a series of equal payments made at the end of each period. For example: What is the present value of $2,000 per year for 10 years assuming an annual interest rate of 9%? For ($n = 10$, $i = 9$%), the PV factor is 6.4177. $2,000 per year for 10 years is the equivalent of $12,835 today ($2,000 × 6.4177).

## TABLE B.4[§]
Future Value of an Annuity of 1

$$f = [(1+i)^n - 1]/i$$

| Periods | | | | | | Rate | | | | | | | Periods |
|---|---|---|---|---|---|---|---|---|---|---|---|---|---|
| | 1% | 2% | 3% | 4% | 5% | 6% | 7% | 8% | 9% | 10% | 12% | 15% | |
| 1 | 1.0000 | 1.0000 | 1.0000 | 1.0000 | 1.0000 | 1.0000 | 1.0000 | 1.0000 | 1.0000 | 1.0000 | 1.0000 | 1.0000 | 1 |
| 2 | 2.0100 | 2.0200 | 2.0300 | 2.0400 | 2.0500 | 2.0600 | 2.0700 | 2.0800 | 2.0900 | 2.1000 | 2.1200 | 2.1500 | 2 |
| 3 | 3.0301 | 3.0604 | 3.0909 | 3.1216 | 3.1525 | 3.1836 | 3.2149 | 3.2464 | 3.2781 | 3.3100 | 3.3744 | 3.4725 | 3 |
| 4 | 4.0604 | 4.1216 | 4.1836 | 4.2465 | 4.3101 | 4.3746 | 4.4399 | 4.5061 | 4.5731 | 4.6410 | 4.7793 | 4.9934 | 4 |
| 5 | 5.1010 | 5.2040 | 5.3091 | 5.4163 | 5.5256 | 5.6371 | 5.7507 | 5.8666 | 5.9847 | 6.1051 | 6.3528 | 6.7424 | 5 |
| 6 | 6.1520 | 6.3081 | 6.4684 | 6.6330 | 6.8019 | 6.9753 | 7.1533 | 7.3359 | 7.5233 | 7.7156 | 8.1152 | 8.7537 | 6 |
| 7 | 7.2135 | 7.4343 | 7.6625 | 7.8983 | 8.1420 | 8.3938 | 8.6540 | 8.9228 | 9.2004 | 9.4872 | 10.0890 | 11.0668 | 7 |
| 8 | 8.2857 | 8.5830 | 8.8923 | 9.2142 | 9.5491 | 9.8975 | 10.2598 | 10.6366 | 11.0285 | 11.4359 | 12.2997 | 13.7268 | 8 |
| 9 | 9.3685 | 9.7546 | 10.1591 | 10.5828 | 11.0266 | 11.4913 | 11.9780 | 12.4876 | 13.0210 | 13.5795 | 14.7757 | 16.7858 | 9 |
| 10 | 10.4622 | 10.9497 | 11.4639 | 12.0061 | 12.5779 | 13.1808 | 13.8164 | 14.4866 | 15.1929 | 15.9374 | 17.5487 | 20.3037 | 10 |
| 11 | 11.5668 | 12.1687 | 12.8078 | 13.4864 | 14.2068 | 14.9716 | 15.7836 | 16.6455 | 17.5603 | 18.5312 | 20.6546 | 24.3493 | 11 |
| 12 | 12.6825 | 13.4121 | 14.1920 | 15.0258 | 15.9171 | 16.8699 | 17.8885 | 18.9771 | 20.1407 | 21.3843 | 24.1331 | 29.0017 | 12 |
| 13 | 13.8093 | 14.6803 | 15.6178 | 16.6268 | 17.7130 | 18.8821 | 20.1406 | 21.4953 | 22.9534 | 24.5227 | 28.0291 | 34.3519 | 13 |
| 14 | 14.9474 | 15.9739 | 17.0863 | 18.2919 | 19.5986 | 21.0151 | 22.5505 | 24.2149 | 26.0192 | 27.9750 | 32.3926 | 40.5047 | 14 |
| 15 | 16.0969 | 17.2934 | 18.5989 | 20.0236 | 21.5786 | 23.2760 | 25.1290 | 27.1521 | 29.3609 | 31.7725 | 37.2797 | 47.5804 | 15 |
| 16 | 17.2579 | 18.6393 | 20.1569 | 21.8245 | 23.6575 | 25.6725 | 27.8881 | 30.3243 | 33.0034 | 35.9497 | 42.7533 | 55.7175 | 16 |
| 17 | 18.4304 | 20.0121 | 21.7616 | 23.6975 | 25.8404 | 28.2129 | 30.8402 | 33.7502 | 36.9737 | 40.5447 | 48.8837 | 65.0751 | 17 |
| 18 | 19.6147 | 21.4123 | 23.4144 | 25.6454 | 28.1324 | 30.9057 | 33.9990 | 37.4502 | 41.3013 | 45.5992 | 55.7497 | 75.8364 | 18 |
| 19 | 20.8109 | 22.8406 | 25.1169 | 27.6712 | 30.5390 | 33.7600 | 37.3790 | 41.4463 | 46.0185 | 51.1591 | 63.4397 | 88.2118 | 19 |
| 20 | 22.0190 | 24.2974 | 26.8704 | 29.7781 | 33.0660 | 36.7856 | 40.9955 | 45.7620 | 51.1601 | 57.2750 | 72.0524 | 102.4436 | 20 |
| 25 | 28.2432 | 32.0303 | 36.4593 | 41.6459 | 47.7271 | 54.8645 | 63.2490 | 73.1059 | 84.7009 | 98.3471 | 133.3339 | 212.7930 | 25 |
| 30 | 34.7849 | 40.5681 | 47.5754 | 56.0849 | 66.4388 | 79.0582 | 94.4608 | 113.2832 | 136.3075 | 164.4940 | 241.3327 | 434.7451 | 30 |
| 35 | 41.6603 | 49.9945 | 60.4621 | 73.6522 | 90.3203 | 111.4348 | 138.2369 | 172.3168 | 215.7108 | 271.0244 | 431.6635 | 881.1702 | 35 |
| 40 | 48.8864 | 60.4020 | 75.4013 | 95.0255 | 120.7998 | 154.7620 | 199.6351 | 259.0565 | 337.8824 | 442.5926 | 767.0914 | 1,779.0903 | 40 |

[§]Used to calculate the future value of a series of equal payments made at the end of each period. For example: What is the future value of $4,000 per year for 6 years assuming an annual interest rate of 8%? For ($n = 6$, $i = 8$%), the FV factor is 7.3359. $4,000 per year for 6 years accumulates to $29,343.60 ($4,000 × 7.3359).

# C Lean Principles and Accounting

## Learning Objectives

### CONCEPTUAL

**C1** Describe lean principles.

### ANALYTICAL

**A1** Compute cycle time and cycle efficiency, and explain their importance to production management.

**A2** Compute days' sales in work in process inventory.

**A3** Compute days' payable outstanding.

### PROCEDURAL

**P1** Record product costs using lean accounting.

**P2** Classify quality costs and prepare a cost of quality report.

## LEAN BUSINESS MODEL

C1 _____
Describe lean principles. Competition forces businesses to improve. One path to improvement is the **lean business model,** whose goals are to use fewer resources to deliver higher-quality products to satisfy customers. Exhibit C.1 shows key aspects of the lean business model. Lean business principles differ from those in traditional manufacturing. Lean business practices like continuous improvement, *just-in-time* inventory systems, and supply chain management aim to cut waste and increase productivity. Lean goals focus on the consumer and overall societal benefits.

**EXHIBIT C.1**

Lean Business Model

| Lean Principles | Lean Practices | Lean Goals |
|---|---|---|
| Value Streams | Continuous Improvement | Customer Satisfaction |
| Pull Production | Just-in-Time | Quality |
| Zero Waste and Zero Defects | Supply Chain Management | Triple Bottom Line |

### Lean Principles

Three key principles of the lean business model involve value streams, pull production, and zero waste and zero defects.

**Value Streams**   Lean businesses aim to provide customers what they want, and when they want it. Customers increasingly want customized products, so manufacturers must produce quickly and without waste. Rather than build standard products in a long assembly line, lean manufacturers use smaller **value streams.** Value streams consist of all the activities needed to create customer value. For example, a food processor might have separate value streams for its trail mix, energy bars, and energy drinks. All of the processes for each product type occur in one value stream. A trail mix value stream is shown in Exhibit C.2.

**EXHIBIT C.2**

Trail Mix Value Stream

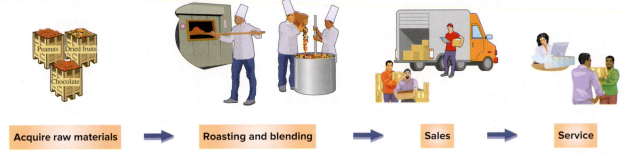

| Acquire raw materials | → | Roasting and blending | → | Sales | → | Service |

**Pull Production**   Lean manufacturing differs from traditional manufacturing. Lean manufacturers use **pull production,** where production begins with a customer order. Goods are "pulled" through the manufacturing process "just-in-time" and delivered directly to the customer after completion.

**Push Production**   Traditional manufacturing uses **push production,** where goods are produced before a customer order and production is based on sales forecasts. Goods are "pushed" into inventory and wait for a customer order. Exhibit C.3 compares push production with pull production. **Push production** has several challenges.

- Inaccurate sales forecasts can cause overproduction. This increases storage costs and risk of obsolescence (decrease in value).
- Inaccurate sales forecasts can cause underproduction. This creates stock-outs and lost sales.
- **Batch sizes (lot sizes),** which are the number of units produced after a machine setup, are high. This makes it hard to produce customized products. Large batch sizes can also produce more defects before the issue is identified and production is stopped.

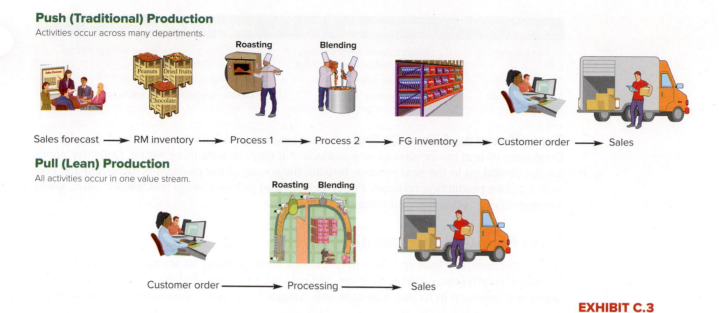

**Push (Traditional) Production**
Activities occur across many departments.

Roasting    Blending

Sales forecast ⟶ RM inventory ⟶ Process 1 ⟶ Process 2 ⟶ FG inventory ⟶ Customer order ⟶ Sales

**Pull (Lean) Production**
All activities occur in one value stream.

Roasting  Blending

Customer order ⟶ Processing ⟶ Sales

**EXHIBIT C.3**

Push Production Compared
with Pull Production

**Pull Production**   To address these issues, many turn to pull production. Pull production follows a lean strategy which includes a focus on reducing (1) cycle time, (2) setup time, and (3) inventory levels.

**Cycle Time**   Cycle time (CT) is the total time a production process takes, starting from putting raw materials into production to completing a finished good. This can be in minutes, such as with fast-food restaurants, or weeks, such as with jet engines. Lean businesses reduce cycle time by producing in smaller batch sizes and making goods to customer order. Smaller batch sizes reduce cycle time because goods spend less time waiting for other goods to finish in the production cycle. Customers get the goods they want more quickly.
Lean businesses focus on improving the following to reduce cycle time.

- *Process time*—Time spent working on and producing the product. Lean businesses reduce process time by simplifying the production process and by eliminating unwanted product features. **Value-added**

- *Inspection time*—Time spent inspecting raw materials received, work in process in production, and finished goods before shipment. Lean businesses emphasize quality materials and processes to reduce inspection time.

- *Move time*—Time spent moving materials and inventory, and employee time spent moving around the production area. Lean businesses reduce move time by strategically placing tools and machinery in the production area. **Non-value-added**

- *Wait time*—Time an order sits before or between production processes. Lean businesses reduce wait time by avoiding raw material order delays, production bottlenecks, and poor production scheduling.

Of the four parts of cycle time, only process time is a **value-added time** activity that adds value to the customer. Inspection, move, and wait time are **non-value-added time** activities because they do not add value to customers.

**Setup Time**   Setup time is the amount of time to prepare a process for production; for example, preparing the roasting process to make trail mix. Setup time includes time spent starting and calibrating machines. Lean businesses want quick setups so they can reduce cycle time when producing goods to customer order in smaller batch sizes.

**Inventory Levels**   Lean businesses believe holding inventory is wasteful and instead use *just-in-time* inventory. The following table compares how traditional and lean manufacturers manage inventory.

| Inventory | Traditional Approach | Lean (Just-in-Time) Approach |
|---|---|---|
| Raw materials .......... | Bought to hold in inventory; enters production based on sales forecast. | Bought after a customer order; enters production immediately after receipt. |
| Work in process......... | Larger; not a priority to reduce. | Reduced as cycle times get faster. |
| Finished goods ......... | Held in inventory until sold. | Delivered to customers after goods are finished. |

## Zero Waste and Zero Defects

Lean businesses aim for zero waste and zero defects. Employees of lean businesses can stop production if they see something wrong. Defective goods are not passed on to the next process. Instead, the source of the problem is identified and corrected before production resumes. Fewer defects lead to lower scrap and rework costs, fewer warranty claims, and increased customer satisfaction.

## Lean Production Example

**Nike** implemented a lean approach to its clothes manufacturing in several countries. Clothes manufacturing requires sewing, ironing, and packing processes. Exhibit C.4 compares Nike's traditional approach to its new lean approach. Several benefits and cost savings are identified.

**EXHIBIT C.4**

Lean Production at Nike

| | Traditional Approach | Lean Approach | Benefits from Lean Approach |
|---|---|---|---|
| Production layout ......... | Sewing, ironing, and packing processes are physically separated. | All processes in the apparel value stream are located together. | Reduced move time of both employees and inventory. |
| Production starts with ....... | Sales forecast. | Customer order. | Less inventory. |
| Quality control............ | End-of-line quality inspection. | Each employee inspects her own output before passing it to the next step. | Fewer defects. |
| Supervision .............. | One supervisor for each process. | One supervisor for the entire value stream. | Reduced overhead costs. |

Source: Distelhorst, Greg; Hainmueller, Jens; and Locke, Richard M. *Does Lean Improve Labor Standards? Management and Social Performance in the Nike Supply Chain,* August 29, 2015, Management Science, Vol. 63, Issue 3.

## Lean Overhead Costs

Traditional manufacturers use methods like *activity-based costing* to allocate overhead costs to products. Lean manufacturers like **Illinois Tool Works** aim to eliminate overhead costs, not allocate them. Focusing on the 20% of its products that generate 80% of its profits, the company produces in separate value streams. Employees are responsible for all activities in their value streams. The company made major operational changes to implement a lean approach and increase profits. The table below shows how those changes reduced overhead costs.

| Operational Change to Produce in Value Streams | Reduced Overhead Costs |
|---|---|
| Eliminate supervisors .............. | Eliminate supervisor salaries and benefits. |
| Eliminate support departments ....... | Costs of quality control, purchasing, customer service, design, maintenance, and scheduling are reduced and directly traced to each value stream. |
| Implement *just-in-time* to eliminate central warehouse ................. | Costs of moving, storing, and controlling inventory are reduced and directly traced to each value stream. |

After eliminating overhead costs, tracing *direct* costs to value streams, and treating any remaining *indirect* costs as period costs, the company no longer allocates costs. It doesn't track cost drivers like number of setups and number of purchase orders that are used in activity-based costing. Profits and employee and customer satisfaction all improved. Source: Tatikonda, L., O'Brien, D., and Tatikonda, R. *Succeeding with 80/20,* Management Accounting, Vol. 80, No.8.

## Supply Chain Management

**Supply chain management** or *logistics* is the control of materials, information, and finances as they move between suppliers, manufacturers, and customers. Lean businesses use supply chain management to ensure raw materials arrive just-in-time for production and customers receive their orders on schedule.

Mihajlo Maricic/Alamy Stock Photo

All types of businesses must manage their supply chains. **Nike** outsources all of its production, and it uses review programs to make sure its suppliers follow ethical practices. **Taco Bell**'s just-in-time preprocessed food deliveries require close coordination and information sharing with its suppliers.

One measure of success in supply chain management is in the demand for its services. A materials handling industry report forecasts over 1.4 million openings for logistics jobs in supply chain management. These include jobs for data analysts, marketers, human resource managers, and fulfillment center employees. Average annual salaries of around $100,000 are common for supply chain managers. The Council of Supply Chain Professionals (cscmp.org) has more information.

## Lean Processes for Service Businesses

Lean principles also apply to retailers and service businesses. **Amazon** applied lean principles when it changed its fulfillment process to use machines for repetitive, low-value-added steps and human employees for high-value, complex work. As a result, the number of defects (incorrect order fulfillments) was reduced. Amazon also applies lean principles to customer service. Employees make quick decisions to satisfy customers. If customers call about a defective product, employees can "stop the line" by removing the product from Amazon's website until the source of the defect is resolved. This lean approach reduces the number of defective products sold and increases customer satisfaction.

**Taco Bell** applies lean principles to food service. By focusing on customer value, management determined "We are in the business of feeding people, not making food." As a result, the company changed from food *processing* to food *assembly*. Ingredients are preprocessed in off-site facilities and shipped just-in-time to restaurants. Employees then assemble ingredients to suit customer orders. The lean approach decreases inventory levels and costs, and it increases quality and customer satisfaction.

---

**Part A**   For each item, identify whether it best applies to lean businesses (L) or traditional businesses (T).

1. Production begins with a sales forecast.
2. Only finished goods are inspected for quality.
3. Uses pull production.
4. Processes are located together.
5. Uses push production.
6. Produces in small batch sizes.

 **C-1**

Lean Production

C1

*Solution*

**1.** T  **2.** T  **3.** L  **4.** L  **5.** T  **6.** L

**Part B**   Identify which of the statements below are true (T) or false (F). Lean businesses aim to:

1. Reduce inventory levels.
2. Increase profits.
3. Produce in large batch sizes.
4. Increase long setup times.
5. Reduce wait time.
6. Reduce inspection time.

*Solution*

**1.** T  **2.** T  **3.** F  **4.** F  **5.** T  **6.** T

Do More: QS C-1, QS C-2, E C-1

## PRODUCTION PERFORMANCE

**A1**

Compute cycle time and cycle efficiency, and explain their importance to production management.

### Cycle Time and Cycle Efficiency

Lean businesses use many nonfinancial measures to evaluate the performance of their production processes. It is important to reduce the time it takes to produce products and to improve efficiency. Cycle time (CT) is the time it takes to produce a good or provide a service. It is computed using the equation in Exhibit C.5.

**EXHIBIT C.5**

Cycle Time

> **Cycle time = Process time + Inspection time + Move time + Wait time**

Process time is the only activity that adds value to the customer (*value-added activity*). Inspection, move, and wait times do not add value to customers (*non-value-added activities*). Lean businesses try to reduce non-value-added time to improve **cycle efficiency (CE).** Cycle efficiency, defined in Exhibit C.6, measures the amount of cycle time spent on value-added activities. A CE of 1 (100%) means a value stream's time is spent entirely on value-added activities. If the CE is low, too much time is being spent on non-value-added activities and the production process should be reviewed with an aim to eliminate waste.

**EXHIBIT C.6**

Cycle Efficiency

$$\text{Cycle efficiency} = \frac{\text{Value-added time}}{\text{Cycle time}}$$

To illustrate, assume that Rocky Mountain Bikes receives and produces an order for 500 mountain bikes. It took the following times to produce this order.

 Process time... 1.8 days

 Inspection time... 0.5 day

 Move time... 0.7 day

 Wait time... 3.0 days

Cycle time is 6.0 days (1.8 + 0.5 + 0.7 + 3.0 days). Cycle efficiency is computed as

$$\text{Cycle efficiency} = \frac{1.8 \text{ days}}{6.0 \text{ days}} = 0.30, \text{ or } 30\%$$

| Time Type | Days | % |
|---|---|---|
| Value-added | 1.8 | 30% |
| Non-value-added | 4.2 | 70 |
| Total | 6.0 | 100% |

Rocky Mountain Bikes's value-added time (its process time, or time spent working on the product) is 30%. The other 70% of time is spent on non-value-added activities. The 30% CE for Rocky Mountain Bikes is low. Employees and managers should try to reduce time spent on non-value-added activities. If the company can reduce its wait time by 2 days, its cycle time will be 4 days (computed as 6 days − 2 days). Its cycle efficiency will then be 0.45 (45%), computed as 1.8 days/4.0 days.

### Days' Sales in Work in Process Inventory

**A2**

Compute days' sales in work in process inventory.

Lean businesses aim to reduce inventory. They typically do not have a separate Raw Materials Inventory account and hold few finished goods. This means the Work in Process Inventory account can be used to measure production efficiency. Work in process inventory reflects delay in getting products to customers, which lean businesses consider wasteful. Getting products to customers sooner by reducing work in process inventory can increase customer satisfaction. To measure production efficiency, we can use **days' sales in work in process inventory,** defined in Exhibit C.7. It's often rounded to the nearest whole day.

**EXHIBIT C.7**

Days' Sales in Work in Process Inventory

$$\text{Days' sales in work in process inventory} = \frac{\text{Work in process inventory}}{\text{Cost of goods sold}} \times 365$$

Axis Co., a computer maker, reports work in process inventory of $503 and cost of goods sold of $45,829. Axis computes its days' sales in work in process inventory as follows.

$$\text{Days' sales in work in process inventory} = \frac{\$503}{\$45,829} \times 365 = 4 \text{ days}$$

Lower days' sales in work in process inventory means the company is completing its production cycle more quickly. Adopting a lean model should result in a lower number of days' sales in work in process inventory. As an example, if Axis Co. adopts a lean model and reduces its work in process inventory by 20%, its days' sales in work in process inventory is 3 days, computed as follows.

$$\text{Days' sales in work in process inventory} = \frac{\$503 \times 80\%}{\$45,829} \times 365 = 3 \text{ days}$$

---

**Part 1**

**NEED-TO-KNOW** C-2

Cycle Time and Cycle Efficiency

**A1**

The following information is for an order produced by Tyler Co. Compute cycle time and cycle efficiency.

| Process time . . . | 8 days | Inspection time . . . | 0.2 day | Move time . . . | 0.4 day | Wait time. . . . | 1.4 days |
|---|---|---|---|---|---|---|---|

**Solution**

Cycle time       = Process time + Inspection time + Move time + Wait time
                 = 8 + 0.2 + 0.4 + 1.4 = <u>10 days</u>

Cycle efficiency = Value-added time/Cycle time
                 = 8/10 = <u>80%</u> → 80% of the company's time is spent on value-added activities.
                       Only process time is considered value-added time.

Do More: QS C-9, QS C-10, E C-6, E C-7, E C-8, E C-9

**Part 2**

Days' Sales in Work in Process Inventory

**A2**

Use the following information to compute days' sales in work in process inventory.

| Work in process inventory . . . . . . . | $2,053 | Cost of goods sold . . . . . . | $46,828 |
|---|---|---|---|

**Solution**

Days' sales in work in process inventory = ($2,053/$46,828) × 365 = <u>16 days</u>

Do More: QS C-11, E C-10, E C-11

---

# LEAN ACCOUNTING

## Key Accounts

Lean businesses usually have fewer transactions to record and use fewer accounts. The key accounts in lean accounting follow.

**P1**

Record product costs using lean accounting.

- **Work in Process Inventory** Lean businesses put raw materials immediately into production, so a separate Raw Materials Inventory account is not used. Raw materials purchases are recorded in Work in Process Inventory.
- **Conversion Costs** Direct labor, indirect labor, and other overhead costs are recorded in this account. In lean businesses, employees work within individual value streams and they do both direct and indirect labor tasks. For example, employees in a trail mix value stream might do roasting, blending, packaging, and cleaning duties. Therefore, all of these costs are accumulated in the Conversion Costs account.

## Conversion Costs

In lean accounting, *budgeted* conversion costs are applied to work in process. For example, if a business budgets for $100,000 of conversion costs and 4,000 production hours in a value stream, the **conversion cost rate** is computed as follows.

$$\text{Conversion cost rate} = \frac{\text{Budgeted conversion costs}}{\text{Budgeted production hours}} = \frac{\$100,000}{4,000 \text{ hours}} = \$25 \text{ per production hour}$$

This rate can be expressed in terms of units of product. For example, if each unit requires 2 production hours, the conversion cost rate is $50 per unit ($25 × 2).

## Accounting Entries

**Point:** Variations of lean accounting exist. Some use "backflush" accounting, where entries are delayed until goods are finished or sold.

Solshine manufactures solar panels. Each solar panel requires $40 of raw materials and $160 of conversion costs. The company produced and sold 200 solar panels for $480 each this period. Actual conversion costs equaled applied conversion costs. The relevant journal entries follow.

| | | | |
|---|---|---|---|
| ① | Work in Process Inventory . . . . . . . . . . . . . . . . . . . . . . . | 8,000 | |
| | Accounts Payable . . . . . . . . . . . . . . . . . . . . . . . . . . | | 8,000 |
| | *Acquired raw materials on credit (200 units × $40).* | | |
| ② | Work in Process Inventory . . . . . . . . . . . . . . . . . . . . . . . | 32,000 | |
| | Conversion Costs . . . . . . . . . . . . . . . . . . . . . . . . . . | | 32,000 |
| | *Apply conversion costs to production (200 units × $160).* | | |
| ③ | Conversion Costs . . . . . . . . . . . . . . . . . . . . . . . . . . . . . | 32,000 | |
| | Various Accounts. . . . . . . . . . . . . . . . . . . . . . . . . . . | | 32,000 |
| | *Record actual conversion costs (given).* | | |

| | | | |
|---|---|---|---|
| ④ | Accounts Receivable . . . . . . . . . . . . . . . . . . . . | 96,000 | |
| | Sales. . . . . . . . . . . . . . . . . . . . . . . . . . . . . . | | 96,000 |
| | *Record sales on credit (200 units × $480).* | | |
| ⑤ | Cost of Goods Sold. . . . . . . . . . . . . . . . . . . . . | 40,000 | |
| | Work in Process Inventory . . . . . . . . . . . | | 40,000 |
| | *Record cost of goods sold (200 × $200).* | | |

① Records raw materials purchased ($40 per panel × 200 panels produced = $8,000) as Work in Process Inventory. Separate raw materials inventory accounts are not used.

② Applies conversion costs ($160 per panel × 200 panels produced = $32,000) to Work in Process Inventory. This applied conversion cost is based on a budgeted amount of conversion costs.

③ Records actual conversion costs to produce 200 solar panels. This amount includes the actual costs of direct labor, indirect labor, and other overhead costs. The various credit accounts in this journal entry would include Salaries Payable, Wages Payable, Utilities Payable, Accumulated Depreciation—Manufacturing Equipment, and others.

④ Records the sale of goods on account (200 panels sold × $480 sales price per panel = $96,000).

⑤ Records the related cost of 200 panels sold (200 × $200 = $40,000). The cost per unit is the sum of $40 of raw materials and $160 of conversion costs. Because lean businesses make goods to order, finished product costs are immediately recorded in Cost of Goods Sold.

**When Finished Goods Inventory Remains**   Lean businesses sometimes end an accounting period with finished but unsold goods. If instead of selling 200 panels, assume Solshine sold 185 panels and had 15 panels left in inventory. It records journal entries ①, ②, and ③ as above; but it records entries ④ and ⑤ as follows. Finished Goods Inventory is increased for the cost of goods *not* sold (15 units × $200). Cost of goods sold is computed as 185 units sold × $200 = $37,000.

| | | | |
|---|---|---|---|
| ④ | Accounts Receivable . . . . . . . . . . . . . . . . . . . . . . . . . . | 88,800 | |
| | Sales. . . . . . . . . . . . . . . . . . . . . . . . . . . . . . . . . . . | | 88,800 |
| | *Record sales on credit (185 units × $480 selling price).* | | |

| | | | |
|---|---|---|---|
| ⑤ | Finished Goods Inventory . . . . . . . . . . . . . . . . | 3,000 | |
| | Cost of Goods Sold. . . . . . . . . . . . . . . . . . . . . | 37,000 | |
| | Work in Process Inventory . . . . . . . . . . | | 40,000 |
| | *Record inventory and cost of goods sold.* | | |

A lean manufacturer incurs $45 per unit in raw materials costs and applies $75 per unit in conversion costs to produce office chairs. Each chair is sold for $170. In the current period, the business produced 500 units and sold 470 units. Prepare the necessary journal entries following lean accounting. Assume actual conversion costs equal applied conversion costs.

**NEED-TO-KNOW** **C-3**

Lean Accounting Entries

**P1**

### Solution

| | | |
|---|---|---|
| Work in Process Inventory . . . . . . . . . . . . . . . . . . . . . . | 22,500 | |
|     Accounts Payable . . . . . . . . . . . . . . . . . . . . . . . | | 22,500 |
| *Acquired raw materials on credit ($45 × 500).* | | |
| Work in Process Inventory . . . . . . . . . . . . . . . . . . . . . . | 37,500 | |
|     Conversion Costs. . . . . . . . . . . . . . . . . . . . . . . | | 37,500 |
| *Apply conversion costs to production ($75 × 500).* | | |
| Conversion Costs . . . . . . . . . . . . . . . . . . . . . . . . . . . | 37,500 | |
|     Various Accounts. . . . . . . . . . . . . . . . . . . . . . . | | 37,500 |
| *Record actual conversion costs.* | | |

| | | |
|---|---|---|
| Accounts Receivable . . . . . . . . . . . . . . . . . . . . . . . . . . . | 79,900 | |
|     Sales . . . . . . . . . . . . . . . . . . . . . . . . . . . . . . . | | 79,900 |
| *Record sales on credit ($170 × 470).* | | |
| Finished Goods Inventory . . . . . . . . . . . . . . . . . . . . . . . | 3,600 | |
| Cost of Goods Sold. . . . . . . . . . . . . . . . . . . . . . . . . . . . | 56,400 | |
|     Work in Process Inventory. . . . . . . . . . . . . . . . . . | | 60,000 |
| *Record ending inventory ($120 × 30) and cost of goods sold ($120 × 470).* | | |

Do More: QS C-3, QS C-4, QS C-5, QS C-6, E C-2, E C-3, E C-4

## Costs of Quality

Lean businesses assess the costs of quality to reduce non-value-added activities. **Costs of quality** are the costs incurred to produce the quality of products that satisfies customers. Exhibit C.8 shows examples of the four different types of quality costs.

**P2**

Classify quality costs and prepare a cost of quality report.

**Costs of Good Quality**

Prevention costs

Appraisal costs

**Costs of Poor Quality**

Internal failure costs

External failure costs

**EXHIBIT C.8**

Types of Quality Costs

**Costs of Good Quality**  Prevention and appraisal costs are incurred before a good or service is provided to a customer. The purpose of these costs is to reduce the chance the customer is provided a defective good or service. These are the costs of trying to ensure that only good-quality items are produced.

- *Prevention* activities focus on quality training and improvement programs to ensure quality is built into the product or service. Working with good suppliers and performing equipment maintenance are other prevention activities.
- *Appraisal* activities include the costs of inspections to ensure that materials and supplies meet specifications and inspections of finished goods.

**Costs of Poor Quality**  Internal and external failure costs are the costs of making poor-quality items.

- *Internal failure costs* are incurred after a company has manufactured a defective product but before that product has been delivered to a customer. Internal failure costs include the costs of reworking products, reinspecting reworked products, and scrap.

- *External failure costs* are incurred after a customer has been provided a defective product or service. Examples of this type of cost include costs of warranty repairs and costs of recalling products. This category also includes lost profits due to dissatisfied customers buying from other companies.

Exhibit C.9 shows a **cost of quality report,** which lists the costs of quality activities by category. In addition to dollar amounts, this report shows the percentage of the total costs of quality in each category. This company spends only 55% (25% + 30%) of its total cost of quality on the activities of good quality. Spending more on prevention and appraisal could reduce the costs of bad quality and reduce the costs of lost profits from dissatisfied customers.

**EXHIBIT C.9**

Cost of Quality Report

| Cost of Quality Report | | | |
|---|---|---|---|
| Quality Category | Cost | Category Total | % of Total Cost of Quality |
| **Prevention** | | | |
| Training . . . . . . . . . . . . . . . . . . | $25,000 | $25,000 | 25% |
| **Appraisal** | | | |
| Inspecting materials . . . . . . . . | 17,500 | | |
| Testing finished goods . . . . . | 12,500 | 30,000 | 30% |
| **Internal failure** | | | |
| Rework . . . . . . . . . . . . . . . . . . | 8,400 | | |
| Scrap . . . . . . . . . . . . . . . . . . . | 7,600 | 16,000 | 16% |
| **External failure** | | | |
| Warranty claims . . . . . . . . . . . | 18,200 | | |
| Product recalls . . . . . . . . . . . . | 10,800 | 29,000 | 29% |
| **Total cost of quality** . . . . . . . . . | | $100,000 | 100% |

## CORPORATE SOCIAL RESPONSIBILITY

Peter Varga/Shutterstock

**Nike** implemented lean processes and achieved increased productivity, lower inventory levels, lower defect rates, and faster production. These improvements benefited the "profit" aspect of the triple bottom line, but lean processes can have other triple bottom line benefits. Nike saw major improvements in compliance with labor rules. Nike increased both profits and working conditions for employees ("people") in its supply chain.

Lean businesses also try to reduce waste. **Apple**'s *Environmental Responsibility Report* shows a focus on the "planet" aspect of the triple bottom line. Apple strives for a **closed-loop supply chain,** where products are built using only renewable resources or recycled material, as shown in Exhibit C.10.

To achieve its goal, Apple works with its suppliers to use 100% recycled tin in the main part of its iPhone. It also has programs to encourage customers to recycle old devices. Robots disassemble millions of iPhones per year to reclaim materials.

**EXHIBIT C.10**

Closed-Loop Supply Chain

Raw materials    Manufacturing    Customer use

Reuse & Recycling

---

**Decision Analysis**     **Days' Payable Outstanding**

**A3** _____

Compute days' payable outstanding.

Companies that buy on credit monitor how long they take to pay creditors. This is particularly important for lean businesses because they usually have long-term contracts with important suppliers. Taking too long to pay could harm important partnerships. Paying too soon, however, means the company has less cash available for other needs. **Days' payable outstanding,** defined in Exhibit C.11, is a measure of how long, on average, a company takes to pay its creditors (it is usually rounded to the nearest whole day).

$$\text{Days' payable outstanding} = \frac{\text{Accounts payable}}{\text{Cost of goods sold}} \times 365$$

**EXHIBIT C.11**

Days' Payable Outstanding

**Nike**'s days' payable outstanding is shown in Exhibit C.12. Its days' payable outstanding is 44 days [($2,612/$21,643) × 365] in the current year. This increased from the two prior years. A company's days' payable outstanding can be compared to its typical credit terms and to its industry competitors. **Under Armour**'s days' payable outstanding was 81 at the end of the current year. A company with 30 days to pay and a days' payable outstanding of 12 days should consider paying its creditors later. On the other hand, a company with 30 days to pay and a days' payable outstanding of 55 days risks hurting its partnerships with key suppliers.

| Under Armour | Current Year |
|---|---|
| Accounts payable | $  618 mil. |
| Cost of goods sold | $2,797 mil. |
| Days' payable | 81 days |

| Company | $ millions | Current Year | One Year Prior | Two Years Prior |
|---|---|---|---|---|
| **Nike** | Accounts payable . . . . . . . . . . . . . . . . . . . | $  2,612 | $  2,279 | $  2,048 |
| | Cost of goods sold. . . . . . . . . . . . . . . . . . . | $21,643 | $20,441 | $19,038 |
| | Days' payable outstanding. . . . . . . . . . . | 44 days | 41 days | 39 days |
| **Under Armour** | Days' payable outstanding. . . . . . . . . . . | 81 days | 72 days | 75 days |

**EXHIBIT C.12**

Days' Payable Outstanding for Two Competitors

Days' payable outstanding varies across industries. **Yum Brands**'s (a restaurant operator) days' payable outstanding has been over 200 days in recent years. **Twitter** has about 52 days' payable outstanding.

## Summary: Cheat Sheet

### LEAN BUSINESS MODEL

| Lean Principles | Lean Practices | Lean Goals |
|---|---|---|
| Value Streams | Continuous Improvement | Customer Satisfaction |
| Pull Production | Just-in-Time | Quality |
| Zero Waste and Zero Defects | Supply Chain Management | Triple Bottom Line |

**Value streams:** Activities that create customer value.
**Pull production:** Production starts with customer order.
**Push production:** Production starts with sales forecast.

### PRODUCTION PERFORMANCE

**Time Components**

Process time  } **Value-added**
Inspection time ⎫
Move time      ⎬ **Non-value-added**
Wait time      ⎭

**Cycle time = Process time + Inspection time + Move time + Wait time**

$$\text{Cycle efficiency} = \frac{\text{Value-added time}}{\text{Cycle time}}$$

*Example:* Process time = 1.8 days, Inspection time = 0.5 day,
Move time = 0.7 day, Wait time = 3.0 days:
Cycle time = 1.8 + 0.5 + 0.7 + 3.0 = 6.0 days

$$\text{Cycle efficiency} = \frac{1.8 \text{ days}}{6.0 \text{ days}} = 0.30 \text{ (or 30\%)}$$

$$\text{Days' sales in WIP} = \frac{\text{Work in process inventory}}{\text{Cost of goods sold}} \times 365$$

### LEAN ACCOUNTING

$$\text{Conversion cost rate} = \frac{\text{Budgeted conversion costs}}{\text{Budgeted production hours}}$$

**Entries for Materials and Conversion Costs**
No separate Raw Materials Inventory account.

**Acquire raw materials on credit**

| Work in Process Inventory . . . . . . . . . . . . . . . . . . . . . . . . . | 8,000 | |
| Accounts Payable. . . . . . . . . . . . . . . . . . . . . . . . . . . . . | | 8,000 |

**Apply conversion costs to production**

| Work in Process Inventory (Conversion cost rate × Units of activity). . . | 32,000 | |
| Conversion Costs . . . . . . . . . . . . . . . . . . . . . . . . . . . . . | | 32,000 |

**Record actual conversion costs**

| Conversion Costs . . . . . . . . . . . . . . . . . . . . . . . . . . . . . . | 32,000 | |
| Various Accounts (Wages Payable, Acc. Dep.-Mfg. Eq., etc) . . . . . | | 32,000 |

| Cost of Quality Report | | | |
|---|---|---|---|
| **Quality Category** | **Cost** | **Category Total** | **% of Total Cost of Quality** |
| **Prevention** | | | |
| Training . . . . . . . . . . . . . . . . . | $25,000 | $25,000 | 25% |
| **Appraisal** | | | |
| Inspecting materials. . . . . . . . . | 17,500 | | |
| Testing finished goods  . . . . . | 12,500 | 30,000 | 30% |
| **Internal failure** | | | |
| Rework . . . . . . . . . . . . . . . . . . | 8,400 | | |
| Scrap . . . . . . . . . . . . . . . . . . . | 7,600 | 16,000 | 16% |
| **External failure** | | | |
| Warranty claims . . . . . . . . . . . | 18,200 | | |
| Product recalls . . . . . . . . . . . . | 10,800 | 29,000 | 29% |
| **Total cost of quality. . . . . . . . .** | | $100,000 | 100% |

$$\text{Days' payable outstanding} = \frac{\text{Accounts payable}}{\text{Cost of goods sold}} \times 365$$

## Key Terms

Batch size (lot size) (C-2)
Closed-loop supply chain (C-10)
Conversion cost rate (C-8)
Costs of quality (C-9)
Cost of quality report (C-10)
Cycle efficiency (CE)  (C-6)

Cycle time (CT) (C-3)
Days' payable outstanding (C-11)
Days' sales in work in process
  inventory (C-6)
Lean business model (C-2)
Non-valued-added time (C-3)

Pull production (C-2)
Push production (C-2)
Setup time (C-3)
Supply chain management (C-5)
Value-added time (C-3)
Value stream (C-2)

**QUICK STUDY**

**QS C-1**
Lean business model   C1

Identify each of the following as applying more to lean (L) or to traditional (T) businesses.
1. Production begins with sales forecasts.
2. Uses "pull" production.
3. Aims for zero defects.
4. Uses large batch sizes.
5. Quality is controlled at each process.
6. Uses just-in-time inventory systems.

**QS C-2**
Lean business model
C1

Identify each of the following as applying more to lean (L) or to traditional (T) businesses.
1. Production begins with a customer order.
2. Reducing defects is *not* a priority.
3. Inventory levels are lower.
4. Wait times are long.
5. Uses small batch sizes.
6. Quality control is only at product completion.
7. Cycle times are shorter.
8. Move times are longer.

**QS C-3**
Lean accounting for
materials   P1

Use lean accounting to prepare the journal entry to record the purchase of $28,000 of raw materials on credit.

**QS C-4**
Lean accounting for
conversion costs   P1

Use lean accounting to prepare journal entries for the following transactions.
1. Applied $43,600 of conversion costs to production.
2. Incurred actual conversion costs of $43,600. Credit "Various Accounts."

**QS C-5**
Lean accounting for cost
of goods sold   P1

Use lean accounting to prepare journal entries for the following transactions.
1. Sold $16,800 of goods on credit.
2. Recorded cost of goods sold of $11,760.

**QS C-6**
Lean accounting for COGS
and inventory   P1

Use lean accounting to prepare journal entries for the following transactions.
1. Sold $33,250 of goods on credit.
2. Recorded cost of goods sold of $23,250, and finished goods inventory of $1,860.

**QS C-7**
Conversion cost rate   P1

A manufacturer budgets annual conversion costs of $1,207,500 and production of 2,100 hours. Compute the conversion cost rate per production hour.

**QS C-8**
Conversion cost rate
P1

A manufacturer budgets annual conversion costs of $1,000,000 and production of 1,600 hours.
1. Compute the conversion cost rate per production hour.
2. Prepare the journal entry to apply conversion costs to an order that used 65 production hours.

**QS C-9**
Cycle time and cycle
efficiency
A1

Compute (a) cycle time and (b) cycle efficiency using the following information.

| Process time | 15 minutes | Move time | 6 minutes |
|---|---|---|---|
| Inspection time | 2 minutes | Wait time | 37 minutes |

Compute (*a*) cycle time, (*b*) value-added time, (*c*) non-value-added time, and (*d*) cycle efficiency using the following information.

| | | | |
|---|---|---|---|
| Process time . . . . . . . . . . . . . . . | 2.10 days | Move time . . . . . . . . . . . . . . . . | 0.75 day |
| Inspection time . . . . . . . . . . . . . | 0.50 day | Wait time . . . . . . . . . . . . . . . . . | 0.15 day |

**QS C-10**
Cycle time and cycle efficiency

**A1**

A company reports work in process inventory of $770 and cost of goods sold of $23,404. Compute days' sales in work in process inventory. Round the answer to the nearest whole day.

**QS C-11**
Days' sales in work in process inventory   **A2**

A lean manufacturer reports the following quality costs. Prepare a cost of quality report.

| | |
|---|---|
| Training machine operators . . . | $ 50,000 |
| Product recalls . . . . . . . . . . . . . | 20,000 |
| Scrap of defective products . . . | 12,000 |
| Inspecting finished goods . . . . | 18,000 |
| Total . . . . . . . . . . . . . . . . . . . . | $100,000 |

**QS C-12**
Cost of quality report

**P2**

A restaurant reports the following quality costs. Prepare a cost of quality report.

| | |
|---|---|
| Training cooks . . . . . . . . . . . . . . . . . . . . . . | $21,000 |
| Scrap of incorrectly prepared food . . . . . . . | 3,000 |
| Inspecting ingredients from suppliers . . . . . | 30,000 |
| Free meals due to customer complaints . . . | 6,000 |
| Total . . . . . . . . . . . . . . . . . . . . . . . . . . . . . | $60,000 |

**QS C-13**
Cost of quality report for service business

**P2**

A company reports accounts payable of $2,055 and cost of goods sold of $18,300. Compute days' payable outstanding. Round the answer to the nearest whole day.

**QS C-14**
Days' payable outstanding

**A3**

A company reports accounts payable of $9,569 and cost of goods sold of $28,155. Compute days' payable outstanding. Round the answer to the nearest whole day.

**QS C-15**
Days' payable outstanding

**A3**

### connect

Identify each of the following production processes as lean (L) or traditional (T).
1. The process produces standard goods, with no customization. Production begins with a sales forecast.
2. The process uses push production in large batch sizes.
3. Production occurs in value streams.
4. The production process begins when a customer makes an order.
5. Raw materials are delivered just-in-time for production to begin.

**EXERCISES**

**Exercise C-1**
Lean business model

**C1**

Use lean accounting to prepare journal entries for the following transactions.
1. Purchased $22,500 of raw materials on credit.
2. Applied conversion costs of $67,500.
3. Incurred actual conversion costs of $67,500. Credit "Various Accounts."
4. Sold $120,000 of goods on credit.
5. Recorded cost of goods sold of $90,000.

**Exercise C-2**
Lean accounting

**P1**

Robo-Pool is a lean manufacturer of robotic pool vacuums. Each unit requires $225 of raw materials and $375 of conversion costs and is sold for $700. During a recent month, the company produced and sold 120 units. Use lean accounting to prepare journal entries for the following transactions.
1. Purchase of raw materials on credit.
2. Applied conversion costs to production.
3. Sold 120 units on credit.
4. Record cost of goods sold.

**Exercise C-3**
Lean accounting

**P1**

**Exercise C-4**

Lean accounting with inventory

**P1**

Robo-Pool is a lean manufacturer of robotic pool vacuums. Each unit requires $225 of raw materials and $375 of conversion costs and is sold for $700. During a recent month the company produced 120 units and sold 100 units. Use lean accounting to prepare journal entries to record each of the following.

1. Purchase of raw materials on credit.
2. Applied conversion costs to production.
3. Sold 100 units on credit.
4. Record ending inventory and cost of goods sold.

**Exercise C-5**

Conversion cost rate

**P1**

Dyzor is a lean manufacturer of wireless sound systems. Its wireless speaker value stream budgets $48,000 of conversion costs and 600 production hours for the next quarter. Each unit requires 2 production hours. Compute the conversion rate per production hour *and* per unit.

**Exercise C-6**

Cycle time and cycle efficiency

**A1**

Oakwood Company produces maple bookcases. The following information is available for the production of a recent order of 500 bookcases.

| | | | |
|---|---|---|---|
| Process time . . . . . . . . . . . . . . | 6 days | Move time . . . . . . . . . . . . . . . . | 3 days |
| Inspection time . . . . . . . . . . . . | 1 day | Wait time . . . . . . . . . . . . . . . . . | 5 days |

1. Compute cycle time.
2. Compute cycle efficiency.
3. Management believes it can reduce move time by 1 day and wait time by 2 days by adopting lean manufacturing techniques. Compute cycle efficiency assuming the predictions are correct.

**Exercise C-7**

Cycle time and cycle efficiency

**A1**

Best Ink produces printers for personal computers. The following information is available for production of a recent order of 500 printers.

| | | | |
|---|---|---|---|
| Process time . . . . . . . . . . . . . . | 16 hours | Move time . . . . . . . . . . . . . . . . | 9 hours |
| Inspection time . . . . . . . . . . . . | 4 hours | Wait time . . . . . . . . . . . . . . . . . | 21 hours |

1. Compute cycle time.
2. Compute cycle efficiency.
3. Management believes it can reduce inspection time by 2 hours and wait time by 8 hours by adopting lean manufacturing techniques. Compute cycle efficiency assuming the predictions are correct.

**Exercise C-8**

Cycle time

**A1**

A manufacturer makes T-shirts in several processes. Information on the components of cycle time follows. Compute (*a*) value-added time, (*b*) inspection time, (*c*) move time, (*d*) wait time, and (*e*) cycle time.

| | | | |
|---|---|---|---|
| Cutting and sewing processing . . . . . . . . . . . . . | 18 min. | Wait time before moving to packaging . . . . . . . | 4 min. |
| Wait time before moving to ironing . . . . . . . . . . | 6 min. | Moving shirts to packaging . . . . . . . . . . . . . . . | 2 min. |
| Moving shirts to ironing . . . . . . . . . . . . . . . . . . | 5 min. | Packaging shirts . . . . . . . . . . . . . . . . . . . . . . . | 10 min. |
| Ironing shirts . . . . . . . . . . . . . . . . . . . . . . . . . . | 8 min. | Quality inspection . . . . . . . . . . . . . . . . . . . . . . | 12 min. |

**Exercise C-9**

Cycle efficiency

**A1**

Management of a T-shirt manufacturer believes if the company applies lean principles, then cycle efficiency can be improved. The following are estimated completion times for different activities in the manufacturing process. Compute cycle efficiency for the (*a*) traditional approach and (*b*) lean approach.

| Activity | Traditional | Lean | Activity | Traditional | Lean |
|---|---|---|---|---|---|
| Cutting and sewing processing . . . . | 18 min. | 18 min. | Wait time before moving to packaging | 8 min. | 2 min. |
| Wait time before moving to ironing | 6 min. | 3 min. | Moving shirts to packaging . . . . . . . . | 6 min. | 1 min. |
| Moving shirts to ironing . . . . . . . . . | 8 min. | 4 min. | Packaging shirts . . . . . . . . . . . . . . . | 10 min. | 10 min. |
| Ironing shirts . . . . . . . . . . . . . . . . . . | 8 min. | 8 min. | Quality inspection . . . . . . . . . . . . . . | 16 min. | 4 min. |

Use the information below to answer the requirements.

| | Current Year | Prior Year |
|---|---|---|
| Work in process inventory.............. | $ 8,640 | $ 13,284 |
| Cost of goods sold.................... | 262,800 | 315,360 |

**Exercise C-10**
Days' sales in work in process inventory
**A2**

1. Compute days' sales in work in process inventory for the current year.
2. Compute days' sales in work in process inventory for the prior year.
3. Did days' sales in work in process inventory increase or decrease from the prior year?

Use the information below to answer the requirements.

| | Current Year |
|---|---|
| Work in process inventory.............. | $ 3,600 |
| Cost of goods sold.................... | 219,000 |

**Exercise C-11**
Days' sales in work in process inventory
**A2**

1. Compute days' sales in work in process inventory for the current year.
2. If the company's work in process inventory were 20% lower, by how many days would days' sales in work in process inventory be reduced? Round to the nearest day.

Orion Motors manufactures cars. Classify each of the following quality costs as either prevention, appraisal, internal failure, or external failure.

| | | | | |
|---|---|---|---|---|
| **1.** Inspecting raw materials | $60,000 | **4.** Warranty claims | $25,000 |
| **2.** Training lean business practices | 55,000 | **5.** Equipment maintenance | 45,000 |
| **3.** Product recalls | 9,000 | **6.** Scrap of defective materials | 6,000 |

**Exercise C-12**
Costs of quality
**P2**

Refer to the information in Exercise C-12. Prepare a cost of quality report.

**Exercise C-13**
Cost of quality report
**P2**

Use the information below to answer the requirements.

| | Current Year | Prior Year |
|---|---|---|
| Accounts payable .................... | $ 1,080 | $ 1,440 |
| Cost of goods sold.................... | 43,800 | 65,700 |

**Exercise C-14**
Days' payable outstanding
**A3**

1. Compute days' payable outstanding for the current year.
2. Compute days' payable outstanding for the prior year.
3. Did the company take longer to pay its creditors in the current year?

Use the information below to answer the requirements.

| | Current Year |
|---|---|
| Accounts payable .................... | $ 19,310 |
| Cost of goods sold.................... | 281,900 |

**Exercise C-15**
Days' payable outstanding
**A3**

1. Compute days' payable outstanding for the current year. Round to the nearest day.
2. If the company's accounts payable were 8% lower, by how many days would days' payable outstanding be reduced? Round to the nearest day.
3. If the company's accounts payable were 8% higher, by how many days would days' payable outstanding be increased? Round to the nearest day.

## PROBLEMS

**Problem C-1**

Lean accounting

P1

Robo-Lawn is a lean manufacturer of robotic lawn mowers. The company budgets $800,000 of conversion costs and 10,000 production hours for this year. The manufacturing of each mower requires 5 production hours and $250 of raw materials. During a recent quarter, the company produced 600 mowers and sold 580 mowers. Each mower is sold for $1,000.

**Required**

1. Compute the conversion cost rate per mower.
2. Prepare journal entries to record (*a*) purchase of raw materials on credit, (*b*) applied conversion costs to production, (*c*) sale of 580 mowers on credit, and (*d*) cost of goods sold and finished goods inventory.

**Problem C-2**

Lean accounting

P1

Auto-Motion is a lean manufacturer of self-driving wheelchairs. The company budgets $680,000 of conversion costs and 2,000 production hours for this year. The manufacturing of each wheelchair requires 25 production hours and raw materials costs of $4,300. The company started and completed 75 wheelchairs during the year and sold 68. Each wheelchair is sold for $15,000. Actual conversion costs equal applied conversion costs.

**Required**

1. Prepare journal entries to record (*a*) the purchase of raw materials on credit to produce 75 units, (*b*) applied conversion costs to the production of 75 units, (*c*) actual conversion costs of $637,500 (credit "Various Accounts"), (*d*) sale of 68 units on credit, and (*e*) ending inventory and cost of goods sold.
2. Compute the ending balances of Work in Process Inventory and Finished Goods Inventory. Assume each of these inventory accounts began the year with a balance of zero.

**Problem C-3**

Cycle time and cycle efficiency

A1

Ruiz Foods makes energy bars using a traditional manufacturing process. Raw materials are stored in inventory and then moved into production. Work in process inventory is moved across the company's three separate departments. The information below in the Traditional column is available for a recent order. If the company adopts lean manufacturing, management believes both move time and wait time can be reduced, as shown in the Lean column.

| Activity | Traditional | Lean |
|---|---|---|
| Process time . . . . . . . . . . . | 24 hours | 24 hours |
| Inspection time . . . . . . . . . | 4 hours | 4 hours |
| Move time . . . . . . . . . . . . . | 6 hours | 3 hours |
| Wait time . . . . . . . . . . . . . . | 2 hours | 1 hour |

**Required**

1. Compute the total amount of non-value-added time under the traditional manufacturing process.
2. Compute cycle efficiency under the traditional manufacturing process. Round to two decimals.
3. Compute the total amount of non-value-added time under the proposed lean manufacturing process.
4. Compute cycle efficiency under the proposed lean manufacturing process. Round to two decimals.
5. Would the proposed lean approach improve cycle efficiency?

## Discussion Questions

**1.** What are the three key principles of the lean business model?

**2.** How does *push* production differ from *pull* production?

**3.** What are three common problems with push production?

**4.** Define *supply chain management*.

**5.** **Apple** wants a closed-loop supply chain. Define a closed-loop supply chain and discuss methods the company uses to meet its goal. **APPLE**

**6.** Can management of a retail company like **Amazon** use lean techniques? Explain.

**7.** Define *setup time* and provide some examples of tasks that are included in setup time.

**8.** Why do lean accounting systems not use separate Raw Materials Inventory accounts?

**9.** Do lean accounting systems use Finished Goods Inventory accounts? Explain.

**10.** Define and describe *cycle time* and identify the components of cycle time.

**11.** Explain the difference between *value-added time* and *non-value-added time*.

**12.** Define and describe *cycle efficiency*.

**13.** Can management of a company like **Samsung** use cycle time and cycle efficiency as useful measures of performance? Explain. **Samsung**

# Index

# Chart of Accounts

Following is a typical chart of accounts, which is used in many assignments. Each company has its own unique set of accounts and numbering system.
*An asterisk denotes a contra account.

## Assets

### Current Assets

101 Cash
102 Petty cash
103 Cash equivalents
104 Short-term investments
105 Fair value adjustment–_____ (ST)
106 Accounts receivable
107 Allowance for doubtful accounts*
108 Allowance for sales discounts*
109 Interest receivable
110 Rent receivable
111 Notes receivable
112 Legal fees receivable
119 Merchandise inventory (or Inventory)
120 _____ inventory
121 Inventory returns estimated
124 Office supplies
125 Store supplies
126 _____ supplies (or Supplies)
128 Prepaid insurance
129 Prepaid interest
131 Prepaid rent
132 Raw materials inventory
133 Work in process inventory, _____
134 Work in process inventory, _____
135 Finished goods inventory
136 Debt investments–Trading (ST)
137 Debt investments–Held-to-maturity (ST)
138 Debt investments–Available-for-sale (ST)
139 Stock investments (ST)

### Long-Term Investments

141 Long-term investments
142 Fair value adjustment–_____ (LT)
144 Investment in _____
145 Bond sinking fund
146 Debt investments–Held-to-maturity (LT)
147 Debt investments–Available-for-sale (LT)
148 Stock investments (LT)
149 Equity method investments

### Plant Assets
### (Property, Plant, & Equipment)

151 Automobiles
152 Accumulated depreciation–Automobiles*
153 Trucks
154 Accumulated depreciation–Trucks*
155 Boats
156 Accumulated depreciation–Boats*
157 Professional library
158 Accumulated depreciation–Professional library*
159 Law library

160 Accumulated depreciation–Law library*
161 Furniture
162 Accumulated depreciation–Furniture*
163 Office equipment
164 Accumulated depreciation–Office equipment*
165 Store equipment
166 Accumulated depreciation–Store equipment*
167 _____ equipment
168 Accumulated depreciation–_____ equipment*
169 Machinery
170 Accumulated depreciation–Machinery*
173 Building _____
174 Accumulated depreciation–Building _____*
175 Building _____
176 Accumulated depreciation–Building _____*
179 Land improvements _____
180 Accumulated depreciation–Land improvements _____*
181 Land improvements _____
182 Accumulated depreciation–Land improvements _____*
183 Land

### Natural Resources

185 Mineral deposit
186 Accumulated depletion–Mineral deposit*

### Intangible Assets

191 Patents
192 Leasehold
193 Franchise
194 Copyrights
195 Leasehold improvements
196 Licenses
197 Right-of-use asset
198 Accumulated amortization–_____*
199 Goodwill

## Liabilities

### Current Liabilities

201 Accounts payable
202 Insurance payable
203 Interest payable
204 Legal fees payable
207 Office salaries payable
208 Rent payable
209 Salaries payable
210 Wages payable
211 Accrued payroll payable

212 Factory wages payable
214 Estimated warranty liability
215 Income taxes payable
216 Common dividend payable
217 Preferred dividend payable
218 State unemployment taxes payable
219 Employee federal income taxes payable
221 Employee medical insurance payable
222 Employee retirement program payable
223 Employee union dues payable
224 Federal unemployment taxes payable
225 FICA taxes payable
226 Estimated vacation pay liability
227 Sales refund payable
228 Loan payable
229 Current portion of long-term debt

### Unearned Revenues

230 Unearned consulting fees (or revenue)
231 Unearned legal fees (or revenue)
232 Unearned property management fees
233 Unearned _____ fees
234 Unearned _____ fees
235 Unearned janitorial revenue
236 Unearned _____ revenue
238 Unearned rent

### Notes Payable

240 Short-term notes payable
241 Discount on short-term notes payable*
244 Current portion of long-term notes payable
245 Notes payable
251 Long-term notes payable
252 Discount on long-term notes payable*

### Long-Term Liabilities

253 Lease liability
255 Bonds payable
256 Discount on bonds payable*
257 Premium on bonds payable
258 Deferred income tax liability

## Equity

### Owner's Equity

301 _____, Capital
302 _____, Withdrawals
303 _____, Capital
304 _____, Withdrawals
305 _____, Capital
306 _____, Withdrawals

### Paid-In Capital

307 Common stock, $ _____ par value
308 Common stock, no-par value
309 Common stock, $ _____ stated value

CA

310 Common stock dividend distributable
311 Paid-in capital in excess of par value, Common stock
312 Paid-in capital in excess of stated value, No-par common stock
313 Paid-in capital from retirement of common stock
314 Paid-in capital, Treasury stock
315 Preferred stock
316 Paid-in capital in excess of par value, Preferred stock

### Retained Earnings

318 Retained earnings
319 Cash dividends (or Dividends)
320 Stock dividends

### Other Equity Accounts

321 Treasury stock, Common*
322 Unrealized gain–Equity
323 Unrealized loss–Equity

# Revenues

401 _____ fees earned
402 _____ revenues
403 _____ revenue
404 Revenues
405 Commissions revenue (or earned)
406 Rent revenue (or Rent earned)
407 Dividends revenue (or Dividends earned)
408 Earnings from investment in _____
409 Interest revenue (or Interest earned)
410 Sinking fund earnings
413 Sales
414 Sales returns and allowances*
415 Sales discounts*
420 Earnings from equity method investments

# Cost of Sales

### Cost of Goods Sold

502 Cost of goods sold
505 Purchases
506 Purchases returns and allowances*
507 Purchases discounts*
508 Transportation-in

### Manufacturing

520 Raw materials purchases
521 Freight-in on raw materials
530 Direct labor
541 Indirect materials
542 Indirect labor
543 Factory insurance expired
544 Factory supervision
545 Factory supplies used
546 Factory utilities
547 Miscellaneous production costs
548 Property taxes on factory building
549 Property taxes on factory equipment
550 Rent on factory building
551 Repairs, factory equipment
552 Small tools written off
560 Depreciation of factory equipment

561 Depreciation of factory building
570 Conversion costs

### Standard Cost Variances

580 Direct material quantity variance
581 Direct material price variance
582 Direct labor efficiency variance
583 Direct labor rate variance
584 Volume variance
585 Controllable variance

# Expenses

### Amortization, Depletion, and Depreciation

601 Amortization expense–_____
602 Amortization expense–_____
603 Depletion expense–_____
604 Depreciation expense–Boats
605 Depreciation expense–Automobiles
606 Depreciation expense–Building _____
607 Depreciation expense–Building _____
608 Depreciation expense–Land improvements _____
609 Depreciation expense–Land improvements _____
610 Depreciation expense–Law library
611 Depreciation expense–Trucks
612 Depreciation expense–_____ equipment
613 Depreciation expense–_____ equipment
614 Depreciation expense–_____
615 Depreciation expense–_____

### Employee-Related Expenses

620 Office salaries expense
621 Sales salaries expense
622 Salaries expense
623 _____ wages expense
624 Employee benefits expense
625 Payroll taxes expense

### Financial Expenses

630 Cash over and short
631 Discounts lost
632 Factoring fee expense
633 Interest expense

### Insurance Expenses

635 Insurance expense–Delivery equipment
636 Insurance expense–Office equipment
637 Insurance expense–_____

### Rental Expenses

640 Rent (or Rental) expense
641 Rent expense–Office space
642 Rent expense–Selling space
643 Press rental expense
644 Truck rental expense
645 _____ rental expense

### Supplies Expenses

650 Office supplies expense
651 Store supplies expense

652 _____ supplies expense
653 _____ supplies expense

### Miscellaneous Expenses

655 Advertising expense
656 Bad debts expense
657 Blueprinting expense
658 Boat expense
659 Collection expense
661 Concessions expense
662 Credit card expense
663 Delivery expense
664 Dumping expense
667 Equipment expense
668 Food and drinks expense
671 Gas and oil expense
672 General and administrative expense
673 Janitorial expense
674 Legal fees expense
676 Mileage expense
677 Miscellaneous expenses
678 Mower and tools expense
679 Operating expense
680 Organization expense
681 Permits expense
682 Postage expense
683 Property taxes expense
684 Repairs expense–_____
685 Repairs expense–_____
687 Selling expense
688 Telephone expense
689 Travel and entertainment expense
690 Utilities expense
691 Warranty expense
692 _____ expense
695 Income tax expense

# Gains and Losses

701 Gain on retirement of bonds
702 Gain on sale of machinery
703 Gain on sale of investments
704 Gain on sale of trucks
705 Gain on _____
706 Foreign exchange gain or loss
801 Loss on disposal of machinery
802 Loss on exchange of equipment
803 Loss on exchange of _____
804 Loss on sale of notes
805 Loss on retirement of bonds
806 Loss on sale of investments
807 Loss on sale of machinery
808 Loss on _____
809 Unrealized gain–Income
810 Unrealized loss–Income
811 Impairment gain
812 Impairment loss
815 Gain on sale of debt investments
816 Loss on sale of debt investments
817 Gain on sale of stock investments
818 Loss on sale of stock investments

# Clearing Accounts

901 Income summary
902 Factory overhead

# BRIEF REVIEW: MANAGERIAL ANALYSES AND REPORTS

## ① Cost Types

| | |
|---|---|
| Variable costs: | Total cost changes in proportion to volume of activity. |
| Fixed costs: | Total cost does not change in proportion to volume of activity. |
| Mixed costs: | Cost consists of both a variable and a fixed element. |

## ② Product Costs

| | |
|---|---|
| Direct materials: | Raw materials costs directly linked to finished product. |
| Direct labor: | Employee costs directly linked to finished product. |
| Overhead: | Production costs indirectly linked to finished product. |

## ③ Costing Systems

| | |
|---|---|
| Job order costing: | Costs assigned to each unique unit or batch of units. |
| Process costing: | Costs assigned to similar products that are mass-produced in a continuous manner. |

## ④ Costing Ratios

Contribution margin ratio = (Sales − Variable costs)/Sales
Predetermined overhead rate = Estimated overhead costs/Estimated activity base
Break-even point in units = Total fixed costs/Contribution margin per unit

## ⑤ Planning and Control Metrics

Cost variance = Actual cost − Standard (budgeted) cost
Sales (revenue) variance = Actual sales − Standard (budgeted) sales

## ⑥ Capital Budgeting

Payback period = Time expected to recover initial investment cost
Accounting rate of return = Annual income/Average investment
Net present value (NPV) = PV of future cash flows − Initial investment cost
NPV rule:  1. Compute net present value (NPV in $).
2. If NPV > 0, then accept project; If NPV < 0, then reject project.
Internal rate  1. Compute internal rate of return (IRR in %).
of return rule: 2. If IRR > hurdle rate, accept project; If IRR < hurdle rate, reject project.

## ⑦ Costing Terminology

| | |
|---|---|
| Relevant range: | Organization's normal range of operating activity. |
| Direct cost: | Cost incurred for the benefit of one cost object. |
| Indirect cost: | Cost incurred for the benefit of more than one cost object. |
| Product cost: | Cost that is necessary and integral to finished products. |
| Period cost: | Cost identified more with a time period than with finished products. |
| Overhead cost: | Cost not separately or directly traceable to a cost object. |
| Relevant cost: | Cost that is pertinent to a decision. |
| Opportunity cost: | Benefit lost by choosing an action from two or more alternatives. |
| Sunk cost: | Cost already incurred that cannot be avoided or changed. |
| Out-of-pocket cost: | Requires a future outlay of cash. |
| Avoidable cost: | Can be eliminated by choosing one alternative over another. |
| Standard cost: | Cost computed using standard price and standard quantity. |
| Budget: | Formal statement of an organization's plans in monetary terms. |
| Break-even point: | Sales level at which an organization earns zero profit. |
| Incremental revenue: | Revenue earned if the organization takes a certain action. |
| Incremental cost: | Cost incurred only if the organization undertakes a certain action. |
| Incremental income: | Incremental revenue minus incremental cost. |
| Transfer price: | Price on transaction between divisions within a company. |

## ⑧ Standard Cost Variances

$$\text{Total materials variance} = \frac{\text{Materials price}}{\text{variance}} + \frac{\text{Materials quantity}}{\text{variance}}$$

$$\text{Total labor variance} = \frac{\text{Labor rate}}{\text{variance}} + \frac{\text{Labor efficiency}}{\text{variance}}$$

Standard overhead rate = Flexible overhead budget at predicted activity level / Standard allocation base at predicted activity level

Standard overhead applied = Actual production × Standard amount of allocation base × Standard overhead rate

Total overhead variance = Actual total overhead − Standard overhead applied
or = Overhead controllable variance + Overhead volume variance

Controllable variance = Actual total overhead − Budgeted (flexible) overhead at units produced

Volume variance = Budgeted (flexible) overhead at units produced − Standard overhead applied

| | |
|---|---|
| Materials price variance | = [AQ × AP] − [AQ × SP] |
| Materials quantity variance | = [AQ × SP] − [SQ × SP] |
| Labor rate variance | = [AH × AR] − [AH × SR] |
| Labor efficiency variance | = [AH × SR] − [SH × SR] |

where AQ is Actual Quantity of materials; AP is Actual Price of materials; AH is Actual Hours of labor; AR is Actual Rate of wages; AVR is Actual Variable Rate of overhead; SQ is Standard Quantity of materials; SP is Standard Price of materials; SH is Standard Hours of labor; SR is Standard Rate of labor; SVR is Standard Variable Rate of overhead.

## ⑨ Sales Variances

| | |
|---|---|
| Sales price variance | = [AS × AP] − [AS × BP] |
| Sales volume variance | = [AS × BP] − [BS × BP] |

where AS = Actual Sales units; AP = Actual sales Price;
BP = Budgeted sales Price; BS = Budgeted Sales units (fixed budget).

---

### Schedule of Cost of Goods Manufactured
#### For *period* Ended *date*

| | | |
|---|---|---|
| Direct materials | | |
| Raw materials inventory, beginning . . . . . . . . . . . . . . . . . . . . . . | $ # | |
| Raw materials purchases. . . . . . . . . . . . . . . . . . . . . . . . . . . . . | # | |
| Raw materials available for use . . . . . . . . . . . . . . . . . . . . . . | # | |
| Less raw materials inventory, ending . . . . . . . . . . . . . . . . . . . | (#) | |
| Direct materials used . . . . . . . . . . . . . . . . . . . . . | | # |
| Direct labor . . . . . . . . . . . . . . . . . . . . . . . . . . . . . . | | # |
| Factory overhead (applied) . . . . . . . . . . . . . . . . . . . . . . . . . | | # |
| Total manufacturing costs . . . . . . . . . . . . . . . . . . . . . . | | # |
| Add work in process inventory, beginning . . . . . . . . . . . . . . | | # |
| Total cost of work in process . . . . . . . . . . . . . . . . . . . . | | # |
| Less work in process inventory, ending . . . . . . . . . . . . . . . . | | (#) |
| Cost of goods manufactured . . . . . . . . . | | $ # |

---

### Contribution Margin Income Statement
#### For *period* Ended *date*

| | | |
|---|---|---|
| Sales . . . . . . . . . . . . . . . . . . . . . . . . . . . . . . . . . . | $ # | |
| Variable costs . . . . . . . . . . . . . . . . . . . . . . . . . . | | # |
| Contribution margin . . . . . . . . . . . . . . . . . . . . . . . | | # |
| Fixed costs . . . . . . . . . . . . . . . . . . . . . . . . . . . . . | | # |
| Income . . . . . . . . . . . . . . . . . . . . . . . . . . . . . . . . . | | $ # |

---

### Flexible Budget
#### For *period* Ended *date*

| | Variable Amount per Unit | Total Fixed Cost | Flexible Budget for Unit Sales of # |
|---|---|---|---|
| Sales . . . . . . . . . . . . . . . . . . . . . . . . . . . . . . . . . . . . . . . | $ # | | $ # |
| Variable costs | | | |
| Examples: Direct materials, Direct labor, Delivery costs, Sales commissions. . . . . . . . . . . . . . . . . | # | | # |
| Total variable costs . . . . . . . . . . . . . . . . . . . . . . . . . | # | | # |
| Contribution margin . . . . . . . . . . . . . . . . . . . . . . . | $ # | | # |
| Fixed costs | | | |
| Examples: Depreciation, Property taxes, Supervisory . . . . . salaries, Administrative salaries, Insurance . . . . . . . . . . | | $ #   # | #   # |
| Total fixed costs . . . . . . . . . . . . . . . . . . . . . . . . . . . . | | $ # | # |
| Income . . . . . . . . . . . . . . . . . . . . . . . . . . . . . . . . . . . | | | $ # |

Total flexible budget costs = Total fixed costs + (Total variable costs per unit × Units of activity level)

Budget variance* = Budget amount − Actual amount
*Applies to both flexible and fixed budgets. F = Favorable variance; U = Unfavorable variance.

### Activity-Based Costing Steps

① Identify activities and assign budgeted costs to activity cost pools.
② Compute an overhead activity rate for each activity cost pool.
③ Allocate overhead costs to cost objects (products).

Activity rate = Budgeted activity cost / Budgeted activity usage

### Performance Measurement

Return on investment = Income / Average assets

Residual income = Income − Target income

### Balanced Scorecard Perspectives
1. Customer   3. Innovation/learning
2. Internal processes   4. Financial

### Variable and Absorption Costing

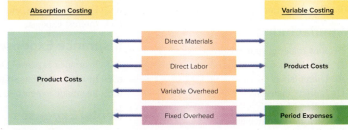

Absorption costing includes fixed overhead in product costs.
Variable costing includes fixed overhead in period expenses.

### Master Budget Sequence

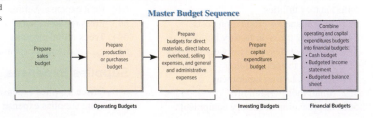

# BRIEF REVIEW: FINANCIAL REPORTS AND TABLES

## Income Statement*
### For *period* Ended *date*

| | | |
|---|---|---|
| Net sales (revenues)........................................... | $ | # |
| Cost of goods sold (cost of sales)............................. | | # |
| Gross margin (gross profit).................................... | | # |
| Operating expenses | | |
|   Examples: depreciation, salaries, wages, rent, utilities,.......... | $ | # |
|     interest, amortization, advertising, insurance,............. | | # |
|     taxes, selling, general and administrative.................. | | # |
| Total operating expenses...................................... | | # |
| Nonoperating gains and losses (unusual and/or infrequent)....... | | # |
| Net income (net profit or earnings)............................ | $ | # |

*A typical chart of accounts is at the end of the text and classifies all accounts by financial statement categories.

## Balance Sheet
### *Date*

### ASSETS

| | | |
|---|---|---|
| **Current assets** | | |
|   Examples: cash, cash equivalents, short-term investments,............ | $ | # |
|     accounts receivable, current portion of notes receivable,........... | | # |
|     inventory, inventory returns estimated, prepaid expenses............ | | # |
|   Total current assets......................................... | $ | # |
| **Long-term investments** | | |
|   Examples: notes receivable, investment in stock, investment in bonds....... | # | |
|   Total long-term investments.................................. | | # |
| **Plant assets** | | |
|   Examples: equipment, machinery, buildings, land................ | # | |
|   Total plant assets, net of depreciation........................ | | # |
| **Intangibles** | | |
|   Examples: patent, trademark, copyright, license, right-of-use, goodwill...... | # | |
|   Total intangible assets, net of amortization................... | | # |
| Total assets.................................................. | $ | # |

### LIABILITIES AND EQUITY

| | | |
|---|---|---|
| **Current liabilities** | | |
|   Examples: accounts payable, wages payable, salaries payable,............ | $ | # |
|     current notes payable, taxes payable, interest payable,............. | | # |
|     unearned revenues, current portion of debt, sales refund payable........ | | # |
|   Total current liabilities..................................... | $ | # |
| **Long-term liabilities** | | |
|   Examples: notes payable, bonds payable, lease liability............ | # | |
|   Total long-term liabilities................................... | | # |
| Total liabilities.............................................. | | # |
| **Equity*** | | |
|   Common stock.............................................. | | # |
|   Paid-in capital in excess of par (or stated value)................ | | # |
|   Retained earnings........................................... | | # |
|   Less treasury stock......................................... | | (#) |
|   Total equity................................................ | | # |
| Total liabilities and equity.................................... | $ | # |

## Statement of Cash Flows
### For *period* Ended *date*

| | | |
|---|---|---|
| Cash flows from operating activities | | |
|   [Prepared using the indirect (see below)† or direct method] | | |
|   Net cash provided (used) by operating activities.................... | $ | # |
| Cash flows from investing activities | | |
|   [List of individual investing inflows and outflows] | | |
|   Net cash provided (used) by investing activities.................... | | # |
| Cash flows from financing activities | | |
|   [List of individual financing inflows and outflows] | | |
|   Net cash provided (used) by financing activities.................... | | # |
| Net increase (decrease) in cash................................. | $ | # |
| Cash (and equivalents) balance at beginning of period............ | | # |
| Cash (and equivalents) balance at end of period................. | $ | # |

Separate schedule or note disclosure of any "Noncash investing and financing transactions" is required.

### †Indirect Method: Cash Flows from Operating Activities

| | | |
|---|---|---|
| Cash flows from operating activities | | |
| Net income................................................... | $ | # |
| Adjustments for operating items not providing or using cash | | |
|   +Noncash expenses and losses............................... | $ | # |
|     *Examples:* Expenses for depreciation, depletion, and amortization; | | |
|     losses from disposal of long-term assets and from retirement of debt | | |
|   −Noncash revenues and gains................................ | | # |
|     *Examples:* Gains from disposal of long-term assets and from | | |
|     retirement of debt | | |
| Adjustments for changes in current assets and current liabilities | | |
|   +Decrease in noncash current operating assets.................... | | # |
|   −Increase in noncash current operating assets.................... | | # |
|   +Increase in current operating liabilities....................... | | # |
|   −Decrease in current operating liabilities....................... | | # |
| Net cash provided (used) by operating activities.................... | $ | # |

## Statement of Retained Earnings
### For *period* Ended *date*

| | | |
|---|---|---|
| Retained earnings, beginning................................... | $ | # |
| Add: Net income.............................................. | | # |
| | | # |
| Less: Dividends............................................... | | # |
|   Net loss (if exists)......................................... | | # |
| Retained earnings, ending...................................... | $ | # |

## Statement of Stockholders' Equity†
### For *period* Ended *date*

| | Common Stock | Capital in Excess of Par | Retained Earnings | Treasury Stock | Total |
|---|---|---|---|---|---|
| Balances, beginning............ | $ # | $ # | $ # | $ # | $ # |
| Net income.................... | | | | | |
| Cash dividends................ | | | | | |
| Stock issuance................ | | | | | |
| Treasury stock purchase....... | | | | | |
| Treasury stock reissuance....... | | | | | |
| Other........................ | | | | | |
| Balances, ending.............. | $ # | $ # | $ # | $ # | $ # |

†Additional columns and account titles commonly include number of shares, preferred stock, unrealized gains and losses on available-for-sale securities, foreign currency translation, and comprehensive income.

## Premium Bond Amortization (Straight-Line) Table*

| Semiannual Period-End | Unamortized Bond Premium† | Bond Carrying Value‡ |
|---|---|---|
| Bond life-start.................. | $ # | $ # |
| ... | : | : |
| ... | : | : |
| Bond life-end................... | 0 | par |

*Bond carrying value is adjusted downward to par and its amortized premium downward to zero over the bond life (carrying value less unamortized bond premium equals par).
†Equals total bond premium less its accumulated amortization.
‡Equals bond par value <u>plus</u> its unamortized bond premium.

## Discount Bond Amortization (Straight-Line) Table*

| Semiannual Period-End | Unamortized Bond Discount† | Bond Carrying Value‡ |
|---|---|---|
| Bond life-start.................. | $ # | $ # |
| ... | : | : |
| ... | : | : |
| Bond life-end ................... | 0 | par |

*Bond carrying value is adjusted upward to par and its amortized discount downward to zero over the bond life (unamortized bond discount plus carrying value equals par).
†Equals total bond discount less its accumulated amortization.
‡Equals bond par value <u>less</u> its unamortized bond discount.

## Effective Interest Amortization Table for Bonds with Semiannual Interest Payment

| Semiannual Interest Period-End | Cash Interest Paid[A] | Bond Interest Expense[B] | Discount or Premium Amortization[C] | Unamortized Discount or Premium[D] | Carrying Value[E] |
|---|---|---|---|---|---|
| # | # | # | # | # | # |
| : | : | : | : | : | : |

[A]Par value multiplied by the semiannual contract rate.
[B]Prior period's carrying value multiplied by the semiannual market rate.
[C]The difference between interest paid and bond interest expense.
[D]Prior period's unamortized discount or premium less the current period's discount or premium amortization.
[E]Par value less unamortized discount or plus unamortized premium.

## Installment Notes Payment Table

| Period Ending Date | Beginning Balance | Debit Interest Expense | + | Debit Notes Payable | = | Credit Cash | Ending Balance |
|---|---|---|---|---|---|---|---|
| # | # | # | | # | | # | # |
| : | : | : | | : | | : | : |

## Bank Reconciliation
### *Date*

| | | | | | |
|---|---|---|---|---|---|
| Bank statement balance........... | $# | | Book balance................................. | | $# |
| Add: Deposits in transit ............. | # | | Add: Interest earned & unrecorded cash receipts .... | | # |
|   Bank errors understating | | |   Book errors understating | | |
|   the balance ................. | # | |   the balance ................. | | # |
| | # | | | | # |
| Less: Outstanding checks............ | # | | Less: Bank fees & NSF checks .................. | | # |
|   Bank errors overstating | | |   Book errors overstating | | |
|   the balance ................. | # | |   the balance ................. | | # |
| **Adjusted bank balance** ............ | $# | | **Adjusted book balance**....................... | | $# |

Balances are equal (reconciled)